新疆统计年鉴

XINJIANG STATISTICAL YEARBOOK

2013

新疆维吾尔自治区统计局・编
Compiled by Statistics Bureau of Xinjiang Uygur Autonomous Region

中国统计出版社
China Statistics Press

图书在版编目(CIP)数据

新疆统计年鉴. 2013 / 新疆维吾尔自治区统计局编.
-- 北京 : 中国统计出版社, 2013.8
ISBN 978-7-5037-6890-3

Ⅰ. ①新… Ⅱ. ①新… Ⅲ. ①统计资料－新疆－2013－年鉴 Ⅳ. ①C832.45-54

中国版本图书馆CIP数据核字(2013)第177499号

新疆统计年鉴—2013

作　　者/新疆维吾尔自治区统计局
责任编辑/佘竞雄
装帧设计/徐鸿梅
出版发行/中国统计出版社
地　　址/北京市丰台区西三环南路甲6号　邮政编码/100073
电　　话/邮购（010）63376909　书店（010）68783171
网　　址/http://csp.stats.gov.cn
印　　刷/新疆统计印刷厂
经　　销/新华书店
开　　本/890mm×1240mm　1/16
字　　数/1400千字
印　　张/50
版　　别/2013年8月第1版
版　　次/2013年8月第1次印刷
定　　价/460.00元（含光盘）

本书附同版本CD-ROM一张，光盘内容以书面文字为准。
如有印装差错，由本社发行部调换。

吉木萨尔 旅游

丝绸明珠 北庭故城

吉木萨尔县位于新疆维吾尔自治区天山北麓东端，准噶尔盆地东南缘，东邻奇台县，西与阜康市接壤，北越卡拉麦里岭和富蕴县相连，南以博格达山分水岭同吐鲁番地区、乌鲁木齐市为界。地势南北高、中间低，地貌可分为南部山区、中部平原、北部沙漠三种类型。主要河流有二工河、西大龙口河、渭户沟河、白杨河等。属温带大陆性气候，冬季长而严寒，夏季短而炎热；春秋季节不明显，干旱少雨，昼夜温差大。

北庭西大寺原貌

五彩湾温泉度假村

北庭园广场恐龙公园

车师古道风景头道桥

吉木萨尔曾是新疆的政治、军事、经济和文化中心，是丝路古道的重要交通枢纽。汉代，这里曾是车师后国的王都，后为汉朝戊(wu)己(ji)校尉—耿恭的驻地，唐代在此设北庭大都护府，元代设尚书省，后改称别失八里，清代称济木萨，光绪二十八年(1902 年)建县，称孚远县，1952 年改称吉木萨尔县。县域总面积 8848 平方公里，地处天山山脉东段北麓，准葛尔盆地东南缘，西距乌鲁木齐 165 公里，东离哈密市 545 公里，国道 216 线、省道 303 线、大奇高速路贯穿全境。

全县矿产资源储量丰厚，有“油盆煤海气库”之称，煤炭资源预测总储量约在 1600 多亿吨，石油预测资源量 8 亿吨，天然气资源量 1000 亿立方米，油页岩储量 50 亿吨。具有天山北坡独有的逆温带气候，目前认证的无公害农产品有大蒜、马铃薯、红花、草莓等 22 种，被誉为“中国四大名蒜之一”:新疆白皮大蒜;“中国高淀粉马铃薯之乡”;被国家工商总局授予“中国红花原产地证明商标”的称号。南部天山冰峰竞秀、森林河谷幽静深远，贯穿天山直达吐鲁番的车师古道、疏勒古城，新地沟、花儿沟、五塘沟、牛圈子沟、渭户沟、车师古道风景优美；中部平原景观历史文化内涵丰富，历史悠久的据今近 2000 年的北庭故城及高昌回鹘佛寺遗址，2012 年 7 月国家文物局将北庭故城遗址列入 “中国世界文化遗产预备名单——丝绸之路中国段”首批申遗名单；北部沙漠奇特景观以空旷神秘的卡拉麦里大漠风光为主题，有野驴、鹅喉羚、比大熊猫还珍贵的全国唯一的普氏野马，7.7 亿年前的古海相沉积水形成的亚洲唯一的、世界罕见的古海温泉，雅丹地貌、古生物化石硅化木、野生动植物资源使旅游者更是感受地质变迁的不可思议，开发前景广阔。

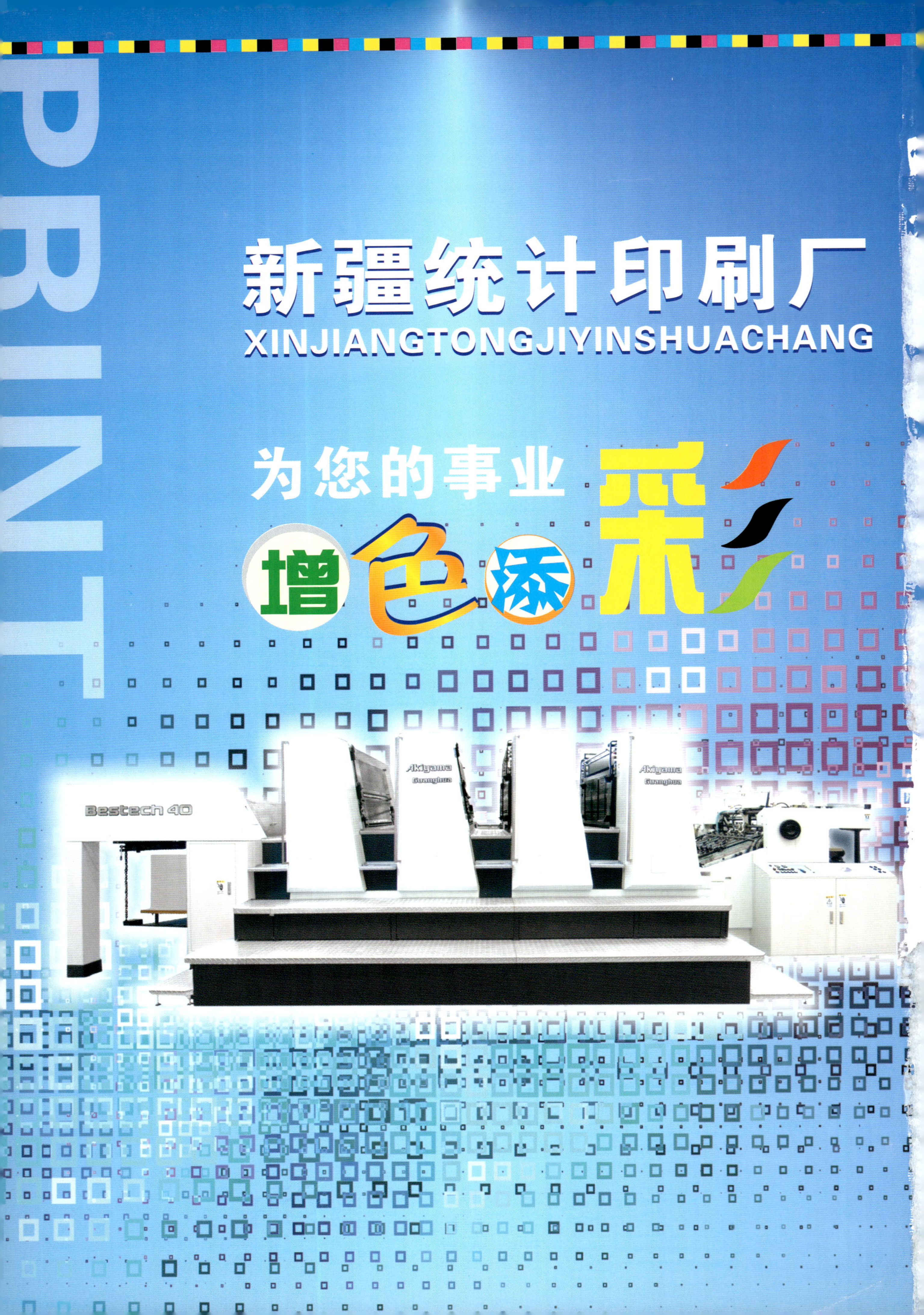
PRINT
新疆统计印刷厂
XINJIANGTONGJIYINSHUACHANG
为您的事业
增色添彩
Bestech 40
Akiyama
Guanghua
Akiyama
Guanghua

《新疆统计年鉴——2013》编辑委员会

XINJIANG STATISTICAL YEARBOOK-2013
NAME LIST OF EDITORIAL BOARD

编者说明

一、《新疆统计年鉴—2013》系统收录了全区和各地、县（市）2012年经济和社会各方面的统计数据，以及重要历史年份和近年全区主要统计数据，并收录了全国及各省市区2012年的主要统计数据，是一部全面反映新疆维吾尔自治区经济和社会发展情况的资料性年刊。

二、全书内容分为：特载（新疆维吾尔自治区2012年国民经济和社会发展统计公报）；综合；国民经济核算；人口与就业；固定资产投资；对外经济贸易和旅游；能源生产和消费；财政、金融和保险；物价指数；人民生活和社会保障；城市概况；自然资源和环境保护；农业；工业；建筑业；运输和邮电；批发和零售、住宿和餐饮业；教育、科技和文化；体育、卫生及其他；各地、州、市主要经济指标排序；附录（各省、市、区主要经济指标排序）。各篇前有简要说明，篇末附有《主要统计指标解释》。

三、本《年鉴》的资料来源，大部分来自年度报表，部分来自抽样调查资料。

四、资料中所使用的度量衡单位均采用国家法定计量单位。

五、本《年鉴》总量指标计算所采用的价格均为现行价格。

六、本《年鉴》伊犁哈萨克自治州的数据包括伊犁州直属县（市）、塔城地区和阿勒泰地区。

七、本《年鉴》使用符号说明："#"表示其中项；"…"表示不足小数位的数据；"空"表示没有或未掌握该指标数据。

八、本《年鉴》在编辑过程中得到自治区内外许多单位和同志们的大力支持，在此深表谢意。限于我们的水平，加之时间仓促，不足之处，敬请各级领导、各界人士和统计战线的同仁批评指正。

Editor's Explanatory Notes

Ⅰ.Xinjiang statistical yearbook 2013 systemly included the economic and social aspects of statistical data by region and throughout the county (city) in 2012,and the main statistical data in historically important years and recent years, and included the major statistical data of provinces and regions in 2012.The book is an annual statistic publication of fully reflect the developmen of economic and social in Xinjiang Uygur Autonomous Region.

Ⅱ.The yearbook comprises such sections as: Special Article (Statistical Bulletin on National Economy and Social Development of Xinjiang Uygur Autonomous Region in the year 2012); general survey; national accounts; population and employment; investment in fixed assets; foreign trade & economic cooperation and tourism; production and consumption of energy; government finance, financial intermediation and insurance; price indices; people's livelihood and social security; general survey of cities; natural resources and environment protection; agriculture; industry; construction; transport and telecommunication services; wholesale & retail trades, hotels and catering services; education, science & technology and culture; sports, public health and others; ranking of main economic indicators by region of Xinjiang; appendix (ranking of main economic indicators by region),etc. Each section is equipped with Explanatory Notes on Main Statistical Indicators at the end.

Ⅲ. The Yearbook of sources are mostly from the annual statements, in part from the sample survey data.

Ⅳ.The units of measurement used in this yearbook are internationally standard measurement units.

Ⅴ.The computation of all the gross indicators in the yearbook is equipped with current prices.

Ⅵ.The data about Yili Kazak Autonomous Prefecture in the present Xinjiang Statistical Yearbook covers counties (cities) direct under Yili Prefecture, Tacheng Prefecture and Altay Prefecture.

Ⅶ.Description of signs or symbols in the yearbook:

"#"stands for interim item; "…" for data with insufficient decimal place ; "blank" for absence of data indicators or ignorance of them.

Ⅷ.In the course of complication, the yearbook has received great support from many units and comrades in and out of Autonomous Region, we acknowledge their help to the book. Mistakes and faults are inevitable to take place for inadequate proficiency and limited time. Leaders, personnel from all walks of life and colleagues from statistical sector are welcome to make their critical comments and suggestions.

目 录 CONTENTS

第一篇 综 合

CHAPTER 1 GENERAL SURVEY

第 二 篇 国民经济核算

CHAPTER 2 NATIONAL ACCOUNTS

第 三 篇 人口与就业

CHAPTER 3 POPULATION AND EMPLOYMENT

第 四 篇 固定资产投资

CHAPTER 4 INVESTMENT IN FIXED ASSETS

第六篇 能源生产和消费
CHAPTER 6 PRODUCTION AND CONSUMPTION OF ENERGY

第 七 篇　财政、金融、保险

CHAPTER 7 GOVERNMENT FINANCE, FINANCIAL INTERMEDIATION AND INSURANCE

第 八 篇　物价指数

CHAPTER 8 PRICE INDICES

第 九 篇 人民生活和社会保障

CHAPTER 9 PEOPLE'S LIVELIHOOD AND SOCIAL SECURITY

第 十 篇 城市概况

CHAPTER 10 GENERAL SURVEY OF CITIES

第 十一 篇 自然资源和环境保护

CHAPTER 11 NATURAL RESOURCES AND ENVIRONMENT PROTECTION

第十二篇 农 业

CHAPTER 12 AGRICULTURE

第 十三 篇 工 业

CHAPTER 13 INDUSTRY

第 十四 篇　建筑业

CHAPTER 14 CONSTRUCTION

第 十五 篇　运输和邮电

CHAPTER 15 TRANSPORT, POSTAL AND TELECOMMUNICATION SERVICES

第十六篇 批发和零售业、住宿和餐饮业
CHAPTER 16 WHOLESALE & RETAIL TRADES, HOTELS AND CATERING SERVICES

第十七篇 教育、科技和文化

CHAPTER 17 EDUCATION, SCIENCE & TECHNOLOGY AND CULTURE

第十八篇　体育、卫生及其他

CHAPTER 18 SPORTS, PUBLIC HEALTH AND OTHERS

第 十九 篇 各地州市主要经济指标排序

CHAPTER 19 RANKING OF MAIN ECONOMIC INDICATORS BY REGION OF XINJIANG

附录： 各省市区主要经济指标排序

APPENDIX: RANKING OF MAIN ECONOMIC INDICATORS BY REGION

新疆统计年鉴
XINJIANG STATISTICAL YEARBOOK

特载

SPECIAL ARTICLE

新疆维吾尔自治区 2012年国民经济和社会发展 统 计 公 报

2012年，自治区党委、人民政府带领全区各族人民，以迎接和学习贯彻党的十八大精神为主要任务，认真落实中央新疆工作座谈会和自治区第八次党代会精神，积极应对国内外环境的复杂变化，牢牢把握"稳中求进、进中求变"的总基调，紧密围绕跨越式发展和长治久安两大历史任务，求真务实、创新变革，加快推进重大基础设施、基础产业和重点民生工程建设，经济社会发展取得新成就，民生建设取得新成效，改革创新取得新突破。

一、综 合

初步核算，全年实现地区生产总值（GDP）7505.31亿元，比上年增长12.0%。其中，第一产业增加值1320.57亿元，增长7.0%；第二产业增加值3481.56亿元，增长13.7%；第三产业增加值2703.18亿元，增长12.3%。

按常住人口计算，人均地区生产总值33796元，增长10.8%。按当年平均汇率折合5356美元。

居民消费价格比上年上涨3.8%，其中，食品价格上涨7.6%。

表 1: 2012 年居民消费价格上涨幅度

单位：%

指 标	涨跌幅度（%）
居民消费价格	3.8
城 市	3.4
农 村	4.7
食 品	7.6
#粮 食	7.3
肉禽及其制品	5.9
油脂类	5.3
蛋 类	2.1
水产品	5.2
菜 类	17.6
烟酒及用品	5.6
衣 着	1.9
家庭设备用品及服务	1.9
医疗保健和个人用品	2.9
交通和通信	-0.5
娱乐教育文化用品及服务	0.1
居 住	2.8

工业生产者出厂价格下降3.1%，其中，轻工业下降5.9%，重工业下降2.6%。工业生产者购进价格下降2.1%。农业生产资料价格上涨 6.2%。农产品生产价格上涨3.2%。固定资产投资价格上涨0.6%。

二、农 业

农作物播种面积7705.82万亩，增长3.1%。其中，粮食播种面积（含薯类）3196.76万亩，增长4.1%；棉花播种面积2581.20万亩，增长5.1%；油料播种面积

363.51万亩，下降8.3%；甜菜播种面积123.95万亩，增长9.5%。

粮食产量(含薯类)1325.68万吨，增长0.4%。棉花产量353.95万吨，增长22.2%。油料产量59.04万吨，下降11.6%。甜菜产量577.19万吨，增长11.2%。水果（含果用瓜）产量1222.10万吨，增长18.0%，其中，园林水果736.74万吨，增长22.5%。

年末牲畜存栏4333.25万头（只）。全年牲畜出栏3737.30万头（只），增长3.6%。肉类总产量134.23万吨，增长5.5%，其中，羊肉产量48.01万吨，增长3.5%；牛肉产量36.16万吨，增长7.0%；猪肉产量30.15万吨，增长1.3%。牛奶产量132.21万吨，增长1.3%。禽蛋产量25.89万吨，增长1.1%。水产品产量12.53万吨，增长7.2%。

年末农业机械总动力1968.27万千瓦，增长9.6%。拥有大中型拖拉机34.26万台，增长16.1%。小型拖拉机33.49万台，下降4.1 %。化肥施用量（折纯）192.27万吨，增长4.9%。农村用电量75.81亿千瓦时，增长5.8%。

三、工业和建筑业

全部工业增加值 2850.06 亿元，比上年增长12.7%。规模以上工业增加值 2724.16 亿元，增长12.7%。

在自治区重点监测的十大产业中，有色工业104.44 亿元，增长 43.4 %；电力工业 257.62 亿元，增长 31.8%；化学工业 280.83 亿元，增长 25.2 %；钢铁工业 96.64 亿元，增长 18.5%；煤炭工业 141.61 亿元，增长 17.4%；纺织工业 40.30 亿元，增长 15.1%；农副食品加工工业 44.66 亿元，增长 11.6%；装备制造工业56.88 亿元，增长 11.3%；石油工业 1386.17 亿元，增长 4.1%；汽车工业 4.78 亿元，增长 3.0 倍。

规模以上工业出口交货值 41.53 亿元，下降31.5%。实现利润总额 841.67 亿元，下降 7.5%。

全社会建筑业增加值 631.50 亿元，比上年增长18.2%。具有资质等级的总承包和专业承包建筑企业总产值 1622.31 亿元，增长 22.9%。

表 2：2012 年工业企业主要产品产量及增速

产品名称	单　位	产　量	比上年增长%
原　煤	万吨	13646.99	13.8
原　油	万吨	2670.68	2.1
天然气	亿立方米	253.01	7.5
原油加工量	万吨	2426.90	1.6
乙　烯	万吨	127.09	22.2
发电量	亿千瓦时	1187.48	35.7
成品糖	万吨	53.64	16.3
卷　烟	亿支	170.00	6.3
罐　头	万吨	69.41	-39.9
#番茄酱	万吨	62.87	-44.1
纱	万吨	40.22	0.8
布	万米	6675.72	-8.6
机制纸及纸板	万吨	41.05	-2.9
化肥(折纯)	万吨	304.17	30.2
十种有色金属	万吨	108.85	1.9 倍
电解铝	万吨	97.07	2.3 倍
粗　钢	万吨	1138.23	27.5
钢　材	万吨	1289.84	30.9
生　铁	万吨	1328.32	22.0
水　泥	万吨	4315.93	36.1
变压器	万千伏安	6194.52	27.6
化学纤维	万吨	44.99	35.9
塑料制品	万吨	139.97	34.4
服　装	万件	2826.38	55.3
轻　革	万平方米	518.04	8.1

四、固定资产投资

全社会固定资产投资6258.38亿元，比上年增长35.1%。其中，城镇投资5593.80亿元，增长35.0%；农村投资664.58亿元，增长36.3%。

在城镇投资中，第一产业投资110.56亿元，增长8.6%；第二产业投资3078.56亿元，增长32.9%；第三产业投资2404.68亿元，增长37.7%。在第二产业中，工业投资2988.09亿元，增长34.6%，其中，制造业投资1523.67亿元，增长40.9%。

在城镇投资中，国有投资3281.07亿元，增长30.8%；民间投资2268.79亿元，增长43.8%。涉及安居富民、定居兴牧、保障性住房建设等民生投资1381.79亿元，增长41.0%。基础设施投资1639.82亿元，增长36.5%。

房地产开发投资606.09亿元，增长17.4%，其中，住宅投资444.27亿元，增长6.7%；办公楼投资12.08亿元，下降22.2%；商业营用房投资97.61亿元，增长70.5%。房屋施工面积6896.54万平方米，增长25.8%；竣工面积1736.19万平方米，增长36.7%。商品房销售面积1430.30万平方米，下降17.2 %；销售额560.45 亿元，下降8.6%。

五、国内贸易

社会消费品零售总额1798.99亿元，比上年增长15.5%，扣除价格因素，实际增长11.8%。

按经营地划分，城镇消费品零售额1642.24亿元，增长15.7%；乡村消费品零售额156.75亿元，增长13.8%。

按行业划分，批发和零售业零售额1553.37亿元，增长14.9%；住宿和餐饮业零售额245.62亿元，增长19.5%。

在限额以上批发和零售业中，食品类零售额增长18.0%，服装、鞋帽、针纺织品类增长15.7%，金银珠宝类增长22.5%，家用电器和音像制品类增长2.4%，家具类增长7.0%，石油及制品类增长22.5%，汽车类增长4.2%。

六、对外经济

货物进出口总额251.71亿美元，比上年增长10.3%。其中，出口193.47亿美元，增长15.0%；进口58.24亿美元，下降2.8%。口岸进出口货运量4112万吨，增长18.6%。

按登记注册类型划分，国有企业进出口68.82亿美元，增长0.1%；集体企业2.74亿美元，增长24.9%；外商投资企业2.44亿美元，下降26.7%；私营企业177.70亿美元，增长15.4%。

新批准设立外商直接投资企业56个，比上年增长12.0%。合同使用外商直接投资项目55个，下降20.3%；实际利用外商直接投资4.08亿美元，增长26.9%。

表 3: 2012 年货物进出口总额及增速

单位：亿美元

指　标	绝对数	比上年增长%
货物进出口总额	251.71	10.3
货物出口额	193.47	15.0
其中：一般贸易	70.09	47.0
加工贸易	1.91	-18.6
边境小额贸易	89.20	1.1
其中：机电产品	44.45	42.3
高新技术产品	2.09	20.6
货物进口额	58.24	-2.8
其中：一般贸易	14.43	-15.5
加工贸易	0.68	1.3 倍
边境小额贸易	40.84	1.6
其中：机电产品	5.46	-21.8
高新技术产品	1.14	-54.1

七、交通、邮电和旅游

铁路货运量6933万吨，比上年增长0.4%；公路货运量61850万吨，增长10.5%；民航货物吞吐量14.30万吨，增长23.3%。

铁路客运量2162万人，增长8.0%；公路客运量52473万人，增长9.5%；民航旅客吞吐量1727.60万人，增长21.4%。

年末铁路营业里程4914公里，增长9.7%；公路里程16.59万公里，增长6.9%，其中，高速公路2276.80公里，增长56.1%。

年末民用汽车保有量211.07万辆（包括三轮车和低速货车），增长24.3%，其中，私人汽车147.46万辆，增长30.3%。

电信业务总量246.67亿元，增长16.0%；邮政业务总量18.17亿元，增长31.3%。年末固定电话用户540.10万户，下降0.1%。固定电话普及率每百人24.5部。新增移动电话用户337.60万户，年末达到2008.50万户，其中，3G移动电话用户397万户。移动电话普及率每百人90.9部。互联网宽带用户255万户，增长22.1%。

接待入境旅游149.80万人次，比上年增长13.1%；旅游外汇收入5.51亿美元，增长18.4%。接待国内旅游4711万人次，增长23.0%；国内旅游收入542亿元，增长31.8%。

八、财政和金融

公共财政预算收入908.97亿元，比上年增长26.2%，其中，税收收入698.93亿元，增长17.8%。地方财政收入1251.64亿元，增长20.3%。全口径财政收入1920.91亿元，增长16.1%。

公共财政预算支出2720.07亿元，增长19.1%。地方财政支出3080.22亿元，增长18.5%。

年末金融机构（含外资）人民币各项存款余额12330.89亿元，比年初增加1943.67 亿元，比上年增长18.7%。其中，单位存款余额6588.72亿元，增长18.2%；个人存款余额5305.81亿元，增长19.7%。

年末金融机构（含外资）人民币各项贷款余额7914.00亿元，比年初增加1640.93亿元，增长26.2%。其中，短期贷款2759.29亿元，增长22.6%；中长期贷款4635.42亿元，增长23.4%。个人消费贷款752.90亿元，增长24.7%。

年末拥有境内上市公司39 家，比上年增加2家，总股本266.68亿股，比上年增长15.1%；股票市价总值2520.93亿元，增长12.9%。全年通过发行、配售股票共筹集资金204.29亿元，增长30.3%。

法人证券公司1家，证券营业部62家，证券交易额4000.32亿元；期货公司2家，期货营业部10家，期货交易额8851.68亿元。

保险公司各项保费收入235.56亿元，比上年增长15.7%。其中，寿险113.68亿元，增长10.5%；财产险93.68亿元，增长19.3%；健康险19.19亿元，增长25.3%；意外伤害险9.02亿元，增长30.3%。

各类保险赔款及给付支出80.12亿元，增长39.4%。其中，财产险赔款50.34亿元，增长47.1%；寿险给付20.33亿元，增长31.1%；健康险赔付7.22亿元，增长15.8%；意外伤害险赔付2.22亿元，增长47.5%。

九、教育和科学技术

年末共有普通高等学校34所，比上年增加2所。全年研究生教育招生5701人，增长14.7%；在校研究生15456人，增长9.6%；毕业生4073人，增长19.1%。本专科招生7.80万人，增长4.9%；在校生26.87 万人，增长3.9%；毕业生6.46万人，增长1.2%。

各类中等职业教育招生8.68万人，下降3.8%；在校生23.53万人，下降3.2%；毕业生7.13万人，增长10.5%。普通高中招生15.53万人，下降0.8%；在校生44.07万人，增长1.8%；毕业生13.51万人，增长4.3%。初中招生31.44万人，下降3.5%；在校生94.32万人，下降3.4 %；毕业生31.95万人，下降2.7%。小学招生33.17万人，增长2.9%；在校生190.08万人，下降1.0%；毕业生32.10万人，下降2.0%。特殊教育招生1137人，增长21.1%；在校生4909人，增长3.7%。幼儿园在园幼儿69.43万人，增长6.6%。

小学学龄儿童净入学率99.8%；小学毕业生升入初中升学率97.9%；初中阶段适龄少年净入学率97.7%；初中毕业升入高中阶段升学率84.7%。

安排自治区级科技计划项目1924项，其中，科技支撑计划167项；高技术研究发展计划114项；科技兴新项目131项；科技成果转化专项资金项目52项；科技中小企业技术创新基金项目134项。共获得省部级以上科技成果236项。

年末拥有县以上部门属研究与技术开发机构118个。其中，自然科学研究与技术开发机构93个，科技信息与文献机构8个，社会与人文科学领域研究与技术开发机构6个，转制科学研究与技术开发机构11个。

年末拥有重点实验室33个，批准成立的工程技术研究中心 19个，其中，国家级4 个。组建期内的工程技术中心73个。自治区科技成果转化基地30个。

年末拥有高新技术企业160个，自治区级高新技术工业园区4个。生产力促进中心61个，其中，国家级示范中心9 个。国家级创新型企业5个，国家级创新型试点企业7个。

年末受理专利申请7044项。其中，受理发明专利申请1679项，占23.8%；获得专利授权3440 项，其中，获得发明专利授权451项，占13.1%。签订技术合同1532项，技术合同成交金额5.49亿元，其中，技术交易额5.33亿元。

十、文化和体育

年末共有艺术表演团体109 个，文化馆116个，公共图书馆105个，博物馆72个，国家综合档案馆109个。拥有广播电台6 座，电视台8 座，广播电视台88座，中、短波广播发射台和转播台64座。广播综合人口覆盖率95.34%。电视综合人口覆盖率95.62%。有线电视用户216.81万户，增长5.4%，其中，有线数字电视用户200.28 万户，增长7.6%。拍摄故事片1 部，译制少数民族语故事片256部。广播电视农村直播卫星用户121.51万户。

建成11个县级全民健身活动中心，16个乡镇农民体育健身工程，5个全国乡镇农民体育健身示范工程，1093个行政村农牧民体育健身工程，2个体育公园和3个全民健身户外活动基地；在国际比赛中荣获金牌3枚，银牌3枚，铜牌1枚，在全国比赛中荣获金牌21枚，银牌24 枚，铜牌44枚；销售体育彩票13.17亿元，增长9.48%，筹集体彩公益金3.30亿元。

十一、人口与人民生活

年末总人口2232.78万人，其中，城镇人口981.98万人，乡村人口1250.80万人。城镇化率44.0%。全年出生人口34.21万人，出生率15.32‰；死亡人口10万人，死亡率4.48 ‰。人口自然增长率10.84‰。

城镇居民人均可支配收入17921元，比上年增长15.5%。人均家庭总收入20195元，增长14.5%，其中，工资性收入14432元，增长14.1%；经营净收入1633元，增长15.6%；财产性收入146元，下降2.4%；转移性收入3984元，增长16.6%。人均消费性支出13892元，增长17.3%，其中，人均食品支出5239元，增长15.5%。

农村居民人均纯收入6394元，比上年增长17.5%，其中，工资性纯收入1008 元，增长25.3%；家庭经营纯收入4239元，增长9.1%；转移性纯收入976元，增长61.8%；财产性纯收入171元，增长16.0%。人均生活消费支出5245元，增长19.3%，其中，人均食品支出1891元，增长19.0%。

十二、劳动就业和社会保险

预计年末就业人员1010.44万人，比上年增加57.10万人，增长6.0%。全年通过各种途径实现城镇就业再就业46.73万人，其中，就业困难人员实现就业7.10万人。消除“零就业”家庭4.35万户，帮助实现就业4.96万人。城镇登记失业率3.4%。

年末参加职工基本养老保险312.16万人，增加20.17万人。其中，在职人员228.86万人，增加14.20万人；离退休人员83.30万人，增加5.97万人。

参加城镇居民社会养老保险31.62万人，增加4.13万人。

参加新型农村社会养老保险497.09万人，增加6.51万人。

参加城镇基本医疗保险629.15万人，增加23.74万人，其中，城镇职工342.56万人，增加19.83万人；城镇居民286.59万人，增加3.91万人。

参加失业保险208.95万人，增加12.23万人。

参加工伤保险225.95万人，增加17.77万人，其中，参加工伤保险农民工40.70万人，增加4.10万人。

参加生育保险217.96万人，增加11.86万人。

城镇居民中有85.70万人得到政府最低生活保障救济。年末各类收养性社会福利单位565个，拥有床位4.14万张，增长9.5%；收养各类人员3.06万人。社区服务机构总数1433个，其中，综合性社区服务中心193个，比上年增加11个。全年销售福利彩票27.67亿元，增长22.8%；筹集公益金8.06亿元，增长22.1%。

直接接受社会捐赠1118.72万元，增长2.5倍。

十三、资源、环境和安全生产

已发现矿种138种。查明有资源储量的矿种97种，其中，能源矿产6种，金属矿产31种，非金属矿产60种。新发现大中型矿产地22处，其中，能源矿产地12 处，金属矿产地10 处。新增查明资源储量23种，其中，煤炭储量3070亿吨。

在监测的19个城市中，有11个城市空气质量达到国家Ⅱ级以上标准；城市空气质量好于Ⅱ级的优良天数占80.6%。首府乌鲁木齐市空气质量好于Ⅱ级的优良天数占79.8%，比上年提高4.2个百分点。

在监测的79 条河流171个断面中，Ⅰ～Ⅲ类优良水质断面比例为 94.7%，提高1.2个百分点；Ⅳ～Ⅴ类轻中度污染水质断面比例为3.0%，下降0.6个百分点；劣Ⅴ类重度污染水质断面比例为2.3 %，下降0.6个百分点。

在监测的32座湖库中，Ⅰ～Ⅲ类优良水质湖库占71.9%，比上年提高9.4个百分点；Ⅳ～Ⅴ类轻中度污染水质湖区占6.2%，下降12.5个百分点；劣Ⅴ类重度污染水质湖库占21.9%，上升3.1个百分点。

省级以上自然保护区29个，保护区总面积2141.06 万公顷，占新疆国土总面积的12.9%，其中，国家级自然保护区9个，自治区级20个。

共发生各类安全生产事故12542起，比上年上升18.0%。死亡2321人，下降3.1%。亿元GDP安全生产事故死亡率0.31，下降13.9 %；工矿商贸十万从业人员生产安全事故死亡率6.2，下降12.7%；道路交通万车死亡率5.07，下降21.6%；煤矿百万吨死亡率0.39，下降49.4%。

注释：

[1]本公报中数据为初步统计数。

[2]地区生产总值（GDP）、各产业增加值及建筑业总产值绝对数按现价计算，增长速度按可比价格计算。

[3]农产品生产价格是指农产品生产者直接出售其产品时的价格

[4]根据2012年政府收支分类科目，一般预算收入及支出调整为公共财政预算收入及支出。

[5]科技、文化、劳动就业和社会保障数据不含兵团。

资料来源：本公报中主要数据来源于自治区统计局和国家统计局新疆调查总队，其他数据来源于相关部门。其中，农业机械动力来源于自治区农机局；利用外资数据来源于自治区商务厅；货物进出口总额及口岸进出口货运量来源于乌鲁木齐海关；铁路客货运量及运输周转量、年末营业里程数据来源于乌鲁木齐铁路局；公路客货运量及公路线路年末营业里程数据来源于自治区交通运输厅；民航客、货运吞吐量来源于新疆（机场）集团有限公司；民用汽车数据来源于自治区公安厅；邮政业务总量数据来源于自治区邮政公司；电信业务数据来源于自治区通讯管理局；国际、国内旅游数据来源于自治区旅游局；财政数据来源于自治区财政厅；金融信贷数据来源于中国人民银行乌鲁木齐中心支行；上市公司数据来源于中国证券监督管理委员会新疆监管局；保险业数据来源于中国保监会新疆监管局；教育数据来源于自治区教育厅；艺术表演团体、博物馆、公共图书馆、文化馆数据来源于自治区文化厅；广播、电视、电影数据来源于自治区广播电视总局；档案数据来源于自治区档案局；体育数据来源于自治区体育局；就业与社会保障数据来源于自治区人力资源和社会保障厅；卫生、新农合数据来源于自治区卫生厅；销售福利彩票及筹集公益金数据来源于自治区福利彩票发行中心；矿产资源数据来源于自治区国土资源厅；环境监测及自然保护区数据来源于自治区环境保护厅；安全生产数据来源于自治区安全监督管理局。

Statistical Communique on the 2012 National Economic & Social Development of the Xinjiang Uygur Autonomous Region

In 2012, under the correct leadership of the Autonomous Region Party Committee and the People's Government, meet and learn the spirit of the eighteen party as the main task, conscientiously implement the central work conference in Xinjiang and the Eighth Party Congress of the autonomous region spirit, actively respond to the complex changes in the domestic and international environment, the general tone firmly grasp great-leap-forward development and long period of stability two historical tasks, truth-seeking, innovation, speeding up major infrastructure, basic industries and key livelihood projects, and made new achievements in economic and social development, people's livelihood construction has made new achievements in reform and innovation to achieve new breakthroughs.

I. General Outlook

According to the Preliminary statistics, the gross domestic product (GDP) of Xinjiang was 750.531 billion yuan,up by 12% over the previous year, of which, the added value of the primary industry was 132.057 billion yuan,up by 7.0%; that of the secondary industry was 348.156 billion yuan,up by 13.7%; and that of the tertiary industry was 270.318 billion yuan,up by 12.3% over the previous year.

The permanent-population-based per-capita GDP reached 33796 yuan, up by 10.8% over the previous year,equivalent to US$ 5356 at current exchange rate.

The total consumer price index of the year was up by 3.8% over the previous year, of which,the price of food was up by 7.6%.

The ex-Factory price index of industrial product was down by 3.1%, of which, light industry was down by 5.9%, heavy industry was down by 2.6%. The purchasing price of industrial product was down by 2.1%. The production price of agriculture products increased up by 6.2%. The price of fixed asset investment was up by 0.6%.

Table 1: Span of rise and decrease on the consumer price indices

unit: %

Items	Span of rise and decrease
Consumer price index	3.8
Rural	3.4
Uban	4.7
Food	7.6
# Grain	7.3
Meal poultry and processed products	5.9
Oil and Fat	5.3
Eggs	2.1
Aquatic products	5.2
Greengrocery	17.6
Tobacco,Liquor and Articles	5.6
Clothing	1.9
Household Facilities, Articles and Services	1.9
Health Care and Personal Articles	2.9
Transportation and Communication	-0.5
Recreation, Education and Culture Articles	0.1
Residence	2.8

II. Agriculture

The total sown areas of farm crops was 77.0582 million mus,up by 3.1% over the previous year; of which, The sown area of grain crops was 31.9676 million mus, up by 4.1%; The sown area of cotton crops was 25.8120 million mus, up by 5.1%; The sown area of oil bearing crops was 3.6351 million mus,down by 8.3%; The sown area of sugar crops was 1.2395 million mus, up by 9.5% over the previous year.

The total output of grain was 1325.68 ten thousand tons,up by 0.4% over the previous year; The output of cotton was 353.95 ten thousand tons,up by 22.2% over the previous year; The output of oil-bearing crops was 59.04 ten thousand tons, down by 11.6%; The output of sugar was 577.19 ten thousand tons,up by 11.2%. The output of fruit was 1222.10 ten thousand tons, up by 18.0%, of which, the output of garden fruit was

736.74ten thousand tons, an increase of 22.5%.

At the end of the year, livestock (only)were 43.3325 million heads. The annual livestock slaughter were 37.3730 heads, up by 3.6%. Total meat output were 1.3423 million tons, up by 5.5%, of which, the mutton output were 480.1 thousand tons, up by 3.5%; the beef output were 361.6 thousan tons, up by 7%; The pork output were 301.5 thousand tons,up by 1.2%. The output of Milk were 1322.1 thousand tons, up by 1.3%. The production of egg were 258.9 thousand tons, up by 1.1%. Aquatic products were 125.3 thousand tons, up by 7.2%.

The year-end total agricultural machinery power was 19.6827 million kilowatt,up by 9.6% over the previous year. There were 34.26 ten thousand large and medium-size tractors,up by 16.1%; and 33.49 ten thousand small-size tractors,down by 4.1%. The consumption of chemical fertilizer was 192.27ten thousand tons(100% equivalent),up by 4.9%. Electricity consumed in rural areas was 7.581 billion kwh, up by 5.8%.

III. Industry and Construction

The total value-added of the industrial sector was 285.006 billion yuan,up by 12.7% over the previous year.The added value of industrial enterprises above designated size was 272.416 billion yuan, up by 12.7%.

Among the ten proportion of industrial enterprises above designated,Minging and processing of non-ferrous metal ores was 10.444 billion yuan, up by 43.4%; Production of electric power was 25.762 billion yuan, up by 31.8%; Manufacture of chemical products was 28.083 billion yuan, up by 25.2%;iron and steel industry was 9.664 billion yuan,up by 18.5; Minging of coal was 14.161 billion yuan, up by 17.4%; Manufacture of textile was 4.030 billion yuan, up by 15.1%; Processing of food from agriculture products was 4.466 billion yuan, up by 11.6%; equipment manufactory industry was 5.688 billion yuan, up by 11.3%; Manufacture of cars was 0.478 billion yuan ,up by three times; oil industry was 138.617 billion, up by 4.1%.

The value of delivered exported goods creat by industrial enterprises above designated size was 4.153 billion yuan, down by 31.5%. The profits achieved to 84.167 billion yuan, down by 7.5%.

The added value of the construction sector was 63.150 billion yuan, up by 18.2% over the previous year, General contracting and special contracting construction enterprises with qualification grade reaped profits of 162.231 billion yuan, up by 22.9%.

Table2: Output of Major Industrial Products 2012

Item	Unit	Output	Increase over 2011(%)
Coal	10 000 tons	13646.99	13.8
Crude oil	10 000 tons	2670.68	2.1
Natural gas	100 million cubic meters	253.01	7.5
Processed oil	10 000 tons	2426.90	1.6
Ethylene	10 000 tons	127.09	22.2
Electricity	100 million kilowatt-hours	1187.48	35.7
Refind sugar	10 000 tons	53.64	16.3
Cigarettes	100 million pieces	170.00	6.3
Can	10 000 tons	69.41	-39.9
#Tomato	10 000 tons	62.87	-44.1
Yarn	10 000 tons	40.22	0.8
Cloth	10 000meters	6675.72	-8.6
Machine-made paper and paperbord	10 000 tons	41.05	-2.9
Chemical fertilizers	10 000 tons	304.17	30.2
Ten non-ferrous	10 000 tons	108.85	1.9times
Electrolytic aluminium	10 000 tons	97.07	2.3 times
Crude steel	10 000 tons	1138.23	27.5
Rolled steel	10 000 tons	1289.84	30.9
Pig Iron	10 000 tons	1328.32	22.0
Cement	kilovolt-ampere	4315.93	36.1
Transformer	10 000 tons	6194.52	27.6
Chemical Fiber	10 000 tons	44.99	35.9
Plastics	10 000 tons	139.97	34.4
Clothing	10 000 sets	2826.38	55.3
Light leather	square meters	518.04	8.1

IV. Investment in Fixed Asset

The completed investment in fixed assets was 625.838 billion yuan,up by 35.1% over the previous year. In terms of urban and rural areas,that in urban areas was 559.380 billion yuan, up by 35.0%; that in rural areas was 66.458 billion yuan, up by 36.3%.

In terms of three industries, the investment in the primary industry was 11.056 billion yuan,up by 8.6%; the investment in the secondary industry was 307.856 billion yuan,up by 32.9%,The tertiary industry investment was 240.468 billion yuan, up by 37.7%. Among the investment in the secondary industry, the investment in industry was 298.809 billion yuan,up by 34.6%, Of which ,the investment in manufature was 152.367 billion yuan ,up by 40.9%.

The investment in the urban fixed assets,centre investment was 328.107 billion yuan,up by 30.8%,local investment was 226.879 billion yuan, up by 43.8%. the people's livelihood project investment, such as Home to Enrich People, Settle to Develop Animal Husbandry, and Affordable Housing Construction, was138.179 billion yuan, up by 41.0%.investment of infrastructure was 163.982 billion yuan,up by 36.5%.

The investment in real estate development was 60.609 billion yuan,up by 17.4% over the previous year. The investment of residential was 44.427 billion yuan,up by 6.7%,The investment of office building was 1.208 billion yuan,down by 22.2%;The commercial business premises was 9.761 billion yuan,up by 70.5%. The floor space of buildings under construction was 68.9654 million square meters, up by 25.8%. The floor space of building completed was 17.3619 million square meters, up by 36.7%. The total sales area of commercial buildings for the whole year reached 14.3030million square meters,down by 17.2%. The total sales of commercial building was 56.045 billion yuan,down by 8.6%.

V. Wholesale and Retail Trades & Hotels and Catering Service

The total retail sales of consumer goods reached 179.899 billion yuan,up by 15.5% over the previous year. Really up by 11.8%.

In terms of urban and rural areas,the retail sales of consumer goods in urban areas reached 164.224 billion yuan,up by15.7%; and the retail sales of consumer goods in rural areas reached 15.675 billion yuan,up by 13.8%.

In terms of different sectors,the sales of the wholesale and retail trade reached 155.337 billion yuan, up by 14.9%; the sales of the accommodation and catering service was 24.562billion yuan,up by 19.5%.

In the enterprises of wholesale retailsale trade, the volume of food retail sales increased by 18.0%;the volume of clothing,shoses & hat and textiles, up by 15.7%; gold, silver and jewelry, up by 22.5%; household appliance and audiovisual products, up by 2.4%; furniture, up by 7.0%; petroleum product, up by 22.5%; automobiles, up by4.2%.

VI. Foreign Economic Cooperation

The total value of import and export reached US$ 25.171 billion,up by 10.3% over the previous year. Of which,the value of export was US$ 19.347 billion, up by 15.0%; and the value of import was US$ 5.824 billion,down by 2.8%. The volume of import and export was 41.12 million tons,up by 18.6%.

In terms of different registration type,the value of import and export in centre enterprises was 6.882 US$ billion,up by 0.1%; the value of import and export in collection enterprises was US$274 million,up by 24.9%; the value of import and export in foreign investment enterprises was US$244 million,down by 26.7%;the value of import and export in private enterprises was US$17.770 billion,up by 15.4%.

The number of newly estabishied foeign directly investment enterprises was 56, up by 12.0% over the previous year. The number of using the projects invested directly by foreign business was 55,down by 20.3%; Foreign directly investment actually utilized this year stood at US$ 408 million, up by 26.9%.

Table3: Total Value of Imports and Exports and Growth Rates

unit: US$ 100 million

Item	2012	Increase over 2011(%)
Total value of imports and exports	251.71	10.3
Total exports	193.47	15.0
#Ordinary trade	70.09	47.0
Processing trade	1.91	-18.6
Frontier small trade	89.20	1.1
#mechanical and electrical products	44.45	42.3
New and high-tech products	2.09	20.6
Total imports	58.24	-2.8
#Ordinary trade	14.43	-15.5
Processing trade	0.68	128.1
Frontier small trade	40.84	1.6
#mechanical and electrical products	5.46	-21.8
New and high-tech products	1.14	-54.1

VII. Transportation,Postal & Telecommunication and Tourism

The freight turnover by railways was 69.33 million tons,up by 0.4%; that by highways 618.50 million tons,up by 10.5%; that by civil aviation 14.30 ten thousands tons,up by 23.3%;

Passenger traffic by railways was 21.62 million passengers,up by 8.0%;that by highways 524.73million passengers,up by 9.5%; that by civil aviation 17.2760 million passengers,up by 21.4%.

At the end of the year, railway in operation reached 4914

kilometers,up by 9.7%; Total civil aviation routes reached 16.59 ten thousand kilometers,up by 6.9%,of which, Length of highways was 22.7680 ten thousand kilometers,up by 56.1%.

At the end of the year, there were 211.07 ten thousand civilian automobiles, up by 24.3%, of which, there were 147.46 ten thousand private automobiles, up by 30.3%.

The total volume of telecommunication was 24.667 billion yuan,up by 16.0% over the previous year. The total volume of post stood at 1.817 billion yuan,up by 31.3%. Number of fixed phone users 5.4010 million,down by 0.1%. The popularization rate of fixed telephone was 24.5 sets/100 persons,The number of newly-increased mobile users was 3.3760 million, Number of mobile phone users 20.0850 million,of which,the number of 3G mobile phone uses was 3.97 million,The popularization rate of mobile telephone was 90.9 sets/100 persons. Year-end Internet customer 2.55 million,up by 22.1%.

Tourists through customs to Xinjiang numbered 149.80 ten thousand, up by 13.1%. Forien exchange income from tourism amounted to US$ 551 million, up by 18.4%. In the year, Xinjiang recevied 4711 ten thousand forien tourists, increased by 23.0% over the previous year. Income from foreign tourists amounted 54.2 billion yuan, up by 31.8%.

VIII. Finance,Banking and Insurance

The public financial budget revenue was 90.897billion yuan, up by 26.2%. Of which, total taxes were 69.893 billion yuan, up by 17.8% over the previous year. The Local government revenue was 125.164 billion yuan, up by 20.3%. The total government revenue was 192.091 billion yuan ,up by 16.1%.

The general budgetary expenditure was 272.007 billion yuan,up by 19.1%.The Local government expenditure reached 308.022 billion yuan,up by 18.5%.

By the end of 2012,savings deposits of all kinds in financial institutions reached 1233.089 billion yuan,increase by 194.367 billion yuan over the year of beginning, up by 18.7% over the previous year. Of which,units savings deposits were 658.872 billion yuan,up by 18.2%; Personal savings deposits were 530.581 billion yuan, up by 19.7%.

Loans of all kinds in financial institutions were 791.40 billion yuan, increase by 164.093 billion yuan over the beginning, up by 26.2%; of which, Loans of short-term were 275.929 billion yuan, up by 22.6%; loan of medium-and long-term were 463.542 billion yuan,up by 23.4%. Individual consumption loans were 75.290 billion yuan, up by 24.7%.

At the end of 2012, there were 39 listed companies, increase by 2 over the previous year; total volume issued were 26.668 billion shares, up by 15.1%; Total market capitalization were 252.093 billion yuan, up by 12.9%. In the year of 2012, the refinancing totaled 20.429 billion yuan,up by 30.3%.

There was 1 Legal person securities companies, 62 securities business department securities ,Transactions of volume were 400.032 billion yuan, 2 Futures Company, 10 futures business department, Total futures trading volume were 885.168 billion yuan.

The total premium of insurance companies reached 23.556 billion yuan,up by 15.7% over the previous year. of the total,life insurance premium was 11.368 billion yuan,up by 10.5%; Property insurance premium 9.368 billion yuan, up by 19.3%; health and casualty insurance premium were 1.919 billion yuan,up by25.3%; that against health and accidental injury were 902 million yuan, up by 30.3%.

Insurance companies paid an indemnity of 8.012 billion yuan as reparation for various property and life insurance programs, up by 39.4%, of which, and that against property was 5.034 billion yuan, up by 47.1%, the indemnity against life insurance was 2.033billion yuan, up by 31.1%; that against health were 722 million yuan, up by 15.8%, and accidental injury were 222million yuan, up by 47.5%.

IX. Education and Scientific Technology

By the end of 2012,there were totally 34 general colleges and universities,an increase by 2.The enrollment of postgraduate students were 5701 new entrants,up by 14.7%; the enrollment of post- graduate students was 15456,up by 9.6%, graduates students were 4073, up by 19.1%. The enrollment of regular under-graduates and college student were 7.80 ten thousand, up by 4.9%; the enrollment of students was 26.87 ten thousand,up by 3.9%, graduates students were 6.46 ten thousand,up by 1.2%.

The enrollment of vocational secondary education was 8.68 ten thousand, down by 3.8%;enrollment were 23.53 ten thousand, down by 3.2%, graduates students were7.13 ten thousand,up by 10.5%. The enrollment of general senior high schools were 155.3 thousand, down by 0.8%; enrollment were 440.7thousand, up by 1.8%; graduates students were 135.1 thousand,up by 4.3%.The enrollment of The junior middle school students were 314.4 thousand,down by 3.5%;enrollment were 943.2 thousand,down by 3.4.with 319.5 thousand graduates, down by 2.7%. Students enrolled in junior secondary schools totaled 331.7 thousand, up by 2.9%; enrollment were

1900.8 thousand, down by 1.0%; with 321.0 thousand graduates, down by 2.0%. Enrollment of special education were 1137,up by 21.1%.enrollment were 4909,up by 3.7%.There were 694.3thousand pre-school children in kindergartens,up by 6.6%.

The enrollment rate of school-age children reached 99.8%. Enrollment rate of junior secondary school-age youth was 97.9%. Junior middle school net enrollment rate of school-age children was 97.7%Promotion rate from junior sendary school to senior secondary school was 84.7%.

In 2012, the autonomous region formulated 1924 sci-tech project plans, undertook 167 project plans of the national level, obtained 114 scientific and technological achievements of the provincial level or above, built 131 scientific research and technological development institutions above the county level .

At the end of the year,There were 118 above the County Department of research and technological development institutions, the natural scientific research and technological development institutions were 93, science and technology information and literature were 8, social sciences and Humanities Research and technological development institutions were 6, research of science and technology development institutions were 11.

By the end of 2012, there were 33 key laboratories, founded 19 engineering and technological research centers, of which, 4 national level. 73 engineering and technological centers which are still at the forming stage, and 30bases for the commercialization of research findings at the level of autonomous region were established.

By the end of 2012, we had 160 high and new tech enterprises, productivity promotion centers were founded, of which, there are 9 state-level demonstration centers, 5 national innovative enterprises and 7 national innovative enterprises under experiment.

There are totally 7044 patent applications, of which, there are 1679 for a patent for invention taking up 23.8%, and 3440 patent licenses, including 451invention patent licenses accounting for 13.1%. 1532 technology contracts were signed, and the turnover reached 549 million yuan, of which, the volume of technology trade was 533 million yuan.

X. Culture, Public Health and Sports

At the end of 2012,there were 109 performance art guoups,there were 116 cutural centers, 105 public library, 72 museums;109 national comprehensive archives.There were 6 radio broadcasting stations, 8 television stations,88 radio and telivision stations. radio broadcasting coverage rate was 95.34%; television coverage rate was 95.62%. Number of users of cable television was 216.81 ten thousand, up by 5.4%, of which, number of Users of digital TV was 200.28ten thousand, up by 7.6%. The Autonomous Region shot 1 feature movie, translated and edited 256 feature movies of minority language.Number of users of radio and television broadcast statellite 121.51 ten thousands.

There were 11 the rural fitnes centers,the farm fitness projects were 16,the national farm fitness projects were 5,the administrative village farmer sport fitness projects were 1093,the sport park were 2. Fitness outdoor activity base were 3.Fitness outdoor activity base were 3 In the international competition Athletes from the Autonomous Region won 3gold medal, 3 silver medal, 1 bronze medal. In the national competition Athletes from the Autonomous Region in matches home and abroad won 21gold medals, 24 silver medals, 44 bronze medals.;Sales of sports lottery were 1.317 billion yuan, raise lottery public welfare fund were 330 million yuan.

XI. Populatin and People's Life

By the end of 2012,the population of autonomous region was 22.3278 million, of which, the population in urban areas was9.8198million, rural areas 12.5080 million; the urbanization rate was 44.0%.The birth population was 34.21 ten thousand, and the birthrate was 15.32‰; the dead population was 10ten thousand, and the deathrate was 4.48‰. The natural growth rate of population was 10.84‰.

The per capital disposable income of urban residents reached 17921 yuan,up by 15.5% over the previous year. The per capital family income reached 20195 yuan,up by 14.5%,Of which, income of salary and wage was 14432 yuan, up by 14.1%, Net operating income were 1633 yuan, up by 15.6%, income of property were 146 yuan, down by 2.4, metastatic income were 3984 yuan, up by 16.6%.per capital annual expenditure was 13892 yuan, up by 17.3%, of which,the per capital annual food expenditure was 5239 yuan, up by 15.5%.

The per capital auunal net income of rural households was 6394 yuan, up by 17.5%, of which, income of salaries and wages was 1008 yuan, up by 25.3%; income from household operations was 4239 yuan, up by 9.1%; Income from transfers was 976 yuan, up by 61.8%; Income from properties was 171yuan, up by 16.0%. Per capita consumption expenditure of rural households was5245 yuan, up by 19.3% over the previous year, of which, the per capital annual food expenditure was 1891 yuan, up by 19.0%.

XII.Employment and Social Security

Number of employed person was 10.1044 million at year-end,an increase by 57.10 ten thousands,up by 6.0%., number of urban employed persons were 46.73 ten thousand, of which,the reemployment of zero-employment workers was 7.10 ten thousand. The elimination of zero employment family 43500 households, helping to realize the employment of 4.96 ten thousand people.Registered unemployment rate in urban areas was 3.4%.

A total of 3.1216 million people participated in basic social endowment insurance programs,an increase by 20.17ten thousands. Among them, 2.2886million were employees, an increase by 14.20 ten thousands. 83.30ten thousand were retirees, an increase of 5.97 ten thousand.

Receive basic social endowment insurance was 31.62 ten thousand, an increase of 4.13 ten thousand.

Receive the new type of rural social endowment insrance was 4.9709 million,an increase of 6.51 ten thousands.

The population covered by basic medical insurance programs was 6.2915 million, an increase of 23.74 ten thousand people. Among them, 3.4256 million were urban workers, 2.8659 million were urban residents,an increase of 3.91 ten thousands.

A total of 2.0895 million people participated in unemployment insurance programs,an increase of 12.23 ten thousand.

Receive the industrial injury insurance was 2.2595 million,an incraese of 17.77 ten thousand,among them,migrant of industrial injury insurance received 40.70 ten thousand an increase of 4.10 ten thousand people.

people participated in the maternity insurance was 2.1796 million,an increase of 11.86 ten thousand.

85.70 ten thousand people recevied basic welfare for urban residents. Number of social welfare institutions were 565 at the end of year, Number of beds were 4.14 ten thousand in social welfare institutions at the end of year, up by 9.5%; Number of inmates were 3.06 ten thousand, The number of community service equipment was 1433. of which, The number of comprehensive community service center were 193, increase by 11 than previous year.Revenue from social welfare lottery tickets were 2.767 billion yuan, up by 22.8%; Social welfare fund were 806 million yuan, up by22.1%. 11.1872 million yuan of donatioas were received from the general public,up by 2.5 times.

XIII. Resources Environment and Safe production

138 mineral products were found, of which, 97mineral products have resources. Of which, there were 6 energy minerals, 31 metal minerals, and 60 non-metal minerals. 22 large-medium orefield were discovered, of which, there were 12 energy resouses mines, 10metal mine.An increase of 23 mineral products have resources,of which,coal resources were 307.0 billion tons.

In the 19 monitored cities, 11 cities had th. air quality reach national standard Grade II. In the Autonomous Region about 80.6% of the year the air quality was better than Grade II. And 79.8% of the year in Urmqi the air quality was better than Grade II,up by 4.2% over the previous year.

Monitoring of water quality on 171 sections of the 79rivers showed that good quality water of standard Grade I ~III accounted for 94.7%, up by 1.2%. Quality water of standard Grade IV~V accounted for 3.0%, down by 0.6%, Quality water of standard Grade V accounted for 2.3%, down by 0.6%.

Monitoring of water quality of 32 lakes and reservoirs showed that good quality water of standard Grade I ~III accounted for 71.9%,up by 9.4%, Quality water of standard Grade IV~V accounted for 6.2%. down by 12.5%, Quality water of standard Grade V accounted for 21.9%, up by 3.1%.

There were 29 national and regional nature reserves. Area of nature reserves were 2141.06ten thousand sqkm, proportion of nature reserves in total area of territory was 12.9%, of which, there were 9 national nature reserves.20 autonomous region nature reserves.

There were 12542 safety accidents occurred, up by18.0%, with 2321person died, decrease of 3.1%. The 100-million-GDP-based death rate in production safety accidents was 0.31, down by 13.9% over the previous year; among every 100 000 employees in trade sectors, 6.20 persons died, down by 12.7%; for every 10 000 vehicles,5.07persons died, down by 21.6%; for every one million tons output of coal mines, 0.39persons died, down by 49.4%.

新疆统计年鉴
XINJIANG STATISTICAL YEARBOOK

1

综　合

GENERAL SURVEY

简要说明

本篇资料的主要内容及来源

综合篇资料主要包括新疆行政区划、国民经济和社会发展资料以及基本单位资料三部分。

行政区划资料由新疆维吾尔自治区民政厅根据国务院批准的、截止到2012年末新疆行政区划变更情况汇总整理并提供；国民经济和社会发展综合资料由新疆维吾尔自治区统计局国民经济综合统计处根据各篇主要指标加工整理而成；基本单位统计资料由新疆维吾尔自治区统计局普查中心依据基本单位年报整理提供。

Brief Introduction

Main Content and Source of Data

This chapter mainly covers three parts: the data of division of administrative areas, grass-roots units and summary data on the national economy and social development.

Data on division of administrative areas are provided by the Bureau of Civil Affairs of Xinjiang Uygur Autonomous Region.Data on grass-roots units and the national economy and social development are compiled and processed by the Department of Comprehensive statistics of the Xinjiang Bureau of Statistics using relevant.Statistical data of basic units by the Xinjiang Uygur Autonomous Region Bureau of Statistics Census Center Based on the basic unit of the annual report consolidation.

1-1 行 政 区 划

Divisions of Administrative Areas in Xinjiang Uygur Autonomous Region

单位：个 (2012 年) (unit)

区划名称	Region	地级区划数 Number of Regions at Prefecture Level	地级市 Cities at Prefecture Level	地区 Administrative Offices	自治州 Autonomous Prefectures	县级区划数 Number of Regions at County level	自治区直辖市 Cities under the Autonomous Region	地州辖市 Cities under the Prefectures
总　计	**Total**	**14**	**2**	**7**	**5**	**101**	**6**	**16**
乌鲁木齐市	Urumqi City	1	1			8		
克拉玛依市	Karamay City	1	1			4		
吐鲁番地区	Turpan Administrative Offices	1		1		3		1
哈密地区	Hami [Kumul] Administrative Offices	1		1		3		1
昌吉回族自治州	Changji Hui Autonomous Prefecture	1			1	7		2
伊犁哈萨克自治州	Ili Kazak Autonomous Prefecture	3		2	1	24		5
伊犁州直属县(市)	Counties (Cities) Direct Under Ili Prefecture	1			1	10		2
塔城地区	Tacheng [Tarbagatai] Administrative Offices	1		1		7		2
阿勒泰地区	Altay Administrative Offices	1		1		7		1
博尔塔拉自治州	Bortala Mongol Autonomous Prefecture	1			1	4		2
巴音郭楞自治州	Bayangol Mongol Autonomous Prefecture	1			1	9		1
阿克苏地区	Aksu Administrative Offices	1		1		9		1
克孜勒苏自治州	Kizilsu Kirgiz Autonomous Prefecture	1			1	4		1
喀什地区	Kashgar [Kaxgar] Administrative Offices	1		1		12		1
和田地区	Hotan Administrative Offices	1		1		8		1
石河子市	Shihezi City					1	1	
阿拉尔市	Aral City					1	1	
图木舒克市	Tumxuk City					1	1	
五家渠市	Wujiaqu City					1	1	
北屯市	Beitun City					1	1	
铁门关市	Tiemenguan City					1	1	

区划名称	Region	县级区划数 Number of Counties: 市辖区 Districts under the Jurisdiction of Cities	县 Counties	#自治县 Autonomous Counties	乡镇级区划数 Number of Regions at Town-ships Level	#镇 Town	#乡 Township	#民族乡 National Township	#街道办事处 Street Communities
总　计	**Total**	**11**	**68**	**6**	**1028**	**263**	**601**	**42**	**163**
乌鲁木齐市	Urumqi City	7	1		87	8	14	1	65
克拉玛依市	Karamay City	4			14		2		12
吐鲁番地区	Turpan Administrative Offices		2		30	11	16	1	3
哈密地区	Hami [Kumul] Administrative Offices		2	1	42	12	25	3	5
昌吉回族自治州	Changji Hui Autonomous Prefecture		5	1	79	39	31	11	9
伊犁哈萨克自治州	Ili Kazak Autonomous Prefecture		19	2	243	72	147	17	24
伊犁州直属县(市)	Counties (Cities) Direct Under Ili Prefecture		8	1	110	23	74	10	13
塔城地区	Tacheng [Tarbagatai] Administrative Offices		5	1	75	32	35	5	8
阿勒泰地区	Altay Administrative Offices		6		58	17	38	2	3
博尔塔拉自治州	Bortala Mongol Autonomous Prefecture		2		21	7	9		5
巴音郭楞自治州	Bayangol Mongol Autonomous Prefecture		8	1	90	26	59	1	5
阿克苏地区	Aksu Administrative Offices		8		95	32	53	2	10
克孜勒苏自治州	Kizilsu Kirgiz Autonomous Prefecture		3		39	6	31	1	2
喀什地区	Kashgar [Kaxgar] Administrative Offices		11	1	173	32	136	3	4
和田地区	Hotan Administrative Offices		7		95	15	76	2	4
石河子市	Shihezi City				7	1	1		5
阿拉尔市	Aral City				5		1		4
图木舒克市	Tumxuk City				3				3
五家渠市	Wujiaqu City				5	2			3
北屯市	Beitun City								
铁门关市	Tiemenguan City								

1-2 县级以上行政区划

Divisions of Administrative Areas at and above County Level

(2012 年)

<table>
<tr><th colspan="3">地、州、市名称
Name of Administrative Offices,
Autonomous Prefectures, Cities</th><th>市、县(市辖区)名称
Names of Cities and Counties (Districts under Cities)</th></tr>
<tr><td colspan="3">乌鲁木齐市
Urumqi City</td><td>天山区、沙依巴克区、新市区、水磨沟区、头屯河区、达坂城区、米东区、乌鲁木齐县
Tianshan District, Shayibak District, Xinshi District, Shui Mogou District, Tou Tunhe District, Da Bancheng District, Midong District, Urumqi County</td></tr>
<tr><td colspan="3">克拉玛依市
Karamay City</td><td>克拉玛依区、独山子区、白碱滩区、乌尔禾区
Karamay District, Dushanzi District, Bai Jiantan District, Urhe District</td></tr>
<tr><td colspan="3">吐鲁番地区
Turpan Administrative Offices</td><td>吐鲁番市、鄯善县、托克逊县
Turpan City, Shanshan [Piqan] County, Toksun County</td></tr>
<tr><td colspan="3">哈密地区
Hami [Kumul] Administrative Offices</td><td>哈密市、巴里坤哈萨克自治县、伊吾县
Hami [Kumul] City, Barkol Kazak Autonomous County, Yiwu[Araturuk] County</td></tr>
<tr><td colspan="3">昌吉回族自治州
Changji Hui Autonomous Prefecture</td><td>昌吉市、阜康市、呼图壁县、玛纳斯县、奇台县、吉木萨尔县、木垒哈萨克自治县
Changji City, Fukang City, Hutubi County, Manas County, Qitai County, Jimsar County, Mori Kazak Autonomous County</td></tr>
<tr><td rowspan="3">伊犁哈萨克自治州
Ili Kazak Autonomous Prefecture</td><td colspan="2">伊犁州直属县(市)
Counties (Cities) Direct Under Ili Prefecture</td><td>伊宁市、奎屯市、伊宁县、察布查尔锡伯自治县、霍城县、巩留县、新源县、昭苏县、特克斯县、尼勒克县
Yining [Gulja] City, Kuytun City , Yining [Gulja] County, Qapqal Xibe AutonomousCounty, Huocheng [Korgas] County, Gongliu [Tokkuzlara] County, Xinyuan [Kunes] County, Zhaosu [Mongolkure] County, Tekes County, Nilka County</td></tr>
<tr><td colspan="2">塔城地区
Tacheng [Tarbagatai] Administrative Offices</td><td>塔城市、乌苏市、额敏县、沙湾县、托里县、裕民县、和布克赛尔蒙古自治县
Tacheng [Qoqek] City, Usu City, Emin [Dorbiljin] County, Shawan County, Toli County, Yumin [Qagantokay] County, Hoboksar Mongol Autonomous County</td></tr>
<tr><td colspan="2">阿勒泰地区
Altay Administrative Offices</td><td>阿勒泰市、布尔津县、富蕴县、福海县、哈巴河县、青河县、吉木乃县
Altay City, Burqin County, Fuyun [Koktokay] County, Fuhai [Burultokay] County, Habahe [Kaba] County, Qinghe [Qinggil] County, Jeminay county</td></tr>
<tr><td colspan="3">博尔塔拉蒙古自治州
Bortala Mongol Autonomous Prefecture</td><td>博乐市、精河县、温泉县、阿拉山口市
Bole [Bortala] City, Jinghe [Jing] County, Wenquan [Arxang] County，Alashankou City</td></tr>
<tr><td colspan="3">巴音郭楞蒙古自治州
Bayangol Mongol Autonomous Prefecture</td><td>库尔勒市、轮台县、尉犁县、若羌县、且末县、焉耆回族自治县、和静县、和硕县、博湖县
Korla City, Luntai [Bugur] County, Yuli [Lopnur] County, Ruoqiang [Qarkilik] County, Qiemo [Qarqan] County, Yanqi Hui Autonomous County, Hejing County, Bohu [Bagrax] County</td></tr>
<tr><td colspan="3">阿克苏地区
Aksu Administrative Offices</td><td>阿克苏市、温宿县、库车县、沙雅县、新和县、拜城县、乌什县、阿瓦提县、柯坪县
Aksu City, Wensu [Onsu] County, Kuqa County, Xayar County, Xinhe [Toksu] County, Baicheng [Bay] County, Wushi [Uqturpan] County, Awat County, Kalpin County</td></tr>
<tr><td colspan="3">克孜勒苏柯尔克孜自治州
Kizilsu Kirgiz Autonomous Prefecture</td><td>阿图什市、阿克陶县、阿合奇县、乌恰县
Artux City, Akto County, Akqi County, Wuqia [Ulugqat] County</td></tr>
<tr><td colspan="3">喀什地区
Kashgar [Kaxgar] Administrative Offices</td><td>喀什市、疏附县、疏勒县、英吉沙县、泽普县、莎车县、叶城县、麦盖提县、岳普湖县、伽师县、巴楚县、塔什库尔干塔吉克自治县
Kashgar [Kaxgar] City, Shufu County, Shule County, Yengisar County, Zepu [Poskam] County, Shache [Yarkant] County, Yecheng [Kagilik] County, Makit County, Yopurga County, Jiashi [Payzawat] County, Bachu [Maralbexi] County, Taxkorgan Tajik Aotonomous County</td></tr>
<tr><td colspan="3">和田地区
Hotan Administrative Offices</td><td>和田市、和田县、墨玉县、皮山县、洛浦县、策勒县、于田县、民丰县
Hotan City, Hotan County, Moyu [Karakax] County, Pishan [Guma] County, Lop County, Qira County, Yutian [Keriya] County, Minfeng [niya] County</td></tr>
<tr><td rowspan="6">自治区直辖县级市</td><td rowspan="6">Municpa-l ity Country-Level City directly under the Central Govern-ment</td><td>石河子市
Shihezi City</td><td></td></tr>
<tr><td>阿拉尔市
Aral City</td><td></td></tr>
<tr><td>图木舒克市
Tumxuk City</td><td></td></tr>
<tr><td>五家渠市
Wujiaqu City</td><td></td></tr>
<tr><td>北屯市
Beitun City</td><td></td></tr>
<tr><td>铁门关市
Tiemenguan City</td><td></td></tr>
</table>

1-3 主要年份平均每天主要社会经济活动
Selected Indicators on Average Daily Social and Economic Activities in Main Years

指　　标	Item	1978	2000	2010	2011	2012
每天创造的财富	**Daily Production**					
新疆生产总值(万元)	Gross Domestic Product (10 000 yuan)	1070.4	37357.8	148971.8	181097.3	205624.9
第一产业	Primary Industry	382.7	7895.3	29551.5	31206.3	36180.0
第二产业	Secondary Industry	502.7	14728.2	71017.8	88380.8	95385.2
工　业	Industry	396.7	11469.3	59216.2	73978.1	78083.8
建筑业	Construction	106.0	3258.9	11801.6	14402.7	17301.4
第三产业	Tertiary Industry	184.9	14734.3	48402.5	61510.1	74059.4
#交通运输仓储和邮政业	Transport, Storage and Post	32.6	4072.1	6095.1	7033.4	9805.5
批发和零售业	Wholesale and Retail Trades	56.7	3016.4	7569.3	10189.0	11689.0
公共财政预算收入(万元)	General Budgetary Revenue in Local Finance (10 000 yuan)	195.6	2166.4	13714.4	19737.8	24903.2
公共财政预算支出(万元)	General Budgetary Expenditure in Local Finance (10 000 yuan)	466.3	5231.6	46545.6	62588.8	74522.4
粮食(吨)	Grain (ton)	10137.3	22153.4	31512.3	32897.3	34515.9
棉花(吨)	Cotton (ton)	150.7	4109.6	6791.8	7938.9	9697.3
油料(吨)	Oil-bearing Crops (ton)	283.0	1647.7	1825.2	1829.0	1617.5
肉类(吨)	Meat (ton)	264.4	2465.8	3335.3	3487.1	3677.5
水产品(吨)	Aquatic Products (ton)	15.6	164.6	277.0	320.3	343.2
布(万米)	Cloth (10 000 m)	76.7	76.9	41.4	20.0	18.3
原煤(吨)	Coal (ton)	29561.9	76682.1	271965.2	328540.0	373889.8
发电量(万千瓦小时)	Electricity (10 000 kwh)	580.0	5013.2	18611.5	23977.8	32533.7
原油(吨)	Crude Oil (ton)	9672.6	50641.9	70086.6	71661.1	73169.3
粗钢(吨)	Crude Steel (ton)	231.8	3005.4	22617.5	24465.2	31184.4
钢材(吨)	Steel Products (ton)	187.1	3596.1	24430.1	26990.1	35338.1
水泥(吨)	Cement (ton)	2141.1	24538.9	65780.8	86896.2	118244.7
每天消费量	**Daily National Consumption**					
最终消费(万元)	Final Consumption Expenditure (10 000 yuan)	757.2	20827.4	78508.6	96406.0	116781.1
居民消费	Resident Consumption	619.3	13488.1	43258.4	53543.3	64949.9
农村居民	Rural Household	330.9	4382.8	12501.7	15350.7	18510.7
城镇居民	Urban Household	288.4	9105.3	30756.7	38192.6	46439.2
政府消费	Government Consumption Expenditure	137.9	7339.3	35250.2	42862.7	51831.2
能源消费量(万吨标准煤)	Energy Consumption (10 000 tons of SCE)		9.1	22.7	27.2	
社会消费品零售总额(万元)	Total Retail Sales of Consumer Goods (10 000 yuan)	599.7	10260.3	36287.1	42660.0	49287.4
每天其他经济活动	**Other Daily Economic Activities**					
资本形成总额(万元)	Gross Capital Formation (10 000 yuan)	504.9	16934.9	92362.1	114036.2	158689.3
固定资产形成	Fixed Capital Formation	363.0	17756.8	88575.3	108188.2	150071.5
存货增加	Increase in Stock	141.9	-821.9	3786.9	5847.9	8617.8
全社会固定资产投资总额	Total investment in Fixed Assets	35.6	16722.7	96977.8	129117.0	171462.5
城　镇	Urban	35.6	15256.2	87166.6	115191.8	153254.9
农　村	Rural		1466.6	98112.6	13925.2	18207.6
能源生产总量(万吨标准煤)	Total Energy Production	3.9	14.8	41.1	45.8	
货运量(万吨)	Freight Traffic (10 000 tons)	16.6	90.7	177.0	192.8	214.4
客运量(万人)	Passenger Traffic (10 000 persons)	2.6	63.5	127.0	138.3	151.5
邮政业务总量(亿元)	Business Volume of Postal Services		162.7	454.2	379.2	497.9
电信业务总量(亿元)	Business Volume of Telecommunication Services		1133.2	15492.3	5826.3	6758.0
进出口总额(万美元)	Total Value of Imports and Exports (USD 10 000)	6.4	620.3	4692.7	6252.7	6596.1
出口额	Exports	2.6	329.9	3479.4	4610.7	5300.5
进口额	Imports	3.8	290.4	1139.3	1642.0	1595.6
实际利用外资额(万美元)	Foreign Capital Actually Used (USD 10 000)		5.3	65.0	91.7	91.7
入境旅游收入(万美元)	Foreign Exchange Earnings from International Tourism	...	26.0	100.9	127.5	150.8
每天婚姻变动	**Daily Marriages Changes**					
结　婚(对)	Marriages (couple)		445	723	774	720
离　婚(对)	Divorces (couple)		162	268	272	286

1-4 主要年份国民经济和社会发展总量与速度指标

指　标	Item	1978
人口与就业	**Population and Employment**	
人口(万人)	**Population (10 000 persons)**	
年末总人口	Population at the Year-end	1233.01
男　性	Male	630.18
女　性	Female	602.83
就业(万人)	**Employment (10 000 persons)**	
就业人员数	Employment	491.25
#在岗职工人数	Staff and Workers	226.69
城镇登记失业人数	Urban Registeration Unemployment	
宏观经济	**Macro Economy**	
国民经济核算(亿元)	**National Accounting (100 million yuan)**	
新疆生产总值	Gross Domestic Product	39.07
第一产业	Primary Industry	13.97
第二产业	Secondary Industry	18.35
第三产业	Tertiary Industry	6.75
支出法新疆生产总值	Gross Domestic Product by Expenditure Approach	
#最终消费	Final Consumption Expenditure	27.64
居民消费	Houshold Consumption Expenditure	22.61
政府消费	Government Consumption Expenditure	5.03
资本形成总额	Gross Capital Formation	18.43
固定资本形成	Gross Fixed Capital Formation	13.25
存货增加	Changes in Inventories	5.18
货物和服务净出口	Net Export of Goods and Services	-7.00
固定资产投资(亿元)	**Investment in Fixed Assets (100 million yuan)**	
全社会固定资产投资总额	Total Investment in Fixed Assets	13.00
城　镇	Urban	13.00
#房地产	Real Estate Development	
农　村	Rural	
全社会施工房屋建筑面积（万平方米）	Floor Space of Buildings under Construction (10 000 sq.m)	
全社会竣工房屋建筑面积（万平方米）	Floor Space of Building Completed (10 000 sq.m)	
消　费	**Consumption**	
社会消费品零售总额(亿元)	Total Retail Sales of Consumer Goods (100 million yuan)	21.89
对外贸易	**Foreign Trade**	
进出口总额(万美元)	Total Value of Imports and Exports	2346
出口额	Exports	937
进口额	Imports	1409
利用外资(万美元)	**Utilization of Foreign Capital (USD 10 000)**	
签订利用外资协议额	Amount of Foreign Capital for Utilization through Signed Contracts or Agreements	
实际利用外资额	Amount of Foreign Capital Actually Utilized	
财政(亿元)	**Public Finance (100 million yuan)**	
公共财政预算收入	Local Financial Governments Intrabudgetary Ordinary Revenue	7.14
#税收收入	Various Taxes	4.34

Principal Aggregate Indicators on National Economic and Social Development and Growth Rates in Main Years

总量指标 Aggregate Data				速度指标(%) Indices and Growth Rates						
				指数(2012 年比以下各年) Index (2012 as percentuage of the following years)				平均增长速度 Average Annual Growth Rate		
2000	2010	2011	2012	1978	2000	2010	2011	1979-2012	2001-2012	2011-2012
1849.41	2181.58	2208.71	2232.78	181.1	120.7	102.3	101.1	1.8	1.6	1.2
957.07	1127.01	1128.75	1145.21	181.7	119.7	101.6	101.5	1.8	1.5	0.8
892.34	1054.57	1079.96	1087.57	180.4	121.9	103.1	100.7	1.8	1.7	1.6
672.50	894.65	953.34	1010.44	205.7	150.3	112.9	106.0	2.1	3.5	6.3
255.75	245.48	270.77	280.33	123.7	109.6	114.2	103.5	0.6	0.8	6.9
11.00	10.99	11.12	11.85		107.7	107.8	106.6		0.6	3.8
1363.56	5437.47	6610.05	7505.31	2939.7	334.7	125.4	112.0	10.5	10.6	12.0
288.18	1078.63	1139.03	1320.57	1130.7	197.1	114.0	107.0	7.4	5.8	6.8
537.58	2592.15	3225.90	3481.56	2751.0	376.5	127.3	113.7	10.2	11.7	2.0
537.80	1766.69	2245.12	2703.18	7792.0	376.3	129.4	112.3	13.7	11.7	13.8
760.20	2865.56	3518.82	4262.51							
492.32	1578.93	1954.33	2370.67							
267.88	1286.63	1564.49	1891.84							
618.12	3371.22	4162.32	5792.16							
648.12	3233.00	3948.87	5477.61							
-30.00	138.22	213.45	314.55							
-14.76	-799.31	-1071.09	-2549.36							
610.38	3539.69	4712.77	6258.38	48141.4	1025.3	176.8	132.8	19.9	21.4	33.0
556.85	3181.58	4204.50	5593.81	43029.3	1004.5	175.8	133.0	19.5	21.2	32.6
57.43	347.72	516.39	606.09		1055.4	174.3	117.4		21.7	32.0
53.53	358.11	508.27	664.58		1241.5	185.6	130.8		23.4	36.2
4485.77	11361.96	16804.88	21626.33		482.1	190.3	128.7		14.0	38.0
2633.23	4649.89	5899.06	7821.44		297.0	168.2	132.6		9.5	29.7
374.50	1324.48	1557.09	1799.00	8218.4	480.4	135.8	115.5	13.8	14.0	16.5
226399	1712834	2282225	2517075	107292.2	1111.8	147.0	110.3	22.8	22.2	21.2
120408	1296981	1682886	1934686	206476.6	1606.8	149.2	115.0	25.2	26.0	22.1
105991	415853	599339	582389	41333.5	549.5	140.0	97.2	19.4	15.3	18.3
9212	30091	55834	61056		662.8	202.9	109.4		17.1	42.4
1923	23742	33485	40795		2121.4	171.8	121.8		29.0	31.1
79.07	500.58	720.43	908.97	12730.7	1149.6	181.6	126.2	15.3	22.6	34.8
64.53	416.23	593.41	698.93	16104.4	1083.1	167.9	117.8	16.1	22.0	29.6

1-4 续表 1

指　　标	Item	1978
公共财政预算支出	Local Financial Governments Intrabudgetary Ordinary Expenditures	17.02
#一般公共服务	General Common Service	
教育与科学技术	Operating Expenses for Education and Operating Expenses for Science and Technology	
社会保障和就业	Operating Expenses for Medical Treatment and Sanitation	
节能环保	Energy Saving and Environmental Protection	
城乡社区事务	Expenses of Community	
农林水事务	Expenses of Agriculture, Forest and Irrigation	
物价总指数(上年=100)	**Price Indices (preceding year=100)**	
居民消费价格总指数	Consumer Price Index	101.2
商品零售价格总指数	Retail Price Index	101.4
工业生产者出厂价格指数	Producer Price Indices for Manufacture Goods	
工业生产者购进价格指数	Purchasing Price Indices of Industrial Products	
固定资产投资价格指数	Investment in Fixed Assets Price Indices	
能源生产与消费(万吨标准煤)	**Production and Consumption of Energy (10 000 tons of SCE)**	
能源生产总量	Total Energy Production	1410.75
能源消费总量	Total Energy Consumption	979.27
产　业	**Industry**	
农　业	**Agriculture**	
农林牧渔业总产值(亿元)	Gross Output Value of Farming, Forestry, Animal Husbandry and Fishery (100 million yuan)	19.12
主要农产品产量(万吨)	Output of Major Farm Products (10 000 tons)	
粮　食	Grain	370.01
棉　花	Cotton	5.50
油　料	Oil-bearing Crops	10.33
甜　菜	Beet Roots	16.37
水　果	Fruits	13.98
肉　类	Meat	9.65
奶　类	Milk	5.25
水产品	Aquatic Products	0.57
工　业	**Industry**	
主要工业产品产量	Output of Major Industrial Products	
纱(万吨)	Yarn (10 000 tons)	2.80
布(亿米)	Cloth (100 million meter)	1.56
绒线(吨)	Knitting Wool (ton)	1239
呢绒(万米)	Woolen Goods (10 000 meter)	189
原盐(万吨)	Crude Salt (10 000 tons)	51.71
机制纸及纸板(万吨)	Machine-Made Paper and Paperboards (10 000 tons)	1.99
成品糖(万吨)	Refined Sugar (10 000 tons)	2.08
原煤(万吨)	Natural Crude Petroleum Coal (10 000 tons)	1079.01
原油(万吨)	Crude Oil (10 000 tons)	353.05
天然气(亿立方米)	Natural Gas (100 million cu.m)	2.51
发电量(亿千瓦小时)	ElectriCity (100 million kwh)	21.17

Continued

总量指标 Aggregate Data				速度指标(%) Indices and Growth Rates						
2000	2010	2011	2012	指数(2012 年比以下各年) Index (2012 as percentuage of the following years)				平均增长速度 Average Annual Growth Rate		
				1978	2000	2010	2011	1979-2012	2001-2012	2011-2012
190.95	1698.91	2284.49	2720.07	15981.6	1424.5	160.1	119.1	16.1	24.8	26.5
	195.57	245.36	303.67			155.3	123.8			24.6
	334.02	426.23	506.87			151.7	118.9			23.2
	166.40	201.64	227.79			136.9	113.0			17.0
	51.02	53.67	64.12			125.7	119.5			12.1
	95.28	140.10	183.49			192.6	131.0			38.8
	220.50	297.59	365.39			165.7	122.8			28.7
99.4	104.3	105.9	103.8							
98.3	104.6	105.1	103.3							
129.4	125.3	114.8	96.9							
115.2	123.9	117.8	97.9							
103.6	104.6	107.1	100.6							
5419.77	15000.47	16703.06								
3316.03	8290.20	9926.50								
487.20	1846.18	1955.39	2275.67	1230.4	209.6	114.8	107.4	7.7	6.4	7.1
808.60	1150.20	1200.75	1259.83	340.5	155.8	109.5	104.9	3.7	3.8	4.7
150.00	247.90	289.77	353.95	6435.5	236.0	142.8	122.1	13.0	7.4	19.5
60.14	66.62	66.76	59.04	571.5	98.2	88.6	88.4	5.3	-0.2	-5.9
292.65	486.97	518.95	577.19	3525.9	197.2	118.5	111.2	11.0	5.8	8.9
151.87	593.85	601.65	736.74	5270.0	485.1	124.1	122.5	12.4	14.1	11.4
90.00	121.74	127.28	134.23	1391.0	149.1	110.3	105.5	8.1	3.4	5.0
78.23	132.82	133.91	136.32	2596.6	174.3	102.6	101.8	10.1	4.7	1.3
6.01	10.11	11.69	12.53	2198.2	208.5	123.9	107.2	9.5	6.3	11.3
33.43	41.58	39.91	40.22	1436.4	120.3	96.7	100.8	8.2	1.6	-1.6
2.81	1.51	0.73	0.67	42.9	23.8	44.4	91.8	-2.5	-11.3	-33.4
1184	741	444	545	44.0	46.0	73.5	122.7	-2.4	-6.3	-14.2
754	326	383	332	175.7	44.0	101.8	86.7	1.7	-6.6	0.9
31.78	174.67	258.05	301.40	582.9	948.4	172.6	116.8	5.3	20.6	31.4
17.65	37.10	42.29	41.05	2062.8	232.6	110.6	97.1	9.3	7.3	5.2
30.76	45.10	46.11	53.64	2578.8	174.4	118.9	116.3	10.0	4.7	9.1
2798.90	9926.72	11991.71	13646.98	1264.8	487.6	137.5	113.8	7.7	14.1	17.3
1848.43	2558.16	2615.63	2670.68	756.5	144.5	104.4	102.1	6.1	3.1	2.2
35.39	249.91	235.38	253.01	10080.1	714.9	101.2	107.5	14.5	17.8	0.6
182.98	679.33	875.19	1187.48	5609.3	649.0	174.8	135.7	12.6	16.9	32.2

1-4 续表 2

指　　标	Item	1978
粗钢(万吨)	Crude Steel (10 000 tons)	8.46
钢材(万吨)	Steel Products (10 000 tons)	6.83
水泥(万吨)	Cement (10 000 tons)	78.15
全部工业总产值(亿元)	Gross industrial Output Value (100 million yuan)	33.91
规模以上工业企业主要经济指标	Principal Financial Indicators of Industrial Enterprises Above Designated Size	
工业总产值	Gross Industrial Output Value	28.43
资产总计	Origninal Value of fixed Assets	
主营业务收入	Revenue from Principal Business	
利润总额(亿元)	Profits (100 million yuan)	4.28
建筑业	**Construction**	
建筑业企业从业人员(万人)	Number of Employed Persons (10 000 persons)	
建筑业企业总产值(亿元)	Gross Output Value (100 million yuan)	
施工房屋面积(万平方米)	Floor Space of Buildings under Construction (10 000 sq.m)	
竣工房屋面积(万平方米)	Floor Space of Buildings Completed (10 000 sq.m)	
交通运输	**Transportation**	
货运量(万吨)	Freight Traffic (10 000 tons)	6064
铁　路	Railways	923
公　路	Highways	4843
管　道	Pipelines	298
航　空	Civil Aviation	0.12
客运量(万人)	Passenger Traffic Volume (10 000 persons)	941
铁　路	Railways	148
公　路	Highways	786
航　空	Civil Aviation	7
邮电通信业	**Postal and Telecommunication Services**	
邮政业务总量(亿元)	Business Volume of Postal Services (100 million yuan)	
电信业务总量(亿元)	Business Volume of Telecommunication Services (100 million yuan)	
函　件(万件)	Number of Letters Delivered (10 000 pieces)	4843
报刊期发数(万份)	Number of Newspapers and Magazines Distributed (10 000 copies)	224
局用交换机容量(万门)	CapaCity of Office Telephone Exchanges (10 000 lines)	
固定电话年末用户(万部)	Local Telephone Subscribers at Year-end (10 000 subscribers)	2.90
移动电话用户(万户)	Number of Mobile Telephone Subscribers (10 000 subscribers)	
旅　游	**Tourism**	
入境旅游过夜者人数(万人)	Number of Tourists (10 000 person-times)	0.01
入境旅游收入(万美元)	Foreign Exchange Eearnings from International Tourism (100 million yuan)	5
金　融	**Finance and Insurance**	
金融机构各项存款(亿元)	Deposits of National Banking System (100 million yuan)	32.07
金融机构各项贷款(亿元)	Loans of National Banking System (100 million yuan)	18.26
教育、科技、文化	**Education, Science & Technology and Culture**	
教　育	**Education**	
专任教师数(人)	Full-time Teachers (person)	
普通高等学校	Regular Institutions of Higher Education	2458

Continued

总量指标 Aggregate Data				速度指标(%) Indices and Growth Rates						
				指数(2012 年比以下各年) Index (2012 as percentuage of the following years)				平均增长速度 Average Annual Growth Rate		
2000	2010	2011	2012	1978	2000	2010	2011	1979-2012	2001-2012	2011-2012
109.70	825.54	892.98	1138.23	13454.3	1037.6	137.9	127.5	15.5	21.5	17.4
131.26	891.70	985.14	1289.84	18884.9	982.7	144.6	130.9	16.7	21.0	20.3
895.67	2400.96	3171.71	4315.93	5522.6	481.9	179.8	136.1	12.5	14.0	34.1
1061.29	5766.51	7105.31	7886.25	23256.4	743.1	136.8	111.0	17.4	18.2	16.9
852.01	5341.90	6720.85	7532.67	26495.5	884.1	141.0	112.1	17.8	19.9	18.7
1708.81	7911.97	9304.95	11669.17		682.9	147.5	125.4		17.4	21.4
821.26	5492.61	6782.25	7510.67		914.5	136.7	110.7		20.3	16.9
90.49	852.43	963.74	888.64	20762.6	982.0	104.2	92.2	17.0	21.0	2.1
26.16	56.48	52.73	63.81		243.9	113.0	121.0		7.7	6.3
234.95	969.47	1327.83	1633.11		695.1	168.5	123.0		17.5	29.8
2241.48	6620.14	8947.71	11026.49		491.9	166.6	123.2		14.2	29.1
1261.42	2891.45	3465.49	4553.97		361.0	157.5	131.4		11.3	25.5
33091	64597	70362	78249	1290.4	236.5	121.1	111.2	7.8	7.4	10.1
4199	6853	6904	6933	751.1	165.1	101.2	100.4	6.1	4.3	0.6
27048	50448	55965	61850	1277.1	228.7	122.6	110.5	7.8	7.1	10.7
1840	7292	7489	9460	3174.5	514.1	129.7	126.3	10.7	14.6	13.9
3.50	3.70	3.90	5.80	4833.3	165.7	156.8	148.7	12.1	4.3	25.2
23191	46346	50461	55298	5876.5	238.4	119.3	109.6	12.7	7.5	9.2
1147	1523	2002	2162	1460.8	188.5	142.0	108.0	8.2	5.4	19.1
21877	44333	47927	52473	6676.0	239.9	118.4	109.5	13.2	7.6	8.8
167	490	532	663	9471.4	397.0	135.3	124.6	14.3	12.2	16.3
5.94	16.58	13.84	18.17		305.9	109.6	131.3		9.8	4.7
41.36	565.47	212.66	246.67				116.0			
7148	2926	3202	2529	52.2	35.4	86.4	79.0	-1.9	-8.3	-7.0
535	307	296	310	138.4	57.9	101.0	104.7	1.0	-4.4	0.5
241.67	928.20	915.10	623.60		258.0	67.2	68.1		8.2	-18.0
191.03	547.50	540.80	540.10	18624.1	282.7	98.6	99.9	16.6	9.0	-0.7
78.00	1359.80	1670.90	2008.50		2575.0	147.7	120.2		31.1	21.5
25.61	101.03	132.50	149.80	1498000.0	584.9	148.3	113.1	32.7	15.9	21.8
9494	36844	46519	55057	1101140.0	579.9	149.4	118.4	31.5	15.8	22.2
1863.48	8870.72	10387.00	12330.89	38449.9	661.7	139.0	118.7	19.1	17.1	17.9
1403.13	4973.16	6270.21	7914.00	43340.6	564.0	159.1	126.2	19.6	15.5	26.1
7924	16506	17256	17570	714.8	221.7	106.4	101.8	6.0	6.9	3.2

1-4 续表 3

指　　标	Item	1978
中等学校	Regular Secondary Schools	44417
小　学	Regular Primary Schools	82616
在校学生数(万人)	Students Enrollment (10 000 persons)	
普通高等学校	Regular Institutions of Higher Education	1.02
中等学校	Regular Secondary Schools	83.86
小　学	Regular Primary Schools	202.88
科　技	**Science and Technology**	
研究与发展经费支出(万元)	Expenditures on Research and Development (10 000 yuan)	
技术市场交易额(万元)	Volume of Transaction in Technical Markets (10 000 yuan)	
文　化	**Culture**	
电视节目制作时间(小时)	Time for TV Programs Production (hour)	
家庭、生活、环境	**Family, People's Livelihood and Environment**	
家　庭	**Family**	
家庭总户数(万户)	Total Number of Households (10 000 households)	
婚　姻	**Marriages and Divorces**	
结婚数(万对)	Number of Marriages (10 000 couples)	
离婚数(万对)	Number of Divorces (10 000 couples)	
居　住	**Housing**	
城镇居民人均住房建筑面积(平方米)	Per capita Gross Floor Space of Urban Residents (sq.m)	
农村居民人均住房面积(平方米)	Per capita Net Floor Space of Rural Residents (sq.m)	
生　活	**People's Livelihood**	
城镇居民人均可支配收入(元)	Per Capita Annual Disposable Income of Urban Households (yuan)	319
农村居民人均纯收入(元)	Per Capita Net Income of Rural Residents (yuan)	119
城乡居民储蓄存款余额(亿元)	Outstanding Amount of Saving Deposits in Urban and Rural Areas (100 million yuan)	6.42
卫　生	**Health Care**	
医院、卫生院(个)	Number of Hospitals (unit)	806
医生(人)	Number of Doctors (person)	16898
医院、卫生院床位数(张)	Number of Hospital Beds (unit)	39179
市政建设	**Municipal Works**	
自来水供应量(亿立方米)	Volume of Tapping Water Supply(100 million cu.m)	
下水道长度(公里)	Length of Sewer Pipelines (km)	
铺装道路长度(公里)	Length of Paved Roads (km)	
环境、灾害	**Environment and Disaster**	
化学需氧量排放量(万吨)	COD Discharge (10 000 tons)	
二氧化硫排放量(万吨)	Sulphur Dioxide Emission (10 000 tons)	
火灾发生数(起)	Number of Fire Disasters (times)	
火灾损失(万元)	Fire Loss (10 000 yuan)	
交通事故发生数(起)	Number of Traffic Accidents (times)	
交通事故损失(万元)	Loss of Traffic Accidents (10 000 yuan)	

Continued

总量指标 Aggregate Data				速度指标(%) Indices and Growth Rates						
				指数(2012 年比以下各年) Index (2012 as percentuage of the following years)				平均增长速度 Average Annual Growth Rate		
2000	2010	2011	2012	1978	2000	2010	2011	1979-2012	2001-2012	2011-2012
89211	128306	132748	134900	303.7	151.2	105.1	101.6	3.3	3.5	2.5
131259	133963	135182	136130	164.8	103.7	101.6	100.7	1.5	0.3	0.8
7.41	26.38	27.28	28.42	2786.3	383.5	107.7	104.2	10.3	11.9	3.8
131.18	168.40	167.52	165.16	196.9	125.9	98.1	98.6	2.0	1.9	-1.0
247.74	193.58	191.95	190.08	93.7	76.7	98.2	99.0	-0.2	-2.2	-0.9
32381	266545	330030	397289		1226.9	149.1	120.4		23.2	22.1
66168	43146	43045	53326		80.6	123.6	123.9		-1.8	11.2
29261	76467	85002	92503		316.1	121.0	108.8		10.1	10.0
481.91	639.86	663.70	675.17		140.1	105.5	101.7		2.8	2.7
16.25	26.40	28.23	26.29		161.8	99.6	93.1		4.1	-0.2
5.90	9.78	9.94	10.43		176.8	106.6	104.9		4.9	3.3
26.75	27.25	28.92	29.03		108.5	106.5	100.4		0.7	3.2
17.25	24.00	26.14	27.18		157.6	113.3	104.0		3.9	6.4
5645	13644	15514	17921	5617.9	317.5	131.3	115.5	12.6	10.1	14.6
1618	4643	5442	6394	5373.1	395.2	137.7	117.5	12.4	12.1	17.4
908.55	3713.47	4421.93	5281.83	82271.5	581.3	142.2	119.4	21.8	15.8	19.3
1352	1712	1742	1759	218.2	130.1	102.7	101.0	2.3	2.2	1.4
45402	48166	48618	49558	293.3	109.2	102.9	101.9	3.2	0.7	1.4
65916	109851	118781	125064	319.2	189.7	113.8	105.3	3.5	5.5	6.7
5.00	7.73	8.09	8.59		171.8	111.1	106.2		4.6	5.4
2008	4372	4592	4956		246.8	113.4	107.9		7.8	6.5
2809	5178	5476	5813		206.9	112.3	106.2		6.2	6.0
	29.60	67.29	67.92			229.5	100.9			51.5
31.10	58.85	76.31	79.61		256.0	135.3	104.3		8.1	16.3
3050	5209	5093	7201		236.1	138.2	141.4		7.4	17.6
2329	3041	5179	8589		368.8	282.4	165.8		11.5	68.1
10048	4949	5182	4942		49.2	99.9	95.4		-5.7	-0.1
4443	864	1036	1233		27.7	142.7	119.0		-10.1	19.4

1-5 主要年份国民经济和社会发展结构指标

Composition Indicators on National Economic and Social Development in Main Years

单位: % (%)

指 标	Item	1978	2000	2010	2011	2012
人口与就业	**Population and Employment**					
人 口	**Population**					
性别结构	Sexual Composition					
男	Male	51.1	51.8	51.3	51.1	51.3
女	Female	48.9	48.2	48.7	48.9	48.7
就 业	**Employment**					
产业结构	Industrial Composition					
第一产业	Primary Industry	72.1	57.7	49.0	48.7	48.7
第二产业	Secondary Industry	14.3	13.8	14.8	15.6	15.6
第三产业	Tertiary Industry	13.6	28.5	36.2	35.7	35.7
宏观经济	**Macro Economy**					
国民核算	**National Accounting**					
新疆生产总值产业结构	Industrial Composition					
第一产业	Primary Industry	35.8	21.1	19.8	17.1	17.6
第二产业	Secondary Industry	47.0	39.4	47.7	48.5	46.4
#工 业	Industry	37.1	30.7	39.8	40.6	38.0
第三产业	Tertiary Industry	17.2	39.5	32.5	34.4	36.0
固定资产投资	**Investment**					
全社会固定资产投资结构	Composition of Total Investment in Fixed Assets					
城 镇	Urban	100	91.2	89.9	89.2	89.4
#房地产	Real Estate Development		10.3	9.8	11.0	9.7
农 村	Rural		8.8	10.1	10.8	10.6
资金来源结构	Composition of Funded Sources					
国家预算内资金	State Budgetary Appropriation	79.0	8.3	16.8	12.2	13.0
国内贷款	Domestic Loans		22.1	15.2	13.0	13.3
利用外资	Foreign Investment		1.6	0.3	0.3	0.3
自筹和其他投资	Fundraising and Other Investment	21.0	68.0	67.7	74.5	73.4
对外经济贸易	**Foreign Economic Trade**					
进出口总额结构	Composition of total Value of Exports and Imports					
出口额	Exports	39.9	53.2	75.7	73.7	76.9
进口额	Imports	60.1	46.8	24.3	26.3	23.1
财 政	**Government Finance**					
公共财政预算收入结构	Composition of Government Revenue					
税收收入	Various Taxes	60.8	81.6	83.2	82.4	76.9
非税收入	Nontax Revenues	39.2	18.4	16.8	17.6	23.1
公共财政预算支出结构	Composition of Government Expenditures					
一般公共服务	General Common Service			11.5	10.7	11.2
教育与科学技术	Operating Expenses for Education and Operating Expenses for Science and Technology			19.7	18.7	18.6
社会保障和就业	Operating Expenses for Medical Treatment and Sanitation			9.8	8.8	8.4
环境保护	Operating Expenses for Environmental Conservation			3.0	2.3	2.4
城乡社区事务	Expenses of Community			5.6	6.1	6.7
农林水事务	Expenses of Agriculture, Forest and Irrigation			13.0	13.0	13.4
其他各项支出	Other Expense			37.4	40.4	39.3
能源生产与消费	**Energy Production and Consumption**					
能源生产总量结构	Composition of Total Energy Production					
原 煤	Coal	60.0	40.6	50.3	55.9	
原 油	Petroleum Crude Oil	35.8	48.7	24.4	22.4	
天然气	Natural Gas	2.4	7.9	22.2	18.7	
水风电	Water, Wind and Electricity	1.8	2.8	3.1	3.0	

1-5 续表 1 Continued

单位: % (%)

指　标	Item	1978	2000	2010	2011	2012
能源消费总量结构	Composition of Total Energy Consumption					
煤　炭	Coal	72.5	63.6	65.8	67.9	
石　油	Petroleum Oil	21.5	23.3	15.8	14.7	
天然气	Natural Gas	3.4	8.6	12.4	12.3	
水电、风电	Hydro-power, Wind Power	2.6	4.5	5.6	5.1	
产　业	**Industrial**					
农　业	**Agriculture**					
农林牧渔业产值结构	Composition of Gross Output Value of AgricultureForestry,Animal Husbandry, Fishery					
农　业	Farming	74.5	74.0	74.6	73.5	73.6
林　业	Forestry	1.8	1.7	1.9	2.0	1.9
牧　业	Animal Husbandry	23.5	23.5	20.4	21.2	21.3
渔　业	Fishery	0.2	0.8	0.7	0.7	0.7
农林牧渔服务业	Agricultural, Forestry, Animal Husbandry, Fishery and Their Services			2.4	2.6	2.5
工　业	**Industry**					
工业总产值规模结构	Composition of Gross Output Value of Industry					
大型企业	Large Enterprises		53.7	55.2	57.1	64.6
中型企业	Medium-sized Enterprises		10.1	24.4	24.4	15.6
小型企业	Small Enterprises		36.2	20.4	18.5	18.9
微型企业						0.9
建筑业	**Construction**					
建筑业总产值结构	Composition of Gross Output Value of Construction Industry					
建筑工程	Construction Projects		88.3	87.2	89.3	89.1
安装工程	Installation Projects		9.1	11.4	9.2	8.7
其　他	Others		2.6	1.4	1.5	2.2
交通运输业	**Transportation**					
货运量结构按运输方式分	By Means of Transportation					
铁　路	Railways	15.2	12.7	10.6	9.8	8.9
公　路	Highways	79.9	81.7	78.1	79.5	79.0
民用航空	Civil Aviation	…	…	…	…	…
管道输油(气)	Pipelines	4.9	5.6	11.3	10.6	12.1
旅游业	**International Tourism**					
来华旅游人数结构	Composition of Tourists					
外国人	Foreigners	100.0	81.4	94.8	94.3	91.0
港澳台同胞	Compatriots form Hong Kong, Macao and Taiwan		18.6	5.2	5.7	9.0
金　融	**Finance**					
金融机构资金来源结构	Composition of Sources of Funds in State Banks					
各项存款	Various Deposits		122.8	110.1	105.3	101.8
应付及暂收款	Payable and Temporary Collection		…	1.5	1.6	1.6
所有者权益	Owner's Right and Interest		0.1	3.6	4.4	4.5
其　他	Others		-22.9	-15.3	-11.3	-7.9
金融机构资金运用结构	Composition of Fund Uses in State Banks					
各项贷款	Loans		92.5	61.8	63.6	65.3
有价证券及投资	Securities and Investment		4.4	5.6	4.7	5.5
系统内资金往来	Funds Tranfer inward Banks		1.6	29.1	23.6	22.7
库存现金	Cash in Stock		1.1	0.7	0.8	0.8
其　他	Others		0.4	2.8	7.3	5.7
教育、科技	**Education and Science**					
教　育	**Education**					
在校学生结构	Composition of Student Enrollment					
大学生	College and University Students	0.4	2.0	6.8	7.0	7.4
中学生	Secondary School Students	29.1	30.8	43.4	43.4	43.0

1-5 续表 2 Continued

单位: % (%)

指　标	Item	1978	2000	2010	2011	2012
小学生	Primary School Students	70.5	67.2	49.8	49.6	49.6
专任教师结构	Full-time Teachers by Type					
大　学	Colleges and Universities	1.9	3.5	5.9	6.0	6.1
中　学	Secondary Schools	34.3	39.1	46.0	46.7	46.7
小　学	Primary Schools	63.8	57.4	48.1	47.3	47.2
科　技	**Science and Technology**					
科学研究与试验发展经费支出结构	Composition of Expenditure on Research and Development					
基础研究	Basic Research		4.7	5.4	6.3	
应用研究	Supplied Research		27.4	23.6	19.9	
实验发展	Experimental Development		67.9	71.0	73.8	
生活、环境	**People's Livelihood and Environment**					
生　活	**People's Livelihood**					
城镇居民消费结构	Consumption Composition of Urban Residents					
食品类	Food		36.4	36.2	38.3	37.7
衣着类	Clothing		13.1	14.8	14.5	14.6
家庭设备、用品及服务	Articles for Daily Use and Others		7.6	6.6	6.7	6.8
医疗保健	Health Care and Medical Services		7.5	6.9	7.7	7.4
交通通讯	Transport and Communication		7.5	12.3	11.6	12.0
教育文化娱乐服务	Education,Cultral and Recreation Services		15.1	9.9	9.5	9.2
居　住	Residence		9.4	8.8	7.5	8.4
杂项商品和服务	Miscellaneous Goods and Services		3.4	4.5	4.2	3.9
农村居民消费结构	Consumption Composition of Rural Residents					
食品类	Food		50.0	40.3	36.1	36.1
衣着类	Clothing		9.2	8.8	8.5	8.2
家庭设备、用品及服务	Articles for Daily Use and Others		3.7	4.0	4.5	4.2
医疗保健	Health Care and Medical Services		6.0	9.1	12.1	8.5
交通和通讯	Transport and Communication		4.9	11.1	5.2	12.3
文教娱乐用品及服务	Education,Cultural and Recreation Services		8.6	4.9	8.6	3.9
居　住	Residence		13.8	20.1	23.3	24.7
其他商品和服务	Other Goods and Services		3.8	1.7	1.7	2.1
卫　生	**Health Care**					
卫生技术人员结构	Doctors by Types					
执业医师(西医师)	(Doctors of Western Medicine)	14.4	76.9	32.0	30.8	30.3
执业助理医师(西医士)	(Paramedics of Western Medicine)	18.7	23.1	7.2	7.1	6.7
注册护士	Registered Nurses	21.1		36.0	37.3	38.4
药剂人员	Pharmacist			5.2	5.0	4.8
技师(士)	Laboratory Technician			6.3	5.9	5.8
其他	Others			13.3	13.9	14.0
环境、灾害	**Environment and Disasters**					
治理工业污染资金使用结构	Uses of Funds Inindustrial Pollution Treatment					
治理废水	Waste Water Treatment		38.2	29.5	15.5	47.9
治理废气	Waste Gas Treatment		40.9	69.3	84.3	51.2
治理固体废物	Solid Wastes Treatment		1.6	1.2		
治理噪声	Noise Abatement		18.4			
其　他	Others		0.9	…	0.2	0.9
火灾事故损失额结构	Composition of Fire Losses Converted into Cash					
特　大	Extraordinarily Serious Fires		15.7			
重　大	Serious Fires		14.3	...		
较　大	Big Fires			0.1	…	27.6
一　般	Ordinary Fires		70.0	99.9	100.0	72.4

1-6 主要年份国民经济和社会发展比例和效益指标

Indicators on Proportions and Efficiency in National Economic and Social Development in Main Years

指　　标	Item	1978	2000	2010	2011	2012
就　业	**Employment**					
城镇登记失业率(%)	Unemployment Rate in Urban Areas (%)		3.8	3.2	3.2	3.7
国民经济核算	**National Accounting**					
人均生产总值(元/人)	Per capita GDP (yuan/person)	313	7372	25034	30087	33796
固定资产投资	**Investment in Fixed Assets**					
全社会固定资产投资相当于新疆生产总值比例(%)	Proportion of Investment in Fixed Assets to GDP of Xinjiang (%)	33.3	44.8	65.1	71.3	83.4
全社会房屋建筑面积竣工率(%)	Rate of Total Floor Space of Buildings Completed in Construction (%)		58.7	40.9	35.1	41.3
消　费	**Consumption**					
人均社会消费品零售额(元)	Per Capita Retail Sales of Consumer Goods(yuan)	179	2066	6104	7094	8101
对外贸易	**Foreign Trade**					
进出口总额相当于新疆生产总值比例(%)	Proportion of Total Value of Imports & Exports to GDP	1.01	13.74	21.32	22.30	21.17
财　政	**Finance**					
公共财政预算收入相当于新疆生产总值比例(%)	Proportion of Local Financial Revenue to GDP of Xinjiang (%)	18.3	5.8	9.2	10.9	12.1
公共财政预算支出相当于新疆生产总值比例(%)	Proportion of Local Financial Expenditure to GDP of Xinjiang (%)	43.6	14.0	31.2	34.6	36.2
利用外资	**Utilization of Foreign Capital**					
实际利用外资额相当于签订利用外资额比例(%)	Proportion of Actually Foreign Direct Investment for Foreign Direct Investment (%)		20.87	78.90	59.97	66.80
能　源	**Energy**					
能源生产弹性系数	Elasticity Ratio of Energy Production	1.20	0.40	1.02	0.94	
电力生产弹性系数	Elasticity Ratio of Electricety Production		0.99	2.02	2.40	
能源消费弹性系数	Elasticity Ratio of Energy Consumption	0.74	0.38	0.96	1.64	
电力消费弹性系数	Elasticity Ratio of Electricity Consumption		0.99	1.96	2.23	

1-6 续表 1 Continued

指　　标	Item	1978	2000	2010	2011	2012
农　业	**Agriculture**					
每公顷播种面积农产品产量（公斤）	Output of Farm Crops per Hectare of Sown Area (kg)					
粮　食	Grain	1650	5595	5771	6003	5990
棉　花	Cotton	375	1485	1697	1769	2057
油　料	Oil-bearing Crops	510	1935	2437	2526	2436
工业（规模以上）	**Industry(Aboue Designated Size)**					
总资产贡献率（%）	Rate of Total Assets to Industrial Output Value (%)		11.2	18.2	18.4	14.5
资产负债率（%）	Assets-Liability Ratio (%)		62.7	50.8	53.8	57.2
成本费用利润率（%）	Rate of Profits to Industrial Cost (%)		12.8	19.3	17.5	14.0
流动资产周转次数（次/年）	Number of Times of Annual of Turnover Circulating Funds (times/year)		1.6	2.2	2.2	2.0
建筑业	**Construction**					
技术装备率（元/人）	Value of Machinery per Laborer (yuan/person)		8582	7145	6812	6568
动力装备率（千瓦/人）	Power of Machines Per Laborer (kw/person)		7	4	4	4
全员劳动生产率(按总产值计算)（元/人）	Overall Labor Productivity (yuan/person) (in terms of gross output value per employee)		74994	176404	226848	249202
交通运输业	**Transportation**					
铁路网密度（公里/万平方公里）	Railway Density (km/10 000 sq.km)	6.19	18.08	26.39	26.91	29.52
公路网密度（公里/万平方公里）	Highway Density (km/10 000 sq.km)	143	208	918	932	997
邮电通信业	**Post and Communications**					
固定电话普及率(部/百人)	PopularizationRate of Telephones (set/100 persons)		15.0	25.4	25.0	24.5
移动电话普及率(部/百人)	Popularization Rate of Mobile Telephone (set/100 persons)			63.0	77.4	90.9
国际旅游	**International Tourism**					
每一来华游客花费(美元)	Expenditure per International Tourist in China (USD)		371	346	351	368

1-6 续表 2 Continued

指　　标	Item	1978	2000	2010	2011	2012
金　融	**Finance**					
金融机构存款相当于新疆生产总值比例(%)	Bank Deposits as Percentage of GDP in Xinjiang (%)	82.08	136.62	163.13	157.14	164.30
金融机构贷款相当于新疆生产总值比例(%)	Bank Loans as Percentage of GDP in Xinjiang (%)	46.74	102.87	91.46	94.86	105.45
教　育	**Education**					
学龄儿童入学率(%)	Rate of School-age Children Enrollment (%)	96.00	97.03	99.78	99.73	99.79
小学升学率(%)	Rate of Graduates of Primary Schools Entering Junior Secondary Schools (%)	88.67	92.01	100.53	99.47	97.94
初中升学率(%)	Rate of Graduates of Junior Secondary Schools Entering Senior Secondary Schools (%)	48.22	30.30	45.40	47.64	48.60
学校教师负担系数(%)	Student-teacher Ratio (in percentage) (%)					
高等学校	Colleges and Universities	4.16	9.34	15.22	14.99	15.29
普通中等	Secondary Schools	19.36	14.92	12.48	12.10	11.70
小学学校	Primary Schools	24.56	18.87	14.45	14.20	13.96
科　技	**Science and Technology**					
研究与开发经费支出相当于新疆生产总值比例(%)	R&D Expenditures as Percentage of GDP (%)		0.38	0.49	0.50	0.53
文　化	**Culture**					
每百万人有艺术表演团体(个)	Number of Troupes per Million Persons(unit)	5.24	4.76	6.08	6.06	6.14
每百万人有公共图书馆(个)	Number of Public Libraries per Million Persons(unit)	0.41	4.33	4.75	4.69	4.70
每百万人有博物馆(个)	Number of Museums per Million Persons(unit)	0.08	1.24	3.27	3.32	3.22
卫　生	**Health Care**					
每万人医院、卫生院数(个)	Number of Hospitals and Health Centers per 10 000 Persons (unit)	0.66	0.73	0.79	0.79	0.79
每万人医生数(人)	Number of Doctors per 10 000 Persons (person)	13.70	24.55	22.25	22.49	22.20
每万人医院、卫生院床位数(张)	Number of Hospital and Health Centers Beds per 10 000 Persons (unit)	31.78	35. 64	50.36	53.93	56.01
医院病床使用率(%)	Utilization Rate of Hospital Beds (%)		66.31	89.19	92.50	86.35
市政建设	**City Construction**					
城市自来水普及率(%)	Percentage of Households with Access to Tap Water (%)	59.0	98.8	99.2	99.2	99.1
城市燃气普及率(%)	Percentage of Households with Access to Tap Gas (%)	11.0	92.8	95.8	96.2	96.6
建成区绿化覆盖率(%)	Green Covrage Rate in Completed Area(%)		29.1	36.4	36.6	35.9
灾　害	**Disasters**					
平均每起火灾损失(元)	Average Loss of per Fire Disaster (yuan)		7635	5422	12529	11928
平均每起交通事故损失(元)	Average Loss of per Traffic Accident (yuan)		4775	1746	2000	2494

1-7 主要年份人均主要工农业产品产量

Per capita Output of Major Industrial and Agricultural Products in Main Years

年份 Year	粮食(公斤) Grain (kg)	棉花(公斤) Cotton (kg)	油料(公斤) Oil-bearing Crops (kg)	甜菜(公斤) Sugar Crops (kg)	水果(公斤) Fruits (kg)	猪牛羊肉(公斤) Pork, Beef and Mutton (kg)	水产品(公斤) Aquatic Products (kg)
1978	303.0	4.5	8.5	13.4	11.4	7.9	0.5
1980	304.1	6.2	13.9	30.3	12.3	9.4	0.5
1985	367.2	13.9	25.3	30.1	36.4	12.8	0.7
1990	453.8	31.4	26.1	150.4	53.6	18.6	1.6
1995	443.3	56.8	30.0	174.9	69.4	27.9	2.7
2000	446.2	82.8	33.2	161.5	83.8	42.4	3.3
2001	427.3	84.3	22.9	244.3	82.8	44.5	3.3
2002	463.3	79.3	23.5	246.9	104.8	46.9	3.4
2003	417.6	83.4	26.1	198.8	113.7	50.4	3.5
2004	425.2	89.9	22.9	176.7	135.6	55.2	3.8
2005	441.5	98.5	19.6	211.0	146.6	60.5	4.0
2006	441.0	131.8	16.2	273.6	169.0	66.5	4.1
2007	418.3	139.9	19.4	283.2	214.7	67.1	4.3
2008	430.2	142.7	26.9	207.7	213.4	47.4	4.4
2009	537.1	117.7	29.8	195.1	263.5	46.5	4.5
2010	530.1	114.2	30.7	224.4	275.1	48.6	4.7
2011	547.0	132.0	30.4	236.4	274.1	50.1	5.3
2012	567.3	159.4	26.6	259.9	331.8	51.5	5.6

年份 Year	布(米) Cloth (m)	机制纸及纸板(公斤) Machine-made Paper and Paperboard (kg)	纱(公斤) Yarn (kg)	原煤(公斤) Coal (kg)	原油(公斤) Crude Oil (kg)	发电量(千瓦小时) Electricity (kwh)	粗钢(公斤) Steel (kg)	水泥(公斤) Cement (kg)
1978	13.0	1.6	2.3	884	289	173	7	64
1980	13.0	1.9	2.5	895	308	186	8	72
1985	16.0	3.1	2.9	1183	369	282	15	149
1990	20.0	6.1	6.8	1408	466	468	23	191
1995	18.0	11.0	14.9	1652	770	731	43	297
2000	15.0	9.7	18.5	1546	1021	1011	61	495
2001	14.0	10.4	16.3	1514	1045	1061	72	527
2002	11.0	12.0	16.7	1639	1077	1123	93	545
2003	8.0	12.2	15.3	1814	1116	1222	106	588
2004	7.0	13.5	15.0	1924	1156	1367	128	623
2005	7.0	14.6	17.2	1962	1212	1545	154	625
2006	8.0	14.5	17.6	2226	1219	1759	194	657
2007	8.0	12.2	19.7	2421	1257	2011	216	742
2008	7.2	14.3	18.8	3201	1285	2315	254	792
2009	7.1	16.6	18.0	4108	1171	2664	305	956
2010	7.0	17.1	19.2	4575	1179	3131	380	1106
2011	2.0	19.3	18.2	5463	1146	3987	407	1445
2012	3.0	18.5	18.1	6145	1203	5351	513	1943

1-8 主要年份人均国民经济主要指标

Per Capita Main Indicators on National Economy in Main Years

指　　标	Item	1978	2000	2010	2011	2012
新疆生产总值(元)	Gross Domestic Product of Xinjiang (yuan)	313	7372	25034	30087	33796
工农业总产值(元)	Gross Output Value of Industry and Agriculture (yuan)	450	8544	35082	41276	45759
工业总产值	Gross Industrial Output Value	278	5856	26574	32368	35512
农林牧渔业总产值	Gross Output Value of Agriculture, Forestry, Animal Husbandry and Fishery	172	2688	8508	8908	10247
固定资产投资总额(元)	Total Investment in Fixed Assets (yuan)	106	3368	16312	21470	28181
公共财政预算收入(元)	General Budgetary Revenue in Local Finance (yuan)	58	436	2307	3282	4093
公共财政预算支出(元)	General Budgetary Expenditure in Local Finance (yuan)	139	1054	7829	10408	12248
主要工农业产品产量	Output of Major Industrial and Agriculturd Produts					
粮食(公斤)	Grain Yield (kg)	303.0	446.2	530.1	547.0	567.3
棉花(公斤)	Cotton Yield (kg)	4.5	82.8	114.2	132.0	159.4
油料(公斤)	Oil-bearing Crops Yield (kg)	8.5	33.2	30.7	30.4	26.6
甜菜(公斤)	Beet Roots Yield (kg)	13.4	161.5	224.4	236.4	259.9
猪牛羊肉(公斤)	Pork, Beef and Mutton Yield (kg)	7.9	42.4	48.6	50.1	51.5
水产品(公斤)	Aquatic Products Yield (kg)	0.5	3.3	4.7	5.3	5.6
水果(公斤)	Fruits Yield (kg)	11.4	83.8	275.1	274.1	331.8
果用瓜(公斤)	Fruit Melon Yield (kg)	36.1	83.3	200.5	197.9	218.6
布(米)	Cloth (m)	13.0	15.0	7.0	2.0	3.0
机制纸和纸板(公斤)	Machine-made Paper and Paperboard (kg)	1.6	9.7	17.1	19.3	18.5
纱(公斤)	Yarn (kg)	2.3	18.5	19.2	18.2	18.1
原煤(公斤)	Coal Output (kg)	884	1546	4575	5463	6145
原油(公斤)	Crude Oil Output (kg)	289	1021	1179	1146	1203
发电量(千瓦小时)	Electric Power (kwh)	173	1011	3131	3987	5351
水泥(公斤)	Cement (kg)	64	495	1106	1445	1943
社会消费品零售总额(元)	Total Retail Sales of Consumer Goods (yuan)	179	2066	6104	7094	8101
海关出口总额(美元)	Value of Exports (USD)	0.8	66.5	789.3	766.7	871.2
高等学校在校学生数(人/万人)	Students Enrollment in Institions of Higher Education (person/10 000 persons)	8.3	41.1	115.1	117.1	127.3
中等专业学校在校学生数(人/万人)	Students Enrollment in Specialized Secondary Schools (person/10 000 persons)	19.2	56.9	69.8	73.2	71.2
普通中学在校学生数(人/万人)	Students Enrollment in Regular Secondary Schools (person/10 000 persons)	654.0	638.0	652.1	638.1	619.8
医院、卫生院床位数(张/万人)	Beds of Medical and Health Centers (unit/10 000 persons)	31.8	35.6	50.4	53.9	56.3
卫生技术人员数(人/万人)	Medical Technical Personnel (person/10 000 persons)	41.4	53.0	56.3	59.5	61.2
#医　生	Doctors	13.7	24.6	22.3	22.5	22.6
城乡居民储蓄存款余额(元)	Urban and Rural Savings Deposits (yuan)	57	4913	17113	20145	23783

1-9 新疆建区以来主要年份国民经济主要指标

年 份 Year	年末总人口（万人） Year-end Population (10 000 persons)	就业人员（万人） Employed Persons (10 000 persons)	新疆生产总值(亿元) Gross Domestic Product of Xinjiang (100 million yuan)	第一产业 Primary Industry	第二产业 Secondary Industry	#工 业 Industry	第三产业 Tertiary Industry	人均新疆生产总值(元) Per Capita GDP (yuan)
1955	511.78	254.58	12.31	6.69	3.22	2.10	2.40	241
1960	686.33	338.32	25.20	9.27	11.06	8.12	4.87	374
1965	789.10	350.25	24.20	12.48	7.32	5.03	4.40	312
1970	976.58	410.33	23.08	10.35	8.67	6.19	4.06	236
1975	1154.53	466.43	28.12	11.21	12.20	8.86	4.71	240
1978	1233.01	491.25	39.07	13.97	18.35	14.48	6.75	313
1980	1283.24	506.35	53.24	21.53	21.44	17.48	10.27	410
1985	1361.14	565.81	112.24	42.89	40.50	32.14	28.85	820
1990	1529.16	617.70	261.44	104.09	83.18	71.50	74.17	1713
1991	1554.57	638.49	335.91	111.86	107.99	84.07	116.06	2101
1992	1580.63	646.94	402.31	114.50	147.64	106.29	140.17	2477
1993	1605.26	655.98	495.25	126.85	205.07	155.92	163.33	2964
1994	1632.70	657.54	662.32	187.69	249.11	190.00	225.52	3888
1995	1661.35	676.00	814.85	240.71	283.97	219.01	290.17	4701
1996	1689.29	684.00	900.93	249.31	313.70	239.07	337.92	5102
1997	1718.08	715.40	1039.85	279.73	385.37	302.50	374.75	5848
1998	1747.35	680.92	1106.95	291.05	395.75	298.53	420.15	6174
1999	1775.00	694.34	1163.17	268.51	420.48	315.86	474.18	6443
2000	1849.41	672.50	1363.56	288.18	537.58	418.63	537.80	7372
2001	1876.19	685.38	1491.60	288.12	573.91	445.60	629.57	7945
2002	1905.19	701.49	1612.65	305.00	603.15	463.59	704.50	8457
2003	1933.95	721.27	1886.35	412.90	719.54	563.57	753.91	9828
2004	1963.11	744.49	2209.09	446.13	914.47	734.10	848.49	11337
2005	2010.35	791.62	2604.14	510.00	1164.80	961.62	929.34	13108
2006	2050.00	811.75	3045.26	527.80	1459.30	1241.33	1058.16	15000
2007	2095.19	830.42	3523.16	628.72	1647.55	1405.11	1246.89	16999
2008	2130.81	847.58	4183.21	691.07	2070.76	1755.35	1421.38	19797
2009	2158.63	866.15	4277.05	759.74	1929.59	1555.84	1587.72	19942
2010	2181.58	894.65	5437.47	1078.63	2592.15	2161.39	1766.69	25034
2011	2208.71	953.34	6610.05	1139.03	3225.90	2700.20	2245.12	30087
2012	2232.78	1010.44	7505.31	1320.57	3481.56	2850.06	2703.18	33796
			平均增长速度(%)					
1956-2012	2.6	2.4	8.2	5.8	9.6	9.9	9.3	5.4
1979-2012	1.8	2.1	10.5	7.4	10.2	10.1	13.7	8.6
2001-2012	1.6	3.5	10.6	5.8	11.7	11.8	11.7	8.9

Main Indicators of National Economic since Xinjing Established in Main Years

全社会固定资产投资总额(亿元) Total Investment in Fixed Assets (100 million yuan)	社会消费品零售总额(亿元) Total Retail Sales of Consumer Goods (100 million yuan)	公共财政预算收入(亿元) General Budgetary Revenue in Local Finance (100 million yuan)	公共财政预算支出(亿元) General Budgetary Expenditure in Local Finance (100 million yuan)	金融机构存款余额(亿元) Deposits of National Banking System (100 million yuan)	金融机构贷款余额(亿元) Loans of National Banking System (100 million yuan)	进出口总额(亿美元) Total Imports And Exports (USD 100 million)	#出口额 Exports	农村居民人均纯收入(元) Annual Per capita Net Income of Rural Residents (yuan)	城镇居民人均可支配收入(元) Annual Per capita Disposable Income of Urban Residents (yuan)
2.62	6.14	1.73	1.83	2.72	3.41	0.51	0.20		
10.59	11.91	6.36	9.58	6.89	15.50	0.73	0.48		
4.03	11.30	4.53	4.89	11.52	9.70	0.14	0.13		
4.50	13.23	3.57	6.05	17.25	14.35	0.02	…		
6.11	16.85	1.01	8.85	26.88	14.71	0.09	0.04		
13.00	21.89	7.14	17.02	32.07	18.26	0.23	0.09	119	319
20.47	29.36	4.03	16.22	38.56	24.74	0.32	0.17	201	427
44.48	57.38	8.47	28.60	82.96	72.68	2.92	1.80	394	735
88.78	104.30	21.78	47.62	221.80	233.72	4.10	3.35	684	1314
124.93	121.52	26.47	50.34	282.21	299.59	4.59	3.63	703	1476
170.03	138.25	26.07	56.09	336.58	380.26	7.50	4.54	740	1952
248.44	168.37	35.13	64.71	397.39	467.81	9.22	4.95	778	2423
285.48	197.11	28.70	71.10	634.44	632.32	10.41	5.76	936	3170
333.34	253.65	38.28	96.40	838.42	843.38	14.28	7.69	1137	4163
387.85	295.36	48.31	114.88	1012.47	1016.20	14.04	5.50	1290	4650
446.81	310.42	54.52	123.35	1180.78	1215.39	14.47	6.65	1500	4845
519.77	327.52	65.39	145.99	1336.58	1318.41	15.32	8.08	1600	5001
534.65	347.40	71.31	166.28	1548.72	1386.78	17.65	10.27	1473	5320
610.38	374.50	79.07	190.95	1863.48	1403.13	22.64	12.04	1618	5645
706.00	406.35	95.09	263.32	1972.55	1584.73	17.71	6.68	1710	6215
813.02	442.88	116.47	361.17	2225.31	1801.15	26.92	13.08	1863	6554
1002.13	421.16	128.22	368.47	2661.65	2099.09	47.72	25.42	2106	7006
1161.52	563.41	155.70	421.04	2959.78	2214.66	56.36	30.47	2245	7503
1352.27	637.78	180.32	519.02	3427.48	2272.08	79.42	50.40	2482	7990
1567.05	727.59	219.46	678.47	4040.78	2412.69	91.03	71.39	2737	8871
1850.84	847.70	285.86	795.15	4614.62	2685.00	137.16	115.03	3183	10313
2259.97	1025.72	361.06	1059.36	5399.34	2826.53	222.17	192.99	3503	11432
2827.24	1177.53	388.78	1346.91	6845.07	3782.92	138.28	108.23	3883	12258
3539.69	1324.48	500.58	1698.91	8870.02	4973.16	171.28	129.70	4643	13644
4712.77	1557.09	720.43	2284.49	10387.00	6270.21	228.22	168.29	5442	15514
6258.38	1798.99	908.97	2720.27	12330.89	7914.00	251.71	193.47	6394	17921
Average Annual Growth Rate (%)									
14.6	10.5	11.6	13.7	15.9	14.6	11.5	12.8		
19.9	13.8	15.3	16.1	19.1	19.6	22.9	25.3	12.4	12.6
21.4	14.0	22.6	24.8	17.1	15.5	22.2	26.0	12.1	10.1

1-9 续表

年 份 Year	主要农产品产量（万吨） Output of Major Farm(10 000 tons)					年末牲畜存栏数（万头（只）） The Year-end Domesticated Animals in Stock (10 000 heads)	
	粮食 Grain	棉花 Cotton	油料 Oil-bearing Crops	甜菜 Beet	水果 Fruit		#羊 Sheep and Goats
1955	147.02	2.51	6.84	0.10	12.33	1640.07	1224.33
1960	197.98	3.19	5.88	7.09	16.10	1911.59	1529.89
1965	261.74	7.59	6.97	15.97	22.35	2697.53	2192.31
1970	303.21	6.46	6.84	21.06	13.70	2431.32	1949.67
1975	310.96	4.67	9.04	15.12	14.25	2436.08	1916.15
1978	370.01	5.50	10.33	16.37	13.98	2476.98	1927.54
1980	386.13	7.92	17.59	38.52	15.62	2672.60	2105.43
1985	496.65	18.78	34.25	40.69	49.25	3016.04	2431.91
1990	676.89	46.88	38.96	224.37	79.88	3496.40	2830.81
1991	672.52	63.95	40.49	256.85	81.10	3494.00	2830.65
1992	706.27	66.76	35.62	329.07	91.89	3495.41	2830.36
1993	720.37	68.00	37.02	236.91	99.82	3514.72	2842.83
1994	666.17	88.21	50.76	299.24	107.52	3599.01	2905.80
1995	730.16	93.50	49.41	288.14	114.43	3724.32	3009.02
1996	818.20	94.04	30.95	354.52	115.99	3863.80	3136.21
1997	825.34	115.00	29.95	388.71	123.67	4007.66	3261.81
1998	830.00	140.00	37.52	513.12	121.48	4223.99	3447.38
1999	838.78	140.75	60.46	354.24	136.42	4396.54	3592.29
2000	808.60	150.00	60.14	292.65	151.87	4524.67	3690.21
2001	796.00	157.00	42.64	455.12	154.25	4603.78	3764.88
2002	875.87	150.00	44.37	466.81	198.20	4781.77	3908.23
2003	801.64	160.00	50.13	381.65	218.34	5026.54	4104.30
2004	828.53	175.25	44.54	344.21	264.22	5206.37	4266.73
2005	877.21	195.70	38.94	419.12	291.26	5333.60	4355.50
2006	895.22	267.53	32.82	555.53	343.14	5339.71	4359.50
2007	867.04	290.00	40.30	586.93	411.98	5023.37	4083.44
2008	909.00	301.55	56.85	438.88	450.87	3746.11	3025.70
2009	1152.00	252.40	63.91	418.41	565.15	3844.75	3127.50
2010	1150.20	247.90	66.62	486.97	593.85	3722.15	3013.37
2011	1200.75	289.77	66.76	518.95	601.65	3697.60	3016.40
2012	1259.83	353.95	59.04	577.19	736.74	4333.25	3502.05
平均增长速度(%)							
1956-2012	3.8	9.1	3.9	16.4	7.4	1.7	1.9
1979-2012	3.7	13.0	5.3	11.0	12.4	1.7	1.8
2001-2012	3.8	7.4	-0.2	5.8	14.1	-0.4	-0.4

Continued

主要畜产品产量（万吨） Output of Major Livestock Products(10 000 tons)			水产品产量（万吨）	主要工业产品产量 Output of Major Industrial Products				
肉类 Meat	羊毛 Wool	奶类 Milk	Output of Aquatic Products (10 000 tons)	原煤（万吨） Crude Coal (10 000 tons)	原油（万吨） Crude Oil (10 000 tons)	天然气（亿立方米） Natural Gas (100 million cu.m)	发电量（亿千瓦时） Volume of Electric Generation (100 million kwh)	钢材（万吨） Steel Rolled (10 000 tons)
6.69			0.07	64.55	3.29	0.01	0.55	0.66
6.08			0.57	473.85	166.23	0.06	3.44	3.63
9.17			0.46	387.00	97.31	0.01	4.46	3.94
8.84		8.53	0.65	558.82	153.60	0.66	7.95	4.21
9.16	3.16	6.35	0.50	716.25	300.19	3.76	13.23	2.20
9.65	3.08	5.25	0.57	1079.01	353.05	2.51	21.17	6.83
12.70	3.31	7.28	0.66	1136.84	390.58	3.53	23.58	8.59
18.37	7.07	19.70	0.90	1600.22	499.00	5.46	38.11	16.73
30.46	5.09	35.64	2.32	2100.00	695.00	5.02	69.79	28.48
32.94	5.19	37.49	2.52	2111.00	762.00	5.54	78.04	33.80
36.02	5.20	39.79	2.66	2204.46	831.66	6.75	86.80	40.30
38.30	5.28	40.85	2.88	2392.29	1065.50	8.43	95.78	45.98
42.81	5.46	44.83	3.53	2633.29	1156.62	9.06	106.17	57.71
52.38	5.66	49.81	4.44	2720.74	1267.83	11.48	120.43	66.55
60.31	5.99	54.22	4.79	2986.00	1457.10	14.06	136.03	86.70
64.40	6.25	58.78	5.24	3021.37	1629.25	21.30	150.58	99.89
75.19	6.48	65.02	5.34	2926.91	1628.38	23.78	157.76	116.19
81.36	6.76	70.43	5.58	2778.15	1739.65	31.06	169.30	117.30
90.00	6.98	78.23	6.01	2798.90	1848.43	35.39	182.98	131.25
97.00	7.30	87.85	6.09	2819.61	1946.95	41.74	197.62	134.42
105.44	7.78	100.71	6.39	3098.67	2036.19	48.52	212.24	173.07
115.00	8.21	119.21	6.73	3482.90	2141.40	50.29	234.62	203.10
128.13	8.91	139.73	7.33	3749.40	2253.02	57.48	266.30	238.52
141.46	9.38	157.84	7.93	3898.81	2408.32	106.64	306.92	326.96
158.21	9.62	185.41	8.45	4518.52	2474.74	164.21	357.15	411.45
160.58	9.34	201.77	8.89	5018.64	2604.31	210.33	416.87	470.94
114.74	9.03	137.40	9.26	6763.41	2715.13	235.89	489.17	576.62
115.31	7.60	125.15	9.70	8812.55	2512.86	245.39	571.31	690.81
121.74	8.69	132.82	10.11	9926.72	2558.16	249.91	679.32	891.70
127.28	9.01	133.91	11.69	11991.71	2615.63	235.38	875.19	985.14
134.23	9.20	136.32	12.53	13646.99	2670.68	253.01	1187.48	1289.84
Average Annual Growth Rate (%)								
5.4			9.5	9.8	12.5	19.5	14.4	14.2
8.1	3.3	10.1	9.5	7.7	6.1	14.5	12.6	16.7
3.4	2.3	4.7	6.3	14.1	3.1	17.8	16.9	21.0

1-10 各时期经济发展主要指标

Major Economic Development Indicators of Each Period

时期	Period	新疆生产总值（亿元） Gross Domestic Product of Xinjiang (100 million yuan)	第一产业 Primary Industry	第二产业 Secondary Industry	#工业 Industry	第三产业 Tertiary Industry	全社会固定资产投资总额（亿元） Total Investment in Fixed Assets (100 million yuan)
“一五”时期	"First Five-year Plan" Period	60.35	33.86	15.54	8.82	10.95	
“二五”时期	"Second Five-year Plan" Period	102.65	43.27	39.48	28.37	19.90	31.42
	1963—1965	64.76	33.56	19.27	13.64	11.93	10.43
“三五”时期	"Third Five-year Plan" Period	111.94	53.53	38.02	27.84	20.39	18.82
“四五”时期	"Fourth Five-year Plan" Period	128.37	54.38	50.55	36.84	23.44	24.72
“五五”时期	"Fifth Five-year Plan" Period	205.39	77.27	91.75	72.34	36.37	69.12
“六五”时期	"Sixth Five-year Plan" Period	405.19	165.70	146.99	117.51	92.50	149.13
“七五”时期	"Seventh Five-year Plan" Period	948.99	356.55	318.96	263.20	273.48	331.97
“八五”时期	"Eighth Five-year Plan" Period	2710.64	781.61	993.78	755.30	935.25	1162.22
“九五”时期	"Ninth Five-year Plan" Period	5574.46	1376.78	2052.88	1574.58	2144.80	2499.46
“十五”时期	"Tenth Five-year Plan" Period	9803.83	1962.15	3975.87	3168.48	3865.81	5034.95
“十一五”时期	"Eleventh Five-year Plan " Period	20466.15	3685.96	9699.35	8119.02	7080.84	12044.80

时期	Period	住宅竣工建筑面积（万平方米） Floor Space of Building Completed (10 000 sq.m)	公共财政预算收入（亿元） General Budgetary Revenue in Local Finance (100 million yuan)	公共财政预算支出（亿元） General Budgetary Expenditure in Local Finance (100 million yuan)	进出口总额（万美元） Total Imports And Exports (USD 10 000)	#出口额 Exports	社会消费品零售总额（亿元） Total Retail Sales of Consumer Goods (100 million yuan)
“一五”时期	"First Five-year Plan" Period		8.65	9.50	20819	10945	31.38
“二五”时期	"Second Five-year Plan" Period		21.39	27.16	26197	17976	53.43
	1963—1965		12.20	11.61	4806	4632	31.92
“三五”时期	"Third Five-year Plan" Period		15.38	21.78	1243	633	63.75
“四五”时期	"Fourth Five-year Plan" Period		11.11	39.78	2922	1217	76.26
“五五”时期	"Fifth Five-year Plan" Period		18.24	54.80	10255	4310	113.51
“六五”时期	"Sixth Five-year Plan" Period	3279.57	27.35	100.30	81536	57445	215.35
“七五”时期	"Seventh Five-year Plan" Period	4175.39	75.48	197.04	190173	142124	323.14
“八五”时期	"Eighth Five-year Plan" Period	4928.74	155.63	338.64	460033	265704	878.89
“九五”时期	"Ninth Five-year Plan" Period	8341.78	318.60	741.45	841181	425462	1655.20
“十五”时期	"Tenth Five-year Plan" Period	12466.98	675.80	1933.02	2281284	1260601	2471.83
“十一五”时期	"Eleventh Five-year Plan " Period	19074.22	1755.75	5578.82	7599235	6173465	5134.21

1-11 各时期经济发展主要指标平均增长率
Growth Rate of Major Economic Development Indicators of Each Period

单位：%　　　　(%)

时 期	Period	新疆生产总值 Gross Domestic Product of Xinjiang	第一产业 Primary Industry	第二产业 Secondary Industry	#工 业 Industry	第三产业 Tertiary Industry	全社会固定资产投资总额 Total Investment in Fixed Assets
"一五"时期	"First Five-year Plan" Period	9.0	5.1	12.6	8.8	18.8	
"二五"时期	"Second Five-year Plan" Period	4.5	2.8	11.0	24.5	-1.3	-14.8
	1963—1965	12.9	17.9	8.4	3.3	5.4	28.4
"三五"时期	"Third Five-year Plan" Period	0.3	-3.1	3.8	4.3	4.8	2.2
"四五"时期	"Fourth Five-year Plan" Period	2.9	…	7.2	7.3	-0.5	6.3
"五五"时期	"Fifth Five-year Plan" Period	10.5	7.4	11.6	14.3	14.5	34.1
"六五"时期	"Sixth Five-year Plan" Period	12.5	13.0	9.2	9.3	17.6	10.9
"七五"时期	"Seventh Five-year Plan" Period	9.8	7.9	8.2	9.2	14.7	14.8
"八五"时期	"Eighth Five-year Plan" Period	11.8	6.7	14.2	13.5	15.0	30.3
"九五"时期	"Ninth Five-year Plan" Period	7.7	5.8	6.8	5.9	10.3	12.9
"十五"时期	"Tenth Five-year Plan" Period	10.0	5.6	10.6	11.3	11.2	17.2
"十一五"时期	"Eleventh Five-year Plan " Period	10.6	5.6	11.8	12.1	11.4	21.2

时 期	Period	住宅竣工建筑面积 Floor Space of Building Completed	公共财政预算收入 General Budgetary Revenue in Local Finance	公共财政预算支出 General Budgetary Expenditure in Local Finance	进出口总额 Total Imports And Exports	#出口额 Exports	社会消费品零售总额 Total Retail Sales of Consumer Goods
"一五"时期	"First Five-year Plan" Period		25.0	30.7	17.8	17.8	18.5
"二五"时期	"Second Five-year Plan" Period		4.7	-0.4	-12.5	-9.6	4.3
	1963—1965		16.8	30.5	-20.4	-13.8	2.3
"三五"时期	"Third Five-year Plan" Period		-4.7	4.3	-34.4	-50.3	3.2
"四五"时期	"Fourth Five-year Plan" Period		-22.3	7.9	40.6	58.0	5.0
"五五"时期	"Fifth Five-year Plan" Period		31.9	12.9	28.4	35.5	11.7
"六五"时期	"Sixth Five-year Plan" Period		16.0	12.0	56.0	60.2	14.3
"七五"时期	"Seventh Five-year Plan" Period	2.3	20.8	10.7	7.0	13.2	12.7
"八五"时期	"Eighth Five-year Plan" Period	3.1	11.9	15.1	28.3	18.1	19.4
"九五"时期	"Ninth Five-year Plan" Period	12.1	15.6	14.6	9.7	9.4	8.1
"十五"时期	"Tenth Five-year Plan" Period	14.0	17.9	22.1	28.5	33.2	11.2
"十一五"时期	"Eleventh Five-year Plan " Period	-1.9	22.7	26.8	16.6	20.8	15.7

1-12 天山北坡经济带主要经济指标

(2012 年)

指　　标	Item	全区合计 Total of the whole region	北坡经济带合计 Total of the economic belt	北坡经济带占全区比重(%) ratio of the economic belt (%)	乌昌合计 Total of Urmqi and Changji	乌昌占全区比重(%) Pencent-age of Urmqi and Changji to total(%)	乌鲁木齐市 Urumqi City
人　口	**Population**						
年末总人口	Total Population at Year-end	2232.78	868.19	38.9	398.01	17.8	257.80
#少数民族人口	Minority Nationalities Population	1385.49	314.95	22.7	108.40	7.8	70.61
城镇人口	Urban Population	981.98	755.18	76.9	370.47	37.7	250.50
乡村人口	Rural Population	1250.80	113.01	9.0	27.54	2.2	7.30
综　合	**General**						
新疆生产总值(亿元)	Gross Domestic Produc in Xinjiang (100 million yuan)	7505.31	5187.48	69.1	2820.30	37.6	2001.74
第一产业	First Industry	1320.57	550.53	41.7	241.74	18.3	25.02
第二产业	Second Industry	3481.56	2600.21	74.7	1217.78	35.0	829.01
#工　业	Industry	2850.06	2227.74	78.2	1026.39	36.0	714.01
第三产业	Tertiary Industry	2703.18	2036.74	75.3	1360.78	50.3	1147.71
新疆生产总值构成(%)	Composition of Gross Domestic Produc in Xinjiang (%)						
第一产业	First Industry	17.6	10.6		8.6		1.2
第二产业	Second Industry	46.4	50.1		43.2		41.4
#工　业	Industry	38.0	42.9		36.4		35.7
第三产业	Tertiary Industry	36.0	39.3		48.2		57.3
财政收入相当于新疆生产总值比重(%)	Ratio of GDP covered by financial Expenditure (%)	12.1	9.5		11.2		12.6
财政支出相当于新疆生产总值比重(%)	Ratio of GDP covered by financial Expenditure (%)	36.2	14.5		15.6		14.8
固定资产投资(亿元)	**Fixed Asset Investment (100 million yuan)**						
#城镇固定资产投资总额	Fixed Asset Value of the town	4987.71	2747.01	55.1	1209.28	24.2	581.22
财政、金融(亿元)	**Finance and Public Money(100 million yuan)**						
公共财政预算收入	Local Financial Income	908.97	495.06	54.5	316.29	34.8	252.01
#各项税收	Various Tax Incomes	698.93	425.43	60.9	270.11	38.6	217.69
公共财政预算支出	Expenditure of Local Finance	2720.07	752.08	27.6	439.33	16.2	295.60
#一般公共服务	General Common Service	303.67	77.42	25.5	43.29	14.3	27.61
教　育	Operating Expenses for Education	473.86	147.54	31.1	75.89	16.0	49.77
社保和就业	Operating Expenses for Medical Treatment and Sanitation	227.79	57.54	25.3	30.94	13.6	23.37
金融机构年末存款余额	Year-end Loan Balance of Finance	12330.89	8487.24	68.8	5607.26	45.5	4819.11
金融机构年末贷款余额	Year-end Deposit Balance of Finance	7914.00	5011.62	63.3	3786.14	47.8	3245.33
物价(上年=100)	**Commodity Price (Preceding year=100)**						
商品零售价格指数	Index of Commodity Retail Price	103.3					102.9
居民消费价格指数	Index of Price for Residents' Consumption	103.8					103.4
人民生活	**People's life**						
在岗职工平均货币工资(元)	Average Staff''s Money Wage (yuan)	45243					52418
农村居民家庭人均纯收入(元)	Annual Per capita Net Income of Rural Residents (yuan)	6394					10356
城乡居民储蓄存款余额(亿元)	Balance of Both Urban and Rural Deposit(100 million yuan)	5281.83	3470.58	65.7	2127.54	40.3	1715.97
建成区绿化覆盖率(%)	Ratio of Green Coverage in Completed Areas(%)	35.88					37.00

Main Economic Indicators for Economic Belt on the Northern Scope of the Tianshan Mountains

克拉玛依市 Karamay City	石河子市 Shihezi City	五家渠市 Wujiaqu City	哈密市 Hami [Kumul] City	吐鲁番市 Turpan City	鄯善县 Shanshan [Piqan] County	托克逊县 Toksun County	伊宁市 Yining [Gulja] City	奎屯市 Kuytun City	伊宁县 Yining [Gulja] County	察布查尔锡伯自治县 Qapqal Xibe Autonomous county	霍城县 Huocheng [Korgas] County	乌苏市 Usu City	沙湾县 Shawan County
28.58	62.00	9.07	46.55	27.58	23.13	11.82	51.53	30.44	42.73	19.43	40.75	22.89	21.64
7.21	3.96	0.33	13.26	22.39	16.62	9.96	33.28	1.59	35.84	12.82	23.71	8.35	7.01
28.58	62.00	9.07	46.55	27.58	17.68	2.49	51.53	30.44	8.83	6.52	21.58	22.89	18.53
					5.45	9.33			33.90	12.91	19.17		3.11
810.71	208.19	94.33	209.44	63.77	140.83	40.05	136.80	105.96	53.36	32.78	73.80	153.46	139.45
4.63	11.36	7.64	20.66	14.37	12.30	7.22	6.36	5.72	21.17	15.78	25.02	45.56	73.43
713.07	119.87	56.17	102.70	20.04	109.35	24.87	36.36	56.53	17.00	7.69	16.39	81.06	30.15
692.07	91.77	42.16	67.55	15.89	95.70	20.33	18.42	45.29	13.79	5.44	12.99	67.21	20.08
93.01	76.96	30.52	86.08	29.36	19.18	7.96	94.08	43.71	15.19	9.31	32.39	26.84	35.87
0.6	5.5	8.1	9.9	22.5	8.7	18.0	4.6	5.4	39.7	48.1	33.9	29.7	52.7
88.0	57.6	59.5	49.0	31.4	77.6	62.1	26.6	53.4	31.9	23.5	22.2	52.8	21.6
85.4	44.1	44.7	32.3	24.9	68.0	50.8	13.5	42.7	25.8	16.6	17.6	43.8	14.4
11.5	37.0	32.4	41.1	46.0	13.6	19.9	68.8	41.3	28.5	28.4	43.9	17.5	25.7
7.1	10.4	7.3	10.6	7.7	7.1	12.1	12.6	12.6	7.3	7.9	4.1	5.2	3.6
8.7	12.9	9.1	14.9	21.9	12.9	29.4	23.9	18.0	37.9	46.0	23.4	13.0	11.7
301.66	175.12	114.25	185.14	33.57	97.42	41.22	101.97	114.18	53.50	41.56	57.69	57.47	42.42
57.26	21.75	6.86	22.26	4.92	10.00	4.84	17.21	13.36	3.88	2.60	3.01	8.01	5.01
50.74	18.58	6.54	19.86	3.78	7.90	3.32	15.65	10.96	3.34	1.62	2.44	6.19	3.90
70.18	26.91	8.56	31.18	13.96	18.11	11.78	32.69	19.09	20.24	15.08	17.24	19.94	16.28
9.17	1.99	0.69	3.59	1.38	2.14	1.35	3.82	1.75	1.62	1.19	1.61	3.04	1.67
16.37	4.25	1.10	4.80	3.35	3.29	2.40	8.10	4.43	6.48	3.26	4.89	3.93	3.74
5.12	1.49	0.56	2.80	1.12	1.11	0.75	3.74	1.11	1.71	1.67	1.87	1.86	1.43
936.72	413.65	83.02	334.97	76.08	75.30	27.53	365.51	197.75	41.01	33.49	58.67	97.36	72.37
142.39	249.21	77.25	180.91	38.86	33.60	21.38	179.39	94.32	48.49	19.60	21.46	65.47	45.01
102.7	103.1		103.1	104.0			103.5	101.4				102.8	
102.9	102.8		103.7	104.3			103.7	102.4				103.9	
73510	44227	46566	46103	43272	61179	47616	38169	41006	30231	33470	33091	28692	37176
13472	12379	12200	9138	6954	6948	6222	10157	10030	9074	8676	9597	13124	15032
231.33	275.64	41.15	184.38	44.78	45.20	16.04	176.89	109.70	21.53	15.70	36.07	59.19	52.04
42.92	42.54	37.01	44.09	22.59	14.45	18.70	39.08	40.15	35.53	29.19	42.41	30.86	33.44

1-12 续表 1

指标	Item	全区合计 Total of the whole region	北坡经济带合计 Total of the economic belt	北坡经济带占全区比重(%) ratio of the economic belt (%)	乌昌合计 Total of Urmqi and Changji	乌昌占全区比重(%) Pencent-age of Urmqi and Changji to total(%)	乌鲁木齐市 Urumqi City
农业	**Agriculture**						
农林牧渔业总产值(亿元)	Value of Farm, Forestry, Herding and Fishery (100 million yuan)	2275.67	1100.09	48.3	306.05	13.4	34.43
农业	Farming	1675.00	702.61	41.9	133.21	8.0	15.22
林业	Forestry	43.04	14.93	34.7	3.34	7.8	0.75
牧业	Animal Husbandry	485.37	326.65	67.3	164.18	33.8	17.61
渔业	Fishery	15.26	6.79	44.5	2.47	16.2	0.70
农林牧渔服务业	Services for Farming, Forestry, Animal Husbandary and Fishery	57.00	49.11	86.2	2.85	5.0	0.15
主要农产品产量(万吨)	Main Rural Products Output (10 000 tons)						
粮食	Grain	1259.83	519.12	41.2	171.50	13.6	15.23
棉花	Cotton	353.95	156.37	44.2	20.43	5.8	0.17
油料	Oil-bearing Crops	59.04	21.73	36.8	8.84	15.0	0.92
甜菜	Beet	577.19	279.58	48.4	64.99	11.3	0.22
水果	Fruit	736.74	232.98	31.6	19.19	2.6	0.89
肉类	Meat	134.23	110.12	82.0	59.15	44.1	6.13
工业	**Industry**						
工业总产值(规模以上)(亿元)	Total Value of Industrial Products (100 million yuan)	7532.67	5757.26	76.4	2755.06	36.6	2150.84
轻工业	Light Industry	892.63	634.37	71.1	331.20	37.1	154.35
重工业	Heavy Industry	6640.04	5122.87	77.2	2423.86	36.5	1996.48
主要工业产品产量	Output of Main Industrial Products						
纱(万吨)	Cotton Yarn (10 000 tons)	37.58	27.75	73.8	3.68	9.8	2.14
布(万米)	Cloth (10 000 m)	3091.00	2469.00	79.9	324.00	10.5	
绒线(吨)	Woolen knitting wool (ton)	359.67	243.67	67.7	243.67	67.7	243.67
呢绒(万米)	Woolen Goods (10 000 m)	331.70	331.70	100.0	88.70	26.7	
原盐(万吨)	Crude Salt (10 000 tons)	256.61	115.39	45.0	10.33	4.0	10.33
成品糖(万吨)	Sugar (10 000 tons)	53.30	26.71	50.1	6.55	12.3	
原煤(万吨)	Crude Coal (10 000 tons)	12395.54	8727.36	70.4	6024.44	48.6	3066.72
原油(万吨)	Crude Oil (10 000 tons)	2670.68	2090.51	78.3	735.00	27.5	735.00
发电量(亿千瓦小时)	Volume of Electric Generation (100 million kwh)	1051.63	834.36	79.3	406.40	38.6	252.43
粗钢(万吨)	Grude steel (10 000 tons)	1138.23	790.72	69.5	770.86	67.7	770.86
钢材(万吨)	Steel Rolled (10 000 tons)	1284.57	929.25	72.3	910.06	70.8	910.06
水泥(万吨)	Cement (10 000 tons)	4025.80	2260.44	56.1	887.06	22.0	491.90
运输邮电业	**Traffic and Telecommunication Sector**						
公路客运量(万人)	Highway Passenger Volume (10 000 persons)	52473	19364	36.9	9643	18.4	3194
公路货运量(万吨)	Highway Cargo Volume (10 000 tons)	61850	39662	64.1	24906	40.3	16142
公路货物周转量(亿吨公里)	Turnover of Highway Cargo (100million tons-km)	946.90	547.87	57.9	337.78	35.7	228.80
邮电业务总量(亿元)	Volume of Postal-Telecommunication (100 million yuan)	264.84	93.34	35.2	75.70	28.6	59.60
国内商业	**Domestic Trades**						
社会消费品零售总额(亿元)	Retail Volume of Social Commodities (100 million yuan)	1798.99	1407.14	78.2	895.41	49.8	739.69
教育、卫生	**Education and Health**						
在校学生数(人)	Number of Registered Students (person)						
高等学校	Institutions of Higher Education	268716	243202	90.5	180549	67.2	158680
中等职业学校	Specialized Secondary School	235277	141938	60.3	85941	36.5	72770
普通中学	Ordinary Middle School	1383886	639494	46.2	233164	16.8	150991
小学	Elementary School	1900844	720747	37.9	263310	13.9	184287
毕业生数(人)	Number of Graduates (person)						
高等学校	Institutions of Higher Education	64591	56884	88.1	43313	67.1	37384
中等职业学校	Specialized Secondary School	71288	45277	63.5	28887	40.5	24776
普通中学	Ordinary Middle School	454590	203498	44.8	73772	16.2	47114
小学	Elementary School	321020	127758	39.8	45239	14.1	30462
医院、卫生院床位数(张)	Number of Sick Beds (unit)	125064	70841	56.6	36448	29.1	26518
卫生技术人员数(人)	Number of Hygiene Technicians (person)	136691	85166	62.3	43639	31.9	32720

Continued

克拉玛依市 Karamay City	石河子市 Shihezi City	五家渠市 Wujiaqu City	哈密市 Hami [Kumul] City	吐鲁番市 Turpan City	鄯善县 Shanshan [Piqan] County	托克逊县 Toksun County	伊宁市 Yining [Gulja] City	奎屯市 Kuytun City	伊宁县 Yining [Gulja] County	察布查尔锡伯自治县 Qapqal Xibe Autonomous county	霍城县 Huocheng [Korgas] County	乌苏市 Usu City	沙湾县 Shawan County
10.59	22.79	15.86	20.88	23.97	20.76	12.04	11.26	1.55	35.18	20.10	22.94	45.22	60.08
3.53	13.59	10.85	13.99	20.13	17.43	8.88	6.76	0.78	18.81	13.39	12.05	33.95	43.08
2.06	0.14	0.10	0.70	0.17	0.12	0.10	0.08	0.01	0.31	0.38	0.34	0.28	0.24
3.58	6.39	3.39	5.75	3.21	3.05	2.86	3.96	0.64	14.82	5.94	9.97	10.45	15.92
0.08	0.42	0.18	0.20	0.04	0.01		0.18		0.67	0.06	0.04	0.09	0.13
1.34	2.25	1.34	0.24	0.42	0.15	0.20	0.28	0.12	0.57	0.33	0.54	0.45	0.71
0.50	3.22	2.19	2.90	0.27	0.41	2.08	11.51	1.08	70.47	38.73	25.45	22.70	20.78
1.24	3.10	1.84	3.28	0.50	0.99	1.53		0.26	0.01	0.97	0.31	10.54	13.17
	0.16	0.18	0.08			0.09	0.17	0.02	0.99	0.63	0.89	0.45	0.93
	0.47	1.18					4.16		13.73	16.44	44.42	3.66	6.57
	3.54	0.43	9.88	41.57	40.42	4.75	35.55		7.82	1.80	8.30	0.24	1.23
1.07	2.41	1.27	2.44	2.11	1.05	0.93	1.27	0.43	4.64	1.82	3.45	3.57	4.50
1693.88	369.95	147.58	157.17	44.25	177.76	49.80	41.64	113.16	41.11	18.27	26.71	41.60	37.26
2.69	99.63	15.76	12.72	3.94	0.47	0.65	19.04	53.50	11.16	7.89	15.27	17.24	25.67
1691.19	270.31	131.82	144.45	40.31	177.30	49.15	22.60	59.67	29.94	10.38	11.45	24.36	11.59
	14.81	0.48	1.07	0.35				3.67				0.94	0.56
	2145.00												
	243.00												
						99.00							
								3.34	4.49		9.40		
			914.25	28.78		1118.23		37.96	256.40	85.87		261.43	
1103.01					156.00							96.50	
46.89	128.18	92.63	57.49	3.72	0.83	23.63	5.54	20.93	4.78		0.73	36.49	
				13.71					0.61				5.54
	2.52			6.97					0.54		3.68		5.48
	289.60		201.20	176.90					182.81	224.70		76.18	116.30
645	1050	1417	354	1295			1445	647	400	235	403	1625	1200
2868	3259	3745	1105	930			1701	492	351	156	477	485	1300
55.42	57.16	22.42	18.98	16.00			30.62	9.84	1.23	1.04	2.28	8.45	8.00
0.49	7.86	0.45	5.75	2.06	1.83	0.64	0.50	0.38	0.09	0.08	0.23	1.32	0.62
48.00	64.98	20.41	49.58	16.41	9.60	3.40	51.25	18.60	10.46	2.31	15.01	10.46	11.63
4198	6067	3012	3788				26946						
802	1826	1815	3314	3138	229	394	9863						
25031	19704	11948	28068	14440	11651	5871	36253	14470	22174	8849	15305	14104	15408
22641	12113	6800	25974	21940	19904	8947	47711	9962	37759	12574	24132	16752	14644
1087	1814	772	399				5581						
315	705	498	534	686	162	200	2760						
7945	6109	2559	8957	4702	4010	2174	11174	4370	7280	2903	4618	4848	5265
4126	2432	1220	4807	3891	3134	1364	7971	1880	5946	2039	3830	3039	2641
1648	5539	868	2159	1054	913	418	4120	944	436	247	540	1261	772
2937	6070	1087	2818	1317	1156	552	4764	1121	1455	579	1038	1607	960

1-12 续表 2

(2012 年)

指　标	Item	昌吉市 Changji City	阜康市 Fukang City	呼图壁县 Hu Tubi County	玛纳斯县 Manas County	奇台县 Qitai County	吉木萨尔县 Jimsar County
人　口	**Population**						
年末总人口	Total Population at Year-end	37.04	16.86	21.73	17.49	24.05	14.09
＃少数民族人口	Minority Nationalities Population	10.19	4.87	5.21	3.43	6.44	4.45
城镇人口	Urban Population	37.04	16.86	20.19	14.01	16.27	11.66
乡村人口	Rural Population			1.54	3.48	7.78	2.43
综　合	**General**						
新疆生产总值(亿元)	Gross Domestic Produc in Xinjiang (100 million yuan)	260.36	118.89	106.87	133.82	85.24	48.13
第一产业	First Industry	33.20	21.89	40.52	57.28	36.56	15.00
第二产业	Second Industry	130.29	72.97	38.33	48.44	28.66	21.42
＃工　业	Industry	110.30	65.08	21.93	39.98	22.96	18.43
第三产业	Tertiary Industry	96.87	24.03	28.02	28.10	20.02	11.71
新疆生产总值构成(%)	Composition of Gross Domestic Produc in Xinjiang (%)						
第一产业	First Industry	12.8	18.4	37.9	42.8	42.9	31.2
第二产业	Second Industry	50.0	61.4	35.9	36.2	33.6	44.5
＃工　业	Industry	42.4	54.7	20.5	29.9	26.9	38.3
第三产业	Tertiary Industry	37.2	20.2	26.2	21.0	23.5	24.3
财政收入相当于新疆生产总值比重(%)	Ratio of GDP covered by financial Expenditure (%)	7.9	9.3	5.0	4.1	6.9	13.5
财政支出相当于新疆生产总值比重(%)	Ratio of GDP covered by financial Expenditure (%)	11.4	16.3	12.2	10.6	21.8	29.3
固定资产投资(亿元)	**Fixed Asset Investment (100 million yuan)**						
＃城镇固定资产投资总额	Fixed Asset Value of the town	108.55	114.08	58.46	50.89	112.13	178.94
财政、金融(亿元)	**Finance and Public Money(100 million yuan)**						
公共财政预算收入	Local Financial Income	20.54	11.07	5.34	5.46	5.85	6.49
＃各项税收	Various Tax Incomes	17.30	8.90	4.42	4.90	5.06	5.87
公共财政预算支出	Expenditure of Local Finance	29.78	19.33	13.05	14.24	18.57	14.10
＃一般公共服务	General Common Service	4.46	2.09	1.18	1.40	1.37	1.30
教　育	Operating Expenses for Education	5.53	3.27	3.23	2.62	4.09	2.25
社保和就业	Operating Expenses for Medical Treatment and Sanitation	1.42	0.92	0.72	0.84	1.09	0.98
金融机构年末存款余额	Year-end Loan Balance of Finance	341.10	87.48	77.76	67.48	75.81	42.78
金融机构年末贷款余额	Year-end Deposit Balance of Finance	240.70	57.19	51.62	44.77	37.53	23.87
物价(上年=100)	**Commodity Price (Preceding year=100)**						
商品零售价格指数	Index of Commodity Retail Price	104.1					
居民消费价格指数	Index of Price for Residents' Consumption	104.1					
人民生活	**People's life**						
在岗职工平均货币工资(元)	Average Staff"s Money Wage (yuan)	44705	44918	35649	42828	38900	49669
农村居民家庭人均纯收入(元)	Annual Per capita Net Income of Rural Residents (yuan)	12136	12236	13114	14580	11133	10855
城乡居民储蓄存款余额(亿元)	Balance of Both Urban and Rural Deposit(100 million yuan)	155.4	49.58	50.03	43.78	41.41	23.90
建成区绿化覆盖率(%)	Ratio of Green Coverage in Completed Areas(%)	39.12	32.85	38.22	37.09	34.00	34.40

Continued

博乐市 Bole [Bortala] City	精河县 Jinghe [Jing] County	农四师 XJPCC No.4 Division	农五师 XJPCC No.5 Division	农六师 XJPCC No.6 Division	农七师 XJPCC No.7 Division	农八师 XJPCC No.8 Division	建工师 XJPCC architectural engineer Division	农十二师 XJPCC No.12 Division	农十三师 XJPCC No.13 Division	兵团直属 Directly under XPCG
26.56	14.43									
8.82	4.60									
26.56	7.82									
	6.61									
126.88	42.62									
29.35	20.49									
30.09	9.75									
20.59	5.77									
67.44	12.38									
23.1	48.1									
23.7	22.9									
16.2	13.5									
53.2	29.0									
4.2	4.6									
12.3	24.8									
90.96	34.61									
5.38	1.95									
4.84	1.63									
15.59	10.58									
1.99	1.01									
3.42	2.97									
1.26	0.60									
119.80	42.49									
63.77	29.50									
103.2										
103.1										
37207	30048									
10003	9716									
54.43	26.44									
36.62	35.07									

1-12 续表 3

指　　标	Item	昌吉市 Changji City	阜康市 Fukang City	呼图壁县 Hu Tubi County	玛纳斯县 Manas County	奇台县 Qitai County	吉木萨尔县 Jimsar County
农　业	**Agriculture**						
农林牧渔业总产值(亿元)	Value of Farm, Forestry, Herding and Fishery (100 million yuan)	40.72	31.58	47.70	52.47	57.14	22.62
农　业	Farming	17.33	14.02	18.12	29.82	22.77	9.73
林　业	Forestry	0.36	0.23	0.37	0.33	0.60	0.56
牧　业	Animal Husbandry	21.66	17.13	27.72	21.25	33.74	12.09
渔　业	Fishery	1.01	0.05	0.35	0.23		0.13
农林牧渔服务业	Services for Farming, Forestry, Animal Husbandary and Fishery	0.36	0.15	1.14	0.84	0.03	0.11
主要农产品产量(万吨)	Main Rural Products Output (10 000 tons)						
粮　食	Grain	22.59	13.87	16.04	14.40	62.76	14.75
棉　花	Cotton	6.27	0.10	5.75	8.08		0.05
油　料	Oil-bearing Crops	1.21	1.86	0.20	0.64	2.09	1.39
甜　菜	Beet	9.88	10.65	6.01	2.43	32.01	2.42
水　果	Fruit	9.16	1.36	0.85	5.06	0.08	1.55
肉　类	Meat	10.36	6.83	9.20	6.80	12.48	4.75
工　业	**Industry**						
工业总产值(规模以上)(亿元)	Total Value of Industrial Products (100 million yuan)	250.79	122.06	50.16	73.95	50.62	51.88
轻工业	Light Industry	81.53	1.50	24.48	45.05	17.41	6.87
重工业	Heavy Industry	169.26	120.56	25.68	28.89	33.20	45.01
主要工业产品产量	Output of Main Industrial Products						
纱(万吨)	Cotton Yarn (10 000 tons)	0.25		1.11	0.19		
布(万米)	Cloth (10 000 m)			324.00			
绒线(吨)	Woolen knitting wool (ton)						
呢绒(万米)	Woolen Goods (10 000 m)	88.70					
原盐(万吨)	Crude Salt (10 000 tons)						
成品糖(万吨)	Sugar (10 000 tons)	2.74				3.81	
原煤(万吨)	Crude Coal (10 000 tons)	808.36	261.36	293.29	37.81	612.81	584.99
原油(万吨)	Crude Oil (10 000 tons)						
发电量(亿千瓦小时)	Volume of Electric Generation (100 million kwh)	51.28	29.74		72.82	0.13	
粗钢(万吨)	Grude steel (10 000 tons)						
钢材(万吨)	Steel Rolled (10 000 tons)						
水泥(万吨)	Cement (10 000 tons)	182.02	38.00			175.14	
运输邮电业	**Traffic and Telecommunication Sector**						
公路客运量(万人)	Highway Passenger Volume (10 000 persons)	2760	551	740	586	817	
公路货运量(万吨)	Highway Cargo Volume (10 000 tons)	4401	512	128	632	978	
公路货物周转量(亿吨公里)	Turnover of Highway Cargo (100million tons-km)	64.90	0.57		8.96	13.20	
邮电业务总量(亿元)	Volume of Postal-Telecommunication (100 million yuan)	5.57	1.72	1.52	1.35	0.96	0.32
国内商业	**Domestic Trades**						
社会消费品零售总额(亿元)	Retail Volume of Social Commodities (100 million yuan)	64.71	21.48	18.26	20.08	17.60	8.44
教育、文化、卫生	**Education, Culture and Health**						
在校学生数(人)	Number of Registered Students (person)						
高等学校	Institutions of Higher Education	40511					
中等职业学校	Specialized Secondary School	10937	1359	1015	755	1285	491
普通中学	Ordinary Middle School	82173	11414	9359	7381	12930	6344
小　学	Elementary School	79023	8129	11055	8901	11652	6715
毕业生数(人)	Number of Graduates (person)						
高等学校	Institutions of Higher Education	9847					
中等职业学校	Specialized Secondary School	3431	634	218	218	161	46
普通中学	Ordinary Middle School	26658	2568	2857	2341	4427	1360
小　学	Elementary School	14777	1572	1911	1739	2298	1311
医院床位数(张)	Number of Sick Beds (unit)	4500	550	919	692	886	522
卫生技术人员数(人)	Number of Hygiene Technicians (person)	3431	664	994	993	694	375

Continued

博尔市 Bole [Bortala] City	精河县 Jinghe [Jing] County	农四师 XJPCC No.4 Division	农五师 XJPCC No.5 Division	农六师 XJPCC No.6 Division	农七师 XJPCC No.7 Division	农八师 XJPCC No.8 Division	建工师 XJPCC architectu-ral engineer Division	农十二师 XJPCC No.12 Division	农十三师 XJPCC No.13 Division	兵团直属 Directly under XPCG
26.46	26.73	57.60	36.18	89.00	70.21	143.35	0.07	14.49	23.20	2.93
19.67	22.14	37.39	29.63	62.97	53.74	106.82	0.07	8.24	15.30	2.40
0.23	0.34	0.63	0.23	0.70	0.68	3.22		0.50	0.15	0.01
5.47	2.87	16.26	3.77	17.43	11.77	18.53		3.81	5.41	0.21
0.03	0.08	0.62	0.09	0.33	0.29	0.55		0.18	0.02	0.04
1.06	1.30	2.69	2.46	7.58	3.72	14.23		1.76	2.32	0.28
26.04	1.91	46.60	9.95	41.08	15.87	11.57	0.03	0.02	2.72	1.40
5.75	8.05	2.87	9.75	15.18	14.77	39.02	0.02	0.01	2.69	0.11
0.07		4.27	0.75	2.08	0.73	0.47	0.01	0.00	0.04	0.40
10.13	0.73	48.81	21.08	7.32	36.79	0.47	0.00	0.00	0.00	0.00
0.19	0.21	18.46	3.68	4.05	3.24	9.08		6.72	11.41	1.46
1.04	0.58	4.35	1.33	5.52	2.46	5.07		0.87	1.32	0.06
39.28	7.54									
13.16	4.39									
26.12	3.15									
1.06	1.12									
	6.06									
2.93										
6.12										
97.27	8.42									
18.35	4.41	12.98	9.89	37.47	22.91	54.03	1.00	15.31	6.26	2.19
		3477	272	1815	576	4599	1953	427	216	18610
10715	6404	15777	10092	17675	10296	21511	6096	5283	4834	6943
13583	9254	18085	10482	19402	10994	24821	7331	5912	6900	2368
		79		558	241	1373	806	139	128	6609
3509	2129	5343	3793	5765	3543	7312	1908	1743	1772	2442
2194	1557	3728	2297	3503	2514	5402	1167	1172	1372	462
1134	508	1537	826	1827	2025	5539	118	230	950	641
1584	587	1545	1040	2584	1961	6056	164	305	1099	909

1-13 法人单位数和产业活动单位数

Number of Legal Entities and Establishment Entities

单位：个 (unit)

年份 Year	地区 Region	法人单位数 Number of Legal Entities	单产业法人 Single Sector	多产业法人 Multi-sector	产业活动单位数 Number of Establishments Entities	#多产业法人的活动单位 Establishments Entities of Multi-sector
	2000	53982	47574	6408		
	2001	66477	60857	5620	114912	54055
	2002	66186	60736	5450	114141	53405
	2003	68203	62895	5308	115782	52887
	2004	63429	58196	5233	112499	54303
	2005	69756	64157	5599	122055	57898
	2006	75447	69724	5723	128165	58441
	2007	79767	73984	5783	132750	58766
	2008	88115	82100	6015	139686	57586
	2009	93673	87408	6265	148845	61437
	2010	96727	90456	6271	151303	60847
	2011	101926	95614	6312	155890	60276
	2012	110109	103664	6445	164313	60649
乌鲁木齐市	Urumqi City	30058	29159	899	33460	4301
克拉玛依市	Karamay City	3329	3068	261	4351	1283
吐鲁番地区	Turpan Administrative Offices	3737	3548	189	4780	1232
哈密地区	Hami [Kumul] Administrative Offices	5436	5082	354	7242	2160
昌吉回族自治州	Changji Hui Autonomous Prefecture	8120	7573	547	11127	3554
伊犁哈萨克自治州	Ili Kazak Autonomous Prefecture	15994	14889	1105	24229	9340
伊犁州直属县(市)	Counties (Cities) Direct Under Ili Prefecture	7336	6868	468	11525	4657
塔城地区	Tacheng [Tarbagatai] Administrative Offices	4004	3716	288	6294	2578
阿勒泰地区	Altay Administrative Offices	4654	4305	349	6410	2105
博尔塔拉蒙古自治州	Bortala Mongol Autonomous Prefecture	3015	2799	216	4341	1542
巴音郭楞蒙古自治州	Bayangol Mongol Autonomous Prefecture	8886	8132	754	12705	4573
阿克苏地区	Aksu Administrative Offices	9045	8378	667	16385	8007
克孜勒苏柯尔克孜自治州	Kizilsu Kirgiz Autonomous Prefecture	2124	1971	153	4173	2202
喀什地区	Kashgar [Kaxgar] Administrative Offices	7932	7292	640	23277	15985
和田地区	Hotan Administrative Offices	8866	8357	509	13092	4735
自治区直辖县级市	Municpality Country-level Gity Directly under the Central Government	3567	3416	151	4959	1543
石河子市	Shihezi City	2665	2574	91	3149	575
阿拉尔市	Aral City	297	275	22	654	379
图木舒克市	Tumxuk City	215	201	14	567	366
五家渠市	Wujiaqu City	390	366	24	589	223

注：2004 年数据不包括农、林、牧、渔业。
Note: Data in 2004 does not include statistics of agriculture,forestry,animal husbandry and fishery.

1-14 按三次产业分的法人单位数及构成

Number of Legal Entities by Three Strata of Industry and Its Composition

年份 Year	地区 Region	法人单位数 Number of Legal Entities	第一产业 Primary Industry	
			绝对数 Value	构成 (%) Composition (%)
	2000	53982		
	2001	66477	3439	5.17
	2002	66186	3421	5.17
	2003	68203	3195	4.68
	2004	63429		
	2005	69756	1449	2.08
	2006	75447	1524	2.02
	2007	79767	1715	2.15
	2008	88115	203	0.23
	2009	93673	2439	2.60
	2010	96727	2842	2.94
	2011	101926	3650	3.58
	2012	110109	4773	4.34
乌鲁木齐市	Urumqi City	30058	205	0.68
克拉玛依市	Karamay City	3329	88	2.64
吐鲁番地区	Turpan Administrative Offices	3737	125	3.34
哈密地区	Hami [Kumul] Administrative Offices	5436	313	5.76
昌吉回族自治州	Changji Hui Autonomous Prefecture	8120	526	6.48
伊犁哈萨克自治州	Ili Kazak Autonomous Prefecture	15994	935	5.85
伊犁州直属县(市)	Counties (Cities) Direct Under Ili Prefecture	7336	297	4.05
塔城地区	Tacheng [Tarbagatai] Administrative Offices	4004	121	3.02
阿勒泰地区	Altay Administrative Offices	4654	517	11.11
博尔塔拉蒙古自治州	Bortala Mongol Autonomous Prefecture	3015	156	5.17
巴音郭楞蒙古自治州	Bayangol Mongol Autonomous Prefecture	8886	768	8.64
阿克苏地区	Aksu Administrative Offices	9045	657	7.26
克孜勒苏柯尔克孜自治州	Kizilsu Kirgiz Autonomous Prefecture	2124	102	4.80
喀什地区	Kashgar [Kaxgar] Administrative Offices	7932	145	1.83
和田地区	Hotan Administrative Offices	8866	664	7.49
自治区直辖县级市	Municpality Country-level Gity Directly under the Central Government	3567	89	2.50
石河子市	Shihezi City	2665	56	2.10
阿拉尔市	Aral City	297	20	6.73
图木舒克市	Tumxuk City	215	6	2.79
五家渠市	Wujiaqu City	390	7	1.79

注：2004 年数据不包括农、林、牧、渔业。
Note: Data in 2004 does not include statistics of agriculture,forestry,animal husbandry and fishery.

1-14 续表 Continued

年 份 Year	地 区 Region	第二产业 Secondary Inclustry		第三产业 Tertiary Industry	
		绝对数 Value	构成(%) Composition	绝对数 Value	构成 (%) Composition (%)
	2000				
	2001	8446	12.71	54592	82.12
	2002	8360	12.63	54405	82.20
	2003	8529	12.51	56479	82.81
	2004	7824	12.34	55605	87.66
	2005	8713	12.49	59594	85.43
	2006	9425	12.49	64498	85.49
	2007	10226	12.82	67826	85.03
	2008	11276	12.80	76636	86.97
	2009	12034	12.85	79200	84.55
	2010	13005	13.45	80880	83.62
	2011	14595	14.32	83681	82.10
	2012	16510	14.99	88826	80.67
乌鲁木齐市	Urumqi City	3704	12.32	26149	87.00
克拉玛依市	Karamay City	536	16.10	2705	81.26
吐鲁番地区	Turpan Administrative Offices	746	19.96	2866	76.69
哈密地区	Hami [Kumul] Administrative Offices	1141	20.99	3982	73.25
昌吉回族自治州	Changji Hui Autonomous Prefecture	1858	22.88	5736	70.64
伊犁哈萨克自治州	Ili Kazak Autonomous Prefecture	2402	15.02	12657	79.14
伊犁州直属县(市)	Counties (Cities) Direct Under Ili Prefecture	1147	15.64	5892	80.32
塔城地区	Tacheng [Tarbagatai] Administrative Offices	684	17.08	3199	79.90
阿勒泰地区	Altay Administrative Offices	571	12.27	3566	76.62
博尔塔拉蒙古自治州	Bortala Mongol Autonomous Prefecture	336	11.14	2523	83.68
巴音郭楞蒙古自治州	Bayangol Mongol Autonomous Prefecture	1395	15.70	6723	75.66
阿克苏地区	Aksu Administrative Offices	1488	16.45	6900	76.29
克孜勒苏柯尔克孜自治州	Kizilsu Kirgiz Autonomous Prefecture	296	13.94	1726	81.26
喀什地区	Kashgar [Kaxgar] Administrative Offices	1177	14.84	6610	83.33
和田地区	Hotan Administrative Offices	533	6.01	7669	86.50
自治区直辖县级市	Municpality Country-level Gity Directly under the Central Government	898	25.18	2580	72.33
石河子市	Shihezi City	593	22.25	2016	75.65
阿拉尔市	Aral City	111	37.37	166	55.89
图木舒克市	Tumxuk City	67	31.16	142	66.05
五家渠市	Wujiaqu City	127	32.56	256	65.64

1-15 按登记注册、机构类型分的法人单位数和产业活动单位数

Number of Legal Entities and Establishment Entities by Status of Registration and Institutions

单位：个 (2012 年) (unit)

类型		法人单位数 Number of Legal Entities	单产业法人 Single Sector	多产业法人 Multisector	产业活动单位数 Number of Establishments Entities	#多产业法人的活动单位 Establishments Entities of Multisector
总计	**Total**	**110109**	**103664**	**6445**	**164313**	**60649**
按登记注册类型分组	**By Status of Registration**					
内资	**Domestic Funded**	**109769**	**103345**	**6424**	**163581**	**60236**
国有	State-owned Enterprises	25967	22170	3797	50767	28597
集体	Collective-owned Enterprises	1162	966	196	2881	1915
股份合作	Cooperative Enterprises	184	170	14	358	188
联营	Joint Ownership Enterprises	112	107	5	202	95
国有联营	State Joint Ownership Enterprises	32	30	2	39	9
集体联营	Collective Joint Ownership Enterprises	36	35	1	42	7
国有与集体联营	Joint State-collective Enterprises	14	13	1	26	13
其他联营	Other Joint Ownership Enterprises	30	29	1	95	66
有限责任公司	Limited Liability Corporations	10667	9926	741	13782	3856
国有独资公司	State Sole Funded Corporations	515	444	71	814	370
其他有限责任公司	Other Limited Liability Corporations	10152	9482	670	12968	3486
股份有限公司	Share-holding Corporations Limited	713	500	213	2877	2377
私营	Private Enterprises	48315	46987	1328	51898	4911
私营独资	Private-funded Enterprises	7164	7070	94	7490	420
私营合伙	Private Partnership Enterprises	1134	1117	17	1183	66
私营有限责任公司	Private Limited Liability Corporations	39180	37986	1194	42316	4330
私营股份有限公司	Private Share-holding Corporations Ltd.	837	814	23	909	95
其他内资	Other Enterprises	22649	22519	130	40816	18297
港澳台商投资	**Enterprises with Funds from Hong Kong, Macao and Taiwan**	**134**	**126**	**8**	**290**	**164**
与港澳台商合资经营	Joint-venture Enterprises	63	61	2	83	22
与港澳台商合作经营	Cooperative Enterprises	4	4		7	3
港澳台商独资	Enterprises with Sole Investment	51	50	1	81	31
港澳台商投资股份有限公司	Enterprises with Sole Investment Share-holding Corporations Ltd.	15	10	5	118	108
其他港、澳、台商投资	Other	1	1		1	
外商投资	**Foreign Funded Enterprises**	**206**	**193**	**13**	**442**	**249**
中外合资经营	Joint-venture Enterprises	95	92	3	111	19
中外合作经营	Cooperation Enterprises	14	13	1	17	4
外资企业	Enterprises with Sole Funds	77	72	5	270	198
外商投资股份有限公司	Share-holding Corporations Ltd.	16	14	2	38	24
其他外商投资	Other	4	2	2	6	4
按机构类型分组	**by Status of Organization**	**110109**	**103664**	**6445**	**164313**	**60649**
企业	Enterprise	64884	61940	2944	81174	19234
事业单位	Institution	13823	12661	1162	26930	14269
机关	Organ	7795	5771	2024	11221	5450
社会团体	Social Organization	3917	3856	61	5148	1292
民办非企业单位	Private Non-enterprises Units	1474	1467	7	1467	
基金会	Foundation	11	11		11	
居委会	Neighborhood Committee	1595	1588	7	1634	46
村委会	Village Commitlee	8746	8662	84	8864	202
其他组织机构	Other Units	7864	7708	156	27864	20156

1-16 按行业分的法人单位数和产业活动单位数
Number of Legal Entities and Establishment Entities by Sector

单位：个 (2012 年) (unit)

类型		法人单位数 Number of Legal Entities	单产业法人 Single Sector	多产业法人 Multi-sector	产业活动单位数 Number of Establishments Entities	#多产业法人的活动单位 Establishments Entities of Multi-sector
总计	**Total**	**110109**	**103664**	**6445**	**164313**	**60649**
农、林、牧、渔业	**Agriculture, Forestry, Animal Husbandry and Fishery**	**4773**	**4506**	**267**	**8973**	**4467**
农业	Farming	1536	1366	170	3571	2205
林业	Forestry	258	245	13	352	107
畜牧业	Animal Husbandry	1352	1318	34	1492	174
渔业	Fishery	63	60	3	76	16
农、林、牧、渔服务业	Services in Support of Agriculture	1564	1517	47	3482	1965
采矿业	**Mining Ores**	**2306**	**2250**	**56**	**2474**	**224**
煤炭开采和洗选业	Mining and Washing of Coal	438	422	16	471	49
石油和天然气开采业	Extraction of Petroleum and Natural Gas	124	112	12	165	53
黑色金属矿采选业	Mining and Processing of Ferrous Metal Ores	663	651	12	681	30
有色金属矿采选业	Mining and Processing of Non-Ferrous Metal Ores	368	365	3	384	19
非金属矿采选业	Mining and Processing of Nonmetal Ores	630	618	12	690	72
其他采矿业	Mining of Other Ores	83	82	1	83	1
制造业	**Manufacture**	**10870**	**10676**	**194**	**11655**	**979**
农副食品加工业	Processing of Food from Agricultural Products	1117	1094	23	1280	186
食品制造业	Manufacture of Foods	461	449	12	489	40
饮料制造业	Manufacture of Beverages	392	383	9	425	42
烟草制品业	Manufacture of Tobacco	1	1		2	1
纺织业	Manufacture of Textile	391	380	11	415	35
纺织服装、鞋、帽制造业	Manufacture of Textile Wearing Apparel, Footware and Caps	124	123	1	132	9
皮革、毛皮、羽毛(绒)及其制品业	Manufacture of Leather, Fur, Feather and Related Products	74	73	1	77	4
木材加工及木、竹、藤、棕、草制品业	Processing of Timber, Manufacture of Wood, bamboo,rattan,palm,and straw products	197	195	2	210	15
家具制造业	Manufacture of Furniture	152	150	2	159	9
造纸及纸制品业	Manufacture of Paper and Paper Products	248	242	6	256	14
印刷业和记录媒介的复制	Printing,Reproduction of Recording Media	325	319	6	343	24
文教体育用品制造业	Manufacture of Articles For Culture, Education and Sport Activities	19	19		20	1
石油加工、炼焦及核燃料加工业	Processing of Petroleum, Coking, Processing of Nuclear Fuel	260	250	10	267	17
化学原料及化学制品制造业	Manufacture of Raw Chemical Materials and Chemical Products	882	859	23	949	90
医药制造业	Manufacture of Medicines	115	112	3	119	7
化学纤维制造业	Manufacture of Chemical Fibers	33	32	1	34	2
橡胶制品业	Manufacture of Rubber	66	65	1	69	4
塑料制品业	Manufacture of Plastics	957	950	7	1007	57
非金属矿物制品业	Manufacture of Non-metallic Mineral Products	2520	2484	36	2726	242
黑色金属冶炼及压延加工业	Smelting and Pressing of Ferrous Metals	179	176	3	182	6
有色金属冶炼及压延加工业	Smelting and Pressing of Non-ferrous Metals	127	124	3	131	7
金属制品业	Manufacture of Metal Products	750	739	11	786	47
通用设备制造业	Manufacture of General Purpose Machinery	421	417	4	436	19

1-16 续表 1 Continued

单位：个 (unit)

类型		法人单位数 Number of Legal Entities	单产业法人 Single Sector	多产业法人 Multi-sector	产业活动单位数 Number of Establishments Entities	#多产业法人的活动单位 Establishments Entities of Multi-sector
专用设备制造业	Manufacture of Special Purpose Machinery	373	368	5	406	38
交通运输设备制造业	Manufacture of Transport Equipment	176	170	6	207	37
电气机械及器材制造业	Manufacture of Electrical Machinery and Equipment	289	284	5	299	15
通信设备、计算机及其他电子设备制造业	Manufacture of Communication Equipment, Computers and Other Electronic Equipment	19	17	2	19	2
仪器仪表及文化、办公用机械制造业	Manufacture of Measuring Instruments and Machinery for Cultural Activity and Office Work	25	25		31	6
工艺品及其他制造业	Manufacture of Artwork and Other Manufacturing	142	141	1	142	1
废弃资源和废旧材料回收加工业	Recycling and Disposal of Waste	35	35		37	2
电力、燃气及水的生产和供应业	**Production and Supply of Electricity,Gas and Water**	**854**	**804**	**50**	**1210**	**406**
电力、热力的生产和供应业	Production and Supply of Electric Power and Heat Power	627	599	28	868	269
燃气生产和供应业	Production and Supply of Gas	79	71	8	112	41
水的生产和供应业	Production and Supply of Water	148	134	14	230	96
建筑业	**Construction**	**2480**	**2264**	**216**	**3334**	**1070**
房屋和土木工程建筑业	Building and Civil Engineering	1167	998	169	1881	883
建筑安装业	Construction Installation	484	452	32	554	102
建筑装饰业	Construction Decoration	523	514	9	554	40
其他建筑业	Other Construction	306	300	6	345	45
交通运输、仓储和邮政业	**Transport,Storage and Postal**	**2883**	**2678**	**205**	**4491**	**1813**
铁路运输业	Railway Transport	32	31	1	39	8
道路运输业	Road Transport	1459	1334	125	1862	528
城市公共交通业	Urban Public Transport	160	146	14	196	50
水上运输业	Water Transport	2	2		2	0
航空运输业	Air Transport	35	33	2	49	16
管道运输业	Pipeline Transport	6	4	2	13	9
装卸搬运和其他运输服务业	Loading,Unloading and Other	853	824	29	920	96
仓储业	Storage	265	260	5	341	81
邮政业	Posts	71	44	27	1069	1025
信息传输、计算机服务和软件业	**Information Transmission Computer Services and Software**	**2211**	**2111**	**100**	**3217**	**1106**
电信和其他信息传输服务业	Telecommunications and Other Information Services	609	526	83	1562	1036
计算机服务业	Computer Services	1413	1396	17	1452	56
软件业	Software industry	189	189		203	14
批发和零售业	**Wholesale and Retail Trades**	**24800**	**23706**	**1094**	**30909**	**7203**
批发业	Wholesalel Trade	16980	16295	685	20590	4295
零售业	Retail Trade	7820	7411	409	10319	2908
住宿和餐饮业	**Hotels and Catering Services**	**1135**	**1063**	**72**	**1556**	**493**
住宿业	Hotels	790	738	52	1060	322
餐饮业	Catering Services	345	325	20	496	171
金融业	**Financial Intermediation**	**865**	**562**	**303**	**3975**	**3413**
银行业	Bank	273	82	191	2544	2462

1-16 续表 2 Continued

单位：个 (unit)

类型		法人单位数 Number of Legal Entities	单产业法人 Single Sector	多产业法人 Multi-sector	产业活动单位数 Number of Establishments Entities	#多产业法人的活动单位 Establishments Entities of Multi-sector
证券业	Securities	16	16		69	53
保险业	Insurance	193	97	96	876	779
其他金融活动	Other Services	383	367	16	486	119
房地产业	**Real Estate**	**4062**	**3823**	**239**	**4548**	**725**
房地产业	Real Estate	4062	3823	239	4548	725
租赁和商务服务业	**Leasing and Business Services**	**6046**	**5827**	**219**	**7088**	**1261**
租赁业	Leasing	462	453	9	514	61
商务服务业	Business Services	5584	5374	210	6574	1200
科学研究、技术服务和地质勘查业	**Scientific Research, Technical Services,and Geological Prospecting**	**3582**	**3402**	**180**	**4797**	**1395**
研究与试验发展	Research and Experimental Development	240	229	11	271	42
专业技术服务业	Technical service industry	1903	1807	96	2327	520
科技交流和推广服务业	Services of science and technology	1016	952	64	1768	816
地质勘查业	Geological prospecting	423	414	9	431	17
水利、环境和公共设施管理业	**Management of Water Conservancy,Enviroment and Public Facilities**	**975**	**868**	**107**	**1960**	**1092**
水利管理业	Management of Water Conservancy	340	266	74	1085	819
环境管理业	Management of Enviroment	258	244	14	397	153
公共设施管理业	Management of and Public Facilities	377	358	19	478	120
居民服务和其他服务业	**Services to Households and other services**	**1583**	**1543**	**40**	**1868**	**325**
居民服务业	Services to Households	591	571	20	771	200
其他服务业	Other services	992	972	20	1097	125
教　育	**Education**	**5298**	**4896**	**402**	**8301**	**3405**
教　育	Education	5298	4896	402	8301	3405
卫生、社会保障和社会福利业	**Health,Social Securities and Social Welfare**	**2688**	**2509**	**179**	**4397**	**1888**
卫　生	Public Health	2281	2115	166	3680	1565
社会保障业	Social Securities	140	132	8	326	194
社会福利业	Social Welfare	267	262	5	391	129
文化、体育和娱乐业	**Culture,Sports and Entertainment**	**1224**	**1177**	**47**	**2181**	**1004**
新闻出版业	Journalism and Publishing Activities	121	118	3	133	15
广播、电视、电影和音像业	Broadcasting,Movies,Television and Audiovisual Activies	312	285	27	761	476
文化艺术业	Culture and Art Activities	550	539	11	985	446
体　育	Sports Activities	97	95	2	130	35
娱乐业	Entertainment	144	140	4	172	32
公共管理和社会组织	**Public Management and Social Organization**	**31474**	**28999**	**2475**	**57379**	**28380**
中国共产党机关	Communist Party of China	1034	927	107	1143	216
国家机构	Government Agencies	10051	7837	2214	17563	9726
人民政协和民主党派	People's Political Consultative Conference and Democratic Parties	132	130	2	133	3
群众团体、社会团体和宗教组织	Non-Government Organizations,Social Organizations and Religion Organizations	9916	9855	61	28042	18187
基层群众自治组织	Grass Roots Self-governing Organizations	10341	10250	91	10498	248

1-17 各地区按机构类型分法人单位数
Number of Legal Entities by Type of Institutions and Region

单位：个 (2012 年) (unit)

地 区	Region	法人单位数 Number of Legal Entities	企业法人 Business Entity	事业法人 Institution Entity	机关法人 Governmint Entity	社会团体 Social Organization	其他 Others
总 计	**Total**	**110109**	**64884**	**13823**	**7795**	**3917**	**19690**
乌鲁木齐市	Urumqi City	30058	25664	1625	839	462	1468
克拉玛依市	Karamay City	3329	2534	199	237	163	196
吐鲁番地区	Turpan Administrative Offices	3737	1664	433	233	179	1228
哈密地区	Hami [Kumul] Administrative Offices	5436	3387	800	368	204	677
昌吉回族自治州	Changji Hui Autonomous Prefecture	8120	4474	1180	614	473	1379
伊犁哈萨克自治州	Ili Kazak Autonomous Prefecture	15994	6604	3621	1839	689	3241
伊犁州直属县(市)	Counties (Cities) DirectUnderIliPrefecture	7336	3591	1679	792	202	1072
塔城地区	Tacheng[Tarbagatai]AdministrativeOffices	4004	1261	917	516	150	1160
阿勒泰地区	Altay Administrative Offices	4654	1752	1025	531	337	1009
博尔塔拉蒙古自治州	Bortala Mongol Autonomous Prefecture	3015	1673	460	277	189	416
巴音郭楞蒙古自治州	BayangolMongolAutonomous Prefecture	8886	5763	1012	653	240	1218
阿克苏地区	Aksu Administrative Offices	9045	4839	1623	679	387	1517
克孜勒苏柯尔克孜自治州	Kizilsu Kirgiz Autonomous Prefecture	2124	897	249	345	68	565
喀什地区	Kashgar [Kaxgar] Administrative Offices	7932	2900	1105	885	423	2619
和田地区	Hotan Administrative Offices	8866	1860	1127	628	324	4927
自治区直辖县级市	Municpality Country-level Gity Directly under the Central Government	3567	2625	389	198	116	239
石河子市	Shihezi City	2665	2120	160	76	95	214
阿拉尔市	Aral City	297	180	72	31	3	11
图木舒克市	Tumxuk City	215	102	62	44	2	5
五家渠市	Wujiaqu City	390	223	95	47	16	9

1-18 按地区和营业状态分企业法人单位数

Number of Business Entities by Region and Operation Status

单位：个　　　　(2012 年)　　　　(unit)

地　区	Region	企业单位数 Number of Business Entities	营业 In Business or Operating	停业(歇业) Closed	筹建 In Preparation	当年关闭 Closed in the Year	当年破产 Bankrupted in the Year	其他 Others
总　计	**Total**	**64884**	**49938**	**4422**	**9335**	**543**	**75**	**571**
乌鲁木齐市	Urumqi City	25664	20364	2509	2404	230	21	136
克拉玛依市	Karamay City	2534	2157	131	230	6		10
吐鲁番地区	Turpan Administrative Offices	1664	1331	73	253	5		2
哈密地区	Hami [Kumul] Administrative Offices	3387	2002	148	1149	36	3	49
昌吉回族自治州	Changji Hui Autonomous Prefecture	4474	3558	224	522	69	23	78
伊犁哈萨克自治州	Ili Kazak Autonomous Prefecture	6604	5278	350	861	64	4	47
伊犁州直属县(市)	Counties (Cities) Direct Under Ili Prefecture	3591	3026	188	280	58	3	36
塔城地区	Tacheng [Tarbagatai] Administrative Offices	1261	1131	72	47	4		7
阿勒泰地区	Altay Administrative Offices	1752	1121	90	534	2	1	4
博尔塔拉蒙古自治州	Bortala Mongol Autonomous Prefecture	1673	1283	138	219	6		27
巴音郭楞蒙古自治州	Bayangol Mongol Autonomous Prefecture	5763	4493	211	990	33	6	30
阿克苏地区	Aksu Administrative Offices	4839	3178	206	1361	49	7	38
克孜勒苏柯尔克孜自治州	Kizilsu Kirgiz Autonomous Prefecture	897	521	91	277	4		4
喀什地区	Kashgar [Kaxgar] Administrative Offices	2900	2501	132	233	18	3	13
和田地区	Hotan Administrative Offices	1860	987	111	615	8	4	135
自治区直辖县级市	Municpality Country-level Gity Directly under the Central Government	2625	2285	98	221	15	4	2
石河子市	Shihezi City	2120	1842	84	190	2		2
阿拉尔市	Aral City	180	149	10	19	2		
图木舒克市	Tumxuk City	102	95	2	5			
五家渠市	Wujiaqu City	223	199	2	7	11	4	

1-19 各地区非公有制企业法人单位数
Number of Business Entities by Region

单位：个 (2012 年) (unit)

地区	Region	全部企业法人单位数 Number of total Enterprises	非公有制企业法人单位数 Number of Non-public Enterprises	非公有制占全部比例(%) As Percentage of Total Enterprises
总计	**Total**	**64884**	**61392**	**94.62**
乌鲁木齐市	Urumqi City	25664	24665	96.11
克拉玛依市	Karamay City	2534	2457	96.96
吐鲁番地区	Turpan Administrative Offices	1664	1553	93.33
哈密地区	Hami [Kumul] Administrative Offices	3387	3191	94.21
昌吉回族自治州	Changji Hui Autonomous Prefecture	4474	4293	95.95
伊犁哈萨克自治州	Ili Kazak Autonomous Prefecture	6604	6009	90.99
伊犁州直属县(市)	Counties (Cities) Direct Under Ili Prefecture	3591	3300	91.90
塔城地区	Tacheng [Tarbagatai] Administrative Offices	1261	1108	87.87
阿勒泰地区	Altay Administrative Offices	1752	1601	91.38
博尔塔拉蒙古自治州	Bortala Mongol Autonomous Prefecture	1673	1526	91.21
巴音郭楞蒙古自治州	Bayangol Mongol Autonomous Prefecture	5763	5432	94.26
阿克苏地区	Aksu Administrative Offices	4839	4618	95.43
克孜勒苏柯尔克孜自治州	Kizilsu Kirgiz Autonomous Prefecture	897	835	93.09
喀什地区	Kashgar [Kaxgar] Administrative Offices	2900	2619	90.31
和田地区	Hotan Administrative Offices	1860	1712	92.04
自治区直辖县级市	Municpality Country-level Gity Directly under the Central Government	2625	2482	94.55
石河子市	Shihezi City	2120	2012	94.91
阿拉尔市	Aral City	180	173	96.11
图木舒克市	Tumxuk City	102	93	91.18
五家渠市	Wujiaqu City	223	204	91.48

1-20 服务业法人单位数和从业人员数
Number of Services to Legal Entities and Employed Persons

年 份 Year	合 计 Total	企 业 Enterprises	行政事业 Administrative	社会团体及其他 Social Organizations and Others
单位数(个) Number of Enterprises				
2009	79200	36738	20616	21846
2010	80880	38226	20636	22018
2011	83681	40854	20729	22098
2012	88826	45569	21021	22236
从业人数(万人) Number of Employed Persons				
2009	173.31	64.48	93.70	15.12
2010	178.72	68.24	95.05	15.43
2011	184.51	73.15	95.76	15.60
2012	194.80	82.11	96.65	16.04

1-21 服务业分行业法人单位数及从业人员数
Number of Services to Legal Entities and Employed Persons by Industry

(2012 年)

行 业	Sector	法人单位数 Number of Legal Entities	从业人数(万人) Employed Persons
总 计	**Total**	**88826**	**194.80**
交通运输、仓储和邮政业	Transport,Storage and Post	2883	13.79
信息传输、计算机服务和软件业	Information Transmission,Comupter Services and Software	2211	3.48
批发和零售业	Wholesale and Retail Trades	24800	26.33
住宿和餐饮业	Hotels and Catering Services	1135	5.57
金融业	Financil Intermediation	865	8.73
房地产业	Real Estate	4062	8.46
租赁和商务服务业	Leasing and Business Services	6046	11.37
科学研究、技术服务和地质勘查业	Scientific Research,Technical Services and Geological Prospecting	3582	7.59
水利、环境和公共设施管理业	Mangement of Water Conservancy,Environment and Public Facilities	975	4.91
居民服务和其他服务业	Services to Households and other Services	1583	2.06
教 育	Education	5298	34.27
卫生、社会保障和社会福利业	Health,Social Securities and Social Welfare	2688	13.25
文化、体育和娱乐业	Culture,Sports and Entertainment	1224	2.88
公共管理和社会组织	Public Mangement and Social Organization	31474	52.12

1-22 各地区服务业法人单位数
Number of Services to Legal Entities by Region

单位：个　　(2012 年)　　(unit)

地区	Region	合计 Total	交通运输仓储及邮政业 Traffic, transport, storage and post	信息传输计算机服务和软件业 Information transmission, Computer, services and software	批发和零售业 Wholesale and retail trade	住宿和餐饮业 Accommodation and Restaurants
总　计	**Total**	**88826**	**2883**	**2211**	**24800**	**1135**
乌鲁木齐市	Urumqi City	26149	975	911	12916	367
克拉玛依市	Karamay City	2705	119	57	1090	33
吐鲁番地区	Turpan Administrative Offices	2866	60	101	330	45
哈密地区	Hami [Kumul] Administrative Offices	3982	209	86	998	35
昌吉回族自治州	Changji Hui Autonomous Prefecture	5736	234	153	864	65
伊犁哈萨克自治州	Ili Kazak Autonomous Prefecture	12657	358	299	1609	199
伊犁州直属县(市)	Counties (Cities) Direct Under Ili Prefecture	5892	182	117	1085	104
塔城地区	Tacheng [Tarbagatai] Administrative Offices	3199	59	84	175	26
阿勒泰地区	Altay Administrative Offices	3566	117	98	349	69
博尔塔拉蒙古自治州	Bortala Mongol Autonomous Prefecture	2523	127	95	654	23
巴音郭楞蒙古自治州	Bayangol Mongol Autonomous Prefecture	6723	227	65	2304	134
阿克苏地区	Aksu Administrative Offices	6900	212	242	1460	61
克孜勒苏柯尔克孜自治州	Kizilsu Kirgiz Autonomous Prefecture	1726	65	14	280	13
喀什地区	Kashgar [Kaxgar] Administrative Offices	6610	104	60	848	77
和田地区	Hotan Administrative Offices	7669	79	22	608	28
自治区直辖县级市	Municpality Country-level Gity Directly under the Central Government	2580	114	106	839	55
石河子市	Shihezi City	2016	90	106	786	46
阿拉尔市	Aral City	166	7		22	1
图木舒克市	Tumxuk City	142	3		10	2
五家渠市	Wujiaqu City	256	14		21	6

1-22 续表 1 Continued

单位：个 (unit)

地　区	Region	金融业 Finance	房地产业 Real estate	租赁和商务服务业 Leasing and Business Services	科学研究技术服务和地质勘察业 Scientific research, technical service and geologic perambulation	水利、环境和公共设施管理业 Management of water conservancy, environment and public establishment
总　计	**Total**	**865**	**4062**	**6046**	**3582**	**975**
乌鲁木齐市	Urumqi City	253	1336	3127	1365	224
克拉玛依市	Karamay City	31	127	276	127	32
吐鲁番地区	Turpan Administrative Offices	22	89	97	61	24
哈密地区	Hami [Kumul] Administrative Offices	67	236	236	162	65
昌吉回族自治州	Changji Hui Autonomous Prefecture	61	281	334	326	106
伊犁哈萨克自治州	Ili Kazak Autonomous Prefecture	121	600	533	570	174
伊犁州直属县(市)	Counties (Cities) Direct Under Ili Prefecture	59	352	293	215	71
塔城地区	Tacheng [Tarbagatai] Administrative Offices	26	103	58	187	42
阿勒泰地区	Altay Administrative Offices	36	145	182	168	61
博尔塔拉蒙古自治州	Bortala Mongol Autonomous Prefecture	34	105	112	108	28
巴音郭楞蒙古自治州	Bayangol Mongol Autonomous Prefecture	68	327	493	202	58
阿克苏地区	Aksu Administrative Offices	62	375	353	259	88
克孜勒苏柯尔克孜自治州	Kizilsu Kirgiz Autonomous Prefecture	16	42	55	60	22
喀什地区	Kashgar [Kaxgar] Administrative Offices	46	245	158	103	49
和田地区	Hotan Administrative Offices	40	85	109	121	72
自治区直辖县级市	Municpality Country-level Gity Directly under the Central Government	44	214	163	118	33
石河子市	Shihezi City	37	145	143	94	13
阿拉尔市	Aral City		22	9	8	10
图木舒克市	Tumxuk City	1	12	5	4	2
五家渠市	Wujiaqu City	6	35	6	12	8

1-22 续表 2 Continued

单位：个 (unit)

地　　区	Region	居民服务和其他服务业 Resident services and other services	教育 Education	卫生、社会保障和社会福利业 Sanitation, social security and social welfare	文化、体育和娱乐业 Culture, Sports and entertainment	公共管理和社会组织 Public management and social organization
总　　计	**Total**	**1583**	**5298**	**2688**	**1224**	**31474**
乌鲁木齐市	Urumqi City	674	855	337	288	2521
克拉玛依市	Karamay City	77	129	30	31	546
吐鲁番地区	Turpan Administrative Offices	49	194	69	27	1698
哈密地区	Hami [Kumul] Administrative Offices	60	261	113	57	1397
昌吉回族自治州	Changji Hui Autonomous Prefecture	96	428	299	85	2404
伊犁哈萨克自治州	Ili Kazak Autonomous Prefecture	113	1179	659	250	5993
伊犁州直属县(市)	Counties (Cities) Direct Under Ili Prefecture	62	700	311	120	2221
塔城地区	Tacheng [Tarbagatai] Administrative Offices	22	270	182	56	1909
阿勒泰地区	Altay Administrative Offices	29	209	166	74	1863
博尔塔拉蒙古自治州	Bortala Mongol Autonomous Prefecture	31	142	79	29	956
巴音郭楞蒙古自治州	Bayangol Mongol Autonomous Prefecture	203	374	243	101	1924
阿克苏地区	Aksu Administrative Offices	75	654	238	138	2683
克孜勒苏柯尔克孜自治州	Kizilsu Kirgiz Autonomous Prefecture	31	64	40	26	998
喀什地区	Kashgar [Kaxgar] Administrative Offices	54	484	284	80	4018
和田地区	Hotan Administrative Offices	61	333	224	61	5826
自治区直辖县级市	Municpality Country-level Gity Directly under the Central Government	59	201	73	51	510
石河子市	Shihezi City	48	151	33	34	290
阿拉尔市	Aral City	4	18	13	5	47
图木舒克市	Tumxuk City	3	15	11	5	69
五家渠市	Wujiaqu City	4	17	16	7	104

主要统计指标解释

行政区划 指国家对行政区域的划分，根据宪法规定，我国的行政区域划分如下：(1)全国分为省、自治区、直辖市；(2)省、自治区分为自治州、县、自治县、市；(3)自治州分为县、自治县、市；(4)县、自治县分为乡、民族乡、镇；(5)直辖市和较大的市分为区、县；(6)国家在必要时设立的特别行政区。

平均增长速度 我国计算平均增长速度有两种方法：一种是习惯上经常使用的"水平法"，又称几何平均法，是以间隔期最后一年的水平同基期水平对比来计算平均每年增长(或下降)速度；另一种是"累计法"，又称代数平均法或方程法，是以间隔期内各年水平的总和同基期水平对比来计算平均每年增长(或下降)速度。在一般正常情况下，两种方法计算的平均每年增长速度比较接近；但在经济发展不平衡、出现大起大落时，两种方法计算的结果差别较大。

本《年鉴》内所列的平均增长速度，均用"水平法"计算。从某年到某年平均增长速度的年份，均不包括基期年在内。如建国四十三年的平均增长速度是以1949年为基期计算的，则写为1950-1992年平均增长速度，其余类推。

国民经济行业分类 自 2012 年定期报表开始使用新的《国民经济行业分类》(GB/T4754-2011)，该分类是由国家统计局组织修订，经国家检验检疫总局和国家标准化委员会批准，于 2011 年 4 月 29 日发布实施。这次修订是在 2002 年分类标准的基础上，参照联合国《全部经济活动的国际标准产业分类》(ISIC/Rev.4)进行的。修订后的《国民经济行业分类》(GB/T4754-2011)共有门类 20 个，大类 96 个，中类 432 个，小类 1094 个。行业门类的数目保持不变，部分门类的名称和顺序作了调整，大类增加 1 个，中类增加 36 个，小类增加 181 个。

企业(单位)登记注册类型 是以在工商行政管理机关登记注册的各类企业为划分对象，以工商行政管理部门对企业登记注册的类型为依据，将企业登记注册类型分为内资企业、港澳台商投资企业和外商投资企业三大类。内资企业包括国有企业、集体企业、股份合作企业、联营企业、有限责任公司、股份有限公司、私营公司和其他企业；港澳台商投资企业和外商投资企业分别包括合资经营企业、合作经营企业、独资经营企业和股份有限公司。对不在工商行政管理部门进行登记注册的行政机关、事业单位和社会团体，主要按其经费来源和管理方式进行划分。

国有企业 指企业全部资产归国家所有，并按《中华人民共和国企业法人登记管理条例》规定登记注册的非公司制的经济组织。不包括有限责任公司中的国有独资公司。

集体企业 指企业资产归集体所有，并按《中华人民共和国企业法人登记管理条例》规定登记注册的经济组织。

股份合作企业 指以合作制为基础，由企业职工共同出资入股，吸收一定比例的社会资产投资组建，实行自主经营，自负盈亏，共同劳动，民主管理，按劳分配与按股分红相结合的一种集体经济组织。

联营企业 指两个及两个以上相同或不同所有制性质的企业法人或事业单位法人，按自愿、平等、互利的原则，共同投资组成的经济组织。联营企业包括国有联营企业、集体联营企业、国有与集体联营企业和其他联营企业。

有限责任公司 指根据《中华人民共和国公司登记管理条例》规定登记注册，由两个以上、五十个以下的股东共同出资，每个股东以其所认缴的出资额对公司承担有限责任，公司以其全部资产对其债务承担责任的经济组织。有限责任公司包括国有独资公司以及其他有限责任公司。

股份有限公司 指根据《中华人民共和国公司登记管理条例》规定登记注册，其全部注册资本由等额股份构成并通过发行股票筹集资本，股东以其认购的股份对公司承担有限责任，公司以其全部资产对其债务承担责任的经济组织。

私营企业 指由自然人投资设立或由自然人控股，以雇佣劳动为基础的营利性经济组织。包括按照《公司法》、《合伙企业法》、《私营企业暂行条例》规定登记注册的私营有限责任公司、私营股份有限公司、私营合伙企业和个人独资企业。

其他企业 指上述企业之外的其他内资经济组织。

与港澳台商合资经营企业 指港澳台地区投资者与内地的企业依照《中华人民共和国中外合资经营企业法》及有关法律的规定，按合同规定的比例投资设立、分享利润和分担风险的企业。

与港澳台商合作经营企业 指港澳台地区投资者与内地企业依照《中华人民共和国中外合作经营企业法》及有关法律的规定，依照合作合同的约定进行投资或提供条件设立、分配利润和分担风险和亏损的企业。

港澳台商独资经营企业 指依照《中华人民共和国外资企业法》及有关法律的规定，在内地由港澳台地区投资者全额投资设立的企业。

港澳台商投资股份有限公司 指根据国家有关规定，经商务部批准设立，并且其中港、澳、台商的股本占公司注册资本的比例达 25% 以上的股份有限公司。凡其中港、澳、台商的股本占公司注册资本的比例小于 25%的，属于内资企业中的股份有限公司。

中外合资经营企业 指外国企业或外国人与中国内地企业依照《中华人民共和国中外合资经营企业法》及有关法律的规定，按合同规定的比例投资设立、分享利润和分担风险的企业。

中外合作经营企业 指外国企业或外国人与中国内地

企业依照《中华人民共和国中外合作经营企业法》及有关法律的规定，依照合作合同的约定进行投资或提供条件设立、分配利润和分担风险和亏损的企业。

外资企业 指依照《中华人民共和国外资企业法》及有关法律的规定，在中国内地由外国投资者全额投资设立的企业。

外商投资股份有限公司 指根据国家有关规定，经商务部批准设立，并且其中外资的股本占公司注册资本的比例达25% 以上的股份有限公司。凡其中外资股本占公司注册资本的比例小于 25%的，属于内资中的股份有限公司。

行政机关、事业单位和社会团体 参照企业登记注册类型，主要按其经费来源和管理方式划分。具体规定如下：

(1)行政机关：包括国家机关和政党机关，原则上均列为“国有”。但有特殊规定的，如供销社等，则列为“集体”。

(2)事业单位：包括经国家机构编制部门和有关业务主管部门批准成立的各类事业单位，不包括实行企业化管理的事业单位。事业单位的划分办法如下：

①由国家财政预算拨款或列入财政预算外资金管理以及经费主要来源于国有主管部门或国有上级单位的事业单位，列为“国有”。

②经费主要来源于集体单位的事业单位，列为“集体”。

③公民个人(或个人合伙)开办的事业单位，列为“私营”。

④上述以外的其他事业单位，如果其经费来源不明确，按管理方式进行归类。

(3)社会团体：包括经民政部门批准成立以及未纳入社会团体管理条例范围的工会、妇联等各类社会团体。社会团体的划分办法如下：

①未纳入民政部社会团体管理条例范围的工会、妇联、共青团、青联、工商联、科协、侨联等社会团体，国家拨款设立的基金会或基金管理组织以及经费主要来源于国有业务主管部门或国有上级单位的社会团体，列为“国有”。

②经费主要来源于集体单位的社会团体，列为“集体”。

③公民个人(或个人合伙)开办的社会团体，划为“私营”。

④上述以外的其他社会团体，如果其经费来源不明确，改按管理方式进行归类。

各个计划时期 表内所用各个“时期”代表的年份如下：恢复时期为 1950 到 1952 年；第一个五年计划时期(简称“一五”时期)为 1953 到 1957 年；第二个五年计划时期(简称“二五”时期)为 1958 到 1962 年；第三个五年计划时期(简称“三五”时期)为 1966 到 1970 年；第四个五年计划时期(简称“四五”时期)为 1971 到 1975 年；第五个五年计划时期(简称“五五”时期)为 1976 到 1980 年；第六个五年计划时期(简称“六五”时期)为 1981 到 1985 年；第七个五年计划时期(简称“七五”时期)为 1986 到 1990 年；第八个五年计划时期(简称“八五”时期)为 1991 到 1995 年；第九个五年计划时期(简称“九五”时期)为 1996 到 2000 年；第十个五年计划时期(简称“十五”时期)为 2001 到 2005 年；第十一个五年计划时期(简称“十一五”时期)为 2006 到 2010 年。第十二个五年计划时期（简称“十二五”时期）为 2011 到 2015 年。

法人单位 指具备：

(1)依法成立、有自己的名称、组织机构和场所、能够独立承担民事责任；

(2)独立拥有和使用（或授权使用）资产、承担负债、有权与其它单位签订合同；

(3)会计上独立核算、能够编制资产负债表。法人单位包括企业法人、事业单位法人、机关法人、社会团体法人和其他法人。

单产业法人 指只在一个地点，主要从事一种生产经营活动的法人单位。

多产业法人 指坐落于两个及两个以上地点、或主要从事两种及两种以上生产经营活动的，按照单位划分规定可以划分为两个或两个以上产业活动单位的法人单位。

产业活动单位 是法人单位的附属单位。产业活动单位应具备下列条件：

(1)在一个场所从事一种或主要从事一种社会经济活动；

(2)相对独立组织生产经营和业务活动；

(3)能够掌握收入和支出等业务核算资料。

服务业 指生产和销售产品的生产部门和企业的集合。在国民经济核算中，将服务业视同为第三产业，即除农业、工业、建筑业以外的其它所有产业部门。

Explanatory Notes on Main Statistical Indicators

Administrative Division refers to the division of administrative areas by the state. The Constitution of the People's Republic of China stipulates that the administrative areas in China are divided as: 1) The whole Country is divided into provinces, autonomous regions and municipalities directly under the central government; 2) Provinces and autonomous regions are divided into autonomous prefectures, counties, autonomous counties and cities; 3) Autonomous prefectures are divided into counties, autonomous counties and cities; 4) Counties and autonomous counties are divided into townships, nationality townships and towns; 5) Municipalities and large cities are divided into districts and counties, 6) The state shall, when necessary, establish special administrative regions.

Average Annual Growth Rate Two methods for calculating average annual growth rate are applied in China,one is often called level approachor the method of calculating geometric average,which is derived by comparing the level of the last year of the interval with that of the beginning year;the other is calledaccumulative approach or algebraic average or equation method,which is derived by the summation of the actual figure of each year in the interval divided by the figure in the base year.Usually the results calculated by the two methods are fairly close, but they differed sharply when uneven economic development occurred with striking fluctuations in growth.

The average annual growth rates listed in this statistical yearbook are calculated by level approach except for the growth rate of investment in fixed assets. The base years are not listed when the years are listed for average annual growth rates. For instance,the average annual growth rate of 43 years since 1949 is listed as average annual growth rate of 1950-1992 without listing the base year 1949.And the analogy of this is also the same for the rest of the years.

Industrial Classification of the National Economy The new Industrial Classification of the National Economy (GB/T 4754-2011) is introduced starting from the compilation of 2012annual statistics. The new revision was based on the 2002 classification and organized by the National Bureau of Statistics taking into consideration of the International Standards of the Industrial Classification of All Economic Activities (ISIC/Rev.4) of the United Nations, and the new Classification was promulgated by the National Administration of Quality Supervision, Inspection and Quarantine on April 29, 2011. The revised version of the Industrial Classification of the National Economy (GB/T 4754-2011) is composed of 20 major divisions, 96 divisions, 432 major groups and 1094 groups, including 1 new divisions, 36 major groups and 181 groups.

Registration Status of Enterprises Enterprises are classified into 3 categories, namely domestic-funded enterprises, enterprises with investment from Hong Kong, Macao and Taiwan, and enterprises with foreign investment, in the light of the registration status of an enterprise in industrial and commercial administration agencies. Domestic-funded enterprises include state-owned enterprises, collective-owned enterprises, cooperative enterprises, joint ownership enterprises, limited liability corporations, share-holding corporations Ltd., private enterprises and other enterprises. Included in the enterprises with investment from Hong Kong, Macao and Taiwan and enterprises with foreign investment are joint-venture enterprises, cooperative enterprises, sole investment enterprises and share-holding corporations Ltd. For government agencies, institutions and social organizations which are not requested to be registered in industrial and commercial administration agencies, they are classified mainly by their sources of funds and way of management.

State-owned Enterprises refer to non-corporation economic units where the entire assets are owned by the state and which have registered in accordance with the Regulation of the People's Republic of China on the Management of Registration of Corporate Enterprises. Excluded from this category are sole state-funded corporations in the limited liability corporations.

Collective-owned Enterprises refer to economic units where the assets are owned collectively and which have registered in accordance with the Regulation of the People's Republic of China on the Management of Registration of Corporate Enterprises.

Cooperative Enterprises refer to a form of collective economic units (enterprises) where capitals come mainly from employees as their shares, with certain proportion of capital from the outside, where production is organized on the basis of independent operation, independent accounting for profits and losses, joint work, democratic management, and a distribution system that integrates remuneration according to work with dividend according to capital share.

Joint Ownership Enterprises refer to economic units established by two or more corporate enterprises or corporate institutions of the same or different ownership, through joint investment on the basis of equality, voluntary participation and mutual benefits. They include state joint ownership enterprises, collective joint ownership enterprises, joint state-collective enterprises, other joint ownership enterprises.

Limited Liability Corporations refer to economic units established with investment from 2-50 investors and registered in accordance with the Regulation of the People's Republic of China on the Management of Registration of Corporations, each investor bearing limited liability to the corporation depending on its share of investment, and the corporation bearing liability to its debt to the maximum of its total assets. Limited liability corporations include exclusive state-funded limited liability corporations and other limited liability corporations.

Share-holding Corporations Ltd. refer to economic units registered in accordance with the Regulation of the People's Republic of China on the Management of Registration of Corporations, with total registered capitals divided into equal shares and raised through issuing stocks. Each investor bears limited liability to the corporation depending on the holding of shares, and the corporation bears liability to its debt to the maximum of its total assets.

Private Enterprises refer to profit-making economic units invested and established by natural persons, or controlled by natural persons using employed labour. Included in this category are private limited liability corporations, private share-holding corporations Ltd., private partnership enterprises and private-funded enterprises registered in accordance with the Corporation Law, Partnership Enterprises Law and Interim Regulations on Private Enterprises.

Other Domestic-funded Enterprises refer to domesticfunded economic units other than those mentioned above.

Joint-venture Enterprises with Funds from Hong Kong, Macao and Taiwan refer to enterprises jointly established by investors from Hong Kong, Macao and Taiwan with enterprises in the mainland of China in accordance with the Law of the People's Republic of China on Sino-foreign Joint Venture Enterprises and other relevant laws, where the share of investment, profits and risks is stipulated in the contract.

Cooperative Enterprises with Funds from Hong Kong Macao and Taiwan established by investors from Hong Kong, Macao and Taiwan with enterprises in the mainland of China in accordance with the Law of the People's Republic of China on Sino-foreign Cooperative Enterprises and other relevant laws, where the investment or provision of facilities, and the share of profits and risks is stipulated in the cooperative contract.

Enterprises with Sole (exclusive) Investment from Hong Kong, Macao and Taiwan refer to enterprises established in the mainland of China with exclusive investment from investors from Hong Kong, Macao and Taiwan in accordance with the Law of the People's Republic of China on Foreign-Funded Enterprises and other relevant laws.

Share-holding Corporations Ltd. with Investment from Hong Kong, Macao and Taiwan refer to share-holding corporations Ltd. established with the approval from the Ministry of Foreign Trades and Economic Relations in line with relevant state regulations, where the share of investment from Hong Kong, Macao or Taiwan businessmen exceeds 25% of the total registered capital of the corporation. In case the share of investment from Hong Kong, Macao or Taiwan is less than 25% of the total registered capital, the enterprise is to be classified as domestic-funded share-holding corporation Ltd.

Joint-venture Enterprises with Foreign Investment refer to enterprises jointly established by foreign enterprises or foreigners with enterprises in the mainland of China in accordance with the Law of the People's Republic of China on Sino-foreign Joint Venture Enterprises and other relevant laws, where the share of investment, profits and risks is stipulated in the contract.

Cooperation Enterprises with Foreign Investment refer to enterprises jointly established by foreign enterprises or foreigners with enterprises in the mainland of China in accordance with the Law of the People's Republic of China on Sino-foreign Cooperative Enterprises and other relevant laws, where the investment or provision of facilities, and the share of profits and risks is stipulated in the cooperative contract.

Enterprises with Sole (exclusive) Foreign Investment refer to enterprises established in the mainland of China with exclusive investment from foreign investors in accordance with the Law of the People's Republic of China on Foreign-Funded Enterprises and other relevant laws.

Shareholding Corporations Ltd. with Foreign Investment refer to share-holding corporations Ltd. established with the approval from the Ministry of Foreign Trades and Economic Relations in line with relevant state regulations, where the share of investment from foreign investors exceeds 25% of the total registered capital of the corporation. In case the share of foreign investment is less than 25% of the total registered capital, the enterprise is to be classified as domestic-funded share-holding corporation Ltd.

Government Agencies, Institutions and Social Organizations are classified into following categories by source of funds and way of management taking reference of the re- gistration status of enterprises:

(1) Government agencies: include state and party agencies, classified in principle as "state-owned". There are exceptions, such as supply and marketing cooperatives which are classified as "collective".

(2) Institutions: include institutions of various types established with the approval by organization and staffing departments of the government, but exclude institutions where enterprise management system is introduced. Institutions are further classified as follows:

(a) Institutions whose main budget is listed in the government budget appropriations or extra-budget funds, or allocated from the budget of their competent government agencies. Such institutions are classified as "state-owned".

(b) Institutions whose budget mainly comes from collective units. Such institutions are classified as "collective".

(c) Social institutions established by individual or a group of citizens, which are classified as private

(d) Institutions other than those mentioned above whose source of budget is not clear. Such institutions are classified by way of management.

(3) Social organizations: include social organizations established with the approval from the Ministry of Civil Affairs, and organizations that are not covered by social organization management regulations such as Trades unions, women's federations etc. Social organizations are further classified as follows:

(a) Social organizations that are not covered by social organization management regulations of the Ministry of Civil Affairs such as Trades unions, women's federations, communist youth leagues, youth associations, industrial and commerce associations, scientists associations, overseas Chinese associations, etc.foundations and fund management organizations established with funds from the state, and social organizations whose funds mainly come from the budget of their competent government agencies. Such institutions are classified as "state-owned".

(b) Social organizations whose budget mainly comes from collective units. Such institutions are classified as "collective".

(c) Social organizations established by individual or a group of citizens, which are classified as "private".

(d) Social organizations other than those mentioned above whose source of budget is not clear. Such organizations are classified by way of management.

Each Plan Period recovery period refer to 1950-1952;the first five-year plan refer to 1953-1957;the second five-year plan refer to 1958-1962;the third five-year plan refer to 1966-1970;the fourth five-year plan refer to 1971-1975;the fifth five-yaer plan refer to 1976-1980;the sixth five-year plan refer to 1981-1985;the seventh five-yaer plan refer to 1986-1990;the eighth five-yaer plan refer to 1991-1995;the ninth five-year plan refer to 1996-2000;the tenth five-year plan refer to 2001-2005;the eleventh five-year plan refer to 2006-2010the twelvth five-yaer plan refer to 2011-2015.

Artificial person refer to unit that have following condition:

(1) legally Estabilished,have own name,organization,location and can undertake a civil case responsibility independently by law.

(2) independently own and use (or authorizable usage)a property,undertake liabilities and can make a bargain with other units.

(3) can independently account and workout balance sheet.artificial person unit Includes business artificial person,artifial person organization,artifial person,meeting group artificial person and other.

Single sector artificial person refer to the unit that have only one location and be engaged in one kind of production mangement activity.

Multi-sector artificial person refer to the unit that have 2 or above 2 locations,or mainly be engaged in 2 kinds or above 2 kinds of production management activity,and who can be diviede 2 or above 2 establishment units.

Establishments unit:refer to the subsidiary unit of artificial person unit.it should have following conditions:

(1) Be engaged in only one kind of social economic activities in excusive conditon.

(2) Opposite independtly organize management and business activity.

(3) Predominate data of business,such as income and expenditure ect.

Service refer to the enterprises and prodution department for production and selling the products.In the national economy accounting,services for the third industry,other said that refers to all sectors except agriculture,industry and construction.

2

国民经济核算

NATIONAL ACCOUNTS

简要说明

本篇资料的主要内容及来源

国民经济核算篇资料包括新疆维吾尔自治区主要年份生产总值的绝对值、构成和指数，居民消费水平，各地、州、市、县生产总值、构成和指数等资料。以上资料是由新疆维吾尔自治区统计局国民经济核算处根据不同产业部门、不同支出构成的特点和资料来源，严格按照国家国民经济核算制度计算的。

本篇所列分地、州（市）、县的数据来自各地、州（市）、县统计局的国民经济核算资料。由于采用分级核算，各地区数据相加不等于全疆总计，地区所辖县、市数据相加不等于地区合计。

本篇中人均地区生产总值按年平均常住人口计算。

Brief Introduction

Main Content and Source of Data

Statistics on national accounts include gross domestic product of Xinjiang Bureau of Statistics, it's composition and indices of gross domestic product, household consumption level, composition and indices of gross domestic product by prefecture, autonomous prefecture, city and county. Data on GDP are calculated by the Department of National Accounts Statistics of the Xinjiang Bureau of Statistics with various approaches in the light of the features of various sectors, various expenditure structures and the data sources and National Accounts system.

Data on the table come from national accounts statistics by prefecture, autonomous prefecture, city and county. Due to the adoption of hierarchical accounting, regional data do not add up to a total area of Xinjiang, under the jurisdiction of county, city is not equal to the sum of the data region total.

Per-capita Gross Domestic Product are calculated at annual permanent population.

2-1 1978-2012年历年新疆生产总值

Gross Domestic Product in Xinjiang(1978-2012)

单位：亿元 (100 million yuan)

年 份 Year	新疆生产总值 Gross Domestic Product	第一产业 Primary Industry	第二产业 Secondary Industry	工 业 Industry	建筑业 Construction	第三产业 Tertiary Industry	#交通运输仓储和邮政业 Transport, Storage and Post	#批发和零售业 Wholesale, and Retail Trades	人均新疆生产总值(元) Per Capita GDP (yuan)
1978	39.07	13.97	18.35	14.48	3.87	6.75	1.19	2.07	313
1979	45.63	16.32	21.43	17.16	4.27	7.88	1.52	2.34	359
1980	53.24	21.53	21.44	17.48	3.96	10.27	1.91	2.91	410
1981	59.41	25.18	22.39	17.93	4.46	11.84	2.25	3.41	450
1982	65.24	28.11	23.35	18.66	4.69	13.78	2.53	3.84	488
1983	78.55	32.84	29.10	23.33	5.77	16.61	3.01	4.75	583
1984	89.75	36.68	31.65	25.45	6.20	21.42	4.01	6.29	661
1985	112.24	42.89	40.50	32.14	8.36	28.85	4.59	8.97	820
1986	129.04	46.00	45.63	36.79	8.84	37.41	5.98	10.48	924
1987	148.50	56.18	50.30	41.16	9.14	42.02	7.73	12.45	1053
1988	192.72	72.27	66.02	53.53	12.49	54.43	11.60	16.11	1347
1989	217.29	78.01	73.83	60.21	13.62	65.45	12.90	17.59	1493
1990	261.44	104.09	83.18	71.50	11.68	74.17	14.63	20.48	1713
1991	335.91	111.86	107.99	84.07	23.92	116.06	22.63	36.88	2101
1992	402.31	114.50	147.64	106.29	41.35	140.17	28.32	39.85	2477
1993	495.25	126.85	205.07	155.92	49.15	163.33	32.58	43.46	2964
1994	662.32	187.69	249.11	190.00	59.11	225.52	44.40	57.67	3888
1995	814.85	240.71	283.97	219.01	64.96	290.17	59.63	73.78	4701
1996	900.93	249.31	313.70	239.07	74.63	337.92	73.74	87.25	5102
1997	1039.85	279.73	385.37	302.50	82.87	374.75	85.70	94.23	5848
1998	1106.95	291.05	395.75	298.53	97.22	420.15	106.87	98.06	6174
1999	1163.17	268.51	420.48	315.86	104.62	474.18	129.60	102.26	6443
2000	1363.56	288.18	537.58	418.63	118.95	537.80	148.63	110.10	7372
2001	1491.60	288.12	573.91	445.60	128.31	629.57	148.38	118.45	7945
2002	1612.65	305.00	603.15	463.59	139.56	704.50	168.58	123.88	8457
2003	1886.35	412.90	719.54	563.57	155.97	753.91	159.43	141.32	9828
2004	2209.09	446.13	914.47	734.10	180.37	848.49	186.70	160.30	11337
2005	2604.14	510.00	1164.80	961.62	203.18	929.34	149.61	145.10	13108
2006	3045.26	527.80	1459.30	1241.33	217.97	1058.16	165.60	163.15	15000
2007	3523.16	628.72	1647.55	1405.11	242.44	1246.89	177.28	187.10	16999
2008	4183.21	691.07	2070.76	1755.35	315.41	1421.38	191.84	222.74	19797
2009	4277.05	759.74	1929.59	1555.84	373.75	1587.72	209.10	253.60	19942
2010	5437.47	1078.63	2592.15	2161.39	430.76	1766.69	222.47	276.28	25034
2011	6610.05	1139.03	3225.90	2700.20	525.70	2245.12	256.72	371.90	30087
2012	7505.31	1320.57	3481.56	2850.06	631.50	2703.18	357.90	426.65	33796

注：根据自治区第三次全国人口普查结果,对2010年人均新疆生产总值数据进行了调整。
Note: According to the results of the third national census of 2010,per capita GDP of Xinjiang data were adjusted.

2-2 1978-2012 年历年新疆生产总值构成

Composition of Gross Domestic Product in Xinjiang(1978-2012)

单位：% (%)

年份 Year	新疆生产总值构成 Composition of Gross Domestic Product	第一产业 Primary Industry	第二产业 Secondary Industry	工业 Industry	建筑业 Construction	第三产业 Tertiary Industry	#交通运输仓储和邮政业 Transport, Storage and Post	#批发和零售业 Wholesale, and Retail Trades
1978	100	35.8	47.0	37.1	9.9	17.2	3.0	5.3
1979	100	35.7	47.0	37.6	9.4	17.3	3.3	5.1
1980	100	40.4	40.3	32.9	7.4	19.3	3.6	5.5
1981	100	42.4	37.7	30.2	7.5	19.9	3.8	5.7
1982	100	43.1	35.8	28.6	7.2	21.1	3.9	5.9
1983	100	41.8	37.1	29.8	7.3	21.1	3.8	6.0
1984	100	40.9	35.2	28.3	6.9	23.9	4.5	7.0
1985	100	38.2	36.1	28.7	7.4	25.7	4.1	8.0
1986	100	35.6	35.4	28.5	6.9	29.0	4.6	8.1
1987	100	37.8	33.9	27.7	6.2	28.3	5.2	8.4
1988	100	37.5	34.3	27.8	6.5	28.2	6.0	8.4
1989	100	35.9	34.0	27.7	6.3	30.1	5.9	8.1
1990	100	39.8	31.8	27.3	4.5	28.4	5.6	7.8
1991	100	33.3	32.1	25.0	7.1	34.6	6.7	11.0
1992	100	28.5	36.7	26.4	10.3	34.8	7.0	9.9
1993	100	25.6	41.4	31.5	9.9	33.0	6.6	8.8
1994	100	28.3	37.6	28.7	8.9	34.1	6.7	8.7
1995	100	29.5	34.9	26.9	8.0	35.6	7.3	9.1
1996	100	27.7	34.8	26.5	8.3	37.5	8.2	9.7
1997	100	26.9	37.1	29.1	8.0	36.0	8.2	9.1
1998	100	26.3	35.7	27.0	8.7	38.0	9.7	8.9
1999	100	23.1	36.1	27.1	9.0	40.8	11.1	8.8
2000	100	21.1	39.4	30.7	8.7	39.5	10.9	8.1
2001	100	19.3	38.5	29.9	8.6	42.2	9.9	7.9
2002	100	18.9	37.4	28.7	8.7	43.7	10.5	7.7
2003	100	21.9	38.1	29.8	8.3	40.0	8.5	7.5
2004	100	20.2	41.4	33.2	8.2	38.4	8.5	7.3
2005	100	19.6	44.7	36.9	7.8	35.7	5.7	5.6
2006	100	17.3	47.9	40.7	7.2	34.8	5.4	5.4
2007	100	17.8	46.8	39.9	6.9	35.4	5.0	5.3
2008	100	16.5	49.5	42.0	7.5	34.0	4.6	5.3
2009	100	17.8	45.1	36.4	8.7	37.1	4.9	5.9
2010	100	19.8	47.7	39.8	7.9	32.5	4.1	5.1
2011	100	17.2	48.8	40.8	8.0	34.0	3.9	5.6
2012	100	17.6	46.4	38.0	8.4	36.0	4.8	5.7

注：本表按当年价格计算。

Note: Data in value terms in this table are calculated at current prices.

2-3 1978-2012 年历年新疆生产总值指数
Indices of Gross Domestic Product in Xinjiang(1978-2012)

(上年=100) (preceding year=100)

年 份 Year	新疆生产总值 Gross Domestic Product	第一产业 Primary Industry	第二产业 Secondary Industry	工 业 Industry	建筑业 Construction	第三产业 Tertiary Industry	#交通运输仓储和邮政业 Transport, Storage and Post	#批发和零售业 Wholesale, and Retail Trades	人均新疆生产总值 Per Capita GDP
1978	109.8	110.2	110.3	112.8	101.8	107.2	102.1	109.3	106.9
1979	112.4	109.8	111.5	111.2	112.6	120.8	121.6	117.5	110.2
1980	107.3	106.0	105.2	108.5	93.1	116.6	115.6	125.5	105.0
1981	108.5	115.2	99.3	99.1	100.3	113.4	119.4	117.9	106.6
1982	109.9	111.2	104.3	104.6	102.8	117.1	118.9	119.8	108.5
1983	113.5	112.1	111.9	112.4	109.8	118.7	113.3	108.8	112.5
1984	114.1	113.6	114.7	115.1	112.9	114.0	100.0	109.2	113.2
1985	116.9	112.9	116.6	116.1	119.0	125.0	100.3	126.6	115.9
1986	111.7	108.3	109.5	111.0	102.5	120.7	124.7	110.0	109.2
1987	110.0	110.7	105.6	108.5	91.4	114.7	119.3	111.0	108.7
1988	109.6	103.3	114.6	113.6	120.2	112.9	118.8	114.7	108.0
1989	106.1	101.8	105.0	106.9	94.5	113.5	112.7	107.5	104.1
1990	111.7	116.0	106.7	106.4	108.6	112.0	106.7	104.5	106.8
1991	114.4	111.2	117.0	113.1	140.6	115.7	128.8	101.6	109.0
1992	113.1	105.5	119.4	112.6	152.8	115.7	124.6	112.6	111.3
1993	110.2	101.1	113.3	111.4	120.3	117.7	118.3	121.3	106.9
1994	112.1	111.2	110.2	111.3	106.3	115.3	109.7	105.6	110.2
1995	109.1	104.9	111.5	113.3	105.0	110.9	119.5	108.9	107.4
1996	106.5	103.5	107.8	107.4	109.5	108.0	113.0	109.6	104.5
1997	108.4	110.8	105.2	103.4	112.0	109.7	119.6	105.8	107.6
1998	107.5	107.2	105.7	103.0	115.0	109.6	117.5	104.9	106.6
1999	107.4	102.7	106.8	106.5	107.7	112.3	114.7	107.9	106.6
2000	108.7	104.8	108.6	109.1	107.3	112.1	114.4	109.6	106.2
2001	108.6	102.8	108.1	107.8	109.0	112.1	109.5	105.0	107.0
2002	108.2	105.0	107.4	107.7	106.3	110.4	114.3	110.3	106.5
2003	111.2	108.2	111.6	111.2	112.8	112.3	115.1	110.9	110.5
2004	111.4	105.7	114.0	114.5	112.2	111.5	115.1	112.6	109.7
2005	110.9	106.5	114.4	115.7	109.7	109.4	109.0	111.9	108.8
2006	111.0	105.7	111.2	112.5	105.0	113.6	107.2	110.5	108.7
2007	112.2	107.1	112.7	114.1	105.4	114.3	106.1	109.1	109.9
2008	111.0	106.4	114.3	114.3	114.1	109.2	108.7	110.3	108.9
2009	108.1	104.5	108.5	106.2	120.9	109.2	107.0	113.4	106.5
2010	110.6	104.5	112.6	113.5	108.3	110.8	107.9	108.3	109.3
2011	112.0	106.5	112.0	111.4	115.0	115.2	117.3	116.6	110.7
2012	112.0	107.0	113.7	112.7	118.2	112.3	124.1	107.8	110.8

注：本表按可比价计算。
Note: Data in this table are calculated at constant prices.

2-4 1978-2012 年历年新疆生产总值指数

Indices of Gross Domestic Product in Xinjiang(1978-2012)

(1978 年=100)

年 份 Year	新疆生产总值 Gross Domestic Product	第一产业 Primary Industry	第二产业 Secondary Industry	工 业 Industry	建筑业 Construction	第三产业 Tertiary Industry	#交通运输仓储和邮政业 Transport, Storage and Post	#批发和零售业 Wholesale, and Retail Trades	人均新疆生产总值 Per Capita GDP
1978	100	100	100	100	100	100	100	100	100
1979	112.4	109.8	111.5	111.2	112.6	120.8	121.6	117.5	110.2
1980	120.6	116.4	117.3	120.7	104.8	140.9	140.6	147.5	115.7
1981	130.9	134.1	116.5	119.6	105.1	159.8	167.9	173.9	123.3
1982	143.9	149.1	121.5	125.1	108.0	187.1	199.6	208.3	133.8
1983	163.3	167.1	136.0	140.6	118.6	222.1	226.1	226.6	150.6
1984	186.3	189.8	156.0	161.8	133.9	253.2	226.1	247.4	170.4
1985	217.8	214.3	181.9	187.8	159.3	316.5	226.8	313.2	197.5
1986	243.3	232.1	199.2	208.5	163.3	382.0	282.8	344.5	215.7
1987	267.6	256.9	210.4	226.2	149.3	438.2	337.4	382.4	234.5
1988	293.3	265.4	241.1	257.0	179.5	494.7	400.8	438.6	253.2
1989	311.2	270.2	253.2	274.7	169.6	561.5	451.7	471.5	263.6
1990	347.6	313.4	270.2	292.3	184.2	628.9	482.0	492.7	281.5
1991	397.7	348.5	316.1	330.6	259.0	727.6	620.8	500.6	306.9
1992	449.8	367.7	377.4	372.3	395.8	841.8	773.5	563.7	341.6
1993	495.7	371.7	427.6	414.7	476.1	990.8	915.1	683.8	365.1
1994	555.7	413.3	471.2	461.6	506.1	1142.4	1003.9	722.1	402.4
1995	606.3	433.6	525.4	523.0	531.4	1266.9	1199.7	786.4	432.1
1996	645.7	448.8	566.4	561.7	581.9	1368.3	1355.7	861.9	451.6
1997	699.9	497.3	595.9	580.8	651.7	1501.0	1621.4	911.9	485.9
1998	752.4	533.1	629.9	598.2	749.5	1645.1	1905.1	956.6	518.0
1999	808.1	547.5	672.7	637.1	807.2	1847.4	2185.1	1032.2	552.2
2000	878.4	573.8	730.6	695.1	866.1	2070.9	2499.8	1131.3	586.4
2001	953.9	589.9	789.8	749.3	944.0	2321.5	2737.3	1187.9	627.4
2002	1032.1	619.4	848.2	807.0	1003.5	2562.9	3128.7	1310.3	668.2
2003	1147.7	670.2	946.6	897.4	1131.9	2878.1	3601.1	1453.1	738.4
2004	1278.5	708.4	1079.1	1027.5	1270.0	3209.1	4144.9	1636.2	810.0
2005	1417.9	754.4	1234.5	1188.8	1393.2	3510.8	4517.9	1830.9	881.3
2006	1573.9	797.4	1372.8	1337.4	1462.9	3988.3	4843.2	2023.1	958.0
2007	1765.9	854.0	1547.1	1526.0	1541.9	4558.6	5138.6	2207.2	1052.8
2008	1960.1	908.7	1768.3	1744.2	1759.3	4978.0	5585.7	2434.5	1146.5
2009	2118.9	949.5	1918.6	1852.4	2127.0	5436.0	5976.7	2760.8	1221.0
2010	2343.5	992.2	2160.3	2102.5	2303.5	6023.1	6448.9	2989.9	1334.6
2011	2624.7	1056.7	2419.5	2342.2	2649.0	6938.6	7564.6	3486.2	1477.4
2012	2939.7	1130.7	2751.0	2639.7	3131.1	7792.0	9387.7	3758.1	1637.0

注：本表按可比价计算。
Note: Data in this table are calculated at constant prices.

2-5 分行业新疆生产总值
Gross Domestic Product by Sector in Xinjiang

指　　标	Item	增加值(亿元) Added Value (100 million yuan)		构　成(%) Composition (%)		指数(上年=100) Indices (preceding year=100)	
		2011	2012	2011	2012	2011	2012
新疆生产总值	**Gross Domestic Product**	**6610.05**	**7505.31**	**100**	**100.0**	**112.0**	**112.0**
第一产业	Primary Industry	1139.03	1320.57	17.2	17.6	106.5	107.0
第二产业	Secondary Industry	3225.90	3481.56	48.8	46.4	112.0	113.7
工　业	Industry	2700.20	2850.06	40.8	38.0	111.4	112.7
建筑业	Construction	525.70	631.50	8.0	8.4	115.0	118.2
第三产业	Tertiary Industry	2245.12	2703.18	34.0	36.0	115.2	112.3
交通运输、仓储和邮政业	Transport, storage and Post	256.72	357.90	3.9	4.8	117.3	124.1
批发和零售业	Wholesale and Retail Trades	371.90	426.65	5.6	5.7	116.6	107.8
住宿和餐饮业	Hotels and Catering Services	77.87	108.39	1.2	1.4	109.0	105.9
金融业	Financial Intermediation	288.77	360.40	4.4	4.8	112.8	123.9
房地产业	Real Estate	176.22	194.38	2.7	2.6	109.1	96.7
其他服务业	Others	1073.64	1255.46	16.2	16.7	116.4	110.6

注：本表按当年价格计算，采用 GB/T4754-2002 国民经济行业分类标准。
Note: Data in value terms in this table are calculated at current prices and adopted the new Industrial Classification of National Economy (GB/T4754-2002).

2-6 新疆生产总值项目结构

Components of Gross Domestic Product in Xinjiang

(2012 年)

指　　标	Item	新疆生产总值 Gross Domestic Product	劳动者报酬 Compensation of Employees	生产税净额 Net Taxes on Production	固定资产折旧 Depreciation of Fixed Assets	营业盈余 Operating Surplus
新疆生产总值(亿元)	**Gross Domestic Product (100 million yuan)**	**7505.31**	**3979.27**	**1140.66**	**1096.08**	**1289.30**
第一产业	Primary Industry	1320.57	1237.78		82.79	
第二产业	Secondary Industry	3481.56	1068.45	845.30	631.83	935.98
工　业	Industry	2850.06	671.92	703.04	579.21	895.89
建筑业	Construction	631.50	396.53	142.26	52.62	40.09
第三产业	Tertiary Industry	2703.18	1673.04	295.36	381.46	353.32
交通运输、仓储和邮政业	Transport, storage and Post	357.90	209.34	29.26	90.95	28.35
信息传输、计算机服务和软件业	Information Transmission, Computer Service and Software	119.77	38.46	8.58	50.16	22.57
批发和零售业	Wholesale and Retail Trades	426.65	172.85	161.35	25.39	67.06
住宿和餐饮业	Hotels and Catering Services	108.39	94.24	6.75	8.27	-0.87
金融业	Financial Intermediation	360.40	118.01	34.44	14.64	193.31
房地产业	Real Estate	194.38	24.50	36.00	100.31	33.57
租赁和商务服务业	Leasing and Business Service	57.28	38.03	5.89	9.58	3.78
科学研究、技术服务和地质勘查业	Scientific Research, Technology Service and Geological Prospecting	66.17	47.97	4.30	5.82	8.08
水利、环境和公共设施管理业	Water Conservancy, Environment and Public Facility Management	36.15	19.69	1.15	15.11	0.20
居民服务和其他服务业	Community Service and Other Services	57.71	50.53	4.89	1.63	0.66
教　育	Education	242.74	227.42	0.62	17.01	-2.31
卫生、社会保障和社会福利业	Health, Social Security and Social Welfare	117.19	104.22	0.71	11.16	1.10
文化、体育和娱乐业	Culture, Sports and Entertainment	29.16	26.20	1.12	3.51	-1.67
公共管理和社会组织	Public Management and Social Organizations	529.29	501.58	0.30	27.92	-0.51

注：本表按当年价格计算。
Note: Data in value terms in this table are calculated at current prices.

2-7 主要年份支出法新疆生产总值
Gross Domestic Product by Expenditure Approach in Xinjiang in Main Years

单位：亿元 (100 million yuan)

年份 Year	支出法新疆生产总值 Gross Domestic Product by Expenditure	最终消费 Final Consumption Expenditures	资本形成总额 Gross Capital Formation	货物和服务净出口 Net Export of Goods and Services	最终消费率(消费率)(%) Final Consumption Rate (%)	资本形成率(投资率)(%) Capital Formation Rate (%)
1978	39.07	27.64	18.43	-7.00	70.7	47.2
1980	53.24	39.82	23.15	-9.73	74.8	43.5
1985	112.24	78.04	58.43	-24.23	69.5	52.1
1986	129.04	92.38	60.26	-23.60	71.6	46.7
1987	148.51	103.77	69.94	-25.20	69.9	47.1
1988	192.72	126.09	98.31	-31.67	65.4	51.0
1989	217.29	137.50	117.84	-38.05	63.3	54.2
1990	261.44	166.77	141.17	-46.50	63.8	54.0
1991	335.91	196.58	169.15	-29.81	58.5	50.4
1992	402.31	221.57	249.26	-68.52	55.1	61.9
1993	495.25	269.92	356.16	-130.83	54.5	71.9
1994	662.32	336.94	487.55	-162.17	50.9	73.6
1995	814.85	444.62	473.71	-103.48	54.6	58.1
1996	900.93	553.90	456.96	-109.93	61.5	50.7
1997	1039.85	611.81	564.92	-136.89	58.8	54.3
1998	1106.95	642.48	685.85	-221.37	58.0	62.0
1999	1163.17	690.57	581.59	-108.99	59.4	50.0
2000	1363.56	760.20	618.12	-14.76	55.8	45.3
2001	1491.60	859.00	771.42	-138.82	57.6	51.7
2002	1612.65	963.71	864.27	-215.33	59.8	53.6
2003	1886.35	1027.22	1119.21	-260.08	54.5	59.3
2004	2209.09	1125.11	1350.47	-266.50	50.9	61.1
2005	2604.14	1266.52	1505.97	-168.35	48.6	57.8
2006	3045.26	1464.53	1654.70	-73.97	48.1	54.3
2007	3513.16	1740.56	1970.06	-197.46	49.5	56.1
2008	4183.21	2073.05	2301.50	-191.34	49.6	55.0
2009	4277.05	2266.20	2549.75	-538.90	53.0	59.6
2010	5437.47	2865.56	3371.22	-799.31	52.7	62.0
2011	6610.05	3518.82	4162.32	-1071.09	53.2	63.0
2012	7505.31	4262.51	5792.16	-2549.36	56.8	77.2

注：2005 年以后数据依据 2008 年经济普查资料已修订。
Note: Since 2005 the data has adjusted according to the economic census in 2008.

2-8 主要年份资本形成总额及其构成
Gross Capital Formation and Its Composition in Main Years

年 份	Year	资本形成总额(亿元) Gross Capital Formation (100 million yuan)	固定资本形成 Gross Fixed Capital Formation	存货增加 Change in Inventories	以资本形成总额为100 Gross Capital Formation=100 固定资本形成(%) Gross Fixed Capital Formation (%)	存货增加(%) Change in Inventories (%)
	1978	18.43	13.25	5.18	71.9	28.1
	1980	23.15	18.14	5.01	78.3	21.7
	1985	58.43	46.78	11.65	80.1	19.9
	1990	141.17	91.50	49.67	64.8	35.2
	1991	169.15	124.77	44.38	73.8	26.2
	1992	249.26	181.17	68.09	72.7	27.3
	1993	356.16	264.90	91.26	74.4	25.6
	1994	487.55	376.95	110.60	77.3	22.7
	1995	473.71	377.91	95.80	79.8	20.2
	1996	456.96	422.87	34.09	92.5	7.5
	1997	564.92	461.41	103.51	81.7	18.3
	1998	685.85	543.78	142.06	79.3	20.7
	1999	581.59	551.72	29.87	94.9	5.1
	2000	618.12	648.12	-30.00	104.9	-4.9
	2001	771.42	720.12	51.30	93.3	6.7
	2002	864.27	856.70	7.57	99.1	0.9
	2003	1119.21	1079.24	39.98	96.4	3.6
	2004	1350.47	1239.50	110.97	91.8	8.2
	2005	1505.97	1384.33	121.63	91.9	8.1
	2006	1654.70	1596.16	58.54	96.5	3.5
	2007	1970.06	1885.24	84.83	95.7	4.3
	2008	2301.50	2285.60	15.90	99.3	0.7
	2009	2549.75	2473.24	76.51	97.0	3.0
	2010	3371.22	3233.00	138.22	95.9	4.1
	2011	4162.32	3948.87	213.45	94.9	5.1
	2012	5792.16	5477.61	314.55	94.6	5.4
“一五”时期	"First Five-year Plan" Period	16.26	14.33	1.94	88.1	11.9
“二五”时期	"Second Five-year Plan" Period	36.39	26.69	9.70	73.3	26.7
	1963—1965	19.40	14.34	5.06	73.9	26.1
“三五”时期	"Third Five-year Plan" Period	30.65	20.96	9.68	68.4	31.6
“四五”时期	"Fourth Five-year Plan" Period	51.70	32.13	19.57	62.1	37.9
“五五”时期	"Fifth Five-year Plan" Period	87.76	62.50	25.26	71.2	28.8
“六五”时期	"Sixth Five-year Plan" Period	191.38	158.48	32.91	82.8	17.2
“七五”时期	"Seventh Five-year Plan" Period	487.52	361.64	125.88	74.2	25.8
“八五”时期	"Eighth Five-year Plan" Period	1735.83	1325.70	410.12	76.4	23.6
“九五”时期	"Ninth Five-year Plan" Period	2907.43	2627.90	279.53	90.4	9.6
“十五”时期	"Tenth Five-year Plan" Period	5611.34	5279.89	331.45	94.1	5.9
“十一五”时期	"Eleventh Five-year Plan " Period	11847.23	11473.23	374.00	96.8	3.2

注：本表按当年价格计算。
Note: Data in value terms in this table are calculated at current prices.

2-9 主要年份最终消费及其构成
Final Consumption Expenditure and Its Composition in Main Years

单位：% (%)

年份	Year	最终消费(亿元) Final Consumption Expenditures (100 million yuan)	居民消费 Household Consumption	农村居民 Rural Household	城镇居民 Urban Household	政府消费 Government Consumption	最终消费=100 Final Consumption Expenditure=100 居民消费 Household Consumption	政府消费 Government Consumption	居民消费=100 Houshold Consumption=100 农村居民 Rural Household	城镇居民 Urban Household
	1978	27.64	22.61	12.08	10.53	5.03	81.8	18.2	53.4	46.6
	1980	39.82	32.78	16.20	16.58	7.04	82.3	17.7	49.4	50.6
	1985	78.04	58.51	26.41	32.10	19.53	75.0	25.0	45.1	54.9
	1990	166.77	121.12	45.67	75.46	45.65	72.6	27.4	37.7	62.3
	1991	196.58	145.55	52.30	93.26	51.02	74.0	26.0	35.9	64.1
	1992	221.57	159.20	55.18	104.02	62.37	71.9	28.1	34.7	65.3
	1993	269.92	197.78	63.96	133.82	72.14	73.3	26.7	32.3	67.7
	1994	336.94	242.79	83.04	159.75	94.15	72.1	27.9	34.2	65.8
	1995	444.62	320.70	108.43	212.27	123.93	72.1	27.9	33.8	66.2
	1996	553.90	397.61	156.07	241.54	156.29	71.8	28.2	39.3	60.7
	1997	611.81	436.67	164.84	271.84	175.14	71.4	28.6	37.7	62.3
	1998	642.48	457.38	175.72	281.66	185.10	71.2	28.8	38.4	61.6
	1999	690.57	475.74	158.98	316.76	214.83	68.9	31.1	33.4	66.6
	2000	760.20	492.32	159.97	332.34	267.88	64.8	35.2	32.5	67.5
	2001	859.00	545.49	176.00	369.49	313.51	63.5	36.5	32.3	67.7
	2002	963.71	615.47	190.85	424.62	348.25	63.9	36.1	31.0	69.0
	2003	1027.22	623.61	202.67	420.94	403.61	60.7	39.3	32.5	67.5
	2004	1125.11	671.28	209.99	461.29	453.84	59.7	40.3	31.3	68.7
	2005	1266.52	764.26	238.98	525.28	502.26	60.3	39.7	31.3	68.7
	2006	1464.53	853.88	253.58	600.31	610.65	58.3	41.7	29.7	70.3
	2007	1740.56	1013.48	295.52	717.96	727.09	58.2	41.8	29.2	70.8
	2008	2073.05	1171.05	340.69	830.36	902.00	56.5	43.5	29.1	70.9
	2009	2266.20	1284.66	385.66	898.99	981.54	56.7	43.3	30.0	70.0
	2010	2865.56	1578.93	456.31	1122.62	1286.63	55.1	44.9	28.9	71.1
	2011	3518.82	1954.33	560.30	1394.03	1564.49	55.5	44.5	28.7	71.3
	2012	4262.51	2370.67	675.64	1695.03	1891.84	55.6	44.4	28.5	71.5
“一五”时期	"First Five-year Plan" Period	42.97	38.62	23.89	14.73	4.35	89.9	10.1	61.9	38.1
“二五”时期	"Second Five-year Plan" Period	71.40	64.02	39.30	24.72	7.38	89.7	10.3	61.4	38.6
	1963—1965	47.00	42.42	30.93	11.49	4.58	90.3	9.7	72.9	27.1
“三五”时期	"Third Five-year Plan" Period	80.09	72.97	49.13	23.84	7.12	91.1	8.9	67.3	32.7
“四五”时期	"Forth Five-year Plan" Period	97.46	83.75	51.78	31.97	13.71	85.9	14.1	61.8	38.2
“五五”时期	"Fifth Five-year Plan" Period	149.77	123.11	65.02	58.09	26.66	82.2	17.8	52.8	47.2
“六五”时期	"Sixth Five-year Plan" Period	289.27	227.00	107.93	119.06	62.28	78.5	21.5	47.5	52.5
“七五”时期	"Seventh Five-year Plan" Period	626.51	464.17	186.47	277.70	162.34	74.1	25.9	40.2	59.8
“八五”时期	"Eighth Five-year Plan" Period	1469.63	1066.03	362.91	703.12	403.60	72.5	27.5	34.0	66.0
“九五”时期	"Ninth Five-year Plan" Period	3258.96	2259.72	815.58	1444.14	999.24	69.3	30.7	36.1	63.9
“十五”时期	"Tenth Five-year Plan" Period	5241.57	3220.11	1018.50	2201.61	2021.46	61.4	38.6	31.6	68.4
“十一五”时期	"Eleventh Five-year Plan " Period	10409.90	5902.00	1731.76	4170.24	4507.90	56.7	43.3	29.3	70.7

注：本表按当年价格计算。
Note: Data in value terms in this table are calculated at current prices.

2-10 各地、州、市、县(市)地区生产总值

单位：万元 (2012 年) (10 000 Yuan)

地　　区	Region	地区生产总值 Gross Regional Product	第一产业 Primary Industry
乌鲁木齐市	**Urumqi City**	**20017386**	**250218**
#乌鲁木齐县	Urumqi County	157484	53306
克拉玛依市	**Karamay City**	**8107054**	**46245**
石河子市	**Shihezi City**	**2081934**	**113665**
吐鲁番地区	**Turpan Administrative Offices**	**2433907**	**339060**
吐鲁番市	Turpan City	637696	143733
鄯善县	Shanshan [Piqan] County	1408343	123063
托克逊县	Toksun County	400516	72264
哈密地区	**Hami [Kumul] Administrative Offices**	**2682518**	**331154**
哈密市	Hami [Kumul] City	2094376	206609
巴里坤哈萨克自治县	Barkol Kazak Autonomous County	363719	85133
伊吾县	Yiwu [Araturuk] County	224330	39411
昌吉回族自治州	**Changji Hui Autonomous Prefecture**	**8185631**	**2167200**
昌吉市	Changji City	2603609	331988
阜康市	Fukang City	1188902	218894
呼图壁县	Hutubi County	1068681	405211
玛纳斯县	Manas County	1338184	572757
奇台县	Qitai County	852361	365624
吉木萨尔县	Jimsar County	481301	149957
木垒哈萨克自治县	Mori Kazak Autonomous County	209652	102929
伊犁哈萨克自治州	**Ili Kazak Autonomous Prefecture**	**12519627**	**3454578**
伊犁州直属县(市)	**Counties (Cities) Direct Under Ili Prefecture**	**5776226**	**1368794**
伊宁市	Yining [Gulja] City	1367965	63567
奎屯市	Kuytun City	1059646	57238
伊宁县	Yining [Gulja] County	533606	211759
察布查尔锡伯自治县	Qapqal Xibe Autonomous County	327753	157752
霍城县	Huocheng [Korgas] County	738012	250206
巩留县	Gongliu [Tokkuztara] County	292924	105469
新源县	Xinyuan [Kunes] County	701452	208465
昭苏县	Zhaosu [Mongolkure] County	295910	135005
特克斯县	Tekes County	170354	76736
尼勒克县	Nilka County	356993	102597

Gross Regional Product by Prefecture, Autonomous Prefecture, City and County

(10 000 yuan)

第二产业 Secondary Industry	工　业 Industry	建筑业 Construction	第三产业 Tertiary Industry	#交通运输、仓储和邮政业 Transport,storage And Post	#批发和零售业 Wholesale, and Retail Trades	人均地区生产总值(元) Per Capita GDP (yuan)
8290099	**7140099**	**1150000**	**11477069**	**2509580**	**1696752**	**59576**
44395	40008	4387	59783	5567	7014	27013
7130736	**6920736**	**210000**	**930073**	**144554**	**106596**	**135018**
1198688	**917676**	**281012**	**769582**	**69400**	**73462**	**64346**
1542558	**1319258**	**223300**	**552289**	**161821**	**37163**	**39068**
200401	158901	41500	293562	75928	23305	23566
1093474	957023	136451	191806	72208	7853	61126
248683	203333	45350	79569	9881	5192	33770
1337700	**902700**	**435000**	**1013664**	**260802**	**161435**	**45613**
1026957	675450	351507	860810	234976	136380	45361
180929	139146	41783	97657	14606	15687	35091
130834	89126	41708	54085	11188	9348	98594
3887740	**3123778**	**763962**	**2130691**	**317287**	**321802**	**51211**
1302901	1103014	199887	968720	185679	110689	54017
729718	650821	78897	240290	31388	41530	71924
383287	219329	163958	280183	39688	72271	48466
484378	399842	84536	281049	26607	53201	52355
286540	229587	56953	200197	22603	39791	39934
214214	184253	29961	117130	7838	16258	37224
34427	24484	9943	72296	3383	9914	23556
4648820	**3414640**	**1234180**	**4416229**	**455292**	**771636**	**26801**
1976460	**1421560**	**554900**	**2430972**	**239310**	**357109**	**21187**
363570	184220	179350	940828	70579	169794	27246
565341	452905	112436	437067	77972	40957	69439
169983	137883	32100	151864	15391	6267	12540
76855	54397	22458	93146	5709	8446	17017
163856	129909	33947	323950	32522	102450	18187
105579	72727	32852	81876	7913	1406	14817
331048	258871	72177	161939	17838	8755	22353
53901	36568	17333	107004	6656	7635	15884
24330	13905	10425	69288	4353	1538	10027
187067	145245	41822	67329	2333	4064	19307

2-10 续表 1

单位：万元

地　　区	Region	地区生产总值 Gross Regional Product	第一产业 Primary Industry
塔城地区	**Tacheng [Tarbagatai] Administrative Offices**	**4862311**	**1711173**
塔城市	Tacheng [Qoqek] City	594874	132881
乌苏市	Usu City	1534588	455638
额敏县	Emin [Dorbiljin] County	558986	186989
沙湾县	Shawan County	1394524	734315
托里县	Toli County	357217	46369
裕民县	Yumin [Qagantokay] County	119435	45887
和布克赛尔蒙古自治县	Hoboksar Mongol Autonomous County	334867	60723
阿勒泰地区	**Altay Administrative Offices**	**1881090**	**374611**
阿勒泰市	Altay City	453683	71260
布尔津县	Burqin County	146780	29230
富蕴县	Fuyun [Koktokay] County	463523	61502
福海县	Fuhai [Burultokay] County	280570	108468
哈巴河县	Habahe [Kaba] County	393800	60528
青河县	Qinghe [Qinggil] County	104327	27395
吉木乃县	Jeminay County	53336	12671
博尔塔拉蒙古自治州	**Bortala Mongolian Autonomous Prefecture**	**1854011**	**570228**
博乐市	Bole [Bortala] City	1268844	293470
精河县	Jinghe [Jing] County	426213	204842
温泉县	Wenquan [Araxang] County	159999	70297
巴音郭楞蒙古自治州	**Bayangol Mongol ian Autonomous Prefecture**	**9075401**	**1554446**
库尔勒市	Korla City	5914147	353996
轮台县	Luntai [Bugur] County	465767	162341
尉犁县	Yuli [Lopnur] County	398899	214732
若羌县	Ruoqiang [Qarkilik] County	600174	159077
且末县	Qiemo [Qarqan] County	182244	80667
焉耆回族自治县	Yanqi Hui Autonomous County	458161	122779
和静县	Hejing County	650822	180312
和硕县	Hoxud County	225105	139628
博湖县	Bohu [Bagrax] County	180006	79302
阿克苏地区	**Aksu Administrative Offices**	**6121381**	**1918479**
阿克苏市	Aksu City	1625336	310572
温宿县	Wensu [Onsu] County	471509	217625
库车县	Kuqa County	1296748	176366

Continued

(10 000 yuan)

第二产业 Secondary Industry	工　业 Industry	建筑业 Construction	第三产业 Tertiary Industry	#交通运输、仓储和邮政业 Transport,storage And Post	#批发和零售业 Wholesale, and Retail Trades	人均地区生产总值(元) Per Capita GDP (yuan)
1788906	**1318626**	**470280**	**1362232**	**135978**	**355157**	**36550**
162171	86113	76058	299822	36704	91148	35836
810562	672084	138478	268388	33875	70090	45684
172957	120203	52754	199040	19296	40469	25505
301492	200816	100676	358717	39535	91854	36156
243314	194234	49080	67534	10297	8648	35658
28543	7229	21314	45005	1892	3757	20141
200803	100651	100152	73341	7470	9191	52323
883454	**674454**	**209000**	**623025**	**80004**	**59370**	**30602**
90685	43985	46700	291738	27047	35902	23928
52824	31924	20900	64726	5316	6394	21617
328757	278757	50000	73264	19792	6485	51161
89387	64987	24400	82715	10751	9231	36063
272503	236203	36300	60769	11614	4541	46454
30355	10955	19400	46577	3460	4079	16125
19292	7992	11300	21373	1468	1475	14110
427976	**275976**	**152000**	**855808**	**132824**	**254562**	**38141**
300914	205866	95048	674461	99404	244923	47917
97540	57740	39800	123831	25072	15960	29510
31461	14334	17127	58241	3893	3324	21248
5839043	**5170543**	**668500**	**1681912**	**230781**	**205248**	**65394**
4692684	4193313	499371	867467	108043	142313	103336
144110	128655	15455	159316	31120	15058	43307
92097	63464	28633	92070	10473	12883	34567
398971	387118	11853	42126	5496	1833	96491
34133	19003	15130	67444	3748	436	28476
132856	88752	44104	202526	36096	17960	32796
290431	259088	31343	180079	62738	7133	32886
32696	21363	11333	52781	7711	5304	29815
33743	18985	14758	66961	5895	7650	29365
2009284	**1472033**	**537250**	**2193618**	**237689**	**279247**	**24248**
489118	356799	132319	825646	93716	141885	33793
116448	57252	59196	137436	6385	16190	19415
775297	615874	159423	345086	81418	39236	27489

2-10 续表 2

单位：万元

地　　区	Region	地区生产总值 Gross Regional Product	第一产业 Primary Industry
沙雅县	Xayar County	394206	126287
新和县	Xinhe [Toksu] County	252803	99606
拜城县	Baicheng [Bay] County	430680	84585
乌什县	Wushi [Uxturpan] County	212128	82101
阿瓦提县	Awat County	427952	215649
柯坪县	Kalpin County	68440	16504
克孜勒苏柯尔克孜自治州	**Kizilsu Kirgiz Autonomous Prefecture**	**610309**	**104520**
阿图什市	Artux City	279690	44560
阿克陶县	Akto County	162872	43177
阿合奇县	Akqi County	58710	8102
乌恰县	Wuqia [Ulugqat] County	106299	8681
喀什地区	**Kashgar [Kaxgar] Administrative Offices**	**5173492**	**1752279**
喀什市	Kashgar [Kaxgar] City	1320127	52000
疏附县	Shufu County	327721	185372
疏勒县	Shule County	497581	165188
英吉沙县	Yengisar County	209782	91047
泽普县	Zepu [Poskam] County	305740	102098
莎车县	Shache [Yarkant] County	574254	306161
叶城县	Yecheng [Kagilik] County	505312	267116
麦盖提县	Makit County	251886	137109
岳普湖县	Yopurga County	208709	70353
伽师县	Jiashi [Payzawat] County	448698	195000
巴楚县	Bachu [Maralbexi] County	452516	170388
塔什库尔干塔吉克自治县	Taxkorgan Tajik Autonomous County	71166	10447
和田地区	**Hotan Administrative Offices**	**1472873**	**457209**
和田市	Hotan City	382731	32412
和田县	Hotan County	190819	75111
墨玉县	Moyu [Karakax] County	253618	116754
皮山县	Pishan [Guma] County	160318	76067
洛浦县	Lop County	157118	49301
策勒县	Qira County	111165	41934
于田县	Yutian [Keriya] County	154788	53214
民丰县	Minfeng [Niya] County	62316	12416

Continued

(10 000 yuan)

第二产业 Secondary Industry	工业 Industry	建筑业 Construction	第三产业 Tertiary Industry	#交通运输、仓储和邮政业 Transport,storage And Post	#批发和零售业 Wholesale, and Retail Trades	人均地区生产总值(元) Per Capita GDP (yuan)
92169	63851	28318	175750	10231	28119	16281
52974	38863	14112	100223	12607	10994	15331
213581	183552	30029	132515	17807	9606	18791
28032	15290	12742	101995	3250	2483	10222
61702	31484	30218	150601	6569	13341	17777
13459	6217	7242	38477	2577	89	14259
174526	**101070**	**73456**	**331263**	**25366**	**16278**	**10887**
65594	42615	22979	169536	18446	7312	10951
55554	31784	23770	64141	1938	1623	7984
15863	9821	6042	34745	1611	1314	13756
42035	21370	20665	55583	3373	3336	18140
1431277	**812605**	**618672**	**1989936**	**159347**	**583182**	**12817**
453675	326589	127086	814452	89417	318682	24042
47071	12300	34771	95278	4152	6705	9681
243745	132350	111395	88648	3541	7507	14466
53452	12479	40973	65283	2923	8042	7538
71715	42646	29069	131927	6795	46761	14566
83887	41500	42387	184206	6136	17824	7140
100349	55108	45241	137847	8918	18968	10849
45287	20077	25210	69490	3589	16959	11170
71146	24689	46457	67210	5179	7364	13241
141517	94209	47308	112181	18946	24982	11328
81815	33000	48815	200313	8921	107632	13321
37619	17658	19961	23100	830	1757	18248
290112	**114584**	**175528**	**725552**	**31010**	**33109**	**7015**
128163	68086	60077	222156	18322	13871	6489
42038	19540	22498	73670	1168	792	6827
21840	5431	16409	115024	4263	8943	4741
23951	4414	19537	60300	1157	1727	5984
26641	6321	20320	81176	1955	2764	6225
14346	1766	12580	54885	1268	1524	7135
18689	3519	15170	82885	2984	3075	6014
13455	4513	8942	36445	2252	794	16442

2-11 各地、州、市、县(市)地区生产总值构成

单位：%　　　　　　(2012 年)

地　　区	Region	地区生产总值 Gross Regional Product	第一产业 Primary Industry
乌鲁木齐市	**Urumqi City**	**100.0**	**1.3**
#乌鲁木齐县	Urumqi County	100.0	33.8
克拉玛依市	**Karamay City**	**100.0**	**0.6**
石河子市	**Shihezi City**	**100.0**	**5.5**
吐鲁番地区	**Turpan Administrative Offices**	**100.0**	**13.9**
吐鲁番市	Turpan City	100.0	22.5
鄯善县	Shanshan [Piqan] County	100.0	8.7
托克逊县	Toksun County	100.0	18.0
哈密地区	**Hami [Kumul] Administrative Offices**	**100.0**	**12.3**
哈密市	Hami [Kumul] City	100.0	9.9
巴里坤哈萨克自治县	Barkol Kazak Autonomous County	100.0	23.4
伊吾县	Yiwu [Araturuk] County	100.0	17.6
昌吉回族自治州	**Changji Hui Autonomous Prefecture**	**100.0**	**26.5**
昌吉市	Changji City	100.0	12.8
阜康市	Fukang City	100.0	18.4
呼图壁县	Hutubi County	100.0	37.9
玛纳斯县	Manas County	100.0	42.8
奇台县	Qitai County	100.0	42.9
吉木萨尔县	Jimsar County	100.0	31.2
木垒哈萨克自治县	Mori Kazak Autonomous County	100.0	49.1
伊犁哈萨克自治州	**Ili Kazak Autonomous Prefecture**	**100.0**	**27.6**
伊犁州直属县(市)	**Counties (Cities) Direct Under Ili Prefecture**	**100.0**	**23.7**
伊宁市	Yining [Gulja] City	100.0	4.6
奎屯市	Kuytun City	100.0	5.4
伊宁县	Yining [Gulja] County	100.0	39.7
察布查尔锡伯自治县	Qapqal Xibe Autonomous County	100.0	48.1
霍城县	Huocheng [Korgas] County	100.0	33.9
巩留县	Gongliu [Tokkuztara] County	100.0	36.0
新源县	Xinyuan [Kunes] County	100.0	29.7
昭苏县	Zhaosu [Mongolkure] County	100.0	45.6
特克斯县	Tekes County	100.0	45.0
尼勒克县	Nilka County	100.0	28.7

Composition of Gross Domestic Product by Prefecture, Autonomous Prefecture, City and County

(%)

第二产业 Secondary Industry	工业 Industry	建筑业 Construction	第三产业 Tertiary Industry	#交通运输、仓储和邮政业 Transport,storage And Post	#批发和零售业 Wholesale, and Retail Trades
41.4	**35.7**	**5.7**	**57.3**	**12.5**	**8.5**
28.2	25.4	2.8	38.0	3.5	4.5
88.0	**85.4**	**2.6**	**11.4**	**1.8**	**1.3**
57.6	**44.1**	**13.5**	**36.9**	**3.3**	**3.5**
63.4	**54.2**	**9.2**	**22.7**	**6.6**	**1.5**
31.4	24.9	6.5	46.1	11.9	3.7
77.6	68.0	9.7	13.7	5.1	0.6
62.1	50.8	11.3	19.9	2.5	1.3
49.9	**33.7**	**16.2**	**37.8**	**9.7**	**6.0**
49.0	32.3	16.8	41.1	11.2	6.5
49.7	38.3	11.5	26.9	4.0	4.3
58.3	39.7	18.6	24.1	5.0	4.2
47.5	**38.2**	**9.3**	**26.0**	**3.9**	**3.9**
50.0	42.4	7.7	37.2	7.1	4.3
61.4	54.7	6.6	20.2	2.6	3.5
35.9	20.5	15.3	26.2	3.7	6.8
36.2	29.9	6.3	21.0	2.0	4.0
33.6	26.9	6.7	23.5	2.7	4.7
44.5	38.3	6.2	24.3	1.6	3.4
16.4	11.7	4.7	34.5	1.6	4.7
37.1	**27.3**	**9.9**	**35.3**	**3.6**	**6.2**
34.2	**24.6**	**9.6**	**42.1**	**4.1**	**6.2**
26.6	13.5	13.1	68.8	5.2	12.4
53.4	42.7	10.6	41.2	7.4	3.9
31.9	25.8	6.0	28.4	2.9	1.2
23.4	16.6	6.9	28.5	1.7	2.6
22.2	17.6	4.6	43.9	4.4	13.9
36.0	24.8	11.2	28.0	2.7	0.5
47.2	36.9	10.3	23.1	2.5	1.2
18.2	12.4	5.9	36.2	2.2	2.6
14.3	8.2	6.1	40.7	2.6	0.9
52.4	40.7	11.7	18.9	0.7	1.1

2-11 续表 1

单位：%

地　　区	Region	地区生产总值 Gross Regional Product	第一产业 Primary Industry
塔城地区	**Tacheng [Tarbagatai] Administrative Offices**	**100.0**	**35.2**
塔城市	Tacheng [Qoqek] City	100.0	22.3
乌苏市	Usu City	100.0	29.7
额敏县	Emin [Dorbiljin] County	100.0	33.5
沙湾县	Shawan County	100.0	52.7
托里县	Toli County	100.0	13.0
裕民县	Yumin [Qagantokay] County	100.0	38.4
和布克赛尔蒙古自治县	Hoboksar Mongol Autonomous County	100.0	18.1
阿勒泰地区	**Altay Administrative Offices**	**100.0**	**19.9**
阿勒泰市	Altay City	100.0	15.7
布尔津县	Burqin County	100.0	19.9
富蕴县	Fuyun [Koktokay] County	100.0	13.3
福海县	Fuhai [Burultokay] County	100.0	38.7
哈巴河县	Habahe [Kaba] County	100.0	15.4
青河县	Qinghe [Qinggil] County	100.0	26.3
吉木乃县	Jeminay County	100.0	23.8
博尔塔拉蒙古自治州	**Bortala Mongolian Autonomous Prefecture**	**100.0**	**30.8**
博乐市	Bole [Bortala] City	100.0	23.1
精河县	Jinghe [Jing] County	100.0	48.1
温泉县	Wenquan [Araxang] County	100.0	43.9
巴音郭楞蒙古自治州	**Bayangol Mongol ian Autonomous Prefecture**	**100.0**	**17.1**
库尔勒市	Korla City	100.0	6.0
轮台县	Luntai [Bugur] County	100.0	34.9
尉犁县	Yuli [Lopnur] County	100.0	53.8
若羌县	Ruoqiang [Qarkilik] County	100.0	26.5
且末县	Qiemo [Qarqan] County	100.0	44.3
焉耆回族自治县	Yanqi Hui Autonomous County	100.0	26.8
和静县	Hejing County	100.0	27.7
和硕县	Hoxud County	100.0	62.0
博湖县	Bohu [Bagrax] County	100.0	44.1
阿克苏地区	**Aksu Administrative Offices**	**100.0**	**31.3**
阿克苏市	Aksu City	100.0	19.1
温宿县	Wensu [Onsu] County	100.0	46.2
库车县	Kuqa County	100.0	13.6

Continued

(%)

第二产业 Secondary Industry	工 业 Industry	建筑业 Construction	第三产业 Tertiary Industry	#交通运输、仓储和邮政业 Transport,storage And Post	#批发和零售业 Wholesale, and Retail Trades
36.8	**27.1**	**9.7**	**28.0**	**2.8**	**7.3**
27.3	14.5	12.8	50.4	6.2	15.3
52.8	43.8	9.0	17.5	2.2	4.6
30.9	21.5	9.4	35.6	3.5	7.2
21.6	14.4	7.2	25.7	2.8	6.6
68.1	54.4	13.7	18.9	2.9	2.4
23.9	6.1	17.8	37.7	1.6	3.1
60.0	30.1	29.9	21.9	2.2	2.7
47.0	**35.9**	**11.1**	**33.1**	**4.3**	**3.2**
20.0	9.7	10.3	64.3	6.0	7.9
36.0	21.7	14.2	44.1	3.6	4.4
70.9	60.1	10.8	15.8	4.3	1.4
31.9	23.2	8.7	29.4	3.8	3.3
69.2	60.0	9.2	15.4	2.9	1.2
29.1	10.5	18.6	44.6	3.3	3.9
36.2	15.0	21.2	40.0	2.8	2.8
23.1	**14.9**	**8.2**	**46.1**	**7.2**	**13.7**
23.7	16.2	7.5	53.2	7.8	19.3
22.9	13.5	9.3	29.0	5.9	3.7
19.7	9.0	10.7	36.4	2.4	2.1
64.3	**57.0**	**7.4**	**18.6**	**2.5**	**2.3**
79.3	70.9	8.4	14.7	1.8	2.4
30.9	27.6	3.3	34.2	6.7	3.2
23.1	15.9	7.2	23.1	2.6	3.2
66.5	64.5	2.0	7.0	0.9	0.3
18.7	10.4	8.3	37.0	2.1	0.2
29.0	19.4	9.6	44.2	7.9	3.9
44.6	39.8	4.8	27.7	9.6	1.1
14.5	9.5	5.0	23.5	3.4	2.4
18.7	10.5	8.2	37.2	3.3	4.2
32.8	**24.0**	**8.8**	**35.9**	**3.9**	**4.6**
30.1	22.0	8.1	50.8	5.8	8.7
24.7	12.1	12.6	29.1	1.4	3.4
59.8	47.5	12.3	26.6	6.3	3.0

2-11 续表 2

单位：%

地　　区	Region	地区生产总值 Gross Regional Product	第一产业 Primary Industry
沙雅县	Xayar County	100.0	32.0
新和县	Xinhe [Toksu] County	100.0	39.4
拜城县	Baicheng [Bay] County	100.0	19.6
乌什县	Wushi [Uxturpan] County	100.0	38.7
阿瓦提县	Awat County	100.0	50.4
柯坪县	Kalpin County	100.0	24.1
克孜勒苏柯尔克孜自治州	**Kizilsu Kirgiz Autonomous Prefecture**	**100.0**	**17.1**
阿图什市	Artux City	100.0	15.9
阿克陶县	Akto County	100.0	26.5
阿合奇县	Akqi County	100.0	13.8
乌恰县	Wuqia [Ulugqat] County	100.0	8.2
喀什地区	**Kashgar [Kaxgar] Administrative Offices**	**100.0**	**33.9**
喀什市	Kashgar [Kaxgar] City	100.0	3.9
疏附县	Shufu County	100.0	56.6
疏勒县	Shule County	100.0	33.2
英吉沙县	Yengisar County	100.0	43.4
泽普县	Zepu [Poskam] County	100.0	33.4
莎车县	Shache [Yarkant] County	100.0	53.3
叶城县	Yecheng [Kagilik] County	100.0	52.9
麦盖提县	Makit County	100.0	54.4
岳普湖县	Yopurga County	100.0	33.7
伽师县	Jiashi [Payzawat] County	100.0	43.5
巴楚县	Bachu [Maralbexi] County	100.0	37.7
塔什库尔干县	Taxkorgan Tajik Autonomous County	100.0	14.7
和田地区	**Hotan Administrative Offices**	**100.0**	**31.0**
和田市	Hotan City	100.0	8.5
和田县	Hotan County	100.0	39.4
墨玉县	Moyu [Karakax] County	100.0	46.0
皮山县	Pishan [Guma] County	100.0	47.4
洛浦县	Lop County	100.0	31.4
策勒县	Qira County	100.0	37.7
于田县	Yutian [Keriya] County	100.0	34.4
民丰县	Minfeng [Niya] County	100.0	19.9

Continued

(%)

第二产业 Secondary Industry	工业 Industry	建筑业 Construction	第三产业 Tertiary Industry	#交通运输、仓储和邮政业 Transport,storage And Post	#批发和零售业 Wholesale, and Retail Trades
23.4	16.2	7.2	44.6	2.6	7.1
21.0	15.4	5.6	39.6	5.0	4.3
49.6	42.6	7.0	30.8	4.1	2.2
13.2	7.2	6.0	48.1	1.5	1.2
14.4	7.4	7.1	35.2	1.5	3.1
19.7	9.1	10.6	56.2	3.8	0.1
28.6	**16.6**	**12.0**	**54.3**	**4.2**	**2.7**
23.5	15.2	8.2	60.6	6.6	2.6
34.1	19.5	14.6	39.4	1.2	1.0
27.0	16.7	10.3	59.2	2.7	2.2
39.5	20.1	19.4	52.3	3.2	3.1
27.7	**15.7**	**12.0**	**38.4**	**3.1**	**11.3**
34.4	24.7	9.6	61.7	6.8	24.1
14.4	3.8	10.6	29.0	1.3	2.0
49.0	26.6	22.4	17.8	0.7	1.5
25.5	5.9	19.5	31.1	1.4	3.8
23.5	13.9	9.5	43.1	2.2	15.3
14.6	7.2	7.4	32.1	1.1	3.1
19.9	10.9	9.0	27.2	1.8	3.8
18.0	8.0	10.0	27.6	1.4	6.7
34.1	11.8	22.3	32.2	2.5	3.5
31.5	21.0	10.5	25.0	4.2	5.6
18.1	7.3	10.8	44.2	2.0	23.8
52.9	24.8	28.0	32.4	1.2	2.5
19.7	**7.8**	**11.9**	**49.3**	**2.1**	**2.2**
33.5	17.8	15.7	58.0	4.8	3.6
22.0	10.2	11.8	38.6	0.6	0.4
8.6	2.1	6.5	45.4	1.7	3.5
14.9	2.8	12.2	37.7	0.7	1.1
17.0	4.0	12.9	51.6	1.2	1.8
12.9	1.6	11.3	49.4	1.1	1.4
12.1	2.3	9.8	53.5	1.9	2.0
21.6	7.2	14.3	58.5	3.6	1.3

2-12 各地、州、市、县(市)地区生产总值指数

(上年=100) (2012 年)

地　　区	Region	地区生产总值 Gross Regional Product	第一产业 Primary Industry
乌鲁木齐市	**Urumqi City**	**117.3**	**105.4**
#乌鲁木齐县	Urumqi County	113.8	111.0
克拉玛依市	**Karamay City**	**106.0**	**105.4**
石河子市	**Shihezi City**	**122.0**	**110.5**
吐鲁番地区	**Turpan Administrative Offices**	**108.8**	**113.1**
吐鲁番市	Turpan City	106.5	115.1
鄯善县	Shanshan [Piqan] County	107.8	114.8
托克逊县	Toksun County	118.4	107.4
哈密地区	**Hami [Kumul] Administrative Offices**	**122.2**	**108.1**
哈密市	Hami [Kumul] City	121.6	109.4
巴里坤哈萨克自治县	Barkol Kazak Autonomous County	118.0	106.4
伊吾县	Yiwu [Araturuk] County	144.8	105.6
昌吉回族自治州	**Changji Hui Autonomous Prefecture**	**114.6**	**106.9**
昌吉市	Changji City	116.5	107.0
阜康市	Fukang City	112.6	106.3
呼图壁县	Hutubi County	116.7	107.1
玛纳斯县	Manas County	112.5	107.9
奇台县	Qitai County	118.8	105.8
吉木萨尔县	Jimsar County	123.2	106.2
木垒哈萨克自治县	Mori Kazak Autonomous County	114.0	106.7
伊犁哈萨克自治州	**Ili Kazak Autonomous Prefecture**	**114.8**	**107.4**
伊犁州直属县(市)	**Counties (Cities) Direct Under Ili Prefecture**	**115.5**	**106.4**
伊宁市	Yining [Gulja] City	113.1	101.3
奎屯市	Kuytun City	117.2	105.7
伊宁县	Yining [Gulja] County	113.3	106.7
察布查尔锡伯自治县	Qapqal Xibe Autonomous County	122.7	108.3
霍城县	Huocheng [Korgas] County	118.8	112.1
巩留县	Gongliu [Tokkuztara] County	117.2	108.6
新源县	Xinyuan [Kunes] County	118.2	103.6
昭苏县	Zhaosu [Mongolkure] County	104.8	99.6
特克斯县	Tekes County	108.1	106.0
尼勒克县	Nilka County	112.3	106.4

Indices of Gross Domestic Product by Prefecture, Autonomous Prefecture, City and County

(preceding year=100)

第二产业 Secondary Industry	工业 Industry	建筑业 Construction	第三产业 Tertiary Industry	#交通运输、仓储和邮政业 Transport,storage And Post	#批发和零售业 Wholesale, and Retail Trades
116.4	**116.6**	**115.0**	**118.3**	**131.5**	**107.9**
113.8	114.5	105.7	116.4	110.0	118.0
105.4	**105.0**	**119.0**	**111.7**	**107.7**	**97.6**
127.4	**119.9**	**161.4**	**116.4**	**109.9**	**102.1**
108.3	**108.2**	**108.6**	**108.0**	**108.9**	**107.9**
98.0	96.6	106.5	110.9	107.7	109.8
107.3	107.4	106.5	106.5	108.2	100.6
124.3	127.5	108.2	109.3	110.1	113.5
132.5	**135.5**	**126.1**	**113.9**	**112.3**	**124.9**
131.5	135.6	123.0	113.1	112.7	118.5
124.4	119.7	142.0	117.8	111.9	149.2
175.3	200.2	139.6	120.6	135.7	225.5
119.4	**119.3**	**119.8**	**114.2**	**114.4**	**112.1**
123.4	125.7	112.1	111.4	112.6	121.4
113.1	112.4	119.8	115.7	110.9	109.8
132.2	142.1	120.9	113.5	113.7	107.6
117.2	115.1	129.8	113.8	108.6	108.2
139.0	142.7	125.8	117.6	118.5	110.1
143.6	148.6	116.5	113.9	119.6	111.5
138.5	151.0	113.0	112.1	112.6	111.9
120.8	**121.0**	**120.0**	**114.0**	**112.1**	**112.3**
122.2	**121.6**	**124.3**	**114.2**	**113.7**	**114.3**
116.6	110.3	126.7	112.4	108.9	111.3
119.1	117.1	129.6	115.8	116.1	113.2
119.1	121.3	106.7	114.8	109.5	104.5
154.9	170.9	114.8	117.4	117.4	158.9
141.7	144.2	131.2	113.1	114.7	106.3
129.5	131.7	124.9	114.4	127.8	131.1
127.9	128.3	126.1	114.2	108.8	119.7
99.1	93.7	117.8	115.5	113.7	138.6
102.5	97.5	115.0	113.2	113.8	112.6
114.7	113.6	118.8	113.5	107.2	111.3

2-12 续表 1

(上年=100)

地　区	Region	地区生产总值 Gross Regional Product	第一产业 Primary Industry
塔城地区	**Tacheng [Tarbagatai] Administrative Offices**	**115.0**	**108.4**
塔城市	Tacheng [Qoqek] City	112.5	106.0
乌苏市	Usu City	122.9	107.7
额敏县	Emin [Dorbiljin] County	110.2	102.0
沙湾县	Shawan County	111.6	108.9
托里县	Toli County	116.2	106.5
裕民县	Yumin [Qagantokay] County	110.7	104.4
和布克赛尔蒙古自治县	Hoboksar Mongol Autonomous County	117.8	108.4
阿勒泰地区	**Altay Administrative Offices**	**112.1**	**106.4**
阿勒泰市	Altay City	112.0	103.5
布尔津县	Burqin County	109.6	105.5
富蕴县	Fuyun [Koktokay] County	116.9	104.2
福海县	Fuhai [Burultokay] County	117.7	113.1
哈巴河县	Habahe [Kaba] County	115.1	106.8
青河县	Qinghe [Qinggil] County	80.3	106.4
吉木乃县	Jeminay County	107.3	77.5
博尔塔拉蒙古自治州	**Bortala Mongolian Autonomous Prefecture**	**119.4**	**107.3**
博乐市	Bole [Bortala] City	122.8	105.7
精河县	Jinghe [Jing] County	115.6	109.3
温泉县	Wenquan [Araxang] County	116.0	107.4
巴音郭楞蒙古自治州	**Bayangol Mongol ian Autonomous Prefecture**	**110.2**	**111.5**
库尔勒市	Korla City	108.3	119.7
轮台县	Luntai [Bugur] County	116.0	108.9
尉犁县	Yuli [Lopnur] County	115.3	107.0
若羌县	Ruoqiang [Qarkilik] County	117.5	130.5
且末县	Qiemo [Qarqan] County	118.2	114.3
焉耆回族自治县	Yanqi Hui Autonomous County	111.2	108.1
和静县	Hejing County	118.0	105.2
和硕县	Hoxud County	110.2	104.1
博湖县	Bohu [Bagrax] County	115.5	107.9
阿克苏地区	**Aksu Administrative Offices**	**114.5**	**109.5**
阿克苏市	Aksu City	112.7	108.4
温宿县	Wensu [Onsu] County	117.0	110.4
库车县	Kuqa County	115.3	107.5

Continued

(preceding year=100)

第二产业 Secondary Industry	工　业 Industry	建筑业 Construction	第三产业 Tertiary Industry	#交通运输、仓储和邮政业 Transport,storage And Post	#批发和零售业 Wholesale, and Retail Trades
122.8	**125.3**	**115.3**	**113.2**	**108.4**	**110.8**
113.0	108.6	118.7	115.4	112.6	114.7
138.5	148.6	110.4	114.0	112.8	110.5
115.0	109.7	129.8	113.9	110.0	109.4
112.1	111.8	113.0	117.0	103.5	113.6
118.3	115.8	130.1	114.5	115.0	110.6
113.7	118.4	112.3	116.1	118.1	108.5
123.2	95.0	169.6	112.1	100.0	106.7
112.8	**110.7**	**119.7**	**114.8**	**113.8**	**111.6**
119.4	112.1	132.4	111.7	109.5	104.6
105.4	113.5	97.6	114.6	110.0	113.5
120.7	116.9	144.9	113.1	108.3	101.8
130.8	154.7	91.7	111.5	124.8	102.7
117.9	117.8	118.6	112.9	107.7	115.6
45.7	17.4	120.7	109.7	147.9	98.3
136.7	142.1	134.1	113.6	138.6	109.8
134.8	**135.2**	**134.0**	**122.4**	**109.2**	**152.0**
130.6	130.7	130.2	128.6	111.4	155.7
144.4	146.2	141.6	110.8	107.7	109.2
135.4	137.1	134.0	117.0	128.5	125.8
108.9	**109.1**	**107.8**	**113.2**	**108.0**	**116.7**
106.9	107.0	106.4	110.4	109.0	116.9
115.2	117.0	99.3	125.7	123.5	118.7
140.3	145.8	127.5	115.5	115.0	116.6
113.8	113.2	133.2	119.9	118.2	131.9
152.3	197.1	117.6	110.4	102.7	123.5
106.4	104.3	111.4	117.5	118.2	118.1
125.4	124.9	129.6	119.0	117.3	132.2
113.8	115.6	110.4	122.0	123.2	117.6
116.4	113.9	119.6	125.5	115.6	122.1
117.0	**116.8**	**117.8**	**116.6**	**112.7**	**115.3**
111.5	110.7	114.1	115.3	113.8	118.7
131.2	142.6	120.0	116.9	123.9	119.6
116.9	116.1	119.6	116.4	110.9	109.3

2-12 续表 2

(上年=100)

地　　区	Region	地区生产总值 Gross Regional Product	第一产业 Primary Industry
沙雅县	Xayar County	117.2	109.1
新和县	Xinhe [Toksu] County	116.8	108.8
拜城县	Baicheng [Bay] County	115.5	107.0
乌什县	Wushi [Uxturpan] County	113.9	107.9
阿瓦提县	Awat County	113.4	111.5
柯坪县	Kalpin County	120.3	112.8
克孜勒苏柯尔克孜自治州	**Kizilsu Kirgiz Autonomous Prefecture**	**118.5**	**109.0**
阿图什市	Artux City	115.0	106.0
阿克陶县	Akto County	119.5	108.0
阿合奇县	Akqi County	132.1	105.8
乌恰县	Wuqia [Ulugqat] County	122.9	109.3
喀什地区	**Kashgar [Kaxgar] Administrative Offices**	**115.7**	**105.8**
喀什市	Kashgar [Kaxgar] City	118.3	108.4
疏附县	Shufu County	114.1	105.6
疏勒县	Shule County	114.5	106.0
英吉沙县	Yengisar County	115.0	103.2
泽普县	Zepu [Poskam] County	119.5	107.0
莎车县	Shache [Yarkant] County	112.1	105.5
叶城县	Yecheng [Kagilik] County	114.5	105.0
麦盖提县	Makit County	112.2	106.3
岳普湖县	Yopurga County	117.8	104.1
伽师县	Jiashi [Payzawat] County	119.6	104.9
巴楚县	Bachu [Maralbexi] County	109.3	108.3
塔什库尔干县	Taxkorgan Tajik Autonomous County	129.9	112.5
和田地区	**Hotan Administrative Offices**	**112.4**	**104.8**
和田市	Hotan City	116.8	110.9
和田县	Hotan County	112.6	110.7
墨玉县	Moyu [Karakax] County	112.6	106.6
皮山县	Pishan [Guma] County	113.0	118.3
洛浦县	Lop County	112.3	114.4
策勒县	Qira County	112.6	107.8
于田县	Yutian [Keriya] County	111.9	110.2
民丰县	Minfeng [Niya] County	112.2	106.1

Continued

(preceding year=100)

第二产业 Secondary Industry	工业 Industry	建筑业 Construction	第三产业 Tertiary Industry	#交通运输、仓储和邮政业 Transport,storage And Post	#批发和零售业 Wholesale, and Retail Trades
132.1	141.8	116.2	117.5	113.1	110.7
137.4	144.2	120.5	116.4	108.7	106.7
117.3	117.2	118.1	118.5	112.3	162.9
115.0	104.0	125.9	119.0	117.1	108.1
114.9	109.9	119.3	115.7	115.3	115.5
146.8	177.0	117.1	112.8	113.0	99.8
131.1	**135.3**	**127.0**	**116.6**	**111.2**	**112.1**
123.2	123.4	123.0	115.1	109.1	90.0
133.2	135.4	131.5	119.4	109.8	116.7
205.2	3034.1	78.8	119.3	112.5	110.9
128.3	116.1	142.9	121.6	113.2	137.4
128.2	**130.3**	**125.6**	**117.5**	**120.5**	**116.0**
118.7	118.5	119.1	118.7	121.1	117.4
143.2	151.0	140.5	119.9	122.7	127.7
125.2	139.2	116.7	117.0	115.0	116.9
142.7	136.8	144.5	117.2	129.3	124.2
144.5	148.6	139.3	119.0	121.4	121.0
127.9	130.5	125.7	117.4	122.3	117.6
142.9	153.6	132.1	115.2	111.6	111.8
119.2	117.8	120.4	117.1	119.3	108.4
125.5	155.2	114.9	123.4	151.2	107.5
143.9	146.5	139.4	124.1	119.3	132.0
121.2	118.8	122.7	106.5	107.1	106.3
148.1	205.7	121.9	116.1	116.2	114.7
121.5	**122.7**	**120.6**	**114.4**	**112.3**	**73.7**
117.1	142.2	102.4	117.5	122.2	81.5
109.6	131.8	95.4	116.3	110.1	103.6
96.4	88.6	99.6	121.9	121.6	59.7
83.7	47.0	112.3	115.0	112.9	109.8
105.5	116.4	102.2	113.3	120.2	105.2
83.9	188.1	76.5	126.5	126.3	105.0
109.6	96.4	111.1	113.6	111.5	110.8
121.2	161.9	101.3	112.4	98.7	128.3

2-13 三次产业贡献率

Share of the Contributions of Three Strata of Industry to the Increase of the GDP

单位：%　　(%)

年 份 Year	新疆生产总值构成 Composition of Gross Domestic Product	第一产业 Primary Industry	第二产业 Secondary Industry	工 业 Industry	建筑业 Construction	第三产业 Tertiary Industry
2001	100.0	12.9	44.0	34.3	9.7	43.1
2002	100.0	12.0	38.2	28.2	10.0	49.8
2003	100.0	13.8	42.7	29.5	13.2	43.5
2004	100.0	9.2	50.5	37.7	12.8	40.3
2005	100.0	11.1	52.9	45.1	7.8	36.0
2006	100.0	10.1	45.8	41.9	3.9	44.1
2007	100.0	10.9	46.2	43.2	2.9	42.9
2008	100.0	10.3	58.5	49.6	8.9	31.2
2009	100.0	9.5	48.6	30.2	18.5	41.8
2010	100.0	7.0	55.4	49.2	6.3	37.6
2011	100.0	10.8	47.8	37.9	9.9	41.4
2012	100.0	11.1	54.4	42.0	12.4	34.5

注：1.三次产业贡献率指各产业增加值增量与 GDP 增量之比。2.本表按不变价格计算。

Note:a) Share of the contributions of the three strata of industry to the increase of the GDP refers to the proportion of the increment of the value-added of each industry to the increment of GDP. b) Data in this table are calculated at constant prices.

2-14 三次产业对地区生产总值增长的拉动

Contribution of the Three Strata of Industry to GDP Growth

单位：百分点　　(percentage points)

年 份 Year	新疆生产总值构成 Composition of Gross Domestic Product	第一产业 Primary Industry	第二产业 Secondary Industry	工 业 Industry	建筑业 Construction	第三产业 Tertiary Industry
2001	8.6	1.1	3.8	2.9	0.8	3.7
2002	8.2	1.0	3.1	2.3	0.8	4.1
2003	11.2	1.5	4.8	3.3	1.5	4.9
2004	11.4	1.1	5.8	4.3	1.5	4.6
2005	10.9	1.2	5.8	4.9	0.9	3.9
2006	11.0	1.1	5.0	4.6	0.4	4.9
2007	12.2	1.3	5.7	5.3	0.4	5.2
2008	11.0	1.1	6.5	5.5	1.0	3.4
2009	8.1	0.8	3.9	2.4	1.5	3.4
2010	10.6	0.7	5.9	5.2	0.7	4.0
2011	12.0	1.3	5.7	4.5	1.2	5.0
2012	12.0	1.3	6.5	5.0	1.5	4.2

注：1.三次产业拉动指 GDP 增长速度与各产业贡献率之乘积。2.本表按不变价格计算。

Note: a) Contribution of the three strata of industry to GDP growth refers to the growth rate of GDP multiplied by the contribution share of every industry. b) Data in this table are calculated at constant prices.

2-15 主要年份居民消费水平及指数
Household Consumption Expenditure and Its Indices in Main Years

年份 Year	居民消费水平(元) Household Consumption (yuan)	农村居民 Rural Households	城镇居民 Urban Households	居民消费水平指数(1952年=100) Index of Residents' Consumption Level (1952=100)	农村居民 Rural Households
1978	181	131	323	140.5	144.5
1980	252	180	417	182.4	184.4
1990	796	447	1508	299.5	236.3
1995	1852	977	3414	344.1	246.5
1996	2266	1387	3836	377.1	312.6
1997	2455	1445	4261	384.6	313.9
1998	2539	1520	4364	396.1	339.3
1999	2606	1358	4841	413.1	319.3
2000	2662	1308	5131	415.2	299.2
2001	2905	1427	5743	434.3	307.6
2002	3228	1525	6483	484.7	325.4
2003	3249	1603	6427	488.6	338.1
2004	3445	1652	6808	502.3	339.8
2005	3814	1884	7221	556.0	385.7
2006	4151	2000	7728	596.2	400.6
2007	4831	2320	8833	661.4	432.7
2008	5521	2686	9882	700.1	452.7
2009	5945	3029	10366	753.6	503.9
2010	7400	3674	12665	894.8	587.6
2011	8895	4495	14663	991.5	644.6
2012	10675	5410	17442	1149.1	749.0

年份 Year	城镇居民 Urban Households	居民消费水平指数(上年=100) Index of Residents' Consumption Level (preceding year=100)	农村居民 Rural Households	城镇居民 Urban Households
1978	99.0	104.7	102.3	102.8
1980	119.3	111.9	107.6	113.1
1990	226.4	103.8	98.8	105.0
1995	257.4	109.0	102.3	112.3
1996	260.7	109.6	126.8	101.3
1997	268.5	102.0	100.4	103.0
1998	268.5	103.0	108.1	100.0
1999	297.8	104.3	94.1	110.9
2000	315.7	100.5	93.7	106.0
2001	338.7	104.6	102.8	107.3
2002	386.8	111.6	105.8	114.2
2003	386.8	100.8	103.9	100.0
2004	396.1	102.8	100.5	102.4
2005	421.1	110.7	113.5	106.3
2006	445.3	107.2	103.9	105.7
2007	489.7	110.9	108.0	110.0
2008	512.3	105.9	104.6	104.6
2009	540.7	107.6	111.3	105.5
2010	627.2	118.7	116.6	116.0
2011	676.7	110.8	109.7	107.9
2012	776.9	115.9	116.2	114.8

2-16 居民消费支出
Household Consumption Expenditure

单位：亿元 (100 million yuan)

项　目	Item	2011	2012
居民消费支出	**Household Consumption Expenditure**	**1954.33**	**2370.67**
食品类支出	Foods	629.50	745.30
衣着类支出	Clothes	209.52	251.08
居住类支出	Residence	113.97	142.63
家庭设备、用品及服务类支出	Family Facilities and Servises	101.71	119.70
医疗保健类支出	Medical and Hygiencic Expenditure	212.38	265.92
交通和通信类支出	Traffic and Telecommunications	197.82	243.08
文教娱乐用品及服务类支出	Teathing, Entertainment and Services	135.31	150.22
金融中介服务虚拟支出	Imaginary Expenditure of Middle Finance Services	116.7	199.63
自由住房服务虚拟支出	Imaginary Expenditure of Freeform Resident Services	135.42	170.88
实物消费支出	Reality Consumption	19.24	16.36
其他商品和服务类支出	Other Goods and Services	82.76	65.87
按城乡分	**By Residence**		
农村居民支出	Agricaltural Households Expenditure	560.30	675.64
食品类支出	Foods	198.11	236.17
衣着类支出	Clothes	46.38	53.69
居住类支出	Residence	41.32	58.99
家庭设备、用品及服务类支出	Family Facilities and Servises	26.47	27.36
医疗保健类支出	Medical and Hygiencic Expenditure	57.80	70.71
交通和通信类支出	Traffic and Telecommunications	66.84	81.73
文教娱乐用品及服务类支出	Teathing, Entertainment and Services	28.62	25.75
金融中介服务虚拟支出	Imaginary Expenditure of Middle Finance Services	34.34	53.69
自由住房服务虚拟支出	Imaginary Expenditure of Freeform Resident Services	48.39	53.79
其他商品和服务类支出	Other Goods and Services	12.03	13.76
城镇居民支出	Non-agricaltural Households Expenditure	1394.03	1695.03
食品类支出	Foods	431.39	509.13
衣着类支出	Clothes	163.14	197.39
居住类支出	Residence	72.65	83.64
家庭设备、用品及服务类支出	Family Facilities and Servises	75.24	92.34
医疗保健类支出	Medical and Hygiencic Expenditure	154.58	195.21
交通和通信类支出	Traffic and Telecommunications	130.98	161.35
文教娱乐用品及服务类支出	Teathing, Entertainment and Services	106.69	124.47
金融中介服务虚拟支出	Imaginary Expenditure of Middle Finance Services	82.36	145.94
自由住房服务虚拟支出	Imaginary Expenditure of Freeform Resident Services	87.03	117.09
实物消费支出	Reality Consumption	19.24	16.36
其他商品和服务类支出	Other Goods and Services	70.73	52.11

主要统计指标解释

国内生产总值(GDP) 指按市场价格计算的一个国家(或地区)所有常住单位在一定时期内生产活动的最终成果。国内生产总值有三种表现形态，即价值形态、收入形态和产品形态。从价值形态看，它是所有常住单位在一定时期内生产的全部货物和服务价值与同期投入的全部非固定资产货物和服务价值的差额，即所有常住单位的增加值之和；从收入形态看，它是所有常住单位在一定时期内创造并分配给常住单位和非常住单位的初次收入之和；从产品形态看，它是所有常住单位在一定时期内最终使用的货物和服务价值与货物和服务净出口价值之和。在实际核算中，国内生产总值有三种计算方法，即生产法、收入法和支出法。三种方法分别从不同的方面反映国内生产总值及其构成。

对于一个地区来说，称为地区生产总值或地区GDP.

三次产业 三产业的划分是世界上较为常用的产业结构分类，但各国的划分不尽一致。我国的三次产业划分是：

第一产业是指农、林、牧、渔业。

第二产业是指采矿业，制造业，电力、煤气及水的生产和供应业，建筑业。

第三产业是指除第一、二产业以外的其他行业。

劳动者报酬 指劳动者因从事生产活动所获得的全部报酬。包括劳动者获得的各种形式的工资、奖金和津贴，既包括货币形式的，也包括实物形式的，还包括劳动者所享受的公费医疗和医药卫生费、上下班交通补贴、单位支付的社会保险费、住房公积金等。

生产税净额 指生产税减生产补贴后的余额。生产税指政府对生产单位从事生产、销售和经营活动以及因从事生产活动使用某些生产要素(如固定资产、土地、劳动力)所征收的各种税、附加费和规费。生产补贴与生产税相反，指政府对生产单位的单方面转移支出，因此视为负生产税，包括政策亏损补贴、价格补贴等。

固定资产折旧 指一定时期内为弥补固定资产损耗按照规定的固定资产折旧率提取的固定资产折旧，或按国民经济核算统一规定的折旧率虚拟计算的固定资产折旧。它反映了固定资产在当期生产中的转移价值。各类企业和企业化管理的事业单位的固定资产折旧是指实际计提的折旧费；不计提折旧的政府机关、非企业化管理的事业单位和居民住房的固定资产折旧是按照统一规定的折旧率和固定资产原值计算的虚拟折旧。原则上，固定资产折旧应按固定资产的重置价值计算，但是目前我国尚不具备对全社会固定资产进行重估价的基础，所以暂时只能采用上述办法。

营业盈余 指常住单位创造的增加值扣除劳动者报酬、生产税净额和固定资产折旧后的余额。它相当于企业的营业利润加上生产补贴，但要扣除从利润中开支的工资和福利等。

支出法国内生产总值 是从最终使用的角度反映一个国家(或地区)一定时期内生产活动最终成果的一种方法，包括最终消费支出、资本形成总额及货物和服务净出口三部分。计算公式为：

支出法国内生产总值=最终消费支出+资本形成总额+货物和服务净出口

最终消费支出 指常住单位为满足物质、文化和精神生活的需要，从本国经济领土和国外购买的货物和服务的支出。它不包括非常住单位在本国经济领土内的消费支出。最终消费支出分为居民消费支出和政府消费支出。

居民消费支出 指常住住户在一定时期内对于货物和服务的全部最终消费支出。居民消费支出除了直接以货币形式购买的货物和服务的消费支出外，还包括以其他方式获得的货物和服务的消费支出，即所谓的虚拟消费支出。居民虚拟消费支出包括如下几种类型：单位以实物报酬及实物转移的形式提供给劳动者的货物和服务；住户生产并由本住户消费了的货物和服务，其中的服务仅指住户的自有住房服务和付酬的家庭雇员提供的家庭和个人服务；金融机构提供的金融媒介服务。

政府消费支出 指政府部门为全社会提供的公共服务的消费支出和免费或以较低的价格向居民住户提供的货物和服务的净支出，前者等于政府服务的产出价值减去政府单位所获得的经营收入的价值，后者等于政府部门免费或以较低价格向居民住户提供的货物和服务的市场价值减去向住户收取的价值。

资本形成总额 指常住单位在一定时期内获得减去处置的固定资产和存货的净额，包括固定资本形成总额和存货变动两部分。

固定资本形成总额 指常住单位在一定时期内获得的固定资产减处置的固定资产的价值总额。固定资产是通过生产活动生产出来的，且其使用年限在一年以上、单位价值在规定标准以上的资产，不包括自然资产。可分为有形固定资本形成总额和无形固定资本形成总额。有形固定资本形成总额包括一定时期内完成的建筑工程、安装工程和设备工器具购置(减处置)价值，以及土地改良、新增役、种、奶、毛、娱乐用牲畜和新增经济林木价值。无形固定资本形成总额包括矿藏的勘探、计算机软件等获得减处置。

存货变动 指常住单位在一定时期内存货实物量变动的市场价值，即期末价值减期初价值的差额，再扣除当期由于价格变动而产生的持有收益。存货增加可以是正值，也可以是负值，正值表示存货上升，负值表示存货下降。存货包括生产单位购进的原材料、燃料和储备物资等存货，以及生产单位生产的产成品、在制品和半成品等存货。

货物和服务净出口 指货物和服务出口减货物和服务进口的差额。出口包括常住单位向非常住单位出售或无偿转让的各种货物和服务的价值；进口包括常住单位从非常住单位购买或无偿得到的各种货物和服务的价值。由于服务活动的提供与使用同时发生，一般把常住单位从非常住单位得到的服务作为进口，非常住单位从常住单位得到的服务作为出口。货物的出口和进口都按离岸价格计算。

Explanatory Notes on Main Statistical Indicators

Gross Domestic Product (GDP) refers to the final products at market prices produced by all resident units in a country (or a region) during a certain period of time. Gross domestic product is expressed in three different forms, i.e. value, income, and products respectively. GDP in its value form refers to the total value of all goods and services produced by all resident units during a certain period of time, minus the total value of input of goods and services of the nature of non-fixed assets; in other term, it is the sum of the value-added of all resident units. GDP in the form of income includes the income created by all resident units and distributed to resident and non-resident units. GDP in the form of products refers to the value of all goods and services for final consumption by all resident units minus the net exports of goods and services during a given period of time. In the practice of national accounting, gross domestic product is calculated with three approaches, i.e. production approach, income approach and expenditure approach, which reflect gross domestic product and its composition from different aspects.

Three Industries Classification of economic activities into three branches of industries is a common practice in the world, although the grouping varies to some extent form country to country. In China economic activities are categorized into following industries:

Primary industry: refers to agriculture, forestry, animal husbandry and fishery.

Secondary industry: refers to mining and quarrying, manufacturing, production and supply of electricity, water and gas, and construction.

Tertiary industry: refers to all other economic activities not included in primary or secondary industry.

Labourers Remuneration refers to the whole payment of various forms earned by the labourers from the productive activities they are engaged in. It includes wages, bonuses and allowances the labourers earned in monetary form and in kind. It also includes the free medical services provided to the labourers and the medicine expenses, traffic subsidies and social insurance, housing fund paid by the employers. As the individual economy is concerned, since the labourers remuneration is not easily distinguished from the operating profit, both are treated as labourers remuneration.

Net Taxes on Production refers to the difference of the taxes on production minus the subsidies on production. The taxes on production refers to the various taxes, extra charges and fees levied on the production units on their production, sale and business activities as well as on the use of some factors of production, such as fixed assets, land and labour force in the production activities they are engaged in. In contrast to the taxes on production, the subsidies on production refer to the unilateral government transfer to the production units and are therefore regarded as negative taxes on production. They include subsidies on the loss due to implementation of government policies, price subsidies, etc.

Depreciation of Fixed Assets refers to the depreciation of fixed assets of a given period, drawn in accordance with the stipulated depreciation rate for the purpose of compensating the wear loss of the fixed assets or the depreciation of fixed assets calculated in a fictitious way in accordance with the stipulated unified depreciation rate in the national economic accounting system. It reflects the value of transfer of the fixed assets in the production of the current period. The depreciation of fixed assets in various enterprises and institutions managed as enterprises refers to the depreciation expenses actually drawn. In government agencies and institutions not managed as enterprises which do not draw the depreciation expenses, as well as for the houses of residents, the depreciation of fixed assets is the imputed depreciation, which is calculated in accordance with the stipulated unified depreciation rate. In principle, the depreciation of fixed assets should be calculated on the basis of the re-purchased value of the fixed assets. However, there is no actual condition to re-evaluate all the fixed assets in China. Therefore, the above-mentioned methods are temporarily adopted at present.

Operating Surplus refers to the balance of the value added created by the resident units deducting the labourers remuneration, net taxes on production and the depreciation of fixed assets. It is equivalent to the business profit of the enterprises plus subsidies on production, but the wages and welfare expenses paid from the profits should be deducted.

GDP by Expenditure Approach refers to the method of measuring the final results of production activities of a country (region) during a given period from the perspective of final use. It includes final consumption, total capital formation and net export of goods and services, i.e:

GDP by expenditure approach = final consumption + total capital formation + net export of goods and services

Final Consumption Expenditure refers to the total expenditure of resident units for purchases of goods and services from domestic economic territory and abroad to meet the require-ments of material, cultural and spiritual life. It excludes the expenditure of non-resident units on consumption in the econo- mic territory of the country. The final consumption is broken down into household consumption and government consum- ption.

Households Consumption Expenditure refers to the total expenditure of resident households on the final consumption of goods and services. In addition to the consumption of goods and services bought by the households directly with money, the households consumption also includes expenditure on goods and services obtained by the households in other ways, i.e. the so-called imputed consumption expenditure, which includes the following: (a) the goods and services provided to the households by the employer in the form of payment in kind and transfer in kind; (b) goods and services produced and consumed by the households themselves, in which the services refer only to the owner- occupied housing and domestic and individual services provided by the paid household workers; (c) financial intermediate services provided by financial institutions; (d) insurance services provided by insurance companies.

Government Consumption Expenditure refers to the expenditure on the consumption of the public services provided by the government to the whole society and the net expenditure on the goods and services provided by the government to the households free of charge or at low prices. The former equals to the output value of the government services minus the value of operating income obtained by the government departments. The latter equals to the market value of the goods and services provided by the government free of charge or at low prices to the households minus the value received by the government from the households.

Total Capital Formation refers to the fixed assets acquired minus those disposed of and the net value of inventory, including the total fixed capital formation and the increase in inventory.

Total Fixed Capital Formation refers to the value of fixed assets acquired minus those disposed of during a given period. Fixed assets are the assets produced through production activities with specified unit value which could be used for over one year, excluding natural assets. Total fixed capital formation can be categorized into total tangible capital formation and total intangible capital formation. The total tangible capital formation include the value of the construction projects, installation projects completed and the equipment, apparatus and instruments purchased as well as the value of land improved, the value of draught animals, breeding stock, animals

for milk, wool and for recreational purpose, and the newly increased forest with economic value during a given period. The total intangible capital formation includes the prospecting of minerals, the acquisition of computer software minus the disposal of them.

Increase in Inventory refers to the market value of the change in inventory of resident units during a given period, i.e. the difference of value between the beginning and the end of the period minus the current gains due to the change in prices. The increase in inventory can be positive or negative. A positive value indicates the increase in inventory while a negative value indicates the decrease in stock. The inventory includes the raw materials, fuels and reserve materials purchased by the production units as well as the inventory of finished products, semi-finished products, work-in-progress, etc.

Net Export of Goods and Services refers to the difference of the exports of goods and services minus the imports of goods and services. The imports include the value of various goods and services sold or gratuitously transferred by the resident units to the non-resident units. The imports include the value of various goods and services purchased or gratuitous- sly acquired by the resident units from the non-resident units. Because the provision of services and the use of them happen simultaneously, the acquisition of services by the resident units from abroad is usually treated as import while the acquisition of services by non-resident units in this country is usually treated as export. The export and import of goods are Valued at free on board(f.o.b) prices.

3

人口与就业

POPULATION AND EMPLOYMENT

简要说明

本篇资料的主要内容及来源

本篇内容主要包括人口、计划生育、就业、工资等资料。人口资料包括全区、各地、州、市、县及兵团人口情况、人口普查的主要数据等。

分地区人口数据为户籍人口，由新疆维吾尔自治区公安厅提供；计划生育资料由新疆维吾尔自治区计划生育委员会提供；失业资料由新疆维吾尔自治区人力资源和社会保障厅提供；全区人口（常住人口）由新疆维吾尔自治区统计局人口与就业统计处根据2012年人口变动调查数据推算；就业和劳动报酬资料由新疆维吾尔自治区统计局人口与就业统计处提供。

Brief Introduction

Main Content and Source of Data

Data in this chapter show the basic condition of population, employment, wages of staff and workers, family planning. Data of population mainly include the condition of population by whole region, prefecture, autonomous prefecture, city, country and Xinjiang Production and Construction Group.

The data on household registered population are provided by Municipal Bureau of Public Security of Xinjiang Uygur Autonomous Region; Data on family planning come from Municipal Family Planning Commission. Data on unemployment are provided by Bureau of Labor and Social Security. Total region population are estimated by the Department of Population and Social Science Technology Statistics of the Xinjiang Bureau of Statistics in accordance with the annual national sample survey on population changes in 2012; The data of population census, employment and wages are provided by the Department of Population and Social Science and Technology Statistic of the Xinjiang Bureau of Statistics.

3-1 主要年份人口数及构成
Population and Its Composition in Main Years

单位：万人、%　　　　(10 000 persons,%)

年份 Year	年末总人口 Total Population (Year-end)	按性别分 By Sex 男 Male 人口数 Population	比重 Proportion	女 Female 人口数 Population	比重 Proportion	按城乡分 By Residence 城镇人口 Urban 人口数 Population	比重 Proportion	乡村人口 Rural 人口数 Population	比重 Proportion
1978	1233.01	630.18	51.11	602.83	48.89	321.40	26.07	911.61	73.93
1980	1283.24	654.90	51.03	628.34	48.97	372.74	29.05	910.50	70.95
1985	1361.14	696.81	51.19	664.33	48.81	582.24	42.78	778.90	57.22
1990	1529.16	785.06	51.34	744.10	48.66	685.96	44.86	843.20	55.14
1995	1661.35	848.12	51.05	813.23	48.95	822.53	49.51	838.82	50.49
1996	1689.29	869.59	51.48	819.70	48.52	846.17	50.09	843.12	49.91
1997	1718.08	883.03	51.40	835.05	48.60	860.76	50.10	857.32	49.90
1998	1747.35	897.90	51.39	849.45	48.61	875.42	50.10	871.93	49.90
1999	1775.00	910.98	51.32	864.02	48.68	929.00	52.34	846.00	47.66
2000	1849.41	957.07	51.75	892.34	48.25	624.18	33.75	1225.23	66.25
2001	1876.19	954.23	50.86	921.96	49.14	633.21	33.75	1242.98	66.25
2002	1905.19	975.46	51.20	929.73	48.80	644.72	33.84	1260.47	66.16
2003	1933.95	994.24	51.41	939.71	48.59	665.11	34.39	1268.84	65.61
2004	1963.11	1008.02	51.30	955.09	48.70	690.11	35.15	1273.00	64.85
2005	2010.35	1029.70	51.22	980.65	48.78	746.85	37.15	1263.50	62.85
2006	2050.00	1050.01	51.22	999.99	48.78	777.77	37.94	1272.23	62.06
2007	2095.19	1072.53	51.19	1022.66	48.81	820.27	39.15	1274.92	60.85
2008	2130.81	1083.94	50.87	1046.87	49.13	844.65	39.64	1286.16	60.36
2009	2158.63	1098.31	50.88	1060.32	49.12	860.21	39.85	1298.42	60.15
2010	2181.58	1127.01	51.66	1054.57	48.34	933.58	42.79	1248.01	57.21
2011	2208.71	1128.75	51.10	1079.96	48.90	961.67	43.54	1247.04	56.46
2012	2232.78	1145.21	51.29	1087.57	48.71	981.98	44.00	1250.80	56.00

3-2 主要年份人口出生率、死亡率、自然增长率
Birth Rate,Death Rate and Natural Growth Rate of Population in Main Years

单位：‰　　　　(‰)

年份 Year	出生率 Birth Rate	死亡率 Death Rate	自然增长率 Natural Growth Rate	年份 Year	出生率 Birth Rate	死亡率 Death Rate	自然增长率 Natural Growth Rate
1978	22.55	7.69	14.86	1998	19.74	6.93	12.81
1980	21.28	7.62	13.66	1999	18.76	6.96	11.80
1985	19.80	6.39	13.41	2000	17.57	5.40	12.17
1986	20.54	6.13	14.41	2001	16.82	5.69	11.13
1987	21.03	5.96	15.07	2002	16.30	5.43	10.87
1988	19.72	5.99	13.73	2003	16.01	5.23	10.78
1989	21.15	5.77	15.38	2004	16.00	5.09	10.91
1990	26.41	7.81	18.60	2005	16.42	5.04	11.38
1991	24.45	7.86	16.59	2006	15.97	5.03	10.94
1992	22.80	7.84	14.96	2007	16.79	5.01	11.78
1993	21.53	7.68	13.85	2008	16.05	4.88	11.17
1994	20.82	7.43	13.39	2009	15.99	5.43	10.56
1995	18.90	6.45	12.45	2010	14.85	4.14	10.71
1996	19.45	6.60	12.85	2011	14.99	4.42	10.57
1997	19.66	6.55	13.11	2012	15.32	4.48	10.84

3-3 新疆人口普查基本情况

Basic Statistics on National Population Census in Xinjiang

单位：万人 (10 000 persons)

指 标	Items	第二次普查(1964 年) 1964 Census	第三次普查(1982 年) 1982 Census	第四次普查(1990 年) 1990 Census	第五次普查(2000 年) 2000 Census	第六次普查(2010 年) 2010 Census
总人口	**Total Population**	**727.01**	**1308.15**	**1515.69**	**1845.95**	**2181.58**
男	Male	389.47	673.22	782.32	955.22	1127.01
女	Female	337.54	634.93	733.37	890.73	1054.57
总户数(万户)	**Total Household (10 000 household)**	**178.00**	**293.79**	**337.41**	**491.66**	**690.29**
家 庭 户	Family Households		292.70	334.89	479.38	670.56
集 体 户	Collective Households		1.09	2.52	12.28	19.73
各年龄组人口	Population by Age Group					
0-5 岁	Age 0-5	121.86	186.70	218.85	165.12	185.03
6-14 岁	Age 6-14	146.77	330.85	282.12	338.18	261.15
15-64 岁	Age 15-64	428.73	742.42	955.49	1256.40	1593.99
65 岁及以上	Aged 65 and Over	29.65	48.18	59.23	86.25	141.41
民族人口	**Nationality Population**					
汉 族	Han Nationality	232.12	528.40	569.54	748.99	882.99
少数民族	Minority Nationalities	494.89	779.75	946.15	1096.96	1298.59
各种文化程度人口	**Population by Educational Level**					
大专及以上	College and Above	4.10	8.37	27.98	94.65	231.53
高中和中专	Senior Secondary School and Specialized Secondary School	15.51	84.28	157.42	224.79	254.56
初 中	Junior Secondary School	50.37	228.63	313.51	508.59	790.62
小 学	Primary School	197.34	442.57	552.55	699.78	656.32
不识字或识字很少	Illiterate and Semi-iliterate	249.03	265.39	198.11	103.68	63.52

注：不识字或识字很少除 1964 年包含 12-14 岁人口外，其他均为 15 岁及以上人口。
Note: Illiterate or semi-illiterate population refers to the population aged above 15 except for the population aged between 12 and 14 in 1964.

3-4 主要年份婚姻登记情况

Number of Marriages Registry in Main Years

单位：万人 (10 000 persons)

指 标	Item	2005	2010	2012
登记结婚(对)	**Registered Marriages (couple)**	**184714**	**264013**	**262864**
初婚(人)	First Marriage (person)	275752	389342	430539
再婚(人)	Remarriage (person)	93676	138684	95189
#男	Male	42576	73863	48202
#再婚中恢复结婚(对)	Resumed Marriages (couple)	6815	11108	9525
登记离婚(对)	**Registered Divorces (couple)**	**74342**	**97817**	**104321**
民政部门批准	Approved by the Civil Administration	47917	69137	73592
法院调判	Mediated by the court	26425	28680	30729
涉外及华侨港澳台居民婚姻	**Marital status of OverseasChinese ,Foreigner and Hong Kong, Macao and Taiwan Compatriots**			
登记结婚(对)	Registered Marriages (couple)	223	235	281
国内公民(人)	Citizen (person)	223	235	281
港澳台居民(人)	Compatriots of Hong Kong, Macao and Taiwan (person)	57	31	23
华 侨(人)	Overseas Chinese (person)	12	13	12
外国人(人)	Foreigner (person)	154	191	246
登记离婚(对)	Registered Divorces (couple)	6	26	36

3-5 各地、州、市、县(市)户数、人口数、土地面积

Household, Population, Land Area by Prefecture, Autonomous Prefecture,City and County

(2012 年)

地区	Region	户数(万户) Number of Households (10 000 households)	年末人口(万人) Population at Year-end (10 000 persons)	#男 Male	平均每户人口(人) Average Persons Per Household (person)	土地面积(平方公里) Land Area (sq.km)
总　计	**Total**	**675.17**	**2232.78**	**1145.21**	**3.31**	**1664897.17**
乌鲁木齐市	**Urumqi City**	**85.75**	**257.80**	**133.61**	**3.01**	**14875.50**
天山区	Tianshan District	18.54	57.63	29.00	3.11	47.31
沙依巴克区	Shayibak District	17.66	53.75	27.32	3.04	38.60
新市区	Xinshi District	18.33	55.62	29.49	3.03	57.07
水磨沟区	Shui Mogou Distric	9.83	30.14	16.11	3.07	10.76
头屯河区	Tou Tunhe District	8.16	23.02	12.28	2.82	20.11
达坂城区	Da Bancheng District	1.46	4.22	2.26	2.89	1111.85
米东区	Midong District	9.68	27.43	14.18	2.83	3789.22
乌鲁木齐县	Urumqi County	2.09	5.99	2.97	2.87	9800.58
克拉玛依市	**Karamay City**	**10.67**	**28.58**	**14.51**	**2.68**	**8654.08**
独山子区	Dushanzi District	2.13	5.63	2.90	2.64	379.11
克拉玛依区	Karamay District	6.97	18.63	9.38	2.67	4231.56
乌尔河区	Urhe District	0.08	0.23	0.12	2.88	1424.65
白碱滩区	Bai Jiantan District	1.49	4.09	2.11	2.74	2618.76
吐鲁番地区	**Turpan Administrative Offices**	**18.99**	**62.53**	**31.65**	**3.29**	**67562.91**
吐鲁番市	Turpan City	7.65	27.58	13.91	3.61	13589.22
鄯善县	Shanshan [Piqan] County	7.70	23.13	11.73	3.00	38281.46
托克逊县	Toksun County	3.64	11.82	6.01	3.25	15692.23
哈密地区	**Hami [Kumul] Administrative Offices**	**20.93**	**59.24**	**30.42**	**2.83**	**142094.88**
哈密市	Hami [Kumul] City	16.32	46.55	23.98	2.85	85587.23
巴里坤哈萨克自治县	Barkol Kazak Autonomous County	3.79	10.41	5.28	2.75	36988.55
伊吾县	Yiwu [Araturuk] County	0.82	2.28	1.16	2.78	19519.10

注：1.全区年末人口数依据 2012 年 1‰人口抽样调查数推算，各地、州、市、县、区人口数据为 2012 年公安年报数据。
2.全疆各地州市土地面积为国土资源厅 2008 年数据。

Note：a) The data of population by prefecture,antonomous prefecture,city and county come from the annual data of public security.
b) The land area of different prefectures and cities come from the Burean of State Land.

3-5 续表 1 Continued

地　区	Region	户 数 (万户) Number of Households (10 000 households)	年末人口 (万人) Population at Year-end (10 000 persons)	#男 Male	平均每户人口 (人) Average Persons Per Household (person)	土地面积 (平方公里) Land Area (sq.km)
昌吉回族自治州	**Changji Hui Autonomous Prefecture**	**47.83**	**140.21**	**71.28**	**2.93**	**73139.75**
昌吉市	Changji City	12.57	37.04	18.74	2.95	7505.12
阜康市	Fukang City	5.73	16.86	8.59	2.94	8534.97
呼图壁县	Hutubi County	7.78	21.73	11.05	2.79	9421.03
玛纳斯县	Manas County	6.33	17.49	8.81	2.76	9597.27
奇台县	Qitai County	7.62	24.05	12.25	3.16	16635.92
吉木萨尔县	Jimsar County	4.89	14.09	7.23	2.88	8144.58
木垒哈萨克自治县	Mori Kazak Autonomous County	2.91	8.95	4.61	3.08	13300.86
伊犁哈萨克自治州	**Ili Kazak Autonomous Prefecture**	**149.83**	**462.84**	**234.80**	**3.09**	**268778.72**
伊犁州直属县(市)	**Counties (Cities) Direct Under Ili Prefecture**	**93.07**	**291.72**	**148.19**	**3.13**	**56381.53**
伊宁市	Yining [Gulja] City	16.54	51.53	25.59	3.12	524.94
奎屯市	Kuytun City	10.98	30.44	15.40	2.77	1109.89
伊宁县	Yining [Gulja] County	11.52	42.73	21.90	3.71	4681.90
察布查尔锡伯自治县	Qapqal Xibe Autonomous County	6.44	19.43	9.88	3.02	4471.95
霍城县	Huocheng [Korgas] County	13.98	40.75	20.83	2.91	5429.83
巩留县	Gongliu [Tokkuztara] County	6.21	20.45	10.49	3.29	4326.90
新源县	Xinyuan [Kunes] County	9.98	31.60	16.16	3.17	6813.74
昭苏县	Zhaosu [Mongolkure] County	6.48	18.91	9.58	2.92	11127.91
特克斯县	Tekes County	5.56	17.19	8.82	3.09	7764.10
尼勒克县	Nilka County	5.38	18.69	9.54	3.47	10130.37
塔城地区	**Tacheng [Tarbagatai] Administrative Offices**	**35.64**	**104.78**	**53.09**	**2.94**	**94698.18**
塔城市	Tacheng [Qoqek] City	5.79	16.94	8.52	2.93	3991.25
乌苏市	Usu City	7.40	22.89	11.66	3.09	14299.86
额敏县	Emin [Dorbiljin] County	8.06	21.92	11.10	2.72	9448.37
沙湾县	Shawan County	7.34	21.64	10.96	2.95	12676.58
托里县	Toli County	2.99	10.02	5.02	3.35	28192.65
裕民县	Yumin [Qagantokay] County	2.10	5.95	3.01	2.83	6112.13
和布克赛尔蒙古自治县	Hoboksar Mongol Autonomous County	1.96	5.42	2.82	2.77	19977.34

3-5 续表 2 Continued

地　　区	Region	户数 (万户) Number of Households (10 000 households)	年末人口 (万人) Year-end Population (10 000 persons)	#男 Male	平均每户人口 (人) Average Persons Per Household (person)	土地面积 (平方公里) Land Area (sq.km)
阿勒泰地区	**Altay Administrative Offices**	**21.12**	**66.34**	**33.52**	**3.14**	**117699.01**
阿勒泰市	Altay City	7.55	23.28	11.78	3.08	10829.06
布尔津县	Burqin County	2.42	7.12	3.59	2.94	10357.35
富蕴县	Fuyun [Koktokay] County	2.75	9.52	4.79	3.46	32186.11
福海县	Fuhai [Burultokay] County	2.36	7.45	3.80	3.16	33250.74
哈巴河县	Habahe [Kaba] County	2.69	8.69	4.41	3.23	8166.58
青河县	Qinghe [Qinggil] County	1.86	6.34	3.19	3.41	15756.87
吉木乃县	Jemnay County	1.49	3.94	1.96	2.64	7152.30
博尔塔拉蒙古自治州	**Bortala Mongol Autonomous Prefecture**	**17.30**	**48.45**	**24.77**	**2.80**	**24934.33**
博乐市	Bole [Bortala] City	9.48	26.56	13.57	2.80	7877.34
精河县	Jinghe [Jing] County	4.94	14.43	7.39	2.92	11175.25
温泉县	Wenquan [Araxang] County	2.88	7.46	3.81	2.59	5881.74
巴音郭楞蒙古自治州	**Bayangol Mongol Autonomous Prefecture**	**43.27**	**137.47**	**70.29**	**3.18**	**470954.25**
库尔勒市	Korla City	17.47	55.15	27.96	3.16	7215.90
轮台县	Luntai [Bugur] County	3.31	11.63	5.89	3.51	14156.61
尉犁县	Yuli [Lopnur] County	3.82	11.06	5.70	2.90	59234.48
若羌县	Ruoqiang [Qarkilik] County	1.13	3.41	1.75	3.02	198793.52
且末县	Qiemo [Qarqan] County	1.85	6.34	3.21	3.43	137831.05
焉耆回族自治县	Yanji Hui Autonomous County	4.42	16.43	8.54	3.72	2440.73
和静县	Hejing County	6.76	19.77	10.26	2.92	34886.74
和硕县	Hoxud County	2.58	7.55	3.88	2.93	12816.49
博湖县	Bohu [Bagrax] County	1.93	6.13	3.10	3.18	3578.73
阿克苏地区	**Aksu Administrative Offices**	**62.85**	**239.69**	**121.59**	**3.81**	**127144.91**
阿克苏市	Aksu City	14.18	49.50	25.08	3.49	13987.61
温宿县	Wensu [Onsu] County	6.48	24.76	12.63	3.82	14202.46
库车县	Kuqa County	11.45	47.06	23.86	4.11	14602.95
沙雅县	Xayar County	6.88	26.40	13.16	3.84	31955.15
新和县	Xinhe [Toksu] County	4.81	17.31	8.71	3.60	5817.82
拜城县	Baicheng [Bay] County	6.92	23.19	11.85	3.35	15553.70
乌什县	Wushi [Uxturpan] County	5.41	21.76	11.15	4.02	9082.00
阿瓦提县	Awat County	5.51	24.58	12.52	4.46	13233.57
柯坪县	Kalpin County	1.21	5.13	2.63	4.24	8709.65

3-5 续表 3 Continued

地　　区	Region	户 数 (万户) Number of Households (10 000 households)	年末人口 (万人) Year-end Population (10 000 persons)	#男 Male	平均每户人口 (人) Average Persons Per Household (person)	土地面积 (平方公里) Land Area (sq.km)
克孜勒苏柯尔克孜自治州	**Kizilsu Kirgiz Autonomous Prefecture**	**14.29**	**56.06**	**28.58**	**3.92**	**72468.08**
阿图什市	Artux City	5.98	25.44	12.98	4.25	16151.17
阿克陶县	Akto County	5.26	20.49	10.48	3.90	24539.86
阿合奇县	Akqi County	1.16	4.26	2.14	3.67	12737.09
乌恰县	Wuqia [Ulugqat] County	1.89	5.87	2.98	3.11	19039.96
喀什地区	**Kashgar [Kaxgar] Administrative Offices**	**103.93**	**415.13**	**209.34**	**3.99**	**137578.51**
喀什市	Kashgar [Kaxgar] City	13.89	48.61	24.18	3.50	199.38
疏附县	Shufu County	8.17	33.85	17.32	4.14	3323.12
疏勒县	Shule County	8.41	34.48	17.46	4.10	2485.31
英吉沙县	Yengisar County	6.50	28.54	14.74	4.39	3223.87
泽普县	Zepu [Poskam] County	6.45	21.09	10.56	3.27	826.90
莎车县	Shache [Yarkant] County	17.91	79.48	39.87	4.44	9066.86
叶城县	Yecheng [Kagilik] County	11.44	47.44	23.87	4.15	29359.29
麦盖提县	Makit County	6.88	26.26	13.14	3.82	10276.57
岳普湖县	Yopurga County	4.35	16.33	8.32	3.75	2700.48
伽师县	Jiashi [Payzawat] County	9.76	40.82	20.70	4.18	6668.59
巴楚县	Bachu [Maralbexi] County	8.98	34.32	17.21	3.32	18903.70
塔什库尔干塔吉克自治县	Taxkorgan Tajik Autonomous County	1.19	3.91	1.97	3.29	50544.44
和田地区	**Hotan Administrative Offices**	**56.71**	**212.34**	**108.28**	**3.74**	**249146.59**
和田市	Hotan City	8.66	33.10	16.72	3.82	495.84
和田县	Hotan County	6.90	27.95	14.30	4.05	40876.80
墨玉县	Moyu [Karakax] County	13.87	53.86	27.59	3.88	25624.02
皮山县	Pishan [Guma] County	7.08	27.03	13.74	3.82	39819.75
洛浦县	Lop County	6.31	25.24	12.87	4.00	14286.97
策勒县	Qira County	4.99	15.63	7.96	3.13	31342.58
于田县	Yutian [Keriya] County	7.64	25.74	13.18	3.37	39126.14
民丰县	Minfeng [Niya] County	1.26	3.79	1.92	3.01	57574.49
自治区直辖县级市	**Municpality Country-LevelCity directly under the Central Govern-ment**	**42.82**	**105.69**	**54.42**	**2.47**	**7267.04**
石河子市	Shihezi City	26.80	62.00	31.64	2.31	459.94
阿拉尔市	Aral City	7.95	18.66	9.95	2.35	4196.00
图木舒克市	Tumxuk City	4.50	15.96	8.25	3.55	1901.10
五家渠市	Wujiaqu City	3.57	9.07	4.58	2.54	710.00

3-6 各地、州、市、县(市)人口自然变动情况

Statistics on Population Natural Changes by Prefecture, Autonomous Prefecture, City and County

单位：‰ (2012 年) (‰)

地　　区	Region	出生率 Birth Rate	#少数民族 Minority Nationalities	死亡率 Death Rate	#少数民族 Minority Nationalities	自然增长率 Natural Growth Rate	#少数民族 Minority Nationalities
乌鲁木齐市	**Urumqi City**	**9.87**	**15.30**	**3.87**	**4.66**	**6.00**	**10.64**
天山区	Tianshan District	8.97	13.79	3.63	3.94	5.34	9.85
沙依巴克区	Shayibak District	9.19	13.95	4.32	4.92	4.87	9.03
新市区	Xinshi District	10.53	13.72	3.42	3.93	7.11	9.79
水磨沟区	Shui Mogou Distric	8.82	20.67	3.42	6.66	5.40	14.01
头屯河区	Tou Tunhe District	8.48	13.42	4.44	6.66	4.04	6.76
达坂城区	Da Bancheng District	10.17	16.17	3.91	3.56	6.26	12.61
米东区	Midong District	12.17	17.78	4.36	5.10	7.81	12.68
乌鲁木齐县	Urumqi County	18.07	22.12	3.91	4.65	14.16	17.47
克拉玛依市	**Karamay City**	**10.24**	**16.65**	**5.47**	**6.39**	**4.77**	**10.26**
独山子区	Dushanzi District	14.59	18.91	8.49	9.25	6.10	9.66
克拉玛依区	Karamay District	8.94	14.64	4.51	5.37	4.43	9.27
乌尔河区	Urhe District	12.30	20.14	3.07	3.84	9.23	16.30
白碱滩区	Bai Jiantan District	10.06	21.22	5.78	6.84	4.28	14.38
吐鲁番地区	**Turpan Administrative Offices**	**24.79**	**29.14**	**12.72**	**14.17**	**12.07**	**14.97**
吐鲁番市	Turpan City	26.82	31.11	20.07	22.10	6.75	9.01
鄯善县	Shanshan [Piqan] County	25.20	31.43	2.61	7.63	22.59	23.80
托克逊县	Toksun County	19.07	20.78	7.59	7.58	11.48	13.20
哈密地区	**Hami [Kumul] Administrative Offices**	**10.35**	**19.02**	**5.05**	**6.58**	**5.30**	**12.44**
哈密市	Hami [Kumul] City	10.19	19.58	4.64	6.29	5.55	13.29
巴里坤哈萨克自治县	Barkol Kazak Autonomous County	10.78	18.74	4.84	4.18	5.94	14.56
伊吾县	Yiwu [Araturuk] County	11.78	14.69	14.37	15.51	-2.59	-0.82
昌吉回族自治州	**Changji Hui Autonomous Prefecture**	**11.49**	**19.90**	**6.05**	**7.12**	**5.44**	**12.78**
昌吉市	Changji City	11.03	17.40	5.04	6.52	5.99	10.88
阜康市	Fukang City	11.72	19.32	6.17	7.86	5.55	11.46
呼图壁县	Hutubi County	11.26	20.99	5.83	7.09	5.43	13.90
玛纳斯县	Manas County	9.99	18.03	4.89	5.39	5.10	12.64
奇台县	Qitai County	12.70	23.65	7.38	6.73	5.32	16.92
吉木萨尔县	Jimsar County	11.85	18.59	8.63	10.26	3.22	8.33
木垒哈萨克自治县	Mori Kazak Autonomous County	12.66	23.18	5.09	6.22	7.57	16.96

3-6 续表 1 Continued

单位：‰ (‰)

地　　区	Region	出生率 Birth Rate	#少数民族 Minority Nationalities	死亡率 Death Rate	#少数民族 Minority Nationalities	自然增长率 Natural Growth Rate	#少数民族 Minority Nationalities
伊犁哈萨克自治州	**Ili Kazak Autonomous Prefecture**	**18.51**	**26.06**	**6.56**	**6.94**	**11.95**	**19.12**
伊犁州直属县(市)	**Counties (Cities) Direct Under Ili Prefecture**	**21.22**	**29.13**	**6.11**	**6.45**	**15.11**	**22.68**
伊宁市	Yining [Gulja] City	22.96	30.57	5.45	5.81	17.51	24.76
奎屯市	Kuytun City	6.14	12.07	7.41	5.75	-1.27	6.32
伊宁县	Yining [Gulja] County	24.03	27.30	8.33	8.81	15.70	18.49
察布查尔锡伯自治县	Qapqal Xibe Autonomous County	19.56	24.59	6.80	8.06	12.76	16.53
霍城县	Huocheng [Korgas] County	21.01	30.64	6.47	7.16	14.54	23.48
巩留县	Gongliu [Tokkuztara] County	24.71	29.61	4.97	4.97	19.74	24.64
新源县	Xinyuan [Kunes] County	22.05	29.82	4.66	4.98	17.39	24.85
昭苏县	Zhaosu [Mongolkure] County	24.42	31.01	4.02	4.27	20.40	26.74
特克斯县	Tekes County	24.28	28.27	3.55	3.72	20.73	24.55
尼勒克县	Nilka County	25.87	31.58	7.34	7.73	18.53	23.85
塔城地区	**Tacheng [Tarbagatai] Administrative Offices**	**13.46**	**19.58**	**8.33**	**9.46**	**5.13**	**10.12**
塔城市	Tacheng [Qoqek] City	13.16	20.91	15.07	16.81	-1.91	4.10
乌苏市	Usu City	12.23	17.40	7.26	8.80	4.97	8.60
额敏县	Emin [Dorbiljin] County	13.51	19.35	5.77	6.87	7.74	12.48
沙湾县	Shawan County	11.05	18.78	6.12	5.95	4.93	12.83
托里县	Toli County	18.65	21.62	8.42	9.68	10.23	11.94
裕民县	Yumin [Qagantokay] County	15.65	22.74	10.32	13.40	5.33	9.34
和布克赛尔蒙古自治县	Hoboksar Mongol Autonomous County	17.11	18.13	8.44	9.20	8.67	8.93
阿勒泰地区	**Altay Administrative Offices**	**14.59**	**19.21**	**5.72**	**6.34**	**8.87**	**12.87**
阿勒泰市	Altay City	11.59	17.79	5.62	6.29	5.97	11.50
布尔津县	Burqin County	15.76	18.61	9.56	10.29	6.20	8.32
富蕴县	Fuyun [Koktokay] County	18.90	21.84	5.97	6.31	12.93	15.53
福海县	Fuhai [Burultokay] County	13.42	19.04	4.28	4.79	9.14	14.25
哈巴河县	Habahe [Kaba] County	15.69	19.27	4.68	5.17	11.01	14.10
青河县	Qinghe [Qinggil] County	18.37	20.47	4.78	5.12	13.59	15.35
吉木乃县	Jemnay County	13.56	15.64	5.38	6.13	8.18	9.51
博尔塔拉蒙古自治州	**Bortala Mongol Autonomous Prefecture**	**12.89**	**20.56**	**7.07**	**8.93**	**5.82**	**11.63**
博乐市	Bole [Bortala] City	17.99	30.43	7.00	8.73	10.99	21.70
精河县	Jinghe [Jing] County	10.40	16.86	6.18	8.63	4.22	8.23
温泉县	Wenquan [Araxang] County	8.45	11.93	8.98	9.66	-0.53	2.27
巴音郭楞蒙古自治州	**Bayangol Mongol Autonomous Prefecture**	**12.98**	**17.39**	**6.69**	**7.62**	**6.29**	**9.77**
库尔勒市	Korla City	8.33	14.50	3.61	4.99	4.72	9.51
轮台县	Luntai [Bugur] County	25.39	30.38	11.71	14.16	13.68	16.22
尉犁县	Yuli [Lopnur] County	11.59	15.49	5.33	5.29	6.26	10.20
若羌县	Ruoqiang [Qarkilik] County	12.03	16.86	4.17	5.53	7.86	11.33
且末县	Qiemo [Qarqan] County	6.13	5.42	3.36	2.97	2.77	2.45
焉耆回族自治县	Yanji Hui Autonomous County	11.95	14.33	4.36	4.52	7.59	9.81
和静县	Hejing County	18.79	28.06	8.11	9.18	10.68	18.88
和硕县	Hoxud County	9.66	14.45	8.06	8.01	1.60	6.44
博湖县	Bohu [Bagrax] County	12.98	17.06	11.49	13.90	1.49	3.16

3-6 续表 2 Continued

单位：‰ (‰)

地　　区	Region	出生率 Birth Rate	#少数民族 Minority Nationalities	死亡率 Death Rate	#少数民族 Minority Nationalities	自然增长率 Natural Growth Rate	#少数民族 Minority Nationalities
阿克苏地区	**Aksu Administrative Offices**	**18.71**	**20.71**	**7.94**	**8.60**	**10.77**	**12.11**
阿克苏市	Aksu City	16.33	22.67	7.22	9.95	9.11	12.72
温宿县	Wensu [Onsu] County	16.56	18.90	4.07	4.09	12.49	14.81
库车县	Kuqa County	25.38	26.58	8.09	8.47	17.29	18.11
沙雅县	Xayar County	23.96	25.11	10.40	10.36	13.56	14.73
新和县	Xinhe [Toksu] County	16.96	17.50	4.10	4.25	12.86	13.25
拜城县	Baicheng [Bay] County	14.77	15.85	5.76	6.13	9.01	9.72
乌什县	Wushi [Uxturpan] County	15.31	15.15	12.68	11.94	2.63	3.21
阿瓦提县	Awat County	15.77	17.10	11.61	13.08	4.16	4.02
柯坪县	Kalpin County	16.54	16.84	4.06	4.14	12.48	12.70
克孜勒苏柯尔克孜自治州	**Kizilsu Kirgiz Autonomous Prefecture**	**47.34**	**48.18**	**19.14**	**19.43**	**28.20**	**28.75**
阿图什市	Artux City	27.47	27.56	11.90	11.80	15.57	15.76
阿克陶县	Akto County	22.66	23.23	8.34	8.62	14.32	14.61
阿合奇县	Akqi County	15.78	16.45	6.58	7.13	9.20	9.32
乌恰县	Wuqia [Ulugqat] County	18.58	19.88	6.45	7.10	12.13	12.78
喀什地区	**Kashgar [Kaxgar] Administrative Offices**	**62.92**	**64.47**	**22.94**	**23.92**	**39.98**	**40.55**
喀什市	Kashgar [Kaxgar] City	25.44	27.85	7.34	7.94	18.10	19.91
疏附县	Shufu County	27.66	27.89	16.92	17.11	10.74	10.78
疏勒县	Shule County	44.15	44.18	13.87	14.46	30.28	29.72
英吉沙县	Yengisar County	50.01	50.49	10.50	10.59	39.51	39.90
泽普县	Zepu [Poskam] County	36.95	40.86	12.16	13.60	24.79	27.26
莎车县	Shache [Yarkant] County	28.71	29.25	17.91	18.28	10.80	10.97
叶城县	Yecheng [Kagilik] County	32.24	33.19	5.05	5.12	27.19	28.07
麦盖提县	Makit County	26.23	24.90	8.73	10.09	17.50	14.81
岳普湖县	Yopurga County	39.80	41.19	26.79	28.34	13.01	12.85
伽师县	Jiashi [Payzawat] County	35.10	35.61	8.07	8.22	27.03	27.39
巴楚县	Bachu [Maralbexi] County	16.88	16.16	3.78	3.38	13.10	12.78
塔什库尔干塔吉克自治县	Taxkorgan Tajik Autonomous County	20.76	20.36	5.57	5.84	15.19	14.52
和田地区	**Hotan Administrative Offices**	**19.34**	**19.77**	**7.25**	**7.40**	**12.09**	**12.37**
和田市	Hotan City	9.85	10.12	4.76	4.83	5.09	5.29
和田县	Hotan County	25.41	25.56	4.28	4.31	21.13	21.25
墨玉县	Moyu [Karakax] County	11.08	11.13	9.32	9.51	1.76	1.62
皮山县	Pishan [Guma] County	16.68	16.85	5.57	5.63	11.11	11.22
洛浦县	Lop County	31.15	31.70	4.47	4.54	26.68	27.16
策勒县	Qira County	22.58	22.81	13.17	13.35	9.41	9.46
于田县	Yutian [Keriya] County	31.85	32.27	9.66	9.84	22.19	22.43
民丰县	Minfeng [Niya] County	17.92	19.30	10.34	11.36	7.56	7.94
自治区直辖县级市	**Municpality Country-LevelCity dire-ctlyunder the Central overn-ment**						
石河子市	Shihezi City	5.78	13.54	6.60	5.18	-0.82	8.36
阿拉尔市	Aral City	8.76	13.96	3.64	1.99	5.12	11.97
图木舒克市	Tumxuk City	10.28	14.05	4.64	11.87	5.64	2.18
五家渠市	Wujiaqu City	6.28	11.96	6.44	3.97	-0.16	7.99

3-7 各地、州、市、县(市)分民族人口数

单位：人 (2012 年)

地区	Region	合计 Total	#少数民族 Minority Nationalities	维吾尔族 Uygur	汉族 Han	哈萨克族 Kazak
乌鲁木齐市	**Urumqi City**	**2578033**	**706051**	**332620**	**1871982**	**69153**
天山区	Tianshan District	576246	218600	148268	357646	13954
沙依巴克区	Shayibak District	537548	120077	63704	417471	8478
新市区	Xinshi District	556204	115299	52084	440905	7354
水磨沟区	Shui Mogou Distric	301441	46492	29043	254949	2969
头屯河区	Tou Tunhe District	230230	51793	24689	178437	1847
达坂城区	Da Bancheng District	42170	23214	2614	18956	6575
米东区	Midong District	274332	91659	11358	182673	4458
乌鲁木齐县	Urumqi County	59862	38916	860	20946	23518
克拉玛依市	**Karamay City**	**285837**	**72144**	**44587**	**213693**	**11753**
独山子区	Dushanzi District	56339	14875	9133	41464	2533
克拉玛依区	Karamay District	186284	44810	27398	141474	7406
乌尔河区	Urhe District	2293	1049	364	1244	70
白碱滩区	Bai Jiantan District	40921	11410	7692	29511	1744
吐鲁番地区	**Turpan Administrative Offices**	**625334**	**489748**	**449774**	**135586**	**304**
吐鲁番市	Turpan City	275777	223939	203576	51838	26
鄯善县	Shanshan [Piqan] County	231311	166181	154551	65130	41
托克逊县	Toksun County	118246	99628	91647	18618	237
哈密地区	**Hami [Kumul] Administrative Offices**	**592354**	**186436**	**107667**	**405918**	**54268**
哈密市	Hami [Kumul] City	465521	132555	98130	332966	12953
巴里坤哈萨克自治县	Barkol Kazak Autonomous County	104106	39214	150	64892	36941
伊吾县	Yiwu [Araturuk] County	22727	14667	9387	8060	4374
昌吉回族自治州	**Changji Hui Autonomous Prefecture**	**1402107**	**377948**	**68025**	**1024159**	**142925**
昌吉市	Changji City	370405	101897	13216	268508	19831
阜康市	Fukang City	168560	48739	10440	119821	14675
呼图壁县	Hutubi County	217267	52068	6290	165199	26091
玛纳斯县	Manas County	174875	34304	6023	140571	19260
奇台县	Qitai County	240530	64396	19378	176134	26675
吉木萨尔县	Jimsar County	140952	44460	7653	96492	11726
木垒哈萨克自治县	Mori Kazak Autonomous County	89518	32084	5025	57434	24667

Population of Major Nationalities by Prefecture, Autonomous Prefecture, City and County

(person)

回 族 Hui	柯尔克孜族 Kirgiz	蒙古族 Mongolian	锡伯族 Xibo	俄罗斯族 Russion	塔吉克族 Tajik	乌孜别克族 Uzbek	塔塔尔族 Tatar	满 族 Manchu	达斡尔族 Daur	其 它 Others
259509	**2002**	**9931**	**5564**	**3670**	**250**	**2019**	**1014**	**10758**	**608**	**8953**
43609	842	2804	1665	1183	109	1137	559	2493	185	1792
37061	463	2595	1335	985	40	399	178	2600	147	2092
45485	466	2179	1464	789	69	278	133	2916	166	1916
10571	109	1004	481	311	16	93	33	1042	42	778
22004	43	611	486	178	11	44	13	956	29	882
13798	10	19	3	10	2	1	5	82	2	93
72862	31	593	123	213	3	12	22	652	33	1299
14119	38	126	7	1		55	71	17	4	101
6968	**147**	**2629**	**938**	**634**	**30**	**307**	**88**	**1216**	**138**	**2709**
1573	8	480	147	158	3	75	8	271	22	464
4528	92	1298	672	420	23	197	54	780	103	1839
17		589	5				1			3
850	47	262	114	56	4	35	25	165	13	403
37973	**2**	**210**	**24**	**55**		**21**	**5**	**296**	**5**	**1079**
19363	1	119	15	40		5	2	141	5	646
11028		76	5	14		16	3	111		336
7582	1	15	4	1				44		97
17655	**22**	**2667**	**178**	**104**		**10**	**32**	**1788**	**11**	**2034**
16513	18	1096	170	86		8	3	1729	11	1838
314	4	1564	8	18		1	29	53		132
828		7				1		6		64
143482	**286**	**6728**	**627**	**729**	**3**	**2390**	**913**	**3264**	**57**	**8519**
62203	98	1569	390	313	3	150	97	1342	32	2653
21190	131	305	65	107		41	58	221	4	1502
17136	3	323	41	98		4	31	171	2	1878
7628	34	120	30	107		21	7	175	13	886
13411	11	1771	70	72		654	458	1187	4	705
20982	6	2610	22	20		474	169	123	2	673
932	3	30	9	12		1046	93	45		222

3-7 续表 1

单位：人

地　区	Region	合　计 Total	#少数民族 Minority Nationalities	维吾尔族 Uygur	汉　族 Han	哈萨克族 Kazak
伊犁哈萨克自治州	**Ili Kazak Autonomous Prefecture**	**4628434**	**2673416**	**783489**	**1955018**	**1223252**
伊犁州直属县(市)	**Counties (Cities) Direct Under Ili Prefecture**	**2917210**	**1833024**	**731717**	**1084186**	**614043**
伊宁市	Yining [Gulja] City	515299	332805	250989	182494	24802
奎屯市	Kuytun City	304402	15854	958	288548	5177
伊宁县	Yining [Gulja] County	427305	358354	198316	68951	52652
察布查尔锡伯自治县	Qapqal Xibe Autonomous County	194312	128208	54303	66104	39529
霍城县	Huocheng [Korgas] County	407483	237115	89996	170368	36197
巩留县	Gongliu [Tokkuztara] County	204494	146965	45257	57529	60629
新源县	Xinyuan [Kunes] County	316002	202855	32008	113147	144244
昭苏县	Zhaosu [Mongolkure] County	189102	137520	18532	51582	92589
特克斯县	Tekes County	171954	135104	19570	36850	73101
尼勒克县	Nilka County	186857	138244	21788	48613	85123
塔城地区	**Tacheng [Tarbagatai] Administrative Offices**	**1047814**	**449476**	**42087**	**598338**	**265779**
塔城市	Tacheng [Qoqek] City	169404	62600	5110	106804	26649
乌苏市	Usu City	228939	83531	17036	145408	22702
额敏县	Emin [Dorbiljin] County	219165	100897	8127	118268	75570
沙湾县	Shawan County	216435	70113	9340	146322	36812
托里县	Toli County	100235	73907	1246	26328	70697
裕民县	Yumin [Qagantokay] County	59468	24006	182	35462	18342
和布克赛尔蒙古自治县	Hoboksar Mongol Autonomous County	54168	34422	1046	19746	15007
阿勒泰地区	**Altay Administrative Offices**	**663410**	**390916**	**9685**	**272494**	**343430**
阿勒泰市	Altay City	232792	94738	5041	138054	77565
布尔津县	Burqin County	71209	49762	1016	21447	40831
富蕴县	Fuyun [Koktokay] County	95153	74321	1950	20832	69242
福海县	Fuhai [Burultokay] County	74516	34040	533	40476	30073
哈巴河县	Habahe [Kaba] County	86945	60741	363	26204	52818
青河县	Qinghe [Qinggil] County	63412	51501	579	11911	48233
吉木乃县	Jemnay County	39383	25813	203	13570	24668
博尔塔拉蒙古自治州	**Bortala Mongol Autonomous Prefecture**	**484491**	**165913**	**64901**	**318578**	**48392**
博乐市	Bole [Bortala] City	265605	88192	42545	177413	20311
精河县	Jinghe [Jing] County	144286	45951	18904	98335	13929
温泉县	Wenquan [Araxang] County	74600	31770	3452	42830	14152
巴音郭楞蒙古自治州	**Bayangol Mongol Autonomous Prefecture**	**1374726**	**595416**	**459041**	**779310**	**1321**
库尔勒市	Korla City	551502	166074	140518	385428	107
轮台县	Luntai [Bugur] County	116255	94493	93898	21762	7
尉犁县	Yuli [Lopnur] County	110640	35380	34268	75260	13
若羌县	Ruoqiang [Qarkilik] County	34118	14642	13047	19476	5
且末县	Qiemo [Qarqan] County	63415	47802	47483	15613	12
焉耆回族自治县	Yanji Hui Autonomous County	164300	94448	55405	69852	36
和静县	Hejing County	197686	93515	52082	104171	1088
和硕县	Hoxud County	75509	27065	12167	48444	35
博湖县	Bohu [Bagrax] County	61301	21997	10173	39304	18

Continued

(person)

回　族 Hui	柯尔克孜族 Kirgiz	蒙古族 Mongolian	锡伯族 Xibo	俄罗斯族 Russion	塔吉克族 Tajik	乌孜别克族 Uzbek	塔塔尔族 Tatar	满　族 Manchu	达斡尔族 Daur	其　它 Others
421091	**21590**	**75534**	**34429**	**5482**	**170**	**7837**	**2796**	**5154**	**5856**	**86736**
314920	**19362**	**34570**	**32355**	**1551**	**138**	**7242**	**1277**	**3972**	**514**	**71363**
37783	661	1973	4931	795	89	4375	513	2074	57	3763
6560	24	1088	263	90	2	17	5	441	38	1191
71999	360	278	262	29	6	724	62	376	6	33284
10619	307	173	20591	102		137	13	95	18	2321
85396	300	775	3270	243	4	211	120	341	340	19922
31711	477	2306	1623	99	1	164	111	288	6	4293
22515	454	176	420	96	5	690	146	149	5	1947
5279	5472	14120	85	40	5	383	281	36	1	697
24008	10600	4634	230	5	19	283	19	81	3	2551
19050	707	9047	680	52	7	258	7	91	40	1394
81840	**2168**	**34596**	**1985**	**3502**	**31**	**406**	**482**	**831**	**5324**	**10445**
13269	1806	1784	1528	2378	1	161	253	241	5136	4284
33854	4	8166	152	137	1	56	32	128	31	1232
7419	304	6196	89	575		123	64	162	61	2207
21635	11	482	42	124	2	22	20	186	22	1415
1093	18	521	60	18	1	21	43	50	8	131
3967	6	152	57	237			9	27	43	984
603	19	17295	57	33	26	23	61	37	23	192
24331	**60**	**6368**	**89**	**429**	**1**	**189**	**1037**	**351**	**18**	**4928**
6855	35	2869	40	197	1	131	324	187	5	1488
4601	6	1613	12	144		3	323	44	3	1166
2199	11	301	11	39		13	88	41	5	421
2580		204	8	32			52	32	3	523
6064	5	452	6			10	49	8		966
1305		880	10	11		31	191	10		251
727	3	49	2	6		1	10	29	2	113
19410	**89**	**28457**	**417**	**195**	**4**	**171**	**19**	**372**	**29**	**3457**
10199	33	12974	294	152	4	102	14	279	13	1272
6091	24	5289	64	40		41	4	64		1501
3120	32	10194	59	3		28	1	29	16	684
70098	**268**	**51144**	**218**	**260**	**4**	**142**	**2**	**1304**	**42**	**11572**
12336	10	5290	190	227	4	80	2	996	16	6298
382		46	4	3				22		131
584		29	2	9		15		36	5	419
1119	1	20	2					9		439
187		20	2			9		5		84
34426	101	3422	2	2		30		81	18	925
7201	142	30887	12	11		8		99	3	1982
7179	2	6954	3	8				27		690
6684	12	4476	1					29		604

3-7 续表 2

单位：人

地区	Region	合计 Total	#少数民族 Minority Nationalities	维吾尔族 Uygur	汉族 Han	哈萨克族 Kazak
阿克苏地区	**Aksu Administrative Offices**	**2396877**	**1923231**	**1888881**	**473646**	**183**
阿克苏市	Aksu City	495002	263465	254851	231537	43
温宿县	Wensu [Onsu] County	247630	193849	187609	53781	12
库车县	Kuqa County	470611	418703	414225	51908	68
沙雅县	Xayar County	263940	221571	218782	42369	6
新和县	Xinhe [Toksu] County	173109	162252	161677	10857	12
拜城县	Baicheng [Bay] County	231909	204645	202393	27264	20
乌什县	Wushi [Uxturpan] County	217556	205576	198375	11980	11
阿瓦提县	Awat County	245821	203283	201185	42538	10
柯坪县	Kalpin County	51299	49887	49784	1412	1
克孜勒苏柯尔克孜自治州	**Kizilsu Kirgiz Autonomous Prefecture**	**560627**	**518863**	**360792**	**41764**	**150**
阿图什市	Artux City	254385	231881	201915	22504	62
阿克陶县	Akto County	204957	196844	147927	8113	19
阿合奇县	Akqi County	42591	38347	1183	4244	35
乌恰县	Wuqia [Ulugqat] County	58694	51791	9767	6903	34
喀什地区	**Kashgar [Kaxgar] Administrative Offices**	**4151345**	**3866387**	**3803463**	**284958**	**382**
喀什市	Kashgar [Kaxgar] City	486127	401676	396961	84451	274
疏附县	Shufu County	338514	333157	332339	5357	6
疏勒县	Shule County	344797	328321	327410	16476	2
英吉沙县	Yengisar County	285399	280566	279814	4833	10
泽普县	Zepu [Poskam] County	210978	174613	168280	36365	9
莎车县	Shache [Yarkant] County	794765	767348	760274	27417	11
叶城县	Yecheng [Kagilik] County	474396	451373	445791	23023	31
麦盖提县	Makit County	262628	214020	212917	48608	5
岳普湖县	Yopurga County	163297	153399	153133	9898	1
伽师县	Jiashi [Payzawat] County	408181	399110	398755	9071	13
巴楚县	Bachu [Maralbexi] County	343222	326453	325686	16769	9
塔什库尔干塔吉克自治县	Taxkorgan Tajik Autonomous County	39041	36351	2103	2690	11
和田地区	**Hotan Administrative Offices**	**2123377**	**2048737**	**2044223**	**74640**	**83**
和田市	Hotan City	330952	294050	292829	36902	23
和田县	Hotan County	279508	277772	277446	1736	3
墨玉县	Moyu [Karakax] County	538598	522857	522628	15741	5
皮山县	Pishan [Guma] County	270270	266284	264163	3986	1
洛浦县	Lop County	252455	247364	247194	5091	30
策勒县	Qira County	156295	153550	153445	2745	2
于田县	Yutian [Keriya] County	257435	252570	252283	4865	17
民丰县	Minfeng [Niya] County	37864	34290	34235	3574	2
自治区直辖县级市	**Municpality Country-LevelCity directly under the Central Govern-ment**	**1056908**	**163249**	**121183**	**893659**	**5291**
石河子市	Shihezi City	619996	39594	8074	580402	4470
阿拉尔市	Aral City	186638	16591	10414	170047	713
图木舒克市	Tumxuk City	159563	103772	102606	55791	1
五家渠市	Wujiaqu City	90711	3292	89	87419	107

Continued

(person)

回 族 Hui	柯尔克孜族 Kirgiz	蒙古族 Mongolian	锡伯族 Xibo	俄罗斯族 Russion	塔吉克族 Tajik	乌孜别克族 Uzbek	塔塔尔族 Tatar	满 族 Manchu	达斡尔族 Daur	其 它 Others
15538	**11183**	**896**	**138**	**132**	**5**	**200**	**9**	**577**	**1**	**5488**
4901	217	624	73	61		41		346		2308
825	4161	34	5	1	3			13		1186
3630	149	83	26	29	2	44	1	98	1	347
2221	11	22	7	21		6		30		465
346	7	13	4	13				42		138
902	1142	36	12			13	1	23		103
1449	5449	13	8			74	3	6		188
1243	18	59	2	7		22	4	19		714
21	29	12	1							39
698	**150826**	**88**	**32**	**6**	**5574**	**173**	**29**	**94**		**401**
284	29204	50	14	6	27	17	1	79		222
205	42949	23	6		5508	101	28	1		77
88	37000	3	2		4			4		28
121	41673	12	10		35	55		10		74
6254	**6701**	**730**	**145**	**99**	**41455**	**4316**	**93**	**539**	**14**	**2196**
1503	340	168	63	63	290	1157	47	248	9	553
75	619	7	2		5	10		1	1	92
295	349	110	4	2	1	13	2	26		107
72	583	13	3	4	20	21	2	22	2	
1063	150	129	10	11	4350	145	1	60		405
988	1161	96	37	9	2736	1782	35	49	1	169
857	1194	49	6	7	2151	1042	1	41		203
643	2	38	1		2	46	1	28		337
108		57	2		2		1	3		92
57	33	31	6			64	2	33		116
566	4	27	5	2	1	36	1	21	1	94
27	2266	5	6	1	31897			7		28
1594	**943**	**187**	**51**	**9**	**1019**	**56**	**7**	**77**		**488**
798	15	89	22	9	7	42	5	36		175
320		1								2
107	1	11	7			5	2	10		81
95	923	23	9		1003	7		1		59
54		27	2					6		51
50		6	3		1	1		2		40
146	3	22	8		4			21		66
24	1	8			4	1		1		14
22784	**323**	**1621**	**178**	**313**	**55**	**14**	**15**	**1209**	**15**	**10248**
19221	141	801	145	239	24	11	15	929	13	5511
1111	179	297	7	17	3	1		62		3787
557		59	2	6	28	1		37		475
1895	3	464	24	51		1		181	2	475

3-8 主要年份分民族人口数

Population by Nationality in Main Years

单位：万人 (10 000 persons)

年 份 Year	维吾尔族 Uygur	汉 族 Han	哈萨克族 Kazak	回 族 Hui	柯尔克孜族 Kirgiz	蒙古族 Mongolian	锡伯族 Xibo
1978	555.53	512.90	82.10	53.12	10.40	10.74	2.55
1980	576.46	531.03	87.68	56.56	10.89	11.32	2.59
1985	629.44	534.92	98.72	59.96	12.35	12.33	2.93
1990	724.95	574.66	113.92	68.89	14.44	14.28	3.42
1995	780.00	631.81	123.77	74.76	15.78	15.28	3.82
1996	791.60	643.28	125.70	76.02	16.05	15.54	3.89
1997	802.00	660.13	127.08	77.06	16.27	15.75	3.90
1998	813.95	674.11	128.70	78.20	16.41	15.91	3.95
1999	825.03	687.15	130.45	79.26	16.64	16.13	4.00
2000	852.33	725.08	131.87	83.93	16.47	16.20	4.05
2001	860.56	742.20	131.92	84.42	17.01	16.19	4.13
2002	869.23	759.57	133.35	85.46	17.13	16.38	4.10
2003	882.35	771.10	135.21	86.67	17.37	16.69	4.03
2004	897.67	780.25	138.16	87.63	17.12	16.96	4.08
2005	923.50	795.66	141.39	89.35	17.15	17.17	4.15
2006	941.38	812.16	143.50	90.96	17.59	17.46	4.19
2007	965.06	823.93	148.39	94.30	18.19	17.71	4.24
2008	983.18	836.33	151.05	95.30	18.64	18.10	4.32
2009	1001.98	841.69	151.48	98.04	18.93	17.96	4.28
2010	1017.15	832.29	151.16	98.40	18.92	17.74	4.23
2011	1037.04	844.42	154.26	100.34	19.40	17.89	4.27
2012	1052.86	847.29	155.75	102.31	19.44	18.08	4.29

年 份 Year	俄罗斯族 Russian	塔吉克族 Tajik	乌孜别克族 Uzbek	塔塔尔族 Tatar	满 族 Manchu	达斡尔族 Daur	其他民族 Others
1978	0.06	2.28	0.77	0.31	0.42	0.41	1.42
1980	0.06	2.41	0.79	0.31	0.50	0.40	2.24
1985	0.43	2.89	0.93	0.33	0.95	0.48	4.49
1990	0.75	3.44	1.14	0.40	1.66	0.56	6.65
1995	0.90	3.82	1.33	0.47	1.99	0.62	7.00
1996	0.92	3.89	1.35	0.47	2.05	0.63	7.90
1997	0.92	3.90	1.35	0.46	2.06	0.63	6.56
1998	0.93	3.96	1.37	0.47	2.09	0.64	6.66
1999	0.94	4.01	1.39	0.48	2.12	0.65	6.75
2000	1.09	4.09	1.36	0.48	2.31	0.66	9.48
2001	1.08	4.12	1.37	0.47	2.30	0.67	9.75
2002	1.12	4.07	1.39	0.48	2.35	0.67	9.89
2003	1.11	4.09	1.46	0.49	2.39	0.67	10.32
2004	1.13	4.35	1.42	0.47	2.41	0.67	10.79
2005	1.12	4.40	1.51	0.47	2.46	0.65	11.37
2006	1.14	4.47	1.60	0.47	2.52	0.66	11.91
2007	1.16	4.48	1.61	0.47	2.56	0.67	12.42
2008	1.16	4.54	1.69	0.49	2.59	0.68	12.74
2009	1.17	4.72	1.67	0.49	2.62	0.69	12.91
2010	1.16	4.69	1.70	0.49	2.61	0.67	13.23
2011	1.16	4.73	1.74	0.49	2.64	0.69	13.59
2012	1.17	4.86	1.77	0.50	2.66	0.68	14.39

3-9 各地、州、市、县(市)按城镇、乡村和农业、非农业分人口数

Population of Urban and Rural, Agriculture and Non-Agriculture by Prefecture, Autonomous Prefecture, City and County

单位：万人　　　　(2012 年)　　　　(10 000 persons)

地区	Region	城镇人口 Urban Population	#非农业人口 Non-agri-cultural Population	乡村人口 Rural Population	农业人口 Agricul-tural Population	非农业人口 Non-agri-cultural Population
乌鲁木齐市	**Urumqi City**	**250.50**	**184.98**	**7.30**	**71.74**	**186.06**
天山区	Tianshan District	57.63	46.73		10.90	46.73
沙依巴克区	Shayibak District	53.75	45.56		8.19	45.56
新市区	Xinshi District	55.62	38.48		17.14	38.48
水磨沟区	Shui Mogou Distric	30.14	19.48		10.66	19.48
头屯河区	Tou Tunhe District	23.02	17.90		5.12	17.90
达坂城区	Da Bancheng District	3.23	1.71	0.99	2.40	1.82
米东区	Midong District	25.75	14.65	1.68	12.54	14.89
乌鲁木齐县	Urumqi County	1.36	0.47	4.63	4.79	1.20
克拉玛依市	**Karamay City**	**28.58**	**28.21**		**0.37**	**28.21**
独山子区	Dushanzi District	5.63	5.63			5.63
克拉玛依区	Karamay District	18.63	18.43		0.20	18.43
乌尔河区	Urhe District	0.23	0.08		0.15	0.08
白碱滩区	Bai Jiantan District	4.09	4.07		0.02	4.07
吐鲁番地区	**Turpan Administrative Offices**	**47.75**	**16.20**	**14.78**	**44.54**	**17.99**
吐鲁番市	Turpan City	27.58	8.39		19.19	8.39
鄯善县	Shanshan [Piqan] County	17.68	5.56	5.45	17.05	6.08
托克逊县	Toksun County	2.49	2.25	9.33	8.30	3.52
哈密地区	**Hami [Kumul] Administrative Offices**	**52.38**	**32.08**	**6.86**	**25.21**	**34.03**
哈密市	Hami [Kumul] City	46.55	29.80		16.75	29.80
巴里坤哈萨克自治县	Barkol Kazak Autonomous County	4.78	1.61	5.63	7.11	3.30
伊吾县	Yiwu [Araturuk] County	1.05	0.67	1.23	1.35	0.93
昌吉回族自治州	**Changji Hui Autonomous Prefecture**	**119.97**	**67.07**	**20.24**	**71.21**	**69.00**
昌吉市	Changji City	37.04	23.55		13.49	23.55
阜康市	Fukang City	16.86	9.60		7.26	9.60
呼图壁县	Hutubi County	20.19	11.74	1.54	9.30	12.43
玛纳斯县	Manas County	14.01	7.17	3.48	9.97	7.52
奇台县	Qitai County	16.27	8.56	7.78	15.15	8.90
吉木萨尔县	Jimsar County	11.66	4.53	2.43	9.44	4.65
木垒哈萨克自治县	Mori Kazak Autonomous County	3.94	1.92	5.01	6.60	2.35

注：1.各地、州、市城镇人口、乡村人口为 2012 年公安年报按行政建制划分的人口数。
　　2.各地、州、市农业人口数均含未落常住户口人员。

Note: a) Population of urban and rural by prefecture,Autonomous prefecture,city and county come from Annual Report on Public Security in 2012
b) Population of agriculture by Prefecture,Autonomous prefecture,city and county included population of without habitual residence.

3-9 续表 1 Continued

单位：万人 (10 000 persons)

地　　区	Region	城镇人口 Urban Population	#非农业人口 Non-agri-cultural Population	乡村人口 Rural Population	农业人口 Agricul-tural Population	非农业人口 Non-agri-cultural Population
伊犁哈萨克自治州	**Ili Kazak Autonomous Prefecture**	**273.62**	**174.34**	**189.22**	**253.63**	**209.21**
伊犁州直属县(市)	**Counties (Cities) Direct Under Ili Prefecture**	**158.02**	**99.18**	**133.70**	**170.94**	**120.78**
伊宁市	Yining [Gulja] City	51.53	34.48		17.05	34.48
奎屯市	Kuytun City	30.44	27.48		2.96	27.48
伊宁县	Yining [Gulja] County	8.83	4.74	33.90	35.76	6.97
察布查尔锡伯自治县	Qapqal Xibe Autonomous County	6.52	4.84	12.91	12.95	6.48
霍城县	Huocheng [Korgas] County	21.58	5.85	19.17	25.60	15.15
巩留县	Gongliu [Tokkuztara] County	3.99	3.06	16.46	16.16	4.29
新源县	Xinyuan [Kunes] County	20.99	7.32	10.61	22.70	8.90
昭苏县	Zhaosu [Mongolkure] County	5.84	5.02	13.07	11.76	7.15
特克斯县	Tekes County	4.18	3.12	13.01	12.35	4.84
尼勒克县	Nilka County	4.12	3.27	14.57	13.65	5.04
塔城地区	**Tacheng [Tarbagatai] Administrative Offices**	**78.93**	**47.98**	**25.85**	**49.39**	**55.39**
塔城市	Tacheng [Qoqek] City	16.94	10.69		6.25	10.69
乌苏市	Usu City	22.89	8.10		14.79	8.10
额敏县	Emin [Dorbiljin] County	11.64	9.36	10.28	8.80	13.12
沙湾县	Shawan County	18.53	12.32	3.11	8.22	13.42
托里县	Toli County	4.42	3.52	5.60	5.95	4.07
裕民县	Yumin [Qagantokay] County	2.02	1.97	3.93	2.98	2.97
和布克赛尔蒙古自治县	Hoboksar Mongol Autonomous County	2.49	2.02	2.93	2.40	3.02
阿勒泰地区	**Altay Administrative Offices**	**36.67**	**27.18**	**29.67**	**33.30**	**33.04**
阿勒泰市	Altay City	23.28	15.12		8.16	15.12
布尔津县	Burqin County	2.01	1.94	5.11	4.39	2.73
富蕴县	Fuyun [Koktokay] County	3.25	2.86	6.27	5.59	3.93
福海县	Fuhai [Burultokay] County	2.88	2.75	4.57	3.58	3.87
哈巴河县	Habahe [Kaba] County	1.92	1.79	6.77	5.63	3.06
青河县	Qinghe [Qinggil] County	1.95	1.53	4.39	4.01	2.33
吉木乃县	Jemnay County	1.38	1.19	2.56	1.94	2.00
博尔塔拉蒙古自治州	**Bortala Mongol Autonomous Prefecture**	**38.82**	**24.11**	**9.63**	**21.90**	**26.55**
博乐市	Bole [Bortala] City	26.56	16.48		10.08	16.48
精河县	Jinghe [Jing] County	7.82	4.46	6.61	8.11	6.32
温泉县	Wenquan [Araxang] County	4.44	3.17	3.02	3.71	3.75
巴音郭楞蒙古自治州	**Bayangol Mongol Autonomous Prefecture**	**109.46**	**62.94**	**28.01**	**71.29**	**66.18**
库尔勒市	Korla City	55.15	34.70		20.45	34.70
轮台县	Luntai [Bugur] County	7.00	2.42	4.63	8.76	2.87
尉犁县	Yuli [Lopnur] County	6.21	4.92	4.85	5.57	5.49
若羌县	Ruoqiang [Qarkilik] County	1.73	1.39	1.68	1.72	1.69
且末县	Qiemo [Qarqan] County	1.83	1.59	4.51	4.12	2.22
焉耆回族自治县	Yanji Hui Autonomous County	12.43	5.33	4.00	10.62	5.81
和静县	Hejing County	17.88	8.24	1.89	11.37	8.40
和硕县	Hoxud County	4.05	2.68	3.50	4.43	3.12
博湖县	Bohu [Bagrax] County	3.18	1.67	2.95	4.25	1.88

3-9 续表 2 Continued

单位：万人 (10 000 persons)

地 区	Region	城镇人口 Urban Population	#非农业人口 Non-agri-cultural Population	乡村人口 Rural Population	农业人口 Agricul-tural Population	非农业人口 Non-agri-cultural Population
阿克苏地区	**Aksu Administrative Offices**	**154.82**	**69.46**	**84.87**	**163.50**	**76.19**
阿克苏市	Aksu City	49.50	27.12		22.38	27.12
温宿县	Wensu [Onsu] County	16.41	6.07	8.35	17.60	7.16
库车县	Kuqa County	33.56	15.31	13.50	30.27	16.79
沙雅县	Xayar County	18.82	5.41	7.58	20.67	5.73
新和县	Xinhe [Toksu] County	5.40	2.74	11.91	13.80	3.51
拜城县	Baicheng [Bay] County	8.82	4.32	14.37	18.08	5.11
乌什县	Wushi [Uxturpan] County	7.69	3.11	14..07	18.08	3.68
阿瓦提县	Awat County	13.68	4.59	10.90	19.05	5.53
柯坪县	Kalpin County	0.94	0.79	4.19	3.57	1.56
克孜勒苏柯尔克孜自治州	**Kizilsu Kirgiz Autonomous Prefecture**	**32.84**	**14.38**	**23.22**	**38.91**	**17.15**
阿图什市	Artux City	25.44	9.03		16.41	9.03
阿克陶县	Akto County	4.27	2.29	16.22	16.93	3.56
阿合奇县	Akqi County	1.25	1.18	3.01	2.37	1.89
乌恰县	Wuqia [Ulugqat] County	1.88	1.88	3.99	3.20	2.67
喀什地区	**Kashgar [Kaxgar] Administrative Offices**	**143.47**	**79.96**	**271.66**	**320.76**	**94.37**
喀什市	Kashgar [Kaxgar] City	48.61	29.23		19.38	29.23
疏附县	Shufu County	3.13	1.99	30.72	30.41	3.44
疏勒县	Shule County	9.94	3.04	24.54	30.19	4.29
英吉沙县	Yengisar County	4.05	3.11	24.49	24.29	4.25
泽普县	Zepu [Poskam] County	5.89	4.92	15.20	14.87	6.22
莎车县	Shache [Yarkant] County	33.18	10.99	46.30	66.51	12.97
叶城县	Yecheng [Kagilik] County	7.73	7.41	39.71	38.45	8.99
麦盖提县	Makit County	6.99	6.60	19.27	18.24	8.02
岳普湖县	Yopurga County	4.70	2.47	11.63	12.79	3.54
伽师县	Jiashi [Payzawat] County	4.67	3.31	36.15	35.94	4.88
巴楚县	Bachu [Maralbexi] County	13.08	5.70	21.24	26.97	7.35
塔什库尔干塔吉克自治县	Taxkorgan Tajik Autonomous County	1.50	1.19	2.41	2.72	1.19
和田地区	**Hotan Administrative Offices**	**69.91**	**28.38**	**142.43**	**175.76**	**36.58**
和田市	Hotan City	33.10	14.16		18.94	14.16
和田县	Hotan County	6.01	0.41	21.94	26.55	1.40
墨玉县	Moyu [Karakax] County	7.67	3.35	46.19	48.60	5.26
皮山县	Pishan [Guma] County	7.58	4.12	19.45	21.20	5.83
洛浦县	Lop County	4.19	1.85	21.05	22.23	3.01
策勒县	Qira County	2.91	1.46	12.72	13.26	2.37
于田县	Yutian [Keriya] County	6.96	2.24	18.78	22.29	3.45
民丰县	Minfeng [Niya] County	1.49	0.79	2.30	2.69	1.10
自治区直辖县级市	**Municpality Country-LevelCity directly under the Central Govern-ment**	**105.69**	**90.61**		**15.08**	**90.61**
石河子市	Shihezi City	62.00	56.95		5.05	56.95
阿拉尔市	Aral City	18.66	11.45		7.21	11.45
图木舒克市	Tumxuk City	15.96	13.55		2.41	13.55
五家渠市	Wujiaqu City	9.07	8.66		0.41	8.66

3-10 各地、州、市采取各种避孕措施情况

Condition of Adopting Various Contraceptives by Prefecture, Autonomous Prefecture, City and County

单位：% (2012 年) (%)

地　　区	Region	男性绝育 Masculine Sterilization	女性绝育 Female Sterilization	宫内节育器 IUD Intrauterine Device	皮下埋植 Subdermal Implant
总　计	**Total**	**0.17**	**4.93**	**79.47**	**0.26**
城　镇	Urban	0.13	2.69	76.08	0.17
农　村	Rural	0.20	6.15	81.32	0.31
乌鲁木齐市	Urumqi City	0.12	2.78	54.21	0.13
克拉玛依市	Karamay City	0.34	4.52	61.69	0.38
吐鲁番地区	Turpan Administrative Offices	0.05	1.92	87.12	0.34
哈密地区	Hami [Kumul] Administrative Offices	0.07	3.71	74.53	0.49
昌吉回族自治州	Changji Hui Autonomous Prefecture	0.14	5.31	77.85	0.36
伊犁州直属县(市)	Counties (Cities) Direct Under Ili Prefecture	0.15	4.00	78.69	0.16
塔城地区	Tacheng [Tarbagatai] Administrative Offices	0.26	7.01	78.15	0.99
阿勒泰地区	Altay Administrative Offices	0.10	3.03	77.31	0.44
博尔塔拉蒙古自治州	Bortala Mongol Autonomous Prefecture	0.46	7.65	72.80	0.63
巴音郭楞蒙古自治州	Bayangol Mongol Autonomous Prefecture	0.70	6.76	80.75	0.11
阿克苏地区	Aksu Administrative Offices	0.19	6.76	85.43	0.43
克孜勒苏柯尔克孜自治州	Kizilsu Kirgiz Autonomous Prefecture	0.01	2.32	91.01	0.08
喀什地区	Kashgar [Kaxgar] Administrative Offices	0.06	3.42	92.53	0.14
和田地区	Hotan Administrative Offices	0.05	9.32	86.48	0.01

地　　区	Region	口服药及注射针 Medicine and Entry Needle	避孕套 Contraceptives	外用药 Drug for Exterior Use	其　他 Other
总　计	**Total**	**0.42**	**14.07**	**0.65**	**0.03**
城　镇	Urban	0.44	20.16	0.28	0.04
农　村	Rural	0.40	10.74	0.86	0.02
乌鲁木齐市	Urumqi City	0.70	41.79	0.19	0.07
克拉玛依市	Karamay City	0.49	32.24	0.33	
吐鲁番地区	Turpan Administrative Offices	0.62	9.70	0.25	
哈密地区	Hami [Kumul] Administrative Offices	0.37	20.71	0.11	0.02
昌吉回族自治州	Changji Hui Autonomous Prefecture	0.35	15.89	0.10	
伊犁州直属县(市)	Counties (Cities) Direct Under Ili Prefecture	0.34	16.36	0.18	0.12
塔城地区	Tacheng [Tarbagatai] Administrative Offices	0.30	13.22	0.06	
阿勒泰地区	Altay Administrative Offices	0.23	18.79	0.10	
博尔塔拉蒙古自治州	Bortala Mongol Autonomous Prefecture	0.41	17.82	0.23	
巴音郭楞蒙古自治州	Bayangol Mongol Autonomous Prefecture	0.14	11.45	0.09	
阿克苏地区	Aksu Administrative Offices	0.70	5.23	1.25	
克孜勒苏柯尔克孜自治州	Kizilsu Kirgiz Autonomous Prefecture	0.99	4.16	1.38	0.05
喀什地区	Kashgar [Kaxgar] Administrative Offices	0.34	1.54	1.97	0.01
和田地区	Hotan Administrative Offices	0.05	3.71	0.38	

注：表 3-10、3-11 根据自治区计生委 2012 年计划生育统计年报整理，不包括兵团。
Note: In table 3-10 and 3-11,data are compiled on statistic annals of the family planning in Xinjiang Uygur Autonomous Region in 2012.

3-11 各地、州、市计划生育及领证情况

Family Planning and Certificate Receiving by Prefecture, Autonomous Prefecture and City

(2012 年)

地区	Region	计划生育率 (%) Family Planning Rate (%)	领证率 (%) Coverage of One-child Certificate (%)	领取计划生育证人数 (人) Number of Persons Receiving Certificates of Honor (person)	领取独生子女证人数 (人) Number of Married Couples with One-child Certificate (person)
总计	**Total**	**99.78**	**34.70**	**659620**	**809143**
城镇	Urban	99.69	48.80	201939	504238
农村	Rural	99.80	27.37	457681	304905
乌鲁木齐市	Urumqi City	99.79	45.69	49862	192557
克拉玛依市	Karamay City	99.87	68.81	10091	46459
吐鲁番地区	Turpan Administrative Offices	99.98	33.44	28781	19186
哈密地区	Hami [Kumul] Administrative Offices	99.61	60.20	12914	47397
昌吉回族自治州	Changji Hui Autonomous Prefecture	99.77	43.00	23194	103473
伊犁州直属县(市)	Counties (Cities) Direct Under Ili Prefecture	99.81	35.73	112286	78693
塔城地区	Tacheng [Tarbagatai] Administrative Offices	99.79	38.23	27679	47254
阿勒泰地区	Altay Administrative Offices	99.77	45.32	31390	22830
博尔塔拉蒙古自治州	Bortala Mongol Autonomous Prefecture	99.62	40.96	11619	19642
巴音郭楞蒙古自治州	Bayangol Mongol Autonomous Prefecture	99.40	33.14	42689	58175
阿克苏地区	Aksu Administrative Offices	99.94	27.70	90960	47675
克孜勒苏柯尔克孜自治州	Kizilsu Kirgiz Autonomous Prefecture	99.92	37.21	31201	9697
喀什地区	Kashgar [Kaxgar] Administrative Offices	99.70	21.62	109810	68104
和田地区	Hotan Administrative Offices	99.80	29.93	77144	48001

3-12 主要年份新疆生产建设兵团人口情况

Population of Xinjiang Production and Construction Group in Main Years

单位：人 (person)

年份 Year	总人口 Total Population	男 Male	女 Female	农业人口 Agricultural Population	非农业人口 Non-Agricultural Population	出生人口 Birth Population	死亡人口 Death Population	出生率 (‰) Birth Rate (‰)	死亡率 (‰) Death Rate (‰)	自然增长率 (‰) Natural Growth Rate (‰)
1978	2119835	1090674	1029161			32749	6203	16.56	3.14	13.42
1980	2200755	1127050	1073705			26972	7162	12.27	3.26	9.01
1990	2143528	1110475	1033053	1132435	1044093	24589	9305	11.48	4.35	7.13
1995	2287896	1194166	1093730	1230151	1057745	22519	10044	9.98	4.45	5.53
2000	2427920	1272719	1155201	1379913	1048007	22674	12525	9.40	5.20	4.20
2001	2453575	1289954	1163621	1325998	1127577	19061	9014	7.80	3.70	4.10
2002	2501189	1311750	1189439	1355526	1145663	18179	9842	7.37	3.99	3.38
2003	2542170	1330666	1211504	1377224	1164946	17218	9914	6.84	3.94	2.90
2004	2563837	1341213	1222624	1413197	1150640	15860	9864	6.21	3.86	2.35
2005	2569756	1346901	1222855	1332458	1237298	16381	11934	6.38	4.65	1.73
2006	2579435	1352541	1226894	1312908	1266527	14687	11858	5.71	4.61	1.10
2007	2584732	1353053	1231679	1316590	1268142	13289	10131	5.15	3.92	1.23
2008	2573077	1344445	1228632	1289450	1283627	14612	11183	5.67	4.34	1.33
2009	2573145	1346229	1226918	1296755	1276390	14447	11285	5.61	4.39	1.22
2010	2607184	1376580	1230604			19205	10572	6.30	4.08	2.22
2011	2613724	1372606	1241118	1244796	1368928	13838	12198	5.33	4.70	0.63
2012	2648636	1390548	1258088	1192468	1456168	14916	14794	5.67	5.62	0.05

3-13 按县、市分列的团场户数、人口数

Household and Population of Regiment Farms by City and County

(2012 年)

团 场	Regiment Farm	户数(户) Number of Households (household)	人口数(人) Population (person)
总 计	**Total**	**629572**	**1784492**
乌鲁木齐市	**Urumqi City**	**22478**	**60520**
沙依巴克区	Shayibake District	9349	26843
104 团	No.104 Regiment Farm	7359	20931
西山农场	Xishan Farm	1990	5912
头屯河区	Tou Tunhe District	13129	33677
三平农场	Sanping Farm	3451	11265
五一农场	MayIst Farm	4143	11032
头屯河农场	Tou Tunhe Farm	5535	11380
克拉玛依市	**Karamay City**	**6765**	**18829**
136 团	No.136 Regiment Farm	3551	10140
137 团	No.137 Regiment Farm	3214	8689
石河子市	**Shihezi City**	**19513**	**54478**
152 团	No.152 Regiment Farm	2645	7921
石河子总场	General Shihezi Farm	16868	46557
吐鲁番地区	**Turpan Administrative Offices**	**1692**	**5818**
吐鲁番市	Turpan City	1692	5818
221 团	No.221 Regiment Farm	1692	5818
哈密地区	**Hami [Kumul] Administrative Offices**	**24927**	**77202**
哈密市	Hami [Kumul] City	20445	63201
红星一场	Red Star No.1 Farm	3371	8584
红星二场	Red Star No.2 Farm	2906	6558
红星四场	Red Star No.4 Farm	2556	7765
黄田农场	Huangtian Farm	3132	10731
火箭农场	Huojian Farm	5312	18857
柳树泉农场	Liu Shuquan Farm	3168	10706
巴里坤哈萨克自治县	Barkol Kazak AutonomousCounty	3485	11541
红山农场	Hongshan Farm	3485	11541
伊吾县	Yiwu [Araturuk] County	997	2460
淖毛湖农场	Zhuo Maohu Farm	997	2460
昌吉回族自治州	**Changji Hui Autonomous Prefecture**	**123477**	**322212**
五家渠市	Wujiaqu City	16655	44246
101 团	No.101 Regiment Farm	3869	11245
102 团	No.102 Regiment Farm	6232	17521
103 团	No.103 Regiment Farm	6554	15480
昌吉市	Changji City	8654	24956
共青团农场	Communist League Farm	3293	10884
军户农场	Junhu Farm	5361	14072
呼图壁县	Hutubi County	29807	77775
105 团	No.105 Regiment Farm	4478	13524
106 团	No.106 Regiment Farm	2977	6138
芳草湖农场	Fang Caohu Farm	22352	58113
玛纳斯县	Manas County	42350	109640
147 团	No.147 Regiment Farm	6127	16035
148 团	No.148 Regiment Farm	9876	26332
149 团	No.149 Regiment Farm	6703	16656
150 团	No.150 Regiment Farm	6631	14176
新湖农场	Xinhu Farm	13013	36441
奇台县	Qitai County	11415	30911
奇台农场	Qitai Farm	10519	27354
北塔山牧场	Bei Tashan Ranch	896	3557
阜康市	Fukang City	9463	22081
222 团	No.222 Regiment Farm	4539	11212
土墩子农场	Tu Dunzi Farm	2051	5190
六运湖农场	Liu Yunhu Farm	2873	5679
吉木萨尔县	Jimsar County	5133	12603
红旗农场	Red Flag Farm	5133	12603
伊犁哈萨克自治州	**Ili Kazak Autonomous Prefecture**	**226511**	**597164**
伊犁州直属县(市)	**Counties (Cities) Direct UnderIli Prefecture**	**71653**	**195931**
奎屯市	Kuytun City	8922	20058
131 团	No.131 Regiment Farm	8922	20058
伊宁县	Yining [Gulja] County	4035	10027
70 团	No.70 Regiment Farm	4035	10027
察布查尔锡伯自治县	Qapqal Xibe Autonomous County	9026	26651
67 团	No.67 Regiment Farm	3589	12529
68 团	No.68 Regiment Farm	3125	7863
69 团	No.69 Regiment Farm	2312	6259
霍城县	Huocheng [Korgas] County	28203	80895
61 团	No.61 Regiment Farm	4099	11392
62 团	No.62 Regiment Farm	5055	15807
63 团	No.63 Regiment Farm	3282	8536
64 团	No.64 Regiment Farm	6922	20692

注：总计中包括农一师的阿拉尔农场、南口农场和幸福城农场，三个农场共计 7121 户、23442 人。

Note: Total in this table includes Alaer,Nankou and Xinfu farms of division 1,there are7121 households and 23442 persons in this three farms.

3-13 续表 1 Continued

团 场	Regiment Farm	户数（户） Number of Households (household)	人口数（人） Popula-Tion (person)
66 团	No.66 Regiment Farm	8845	24468
巩留县	Gongliu [Tokkuztara] County	2822	7220
73 团	No.73 Regiment Farm	2822	7220
新源县	Xinyuan [Kunes] County	8032	20715
71 团	No.71 Regiment Farm	4117	11018
72 团	No.72 Regiment Farm	3915	9697
昭苏县	Zhaosu [Mongolkure] County	7643	21449
74 团	No.74 Regiment Farm	1176	3063
75 团	No.75 Regiment Farm	1085	2821
76 团	No.76 Regiment Farm	3435	9158
77 团	No.77 Regiment Farm	1947	6407
特克斯县	Tekes County	1642	4381
78 团	No.78 Regiment Farm	1642	4381
尼勒克县	Nilka County	1328	4535
79 团	No.79 Regiment Farm	1328	4535
塔城地区	**Tacheng [Tarbagatai] Administrative Offices**	**138463**	**357794**
塔城市	Tacheng City	4978	14661
163 团	No.163 Regiment Farm	3068	9067
164 团	No.164 Regiment Farm	1910	5594
额敏县	Emin [Dorbiljin] County	11134	30217
165 团	No.165 Regiment Farm	1676	5254
166 团	No.166 Regiment Farm	2393	7556
167 团	No.167 Regiment Farm	1969	5498
168 团	No.168 Regiment Farm	3873	8731
团结农场	Tuanjie Farm	1223	3178
乌苏市	Usu City	52788	138275
123 团	No.123 Regiment Farm	9143	23573
124 团	No.124 Regiment Farm	8180	19244
125 团	No.125 Regiment Farm	7083	18272
126 团	No.126 Regiment Farm	3929	12280
127 团	No.127 Regiment Farm	5341	14771
128 团	No.128 Regiment Farm	5494	15998
129 团	No.129 Regiment Farm	6059	16113
130 团	No.130 Regiment Farm	7559	18024
沙湾县	Shawan County	64397	159775
121 团	No.121 Regiment Farm	15175	38829
133 团	No.133 Regiment Farm	8050	22383
134 团	No.134 Regiment Farm	8624	19145
141 团	No.141 Regiment Farm	3879	9066
142 团	No.142 Regiment Farm	9600	26065
143 团	No.143 Regiment Farm	14024	32429
144 团	No.144 Regiment Farm	5045	11858
托里县	Toli County	827	2793
170 团	No.170 Regiment Farm	827	2793
裕民县	Yumin [Qagantokay] County	1962	5302
161 团	No.161 Regiment Farm	1962	5302
和布克赛尔蒙古自治县	Hoboksar Mongol Autonomous County	2377	6771
184 团	No.184 Regiment Farm	2377	6771
阿勒泰地区	**Altay Administrative Offices**	**16395**	**43439**
阿勒泰市	Altay City	3334	9658
181 团	No.181 Regiment Farm	3334	9658
福海县	Fuhai [Burultokay] County	11003	28165
182 团	No.182 Regiment Farm	1626	4649
183 团	No.183 Regiment Farm	3123	8045
187 团	No.187 Regiment Farm	2286	6018
188 团	No.188 Regiment Farm	3968	9453
哈巴河县	Habahe [Kaba] County	1193	3256
185 团	No.185 Regiment Farm	1193	3256
吉木乃县	Jeminay County	865	2360
186 团	No.186 Regiment Farm	865	2360
博尔塔拉蒙古自治州	**Bortala Mongol Autonomous Prefecture**	**29870**	**91002**
博乐市	Bole [Bortala] City	18039	57289
81 团	No.81 Regiment Farm	3394	10899
84 团	No.84 Regiment Farm	2132	7325
86 团	No.86 Regiment Farm	4822	15038
89 团	No.89 Regiment Farm	4855	14981
90 团	No.90 Regiment Farm	2836	9046
精河县	Jinghe [Jing] County	8738	25225
83 团	No.83 Regiment Farm	7266	21492
91 团	No.91 Regiment Farm	1472	3733
温泉县	Wenquan [Araxang] County	3093	8488
87 团	No.87 Regiment Farm	1587	4284

3-13 续表 2 Continued

团场	Regiment Farm	户数(户) Number of Households (household)	人口数(人) Population (person)	团场	Regiment Farm	户数(户) Number of Households (household)	人口数(人) Population (person)
88 团	No.88 Regiment Farm	1506	4204	乌什县	Wushi [Uxturpan] County	2412	5938
巴音郭楞蒙古自治州	**Bayangol Mongol Autonomous Prefecture**	**49341**	**136364**	4 团	No.4 Regiment Farm	2412	5938
库尔勒市	Korla City	10748	30412	阿瓦提县	Awat County	4929	14507
29 团	No.29 Regiment Farm	7836	21602	3 团	No.3 Regiment Farm	4929	14507
30 团	No.30 Regiment Farm	2912	8810	克孜勒苏柯尔克孜自治州	**Kizilsu Kirgiz Autonomous Prefecture**	**1199**	**4538**
尉犁县	Yuli [Lopnur] County	11599	32034	阿图什市	Artux City	926	3668
31 团	No.31 Regiment Farm	3250	8778	红旗农场	Red Flag Farm	926	3668
33 团	No.33 Regiment Farm	4903	12604	乌恰县	Wuqia [Ulugqat] County	273	870
34 团	No.34 Regiment Farm	3446	10652	托云牧场	Tuoyun Ranch	273	870
若羌县	Ruoqiang [Qarkilik] County	2462	7632	喀什地区	**Kashgar [Kaxgar] Administrative Offices**	**49986**	**185521**
36 团	No.36 Regiment Farm	2462	7632	疏勒县	Shule County	2141	6178
焉耆回族自治县	Yanji Hui Autonomous County	4531	10869	41 团	No.41 Regiment Farm	2141	6178
27 团	No.27 Regiment Farm	4531	10869	英吉莎县	Yengisar County	426	1530
和静县	Hejing County	12996	35429	东风农场	Dong Feng Farm	426	1530
21 团	No.21 Regiment Farm	3835	10349	叶城县	Yecheng [Kagilik] County	335	1265
22 团	No.22 Regiment Farm	6248	17504	叶城牧场	Yechen Ranch	335	1265
223 团	No.223 Regiment Farm	2913	7576	麦盖提县	Makit County	9192	30293
和硕县	Hoxud County	4115	11675	45 团	No.45 Regiment Farm	7951	26766
24 团	No.24 Regiment Farm	4115	11675	46 团	No.46 Regiment Farm	1241	3527
博湖县	Bohu [Bagrax] County	2145	5328	岳普湖县	Yopurga County	1268	3160
25 团	No.25 Regiment Farm	2145	5328	42 团	No.42 Regiment Farm	1268	3160
且末县	Qiemo County	745	2985	伽师县	Jiashi [Payzawat] County	3598	11536
38 团	No.38 Regiment Farm	745	2985	伽师总场	General Jiashi Farm	3598	11536
阿克苏地区	**Aksu Administrative Offices**	**55375**	**168699**	巴楚县	Bachu [Maralbexi] County	33026	131559
阿克苏市	Aksu City	39504	119922	44 团	No.44 Regiment Farm	6996	25472
1 团	No.1 Regiment Farm	6775	20595	48 团	No.48 Regiment Farm	2038	6566
2 团	No.2 Regiment Farm	3457	10119	49 团	No.49 Regiment Farm	4150	14888
7 团	No.7 Regiment Farm	3840	11445	50 团	No.50 Regiment Farm	5530	18930
8 团	No.8 Regiment Farm	3346	10001	51 团	No.51 Regiment Farm	9322	44698
10 团	No.10 Regiment Farm	5400	16020	53 团	No.53 Regiment Farm	4990	21005
11 团	No.11 Regiment Farm	3193	9203	和田地区	**Hotan Administrative Offices**	**11317**	**38703**
12 团	No.12 Regiment Farm	2639	8043	墨玉县	Moyu [Karakax] County	4188	13116
13 团	No.13 Regiment Farm	3862	13906	47 团	No.47 Regiment Farm	1464	4045
14 团	No.14 Regiment Farm	2662	7827	224 团	No.224 Regiment Farm	2724	9071
16 团	No.16 Regiment Farm	4330	12763	皮山县	Pishan [Guma] County	6369	23670
温宿县	Wensu [Onsu] County	8530	28332	皮山农场	Pishan Farm	6369	23670
5 团	No.5 Regiment Farm	5768	18598	策勒县	Qira County	760	1917
6 团	No.6 Regiment Farm	2762	9734	一牧场	No.1Ranch	760	1917

3-14 主要年份按三次产业分的就业人员

Number of Employed Persons by Three Strata of Industry in Main Years

单位：万人 (10 000 persons)

年 份 Year	经济活动人口 Economically Active Population	就业人员合计 Total Number of Employed persons	第一产业 Primary Industry	第二产业 Secondary Industry
1978		491.25	353.99	70.42
1980		506.35	354.49	75.12
1985		565.81	363.24	89.64
1990		617.70	378.47	107.42
1995		676.00	388.16	124.21
1996		684.00	390.98	119.39
1997		715.40	421.30	105.40
1998		680.92	387.80	106.22
1999		694.34	385.57	104.51
2000		672.50	387.90	92.70
2001	697.45	685.38	388.19	92.19
2002	714.17	701.49	391.84	95.82
2003	734.02	721.27	397.20	95.69
2004	755.36	744.49	403.31	98.49
2005	802.75	791.62	408.00	122.81
2006	823.73	811.75	414.45	111.28
2007	842.12	830.42	417.73	118.34
2008	859.35	847.58	421.32	120.05
2009	878.01	866.15	427.48	127.28
2010	905.64	894.65	438.13	132.75
2011	964.46	953.34	463.91	149.04
2012	1022.29	1010.44	492.36	157.71

年 份 Year		构成(合计=100) (%) Composition in Percentage (total=100)(%)		
	第三产业 Tertiary Industry	第一产业 Primary Industry	第二产业 Secondary Industry	第三产业 Tertiary Industry
1978	66.84	72.06	14.33	13.61
1980	76.74	70.01	14.84	15.15
1985	112.93	64.20	15.84	19.96
1990	131.81	61.27	17.39	21.34
1995	163.63	57.42	18.37	24.21
1996	173.63	57.16	17.45	25.39
1997	188.70	58.89	14.73	26.38
1998	186.90	56.95	15.60	27.45
1999	204.26	55.53	15.05	29.42
2000	191.90	57.68	13.78	28.54
2001	205.00	56.64	13.45	29.91
2002	213.83	55.86	13.66	30.48
2003	228.38	55.07	13.27	31.66
2004	242.69	54.17	13.23	32.60
2005	260.81	51.54	15.51	32.95
2006	286.02	51.06	13.71	35.23
2007	294.35	50.30	14.25	35.45
2008	306.21	49.71	14.16	36.13
2009	311.39	49.35	14.70	35.95
2010	323.77	48.97	14.84	36.19
2011	340.39	48.66	15.63	35.71
2012	360.37	48.73	15.61	35.66

3-15 分地区全部就业人员(年末数)

Number of Employed Persons at Year-end by Region

单位：人 (2012 年) (person)

项 目 Item	合 计 Total	私 营 Private	个 体 Self-employed Individuals
总 计 Total	**10104431**	**851418**	**972038**
乌鲁木齐市 Urumqi City	1181164	197347	192926
克拉玛依市 Karamay City	238160	27979	36712
石河子市 Shihezi City	167431	31658	28691
吐鲁番地区 Turpan Administrative Offices	404793	33270	34156
哈密地区 Hami [Kumul] Administrative Offices	248544	20210	32750
昌吉回族自治州 Changji Hui Autonomous Prefecture	807922	104034	82551
伊犁哈萨克自治州 Ili Kazak Autonomous Prefecture	2117998	141200	186081
伊犁州直属县(市) Counties (Cities) Direct Under Ili Prefecture	1175135	68616	106927
塔城地区 Tacheng [Tarbagatai] Administrative Offices	613310	40994	47837
阿勒泰地区 Altay Administrative Offices	329553	31590	31317
博尔塔拉蒙古自治州 Bortala Mongol Autonomous Prefecture	246497	25599	24518
巴音郭楞蒙古自治州 Bayangol Mongol Autonomous Prefecture	629791	84366	88274
阿克苏地区 Aksu Administrative Offices	1202344	80088	97817
克孜勒苏柯尔克孜自治州 Kizilsu Kirgiz Autonomous Prefecture	243750	10900	11363
喀什地区 Kashgar [Kaxgar] Administrative Offices	1770600	66718	96087
和田地区 Hotan Administrative Offices	845437	28049	60112

3-16 主要年份城镇登记失业人数及失业率

Number of Registered Unemployed Persons in Urban Areas and Unemployment Rate in Main Years

单位：万人（%） (10 000 persons)

年 份 Year	城镇登记失业人数 Number of Registered Unemployment Persons in Urban Area	城镇登记失业率(%) Registered Unemployment Rate in Urban Areas (%)	年 份 Year	城镇登记失业人数 Number of Registered Unemployment Persons in Urban Area	城镇登记失业率(%) Registered Unemployment Rate in Urban Areas (%)
1980	13.55	7.5	2001	12.07	3.7
1985	4.04	1.9	2002	12.68	3.6
1990	9.60	3.8	2003	12.75	3.8
1991	9.95	3.8	2004	10.87	3.8
1992	9.81	3.7	2005	11.13	3.9
1993	9.50	3.6	2006	11.98	3.9
1994	10.00	3.8	2007	11.70	3.9
1995	10.24	3.9	2008	11.77	3.7
1996	9.81	3.8	2009	11.86	3.8
1997	10.20	3.8	2010	10.99	3.2
1998	11.06	3.9	2011	11.12	3.2
1999	10.30	3.7	2012	11.85	3.4
2000	11.00	3.8			

3-17 各地、州、市城镇登记失业率

Registered Unemployment Rate in Urban Area by Prefecture, Autonomous Prefecture and City

单位：%

地 区	Region	2011	2012
总 计	**Total**	**3.22**	**3.39**
乌鲁木齐市	Urumqi City	3.93	3.48
克拉玛依市	Karamay City	0.71	0.69
石河子市	Shihezi City	1.98	2.01
吐鲁番地区	Turpan Administrative Offices	3.28	3.19
哈密地区	Hami [Kumul] Administrative Offices	2.93	2.70
昌吉回族自治州	Changji Hui Autonomous Prefecture	3.23	2.75
伊犁州直属县(市)	Counties (Cities) Direct Under Ili Prefecture	3.82	2.76
塔城地区	Tacheng [Tarbagatai] Administrative Offices	0.71	0.99
阿勒泰地区	Altay Administrative Offices	2.80	2.70
博尔塔拉蒙古自治州	Bortala Mongol Autonomous Prefecture	3.98	3.72
巴音郭楞蒙古自治州	Bayangol Mongol Autonomous Prefecture	2.75	2.89
阿克苏地区	Aksu Administrative Offices	2.73	2.42
克孜勒苏柯尔克孜自治州	Kizilsu Kirgiz Autonomous Prefecture	2.89	2.09
喀什地区	Kashgar [Kaxgar] Administrative Offices	5.50	3.98
和田地区	Hotan Administrative Offices	2.81	2.35

3-18 各地区按行业分城镇单位就业人员(年末数)

Number of Employed Persons in Urban Units at Year-end by Sectors and Region

单位：人 (2012 年) (person)

项 目	Item	合 计 Total	国有单位 State-owned Units	城镇集体 Urban Collective-Owned Units	其他单位 Units of Other Types Of Ownership
总 计	**Total**	**2887710**	**2008191**	**33861**	**845658**
按国民经济行业分组	**Grouped by Sectors**				
农林牧渔业	Farming, Forestry, Animal Husbandry and Fishery	562081	541212	52	20817
采 矿 业	Mining	188505	41648	633	146224
制 造 业	Manufacturing	305850	32464	3888	269498
电力、燃气及水的生产和供应业	Production and Supply of Electricity, Gas and Water	75908	32995	142	42771
建 筑 业	Construction	223839	62695	5372	155772
批发和零售业	Wholesale and Retail Trades	82209	28609	4786	48814
交通运输、仓储和邮政业	Traffic Transport, Storage and Post	125981	95592	1225	29164
住宿和餐饮业	Hotels and Catering Services	28012	13493	957	13562
信息传输、计算机服务和软件业	Information Transmission, Computer Servcie and Software	26395	10108	308	15979
金 融 业	Financial Intermediation	81278	29471	9956	41851
房地产业	Real Estate	31876	8094	573	23209
租赁和商务服务业	Leasing and Business Services	53533	29571	3818	20144
科学研究、技术服务和地质勘查业	Scientific Research, Technical Service and Geological Prospecting	60677	53105	137	7435
水利、环境和公共设施管理业	Management of Water Conservancy, Environment and PublicFacility	54227	50459	1	3767
居民服务和其他服务业	Services to households and Other Services	5974	4596	388	990
教 育	Education	359779	356814	121	2844
卫生、社会保障和社会福利业	Health, Social Security and Social Welfare	157753	155472	1494	787
文化、体育和娱乐业	Culture, Sports and Entertainment	29474	27513		1961
公共管理和社会组织	Public Management and Social Organizations	434359	434280	10	69
按地区分	**By Region**				
乌鲁木齐市	Urumqi City	652679	391532	9223	251924
克拉玛依市	Karamay City	172142	58832	2019	111291
吐鲁番地区	Turpan Administrative Offices	79505	51602	597	27306
哈密地区	Hami [Kumul] Administrative Offices	92513	61923	783	29807
昌吉回族自治州	Changji Hui Autonomous Prefecture	206277	136980	3005	66292
伊犁哈萨克自治州	Ili Kazak Autonomous Prefecture	616041	504491	5570	105980
伊犁州直属县(市)	Counties (Cities) Direct Under Ili Prefecture	281325	210218	3199	67908
塔城地区	Tacheng [Tarbagatai] Administrative Offices	217969	195002	1608	21359
阿勒泰地区	Altay Administrative Offices	116747	99271	763	16713
博尔塔拉蒙古自治州	Bortala Mongol Autonomous Prefecture	95695	87365	849	7481
巴音郭楞蒙古自治州	Bayangol Mongol Autonomous Prefecture	205204	140294	2627	62283
阿克苏地区	Aksu Administrative Offices	209609	148458	2206	58945
克孜勒苏柯尔克孜自治州	Kizilsu Kirgiz Autonomous Prefecture	46910	44922	415	1573
喀什地区	Kashgar [Kaxgar] Administrative Offices	224851	176741	5671	42439
和田地区	Hotan Administrative Offices	98944	90595	617	7732
石河子市	Shihezi City	98279	52729	279	45271
阿拉尔市	Aral City	42240	29982		12258
图木舒克市	Tumxuk City	17412	14713		2699
五家渠市	Wujiaqu City	29409	17032		12377

3-19 各地区城镇单位在岗职工（含劳务派遣工）人数

Number of Staff and Workers(including the dispatched workers) in Urban Units at Year-end by Region

单位：万人 (10 000 persons)

年 份 Year	地 区 Region	合 计 Total	国有单位 State-owned Units	城镇集体 Urban Collective-owned Units	其他单位 Units of Other Types of Ownership
	2002	242.26	189.26	9.31	43.69
	2003	237.94	184.02	7.55	46.37
	2004	235.97	182.80	6.43	46.74
	2005	237.84	181.92	5.96	49.96
	2006	238.95	182.91	5.19	50.85
	2007	239.45	181.46	4.58	53.41
	2008	239.16	180.29	3.64	55.23
	2009	239.54	175.90	3.54	60.10
	2010	245.48	178.40	3.00	64.08
	2011	270.77	187.78	3.00	79.99
	2012	280.33	195.47	3.26	81.60
乌鲁木齐市	Urumqi City	63.88	38.66	0.91	24.31
克拉玛依市	Karamay City	16.76	5.73	0.19	10.84
吐鲁番地区	Turpan Administrative Offices	7.57	4.91	0.05	2.61
哈密地区	Hami [Kumul] Administrative Offices	9.00	6.09	0.05	2.86
昌吉回族自治州	Changji Hui Autonomous Prefecture	19.87	13.38	0.29	6.20
伊犁哈萨克自治州	Ili Kazak Autonomous Prefecture	60.40	49.63	0.56	10.21
伊犁州直属县(市)	Counties (Cities) Direct Under Ili Prefecture	27.77	20.85	0.32	6.60
塔城地区	Tacheng [Tarbagatai] Administrative Offices	21.46	19.28	0.16	2.02
阿勒泰地区	Altay Administrative Offices	11.17	9.50	0.08	1.59
博尔塔拉蒙古自治州	Bortala Mongol Autonomous Prefecture	9.38	8.57	0.08	0.73
巴音郭楞蒙古自治州	Bayangol Mongol Autonomous Prefecture	19.18	13.01	0.27	5.90
阿克苏地区	Aksu Administrative Offices	20.91	14.81	0.22	5.88
克孜勒苏柯尔克孜自治州	Kizilsu Kirgiz Autonomous Prefecture	4.27	4.09	0.04	0.14
喀什地区	Kashgar [Kaxgar] Administrative Offices	21.64	17.11	0.52	4.01
和田地区	Hotan Administrative Offices	8.84	8.13	0.05	0.66
石河子市	Shihezi City	9.80	5.25	0.03	4.52
阿拉尔市	Aral City	4.22	2.99		1.23
图木舒克市	Tumxuk City	1.74	1.47		0.27
五家渠市	Wujiaqu City	2.87	1.64		1.23

3-20 分行业城镇单位在岗职工(含劳务派遣工)人数

Number of Staff and Workers(including the dispatched workers) in Urban Units at Year-end by Sectors

单位：人 (2012 年) (person)

项目	Item	合计 Total	国有单位 State-owned Units	城镇集体 Urban Collective-owned Units	其他单位 Units of Other Types of Ownership
总计	**Total**	**2803299**	**1954759**	**32565**	**815975**
农林牧渔业	**Farming, Forestry, Animal Husbandry and Fishery**	**549662**	**528880**	**52**	**20730**
农业	Farming	450668	436512	35	14121
林业	Forestry	7559	6513		1046
畜牧业	Animal Husbandry	71388	67776	9	3603
渔业	Fishery	253	189		64
农林牧渔服务业	Services in Support of Agriculture	19794	17890	8	1896
采矿业	**Mining**	**185765**	**41248**	**633**	**143884**
#煤炭开采和洗选业	Mining and Washing of Coal	53452	4258	500	48694
石油和天然气开采业	Extraction of Petroleum and Natural Gas	75314			75314
黑色金属矿采选业	Mining and Processing of Ferrous Metal Ores	6813	342		6471
有色金属矿采选业	Mining and Processing of Non-Ferrous Metal Ores	6694	564		6130
非金属矿采选业	Mining and Processing of Nonmetal Ores	3273	1034	130	2109
开采辅助活动	Mining Activities	40207	35050	3	5154
其他采矿业	Mining of Other Ores	12			12
制造业	**Manufacturing**	**300560**	**32122**	**3805**	**264633**
#农副食品加工业	Processing of Food from Agriculture Products	21892	1192	20	20680
食品制造业	Manufacture of Food	15336	706	126	14504
酒、饮料和精制茶制造业	Manufacture of Beverage	12099	384	50	11665
烟草制品业	Manufacture of Tobacco	980	980		
纺织业	Manufacture of Textile	22975	3080	34	19861
纺织服装、服饰业	Manufacture of Textile Wearing Apparel, Footware and Caps	1835	247	67	1521
皮革、毛皮、羽毛及其制品和制鞋业	Manufacture of Leather, Fur, Feather and Related Products	230		5	225
木材加工和木、竹、藤、棕、草制品业	Processing of Timber, Manufacture of Wood, Bamboo, Rattan, Palm and Straw Products	567	4	9	554
家具制造业	Manufacture of Furniture	108	51	15	42
造纸及纸制品业	Manufacture of Paper and Paper Products	4544	26	107	4411
印刷业和记录媒介的复制业	Printing and Record Medium Reproduction	3600	1845	59	1696
文教、工美、体育和娱乐用品制造业	Manufacture of Articles For Culture, Education and Sport Activities	172		5	167
石油加工、炼焦及核燃料加工业	Oil processing, Refining and Nuclear-fuel processing	39998	10552	6	29440
化学原料及化学制品制造业	Raw Chemical Materials and Chemical Products	44129	3247	695	40187
医药制造业	Manufacture of Medicines	3302	539		2763
化学纤维制造业	Manufacture of Chemical Fibers	3049			3049
橡胶和塑料制品业	Plastic Products	11989	325	325	11339
非金属矿物制品业	Manufacture of Non-metal Mineral Products	37383	2498	1137	33748
黑色金属冶炼及压延加工业	Smelting and Pressing of Ferrous Metals	34167	358	743	33066
有色金属冶炼及压延加工业	Smelting and Pressing of Nonferrous Metals	11740	774	86	10880
金属制品业	Smelting and Pressing of Ferrous Metals	6140	1248	115	4777
通用设备制造业	Manufacturing of Equipment for General Purpose	1714	120	13	1581
专用设备制造业	Manufacture of Special Purpose Machinery	4050	1454	63	2533

3-20 续表 1 Continued

单位：人 (person)

项　目	Item	合 计 Total	国有单位 State-owned Units	城镇集体 Urban Collective-owned Units	其他单位 Units of Other Types of Ownership
汽车制造业	Manufacture of Metal Car	2247	399		1848
铁路、船舶、航空航天和其他运输设备制造业	Manufacture of Transport Equipment	1775	1775		
电气机械和器材制造业	Manufacture of Electrical Machinery and Equipment	6072	190	55	5827
计算机、通信和其他电子设备制造业	Manufacture of Communication Equipment, Computers and Other Electronic Equipment	4335			4335
仪器仪表制造业	Manufacture of Measuring Instruments	178			178
其他制造业	Other Electronic Equipment	3118			3118
废弃资源综合利用业	Recycling and Disposal of Waste	72	29		43
金属制品、机械和设备修理业	Manufacture of Electrical Machinery and Equipment	764	99	70	595
电力、燃气及水的生产和供应业	**Production and Distribution of Electricity, Gas and Water**	**75293**	**32856**	**142**	**42295**
电力、热力的生产和供应业	Production and Distribution of Electric Power, Thermal Power	63926	28142	52	35732
燃气生产和供应业	Production and Distribution of Gas	3416	54		3362
水的生产和供应业	Production and Distribution of Water	7951	4660	90	3201
建 筑 业	**Construction**	**216673**	**60666**	**5079**	**150928**
房屋建筑业	Construction of Buildings	132499	28263	2185	102051
土木工程建筑业	Construction of Civil Engineering	65149	25725	2068	37356
建筑安装业	Building Installation	14295	2505	822	10968
建筑装饰和其他建筑业	Other Construction	4730	4173	4	553
批发和零售业	**Wholesale and Retail Trades**	**80560**	**28075**	**4242**	**48243**
批发业	Wholesale Trades	51544	20409	3781	27354
零售业	Retail Trades	29016	7666	461	20889
交通运输、仓储和邮政业	**Transport Storage and Post**	**125538**	**95222**	**1217**	**29099**
铁路运输业	Railway Transport	41961	41943		18
道路运输业	Road Transportat	41437	19911	315	21211
航空运输业	Air Transportat	11854	5951		5903
管道运输业	Via Pipe Transportat	5341	4984		357
装卸搬运和运输代理业	Loading and Discharging; Other Transportation Service	9128	7054	897	1177
仓储业	Storage	3914	3476	5	433
邮政业	Post	11903	11903		
住宿和餐饮业	**Hotels and Catering Services**	**26988**	**12822**	**944**	**13222**
住宿业	Hotels	21486	10845	857	9784
餐饮业	Catering Services	5502	1977	87	3438
信息传输、软件和信息技术服务业	**Information Transmission, Computer Service and Software**	**26101**	**9987**	**308**	**15806**
电信、广播电视和卫星传输服务	Telecommunication and Other I.T Transmission Service	23847	9752	308	13787
互联网和相关服务	Computer Service	799	75		724
软件和信息技术服务业	Software	1455	160		1295
金 融 业	**Financial Intermediation**	**65161**	**27566**	**9783**	**27812**
货币金融服务业	Banking	48390	23615	9385	15390
资本市场服务业	Security Activities	997	224		773
保险业	Insurance	15359	3633	364	11362

3-20 续表 2 Continued

单位：人 (person)

项　目	Item	合 计 Total	国有单位 State-owned Units	城镇集体 Urban Collective-owned Units	其他单位 Units of Other Types of Ownership
其他金融活动	Other Finance Activities	415	94	34	287
房地产业	**Real Estate**	**31066**	**7656**	**543**	**22867**
#房地产开发经营	Development and Management of Real Estate	12878	1058	60	11760
物业管理	Real Estate Management	15216	5350	253	9613
房地产中介服务	Agency Service for Real Estate	715	272	5	438
租赁和商务服务业	**Leasing and Business Service**	**52041**	**28777**	**3812**	**19452**
租赁业	Leasing	947	553		394
商务服务业	Business Service	51094	28224	3812	19058
科学研究、技术服务和地质勘查业	**Scientific Research, Technology Service and Geological Prospecting**	**58494**	**51663**	**50**	**6781**
研究与试验发展	Research and Experiment Development	6598	6396		202
专业技术服务业	Professional Technique Service	42194	35843	50	6301
科技交流和推广服务业	Services of Science and Technology Exchanges and Promotion	9702	9424		278
水利、环境和公共设施管理业	**Management of Water Conservancy, Environment and Public Facility**	**51884**	**48143**	**1**	**3740**
水利管理业	Management of Water Conservance	20581	20542		39
生态保护和环境治理业	Environmental Management	2861	2679		182
公共设施管理业	Management of Public Facilities	28442	24922	1	3519
居民服务、修理和其他服务业	**Service to Households and Other Services**	**5916**	**4590**	**383**	**943**
居民服务业	Services to Households	4808	3985	115	708
机动车、电子产品和日用产品修理业	Repair of motor car,electruical products	713	348	181	184
其他服务业	Other Services	395	257	87	51
教　育	**Education**	**354105**	**351209**	**121**	**2775**
#初等教育	Junior Education	132200	131521		679
中等教育	Secondary Education	172583	172100	15	468
高等教育	Senior Education	28665	28665		
卫生和社会工作	**Health, Social Security and Social Welfare**	**152973**	**150786**	**1440**	**747**
卫　生	Health	147107	144964	1440	703
社会工作	Social Security	5866	5822		44
文化、体育和娱乐业	**Culture, Sports and Entertainment**	**28960**	**27011**		**1949**
新闻和出版业	Journalism and Publishing Activities	6265	4570		1695
广播、电视、电影和影视录音制作业	Broadcasting, Movies, Televisions and Audiovisual Activities	10599	10592		7
文化艺术业	Culture and Art Activities	10640	10540		100
体　育	Sports	966	924		42
娱乐业	Entertainment	490	385		105
公共管理、社会保障和社会组织	**Public Management and Social Organization**	**415559**	**415480**	**10**	**69**
#中国共产党机关	Organs of Communist Party of China	21079	21079		
国家机构	Government Agencies	381999	381920	10	69
人民政协和民主党派	People's Political Consultative Conference and Democratic Parties	2579	2579		
社会保障	Social Security	3855	3855		
群众社团、社会团体和其他成员组织	Non-Governmental Organizations, Social Organizations and Religion Organizations	6047	6047		

3-21 各地、州、市分行业城镇单位在岗职工(含劳务派遣工)人数

Number of Staff and Workers in Urban Units at Year-end by Sector and Prefecture, Autonomous Prefecture and City(including the dispatched workers)

单位：人　　(2012 年)　　(person)

年份 Year	地区 Region	合计 Total	农林牧渔业 Farming, Forestry, Animal Husbandry and Fishery	采矿业 Mining	制造业 Manufacturing	电力、热力、燃气及水的生产和供应业 Production and Distribution of Power, Gas and Water
总　　计	**Total**	**2803299**	**549662**	**185765**	**300560**	**75293**
乌鲁木齐市	Urumqi City	638760	10872	19207	88538	20459
克拉玛依市	Karamay City	167545	8540	74708	29146	68
吐鲁番地区	Turpan Administrative Offices	75708	3160	26548	8026	2360
哈密地区	Hami [Kumul] Administrative Offices	90027	19314	14892	6060	3465
昌吉回族自治州	Changji Hui Autonomous Prefecture	198708	56653	6449	34689	7020
伊犁哈萨克自治州	Ili Kazak Autonomous Prefecture	604025	234012	14677	44136	13108
伊犁州直属县(市)	Counties (Cities) Direct Under Ili Prefecture	277749	69172	3443	31984	7357
塔城地区	Tacheng [Tarbagatai] Administrative Offices	214575	120975	5866	9644	3142
阿勒泰地区	Altay Administrative Offices	111701	43865	5368	2508	2609
博尔塔拉蒙古自治州	Bortala Mongol Autonomous Prefecture	93837	43656	246	4140	2265
巴音郭楞蒙古自治州	Bayangol Mongol Autonomous Prefecture	191774	44459	19852	20812	4751
阿克苏地区	Aksu Administrative Offices	209096	38970	8778	17447	5941
克孜勒苏柯尔克孜自治州	Kizilsu Kirgiz Autonomous Prefecture	42672	2206	11	761	464
喀什地区	Kashgar [Kaxgar] Administrative Offices	216407	17381	184	8491	6157
和田地区	Hotan Administrative Offices	88404	13078	213	836	2364
石河子市	Shihezi City	98027	12319		24827	4601
阿拉尔市	Aral City	42237	28094		3080	351
图木舒克市	Tumxuk City	17409	9132		1292	496
五家渠市	Wujiaqu City	28663	7816		8279	1423

年份 Year	地区 Region	建筑业 Construction	批发和零售业 Wholesale and Retail	交通运输、仓储和邮政业 Trades Transport Storage and Post	住宿和餐饮业 Hotels and Catering Services	信息传输、软件和信息技术服务业 Information Transmission, Computer Servcie and Software
总　　计	**Total**	**216673**	**80560**	**125538**	**26988**	**26101**
乌鲁木齐市	Urumqi City	107767	34416	88219	14518	8953
克拉玛依市	Karamay City	13260	1762	2559	730	1325
吐鲁番地区	Turpan Administrative Offices	1117	1559	1514	453	921
哈密地区	Hami [Kumul] Administrative Offices	1349	1927	1291	960	990
昌吉回族自治州	Changji Hui Autonomous Prefecture	7208	4097	3234	389	1463
伊犁哈萨克自治州	Ili Kazak Autonomous Prefecture	15164	11873	10978	5842	4827
伊犁州直属县(市)	Counties (Cities) Direct Under Ili Prefecture	7512	8289	6409	3480	2453
塔城地区	Tacheng [Tarbagatai] Administrative Offices	4261	2269	2324	727	1096
阿勒泰地区	Altay Administrative Offices	3391	1315	2245	1635	1278
博尔塔拉蒙古自治州	Bortala Mongol Autonomous Prefecture	1155	1559	1651	455	604
巴音郭楞蒙古自治州	Bayangol Mongol Autonomous Prefecture	6879	4544	4545	1243	1792
阿克苏地区	Aksu Administrative Offices	10635	7357	3137	581	1697
克孜勒苏柯尔克孜自治州	Kizilsu Kirgiz Autonomous Prefecture	1249	362	1055	85	344
喀什地区	Kashgar [Kaxgar] Administrative Offices	22157	7209	5008	883	1077
和田地区	Hotan Administrative Offices	1850	1129	1027	343	874
石河子市	Shihezi City	22020	1174	1107	476	1189
阿拉尔市	Aral City	1688	1134	7		
图木舒克市	Tumxuk City	1907	24		30	
五家渠市	Wujiaqu City	1268	434	206		45

3-21 续表 Continued

单位：人　　　　(person)

年份 Year	地区 Region	金融业 Financial Intermedia-tion	房地产业 Real Estate	租赁和商务服务业 Leasing and Business Services	科学研究、技术服务业 Scientific Research, Technology Service and Geological Prospecting	水利、环境和公共设施管理业 Management of Water Conservancy, Environment and Public Facility
总　计	Total	**65161**	**31066**	**52041**	**58494**	**51884**
乌鲁木齐市	Urumqi City	18643	12587	19208	22313	5949
克拉玛依市	Karamay City	2850	3528	5385	777	1042
吐鲁番地区	Turpan Administrative Offices	1720	183	532	1228	802
哈密地区	Hami [Kumul] Administrative Offices	2753	369	722	2599	3759
昌吉回族自治州	Changji Hui Autonomous Prefecture	4974	2588	2860	4646	5867
伊犁哈萨克自治州	Ili Kazak Autonomous Prefecture	11841	4243	4805	9913	10104
伊犁州直属县(市)	Counties (Cities) Direct Under Ili Prefecture	6447	3314	3582	4628	4776
塔城地区	Tacheng [Tarbagatai] Administrative Offices	3067	525	570	2383	3346
阿勒泰地区	Altay Administrative Offices	2327	404	653	2902	1982
博尔塔拉蒙古自治州	Bortala Mongol Autonomous Prefecture	1588	385	5350	1268	1439
巴音郭楞蒙古自治州	Bayangol Mongol Autonomous Prefecture	4071	1462	3166	3711	5004
阿克苏地区	Aksu Administrative Offices	5273	1980	2931	3302	6071
克孜勒苏柯尔克孜自治州	Kizilsu Kirgiz Autonomous Prefecture	899	89	644	2091	538
喀什地区	Kashgar [Kaxgar] Administrative Offices	3687	2655	1442	3295	4515
和田地区	Hotan Administrative Offices	2281	149	578	1760	1346
石河子市	Shihezi City	3565	197	4025	1019	1873
阿拉尔市	Aral City			128	151	2655
图木舒克市	Tumxuk City			117	19	266
五家渠市	Wujiaqu City	1016	651	148	402	654

年份 Year	地区 Region	居民服务、修理和其他服务业 Service to Households and Other Services	教育 Education	卫生社会工作 Health, Social Security and Social Welfare	文化、体育和娱乐业 Culture, Sports and Entertainment	公共管理、社会保障和社会组织 Public Management and Social Organizations
总　计	Total	**5916**	**354105**	**152973**	**28960**	**415559**
乌鲁木齐市	Urumqi City	1651	49927	33215	11903	70415
克拉玛依市	Karamay City	85	6598	3081	466	11635
吐鲁番地区	Turpan Administrative Offices		9246	3160	549	12630
哈密地区	Hami [Kumul] Administrative Offices	249	9864	5023	962	13479
昌吉回族自治州	Changji Hui Autonomous Prefecture		21705	10839	1035	22992
伊犁哈萨克自治州	Ili Kazak Autonomous Prefecture	665	78869	31714	4702	92552
伊犁州直属县(市)	Counties (Cities) Direct Under Ili Prefecture	600	45197	18710	2563	47833
塔城地区	Tacheng [Tarbagatai] Administrative Offices	23	21198	8195	1212	23752
阿勒泰地区	Altay Administrative Offices	42	12474	4809	927	20967
博尔塔拉蒙古自治州	Bortala Mongol Autonomous Prefecture	8	9681	4024	808	13555
巴音郭楞蒙古自治州	Bayangol Mongol Autonomous Prefecture	105	21230	10947	1062	32139
阿克苏地区	Aksu Administrative Offices	132	33648	12724	1634	46858
克孜勒苏柯尔克孜自治州	Kizilsu Kirgiz Autonomous Prefecture	2738	10719	6614	971	10832
喀什地区	Kashgar [Kaxgar] Administrative Offices	130	62192	17090	2743	50111
和田地区	Hotan Administrative Offices	96	26220	6776	1357	26127
石河子市	Shihezi City	55	7720	5079	531	6250
阿拉尔市	Aral City		2858	1036	117	938
图木舒克市	Tumxuk City		1551	492		2083
五家渠市	Wujiaqu City	2	2077	1159	120	2963

3-22 分行业城镇单位女性就业人员（年末数）
Number of Female Employed in Urban Units at Year-end by Sectors

单位：人 (2012 年) (person)

项 目	Item	合 计 Total	国有单位 State-owned Units	城镇集体 Urban Collective-owned Units	其他单位 Units of Other Types of Ownership
总 计	**Total**	**1161242**	**877867**	**11693**	**271682**
农林牧渔业	Farming, Forestry, Animal Husbandry and Fishery	246687	238103	15	8569
采 矿 业	Mining	53173	8990	42	44141
制 造 业	Manufacturing	97621	11313	1384	84924
电力、热力、燃气及水生产和供应业	Production and Distribution of Electricity, Gas and Water	23040	9628	38	13374
建 筑 业	Construction	29313	6867	756	21690
批发和零售业	Wholesale and Retail Trades	32938	10798	1542	20598
交通运输、仓储和邮政业	Transport, Storage and Post	37794	27381	590	9823
住宿和餐饮业	Hotels and Catering Services	15640	7694	512	7434
信息传输、软件和信息技术服务业	Information Transmission, Computer Servcie and Software Industries	12195	4474	86	7635
金 融 业	Financial Intermediation	45674	15153	4258	26263
房地产业	Real Estate	14223	3850	211	10162
租赁和商务服务业	Leasing and Business Services	23072	12292	888	9892
科学研究、技术服务业	Scientific Research, Technology Service and Geological Prospecting	20361	18463	39	1859
水利、环境和公共设施管理业	Management of Water Conservancy, Environment and Public Facility	23640	21861		1779
居民服务、修理和其他服务业	Services to households and Other Services	3278	2713	213	352
教 育	Education	218388	216663	72	1653
卫生和社会工作	Health, Social Security and Social Welfare	106066	104517	1044	505
文化、体育和娱乐业	Culture, Sports and Entertainment	13546	12543		1003
公共管理、社会保障和社会组织	Public Management and Social Organizations	144593	144564	3	26

3-23 城镇单位在岗职工工资总额及构成
Total Wages of Staff and Workers and Its Composition in Urban Units

年份 Year	地区 Region	工资总额（万元） Total wages Bill(10 000 yuan)				构成(总计=100)(%) composition (total=100)(%)		
		合计 Total	国有单位 State-owned Units	城镇集体单位 Urban Collective-owned Units	其他单位 Units of Other Types of Ownership	国有单位 State-owned Units	城镇集体单位 Urban Collective -owned Units	其他单位 Units of Other Types of owner-ship
	1978	159409	148278	11131		93.0	7.0	
	1980	212446	196711	15735		92.6	7.4	
	1985	339110	304999	33789	322	89.9	10.0	0.1
	1990	668808	601300	65858	1650	90.0	9.8	0.2
	1995	1677257	1521670	135990	19597	90.7	8.1	1.2
	2000	2344694	2007823	125510	211361	85.6	5.4	9.0
	2001	2677431	2092155	105861	479415	78.1	4.0	17.9
	2002	2915398	2211411	93605	610382	75.9	3.2	20.9
	2003	3315399	2497369	77460	740570	75.3	2.3	22.4
	2004	3563312	2691462	78224	793626	75.5	2.2	22.3
	2005	3874068	2871542	75971	926555	74.1	2.0	23.9
	2006	4429959	3318694	77978	1033287	74.9	1.8	23.3
	2007	5332395	3951882	82215	1298298	74.1	1.5	24.4
	2008	6198976	4428784	84187	1686005	71.4	1.4	27.2
	2009	6912058	4796811	91488	2023759	69.4	1.3	29.3
	2010	8286857	5669760	105413	2511684	68.4	1.3	30.3
	2011	11034557	7021538	140410	3872609	63.6	1.3	35.1
	2012	13662181	8543738	174136	4944307	62.5	1.3	36.2
乌鲁木齐市	Urumqi City	3845062	2219341	54210	1571511	57.7	1.4	40.9
克拉玛依市	Karamay City	1245479	429543	7016	808920	34.5	0.6	64.9
吐鲁番地区	Turpan Administrative Offices	395416	258368	1763	135285	65.3	0.4	34.2
哈密地区	Hami [Kumul] Administrative Offices	395047	237380	1729	155938	60.1	0.4	39.5
昌吉回族自治州	Changji Hui Autonomous Prefecture	909379	588329	14650	306400	64.7	1.6	33.7
伊犁哈萨克自治州	Ili Kazak Autonomous Prefecture	2225596	1658013	28083	539499	74.5	1.3	24.2
伊犁州直属县(市)	Counties (Cities) Direct Under Ili Prefecture	1086007	736322	15293	334392	67.8	1.4	30.8
塔城地区	Tacheng [Tarbagatai] Administrative Offices	763184	636056	7292	119836	83.3	1.0	15.7
阿勒泰地区	Altay Administrative Offices	376404	285635	5498	85271	75.9	1.5	22.7
博尔塔拉蒙古自治州	Bortala Mongol Autonomous Prefecture	331083	289043	16678	25362	87.3	5.0	7.7
巴音郭楞蒙古自治州	Bayangol Mongol Autonomous Prefecture	1009348	529991	12845	466512	52.5	1.3	46.2
阿克苏地区	Aksu Administrative Offices	884094	535027	12418	336649	60.5	1.4	38.1
克孜勒苏柯尔克孜自治州	Kizilsu Kirgiz Autonomous Prefecture	169011	165109	1038	2864	97.7	0.6	1.7
喀什地区	Kashgar [Kaxgar] Administrative Offices	898442	711760	16441	170241	79.2	1.8	18.9
和田地区	Hotan Administrative Offices	429215	393929	4341	30945	91.8	1.0	7.2
石河子市	Shihezi City	617312	323394	2924	290994	52.4	0.5	47.1
阿拉尔市	Aral City	119527	87663		31864	73.3		26.7
图木舒克市	Tumxuk City	63471	52312		11159	82.4		17.6
五家渠市	Wujiaqu City	124700	64536		60164	51.8		48.2

注：含劳务派遣工.
Note: Including the dispatched workers.

3-24 主要年份城镇单位在岗职工工资总额指数
Indices of Total Wages of Staff and Workers in Urban Units in Main Years

年份 Year	指数(上年=100) Indices (preceding year=100)				指数(1978 年=100) Indices (1978=100)			
	合计 Total	国有单位 State-owned Units	城镇集体单位 Urban Collective-owned Units	其他单位 Units of Other Types of Ownership	合计 Total	国有单位 State-owned Units	城镇集体单位 Urban Collective-owned Units	其他单位 Units of Other Types of Ownership
1978	114.2	114.5	109.6		100.0	100.0	100.0	
1980	120.5	120.1	125.2		133.3	132.7	141.4	
1985	117.4	117.5	116.0	167.5	212.7	205.7	303.6	100.0
1990	116.6	116.3	126.9	132.6	419.6	405.5	591.7	513.4
1995	126.3	126.8	119.3	146.6	1052.2	1026.2	1221.7	6097.7
2000	110.7	108.1	91.4	171.0	1470.9	1354.1	1127.6	65762.7
2001	114.2	104.2	84.3	226.8	1679.6	1411.0	951.0	149164.7
2002	108.9	105.7	88.4	127.3	1828.9	1491.4	840.9	189913.4
2003	113.7	112.9	82.8	121.3	2079.8	1684.2	695.9	230420.0
2004	107.5	107.8	101.0	107.2	2235.3	1815.1	702.8	246927.8
2005	108.7	106.7	97.1	116.7	2430.3	1936.6	682.5	288287.3
2006	114.3	115.6	102.6	111.5	2779.0	2238.2	700.5	321896.3
2007	120.4	119.1	105.4	125.6	3345.1	2665.2	738.6	403198.1
2008	116.3	112.1	102.4	129.9	3888.7	2986.8	756.3	523604.0
2009	111.5	108.3	108.7	120.0	4336.1	3235.0	821.9	628496.6
2010	119.9	118.2	115.2	124.1	5198.5	3823.7	947.0	780026.1
2011	133.2	123.8	133.2	154.2	6922.2	4735.4	1261.4	1202673.7
2012	123.8	121.7	124.0	127.7	8570.5	5762.0	1564.4	1535499.1

注：2000 年起职工工资总额指数由在岗职工工资总额计算而得。
Note:. Since 2000,total wages of staff and worders were caculated by indices of total wages of stuff and workers.

3-25 主要年份城镇单位在岗职工工资情况
Wages of Full-Employed Staff and Workers in Urban Units in Main Years

年份 Year	在岗职工工资总额(亿元) Total Wages of staff and workers (100 million yuan)	国有单位 State-owned Units	城镇单位 Urban Collective-owned Units	其他单位 Units of Other Types of Ownership	在岗职工平均工资(元) Average Wage of Staff and Workers (yuan)	国有单位 State-owned Units	城镇单位 Urban Collective-owned Units	其他单位 Units of Other Types of Ownership
1999	211.86	185.77	13.73	12.36	7611	7614	6815	8681
2000	234.47	200.78	12.55	21.14	8717	8731	7489	9498
2001	267.74	209.22	10.59	47.94	10278	10145	8197	11594
2002	291.54	221.14	9.36	61.04	11605	11435	9353	12767
2003	331.54	249.74	7.75	74.06	13255	13199	9966	13937
2004	356.33	269.15	7.82	79.36	14484	14477	11594	14870
2005	387.41	287.15	7.60	92.66	15558	15364	12738	16503
2006	443.00	331.87	7.80	103.33	17819	17704	14209	18566
2007	533.24	395.19	8.22	129.83	21434	21369	17780	21921
2008	619.90	442.88	8.42	168.60	24687	24016	22060	26815
2009	691.21	479.68	9.15	202.38	27753	26872	22862	30409
2010	828.69	566.98	10.54	251.17	32361	31390	31997	34807
2011	1103.46	702.15	14.04	387.26	38820	36752	40102	43177
2012	1366.22	854.37	17.41	494.43	45243	43115	47248	49380

3-26 各地区按行业分城镇单位就业人员平均工资
Average Wage of Employed Persons in Urban Units by Sector in Detail

单位：元 (2012 年) (yuan)

项　　目	Item	2011 年	2012 年
总　计	**Total**	**38238**	**44576**
按行业分	**Grouped by Industrial Sector**		
农、林、牧、渔业	Farming, Forestry, Animal Husbandry and Fishery	22678	26323
采 矿 业	Mining	63085	76486
制 造 业	Manufacturing	39883	47371
电力、热力、燃气及水生产和供应业	Production and Distribution of Electricity, Gas and Water	50591	53796
建筑业	Construction	35558	41232
批发和零售业	Mining	40300	45733
交通运输、仓储和邮政业	Mining and Washing of Coal	53243	62427
住宿和餐饮业	Extraction of Petroleum and Natural Gas	28136	32468
信息传输、软件和信息技术服务业	Information Transmission, Computer Services and Software	48034	54862
金融业	Financial Intermediation	59732	69445
房地产业	Real Estate	31948	36266
租赁和商务服务业	Leasing and Business Services	27185	35016
科学研究、技术服务业	Scientific Research, Technology Service	45501	50555
水利、环境和公共设施管理业	Management of Water Conservancy, Environment and Public Facilities	28561	32060
居民服务、修理和其他服务业	Services to households and Other Services	30968	27376
教育	Education	40697	47187
卫生和社会工作	Health and Social Security	38552	44864
文化、体育和娱乐业	Culture, Sports and Entertainment	38062	45049
公共管理、社会保障和社会组织	Public Management and Social Organization	39862	45071
按地区分	**By Region**		
乌鲁木齐市	Urumqi City	45039	51906
克拉玛依市	Karamay City	57385	71896
吐鲁番地区	Turpan Administrative Offices	44187	49659
哈密地区	Hami [Kumul] Administrative Offices	37787	43990
昌吉回族自治州	Changji Hui Autonomous Prefecture	36389	42217
伊犁哈萨克自治州	Ili Kazak Autonomous Prefecture	29019	34149
伊犁州直属县(市)	Counties (Cities) Direct Under Ili Prefecture	30666	36391
塔城地区	Tacheng [Tarbagatai] Administrative Offices	27824	32594
阿勒泰地区	Altay Administrative Offices	27361	31636
博尔塔拉蒙古自治州	Bortala Mongol Autonomous Prefecture	28149	33516
巴音郭楞蒙古自治州	Bayangol Mongol Autonomous Prefecture	36593	44130
阿克苏地区	Aksu Administrative Offices	34965	41728
克孜勒苏柯尔克孜自治州	Kizilsu Kirgiz Autonomous Prefecture	31512	38589
喀什地区	Kashgar [Kaxgar] Administrative Offices	34278	40719
和田地区	Hotan Administrative Offices	36376	45529
石河子市	Shihezi City	38885	44194
阿拉尔市	Aral City	35190	38145
图木舒克市	Tumxuk City	30511	36937
五家渠市	Wujiaqu City	32855	45807

3-27 主要年份城镇单位在岗职工平均货币工资
Average Money Wage of Staff and Workers in Urban Units in Main Years

单位：元 (yuan)

年份 Year	全部职工 Full Staff and Workers	国有单位 State-owned Units	城镇集体单位 Urban Collective-owned Units	其他单位 Units of Other Types of Ownership
1978	717	726	614	
1980	882	904	676	
1985	1277	1310	1038	1707
1990	2272	2345	1765	2498
1995	5348	5431	4509	5973
2000	8717	8731	7489	9498
2001	10278	10145	8197	11594
2002	11605	11435	9353	12767
2003	13255	13199	9966	13937
2004	14484	14477	11594	14870
2005	15558	15364	12738	16503
2006	17819	17704	14209	18566
2007	21434	21369	17780	21921
2008	24687	24016	22060	26815
2009	27753	26872	22862	30409
2010	32361	31390	31997	34807
2011	38820	36752	40102	43177
2012	45243	43115	47248	49380

3-28 主要年份城镇单位在岗职工平均工资指数
Indices of Average Wage of Staff and Workers in Urban Units in Main Years

(上年=100) (preceding year=100)

年份 Year	货币工资 Money Wage				实际工资 Real Wage			
	合计 Total	国有单位 State-owned Units	城镇集体单位 Urban Collective-owned Units	其他单位 Units of Other Types of Ownership	合计 Total	国有单位 State-owned Units	城镇集体单位 Urban Collective-owned Units	其他单位 Units of Other Types of Ownership
1978		105.2				103.9		
1980	114.5	115.3	108.3		109.3	110.0	103.4	
1985	115.7	116.0	112.5	124.6	105.9	106.0	102.7	113.7
1990	113.2	113.3	113.6	96.5	108.3	108.4	108.7	92.3
1995	125.8	125.7	125.8	120.9	105.7	105.6	105.7	101.6
2000	114.5	114.7	109.9	109.4	115.2	115.4	110.6	110.1
2001	117.9	116.2	109.5	122.1	113.4	111.7	105.3	117.4
2002	112.9	112.7	114.1	110.1	113.6	113.4	114.8	110.8
2003	114.2	115.4	106.6	109.2	113.6	114.8	106.1	108.7
2004	109.3	109.7	116.3	106.7	107.0	107.4	113.9	104.5
2005	107.4	106.1	109.9	111.0	106.7	105.4	109.1	110.2
2006	114.5	115.2	111.5	112.5	113.7	114.4	110.7	111.7
2007	120.3	120.7	125.1	118.1	114.0	114.4	118.6	111.9
2008	115.2	112.4	124.1	122.3	106.6	104.0	114.8	113.1
2009	112.4	111.9	103.6	113.4	111.6	111.1	102.9	112.6
2010	116.6	116.8	140.0	114.5	111.8	112.0	134.2	109.7
2011	120.0	117.1	125.3	124.0	113.3	110.6	118.3	117.1
2012	116.5	117.3	117.8	114.4	112.2	113.0	113.5	110.2

3-29 各地、州、市分行业城镇单位在岗职工(含劳务派遣工)平均货币工资

Average Money Wage of Staff and Workers in Urban Units by Sector and Prefecture, Autonomous Prefecture and City(including the dispatched workers)

单位：元 (2012 年) (yuan)

年 份 Year	地 区 Region	合 计 Total	农林牧渔业 Farming, Forestry, Animal Husbandry and Fishery	采 矿 业 Mining	制 造 业 Manufacturing	电力、热力、燃气及水的生产和供应业 Production and Distribution of Power, Gas and Water
总 计	**Total**	**45243**	**26553**	**77082**	**47650**	**54041**
乌鲁木齐市	Urumqi City	52418	31821	75403	52091	56721
克拉玛依市	Karamay City	73510	31134	91778	71139	74632
吐鲁番地区	Turpan Administrative Offices	51343	22307	66827	39044	73097
哈密地区	Hami [Kumul] Administrative Offices	44480	27446	60467	43674	67127
昌吉回族自治州	Changji Hui Autonomous Prefecture	42707	34290	57272	39120	54292
伊犁哈萨克自治州	Ili Kazak Autonomous Prefecture	34435	22513	47736	40447	54502
伊犁州直属县(市)	Counties (Cities) Direct Under Ili Prefecture	36525	23861	43679	41420	53005
塔城地区	Tacheng [Tarbagatai] Administrative Offices	32926	24912	49114	39458	57017
阿勒泰地区	Altay Administrative Offices	32116	13708	49007	31100	55826
博尔塔拉蒙古自治州	Bortala Mongol Autonomous Prefecture	33823	25246	36659	28015	48412
巴音郭楞蒙古自治州	Bayangol Mongol Autonomous Prefecture	45609	27079	80814	48916	47813
阿克苏地区	Aksu Administrative Offices	41760	23242	70598	46594	56992
克孜勒苏柯尔克孜自治州	Kizilsu Kirgiz Autonomous Prefecture	40090	36941	35500	26194	42325
喀什地区	Kashgar [Kaxgar] Administrative Offices	41604	30805	32889	28982	44562
和田地区	Hotan Administrative Offices	48887	26242	58549	42345	46079
石河子市	Shihezi City	44227	46916		42492	44858
阿拉尔市	Aral City	38148	33801		33563	39050
图木舒克市	Tumxuk City	36937	30747		38496	52956
五家渠市	Wujiaqu City	46566	28760		57415	58828

年 份 Year	地 区 Region	建 筑 业 Construction	批发和零售业 Wholesale and Retail	交通运输、仓储和邮政业 Trades Transport, Storage and Post	住宿和餐饮业 Hotels and Catering Services	信息传输、软件和信息技术服务业 Information Transmission, Computer Servcie and Software
总 计	**Total**	**41670**	**46175**	**62581**	**32701**	**55166**
乌鲁木齐市	Urumqi City	40937	51133	72928	37504	60856
克拉玛依市	Karamay City	49845	58252	47964	36179	68328
吐鲁番地区	Turpan Administrative Offices	31112	55255	35139	25221	46781
哈密地区	Hami [Kumul] Administrative Offices	32479	58569	45888	25907	58950
昌吉回族自治州	Changji Hui Autonomous Prefecture	45596	46216	33951	27477	40965
伊犁哈萨克自治州	Ili Kazak Autonomous Prefecture	36058	34420	37568	26093	42631
伊犁州直属县(市)	Counties (Cities) Direct Under Ili Prefecture	40329	32493	34072	25154	43308
塔城地区	Tacheng [Tarbagatai] Administrative Offices	29963	34061	44752	19740	42885
阿勒泰地区	Altay Administrative Offices	35683	46897	40411	30641	41103
博尔塔拉蒙古自治州	Bortala Mongol Autonomous Prefecture	34029	47735	39374	33109	60939
巴音郭楞蒙古自治州	Bayangol Mongol Autonomous Prefecture	49055	46460	35726	25721	60473
阿克苏地区	Aksu Administrative Offices	52066	35760	38114	29595	64004
克孜勒苏柯尔克孜自治州	Kizilsu Kirgiz Autonomous Prefecture	19181	24310	38588	30605	31595
喀什地区	Kashgar [Kaxgar] Administrative Offices	40663	43133	34843	26024	63001
和田地区	Hotan Administrative Offices	49649	41387	43083	29435	37686
石河子市	Shihezi City	39461	54841	56907	30967	59239
阿拉尔市	Aral City	41570	49636	11143		
图木舒克市	Tumxuk City	43008	63292		28800	
五家渠市	Wujiaqu City	41259	45444	40414		37533

3-29 续表 Continued

单位：元 (yuan)

年 份 Year	地 区 Region	金融业 Financial Intermedition	房地产业 Real Estate	租赁和商务服务业 Leasing and Business Services	科学研究、技术服务 Scientific Research, Technology Service	水利、环境和公共设施管理业 Management of Water Conservancy, Environment and Public Facility
总 计	**Total**	**79997**	**36631**	**35328**	**51293**	**32938**
乌鲁木齐市	Urumqi City	112848	44674	48178	58974	42415
克拉玛依市	Karamay City	82992	25905	40876	47392	38060
吐鲁番地区	Turpan Administrative Offices	66374	27694	22662	36510	37933
哈密地区	Hami [Kumul] Administrative Offices	73470	25399	37183	54761	25904
昌吉回族自治州	Changji Hui Autonomous Prefecture	74651	37909	22645	44307	37505
伊犁哈萨克自治州	Ili Kazak Autonomous Prefecture	66062	30528	24032	45537	30583
伊犁州直属县(市)	Counties (Cities) Direct Under Ili Prefecture	65602	30261	22220	45529	27017
塔城地区	Tacheng [Tarbagatai] Administrative Offices	65019	34450	28988	45476	33978
阿勒泰地区	Altay Administrative Offices	68723	27622	30730	45602	33414
博尔塔拉蒙古自治州	Bortala Mongol Autonomous Prefecture	88363	32611	13711	59221	40180
巴音郭楞蒙古自治州	Bayangol Mongol Autonomous Prefecture	76480	24307	34423	49369	24496
阿克苏地区	Aksu Administrative Offices	61725	30927	26745	45134	26424
克孜勒苏柯尔克孜自治州	Kizilsu Kirgiz Autonomous Prefecture	39068	31841	18800	42466	43257
喀什地区	Kashgar [Kaxgar] Administrative Offices	38285	26451	28120	35551	35107
和田地区	Hotan Administrative Offices	56100	26363	39771	53419	40413
石河子市	Shihezi City	66553	54367	31169	60867	42763
阿拉尔市	Aral City			34516	41067	26437
图木舒克市	Tumxuk City			34175	45684	34792
五家渠市	Wujiaqu City	78306	50946	45662	59328	30778

年 份 Year	地 区 Region	居民服务、修理和其他服务业 Services to households and Other Services	教 育 Education	卫生和社会事业 Health, Social Security and Social Welfare	文化、体育和娱乐业 Culture, Sports and Entertainment	公共管理、社会保障和社会组织 Public Administration and Social Organizations
总 计	**Total**	**27351**	**47644**	**45625**	**45531**	**46319**
乌鲁木齐市	Urumqi City	43012	47271	53729	48263	49371
克拉玛依市	Karamay City	44370	72063	76555	78298	63004
吐鲁番地区	Turpan Administrative Offices		46896	45640	44856	44480
哈密地区	Hami [Kumul] Administrative Offices	27996	46406	43224	37923	44129
昌吉回族自治州	Changji Hui Autonomous Prefecture		52607	45868	48008	48282
伊犁哈萨克自治州	Ili Kazak Autonomous Prefecture	23475	43792	39731	38914	42850
伊犁州直属县(市)	Counties (Cities) Direct Under Ili Prefecture	22968	42326	36815	38704	40677
塔城地区	Tacheng [Tarbagatai] Administrative Offices	32417	45514	43928	38775	46131
阿勒泰地区	Altay Administrative Offices	25214	46184	43773	39680	44095
博尔塔拉蒙古自治州	Bortala Mongol Autonomous Prefecture	36600	46831	45690	45122	42790
巴音郭楞蒙古自治州	Bayangol Mongol Autonomous Prefecture	39982	47073	42611	43796	44421
阿克苏地区	Aksu Administrative Offices	33926	42345	40514	42538	42041
克孜勒苏柯尔克孜自治州	Kizilsu Kirgiz Autonomous Prefecture	15873	48449	30924	42762	48592
喀什地区	Kashgar [Kaxgar] Administrative Offices	38260	47408	41568	40019	43224
和田地区	Hotan Administrative Offices	51115	54726	50256	51164	55380
石河子市	Shihezi City	39893	55949	53892	51318	58344
阿拉尔市	Aral City		59382	59351	56914	54542
图木舒克市	Tumxuk City		42302	45158		48622
五家渠市	Wujiaqu City	63500	48128	53426	49353	54744

3-30 各地、州、市、县(市) 城镇单位在岗职工(含劳务派遣工)平均货币工资

Average Wages of Fully Employed Staff and Workers in Urban Units (including the dispatched workers) by Prefecture, Autonomous Prefecture, City and County

单位：元　　(2012 年)　　(yuan)

地　区	Region	合　计 Total	国有单位 State-owned Units	城镇集体单位 Urban Collective-owned Units	其他单位 Units of Other Types of Ownership
总　计	**Total**	**45243**	**43115**	**47248**	**49380**
乌鲁木齐市	**Urumqi City**	**52418**	**55487**	**51965**	**48633**
天山区	Tianshan District	51540	57086	42317	44351
沙依巴克区	Shayibak District	47616	47349	43879	48013
新市区	Xinshi District	51890	51164	77724	52036
水磨沟区	Shui Mogou Distric	43175	45115	25540	41492
头屯河区	Tou Tunhe District	46130	38990	51805	55409
达坂城区	Da Bancheng District	55940	42973	43320	59626
米东区	Midong District	56170	65249	45911	48504
乌鲁木齐县	Urumqi County	44553	41980	47248	49380
克拉玛依市	**Karamay City**	**73510**	**74218**	**33139**	**73916**
独山子区	Dushanzi District	71514	66245	33133	75075
克拉玛依区	Karamay District	76093	77892	31771	75545
乌尔河区	Urhe District	48636	58990	34000	57474
白碱滩区	Bai Jiantan District	34988	32414	102667	47102
吐鲁番地区	**Turpan Administrative Offices**	**51343**	**52741**	**34563**	**49164**
吐鲁番市	Turpan City	43272	44616	21076	41221
鄯善县	Shanshan [Piqan] County	61179	61337	82784	60508
托克逊县	Toksun County	47616	48300	33301	47304
哈密地区	**Hami [Kumul] Administrative Offices**	**44480**	**39799**	**33433**	**54425**
哈密市	Hami [Kumul] City	46103	40978	25241	54294
巴里坤哈萨克自治县	Barkol Kazak Autonomous County	35181	33699	51365	63450
伊吾县	Yiwu [Araturuk] County	46620	47251	27823	30000
昌吉回族自治州	**Changji Hui Autonomous Prefecture**	**42707**	**42010**	**54973**	**43631**
昌吉市	Changji City	44705	45795	85458	42591
阜康市	Fukang City	44918	43070	27817	47046
呼图壁县	Hutubi County	35649	33364	85214	40813
玛纳斯县	Manas County	42828	42241	23011	47568
奇台县	Qitai County	38900	39214	48136	37536
吉木萨尔县	Jimsar County	49669	48744	56783	52445
木垒哈萨克自治县	Mori Kazak Autonomous County	49583	49536	57019	48737
伊犁哈萨克自治州	**Ili Kazak Autonomous Prefecture**	**34435**	**33047**	**49660**	**38828**
伊犁州直属县(市)	**Counties (Cities) Direct Under Ili Prefecture**	**36525**	**35054**	**45245**	**39858**
伊宁市	Yining [Gulja] City	38169	38599	36374	37560
奎屯市	Kuytun City	41006	41060	38116	41058
伊宁县	Yining [Gulja] County	30231	26408	15023	41586
察布查尔锡伯自治县	Qapqal Xibe Autonomous County	33470	33413	43403	32995
霍城县	Huocheng [Korgas] County	33091	31275	43761	44886
巩留县	Gongliu [Tokkuztara] County	37152	36941	59522	

3-30 续表 1 Continued

单位：元 (yuan)

地　区	Region	合 计 Total	国有单位 State-owned Units	城镇集体单位 Urban Collective-owned Units	其他单位 Units of Other Types of Ownership
新源县	Xinyuan [Kunes] County	38545	38038	72082	38867
昭苏县	Zhaosu [Mongolkure] County	33501	33110	66847	32017
特克斯县	Tekes County	36963	37135	78354	27520
尼勒克县	Nilka County	38978	33101	64994	55323
塔城地区	**Tacheng [Tarbagatai] Administrative Offices**	**32926**	**32377**	**47043**	**35472**
塔城市	Tacheng [Qoqek] City	39646	36472	42787	56567
乌苏市	Usu City	28692	26960	34350	43044
额敏县	Emin [Dorbiljin] County	22973	22016	80821	30456
沙湾县	Shawan County	37176	39640	65854	26150
托里县	Toli County	45990	48733	24486	33105
裕民县	Yumin [Qagantokay] County	32724	32884	28227	18000
和布克赛尔蒙古自治县	Hoboksar Mongol Autonomous County	30784	26957	48302	42843
阿勒泰地区	**Altay Administrative Offices**	**32116**	**30001**	**75836**	**40097**
阿勒泰市	Altay City	32933	32512	64629	34267
布尔津县	Burqin County	30646	29255	72143	33784
富蕴县	Fuyun [Koktokay] County	29671	21191	100594	50101
福海县	Fuhai [Burultokay] County	30117	29024	92321	38670
哈巴河县	Habahe [Kaba] County	35167	31943	72340	44051
青河县	Qinghe [Qinggil] County	35741	35368	73350	34684
吉木乃县	Jeminay County	32291	31659	47083	37445
博尔塔拉蒙古自治州	**Bortala Mongol Autonomous Prefecture**	**33823**	**33427**	**40610**	**34690**
博乐市	Bole [Bortala] City	37207	37029	67091	38014
精河县	Jinghe [Jing] County	30048	28821	38638	27149
温泉县	Wenquan [Araxang] County	26536	26227	81370	24262
巴音郭楞蒙古自治州	**Bayangol Mongol Autonomous Prefecture**	**45609**	**39403**	**54777**	**55239**
库尔勒市	Korla City	50482	44236	43892	56188
轮台县	Luntai [Bugur] County	38946	37276	95947	49568
尉犁县	Yuli [Lopnur] County	37640	37205	60326	33257
若羌县	Ruoqiang [Qarkilik] County	69593	47015	167844	104793
且末县	Qiemo [Qarqan] County	37799	37103	36734	48939
焉耆回族自治县	Yanji Hui Autonomous County	36932	36558	74993	35363
和静县	Hejing County	36509	32513	26013	43256
和硕县	Hoxud County	30429	30049	54845	29818
博湖县	Bohu [Bagrax] County	36044	35708	83360	28045
阿克苏地区	**Aksu Administrative Offices**	**41760**	**38675**	**57598**	**47275**
阿克苏市	Aksu City	45613	43725	31315	48689
温宿县	Wensu [Onsu] County	29457	30245	39879	27187
库车县	Kuqa County	45202	35850	63492	55435
沙雅县	Xayar County	36037	32671	65730	42014
新和县	Xinhe [Toksu] County	41221	38968	73902	46782

3-30 续表 2 Continued

单位：元 (yuan)

地　　区	Region	合计 Total	国有单位 State-owned Units	城镇集体单位 Urban Collective-owned Units	其他单位 Units of Other Types of Ownership
拜城县	Baicheng [Bay] County	49090	41470	85743	57986
乌什县	Wushi [Uxturpan] County	37807	38762	50622	24383
阿瓦提县	Awat County	38692	40058	43944	32918
柯坪县	Kalpin County	39889	40031	32440	23200
克孜勒苏柯尔克孜自治州	**Kizilsu Kirgiz Autonomous Prefecture**	**40090**	**40804**	**25943**	**22136**
阿图什市	Artux City	39582	40726	25511	22978
阿克陶县	Akto County	52029	53101	25937	10910
阿合奇县	Akqi County	27244	27271	27360	19833
乌恰县	Wuqia [Ulugqat] County	39046	39140	27053	32028
喀什地区	**Kashgar [Kaxgar] Administrative Offices**	**41604**	**42511**	**31865**	**39259**
喀什市	Kashgar [Kaxgar] City	40553	41567	20964	39869
疏附县	Shufu County	44740	45665	22298	19669
疏勒县	Shule County	41608	42897	31743	24206
英吉沙县	Yengisar County	40181	39860	51371	34967
泽普县	Zepu [Poskam] County	38266	39486	27754	25597
莎车县	Shache [Yarkant] County	43869	44277	38204	32375
叶城县	Yecheng [Kagilik] County	50348	53785	33123	39642
麦盖提县	Makit County	35305	35402	28192	40945
岳普湖县	Yopurga County	43354	43438	37697	
伽师县	Jiashi [Payzawat] County	38935	38779	53736	21000
巴楚县	Bachu [Maralbexi] County	38437	39166	18074	23440
塔什库尔干塔吉克自治县	Taxkorgan Tajik Autonomous County	52115	52115		
和田地区	**Hotan Administrative Offices**	**48887**	**49088**	**81133**	**44125**
和田市	Hotan City	51671	53648	63317	40602
和田县	Hotan County	55310	54150	#DIV/0!	79878
墨玉县	Moyu [Karakax] County	47309	47419	#DIV/0!	45156
皮山县	Pishan [Guma] County	37871	37248	126897	34524
洛浦县	Lop County	52574	52760	48051	43596
策勒县	Qira County	50110	48202	130110	54833
于田县	Yutian [Keriya] County	53480	54657		31501
民丰县	Minfeng [Niya] County	51050	51381	39053	41683
自治区直辖县级市	**Municpality Country-LevelCity Directly under the Central Government**	**43049**	**41929**	**113798**	**44434**
石河子市	Shihezi City	44227	44274	113798	43905
阿拉尔市	Aral City	38148	39695		34452
图木舒克市	Tumxuk City	36937	36160		41073
五家渠市	Wujiaqu City	46566	39566		57474

3-31 分地区分行业城镇私营单位平均工资

Average Wage of Employed Persons in Urban Private Unites by Sector and Region

单位：元 (yuan)

项　　目	Item	2011 年	2012 年
总　计	**Total**	**24771**	**29486**
农、林、牧、渔业	Farming, Forestry, Animal Husbandry and Fishery	19691	23683
采矿业	Farming	32945	40581
制造业	Forestry	24004	28876
电力、煤气及水的生产和供应	Animal Husbandry	21488	28189
建筑业	Fishery	29929	37844
批发和零售业	Services in Support of Agriculture	21581	24048
交通运输、仓储和邮政业	Mining	25992	28966
住宿和餐饮业	Mining and Washing of Coal	19907	23806
信息传输、计算机服务和软件	Extraction of Petroleum and Natural Gas	20089	25610
金融业	Financial Intermediation	31007	28851
房地产业	Manufacture of Food	26365	31252
租赁和商务服务业	Manufacture of Beverage	20673	23595
科学研究、技术服务和地质勘查业	Scientific Research, Technology Service and Geological Prospecting	25645	30500
水利、环境和公共设施管理	Manufacture of Textile	19232	22446
居民服务和其他服务业	Services to households and Other Services	17760	21843
教　育	Education	20267	23493
卫生、社会保障和社会福利	Health, Social Security and Social Welfare	23299	26461
文化、体育和娱乐业	Culture, Sports and Entertainment	20385	18168
按地区分	**By Region**		
乌鲁木齐市	Urumqi City	27274	26485
克拉玛依市	Karamay City	39609	28404
吐鲁番地区	Turpan Administrative Offices	27899	22152
哈密地区	Hami [Kumul] Administrative Offices	34519	26144
昌吉回族自治州	Changji Hui Autonomous Prefecture	32118	27225
伊犁州直属县(市)	Counties (Cities) Direct Under Ili Prefecture	30869	25788
塔城地区	Tacheng [Tarbagatai] Administrative Offices	22758	15279
阿勒泰地区	Altay Administrative Offices	32928	26361
博尔塔拉蒙古自治州	Bortala Mongol Autonomous Prefecture	28498	23856
巴音郭楞蒙古自治州	Bayangol Mongol Autonomous Prefecture	26231	22678
阿克苏地区	Aksu Administrative Offices	34061	26056
克孜勒苏柯尔克孜自治州	Kizilsu Kirgiz Autonomous Prefecture	25941	21197
喀什地区	Kashgar [Kaxgar] Administrative Offices	22076	18490
和田地区	Hotan Administrative Offices	32121	24381
生产建设兵团	Xinjiang Production and Construction Group	35315	26359

主要统计指标解释

人口数 指一定时点、一定地区范围内的有生命的个人的总和。

年度统计的年末人口数指每年12月31日24时的人口数。

户籍人口 指公民依照《中华人民共和国户口登记条例》已在其经常居住地的公安户籍管理机关登记了常住户口的人。

常住人口 指在某地区实际居住半年以上的人口。

城镇人口和乡村人口 城镇人口是指居住在城镇范围内的全部常住人口；乡村人口是除上述人口以外的全部人口。

出生率(又称粗出生率) 指在一定时期内(通常为一年)一定地区的出生人数与同期内平均人数(或期中人数)之比，用千分率表示。本资料中的出生率指年出生率，其计算公式为：

出生率＝年出生人数／年平均人数×1000‰

式中：出生人数指活产婴儿，即胎儿脱离母体时(不管怀孕月数)，有过呼吸或其他生命现象。年平均人数指年初、年底人口数的平均数，也可用年中人口数代替。

死亡率(又称粗死亡率) 指在一定时期内(通常为一年)一定地区的死亡人数与同期平均人数(或期中人数)之比，用千分率表示。本资料中的死亡率指年死亡率，其计算公式为：

死亡率＝年死亡人数／年平均人数×1000‰

人口自然增长率 指在一定时期内(通常为一年)人口自然增加数(出生人数减死亡人数)与该时期内平均人数(或期中人数)之比，一般用千分率表示。计算公式为：

人口自然增长率＝(本年出生人数－本年死亡人数)／年平均人数×1000‰＝人口出生率－人口死亡率

经济活动人口 指在16岁以上，有劳动能力，参加或要求参加社会经济活动的人口；包括就业人员和失业人员。

就业人口 指16周岁及以上从事一定的社会劳动并取得劳动报酬或经营收入的人员。这一指标反应了一定时期内全部劳动力资源的实际利用情况，是研究我国基本国情国力的重要指标。

单位就业人员 指期末最后一日24时在各类单位中工作，并取得工资或其他形式劳动报酬的人员数。该指标为时点指标，不包括最后一日当天及以前已经与单位解除劳动合同关系的人员，是在岗职工、劳务派遣人员及其他从业人员之和。从业人员不包括：

(1)离开本单位仍保留劳动关系，并定期领取生活费的人员；

(2)利用课余时间打工的学生及在本单位实习的各类在校学生；

(3)本单位因劳务外包而使用的人员。

国有单位 指资产归国家所有的经济组织。包括按《中华人民共和国企业法人登记管理条例》规定登记注册的非公司制的经济组织，以及中央、地方各级国家机关、事业单位和社会团体。

集体单位 指生产资料归集体所有，并按《中华人民共和国企业法人登记管理条例》规定登记注册的经济组织。

其他单位 包括股份合作单位、联营单位、有限责任公司、股份有限公司、港澳台商投资单位以及外商投资单位等其他登记注册类型单位。

城镇私营和个体就业人员 城镇私营就业人员指在工商管理部门注册登记，其经营地址设在县城关镇(含城关镇)以上的私营企业就业人员，包括私营企业投资者和雇工。城镇个体就业人员指在工商管理部门注册登记，并持有城镇户口或在城镇长期居住，经批准从事个体工商经营的就业人员，包括个体经营者和在个体工商户劳动的家庭帮工和雇工。

在岗职工 指在本单位工作且与本单位签订劳动合同，并由单位支付各项工资和社会保险、住房公积金的人员，以及上述人员中由于学习、病伤、产假等原因暂未工作仍由单位支付工资的人员。在岗职工还包括：

(1)应订立劳动合同而未订立劳动合同人员(如使用的农村户籍人员)；

(2)处于试用期人员；

(3)编制外招用的人员；

(4)派往外单位工作，但工资仍由本单位发放的人员(如挂职锻炼、外派工作等情况)。

工资总额 指根据《关于工资总额组成的规定》(1990年1月1日国家统计局发布的一号令)进行修订，在报告期内(季度或年度)直接支付给本单位全部从业人员的劳动报酬总额。包括计时工资、计件工资、奖金、津贴和补贴、加班加点工资、特殊情况下支付的工资，是在岗职工工资总额、劳务派遣人员工资总额和其他从业人员工资总额之和。

工资总额是税前工资，包括单位从个人工资中直接为其代扣或代缴的房费、水费、电费、住房公积金和社会保险基金个人缴纳部分等。

工资总额不论是计入成本的还是不计入成本的，不论是以货币形式支付的还是以实物形式支付的，均应列入工资总额的计算范围。

平均工资 指单位就业人员在一定时期内平均每人所得的货币工资额。它表明一定时期职工工资收入的高低程度，是反映就业人员工资水平的主要指标。计算公式为:

平均工资＝报告期实际支付的全部就业人员工资总额／报告期全部就业人员平均人数

平均工资指数 指报告期就业人员平均工资与基期就业人员平均工资的比率，是反映不同时期就业人员货币工资水平变动情况的相对数。计算公式为：

平均工资指数＝报告期就业人员平均工资／基期就业人员平均工资

平均实际工资指数 就业人员平均实际工资指扣除物价变动因素后的就业人员平均工资。就业人员平均实际工资指数是反映实际工资变动情况的相对数，表明就业人员实际工资水平提高或降低的程度。计算公式为：

平均实际工资指数＝报告期就业人员平均工资指数／报告期城镇居民消费价格指数×100%

城镇登记失业人员 指有非农业户口，在一定的劳动年龄内（16周岁至退休年龄），有劳动能力，无业而要求就业，并在当地劳动保障部门进行失业登记的人员。

城镇登记失业率 指城镇登记失业人员与城镇单位就业人员（扣除使用的农村劳动力、聘用的离退休人员、港澳台及外方人员）、城镇单位中不在岗职工、城镇私营业主、个体户主、城镇私营企业和个体就业人员、城镇登记失业人数之和的比。计算公式为：

城镇登记失业率=城镇登记失业人数／{(城镇单位就业人数-使用的农村劳动力-聘用的离退休人员-聘用的港澳台及外方人员)+ 不在岗职工+城镇私营业主+城镇个体户主+城镇私营企业及个体就业人员+城镇登记失业人数)}×100%

Explanatory Notes on Main Statistical Indicators

Total Population refers to the total number of people alive at a certain point of time within a given area.

The annual statistics on total population is taken at midnight, the 3lst of December.

The household register population refers to citizens in accordance with the "people's Republic of Household Registration Ordinance" has been registered permanent residence.

The resident population refers to the practical living more than half year of the population.

City,Town and County Population City ,Town Population total population under the jurisdiction of City and tom. County Population refers to total population of country under the jurisdiction of County).

Birth Rate(or Crude Birth Rate) refers to the ratio of the number of births to the average population during a certain period of time(usually a year) which is often expressed in‰. The following formula is used:

Brith Rate= Number of Births/Annual Average Number of Population

Number of births refers to live births i.e. the births when babies had showed any vital phenomena regardless of the length of pregnancy.

Annual average number of population is the average of the number of population at the beginning of the year and that at the end of the year. Sometimes it is substituted for with the mid year population.

Death Rate(or Crude Death Rate) refers to the ratio of the number of deaths to the average population (or mid year population) during a certain period of time (usually a year) which is often expressed in‰. The following formula is used:

Death Rate =Number of Deaths/ Annual Average Number of Population

Natural Growth Rate of Population refers to the ratio of natural increase in population(number of births minus number of deaths)in a certain period of time(usually a year)to the average population(or mid year population)of the same period which is often expressed in‰. The following formula is applied:

Natural Growth Rate of Population= Number of Births-Number of Deaths / Average Number of Population

Natural Growth Rate of Population=Birth Rate-Death Rate

Economically Active Population refers to the population aged 16 and over who are capable to work, are participating in or willing to participate in economic activities, including employed persons and unemployed persons.

Employed Population refers to population aged 15 or over engaging in social labour which generates income.

Persons Employed in Various Units Persons Employed in Various Units refer to the total number of employees who work at various units and obtain wages or other forms of payment at the end of the reference period. This indicator is a kind of time point index and it equals to the sum of the number of employed staff and workers, labor dispatch personnel and other employed persons. Employed persons do not include:

1) persons who have left their working units while keeping their labour contract (employment relation) unchanged and receiving regular alimony;

2)students who do part-time jobs in spare time and all kinds of enrolled students who do internship in various units;

3)persons employed due to labor outsourcing;

4)persons who dissolve labor contracts with their units on the last day of reference period or before.

State-owned Units refer to economic units whose assets are owned by the state.Included are non-corporation units registered according to Regulation of the People’s Republic of China on the Registration of Enterprises and Corporation ,state argans,institutions and social organizations at the central and local levels.

Collective-owned Units refer to economic units registered according to Regulation of the People’s Republic of China on the Registration of Enterprises and Corporations where the means of production are collectively owned.

Units of Other Types of Ownership refer to units registered with other types of ownership,including cooperative units,joint ownership units,limited companies,share holding corporation,units invested by entrepreneurs from Hong Kong, Macao,and Taiwan,and foreign-invested units.

Persons Employed in Private Enterprises and Self-Employed Individuals in Urban Areas Persons employed in private enterprises refer to the persons employed in the private enterprises which have been registered at the departments of industrial and commercial administration and are situated at a County town (i.e. a town where the County government is located) for business operation or at urban areas with the level higher than a County town. The self-employed individuals in urban areas refer to persons who hold the certificates of residence in urban areas or have resided in the urban areas for a long time and have been registered at the departments of industrial and commercial administration and approved to be engaged in individual industrial or commercial business, including self-employed persons as well as helpers and hired labourers who work in the individual households engaged in industrial or commercial business.

Staff and Workers refer to the persons who work in(and receive payment therefrom)enterprises and institutions of state ownership, collective ownership, joint ownership, share holding, foreign ownership, and ownership by entrepreneurs from Hong Kong, Macao, and Taiwan, and other types of ownership and their affiliated units, excluding the retired persons invited to work in the units again, teachers in the schools run by the local people and foreigners and persons coming from Hong Kong, Macao and Taiwan and working in the state-owned economic units. (Number of staff and workers in this yearbook include only fully employed staff and workers, excluding those who have left their working units while keeping their labour contract/employment relation unchanged).

Total Wage Bill It is revised according to the "Provision of Composition of Total Wages" (Order No.1 by National Bureau of Statistics on January, 1st, ,1990), total wage bill refers to the total remuneration payment to all employed persons in various units during the reporting period (by quarter or by year), including hourly-paid wages, piece-rate wages, bonuses, allowance and subsidies, overtime wages and wages paid under special circumstances. It equals to the sum of total wages of employed staff and workers, dispatch labors and other employed persons.

Total wage bill is pre-tax wages, including the room charges, utility bills, housing funds and social insurance paid or withheld by employee's units.

Total wage bill, whether or not included in cost, whether or not paid in money or in kind, shall be included in the calculation of total wage.

Average Wage refers to the average wage in money terms per person during a certain period of time for staff and workers in enterprises, institutions, and government agencies, which reflects the general level of wage income during a certain period of time and is calculated as follows:

Average Wage =Total Wage Bill of Empioyed perons At Reference Time / Average Number of persons Employed at Reference Time

Average Wage Indices refers to the ratio of average wage of employed persons the reference period to that at the base period, which reflects the change of wage of employed persons at the different period. It is calculated as follows:

Average Wage Indices = Average Wage of Employed Persons at Reference Time / Average Wage of Persons Employeds at Base Period *100%

Average Real Wage Indices average real wage of employed persons refers to the average wage of employed persons after removing the effects of the price changes and average real wage indices of employed persons refers to the change of real wage, which reflects the relative increasing or decreasing level of real wage of employed persons ,which is calculated as follows:

Average Real Wage Indices =Average Wage Indices of Employed Persons at the Reference Time / Urban Consumer Price Indices at Reference Time *100%

Registered Unemployed Persons in Urban Areas refer to the persons with non-agricultural household registration at certain working ages (16 years old to retirement age), who are capable of working, unemployed and willing to work, and have been registered at the local employment service agencies to apply for a job.

Registered Unemployment Rate in Urban Areas refers to the ratio of the number of the registered unemployed persons to the sum of the number of persons employed in various units (minus the employed rural labour force, re-employed retirees, and Hong Kong, Macao, Taiwan or foreign employees), laid-off staff and workers in urban units, owners of private enterprises in urban areas, owners of self-employed individuals in urban areas, employees of private enterprises in urban areas, employ-yee of self-employed individuals in urban areas, and the registered unemployed persons in urban areas. The formula is as follows:

$$\text{Registered unemployment rate in urban areas} = \frac{\text{number of registered urban unemployed persons}}{\begin{array}{c}\text{number of persons employed in urban units - employed rural labour force}\\ \text{re-employed retirees - Hong Kong, Macao, Taiwan or foreign employees}\\ \text{+ laid-off staff and workers + owners of urban private enterprises + owners of}\\ \text{urban self-employed individuals + employees of urban private enterprises + employees of}\\ \text{urban self-employed individuals + registered unemployed persons in urban areas}\end{array}} \times 100\%$$

新疆统计年鉴
XINJIANG STATISTICAL YEARBOOK

4

固定资产投资

INVESTMENT IN FIXED ASSETS

简要说明

本篇资料的主要内容及来源

本篇资料包括主要年份全社会固定资产投资及其主要分组；2012年及同期的全区固定资产投资及其细化分组；2012年新增主要产品生产能力(或效益)；房地产开发企业基本情况；农村非农户及农户固定资产投资情况

农村固定资产投资来自国家统计局新疆调查总队商业和投资建筑业调查处；其余资料均来自新疆维吾尔自治区统计局固定资产投资统计处。

本篇资料的统计范围，2011年及以前年份，固定资产投资统计起点为50及50万元以上；2012年开始，按照国家统计局相关规定，固定资产投资统计起点调整为500万元及以上。

本篇的统计调查方法除农户固定资产投资统计采用抽样调查方法外，其他均为全面调查。

Brief Introduction

Main Content and Source of Data

Statistics in this chapter cover the total investment in fixed assets of the whole society and its composition, total investment in fixed assets and its refining grouping by region in 2012;newly increased production capacity of major production in 2012; basic condition of enterprises for real estate development, basic condition of individual investment in fixed assets of farm households and non-farm households.

The data of individual investment in fixed assets in rural areas come from the Trade and Fixed Assets and Construction Census Division of NBS Survey Office in Xinjiang; Others data come from the Division of Investment in Fixed Assets, Xinjiang Bureau of Statistics.

Scope of statistics: Before and in 2011,the starting point of fixed assets is changed from RMB 500,000 and above; From 2012,the stating point of fixed assets is changed to RMB 5 million according to relevant regulations of National Bureau of Statistics.

All data on the investment in fixed assets are collected by the statistical reporting system with complete enumeration, except data on the investment in fixed assets in rural areas which are collected through sample surveys.

4-1 1978-2012 年历年全社会固定资产投资
Total Investment in Fixed Assets in the Whole Country by Period (1978-2012)

单位：万元 (10 000 yuan)

年份 Year	合计 Total	城镇 Urban Area	#房地产 Real Estate Development	农村 Rural Area	非农户 Non-Farm Households	农村个人 Farm Individuals
1978	129999	129999				
1979	138253	138253				
1980	204652	203489		1163		1163
1981	183986	171706		12280	10000	2280
1982	247382	233668		13714	9693	4021
1983	277923	262027		15896	8804	7092
1984	337250	305713		31537	11089	20448
1985	444758	408435		36323	11528	24795
1986	484658	443631		41027	13934	27093
1987	512479	469898		42581	14714	27867
1988	684119	622041		62078	16848	45230
1989	750698	664243		86455	18841	67614
1990	887775	791555	9456	96220	20578	75642
1991	1249325	1130155	16886	119170	26946	92224
1992	1700326	1571456	23941	128870	33202	95668
1993	2484352	2336810	53616	147542	40738	106804
1994	2854786	2614211	86244	240575	70349	170226
1995	3333404	3035386	171238	298018	92118	205900
1996	3878472	3495942	156232	382530	111936	270594
1997	4468148	3987127	169906	481021	131063	349958
1998	5197673	4709794	148577	487879	136402	351477
1999	5346468	4847597	234481	498871	150744	348127
2000	6103843	5568492	574347	535351	171862	363489
2001	7059970	6469753	979184	590217	210040	380177
2002	8130223	7474024	877060	656199	252891	403308
2003	10021256	9213289	1024908	807967	327137	480830
2004	11615245	10608048	1125577	1007197	463358	543839
2005	13522757	12232255	1016618	1290502	573585	716917
2006	15670521	14180110	1208786	1490411	699084	791327
2007	18508415	16591894	1683160	1916521	1080611	835910
2008	22599746	20256393	2286267	2343353	1412796	930557
2009	28272359	25358648	2358805	2913711	1874325	1039386
2010	35396941	31815829	3477185	3581112	2395698	1185414
2011	47127699	42044959	5163895	5082740	3211176	1871564
2012	62583830	55938065	6060939	6645765	3637772	3007993

4-2 全社会固定资产投资

Total Investment in Fixed Assets in the Whole Country

单位：万元 (2012 年) (10 000 yuan)

项 目	Item	合 计 Total	城 镇 Urban	#房地产 Real Estate Development
投资总额	**Total Investment**	**62583830**	**55938065**	**6060939**
#住 宅	Residential Buildings	11373544	9240768	4442667
#国有经济控股	State-holding	34961647	32745941	1038863
按构成分	**Grouped by Use of Funds**			
建筑工程	Construction	39278692	35061891	4713051
安装工程	Installation	4507946	4292334	464374
设备工器具购置	Purchase of Equipment and Instruments	14260205	12433587	89271
其他费用	Other Expenses	4536987	4150253	794243
按三次产业分	**Grouped by Three Strata of Industry**			
第一产业	Primary Industry	2939876	1105634	
第二产业	Secondary Industry	33600397	30785612	
第三产业	Tertiary Industry	26043557	24046819	6060939
按登记注册类型分	**Grouped by Types of Registration**			
内资企业	Domestic Fund Enterprises	58893792	55403798	6051667
国 有	State-owned	25877707	23869145	197390
集 体	Collective-owned	84530	66050	1500
股份合作	Share-holding Cooperative	74596	74596	1258
联营企业	Joint Ownership Enterprises	104771	100321	
国有联营企业	State Joint Ownership Enterprises	71363	69911	
集体联营企业	Collective-owned Joint Ownership Enterprises	4210	4210	
国有与集体联营企业	State and Collective-owned Joint Ownership Enterprises	10288	7400	
其他联营企业	Others	18910	18800	
有限责任公司	Limited Liability Corporations	16182314	15481537	2864313
国有独资公司	State-funded Corporations	1113114	1105903	266477
其他有限责任公司	Other Limited Liability Corporations	15069200	14375634	2597836
股份有限公司	Share-holding Corporations Ltd	5956362	5663193	44516
私营企业	Private Enterprises	9719196	9379249	2893136
其他企业	Others	894316	769707	49554
港澳台商投资企业	Funds from Hongkong,Macao and Taiwan	167158	139409	9272

4-2 续表 1 Continued

单位：万元 (10 000 yuan)

项　目	Item	农　村 Rural	非农户 Non-Rural Households	农村个人 Rural Individuals
投资总额	**Total Investment**	**6645765**	**3637772**	**3007993**
#住　宅	Residential Buildings	2132776	682991	1449785
#国有经济控股	State-holding	2215706	2215706	
按构成分	**Grouped by Use of Funds**			
建筑工程	Construction	4216801	2681289	1535512
安装工程	Installation	215612	215391	221
设备工器具购置	Purchase of Equipment and Instruments	1826618	576768	1249850
其他费用	Other Expenses	386734	164324	222410
按三次产业分	**Grouped by Three Strata of Industry**			
第一产业	Primary Industry	1834242	607559	1226683
第二产业	Secondary Industry	2814785	1380541	1434244
第三产业	Tertiary Industry	1996738	1649672	347066
按登记注册类型分	**Grouped by Types of Registration**			
内资企业	Domestic Fund Enterprises	3489994	3489994	
国　有	State-owned	2008562	2008562	
集　体	Collective-owned	18480	18480	
股份合作	Share-holding Cooperative			
联营企业	Joint Ownership Enterprises	4450	4450	
国有联营企业	State Joint Ownership Enterprises	1452	1452	
集体联营企业	Collective-owned Joint Ownership Enterprises			
国有与集体联营企业	State and Collective-owned Joint Enterprises	2888	2888	
其他联营企业	Others	110	110	
有限责任公司	Limited Liability Corporations	700777	700777	
国有独资公司	State-funded Corporations	7211	7211	
其他有限责任公司	Other Limited Liability Corporations	693566	693566	
股份有限公司	Share-holding Corporations Ltd	293169	293169	
私营企业	Private Enterprises	339947	339947	
其他企业	Others	124609	124609	
港澳台商投资企业	Enterprises With Funds from Hong Kong, Macao and Taiwan	27749	27749	

4-2 续表 2 Continued

单位：万元 (10 000 yuan)

项　目	Item	合 计 Total	城 镇 Urban	#房地产 Real Estate Development
合资经营企业(港或澳、台资)	Joint-venture Enterprises (Hongkong,Macao and Taiwan)	39692	34785	6838
合作经营企业(港或澳、台资)	Cooperation Enterprises (Hongkon,Macao and Taiwan)	9834		
港、澳、台商独资经营企业	Enterprises With Sole Investment	51794	46794	2434
港、澳、台商投资股份有限公司	Share-holding Corporation Ltd.	58580	57830	
其他港、澳、台商投资企业	Others	7258		
外商投资企业	Foreign Funded Enterprises	305565	300056	
中外合资经营企业(港或澳、台资)	Joint-venture Enterprises (Hongkong,Macao and Taiwan)	98068	98068	
中外合作经营企业(港或澳、台资)	Cooperation Enterprises (Hongkon,Macao and Taiwan)	35635	35635	
外资企业	Enterprises With Sole Funds	107862	107822	
外商投资股份有限公司	Share-holding Corporations Ltd.	55031	55031	
其他外商投资企业	Others	8969	3500	
个体经营	Individual Operate	3217315	94802	
#个 体 户	Self-employed Personel	196887	92102	
个人合伙	Individual Partnership	12435	2700	
按隶属关系分	**By Administrative Relationship**			
中 央	Central Government	14431900	13651515	353962
地 方	Local	48151930	42286550	5706977
资金来源小计	**All Sources**	**66725427**	**59825190**	**7979461**
国家预算内资金	State Budget Funds	8684685	7652454	
国内贷款	Domestic Loans	8897975	7968864	908749
债　券	Bonds	59736	59304	
利用外资	Foreign Investment	91197	81597	
自筹资金	Self-raising Funds	40114052	36089714	2976896
其他资金来源	Others	8877782	7973257	4093816
本年新增固定资产	**Newly Increased Fixed Assets**	**39474336**	**33548268**	**4329468**
房屋施工面积(万平方米)	**Floor Space of Buildings (10 000 sq.m)**	**21626.33**	**18018.76**	**6896.55**
#住 宅	Residential Buildings	14159.68	11188.62	5482.59
房屋竣工面积(万平方米)	**Floor Space of Buildings Completed (10 000 sq.m)**	**7821.44**	**4827.97**	**1736.17**
#住 宅	Residential Buildings	6152.03	3608.10	1438.43

4-2 续表 3 Continued

单位：万元 (10 000 yuan)

项　目	Item	农　村 Rural	非农户 Non-Rural Households	农村个人 Rural Individuals
合资经营企业(港或澳、台资)	Joint-venture Enterprises (Hongkong,Macao and Taiwan)	4907	4907	
合作经营企业(港或澳、台资)	Cooperation Enterprises (Hongkon,Macao and Taiwan)	9834	9834	
港、澳、台商独资经营企业	Enterprises With Sole Investment	5000	5000	
港、澳、台商投资股份有限公司	Share-holding Corporation Ltd.	750	750	
其他港、澳、台商投资企业	Others	7258	7258	
外商投资企业	Foreign Funded Enterprises	5509	5509	
中外合资经营企业(港或澳、台资)	Joint-venture Enterprises (Hongkong,Macao and Taiwan)			
中外合作经营企业(港或澳、台资)	Cooperation Enterprises (Hongkon,Macao and Taiwan)			
外资企业	Enterprises With Sole Funds	40	40	
外商投资股份有限公司	Share-holding Corporations Ltd.			
其他外商投资企业	Others	5469	5469	
个体经营	Individual Operate	3122513	114520	3007993
#个 体 户	Self-employed Personel	104785	104785	
个人合伙	Individual Partnership	9735	9735	
按隶属关系分	**By Administrative Relationship**			
中 央	Central Government	780385	780385	
地 方	Local	5865380	2857387	3007993
资金来源小计	**All Sources**	**6900237**	**3892244**	**3007993**
国家预算内资金	State Budget Funds	1032231	1032231	
国内贷款	Domestic Loans	929111	406590	522521
债 券	Bonds	432	432	
利用外资	Foreign Investment	9600	9600	
自筹资金	Self-raising Funds	4024338	2135673	1888665
其他资金来源	Others	904525	307718	596807
本年新增固定资产	**Newly Increased Fixed Assets**	**5926068**	**2918075**	**3007993**
房屋施工面积(万平方米)	**Floor Space of Buildings (10 000 sq.m)**	**3607.57**	**1384.06**	**2223.51**
#住 宅	Residential Buildings	2971.06	859.91	2111.15
房屋竣工面积(万平方米)	**Floor Space of Buildings Completed (10 000 sq.m)**	**2993.47**	**881.48**	**2111.99**
#住 宅	Residential Buildings	2543.93	544.29	1999.64

4-3 按构成分全社会固定资产投资

Structure of Total Investment in Fixed Assets in the whole Country

单位：万元 (10 000 yuan)

年份 Year	地区 Region	合计 Total	建筑工程 Construction Works	安装工程 Installation Works	设备工具器具购置 Purchase of Equipment and Instruments	其他费用 Others
	1978	129999	86667		35686	7646
	1985	444758	323395		93254	28109
	1990	887775	571461		274647	41667
	1995	3333404	2145762		810995	376647
	1996	3878472	2245924	278445	929463	424640
	1997	4468148	2725428	310687	988070	443963
	1998	5197673	3435120	278895	920992	562666
	1999	5346468	3245779	344130	1039617	716942
	2000	6103843	3833328	416759	1254077	599679
	2001	7059970	4232768	454765	1616907	755530
	2002	8130223	4815707	593242	1787899	933375
	2003	10021256	6075091	690459	2030335	1225371
	2004	11615245	7133323	806705	2304931	1370286
	2005	13522757	8499303	993311	2637777	1392366
	2006	15670521	9776613	1014851	3166617	1712440
	2007	18508415	10667717	1517359	4312525	2010814
	2008	22599746	13071829	1773200	5488261	2266456
	2009	28272359	17511739	1938944	5855684	2965992
	2010	35396941	22224487	1943535	7960420	3268499
	2011	47127699	29541315	3362813	10626129	3597442
	2012	62583830	39278692	4507946	14260205	4536987
乌鲁木齐市	Urumqi City	8276320	5231929	584060	1641669	818662
克拉玛依市	Karamay City	3274858	2136746	356777	543850	237485
吐鲁番地区	Turpan Administrative Offices	1756596	881686	160542	615621	98747
哈密地区	Hami [Kumul] Administrative Offices	3017682	1319046	248299	1275901	174436
昌吉回族自治州	Changji Hui Autonomous Prefecture	7334746	4398201	412514	2126130	397901
伊犁哈萨克自治州	Ili Kazak Autonomous Prefecture	10925718	7271042	710725	1982580	961371
伊犁州直属县(市)	Counties (Cities) Direct Under Ili Prefecture	6143187	3861187	455218	1194789	631993
塔城地区	Tacheng [Tarbagatai] Administrative Offices	2822109	2117206	175580	402129	127194
阿勒泰地区	Altay Administrative Offices	1960422	1292649	79927	385662	202184
博尔塔拉蒙古自治州	Bortala Mongol Autonomous Prefecture	1556881	1005827	61920	368199	120935
巴音郭楞蒙古自治州	Bayangol Mongol Autonomous Prefecture	5444520	3789920	498317	806047	350236
阿克苏地区	Aksu Administrative Offices	4005680	2326357	413485	1083461	182377
克孜勒苏柯尔克孜自治州	Kizilsu Kirgiz Autonomous Prefecture	792344	589314	32800	150631	19599
喀什地区	Kashgar [Kaxgar] Administrative Offices	4963534	3645634	386230	714891	216779
和田地区	Hotan Administrative Offices	1512085	1282489	34852	95600	99144
石河子市	Shihezi City	1978613	712412	273428	846172	146601
阿拉尔市	Aral City	738855	490122	85201	135550	27982
图木舒克市	Tumxuk City	307443	231448	6058	47962	21975
五家渠市	Wujiaqu City	1423501	746120	187194	430794	59393
跨地区投资	Trans-regional Investment	2266461	1684887	55323	145297	380954

注：各地区投资中不包括农村个人投资。
Note: Investment classified in different regions does not include rural individual investment.

4-4 全社会固定资产投资资金来源情况

Sources of Funds of Total Investment in Fixed Assets in the Whole Country

单位：万元 (10 000 yuan)

年份 地区	Year Region	合计 Total	国家预算内资金 State Budget	国内贷款 Domestic Loans	债券 Bonds	利用外资 Foreign Investment	自筹及其他资金 Self-raising Fund And Others
	1978	129999	102693				27306
	1985	444758	117439	72227		7708	247384
	1990	887775	105423	294985		40927	446440
	1995	3333404	98004	818914		307619	2108867
	1996	3878472	128725	756412		324532	2668803
	1997	4468148	269106	749345		109629	3340068
	1998	5197673	384195	1116497		133936	3563045
	1999	5346468	512364	1097949	12376	93895	3629884
	2000	6103843	506867	1346175	19429	99942	4131430
	2001	7059970	545176	1321317	8340	64834	5120303
	2002	8130223	1323660	1607535	30504	62992	5105532
	2003	10021256	1626261	1896104	21586	95287	6382018
	2004	11490824	1799593	1555105	46095	87388	8002643
	2005	13543432	2093022	1677020	15428	109968	9647994
	2006	15773966	2119253	1854512	8193	88675	11703333
	2007	19070184	2258779	2480410	5526	110034	14215435
	2008	22725814	3388141	3020001	3410	90233	16224029
	2009	30345365	5813486	5246186	54636	94000	19137057
	2010	37844438	6347565	5750361	11544	120367	25614601
	2011	51265602	6266348	6679368	22559	137967	38159360
	2012	66725427	8684685	8897975	59736	91197	48991834
乌鲁木齐市	Urumqi City	9706411	734774	2122779	1889		6846969
克拉玛依市	Karamay City	3449489	167963	281767		30000	2969759
吐鲁番地区	Turpan Administrative Offices	1866989	134153	418651		11247	1302938
哈密地区	Hami [Kumul] Administrative Offices	2708242	267819	323703	6593		2110127
昌吉回族自治州	Changji Hui Autonomous Prefecture	8057014	660935	1213448	500	11335	6170796
伊犁哈萨克自治州	Ili Kazak Autonomous Prefecture	11530214	2013045	871588	6822	23316	8615443
伊犁州直属县(市)	Counties (Cities) Direct Under Ili Prefecture	6458748	918022	550349	956	2467	4986954
塔城地区	Tacheng [Tarbagatai] Administrative Offices	3378183	634950	163361	5464	2000	2572408
阿勒泰地区	Altay Administrative Offices	1693283	460073	157878	402	18849	1056081
博尔塔拉蒙古自治州	Bortala Mongol Autonomous Prefecture	1600914	293019	55491			1252404
巴音郭楞蒙古自治州	Bayangol Mongol Autonomous Prefecture	5524834	412020	640453		2000	4470361
阿克苏地区	Aksu Administrative Offices	4325616	598135	573757			3153724
克孜勒苏柯尔克孜自治州	Kizilsu Kirgiz Autonomous Prefecture	733788	208906	102000			422882
喀什地区	Kashgar [Kaxgar] Administrative Offices	5628077	1606996	63082	432	9799	3947768
和田地区	Hotan Administrative Offices	1650057	811358	37165	3500		798034
石河子市	Shihezi City	1950984	33100	323253			1594631
阿拉尔市	Aral City	632207	72994	96155			463058
图木舒克市	Tumxuk City	260513	121303	5545			133665
五家渠市	Wujiaqu City	1561099	85840	67607		3500	1404152
跨地区投资	Trans-regional Investment	2530986	462325	1179010	40000		849651

注：1.自 2004 年起资金来源为本年实际到位资金。2.各地区资金来源中不包括农村个人资金。
Note: a) Sources of capital caculated on actual arrived investment from 2004. b) Sources of Capital from different regions excludes rural individdual fund.

4-5 按行业分全社会固定资产投资

Total Investment in Fixed Assets in the Whole Country by Sector

单位：万元 (10 000 yuan)

行业	Sector	2011	2012
总计	**Total**	**47127699**	**62583830**
农、林、牧、渔业	**Agriculture, Forestry, Animal Husbandry and Fishery**	**2377851**	**2939876**
农业	Agriculture	361651	316170
林业	Forestry	173081	153960
畜牧业	Animal Husbandry	195970	268860
渔业	Fishing	4401	2275
农、林、牧、渔服务业	Services in Support of Agriculture	941809	971928
采矿业	**Mining**	**6518237**	**7487174**
#煤炭开采和洗选业	Mining and Washing of Coal	1333439	1719835
石油和天然气开采业	Extraction of Petroleum and Natural Gas	4313859	4405085
黑色金属矿采选业	Mining and Processing of Ferrous Metals Ores	307947	309489
#铁矿采选	Mining and Processing of Iron Ore	282066	291779
有色金属矿采选业	Mining and Processing of Non-ferrous Metals Ores	439009	604555
#常用有色金属矿采选	Mining and Processing of Common Non-ferrous Metal	334930	489263
非金属矿采选业	Mining and Processing of Nonmetal Ores	113173	147654
#土砂石开采	Mining of Earth and Gravel	64469	90997
化学矿采选	Extracting of Chemical Ore	40422	6280
制造业	**Manufacturing**	**11568245**	**15901587**
#农副食品加工业	Processing of Food from Agricultural Products	422099	690933
食品制造业	Manufacture of Food	351975	544558
烟草制品业	Manufacture of Tobacco	77838	54155
纺织业	Manufacture of Textile	473103	435812
皮革、毛皮、羽绒及其制品业	Leather, Fur, Feather and Related Products Manufacturing		859
木材加工和木、竹、藤、棕、草制品业	Processing of Timber, Wood, Bamboo, Cane, Grass Products	52916	58514
家具制造业	Furniture Manufacturing	10130	21183
造纸及纸制品业	Paper and Paper Products Manufacturing	161811	116885
印刷和记录媒介复制业	Printing and Copying of Medium for Record	13777	35451
石油加工及炼焦业	Oil Processing, Coking and Nuclear Fuel Processing	1250754	1447755
#精炼石油产品制造	Manufacture of Oil Products	697361	791839
炼焦	Coking	553393	655916
化学原料及化学制品制造业	Raw Chemical Material and Chemical Products	2387322	2888806
#基础化学原料制造	Basic Chemical Material	1166221	1208988
肥料制造	Fertilizer Making	523466	561291
医药制造业	Medicine Manufacturing	120057	295711
#中药饮片加工	Processing of Chinese Herbs and Tablet	8175	10403
中成药制造	Manufacture of Chinese Herbs and Patent Medicine	7397	18972
化学纤维制造业	Chemical Fiber Manufacturing	146273	89202
橡胶和塑料制品业	Manufacture of Rubber and Plastics	8175	339221
橡胶制品业	Manufacture of Rubber	51034	38273
塑料制品业	Manufacture of Plastic	181500	300948

注：该表门类包括农村个人投资，大类未包括。
Note: The major category contains rural individual investment while sub-category excludes it.

4-5 续表 1 Continued

单位：万元 (10 000 yuan)

行　业	Sector	2011	2012
非金属矿物制品业	Manufacture of Non-metallic Mineral Products	2223317	2796123
#水泥、石灰和石膏的制造	Cement Manufacturing	1147369	1288059
黑色金属冶炼及压延加工业	Smelting and Pressing of Non-Ferrous Metals	1111071	2209612
#钢压延加工	Steel Rolling	133192	424172
有色金属冶炼及压延加工业	Smelting and Pressing of Nonferrous Metals	1560191	2055339
#常用有色金属冶炼	Smeltering of Common Non-ferrous Metal	1534710	1710794
金属制品业	Manufacture of Metal Products	252552	332819
通用设备制造业	Manufacture of General Purpose Machinery	68925	188365
专用设备制造业	Manufacture of Special Purpose Machinery	182358	198432
汽车制造	Manufacture of Car	68378	218202
电气机械及器材制造业	Manufacture of Electricial Equipment and Machinery	194847	160224
电力、热力、燃气及水的生产和供应业	**Production and Supply of Electricity Gas and Water**	**5700481**	**7815608**
电力、热力的生产和供应业	Production and Supply of Electric Power and Heat Power	4755198	6534845
电力生产	Production of Electric Power	3771666	5025890
电力供应	Distribution of Electric Power	723663	865387
热力生产和供应	Production and Supply of Heat Power	259869	643568
燃气生产和供应业	Production and Supply of Gas	625197	852032
水的生产和供应业	Production and Supply of Water	320086	428731
#自来水的生产和供应	Production and Distribution of Running Water	243487	325050
污水处理及其再生利用	Treatment and Recycle of Waste Water	74853	82826
建筑业	**Construction**	**866512**	**2396028**
#房屋和土木工程建筑业	Construction of Buildings and Givil Engineering	722749	910907
建筑安装业	Building Installation	12922	16641
交通运输、仓储和邮政业	**Transport, Storage and Post**	**3940920**	**4421504**
铁路运输业	Railway Transport	814209	930826
道路运输业	Road Transport	2199116	2384540
#城市公共交通业	Urban Public Transport	53317	82673
航空运输业	Air Transport	34130	53335
管道运输业	Via Pipeline Transport	280873	50908
装卸搬运和其他运输服务业	Loading, Unloading and Other Transport Services	25172	18919
仓储业	Storage	244189	638585
邮政业	Post	16744	5246
信息传输、软件和信息技术服务业	**Information Transmission, Computer Services and Software**	**481474**	**444177**
#电信、广播电视和卫星传输服务	Telecommunication and Other Information Transmission Services	473099	404589
#电　信	Telecommunication	457363	384433
批发和零售业	**Wholesal and Retail Trades**	**468815**	**865063**
批发业	Wholesale Trade	260950	458366
零售业	Retail Trade	207865	406697
住宿和餐饮业	**Hotels and Catering Services**	**212911**	**394495**
住宿业	Hotels	196139	309975
#旅游饭店	Tourist Restaurant	138411	248567
餐饮业	Catering Service	16772	77124
金融业	**Financial Intermediation**	**51154**	**32070**

4-5 续表 2 Continued

单位：万元 (10 000 yuan)

行　业	Sector	2011	2012
银行业	Banks	46792	26082
保险业	Insurance	1200	758
其他金融活动	Other Financial Activities	3162	1230
房地产业	**Real Estate**	**9935788**	**12779833**
#房地产开发与经营业	Real Estate Development and Operation	5706972	6671772
物业管理	Real Estate Management	12526	42259
租赁和商务服务业	**Leasing and Business Services**	**172723**	**197044**
租赁业	Leasing	10645	20216
商务服务业	Business Service	153226	176828
科学研究和技术服务业	**Scientific Research, Technical Service and Geological Prospecting**	**186848**	**188774**
研究与试验发展	Research and Experimental Development	585	13182
专业技术服务业	Professional Technical Service	55561	145696
科技推广和应用服务业	Services of Science and Technology Exchanges and Promotion	20230	29896
水利、环境和公共设施管理业	**Management of Water Conservancy, Environment and Public Facilities**	**2032966**	**3425828**
水利管理业	Management of Water Conservancy	735946	1046318
生态保护和环境治理业	Environmental Management	123440	150328
公共设施管理业	Management of Public Facilities	1173443	2229182
#市政设施管理	Management of Public Facilities	911840	1732498
绿化管理	Urban Greening Management	172685	139553
公园和游览景区管理	Scenic-Spot Management	88918	213676
居民服务、修理和其他服务业	**Services to Households and Other Services**	**48747**	**108870**
教　育	**Education**	**662563**	**974774**
#初等教育	Junion Education	116519	155797
中等教育	Secondary Education	299962	553117
高等教育	Senior Education	67151	84042
卫生和社会工作	**Health, Social Security and Social Welfare**	**351039**	**400699**
卫　生	Health Care	284314	320524
#医　院	Hospital	206077	234936
专科疾病防治活动	Control Over Special Diseases	1130	
疾病预防控制及防疫活动	Prevention and Control of Diseases	1461	2773
社会保障业	Social Security	32593	13873
文化、体育和娱乐业	**Culture, Sports and Entertainment**	**181151**	**351896**
新闻和出版业	Journalism and Publishing Activities	4556	7000
广播、电视、电影和影视录音制作	Broadcasting,Movies,Televisions and Audiovisual Activites	12396	27722
文化艺术业	Culture and Art Activities	95277	202491
体　育	Sports	19246	104391
娱乐业	Entertainment	49676	10292
公共管理、社会保障和社会组织	**Public Management and Social Organization**	**1369274**	**1458530**
中国共产党机关	Orgars of Communist Party of China	30419	18538
国家机构	Govemment Agencies	1312136	1310277
人民政协、民主党派	People's Political Consultative Conference and Democratic Parties	200	550
群众团体、社会团体和其他成员组织	Non-Governmental Institutions,Social Organizations and Religion Organizations	5973	91446
基层群众自治组织	Grass Roots Self-governing Organizations	20546	23846

4-6 全社会房屋施工面积、竣工面积

Floor Space of Buildings under Construction and Completed in Whole Country

单位：万平方米 (10 000 sq.m)

年份 Year	地区 Region	施工面积 Floor Space of Buildings under Construction	#住宅 Residential Buildings	竣工面积 Floor Space of Buildings Completed	#住宅 Residential Buildings	房屋建筑面积竣工率(%) Rate of Floor Space of Building Completed (%)	#住宅 Residential Buildings
	1985	1670.30	945.76	1327.69	816.26	79.5	86.3
	1990	1740.94	1074.98	1337.06	912.57	76.8	84.9
	1995	2420.38	1368.84	1634.33	1064.14	67.5	77.7
	1996	2952.02	1901.01	2095.58	1441.22	71.0	75.8
	1997	2574.79	1732.19	1903.96	1393.11	73.9	80.4
	1998	2946.76	2057.08	2148.75	1604.68	72.9	78.0
	1999	3439.11	2470.41	2618.98	2020.89	76.2	81.8
	2000	4485.77	2509.17	2633.23	1881.88	58.7	75.0
	2001	4940.70	3282.51	3386.60	2411.78	68.5	73.5
	2002	3986.81	2358.04	2706.44	1790.82	67.9	75.9
	2003	5004.13	2863.92	3599.74	2347.04	71.9	82.0
	2004	5290.77	2999.85	4273.02	2298.56	80.8	76.6
	2005	6677.06	4522.20	4705.07	3618.78	70.5	80.0
	2006	7854.43	5694.75	4773.93	3785.46	60.8	66.5
	2007	8028.32	5915.83	5441.23	4458.77	67.8	75.4
	2008	8317.15	5938.78	5184.01	4125.67	62.3	69.5
	2009	9511.02	6344.39	4598.79	3412.43	48.4	53.8
	2010	11361.96	7640.58	4649.89	3291.89	40.9	43.1
	2011	16804.88	11357.36	5899.06	4504.94	35.1	39.7
	2012	21626.33	14159.68	7821.44	6152.03	36.2	43.4
乌鲁木齐市	Urumqi City	3555.29	2498.95	939.60	701.32	26.4	28.1
克拉玛依市	Karamay City	487.27	310.55	107.29	76.02	22.0	24.5
吐鲁番地区	Turpan Administrative Offices	276.78	139.50	29.30	26.94	10.6	19.3
哈密地区	Hami [Kumul] Administrative Offices	608.95	469.07	239.71	204.81	39.4	43.7
昌吉回族自治州	Changji Hui Autonomous Prefecture	1339.69	1026.35	331.59	241.54	24.8	23.5
伊犁哈萨克自治州	Ili Kazak Autonomous Prefecture	3539.85	2238.30	1258.23	925.65	35.5	41.4
伊犁州直属县(市)	Counties (Cities) Direct Under Ili Prefecture	2011.28	1131.36	620.89	430.52	30.9	38.1
塔城地区	Tacheng [Tarbagatai] Administrative Offices	961.53	669.88	402.36	308.25	41.8	46.0
阿勒泰地区	Altay Administrative Offices	567.04	437.06	234.98	186.88	41.4	42.8
博尔塔拉蒙古自治州	Bortala Mongol Autonomous Prefecture	573.08	394.01	189.48	144.24	33.1	36.6
巴音郭楞蒙古自治州	Bayangol Mongol Autonomous Prefecture	1742.27	1154.63	493.50	366.02	28.3	31.7
阿克苏地区	Aksu Administrative Offices	1426.16	875.69	487.62	341.83	34.2	39.0
克孜勒苏柯尔克孜自治州	Kizilsu Kirgiz Autonomous Prefecture	351.71	207.35	190.90	146.78	54.3	70.8
喀什地区	Kashgar [Kaxgar] Administrative Offices	2166.35	1200.44	313.34	277.91	14.5	23.2
和田地区	Hotan Administrative Offices	1782.55	723.94	756.04	469.15	42.4	64.8
石河子市	Shihezi City	599.72	289.51	103.18	26.86	17.2	9.3
阿拉尔市	Aral City	292.65	131.40	130.84	86.71	44.7	66.0
图木舒克市	Tumxuk City	195.89	131.46	55.99	47.31	28.6	36.0
五家渠市	Wujiaqu City	463.12	255.89	82.84	69.30	17.9	27.1
跨地区投资	Trans-regional Investment	1.49	1.49				

注：分地区房屋施工面积、竣工面积未包括农村个人。
Note: Floor space under construction and completed floor space by sectors exclude those in rural areas.

4-7 按构成及建设性质分城镇固定资产投资

Investment in Fixed Assets in Urban Area by Composition of Funds and Type of Construction

单位：万元 (10 000 yuan)

年份 Year	地区 Region	合计 Total	按构成分 By Composition of Funds 建筑安装工程 Construction and Installation	设备工具器具购置 Purchase of Equipment and Instruments	#用于更新的设备 Update Equipment	其他费用 Others
	1978	129999	86667	35686		7646
	1985	408435	314651	67295	5499	26489
	1990	782099	516443	224673	25153	40983
	1995	2864148	1817364	754369	64612	292415
	1996	3339710	2167304	825067	66119	347339
	1997	3817221	2600884	858958	61094	357379
	1998	4561217	3333948	792449	71986	434820
	1999	4613116	3294346	831951	82363	486819
	2000	4994145	3531280	1103399	104850	359466
	2001	5490569	3638754	1392920	186605	458895
	2002	6596964	4379556	1558818	181920	658590
	2003	8188381	5599787	1718853	105728	869741
	2004	9482471	6451184	2047000	232343	984287
	2005	11215637	7926905	2230165	145514	1058567
	2006	12971324	8943879	2686125	188170	1341320
	2007	14908734	9646247	3746476	177062	1516011
	2008	17970126	11542024	4772937	311014	1655165
	2009	22999843	15632380	5026513	552733	2340950
	2010	28338644	18973774	6938417	346525	2426453
	2011	36881064	25313983	9102251	726850	2464830
	2012	49877126	34176800	12344316	1048785	3356010
乌鲁木齐市	Urumqi City	5812238	3712899	1595982	237790	503357
克拉玛依市	Karamay City	3016611	2250615	540098	102097	225898
吐鲁番地区	Turpan Administrative Offices	1722084	1014406	614245	52591	93433
哈密地区	Hami [Kumul] Administrative Offices	2817495	1397888	1263028	20613	156579
昌吉回族自治州	Changji Hui Autonomous Prefecture	6280548	4019948	1947373	138380	313227
伊犁哈萨克自治州	Ili Kazak Autonomous Prefecture	8486050	5948866	1813683	170155	723501
伊犁州直属县(市)	Counties (Cities) Direct Under Ili Prefecture	4551987	3013218	1074839	115721	463930
塔城地区	Tacheng [Tarbagatai] Administrative Offices	2213131	1772979	365869	43909	74283
阿勒泰地区	Altay Administrative Offices	1720932	1162669	372975	10525	185288
博尔塔拉蒙古自治州	Bortala Mongol Autonomous Prefecture	1369994	933279	342205	49278	94510
巴音郭楞蒙古自治州	Bayangol Mongol Autonomous Prefecture	4788552	3716995	795335	30364	276222
阿克苏地区	Aksu Administrative Offices	2983155	1957179	932565	98519	93411
克孜勒苏柯尔克孜自治州	Kizilsu Kirgiz Autonomous Prefecture	685058	526033	145702	78965	13323
喀什地区	Kashgar [Kaxgar] Administrative Offices	4490274	3622629	695069	27974	172576
和田地区	Hotan Administrative Offices	1430713	1245428	90109	38674	95176
石河子市	Shihezi City	1751156	780470	845172		125514
阿拉尔市	Aral City	583934	426875	132728	1215	24331
图木舒克市	Tumxuk City	250296	194726	40922		14648
五家渠市	Wujiaqu City	1142507	688354	404803		49350
跨地区投资	Trans-regional Investment	2266461	1740210	145297	2170	380954

注：城镇投资额未含房地产投资，以下同。
Note: Urban Investment exclude real estate, the following the same as follows.

4-7 续表 Continued

单位：万元 (10 000 yuan)

年份 Year	地区 Region	按建设性质分 By Type of Construction 新建 New Construction	扩建 Expansion	改建 Reconstruction	其他 Others
	1978	93462	34399		2138
	1985	110236	160639	116006	21554
	1990	299356	148222	277007	57514
	1995	1067281	886882	646081	263904
	1996	1240585	820966	967022	311137
	1997	1405259	911902	1155121	344939
	1998	1648622	1017786	1338994	555815
	1999	1381764	1226797	1326775	677780
	2000	1410065	1424339	1558514	601227
	2001	891146	2373927	1614961	610535
	2002	1429874	2687996	1984657	494437
	2003	2207269	3128374	2237752	614986
	2004	2358662	3595847	2781101	746861
	2005	3397472	3657464	3063457	1097244
	2006	3633284	5436397	2430373	1471270
	2007	3759028	7439715	2386806	1323185
	2008	5350574	8078708	2759536	1781308
	2009	9465044	7634515	4113649	1786635
	2010	13612835	8408038	4177527	2140244
	2011	19799225	9910989	4216233	2954617
	2012	29842768	12229771	4387038	3417549
乌鲁木齐市	Urumqi City	2316029	2700682	482765	312762
克拉玛依市	Karamay City	2606982	68386	274753	66490
吐鲁番地区	Turpan Administrative Offices	1025591	528798	84262	83433
哈密地区	Hami [Kumul] Administrative Offices	1323613	1306208	71829	115845
昌吉回族自治州	Changji Hui Autonomous Prefecture	4842715	408371	674677	354785
伊犁哈萨克自治州	Ili Kazak Autonomous Prefecture	4520721	2447335	727054	790940
伊犁州直属县(市)	Counties (Cities) Direct Under Ili Prefecture	2902406	1082679	284840	282062
塔城地区	Tacheng [Tarbagatai] Administrative Offices	1110117	488697	332481	281836
阿勒泰地区	Altay Administrative Offices	508198	875959	109733	227042
博尔塔拉蒙古自治州	Bortala Mongol Autonomous Prefecture	525559	480872	141187	222376
巴音郭楞蒙古自治州	Bayangol Mongol Autonomous Prefecture	3654197	661512	131276	341567
阿克苏地区	Aksu Administrative Offices	1897015	754382	93804	237954
克孜勒苏柯尔克孜自治州	Kizilsu Kirgiz Autonomous Prefecture	453995	140355	83505	7203
喀什地区	Kashgar [Kaxgar] Administrative Offices	3421603	693645	177134	197892
和田地区	Hotan Administrative Offices	107967	874373	176821	271552
石河子市	Shihezi City	1354132	213815	63781	119428
阿拉尔市	Aral City	407297	33330	19975	123332
图木舒克市	Tumxuk City	44823	62447	18803	124223
五家渠市	Wujiaqu City	637929	425260	31551	47767
跨地区投资	Trans-regional Investment	702600	430000	1133861	

4-8 分行业城镇固定资产投资主要指标
Main Indicators of Investment in Fixed Assets in Urban Area by Sector

(2012 年)

行　业	Sector	投资额(万元) Total Investment (10 000 yuan)	#地方 Local	施工项目个数(个) Number of Projects under Construction (unit)	竣工项目个数(个) Number of Projects Completed (unit)	本年新增固定资产(万元) Newly Increased Fixed Assets (10 000 yuan)
总　计	**Total**	**49877126**	**36579573**	**9879**	**5799**	**29218800**
农、林、牧、渔业	**Agriculture, Forestry, Animal Husbandry and Fishery**	**1105634**	**929972**	**707**	**502**	**939187**
农　业	Agriculture	185072	177856	118	66	123658
林　业	Forestry	111670	104595	88	66	89842
畜牧业	Animal Husbandry	128298	116866	78	54	91025
渔　业	Fishing	925	925	2	2	925
农、林、牧、渔服务业	Service in Support of Agriculture	679669	529730	421	314	633737
采矿业	**Mining**	**7324221**	**2490875**	**359**	**191**	**4702036**
#煤炭开采和洗选业	Mining and Washing of Coal	1606501	1434493	126	51	688655
石油和天然气开采业	Extraction of Petroleum and Natural Gas	4405085	5822	13	8	3114623
黑色金属矿采选业	Mining and Processing of Ferrous Metals Ores	302625	290725	68	38	185639
#铁矿采选	Mining and Processing of Iron Ore	284915	273015	60	35	173709
有色金属矿采选业	Mining and Processing of Non-ferrous Metals Ores	572781	543316	93	55	383268
#常用有色金属矿采选	Mining and Processing of Common Non-ferrous Metal	461096	442749	61	39	289475
非金属矿采选业	Mining and Processing of Nonmetal Ores	136673	135589	47	31	76826
#土砂石开采	Mining of Earth and Gravel	86917	86833	25	15	43390
制造业	**Manufacturing**	**15236716**	**14168377**	**1900**	**945**	**7831478**
#农副食品加工业	Processing of Food from Agricultural Products	642178	601253	216	128	476950
食品制造业	Manufacture of Foods	533908	523609	56	31	188827
酒、饮料和精制茶制造业	Manufacture of Tobacco,Wine and Tea	220220	218621	62	27	137473
烟草制品业	Manufacture of Tobacco	54155	54155	1		
纺织业	Manufacture of Textile	409520	389748	74	36	208839
纺织服装、服饰业	Manufacture of Textile Wearing Apparel, Footware and Caps	3457	3457	2		
皮革、毛皮、羽毛及其制品和制鞋业	Manufacture of Leather,Fur,Feather and Related Products	859	859	2	2	2770
木材加工和木、竹、藤、棕、草制品业	Processing of Timber, Wood, Bamboo, Cane, Grass Products	51064	51064	20	11	41720
造纸和纸制品业	Manufacture of Paper and Paper Products	111725	105687	25	14	55699
印刷和记录媒介复制业	Printing,Reproduction,of Recording Media	34981	34981	14	6	23347
石油加工、炼焦和核燃料加工业	Processing of Petroleum,Coking	1361308	1227212	89	35	878531
#精炼石油产品制造	Manufacture of Oil Products	790839	679077	46	18	647387
炼　焦	Coking	570469	548135	43	17	231144
化学原料和化学制品制造业	Manufacture of Raw Chemical Material and Chemical Products	2781109	2475257	162	66	1472920

4-8 续表 1 Continued

行业	Sector	投资额（万元）Total Investment (10 000 yuan)	#地方 Local	施工项目个数（个）Number of Projects under Construction (unit)	竣工项目个数（个）Number of Projects Completed (unit)	本年新增固定资产（万元）Newly Increased Fixed Assets (10 000 yuan)
医药制造业	Manufacture of Medicine	293211	267238	33	13	33413
化学纤维制造业	Manufacture of Chemical Fibers	83402	83402	9	7	131174
橡胶和塑料制品业	Manufacture of Rubber and Plastic Products	324961	311859	111	64	306532
非金属矿物制品业	Manufactureof Non-metallicMineral Products	2533108	2339257	556	298	1551329
#水泥、石灰和石膏制造	Cement Manufacturing	1183156	1030553	95	41	620878
玻璃制造	Manufacture of Glasses	67267	65724	15	9	68343
黑色金属冶炼和压延加工业	Smelting and Pressing of Ferrous Metals	2194738	1928223	103	55	831599
#炼　铁	Coking	536492	313277	33	21	362869
炼　钢	Smelting	1102011	1096711	25	9	234190
有色金属冶炼和压延加工业	Smelting and Pressing of Nonferrous Metals	2052355	2046878	52	20	930793
金属制品业	Manufacture of Metal Products	315218	310305	90	46	188088
通用设备制造业	Manufacture of General Purpose Machinery	182279	179279	53	20	73443
专用设备制造业	Manufacture of Special Purpose Machinery	185383	184745	56	19	97334
汽车制造业	Manufacture of Car	215392	193557	10	4	24630
电气机械和器材制造业	Manufacture of Electric Equipment and Machinery	157385	150931	45	16	48329
计算机、通信和其他电子设备制造业	Manufacture of Communication Equipment, Comuputer and othe Elctronic Equipment	114900	114900	7	1	5000
电力、热力、燃气及水生产和供应业	**Production and Supply of Electricity,Gas and Water**	**7372980**	**4969397**	**938**	**544**	**3950503**
电力、热力生产和供应业	Production and Supply of Electricity Power and Heat Power	6168010	3850062	646	362	3283119
电力生产	Production of Electric Power	4746152	3137505	221	68	2220145
电力供应	Supply of Electric Power	799403	363794	263	184	681123
热力生产和供应	Production and Supply of Heat Power	622455	348763	162	110	381851
燃气生产和供应业	Production and Supply of Gas	802359	766883	114	70	395167
水的生产和供应业	Production and Supply of Water	402611	352452	178	112	272217
#自来水生产和供应	Production and Distribution of Running Water	305797	268731	125	78	174650
污水处理及其再生利用	Treatment and Recycle of Waste Water	78525	65432	39	26	92280
建筑业	**Construction**	**851695**	**510073**	**256**	**179**	**600759**
#房屋建筑业	Construction of Buildings	266432	212362	100	71	243262
土木工程建筑业	Buildings and Givil Engineering Construction	534304	246752	128	82	300501
建筑安装业	Building Installation	16641	16641	8	7	15003
批发和零售业	**Wholesale&Retail Trades**	**831863**	**737139**	**261**	**139**	**421650**
批发业	Wholesale Trades	433336	372396	112	49	232433

4-8 续表 2 Continued

行业	Sector	投资额(万元) Total Investment (10 000 yuan)	#地方 Local	施工项目个数(个) Number of Projects under Construction (unit)	竣工项目个数(个) Number of Projects Completed (unit)	本年新增固定资产(万元) Newly Increased Fixed Assets (10 000 yuan)
零售业	Retail Trades	398527	364743	149	90	189217
交通运输、仓储和邮政业	**Transport Storage and Post**	**3802530**	**2377180**	**608**	**366**	**1615611**
#铁路运输业	Railway Transport	928689	26820	28	6	77609
道路运输业	Road Transport	2142596	1756837	457	288	1133799
航空运输业	Air Transportation	53335	33152	8	4	32725
管道运输业	Via Pipelines Transport	50908	5559	7	5	14661
仓储业	Storage	602487	532176	97	54	331537
邮政业	Post	5246	5246	5	5	7866
住宿和餐饮业	**Hotels and Catering Services**	**371715**	**349384**	**141**	**78**	**217103**
住宿业	Hotels	298511	276180	112	60	184523
#旅游饭店	Tourist Restaurant	239623	222572	73	36	126857
餐饮业	Catering Services	73204	73204	29	18	32580
信息传输、软件和信息技术服务业	**Information Transmission, Computer Services and Software**	**444177**	**123607**	**77**	**66**	**486820**
#电信、广播电视和卫星传输服务	Telecommunication and Other Information Transmission Services	404589	113085	70	62	480917
电　信	Telecommunication	384433	94179	56	54	465545
金融业	**Financial Intermediation**	**30370**	**30370**	**19**	**10**	**23542**
#货币金融服务	Services of Intermediation	24882	24882	16	9	19062
资本市场服务	Services of Capital Market	4000	4000	1	1	4000
保险业	**Insurance**	**758**	**758**	**1**		
房地产业	**Real Estate**	**5993429**	**4132741**	**1524**	**930**	**4370636**
#房地产开发经营	Real Estate Development and Operation	591187	587067	205	137	446883
物业管理	Management of Real Estate	42259	41709	8	6	37219
其他房地产业	Other Real Estate	5304945	3448927	1289	773	3851202
租赁和商务服务业	**Leasing and Business Services**	**194833**	**193413**	**62**	**27**	**94448**
租赁业	Leasing	19816	19816	5	1	1500
商务服务业	Business Service	175017	173597	57	26	92948
科学研究和技术服务业	**Scientific Research, Technical Service and Geological Prospecting**	**186717**	**177404**	**74**	**54**	**178143**
研究和试验发展	Research and Experiment Development	13182	7627	5	4	7347
专业技术服务业	Professional Technical Service	144639	142681	49	35	147720
科技推广和应用服务业	Services of Science and Technology Exchanges and Difussion	28896	27096	20	15	23076

4-8 续表 3 Continued

行　　业	Sector	投资额 (万元) Total Investment (10 000 yuan)	#地 方 Local	施工项目个数 (个) Number of Projects under Construction (unit)	竣工项目个数 (个) Number of Projects Completed (unit)	本年新增固定资产 (万元) Newly Increased Fixed Assets (10 000 yuan)
水利、环境和公共设施管理业	**Management of Water Conservancy, Environment and Public Facilities**	**3109419**	**2672515**	**1097**	**674**	**1759402**
水利管理业	Management of Water Conservancy	802127	730125	360	231	467438
生态保护和环境治理业	Environmental Management	138379	136719	35	24	88858
公共设施管理业	Management of Public Facilities	2168913	1805671	702	419	1203106
市政设施管理	Management of Public Facilities	1704813	1372368	485	286	924140
环境卫生管理	Management of Enviroment	63450	58853	50	30	40452
城乡市容管理	Management of Apperance City	73022	73022	26	20	65926
绿化管理	Management of Urban Greening	128965	121958	67	49	101701
公园和游览景区管理	Scenic-Spot Management	198663	179470	74	34	70887
居民服务、修理和其他服务业	**Resident Service and Other Services**	**92759**	**77856**	**66**	**31**	**69504**
教　育	**Education**	**939644**	**823280**	**650**	**409**	**625238**
#初等教育	Elementary Education	136503	133368	132	93	95668
中等教育	Secondary Education	546601	453251	352	213	343356
高等教育	Higher Education	84042	80642	23	14	71422
卫生和社会工作	**Health, Social Security and Social Welfare**	**392405**	**347070**	**268**	**147**	**310505**
卫　生	Health Care	314090	275881	198	113	263993
#医　院	Hospital	234493	199293	128	66	179230
社会工作	Mangement of Social	78315	71189	70	34	46512
文化、体育和娱乐业	**Culture, Sports and Entertainment**	**338564**	**306528**	**183**	**99**	**190335**
新闻和出版业	Journalism and Publishing Activities	7000	7000	1	1	7000
广播、电视、电影和影视录音制作业	Broadcasting,Movies,Televisions and Audiovisual Activites	27722	26167	21	11	18770
文化艺术业	Cultural and Art Activities	191229	166917	113	64	104099
体　育	Sports	103491	98049	43	21	56939
娱乐业	Entertainment	9122	8395	5	2	3527
公共管理、社会保障和社会组织	**Public Management and Social Organization**	**1257455**	**1162392**	**689**	**408**	**831900**
中国共产党机关	Organ of Communist Party of China	18425	17725	15	10	17505
国家机构	Government Agencies	1157722	1072649	622	376	766954
人民政协、民主党派	People's Political Consultative Conference and Democratic Parties	550	550	1		550
社会保障	Social Security	10193	9818	9	2	1250
群众团体、社会团体和其他成员组织	Non-Governmental Institutions,Social Organizations and Religion Organizations	50159	41244	28	12	29282
基层群众自治组织	Grass Roots Self-governing Organizations	20406	20406	14	8	16359

4-9 分行业城镇固定资产投资资金来源情况

单位：万元 (2012 年)

行　业	Sector	本年资金来源小计 Sub-total Funds This Year
总　计	**Total**	**51845729**
农、林、牧、渔业	**Agriculture, Forestry, Animal Husbandry and Fishery**	**1105063**
农　业	Agriculture	195261
林　业	Forestry	103087
畜牧业	Animal Husbandry	129466
渔　业	Fishing	725
农、林、牧、渔服务业	Service in Support of Agriculture	676524
采矿业	**Mining**	**7859650**
#煤炭开采和洗选业	Mining and Washing of Coal	1817080
石油和天然气开采业	Extraction of Petroleum and Natural Gas	4443899
黑色金属矿采选业	Mining and Processing of Ferrous Metals Ores	552983
#铁矿采选	Mining and Processing of Iron Ore	529193
有色金属矿采选业	Mining and Processing of Non-ferrous Metals Ores	613122
#常用有色金属矿采选	Mining and Processing of Common Non-ferrous Metal	470811
非金属矿采选业	Mining and Processing of Nonmetal Ores	141846
#土砂石开采	Mining of Earth and Gravel	94270
制造业	**Manufacturing**	**15724678**
#农副食品加工业	Processing of Food from Agricultural Products	660895
食品制造业	Manufacture of Foods	636289
酒、饮料和精制茶制造业	Manufacture of Tobacco,Wine and Tea	224863
烟草制品业	Manufacture of Tobacco	54156
纺织业	Manufacture of Textile	495422
纺织服装、服饰业	Manufacture of Textile Wearing Apparel,Footware and Caps	3500
皮革、毛皮、羽毛及其制品和制鞋业	Manufacture of Leather,Fur,Feather and Related Products	859
木材加工和木、竹、藤、棕、草制品业	Processing of Timber, Wood, Bamboo, Cane, Grass Products	54169
造纸和纸制品业	Manufacture of Paper and Paper Products	111122
印刷和记录媒介复制业	Printing,Reproduction,of Recording Media	36574
石油加工、炼焦和核燃料加工业	Processing of Petroleum,Coking	1611974
#精炼石油产品制造	Manufacture of Oil Products	978477
炼　焦	Coking	633497

Sources of Funds of Investment in Fixed Assets in Urban Area by Sector

(10 000 yuan)

国家预算内资金 State Budget	国内贷款 Domestic Loans	债券 Bonds	利用外资 Foreign Investment	自筹资金 Self-raising Funds	其他资金来源 Others
7652454	**7060115**	**59304**	**81597**	**33112818**	**3879441**
421003	**19111**		**6360**	**544304**	**114285**
61190			3500	94301	36270
58307			2060	28731	13989
24568	1192			92451	11255
168				557	
276770	17919		800	328264	52771
19133	**671905**		**6335**	**6805757**	**356520**
4276	212857		6335	1560455	33157
1222	335556			3881831	225290
200	27622			484274	40887
200	27622			464584	36787
12405	40310			528597	31810
5000	39900			399671	26240
	22880			93590	25376
	22880			61604	9786
102191	**2012324**	**5100**	**39799**	**13278036**	**287228**
14086	38331			584160	24318
650	4050			626089	5500
310	13010			206398	5145
				54156	
7946	61845			416926	8705
				3500	
				859	
	2500			51423	246
6433	15180	5100		80968	3441
3000	5000			20916	7658
29470	73550		30000	1444561	34393
29470	21194		30000	863420	34393
	52356			581141	

4-9 续表 1

单位：万元

行　业	Sector	本年资金来源小计 Sub-total Funds This Year
化学原料和化学制品制造业	Manufacture of Raw Chemical Material and Chemical Products	2764744
医药制造业	Manufacture of Medicine	168100
化学纤维制造业	Manufacture of Chemical Fibers	78148
橡胶和塑料制品业	Manufacture of Rubber and Plastic Products	322331
非金属矿物制品业	Manufacture of Non-metallic Mineral Products	2605388
#水泥、石灰和石膏制造	Cement Manufacturing	1215866
玻璃制造	Manufacture of Glasses	59536
黑色金属冶炼和压延加工业	Smelting and Pressing of Ferrous Metals	2151764
#炼 铁	Coking	499965
炼 钢	Smelting	1070447
有色金属冶炼和压延加工业	Smelting and Pressing of Nonferrous Metals	2140628
金属制品业	Manufacture of Metal Products	320283
通用设备制造业	Manufacture of General Purpose Machinery	191346
专用设备制造业	Manufacture of Special Purpose Machinery	183337
汽车制造业	Manufacture of Car	227306
电气机械和器材制造业	Manufacture of Electric Equipment and Machinery	179008
计算机、通信和其他电子设备制造业	Manufacture of Communication Equipment,Comuputer and othe Elctronic	118301
电力、热力、燃气及水生产和供应业	**Production and Supply of Electricity,Gas and Water**	**7721863**
电力、热力生产和供应业	Production and Supply of Electricity Power and Heat Power	6493251
电力生产	Production of Electric Power	4971564
电力供应	Supply of Electric Power	817203
热力生产和供应	Production and Supply of Heat Power	704484
燃气生产和供应业	Production and Supply of Gas	824006
水的生产和供应业	Production and Supply of Water	404606
#自来水生产和供应	Production and Distribution of Running Water	312201
污水处理及其再生利用	Treatment and Recycle of Waste Water	73344
建筑业	**Construction**	**839742**
#房屋建筑业	Consturction of Buildings	260685
土木工程建筑业	Buildings and Givil Engineering Construction	534293
建筑安装业	Building Installation	16641
批发和零售业	**Wholesale&Retail Trades**	**854919**
批发业	Wholesale Trades	437030

Continued

(10 000 yuan)

国家预算内资金 State Budget	国内贷款 Domestic Loans	债券 Bonds	利用外资 Foreign Investment	自筹资金 Self-raising Funds	其他资金来源 Others
4469	1150743			1576982	32550
6660	14700			145836	904
	16780			60518	850
	21386			291637	9308
12577	144231			2356144	92436
2000	119645			1076671	17550
	4000			55536	
10015	201343			1904217	36189
	86851			393014	20100
	74183			992176	4088
	198745			1941442	441
	2500			311840	5943
315	4480			185211	1340
1200	7150			173987	1000
	15000			212306	
4640	8300			165518	550
420	13500			104381	
675981	**1984253**	**600**	**3537**	**4963831**	**93661**
474631	1943620			4018424	56576
131064	1376302			3433540	30658
137331	401448			264326	14098
206236	165870			320558	11820
72724	10690			722463	18129
128626	29943	600	3537	222944	18956
90196	18326	600	2800	186151	14128
29313	8617			32914	2500
285874	**268777**			**260623**	**24468**
124399	29206			94760	12320
151500	239571			134370	8852
6832				9809	
19437	**8608**			**748133**	**78741**
4698	3812			384968	43552

4-9 续表 2

单位：万元

行业	Sector	本年资金来源小计 Sub-total Funds This Year
零售业	Retail Trades	417889
交通运输、仓储和邮政业	Transport Storage and Post	**4099406**
#铁路运输业	Railway Transport	798883
道路运输业	Road Transport	2494880
航空运输业	Air Transportation	58956
管道运输业	Via Pipelines Transport	50691
仓储业	Storage	672313
邮政业	Post	4763
住宿和餐饮业	**Hotels and Catering Services**	**398048**
住宿业	Hotels	325508
#旅游饭店	Tourist Restaurant	257608
餐饮业	Catering Services	72540
信息传输、软件和信息技术服务业	**Information Transmission, Computer Services and Software**	**406197**
#电信、广播电视和卫星传输服务	Telecommunication and Other Information Transmission Services	365455
#电信	Telecommunication	343763
金融业	**Financial Intermediation**	**29968**
#货币金融服务	Services of Intermediation	25128
资本市场服务	Services of Capital Market	3600
保险业	**Insurance**	**510**
房地产业	**Real Estate**	**6007314**
#房地产开发经营	Real Estate Development and Operation	600065
物业管理	Management of Real Estate	39484
其他房地产业	Other Real Estate	5314097
租赁和商务服务业	**Leasing and Business Services**	**206043**
租赁业	Leasing	20357
商务服务业	Business Service	185686
科学研究和技术服务业	**Scientific Research, Technical Service and Geological Prospecting**	**193568**
研究和试验发展	Research and Experiment Development	14377
专业技术服务业	Professional Technical Service	148961
科技推广和应用服务业	Services of Science and Technology Exchanges and Difussion	30230

Continued

(10 000 yuan)

国家预算内资金 State Budget	国内贷款 Domestic Loans	债券 Bonds	利用外资 Foreign Investment	自筹资金 Self-raising Funds	其他资金来源 Others
14739	4796			363165	35189
1290796	**1193247**	**40000**	**7306**	**1247820**	**320237**
344762	277030	40000		91771	45320
706164	815047		7306	707970	258393
	7500			42891	8565
	42472			8219	
238320	51198			374836	7959
550				4213	
10928	**12460**		**1730**	**334442**	**38488**
8841	11800		1730	271491	31646
7200	8300		1730	221530	18848
2087	660			62951	6842
24146				**377684**	**4367**
21641				339447	4367
16540				324823	2400
1748				26210	2010
1018				22100	2010
				3600	
				510	
1787574	**180084**	**5076**		**2299997**	**1734583**
199418	5700	402		338062	56483
1071	17000			12035	9378
1573349	157384	4674		1927865	1650825
26171	**5110**			**166789**	**7973**
	2000			18357	
26171	3110			148432	7973
29512	**6935**			**89602**	**67519**
2500	2805			9072	
19219	3130			64542	62070
7793	1000			15988	5449

4-9 续表 3

单位：万元

行　　业	Sector	本年资金来源小计 Sub-total Funds This Year
水利、环境和公共设施管理业	**Management of Water Conservancy, Environment and Public Facilities**	**3292067**
水利管理业	Management of Water Conservancy	831033
生态保护和环境治理业	Environmental Management	138731
公共设施管理业	Management of Public Facilities	2322303
市政设施管理	Management of Public Facilities	1721228
环境卫生管理	Management of Enviroment	69589
城乡市容管理	Management of Apperance City	74015
绿化管理	Management of Urban Greening	115567
公园和游览景区管理	Scenic-Spot Management	341904
居民服务、修理和其他服务业	**Resident Service and Other Services**	**96466**
教　育	**Education**	**991105**
#初等教育	Elementary Education	142885
中等教育	Secondary Education	589122
高等教育	Higher Education	98128
卫生和社会工作	**Health, Social Security and Social Welfare**	**380174**
卫　生	Health Care	295900
#医院	Hospital	220620
社会工作	Mangement of Social	84274
文化、体育和娱乐业	**Culture, Sports and Entertainment**	**354809**
新闻和出版业	Journalism and Publishing Activities	6719
广播、电视、电影和影视录音制作业	Broadcasting,Movies,Televisions and Audiovisual Activites	25070
文化艺术业	Cultural and Art Activities	202026
体　育	Sports	112422
娱乐业	Entertainment	8572
公共管理、社会保障和社会组织	**Public Management and Social Organization**	**1284649**
中国共产党机关	Organ of Communist Party of China	23173
国家机构	Government Agencies	1175401
人民政协、民主党派	People's Political Consultative Conference and Democratic Parties	680
社会保障	Social Security	10898
群众团体、社会团体和其他成员组织	Non-Governmental Institutions,Social Organizations and Religion Organizations	52653
基层群众自治组织	Grass Roots Self-governing Organizations	21844

Continued

(10 000 yuan)

国家预算内资金 State Budget	国内贷款 Domestic Loans	债券 Bonds	利用外资 Foreign Investment	自筹资金 Self-raising Funds	其他资金来源 Others
1288867	**576643**	**513**	**16530**	**1116673**	**292841**
566550	19657	513	3081	214689	26543
63737	18393			49251	7350
658580	538593		13449	852733	258948
437384	510026		10524	543633	219661
44105	2194		2413	18755	2122
32018				35743	6254
60972	962			42679	10954
84101	25411		512	211923	19957
35714	**2565**			**49837**	**8350**
582809	**54914**	**6589**		**163323**	**183470**
95609				20475	26801
364454	35150	4700		67811	117007
31174	16634	1889		31410	17021
188216	**25182**	**146**		**104009**	**62621**
130784	18237	146		89804	56929
103708	18237	146		68826	29703
57432	6945			14205	5692
147849	**11690**			**171655**	**23615**
	2060			4659	
16465				8180	425
85723	8930			86683	20690
45661	700			63661	2400
				8472	100
714505	**26307**	**1280**		**364093**	**178464**
16002				923	6248
661451	26307	1280		337818	148545
				680	
2296				4762	3840
22651				15855	14147
12105				4055	5684

4-10 各地、州、市、县(市)城镇固定资产投资和新增固定资产

Total Investment and Newly Increased Fixed Assets in Urban Area by Prefecture, Autonomous Prefecture, City and County

单位：万元 (2012 年) (10 000 yuan)

地区 Region	投资总额 Total Investment	第一产业 Primary Industry	第二产业 Secondary Industry	第三产业 Tertiary Industry	新增固定资产 Newly Increased Fixed Assets	房屋建筑面积(万平方米) Floor Space of Buildings (10 000 sq.m) 施工面积 Floor Space Under Construction	竣工面积 Floor Space Completed
总计 Total	**49877126**	**1105634**	**30785612**	**17985880**	**29218800**	**11122.21**	**3091.80**
按隶属关系分 **By Administrative Relationship**							
中央 Central Government	13297553	175662	8646890	4475001	8531366	2412.43	1039.63
地方 Local	36579573	929972	22138722	13510879	20687434	8709.78	2052.17
按区域分 **Grouped by Region**							
乌鲁木齐市 Urumqi City	**5812238**	**25622**	**3272271**	**2514345**	**4392759**	**1016.17**	**250.62**
天山区 Tianshan District	693221		458207	235014	586959	106.47	40.36
沙依巴克区 Shayibak District	697591	783	195841	500967	502815	187.70	11.39
新市区 Xinshi District	2021642		1444253	577389	1177010	215.88	7.97
水磨沟区 Shui Mogou District	643696	700	16858	626138	282087	143.17	78.82
头屯河区 Tou Tunhe District	590170	14555	244192	331423	555998	259.10	74.53
达坂城区 Da Bancheng District	336489	2199	332632	1658	266124	14.20	
米东区 Midong District	700826	3895	490944	205987	942946	82.73	31.11
乌鲁木齐县 Urumqi County	128603	3490	89344	35769	78820	6.92	6.44
克拉玛依市 Karamay City	**3016611**	**9391**	**2530718**	**476502**	**2641388**	**167.74**	**44.25**
独山子区 Dushanzi District	80991		53098	27893	281266	6.36	
克拉玛依区 Karamay District	2754557	9391	2339584	405582	2274873	126.19	35.79
乌尔禾区 Urhe District	113427		94189	19238	49714	13.51	8.46
白碱滩区 Bai Jiantan District	67636		43847	23789	35535	21.68	
吐鲁番地区 Turpan Administrative Offices	**1722084**	**22796**	**1455604**	**243684**	**856344**	**237.42**	**28.01**
吐鲁番市 Turpan City	335671	11025	223248	101398	188713	148.15	9.23
鄯善县 Shanshan [Piqan] County	974224	11771	860187	102266	649607	32.42	9.63
托克逊县 Toksun County	412189		372169	40020	18024	56.85	9.15
哈密地区 Hami [Kumul] Administrative Offices	**2817495**	**39432**	**2274295**	**503768**	**930886**	**345.69**	**126.73**
哈密市 Hami [Kumul] City	1851445	16590	1454374	380481	475996	309.31	110.12
巴里坤哈萨克自治县 Barkol Kazak Autonomous County	407845	9044	340342	58459	329843	29.24	14.67
伊吾县 Yiwu [Araturuk] County	558205	13798	479579	64828	125047	7.14	1.94
昌吉回族自治州 Changji Hui Autonomous Prefecture	**6280548**	**178474**	**4628320**	**1473754**	**2622700**	**776.67**	**173.98**
昌吉市 Changji City	1085526	37535	383024	664967	306461	334.17	18.33
阜康市 Fukang City	1140798	22908	990348	127542	198778	53.67	33.14

4-10 续表 1 Continued

单位：万元 (10 000 yuan)

地区 Region	投资总额 Total Investment	第一产业 Primary Industry	第二产业 Secondary Industry	第三产业 Tertiary Industry	新增固定资产 Newly Increased Fixed Assets	房屋建筑面积(万平方米) Floor Space of Buildings (10 000 sq.m) 施工面积 Floor Space Under Construction	竣工面积 Floor Space Completed
呼图壁县 Hutubi County	584646	69257	385627	129762	365479	111.24	34.70
玛纳斯县 Manas County	508919	35845	247776	225298	517485	195.66	73.68
奇台县 Qitai County	1121341	12929	845134	263278	1098330	74.86	14.13
吉木萨尔县 Jimsar County	1789355		1749279	40076	96121		
木垒哈萨克自治县 Mori Kazak Autonomous County	49963		27132	22831	40046	7.07	
伊犁哈萨克自治州 Ili Kazak Autonomous Prefecture	**8486050**	**302395**	**5057868**	**3125787**	**4895556**	**1947.76**	**694.97**
伊犁州直属县(市) Counties (Cities) Direct Under Ili Prefecture	**4551987**	**56563**	**2995038**	**1500386**	**2050782**	**956.49**	**241.22**
伊宁市 Yining [Gulja] City	1019719	3600	667356	348763	257656	107.36	29.69
奎屯市 Kuytun City	1141756	6070	759109	376577	832627	162.73	50.39
伊宁县 Yining [Gulja] County	534953	7349	439498	88106	119423	64.10	14.22
察布查尔锡伯自治县 Qapqal Xibe Autonomous County	415592	8984	350951	55657	155498	54.79	23.51
霍城县 Huocheng [Korgas] County	576869	6010	279426	291433	267855	249.17	43.64
巩留县 Gongliu [Tokkuztara] County	179118	11120	78216	89782	79643	42.75	20.76
新源县 Xinyuan [Kunes] County	301478	7388	203383	90707	148590	138.21	13.04
昭苏县 Zhaosu [Mongolkure] County	72951	1192	19100	52659	60635	22.91	11.88
特克斯县 Tekes County	120527	4340	62663	53524	70428	13.24	10.89
尼勒克县 Nilka County	189024	510	135336	53178	58427	101.23	23.20
塔城地区 Tacheng [Tarbagatai] Administrative Offices	**2213131**	**119402**	**1186340**	**907389**	**1784483**	**671.21**	**282.63**
塔城市 Tacheng [Qoqek] City	186263	22377	46845	117041	202941	84.55	47.59
乌苏市 Usu City	574724	32497	392600	149627	438272	103.59	48.19
额敏县 Emin Ciunty	359966	30949	143753	185264	279274	154.50	73.78
沙湾县 Shawan County	424165	22502	142328	259335	332320	269.56	84.47
托里县 Toli County	229363	5528	159542	64293	141203	25.99	13.84
裕民县 Yumin [Qagantokay] County	36672	3420	9249	24003	22590	7.95	3.26
和布克赛尔蒙古自治县 Hoboksar Mongol Autonomous County	401978	2129	292023	107826	367883	25.07	11.50
阿勒泰地区 Altay Administrative Offices	**1720932**	**126430**	**876490**	**718012**	**1060291**	**320.06**	**171.12**
阿勒泰市 Altay City	395846	23752	100784	271310	233042	134.15	34.81
布尔津县 Burqin County	191709	27822	126367	37520	218959	30.68	28.90
富蕴县 Fuyun [Koktokay] County	419484	4229	326755	88500	128459	27.00	15.02
福海县 Fuhai [Burultokay] County	165558	28122	38380	99056	108825	49.99	25.27

4-10 续表 2 Continued

单位：万元 (10 000 yuan)

地区 Region	投资总额 Total Investment	第一产业 Primary Industry	第二产业 Secondary Industry	第三产业 Tertiary Industry	新增固定资产 Newly Increased Fixed Assets	房屋建筑面积(万平方米) Floor Space of Buildings (10 000 sq.m) 施工面积 Floor Space Under Construction	竣工面积 Floor Space Completed
哈巴河县 Habahe [Kaba] County	234995	23481	88750	122764	184224	46.64	43.62
青河县 Qinghe [Qinggil] County	194715	8188	147855	38672	95751	15.51	10.00
吉木乃县 Jeminay County	118625	10836	47599	60190	91031	16.09	13.50
博尔塔拉蒙古自治州 Bortala Mongol Autonomous Prefecture	**1369994**	**66719**	**503429**	**799846**	**1043867**	**416.88**	**142.85**
博乐市 Bole [Bortala] City	909624	45947	317712	545965	683364	258.26	97.98
精河县 Jinghe [Jing] County	346146	11288	171513	163345	276141	114.99	16.45
温泉县 Wenquan [Araxang] County	114224	9484	14204	90536	84362	43.63	28.42
巴音郭楞蒙古自治州 Bayangol Mongol Autonomous Prefecture	**4788552**	**78386**	**3716472**	**993694**	**2341180**	**891.82**	**282.30**
库尔勒市 Korla City	2715379	500	2416403	298476	1200839	189.73	89.13
轮台县 Luntai [Bugur] County	288760	12843	180979	94938	174589	49.37	25.45
尉犁县 Yuli [Lopnur] County	122461	5521	48984	67956	64237	46.82	21.48
若羌县 Ruoqiang [Qarkilik] County	442801	15874	299000	127927	347490	159.60	51.27
且末县 Qiemo [Qarqan] County	176658	10413	78032	88213	143393	187.31	23.75
焉耆回族自治县 Yanqi Hui Autonomous County	166179	19965	75018	71196	43903	43.72	20.26
和静县 Hejing County	693150	5327	543394	144429	292081	100.00	23.09
和硕县 Hoxud County	126554	4755	52640	69159	46467	81.11	14.79
博湖县 Bohu [Bagrax] County	56610	3188	22022	31400	28181	34.16	13.08
阿克苏地区 Aksu Administrative Offices	**2983155**	**54813**	**1844932**	**1083410**	**1720077**	**794.29**	**220.72**
阿克苏市 Aksu City	780126	14952	441419	323755	438472	431.14	74.86
温宿县 Wensu [Onsu] County	302088	6341	163068	132679	72678	30.56	16.41
库车县 Kuqa County	883180	8501	601766	272913	465986	119.66	79.88
沙雅县 Xayar County	226769		203096	23673	191936	20.33	2.41
新和县 Xinhe [Toksu] County	172558	9315	87843	75400	131838	71.35	
拜城县 Baicheng [Bay] County	353076		259262	93814	250641		
乌什县 Wushi [Uxturpan] County	61056	9068	4067	47921	43622	45.31	17.62
阿瓦提县 Awat County	156288	2564	68859	84865	89158	68.73	29.54
柯坪县 Kalpin County	48014	4072	15552	28390	35746	7.21	
克孜勒苏柯尔克孜自治州 Kizilsu Kirgiz Autonomous Prefecture	**685058**	**10083**	**507132**	**167843**	**318613**	**239.20**	**126.81**
阿图什市 Artux City	259354	4000	184583	70771	89192	86.49	37.75
阿克陶县 Akto County	208601	6083	146187	56331	102050	99.87	67.94

4-10 续表 3 Continued

单位：万元 (10 000 yuan)

地 区 Region	投资总额 Total Investment	第一产业 Primary Industry	第二产业 Secondary Industry	第三产业 Tertiary Industry	新增固定资产 Newly Increased Fixed Assets	房屋建筑面积(万平方米) Floor Space of Buildings (10 000 sq.m) 施工面积 Floor Space Under Construction	竣工面积 Floor Space Completed
阿合奇县 Akqi County	74457		74088	369	16769	21.09	
乌恰县 Wuqia [Ulugqat] County	142646		102274	40372	110602	31.75	21.12
喀什地区 Kashgar [Kaxgar] Administrative Offices	**4490274**	**185705**	**1525096**	**2779473**	**3373820**	**1761.08**	**164.98**
喀什市 Kashgar [Kaxgar] City	958522	5710	178405	774407	647059	101.73	5.11
疏附县 Shufu County	167938	1000	65016	101922	87667	301.56	67.89
疏勒县 Shule County	790240	34588	409917	345735	539137	137.54	16.30
英吉沙县 Yengisar County	412442	24315	195653	192474	305047	146.18	
泽普县 Zepu [Poskam] County	238525	9010	60774	168741	211618	158.83	
莎车县 Shache [Yarkant] County	229517	10042	50815	168660	209168	299.77	2.09
叶城县 Yecheng [Kagilik] County	368344	11966	100627	255751	289923	132.79	
麦盖提县 Makit County	229423	28630	50521	150272	139954	73.45	15.57
岳普湖县 Yopurga County	248214	18643	116170	113401	235704	6.58	3.54
伽师县 Jiashi [Payzawat] County	346087	36593	123355	186139	213107	144.50	10.46
巴楚县 Bachu [Maralbexi] County	318022	1092	93171	223759	312436	257.29	44.02
塔什库尔干塔吉克自治县 Taxkorgan Tajik Autonomous County	183000	4116	80672	98212	183000	0.86	
和田地区 Hotan Administrative Offices	**1430713**	**95046**	**268593**	**1067074**	**1152452**	**1536.59**	**564.43**
和田市 Hotan City	398444	10055	37535	350854	303437	938.51	138.77
和田县 Hotan County	189749	18907	66569	104273	93804	32.26	11.68
墨玉县 Moyu [Karakax] County	255233	16163	50972	188098	200395	110.79	68.28
皮山县 Pishan [Guma] County	128472	10312	11641	106519	118899	89.66	52.43
洛浦县 Lop County	135616	9766	35769	90081	171373	217.27	195.10
策勒县 Qira County	104899	15118	7337	82444	84134	70.20	45.56
于田县 Yutian [Keriya] County	165015	9450	52203	103362	132629	48.19	38.76
民丰县 Minfeng [Niya] County	53285	5275	6567	41443	47781	29.71	13.85
自治区直辖县级市 Municpality Country-LevelCity directly	**3727893**	**36772**	**2890882**	**800239**	**2401158**	**989.41**	**271.16**
石河子市 Shihezi City	1751156	11727	1482922	256507	1151154	352.11	81.19
阿拉尔市 Aral City	583934	5519	331115	247300	330283	250.64	103.13
图木舒克市 Tumxuk City	250296	5990	66362	177944	111202	165.90	49.50
五家渠市 Wujiaqu City	1142507	13536	1010483	118488	808519	220.76	37.34
跨地区投资 Trans-regional Investment	**2266461**		**310000**	**1956461**	**528000**	**1.49**	

4-11 各地、州、市分行业城镇固定资产投资

单位：万元 (2012 年)

行业 Sector	合计 Total	乌鲁木齐市 Urumqi City	克拉玛依市 Karamay City	吐鲁番地区 Turpan Administrative Offices	哈密地区 Hami [Kumul] Administrative Offices	昌吉回族自治州 Changji Hui Autonomous Prefecture	伊犁哈萨克自治州 Ili Kazak Autonomous Prefecture	伊犁州直属县(市) Counties (Cities) Direct Under Ili Prefecture
总计 Total	**49877126**	**5812238**	**3016611**	**1722084**	**2817495**	**6280548**	**8486050**	**4551987**
农、林、牧、渔业 Farming, Forestry, Animal Husbandry and Fishery	1105634	25622	9391	22796	39432	178474	302395	56563
采矿业 Mining	7324221	43496	1906041	604170	678922	561753	645738	352041
制造业 Manufacturing	15236716	1794669	387709	490568	331045	3610382	2634914	1807197
电力、热力、燃气及水生产和供应业 Production and Supply of Electricity, Gas and Water	7372980	1052539	110326	360866	1264328	456185	1743026	809674
建筑业 Construction	851695	381567	126642				34190	26126
交通运输、仓储及邮政业 Transport, Storage, Postal and Telecommunications Services	3802530	354763	14378	27769	66658	370316	441990	265959
信息传输、软件和信息技术服务业 Information Transmission, Computer Services and Software	444177	294100	9433		4023	2371	39458	14014
批发和零售业 Wholesale&Retail Trades	831863	156675	105309	19043	18510	39102	175986	118112
住宿和餐饮业 Hotels and Catering Services	371715	34756	9240	11912	5043	65137	66993	25120
金融业 Financial Intermediation	30370						4819	
房地产业 Real Estate	5993429	489537	65107	58886	239367	567892	1065866	444053
租赁和商务服务业 Leasing and Business Services	194833	19908	12616			42833	37522	24922
科学研究和技术服务业 Scientific Research, Technical Service and Geological Prospection	186717	11310	64399	1455	690	11205	65372	4052
水利、环境和公共设施管理业 Management of Water Conservancy, Environment and Public Facilities	3109419	835184	3562	36341	57223	223571	708504	341271
居民服务、修理和其他服务业 Service to Households and Others Services	92759	11550	6275	578	3281	8135	13191	8400
教育 Education	939644	132809	49926	18705	31854	22652	174331	93697
卫生和社会工作 Health, Social Securities and Social Welfare	392405	58577	23797	4891	18779	25608	60019	33619
文化、体育和娱乐业 Culture, Sports and Entertainment	338564	13052	41988	3614	5909	73404	83851	30793
公共管理、社会保障和社会组织 Public Management and Social Organization	1257455	102124	70472	60490	52431	21528	187885	96374

Investment in Fixed Assets in Urban Area by Sectors in Prefecture, Autonomous Prefecture and City

(10 000 yuan)

塔城地区 Tacheng [Tarbagatai] Administrative Offices	阿勒泰地区 Altay Administrative Offices	博尔塔拉蒙古自治州 Bortala Mongol Autonomous Prefecture	巴音郭楞蒙古自治州 Bayangol Mongol Autonomous Prefecture	阿克苏地区 Aksu Administrative Offices	克孜勒苏柯尔克孜自治州 Kizilsu Kirgiz Autonomous Prefecture	喀什地区 Kashgar [Kaxgar] Administrative Offices	和田地区 Hotan Administrative Offices	石河子市 Shihezi City	阿拉尔市 Aral City	图木舒克市 Tumxuk City	五家渠市 Wujiaqu City	跨地区投资 Trans-regional Investment
2213131	**1720932**	**1369994**	**4788552**	**2983155**	**685058**	**4490274**	**1430713**	**1751156**	**583934**	**250296**	**1142507**	**2266461**
119402	126430	66719	78386	54813	10083	185705	95046	11727	5519	5990	13536	
173531	120166	47005	2291916	93108	12452	89176	40444					310000
577936	249781	258940	1090687	1282196	237131	1062606	141592	854903	194144	41858	823372	
427052	506300	176537	329919	395639	159637	261459	86557	627376	136971	24504	187111	
7821	243	20947	3950	73989	97912	111855		643				
88576	87455	60681	97926	40123	11070	187427	112049	31542	16056		13321	1956461
18705	6739	6629	2124	5360	1340	68596	10743					
50696	7178	23968	64144	59383	5108	113797	5217	16500	19521	500	9100	
26322	15551	2125	25395	13656	7650	86821	16743	8348	9466	5730	2700	
3973	846	564	5800	3297		15890						
405816	215997	340973	387929	630700	55464	1203527	502446	88589	125606	123923	47617	
5600	7000	2933	10662	438	2220	61029	4672					
3753	57567	2258	4408	320	4617	13425	5508	1750				
138392	228841	254730	224126	134030	17871	327560	101086	67596	52404	28689	36942	
4791		2933	1965	7957	654	24314	6127	3106	2134		559	
49408	31226	27077	46561	93100	28712	148967	129575	8476	14244	7906	4749	
21124	5276	7952	18871	12502	6906	107027	33976	6701	3490	2309	1000	
40254	12804	6299	27034	11029	2500	48565	12545	4150	2248	676	1700	
49979	41532	60724	76749	71515	23731	372528	126387	19749	2131	8211	800	

4-12 城镇固定资产投资效果指标
Investment Result of Urban Investment

指 标	Item	2011	2012
建设周期(年)	Construction Cycle (year)	4	4
计划总投资(万元)	Total Planned Investment (10 000 yuan)	131077233	180099700
本年完成投资(万元)	Completed Invetsment for the Current Year (10 000 yuan)	36881064	49877126
本年新增固定资产(万元)	Newly Increased Fixed Assets for the Current Year (10 000 yuan)	20864406	29218800
固定资产交付使用率(%)	Rate of Projects of Fixed Assets Completed and Put into Operation (%)	56.6	58.6
施工项目个数(个)	Number of Projects under Construction (unit)	10382	9879
竣工项目个数(个)	Number of Projects Completed (unit)	6528	5799
建设项目投产率(%)	Rate of Projects Completed&Put into Use (%)	62.9	58.7
施工面积(万平方米)	Construction Area (10 000 sq.m)	8204.64	11122.21
#住 宅	Residential Buildings	4309.17	5706.03
竣工面积(万平方米)	Completed Area (10 000 sq.m)	2358.37	3091.80
#住 宅	Residential Buildings	1513.57	2169.67
房屋面积竣工率(%)	Rate of Floor Space of Buildings Completed (%)	28.7	27.8
#住 宅	Residential Buildings	35.1	38.0

4-13 主要年份房地产开发企业基本情况
Basic Condition of Enterprises for Real Estate Development in Main Years

指　标	Item	2005	2010	2012
企业单位数(个)	**Number of Enterprises (unit)**	**756**	**1233**	**1509**
#亏损企业	Loss- Suffering Enterprises	410	606	869
主要财务指标 (万元)	**Main Financial Indices (10 000 yuan)**			
年末资产负债情况	Situation of Year-end Liabilities			
资产总计	Total Assets	4861415	12591584	22518080
固定资产累计折旧	Accumulated Depreciation of Fixed Assets	81096	156739	238825
#本年折旧	Depreciation for the Current Year	17981	34814	58997
负债总计	Total Liabilities	2932694	9422446	17260594
所有者权益合计	Total of Owner's Right and Interest	1928721	3169138	5257486
实收资本	Total of Actual Capital	970103	2109245	3848658
#国家资本	State-owned Capital	59976	162505	
损益情况	Situation of Profit and Loss			
经营收入总计	Total Income of Business	1084796	4119413	5505493
#土地转让收入	Income of Land Transfer	11295	19029	23648
商品房销售收入	Sales Income of Commercial Flat	1047965	4022490	5334513
房屋出租收入	Income of Renting House	15773	39343	62549
其他收入	Others	9763	38550	84783
经营成本	Operating Cost	871320	3040741	3980185
经营税金及附加	Operating Tax and Extra Charges	63562	295011	414382
销售费用	Expenses of sales	27319	100896	174916
其他业务利润	Other Business Profits	9161	28592	148522
管理费用及财务费用	Expenses of Both Management and Finance	80949	257405	433803
投资收益及营业外收入	Income of Investment earnings and Extra-business	7829	14881	133026
营业外支出	Expenditure of Extra-business	3456	14909	32538
利润总额	Total Profits	34320	454814	644250

注：2004 年以后，企业个数包括了没有开发量的企业数，而往年未包括。
Note: Urban Investment exclude real estate, the following the same as follows.

4-14 主要年份房地产投资主要指标
Main Indicators of Real Estate Investment in Main Years

指 标	Item	2005	2010	2012
本年购置土地面积(万平方米)	**Land Area Purchased for the Current Year (10 000 sq. m)**	**447.30**	**557.69**	**760.67**
房地产开发投资额(万元)	**Total Investment of Real-Estate Development (10 000 yuan)**	**1016618**	**3477185**	**6060939**
按中央和地方分	Grouped by Central and Local			
中央企业	Central Enterprises	54128	175564	353962
地方企业	Local Enterprises	962490	3301621	5706977
按投资构成分	Classified by Use of Funds			
建筑工程	Construction Works	810003	2742491	4713051
安装工程	Works of Installation	49559	161703	464374
设备工器具购置	Purchase of Equipment and Instruments	14135	51777	89271
其他费用	Other Expenses	142921	521214	794243
#土地购置费	Expenses of Land Purchase	94230	313568	382920
按工程用途分	Grouped by Purpose of Projects			
住 宅	Residential buildings	679521	2815620	4442667
办公楼	Office Building	40977	102895	120840
商业营业用房	Houses for Commercial and Business Purpose	247033	380275	976135
其 他	Others	49087	178395	521297
本年资金来源小计 (万元)	**Sub-total of Capital Sources for the Current Year (10 000 yuan)**	**1137693**	**5380739**	**7979461**
国内贷款	Domestic Loans	113887	684191	908749
利用外资	Foreign Investment	160		
自筹资金	Self-raising Funds	479948	1397982	2976896
其它资金	Others	543698	3298566	4093816

4-15 按用途分房地产开发企业（单位）投资完成额

Investment Actually Completed by Enterprises for Real Estate Development by Use

单位：万元　　　　(10 000 yuan)

年份 Year	地区 Region	企业个数（个） Number of Enterprises (unit)	本年完成投资 Investment Completed This Year	住宅 Residential Buildings	#别墅、高档公寓 Villas, High-grade Apartments
	1996	139	156232	80728	
	1997		169906	81886	1668
	1998		148577	95225	1000
	1999	165	234481	174446	2994
	2000	209	574347	500381	2390
	2001	293	979184	757490	3126
	2002	335	877060	570643	11001
	2003	492	1024908	547770	20212
	2004	709	1125577	599276	29585
	2005	756	1016618	679521	26634
	2006	824	1208786	899482	48542
	2007	909	1683160	1390360	57776
	2008	1130	2286267	1937460	94256
	2009	1159	2358805	1882530	148916
	2010	1233	3477185	2815620	194136
	2011	1421	5163895	4163926	258846
	2012	1509	6060939	4442667	368122
乌鲁木齐市	Urumqi City	387	2338304	1840785	119759
克拉玛依市	Karamay City	37	253332	211212	14199
吐鲁番地区	Turpan Administrative Offices	23	25784	11291	
哈密地区	Hami [Kumul] Administrative Offices	95	158701	112603	2492
昌吉回族自治州	Changji Hui Autonomous Prefecture	131	387220	306223	21550
伊犁哈萨克自治州	Ili Kazak Autonomous Prefecture	292	1079378	785072	10097
伊犁州直属县(市)	Counties (Cities) Direct Under Ili Prefecture	166	764916	546204	6609
塔城地区	Tacheng [Tarbagatai] Administrative Offices	48	160286	128676	1028
阿勒泰地区	Altay Administrative Offices	78	154176	110192	2460
博尔塔拉蒙古自治州	Bortala Mongol Autonomous Prefecture	48	92072	56662	1269
巴音郭楞蒙古自治州	Bayangol Mongol Autonomous Prefecture	150	553463	405121	160648
阿克苏地区	Aksu Administrative Offices	133	319972	215004	
克孜勒苏柯尔克孜自治州	Kizilsu Kirgiz Autonomous Prefecture	14	40005	31722	
喀什地区	Kashgar [Kaxgar] Administrative Offices	89	227334	97701	
和田地区	Hotan Administrative Offices	4	12168	5087	
石河子市	Shihezi City	58	226135	161589	
阿拉尔市	Aral City	14	46572	37432	
图木舒克市	Tumxuk City	9	22564	9694	
五家渠市	Wujiaqu City	25	277935	155469	38108

4-15 续表 Continued

单位：万元 (10 000 yuan)

年 份 Year	地 区 Region	办公楼 Office buildings	商业营业用房 Houses for Business Use	其 他 Other
	1996	18108	42562	14834
	1997	25347	41935	20738
	1998	17394	22027	13931
	1999	9133	27068	23834
	2000	13171	42601	18194
	2001	41911	111028	68755
	2002	81119	153498	71800
	2003	81497	286896	108745
	2004	77843	390566	57892
	2005	40977	247033	49087
	2006	28233	236945	44126
	2007	27629	205590	59581
	2008	56358	221418	71031
	2009	81926	281946	112403
	2010	102895	380275	178395
	2011	155400	572602	271967
	2012	120840	976135	521297
乌鲁木齐市	Urumqi City	56528	178996	261995
克拉玛依市	Karamay City	4504	26894	10722
吐鲁番地区	Turpan Administrative Offices	1027	10589	2877
哈密地区	Hami [Kumul] Administrative Offices	6593	29450	10055
昌吉回族自治州	Changji Hui Autonomous Prefecture	6103	47093	27801
伊犁哈萨克自治州	Ili Kazak Autonomous Prefecture	14575	207323	72408
伊犁州直属县(市)	Counties (Cities) Direct Under Ili Prefecture	11792	161527	45393
塔城地区	Tacheng [Tarbagatai] Administrative Offices	20	13979	17611
阿勒泰地区	Altay Administrative Offices	2763	31817	9404
博尔塔拉蒙古自治州	Bortala Mongol Autonomous Prefecture	1568	21810	12032
巴音郭楞蒙古自治州	Bayangol Mongol Autonomous Prefecture	16075	96191	36076
阿克苏地区	Aksu Administrative Offices	4258	87365	13345
克孜勒苏柯尔克孜自治州	Kizilsu Kirgiz Autonomous Prefecture	1100	5059	2124
喀什地区	Kashgar [Kaxgar] Administrative Offices	6464	93327	29842
和田地区	Hotan Administrative Offices		1250	5831
石河子市	Shihezi City	1758	30868	31920
阿拉尔市	Aral City		9140	
图木舒克市	Tumxuk City	7	12728	135
五家渠市	Wujiaqu City	280	118052	4134

4-16 房地产开发企业（单位）资金来源
Sources of Funds of Enterprises for Real Estate Development

单位：万元 (10 000 yuan)

年 份 Year	地 区 Region	合 计 Total	国内贷款 Domestic Loans	利用外资 Foreign Investment	自筹资金 Self-raising Funds	其他资金来源 Others
	1996	154995	51048	742	45104	58101
	1997	161399	51443	500	60573	48883
	1998	151094	22419	500	49427	78748
	1999	244252	29665	5770	73899	134918
	2000	701332	113823	600	232768	354141
	2001	890102	106794	1278	303975	478055
	2002	1064031	158511		455707	449813
	2003	1117659	208348		448441	460870
	2004	1215850	125553		546282	544015
	2005	1137693	113887	160	479948	543698
	2006	1446593	145340		478871	822382
	2007	2243755	217380		766344	1260031
	2008	2427323	253427		961343	1212553
	2009	3683795	453692	50	915219	2314834
	2010	5380739	684191		1397982	3298566
	2011	6843313	731550	1666	2314233	3795864
	2012	7979461	908749		2976896	4093816
乌鲁木齐市	Urumqi City	3314323	464090		869630	1980603
克拉玛依市	Karamay City	437093	82582		236844	117667
吐鲁番地区	Turpan Administrative Offices	35541	2360		26642	6539
哈密地区	Hami [Kumul] Administrative Offices	224968	26895		62819	135254
昌吉回族自治州	Changji Hui Autonomous Prefecture	641987	80576		157887	403524
伊犁哈萨克自治州	Ili Kazak Autonomous Prefecture	1242522	52063		655574	534885
伊犁州直属县(市)	Counties (Cities) Direct Under Ili Prefecture	925903	36610		439744	449549
塔城地区	Tacheng [Tarbagatai] Administrative Offices	182009	2209		135655	44145
阿勒泰地区	Altay Administrative Offices	134610	13244		80175	41191
博尔塔拉蒙古自治州	Bortala Mongol Autonomous Prefecture	112028			52395	59633
巴音郭楞蒙古自治州	Bayangol Mongol Autonomous Prefecture	602498	59816		217429	325253
阿克苏地区	Aksu Administrative Offices	358343	47494		187738	123111
克孜勒苏柯尔克孜自治州	Kizilsu Kirgiz Autonomous Prefecture	38305			30853	7452
喀什地区	Kashgar [Kaxgar] Administrative Offices	297889	28980		176202	92707
和田地区	Hotan Administrative Offices	15742			15742	
石河子市	Shihezi City	297635	24250		98111	175274
阿拉尔市	Aral City	36142			31182	4960
图木舒克市	Tumxuk City	15325			9104	6221
五家渠市	Wujiaqu City	309120	39643		148744	120733

4-17 房地产开发企业（单位）施工、销售和待售情况

单位：万平方米

年 份 Year	地 区 Region	本年施工房屋面积 Floor Space of Building under Construction This Year	#住宅 Residential Buildings	#商业营业用房 Houses for Business Use	本年新开工房屋面积 Floor Space Started This Year	#住宅 Residential Buildings	#商业营业用房 Houses for Business Use
	1996	224.90	150.80	41.67	103.87	69.84	19.52
	1997	222.20	144.50	47.68	90.24	70.08	12.81
	1998	252.61	188.38	40.72	133.26	120.95	6.35
	1999	343.38	295.62	34.33	212.73	194.77	12.48
	2000	771.86	665.30	74.20	453.63	397.77	43.00
	2001	1433.54	1207.89	150.63	912.06	778.55	97.24
	2002	1246.89	946.11	204.52	577.04	433.57	98.13
	2003	1382.14	962.89	298.51	782.78	557.28	175.73
	2004	1333.03	863.19	357.53	771.47	550.66	178.43
	2005	1371.15	941.58	340.63	793.55	639.98	130.90
	2006	1567.70	1188.61	307.19	1035.59	875.99	131.90
	2007	2053.76	1715.00	271.52	1347.11	1216.39	101.82
	2008	2639.06	2247.80	259.78	1703.86	1500.75	129.11
	2009	3064.41	2560.67	305.81	1718.17	1482.86	158.07
	2010	3980.80	3317.68	410.96	2177.24	1852.88	214.50
	2011	5481.44	4574.72	543.12	2974.51	2510.68	304.46
	2012	6896.54	5482.59	841.24	2823.64	2149.35	421.32
乌鲁木齐市	Urumqi City	2500.45	1998.18	169.85	710.90	544.52	48.78
克拉玛依市	Karamay City	319.34	284.55	23.40	220.11	197.78	15.77
吐鲁番地区	Turpan Administrative Offices	39.35	18.88	16.65	24.35	10.16	14.18
哈密地区	Hami [Kumul] Administrative Offices	259.41	212.82	30.51	68.73	55.53	7.46
昌吉回族自治州	Changji Hui Autonomous Prefecture	477.49	415.53	42.52	201.75	158.14	31.11
伊犁哈萨克自治州	Ili Kazak Autonomous Prefecture	1109.82	848.37	212.68	512.53	367.47	117.77
伊犁州直属县(市)	Counties (Cities) Direct Under Ili Prefecture	719.18	521.86	161.97	354.12	233.90	97.89
塔城地区	Tacheng [Tarbagatai] Administrative Offices	182.40	164.42	12.31	72.45	62.56	9.11
阿勒泰地区	Altay Administrative Offices	208.24	162.09	38.40	85.96	71.01	10.77
博尔塔拉蒙古自治州	Bortala Mongol Autonomous Prefecture	138.23	92.63	39.40	67.45	43.64	18.17
巴音郭楞蒙古自治州	Bayangol Mongol Autonomous Prefecture	786.19	642.25	95.98	340.54	264.45	50.37
阿克苏地区	Aksu Administrative Offices	407.09	323.54	69.65	262.61	207.40	47.07
克孜勒苏柯尔克孜自治州	Kizilsu Kirgiz Autonomous Prefecture	51.43	43.65	5.42	40.47	36.30	3.77
喀什地区	Kashgar [Kaxgar] Administrative Offices	238.90	164.48	54.99	91.89	67.62	18.28
和田地区	Hotan Administrative Offices	15.22	12.95	0.76	5.05	2.91	0.68
石河子市	Shihezi City	247.62	183.48	36.07	116.11	77.21	21.18
阿拉尔市	Aral City	38.22	32.48	5.74	18.73	17.51	1.22
图木舒克市	Tumxuk City	25.42	15.85	9.23	11.13	5.14	5.68
五家渠市	Wujiaqu City	242.36	192.95	28.39	131.29	93.57	19.83

Condition of Under Construction, Sale and Idle of Enterprises for Real Estate Development

(10 000 sq.m)

本年竣工房屋面积 Floor Space of Buindings Completed This Year	#住宅 Residential Buildings	#商业营业用房 Houses for Business Use	本年房屋销售面积 Floor Space of Building Sold This Year	#住宅 Residential Buildings	#商业营业用房 Houses for Business Use	房屋销售额(万元) Sales Value of Buildings (10 000 yuan)	#住宅 Residential Buildings	#商业营业用房 Houses for Business Use
81.19	64.51	8.14	45.60	41.29	2.91	67514	57024	5883
93.56	73.32	6.93	55.43	52.48	0.98	75110	67585	1569
94.28	79.92	6.23	83.29	75.97	3.46	118386	98803	8544
159.99	143.93	13.52	127.48	120.44	4.67	177683	158304	12599
330.11	298.79	23.07	262.52	250.95	9.82	373801	333166	35153
633.25	559.91	57.01	419.87	381.67	31.77	643814	537818	90441
727.21	616.12	85.03	506.66	455.68	46.34	879287	658157	208821
791.14	626.50	126.42	587.02	516.48	53.44	1066640	768012	224579
704.25	511.61	156.54	635.53	538.33	81.27	1106143	784408	281856
717.43	553.48	121.37	687.20	606.48	68.16	1235410	915191	288747
679.06	551.63	104.13	892.41	806.46	73.96	1658176	1358136	265450
890.55	798.12	72.07	1144.34	1078.28	51.57	2381520	2113425	211508
1049.29	943.40	67.30	954.35	886.35	51.22	2137859	1861169	212861
1032.72	900.87	76.28	1406.55	1326.67	65.81	3662638	3271682	317310
1012.90	859.92	98.40	1564.90	1450.02	94.42	4830392	4164140	523153
1270.48	1108.02	109.66	1728.23	1570.56	123.12	6133128	5162366	779898
1736.19	1438.43	177.43	1430.30	1274.79	116.33	5604508	4581386	759812
684.12	564.91	37.27	402.93	363.65	15.36	2209166	1858457	149501
62.86	56.41	4.41	69.06	62.81	2.24	195975	172209	14302
1.30	0.82	0.47	3.25	2.74	0.52	8960	6451	2509
110.96	100.13	7.73	47.83	43.18	3.23	170586	139061	24590
123.98	113.33	7.51	194.44	184.08	9.06	661848	594986	62905
261.50	214.97	33.57	263.27	237.72	23.56	831250	692268	131280
182.82	150.57	24.82	183.35	163.18	18.79	635337	517802	111045
50.40	43.29	2.45	29.65	28.65	0.54	87097	83148	3029
28.28	21.11	6.30	50.27	45.89	4.23	108816	91318	17206
34.08	25.38	8.64	38.40	30.14	8.26	134673	82172	52501
192.67	158.46	24.92	138.38	128.97	8.59	418511	357043	59632
102.04	73.52	27.15	78.12	58.03	19.09	253750	144476	107737
10.06	7.32	1.16	13.47	10.02	1.90	42393	16538	24069
56.36	51.56	2.59	31.92	25.85	4.62	118625	80780	31771
0.18	0.18	0.00	10.47	9.76	0.43	30780	27836	1968
21.99	11.13	8.92	61.87	55.81	4.78	275333	229799	23994
24.34	19.69	4.65	17.96	13.03	4.93	61418	36087	25331
4.25	2.75	1.47	4.34	2.03	2.30	15315	3410	11880
45.50	37.87	6.97	54.59	46.97	7.46	175925	139813	35842

4-17 续表 Continued

单位：万平方米 (10 000 sq.m)

年 份 Year	地 区 Region	房屋待售面积 Floor Space At Idle	# 住宅 Residential Buildings	# 商业营业用房 Houses for Business Use
	1996	33.20	27.41	4.44
	1997	36.33	25.58	3.76
	1998	27.20	20.33	2.78
	1999	63.01	49.00	8.91
	2000	69.75	58.92	6.35
	2001	200.46	169.78	20.26
	2002	353.23	285.87	51.33
	2003	422.11	313.93	84.81
	2004	400.40	248.38	125.31
	2005	460.99	269.07	151.02
	2006	406.25	208.02	157.83
	2007	289.22	115.39	150.68
	2008	389.70	245.81	119.10
	2009	419.83	254.36	121.41
	2010	348.98	195.47	106.55
	2011	367.02	220.45	92.77
	2012	459.21	277.72	93.42
乌鲁木齐市	Urumqi City	156.76	62.06	29.24
克拉玛依市	Karamay City	3.18	0.90	1.47
吐鲁番地区	Turpan Administrative Offices	3.67	1.72	1.95
哈密地区	Hami [Kumul] Administrative Offices	14.51	10.32	2.98
昌吉回族自治州	Changji Hui Autonomous Prefecture	36.85	31.49	3.96
伊犁哈萨克自治州	Ili Kazak Autonomous Prefecture	82.05	61.69	11.64
伊犁州直属县(市)	Counties (Cities) Direct Under Ili Prefecture	40.33	26.96	6.87
塔城地区	Tacheng [Tarbagatai] Administrative Offices	30.05	28.37	1.03
阿勒泰地区	Altay Administrative Offices	11.67	6.36	3.75
博尔塔拉蒙古自治州	Bortala Mongol Autonomous Prefecture	4.97	2.66	2.31
巴音郭楞蒙古自治州	Bayangol Mongol Autonomous Prefecture	52.31	36.23	15.12
阿克苏地区	Aksu Administrative Offices	51.70	37.98	13.01
克孜勒苏柯尔克孜自治州	Kizilsu Kirgiz Autonomous Prefecture	0.32	0.15	0.17
喀什地区	Kashgar [Kaxgar] Administrative Offices	23.84	13.05	3.62
和田地区	Hotan Administrative Offices	1.38	1.12	0.27
石河子市	Shihezi City	10.02	5.97	2.64
阿拉尔市	Aral City	11.34	7.11	4.23
图木舒克市	Tumxuk City	0.22	0.03	0.18
五家渠市	Wujiaqu City	6.09	5.24	0.63

4-18 新增主要产品生产能力
Newly Increased Production Capacity of Major Products

项　目	Item	2011	2012
原煤开采(万吨/年)	Coal Mining (10 000 tons/year)	2706.00	1356.60
焦炭(万吨/年)	Coke (10 000 tons/year)	190.00	697.50
天然原油开采(万吨/年)	Petroleum Extractin (10 000 tons/year)	1092.80	243.46
天然气开采(亿立方米/年)	Natural Gas Extraction (100 million cu.m/year)	23.00	16.00
石油加工	Petroleum Processing		
裂化设备能力(处理万吨/年)	Cracking Equipment Capabillity(handle 10 000 tons/year)	8.00	10.30
铁矿石开采(原矿) (万吨/年)	Iron-Ore Mining (10 000 tons/year)	907.60	226.90
铁矿选矿处理原矿量(万吨/年)	Iron-ore Dressing (10 000 tons/year)	62.50	428.20
铁矿石成品矿(万吨/年)	Eed Products of Iron Ore Mine(10 000 tons/year)	86.00	226.00
生铁(万吨/年)	Pig Iron(10 000 tons/year)	520.60	356.80
粗钢(万吨/年)	Crude Steel(10 000 tons/year)	270.00	311.50
铜采矿(原矿)(万吨/年)	Copper Ore Mining (10 000 tons/year)	92.15	60.51
铜选矿	Copper Ore Dressing		
处理原矿(万吨/年)	Raw Ore Treatment (10 000 tons/year)	152.52	50.70
铅锌采矿(原矿) (万吨/年)	Plumbum/Zinc Ore Mining (10 000 tons/year)	5.00	95.00
铝加工(吨/年)	Aluminium Processing (ton/year)	74000	112193
黄金(公斤/年)	Gold (kg/year)	394	335.34
发电机组容量(万千瓦)	Capacity of Generating Setes (10 000 kw/year)		
水力发电	Hydropower	37.05	91.15
火力发电	Thermal Power	237.32	400.20
其他发电	Others	68.15	0.80
输电线路长度(11 万伏及以上)(公里)	Transmission Line (110 000V)(km)	2881.84	5460.46
水泥(万吨/年)	Cement (10 000 tons/year)	2071.80	2685.30

4-18 续表 Continued

项　　目	Item	2011	2012
石墨及炭素制品(吨/年)	Graphite and Carbon Products(ton/year)	332895	303000
电石(吨/年)	Calcium Carbide (ton/year)	1810000	909000
农用氮、磷、钾化学肥料(吨/年)	Farm-use Nitrogen, Phosphorus and Potassium Fertilizer (ton/year)		
氮肥	Nitrogen Fertilizer	962907	591320
磷肥	Phoshate Fertilizer	14500	10526
钾肥	Potash Fertilizer	1209000	1000
塑料树脂及共聚物(吨/年)	Plastic Colophony and Polymer (ton/year)	437010	600000
化学纤维(吨/年)	Chemical Fiber (ton/year)	113000	85000
粘胶纤维(吨/年)	Viscose Fiber(ton/year)	100000	50000
棉纺锭(锭)	Cotton Spindle (spindle)	160000	305720
酒(万吨/年)	Liquors (10 000 tons/year)	1.98	10.40
其他酒	Others	1.98	5.70
新建公路(公里)	Length of New Highways (km)	2140.11	1473.11
二级公路	Second Class highway	202.73	52.08
改建公路(公里)	Length of Reconstructed Highways(km)	7691.18	7239.27
二级公路	Second Class highway	1524.96	598.80
新建独立公路桥梁(延长米)	New-Built Separate Highway and Bridge (Extended Length m)	2084.54	5294.69
(座)	(unit)	5	9
新(扩)建客、货运站(个)	Number of newly-Built or Expanded Passenger and Freight Stations (unit)	14	9
(平方米)	(sq.m)	22802	45863
城市自来水供水能力(万吨/日)	Capacity of City Tap Water Supply (10 000 tons/day)	17.25	27.19
城市污水处理能力(万吨/日)	Disposal Capacity of Sewer (10 000 tons/day)	11.36	19.75

4-19 农村非农户固定资产投资情况
Investment in Fixed Assets of Non-Rural Households in Rural Areas

单位：万元 (10 000 yuan)

指标	Item	2011	2012
新增固定资产	**Newly Increased Investment in Fixed Assets**	**2158777**	**2918075**
固定资产投资完成额	**Completed Investment in Fixed Assets**	**3211176**	**3637772**
按投资构成分	By Use of Funds		
建筑工程	Construction Works	2234227	2681289
安装工程	Installation Works	147782	215391
设备工器具购置	Purchase of Equipment and Instruments	672389	576768
#用于更新的设备	Renew of Equipment and Instruments	48911	82003
其　他	Others	156778	164324
按投资方向分	By Sector of Investment		
农、林、牧、渔业	Agriculture, Forestry, Animal Husbandry and Fishing	658798	607559
采矿业	Mining	207420	162953
制造业	Manufacturing	749671	664789
电力、热力、燃气及水的生产及供应业	Production and Supply of Electricity Gas and Water	279839	442628
建筑业	Construction	150305	110171
交通运输、仓储和邮政业	Transport, Storage and Post	208751	280179
信息传输、软件和信息技术服务业	Information Transmission, Computer Servcies and Software	200	
批发和零售业	Wholesale and Retail Trades	13142	33200
住宿和餐饮业	Hotel and Catering Service	9791	15384
金融业	Financial Intermediation	2120	1700
房地产业	Real Estate	367474	725465
租赁和商务服务业	Leasing and Business Service Industries	7570	2211
科学研究和技术服务业	Scientific Research, Technology Service and Geological Prospecting	8602	2057
水利、环境和公共设施管理业	Water Conservancy, Environment and Public Facility Management	208970	316409
居民服务、修理和其他服务业	Community Service and Other Services	1300	15236
教　育	Education	36501	35130
卫生和社会工作	Health, Social Security and Social Welfare	11149	8294
文化、体育和娱乐业	Culture, Sports and Entertainment	6757	13332
公共管理、社会保障和社会组织	Public Management and Social Organizations	282816	201075
资金来源	**Sub-total Funds**	**3614758**	**3892244**
国家预算内资金	State Budgetary Funds	1001746	1032231
国内贷款	Domestic Loans	177709	406590
债　券	Bonds	822	432
利用外资	Foreign Investment	6308	9600
自筹资金	Self-raising Funds	2045605	2135673
其他资金	Others	382568	307718
本年施工房屋面积(万平方米)	**Floor Space of Buildings Under Construction (10 000 sq.m)**	**1223.34**	**1384.06**
#住　宅	Residential Building	744.25	859.91
本年竣工房屋面积(万平方米)	**Floor Space of Completed Building (10 000 sq.m)**	**547.39**	**881.48**
#住　宅	Residential Building	322.04	544.29

4-20 农户固定资产投资情况

Investment in Fixed Assets of Rural Households in Rural Areas

单位:万元 (抽样调查 Sampled Survey) (10 000 yuan)

指 标	Item	2011	2012
新增固定资产原值	**Newly Increased Investment in Fixed Assets**	**1871564**	**3007993**
固定资产投资完成额	**Complete Investment in Fixed Assets**	**1871564**	**3007993**
按投资来源分	By Source of Fund		
国内贷款	Domestic Loans	317899	522521
自筹资金	Self-raising Funds	1440585	1888665
其他资金	Others	113080	596807
按投资构成分	By Use of Funds		
建筑工程	Construction	899078	1535512
#水 利	Water Conservancy	34617	36515
房 屋	Building	859660	1485499
#住 宅	Residential Building	780935	1449785
安装工程	Works of Installation		221
设备工、器具购置	Purchase of Equipment And Instruments	798264	1249850
#生产设备	Production of Equipment	618222	1149292
其 它	Others	174222	222410
按投资方向分	By Sector of Funds		
第一产业	Primary	700939	1226683
第二产业	Secondary	105229	1434244
第三产业	Tertiary	1065396	347066
按具体投资项目分	By Project of Investment		
房 屋	Building	859660	1485499
#住 宅	Residential Building	780935	1449785
道 路	Road	137	
设 备	Equipment	798264	1249850
水 利	Water Conservancy	34617	36516
其 他	Others	178886	236128
本年施工房屋面积(万平方米)	**Floor Space of Buildings Under Construction (10 000 sq.m)**	**1895.46**	**2223.51**
#住 宅	Residential Building	1729.22	2111.15
本年竣工房屋面积(万平方米)	**Floor Space of Completed Building (10 000 sq.m)**	**1722.82**	**2111.99**
#住 宅	Residential Building	1561.31	1999.64
调查户总人口(人)	**Total Number of Households (person)**	**6655**	**6718**

主要统计指标解释

全社会固定资产投资 以货币形式表现的在一定时期内全社会建造和购置固定资产的工作量以及与此有关的费用的总称。该指标是反映固定资产投资规模、结构和发展速度的综合性指标,又是观察工程进度和考核投资效果的重要依据。全社会固定资产投资按登记注册类型可分为国有、集体、联营、股份制、私营和个体、港澳台商、外商、其他等。

城镇固定资产投资 指城镇各种登记注册类型的企业、事业、行政单位及个体户进行的计划总投资500万元以上的建设项目投资和房地产开发投资。县城及以上区域内发生的投资，县及县以上各级政府及主管部门直接领导、管理的建设项目和企业事业单位的投资均为城镇固定资产投资。

固定资产投资（不含农户） 包含原口径的城镇固定资产投资加上农村企事业组织项目投资，该口径自2011年起开始使用。

房地产开发投资 指各种登记注册类型的房地产开发法人单位统一开发的包括统代建、拆迁还建的住宅、厂房、仓库、饭店、宾馆、度假村、写字楼、办公楼等房屋建筑物和配套的服务设施，土地开发工程（如道路、给水、排水、供电、供热、通讯、平整场地等基础设施工程）和土地购置的投资；不包括单纯的土地开发和交易活动。

农村投资 包括在农村区域范围内进行固定资产投资活动的企业、事业、行政单位及农户投资。

建设总规模 是指在报告期内所有施工项目的计划总投资。这个指标和施工项目相对应。

在建总规模 是指在报告期末所有在建项目的计划总投资。

在建净规模 是指报告期末所有在建项目建成投产尚需的投资总量。

在建净规模＝在建总规模－未投产项目（期末在建）累计完成投资。

固定资产投资的资金来源 根据固定资产投资的资金来源不同，分为国家预算内资金、国内贷款、利用外资、自筹资金和其他资金。

(1)国家预算内资金: 国家预算包括一般预算、政府性基金预算、国有资本经营预算和社保基金预算。各类预算中用于固定资产投资的资金全部作为国家预算资金填报，其中一般预算中用于固定资产投资的部分包括基建投资、车购税、灾后恢复重建基金和其他财政投资。各级政府债券也应归入国家预算资金。

(2)国内贷款: 指报告期内向银行及非银行金融机构借入的各种国内借款，包括银行利用自有资金及吸收存款发放的贷款、上级主管部门拨入的国内贷款、国家专项贷款（包括煤代油贷款、劳改煤矿专项贷款等），地方财政专项资金安排的贷款、国内储备贷款、周转贷款等。

(3)利用外资: 指报告期收到的用于固定资产建造和购置的境外资金(包括设备、材料、技术在内)。包括对外借款(外国政府贷款、国际金融组织贷款、出口信贷、外国银行商业贷款、对外发行债券和股票)、外商直接投资、外商其他投资(包括利用外商投资收益在国内进行固定资产再投资活动的资金)。不包括我国自有外汇资金(国家外汇、地方外汇、留成外汇、调剂外汇和国内银行自有资金发放的外汇贷款等)。计算利用外资时，需要折算成人民币，折算时所使用的外汇汇率按现汇汇率计算，即按报告期末的汇率计算。

(4)自筹资金: 指固定资产投资单位在报告期收到的，由各企、事业单位筹集用于固定资产投资的资金，包括各类企事业单位的自有资金和从其他单位筹集的用于固定资产投资的资金，但不包括各类财政性资金、从各类金融机构借入资金和国外资金。

(5)其他资金: 指在报告期收到的除以上各种资金之外的用于固定资产投资的资金，包括社会集资、个人资金、无偿捐赠的资金及其他单位拨入的资金等。

固定资产投资按国民经济行业分 根据建设项目建成投产后的主要产品种类或主要用途及社会经济活动种类来划分，不能根据项目单位本身的行业类别来划分。如果项目投产后有几种产品，应根据主要产品来确定行业类别。一般情况下，一个建设项目只能属于一种国民经济行业。

固定资产投资按建设性质分 按整个建设项目情况来确定。建设项目的性质一般分为新建、扩建、改建和技术改造、单纯建造生活设施、迁建、恢复、单纯购置。房地产开发单位、农户投资不划分建设性质。

(1)新建 指从无到有“平地起家”开始建设的项目。现有企业、事业、行政单位投资的项目一般不属于新建。但如有的单位原有基础很小，经过建设后新增的固定资产价值超过该企业、事业、行政单位原有固定资产价值（原值）三倍以上的，也应作为新建。

(2)扩建 指在厂内或其他地点，为扩大原有产品的生产能力(或效益)或增加新的产品生产能力，而增建的生产车间(或主要工程)、分厂、独立的生产线的企业、事业单位。行政、事业单位在原单位增建业务性用房(如学校增建教学用房、医院增建门诊部、病房等)也作为扩建。

现有企、事业单位为扩大原有主要产品生产能力或增加新的产品生产能力，增建一个或几个主要生产车间(或主要工程)、分厂，同时进行一些更新改造工程的，也应作为扩建。

(3)改建和技术改造　指现有企业、事业单位对原有设施进行技术改造或更新(包括相应配套的辅助性生产、生活福利设施) 的建设项目。改建项目包括现有企业、事业单位为适应市场变化的需要，而改变企业的主要产品种类(如军工企业转民产品等) 的建设项目，原有产品生产作业线由于各工序(车间)之间能力不平衡，为填平补齐充分发挥原有生产能力而增建不增加本企业主要产品设计能力的车间的建设项目。技术改造是指企业、事业单位在现有基础上，用先进的技术代替落后的技术，用先进的工艺和装备代替落后的工艺和装备，以改变企业落后的技术经济面貌，实现以内涵为主的扩大再生产，达到提高产品质量、促进产品更新换代、节约能源、降低消耗、扩大生产规模、全面提高社会经济效益的目的。技术改造具体包括以下内容：机器设备和工具的更新改造；生产工艺改革、节约能源和原材料的改造；厂房建筑和公共设施的改造；保护环境进行的“三废”治理改造；劳动条件和生产环境的改造等。

固定资产投资按构成分

(1)建筑工程　指各种房屋、建筑物的建造工程，又称建筑工作量。这部分投资额必须兴工动料，通过施工活动才能实现，是固定资产投资额的重要组成部分。

(2)安装工程　指各种设备、装置的安装工程，又称安装工作量。

在安装工程中，不包括被安装设备本身价值。

(3)设备工具器具购置　指建设单位或企、事业单位购置或自制的，达到固定资产标准的设备、工具、器具的价值。新建单位及扩建单位的新建车间，按照设计或计划要求购置或自制的全部设备、工具、器具，不论是否达到固定资产标准均计入“设备工具器具购置”中。

(4)其他费用　指在固定资产建造和购置过程中发生的，除上述几项内容以外的各种应分摊计入固定资产的费用。

施工项目个数　是指本年正式进行过建筑或安装施工活动的建设项目个数。包括本年新开工项目，以前年度开工跨入本年继续施工项目，本年全部建成投产项目、以前年度全部停缓建在本年恢复施工的项目，本年进行过施工又在本年内全部停缓建的项目。施工项目个数可以反映一定时期固定资产投资的实际规模，与同期全部建成投产项目个数相比，可以从建设速度的角度反映固定资产投资的效果。

投产项目个数　指报告期内按设计文件规定建成主体工程和相应配套的辅助设施，形成生产能力或工程效益，经过验收合格，并且已正式投入生产或交付使用的建设项目。

新增生产能力(或工程效益)　指通过固定资产投资活动而增加的设计能力(或工程效益)，主要指标包括建设规模、本年施工规模、自开始建设累计新增生产能力（或工程效益）、本年新增生产能力（或工程效益）等。

房屋施工面积　指报告期内施工的全部房屋建筑面积。包括本期新开工的面积、上期跨入本期继续施工的房屋建筑面积、上期停缓建在本期恢复施工的房屋建筑面积、本期竣工的房屋建筑面积以及本期施工后又停缓建的房屋建筑面积。多层建筑应填各层建筑面积之和。

房屋竣工面积　指在报告期内房屋建筑按照设计要求已经全部完工，达到住人和使用条件，经验收鉴定合格或达到竣工验收标准，可正式移交使用的各栋房屋建筑面积的总和。

新增固定资产　是指已经完成建造和购置过程，并已交付生产或使用单位的固定资产的价值，包括已经建成投入生产或交付使用的工程投资和达到固定资产标准的设备、工具、器具的投资及有关应摊入的费用。该指标是表示固定资产投资成果的价值指标，也是反映建设进度，计算固定资产投资效果的重要指标。

建设项目投产率　指一定时期内全部建成投产项目个数与同期施工项目个数的比率。该指标是从建设单位建设速度的角度反映投资效果的指标。

固定资产交付使用率　指一定时期新增固定资产与同期完成投资额的比率。该指标是反映固定资产动用速度，衡量建设过程中宏观投资效果的综合指标。由于新增固定资产是较长时期内形成的结果，而投资额则是当年完成的，因此，该指标一般适宜于反映较长时期内固定资产的动用情况。

商品房销售面积　指报告期内出售商品房屋的合同总面积（即双方签署的正式买卖合同中所确定的建筑面积）。由现房销售面积和期房销售面积两部分组成。

商品房销售额　指报告期内出售商品房屋的合同总价款（即双方签署的正式买卖合同中所确定的合同总价）。该指标与商品房销售面积同口径，由现房销售额和期房销售额两部分组成。

Explanatory Notes on Main Statistical Indicators

Total Investment in Fixed Assets in the Whole Country refers to the volume of activities in construction and purchases of fixed assets and related fees, expressed in monetary terms. It is a comprehensive indicatorwhich shows the size, structure and growth of the investment in fixed assets, providing basis for observing the progress of construction projects and evaluating results of investment. Total investment in fixed assets in the whole country includes, by type of ownership, the investment by the state-owned units, collective units, individuals, joint ownership units, share-holding units, as well as investment by businessmen from foreign countries and from Hong Kong, Macau and Taiwan, and by other units.

Urban Investment in Fixed Assets refer to construction projects involving a total planned (or required) investment of 5 million yuan and over by urban enterprises and institutions of various types of ownership, by administrative units and by individuals, investment in real estate development, and housing investment by individuals in urban areas and in industrial and mining areas. In other words, all investments that take place in county towns and urban areas, investment in construction projects under the direct leadership and management of government agencies at and above county levels and investments by enterprises and institutions at and above county levels are covered in urban investment in fixed assets. Investment in Fixed Assets (Excluding Rural Households) refers to the urban investment in fixed assets under the previous statistical coverage plus project investments by rural enterprises and institutions.

Investment in Fixed Assets (Excluding Rural Households) refers to the urban investment in fixed assets under the previous statistical coverage plus project investments by rural enterprises and institutions.

Investment in Real Estate Development refers to the investment by the real estate development companies, commercial buildings construction companies and other real estate development units of various types of ownership in the construction of house buildings, such as residential buildings, factory buildings, warehouses, hotels, guesthouses, holiday villages, office buildings, and the complementary service facilities and land development projects, such as roads, water supply, water drainage, power supply, heating, telecommunications, land leveling and other projects of infrastructure. It excludes the activities in pure land transactions.

Investment in Rural Areas refers to investment in fixed assets by enterprises, institutions and individuals in rural areas.

Total Size of Construction refers to the planned total investment for all construction projects during the reference period.

Total Size of Investment in Projects under Construction refers to the planned total investment of all projects under construction at the end of the reference period.

Net Size of Investment in Projects under Construction refers to the required investment of all projects under construction at the end of the reference period.

Net Size of Investment = Total Size of Investment – accumulated completed investment of projects under construction

Sources of Funds for Investment in Fixed Assets include fund from state budget, domestic loans, foreign investment, self-raised funds, and others depending on the source of investment. (1) Fund from state budget consists of budgetary appropriation and loans from state budget. More specifically, it includes, from the budget of the central government, capital construction fund (operation fund and non-operational fund), special expenses (e.g. expenses on substituting petroleum with coal), loans from repayment, discount fund, expenses on innovation and trial production of new products, expenses on urban construction, expenses on temporary construction by Trades departments, development fund for less developed areas, as well as local budgetary fund transferred from the central budget. (2) Domestic loans refer to loans of various forms borrowed by investing units from banks and non-bank financial institutions during the reference period for the purpose of investment in fixed assets, including loans issued by banks from their self-owned funds and deposit, loans appropriated by higher responsible authorities, special loans by government (including loan for substituting petroleum with coal, special loan for reform-through-labour coal mines), loans arranged by local government from special funds, domestic reserve loan, and working loan, etc. (3) Foreign Investment refers to foreign funds received during the reference period for the construction and purchase of investment in fixed assets (covering equipment, materials and technology), including foreign borrowings (loans from foreign governments and international financial institutions, export credit, commercial loans from foreign banks, issue of bonds and stocks overseas), foreign direct investment and other foreign investment. Excluded in this category are capitals in foreign exchanges owned by China (foreign exchanges owned by the central and local governments, foreign exchanges retained by enterprises, foreign exchanges by enterprises through regulating mechanism, loans in foreign exchanges issued by the Bank of China with its own fund, etc.). In calculating the utilization of foreign capitals, foreign currencies are converted into Chinese Renminbi applying the current exchange rate when the foreign capitals are actually used. (4) Self-raised funds refer to extra-budgetary funds for investment in fixed assets received by investing units from central government ministries, local governments, enterprises and institutions, including their self-raised funds. (5) Others refer to funds for investment in fixed assets received from the sources other than those listed above, including capitals raised through issuing bonds by enterprises or financial institutions, funds raised from individuals and through donations, and funds transferred from other units.

Investment in Fixed Assets by Sector The classification of construction projects by sector is determined by the major products or the purpose of the projects when they are put into production or use, and by the nature of their social economic activities. In general, one project or one enterprise or institution can only be classified into one sector.

Investment in Fixed Assets by Type of Construction The construction projects in general can be classified, by the type of construction, into new construction, expansion, reconstruction and technical transformation, moving and restoration. However, investment by type of construction is not applied to investment by real-estate development units, investment in rural areas and investment in housing by urban individuals.

(1) New construction in general refers to newly constructed enterprises, institutions, administrative agencies or independent projects from scratch. Construction in the existing enterprises, institutions or agencies is not considered as new construction. In case the assets of the existing unit is quite small, and the value of newly added fixed assets exceeds the original value of assets by three times, the expansion will be considered as new construction.

(2) Expansion refers to construction of new major production workshop, branch factory or independent production line within a factory or in other locations, for the purpose of increasing the production capacity (or improving efficiency) of the original products. Newly constructed houses for the operation of institutions and administrative organizations (such as the newly constructed buildings for teaching in schools, buildings for clinics or wards in hospitals, etc.) are also classified as expansion.Also included in the expansion are investments by existing enterprises or institutions in building major production line(s) or branch factory(ies) along with some work on innovation, for the purpose of expending the production capacity of original products or producing new products.

(3) Reconstruction refers to construction projects by existing enterprises or institutions in innovation or technical transformation of the old facilities (including auxiliary production equipment and welfare facilities). Also considered as reconstruction is the construction of new workshops by the existing enterprises or institutions to change the variety of products to meet the market demand (such as the production of civil products by defence industries), or to bring the designed production capacity into full play through a more balanced production process on production lines. Technical transformation refers to replacement of old technology or equipment by new technology or equipment, in order to expand the reproduction through improvement of technology contents in production, to improve product quality, to promote new products, to save energy and reduce consumption and to improve overall social-economic efficiency. Contents of technical transformation include: updating of machinery, equipment and tools; reforming production process by using energy or materials saving technology; construction of factory workshops and transformation of public facilities; improvement of working conditions and environment, etc.

Investment in Fixed Assets by Structure By their contents, investment activities are classified into 3 categories, i.e. construction and installation, purchase of equipment and instrument, and other expenses.(1) Construction and installation (work volume of construction and installation) refers to the construction of various houses and buildings and installation of various kinds of equipment and instruments. They include construction of various houses; equipment foundations, industrial kilns and stoves, and metal structure work; preparation works for project construction, and clearing up works post project construction; pavement of railways and roads, drilling of mines and putting up of oil pipes; construction of projects of water conservancy; construction of underground air-raid shelters and construction of other special projects; value of equipment for heating, sanitation, ventilation, lighting, gas, painting, etc. that are covered by the budget of housing projects; laying out of various pipelines (for steam, compressed air, petroleum, tap water and sewage) and lines for electric power and for communications;

installation of various machinery equipment, testing operation for pre-testing the quality of installation projects, and land and other development work conducted by real estate developers for commercial housing. The value of equipment installed is not included in the value of installation projects.(2) Purchase of equipment and instruments refers to the total value of equipment, tools, and instruments purchased or self-produced which come up to standards for fixed assets by the construction units or investing enterprises or institutions. Equipment, tools and instruments purchased or self-produced for new workshops by newly established or expanded units are categorized as "purchase of equipment and instruments" no matter whether they come up to the standards for fixed assets.(3) Other expenses refer to expenses occurring during the construction or purchase of fixed assets other than those mentioned above.

Projects under Construction refer to number of all projects construction activities newly started in current year or left-over from the previous year in the reference period. All projects that have construction activities undertaken during the reference period are reported as projects under construction irrespective of the length of construction work. The number of projects under construction can reflect the actual size of investment in fixed assets during a given period, and when compared with the number of projects completed and put into use during the same period, it demonstrates the results of investment in fixed assets. Depending on the nature of const ruction activities, projects under construction can also be classified into projects under construct ion in current y ear, winding-up projects in current year and stopped or suspended projects in previous years (with preservation work in current year).

Projects Completed and Put into Use refer to projects have been completed in accordance with the design documents, rusulting in forming production capacity (efficiency) and have been checked and accepted after relevant tests,and have been formaally delivered for use.

Newly Increased Production Capacity (or Project Efficiency) refers to the increase in design capacity (or project efficiency) through investment in fixed assets, The main indicator include:construction scal,scale of projects under production capacity since the start of projects and the newly increased production capacity(project efficiency) of current year.

The newly increased product ion capaCity (project efficiency) are usually expressed in one of the following forms: (1) output of products, i.e. the output that the project can produce during a given period (usually a year). For instance, the capaCity in coal mining is expressed in 10, 000 tons/year , the capaCity in producing chemical pesticides expressed in ton/year, the capaCity in producing tractors in tractor/year, etc. For some chemical products where the effective contents differ significantly, the production capaCity is expressed as the designed effective content equivalent, such as in the case of sulphuric acid, soda ash, caustic soda, etc; (2) raw materials processing capaCity, i.e. the volume of raw materials that could be processed by the project per day (or per hour), such as tons of materials processed per day by a sugar refining project or edible vegetable oil project, or tons of urban sewage processed per day; (3) number or capaCity of major equipment increased, such as number of cotton or silk looms increased, wool spindles in-creased, or capaCity (in kilowatt s) of power generators increased; (4) saved raw materials, fuels or power, which are mainly used for the efficiency of innovation and transformation projects; and (5) physical measures (volume, capaCity, area, and length) of construction, which is typical for non industrial projects, for instance, the length of new railways or highways, the capaCity of reservoirs, the floor space of housing projects, capaCity f or new students in schools or beds in hospitals, areas under new irrigation project, etc. Features of projects sometimes call for combined use of two or more measurement to reflect the increased production capaCity (or project efficiency), for instance, the new capaCity for the production of internal combustion engines are expressed in set s per year and kilowatts per year simultaneously. To standardize the nomenclature and unit of measurement for new production capaCity (or project efficiency), the National Bureau of Statistics has developed Nomenclature for New Production CapaCity (Project Efficiency) and Nomenclature for Saving Raw Materials, Fuels and Power. All reporting units with investment activities are required to follow these two nomenclatures in reporting statistics on new production capaCity (project efficiency).

Floor Space of Buildings under Construction refers to total floor space of the horizontal section of outer walls above the plinth of the building, including the effective area and the area occupied by the structure. This indicator is one of the important indicators in physical terms to reflect the scale and accomplishment of the construction industry, and important basis for monitoring the pr ogress, calculating the cost, analyzing the efficiency and studying the sup ply of building materials in relation with the construction projects.

Floor Space of Residential Buildings refers to the floor space of the residential buildings among the total space of buildings under construction or completed.

Newly Increased Fixed Assets refer to the newly in-creased value of fixed assets, constructed or purchased, that have been transfer red to the investors. This is an indicator that demonstrates the results of investment in fixed assets in monetary terms, and an important indicator to reflect the speed of construct ion and to calculate the efficiency of investment.

Rate of Construction Projects Completed and Put into Use refers to the ratio of the number of construction projects completed and put into use in certain period of time to the number of projects under construction in the same period. This reflects the investment efficiency from the perspective of the speed of projects construction.

Rate of Projects of Fixed Assets Completed and Put into Operation refers to the ratio of the newly increased fixed assets to the total investment made in the same period. This is a comprehensive indicator reflecting the speed of the employment of fixed assets and the investment efficiency at the macro-level. As the newly increase fixed assets is the result of a long period while the investment is completed in the current year, this indicator is expected to be used to reflect the employment of fixed assets over a long period of time.

Area of Commercialized Housing Sold refers to total contracted area of commercialized housing (i.e. area of floor space as designated in the formal contracts signed by both sides) during the reference time. It constitutes floor space of completed housing and floor space of future housing.

Value of Commercialized Housing Sold refers to the total contracted value (i.e. value of sales/purchase for selling/purchase of commercialized housing as designated in the contract signed by both sides) during the reference time. This indicator has the same coverage as the area of commercialized housing sold, which constitutes floor space of completed housing and floor space of housing yet to be completed.

5

对外经济贸易和旅游

FOREIGN TRADE & ECONOMIC COOPERATION AND TOURISM

简要说明

本篇资料的主要内容及来源

本篇内容包括海关进出口额、主要进出口商品数量及金额、对外承包工程和劳务合作、利用外资、外国和港澳台地区在新疆直接投资情况、新疆在国外和港澳台地区直接投资、经济技术开发（合作）主要情况、旅游情况等。

海关进出口额、利用外资、旅游资料由新疆维吾尔自治区统计局贸易外经统计处分别根据乌鲁木齐海关、新疆维吾尔自治区对外经济贸易厅、新疆维吾尔自治区工商管理局和新疆维吾尔自治区旅游局的有关资料加工整理。

Brief Introduction

Main Content and Source of Data

Data in this chapter cover mainly total imports and exports at customs, main imports and exports in volume and value, contracted projects and labor services cooperation, utilization of foreign capital, basic condition of direct investment in Xinjiang by foreign countries and compatriots from Hong Kong, Macao and Taiwan, main condition of economic and technological development and cooperation zones, condition of tourism.

Data on imports and exports, utilization of foreign capitals, tourism are collected and processed by the Department of Trade Statistics, the Xinjiang Bureau of Statistics in accordance with the data from custom of Urumqi, Foreign Economic and Trade Commission of Xinjiang, Xinjiang Administration for Industry and Commerce, Tourist Bureau of Xinjiang.

5-1 进出口贸易总额
Total Value of Imports and Exports

单位：万美元 (USD 10 000)

年份 Year	地区 Region	进出口总额 Total Imports and Exports	出口额 Exports	#一般贸易 Ordinary Trade	#边境贸易 Border Trade	进口额 Imports	#一般贸易 Ordinary Trade	#边境贸易 Border Trade
1978		2346	937			1409		
1985		29197	18020			11177		
1990		41025	33530		3506	7495		3416
1995		142798	76880	44550	27562	65918	17640	41888
1996		140367	54975	30281	18647	85392	25982	54484
1997		144667	66547	36061	22962	78120	24061	52031
1998		153214	80789	32268	37599	72425	20972	49354
1999		176534	102743	37120	57329	73791	25723	44976
2000		226399	120408	55060	58020	105991	28020	73950
2001		177148	66849	29523	18418	110299	24895	79661
2002		269186	130849	54404	47218	138337	26028	107152
2003		477198	254221	71115	160411	222977	72510	143504
2004		563563	304658	50194	223782	258905	101540	147058
2005		794189	504024	88036	386237	290165	108894	167648
2006		910327	713923	158842	522038	196404	61915	126429
2007		1371623	1150311	294000	806885	221312	75418	134778
2008		2221680	1929925	290237	1576911	291755	92279	187279
2009		1382771	1082325	168078	754206	300446	128702	157390
2010		1712834	1296981	208909	767478	415853	154567	236745
2011		2282225	1682886	476788	881882	599339	170863	401754
2012		2517075	1934686	700915	891987	582389	144347	408382
乌鲁木齐市	Urumqi City	1039689	806398			233291		
克拉玛依市	Karamay City	23896	14146			9750		
石河子市	Shihezi City	76842	72791			4051		
吐鲁番地区	Turpan Administrative Offices	3459	2272			1187		
哈密地区	Hami [Kumul] Administrative Offices	2624	1683			941		
昌吉回族自治洲	Changji Hui Autonomous Prefecture	210932	199254			11678		
伊犁哈萨克自治州	Ili Kazak Autonomous Prefecture	706758	505848			200910		
伊犁州直属县(市)	Counties (Cities) Direct Under Ili Prefecture	571024	375891			195133		
塔城地区	Tacheng [Tarbagatai] Administrative Offices	44822	39328			5494		
阿勒泰地区	Altay Administrative Offices	90912	90629			283		
博尔塔拉蒙古自治州	Bortala Mongol Autonomous Prefecture	245749	134605			111144		
巴音郭楞蒙古自治州	Bayangol Mongol Autonomous Prefecture	16687	13348			3339		
阿克苏地区	Aksu Administrative Offices	55347	53573			1774		
克孜勒苏柯尔克孜自治州	Kizilsu Kirgiz Autonomous Prefecture	26066	22720			3346		
喀什地区	Kashgar [Kaxgar] Administrative Offices	108297	107358			939		
和田地区	Hotan Administrative Offices	729	690			39		

注：1998 年以前的资料由外经贸厅提供，1998 年以后资料由乌鲁木齐海关提供(5-2、5-3、5-4 表相同)。
Note: The data prior to 1998 is offered by the Bureau of Foreign Economic and Trades , data after 1998 is offered by Urumqi Customs (The same in the 5-2, 5-3, 5-4 tables).

5-2 主要进出口商品数量和金额
Main Imports and Exports in Volume and Value

项　目	Item	2011		2012	
		数　量 Volume	金　额 (万美元) Value (USD 10 000)	数　量 Volume	金　额 (万美元) Value (USD 10 000)
主要出口商品	**Main Export Commodities**				
棉纱(吨)	Cotton Yarn (ton)	2849	1478	2750	1268
棉机织物(万米)	Cotton Woven Fabrics(10 000 m)	18749	24153	18315	26287
肠衣(吨)	Casings (ton)	491	2809	458	2603
番茄酱(万吨)	Tomato Jam (10 000 tons)	68	50926	58	44179
电视机(万台)	TV Sets (10 000 sets)	20	262	31	471
地毯(吨)	Carpets (ton)	2619	1442	2552	1418
药材(吨)	Medical Materials (ton)	91	56	287	96
鞋　类	Shoes		190232		213716
主要进口商品	**Main Import Commodities**				
羊毛及条(吨)	Wool and Wool Tops (ton)	9476	800	5535	620
钢材(万吨)	Rolled Steel (10 000 tons)	16	16677	21	16875
纸及纸板(未切成型的)(吨)	Paper and Paperboard in Rolls (ton)	57	12.0	10	8.6
原木(万立方米)	Logs (10 000 cu.m)	1.0	170	0.7	107
医疗仪器及器械	Medical Equipment and Apparatus		4441		4184
肥料(万吨)	Fertilizers (10 000 tons)	3	1328	2	662
原油(万吨)	Crude Oil (10 000 tons)	370	283746	371	307388
成品油(万吨)	Oil Product (10 000 tons)	71	44792	34	22220
牛皮革及马皮革(吨)	Cattle and Horse Leather (ton)	15203	1774	23651	2681

5-3 新疆同各国(地区)海关进出口总额

Value of Xinjiang's Imports and Exports by Countries(Region) of Destination

单位：万美元 (USD 10 000)

国别(地区)	Country (Territory)	2011			2012		
		进出口总额 Total Value Imports and Exports	出口额 Exports	进口额 Imports	进出口总额 Total Value Imports and Exports	出口额 Exports	进口额 Imports
合 计	**Total**	**2282225**	**1682886**	**599339**	**2517075**	**1934686**	**582389**
亚 洲	**Asia**	**1885418**	**1402547**	**482871**	**2022402**	**1526269**	**496133**
阿富汗	Afghanistan	365	355	10	262	254	8
巴 林	Bahrain	166	166		963	511	452
孟加拉国	Bangladesh	910	910		1670	1670	
不 丹	Bhutan	314	314		50	50	
文 莱	Brunei	124	124		946	946	
缅 甸	Myanmar	150	150		374	374	
柬埔寨	Cambodia	863	863		832	832	
塞浦路斯	Cyprus	13	13		117	117	
朝 鲜	Korea DPR	95	95		628	236	392
香 港	Hong Kong, China	4483	4176	307	9075	8949	126
印 度	India	7524	5729	1795	19460	16016	3444
印度尼西亚	Indonesia	4306	3897	409	20116	19915	201
伊 朗	Iran	5167	4488	679	4139	4052	87
伊拉克	Iraq	258	62	196	1149	1071	78
以色列	Israel	2455	2164	291	3449	3035	414
日 本	Japan	22299	8649	13650	22871	10993	11878
约 旦	Jordan	396	396		1510	1510	
科威特	Kuwait	70	70		623	623	
老 挝	Laos	7	7		136	136	
黎巴嫩	Lebanon	355	355		714	714	
马来西亚	Malaysia	12087	11645	442	35437	33847	1590
马尔代夫	Maldives				53	53	
蒙 古	Mongolia	42105	34755	7350	34356	25474	8882
尼泊尔联邦民主共和国	Nepal	66	66		86	85	1
阿 曼	Aman	431	431		852	849	3
巴基斯坦	Pakistan	38202	37983	219	13965	13696	269
巴勒斯坦	Palestine	52	52		18	18	
菲律宾	Philppines	2279	1908	371	4066	3799	267
卡塔尔	Qatar	125	125		589	589	
沙特阿拉伯	Saudi Arbia	4602	4478	124	9512	9397	115
新加坡	Singapore	4188	3209	979	11429	9675	1754
韩 国	Korea Rep.	8513	4255	4258	24693	19793	4900
斯里兰卡	Sri Lanka	446	427	19	830	787	43
叙利亚	Syria	154	146	8	186	183	3
泰 国	Thailand	4646	4549	97	10249	10094	155
土耳其	Turkey	2830	1420	1410	4798	2299	2499
阿联酋	United Arad Emirates	6230	6116	114	11046	11007	39
也 门	Yemen	962	962		1902	1902	
越 南	Vietnam	5576	5495	81	6113	6049	64
中华人民共和国	P.R.China	423		423	1178		1178
台湾省	Taiwan,China	2766	2238	528	3603	3214	389
东帝汶	Timor Lestor				24	24	
哈萨克斯坦	Kazakhstan	1059664	666499	393165	1116736	713941	402795
吉尔吉斯斯坦	Kirghizia	380556	372071	8485	403899	398808	5091
塔吉克斯坦	Tadzhikistan	172229	168395	3834	140738	136722	4016
土库曼斯坦	Turkmenistan	11824	10640	1184	13849	13488	361
乌兹别克斯坦	Uzbekistan	74142	31699	42443	83111	38472	44639
非 洲	**Africa**	**23160**	**22282**	**878**	**90661**	**85697**	**4964**
阿尔及利亚	Algeria	2108	2108		2087	2087	

5-3 续表 1 Continued

单位：万美元 (USD 10 000)

国 别 (地 区)	Country (Territory)	2011			2012		
		进出口总额 Total Value Imports and Exports	出口额 Exports	进口额 Imports	进出口总额 Total Value Imports and Exports	出口额 Exports	进口额 Imports
安哥拉	Angola	447	447		6096	6091	5
贝 宁	Benin	265	265		5571	1202	4369
博茨瓦纳	Botswana				41	41	
布隆迪	Burundi	30	30		5	5	
喀麦隆	Cameroon	423	423		1120	1120	
佛得角	Cape Verde				81	81	
科摩罗	Comoros				51	51	
刚果（布）	Congo	18	18		180	180	
吉布提	Djibouti	67	67		551	551	
埃及	Egypt	2749	2436	313	2274	2273	1
赤道几内亚	Eq. Guinea	43	43		59	59	
埃塞俄比亚	Ethiopia	513	513		4977	4977	
加 纳	Ghana	1583	1583		13293	13293	
冈比亚	Gambia	21	21		94	94	
加 蓬	Gabon	143	33	110	239	239	
几内亚	Guinea	77	77		1933	1933	
科特迪瓦	Cote d'lvoire	297	297		1108	1108	
肯尼亚	Kenya	287	287		2696	2696	
利比里亚	Liberia	4	4		74	74	
利比亚	Libya	28	28		426	426	
马达加斯加	Madagascar	47	47		123	123	
马拉维	Malawi	12	12		230	230	
马 里	Mali	338	338		690	175	515
毛里塔尼亚	Mauritania	21	21		185	185	
毛里求斯	Mauritius	589	589		672	672	
摩洛哥	Morocco	392	392		1946	1946	
莫桑比克	Mozambique	73	69	4	944	939	5
纳米比亚	Namibia	30	30		260	260	
尼日尔	Niger				297	297	
尼日利亚	Nigeria	4082	4082		7493	7479	14
留尼汪	Reunion				55	55	
卢旺达	Rwanda				21	21	
圣多美和普林西比	Sao Tome & Principe	2	2		3	3	
塞内加尔	Senegal	507	507		1873	1873	
塞拉利昂	Sierra Leone	97	97		278	278	
索马里	Somalia	2	2		40	40	
南 非	South Africa	3578	3133	445	13568	13517	51
苏 丹	Sudan	3079	3079		4319	4319	
坦桑尼亚	Tanzania	479	475	4	1684	1684	
多 哥	Togo	374	374		10689	10689	
突尼斯	Tunisia	64	64		946	942	4
乌干达	Uganda				389	389	
布基纳法索	Burkina Faso				3	3	
刚果（金）	Congo DR	154	154		408	408	
赞比亚	Zambia	128	128		295	295	
莱索托	Lesotho				10	10	
津巴布韦	Zimbabwe	7	5	2	131	131	
马约特	Mayotte	2	2		111	111	
梅利利亚	Melilla				10	10	
斯威士兰	Swaziland				1	1	
厄立特里亚	Eritrea				31	31	

5-3 续表 2 Continued

单位：万美元 (USD 10 000)

国 别 (地 区)	Country (Territory)	2011			2012		
		进出口总额 Total Value Imports and Exports	出口额 Exports	进口额 Imports	进出口总额 Total Value Imports and Exports	出口额 Exports	进口额 Imports
欧 洲	**Europe**	**260755**	**171352**	**89403**	**234045**	**179937**	**54108**
比利时	Belgium	4718	4243	475	5768	5603	165
丹 麦	Denmark	730	470	260	1353	628	725
英 国	United Kingdom	10802	9889	913	16642	15687	955
德 国	Germany	39035	16705	22330	31451	19868	11583
法 国	France	6626	4300	2326	7282	5512	1770
爱尔兰	Ireland	468	253	215	585	292	293
意大利	Italy	18718	13267	5451	10810	8094	2716
卢森堡	Luxembourg			429	84	79	5
荷 兰	Netherlands	9940	9511	58	13631	13064	567
希 腊	Greece	443	385		932	928	4
葡萄牙	Portugal	359	356	3	730	729	1
西班牙	Spain	4087	3907	180	8364	8263	101
阿尔巴尼亚	Albania	23	23		61	61	
安道尔	Andorra	1	1		919	919	
奥地利	Austria	971	469	502	695	416	279
保加利亚	Bulgaria	145	145		437	437	
芬 兰	Finland	10233	279	9954	3254	898	2356
直布罗陀	Gibraltar				10	10	
匈牙利	Hungary	96	96		72	72	
冰 岛	Iceland	3	3				
马耳他	Malta	632	632		2060	2060	
摩纳哥	Monaco				336	336	
挪 威	Norway	543	471	72	830	688	142
波 兰	Poland	2447	2442	5	6812	6560	252
罗马尼亚	Romania	597	585	12	1719	1602	117
瑞 典	Sweden	1545	365	1180	2454	651	1803
瑞 士	Switzerland	3872	943	2929	4712	1004	3708
爱沙尼亚	Estonia	71	70	1	51	42	9
拉脱维亚	Latvia	188	188		202	202	
立陶宛	Lithuania	395	394	1	512	512	
格鲁吉亚	Georgia	285	264	21	1141	1107	34
亚美尼亚	Armenia	587	587		328	328	
阿塞拜疆	Azerbaijan	43960	43439	521	26057	25905	152
白俄罗斯	Byelorussia	641	59	582	276	30	246
摩尔多瓦	Moldavia	9	9		191	191	
俄罗斯联邦	Russia	92778	51892	40886	64442	38491	25951
乌克兰	Ukraine	3897	3808	89	17139	17076	63
斯洛文尼亚	Slovenia	191	191		436	436	
克罗地亚	Croatia	131	131		209	209	
捷 克	Czech	545	539	6	742	631	111
斯洛伐克	Slovak	5	5		73	73	
前南马其顿	Macedonia				4	4	
波 黑	Bosnia & Herzegovina				20	20	
塞尔维亚	Serbia	37	35	2	197	197	
黑 山	Montenegro	1	1		22	22	
拉丁美洲	**Latin America**	**12746**	**12580**	**166**	**42529**	**41901**	**628**
阿根廷	Argentina	2407	2388	19	3023	3014	9
阿鲁巴	Aruba				21	21	
巴哈马	Bahamas	3	3		319	319	
巴巴多斯	Barbados	11	11		97	97	

5-3 续表 3 Continued

单位：万美元 (USD 10 000)

国别（地区）	Country (Territory)	2011			2012		
		进出口总额 Total Value Imports and Exports	出口额 Exports	进口额 Imports	进出口总额 Total Value Imports and Exports	出口额 Exports	进口额 Imports
伯利兹	Belize	5	5		16	16	
多民族玻利维亚国	Bolivia				2	2	
巴　西	Brazil	2206	2158	48	12305	11897	408
智　利	CaymanIs	1293	1293		2708	2682	26
哥伦比亚	Colombia	514	514		1077	1077	
多米尼克	Dominica				36	36	
哥斯达黎加	Costa Rica	71	71		165	165	
古　巴	Cuba	4			714	714	
库腊索岛	Curacao			4	29	29	
多米尼加共和国	Dominica Rep	29	23	6	127	119	8
厄瓜多尔	Ecuador	208	208		1605	1605	
法属圭亚那	French Guyana				6	6	
格林纳达	Granada	12	12		44	44	
危地马拉	Guatemala	77	77		261	260	1
圭亚那	Guyana				177	177	
海　地	Haiti	91	91		155	155	
洪都拉斯	Honduras	35	35		896	896	
牙买加	Jamaica	316	316		2949	2949	
马提尼克	Martinique				10	10	
墨西哥	Mexico	1310	1224	86	3902	3726	176
尼加拉瓜	Nicaragua	6	6		10	10	
巴拿马	Panama	2498	2498		6255	6255	
巴拉圭	Paraguay	146	146		726	726	
秘　鲁	Peru	809	806	3	974	974	
波多黎各	Puerto Rico	42	42		55	55	
圣卢西亚	Saint Lucia				63	63	
圣马丁岛	Saint Martin Is				5	5	
萨尔瓦多	EL Salvador	15	15		500	500	
苏里南	Surinam	33	33		79	79	
特立尼达和多巴哥	Trinidad and Tobago	9	9		68	68	
乌拉圭	Uruguay	314	314		1400	1400	
委内瑞拉	Venezuela	282	282		1740	1740	
荷属安的列斯群岛	Andreas Is (N)				10	10	
北美洲	**North America**	**89951**	**68498**	**21453**	**111901**	**88853**	**23048**
加拿大	Canada	5814	5022	792	9894	9167	727
美　国	United States	84137	63476	20661	102007	79686	22321
大洋洲	**Oceanic**	**10195**	**5627**	**4568**	**15537**	**12029**	**3508**
澳大利亚	Australia	8826	4781	4045	13412	10089	3323
斐　济	Fiji	28	28		123	123	
新喀里多尼亚	New Caledonia (Fr)	12	12		41	41	
瓦努阿图	Vanuatu				20	20	
新西兰	New Zealand	1161	781	380	1079	894	185
巴布亚新几内亚	Papua New Guinea	159	16	143	177	177	
社会群岛	Society Is				10	10	
所罗门群岛	Solomon Is	5	5		5	5	
汤　加	Tonga				64	64	
萨摩亚	Samoa	4	4		246	246	
基里巴斯	Kiribati				339	339	
图瓦卢	Tuvalu				16	16	
法属波利尼西亚	Polynesia (F)				5	5	

5-4 按贸易方式和登记注册类型分的海关进出口额

Total Value of Imports and Exports by Customs Regime and Registration (Customs Statiatics)

单位：万美元 (USD 10 000)

项目	Item	2011			2012		
		进出口总额 Total Imports and Exports	出口额 Exports	进口额 Imports	进出口总额 Total Imports and Exports	出口额 Exports	进口额 Imports
总计	**Total**	**2282225**	**1682886**	**599339**	**2517075**	**1934686**	**582389**
按贸易方式分	**By Customs Regime**						
一般贸易	Ordinary Trades	647651	476788	170863	845263	700915	144347
加工贸易	Processing Trades	26470	23493	2977	25911	19120	6791
边境小额贸易	Petty-volume Border Trades	1283636	881882	401754	1300369	891987	408382
其它贸易	Other Trades	324468	300723	23745	345532	322664	22869
按登记注册类型分	**By Registration Status**						
国有经济	State-owned Units	687378	198333	489045	688244	194449	493795
集体经济	Collective-owned Units	21965	15929	6036	27439	15651	11788
私营经济	Private-owned Units	1539587	1449389	90198	1776970	1706386	70584
三资企业	Three Kinds of Ventures	33290	19230	14060	24422	18200	6222
其它经济	Other Types of Ownership	5	5				

5-5 主要年份人民币对主要外币年平均汇价(中间价)

Average Exchange Rate of RMB Yuan Against Main Convertible Currences in Main Years (Medium Rate)

单位：人民币元 (RMB yuan)

年份 Year	100 美元 100 US Dollars	100 日元 100 JapaneseYen	100 港元 100 Hong Kong Dollars	100 欧元 100 Euros
1985	293.66	1.25	37.57	
1990	478.32	3.32	61.39	
1995	835.10	8.92	107.96	
1996	831.42	7.64	107.51	
1997	828.98	6.86	107.09	
1998	827.91	6.35	106.88	
1999	827.83	7.29	106.66	
2000	827.84	7.69	106.18	
2001	827.70	6.81	106.08	
2002	827.70	6.62	106.07	800.58
2003	827.70	7.15	106.24	936.13
2004	827.68	7.66	106.23	1029.00
2005	819.17	7.45	105.30	1019.53
2006	797.18	6.86	102.62	1001.90
2007	760.40	6.46	97.46	1041.75
2008	694.51	6.74	89.19	1022.27
2009	683.10	7.29	88.12	952.70
2010	676.95	7.73	87.13	897.25
2011	645.88	8.11	82.97	900.11
2012	631.25	7.90	81.38	810.67

5-6 对外承包工程和劳务合作
Contracted Projects in Foreign Countries or Territories

单位：个、万美元 (unit,USD 10 000)

项　　目	Item	2011	2012
承包工程	**Contracted Projects**		
新签合同数	Number of Newly Signed Contracts	51	154
新签合同金额	Newly Signed Contracted Value	46987	224107
实际营业额	Actual Business Volume	97167	147047

5-7 外商直接投资
Direct Foreign Investments

单位：个、万美元 (unit, USD 10 000)

指　　标	Item	2011			2012		
		项　目 Number of Projects	合同金额 Contract Value	实际使用金额 Used Value	项　目 Number of Projects	合同金额 Contract Value	实际使用金额 Used Value
总　　计	**Total**	**69**	**55834**	**33485**	**55**	**61056**	**40795**
独资经营企业	Foreign Investment Enterprises	45	35214	11394	32	22841	13536
合资经营企业	Joint Ventures Enterprises	23	8701	9206	22	23419	12413
合作经营企业	Cooperative Operation Enterprises	1	1238	3587	1	2734	13
股份制企业	Share-holding Corporations Ltd.		10681	9298		12062	14833

5-8 外国和港澳台地区在华直接投资情况

Basic Conditions of Direct Investment in China by Foreign Countries and Compatriots from Hongkong，Macao and Taiwan

单位：个、万美元 (2012 年) (unit, USD 10 000)

项　目	Item	签订协议情况 Signed Agreements		客商实际投资额	年末实有企业个数
		合同数 Number of Contracts	客商投资额 Actually Used Amount of Region Investment	Used Amount of Foreign Investment	Number of Enterprises at Year-end
总　计	**Total**	**55**	**61056**	**40795**	**525**
按投资方式分	**Grouped by Investment Mode**				
独资经营企业	Foreign Investment Enterprises	32	22841	13536	235
合资经营企业	Joint Ventures Enterprises	22	23419	12413	253
合作经营企业	Cooperative Operation Enterprises	1	2734	13	29
外商投资股份制企业	Foreign Investment Share Enterprises		12062	14833	8
按国民经济行业分	**Grouped by Economic Sector**				
农、林、牧、渔业	Farming, Forestry, Animal Husbandry and Fishery	5	2071	3786	36
采矿业	Mining and Quarrying	1	5523	6045	28
制造业	Manufacturing	12	16366	10648	227
电力、煤气及水的生产和供应业	Production and Distribution of Electricity, Gas and Water			288	29
建筑业	Construction			266	15
交通运输、仓储及邮电通讯业	Transport, Storage, Post and Telecommunications	1	13121	14610	49
信息传输、计算机服务和软件业	Information Transmission, Computer Service and Software				320
批发和零售业	Wholesale and Retail Trades	22	13593	2644	360
住宿和餐饮业	Accommodation and Catering Service	3	9	10	67
金融业	Financial Intermediation	1	1112		33
房地产业	Real Estate			257	19
租赁和商务服务业	Leasing and Business Services	8	9067	1572	67
科学研究、技术服务和地质勘察业	Scientific Research, Technical Service and Geological Prospecting	2	162	620	29
水利、环境和公共设施管理业	Water Conservancy, Environment and Public Facility Management				6
居民服务和其他服务业	Services to Households and Other Services		32	49	20
教　育	Education				2
文化、体育和娱乐业	Culture,Sports and Entertainment				3
按国别、地区分	**By Country or Territory**				
中国香港	Hong Kong，China	24	34816	16848	211
中国台湾	Taiwan，China		-140	229	20
日　本	Japan	1	166		11
美　国	United States	4	538	67	30
加拿大	Canada			11	9
丹　麦	Denmark				3
意大利	Italy				2
德　国	Federal Republic of Germany	1	96		4
土耳其	Turkey	5	359	20	17
英　国	United Kingdom	1	-675	231	3
泰　国	Thailand				2
新加坡	Singapore	2	1475	391	12
澳大利亚	Australia	2	467		12
独联体	Commonwealth of Independent States	9	227	501	83
马来西亚	Malaysia				2
韩　国	Republic of Korea	3	14	4	22

5-9 各地、州、市利用外商直接投资情况
Conditions of Foreign Direct Investment Used by Prefecture, Autonomous Prefecture and City

单位：个、万美元 (unit, USD 10 000)

地 区	Region	2011			2012		
		签订合同数 Number of Contracts	合同金额 Contract Value	实际使用投资 Amount of Foreingn Capital Actually Used	签订合同数 Number of Contracts	合同金额 Contract Value	实际使用投资 Amount of Foreign Capital Actually Used
总 计	**Total**	**69**	**55834**	**33485**	**55**	**61056**	**40795**
乌鲁木齐市	Urumqi City	38	10331	11702	35	24166	17572
克拉玛依市	Karamay City	1	3320	1500	1	52	1720
石河子市	Shihezi City	11	15702	8384	5	14393	4406
吐鲁番地区	Turpan Administrative Offices				1	545	300
哈密地区	Hami [Kumul] Administrative Offices	2	4876	2012		583	2333
昌吉回族自治州	Changji Hui Autonomous Prefecture	4	7033	3629	4	7850	4174
伊犁哈萨克自治州	Ili Kazak Autonomous Prefecture	4	1653	2496	3	2525	3819
伊犁州直属县(市)	Counties (Cities) Direct Under Ili Prefecture	3	773	1609	3	2736	1873
塔城地区	Tacheng [Tarbagatai] Administrative Offices	1	880			-211	675
阿勒泰地区	Altay Administrative Offices			887			1271
博尔塔拉蒙古自治州	Bortala Mongol Autonomous Prefecture				1	2393	
巴音郭楞蒙古自治州	BayangolMongol Autonomous Prefecture	2	5300	2470	2	4784	2858
阿克苏地区	Aksu Administrative Offices	3	6089	586	2	1273	2922
克孜勒苏柯尔克孜自治州	Kizilsu Kirgiz Autonomous Prefecture			661		2323	11
喀什地区	Kashgar [Kaxgar] Administrative Offices	4	1530		1	169	680
和田地区	Hotan Administrative Offices			45			

5-10 新疆在外国和港澳台地区直接投资
Direct Investment in Foreign Countries and Hong Kong, Macao and Taiwan Made by Xinjiang Partner

单位：个、万美元 (unit, USD 10 000)

年 份 Year	投资额 Investment	年 份 Year	投资额 Investment
2005	5280	2010	47809
2008	6863	2011	41803
2009	28619	2012	25920

5-11 主要年份旅游事业发展情况
Development of Tourism in Main Years

项　　目	Item	1995	2000	2012
旅行社总数（个）	**Total Number of Travel Agencies (unit)**	**79**	**130**	**413**
入境旅游人数（人）	**Total Number of Overseas Vistor Arrivals (person)**	**203579**	**256082**	**1498025**
外国人	Foreigners	185514	208374	1363266
#日　本	Japan	43983	51974	26992
新加坡	Singapore	2048	5137	10331
美　国	United States	5595	10231	29235
英　国	United Kingdom	2422	3702	10348
法　国	France	3062	5218	12671
德　国	Federal Republic of Germany	4892	6310	9098
独联体	Commonwealth of Independent States	93578	76966	1062004
香港同胞	Compatriots from Hong Kong		12710	42994
澳门同胞	Compatriots from Macao		1387	4168
台湾同胞	Compatriots from Taiwan	8816	33611	87957
按地区分	**By Regions**			
乌鲁木齐市	Urumqi City	63275	144830	364299
克拉玛依市	Karamay City		505	3296
石河子市	Shihezi City		532	1412
吐鲁番地区	Turpan Administrative Offices	27230	43641	54615
哈密地区	Hami [Kumul] Administrative Offices	1220	624	28610
昌吉回族自治州	Changji Hui Autonomous Prefecture	224	213	16833
伊犁哈萨克自治州	Ili Kazak Autonomous Prefecture	68948	18204	869682
伊犁州直属县(市)	Counties (Cities) Direct Under Ili Prefecture	67651	15356	738682
塔城地区	Tacheng [Tarbagatai] Administrative Offices	1297	298	32439
阿勒泰地区	Altay Administrative Offices		2550	98561
博尔塔拉蒙古自治州	Bortala Mongol Autonomous Prefecture	354	672	50786
巴音郭楞蒙古自治州	BayangolMongol Autonomous Prefecture	1738	7313	21052
阿克苏地区	Aksu Administrative Offices	5737	6028	7050
克孜勒苏柯尔克孜自治州	Kizilsu Kirgiz Autonomous Prefecture	2485	2100	17240
喀什地区	Kashgar [Kaxgar] Administrative Offices	31102	27510	45883
和田地区	Hotan Administrative Offices	1266	3910	17267
国内旅游人数（万人）	**Number of Domestic Visitors (10 000 persons)**	**514**	**758**	**4711**
疆内居民出境游（人）	**Number of Domestic Resident Outbound Visitors (person)**	**591**	**4535**	**28895**
旅游收入	**Income of Tourism**			
入境旅游收入(万美元)	Foreign Exchange Earnings from International Tourism (USD 10 000)	5268	9494	55057
国内旅游收入(亿元)	Earnings from Domestic Tourism (100 million yuan)	7.10	62.67	541.75

5-12 各地、州、市旅行社及旅游宾馆(酒店)基本情况

Accommodation of Travel Agencies and Tourist Hotels by Prefecture, Autonomous Prefecture and City

(2012 年)

地区	Region	旅行社 (个) Number of Travel Agencies (unit)	星级宾馆 (个) Number of Tourist Hotels (unit)	客房 (间) Number of Rooms (unit)	床位 (张) Number of Beds (unit)
总计	**Total**	**413**	**472**	**48677**	**92431**
乌鲁木齐市	Urumqi City	229	83	13314	22770
克拉玛依市	Karamay City	15	16	1401	2390
石河子市	Shihezi City	5	15	1835	4410
吐鲁番地区	Turpan Administrative Offices	4	27	2200	4224
哈密地区	Hami [Kumul] Administrative Offices	10	17	1965	3710
昌吉回族自治洲	Changji Hui Autonomous Prefecture	11	33	1845	4017
伊犁哈萨克自治州	Ili Kazak Autonomous Prefecture	73	130	11571	25067
伊犁州直属县(市)	Counties (Cities) Direct Under Ili Prefecture	31	60	5098	9871
塔城地区	Tacheng [Tarbagatai] Administrative Offices	5	14	960	1817
阿勒泰地区	Altay Administrative Offices	37	56	5513	13379
博尔塔拉蒙古自治州	Bortala Mongol Autonomous Prefecture	5	13	943	1677
巴音郭楞蒙古自治州	Bayangol Mongol Autonomous Prefecture	19	42	4478	8265
阿克苏地区	Aksu Administrative Offices	10	37	3913	6790
克孜勒苏柯尔克孜自治州	Kizilsu Kirgiz Autonomous Prefecture	3	4	255	492
喀什地区	Kashgar [Kaxgar] Administrative Offices	27	36	3507	6236
和田地区	Hotan Administrative Offices	2	19	1450	2383

5-13 各地、州、市旅游收入情况

Income of Tourism by Prefecture, Autonomous Prefecture and City

(2012 年)

地　区	Region	入境旅游收入 (万美元) Foreign Exchange Earnings from International Tourism (USD 10 000)	国内旅游收入 (万元) Earnings from Domestic Tourism (10 000 yuan)
总　计	**Total**	**55057**	**5417546**
乌鲁木齐市	Urumqi City	19855	2199247
克拉玛依市	Karamay City	125	150392
石河子市	Shihezi City	60	197496
吐鲁番地区	Turpan Administrative Offices	3455	374542
哈密地区	Hami [Kumul] Administrative Offices	1210	206597
昌吉回族自治州	Changji Hui Autonomous Prefecture	528	218097
伊犁哈萨克自治州	Ili Kazak Autonomous Prefecture	22380	1081546
伊犁州直属县(市)	Counties (Cities) Direct Under Ili Prefecture	19688	429449
塔城地区	Tacheng [Tarbagatai] Administrative Offices	674	119548
阿勒泰地区	Altay Administrative Offices	2018	532549
博尔塔拉蒙古自治州	Bortala Mongol Autonomous Prefecture	910	50536
巴音郭楞蒙古自治州	BayangolMongol Autonomous Prefecture	1268	307917
阿克苏地区	Aksu Administrative Offices	400	140124
克孜勒苏柯尔克孜自治州	Kizilsu Kirgiz Autonomous Prefecture	801	21224
喀什地区	Kashgar [Kaxgar] Administrative Offices	3155	360503
和田地区	Hotan Administrative Offices	910	109325

5-14 入境旅游收入及构成
Foreign Exchange Earnings from International Tourism and Composition

单位：万美元、% (USD 10 000,%)

指标	Item	2011 金额 Value	2011 比重 Percentage	2012 金额 Value	2012 比重 Percentage
总计	**Total**	**46519**	**100**	**55057**	**100**
长途交通费	Long Distance Transportation	11304	24.3	21087	38.3
民航	Air	3442	7.4	12828	23.3
铁路	Railway	3954	8.5	2533	4.6
汽车	Highway	3908	8.4	5726	10.4
游览	Visiting	1489	3.2	2973	5.4
住宿	Accommodation	3582	7.7	6717	12.2
餐饮	Catering	2000	4.3	2753	5.0
商品销售	Commodity Sales	17677	38.0	11011	20
娱乐	Entertainment			3909	7.1
邮电通信	Post and Communication Services	1303	2.8	1376	2.5
市内交通	Local Transportation	1861	4.0	1817	3.3
其他服务	Other Services	7303	15.7	3414	6.2

5-15 接待外国旅游人数(按国别分)
Number of Foreign Tourists Received by Country

单位：人 (person)

国别	Country	2011	2012	国别	Country	2011	2012
总计	**Total**	**1248983**	**1363266**	德国	Federal Republic of Germany	7412	9098
亚洲	**Asia**	**957530**	**1041182**	法国	France	10197	12671
印度	India	1310	1230	意大利	Italy	2619	4028
印度尼西亚	Indonesia	949	1714	西班牙	Spain	1420	1885
日本	Japan	28085	26992	瑞典	Sweden	1529	1599
马来西亚	Malaysia	5257	11930	瑞士	Switzerland	2189	2750
蒙古	Mongolia	41246	62303	独联体(欧洲部分)	Commonwealth of Independent States (Europe)	197531	212420
菲律宾	The Philppines	321	536	其他	Others	6505	5896
新加坡	Singapore	6992	10331	北美洲	**North America**	**39097**	**41279**
韩国	Republic of Korea	17841	23768	加拿大	Canada	6880	9185
泰国	Thailand	3108	3539	美国	United States	25965	29235
巴基斯坦	Pakistan	41325	43997	其他	Others	6252	2859
哈萨克斯坦		769873	813385	大洋洲	**Oceania**	**8636**	**14402**
其他	Others	41223	41457	澳大利亚	Australia	6135	9730
非洲	**Africa**	**765**	**816**	新西兰	New Zealand	1438	3931
欧洲	**Europe**	**238190**	**260695**	其他	Others	1063	741
英国	United Kingdom	8788	10348	其他小计	**Other sub-total**	**4765**	**4892**

注：表中独联体仅指独联体在欧洲部分的国家。
Note: Commonwealth of Independent State in the table only refer to the part of the countries in Europe.

主要统计指标解释

货物进出口总额 指实际进出我国国境的货物总金额。包括对外贸易实际进出口货物，来料加工装配进出口货物，国家间、联合国及国际组织无偿援助物资和赠送品，华侨、港澳台同胞和外籍华人捐赠品，租赁期满归承租人所有的租赁货物，进料加工进出口货物，边境地方贸易及边境地区小额贸易进出口货物(边民互市贸易除外)，中外合资企业、中外合作经营企业、外商独资经营企业进出口货物和公用物品，到、离岸价格在规定限额以上的进出口货样和广告品(无商业价值、无使用价值和免费提供出口的除外)，从保税仓库提取在中国境内销售的进口货物，以及其他进出口货物。该指标可以观察一个国家在对外贸易方面的总规模。我国规定出口货物按离岸价格统计，进口货物按到岸价格统计。

利用外资 指我国各级政府、部门、企业和其他经济组织通过对外借款、吸收外商直接投资以及用其他方式筹措的境外现汇、设备、技术等。

外商直接投资 是指外国投资者在我国境内通过设立外商投资企业、合伙企业、与中方投资者共同进行石油资源的合作勘探开发以及设立外国公司分支机构等方式进行投资。

外国投资者可以用现金、实物、无形资产、股权等投资，还可以用从外商投资企业获得的利润进行再投资。

对外承包工程 指我国境内企业法人或者其他经济组织按照国际通行做法，在国外及港澳台地区承揽、实施工程建设项目的勘察、设计、施工、监理、设备材料采购、安装调试、工程咨询、工程管理等经营活动。

对外劳务合作 指我国境内企业法人与国（境）外允许招收或雇用外籍劳务人员的公司、中介机构或私人雇主签订合同，并按合同约定的条件有组织地招聘、选拔、派遣我国公民到国（境）外为外方雇主提供劳务服务并进行管理的经济活动。

旅游人数 包括入境游客、出境人数和国内游客。

(1) 入境游客 指报告期内来中国（大陆）观光、度假、探亲访友、就医疗养、购物、参加会议或从事经济、文化、体育、宗教活动的外国人、港澳台同胞等游客人数。

(2)出境人数：指中国（大陆）居民因公或因私出境前往其他国家、中国香港特别行政区、澳门特别行政区和台湾省观光、度假、探亲访友、就医疗养、购物、参加会议或从事经济、文化、体育、宗教活动的人数，即出境游客。统计时，按每出境一次统计1人次。

(3)国内游客：指在报告期内在中国（大陆）观光游览、度假、探亲访友、就医疗养、购物、参加会议或从事经济、文化、体育、宗教活动的中国（大陆）居民人数，其出游的目的不是通过所从事的活动谋取报酬。统计时，国内游客按每出游一次统计1人次。

国际旅游(外汇)收入 指入境游客在中国（大陆）境内旅行、游览过程中用于交通、参观游览、住宿、餐饮、购物、娱乐等全部花费。

国内旅游收入 又称旅游总花费。指国内游客在国内旅行、游览过程中用于交通、参观游览、住宿、餐饮、购物、娱乐等全部花费。

星级饭店 指设备、设施、服务符合《旅游饭店星级的划分与评定》（GB/T14308-2003），通过相关旅游管理部门评定，并取得星级饭店称号的饭店（含预备星级饭店）。

Explanatory Notes on Main Statistical Indicators

Total Imports and Exports at Customs refer to the real value of commodities imported and exported across the border of China. They include the actual imports and exports through foreign trade, imported and exported goods under the processing and assembling trades and materials, supplies and gifts as aid given gratis between governments and by the United Nations and other international organizations, and contributions donated by overseas Chinese, compatriots in Hong Kong and Macao and Chinese with foreign citizenship, leasing commodities owned by tenant at the expiration of leasing period, the imported and exported commodities processed with imported materials, commodities trading in border areas (excluding mutual exchange goods), the imported and exported commodities and articles for public use of the Sino-foreign joint ventures, cooperative enterprises and ventures with sole foreign investment. Also included is import or export of samples and advertising goods for which CIF or FOB value are beyond the permitted ceiling (excluding goods of no trading or use value and free commodities for export), imported goods sold in China from bonded warehouses and other imported or exported goods. The indicator of the total imports and exports at customs can be used to observe the total size of external trade in a country. In accordance with the stipulation of the Chinese government, imports are calculated at CIF, while exports are calculated at FOB.

Utilization of Foreign Capitals refers to remittance, equipment and technology financed from abroad, by loans, foreign direct investment and other forms undertaken by the Chinese governments at all levels, by various departments, enterprises and other economic units.

Foreign Direct Investment refers to the investments inside China by foreign enterprises and economic organizations or individuals (including overseas Chinese, compatriots from Hong Kong, Macao and Taiwan, and Chinese enterprises registered abroad), following the relevant policies and laws of China, for the establishment of ventures exclusively with foreign own investment, Sino-foreign joint ventures and cooperative enterprises or for co-operative exploration of resources with enterprises or economic organizations in China. It includes the re- investment of the foreign entrepreneurs with the profits gained from the investment and the funds that enterprises borrow from abroad in the total investment of projects which are approved by the relevant department of the government.

Overseas Contracted Project refers to in accordance with the international common practice, domestic corporates or other economic organizations contract and implement construction projects in foreign countries, Hong Kong SAR, Macao SAR and Taiwan province including reconnaissance, design, construction, supervision, purchasing of equipment and materials, installation and testing, engineering consulting and project management.

Overseas Labour Services refer to domestic corporates which signed contracts with overseas corporations, intermediary agencies and private employers which are allowed to recruit or hire foreign labour forces, they will send Chinese citizens to go abroad to provide labour services to foreign employers through organized recruitment and selection according to the signed contracts and relevant management activities.

Number of Tourists include international tourists entering into China, Chinese residents going abroad and domestic tourists.

(1) International tourists refer to foreigners, overseas Chinese, Chinese compatriots from Hong Kong, Macao and Taiwan coming to China for sightseeing, visits, tours, family reunions, vacations, study tours, conferences and other activities of a business, scientific and technological, cultural, educational and religious nature. It does not include representatives and employees of resident institutions of foreign countries in China such as embassies, consulates, news agencies and offices of foreign companies and organizations, nor does it include long-term foreign experts or students residing in China, or persons in transition without spending a night in China.

(2) Chinese residents going abroad refer to Chinese residents going abroad for short terms for either public business or private purposes. Chinese employees working on international transport carriers are included in those going abroad for public business purpose, not in those for private purpose.

(3) Domestic tourists refer to residents of the mainland of China who stay for one night at least but no more than 6 months at tourist facilities in other places than their permanent residence within the territory of the mainland China, including foreigners, overseas Chinese and Chinese compatriots from Hong Kong, Macao and Taiwan who have resided in China for over one year.

Foreign Exchange Earnings from International Tourism refer to the total expenditures of foreigners, overseas Chinese, Chinese compatriots from Hong Kong, Macao and Taiwan during their stay in the mainland of China, which are earnings of foreign exchange from international tourism from the point of view from China.

Earning from domestic travel refer to the domestic tourists during their stay in the mainland of China ,which are earnings of transportaion,inviting,hoteling,catering,shopping and entertainment.

Start-Hotels refer to hotels that are able, with the approval of departments concerned, to accommodate foreigners, overseas Chinese, Chinese compatriots from Hong Kong, Macao and Taiwan Province.

新疆统计年鉴

XINJIANG STATISTICAL YEARBOOK

6

能源生产和消费

PRODUCTION AND CONSUMPTION OF ENERGY

简要说明

本篇资料的主要内容及来源

本篇包括的主要内容有能源生产、消费总量及品种构成，综合能源平衡表和主要能源品种单项平衡表，分行业、分主要能源品种的消费量，能源生产和消费弹性系数，能源加工转换效率及生活用能源消费量等。

从2006年度开始，能源生产、消费等指标需经国家审定后方可公布，因国家审定、公布各省的这部分指标数据为每年的八月份，时间在年鉴出版时间之后，为此，这部分数据采取错年上，即2012年上2011年数据。

本篇资料由新疆维吾尔自治区统计局能源与资源统计处依据能源年报整理提供。

Brief Introduction

Main Content and Source of Data

Data in this chapter cover mainly the energy production and consumption and their composition, the overall balance of energy and the balance by different types of energy, the consumption of energy by sector and by types of energy the elasticity ratio of energy production and consumption, efficiency of energy conversion and the consumption of energy for non-production uses.

Since 2006, data on production and consumption of energy are announced after NBS authorized. Time of publication is August every year. So the data on energy in 2011 Statistical Yearbook is data in 2012.

Data in this chapter are provided and processed in accordance with the statistical reporting scheme on energy by the Department of Industry and Transport of the Xinjiang Bureau of Statistics.

6-1 主要年份能源生产总量及构成

Total Production of Energy and Its Composition in Main Years

年 份 Year	能源生产总量 (万吨标准煤) Total Energy Production (10 000 tons of SCE)	占能源生产总量的比重(%) Percentage of Total Energy Production (%)			
		原 煤 Coal	原 油 Crude Oil	天然气 Natural Gas	水风电 Hydro- Power and Wind Power
1978	1410.75	60.0	35.8	2.4	1.8
1980	1527.72	58.4	36.5	3.1	2.0
1985	2092.47	60.0	34.1	3.5	2.4
1990	2801.57	58.8	35.8	2.4	3.0
1995	4266.06	50.1	43.5	3.6	2.8
2000	5419.77	40.6	48.7	7.9	2.8
2001	5720.04	38.7	48.6	9.7	3.0
2002	6156.05	39.5	47.3	10.5	2.7
2003	6657.43	41.1	46.0	10.2	2.7
2004	7112.95	41.4	45.3	10.7	2.6
2005	8175.74	37.9	42.1	17.3	2.7
2006	9528.72	37.3	37.1	22.9	2.7
2007	10735.84	36.7	34.7	26.0	2.6
2008	12669.13	41.9	30.6	24.8	2.7
2009	13542.33	46.5	26.5	24.1	2.9
2010	15000.47	50.3	24.4	22.2	3.1
2011	16703.06	55.9	22.4	18.7	3.0

注：电力折算标准煤的系数根据当年平均发电煤耗计算，并将历史资料做了调整，下表同。
Note: The coefficient for conversion of electric power into SCE (standard coal equivalent) is calculated on the basic of the data on the average coal consumption in generating electric power in the same year. The same is as in the following tables.

6-2 主要年份能源消费总量及构成

Total Consumption of Energy and Its Composition in Main Years

年 份 Year	能源消费总量 (万吨标准煤) Total Energy Consumption (10 000 tons of SCE)	占能源消费总量的比重(%) As percentage of Total Energy Consumption (%)			
		煤 炭 Coal	石 油 Crude Oil	天然气 Natural Gas	水风电 Hydro- Power and Wind Power
1978	979.27	72.5	21.5	3.4	2.6
1980	1026.45	71.3	21.1	4.6	3.0
1985	1410.84	72.0	19.3	5.1	3.6
1990	1924.38	69.6	22.5	3.5	4.4
1995	2733.04	66.2	23.8	5.6	4.4
2000	3316.03	63.6	23.3	8.6	4.5
2001	3496.44	60.4	21.6	13.2	4.8
2002	3622.40	62.2	20.5	12.7	4.6
2003	4064.43	60.3	21.7	13.1	4.9
2004	4784.83	61.0	20.1	15.0	3.9
2005	5506.49	56.1	26.2	13.7	4.0
2006	6047.27	56.7	24.7	14.3	4.3
2007	6575.92	57.8	23.9	14.1	4.2
2008	7069.39	61.7	20.3	13.1	4.9
2009	7525.56	65.9	16.9	12.0	5.2
2010	8290.20	65.8	15.8	12.4	5.6
2011	9926.50	67.9	14.7	12.3	5.1

6-3 主要年份综合能源平衡表
Overall Energy Balance Sheet in Main Years

单位:万吨标准煤 (10 000 tons of SCE)

项 目	Item	1990	2000	2005	2010	2011
可供消费的能源总量	**Total Energy Available for Consumption**	**2045.32**	**3430.05**	**5349.17**	**8285.44**	**9895.23**
一次能源生产量	Primary Energy Output	2801.57	5419.77	8175.74	15000.47	16703.06
进口量	Imports		107.39	130.80	1417.54	1671.54
外省调入量	Inflow from other Provinces (Autonomons Regions and Municipalities)	2.26	25.59	58.17	175.17	
出口量(-)	Exports (-)	4.84	31.90	60.80	18.49	26.31
本区调出量(-)	Outflow (-)	694.89	2144.79	3172.41	8119.06	8301.65
年初年末库存差额	Stock Changes in the Year	-58.78	53.99	95.71	-171.00	-151.41
能源消费总量	**Total Energy Consumption**	**1924.45**	**3316.03**	**5506.49**	**8290.20**	**9926.50**
在总量中:	Consumption by Sector					
农、林、牧、渔、水利业	Farming, Forestry, Animal Husbandry, Fishery and Water Conservancy	134.91	274.97	314.25	416.74	468.70
工 业	Industry	1095.22	1860.26	3440.83	5903.00	7278.59
建筑业	Construction	41.16	81.73	43.22	75.86	98.02
交通运输和邮电通讯业	Transportation, Post and Telecommunications Services	99.72	189.76	413.77	635.41	678.79
商业、饮食、物资供销和仓储业	Commerce, Catering Services, Materials Supply, Marketing and Storage	26.28	93.83	138.39	182.27	195.28
其 他	Others	99.12	164.57	177.51	218.02	234.40
生活消费	Residential Consumption	428.04	650.91	978.54	858.90	972.76
在总量中:	Consumption by Usage					
终端消费	End-use Consumption	1825.44	3148.77	5086.96	7300.36	8813.08
#工 业	Industry	996.27	1692.96	3021.27	5027.82	6265.99
加工转换损失量	Losses During the Process of Energy Conversion	27.90	91.25	228.26	634.69	763.46
#炼 焦	Coking	13.00	72.05	77.60	289.29	356.58
炼 油	Petroleum Refining	13.16	75.99	62.18	70.58	109.15
损失量	Energy Losses	71.05	76.05	191.27	310.06	349.97
平衡差额	**Balance**	**120.87**	**114.02**	**-157.32**	**27.18**	**-31.28**

注：1.村办工业包括在工业中(下同)。
2.电力、热力按等价热值折算，因此加工转换损失量中不包括发电、供热损失量。
3.进口量包括新疆飞机在国外加油量，出口量包括外国飞机在新疆的加油量。

Note: a) Data on industry includes the data of village-run industry. (The same is as in the following tables).
b) Electric power and heat are converted on the basic of equal caloric value. Therefore, losses in processing and transformation exclude losses in power generation and heating.
c) Data on imports include the petroleum consumed by the Xinjiang airplanes in refueling abroad. Data on exports include the petroleum consumed by the foreign airplanes in refueling in Xinjiang.

6-4 主要年份石油平衡表
Petroleum Balance Sheet in Main Years

单位:万吨 (10 000 tons)

项 目	Item	1990	2000	2005	2010	2011
可供量	**Total Energy Available for Consumption**	**333.19**	**616.14**	**1021.31**	**869.02**	**968.64**
生产量	Output	701.26	1848.43	2408.32	2558.16	2615.63
进口量	Imports		75.16	91.54	993.43	1174.17
外省调入量	Inflow from other Provinces (Autonomons Regions and Municipalities)	1.44	10.85	14.85		
出口量(-)	Exports (-)	3.29	11.17	5.18	1.08	1.58
本区调出量(-)	Outflow (-)	353.59	1285.38	1525.72	2682.12	2806.87
年初年末库存差额	Stock Changes in the Year	-12.63	-21.75	37.50	0.63	-12.71
消费量	**Total Energy Consumption**	**300.16**	**527.71**	**1014.84**	**869.02**	**970.64**
在消费量中:	Consumption by Sector					
农、林、牧、渔、水利业	Farming, Forestry, Animal Husbandry, Fishery and Water Conservancy	42.46	63.65	70.68	71.27	74.30
工 业	Industry	171.96	273.95	611.18	298.42	369.97
建筑业	Construction	16.87	32.10	15.36	23.81	26.37
交通运输和邮电通讯业	Transportation, Post and Telecommunications Services	48.30	86.89	210.00	360.79	381.33
商业、饮食、物资供销和仓储业	Commerce, Catering Services, Materials Supply, Marketing and Storage	3.66	18.78	31.91	40.15	41.55
其 他	Others	8.48	32.70	46.20	44.91	46.91
生活消费	Residential Consumption	8.43	19.64	29.51	29.67	30.21
在消费量中:	Consumption by Sector					
终端消费	Final Consumption	257.06	457.99	936.88	687.45	802.77
#工 业	Industry	128.86	204.23	533.22	197.11	272.70
中间消费(用于加工转换)	Intermediate Consumption	15.69	17.34	47.37	101.31	97.27
#发 电	Power Generation	15.69	2.10	8.65	13.31	8.79
供 热	Heating		1.24	1.04	27.43	17.60
此外:当年炼油投入量	Petroleum Refining Input	464.29	1001.32	1531.68	2182.96	2482.08
平衡差额	**Balance**	**33.03**	**88.43**	**6.47**		**-2.00**

注:1.生产量为原油产量。
2.进口量包括新疆飞机在国外加油量,出口量包括外国飞机在新疆的加油量。

Note: a) Data on output refer to the output of crude oil.
b) Data on imports include the petroleum consumed by the Xinjiang Airplanes in refueling abroad. Data on exports include the petroleum consumed by the foreign airplanes in refueling in Xinjiang.

6-5 主要年份煤炭平衡表
Coal Balance Sheet in Main Years

单位:万吨 (10 000 tons)

项 目	Item	1990	2000	2005	2010	2011
可供量	**Total Energy Available for Consumption**	**1816.32**	**2702.81**	**3702.32**	**8106.35**	**9705.55**
生产量	Output	2100.20	2798.90	3942.29	9926.73	11991.71
外省调入量	Inflow from other Provinces (Autonomons Regions and Municipalities)		10.70	30.40	213.43	
进口量	Imports			0.03	0.52	1.81
出口量(-)	Exports (-)	0.01	0.22	0.01		0.08
本区调出量(-)	Outflow (-)	232.76	203.12	323.47	1916.20	2075.63
年初年末库存差额	Stock Changes in the Year	-51.11	96.55	53.08	-118.13	-212.26
消费量	**Total Energy Consumption**	**1716.11**	**2702.40**	**3859.91**	**8106.35**	**9745.08**
在消费量中:	Consumption by Sector					
农、林、牧、渔、水利业	Farming, Forestry, Animal Husbandry, Fishery and Water Conservancy	23.96	100.00	103.30	101.00	101.30
工 业	Industry	1080.07	1801.40	3110.44	7593.35	9230.48
建筑业	Construction	11.67	26.00	17.00	19.00	21.00
交通运输和邮电通讯业	Transportation, Post and Telecommunications Services	25.42	55.00	56.60	50.00	49.30
商业、饮食、物资供销和仓储业	Commerce, Catering Services, Materials Supply, Marketing and Storage	20.50	40.00	31.78	47.00	45.00
其 他	Others	79.48	90.00	40.00	44.00	42.00
生活消费	Residential Consumption	479.37	590.00	500.79	252.00	256.00
在消费量中:	Consumption by Sector					
终端消费	Final Consumption	1163.46	1502.63	1503.83	2350.51	2569.26
#工 业	Industry	523.06	601.63	754.36	1837.51	2054.66
中间消费(用于加工转换)	Intermediate Consumption	525.51	1199.77	2356.08	5755.84	7175.82
#发 电	Power Generation	372.01	849.20	1363.96	2501.72	3368.56
供 热	Heating	32.32	204.46	585.51	1096.50	1233.00
炼 焦	Coking	111.39	137.77	380.90	1988.54	2365.07
平衡差额	**Balance**	**100.21**	**0.41**	**-157.59**		**-39.53**

注：生产量为原煤产量。
Note: Data on output refer to the output of crude coal.

6-6 主要年份电力平衡表
Electricity Balance Sheet in Main Years

单位:亿千瓦小时 (100 million kwh)

项目	Item	1990	2000	2005	2010	2011
可供量	**Total Energy Available for Consumption**	**69.79**	**182.98**	**310.14**	**661.96**	**839.10**
生产量	Output	69.79	182.98	310.14	665.06	875.19
水　电	Hydropower	14.25	30.54	46.49	97.07	114.57
风　电	Wind Power	0.08	1.73	2.32	30.02	28.26
火　电	Thermal Power	55.46	150.71	261.33	538.63	732.36
消费量	**Total Energy Consumption**	**69.79**	**182.98**	**310.14**	**661.96**	**839.10**
在消费量中：	Consumption by Sector					
农、林、牧、渔、水利业	Farming, Forestry, Animal Husbandry, Fishery and Water Conservancy	9.16	22.30	28.72	61.12	74.86
工　业	Industry	48.86	118.85	221.67	494.94	639.34
建筑业	Construction	1.18	3.50	1.44	6.86	9.91
交通运输和邮电通讯业	Transportation, Post and Telecommunications Services	1.48	4.00	4.74	6.68	7.69
商业、饮食、物资供销和仓储业	Commerce, Catering Services, Materials Supply, Marketing and Storage	0.81	6.90	11.09	16.74	19.10
其　他	Others	4.08	9.83	15.38	28.52	33.05
生活消费	Residential Consumption	4.22	17.60	27.10	47.10	55.15
在消费量中：	Consumption by Sector					
终端消费	Final Consumption	65.74	170.86	282.42	608.71	768.44
#工　业	Industry	44.81	106.73	193.95	441.69	568.68
输配电损失量	Losses in Transmission	4.05	12.12	27.72	53.25	70.66

6-7 分行业能源消费总量和主要能源消费量

(2011 年)

行业	Sector	能源消费总量(万吨标准煤) Total Energy Consumption (10 000 tons of SCE)	煤炭消费量(万吨) Coal Consumption (10 000 tons)	焦炭消费量(万吨) Coke Consumption (10 000 tons)
消费总量	**Total Consumption**	**9926.50**	**9745.08**	**880.23**
农、林、牧、渔业	**Farming, Forestry, Animal Husbandry, and Fishery**	**468.70**	**101.30**	
工　业	**Industry**	**7278.59**	**9230.48**	**880.23**
采矿业	**Mining and Quarrying**	**1270.97**	**491.83**	**23.78**
煤炭开采和洗选业	Mining and Washing of Coal	331.16	379.77	20.30
石油和天然气开采业	Extraction of Petroleum and Natural Gas	823.79	56.32	
黑色金属矿采选业	Mining and Processing of Ferrous Metals Ores	64.27	27.53	1.03
有色金属矿采选业	Mining and Processing of Nonferrous Metals Ores	38.75	14.99	2.45
非金属矿采选业	Mining and Processing of Non-metal Ores	12.50	13.06	
其他采矿业	Mining of Other Ores	0.50	0.16	
制造业	**Manufacturing**	**5081.29**	**5124.00**	**856.45**
农副食品加工业	Processing of Food from Agricultural Products	114.56	128.11	3.07
食品制造业	Manufacture of Food	75.31	73.31	
饮料制造业	Manufacture of Beverage	20.01	14.41	
烟草制品业	Manufacture of Tobacco	1.06	0.85	
纺织业	Manufacture of Textile	65.68	23.28	
纺织服装、鞋、帽制造业	Manufacture of Textile Wearing Apparel,Footware and Caps	0.32		
皮革、毛皮、羽绒及其制品业	Manufacture of Leather, Fur, Feather and Related Products	0.45	0.37	
木材加工及木、竹、藤、棕、草制品业	Timber Production, Wood, Bamboo, Cane and Grass	11.01	9.41	
家具制造业	Manufacture of Furniture	1.20	0.74	
造纸及纸制品业	Manufacture of Paper and Paper Products	29.75	31.70	
印刷业和记录媒介的复制	Printing and Copying of Medium for Record	1.06	0.12	
石油加工、炼焦及核燃料加工业	Processing of Oil Processing, Coking and Nuclear Fuel	1317.95	2350.20	

Consumption of Total Energy and Its Main Varieties by Sector

原油消费量 (万吨) Crude Oil Consumption (10 000 tons)	汽油消费量 (万吨) Gasoline Consumption (10 000 tons)	煤油消费量 (万吨) Kerosene Consumption (10 000 tons)	柴油消费量 (万吨) Diesel Oil Consumption (10 000 tons)	燃料油消费量 (万吨) Fuel Oil Consumption (10 000 tons)	天然气消费量 (亿立方米) Natural Gas Consumption (100 million cu.m)	电力消费量 (亿千瓦小时) Electricity Consumption (100 million kwh)
2598.46	**138.84**	**37.32**	**390.52**	**2.40**	**95.01**	**839.10**
	9.88	**0.42**	**63.00**		**0.02**	**74.86**
2527.86	**6.41**	**0.03**	**67.23**	**2.40**	**83.61**	**639.34**
86.24	**2.67**		**53.10**		**54.85**	**75.23**
	0.54		19.71			25.00
86.24	1.86		24.77		54.51	34.84
	0.09		7.04		0.33	8.24
	0.15		0.85			6.39
	0.03		0.72			0.67
			0.01			0.10
2441.60	**2.59**	**0.03**	**12.95**	**2.36**	**27.32**	**406.89**
	0.25		0.35		0.05	6.61
	0.17		0.30		0.14	4.86
	0.08		0.04		0.02	1.61
	0.01		0.01			0.12
	0.10		0.04			12.95
	0.02		0.01			0.03
	0.01		0.01			0.05
			0.06			0.94
	0.02		0.01			0.15
	0.02		0.04	0.09	0.01	2.37
	0.05		0.01			0.14
2441.60	0.27	0.02	0.87	2.27	12.16	43.65

6-7 续表

行业	Sector	能源消费总量(万吨标准煤) Total Energy Consumption (10 000 tons of SCE)	煤炭消费量(万吨) Coal Consumption (10 000 tons)	焦炭消费量(万吨) Coke Consumption (10 000 tons)
化学原料及化学制品制造业	Manufacture of Raw Chemical Material and Chemical Products	1230.10	854.37	202.67
医药制造业	Manufacture of Medicine	5.84	6.41	
化学纤维制造业	Manufacture of Chemical Fiber	85.34	96.90	
橡胶制品业	Manufacture of Rubber Products	3.17	2.91	
塑料制品业	Manufacture of Plastic Products	15.52	2.80	
非金属矿物制品业	Manufacture of Non-metallic Mineral Products	594.43	555.39	5.21
黑色金属冶炼及压延加工业	Smelting and Pressing of Ferrous Metals	1270.73	887.53	636.00
有色金属冶炼及压延加工业	Smelting and Pressing of Non-ferrous Metals	171.38	35.64	5.45
金属制品业	Metal Products Manufacturing	11.28	2.84	3.82
通用设备制造业	Manufacture of General Purpose Machinery	2.99	0.91	0.20
专用设备制造业	Manufacture of Special Purpose Machinery	2.51	0.28	0.03
交通运输设备制造业	Manufacture of Transport Equipment	1.15	0.01	
电气机械及器材制造业	Manufacture of Electric Equipment and Machinery	7.51	2.75	
通信设备、计算机及其他电子设备制造业	Communication Equipment, Computer and Other Electronic Equipment	36.74	40.25	
仪器仪表及文化办公用机械制造业	Manufacture of Equipment, Meter, Culture and Office Machinery	0.08		
工艺品及其他制造业	Manufacture of Artwork and Other Manufacturing Sector	0.74	0.02	
废弃资源和废旧材料回收加工业	Recycling and Disposal of Waste	3.42	2.47	
电力、燃气及水的生产和供应业	**Electric Power, Gas and Water Production and Supply**	**926.33**	**3614.65**	
电力、热力的生产和供应业	Production and Distribution of Power, Steam and Hot Water	913.09	3607.79	
燃气生产和供应业	Production and Supply of Gas	5.82	3.22	
水的生产和供应业	Production and Supply of Water	7.41	3.64	
建筑业	**Construction**	**98.02**	**21.00**	
交通运输、仓储及邮电通信业	**Transportation, Storage, Post & Telecommunications Services**	**678.79**	**49.30**	
批发和零售贸易业、餐饮业	**Wholesale, Retail Trades and Catering Services**	**195.28**	**45.00**	
其他行业	**Others**	**234.40**	**42.00**	
生活消费	**Household Consumption**	**972.76**	**256.00**	

Continued

原油消费量(万吨) Crude Oil Consumption (10 000 tons)	汽油消费量(万吨) Gasoline Consumption (10 000 tons)	煤油消费量(万吨) Kerosene Consumption (10 000 tons)	柴油消费量(万吨) Diesel Oil Consumption (10 000 tons)	燃料油消费量(万吨) Fuel Oil Consumption (10 000 tons)	天然气消费量(亿立方米) Natural Gas Consumption (100 million cu.m)	电力消费量(亿千瓦小时) Electricity Consumption (100 million kwh)
	0.46		2.46		14.23	151.01
	0.03		0.02		0.01	0.25
	0.03		0.07			6.33
			0.01			0.30
	0.12		0.06		0.04	3.31
	0.34	0.01	6.80		0.50	58.23
	0.14		1.18		0.06	56.66
	0.06		0.33		0.01	43.26
	0.12		0.11		0.04	1.13
	0.09		0.04			0.42
	0.08		0.04			0.45
	0.03		0.01		0.01	0.09
	0.05		0.02		0.01	1.53
	0.02		0.02			9.83
	0.01		0.01			0.01
	0.01		0.01			0.13
			0.01			0.47
0.02	**1.15**		**1.18**	**0.04**	**1.44**	**157.21**
0.02	1.05		1.08	0.04	1.12	154.93
	0.03		0.07		0.30	0.59
	0.07		0.03		0.02	1.69
	3.30	**0.17**	**14.45**		**0.03**	**9.91**
70.60	**76.00**	**36.00**	**189.00**		**3.70**	**7.69**
	10.80	**0.06**	**25.70**		**1.45**	**19.10**
	20.80	**0.30**	**24.40**		**0.49**	**33.05**
	11.65	**0.34**	**6.74**		**5.71**	**55.15**

6-8 主要年份能源生产弹性系数
Elasticity Ration of Energy Production in Main Years

年 份 Year	能源生产比上年增长(%) Growth Rate of Energy Production Over Preceding Year(%)	电力生产比上年增长(%) Growth Rate of Electricity Production over Preceding Year(%)	新疆生产总值比上年增长(%) Growth Rate of Gross Domestic Product (GDP) Over Preceding Year(%)	能源生产弹性系数 Elasticity Coefficient of Energy Production	电力生产弹性系数 Elasticity Ratio of Electricity Production
1980	7.8	3.6	7.2	1.08	0.50
1985	11.6	11.5	16.9	0.69	0.68
1990	5.8	10.8	11.7	0.50	0.92
1995	7.8	13.4	9.0	0.87	1.49
2000	3.3	8.1	8.2	0.40	0.99
2001	5.5	8.0	8.1	0.68	0.99
2002	7.6	7.4	8.1	0.94	0.91
2003	8.1	10.5	10.8	0.75	0.97
2004	6.8	13.3	11.1	0.61	1.20
2005	14.9	16.6	10.9	1.37	1.52
2006	16.6	15.2	11.0	1.51	1.38
2007	12.7	16.7	12.2	1.04	1.37
2008	18.0	16.0	11.0	1.64	1.45
2009	6.9	14.3	8.1	0.85	1.77
2010	10.8	21.4	10.6	1.02	2.02
2011	11.3	28.8	12.0	0.94	2.40

注：新疆生产总值增速按可比价格计算，下表同。
Note: The growth rate of GDP in Xinjiang is calculated at comparable prices and the same as in the following tables.

6-9 主要年份能源消费弹性系数
Elasticity Ration of Energy Consumption in Main Years

年 份 Year	能源消费比上年增长(%) Growth Rate of Energy Consumption Over Preceding Year(%)	电力消费比上年增长(%) Growth Rate of Electricity Consumption over Preceding Year(%)	新疆生产总值比上年增长(%) Growth Rate of Gross Domestic Product (GDP) Over Preceding Year(%)	能源消费弹性系数 Elasticity Ration of Energy Consumption	电力消费弹性系数 Elasticity Ration of Electricity Consumption
1980	4.5	3.6	7.2	0.63	0.50
1985	13.6	11.5	16.9	0.80	0.68
1990	9.3	10.8	11.7	0.79	0.92
1995	4.9	13.4	9.0	0.54	1.49
2000	3.1	8.1	8.2	0.38	0.99
2001	5.4	8.0	8.1	0.67	0.99
2002	3.6	7.4	8.1	0.44	0.91
2003	12.2	10.5	10.8	1.13	0.97
2004	17.7	13.3	11.1	1.59	1.20
2005	15.1	16.6	10.9	1.39	1.52
2006	9.8	14.8	11.0	0.89	1.35
2007	8.7	16.0	12.2	0.71	1.31
2008	7.5	16.0	11.0	0.68	1.45
2009	6.5	14.3	8.1	0.80	1.77
2010	10.2	20.8	10.6	0.96	1.96
2011	19.7	26.8	12.0	1.64	2.23

6-10 主要年份能源加工转换效率

Efficiency of Energy Procession and Conversion in Main Years

单位：%　　(%)

年　份 Year	总效率 Total Efficiency	发　电 Electricity Generation	供　热 Heating	炼　焦 Coking	炼　油 Petroleum Refining
1980	73.9	21.2		72.0	96.9
1985	74.9	21.1		75.5	98.1
1990	73.9	20.9	69.4	85.5	98.0
1995	72.7	23.6	71.2	78.6	96.6
2000	73.6	26.6	75.0	89.4	94.7
2001	73.7	26.1	74.6	78.2	97.4
2002	73.6	26.8	73.5	83.4	96.8
2003	73.8	26.0	78.0	92.0	97.9
2004	70.2	25.9	70.3	78.8	96.2
2005	72.3	27.0	77.7	75.7	97.1
2006	74.8	27.8	76.7	85.0	97.6
2007	73.3	28.6	73.5	86.3	96.4
2008	73.8	30.0	76.6	84.8	96.6
2009	73.5	30.4	77.4	82.2	96.3
2010	75.6	33.5	76.8	81.5	96.1
2011	74.8	34.9	75.6	81.2	97.0

6-11 主要年份平均每天各种能源消费量

Average Daily Energy Consumption by Type of Energy in Main Years

能源品种	Variey of Energy	1990	2000	2005	2010	2011
总计(万吨标准煤)	**Total (10 000 tons of SCE)**	**5.41**	**9.09**	**15.09**	**22.71**	**27.20**
煤炭(万吨)	Coal (10 000 tons)	5.04	7.48	10.58	22.21	26.70
焦炭(万吨)	Coke (10 000 tons)	0.16	0.20	0.50	1.78	2.41
原油(万吨)	Crude Oil (10 000 tons)	1.33	2.94	4.46	6.32	7.12
燃料油(万吨)	Fuel Oil (10 000 tons)	0.25	0.16	0.50	0.04	0.01
汽油(万吨)	Gasoline (10 000 tons)	0.20	0.28	0.29	0.36	0.38
煤油(万吨)	Kerosene (10 000 tons)	0.01	0.06	0.07	0.09	0.10
柴油(万吨)	Diesel Oil (10 000 tons)	0.24	0.43	0.83	1.00	1.07
天然气(万立方米)	Natural Gas (10 000 cu.m)	137.53	642.19	1546.85	2195.89	2603.01
电力(亿千瓦时)	Electricity (100 million kwh)	0.19	0.50	0.85	1.81	2.30

6-12 主要年份分品种生活能源年消费总量

Average Annual Energy Consumption for Household by Variety in Main Years

年 份 Year	合 计 (万吨标准煤) Total (10 000 tons of SCE)	煤 炭 (万吨) Coal (10 000 tons)	煤 油 (万吨) Kerosene (10 000 tons)	液化石油气 (万吨) Liquefied Petroleum Gas (10 000 tons)	天然气 (亿立方米) Natural Gas (100 million cu.m)	热 力 (万百万千焦) Heat (10 billion kilo-joule)	电 力 (亿千瓦小时) Electricity (100 million kwh)
1980	330.44	404.10					1.70
1985	355.65	421.72	0.71	3.00			2.38
1990	428.04	479.37	0.58	5.35		160.02	4.22
1995	499.84	527.00	0.50	8.94		177.29	10.11
2000	650.91	590.00	0.75	10.89	0.13	1611.81	17.60
2001	703.97	600.00	0.67	12.31	0.46	2209.66	19.50
2002	752.10	610.00	0.10	14.22	0.32	3112.58	19.20
2003	782.21	625.04		16.62	0.60	3191.14	20.37
2004	901.88	605.00		17.00	1.00	3363.45	24.26
2005	978.54	500.79	0.55	12.96	1.92	6219.00	27.10
2006	612.66	211.00	0.55	14.10	2.60	5008.00	31.90
2007	652.36	213.00	0.42	14.53	2.70	5097.43	33.52
2008	752.73	232.20	0.35	11.60	2.89	7371.00	38.55
2009	855.56	255.00	0.35	13.50	3.90	9073.84	42.62
2010	858.90	252.00	0.34	12.30	4.60	10511.04	47.10
2011	972.76	256.00	0.34	11.42	5.71	12103.27	55.15

注：表 6-12 和 6-13 中，2006 年以前数据未按新口径进行调整。
Note: Figures in table6-12 and6-13 did not adjusted at new coverage, except for figures in 2006.

6-13 主要年份每人年平均生活用能源

Annual Per-Capital Energy Consumption of Households in Main Years

年 份 Year	平均每人生活消费能源 (公斤标准煤/人) Annual Per Capita Consumption for Household (kg of SCE/person)	煤 炭 (公斤) Coal (kg)	电 力 (千瓦小时) Electricity (kwh)	煤 油 (公斤) Kerosene (kg)	液化石油气 (公斤) Liquefied Petroleum Gas (kg)	天然气 (立方米) Natural Gas (cu.m)
1980	258	315	13.25			
1985	261	310	17.49	0.52	2.20	
1990	268	313	27.60	0.38	3.50	
1995	301	317	65.60	0.30	5.33	
2000	353	320	95.33	0.41	5.90	0.70
2001	375	320	103.93	0.36	6.56	2.45
2002	395	320	100.78	0.05	7.46	1.68
2003	404	323	105.33		8.59	3.10
2004	459	308	123.58		8.66	5.09
2005	487	249	134.80	0.27	6.45	9.55
2006	302	104	157.13	0.27	6.95	12.81
2007	311	102	159.99	0.20	6.93	12.89
2008	352	109	180.92	0.16	5.44	13.56
2009	396	118	197.44	0.16	6.25	18.07
2010	394	116	215.92	0.16	5.64	21.09
2011	440	116	249.69	0.15	5.17	25.85

6-14 各地、州、市规模以上工业企业能源消费量

Energy Consumption of Industry above Designated Size by Prefecture, Autonomous Prefecture and City

(2011 年)

能源品种	Item	合 计 Total	乌鲁木齐市 Urumqi City	克拉玛依市 Karamay City	吐鲁番地区 Turpan Administrative Offices
原煤(吨)	Coal (ton)	84236275	19799156	3328448	3891855
洗精煤(吨)	Washed Coal(ton)	6427520	4076193		
其他洗煤(吨)	Other Washed Coal (ton)	176386	96193		
焦炭(吨)	Coke (ton)	8582316	3360447		1125272
焦炉煤气(万立方米)	Coke Oven Gas (10 000 cu.m)	238497	164987		18522
高炉煤气(万立方米)	High Oven Gas (10 000 cu.m)	1012737	1012737		
天然气(万立方米)	Natural Gas (10 000 cu.m)	815964	111762	294094	73888
原油(吨)	Coal (ton)	24568554	5706842	13882512	108623
汽油(吨)	Gasoline (ton)	44116	12614	10322	1267
煤油(吨)	Kerosene (ton)	153	91		
柴油(吨)	Diesel Oil (ton)	639967	49000	207257	41105
燃料油(吨)	Fuel Oil (ton)	23936	20575	401	1383
液化石油气(吨)	Liquefied Petroleum Gas (ton)	224907	75	137487	18972
炼厂干气(吨)	Refinary Dry Gas (ton)	1088999	141745	753271	
其他石油制品(吨)	Other Oil Product (ton)	1072704	758117	75543	53359
热力(百万千焦)	Heat (million KJ)	83621503	23849741	26707833	1796181
电力(万千瓦时)	Electricity (10 000 kwh)	6116168	1616461	462334	331023
其他燃料(吨标准煤)	Other (ton of SCE)	106577	14845		5319
能源合计(吨标准煤)	Energy Total (ton of SCE)	139693397	37677496	29433536	6076522

能源品种	Item	哈密地区 Hami [kumul] Administrative Offices	昌吉回族自治州 Changji Hui Autonomous Prefecture	博尔塔拉蒙古自治州 Bortala Mongol Autonomous Prefecture	伊犁州直属县(市) Counties (Cities) Direct Under Ili Prefecture
原煤(吨)	Coal (ton)	4586526	22248624	555116	4614380
洗精煤(吨)	Washed Coal (ton)		128005		754517
其他洗煤(吨)	Other Washed Coal (ton)	9359			
焦炭(吨)	Coke (ton)	177362	675509	155743	825656
焦炉煤气(万立方米)	Coke Oven Gas (10 000 cu.m)		32744		21548
高炉煤气(万立方米)	High Oven Gas (10 000 cu.m)				
天然气(万立方米)	Natural Gas (10 000 cu.m)		6077		144
原油(吨)	Coal (ton)		48921		
汽油(吨)	Gasoline (ton)	2200	3016	400	2787
煤油(吨)	Kerosene (ton)		59		4
柴油(吨)	Diesel Oil (ton)	48726	140932	2435	16329
燃料油(吨)	Fuel Oil (ton)				
液化石油气(吨)	Liquefied Petroleum Gas (ton)		2	3	4
炼厂干气(吨)	Refinary Dry Gas (ton)				
其他石油制品(吨)	Other Oil Product (ton)		11061	542	31202
热力(百万千焦)	Heat (million KJ)	2548	2150789	116070	537135
电力(万千瓦时)	Electricity (10 000 kwh)	214468	518708	26813	456294
其他燃料(吨标准煤)	Other (ton of SCE)				
能源合计(吨标准煤)	Energy Total (ton of SCE)	3805480	18101436	589964	5766661

注：各地区数含兵团工业在内。
Note:Figures in different prefectures include data of XPCG enterprises.

6-14 续表 Continued

名　称	Variey of Energy	塔城地区 Tacheng [Tarbagatai] Administrative Office	阿勒泰地区 Altay Administrative Offices	巴音郭楞蒙古自治州 Bayangol Mongol Autonomous Prefecture	阿克苏地区 Aksu Administrative Offices
原煤(吨)	Coal (ton)	2909084	800619	3178461	5767285
洗精煤(吨)	Washed Coal (ton)			84768	732532
其他洗煤(吨)	Other Washed Coal (ton)			18019	52815
焦炭(吨)	Coke (ton)	34862	162809	694785	46990
焦炉煤气(万立方米)	Coke Oven Gas (10 000 cu.m)				225
高炉煤气(万立方米)	High Oven Gas (10 000 cu.m)				
天然气(万立方米)	Natural Gas (10 000 cu.m)			223890	89753
原油(吨)	Coal (ton)			599519	4222138
汽油(吨)	Gasoline (ton)	1203	1699	4450	1668
煤油(吨)	Kerosene (ton)				
柴油(吨)	Diesel Oil (ton)	7465	54350	35309	18299
燃料油(吨)	Fuel Oil (ton)			1167	
液化石油气(吨)	Liquefied Petroleum Gas (ton)	6		55180	8
炼厂干气(吨)	Refinary Dry Gas (ton)			31836	162147
其他石油制品(吨)	Other Oil Product (ton)			16032	126739
热力(百万千焦)	Heat (million KJ)	1258248		12484694	3370008
电力(万千瓦时)	Electricity (10 000 kwh)	155727	107078	364250	228520
其他燃料(吨标准煤)	Other (ton of SCE)			18437	39460
能源合计(吨标准煤)	Energy Total (ton of SCE)	2376788	951757	7870491	13422247

名　称	Variey of Energy	克孜勒苏柯尔克孜自治州 Kizilsu Kirgiz Autonomous Prefecture	喀什地区 Kashgar [kaxgar] Administrative Offices	和田地区 Hotan Administrative Offices	石河子市 Shihezi City
原煤(吨)	Coal (ton)	137523	1289372	232823	7835849
洗精煤(吨)	Washed Coal (ton)				
其他洗煤(吨)	Other Washed Coal (ton)				
焦炭(吨)	Coke (ton)	13136	136467		1173201
焦炉煤气(万立方米)	Coke Oven Gas (10 000 cu.m)				
高炉煤气(万立方米)	High Oven Gas (10 000 cu.m)				
天然气(万立方米)	Natural Gas (10 000 cu.m)	6863	4256	39	4526
原油(吨)	Coal (ton)				
汽油(吨)	Gasoline (ton)	93	818	478	750
煤油(吨)	Kerosene (ton)				
柴油(吨)	Diesel Oil (ton)	2860	3192	759	10221
燃料油(吨)	Fuel Oil (ton)	15		1	394
液化石油气(吨)	Liquefied Petroleum Gas (ton)	1	13161		
炼厂干气(吨)	Refinary Dry Gas (ton)				
其他石油制品(吨)	Other Oil Product (ton)	39			
热力(百万千焦)	Heat (million KJ)				10022085
电力(万千瓦时)	Electricity (10 000 kwh)	19006	62983	31070	1110016
其他燃料(吨标准煤)	Other (ton of SCE)		28517		
能源合计(吨标准煤)	Energy Total (ton of SCE)	231344	1276225	218669	8398651

主要统计指标解释

能源生产总量 指一定时期内，一个地区一次能源生产量的总和。该指标是观察一个地区能源生产水平、规模、构成和发展速度的总量指标。一次能源生产量包括原煤、原油、天然气、水电、核能及其他动力能(如风能、地热能等)发电量，不包括低热值燃料生产量、生物质能、太阳能等的利用和由一次能源加工转换而成的二次能源产量。

能源消费总量 指一定时期内，一个地区和居民生活消费的各种能源的总和，该指标是观察能源消费水平、构成和增长速度的总量指标。能源消费总量包括原煤和原油及其制品、天然气、电力，不包括低热值燃料、生物质能和太阳能等的利用。能源消费总量分为终端能源消费量、能源加工转换损失量和能源损失量三部分。

(1)终端能源消费量：指一定时期内，一个地区生产和生活消费的各种能源在扣除了用于加工转换二次能源消费量和损失量以后的数量。

(2)能源加工转换损失量：指一定时期内，一个地区投入加工转换的各种能源数量之和与产出各种能源产品之和的差额，该指标是观察能源在加工转换过程中损失量变化的指标。

(3)能源损失量：指一定时期内，能源在输送、分配、储存过程中发生的损失和由客观原因造成的各种损失量，不包括各种气体能源放空、放散量。

能源生产弹性系数 是研究能源生产增长速度与国民经济增长速度之间关系的指标。计算公式为：

能源生产弹性系数＝能源生产总量年平均增长速度／国民经济年平均增长速度

国民经济年平均增长速度，可根据不同的目的或需要，用国民生产总值、国内生产总值等指标来计算，本年鉴是采用国内生产总值指标计算的。

电力生产弹性系数 是研究电力生产增长速度与国民经济增长速度之间关系的指标。一般来说，电力的发展应当快于国民经济的发展，也就是说电力应超前发展。计算公式为：

电力生产弹性系数＝电力生产量年平均增长速度／国民经济年平均增长速度

能源消费弹性系数 是反映能源消费增长速度与国民经济增长速度之间比例关系的指标。计算公式为：

能源消费弹性系数＝能源消费量年平均增长速度／国民经济年平均增长速度

电力消费弹性系数 反映电力消费增长速度与国民经济增长速度之间比例关系的指标。计算公式为：

电力消费弹性系数＝电力消费量年平均增长速度／国民经济年平均增长速度

能源加工转换效率 指一定时期内，能源经过加工、转换后，产出的各种能源产品的数量与同期内投入加工转换的各种能源数量的比率。该指标是观察能源加工转换装置和生产工艺先进与落后、管理水平高低等的重要指标。计算公式为：

能源加工转换效率＝能源加工转换产出量／能源加工转换投入量×100%

单位国内生产总值能耗 指一定时期内，一个国家或地区每生产一个单位的国内生产总值所消耗的能源。计算公式为：

单位国内生产总值能耗=能源消费总量/国内生产总值

单位国内生产总值电耗 指一定时期内，一个国家或地区每生产一个单位的国内生产总值所消耗的电力。计算公式为：

单位国内生产总值电耗=全社会用电量/国内生产总值

单位工业增加值能耗 指一定时期内，一个国家或地区每生产一个单位的工业增加值所消耗的能源。计算公式为：

单位工业增加值能耗=工业能源消费量/工业增加值

Explanatory Notes on Main Statistical Indicators

Total Energy Production refers to the total production of primary energy by all energy producing enterprises in the country in a given period of time. It is a comprehensive indicator to show the level, scale, composition and pace of development of energy production of the country. The production of primary energy includes that of coal, crude oil, natural gas, hydro-power and electricity generated by nuclear energy and other means such as wind power and geothermal power. However, it does not include the production of fuels of low calorific value, bio-energy, solar energy and secondary energy converted from primary energy.

Total Energy Consumption refers to the total consumption of energy of various kinds by the production sectors and the households in the country in a given period of time. It is a comprehensive indicator to show the scale, composition and pace of increase of energy consumption. Total energy consumption includes that of coal, crude oil and their products, natural gas and electricity. However, it does not include the consumption of fuel of low calorific value, bio-energy and solar energy. Total energy consumption can be divided into three parts: end-use energy consumption; loss during the process of energy conversion; and energy loss.

(1)End-use Energy Consumption: It refers to the total energy consumption by the production sectors and the households in the country (region) in a given period of time. It does not include the consumption during the conversion of primary energy into secondary energy and the loss in the process of energy conversion.

(2)Loss During the Process of Energy Conversion: It refers to the total input of various kinds of energy for conversion, minus the total output of various kinds of energy in the country in a given period of time. It is an indicator to show the loss that occurs during the process of energy conversion.

(3)Energy Loss: It refers to the total of the loss of energy during the course of energy transport, distribution and storage and the loss caused by any objective reason in a given period of time. The loss of various kinds of gas due to gas discharges and stocktaking is not included.

Elasticity Ratio of Energy Production is an indicator to show the relationship between the growth rate of energy production and the growth rate of the national economy. The formula is:

$$\text{Elasticity Ratio of Energy Production} = \frac{\text{Average Annual Growth Rate of Energy Production}}{\text{Average Annual Growth Rate of National Economy}}$$

The average annual growth rate of the national economy can be measured by indicators such as the Gross National Product and the Gross Domestic Product, depending on the purposes or needs. The Gross Domestic Product has been used in the calculation of the ratio in this Yearbook.

Elasticity Ratio of Electricity Production is an indicator to show the relationship between the growth rate of electricity production and the growth rate of the national economy. Generally speaking, the growth rate of electricity production should be higher than that of the national economy.

Its formula is:

$$\text{Elasticity Ratio of Electricity Production} = \frac{\text{Average Annual Growth Rate of Electricity Production}}{\text{Average Annual Growth Rate of National Economy}}$$

Elasticity Ratio of Energy Consumption is an indicator to show the relationship between the growth rate of energy consumption and the growth rate of the national economy. The formula is:

$$\text{Elasticity Ratio of Energy Consumption} = \frac{\text{Average Annual Growth Rate of Energy Consumption}}{\text{Average Annual Growth Rate of National Economy}}$$

Elasticity Ratio of Electricity Consumption is an indicator to show the relationship between the growth rate of electricity consumption and the growth rate of the national economy. The formula is:

$$\text{Elasticity Ratio of Electricity Consumption} = \frac{\text{Average Annual Growth Rate of Electricity Consumption}}{\text{Average Annual Growth Rate of National Economy}}$$

Efficiency of Energy Processing and Conversion refers to the ratio of the total output of energy products of various kinds after processing and conversion to the total input of energy of various kinds for processing and conversion in the same reference period. It is an important indicator to show the current conditions of energy processing and conversion equipment, production technique and management. The formula is:

$$\text{Efficiency of Energy Processing \& Conversion} = \frac{\text{Output of Energy After Processing \& Conversion}}{\text{Input of Energy for Processing \& Conversion}} \times 100\%$$

Energy Consumption per Unit of GDP refers to the energy consumption per unit of Gross Domestic Product in a country or the Gross Regional Product in a region in the same reference period. The formula is:

$$\text{Energy Consumption per Unit of GDP} = \frac{\text{Total Energy Consumption}}{\text{Gross Domestic Product}}$$

Electricity Consumption per Unit of GDP refers to the electricity consumption per unit of Gross Domestic Product in a country or the Gross Regional Product in a region in the same reference period. The formula is:

$$\text{Electricity Consumption per Unit of GDP} = \frac{\text{Total Electricity Consumption}}{\text{Gross Domestic Product}}$$

Energy Consumption per Unit of Industrial Value-added refers to the energy consumption per unit of industrial value-added in a country or region in the same reference period. The formula is:

$$\text{Energy Consumption per Unit Of Industrial Value-added} = \frac{\text{energy consumption of industry}}{\text{Industrial Value-added}}$$

新疆统计年鉴
XINJIANG STATISTICAL YEARBOOK

7

财政、金融和保险

GOVERNMENT FINANCE, FINANCIAL INTERMEDIATION AND INSURANCE

简要说明

本篇资料的主要内容及来源

本篇反映自治区财政、金融和保险业发展情况,有以下三个部分：一是地方财政预算收支情况；二是金融机构存贷等活动情况；三是保险业务情况。

地方财政预算收支情况取自新疆维吾尔自治区财政厅年度决算；金融资料来自中国人民银行乌鲁木齐中心支行金融机构信贷统计月报及年报；保险业务情况资料取自中国保险监督管理委员会新疆监管局编制的保险统计资料。

本篇章数据由新疆维吾尔自治区统计局国民经济综合统计处根据上述部门所提供的资料整理。

Brief Introduction

Main Content and Source of Data

The data in this chapter show the development of Xinjiang Uygur Autonomous region government finance, banking and insurance, in the following three aspects:(1)The government revenue and expenditure;(2)The financial activities of banking institutions;(3)The business of insurance.

Data on the government revenue and expenditure come from the final state financial accounts, Data on financial intermediation come from the credit funds sheet of financial institutions of Urumqi municipal sub-branches, People's Bank of China; Data on insurance come from Xinjiang Insurance Regulatory Bureau of China Insurance Regulatory Commission.

Data in this chapter are compiled and collected by the Division of comprehensive of the Xinjing Bureau of Statistics on the basis of data from the relative departments.

7-1 主要年份公共财政预算收支及增长速度
The General Budgetary Revenue & Expenses and Growth Rate of Local Finance in Main Years

单位：万元 (10 000 yuan)

年 份 Year	公共财政预算收入 General Budgetary Revenue in Local Finance	公共财政预算支出 General Budgetary Expenditure in Local Finance	收支差额 Balance	指数(上年=100) Indices (precding year=100)	
				公共财政预算收入 General Budgetary Revenue in Local Finance	公共财政预算支出 General Budgetary Expenditure in Local Finance
1978	71416	170169	-98753	196.5	153.3
1980	40309	162159	-121850	73.4	95.4
1985	84663	286031	-201368	117.2	122.6
1990	217784	476210	-258426	118.9	114.2
1995	382818	964021	-581203	133.4	135.6
2000	790724	1909529	-1118805	110.9	114.8
2001	950933	2633232	-1682299	120.3	137.9
2002	1164724	3611729	-2447005	122.5	137.2
2003	1282218	3684676	-2402458	110.1	102.0
2004	1557040	4210446	-2653406	121.4	114.3
2005	1803184	5190179	-3386995	115.8	123.3
2006	2194628	6784723	-4590095	121.7	130.7
2007	2858600	7951540	-5092940	130.3	117.2
2008	3610616	10593638	-6983022	126.3	133.2
2009	3887848	13469125	-9581277	107.7	127.1
2010	5005759	16989126	-11983367	128.8	126.1
2011	7204324	22844864	-15640540	143.9	134.5
2012	9089655	27200673	-18111018	126.2	119.1

7-2 主要年份公共财政预算收入占新疆生产总值的比重
Ration of the General Budgetary Revenue in Local Finance to GDP of Xinjiang in Main Years

单位：亿元 (100 million yuan)

年 份 Year	公共财政预算收入 General Budgetary Revenue in Local Finance	新疆生产总值 Gross Domestic Product in Xinjiang	公共财政预算收入相当于新疆生产总值的比例(%) Proportion of Local Financial Revenue to GDP of Xinjiang (%)
1978	7.14	39.07	18.27
1980	4.03	53.24	7.57
1985	8.47	112.24	7.56
1990	21.78	261.44	8.34
1995	38.28	814.85	4.70
2000	79.07	1363.56	5.80
2001	95.09	1491.60	6.37
2002	116.47	1612.65	7.22
2003	128.22	1886.35	6.79
2004	155.70	2209.09	7.05
2005	180.32	2604.14	6.92
2006	219.46	3045.26	7.21
2007	285.86	3523.16	8.11
2008	361.06	4183.21	8.63
2009	388.78	4277.05	9.09
2010	500.58	5437.47	9.21
2011	720.43	6610.05	10.90
2012	908.97	7505.31	12.11

7-3 地方财政收支情况

Statistics on Total Government Revenue and Expenditures in Local Finance

单位：万元 (10 000 yuan)

项　　目	Item	2011	2012
收入合计	**Total Revenue**	**1040.42**	**1251.64**
公共财政预算收入	General Budgetary Revenue in Local Finance	720.43	908.97
税收收入	Taxes Revenue	593.41	698.93
增值税	Value-added Tax	96.70	100.57
营业税	Business Tax	209.84	259.30
企业所得税（含退税）	Corporate Income Tax	63.43	79.99
个人所得税	Individual Income Tax	38.34	35.89
资源税	Resources Tax	65.01	69.35
城市维护建设税	City Maintenance and Construction Tax	41.26	44.99
房产税	House Property Tax	14.67	18.82
契　税	Contract Tax	21.86	26.22
其他税收收入	Other Revenues	42.30	63.80
非税收入	Non-tax Revenues	127.02	210.04
专项收入	Special Program Receipts	46.39	89.40
行政性收费收入	Charge of Administrative and Institutional Units	36.56	42.58
罚没收入	Penalty Receipts	14.00	18.16
其他收入	Other Revenues	30.07	59.90
基金预算收入	Fund Budgetary Revenues	319.99	342.67
支出合计	**Total Expenditures**	**2599.67**	**3080.22**
公共财政预算支出	General Budgetary Expenditure in Local Finance	2284.49	2720.07
一般公共服务	Expenditure for General Public Services	245.36	303.67
教　育	Expenditure for Education	399.80	473.86
科学技术	Expenditure for Science and Technology	26.43	33.01
文化体育与传媒	Expenditure for Culture Sports and Media	47.70	68.23
社会保障和就业	Expenditure for Social Safety Net and Employment Effort	201.64	227.79
医疗卫生	Expenditure for Medical and Health Care	132.43	145.88
节能环保	Expenditure for Environmental Protection	53.67	64.12
城乡社区事务	Expenditure for Urban and Rural Community Affairs	140.10	183.49
农林水事务	Expenditure for Agriculture, Forestry and Water Conservancy	297.59	365.39
交通运输	Expenditure for Transportation	206.83	226.47
资源勘探电力信息等事务	Expenditure for Miming and Quarrying,Electriaty and Information Technology	47.60	60.45
其他各项支出	Other Expenditures	485.34	567.71
基金预算支出	Fund Budgetary Expenditure	315.18	360.15

7-4 各地、州、市、县(市)公共财政预算收支

Government Revenue and Expenditures by Prefecture, Autonomous Prefecture, City and County

单位：万元 (2012 年) (10 000 yuan)

地 区	Region	收 入 Revenue	支 出 Expenditures
总 计	**Total**	**9089655**	**27200673**
自治区本级	Autonomous regional Level	1331410	7200111
乌鲁木齐市	**Urumqi City and Changji Prefecture**	**2520052**	**2956004**
乌鲁木齐市本级	Urumqi and Changji Level	1410387	1792055
乌鲁木齐县	Urumqi County	36843	76186
天山区	Tianshan District	218258	220165
沙依巴克区	Shayibak District	157829	181662
新市区	Xinshi District	204970	142654
水磨沟区	Shui Mogou District	170371	183922
头屯河区	Tou Tunhe District	85481	65222
米东区	Midong District	183158	226714
达坂城区	Da Bancheng District	52755	67424
昌吉回族自治州	**Changji Hui Autonomous Prefecture**	**642809**	**1437355**
昌吉州本级	Changji Prefecture Level	76061	236561
昌吉市	Changji City	205356	297840
阜康市	Fukang City	110723	193288
呼图壁县	Hutubi County	53359	130456
玛纳斯县	Manas County	54634	142355
奇台县	Qitai County	58501	185744
吉木萨尔县	Jimsar County	64925	141005
木垒哈萨克自治县	Mori Kazak Autonomous County	19250	110106
克拉玛依市	**Karamay City**	**572603**	**701753**
市本级	City Level	354317	392329
克拉玛依区	Karamay District	130557	150721
独山子区	Dushanzi District	54803	95538
白碱滩区	Bai Jiantan District	24489	47128
乌尔河区	Urhe District	8437	16037
吐鲁番地区	**Turpan Administrative Offices**	**252207**	**521607**
地区本级	Prefecture Level	54587	83123
吐鲁番市	Turpan City	49222	139574
鄯善县	Shanshan [Piqan] County	100028	181130
托克逊县	Toksun County	48370	117780
哈密地区	**Hami [Kumul] Administrative Offices**	**303845**	**681438**
地区本级	Prefecture Level	28568	164865
哈密市	Hami [Kumul] City	222574	311838
巴里坤哈萨克自治县	Barkol Kazak Autonomous County	28388	125521
伊吾县	Yiwu [Araturuk] County	24315	79214
伊犁哈萨克自治州	**Ili Kazak Autonomous Prefecture**	**1136329**	**4263143**
伊犁州直属县(市)	**Counties (Cities) Direct Under Ili Prefecture**	**561683**	**2094391**
州本级	Autonomous Prefecture Level	36241	292622
伊宁市	Yining [Gulja] City	172123	326906
奎屯市	Kuytun City	133614	190875
伊宁县	Yining [Gulja] County	38764	202435
察布查尔锡伯自治县	Qapqal Xibe Autonomous County	26000	150828
霍城县	Huocheng [Korgas] County	30060	172420

7-4 续表 1 Continued

单位：万元　　(10 000 yuan)

地　　区	Region	收 入 Revenue	支 出 Expenditures
巩留县	Gongliu [Tokkuztara] County	14400	148600
新源县	Xinyuan [Kunes] County	51228	192487
昭苏县	Zhaosu [Mongolkure] County	10017	127879
特克斯县	Tekes County	13099	142895
尼勒克县	Nilka County	36137	146444
塔城地区	**Tacheng [Tarbagatai] Administrative Office**	**320435**	**1122564**
地区本级	Prefecture Level	6240	100359
塔城市	Tacheng [Qoqek] City	29407	140461
乌苏市	Usu City	80073	199352
额敏县	Emin [Dorbiljin] County	24372	147333
沙湾县	Shawan County	50117	162837
托里县	Toli County	25453	126817
裕民县	Yumin [Qagantokay] County	4738	87044
和布克赛尔蒙古自治县	Hoboksar Mongol Autonomous County	100035	158361
阿勒泰地区	**Altay Administrative Offices**	**254211**	**1046188**
地区本级	Prefecture Level	25666	122624
阿勒泰市	Altay City	33777	182813
布尔津县	Burqin County	16893	96992
富蕴县	Fuyun [Koktokay] County	88577	192049
福海县	Fuhai [Burultokay] County	21489	108055
哈巴河县	Habahe [Kaba] County	50007	135413
青河县	Qinghe [Qinggil] County	13700	121464
吉木乃县	Jeminay County	4102	86778
博尔塔拉蒙古自治州	**Bortala Mongol Autonomous Prefecture**	**103878**	**478568**
州本级	Autonomous Prefecture Level	24557	133060
博乐市	Bole [Bortala] City	53849	155861
精河县	Jinghe [Jing] County	19464	105794
温泉县	Wenquan [Araxang] County	6008	83853
巴音郭楞蒙古自治州	**Bayangol Mongol Autonomous Prefecture**	**604892**	**1501148**
州本级	Autonomous Prefecture Level	55573	220520
库尔勒市	Korla City	261012	368606
轮台县	Luntai [Bugur] County	70065	129126
尉犁县	Yuli [Lopnur] County	17554	98729
若羌县	Ruoqiang [Qarkilik] County	66489	109488
且末县	Qiemo [Qarqan] County	23484	100447
焉耆回族自治县	Yanqi Hui Autonomous County	21532	105593
和静县	Hejing County	68700	210973
和硕县	Hoxud County	10644	83727
博湖县	Bohu [Bagrax] County	9839	73939
阿克苏地区	**Aksu Administrative Offices**	**721656**	**1869077**
地区本级	Prefecture Level	24791	216857
阿克苏市	Aksu City	126117	238065
温宿县	Wensu [Onsu] County	31018	176041

7-4 续表 2 Continued

单位：万元 (10 000 yuan)

地　　区	Region	收 入 Revenue	支 出 Expenditure
库车县	Kuqa County	280650	372756
沙雅县	Xayar County	100959	183832
新和县	Xinhe [Toksu] County	41729	129835
拜城县	Baicheng [Bay] County	89751	187880
乌什县	Wushi [Uxturpan] County	10151	135916
阿瓦提县	Awat County	12417	154910
柯坪县	Kalpin County	4073	72985
克孜勒苏柯尔克孜自治州	**Kizilsu Kirgiz Autonomous Prefecture**	**70862**	**716335**
州本级	Autonomous Prefecture Level	6837	133235
阿图什市	Artux City	20013	171621
阿克陶县	Akto County	19672	198412
阿合奇县	Akqi County	6613	92392
乌恰县	Wuqia [Ulugqat] County	17727	120675
喀什地区	**Kashgar [Kaxgar] Administrative Offices**	**377973**	**2921788**
地区本级	Prefecture Level	14974	214417
喀什市	Kashgar [Kaxgar] City	131406	410178
疏附县	Shufu County	17018	190328
疏勒县	Shule County	28006	176554
英吉沙县	Yengisar County	12550	179983
泽普县	Zepu [Poskam] County	20503	163919
莎车县	Shache [Yarkant] County	32000	444960
叶城县	Yecheng [Kagilik] County	31049	300907
麦盖提县	Makit County	16580	151035
岳普湖县	Yopurga County	10073	129322
伽师县	Jiashi [Payzawat] County	30710	249802
巴楚县	Bachu [Maralbexi] County	22954	216551
塔什库尔干塔吉克自治县	Taxkorgan Tajik Autonomous County	10150	93832
和田地区	**Hotan Administrative Offices**	**111841**	**1512549**
地区本级	Prefecture Level	7327	144972
和田市	Hotan City	38113	201614
和田县	Hotan County	12166	172567
墨玉县	Moyu [Karakax] County	15001	279574
皮山县	Pishan [Guma] County	10423	167506
洛浦县	Lop County	7568	161094
策勒县	Qira County	6282	125306
于田县	Yutian [Keriya] County	8369	190148
民丰县	Minfeng [Niya] County	6592	69768
自治区直辖县级市	**Municpality Country-LevelCity directly under the Central Govern-ment**	**339298**	**439797**
石河子市	Shihezi City	217520	269061
阿拉尔市	Aral City	32269	48056
图木舒克市	Tumxuk City	14252	27441
五家渠市	Wujiaqu City	68623	85556
北屯市	Beitun City	6634	9683

7-5 1978-2012 年历年金融机构各项存款和各项贷款余额
Balance of Deposits and Loans of National Banking System (1978-2012)

单位：亿元 (100 million yuan)

年份 Year	各项存款合计 Total Deposits	#单位存款 Deposits by Units	#储蓄存款 Savings Deposit	各项贷款合计 Total Loans
1978	32.07	6.86	6.42	18.26
1979	33.44	7.03	7.21	21.19
1980	38.56	9.60	9.52	24.74
1981	45.59	12.21	12.29	28.84
1982	53.47	15.23	15.30	32.86
1983	61.94	17.95	19.01	38.85
1984	73.63	23.35	24.31	52.02
1985	82.96	29.87	29.55	72.68
1986	102.75	38.15	40.37	93.18
1987	124.93	44.13	53.25	111.14
1988	141.10	47.41	66.25	139.43
1989	167.03	52.76	83.33	173.02
1990	221.80	71.23	114.13	233.72
1991	282.21	92.78	145.01	299.59
1992	336.58	119.51	175.62	380.26
1993	397.39	129.98	220.45	467.81
1994	634.44	214.13	347.71	632.32
1995	838.42	274.24	477.18	843.38
1996	1012.47	364.51	575.79	1016.20
1997	1180.78	442.76	676.13	1215.39
1998	1336.58	461.02	759.14	1318.41
1999	1548.72	544.22	824.68	1386.78
2000	1863.48	702.21	908.55	1403.13
2001	1972.55	691.74	994.00	1584.73
2002	2225.31	705.82	1137.87	1801.15
2003	2661.65	763.49	1371.59	2099.09
2004	2959.78	832.50	1534.67	2214.66
2005	3427.48	909.45	1816.38	2272.08
2006	4040.78	1106.42	2035.63	2412.69
2007	4614.62	1452.25	2054.91	2685.00
2008	5399.34	1473.24	2550.95	2826.53
2009	6845.07	2043.54	3049.91	3782.92
2010	8870.72	2791.72	3713.47	4973.16
2011	10387.00	5573.38	4421.93	6270.21
2012	12330.89	6588.72	5281.83	7914.00

注：单位存款 2010 年及以前年份为企业存款。
Note: Before 2010 the deposits of units refer to the deposits of enterprises.

7-6 金融机构和人员数
Number of Financial Institutions and Staff

单位：个、人 (2012 年) (unit, person)

项　目	Item	合　计 Total		自治区级 Level of Autonomous Region		地区级 Prefectural Level	
		机构 Institutions	人员 Employees	机构 Institutions	人员 Employees	机构 Institutions	人员 Employees
总　计	**Total**	**3521**	**62070**	**19**	**5005**	**155**	**15834**
人民银行	**The People's Bank of China**	**69**	**3501**	**1**	**443**	**14**	**1782**
银监会新疆监管局	**China Banking Regulatory Commission Xingjiang Bureau**	**51**	**928**	**1**	**148**	**14**	**643**
中资全国性大型银行	**Large National Bank of Chinese Investment**	**1977**	**36729**	**8**	**3527**	**82**	**9973**
工商银行	Industrial and Commercial Bank	293	8409	1	749	15	2852
农业银行	Agricultural Bank	375	8058	1	347	15	2325
兵团分行	XPCG Branch	249	4028	1	261	4	721
中国银行	Bank of China	274	5244	1	910	14	1050
建设银行	Bank of Construction	200	5579	1	695	14	1969
国家开发银行	State Development Bank	1	162	1	162		
交通银行	Bank of Communication	31	877	1	277	3	130
邮政储蓄银行	Postal Savings Bank	554	4372	1	126	17	926
中资全国性中小银行	**Small and Medium-sized National Bank of Chinese Investment**	**167**	**5091**	**5**	**569**	**28**	**1965**
中国进出口银行	Export and Import Bank of China	1	32	1	32		
农业发展银行	Agricultural Development Bank	89	2275	1	163	17	739
中信银行	China Citic Bank	6	231			1	135
光大银行	Guang Da Bank	2	105			1	93
华夏银行	Hua Xia Bank	7	239			1	137
广发银行	GuangFa Bank	1	101			1	101
招商银行	Merchants Bank	11	445			1	237
浦发银行	Shanghai PuDong Development Bank	11	361	1	175	2	46
兴业银行	Xing Ye Bank	10	404	1	189		
昆仑银行	KunLun Bank	29	898	1	10	4	477
中资区域性中小型银行	**Small and Medium-sized Regional Bank of Chinese Investment**	**175**	**2977**			**12**	**1091**
城市商业银行	City Commercial Bank	124	2322			11	1055
农村商业银行	Rural Commercila Bank	4	96			1	36
村镇银行	County Bank	25	301				
农村合作银行	Rural Cooperation Bank	22	258				
外资银行	**Foreign Bank**	**2**	**77**			**1**	**67**
农村信用社	**Rural Credit Cooperative**	**1073**	**12336**	**1**	**200**		
财务公司	**Finance Company**	**1**	**13**			**1**	**13**
信托投资公司	**Trust and Investment Company**	**2**	**217**			**2**	**217**
金融租赁公司	**Financial Leasing Company**	**1**	**83**			**1**	**83**
资产管理公司	**Assets Management Company**	**3**	**118**	**3**	**118**		

7-6 续表 Continued

单位：个、人 (unit, person)

项目	Item	县级 County Level		营业网点 Business Outlets	
		机构 Institutions	人员 Employees	机构 Institutions	人员 Employees
总计	**Total**	**963**	**21563**	**2384**	**19668**
人民银行	**The People's Bank of China**	**54**	**1276**		
银监会新疆监管局	**China Banking Regulatory Commission Xingjiang Bureau**	**36**	**137**		
中资全国性大型银行	**Large National Bank of Chinese Investment**	**679**	**13213**	**1208**	**10016**
工商银行	Industrial and Commercial Bank	221	4136	56	672
农业银行	Agricultural Bank	124	2910	235	2476
兵团分行	XPCG Branch	52	1173	192	1873
中国银行	Bank of China	38	870	221	2414
建设银行	Bank of Construction	98	1845	87	1070
国家开发银行	State Development Bank				
交通银行	Bank of Communication	27	470		
邮政储蓄银行	Postal Savings Bank	119	1809	417	1511
中资全国性中小银行	**Small and Medium-sized National Bank of Chinese Investment**	**98**	**1842**	**36**	**715**
中国进出口银行	Export and Import Bank of China				
农业发展银行	Agricultural Development Bank	71	1373		
中信银行	China Citic Bank			5	96
光大银行	Guang Da Bank	1	12		
华夏银行	Hua Xia Bank			6	102
广发银行	GuangFa Bank				
招商银行	Merchants Bank			10	208
浦发银行	Shanghai PuDong Development Bank	1	20	7	120
兴业银行	Xing Ye Bank	1	26	8	189
昆仑银行	KunLun Bank	24	411		
中资区域性中小型银行	**Small and Medium-sized Regional Bank of Chinese Investment**	**12**	**373**	**151**	**1513**
城市商业银行	City Commercial Bank	1	14	112	1253
农村商业银行	Rural Commercila Bank	3	60		
村镇银行	County Bank	7	206	18	95
农村合作银行	Rural Cooperation Bank	1	93	21	165
外资银行	**Foreign Bank**	**1**	**10**		
农村信用社	**Rural Credit Cooperative**	**83**	**4712**	**989**	**7424**
财务公司	**Finance Company**				
信托投资公司	**Trust and Investment Company**				
金融租赁公司	**Financial Leasing Company**				
资产管理公司	**Assets Management Company**				

7-7 金融机构人民币信贷资金平衡表
Balance Sheet of Credit Funds of Financial Institutions

单位：亿元 (100 million yuan)

项目	Item	2012
资金来源合计	**All Sources**	**12114.06**
各项存款	Total Deposits	12330.89
单位存款	Deposits by Enterprises	6588.72
活期存款	Current Deposits	4657.05
定期存款	Time Deposits	1148.56
个人存款	Personal Desposits	5305.81
#储蓄存款	Savings Desposits	5281.83
其他存款	Other Desposits	436.36
中长期借款	Medium and Long-term Loans	70.26
应付及暂收款	Payable and Temporary Collection	198.34
同业往来(来源方)	Inter-bank Transactions	99.86
外汇买卖(来源方)	Foreign Exchange Trading	195.48
各项准备金	Various Preparations	185.39
所有者权益	Owner's Right and Interest	541.63
其　他	Others	-1507.79
资金运用合计	**All Uses**	**12114.06**
各项贷款	Total Loans	7914.00
#境内贷款	Domestic Loans	7913.80
短期贷款	Short-term Loans	2759.29
个人贷款及透支	Personal loans and overdrafts	551.90
#个人消费贷款	Personal Consumption Loans	26.84
单位贷款及透支	Unit loans and overdrafts	1953.58
#经营贷款	Loans to Business	1912.63
固定资产贷款	Loans to fixed Assets	40.95
普通并购贷款	The General Loans	0.21
银团贷款	Syndicated Loans	112.60
贸易融资	Trade finance	141.01
中长期贷款	Medium & Long-term Loans	4635.42
个人贷款	Personal loans	1091.15
#个人消费贷款	Personal Consumption Loans	726.06
单位普通贷款	Common Unit Loans	2814.06
#经营贷款	Loans to Business	653.15
固定资产贷款	Loans to fixed Assets	2160.91
普通并购贷款	Ordinary　Loans	14.15
银团贷款	Syndicated Loans	689.47
贸易融资	Foreign Trades Finance	25.34
境外筹资转贷款	Overseas Financing Loans	1.25
融资租赁	Finance leasing	214.37
票据融资	Bills financing	302.40
各项垫付	The various funds	2.33
境外贷款	Foreign Loans	0.21
有价证券、股权及投资	Portfolio Investment	671.51
系统内资金往来(运用方)	Capital Transaction inside the System	2752.05
同业往来(运用方)	Trade Current Account	243.60
外汇买卖（运用方）	Foreign Exchang Trading	195.76
固定资产	Fixed assets	151.79
其　他	Others	185.35

7-8 各地区金融机构存贷款年底余额
Deposits and Loans of Financial Institution by Region

单位：亿元 (2012 年) (100 million yuan)

项　　目	Item	各项存款余额 Balance of Deposits	#单位存款 #Deposits by Units	各项贷款余额 Banlance of Loans	#中长期贷款 #Medium and Long-term
总　计	**Total**	**12330.89**	**6588.72**	**7914.00**	**4635.42**
乌鲁木齐市	Urumqi City	4817.66	2781.46	3245.33	1866.87
克拉玛依市	Karamay City	936.72	700.14	142.39	68.18
吐鲁番地区	Turpan Administrative Offices	178.91	67.94	93.84	52.47
哈密地区	Hami [Kumul] Administrative Offices	372.52	168.20	191.83	131.69
昌吉回族自治州	Changji Hui Autonomous Prefecture	788.15	358.62	540.81	257.11
博尔塔拉蒙古自治州	Bortala Mongol Autonomous Prefecture	225.85	111.25	113.15	36.46
巴音郭楞蒙古自治州	Bayangol Mongol Autonomous Prefecture	789.43	338.03	446.56	192.51
阿克苏地区	Aksu Administrative Offices	837.58	370.07	448.50	199.54
克孜勒苏柯尔克孜自治州	Kizilsu Kirgiz Autonomous Prefecture	112.66	65.99	36.09	17.16
喀什地区	Kashgar [Kaxgar] Administrative Offices	854.06	463.99	312.07	171.96
和田地区	Hotan Administrative Offices	331.79	195.86	79.48	45.30
伊犁哈萨克自治州直属	Ili Kazak Autonomous Prefecture	874.84	410.30	440.90	214.91
塔城地区	Tacheng [Tarbagatai] Administrative Offices	380.85	144.05	197.68	66.81
阿勒泰地区	Altay Administrative Offices	280.02	146.24	118.07	66.46
石河子市	Shihezi City	413.65	135.38	249.21	77.82

7-9 个人消费贷款情况
Basic Conditions of Personal Consumption Loans

单位：亿元 (100 million yuan)

项　　目	Item	2011	2012
个人消费贷款	**Personal Consumption Loans**	**603.81**	**752.90**
短期个人消费贷款	Short-term Loans for Personal Consumption	22.00	26.84
住房贷款	Housing Loans	0.83	0.93
汽车贷款	Auto Loans	0.13	0.19
其他贷款	Other Loans	13.10	13.85
个人卡透支	Personalized Card is Overdrawn	7.94	11.63
长期个人消费贷款	Long-term Loans for Personal Consumption	581.81	726.06
住房贷款	Housing Loans	496.23	626.25
汽车贷款	Auto Loans	16.32	14.79
助学贷款	Student Loans	0.73	0.67
其他贷款	Other Loans	65.36	80.52

7-10 主要年份国内保险业务情况
Conditions of Domestic Insurance Service in Main Years

单位：亿元 (100 million yuan)

年 份 Year	承保额 Amount Insured		保 费 Premium		赔款及给付 Claim and Payment	
	财产险 Property Insurance	人身险 Life Insurance	财产险 Property Insurance	人身险 Life Insurance	财产险 Property Insurance	人身险 Life Insurance
1980	4		0.01			
1985	70	2	0.40	0.01	0.15	…
1990	241	41	1.04	0.53	0.47	0.08
1995	613	168	4.59	2.06	2.38	0.41
2000	1612	1711	12.49	15.72	5.99	3.72
2001	2112	1371	14.17	19.98	7.43	4.37
2002	2283	3524	16.48	35.25	7.84	5.02
2003	5588	1362	19.12	43.06	10.36	7.10
2004	6401	1735	20.04	48.09	10.65	7.70
2005	8949	9418	20.93	51.57	12.60	7.65
2006	8333	27028	24.61	60.79	12.92	10.34
2007	12188	13081	34.67	70.95	18.78	18.64
2008	13641	17555	44.25	108.26	23.61	20.79
2009	16296	19819	51.82	104.87	26.60	21.51
2010	17431	18129	63.00	127.92	29.21	20.12
2011	23575	13649	78.51	125.11	34.24	23.24
2012	29356	12729	93.68	141.88	50.34	29.77

7-11 保险业务经济技术指标
Economic and Technical Indicators of Insurance Company

单位：万元 (10 000 yuan)

项 目	Item	保 费 Premium		赔款及给付 Claim and Payment	
		2011	2012	2011	2012
财产保险业务	**Property Insurance Companies**	**785100**	**936810**	**342350**	**503434**
企业财产险	Insurance of Enterprise Property	54112	61255	17104	27237
家庭财产险	Insurance of Family Property	6534	7340	735	860
机动车辆险	Insurance of Mobile Vehicles	492578	604686	225335	324210
工程保险	Engineering Insurance	25790	9108	5771	4482
责任保险	Insurance of Liability	30346	38971	8030	12579
信用保险	Insurance of Credit		107		
保证保险	Insurance of Guaranty	13128	10228	1427	1381
船舶险	Insurance of Snip	5	7		
货物运输险	Insurance of Cargo Transportation	10153	11968	1635	1629
特殊风险保险	Special insurance against risk	62	763	748	181
农业保险	Insurance of Agriculture	152358	192333	81570	130884
其他险	Other Insurance	33	45	-4	-9
人身保险业务	**Life Insurance Companies**	**1251055**	**1418794**	**232443**	**297733**
寿 险	Life Insurance	1028580	1136769	155002	203272
健康险	Health Insurance	153246	191851	62381	72247
人身意外伤害险	Unforeseen Human Injury Insurance	69229	90174	15059	22214

7-12　新疆辖区保险机构
Number of Insurance Institutions in Xinjiang

单位：个　　(2012 年)　　(unit)

项　目	Item	机构数 Number of Institution	自治区分公司 Xinjiang Branch Company
总　计	**Total**	**1566**	**28**
中国人民财产保险股份有限公司	The People's Insurance Corporation Ltd.of china	458	1
中国人寿保险股份有限公司	The Life Insurance Corporation Ltd.of China	377	1
中国大地财产保险股份有限公司	Da Di Property Insurance Corporation Ltd of China	13	1
中华联合财产保险股份有限公司	The Pacific Insurance Corporation Ltd.Property Insruance Company of China	233	1
中国太平洋财产保险股份有限公司	The Pacific Insurance Corporation Ltd., Property Insurance Company of China	21	1
中国太平洋人寿保险股份有限公司	The Pacific Insurance Corporation Ltd.,Life Insurance Company of China	30	1
中国平安财产保险股份有限公司	The Ping An Insurance Corporation Ltd., Property Insurance Company of China	52	1
中国平安人寿保险股份有限公司	The Ping An Insurance Corporation Ltd.,Life Insurance Company of China	68	1
新华人寿保险股份有限公司	Xin Hua Life Insurance Corporation Ltd.	45	1
泰康人寿保险股份有限公司	Tai Kang Life Insurance Corporation Ltd.	63	1
天安保险股份有限公司	Tian An Property Insurance Corporation Ltd.	14	1
永安财产保险股份有限公司	Yong An Property Insurance Corporation Ltd.	51	1
太平人寿保险有限公司	Taiping Life Insurance Corporation Ltd.	7	1
中银保险有限公司	Zhongyin Insurance Corporation Ltd.	1	1
生命人寿保险股份有限公司	The Life Insurance Corporation Ltd.	4	1
永诚财产保险股份有限公司	Yong chen Insurance Corporation Ltd.	4	1
平安养老保险股份有限公司	The Pingan Old-age Pension Insurance Company	1	1
合众人寿保险股份有限公司	Union Life Insurance Corporation Ltd.	12	1
中国人民健康保险股份有限公司	PICC Health Insurance Corporation Ltd.	6	1
阳光财产保险股份有限公司	Sunshine Property Insurance Corporation Ltd.	30	1
都邦财产保险股份有限公司	Du-bang Property Insurance Corporation Ltd.	1	1
渤海财产保险股份有限公司	Bohai Property Insurance Corporation Ltd.	5	1
中国人民人寿保险股份有限公司	PICC Life Insurance Corporation Ltd.of China	19	1
中国人寿财产保险股份有限公司	The Life Insurance Corporation Ltd.,Property Insurance Company	8	1
泰康养老保险股份有限公司	The Taikang Old-age Pension Insurance Company	1	1
阳光人寿保险股份有限公司	The Sun of Life Insurance Corporation Ltd.	8	1
信达财产保险股份有限公司	Xinda Property Insurance Corporation Ltd.	4	1
安邦财产保险股份有限公司	An Bang Property Insurance Corporation Ltd.	30	1

7-12 续表 Continued

单位：个 (2012 年) (unit)

项　　目	Item	地区级中心支公司 Branch Company at Prefecture Level	县级支公司 Branch Company at County Level	营销服务部 Marke-Ting Depart-ment
总　计	**Total**	**191**	**465**	**882**
中国人民财产保险股份有限公司	The People's Insurance Corporation Ltd.of china	15	98	344
中国人寿保险股份有限公司	The Life Insurance Corporation Ltd.of China	15	68	293
中国大地财产保险股份有限公司	Da Di Property Insurance Corporation Ltd of China	2	1	9
中华联合财产保险股份有限公司	The Pacific Insurance Corporation Ltd.Property Insruance Company of China	15	145	72
中国太平洋财产保险股份有限公司	The Pacific Insurance Corporation Ltd., Property Insurance Company of China	9	11	
中国太平洋人寿保险股份有限公司	The Pacific Insurance Corporation Ltd.,Life Insurance Company of China	8	20	1
中国平安财产保险股份有限公司	The Ping An Insurance Corporation Ltd., Property Insurance Company of China	15	32	4
中国平安人寿保险股份有限公司	The Ping An Insurance Corporation Ltd.,Life Insurance Company of China	12	15	40
新华人寿保险股份有限公司	Xin Hua Life Insurance Corporation Ltd.	10	12	22
泰康人寿保险股份有限公司	Tai Kang Life Insurance Corporation Ltd.	11	17	34
天安保险股份有限公司	Tian An Property Insurance Corporation Ltd.	6		7
永安财产保险股份有限公司	Yong An Property Insurance Corporation Ltd.	14	4	32
太平人寿保险有限公司	Taiping Life Insurance Corporation Ltd.	4	2	
中银保险有限公司	Zhongyin Insurance Corporation Ltd.			
生命人寿保险股份有限公司	The Life Insurance Corporation Ltd.	1	1	1
永诚财产保险股份有限公司	Yong chen Insurance Corporation Ltd.	2		1
平安养老保险股份有限公司	The Pingan Old-age Pension Insurance Company			
合众人寿保险股份有限公司	Union Life Insurance Corporation Ltd.	7	4	
中国人民健康保险股份有限公司	PICC Health Insurance Corporation Ltd.	1		4
阳光财产保险股份有限公司	Sunshine Property Insurance Corporation Ltd.	8	15	6
都邦财产保险股份有限公司	Du-bang Property Insurance Corporation Ltd.			
渤海财产保险股份有限公司	Bohai Property Insurance Corporation Ltd.	4		
中国人民人寿保险股份有限公司	PICC Life Insurance Corporation Ltd.of China	10	8	
中国人寿财产保险股份有限公司	The Life Insurance Corporation Ltd.,Property Insurance Company	7		
泰康养老保险股份有限公司	The Taikang Old-age Pension Insurance Company			
阳光人寿保险股份有限公司	The Sun of Life Insurance Corporation Ltd.	2	5	
信达财产保险股份有限公司	Xinda Property Insurance Corporation Ltd.	2	1	
安邦财产保险股份有限公司	An Bang Property Insurance Corporation Ltd.	11	6	12

7-13 新疆辖区保险事业发展情况
Statistics on Development of Insurance in Xinjiang

单位：万元 (2012 年) (10 000 yuan)

项 目	Item	承保额（亿元） Amount Insured (100 million yuan)	保 费 Premium	赔款及给付 Claim and Payment
总 计	**Total**	**42085.38**	**2355603.69**	**801167.08**
产险公司小计	**Sub-total**	**32325.83**	**1024726.78**	**542288.60**
中国人民财产保险股份有限公司	The People's Insurance Corporation Ltd.of China	14443.51	527276.52	264508.99
中华联合财产保险股份有限公司	The Property Insurance Corporation Ltd.XPCG	7523.64	252470.23	147629.77
中国平安财产保险股份有限公司	The Ping An Insurance Corporation Ltd., Property Insurance Company of China	4729.97	97866.34	50428.40
中国太平洋财产保险股份有限公司	The Pacific Insurance Corporation Ltd., Property Insurance Company of China	2750.30	54313.33	36987.10
永安财产保险股份有限公司	Yong An Property Insurance Corporation Ltd.	691.92	22851.97	14046.43
天安保险股份有限公司	Tian An Property Insurance Corporation Ltd.	212.27	7768.79	4619.66
安邦财产保险股份有限公司	An Bang Property Insurance Corporation Ltd.	76.15	6262.88	1064.59
中国大地财产保险股份有限公司	Da Di Property Insurance Corporation Ltd.	363.01	9318.52	4877.50
阳光财产保险股份有限公司	Sunshine Property Insurance Corporation Ltd.	529.31	23656.59	11320.06
都邦财产保险股份有限公司	Du-bang Property Insurance Corporation Ltd.	152.94	1425.45	529.49
渤海财产保险股份有限公司	Bohai Property Insurance Corporation Ltd.	40.30	2854.02	1477.59
永诚财产保险股份有限公司	Yongcheng Property Insurance Corporation Ltd.	312.86	2968.13	1254.48
中银财产保险股份有限公司	Zhongyin Property Insurance Corporation Ltd.	142.40	2265.93	149.08
信达财产保险股份有限公司	Xinda Property Insurance Corporation Ltd.	114.57	3065.65	1154.99
中国人寿财产保险股份有限公司	The Life Insurance Corporation Ltd.,Property Insurance Company	242.68	10362.43	2240.47
寿险公司小计	**Sub-total**	**9759.56**	**1330876.91**	**258878.48**
中国人寿保险股份有限公司	The Life Insurance Corporation Ltd.of China	4742.70	505942.17	172288.41
中国平安人寿保险股份有限公司	The Ping An Insurance Corporation Ltd.,Life Insurance Company of China	1009.35	173729.70	38682.55
中国太平洋人寿保险股份有限公司	The Pacific Insurance Corporation Ltd.,Life Insurance Company of China	617.18	216579.74	16107.28
新华人寿保险股份有限公司	Xin Hua Life Insurance Corporation Ltd.	416.64	166111.01	8636.86
泰康人寿保险股份有限公司	Tai Kang Life Insurance Corporation Ltd.	791.53	98536.38	7423.24
中国人民人寿保险股份有限公司	PICC Life Insurance Corporation Ltd.of China	436.91	55733.01	2653.37
太平人寿保险有限公司	Taiping Life Insurance Corporation Ltd.	49.83	44687.64	1960.94
中国人民健康保险股份有限公司	PICC Health Insurance Corporation Ltd.	814.78	19318.04	6617.69
合众人寿保险股份有限公司	Union Life Insurance Corporation Ltd.	66.62	23203.86	848.98
平安养老保险股份有限公司	The Pingan Old-age Pension Insurance Company	725.34	7173.42	2404.78
阳光人寿保险股份有限公司	The Sun of Life Insurance Corporation Ltd.	73.55	7829.81	368.04
生命人寿保险股份有限公司	The Life Insurance Corporation Ltd.	15.14	12032.13	886.34

7-14 各地区保险业务情况
Conditions of Insurance Service by Region

单位：万元　　(2012 年)　　(10 000 yuan)

地 区	Region	全部业务 All Insurance Business 保费收入 Premium Income	全部业务 比上年增长(%) Increase Rate Over preceding year(%)	财产保险公司业务 Property Insurance Business 保费收入 Premium Income	财产保险公司业务 比上年增长(%) Increase Rate Over preceding year(%)
总 计	**Total**	**2355604**	**15.7**	**1024727**	**20.7**
乌鲁木齐市	Urumqi City	776081	15.8	263025	15.1
昌吉回族自治州	Changji Hui Autonomous Prefecture	226928	17.9	107925	25.7
伊犁州直属县(市)	Counties (Cities) Direct Under Ili Prefecture	148621	18.1	74082	21.2
克拉玛依市	Karamay City	128802	8.2	44566	8.3
博尔塔拉蒙古自治州	Bortala Mongol Autonomous Prefecture	57510	14.7	27523	18.5
石河子市	Shihezi City	120080	17.0	55939	31.0
奎屯市	Kuytun City	61821	21.3	30840	37.3
阿勒泰地区	Altay Administrative Offices	52540	12.8	25707	24.0
塔城地区	Tacheng [Tarbagatai] Administrative Offices	81311	11.0	32459	19.4
克孜勒苏柯尔克孜自治州	Kizilsu Kirgiz Autonomous Prefecture	11670	16.4	8391	15.5
和田地区	Hotan Administrative Offices	39555	25.0	27052	27.6
喀什地区	Kashgar [Kaxgar] Administrative Offices	136060	11.7	85888	15.6
巴音郭楞蒙古自治州	Bayangol Mongol Autonomous Prefecture	193118	15.9	88201	23.3
阿克苏地区	Aksu Administrative Offices	178157	20.0	96544	28.6
吐鲁番地区	Turpan Administrative Offices	51519	14.8	23682	14.6
哈密地区	Hami [Kumul] Administrative Offices	91831	12.4	32903	25.2

地 区	Region	人寿保险公司业务 Life Insurance Business 保费收入 Premium Income	人寿保险公司业务 比上年增长(%) Increase Rate Over preceding year(%)	保险密度(元) Insurance Density (yuan)	保险深度(%) Insurance Depth(%)
总 计	**Total**	**1330877**	**12.1**	**1055**	**3.13**
乌鲁木齐市	Urumqi City	513056	16.2	3010	3.88
昌吉回族自治州	Changji Hui Autonomous Prefecture	119003	11.7	1618	2.77
伊犁州直属县(市)	Counties (Cities) Direct Under Ili Prefecture	74539	15.2	569	1.30
克拉玛依市	Karamay City	84236	8.1	4507	1.59
博尔塔拉蒙古自治州	Bortala Mongol Autonomous Prefecture	29987	11.5	1187	3.10
石河子市	Shihezi City	64141	7.1	1937	5.77
奎屯市	Kuytun City	30981	8.7	2031	5.83
阿勒泰地区	Altay Administrative Offices	26833	3.9	792	2.79
塔城地区	Tacheng [Tarbagatai] Administrative Offices	48852	6.1	776	1.67
克孜勒苏柯尔克孜自治州	Kizilsu Kirgiz Autonomous Prefecture	3279	18.7	208	1.91
和田地区	Hotan Administrative Offices	12503	19.6	186	2.69
喀什地区	Kashgar [Kaxgar] Administrative Offices	50172	5.6	328	2.63
巴音郭楞蒙古自治州	Bayangol Mongol Autonomous Prefecture	104917	10.3	1405	2.13
阿克苏地区	Aksu Administrative Offices	81613	11.2	743	2.91
吐鲁番地区	Turpan Administrative Offices	27837	15.0	824	2.12
哈密地区	Hami [Kumul] Administrative Offices	58928	6.3	1550	3.42

主要统计指标解释

地方财政收入 指国家财政参与社会产品分配所得的收入，是实现国家职能的财力保证。包括地方公共财政预算收入和基金预算收入。

公共财政预算收入 是通过一定的形式和程序，由各级财政部门组织并纳入预算管理的各项收入。

基金预算收入 是按规定收取，转入或通过当年财政安排，由财政管理并具有指定用途的政府性基金预算收入等。

税收收入 包括增值税、营业税、企业所得税、个人所得税、资源税、城市维护建设税、房产税、印花税、城镇土地使用税、土地增值税、车船税、耕地占用税、契税等。

非税收收入 包括专项收入、行政事业性收费、罚没收入和其他收入。

地方财政支出 是以国家为主体，以财政的事权为依据进行的一种财政资金分配活动，集中反映了国家的职能活动范围及其所发生的耗费，包括地方公共财政预算支出和基金预算支出。

公共财政预算支出 是各级财政部门对集中的一般预算收入有计划地分配和使用而安排的支出。

基金预算支出 是各级财政部门用基金预算收入安排的支出。

一般公共服务支出 指政府提供基本公共管理与服务的支出，包括人大事务、政协事务、政府办公厅（室)及相关机构事务、发展与改革事务、统计信息事务、财政事务、税收事务、审计事务、海关事务、人力资源事务、纪检监察事务、人口与计划生育事务、 商贸事务、知识产权事务、工商行政管理事务、国土资源事务、 海洋管理事务、 测绘事务、地震事务、气象事务、民族事务、宗教事务、港澳台侨事务、档案事务、共产党事务、民主党派事务及工商联事务、群众团体事务、彩票事务等。

教育支出 指政府教育事务支出，包括教育行政管理、学前教育、小学教育、初中教育、普通高中教育、普通高等教育、初等职业教育、中专教育、技校教育、职业高中教育、高等职业教育、广播电视教育、留学生教育、特殊教育、干部继续教育、教育机关服务等。

科学技术支出 指用于科学技术方面的支出，包括科学技术管理事务、基础研究、应用研究、技术研究与开发、科技条件与服务、社会科学、科学技术普及、科技交流与合作等。

文化教育与传媒支出 指政府在文化、文物、体育、广播影视、新闻出版等方面的支出。

社会保障和就业支出 指政府在社会保障与就业方面的支出，包括社会保障和就业管理事务、民政管理事务、财政对社会保险基金的补助、补充全国社会保障基金、行政事业单位离退休、企业改革补助、就业补助、抚恤、退役安置、社会福利、残疾人事业、城市居民最低生活保障、其他城镇社会救济、农村社会救济、自然灾害生活救助、红十字事务等。

医疗卫生支出 指政府医疗卫生方面的支出，包括医疗卫生管理事务支出、医疗服务支出、医疗保障支出、疾病预防控制支出、卫生监督支出、妇幼保健支出、农村卫生支出等。

节能环保支出 指政府环境保护支出，包括环境保护管理事务支出、环境监测与监察支出、污染治理支出、自然生态保护支出、天然林保护工程支出、退耕还林支出、风沙荒漠治理支出、退牧还草支出、已垦草原退耕还草、能源节约利用、污染减排、可再生能源和资源综合利用等支出。

交通运输支出 指政府交通运输和邮政业方面的支出，包括公路运输支出、水路运输支出、铁路运输支出、民用航空运输支出、邮政业支出等。

城乡社区事务支出 指政府城乡社区事务支出，包括城乡社区管理事务支出、城乡社区规划与管理支出、城乡社区公共设施支出、城乡社区住宅支出、城乡社区环境卫生支出、建设市场管理与监督支出等。

农林水事务支出 指政府农林水事务支出，包括农业支出、林业支出、水利支出、扶贫支出、农业综合开发支出等。

信贷资金 指金融机构以信用方式积聚和分配的货币资金。金融机构信贷资金的来源有各项存款、金融债券、对国际金融机构负债、流通中现金、其他项目等；信贷资金的运用有各项贷款、有价证券及投资、金银占款、外汇占款、财政借款及在国际金融机构中的资产等。

存款 指企业、机关、团体或居民根据资金必须收回的原则，把货币资金存入银行或其他信贷机构保管并取得一定利息的一种信用活动形式。根据存款对象或性质的不同可划分为企业存款、财政存款、机关团体存款、城乡储蓄存款、农业存款、信托及委托类存款、其他存款等科目。它是银行信贷资金的主要来源。

贷款 指银行或其他信用机构根据资金必须归还的原则，按一定利率，为企业、个人等提供资金的一种信用活动形式。我国银行贷款分为短期贷款、委托及信托类贷款、其他类贷款等

保险金额 指保险人承担赔偿或者给付保险金责任的最高限额。

保费 指投保人为取得保险人在约定范围内所承担赔偿责任而支付给保险人的费用。

赔款 指保险人根据保险合同的规定，向被保险人支付的赔偿保险责任损失的金额。

给付 包括死伤医疗给付和满期给付。死伤医疗给付是指保险人根据人寿保险及长期健康保险合同的规定，因被保险人在保险期内发生保险责任范围内的保险事故支付给被保险人(或受益人)的金额。满期给付是指被保险人生存期满，保险人按人寿保险合同规定支付给被保险人的满期保险金额。

Explanatory Notes on Main Statistical Indicators

Local Government Revenue refer to the revenue from participation of national finance in social product allocation. It is a financial guarantee to realize national functions, and includes local public budgetary financial revenue and fund budget revenue.

Local Public Budgetary Financial Revenue refers to the revenue organized by finance authorities at all levels in certain form and through certain procedures and involved in budgetary management.

Fund Budget Revenue refers to governmental fund budget revenues collected, transferred in or arranged by government finance the same year in accordance with regulations, governed by government finance and for specific use of purpose.

Tax Revenue includes value—added tax, business tax ,corporate income tax ,individual income tax, resource tax, urban maintenance and construction tax ,house property tax ,stamp tax,urban and use tax,1and value—added tax,tax on vehicles and boat operation, arable land occupation tax, deed etc.

Non-tax Revenue includes special revenues, administrative charges ,fines,and other revenues.

Local Financial Expenditure refers to a sort of allocation activity of financial funds by the state based on the position of finance It is a concentrated reflection of the functional activity scope of the state and the expenditure incurred by it. It includes local public budgetary financial expenditure and fund budget expenditure.

Local Public Budgetary Financial Expenditure refers to the expenditure arranged by finance authorities at all levels during their planned distribution and use of the general budgetary revenue gathered.

Fund Budget Expenditure refers to the expenditure arranged by finance authorities at all level with the fund budget revenue.

Expenditure for General Public Services refers to the spending on the basic public management and services provided by governments,including the expense on affairs of people's congress,affairs of People's Political Consultative Conference. Affairs of government general offices and relative institutions, affairs of development and reform ,affairs of statistical information. affairs of finance, affairs of taxation, affairs of audit, affairs of customs affairs of human resources. affairs of discipline inspection and supervision, affairs of population and family Ling, affairs of commerce and trade, affairs of intellectual Planning affairs of administration for industry and commerce, affairs of land and resources, affairs of oceanic administration .affairs of surveying and mapping ,affairs of earthquake, weather affairs ,ethnic affairs, religious affairs, affairs of Hong Kong, Macao , Taiwan, and overseas Chinese, affairs of archives administration, affairs Of Chinese Communist Party. affairs of democratic parties and federation of industry and commerce, affairs of mass organizations, and affairs of lottery tickets, etc.

Expenditure for Education refers to the spending of government on education,including the expense on the administration of education pre-school education, primary education, junior high school education, senior high school education,regular higher education, primary vocational education,secondary vocational education, technical school education,vocational senior high school education and higher vocational education, radio and television education, student abroad education, special education,continuing education for management personnel, and services for education authorities, etc.

Expenditure for Science and Technology refers to the spending on science and technology(S&T), including the expense on the administration of S&T,basic research,applied research, research and development, conditions and services of S&T. popularization of social science and S&T. exchanges and cooperation of S&T. etc.

Expenditure for Cultural Education and Media refers to the spending on culture, cultural relics, sports, radio, film, television, press and publication, etc.

Expenditure for Social Security and Employment refers to the spending on social security and employment, including the expense on social security and employment administration affairs, civil affairs, budgetary subsidy on the social insurance funds, subsidy on National Social Security Fund. Retirees of administrative units and institutions, subsidy on enterprise reform, subsidy on employment effort, pension, placement of ex—service man, social welfare, the handicapped undertakings, the system of cost of living allowances for urban residents, other urban social relief, rural social relief, living relief of natural disasters, affairs of Red Cross, etc.

Expenditure for Medical Service and Health Care refers to the spending on medical service and health care including the expense on affairs of medical and health administration. medical services, medical guarantee, disease prevention and control, health inspection and supervision, women and children's health care, rural health care, etc.

Expenditure for Energy Saving and Environmental Protection refers to the spending of government on environmental protection,including the expense on administration of environmental protection. environment monitoring and supervision, pollution control, natural ecology protection, project of virgin forest protection, reforesting farmland, control of sources of dust storms, returning pastureland to grassland, returning cultivated land to grassland, energy conservation and utilization, emissions reduction, comprehensive utilization of renewable energy and resources, etc.

Expenditure for Transportation refers to the spending of government on transportation and postal services, including the expense on highway transportation, waterway transportation, railway transportation, civil aviation transportation and postal services, etc.

Expenditure for Urban and Rural Community Affairs refers to the spending of government on urban and rural community affairs, including the expense on administration of urban and rural communities, planning and management of urban and rural communities, public facilities in urban and rural communities, residential houses in urban and rural communities, sanitation in urban and rural communities, management and supervision of construction markets, etc.

Expenditure for Agriculture, Forestry and Water Conservancy Affairs refers to the spending of government on agriculture, forestry and water conservancy affairs, including the expense on agriculture affairs, forestry affairs, water conservancy affairs, poverty alleviation and comprehensive agricultural development, etc.

Credit Funds refer to the funds issued as loans by banking institutions. The sources of credit funds of the banking institutions included deposits, liabilities to international financial institutions, currency in circulation, self-owned funds and current retained profits, etc. The credit funds can be used in forms of loans, gold, foreign exchange, government debt and assets in the international financial institutions.

Deposit is a form of credit by which enterprises, institutions, organizations or households can put money into banks and other credit institutions for safekeeping and interest earning under the principle of free withdrawal. According to different depositors, deposits are divided into enterprise deposits, treasury deposits, deposits of government agencies and organizations, capital construction deposits, urban savings deposits, rural deposits and other deposits. Deposits are major sources of the credit funds of banks.

Loan is a form of credit by which banks and other credit institutions provide funds at certain interest rate to enterprises and individuals in the light of the principle of unconditional repayment. Loans from Chinese banks include circulating capital loans, fixed assets loans, loans to urban and rural individuals engaged in industrial and commercial business and agricultural loans.

Amount Insured refers to the maximum that the insurant will get for the claim of the case insured.

Premium is the fee paid by the insurant to the insurer to obtain the obligation of compensation from the insurance within the agreed terms.

Settled Claim is the compensation paid by the insurer to the insurant in accordance with the insurance contract.

Payment includes payment for death, injury or medical treatment and mature payment. Payment for death, injury or medical treatment refers to the money paid to the insurant (or the beneficiary) in accordance with the life or health insurance contract when the insurant encounters accidents within the insured period covered in the contract. Mature payment refers to the mature payment to the insurant in accordance with the life insurance contract at the end of the insured period.

新疆统计年鉴
XINJIANG STATISTICAL YEARBOOK

8

价格指数

PRICE INDICES

简要说明

本篇资料的主要内容及来源

本篇价格指数资料，反映生产、流通、消费与投资环节的价格变动趋势和变动幅度，主要包括居民消费价格指数、商品零售价格指数、农业生产资料价格指数、工业生产者出厂价格指数、工业生产者购进价格指数、固定资产投资价格指数。

居民消费价格指数、商品零售价格指数和农业生产资料价格指数出自国家统计局新疆调查总队消费价格调查处；工业生产者出厂价格指数、工业生产者购进价格指数、固定资产投资价格指数出自国家统计局新疆调查总队生产投资价格调查处。

Brief Introduction

Main Content and Source of Data

Data on the price indices in this chapter show the changing trend and the change rates in production, circulation, consumption and investment, including mainly consumer price indices of residents, retail price indices, price indices of agricultural means of production, purchasing price indices of farm products, producers' price indices of industrial products, purchasing price indices of raw materials, fuels and power, price indices of investment in fixed assets, and real estate price indices.

Data on the consumer price index, retail price index and price indices of agriculture production come from Division of Consumer Price of NBS Survey Office in Xinjiang; Data on the price indices of industrial products, indices of purchasing price of raw materials, fuels and power, price indices of investment in fixed assets, price indices for real estate come from Division of Consumer Price of NBS Survey Office in Xinjiang.

8-1 主要年份各种物价指数

Price Indices in Main Years

年 份 Year	居民消费价格指数 Consumer Price Index	城市居民消费价格指数 Urban Household	农村居民消费价格指数 Rural Household	商品零售价格指数 Retail Price Index
上年=100 **Preceding year=100**				
1978	101.2	101.4	100.3	101.4
1980	102.8	104.1	102.0	104.2
1985	107.8	109.5	106.4	108.1
1990	105.0	104.5	105.9	104.1
1995	119.7	118.4	122.5	116.7
2000	99.4	100.1	97.6	98.3
2001	104.0	104.0	103.8	102.5
2002	99.4	98.9	100.9	97.9
2003	100.4	100.5	100.2	99.2
2004	102.7	102.1	104.5	100.7
2005	100.7	100.6	101.2	99.4
2006	101.3	101.0	102.0	101.8
2007	105.5	104.6	107.2	105.1
2008	108.1	107.3	109.5	108.5
2009	100.7	100.2	102.0	100.4
2010	104.3	103.6	105.8	104.6
2011	105.9	105.5	106.8	105.1
2012	103.8	103.4	104.7	103.3
1978 年=100 **Year 1978 =100**				
1978	100.0	100.0	100.0	100.0
1980	105.1	106.6	103.8	107.8
1985	120.9	125.6	117.9	124.2
1990	194.3	206.0	184.0	197.6
1995	392.7	422.7	364.2	381.0
2000	436.5	471.9	398.6	397.9
2001	454.0	490.8	413.8	407.8
2002	451.3	485.4	417.5	399.3
2003	453.1	487.8	418.3	396.1
2004	465.3	498.1	437.1	398.9
2005	468.6	501.1	442.3	396.5
2006	474.7	506.1	451.1	403.6
2007	500.8	529.4	483.6	424.2
2008	541.4	568.0	529.5	460.3
2009	545.2	569.1	540.1	462.1
2010	568.6	589.6	571.4	483.4
2011	602.1	622.0	610.3	508.1
2012	625.0	643.1	639.0	524.9

8-2 居民消费价格分类指数
Consumer Price Indices by Category

(上年=100) (2012 年) (preceding year=100)

项　　目	Item	全　区 Autonomous Region	城　市 Urban Indices	农　村 Rural Indices
居民消费价格总指数	**Consumer Price Index**	**103.8**	**103.4**	**104.7**
食　品	**Food**	**107.6**	**107.3**	**108.1**
粮　食	Grain	107.3	107.3	107.2
大　米	Rice	103.5	102.5	104.7
面　粉	Flour	109.2	107.8	110.4
粮食制品	Grain Products	109.9	110.9	104.8
其　它	Others	100.6	101.0	100.3
淀　粉	Starches and Tubers	108.0	108.3	107.7
干豆类及豆制品	Beans and Its Products	104.5	102.3	108.2
油　脂	Oil or Fat	105.3	105.7	104.8
肉禽及其制品	Meat, Poultry and Processed Products	105.9	105.8	106.0
蛋	Eggs	102.1	101.2	103.4
水产品	Aquatic Products	105.2	104.4	106.3
菜	Vegetables	117.6	116.2	119.9
鲜　菜	Fresh Vegetables	119.1	117.6	121.4
干菜及菜制品	Dried Vegetables and Vegetable Products	100.1	103.4	93.1
薯　类	Tubers	93.7	93.4	94.2
调味品	Flavoring	103.6	103.9	103.2
糖	Carbohydrate	104.3	105.7	102.8
食　糖	Sugar	101.2	102.6	100.0
糖　果	Candy	108.7	110.0	107.2
巧克力制品	Chocolate Goods	99.0	105.7	91.9
糖类小食品	Carbohydrate Products	108.0	103.6	114.4
茶及饮料	Tea and Beverages	104.4	104.4	104.4
干鲜瓜果	Dried and Fresh Melons and Fruits	108.1	107.9	108.5
鲜瓜果	Fresh Fruits	107.8	105.9	110.9
干(坚)果	Drie (nut) Fruits	109.0	112.2	101.5
糕点饼干	Cake and Biscuit	104.4	102.8	108.4
液体乳及乳制品	Milk and Its Products	104.8	104.5	105.6
在外用膳食品	Dining Out	109.0	109.1	108.9
主　食	Staple Food	109.8	110.2	107.8
炒　菜	Fried Dishes	102.6	102.5	103.0
地方小吃	Local Snack	121.8	122.1	120.8
其他	Others	105.8	103.2	111.7
其他食品	Other Foods	105.8	103.2	111.7
烟　酒	**Tobacco, Liquor**	**105.6**	**104.3**	**107.8**
烟　草	Tobacco	101.1	100.7	101.9
酒	Liquor	110.2	108.3	113.3
衣　着	**Clothing**	**101.9**	**101.8**	**102.1**
服　装	Garments	101.8	101.8	101.8
衣着材料	Clothing Material	106.5	107.2	105.8
棉　布	Cotton Cloth	111.2	111.0	111.4

8-2 续表 Continued

(上年=100) (preceding year=100)

项 目	Item	全 区 Autonomous Region	城 市 Urban Areas	农 村 Rural Areas
化纤布	Chemical Fiber Cloth	106.2	107.1	105.4
毛 线	Wool	104.8	106.7	102.5
其 他	Others	101.9	102.3	101.6
鞋袜帽	Footwear and Hats	101.2	101.2	101.2
鞋	Shoes	100.9	101.3	100.2
袜 子	Socks and Stockings	102.7	101.2	105.5
帽 子	Hats	100.2	100.1	100.2
衣着加工服务费	Clothing Processing	109.4	108.1	110.7
家庭设备用品及维修服务	**Household Facilities,Articles and Services**	**101.9**	**100.9**	**103.9**
耐用消费品	Durable Consumer Goods	100.4	100.1	101.1
家 具	Furniture	102.0	102.2	101.6
家庭设备	Household Facilities	99.5	98.8	100.7
室内装饰品	Interior Decorations	100.4	99.6	101.9
床上用品	Bed Articles	98.7	97.1	101.7
家庭日用杂品	Daily Use Household Articles	101.2	99.8	104.7
家庭服务及加工维修服务	Household Service and Mainteance and Renovation	114.4	111.3	120.7
医疗保健和个人用品	**Health Care and Personal Articles**	**102.9**	**102.5**	**103.8**
医疗保健	Health Cares	102.6	102.4	103.4
医疗器具及用品	Medical Instruments and Articles	102.1	102.7	101.2
中药材及中成药	Traditional Chinese Medicine	107.3	105.6	112.6
西 药	Western Medicine	101.9	102.5	100.1
保健器具及用品	Constitutional Appliances and Articles	102.1	103.0	99.1
医疗保健服务	Medical and Health Service	100.4	100.1	101.8
个人用品及服务	Personal Articles and Services	103.3	102.7	104.0
交通和通信	**Transportation and Communication**	**99.5**	**99.0**	**100.4**
交 通	Transportation	102.3	101.3	104.0
通 信	Communication	96.7	96.9	96.4
娱乐教育文化用品及服务	**Recreation, Education, Culture Articles**	**100.1**	**99.5**	**101.2**
文娱用耐用消费品及服务	Durable Consumer Goods for Cultural and Recreationl Use and Services	92.9	92.5	93.7
教 育	Education	102.3	101.4	104.2
文化娱乐	Culture and Recreation Articles	101.2	100.9	101.8
文化娱乐用品	Cultural and Recreational Articles	99.0	98.3	100.7
书报杂志	Newspapers and Magazines	100.5	99.9	101.8
文娱费	Expenditure on Culture and Recreation	103.6	103.9	103.0
旅 游	Touring and Outing	101.1	101.4	100.6
居 住	**Housing**	**102.8**	**102.3**	**103.7**
建房及装修材料	Building and Building Decoration Materials	97.5	96.7	99.2
住房租金	Renting	102.7	102.8	102.6
自有住房	Private Housing	104.2	103.6	105.2
水、电、燃料	Water, Electricity and Fuels	102.2	103.0	101.3
服务项目价格指数	**Services**	**102.9**	**102.2**	**104.5**

8-3 各市县居民消费价格分类指数

(上年=100) (2012 年)

项　　目	Item	乌鲁木齐市 Urumqi City	喀什市 Kashgar [Kaxgar] City	伊宁市 Yining [Gulja] City	和田市 Hotan City	克拉玛依市 Karamay City	哈密市 Hami [Kumul] City
居民消费价格总指数	**Consumer Price Index**	**103.4**	**104.6**	**103.7**	**104.8**	**102.9**	**103.7**
食　品	**Food**	**107.7**	**108.9**	**108.1**	**109.3**	**107.0**	**106.1**
粮　食	Grain	108.5	107.2	107.9	105.0	104.8	107.1
大　米	Rice	103.6	101.1	101.3	101.7	100.6	106.7
面　粉	Flour	110.7	108.6	106.6	106.2	107.1	108.4
粮食制品	Grain Products	114.7	120.4	120.1	110.1	105.7	106.9
其　它	Others	93.6	96.7	97.5	101.3	113.3	101.9
淀　粉	Starches and Tubers	111.3	103.2	106.6	114.7	97.6	102.0
干豆类及豆制品	Beans and Its Products	103.9	99.0	93.0	99.6	100.2	98.1
油　脂	Oil or Fat	109.8	100.9	103.7	100.6	109.2	103.4
肉禽及其制品	Meat, Poultry and Their Products	107.1	105.7	107.6	105.1	105.1	106.6
蛋	Eggs	101.3	102.2	98.9	104.0	100.7	101.8
水产品	Aquatic Products	107.1	102.9	99.9	99.8	101.8	104.1
菜	Vegetables	114.2	120.0	114.9	122.2	120.9	110.9
鲜　菜	Fresh Vegetables	115.4	121.2	117.9	124.1	124.0	113.2
干菜及菜制品	Dried Vegetables and Vegetable Products	105.4	108.4	106.7	100.8	96.4	99.1
薯　类	Tubers	89.8	91.8	99.3	100.6	98.9	85.0
调味品	Flavoring	104.3	105.6	105.5	105.0	100.1	103.7
糖	Carbohydrate Products	111.3	100.9	111.3	104.7	105.9	101.7
食　糖	Sugar	103.2	91.8	102.7	104.8	110.2	104.1
糖　果	Candy	114.3	108.1	119.6	105.7	107.0	101.2
巧克力制品	Chocolate Goods	113.6	91.8	107.9	101.6	102.4	103.0
糖类小食品	Carbohydrate	107.7	104.6	109.1	103.6	103.0	93.3
茶及饮料	Tea and Beverages	102.0	105.6	103.1	108.0	110.4	111.9
干鲜瓜果	Dried and Fresh Melons and Fruits	111.1	103.9	117.5	112.8	92.8	94.6
鲜瓜果	Fresh Fruits	108.4	107.2	120.9	113.5	89.4	89.8
干(坚)果	Dried(nut)Fruits	117.7	97.7	108.5	111.1	106.5	102.9
糕点饼干面包	Cake, Cookie	102.2	104.5	102.0	109.0	100.0	102.9
液体乳及乳制品	Milk and Its Products	104.8	105.7	103.4	102.8	105.8	105.5
在外用膳食品	Dining Out	105.6	122.2	109.3	117.1	113.3	112.8
主　食	Staple Food	109.4	114.5	118.2	121.5	103.0	113.7
炒　菜	Fried Dishes	98.7	112.8	100.1	113.7	106.7	115.7
地方小吃	Local Snack	118.9	144.2	112.2	123.0	134.1	105.7
其　他	Others	101.7	106.9	101.2	107.1	102.7	116.1
其他食品	Other Foods	101.7	106.9	101.2	107.1	102.7	116.1
烟　酒	**Tobacco, Liquor**	**105.7**	**108.8**	**108.3**	**109.3**	**99.8**	**101.1**
烟　草	Tobacco	102.8	100.0	100.0	100.0	100.0	100.4
酒	Liquor	109.0	118.5	114.8	117.5	99.6	101.7
衣　着	**Clothing**	**102.3**	**102.3**	**103.1**	**103.1**	**102.0**	**101.9**
服　装	Garments	102.7	102.0	103.3	100.7	100.4	99.1
衣着材料	Clothing Material	115.7	106.9	101.9	108.0	103.4	106.8
棉　布	Cotton Cloth	114.8	98.0	100.0	113.0	113.0	113.2

Consumer Price Indices by Category in Cities and Counties

(preceding year=100)

昌吉市 Changji City	库尔勒市 Korla City	阿克苏市 Aksu City	焉耆回族自治县 Yanqi Hui Autonomous County	塔城市 Tacheng [Qoqek] City	阿勒泰市 Altay City	乌苏市 Usu City	博乐市 Bole [Bortala] City	吐鲁番市 Turpan City	库车县 Kuqa County	阿图什市 Artux City	莎车县 Shache [Yarkant] County	奎屯市 Kuytun City	石河子市 Shihezi City
104.1	**102.6**	**102.2**	**103.4**	**103.9**	**104.3**	**103.9**	**103.1**	**104.3**	**104.2**	**105.1**	**105.4**	**102.4**	**102.8**
108.8	**105.8**	**104.2**	**104.8**	**106.5**	**110.3**	**109.0**	**104.9**	**109.8**	**103.2**	**109.8**	**109.5**	**103.2**	**107.1**
109.4	105.3	95.7	105.9	104.8	109.7	106.5	103.6	104.5	101.5	105.2	111.4	106.8	101.1
108.6	107.3	88.9	98.1	102.3	107.1	104.3	103.4	105.5	94.9	100.0	110.7	112.5	96.8
111.4	100.9	100.2	111.9	111.2	108.0	108.8	108.3	108.6	105.9	108.5	114.8	101.7	104.2
105.2	107.3	103.0	109.7	103.7	122.1	107.6	100.4	97.3	106.0	103.6	100.1	106.3	103.6
103.2	107.2	94.7	105.6	97.8	100.1	100.0	86.4	97.4	100.9	121.9	108.9	103.2	101.4
108.8	110.4	103.0	100.3	105.6	120.0	102.1	99.7	100.0	99.8	136.7	113.2	102.9	100.7
102.9	109.0	102.5	101.1	106.1	103.4	102.2	111.7	103.1	102.3	116.4	107.3	94.9	92.2
106.8	108.9	94.5	104.9	106.9	96.7	107.4	115.9	105.9	98.5	103.6	103.1	100.1	100.3
107.8	105.7	98.4	103.3	108.2	111.4	108.7	105.5	109.0	106.1	109.1	103.2	102.5	107.0
110.0	96.8	97.3	100.2	98.9	109.7	104.3	104.3	103.3	104.0	102.8	104.5	88.7	98.6
103.8	101.1	99.2	100.5	100.5	113.4	101.7	101.8	116.1	110.2	103.1	101.0	99.1	109.4
109.9	112.3	130.1	108.3	111.4	120.5	120.3	100.3	119.4	103.4	119.3	118.8	107.4	116.2
109.8	114.2	133.5	110.6	117.8	125.1	125.6	106.9	127.0	102.5	119.7	120.1	107.6	119.0
111.2	103.0	104.2	102.9	100.1	106.7	99.9	70.8	99.7	103.8	108.2	92.5	102.1	100.6
96.7	90.3	84.4	88.9	76.5	98.7	109.7	88.3	89.7	116.2	120.8	97.7	97.4	111.7
101.9	104.7	101.8	99.7	104.2	107.5	100.0	99.9	107.9	96.8	117.0	103.1	100.0	99.0
108.2	104.0	101.1	102.7	103.4	101.3	109.3	100.5	93.2	104.0	97.9	116.3	102.9	99.7
108.1	99.6	97.2	96.1	93.2	102.7	107.9	86.5	77.6	112.1	100.3	97.9	105.6	100.8
110.1	105.9	104.1	112.7	112.7	100.0	115.1	109.2	102.1	105.0	99.0	110.1	101.3	99.2
103.6	105.7	101.1	99.7	100.0	100.3	100.0	109.3	96.1	83.0	93.6	82.6	100.5	98.3
102.3	102.2	100.0	99.4	101.6	103.2	112.5	100.4	115.6	90.3	93.2	173.4	100.0	100.0
102.1	100.7	102.8	104.8	107.9	103.5	102.3	107.9	99.2	103.6	98.4	105.1	100.0	100.4
109.4	107.2	114.5	100.3	100.6	110.7	108.6	111.0	109.5	96.6	113.0	111.5	103.3	106.9
101.1	108.3	121.2	100.3	96.6	110.0	105.0	115.3	111.1	91.9	115.8	123.4	97.7	109.0
124.8	103.5	94.9	100.3	112.3	113.1	119.1	100.3	106.0	110.4	104.6	89.4	114.3	99.3
104.1	103.9	101.5	110.8	106.0	102.5	103.1	111.0	119.8	100.6	103.5	112.1	107.2	100.9
108.3	102.8	102.7	105.5	103.8	103.6	106.2	111.4	102.8	100.4	105.9	112.4	109.0	103.4
113.3	104.7	104.7	109.3	105.3	110.8	111.7	93.3	115.4	106.7	111.3	113.0	104.6	112.6
114.0	105.0	100.3	111.4	107.8	113.5	103.5	95.3	107.7	101.7	105.8	112.6	102.1	120.0
109.9	100.0	105.2	108.4	100.0	102.3	102.3	89.7	122.3	102.3	119.4	97.6	104.5	101.7
116.5	117.4	114.5	108.6	114.2	122.8	134.0	96.7	121.5	120.4	110.8	129.2	107.7	131.3
104.8	101.7	99.3	110.8	119.9	100.0	100.0	109.3	108.5	102.1	105.0	123.1	100.0	101.8
104.8	101.7	99.3	110.8	119.9	100.0	100.0	109.3	108.5	102.1	105.0	123.1	100.0	101.8
103.0	**102.5**	**103.6**	**106.5**	**112.4**	**105.9**	**108.4**	**104.7**	**109.3**	**110.8**	**107.6**	**107.2**	**102.2**	**100.2**
100.5	100.1	100.0	106.2	100.0	99.6	100.0	99.9	100.3	97.8	100.0	104.9	100.0	100.8
105.9	105.4	107.9	106.7	121.6	112.7	116.5	109.8	117.7	124.3	114.8	109.9	104.2	99.6
103.7	**99.0**	**102.4**	**103.3**	**101.2**	**104.7**	**102.3**	**104.2**	**98.8**	**107.6**	**104.4**	**99.0**	**101.6**	**100.9**
103.9	98.8	98.2	104.4	100.7	103.2	102.6	103.7	99.4	106.2	105.0	98.2	101.0	101.5
101.6	101.1	109.1	102.2	109.4	112.6	109.3	113.7	109.3	103.0	98.4	100.7	100.3	100.8
103.1	101.2	124.9	103.8	110.0	111.2	108.2	131.4	114.0	117.4	94.4	100.7	100.4	100.0

8-3 续表

(上年=100)

项　目	Item	乌鲁木齐市 Urumqi City	喀什市 Kashgar [Kaxgar] City	伊宁市 Yining [Gulja] City	和田市 Hotan City	克拉玛依市 Karamay City	哈密市 Hami [Kumul] City
化纤布	Chemical Fiber Cloth	120.2	100.0	100.0	100.0	85.5	103.5
毛　线	Wool	112.3	125.3	106.7	104.5	100.1	109.4
其　他	Others	100.0	100.0	100.0	112.1	104.9	100.0
鞋袜帽	Footgear and Hats	100.2	99.8	102.7	105.6	104.2	102.5
鞋	Shoes	100.3	99.7	103.0	105.4	104.9	101.4
袜　子	Socks and Stockings	100.0	100.0	100.1	106.7	100.6	108.6
帽　子	Hats	99.2	100.0	100.0	103.1	101.0	100.0
衣着加工服务费	Clothing Manufacturing Services	102.5	118.3	103.1	117.2	111.9	115.4
家庭设备用品及维修服务	**Household Facilities and Articles and Services**	**101.7**	**102.0**	**101.2**	**99.8**	**101.0**	**102.3**
耐用消费品	Durable Consumer Goods	100.9	99.7	99.9	99.5	99.2	97.3
家　具	Furniture	104.0	99.1	99.8	103.8	100.5	100.4
家庭设备	Household Facilities	98.8	100.1	99.9	96.5	98.3	95.9
室内装饰品	Interior Decorations	98.9	100.0	101.1	97.7	99.6	100.4
床上用品	Bed Articles	91.7	100.0	104.7	98.8	100.0	99.3
家庭日用杂品	Daily Use Household Articles	102.5	103.1	99.9	101.4	100.3	107.8
家庭服务及加工维修服务	Household Services and Maintenance and Renovation	116.7	113.1	107.5	100.0	112.7	113.4
医疗保健和个人用品	**Health Care and Personal Articles**	**102.8**	**105.7**	**101.8**	**102.3**	**102.3**	**104.1**
医疗保健	Health Cares	102.9	108.6	102.4	101.7	102.7	103.6
医疗器具及用品	Medical Appliances and Articles	100.6	102.7	103.7	100.0	102.1	106.7
中药材及中成药	Traditional Chinese Medicine	103.2	122.9	107.7	106.3	107.3	101.0
西　药	Western Medicine	103.4	104.3	100.3	100.9	102.0	106.6
保健器具及用品	Constitutional Appliances and Articles	106.0	104.5	100.0	100.0	99.6	105.0
医疗保健服务	Medical and Health Service	100.0	100.0	101.4	100.0	99.9	100.0
个人用品及服务	Personal Articles and Services	102.4	101.7	100.8	103.6	102.0	104.8
交通和通信	**Transportation and Communication**	**98.0**	**100.7**	**98.8**	**100.0**	**98.6**	**98.5**
交　通	Transportation	100.4	103.1	99.6	103.9	100.4	101.6
通　信	Communication	95.4	97.6	98.2	96.6	96.6	94.5
娱乐教育文化用品及服务	**Recreation, Education and Culture Articles and Services**	**100.8**	**100.7**	**100.3**	**98.5**	**98.1**	**99.8**
文娱用耐用消费品及服务	Durable Consumer Goods for Cultural and Recreationl Use and Services	87.8	93.0	92.9	93.5	95.4	90.7
教　育	Education	101.7	104.4	101.0	100.1	100.6	102.0
文化娱乐	Culture and Recreation Articles	104.7	97.9	98.1	100.8	99.5	100.1
文化娱乐用品	Cultural and Recreational Articles	98.0	99.7	97.6	100.8	98.2	99.9
书报杂志	Newspapers and Magazines	100.0	98.5	100.0	100.0	100.9	100.0
文娱费	Expenditure on Culture and Recreation	116.1	94.8	96.9	101.1	100.4	100.4
旅　游	Touring and Outing	103.4	98.2	105.9	95.0	96.9	109.7
居　住	**Residence**	**100.4**	**100.7**	**100.7**	**105.0**	**102.9**	**106.2**
建房及装修材料	Building and Building Decoration Materials	95.4	96.1	97.3	93.4	97.6	93.9
住房租金	Renting	103.7	99.5	100.0	103.1	100.0	113.8
自有住房	Private Housing	100.5	102.5	102.1	109.3	106.7	106.7
水、电、燃料	Water, Electricity and Fuels	102.1	102.6	102.3	102.4	100.8	104.1
服务项目价格指数	**Services**	**101.9**	**102.8**	**101.3**	**104.2**	**102.4**	**106.5**

Continued

(preceding year=100)

昌吉市 Changji City	库尔勒市 Korla City	阿克苏市 Aksu City	焉耆回族自治县 Yanqi Hui Autonomous County	塔城市 Tacheng [Qoqek] City	阿勒泰市 Altay City	乌苏市 Usu City	博乐市 Bole [Bortala] City	吐鲁番市 Turpan City	库车县 Kuqa County	阿图什市 Artux City	莎车县 Shache [Yarkant] County	奎屯市 Kuytun City	石河子市 Shihezi City
99.5	100.0	105.9	100.4	100.0	105.7	125.6	106.0	112.6	100.3	101.2	100.5	100.0	100.0
103.0	102.3	97.9	104.8	114.9	103.3	100.0	105.0	105.6	101.2	100.0	100.6	100.6	100.2
100.0	100.0	102.3	100.0	100.0	126.3	100.0	101.9	97.1	87.0	100.0	101.0	100.0	102.6
102.9	97.2	97.3	100.3	100.6	101.5	100.4	102.2	93.8	111.9	103.0	99.3	103.2	99.8
103.3	96.7	98.4	100.2	100.0	101.9	100.6	101.9	87.4	108.2	102.3	99.8	104.5	99.5
101.2	100.6	95.1	101.0	105.5	100.0	100.0	102.1	120.7	132.1	107.8	100.1	100.0	100.8
100.0	102.5	90.6	100.0	100.0	100.0	100.0	108.4	103.4	120.7	100.0	83.1	100.0	98.9
105.3	109.1	127.8	106.4	133.0	132.8	100.0	104.8	105.8	112.3	113.2	106.7	101.0	100.6
102.4	**100.1**	**101.3**	**101.6**	**101.9**	**101.3**	**102.6**	**100.9**	**104.1**	**103.6**	**108.0**	**108.4**	**101.9**	**100.1**
101.2	98.8	100.2	103.8	99.9	100.6	100.0	97.8	103.2	97.6	103.1	102.7	99.4	99.9
103.6	100.7	101.4	109.0	100.0	100.9	100.0	99.8	101.4	97.0	106.2	102.7	98.3	100.6
100.8	98.0	99.4	100.8	99.8	100.5	100.0	96.4	103.9	98.3	100.9	102.7	100.1	99.5
100.5	101.4	101.4	99.9	100.0	100.0	100.0	101.8	107.6	101.6	100.0	104.5	106.7	99.6
100.9	99.7	100.3	101.0	100.0	103.2	100.0	100.2	100.6	103.3	106.2	100.6	104.1	101.8
102.6	100.3	100.9	98.9	100.7	99.2	107.3	107.4	102.6	103.1	101.5	108.4	100.7	100.1
112.6	106.4	106.4	100.0	121.3	110.5	103.2	99.2	108.4	131.8	145.9	140.0	107.0	100.0
102.3	**100.8**	**100.1**	**102.5**	**103.3**	**101.7**	**100.0**	**103.7**	**108.4**	**103.1**	**102.4**	**105.6**	**101.7**	**102.6**
100.6	101.0	99.3	103.2	103.6	99.9	98.1	104.5	111.8	101.7	102.8	105.9	100.6	103.5
100.0	107.4	101.1	102.0	111.0	100.0	101.3	113.5	101.6	98.8	96.9	101.4	102.4	104.3
102.3	102.2	103.4	111.6	113.6	100.8	96.4	104.2	144.1	100.4	109.8	120.4	101.7	102.3
99.4	100.1	96.6	99.3	99.7	99.0	97.5	105.6	103.7	100.7	101.2	98.1	99.9	106.6
103.0	100.9	95.8	101.3	101.7	100.0	98.5	98.5	96.0	99.1	100.0	99.4	101.5	105.1
100.0	100.0	100.5	100.0	101.1	100.0	100.8	99.9	103.2	107.1	100.0	102.5	100.0	100.0
105.7	100.6	101.4	101.5	102.4	105.0	102.6	102.6	103.2	105.2	101.7	105.3	103.2	101.1
99.5	**100.6**	**100.8**	**101.5**	**101.4**	**96.2**	**96.7**	**98.1**	**98.2**	**97.6**	**98.1**	**102.1**	**99.6**	**99.8**
102.3	103.4	102.4	105.6	102.4	99.2	106.1	99.7	104.8	101.8	103.1	103.4	100.3	100.9
96.7	96.3	98.2	98.3	100.0	92.6	87.7	96.5	91.8	90.5	92.6	100.7	99.0	98.4
100.1	**99.6**	**99.8**	**102.1**	**100.4**	**98.2**	**100.2**	**102.6**	**94.2**	**104.0**	**100.8**	**99.5**	**100.2**	**99.3**
93.6	97.0	94.8	91.9	90.6	88.0	87.7	96.7	88.6	97.9	93.0	97.8	99.9	95.5
101.1	101.0	103.0	107.0	103.5	100.0	110.7	103.5	100.8	107.8	103.3	100.4	100.3	100.2
101.3	101.0	99.7	99.5	99.3	101.2	100.0	106.1	94.5	104.6	101.4	103.2	99.4	99.1
102.1	100.2	98.7	98.0	97.8	98.3	99.9	100.9	101.8	101.7	99.9	104.6	97.3	98.1
99.9	99.9	100.2	101.5	100.0	102.3	100.0	100.5	98.6	100.6	102.9	104.1	100.0	100.0
102.4	103.9	100.4	99.4	100.4	105.3	100.0	118.6	78.9	111.8	101.8	100.0	101.9	100.0
101.7	99.1	100.0	107.2	114.6	104.9	100.0	108.6	77.4	103.7	102.9	94.6	101.2	102.2
101.9	**103.6**	**101.4**	**103.3**	**103.4**	**102.2**	**102.2**	**101.9**	**101.7**	**108.2**	**102.2**	**103.8**	**105.6**	**100.4**
99.9	95.9	98.0	102.6	91.8	101.7	96.8	101.3	99.5	86.4	100.9	104.8	101.4	99.7
102.4	107.3	101.2	103.0	100.0	101.3	100.0	102.8	100.0	102.9	101.8	112.9	102.9	100.4
102.6	105.7	102.8	103.9	108.0	101.2	104.8	101.8	102.9	118.0	102.9	104.2	108.8	100.0
100.0	101.6	99.1	102.0	99.7	107.2	101.3	103.4	99.4	99.8	101.5	100.5	99.6	104.9
102.5	**103.3**	**103.0**	**103.3**	**104.9**	**102.6**	**103.3**	**102.2**	**101.4**	**108.4**	**103.6**	**104.3**	**104.1**	**100.6**

8-4 商品零售价格分类指数
Retail Price Indices by Category

(上年=100) (2012 年) (preceding year=100)

项　目	Item	全　区 Autonomous Region	城　市 Urban Indices	农　村 Rural Indices
商品零售价格总指数	**Retail Price Index**	**103.3**	**103.0**	**104.0**
食　品	**Food**	**107.9**	**107.5**	**108.7**
粮　食	Grain	107.1	107.3	106.8
油　脂	Oil or Fat	105.7	106.3	104.7
肉禽及其制品	Meat, Poultry and Processed Products	106.5	106.5	106.6
猪　肉	Pork	99.6	99.1	100.7
牛　肉	Beef	106.8	106.2	107.9
羊　肉	Mutton	109.9	110.8	107.8
鸡	Chicken	104.2	104.2	104.4
鲜　蛋	Fresh Eggs	101.3	100.7	102.8
水产品	Aquatic Products	105.6	105.3	106.3
鲜瓜果	Fresh Melons and Fruits	108.5	107.5	110.8
糕点、饼干、面包	Cake、Biscuit and Bread	104.1	102.5	108.7
饮料、烟酒	**Beverages, Tobacco and Liquor**	**105.9**	**105.3**	**107.2**
茶及饮料	Tea and Beverages	103.7	104.0	103.3
#饮　料	Beverages	103.5	103.8	102.7
烟　草	Tobacco	102.5	102.7	102.0
酒	Liquor	110.4	108.7	114.6
服装鞋帽	**Garments, Shoes and Hats**	**101.5**	**101.5**	**101.4**
服　装	Garments	101.9	102.0	101.7
鞋袜帽	Footgear and Hats	100.7	100.5	101.0
#鞋	Shoes	100.3	100.6	99.7
纺织品	**Textiles**	**101.8**	**100.8**	**104.2**
棉　布	Cotton Cloth	111.6	111.4	111.8
化纤布	Chemical Fiber Cloth	113.4	115.6	106.6
毛　线	Wool	108.2	110.6	103.2
其　他	Others	100.9	100.8	101.2
家用电器及音响器材	**Household Appliances,Music and Video Equipment**	**95.9**	**95.4**	**96.8**
家庭设备	Household Facilities	99.5	98.9	100.8
文娱用耐用消费品	Durable Consuming Goods for Entertainment	91.1	90.6	92.0
专业音像器材	Sound Apparatus	99.1	99.2	98.8

8-4 续表 Continued

(上年=100) (preceding year=100)

项　目	Item	全　区 Autonomous Region	城　市 Urban Indices	农　村 Rural Indices
文化办公用品	**Cultural and Office Goods**	**98.5**	**97.2**	**101.1**
日用品	**Articles for Daily Use**	**102.9**	**102.6**	**103.5**
日用百货	General Merchandise for Daily Use	101.1	99.7	103.3
日用杂品	Miscellaneous for Daily Use	101.5	100.3	103.9
洗涤用品	Washing and Cleaning Goods	106.4	106.5	105.8
其他日用品	Other Daily-use Goods	100.9	100.7	101.4
体育娱乐用品	**Sports and Entertainment Goods**	**98.5**	**97.4**	**101.5**
体育用品	Sports Articles	101.0	100.3	102.8
娱乐用品	Recreational Articles	96.4	95.1	100.3
交通、通信用品	**Traffic and Telecommunication Goods**	**91.8**	**91.2**	**93.3**
交通运输机械	Traffic and Transport Machinery	98.5	98.3	98.8
通信器材	Telecommunication Apparatus	83.7	82.1	87.2
家　具	**Furniture**	**103.3**	**103.8**	**101.8**
化妆品	**Cosmetics**	**102.2**	**102.0**	**102.6**
金银珠宝	**Gold and Silver Jewelry**	**103.8**	**104.0**	**103.0**
中西药品及医疗保健用品	**Chinese and Western Medicine, Medical-care and Healthy Goods**	**104.1**	**103.3**	**105.8**
医疗器具及用品	Medical-care Apparatus and Goods	101.1	101.3	100.7
中药材及中成药	Chinese Herbs and Patent Medicine	108.4	104.4	115.0
西　药	Western Medicine	102.0	102.7	100.1
保健器具及用品	Healthy Devices and Goods	103.4	104.6	98.9
书报杂志及电子出版物	**Books, Magazines and Electronic Publications**	**103.4**	**103.8**	**102.4**
教材及参考书	Texts and Reference Books	106.1	106.5	105.3
书报杂志	Newspapers and Magazines	100.3	99.9	101.6
电子音像制品	Electronic Audio and Video Products	104.9	107.7	98.4
燃　料	**Fuels**	**103.8**	**104.3**	**102.7**
煤炭及制品	Coal and Its Products	103.7	105.9	101.4
石油及制品	Oil and Its Products	103.9	103.9	103.7
建筑材料及五金电料	**Building Apparatus, Hardwares and Electrical Apparatus**	**97.7**	**96.9**	**99.2**
建筑装璜材料	Building Decoration Materials	96.5	95.2	98.8
五金电料	Hardwares and Electrical Apparatus	101.1	101.6	100.3

8-5 各市县商品零售价格分类指数

(上年=100) (2012 年)

项 目	Item	乌鲁木齐市 Urumqi City	喀什市 Kashgar [Kaxgar] City	伊宁市 Yining [Gulja] City	和田市 Hotan City	克拉玛依市 Karamay City	哈密市 Hami [Kumul] City
商品零售价格总指数	**General Retail Price Index**	**102.9**	**103.9**	**103.5**	**104.1**	**102.7**	**103.1**
食 品	**Food**	**107.7**	**109.3**	**108.1**	**109.3**	**106.8**	**106.0**
粮 食	Grain	108.6	107.4	107.8	104.4	104.7	107.2
油 脂	Oil or Fat	108.9	100.6	103.5	100.8	109.2	103.4
肉禽及其制品	Meat, Poultry and Their Products	107.2	105.4	107.6	105.6	104.7	106.7
猪 肉	Pork	99.8	95.5	99.4	97.4	100.0	96.1
牛 肉	Beef	105.6	105.5	109.6	100.9	106.5	109.2
羊 肉	Mutton	111.0	107.5	114.7	110.1	112.0	112.2
鸡	Chicken	106.5	105.1	103.2	101.2	102.1	101.6
鲜 蛋	Fresh Egg	100.7	101.8	98.3	103.8	100.4	101.1
水产品	Aquatic Products	107.2	106.7	99.7	99.6	101.8	103.7
鲜瓜果	Fresh Fruits	108.4	107.2	120.9	113.5	89.4	89.8
糕点、饼干、面包	Cake、Biscuit and Bread	102.2	104.3	102.1	109.0	100.0	102.8
饮料、烟酒	**Beverages, Tobacco and Liquor**	**105.4**	**105.6**	**106.7**	**110.4**	**103.7**	**103.3**
茶及饮料	Tea and Beverages	102.1	106.2	103.1	110.3	110.0	111.9
#饮 料	Beverages	102.4	102.6	103.9	105.6	110.5	108.9
烟 草	Tobacco	102.8	100.0	100.0	100.0	100.0	100.4
酒	Liquor	108.9	117.1	113.4	117.5	99.6	101.7
服装鞋帽	**Garments, Shoes and Hats**	**101.9**	**101.0**	**103.0**	**102.4**	**101.6**	**100.5**
服 装	Garments	102.7	101.5	103.3	100.7	100.4	99.1
鞋袜帽	Footgear and Hats	100.2	99.8	102.7	106.1	104.1	102.3
#鞋	Shoes	100.3	99.7	103.0	106.0	104.9	101.4
纺织品	**Textiles**	**99.8**	**104.0**	**102.5**	**103.9**	**100.7**	**103.5**
棉 布	Cotton Cloth	114.8	98.0	100.0	113.0	113.0	113.2
化纤布	Chemical Fiber Cloth	120.2	100.0	100.0	100.0	85.5	103.5
毛 线	Wool	112.3	125.3	106.7	104.5	100.1	109.4
其 他	Others	100.0	100.0	100.0	112.1	104.9	100.0
家用电器及音响器材	**Household Appliances, Music and Sound Apparatus**	**94.9**	**96.0**	**97.1**	**95.1**	**97.4**	**92.3**
家庭设备	Household Facilities	98.9	100.9	99.9	96.2	98.2	95.9
文娱用耐用消费品	Durable Consuming Goods for Entertainment	88.8	90.0	92.8	92.6	95.9	87.9
专业音像器材	Sound Apparatus	99.5	98.3	97.3	104.4	100.0	93.7

Retail Price Indices by Category in Cities and Counties

(preceding year=100)

昌吉市 Changji City	库尔勒市 Korla City	阿克苏市 Aksu City	焉耆回族自治县 Yanqi Hui Autonomous County	塔城市 Tacheng [Qoqek] City	阿勒泰市 Altay City	乌苏市 Usu City	博乐市 Bole [Bortala] City	吐鲁番市 Turpan City	库车县 Kuqa County	阿图什市 Artux City	莎车县 Shache [Yarkant] County	奎屯市 Kuytun City	石河子市 Shihezi City
104.1	**102.0**	**101.4**	**103.1**	**102.6**	**103.9**	**102.8**	**103.2**	**104.0**	**101.8**	**104.0**	**105.1**	**101.4**	**103.1**
108.8	**106.2**	**103.6**	**104.7**	**106.1**	**110.4**	**108.6**	**104.8**	**110.1**	**103.1**	**109.7**	**110.0**	**103.2**	**107.6**
110.0	104.9	95.9	106.3	104.8	109.7	106.7	100.9	104.4	101.6	104.9	110.1	106.3	101.0
107.7	111.1	94.6	105.4	106.9	97.0	107.4	117.1	105.8	98.5	102.6	103.1	99.3	100.3
107.6	105.2	98.5	103.3	108.2	112.0	108.0	105.7	109.0	105.2	108.9	103.8	103.6	107.3
97.4	95.8	96.5	102.6	101.8	102.0	92.8	100.9	100.6	101.3	107.1	100.5	98.5	102.5
110.7	104.5	100.1	104.3	113.5	108.5	107.4	105.8	109.5	105.1	106.1	107.8	117.8	113.3
108.7	113.6	104.9	102.5	113.3	112.9	112.1	102.4	113.7	112.9	109.0	100.8	104.7	111.9
107.0	96.3	82.3	100.9	112.7	108.3	107.0	104.5	99.2	102.4	114.2	101.7	96.2	110.3
109.2	96.4	99.0	99.4	98.6	109.3	103.5	99.5	103.4	104.3	102.7	103.8	97.2	97.1
103.7	102.6	99.1	99.0	100.5	114.3	101.4	102.9	116.1	109.9	103.1	101.5	98.7	109.8
101.1	108.3	121.2	100.3	96.6	110.0	105.0	115.3	111.1	91.9	115.8	123.4	97.7	109.0
103.9	104.3	101.5	110.5	106.0	102.6	101.9	112.1	119.8	100.7	103.6	110.9	107.7	100.8
102.9	**101.6**	**103.6**	**106.4**	**108.8**	**106.1**	**106.7**	**104.4**	**103.8**	**109.7**	**103.0**	**106.5**	**101.8**	**100.6**
102.0	100.8	102.5	105.4	107.9	104.6	102.2	108.4	99.2	103.9	97.7	104.5	100.0	100.5
102.4	100.7	102.4	104.1	101.1	104.8	103.0	106.9	99.0	108.2	106.2	101.6	100.0	99.9
100.5	99.3	100.0	106.0	100.0	99.8	100.0	99.5	101.1	98.3	100.0	105.1	100.0	101.6
106.1	104.7	107.9	107.3	121.6	112.7	115.2	107.8	117.7	124.4	112.9	109.0	105.2	99.9
103.6	**98.4**	**97.1**	**103.3**	**100.7**	**101.9**	**101.3**	**103.5**	**97.9**	**109.9**	**103.3**	**98.6**	**102.3**	**101.4**
103.9	98.6	97.1	105.1	100.7	102.9	102.7	103.6	99.6	105.8	103.5	98.4	101.4	102.3
103.0	97.9	96.9	100.3	100.6	100.6	100.4	103.7	93.8	117.0	103.5	99.4	103.6	99.9
103.3	96.7	98.4	100.2	100.0	101.2	100.5	102.4	87.4	108.2	102.1	100.3	104.8	99.8
101.3	**100.0**	**106.3**	**101.8**	**103.5**	**108.0**	**104.9**	**108.1**	**105.5**	**101.3**	**102.1**	**100.7**	**100.1**	**101.8**
103.1	101.2	124.9	103.8	110.0	111.2	108.2	131.4	114.0	117.4	94.4	100.7	100.4	100.0
99.5	100.0	105.9	100.4	100.0	105.7	125.6	106.0	112.6	100.3	101.2	100.5	100.0	100.0
103.0	102.3	97.9	104.8	114.9	103.3	100.0	105.0	105.6	101.2	100.0	100.6	100.6	100.2
100.0	100.0	102.3	100.0	100.0	126.3	100.0	101.9	97.1	87.0	100.0	101.0	100.0	102.6
98.1	**97.1**	**97.5**	**97.3**	**94.4**	**94.5**	**94.0**	**96.5**	**97.9**	**97.9**	**97.2**	**99.8**	**99.2**	**96.8**
100.8	97.7	99.4	100.8	99.8	100.2	100.0	97.4	103.8	98.0	100.7	101.9	100.9	99.6
94.3	96.1	94.8	91.1	87.7	86.5	85.4	95.1	86.8	97.9	91.9	97.0	97.8	93.1
95.6	98.8	105.4	100.3	100.0	100.0	100.0	98.3	100.0	97.8	100.0	100.0	96.4	100.0

8-5 续表

(上年=100)

项　目	Item	乌鲁木齐市 Urumqi City	喀什市 Kashgar [Kaxgar] City	伊宁市 Yining [Gulja] City	和田市 Hotan City	克拉玛依市 Karamay City	哈密市 Hami [Kumul] City
文化办公用品	**Cultural and Office Appliances**	**96.1**	**99.9**	**98.0**	**98.5**	**98.0**	**98.6**
日用品	**Articles for Daily Use**	**103.6**	**100.0**	**101.9**	**101.7**	**100.4**	**105.7**
日用百货	General Merchandise for Daily Use	97.1	100.9	98.1	99.4	99.4	100.8
日用杂品	Miscellaneous for Daily Use	100.1	100.8	99.8	100.1	100.6	102.4
洗涤用品	Washing and Cleaning Goods	107.7	99.5	108.4	105.1	101.4	113.1
其他日用品	Other Daily-use Goods	100.9	99.2	101.1	101.7	100.0	98.7
体育娱乐用品	**Sports and Entertainment Goods**	**95.8**	**97.7**	**99.8**	**99.2**	**100.9**	**100.7**
体育用品	Sports Articles	100.2	98.3	100.3	98.4	99.8	105.8
娱乐用品	Recreational Articles	92.3	97.1	99.5	100.2	101.9	94.0
交通、通信用品	**Traffic and Telecommunication Goods**	**87.4**	**95.4**	**94.2**	**96.2**	**97.1**	**93.0**
交通运输机械	Traffic and Transport Machinery	97.8	99.0	100.0	99.1	100.0	97.3
通信器材	Telecommunication Apparatus	75.7	89.5	89.2	92.1	93.9	87.0
家　具	**Furniture**	**105.7**	**99.1**	**99.8**	**104.0**	**100.5**	**100.5**
化妆品	**Cosmetics**	**102.2**	**98.8**	**103.2**	**101.4**	**101.3**	**104.9**
金银珠宝	**Gold and Silver Jewelry**	**101.5**	**100.0**	**105.1**	**101.8**	**102.2**	**112.0**
中西药品及医疗保健用品	**Chinese and Western Medicine, Medical-care and Healthy Goods**	**103.6**	**110.3**	**103.1**	**102.2**	**103.2**	**104.6**
医疗器具及用品	Medical-care Apparatus and Goods	100.6	102.7	103.7	100.0	102.1	106.7
中药材及中成药	Chinese Herbs and Patent Medicine	103.3	123.8	107.8	106.3	107.3	101.0
西　药	Western Medicine	103.4	104.7	100.3	101.0	102.1	107.4
保健器具及用品	Healthy Devices and Goods	106.0	103.3	100.0	100.0	99.7	105.0
书报杂志及电子出版物	**Books, Magazines and Electronic Publications**	**105.5**	**100.5**	**99.3**	**100.2**	**101.1**	**99.0**
教材及参考书	Texts and Reference Books	110.6	102.6	101.1	100.6	101.6	100.0
书报杂志	Newspapers and Magazines	100.0	98.5	100.0	100.0	100.9	100.0
电子音像制品	Electronic Audio and Video Products	113.3	100.0	93.9	100.0	100.0	94.4
燃　料	**Fuels**	**104.7**	**103.8**	**103.0**	**106.1**	**103.9**	**108.9**
煤炭及制品	Coal and Its Products	104.2	105.4	107.6	110.0	106.9	119.6
石油及制品	Oil and Its Products	104.7	103.2	102.5	105.1	102.4	103.7
建筑材料及五金电料	**Building Apparatus, Hardwares and Electrical Apparatus**	**96.2**	**96.1**	**97.6**	**96.5**	**98.4**	**97.0**
建筑装璜材料	Building Decoration Materials	94.5	94.7	96.7	94.0	96.9	94.6
五金电料	Hardwares and Electrical Apparatus	101.4	101.7	101.0	102.6	101.4	101.7

Continued

(preceding year=100)

昌吉市 Changji City	库尔勒市 Korla City	阿克苏市 Aksu City	焉耆回族自治县 Yanqi Hui Autonomous County	塔城市 Tacheng [Qoqek] City	阿勒泰市 Altay City	乌苏市 Usu City	博乐市 Bole [Bortala] City	吐鲁番市 Turpan City	库车县 Kuqa County	阿图什市 Artux City	莎车县 Shache [Yarkant] County	奎屯市 Kuytun City	石河子市 Shihezi City
97.7	**99.2**	**97.1**	**98.6**	**99.6**	**95.8**	**100.0**	**100.0**	**98.4**	**100.0**	**99.7**	**104.7**	**96.5**	**99.1**
101.6	**101.2**	**101.6**	**101.9**	**100.1**	**100.2**	**100.7**	**106.0**	**102.3**	**104.5**	**101.4**	**106.5**	**101.4**	**100.0**
102.6	102.1	103.8	103.6	98.2	97.4	100.0	100.9	103.6	105.0	102.4	106.1	101.7	100.1
103.1	99.9	103.1	100.0	100.1	99.3	103.6	107.4	99.7	104.9	100.1	107.1	101.7	99.9
100.6	101.5	102.1	101.9	102.6	104.6	100.0	112.0	102.3	102.8	101.2	109.7	100.0	100.1
102.2	100.6	98.1	100.8	100.5	99.7	100.0	100.1	103.3	106.2	100.0	97.7	101.7	99.4
100.7	**100.8**	**99.1**	**100.4**	**97.5**	**100.0**	**100.4**	**100.2**	**110.2**	**99.4**	**100.1**	**100.5**	**101.1**	**99.5**
100.6	103.0	94.3	100.0	95.4	100.0	101.3	100.2	116.3	99.9	100.1	99.4	100.9	100.7
100.7	97.9	101.1	100.8	99.4	100.0	100.0	100.2	100.1	98.8	100.0	101.7	101.3	98.2
96.1	**97.7**	**97.1**	**94.1**	**98.4**	**92.5**	**88.7**	**94.8**	**86.9**	**91.6**	**89.9**	**94.9**	**98.4**	**97.7**
98.1	100.0	98.5	100.0	97.6	96.9	100.0	98.8	99.1	97.1	100.3	100.2	100.0	99.1
93.7	92.8	94.8	91.2	99.9	88.4	79.4	89.7	80.5	85.9	80.4	91.0	97.3	95.8
103.3	**100.5**	**101.5**	**108.4**	**100.0**	**101.3**	**100.0**	**99.9**	**101.4**	**98.4**	**108.1**	**102.8**	**96.5**	**100.6**
103.8	**100.6**	**100.4**	**101.5**	**101.3**	**101.8**	**104.3**	**104.4**	**101.8**	**100.9**	**101.5**	**107.6**	**101.7**	**98.6**
123.0	**101.3**	**107.6**	**99.4**	**102.0**	**106.1**	**103.0**	**98.9**	**103.1**	**105.6**	**97.2**	**102.0**	**100.9**	**104.2**
100.9	**101.3**	**99.0**	**104.2**	**107.3**	**99.8**	**97.3**	**104.4**	**113.5**	**100.4**	**102.9**	**107.2**	**100.7**	**104.9**
100.0	107.4	101.1	102.0	111.0	100.0	101.3	113.5	101.6	98.8	96.9	101.4	102.4	104.3
102.5	102.7	103.4	110.7	113.6	99.9	96.3	103.3	140.5	100.4	108.9	122.2	101.6	102.3
99.5	100.0	96.6	99.5	99.7	99.7	97.7	105.6	102.7	101.5	101.1	99.8	99.9	107.0
103.1	100.8	95.8	101.3	101.7	100.0	98.2	97.1	96.2	98.4	100.0	99.5	100.3	104.4
100.2	**100.8**	**101.6**	**112.2**	**98.0**	**100.8**	**106.6**	**100.3**	**99.5**	**106.7**	**103.7**	**103.1**	**100.0**	**99.9**
100.6	102.6	100.7	119.2	100.0	100.0	115.6	100.2	100.2	119.4	103.7	101.2	100.0	100.0
99.9	100.0	100.2	100.9	100.0	102.2	100.0	100.4	98.6	100.6	104.4	105.2	100.0	100.0
100.6	100.6	103.4	98.5	86.0	100.0	100.0	100.3	100.0	100.0	100.0	100.0	100.0	99.3
101.2	**101.8**	**102.0**	**105.6**	**102.6**	**103.3**	**103.5**	**108.7**	**100.1**	**97.9**	**104.2**	**102.5**	**101.0**	**102.1**
102.8	98.6	103.7	109.7	88.5	102.9	103.9	121.2	96.0	93.9	106.6	103.0	103.1	102.3
101.1	102.8	101.5	103.1	107.5	103.5	103.2	103.6	103.1	101.7	103.5	102.2	99.9	102.1
98.6	**98.1**	**98.3**	**100.8**	**92.6**	**100.7**	**97.1**	**100.9**	**103.2**	**91.7**	**100.8**	**102.7**	**102.1**	**99.7**
97.6	95.2	97.9	101.4	92.0	101.0	94.8	101.4	99.5	86.2	101.1	104.2	101.9	99.5
102.3	104.7	100.1	99.2	101.5	100.0	100.0	100.0	111.5	97.4	100.1	97.7	103.1	100.0

8-6 主要年份农业生产资料价格分类指数
Price Indices for Means of Agricultural Production by Category in Main Years

(上年=100) (preceding year=100)

项目	Item	2005	2010	2012
农业生产资料价格指数	**Price Indices for Means of Agricultural Production**	**105.3**	**103.1**	**106.2**
农用手工工具	Farm Handtools	104.9	101.0	101.5
饲料类	Forage	101.3	114.0	107.7
产品畜	Commodity Animals	89.4	127.1	109.6
半机械化农具	Semi-mechanized Farm Tools	100.9	101.7	101.2
机械化农具	Mechanized Farm Machinery	102.5	100.1	101.6
化学肥料	Chemical Fertilizer	110.2	95.3	107.6
农药及农药械	Pesticide and Its Appliances	102.8	101.7	100.7
农用机油	Oil for Farm Machinery	111.0	110.1	103.2
其他农业生产资料	Other Means of Agricultural Production	105.5	100.7	108.0
农业生产服务	Service for Agriculture Production		102.0	105.4

8-7 各市县农业生产资料价格指数
Price Indices for Means of Agricultural Production in Cities and Counties

(上年=100) (2012 年) (preceding year=100)

项目	Item	塔城市 Kashgar [Kaxgar] City	阿勒泰市 Altay City	乌苏市 Usu City	博乐市 Bole [Bortala] City	吐鲁番市 Turpan City	库车县 Kuqa County	阿图什市 Artux City	莎车县 Shache [Yarkant] County	焉耆回族自治县 Yanqi Hui Autonomous County
农业生产资料价格指数	**Price Indices for Means of Agricultural Production**	**104.5**	**103.6**	**108.7**	**102.7**	**105.3**	**99.8**	**107.6**	**108.0**	**106.4**
农用手工工具	Farm Handtools	100.9	102.7	100.0	101.4	99.2	103.8	100.0	101.8	101.6
饲料类	Forage	103.0	105.7	124.9	99.9	106.3	79.5	108.5	113.5	109.8
产品畜	Commodity Animals	107.6	114.2	129.8	114.8	125.2	98.4	118.7	103.1	108.0
半机械化农具	Semi-mechanized Farm Tools	103.0	104.0	100.0	100.2	100.0	101.8	100.0	99.8	105.7
机械化农具	Mechanized Farm Machinery	98.8	102.7	100.0	100.5	100.0	100.0	100.1	102.1	105.0
化学肥料	Chemical Fertilizer	103.3	101.2	108.6	103.1	103.5	107.1	110.2	111.9	106.5
农药及农药械	Pesticide and Its Appliances	101.6	103.6	100.0	101.3	104.1	100.3	101.0	98.7	101.4
农用机油	Oil for Farm Machinery	111.1	102.3	103.1	103.9	105.6	101.4	111.0	100.0	106.0
其他农业生产资料	Other Means of Agricultural Production	100.0	104.5	103.8	100.3	106.8	100.3	102.2	110.2	111.0
农业生产服务	Service for Agriculture Production	112.9	104.0	103.3	102.8	104.1	104.2	107.4	106.9	101.3

8-8 主要年份工业生产者出厂价格分类指数
Producer Price Indices for Manufactured Goods by Category in Main Years

(上年=100) (preceding year=100)

项　目	Item	2005	2010	2012
全部工业品	**Total Industrial Products**	**116.6**	**125.3**	**96.9**
按轻、重工业分	**By Light and Heavy Industry**			
轻工业	Light Industry	99.6	108.9	94.1
以农产品为原料	Using Farm Produces as Raw Materials	98.4	111.2	95.6
以非农产品为原料	Using Non-farm Produces as Raw Materials	101.9	104.6	86.1
重工业	Heavy Industry	122.5	128.7	97.4
采　掘	Mining and Quarrying	136.2	153.1	97.9
原　料	Raw Materials	114.2	114.0	98.1
加　工	Processing	104.1	105.6	94.2
按部类分	**By Sector**			
生产资料	Means of Production	118.4	127.1	96.6
采　掘	Mining and Quarrying	136.0	151.9	97.9
原　料	Raw Materials	114.3	115.1	97.3
加　工	Processing	100.4	107.3	93.0
生活资料	Consumer Goods	101.3	104.1	100.8
食　品	Food	101.7	104.4	100.8
衣　着	Clothing	96.4	101.5	100.0
一般日用品	Articles for Daily Use	101.1	101.4	101.3
耐用消费品	Durable Consumer Goods	99.2	102.3	100.3
按工业部门分	**Division of Industrial Setors**			
冶金工业	Metallurgical Industry	101.9	114.4	92.6
电力工业	Power Industry	100.9	100.7	100.5
煤炭及炼焦工业	Coal and Coking Industry	109.4	104.0	103.1
石油工业	Petroleum Industry	130.5	141.6	99.8
化学工业	Chemical Industry	106.1	112.1	88.8
机械工业	Machine Manufacturing Industry	112.4	97.4	94.8
建筑材料工业	Building Materials Industry	99.4	101.1	92.7
森林工业	Timber Industry	99.9	101.7	101.4
食品工业	Food Industry	101.1	104.9	101.2
纺织工业	Textile Industry	92.1	122.8	85.2
缝纫工业	Tailoring Industry	96.3	101.5	100.0
皮革工业	Leather Industry	100.0	101.1	106.8
造纸工业	Paper Industry	102.6	127.8	94.7
文教艺术用品工业	Cultural, Educational and Handicrafts Articles	99.7	101.1	101.6
其他工业	Other Industry	104.0	107.7	99.5

8-9 主要年份工业生产者购进价格分类指数

Purchasing Prices Indices for Raw Material, Fuels and Power by Category in Main Years

(上年=100) (preceding year=100)

项　　目	Iterm	2005	2010	2012
全部原材料价格指数	**Total of Raw Material**	**110.7**	**123.9**	**97.9**
燃料、动力类	Fuel and Power	132.0	137.6	98.6
黑色金属材料类	Ferrous Metals	113.8	105.0	91.5
#钢　材	Rolled Steel	112.9	102.5	95.7
其　他	Others	114.9	112.3	83.8
有色金属材料及电线类	Nonferrous Metals and Wire Type	108.5	139.6	95.3
化工原料类	Raw Chemistry Material	113.0	106.8	99.7
木材及纸浆类	Timber and Paper Pulp	102.0	104.0	103.3
建筑材料及非金属类	Building Material and Non-metal Ore	103.9	103.0	98.9
其他工业原材料及半成品类	Other Industrial Raw Material and Semi-finished Category	105.5	101.1	98.8
农副产品类	Agricultural Products	91.9	118.7	98.9
纺织原料类	Textile Raw Materials	93.0	144.2	94.3

8-10 主要年份固定资产投资价格指数

Price Indices for Investment in Fixed Assets in Main Years

(上年=100) (preceding year=100)

项　　目	Item	2005	2010	2012
固定资产投资价格指数	**Investment in Fixed Assets**	**102.8**	**104.6**	**100.6**
建筑安装工程	**Construction and Installtion**	**102.7**	**105.9**	**101.5**
人工费	Manpower Expenses	103.8	110.6	109.6
材料费	Material Expenses	102.3	104.8	98.4
#钢　材	Rolled Steel	101.7	104.4	96.5
木　材	Timber	102.5	104.8	104.6
水　泥	Cement	100.1	104.7	95.5
地方材料	Local Material	102.0	104.6	100.3
化工材料	Chemical Material	109.1	104.9	102.6
电　料	Electrical Wire	104.0	105.1	99.8
其他材料	Other Material	99.9	101.7	102.5
机械使用费	Expenses of Machine Use	102.3	103.3	104.0
设备工器具	**Purchase of Equipment,Tools and Instruments**	**104.8**	**100.4**	**97.3**
其他费用	**Others**	**100.0**	**105.2**	**101.1**

主要统计指标解释

居民消费价格指数　简称CPI，是反映一定时期内城乡居民所购买的生活消费品价格和服务项目价格变动趋势和程度的相对数，是对城市居民消费价格指数和农村居民消费价格指数进行综合汇总计算的结果。该指数可以观察和分析消费品的零售价格和服务价格变动对城乡居民实际生活费支出的影响程度。

商品零售价格指数　是反映一定时期内城乡商品零售价格变动趋势和程度的相对数。商品零售物价的变动直接影响到城乡居民的生活支出和国家的财政收入，影响居民购买力和市场供需的平衡，影响到消费与积累的比例关系。因此，该指数可以从一个侧面对上述经济活动进行观察和分析。

农业生产资料价格指数　指反映一定时期内农业生产资料价格变动趋势和程度的相对数。其编制目的是了解农业生产中物质资料投入价格的变动状况，服务于国民经济核算。1994年以前，农业生产资料价格指数仅仅是商品零售价格指数的一个类别，此后，从商品零售价格指数中分离出来，单独编制。

工业生产者出厂价格指数　简称PPI，是反映一定时期内全部工业产品出厂价格（工业企业产品第一次出售时的价格）总水平的变动趋势和程度的相对数，包括工业企业售给本企业以外所有单位的各种产品和直接售给居民用于生活消费的产品。该指数可以观察出厂价格变动对工业总产值及增加值的影响。

工业生产者购进价格指数　是反映工业企业作为生产投入而从物资交易市场和能源、原材料生产企业购买原材料、燃料和动力产品时，所支付的价格水平变动趋势和程度的相对数。是扣除工业企业物质消耗成本承担价格变动影响的重要依据。

固定资产投资价格指数　是反映一定时期内固定资产投资品及费用项目的价格变动趋势和程度的相对数。固定资产投资额是由建筑安装工程投资完成额、设备工器具购置投资完成额和其他费用投资完成额三部分组成的。编制固定资产投资价格指数应首先分别编制上述三部分投资的价格指数，然后采用加权算术平均法求出固定资产投资价格总指数。

该指数可以准确地反映固定资产投资中涉及的各类投资品和取费项目价格变动趋势和变动幅度，消除按现价计算的固定资产投资指标中的价格变动因素，真实地反映固定资产投资的规模、速度、结构和效益，为国家科学地制定、检查固定资产投资计划并提高宏观调控水平，为完善国民经济核算体系提供科学的、可靠的依据。

Explanatory Notes on Main Statistical Indicators

Consumer Price Indices reflect the trend and degree of changes in prices of consumer goods and services purchased by urban and rural households during a given period.They are obtained by combining Consumer Price Indices of Urban Household and Consumer Price Indices of Rural Household. The Indices enable the observation and analysis of the degree of impact of the changes in the prices of retailed goods and services on the actual living expenses of urban and rural residents

Retail Price Indices reflect the trend and degree of change in retail prices of commodities during a given period. The change in retail prices of commodities is related to government revenue, the equilibrium of market supply and demand, and the ratio of consumption to accumulation. Therefore, the retail price indices are useful from an oblique perspective for observing and analyzing the changes of the above economic activities.

Price Indices for Means of Agricultural Production reflect the trend and degree of changes in the prices of the means of agricultural production during a given period. Compilation of these indices helps to understand the price changes of material input in agricultural production and facilitate the compilation of national accounts. Before 1994, price indices for means of agricultural production were a sub-category in the retail price indices for commodities, and it has been compiled separately since 1994.

Producer Price Indices for Industrial Products reflect the trend and degree of changes in general ex-factory prices of all manufactured goods during a given period, including sales of manufactured goods by an industrial enterprise to all units outside the enterprise, as well as sales of consumer goods to residents. It can be used to analyze the impact of ex-factory prices on gross output value and value-added of the industrial sector.

Purchasing Price Indices for Industrial Producers reflect changes in the level and degree of prices paid by industrial enterprises when they purchase production input such as raw materials, fuels and power from the market or from other energy or raw materials producing enterprises. These indices provide an important basis for measuring the material consumption of industrial enterprises after removing the influence of price changes.

At present, products in 9 categories, including fuels and power, ferrous metals, non-ferrous metals, chemicals, building materials, are covered in China for the survey to produce indices for purchasing' prices for industrial producers.

Price Indices for Investment in Fixed Assets reflect the trend and degree of changes in prices of investment goods and projects in fixed assets during a given period. The investment in fixed assets consists of three components, namely the investment in construction and installation, the investment in purchases of equipment and instrument, and the investment in other items. Price indices for investment in fixed assets are calculated as the weighted arithmetic mean of the price indices for the three components of investment in fixed assets.

Removing the factor of price change in the aggregates of investment at current prices, this indicator shows the changes in the prices of commodities and fees involved in the investment of fixed assets, and can be used to observe the actual size, growth, structure, and efficiency of investment in fixed assets and provides reliable and scientific data for government planning, management, decision-making, and further improving the current national accounting system..

新疆统计年鉴
XINJIANG STATISTICAL YEARBOOK

9

人民生活和社会保障
PEOPLE'S LIVELIHOOD AND SOCIAL SECURITY

简要说明

本篇资料的主要内容及来源

本篇资料反映新疆城乡人民生活现状及变化以及城乡居民社会保障情况，主要包括居民家庭基本情况、家庭收入、支出情况、主要商品购买数量及支出金额、居住状况和耐用消费品的拥有量及城乡居民社会保险情况等。

居民生活状况的数据来源于国家统计局新疆调查总队住户调查处。

居民社会保险情况数据来源于新疆维吾尔自治区人力资源和社会保障厅。

Brief Introduction

Main Content and Source of Data

Data in this chapter show the condition of people's livelihood in Xinjiang and social security in urban and rural, including mainly basic condition of people's household, income of households, income and expenditure of the household, the quantity and the expenditure on major commodities purchased, the housing condition and the possession of the durable consumer goods, etc.

Data on the livelihood of residents are from the Department of Urban households Survey , NBS Survey office in Xinjiang.

Data on social security of residents are from Bureau of Human Resources and Social Security of Xinjiang Uygur Autonomous Region.

9-1 主要年份人民物质文化生活情况

People's Material and Cultural Living Conditions in Main Years

项　目	Item	2000	2005	2010	2012
就 业	**Employment**				
城镇居民家庭每户就业人口(人)	Average Number of Employed Persons Per Urban Household (person)	1.55	1.48	1.54	1.49
农村居民家庭每户整半劳动力(人)	Average Number of Full/Semi Laborer Per (person)	3.06	2.92	3.14	2.85
每一农村劳动力负担人数(人)	Number of Dependents Per Laborer of Rural Household (person)	1.74	1.62	1.47	1.51
每一城镇就业者负担人数(人)	Number of Dependents Per Employee of Urban Household (person)	2.03	2.04	1.94	1.95
城镇登记失业率(%)	Registered Urban Unemployment Rate (%)	3.8	3.9	3.2	3.4
收入与支出	**Income and Expenditure**				
城镇居民家庭人均可支配收入(元)	Annual Per capita Disposable Income of Urban Household Residents (yuan)	5645	7990	13644	17921
农村居民家庭人均纯收入(元)	Annual per Capita Net Income of Rural Household (yuan)	1618	2482	4643	6394
城镇居民人均消费性支出(元)	Annual Per capita Net Income of Rural Household (yuan)	4423	6208	10197	13892
农村居民人均生活消费支出(元)	Annual per Capita Living Expencliture of Urban (yuan)	1236	1924	3458	5245
人均储蓄存款余额(元)	Per Capita Balance of Saving Deposit (yuan)	4913	9035	17113	23781
生活质量(元)	**Annual Per capita Consumption (yuan)**				
居民家庭恩格尔系数 (%)	Household's Engel;s Coefficient (%)				
城 镇	Urban	36.4	36.4	36.2	37.7
农 村	Rural	50.0	41.8	40.3	36.1
居住条件	Residence Condition				
城镇人均住房建筑面积(平方米)	Per Capita Building Space in Urban Area (sq.m)	26.75	26.02	27.25	29.03
农村人均住房面积(平方米)	Per Capita Living Space in Rural Area (sq.m)	17.25	21.23	24.00	27.18
交 通	Traffic				
城镇每百户拥有汽车(辆)	Number of Automobile per 100 Households in Urban Areas (unit)	0.82	2.81	8.63	15.58
农村每百户拥有摩托车(辆)	Number of Motor Cycles Per 100 Rural Household (unit)	18.33	45.42	62.84	79.87
通信条件	Communication Condition				
电话普及率(固定电话)(部/百人)	Telephone Popularization Rate (Fixed Telephone)(set/100 persons)	15.0	30.8	25.4	24.5
移动电话普及率(部/百人)	Popularization Rate of Mobile Telephone (set/100 persons)	4.3	26.7	63.0	90.9
城镇公用事业	Public Utilities in Urban Areas				
自来水普及率 (%)	Coverage Rate of Population with Access to Tap Water (%)	98.8	97.9	99.2	99.1

9-1 续表 Continued

项　　目	Item	2000	2005	2010	2012
燃气普及率 (%)	Coverage Rate of Population with Access to Gas(%)	92.8	89.3	95.8	96.6
文化、教育和卫生	**Culture,Education and Health Care**				
文 化	Culture				
广播综合人口覆盖率 (%)	Radio Coverage Rate of Population (%)	89.77	93.14	94.90	95.34
电视综合人口覆盖率 (%)	TV Coverage Rate of Population (%)	92.15	92.78	95.28	95.62
每百户彩色电视机拥有量 (部/百户)	Number of Color TV Per 100 Household (set/100 Households)				
城 镇	Urban	102.57	105.70	105.61	106.72
农 村	Rural	31.87	61.81	89.87	96.90
居民家庭文教娱乐支出比重 (%)	Percentage of Household Expenditure on Education, Culture and Entertainment				
城 镇	Urban	13.58	11.94	9.93	9.22
农 村	Rural	3.76	3.70	4.92	4.36
教 育	Education				
各级普通学校毕业生升学率 (%)	Rate of Entering Higher School				
高中升学率	Promotion Rate from Senion Secondary Schools to Higher Education	80.46	64.84	84.59	85.34
初中升学率	Promotion Rate from Junior Secondary Schools to Senior Secondary Schools	30.30	39.13	45.40	48.60
小学升学率	Promotion Rate from Primary Schools to Junior Secondary Schools	92.01	99.33	100.53	97.94
卫 生	Public Health				
每万人有医院、卫生院床位(张)	Number of Hospital Beds per 10 000 Population (unit)	35.6	37.8	50.4	56.0
每万人有医生数(人)	Number of Doctors per 10 000 Population (person)	24.6	20.6	22.3	22.6
居民家庭医疗保健支出比重 (%)	Percentage of Resident Expenditure on Health Care				
城 镇	Urban	7.48	8.04	6.94	7.40
农 村	Rural	2.61	3.93	9.10	9.39
社会保障	Social Security				
参加城镇职工基本养老保险人数 (万人)	Number of Employees Joining Urban Basic Pension Insurance (10 000persons)	140.34	181.87	259.67	312.16
参加城镇职工基本医疗保险人数 (万人)	Number of Persons Joining Urban Basic Medical Care System (10 000persons)	88.20	211.85	296.72	342.56
参加失业保险人数 (万人)	Number of Employees Joining Unemploy ment Insurance (10 000persons)	122.10	140.82	180.29	208.95
参加工伤保险人数 (万人)	Number of Employees Joining Injury Insurance (10 000persons)		79.51	184.13	225.95
参加生育保险人数 (万人)	Number of persons Joining Maternity Insurance (10 000persons)		103.48	188.23	217.96

9-2 主要年份城乡居民储蓄存款年底余额和年增加额
Savings Deposit of Urban and Rural Households at Year-end in Main Years

单位：亿元 (100 million yuan)

年 份 Year l	年末余额 Total	年增加额 Year-on-year Increase	年 份 Year l	年末余额 Total	年增加额 Year-on-year Increase
1978	6.42		2004	1534.67	162.85
1980	9.52	2.31	2005	1816.38	281.71
1985	29.55	5.24	2006	2035.63	219.25
1990	114.13	35.68	2007	2054.91	19.29
1995	477.18	129.47	2008	2550.95	499.45
2000	908.55	83.86	2009	3049.91	498.79
2001	994.00	85.46	2010	3713.47	662.61
2002	1137.87	143.85	2011	4421.93	709.38
2003	1371.59	233.81	2012	5281.83	859.21

9-3 主要年份城乡居民家庭人均收入及指数
Per Capita Annual Income of Urban and Rural Households and the Related Index in Main Years

年 份 Year	农村居民家庭人均纯收入 Per capita Annual Net Income of Rural Households		城镇居民家庭人均年可支配收入 Per capita Annual Disposable Income of Urban Households		农村居民家庭恩格尔系数 (%) Engel's Coefficient of Rural Households (%)	城镇居民家庭恩格尔系数 (%) Engel's Coefficient of Urban Households (%)
	绝对数（元） Value (yuan)	指数(1978=100) Index	绝对数（元） Value (yuan)	指数(1978=100) Index		
1978	119	100.0	319	100.0		
1980	201	168.9	427	133.9	60.8	57.3
1985	394	331.1	735	230.4	57.9	46.8
1990	684	574.8	1314	411.8	53.7	47.8
1995	1137	955.5	4163	1172.3	50.1	44.8
2000	1618	1359.3	5645	1589.4	50.0	36.4
2001	1710	1437.0	6215	1749.9	50.4	34.8
2002	1863	1564.9	6554	1979.1	49.0	33.9
2003	2106	1768.3	7006	2115.7	45.5	35.9
2004	2245	1885.0	7503	2265.9	45.2	36.1
2005	2482	2084.0	7990	2412.9	41.8	36.4
2006	2737	2300.0	8871	2679.0	39.9	35.5
2007	3183	2674.8	10313	3114.5	39.9	35.1
2008	3503	2943.7	11432	3452.4	42.5	37.3
2009	3883	3263.0	12258	3701.8	41.6	36.3
2010	4643	3901.7	13644	4120.0	40.3	36.2
2011	5442	4573.1	15514	4684.4	36.1	38.3
2012	6394	5373.4	17921	5410.5	36.1	37.7

注：1992 年以前城镇居民人均年可支配收入为人均年生活费收入。
Note: Per capita disposal income of urban households before the year 1992 is Per capita annual income as life expense.

9-4 主要年份城镇居民家庭生活基本情况
Basic Living Conditions of Urban Households in Main Years

(抽样调查 Sampled Survey)

项　　目	Item	2000	2005	2010	2012
调查户数（户）	**Number of Households Surveyed (household)**	**790**	**1380**	**1560**	**1460**
平均每户家庭人口(人)	**Average Household Size (person)**	**3.15**	**3.02**	**2.98**	**2.91**
平均每户就业人口(人)	**Average Number of Employed Persons Per Household (person)**	**1.55**	**1.48**	**1.54**	**1.49**
平均每户就业面（%）	**Proportion of Employment per Household (%)**	**49.21**	**49.01**	**51.68**	**51.20**
平均每一就业者负担人数(包括就业者本人)(人)	**Number of Dependents Per Employee (including the employee himself or herself) (person)**	**2.03**	**2.04**	**1.94**	**1.95**
平均每人全部年收入(元)	**Per Capita Annual Income (yuan)**	**5686.52**	**8693.67**	**15421.59**	**20194.55**
#可支配收入	Disposable Income	5644.86	7990.15	13643.77	17920.68
工资性收入	Income from Wages and Salaries	4128.29	6553.47	11327.91	14432.12
工资及补贴收入	Salary & Subsidy	4027.36	6331.74	11208.19	14273.38
其他劳动收入	Part-time Income	100.93	221.73	119.72	158.74
经营净收入	Net Business Income	230.29	522.14	1131.78	1633.22
财产性收入	Income from Porperties	38.03	54.51	151.94	145.50
转移性收入	Income from Transfer	1243.55	1563.54	2809.96	3983.71
平均每人消费性支出(元)	**Per Capita Annual Consumption Expenditures (yuan)**	**4422.92**	**6207.52**	**10197.09**	**13891.72**
平均每人消费性支出构成(%)(人均消费支出=100)	**Composition of Per Capita Annual Consumption (%)**	**100**	**100**	**100**	**100**
食　品	Food	36.38	36.37	36.23	37.71
衣　着	Clothing	13.05	13.31	14.84	14.62
家庭设备用品及服务	Household Facilities,Articles and Service	9.29	4.99	6.57	6.84
医疗保健	Health Care and Medical Service	7.48	8.04	6.94	7.40
交通通讯	Transport and Communication	7.48	12.20	12.32	11.95
教育文化娱乐服务	Education , Cultural and Recreation Services	13.58	11.94	9.93	9.22
居　住	Residence	7.76	9.21	8.81	8.40
其他商品和服务	Miscellaneous Goods and Services	4.98	3.94	4.36	3.86

9-5 城镇居民家庭基本情况
Basic Conditions of Urban Households

(2012 年) (抽样调查 Sampled Survey)

项目	Item	全区 Whole Region	最低收入户 Lowest Income Households	#困难户 Poor Households	低收入户 Low Income Households
调查户数(户)	Number of Households Surveyed (household)	1460	148	74	145
比重(%)	Proportion (%)	100	10	5	10
平均每户家庭人口(人)	Average Household Size (person)	2.91	3.96	4.23	3.21
平均每户就业人口(人)	Average Number of Employees per Household (person)	1.49	1.23	1.14	1.55
平均每户就业面(%)	Proportion of Employment per Household (%)	51.20	31.06	26.95	48.29
平均每一就业者负担人数(包括就业者本人)(人)	Number of Dependents per Employee (Including the employee himself or herself) (person)	1.95	3.22	3.71	2.07
平均每人全部年收入(元)	Per Capita Annual Income (yuan)	20194.55	7072.02	5816.30	11692.02
平均每人可支配收入(元)	Per Capita Disposable Income (yuan)	17920.68	6148.36	5131.41	10156.18
平均每人消费性支出(元)	Per Capita Annual Consumption Expenditure (yuan)	13891.72	6620.27	6011.87	8897.41

项目	Item	中等偏下户 Lower Middle Income Households	中等收入户 Middle Income Households	中等偏上户 Upper Middle Income Households	高收入户 High Income Households	最高收入户 Highest Income Households
调查户数(户)	Number of Households Surveyed (household)	291	291	291	147	147
比重(%)	Proportion (%)	20	20	20	10	10
平均每户家庭人口(人)	Average Household Size (person)	3.12	2.89	2.60	2.33	2.15
平均每户就业人口(人)	Average Number of Employees per Household (person)	1.65	1.58	1.45	1.41	1.30
平均每户就业面(%)	Proportion of Employed Persons per Household (%)	58.88	54.67	55.77	60.52	60.47
平均每一就业者负担人数(包括就业者本人)(人)	Number of Dependents per Employee (Including the employee himself or herself) (person)	1.89	1.83	1.79	1.65	1.65
平均每人全部年收入(元)	Per Capita Annual Income (yuan)	16004.34	20704.85	26507.66	33189.02	43268.57
平均每人可支配收入(元)	Per Capita Disposable Income (yuan)	14023.62	18337.10	23533.65	29817.89	39236.07
平均每人消费性支出(元)	Per Capita Annual Consumption Expenditure (yuan)	11593.10	13763.03	17882.40	22509.20	25319.35

9-6 城镇居民家庭平均每人全年消费性支出

Per Capita Annual Living Expenditure of Urban Households

单位：元 (2012 年) (抽样调查 Sampled Survey) (yuan)

项 目	Item	总平均 Total Average	最低收入户 Lowest Income Households	#困难户 Poor Households	低收入户 Low Income Households
消费性支出	**Consumption Expenditures**	**13891.72**	**6620.27**	**6011.87**	**8897.41**
食 品	Food	5238.89	3210.42	3026.21	3891.00
#粮 食	Grain	494.46	535.98	554.12	468.29
肉禽及其制品	Meat, Poultry and Processed Products	1205.88	994.07	1001.17	939.16
蛋 类	Eggs	91.01	63.66	63.10	90.92
水产品	Aquatic Products	115.34	50.52	37.56	89.27
奶及奶制品	Milk and Processed Products	237.05	109.17	100.58	176.03
衣 着	Clothing	2031.14	769.54	722.30	1262.29
#服 装	Garments	1458.13	527.16	504.06	882.65
家庭设备用品及服务	Household Appliances and Services	950.17	313.00	300.58	526.89
#耐用消费品	Durable Consumer Goods	303.05	57.68	57.20	143.53
医疗保健	Health Care and Medical Services	1027.60	435.02	265.93	598.12
交通通讯	Transport and Communication Services	1660.27	675.01	841.19	817.65
教育文化娱乐服务	Education , Cultural and Recreation Services	1280.81	473.96	251.11	812.71
#文化娱乐用品	Recreation Articles	359.49	74.03	57.54	183.80
居 住	Residence	1166.59	640.69	532.84	709.42
#住 房	Housing	402.96	198.27	129.94	139.63
其他商品和服务	Miscellaneous Goods and Services	536.24	102.62	71.71	279.31

项 目	Item	中等偏下户 Lower Middle Income Households	中等收入户 Middle Income Households	中等偏上户 Upper Middle Income Households	高收入户 High Income Households	最高收入户 Highest Income Households
消费性支出	**Consumption Expenditures**	**11593.10**	**13763.03**	**17882.40**	**22509.20**	**25319.35**
食 品	Food	4687.82	5265.75	6164.33	7669.54	8300.08
#粮 食	Grain	448.53	475.52	487.22	593.52	545.06
肉禽及其制品	Meat, Poultry and Processed Products	1057.00	1238.35	1330.74	1611.35	1688.56
蛋 类	Eggs	82.92	88.97	106.89	116.54	111.24
水产品	Aquatic Products	112.33	126.95	122.04	165.10	196.46
奶及奶制品	Milk and Processed Products	231.28	244.37	311.06	330.80	317.12
衣 着	Clothing	1800.51	2027.49	2838.21	3145.25	3456.63
#服 装	Garments	1279.83	1438.83	2110.45	2271.49	2471.97
家庭设备用品及服务	Household Appliances and Services	734.88	937.19	1296.11	1733.52	1949.94
#耐用消费品	Durable Consumer Goods	157.45	308.39	469.15	577.05	807.26
医疗保健	Health Care and Medical Services	804.78	1060.87	1277.09	1977.67	1857.02
交通通讯	Transport and Communication Services	1135.25	1599.35	2402.66	2721.15	3945.49
教育文化娱乐服务	Education , Cultural and Recreation Services	1080.33	1335.27	1747.89	1997.82	2269.40
#文化娱乐用品	Recreation Articles	298.21	367.97	515.76	578.93	791.38
居 住	Residence	995.30	1053.26	1371.79	2135.84	2242.69
#住 房	Housing	286.68	304.92	506.99	1007.35	939.74
其他商品和服务	Miscellaneous Goods and Services	354.22	483.85	784.32	1128.42	1298.10

9-7 城镇居民家庭平均每人全年消费性支出构成
Composition of Per Capita Living Expenditure of Urban Households

单位：% (2012 年) (抽样调查 Sampled Survey) (%)

项目	Item	总平均 Total Average	最低收入户 Lowest Income Households	#困难户 Poor Households	低收入户 Low Income Households
消费性支出	**Consumption Expenditures**	**100**	**100**	**100**	**100**
食品	Food	37.71	48.49	50.34	43.73
衣着	Clothing	14.62	11.62	12.01	14.19
家庭设备用品及服务	Household Facilities, Articles and Services	6.84	9.68	8.86	7.97
医疗保健	Health Care and Medical Services	7.40	4.73	5.00	5.92
交通通讯	Transport and Communication Services	11.95	6.57	4.42	6.72
教育文化娱乐服务	Education , Cultural and Recreation Services	9.22	10.20	13.99	9.19
居住	Residence	8.40	7.16	4.18	9.13
其他商品和服务	Miscellaneous Goods and Services	3.86	1.55	1.19	3.14

项目	Item	中等偏下户 Lower Middle Income Households	中等收入户 Middle Income Households	中等偏上户 Upper Middle Income Households	高收入户 High Income Households	最高收入户 Highest Income Households
消费性支出	**Consumption Expenditures**	**100**	**100**	**100**	**100**	**100**
食品	Food	40.44	38.26	34.07	32.78	40.44
衣着	Clothing	15.53	14.73	13.97	13.65	15.53
家庭设备用品及服务	Household Facilities, Articles and Services	8.59	7.65	9.49	8.86	8.59
医疗保健	Health Care and Medical Services	6.34	6.81	7.70	7.70	6.34
交通通讯	Transport and Communication Services	6.94	7.71	8.79	7.33	6.94
教育文化娱乐服务	Education , Cultural and Recreation Services	9.79	11.62	12.09	15.58	9.79
居住	Residence	9.32	9.70	8.88	8.96	9.32
其他商品和服务	Miscellaneous Goods and Services	3.06	3.52	5.01	5.13	3.06

9-8 主要年份城镇居民家庭年人均购买的主要商品数量
Per Capita Annual Purchases of Major Commodities of Urban Households in Main Years

(抽样调查 Sampled Survey)

项 目	Item	2000	2005	2010	2012
粮食(千克)	Grain (kg)	81.91	88.38	89.76	103.48
鲜菜(千克)	Fresh Vegetables (kg)	90.56	109.45	96.15	100.05
食用植物油(千克)	Edible Vegetable Oil (kg)	9.69	11.01	10.94	11.76
猪肉(千克)	Pork (kg)	5.17	6.37	7.33	6.84
牛肉(千克)	Beef (kg)	3.62	3.51	3.86	5.17
羊肉(千克)	Mutton(kg)	13.06	11.99	9.87	10.77
禽类(千克)	Poultry (kg)	6.11	6.71	8.14	8.37
鲜蛋(千克)	Fresh Eggs (kg)	7.39	7.44	7.91	8.91
水产品(千克)	Aquatic Products (kg)	4.35	4.98	5.27	4.85
鲜乳品(千克)	Fresh Dairy Products (kg)	18.44	26.26	21.80	23.98
鲜瓜果(千克)	Fresh Fruits & Melons(kg)	64.31	66.99	57.36	69.46
服装(件)	Clothes(piece)	6.36	7.51	8.60	9.42
管道天然气(立方米)	Natural Gas (cu.m)	1.93	22.12	39.68	65.10
煤炭(千克)	Coal (kg)	123.78	133.57	84.07	49.78

9-9 主要年份城镇居民家庭平均每百户年底耐用消费品拥有量
Number of Major Durable Consumer Goods Owned Per-100 Urban Households at Year-end in Main Years

项 目	Item	2000	2005	2010	2012
摩托车(辆)	Motorcycle (unit)	8.53	16.04	18.53	14.22
助力车(辆)	Aided Power Bicycle (unit)		2.29	8.60	15.77
家用汽车(辆)	Automobil (unit)	0.82	2.81	8.63	15.58
洗衣机(台)	Washing Machine (unit)	95.48	88.53	93.43	97.63
电冰箱(台)	Refrigerator (unit)	81.76	79.72	90.20	96.99
彩色电视机(台)	Color TV Set (set)	102.57	105.70	105.61	106.72
计算机(台)	Household Computer (set)	5.68	23.86	47.68	65.75
组合音响(套)	Hi-Fi Stereo Component System (set)	17.53	16.10	15.06	15.99
摄相机(架)	Pickug Camera (set)	1.02	3.12	4.57	8.52
照相机(架)	Camera (set)	33.71	37.42	26.83	33.79
钢琴(架)	Piano (set)	1.38	2.23	2.04	2.63
其他中高档乐器(件)	Other Medium and High Grade Musical Instrument (piece)	9.09	5.97	6.54	6.21
微波炉(台)	Oven (unit)	5.39	19.68	34.84	41.58
空调器(台)	Air Conditioner (unit)	2.78	7.02	12.42	13.73
淋浴热水器(台)	Shower (unit)	47.91	59.58	74.27	79.50
消毒碗柜(台)	Disinfectant Machine (unit)		4.56	3.80	5.41
健身器材(台)	Healthy Equipment (unit)	2.35	3.89	2.65	1.36
固定电话(部)	Telephone (unit)	71.69	87.23	82.42	78.33
移动电话(部)	Mobile Phone (unit)	4.81	108.61	159.79	192.21
接入有线电视电视机(台)	Cable Tv (unit)		97.86	88.34	85.32
接入互连网计算机(台)	Internet Computer (unit)		12.43	32.20	51.93
接入互连网移动电话(台)	Internet Mobile Phone (unit)		0.52	7.89	23.37

9-10 按收入等级分城镇居民家庭平均每人全年购买商品数量
Per Capita Annual Purchases of Major Commodities of Urban Households by Level of Income

(2012 年) (抽样调查 Sampled Survey)

项目	Item	总平均 Total Average	最低收入户 Lowest Income Households	#困难户 Poor Households	低收入户 Low Income Households
粮 食(千克)	Grain (kg)	103.48	124.55	133.38	99.14
油脂类(千克)	Oil and Fats (kg)	11.81	11.76	12.41	11.32
食用植物油(千克)	Edible Vegetable Oil (kg)	11.76	11.72	12.37	11.28
肉 类(千克)	Meat (kg)	26.00	21.23	21.04	20.47
猪 肉	Pork	6.84	2.08	1.38	5.75
牛 肉	Beef	5.17	3.60	2.12	4.37
羊 肉	Mutton	10.77	14.37	16.50	8.36
禽 类(千克)	Poultry (kg)	8.37	4.23	3.78	7.08
蛋 类(千克)	Fresh Eggs (kg)	9.55	7.07	7.24	9.47
鱼 (千克)	Fish (kg)	4.44	2.45	1.92	3.55
虾 (千克)	Shrimp (kg)	0.41	0.10	0.07	0.27
鲜 菜(千克)	Fresh Vegetables (kg)	100.05	79.11	74.95	85.32
酒 类(千克)	Liquor (kg)	3.38	0.88	0.68	2.60
白 酒	Liquor	1.07	0.23	0.18	0.79
果 酒	Fruit Wine	0.17	0.03	0.01	0.09
啤 酒	Beer	2.14	0.62	0.49	1.72
鲜 果(千克)	Fresh Fruits (kg)	36.27	23.71	21.38	27.90
鲜 瓜(千克)	Fresh Melon (kg)	33.19	27.07	28.18	24.25
糕 点(千克)	Cake (kg)	4.31	1.95	1.68	3.35
鲜乳品(千克)	Fresh Dairy Products (kg)	23.98	15.70	16.41	19.20
奶 粉(千克)	Milk Powder (kg)	0.24	0.13	0.07	0.12
酸 奶(千克)	Yogurt (kg)	4.30	2.03	1.71	3.35
服 装(件)	Clothing (piece)	9.42	4.76	4.57	7.05
鞋 类(双)	Shoes (pair)	3.00	2.13	2.01	2.66
水(吨)	Water (ton)	28.18	26.69	23.75	17.27
电(度)	Electricity (kw)	328.60	216.51	187.67	282.97
煤 炭(千克)	Coal (kg)	49.78	130.40	126.36	43.53
罐装液化石油气(千克)	Liquefied Gas (kg)	5.08	5.12	6.09	4.65
管道天然气(立方米)	Gas Pipeline (cu.m)	65.10	43.33	49.29	28.45

9-10 续表 Continued

项　　目	Item	中等偏下户 Lower Middle Income Households	中等收入户 Middle Income Households	中等偏上户 Upper Middle Income Households	高收入户 High Income Households	最高收入户 Highest Income Households
粮　食(千克)	Grain (kg)	93.38	100.29	99.40	115.83	101.58
油脂类(千克)	Oil and Fats (kg)	11.37	12.06	12.88	12.74	9.67
食用植物油(千克)	Edible Vegetable Oil (kg)	11.35	11.99	12.79	12.72	9.65
肉　类(千克)	Meat (kg)	23.10	26.63	28.75	34.04	36.42
猪　肉	Pork	6.20	6.60	9.54	10.60	10.46
牛　肉	Beef	4.47	5.68	6.02	6.39	7.20
羊　肉	Mutton	9.16	11.21	9.88	12.89	10.53
禽　类(千克)	Poultry (kg)	7.78	8.00	10.68	11.34	13.10
蛋　类(千克)	Fresh Eggs (kg)	8.64	9.22	11.43	12.24	11.01
鱼　(千克)	Fish (kg)	4.30	4.80	5.10	6.04	6.00
虾　(千克)	Shrimp (kg)	0.42	0.50	0.40	0.61	0.81
鲜　菜(千克)	Fresh Vegetables (kg)	92.47	102.93	111.60	122.53	129.97
酒　类(千克)	Liquor (kg)	3.96	3.91	3.79	4.49	4.37
白　酒	Liquor	1.04	1.33	1.42	1.70	1.14
果　酒	Fruit Wine	0.17	0.21	0.20	0.27	0.30
啤　酒	Beer	2.74	2.37	2.17	2.51	2.92
鲜　果(千克)	Fresh Fruits (kg)	33.40	36.28	41.68	47.25	59.79
鲜　瓜(千克)	Fresh Melon (kg)	30.94	39.28	33.46	40.09	41.84
糕　点(千克)	Cake (kg)	4.13	4.63	5.64	5.26	6.26
鲜乳品(千克)	Fresh Dairy Products (kg)	21.78	25.11	27.58	36.17	29.72
奶　粉(千克)	Milk Powder (kg)	0.28	0.27	0.42	0.16	0.17
酸　奶(千克)	Yogurt (kg)	4.25	4.65	5.15	5.25	6.73
服　装(件)	Clothing (piece)	9.75	8.98	12.17	12.96	12.63
鞋　类(双)	Shoes (pair)	3.04	2.83	3.43	3.52	4.09
水(吨)	Water (ton)	23.66	26.26	31.76	37.87	49.20
电(度)	Electricity (kw)	321.67	353.04	340.57	445.87	422.79
煤　炭(千克)	Coal (kg)	65.27	34.38	18.85	5.99	12.21
罐装液化石油气(千克)	Liquefied Gas (kg)	4.69	5.45	5.74	5.26	4.12
管道天然气(立方米)	Gas Pipeline (cu.m)	47.14	76.28	48.63	118.24	172.66

9-11 按收入等级分城镇居民家庭平均每百户年底耐用消费品拥有量
Ownership of Durable Consumer Goods Per100 Urban Households at Year-end by Level of Income

(2012 年) (抽样调查 Sampled Survey)

项目	Item	总平均 Total Average	最低收入户 Lowest Income Households	#困难户 Poor Households	低收入户 Low Income Households
摩托车(辆)	Motorcycle(unit)	14.22	21.87	15.90	17.42
助力车(辆)	Aided Power Bicycle (unit)	15.77	19.79	15.49	15.55
家用汽车(辆)	Automobile(unit)	15.58	5.70	9.43	9.12
洗衣机(台)	Washing Machine (unit)	97.63	97.82	97.28	95.48
电冰箱(台)	Refrigerator (unit)	96.99	86.18	75.82	91.01
彩色电视机(台)	Color TV (set)	106.72	100.40	100.39	101.78
计算机(台)	Household Computer (set)	65.75	31.55	27.43	57.30
组合音响(套)	Hi-Fi Stereo Sound System (set)	15.99	9.01	5.53	15.20
摄像机(架)	Pickup Camera (set)	8.52	0.40	0.77	7.92
照相机(架)	Camera (set)	33.79	8.77	3.61	24.32
钢琴(架)	Piano (set)	2.63			
其他中高档乐器(件)	Other Medium and High Grade Musical Instrument (piece)	6.21	1.23	0.39	8.03
微波炉(台)	Microwave Oven (unit)	41.58	11.59	5.06	32.22
空调器(台)	Air Conditioner (unit)	13.73	1.84	2.40	7.02
淋浴热水器(台)	Water Heater for Shower (unit)	79.50	50.29	33.79	70.77
消毒碗柜(台)	Disinfectant Machine (unit)	5.41	1.43	0.77	2.45
健身器材(件)	Health Equipment (unit)	1.36			0.20
固定电话(部)	Fixed Telephone (unit)	78.33	65.86	68.86	75.09
移动电话(部)	Mobile Telephone (unit)	192.21	135.61	112.65	188.43
接入有线电视电视机(台)	Cable Tv (unit)	85.32	52.37	42.51	84.90
接入互连网计算机(台)	Internet Computer (unit)	51.93	17.73	15.53	44.75
接入互连网移动电话(台)	Internet Mobile Phone (unit)	23.37	6.88	8.42	15.05

项目	Item	中等偏下户 Lower Middle Income Households	中等收入户 Middle Income Households	中等偏上户 Upper Middle Income Households	高收入户 High Income Households	最高收入户 Highest Income Households
摩托车(辆)	Motorcycle(unit)	11.40	15.57	10.64	7.67	19.74
助力车(辆)	Aided Power Bicycle (unit)	15.87	12.79	16.85	15.70	15.63
家用汽车(辆)	Automobile(unit)	11.57	16.08	20.35	20.69	27.14
洗衣机(台)	Washing Machine (unit)	98.45	97.91	97.02	99.78	96.13
电冰箱(台)	Refrigerator (unit)	96.43	98.32	103.14	103.01	95.52
彩色电视机(台)	Color TV (set)	105.53	107.89	105.60	109.83	118.67
计算机(台)	Household Computer (set)	68.85	68.09	69.07	76.67	84.46
组合音响(套)	Hi-Fi Stereo Sound System (set)	17.14	13.43	18.27	20.38	18.48
摄像机(架)	Pickup Camera (set)	5.32	9.23	12.08	12.61	12.47
照相机(架)	Camera (set)	31.90	39.62	37.40	42.07	48.68
钢琴(架)	Piano (set)	2.31	4.24	4.03	3.11	2.52
其他中高档乐器(件)	Other Medium and High Grade Musical Instrument (piece)	6.47	6.72	6.30	7.57	6.52
微波炉(台)	Microwave Oven (unit)	38.25	44.36	45.71	59.52	59.81
空调器(台)	Air Conditioner (unit)	13.39	14.89	18.34	14.42	23.75
淋浴热水器(台)	Water Heater for Shower (unit)	78.34	79.73	90.00	94.79	87.17
消毒碗柜(台)	Disinfectant Machine (unit)	3.85	6.29	6.48	7.92	9.96
健身器材(件)	Health Equipment (unit)	0.11	2.89	1.39	1.60	3.43
固定电话(部)	Fixed Telephone (unit)	77.12	83.37	77.26	83.63	84.30
移动电话(部)	Mobile Telephone (unit)	203.66	203.42	196.11	196.61	200.01
接入有线电视电视机(台)	Cable Tv (unit)	88.86	87.19	90.90	90.04	96.04
接入互连网计算机(台)	Internet Computer (unit)	56.80	56.30	51.62	61.86	69.13
接入互连网移动电话(台)	Internet Mobile Phone (unit)	26.70	30.29	24.12	21.98	29.88

9-12 按收入等级分城镇居民家庭年末住房情况
Living Conditions of Urban Households by level of Income at Year-end

(2012 年) (抽样调查 Sampled Survey)

项　　目	Item	总平均 Total Average	最低收入户 Lowest Income Households	#困难户 Poor Households	低收入户 Low Income Households
家庭居住人口数(人/户)	Number of Permanent Residents (person/household)	2.91	3.96	4.23	3.21
现住房总建筑面积(平方米/人)	Floor Space of Buildings (Sq.m/person)	29.03	23.89	20.05	23.44
现住房屋总使用面积(平方米/人)	Floor Space of Using(Sq.m/person)	21.78	17.92	15.04	17.58
房屋产权 (%)	House Ownership (%)				
租赁公房	Renting of Publicly-Funded House	1.97	6.59	8.78	4.37
租赁私房	Renting of Private House	3.15	4.79	6.29	5.17
原有私房	Original Private House	8.82	38.94	45.61	12.59
房改私房	Private House Obtained from House Reform	48.07	27.65	24.07	44.28
商品房	Commercial House	33.80	19.95	11.22	29.31
其他	Others	4.19	2.08	4.03	4.27
住宅建筑式样 (%)	Architectural Style of Dwelling (%)				
单栋住宅	Building	0.01			
四居室	Four-Room House	1.37			0.76
三居室	Three-Room House	34.32	29.57	27.03	27.19
二居室	Two-Room House	43.09	16.55	10.93	42.66
一居室	One-Room House	4.46	5.97	3.57	7.32
普通楼房	Ordinary Multi-Storey Building	5.98	2.47	2.60	5.35
平房及其他	A Single-Storey House and Others	10.77	45.45	55.88	16.72
装修状况 (%)	Decoration Situation (%)				
有装修	Decoration	67.59	42.34	36.76	60.22
未装修	Without Decoration	32.41	57.66	63.24	39.78
饮水情况 (%)	Condition of Drinking Water (%)				
# 自来水	Tap Water	98.58	97.19	96.27	96.44
纯净水	Purified　Water	0.28			
井、河水	Well Water、River Water	1.12	2.81	3.73	3.56
用水情况 (%)	By Tap Water Facilities (%)				
独用自来水	Tap Water Owner Per Household	98.78	97.19	96.27	96.13
公用自来水	Public Tap Water	0.07			
井、河水	Well Water、River Water	1.10	2.81	3.73	3.36
卫生设备 (%)	By Health Facilities (%)				
无卫生设备	Without Toilet Room	4.42	11.41	16.78	9.28
有厕所浴室	Bathroom and Toilet Room Owned by Household	79.21	47.55	33.79	70.77
有厕所无浴室	Toilet Room Owned by Household and Without bathroom	15.15	33.20	43.84	18.93
公用	Public Toilet Room	1.23	7.85	5.59	1.01
取暖设备 (%)	By Heating Facilities (%)				
无取暖设备	Without Heating Facilities				
暖气	Warm Gas	89.82	55.62	45.82	84.83
其他	Other	10.14	44.38	54.18	15.17
炊用燃料使用情况 (%)	By Fuel Types (%)				
管道天然气	Pipeline gas	67.26	41.97	31.54	59.99
罐装液化石油气	LPG	23.02	15.62	13.09	24.80
煤炭	Coal	9.51	42.01	54.60	15.21
其他	Others	0.18	0.40	0.78	
通信设备使用情况	By General Equipment Usage				
固定电话(部/百户)	Fixed Telephone (unit /100 Households)	78.33	65.86	68.86	75.09
移动电话(部/百户)	Mobile Telephone (unit /100 Households)	192.21	135.61	112.65	188.43
使用互联网(条/百户)	The use of Internet (unit /100 Households)	51.93	17.73	15.53	44.75

9-12 续表 Continued

项　目	Item	中等偏下户 Lower Middle Income Households	中等收入户 Middle Income Households	中等偏上户 Upper Middle Income Households	高收入户 High Income Households	最高收入户 Highest Income Households
家庭居住人口数(人/户)	Number of Permanent Residents	3.12	2.89	2.60	2.33	2.15
现住房总建筑面积(平方米/人)	Floor Space of Buildings (Sq.m/person)	25.95	28.74	32.58	38.47	40.16
现住房屋总使用面积(平方米/人)	Floor Space of Using(Sq.m/person)	19.47	21.56	24.44	28.86	30.13
房屋产权 (%)	House Ownership (%)					
租赁公房	Renting of Publicly-Funded House	1.91	0.44	1.52		0.47
租赁私房	Renting of Private House	3.40	2.55	3.15	0.95	2.27
原有私房	Original Private House	6.85	3.66	2.96	2.19	4.28
房改私房	Private House Obtained from House Reform	45.37	52.39	53.21	55.47	54.05
商品房	Commercial House	39.52	38.42	34.43	33.91	30.82
其他	Others	2.95	2.54	4.73	7.49	8.10
住宅建筑式样 (%)	Architectural Style of Dwelling (%)					
单栋住宅	Building			0.07		
四居室	Four-Room House	1.71	2.14	1.58	1.03	1.21
三居室	Three-Room House	24.93	34.94	39.34	47.59	42.12
二居室	Two-Room House	52.15	46.61	43.87	43.17	45.24
一居室	One-Room House	5.58	3.41	4.97	1.15	2.01
普通楼房	Ordinary Multi-Storey Building	7.76	7.65	5.51	4.85	5.47
平房及其他	A Single-Storey House and Others	7.87	5.25	4.66	2.21	3.96
装修状况 (%)	Decoration Situation (%)					
有装修	Decoration	74.43	63.66	74.25	76.96	75.01
未装修	Without Decoration	25.57	36.34	25.75	23.04	24.99
饮水情况 (%)	Condition of Drinking Water (%)					
# 自来水	Tap Water	98.09	99.32	99.65	98.62	100.00
纯净水	Purified Water	0.21	0.21	0.23	1.38	
井、河水	Well Water、River Water	1.70	0.47			
用水情况 (%)	By Tap Water Facilities (%)					
独用自来水	Tap Water Owner Per Household	98.20	99.40	100.00	100.00	99.72
公用自来水	Public Tap Water	0.11	0.12			0.28
井、河水	Well Water、River Water	1.70	0.47			
卫生设备 (%)	By Health Facilities (%)					
无卫生设备	Without Toilet Room	4.06	3.64	2.38	1.72	0.28
有厕所浴室	Bathroom and Toilet Room Owned by Household	78.34	79.73	89.47	94.79	88.24
有厕所无浴室	Toilet Room Owned by Household and Without bathroom	17.45	15.88	7.63	3.50	11.49
公用	Public Toilet Room	0.16	0.75	0.52		
取暖设备 (%)	By Heating Facilities (%)					
无取暖设备	Without Heating Facilities					
暖气	Warm Gas	92.24	94.69	96.06	99.21	96.28
其他	Other	7.76	5.12	3.94	0.79	3.72
炊用燃料使用情况 (%)	By Fuel Types (%)					
管道天然气	Pipeline gas	69.26	70.18	70.44	75.03	79.15
罐装液化石油气	LPG	23.79	24.43	25.06	23.14	20.58
煤炭	Coal	6.94	5.09	4.50	0.79	0.28
其他	Others		0.11		1.04	
通信设备使用情况	By General Equipment Usage					
固定电话(部/百户)	Fixed Telephone (unit /100 Households)	77.12	83.37	77.26	83.63	84.30
移动电话(部/百户)	Mobile Telephone (unit /100 Households)	203.66	203.42	196.11	196.61	200.01
使用互联网(条/百户)	The use of Internet (unit /100 Households)	56.80	56.30	51.62	61.86	69.13

9-13 城镇居民家庭就业情况
Employment Conditions of Urban Households

(抽样调查 Sampled Survey)

项　目	Item	2011	2012
调查户数(户)	**Number of Households Surveyed (household)**	**1460**	**1460**
平均每户家庭人口数(人)	**Average Household Size (person)**	**2.91**	**2.91**
有收入者人数	Number of person having income	1.89	1.91
就业人数	Number of person Employed	1.49	1.49
国有经济单位职工人数	Employed Person in State-owned Units	0.85	0.84
城镇集体经济单位职工人数	Employed Person in Collective-owned Units	0.04	0.03
其他各种经济类型单位职工	Employed Person in Other Varions Economic Units	0.09	0.08
城镇个体经营者人员数	Number of Employed Person by himself in Town	0.17	0.18
城镇个体被雇人员数	Number of Employed Person in Town	0.28	0.30
离退休再就业人员	Retired and resigned person reemployed	0.01	0.01
其他就业人员	Person employed in other way	0.05	0.04
离退休人员	Number of Retired and Resinged Person	0.36	0.39
其他有收入者人数	Number of other person having income	0.04	0.04
无收入者人数	Number of person having no income	1.03	1.00

9-14 主要年份农村居民家庭基本情况
Basic Conditions of Rural Households in Main Years

(抽样调查 Sampled Survey)

项　　目	Item	2000	2005	2010	2012
调查户数(户)	**Number of Households Surveyed(household)**	**1500**	**1550**	**1550**	**1550**
调查户人口(人)	**Number of Residents Surveyed (person)**	**7999**	**7315**	**7169**	**6639**
平均每户常住人口	Average Number of Permanent Residents per Household	5.33	4.72	4.63	4.28
平均每户整半劳动力	Average Number of Full/semi Labour Force per Household	3.06	2.92	3.14	2.85
平均每个劳动力负担人口(含本人)	Average Number of Dependents per Labour Force (Including the laborer himself and herself)	1.74	1.62	1.47	1.51
平均每人经营耕地面积(亩)	Average Number of Management of Cultivated Land Area(Mu)	4.20	4.20	4.76	5.76
年内每户新建(购)房屋面积(平方米)	Space of Rooms per Household Newly Built Within the Year (sq.m)	2.03	6.45	3.68	1.69
年底人均居住面积(平方米)	Per Capita Net Living Rooms Space in Rural Area (sq.m)	17.25	21.13	24.00	27.18
平均每人年收入(元)	**Per Capita Annual Income(yuan)**				
总收入	Total Income	3129.35	4604.90	8806.87	13675.26
工资性收入	Income from Wages and Salaries	104.58	195.51	556.26	1007.94
家庭经营收入	Income from Household Operations	2926.75	4252.96	7795.26	11473.81
财产性收入	Income from Properties	40.42	33.87	126.53	170.72
转移性收入	Income from Transfers	57.60	122.56	328.82	1022.80
现金收入	Cash Income	2444.30	3921.17	7517.22	12596.05
工资性收入	Income from Wages and Salaries	104.46	195.51	556.26	1007.94
家庭经营收入	Income from Household Operations	2245.31	3580.44	6525.27	10422.49
财产性收入	Income from Properties	37.87	22.84	106.87	143.04
转移性收入	Income from Transfers	56.66	122.38	328.82	1022.58
平均每人年支出(元)	**Per Capita Annual Expenditures(yuan)**				
总支出	Total Expenditure	2819.77	4302.26	8241.28	13541.28
家庭经营费用支出	Expenditure for Household Operations	1198.23	1928.63	3800.24	6682.45
购置生产性固定资产	Purchase of Productive Fixed Assets	115.19	258.79	568.14	1014.37
税费支出	Taxes and Fees	177.24	14.36	7.83	6.35
生活消费支出	Expenditure on Household Consumption	1236.45	1924.41	3458.14	5245.28
转移性和财产性支出	Expenditure for Transfer and Property	92.66	176.07	406.93	588.86
现金支出	Cash Expenditure	2353.45	3855.34	7464.48	12877.65
家庭经营费用支出	Expenditure for Household Operations	1100.43	1823.95	3643.29	6535.47
购置生产性固定资产	Purchase of Productive Fixed Assets	115.19	258.79	568.14	1014.37
税费支出	Taxes and Fees	177.22	14.36	7.83	6.35
生活消费支出	Expenditure on Household Consumption	871.37	1582.17	2838.29	4728.78
转移性和财产性支出	Expenditure for Transfer and Property	89.24	176.07	406.93	588.72
平均每人年纯收入(元)	**Per Capita Annual Net Income (yuan)**	**1618.08**	**2482.15**	**4642.67**	**6393.70**
工资性收入	Income from Wages and Salaries	104.58	195.51	556.26	1007.94
家庭经营纯收入	Income from Household Business	1451.33	2140.76	3649.98	4239.16
财产性收入	Income from Properties	40.43	33.87	126.52	170.72
转移性收入	Income from Transfers	21.74	112.01	309.91	975.88

9-15 农村居民家庭人均年总收入、纯收入和构成

Per Capita Annual Gross and Net Income and Its Composition of Rural Households

单位：元　　(抽样调查 Sampled Survey)　　(yuan)

项　目	Item	2011	2012	构成(%) Composition 2011	构成(%) Composition 2012
全年总收入	**Annual Gross Income**	**11590.94**	**13675.26**	**100**	**100**
工资性收入	Income from Wages and Salaries	804.73	1007.94	6.94	7.37
家庭经营收入	Income from Household Operations	9988.44	11473.81	86.18	83.90
财产性收入	Income from Transfers	147.14	170.72	1.27	1.25
转移性收入	Income from Properties	650.63	1022.80	5.61	7.48
全年总支出	**Annual Gross Expenditure**	**11250.23**	**13541.28**	**100**	**100**
#家庭经营费用支出	Expenditure for Household Business	5620.97	6682.45	49.96	49.35
生活消费支出	Expenditure for Consumption	4397.82	5245.28	39.09	38.74
全年纯收入	**Annual Net Income**	**5442.15**	**6393.70**	**100**	**100**
工资性收入	Income from Wages and Salaries	804.73	1007.94	14.79	15.76
家庭经营纯收入	Income from Household Operations	3887.15	4239.16	71.43	66.30
财产性纯收入	Income from Transfers	147.14	170.72	2.70	2.67
转移性收入	Income from Properties	603.13	975.88	11.08	15.26

9-16 主要年份农村居民家庭平均每人总收入和纯收入

Per Capita Annual Gross and Net Income of Rural Households in Main Years

单位：元　　(抽样调查 Sampled Survey)　　(yuan)

项　目	Item	2000	2005	2010	2012
总 收 入	**Gross Income**	**3129.35**	**4604.9**	**8806.87**	**13675.26**
基本收入	Basic Income	3031.33	4448.47	8351.52	12481.75
工资性收入	Income from Wages and Salaries	104.58	195.51	556.26	1007.94
家庭经营收入	Income from Household Operations	2926.75	4252.96	7795.26	11473.81
财产性收入	Income from Transfers	98.02	156.43	126.53	170.72
转移性收入	Income from Properties			328.82	1022.80
纯 收 入	**Net Income**	**1618.08**	**2482.15**	**4642.67**	**6393.70**
基本收入	Basic Income	1555.91	2336.27	4206.24	5247.11
工资性收入	Income from Wages and Salaries	104.58	195.51	556.26	1007.94
家庭经营纯收入	Income from Household Operations	1451.33	2140.76	3649.98	4239.16
农业收入	Farming	1109.39	1618.33	2670.60	3048.71
林业收入	Forestry	22.51	61.65	172.01	171.37
牧业收入	Animal Husbandry	171.18	245.10	469.08	553.95
渔业收入	Fishery				0.06
工业收入	Industry	6.35	18.84	34.65	21.12
建筑业收入	Construction	4.31	15.22	22.71	70.25
交通、运输和邮电业收入	Transportation, Post and Telecommunications Services	26.48	30.06	94.88	94.71
批发和零售贸易业、饮食业收入	Wholesale, Retail Trades and Catering Services	23.8	86.86	128.47	200.58
社会服务业收入	Services Trades	15.01	9.43	22.70	59.95
文教卫生业收入	Cultural, Education, Medicines and Medical Services			10.53	8.08
其他行业收入	Others	72.30	55.27	24.36	10.38
转移性和财产性收入	Income from Transfers and Properties	62.17	145.88	436.43	1146.59

9-17 主要年份农村居民家庭人均主要消费品消费量
Per Capita Consumption of Major Consumer Goods of Rural Households in Main Years

单位:千克　　(抽样调查 Sampled Survey)　　(kg)

项　目	Item	2000	2005	2010	2012
粮食(原粮)	Grain(Unprocessed)	244.83	235.66	236.10	227.62
#小 麦	Wheat	199.83	188.38	191.28	181.89
稻 谷	Rice	15.19	19.93	23.20	32.11
豆类及豆制品	Soybeans and Processed Products	0.50	0.83	0.56	0.44
蔬　菜	Fresh Vegetable	89.24	67.89	77.72	77.13
食　油	Edible Oil	9.64	10.90	10.74	12.85
#植物油	Vegetable Oil	9.56	10.79	10.69	12.82
肉禽及制品	Meats,Poultry and Processed Products	12.41	14.31	15.38	20.80
#猪 肉	Pork	1.95	0.67	1.04	1.33
牛 肉	Beef	1.95	2.56	2.32	4.38
羊 肉	Mutton	7.03	8.99	9.18	11.70
家 禽	Poultry	1.36	1.70	2.27	3.00
蛋及制品	Eggs and Processed Products	1.20	1.00	1.92	3.62
食　糖	Sugar	0.42	0.45	0.49	0.52
酒	Liquor	1.12	1.27	1.06	1.91
水果及制品	Fruits and Processed Products	46.89	34.81	25.30	22.45
茶　叶	Tea	0.37	0.45	0.43	0.57

9-18 主要年份农村居民家庭平均每百户耐用消费品拥有量
Number of Durable Consumer Goods Owned by Per100 Rural Households in Main Years

(抽样调查 Sampled Survey)

项　目	Item	2000	2005	2010	2012
洗衣机(台)	Washing Machine (unit)	20.87	28.26	47.94	77.35
电冰箱(台)	Refrigerator (unit)	9.93	20.13	43.48	68.77
空调机(台)	Air Conditioner (unit)		0.39	0.65	1.35
抽油烟机(台)	Exhaust Fan(unit)	1.13	1.23	2.77	5.74
自行车(辆)	Bicycle (unit)	136.60	80.97	78.52	66.19
摩托车(辆)	Motorcycle (unit)	18.33	45.42	62.84	79.87
电话机(部)	Telephone(unit)	15.07	36.26	38.97	29.87
移动电话(部)	Mobile phone (unit)	0.33	21.29	84.32	147.29
黑白电视机(台)	Black and White TV (set)	59.33	35.16	11.61	4.19
彩色电视机(台)	Color TV (set)	31.87	61.81	89.87	96.90
照像机(架)	Camera (set)	2.20	3.23	3.29	3.42
影碟机(台)	Video Disc Player (set)	3.60		31.94	34.00
微波炉(台)	Microwave Oven (unit)			1.81	4.65

9-19 农村居民人均生活消费支出及构成
Composition of Per Capita Living Expenditure of Rural Households

单位：元　　(抽样调查 Sampled Survey)　　(yuan)

项　　目	Item	2011	2012	构成(%) Composition(%) 2011	构成(%) Composition(%) 2012
生活消费支出	**Expenditure for Consumption**	**4397.82**	**5245.28**	**100**	**100**
食　品	Food	1589.46	1890.96	36.14	36.05
#主　食	Staple Food	422.70	459.32	9.61	8.76
副食及其他食品	Non-staple Food and others	992.34	1149.56	22.56	21.92
衣　着	Clothing	372.10	429.92	8.46	8.20
居　住	Residence	1025.28	1298.44	23.32	24.75
家庭设备、用品及服务	Household Facilities,Articles and Services	198.57	219.10	4.52	4.18
交通和通讯	Transport and Communications	530.59	646.37	12.06	12.32
文教娱乐用品及服务	Cultural, Education ,Recreation and Services	229.66	206.15	5.22	3.93
医疗保健	Health Care and Medical Services	376.87	444.15	8.57	8.47
其他商品和服务	Other Commodities and Services	75.28	110.20	1.71	2.10

9-20 农村居民家庭平均每百户耐用消费品拥有量
Number of Durable Consumer Goods Owned by Per100 Rural Households

(抽样调查 Sampled Survey)

项　　目	Item	2011	2012
自行车(辆)	Bicycle (unit)	62.58	66.19
黑白电视机(台)	Black and White TV (set)	4.58	4.19
彩色电视机(台)	Color TV (set)	99.03	96.90
抽油烟机(台)	Exhaust Fan(unit)	4.58	5.74
照像机(架)	Camera (set)	2.90	3.42
移动电话(部)	Mobile phone (unit)	141.87	147.29
洗衣机(台)	Washing Machine (unit)	72.77	77.35
电冰箱(台)	Refrigerator (unit)	63.94	68.77
摩托车(辆)	Motorcycle (unit)	77.23	79.87
影碟机(台)	Video Disc Player (set)	31.48	34.00
微波炉(台)	Microwave Oven (unit)	3.87	4.65

9-21 农村居民家庭人均商品性和自给性生活消费品支出
Per Capita Self-Sufficiency and Consumption on Commodity Goods of Living Expenditure in Rural Households

(抽样调查 Sampled Survey)

项目	Item	2011			2012		
		合计 Total	货币性 In Money	实物性 In Kind	合计 Total	货币性 In Money	实物性 In Kind
生活消费支出合计(元/人)	**Expenditure for Consumption (yuan/person)**	**4397.82**	**3889.69**	**508.13**	**5245.28**	**4728.78**	**516.51**
食　品	Food	1589.46	1138.12	451.34	1890.96	1391.06	499.90
衣　着	Clothing	372.10	368.37	3.73	429.92	426.57	3.35
居　住	Residence	1025.28	976.36	48.92	1298.44	1289.21	9.23
家庭设备、用品及服务	Household Appliances and Services	198.57	194.43	4.14	219.10	215.07	4.03
交通和通讯	Transportation and Communications	530.59	530.59		646.37	646.37	
文教娱乐用品及服务	Cultural, Education and Recreational Articles and Services	229.66	229.66		206.15	206.15	229.66
医疗保健	Health Care and Medical Services	376.87	376.87		444.15	444.15	
其他商品和服务	Other Commodities and Services	75.28	75.28		110.20	110.20	
生活消费支出构成(%)	**Composition of Living Expenditures (%)**	**100**	**100**	**100**	**100**	**100**	**100**
食　品	Food	36.14	29.26	88.82	36.05	29.42	96.79
衣　着	Clothing	8.46	9.47	0.73	8.20	9.02	0.65
居　住	Residence	23.32	25.10	9.64	24.75	27.26	1.79
家庭设备、用品及服务	Household Facilities,Articles and Services	4.52	5.00	0.81	4.18	4.55	0.78
交通和通讯	Transportation and Communications	12.06	13.64		12.32	13.67	
文教娱乐用品及服务	Cultural, Education and Recreational Articles and Services	5.22	5.90		3.93	4.36	
医疗保健	Health Care and Medical Services	8.57	9.69		8.47	9.39	
其他商品和服务	Other Commodities and Services	1.71	1.94		2.10	2.33	
生活消费支出中货币性和实物性比重(%)	**Percentage of Expenditure for Consumption in Money and Kind (%)**	**100**	**88.45**	**11.55**	**100**	**90.15**	**9.85**
食　品	Food	100	71.60	28.40	100	73.56	26.44
衣　着	Clothing	100	99.00	1.00	100	99.22	0.78
居　住	Residence	100	95.23	4.77	100	99.29	0.71
家庭设备、用品及服务	Household Facilities,Articles and Services	100	97.92	2.08	100	98.16	1.84
交通和通讯	Transportation and Communications	100			100		
文教娱乐用品及服务	Cultural, Education and Recreational Articles and Services	100			100		
医疗保健	Health Care and Medical Services	100			100		
其他商品和服务	Other Commodities and Services	100			100		

9-22 分地区农村居民家庭人均总收入和纯收入

单位：元 (2012 年)

项目 Item	自治区 Autonomous Region	乌鲁木齐市 Urumqi City	吐鲁番地区 Turpan Administrative Offices	哈密地区 Hami [Kumul] Administrative Offices
调查县、市(个) **Number of Counties and Cities Surveyed (unit)**	**33**	**3**	**2**	**2**
调查户数(户) **Number of Households Surveyed (household)**	**1550**	**300**	**180**	**180**
常住人口(人) **Number of Permanent Residents In the Households Surveyed (person)**	**6639**	**1095**	**827**	**628**
总收入 **Annual Gross Income**	**13675.26**	**17563.74**	**12411.13**	**13190.19**
工资性收入 Income from Wages and Salaries	1007.94	2622.52	1254.49	2424.30
在非企业组织中劳动得到的 From Non-enterprise Organization	197.49	321.99	167.16	593.83
在本地企业中劳动得到的 From Local Enterprise	489.65	2239.59	895.38	973.51
常住人口外出从业得到的 Out of Migrant Workers	320.80	60.94	191.95	856.96
家庭经营收入 Income From Household Business	11473.81	13944.41	10168.75	9004.78
农业收入 Farming	8327.85	7591.85	7365.62	6051.40
林业收入 Forestry	248.75	165.42	9.44	32.25
牧业收入 Animal Husbandry	1965.10	4191.68	1347.91	2149.84
渔业收入 Fishery	0.06			
工业收入 Industry	78.12			8.17
建筑业收入 Construction	146.08			87.51
交通、运输和邮电业收入 Transportation, Post and Telecommunications Services	236.41	1184.18	137.52	194.12
批发和零售贸易、餐饮业收入 Wholesale, Retail Trades and Catering Services	315.47	676.55	1239.92	377.73
社会服务业收入 Social Services	84.31	134.73	66.44	61.47
文教卫生业收入 Cultural, Education, Medicines and Medical Services	31.36		1.90	
其他家庭经营收入 Others	39.75			40.60
财产性收入 Income from Properties	170.72	344.12	314.68	313.49
#利 息 Interest	2.67	9.34		11.41
租 金 Rent	24.65	164.62	84.30	76.16
转移性收入 Income from Transfer	1022.80	652.69	673.22	1447.61
全年家庭人均纯收入 **Annual Net Income**	**6393.70**	**10031.55**	**7105.35**	**8389.48**

Per Capita Annual Gross and Net Income of Rural Households by Region

(抽样调查 Sampled Survey) (yuan)

	昌吉回族自治州 Changji Hui Autonomous Prefecture	伊犁州直属县(市) Counties (Cities) Direct Under Ili Prefecture	塔城地区 Tacheng [Tarbagatai] Administrative Offices	阿勒泰地区 Altay Administrative Offices	博尔塔拉蒙古自治州 Bortala Mongol Autonomous Prefecture	巴音郭楞蒙古自治州 Bayangol Mongol Autonomous Prefecture	阿克苏地区 Aksu Administrative Offices	克孜勒苏克尔克孜自治州 Kizilsu Kirgiz Autonomous Prefecture	喀什地区 Kashgar [Kaxgar] Adminis-trative Offices	和田地区 Hotan Adminis-trative Offices
	4	**5**	**5**	**6**	**2**	**4**	**6**	**3**	**7**	**4**
	400	**240**	**200**	**300**	**200**	**400**	**410**	**240**	**560**	**400**
	1314	**1031**	**717**	**1179**	**706**	**1577**	**1761**	**1189**	**2625**	**1700**
	34396.55	**15353.08**	**33489.35**	**12196.28**	**32581.92**	**16324.78**	**12483.47**	**4812.29**	**8559.03**	**6490.56**
	1925.18	1770.37	739.51	924.73	939.30	1144.97	597.72	663.04	769.42	930.51
	133.99	589.05	164.65	322.43	339.88	346.21	176.44	87.63	105.25	202.82
	1633.14	881.64	484.22	547.97	445.97	702.06	402.65	151.07	283.32	242.91
	158.04	299.68	90.65	54.33	153.45	96.70	18.62	424.34	380.85	484.78
	30743.15	11928.44	31804.10	10273.84	30596.76	13812.37	11060.37	3454.08	6947.51	4541.68
	26824.75	7140.68	28841.56	6241.33	27480.22	10876.97	8516.34	1598.63	4833.02	1855.01
	24.16	78.41	13.23	15.21	43.86	77.71	573.59	73.79	226.91	414.17
	2773.39	3311.06	1919.92	3431.35	2334.17	2458.99	1789.05	1251.92	1366.70	1282.89
				0.50			0.05			
	52.93	16.29		144.16	2.10	17.26	20.78	45.08		246.32
		20.30	707.39	25.06	9.95		11.71	0.52	88.93	176.39
	784.25	489.04	105.09	236.86	351.50	165.82	22.78	274.39	116.28	197.41
	222.63	568.21	21.46	130.53	371.54	195.49	109.96	168.89	114.12	235.26
	53.38	54.80	11.89	20.88		14.19	5.52	28.13	100.98	124.28
	2.33	224.69	21.63							0.12
	5.35	24.96	0.11	21.82	0.47	5.96	10.26	12.72	100.25	9.82
	451.68	258.55	283.76	238.47	368.65	612.77	121.30	2.05	56.99	21.56
	21.21		13.09		21.79		1.74		0.27	
	96.97	32.88		43.73	34.73	34.62	1.30		0.04	
	1276.54	1395.72	661.98	759.24	677.21	754.67	704.08	693.13	785.11	996.81
	11470.40	**7449.66**	**9895.84**	**6242.86**	**9433.55**	**9935.97**	**6891.39**	**3081.37**	**4708.23**	**4260.03**

9-23 分地区农村居民家庭平均每人总支出

单位：元 (2012 年)

项目 Item	自治区 Autonomous Region	乌鲁木齐市 Urumqi City	吐鲁番地区 Turpan Administrative Offices	哈密地区 Hami [Kumul] Administrative Offices	昌吉回族自治州 Changji Hui Autonomous Prefecture
全年总支出 **Annual Total Expenditure**	**13541.28**	**16652.21**	**12166.25**	**12424.48**	**35971.97**
家庭经营费用支出 **Expenditure for Household Business**	**6682.45**	**6730.61**	**4466.57**	**4027.86**	**21161.75**
农业生产 Farming	4989.68	3576.44	2663.85	2554.47	18900.21
林业生产 Forestry	76.76	44.52	6.58	10.78	58.75
牧业生产 Animal Husbandry	1242.77	2589.53	1234.31	1213.10	1584.14
渔业生产 Fishery	…		0.06		0.06
工业生产 Industry	36.88			7.03	12.14
建筑业生产 Construction	53.51	0.07		26.67	4.29
交通、运输和邮电业支出 Transportation, Post and Telecommunications Services	105.73	308.82	49.43	93.40	400.28
批发和零售贸易、餐饮业支出 Wholesale, Retail Trades and Catering Services	105.23	181.77	486.00	82.47	171.86
社会服务业支出 Social Services	22.34	24.53	25.41	29.40	28.59
文教卫生业支出 Cultural, Education, Medicines and Medical Services	20.69	0.53	0.28		
其他经营支出 Others	28.86	4.41	0.65	10.53	1.43
购置生产用固定资产支出 **Expenditure for Productive Fixed Assets**	**1014.37**	**585.53**	**710.74**	**399.67**	**2275.94**
税费支出 **Taxes and Fee**	**6.35**	**4.48**	**3.57**		**14.54**
生活消费支出 **Expenditure for Consumption**	**5245.28**	**8398.49**	**6132.65**	**7350.15**	**10410.74**
食品 Food	1890.96	2753.71	2393.04	2180.03	3191.94
#主食 Staple Food	459.32	506.73	501.64	349.17	397.92
副食及其他食品 Non-staple Food and Others	1149.56	1742.57	1620.22	1530.56	1829.50
衣着 Clothing	429.92	695.25	568.12	732.49	778.28
居住 Residence	1298.44	2151.57	930.57	1646.04	2204.62
家庭设备、用品及服务 Household Facilities, Articles and Services	219.10	381.63	254.07	394.77	426.79
交通和通讯 Transportation and Communications	646.37	1021.60	841.50	1018.69	1833.31
文化教育娱乐用品及服务 Cultural, Education and Recreational Articles and Services	206.15	398.24	349.75	348.20	700.89
医疗保健 Health Care and Medical Services	444.15	852.89	717.23	875.93	950.99
其他商品和服务 Other Commodities and Services	110.20	143.59	78.36	154.00	323.92

Per Capita Total Expenditure of Rural Household by Region

(抽样调查 Sampled Survey) (yuan)

伊犁州直属县(市) Counties (Cities) Direct Under Ili Prefecture	塔城地区 Tacheng [Tarbagatai] Administrative Offices	阿勒泰地区 Altay Administrative Offices	博尔塔拉蒙古自治州 Bortala Mongol Autonomous Prefecture	巴音郭楞蒙古自治州 Bayangol Mongol Autonomous Prefecture	阿克苏地区 Aksu Administrative Offices	克孜勒苏克尔克孜自治州 Kizilsu Kirgiz Autonomous Prefecture	喀什地区 Kashgar [Kaxgar] Administrative Offices	和田地区 Hotan Administrative Offices
17834.45	**37593.67**	**11974.68**	**35132.84**	**12668.85**	**12999.24**	**4133.08**	**7948.36**	**6330.03**
7169.17	**22392.60**	**4990.51**	**22435.85**	**5899.20**	**5038.78**	**1476.30**	**3658.64**	**2038.42**
3748.62	20817.34	3495.35	20082.92	4444.73	3672.11	688.15	2678.47	779.25
32.39	52.56	7.96	69.38	17.45	150.79	14.52	45.76	92.03
2665.18	1066.87	1326.70	1588.37	1330.99	1154.14	598.98	754.60	693.59
		0.10	0.41		0.02			
2.30		29.00		3.70	9.59	53.39	0.04	141.51
7.08	367.98	23.89	35.10		4.01		19.44	100.81
162.35	62.09	69.57	280.25	52.15	3.81	98.06	39.05	57.72
381.77	6.83	32.48	343.84	40.66	20.81	21.77	60.45	98.51
18.81	2.73	2.39		7.83	18.82		27.13	23.76
148.60	16.11		25.14		0.84	0.42	0.84	
2.07	0.08	3.07	10.45	1.70	3.84	1.00	32.86	51.25
807.13	**3619.93**	**749.26**	**624.24**	**528.62**	**1044.37**	**187.46**	**361.62**	**334.01**
	6.66		**12.95**	**1.73**	**23.12**		**0.45**	**1.76**
8849.92	**10289.79**	**5670.53**	**10410.66**	**5846.03**	**6579.16**	**2311.53**	**3790.70**	**3819.88**
2193.73	2783.65	1835.08	2966.54	2239.93	1878.79	1094.92	1561.96	1406.90
472.24	378.71	424.89	515.58	532.55	418.71	402.19	539.29	364.45
1324.91	1590.98	1093.44	1689.38	1402.27	1167.21	682.38	1012.26	923.18
517.76	861.86	651.22	700.14	503.11	631.24	177.50	391.62	363.10
3511.29	2258.46	982.55	2995.89	1139.36	1914.21	493.64	972.03	1143.93
382.66	465.38	259.57	463.14	245.39	272.31	66.32	132.87	219.95
921.37	2092.18	919.49	1570.07	873.56	943.81	222.97	302.66	387.26
510.68	578.34	196.73	776.20	213.37	154.25	28.40	59.36	34.09
607.33	960.83	750.52	617.22	573.53	612.45	165.36	240.65	223.93
205.10	289.09	75.35	321.48	57.78	172.10	2.97	28.33	40.72

9-24 分地区农村居民家庭人均现金收支

单位：元 (2012 年)(抽样调查 Sampled Survey)

项目	Item	自治区 Autonomous Region	乌鲁木齐市 Urumqi City	吐鲁番地区 Turpan Administrative Offices	哈密地区 Hami [Kumul] Administrative Offices
期内现金收入	**Annual Total Income In Cash**	**12596.05**	**17141.05**	**12323.61**	**12657.97**
工资性收入	Income from Wages and Salaries	1007.94	2622.52	1254.49	2423.99
在非企业组织中劳动得到的	From Non-enterprise Organization	197.49	321.99	167.16	593.52
在本地企业中劳动得到的	From Local Enterprises	489.65	2239.59	895.38	973.51
常住人口外出从业得到的	Out of Migrant Workers	320.80	60.94	191.95	856.96
家庭经营收入	Income of Household Operation	10422.49	13532.50	10207.79	8493.35
农业现金收入	Cash Income from Farming	7423.52	7336.82	7670.02	5687.46
#出售农产品收入	Sale of Agricultural Products	7037.59	7253.87	7447.56	5593.55
林业现金收入	Cash Income from Forestry	234.65	165.42	9.44	32.25
#出售林业产品收入	Sale of Forestry Products	233.21	165.42	9.37	31.31
牧业现金收入	Cash Income from Animal Husbandry	1832.23	4034.81	1082.56	2002.38
#出售牧业产品收入	Sale of Animal Husbandry Products	1807.53	4024.96	1068.88	1929.05
工业收入	Income from Industry	78.12			8.17
#出售工业产品收入	Sale of Industrial Products	39.49			
工业服务性收入	Income from Industrial services	38.63			8.17
建筑业收入	Income from Construction	146.08			87.51
#出售建筑业产品收入	Sale of Constructive Products	0.30			0.75
建筑业服务性收入	Income from Constructive services	145.78			86.75
交通、运输、邮电业收入	Income from Transport,Post and Telecommunication Servies	236.41	1184.18	137.52	194.12
批零贸易业、饮食业收入	Income from Wholesale and Retail Trades and Catering Servies	315.47	676.55	1239.92	377.73
社会服务业收入	Income from Social Services	84.31	134.73	66.44	61.47
文教卫生业收入	Income from Culture,Edcuation and Health Care	31.36		1.90	
其他行业收入	Others	39.75			40.56
财产性收入	Property Income	143.04	344.12	192.36	296.91
#利 息	Interest	2.67	9.34		11.41
租 金	Rent	24.65	164.62	84.30	76.16
转移性收入	Transfer Income	1022.58	641.91	668.97	1443.71
非收入所得	**Non-income Gain**	**4546.01**	**3173.45**	**3119.37**	**4421.85**
#从银行信用社得到的贷款	Credit	2183.53	436.93	1615.53	1263.58
借入款	Borrowed Money	804.15	247.68	570.39	527.26
收回借出款	Recall Loaned Money	145.15	295.20	3.21	431.28
从银行信用社取回存款	Take Deposit back	621.30	278.75	238.48	916.07
出售财产所得款	Sold Property	263.44	96.93	364.80	1.84
期内现金支出	**Annual Expenditure in Cash**	**12877.65**	**16286.39**	**11745.04**	**11888.33**
生产费用支出	Producing Expenditure	7553.79	7319.38	5179.65	4345.22
#家庭经营费用支出	Expenditure for Household Business	6535.47	6731.02	4460.50	3918.34
农业生产支出	Farming	4954.11	3578.77	2663.85	2521.00
林业生产支出	Forestry	76.76	44.52	6.49	10.78
牧业生产支出	Animal Husbandry	1131.35	2587.60	1228.33	1137.06

Per Capita Income and Expenditure in Cash of Rural Household by Region

(yuan)

昌吉回族自治州 Changji Hui Autonomous Prefecture	伊犁州直属县(市) Counties (Cities) Direct Under Ili Prefecture	塔城地区 Tacheng [Tarbagatai] Adminis-trative Offices	阿勒泰地区 Altay Adminis-trative Offices	博尔塔拉蒙古自治州 Bortala Mongol Autonomous Prefecture	巴音郭楞蒙古自治州 Bayangol Mongol Autonomous Prefecture	阿克苏地区 Aksu Adminis-trative Offices	克孜勒苏克尔克孜自治州 Kizilsu Kirgiz Autonomous Prefecture	喀什地区 Kashgar [Kaxgar] Adminis-trative Offices	和田地区 Hotan Adminis-trative Offices
32078.68	**14346.81**	**33117.09**	**11407.36**	**32028.39**	**15853.06**	**10427.27**	**4096.78**	**7375.07**	**5096.96**
1909.71	1770.37	739.51	924.73	939.30	1144.97	597.72	663.04	769.42	930.51
124.48	589.05	164.65	322.43	339.88	346.21	176.44	87.63	105.25	202.82
1627.18	881.64	484.22	547.97	445.97	702.06	402.65	151.07	283.32	242.91
158.04	299.68	90.65	54.33	153.45	96.70	18.62	424.34	380.85	484.78
28425.94	11012.14	31440.41	9521.87	30107.44	13491.54	9022.81	2739.45	5773.44	3156.38
24899.20	6279.22	28562.98	5725.95	27454.39	10758.97	6726.32	998.02	3757.15	804.91
23295.05	5893.78	27305.85	5120.71	26651.32	10346.33	6013.90	866.82	3463.46	720.16
23.97	102.11	13.23	14.55	43.86	75.27	452.15	73.79	216.12	362.75
23.90	101.99	13.23	2.43	43.86	75.27	448.16	73.79	214.36	361.46
2387.27	3232.52	1834.81	3195.51	1870.68	2258.60	1662.95	1137.91	1279.31	999.13
2385.08	3142.61	1831.56	3120.08	1870.68	2258.60	1637.34	1137.91	1268.03	989.69
52.93	16.29		144.16	2.10	17.26	20.78	45.08		246.32
43.24	1.48		36.65	2.10	3.62		0.97		152.28
9.68	14.81		107.51		13.64	20.78	44.11		94.04
	20.30	707.39	25.06	9.95		11.71	0.52	88.93	176.39
				0.56				0.95	
	20.30	707.39	25.06	9.39		11.71	0.52	87.97	176.39
784.25	489.04	105.09	236.86	351.50	165.82	22.78	274.39	116.28	197.41
222.63	568.21	21.46	130.53	371.54	195.49	109.96	168.89	114.12	235.26
53.38	54.80	11.89	20.88		14.19	5.52	28.13	100.98	124.28
2.33	224.69	21.63							0.12
	24.96		21.82		5.96	10.26	12.72	100.25	9.82
527.16	168.57	275.18	202.17	304.70	461.87	102.89	1.16	47.35	13.26
21.21		13.09		21.79		1.74		0.27	
96.97	32.88		43.73	34.73	34.62	1.30		0.04	
1215.88	1395.72	661.98	758.59	676.94	754.67	703.86	693.13	784.86	996.81
17661.79	**4571.24**	**15867.39**	**4241.75**	**7887.84**	**2949.70**	**4723.44**	**719.10**	**1838.43**	**686.98**
10572.20	2009.99	8590.97	3119.37	4432.92	2389.66	2523.89	355.34	1338.95	436.35
2015.23	966.93	4166.11	349.83	1296.50	131.43	435.08	186.91	74.53	78.32
709.79	103.41	293.70	94.55	254.26	22.38	83.18			22.28
2498.50	608.94	2172.04	431.65	1397.66	164.99	778.67	4.27	233.94	2.47
586.90	198.02	352.01	20.41	81.42	86.74	529.49	48.02	43.39	61.27
35300.44	**17311.70**	**37314.46**	**11429.01**	**34958.84**	**12224.42**	**12549.70**	**3620.21**	**7117.77**	**5631.79**
23509.88	7802.67	25953.29	5644.22	22972.78	6360.02	6034.60	1498.66	3793.76	2262.08
21021.88	6977.08	22333.36	4888.34	22347.14	5831.40	4990.10	1311.20	3432.14	1928.07
18876.52	3737.00	20817.34	3484.83	20082.92	4410.73	3671.85	644.42	2620.77	736.56
58.75	32.39	52.56	7.96	69.38	17.45	150.79	14.52	45.76	92.03
1467.95	2484.71	1007.62	1235.05	1499.65	1297.18	1105.72	477.62	585.79	625.92

9-24 续表

单位：元

项　目	Item	自治区 Autonomous Region	乌鲁木齐市 Urumqi City	吐鲁番地区 Turpan Administrative Offices	哈密地区 Hami [Kumul] Administrative Offices
渔业生产支出	Fishery	…		0.06	
工业生产支出	Industry	36.88			7.03
建筑业生产支出	Construction	53.51	0.07		26.67
交通运输支出	Transportation	105.73	308.82	49.43	93.40
批发和零售贸易、餐饮业	Wholesale Retail Trades and Catering services	105.23	181.77	486.00	82.47
社会服务业支出	Social Services	22.34	24.53	25.41	29.40
文教卫生业	Cultural, Education, Medicines and Medical Services	20.69	0.53	0.28	
其他经营支出	Others	28.87	4.41	0.65	10.53
购置生产性固定资产支出	Expenditure for Productive Fixed Assets	1014.37	585.53	710.74	399.67
税费支出	Taxes and Fee	6.35	4.48	3.57	
生活消费支出	Expenditure for Consumption	4728.78	8032.32	5717.51	6923.57
财产性支出	Expenditure for Properties	9.86	34.87	80.86	0.47
转移性支出	Expenditure for Transfers	578.86	895.35	763.45	619.07
非消费性现金付出	**Expenditure for Non-consumption**	**3376.81**	**1997.66**	**2256.10**	**3507.34**
#归还银行信用社贷款	Loan Returned to Bank	1552.89	705.01	781.25	939.30
借出款	Lending Money	75.22	54.64	86.39	109.77
归还借款	Return Borrowed Money	607.58	307.82	501.33	690.13
存入银行信用社	Deposit	604.46	107.69	208.93	614.17
期末金融资产余额	**Balance of Financial Assets in Year-end**	**3475.36**	**6476.43**	**3964.89**	**4862.61**
#手存现金	Cash	961.67	879.76	1184.61	1572.21
银行存款	Deposit	2503.68	5592.26	2780.28	3270.00
期末债务余额	**Balance of Debt in Year-end**	**1630.99**	**4364.35**	**2749.47**	**2391.28**
#银行、信用社贷款	Loan from Bank and Credit Cooperatives	1183.12	3539.48	1801.51	1575.36
个人借(欠)款	Borrowed Money from Individual	425.10	604.20	773.16	806.51
生活消费支出的现金	**Expenditure for Consumption**	**4728.78**	**8032.32**	**5717.51**	**6923.57**
食　品	Food	1391.06	2387.55	1979.36	1753.45
#主　食	Staple Food	241.47	505.56	501.28	272.62
副　食	Non-staple Food	867.50	1377.58	1206.89	1180.51
衣 着	Clothing	426.57	695.25	566.73	732.49
居 住	Residence	1289.21	2151.57	930.57	1646.04
家庭设备、用品及服务	Household Facilities, Articles and Services	215.07	381.63	254.00	394.77
交通和通讯	Transportation and Communications	646.37	1021.60	841.50	1018.69
文化教育、娱乐用品及服务	Cultural, Education and Recreational Articles and Services	206.15	398.24	349.75	348.20
#文化教育、娱乐用品	Cultural, Education and Recreational Articles	63.57	136.54	56.28	75.91
文化教育、娱乐服务	Cultural, Education and Recreational Services	142.58	261.70	293.48	272.29
医疗保健	Health Care and Medical Services	444.15	852.89	717.23	875.93
其他商品和服务	Other Commodities and Services	110.20	143.59	78.36	154.00
在生活消费支出的现金中	Expenditure for Consumption				
商品性支出	Commodities	3469.78	5838.54	3923.05	4909.03
服务支出	Services	1258.99	2193.78	1794.46	2014.54

Continued

(yuan)

昌吉回族自治州 Changji Hui Autonomous Prefecture	伊犁州直属县(市) Counties (Cities) Direct Under Ili Prefecture	塔城地区 Tacheng [Tarbagatai] Adminis-trative Offices	阿勒泰地区 Altay Adminis trative Offices	博尔塔拉蒙古自治州 Bortala Mongol Autonomous Prefecture	巴音郭楞蒙古自治州 Bayangol Mongol Autonomous Prefecture	阿克苏地区 Aksu Adminis-trative Offices	克孜勒苏克尔克孜自治州 Kizilsu Kirgiz Autonomous Prefecture	喀什地区 Kashgar [Kaxgar] Adminis-trative Offices	和田地区 Hotan Adminis-trative Offices
0.06			0.10	0.41		0.02			
12.14	2.30		29.00		3.70	9.59	53.39	0.04	141.51
4.29	7.08	367.98	23.89	35.10		4.01		19.44	100.81
400.28	162.35	62.09	69.57	280.25	52.15	3.81	98.06	39.05	57.72
171.86	381.77	6.83	32.48	343.84	40.66	20.81	21.77	60.45	98.51
28.59	18.81	2.73	2.39		7.83	18.82		27.13	23.76
	148.60	16.11		25.14		0.84	0.42	0.84	
1.43	2.07	0.08	3.07	10.45	1.70	3.84	1.00	32.86	51.25
2275.94	807.13	3619.93	749.26	624.24	528.62	1044.37	187.46	361.62	334.01
14.54		6.66		12.95	1.73	23.12		0.45	1.76
9883.32	8519.25	10069.84	5232.97	10325.37	5469.70	6178.40	1963.76	3186.61	3231.99
4.56				198.26		8.98	4.40	8.00	2.87
1888.14	989.78	1284.68	551.82	1449.47	392.98	304.60	153.40	128.94	133.09
14785.68	**4155.21**	**15784.64**	**3594.87**	**6627.30**	**2407.67**	**2917.97**	**506.41**	**1105.65**	**532.17**
5969.02	1773.60	8827.15	1898.88	3696.81	1797.18	1462.70	37.16	541.38	274.04
329.57	76.25	202.93	30.51	405.30	35.18	53.01	9.99	13.82	11.81
2619.52	721.69	1621.08	350.07	1394.37	76.08	327.45	37.01	159.80	116.60
4670.09	548.15	4010.96	882.30	156.63	89.09	547.64	339.02	251.86	10.13
10274.91	**3184.58**	**7780.70**	**4649.32**	**13214.70**	**5102.16**	**1807.96**			
686.75	849.62	685.31	1519.06	865.12	2476.38	606.28			
9588.16	2286.25	7095.39	3130.27	12349.59	2625.78	1189.76			
6035.52	**3603.88**	**1664.40**	**2904.88**	**2284.55**	**1930.34**	**665.84**			
5419.16	2553.47	1441.06	2440.89	1324.77	1386.81	428.05			
614.98	993.17	223.35	419.52	959.78	483.26	236.86			
9883.32	**8519.25**	**10069.84**	**5232.97**	**10325.37**	**5469.70**	**6178.40**	**1963.76**	**3186.61**	**3231.99**
2667.31	1873.13	2563.70	1398.04	2890.85	1864.72	1481.02	826.67	1088.28	857.81
304.67	345.57	375.32	393.79	498.67	415.78	264.76	210.40	169.70	99.58
1398.13	1130.97	1374.42	687.51	1630.60	1143.83	923.38	546.49	806.94	638.95
778.28	517.76	861.86	651.22	700.14	501.99	631.24	177.41	383.05	359.72
2201.83	3501.22	2258.46	982.55	2986.29	1139.36	1911.21	476.60	956.91	1128.19
426.79	382.66	465.38	259.06	463.14	245.39	272.31	63.37	127.38	200.28
1833.31	921.37	2092.18	919.49	1570.07	873.56	943.81	222.97	302.66	387.26
700.89	510.68	578.34	196.73	776.20	213.37	154.25	28.40	59.36	34.09
196.36	116.35	218.09	60.09	148.00	82.85	43.70	10.70	20.25	21.90
504.53	394.33	360.25	136.65	628.20	130.51	110.56	17.70	39.11	12.20
950.99	607.33	960.83	750.52	617.22	573.53	612.45	165.36	240.65	223.93
323.92	205.10	289.09	75.35	321.48	57.78	172.10	2.97	28.33	40.72
6531.33	6144.66	7424.80	3664.03	7492.73	4028.49	4437.14	1471.03	2493.86	2711.44
3351.99	2374.59	2645.04	1568.94	2832.64	1441.21	1741.26	492.73	692.75	520.55

9-25 农村居民家庭人均纯收入分组
Rural Households Grouped by Per Capita Annual Net Income

(2012 年) (抽样调查 Sampled Survey)

项 目	Item	合 计 Total	0-400 元 0-400 yuan	400-600 元 400-600 yuan	600-800 元 600-800 yuan	800-1000 元 800-1000 yuan	1000-1200 元 1000-1200 yuan
调查户数(户)	**Number of Households Surveyed (household)**	**1550**	**28**	**3**	**9**	**11**	**18**
构成(%)	Percentage (%)	100	1.81	0.19	0.58	0.71	1.16
常住人口(人)	**Number of Permanent Residents in the Households Surveyed (person)**	**6639**	**90**	**11**	**41**	**62**	**87**
构成(%)	Percentage (%)	100	1.35	0.17	0.62	0.94	1.31
人均纯收入(元)	**Per Capita Net Income (yuan)**	**6393.70**	**-1943.15**	**430.01**	**696.76**	**905.80**	**1097.56**

项 目	Item	1200-1500 元 1200-1500 yuan	1500-1700 元 1500-1700 yuan	1700-2000 元 1700-2000 yuan	2000-2500 元 2000-2500 yuan	2500-3000 元 2500-3000 yuan
调查户数(户)	**Number of Households Surveyed (household)**	**44**	**16**	**58**	**84**	**99**
构成(%)	Percentage (%)	2.84	1.03	3.74	5.42	6.39
常住人口(人)	**Number of Permanent Residents in the Households Surveyed (person)**	**214**	**78**	**278**	**402**	**524**
构成(%)	Percentage (%)	3.23	1.17	4.18	6.06	7.88
人均纯收入(元)	**Per Capita Net Income (yuan)**	**1374.63**	**1628.61**	**1850.71**	**2271.11**	**2736.88**

项 目	Item	3000-3500 元 3000-3500 yuan	3500-4000 元 3500-4000 yuan	4000-4500 元 4000-4500 yuan	4500-5000 元 4500-5000 yuan	5000 元以上 over 5000 yuan
调查户数(户)	**Number of Households Surveyed (household)**	**109**	**106**	**92**	**71**	**802**
构成(%)	Percentage (%)	7.03	6.84	5.94	4.58	51.74
常住人口(人)	**Number of Permanent Residents in the Households Surveyed (person)**	**530**	**486**	**412**	**318**	**3107**
构成(%)	Percentage (%)	7.98	7.32	6.20	4.79	46.79
人均纯收入(元)	**Per Capita Net Income (yuan)**	**3256.52**	**3745.74**	**4243.41**	**4736.42**	**10415.18**

9-26 主要年份农村居民家庭房屋使用情况
Housing Conditions of Rural Households in Main Years

(抽样调查 Sampled Survey)

项 目	Item	2000	2005	2010	2012
本年新建(购)房屋	**Houses Newly built This Year**				
面积(平方米/人)	Per Capita Floor Space of Houses (sq.m/person)	0.38	1.37	0.73	1.52
价值(元/平方米)	Value of Houses (yuan/sq.m)	169.37	225.20	442.00	626.67
住房结构(平方米/人)	Structure of Houses (sq.m/person)				
#钢筋混凝土结构	Reinforced Concrete Structure	0.03	0.08	0.22	0.35
砖木结构	Brick and Wood Structure	0.16	1.04	0.50	1.29
年末住房情况	**Houses at Year-end**				
住房面积(平方米/人)	Per Capita Floor Space of Houses (sq.m/person)	17.25	21.23	24.00	27.18
住房价值(元/平方米)	Value of Houses (yuan/sq.m)	120.86	160.99	252.79	488.79
住房结构(平方米/人)	Structure of House (sq.m/person)				
#钢筋混凝土结构	Reinforced Concrete Structure	0.53	0.98	1.83	2.80
砖木结构	Brick and Wood Structure	2.75	6.48	10.95	14.19

9-27 主要年份城乡新建住宅面积和居民住房情况
Floor Space of Newly Built Residential Buildings and Housing Conditions of Urban and Rural Residents in Main Years

年 份 Year	城镇新建住宅面积(万平方米) Floor Space of Newly Built Residential Buildings In Urban Areas (10 000 sq.m)	农村新建住宅面积(万平方米) Floor Space of Newly Built Residential Buildings in Rural Areas (10 000 sq.m)	城镇人均使用面积(平方米) Per Capita Gross Living Space in Urban Areas (sq.m)	城镇人均建筑面积(平方米) Per Capita Floor Space of Residential Building in Urban Areas (sq.m)	农村人均居住面积(平方米) Per Capita Floor Space of Residential Building in Rural Areas (sq.m)
1985	353.26	463.00	10.70	14.27	12.75
1990	381.61	593.96	13.55	18.07	14.04
1995	567.54	496.60	16.57	22.09	16.12
1996	683.51	757.71	17.61	23.48	16.12
1997	673.58	719.53	13.62	18.16	16.13
1998	874.97	729.71	18.95	25.27	16.20
1999	1315.89	705.00	19.76	26.35	16.90
2000	1327.29	554.59	20.06	26.75	17.25
2001	1517.22	894.56	20.60	27.47	18.04
2002	1256.72	534.10	18.17	23.78	18.56
2003	1546.23	800.81	17.91	23.36	18.62
2004	1565.72	732.84	18.82	24.44	19.10
2005	2226.97	1391.81	20.15	26.02	21.23
2006	2212.08	1573.38	20.33	26.31	21.96
2007	2491.60	1967.17	20.38	27.17	22.45
2008	2584.23	1541.44	20.47	27.29	22.79
2009	1994.28	1418.15	20.42	27.16	23.45
2010	2028.26	1263.63	20.49	27.25	24.00
2011	2621.59	1883.35	21.70	28.92	26.14
2012	3608.10	2543.93	21.78	29.03	27.18

9-28 分地区农村居民家庭平均每人粮食收支情况
Per Capita Grain Balance of Debit and Credit by Region

单位：公斤 (2012 年)(抽样调查 Sampled Survey) (kg)

项 目	Item	自治区 Autonomous Region	乌鲁木齐市 Urumqi City	吐鲁番地区 Turpan Administrative Offices	哈密地区 Hami [Kumul] Administrative Offices
粮食收入合计	**Total of Debit**	**1604.23**	**1333.06**	**212.66**	**664.91**
家庭经营生产的	From Household Business	1406.65	765.55	7.33	503.83
购 入	Purchases	197.51	567.51	205.30	160.94
其他粮食收入	Others	0.08		0.03	0.14
粮食支出合计	**Total of Expenditure**	**1441.09**	**1256.33**	**210.44**	**596.08**
主食用粮	Staple Food	227.62	187.97	191.88	146.82
出 售	Sales	1015.69	687.44	2.33	335.60
种 籽	Seeds	43.16	20.81	0.99	26.77
饲 料	Fodder	151.02	360.12	15.23	86.86
其他粮食支出	Others	3.60			0.03

项 目	Item	昌吉回族自治州 Changji Hui Autonomous Prefecture	伊犁州直属县(市) Counties (Cities) Direct Under Ili Prefecture	塔城地区 Tacheng [Tarbagatai] Adminis-trative Offices	阿勒泰地区 Altay Adminis-trative Offices	博尔塔拉蒙古自治州 Bortala Mongol Autonomous Prefecture
粮食收入合计	**Total of Debit**	**4375.55**	**2318.44**	**4407.69**	**947.49**	**5036.89**
家庭经营生产的	From Household Business	3952.28	2094.97	4091.11	684.49	4700.02
购 入	Purchases	423.27	223.47	316.58	261.59	336.87
其他粮食收入	Others					
粮食支出合计	**Total of Expenditure**	**3641.04**	**1965.68**	**4186.82**	**912.90**	**5107.80**
主食用粮	Staple Food	182.43	198.60	167.82	173.39	193.21
出 售	Sales	3092.57	1556.91	3821.69	589.52	4702.14
种 籽	Seeds	117.28	20.30	95.09	50.61	45.46
饲 料	Fodder	248.76	189.87	102.22	99.38	166.98
其他粮食支出	Others					

项 目	Item	巴音郭楞蒙古自治州 Bayangol Mongol Autonomous Prefecture	阿克苏地区 Aksu Adminis-trative Offices	克孜勒苏克尔克孜自治州 Kizilsu Kirgiz Autonomous Prefecture	喀什地区 Kashgar [Kaxgar] Adminis-trative Offices	和田地区 Hotan Adminis-trative Offices
粮食收入合计	**Total of Debit**	**707.54**	**961.07**	**669.73**	**840.35**	**788.63**
家庭经营生产的	From Household Business	408.48	776.05	497.06	757.03	723.02
购 入	Purchases	299.06	184.93	172.66	83.18	65.61
其他粮食收入	Others		0.09		0.13	
粮食支出合计	**Total of Expenditure**	**555.34**	**714.10**	**552.15**	**656.02**	**458.32**
主食用粮	Staple Food	212.36	194.45	177.63	254.82	217.65
出 售	Sales	148.56	403.96	197.21	215.01	130.54
种 籽	Seeds	19.84	25.23	28.42	34.12	17.43
饲 料	Fodder	174.58	90.47	148.89	140.29	91.01
其他粮食支出	Others				11.77	1.69

9-29 主要年份农村居民家庭平均每户饲养畜禽、其他小动物生产情况
Output of Livestock, Poultry and Other Small Animals Per Rural Households in Main Years

单位：公斤　　(抽样调查)(Sampled Surrey)　　(kg)

年份 Year	出售自宰猪肉产量 Output of Pork Sold and Self-slaugutered	出售自宰羊肉产量 Output of Mutton Sold and Self-slaughtered	羊毛产量 Output of Wool	牛羊奶产量 Output of Cow and Sheep Milk	出售自宰家禽产量 Output of Poultry Sold and Self-slaughtered	禽蛋产量 Output of Poultry and Eggs	蚕茧产量 Output of Silkworm
1985	16.76	47.54	10.51	51.53		13.95	0.26
1990	24.97	45.72	15.86	67.16		17.68	1.26
1995	23.42	61.41	14.86	66.16	28.86	23.14	1.69
1996	23.10	62.09	7.61	34.93	7.61	8.20	0.89
1997	12.46	73.78	7.37	33.57	9.87	7.97	1.08
1998	10.18	84.42	5.40	42.53	7.39	8.78	1.58
1999	12.91	100.45	4.06	34.92	7.65	13.90	1.38
2000	16.48	94.55	5.49	34.27	13.03	25.26	1.01
2001	13.24	91.54			16.92	35.71	
2002	11.01	110.97			16.09	41.07	
2003	13.16	86.23	4.51	91.91	12.48	37.10	0.66
2004	10.30	105.20	4.09	89.54	12.75	6.03	0.23
2005	8.29	107.11	6.28	134.36	14.95	49.14	0.23
2006	4.28	114.78	6.91	112.72	12.33	71.07	0.14
2007	2.70	112.08	7.05	144.28	12.25	40.59	0.02
2008	9.39	105.70	5.06	169.98	18.43	62.33	0.03
2009	9.64	102.68	5.19	136.18	25.58	67.18	
2010	11.64	108.72	4.05	145.32	19.16	36.26	
2011	22.81	105.84	5.79	83.25	23.02	58.02	
2012	23.43	137.38	2.97	46.67	18.29	39.97	

注：因调查户调整，部分指标数据与往年相比变动较大。
Note:Beceucse of Households Surveyed adjustment, Parts of Index sign data quite changed compared to last yesr.

9-30 主要年份农村居民家庭平均每户饲养畜禽、其他小动物出售量
Quantities of Livestock, Poultry and Other Small Animals Sold Per Rural Households in Main Years

(抽样调查) (Sampled Surrey)

年份 Year	猪(头) Pork (head)	牛(头) Cattle (head)	羊(只) Sheep (head)	家禽(只) Poultry (head)	蛋类(公斤) Eggs (kg)	羊毛(公斤) Wool (kg)	牛羊奶(公斤) Milk (kg)
1985	0.10		1.94	3.30	7.68	6.87	5.68
1990	0.22	0.11	1.50	4.15	8.25	9.63	17.47
1995	0.17	0.22	2.21	11.69	17.28	5.80	26.76
1996	0.24	0.14	2.14	1.98	3.08	3.13	12.43
1997	0.11	0.16	2.74	3.00	3.51	4.16	11.56
1998	0.07	0.15	3.47	2.14	4.30	2.23	18.04
1999	0.08	0.25	3.89	2.70	9.23	1.67	12.75
2000	0.14	0.39	3.81	4.89	21.27	1.82	21.30
2001	0.12	0.37	3.85	7.55	31.60	1.43	39.77
2002	0.11	0.35	4.61	6.64	34.55	1.95	55.33
2003	0.18	0.35	4.14	3.60	33.55	1.81	73.94
2004	0.12	0.32	4.55	4.28	3.01	1.86	77.30
2005	0.09	0.39	6.03	4.42	46.51	4.54	117.65
2006	0.06	0.59	7.21	4.12	68.19	5.19	91.42
2007	0.03	0.65	6.03	3.54	38.11	5.43	123.35
2008	0.11	0.56	4.92	6.35	59.54	3.28	148.16
2009	0.12	0.43	4.62	9.63	63.91	3.06	119.28
2010	0.12	0.39	4.32	6.12	33.01	2.88	129.76
2011	0.43	0.41	4.47	7.17	54.03	4.71	71.60
2012	0.27	0.54	4.96	25.87	43.49	5.42	51.16

9-31 社会保险基本情况
Basic Conditions on Social Insurance

指　标	Item	2011	2012
基本养老保险	**Basic Endowment Insurance**		
职工基本养老保险	Employee Basic Pension Insurance		
年末参保人数(万人)	Contributors at Year-end (10 000 persons)	291.99	312.16
#参保职工	Staff and Workers	214.66	228.86
离退休人员	Number of Retirees	77.33	83.30
新型农村社会养老保险	New Rural Old-age Insurance		
年末参保人数(万人)	Contributors at Year-end (10 000 persons)	490.58	497.09
享受待遇人数（万人）	Beneficiaries at Year-end (10000 persons)	84.68	88.29
城镇居民社会养老保险	Urban Employee Basic Pension Insurance		
年末参保人数(万人)	Contributors at Year-end (10 000 persons)	27.49	31.62
享受待遇人数（万人）	Beneficiaries at Year-end (10000 persons)	4.48	5.14
基本医疗保险	**Basic Medical Care Insurance**		
职工基本医疗保险	Employee Basic Medical Care Insurance		
年末参保人数(万人)	Contributors at Year-end (10 000 persons)	322.73	342.56
城镇居民基本医疗保险	Urban Employee Basic Medical Care Insurance		
年末参保人数(万人)	Contributors at Year-end (10 000 persons)	282.68	286.59
工伤保险	**Work Injury Insurance**		
年末参保人数(万人)	Contributors at Year-end (10 000 persons)	208.18	225.95
年末享受待遇人次数（万人次）	Beneficiaries at Year-end (10 000 persons)	1.42	1.77
失业保险	**Unemployment Insurance**		
年末参保人数(万人)	Year-end Contributors (10 000 persons)	196.72	208.95
年末享受待遇人数（万人）	Beneficiaries at Year-end (10 000 persons)	5.55	4.93
生育保险	**Maternity Insurance**		
年末参保人数(万人)	Contributors at Year-end (10 000 persons)	206.14	217.96
年末享受待遇人次数（万人次）	Beneficiaries at Year-end (10000 persons)	5.26	8.09

注：基本医疗保险数据不含新型农村合作医疗。
Note: Statistics on basic endowment insuranse didn't coner data on new rural old-age insurance.

9-32 各地、州、市社会保险年末参保人数

Number of Social Insured Persons at the Year-end by Prefecture, Autonomous Prefecture and City

单位：万人 (10 000 persons)

年份 Year	地区 Region	基本养老保险 Basic Endowment Insurance 职工基本养老保险 Employee Basic Pension Insurance	新型农村社会养老保险 New Rural Old-age Insurance	城镇居民社会养老保险 Urban Non-employment Social Pension Insurance	基本医疗保险 Basic Medical Care Insurance 职工基本医疗保险 Employee Basic Medical Care Insurance
	2001	148.08			116.17
	2002	152.06			148.12
	2003	160.04			176.37
	2004	173.76			195.97
	2005	181.88			211.85
	2006	191.97			227.15
	2007	205.00			244.78
	2008	222.17			263.54
	2009	232.08			279.09
	2010	259.67			296.72
	2011	291.99	490.58	27.49	322.73
	2012	312.16	497.09	31.62	342.56
乌鲁木齐市	Urumqi City	102.93	10.36	1.09	106.12
克拉玛依市	Karamay City	5.22	0.10	0.08	17.52
吐鲁番地区	Turpan Administrative Offices	5.61	21.25	0.57	8.14
哈密地区	Hami [Kumul] Administrative Offices	10.15	8.37	0.28	10.65
昌吉回族自治州	Changji Hui Autonomous Prefecture	21.57	29.91	0.85	23.83
伊犁州直属县(市)	Counties (Cities) Direct Under Ili Prefecture	24.96	53.05	5.82	26.58
塔城地区	Tacheng [Tarbagatai] Administrative Offices	12.30	20.06	1.79	12.57
阿勒泰地区	Altay Administrative Offices	8.09	12.72	1.09	11.58
博尔塔拉蒙古自治州	Bortala Mongol Autonomous Prefecture	5.47	7.29	0.44	6.13
巴音郭楞蒙古自治州	Bayangol Mongol Autonomous Prefecture	22.09	20.59	1.63	25.62
阿克苏地区	Aksu Administrative Offices	12.14	63.47	3.03	17.80
克孜勒苏柯尔克孜自治州	Kizilsu Kirgiz Autonomous Prefecture	3.46	17.12	1.15	7.54
喀什地区	Kashgar [Kaxgar] Administrative Offices	14.95	140.04	10.75	24.71
和田地区	Hotan Administrative Offices	5.56	92.76	3.05	10.86

注：基本医疗保险数据不含新型农村合作医疗。
Note: Data of basic medical care insurance did not include new cooperative health care in agricultural and pastoral areas.

9-32 续表 Continued

单位：万人 (10 000 persons)

年 份 Year	地 区 Region	基本医疗保险 Basic Medical Care Insurance 城镇居民基本医疗保险 Urban Non-employment Basic Medical Insurance	工伤保险 Work Injury Insurance	失业保险 Unemployment Insurance	生育保险 Maternity Insurance
	2001		30.53	126.47	30.52
	2002		29.45	131.29	29.72
	2003		41.08	135.12	32.16
	2004		60.93	138.58	59.23
	2005		79.51	140.82	103.48
	2006		102.40	145.04	135.90
	2007		132.55	151.55	151.60
	2008	175.07	151.08	162.76	165.02
	2009	256.90	167.70	169.60	176.07
	2010	274.60	184.13	180.29	188.23
	2011	282.68	208.18	196.72	206.14
	2012	286.59	225.95	208.95	217.96
乌鲁木齐市	Urumqi City	55.77	71.27	72.08	61.52
克拉玛依市	Karamay City	7.80	16.31	4.74	15.24
吐鲁番地区	Turpan Administrative Offices	9.55	6.23	4.51	5.13
哈密地区	Hami [Kumul] Administrative Offices	9.89	9.38	6.38	6.47
昌吉回族自治州	Changji Hui Autonomous Prefecture	21.26	23.97	14.23	18.23
伊犁州直属县(市)	Counties (Cities) Direct Under Ili Prefecture	32.95	15.62	14.69	17.32
塔城地区	Tacheng [Tarbagatai] Administrative Offices	10.91	6.66	6.22	7.54
阿勒泰地区	Altay Administrative Offices	12.45	7.69	5.41	6.58
博尔塔拉蒙古自治州	Bortala Mongol Autonomous Prefecture	7.09	4.70	3.67	4.30
巴音郭楞蒙古自治州	Bayangol Mongol Autonomous Prefecture	21.10	16.71	16.06	16.36
阿克苏地区	Aksu Administrative Offices	27.03	9.06	9.34	10.79
克孜勒苏柯尔克孜自治州	Kizilsu Kirgiz Autonomous Prefecture	6.53	4.31	3.72	4.37
喀什地区	Kashgar [Kaxgar] Administrative Offices	46.11	15.16	14.97	16.51
和田地区	Hotan Administrative Offices	18.14	6.56	6.37	7.41

主要统计指标解释

一、城镇住户

城镇家庭人口 指居住在一起，经济上合在一起共同生活的家庭成员。凡计算为家庭人口的成员其全部收支都包括在本家庭中。

城镇就业面 指就业人口占家庭人口的百分比。

城镇就业者负担人数 指家庭人口与就业人口之比。

城镇家庭总收入 指家庭成员得到的工资性收入、经营净收入、财产性收入、转移性收入之和，不包括出售财物收入和借贷收入。

城镇居民家庭可支配收入 指家庭成员得到可用于最终消费支出和其它非义务性支出以及储蓄的总和，即居民家庭可以用来自由支配的收入。它是家庭总收入扣除交纳的所得税、个人交纳的社会保障支出以及记账补贴后的收入。计算公式为：

城镇居民家庭可支配收入=家庭总收入-交纳个人所得税-个人交纳的社会保障支出-记帐补贴

城镇家庭总支出 指家庭除借贷支出以外的全部实际支出。包括现金消费支出、财产性支出、转移性支出、社会保障支出、购房与建房支出。

城镇家庭消费性支出 指家庭用于日常生活的支出，包括食品、衣着、家庭设备用品及服务、医疗保健、交通和通信、娱乐教育文化服务、居住、其他商品和服务等八大类支出。

城镇家庭服务性消费支出 指家庭用于支付社会提供的各种非商品性服务费用。

城镇家庭收入分组方法 是将所有调查户依户人均可支配收入由低到高排队，按10%，10%，20%，20%，20%，10%，10%的比例依次分成：最低收入户、较低收入户、中等偏下收入户、中等收入户、中等偏上收入户、较高收入户、最高收入户等七组。总体中最低5%的户为困难户。

恩格尔系数 指食物支出金额在消费性总支出金额中所占的比例。计算公式为：

恩格尔系数=食品支出金额/生活消费总支出金额×100%

二、农村住户

总收入 指调查期内农村住户和住户成员从各种来源渠道得到的收入总和。按收入的性质划分为工资性收入、家庭经营收入、财产性收入和转移性收入。

工资性收入 指农村住户成员受雇于单位或个人，靠出卖劳动所而获得的收入。

家庭经营收入 指农村住户以家庭为生产经营单位进行生产筹划和管理而获得的收入。农村住户家庭经营活动按行业划分为农业、林业、牧业、渔业、工业、建筑业、交通运输业邮电业、批发和零售贸易餐饮业、社会服务业、文教卫生业和其他家庭经营。

财产性收入 指金融资产或有形非生产性资产的所有者向其他机构单位提供资金或将有形非生产性资产供其支配，作为回报而从中获得的收入。

转移性收入 指农村住户和住户成员无须付出任何对应物而获得的货物、服务、资金或资产所有权等，不包括无偿提供的用于固定资本形成的资金。一般情况下，是指农村住户在二次分配中的所有收入。

现金收入 指农村住户和住户成员在调查期内得到以现金形态表现的收入。按来源分成工资性收入、家庭经营现金收入、财产性收入、转移性收入。

纯收入 指农村住户当年从各个来源得到的总收入相应地扣除所发生的费用后的收入总和。计算方法：

农村居民家庭纯收入=总收入-家庭经营费用支出-税费支出-生产性固定资产折旧-赠送农村外部亲友支出

纯收入主要用于再生产投入和当年生活消费支出，也可用于储蓄和各种非义务性支出。"农民人均纯收入"按人口平均的纯收入水平，反映的是一个地区农村居民的平均收入水平。

总支出 指农村住户用于生产、生活和再分配的全部支出。包括家庭经营费用支出、购置生产性固定资产支出、税费支出、生活消费支出、财产性支出和转移性支出。

三、社会保险

城镇职工基本养老保险

1.参加保险职工人数: 指报告期末按照国家法律、法规和有关政策规定参加基本养老保险并在社保经办机构已建立缴费记录档案的职工人数。包括中断缴费但未终止养老关系的职工人数，不包括只登记未建立缴费记录档案的人数。

2.参加保险离退休人员人数: 指报告期末参加基本养老保险的离休、退休和退职人员的人数。

3.基本养老保险基金收入: 指根据国家有关规定，由纳入基本养老保险范围的缴费单位和个人按照国家规定的缴费基数和缴费比例缴纳的养老保险基金，以及通过其他方式取得的形成基金来源的收入。包括单位和职工个人缴纳的基本养老保险费、基本养老基金利息收入、上级补助收入、下级上解收入、转移收入、财政补贴和其他收入。

4.基本养老保险基金支出: 指按照国家政策规定的开支范围和开支标准从基本养老保险基金中支付给参加基本养老保险的个人的养老金、丧葬抚恤补助，以及由于保险关系转移、上下级之间调剂资金等原因而发生的支出。包括:离休金、退休金、退职金、各种补贴、医疗费、死亡丧葬补助费、抚恤救济费、社会保险经办机构管理费、补助下级支出、上解上级支出、转移支出、其他支出等。

5. 基本养老保险基金累计结余：指截止报告期末基本养老基金收支相抵后的累计余额。

基本医疗保险

1.参保人数：指报告期末按国家有关规定参加基本医疗保险的人数。

2.基金收入：指由用人单位和个人按照国家规定的缴费基数、缴费比例或缴费标准缴纳的基本医疗保险基金，财政补助资金以及通过其他方式取得的形成基金来源的款项，包括：单位缴纳收入、个人缴纳收入、财政补助收入（含医疗救助补助个人收入）、财政补贴收入、利息收入和其他收入。

3.基金支出：指按照国家政策规定的开支范围和开支标准从社会统筹基金中支付给参加基本医疗保险的职工和退休人员的医疗保险待遇支出，和从个人帐户基金中支付给参加基本医疗保险的职工和退休人员的医疗费用支出，以及其他支出。包括：住院医疗费用支出、门急诊医疗费用支出、个人账户基金支出、其他支出。

4.基金累计结余：指截止报告期末基本医疗保险基金累计结余金额。

失业保险

1.参加保险人数：指报告期末按照国家法律、法规和有关政策规定参加了失业保险的城镇企业、事业单位的职工及地方政府规定参加失业保险的其他人员的人数。

2.失业保险基金收入：指报告期内筹集的失业保险基金的总额，包括失业保险费收入、利息收入、财政补贴收入、其他收入、转移收入、上级补助收入、下级上解收入。

3.失业保险基金支出：指报告期内为保障失业人员基本生活、促进其再就业等支出的基金总额，包括失业保险金支出、医疗补助金支出、丧葬补助金和抚恤金支出、职业培训和职业介绍补贴支出、农民合同制工人一次性生活补助支出、其他支出、转移支出、上级补助支出、下级上解支出。

4.基金累计结余：指截止报告期末失业保险基金收支相抵后的累计余额。

工伤保险

1.参加保险人数：指报告期末依据国家有关规定参加工伤保险的职工人数和有雇工的个体工商户的雇工数。

2.享受保险待遇人数：指年初至报告期末因工伤或职业病而享受工伤保险待遇的人数。为享受工伤医疗待遇中未评定等级的人数、享受伤残待遇人数以及享受因工死亡待遇人数之和。

3.基金收入：指根据国家有关规定，由参加工伤保险的单位按国家规定的缴费基数和缴费比例缴纳的工伤保险基金，以及通过其他形式取得的形成基金来源的款项。包括：单位缴纳的社会统筹基金收入、财政补贴收入、利息收入、其他收入。

4.基金支出：指按照国家政策规定的开支范围和开支标准从工伤保险基金中支付给参加工伤保险的人员及供养直系亲属工伤保险待遇支出及其他支出。包括工伤医疗费、伤残补助金、工亡补助金、护理费、丧葬补助费、工伤预防费用、职业康复费用和其他支出。

5.基金累计结余：指截止报告期末工伤保险基金累计结余金额。

生育保险

1.参保人数：指报告期末依据有关规定参加生育保险的人数。

2.基金收入：指根据国家有关规定，由参加生育保险的单位按照国家规定的缴费基数和缴费比例缴纳的生育保险基金，以及通过其他方式取得的形成基金来源的款项，包括：单位缴纳的基金收入、利息收入和其他收入。

3.基金支出：指按照国家政策规定的开支范围和开支标准，从生育保险基金中支付给参加生育保险的职工，因妊娠、分娩和计划生育手术而享受的待遇及其他支出。包括：生育津贴、医疗费用支出及其他支出。

4.基金累计结余：指截止报告期末生育保险基金累计结余金额。

Explanatory Notes on Main Statistical Indicators

I. Urban Households

Population of Urban Households refer to members of households living and sharing economically together in the urban areas. All the income and expenditure of all the members of such households are included in the income and expenditure of the household.

Proportion of Urban Employment refers to the proportion of employed population to the population of urban households.

Number of Dependents per Urban Employee refers to the ratio between number of persons in an urban household and the number of employed persons.

Total Income of Urban Households refers to the sum of wage income; net business income; income from properties; and income from transfers of members of the households. Income from selling of properties and income from borrowing are not included.

Disposable Income of Urban Households refers to the actual income at the disposal of members of the households which can be used for final consumption, other non-compulsory expenditure and savings. This equals to total income minus income tax, personal contribution to social security and subsidy for keeping diaries in being a sample household. The following formula is used:

Disposable Income of Urban Households= total household income - income tax - personal contribution to social security - subsidy for keeping diaries for a sampled household

Total Expenditure of Urban Households refers to all actual expenditure of households except expenditure on lending. It includes cash expenditure; property expenditure, transfer expenditure, social insurance expenditure and expenditure on house purchasing or house building.

Consumption Expenditure of Urban Households in Cash refers to total cash expenditure of households for consumption in daily life, including expenditure on the eight categories of food; clothing; housing; household appliances; transport and communications; education; cultural and recreational activities and medical care.

Consumption Expenditure of Urban Households on Services refers to non-commodity service expenditure of households on various kinds of cultural and living activities provided by society.

Urban Households by Income Group All households in the sample are grouped by per capita disposable income of the household, into groups of lowest income, low income, lower middle income, middle income, upper middle income, high income and highest income, each group consisting of 10%, 10%, 20%, 20%, 20%, 10% and 10% of all households respectively. The lowest 5% of households are also referred to as poor households.

Engel's Coefficient refers to the percentage of expenditure on food to the total consumption in cash, using the following formula:

$$\text{Engel's Coefficient} = \frac{\text{expenditure on food}}{\text{total consumption expenditure}} \times 100\%$$

II. Rural Household

Total Income refers to the sum of income earned from various sources by the rural households and their members during the reference period, and is classified as income from wages and salaries, income from household operations, income from properties and income from transfers.

Income from Wages and Salaries refers to income from labour earned by the members of rural households employed by other units or individuals.

Income from Household Operations refers to income by the rural households as units of production and operation. Operations by rural households are classified according to their economic activities namely agriculture, forestry, animal husbandry, fishery, manufacturing, construction, transportation, post and telecommunications, wholesale, retail and catering, social service, culture, education, health, and other household operations.

Income from Properties refers to the income received as returns by owners of financial assets or tangible non-productive assets by providing capitals or tangible non-productive assets to other institutional units.

Income from Transfers refers to the receipt by rural households and their members of goods, services, capital or rights of assets without giving or repaying accordingly, excluding capital provided to them for the formation of fixed assets. In general, it refers to all income received by rural households through redistribution.

Cash Income refers to income received by rural households and their members in the form of cash during the reference period. It is classified, by source of income, into income from wages and salaries, cash income from household operations, income from properties and income from transfers.

Net Income refers to the total income of rural households from all sources minus all corresponding expenses. The formula for calculation is as follows:

Net income of rural households = total income - household operation expenses - taxes and fees-depreciation of fixed assets for production - gifts to rural relatives.

Net income is mainly used as input for reinvestment in production and as consumption expenditure of the year, and also used for savings and non-compulsory expenses of various forms. "Per capita net income of farmers" is the level of net income averaged by population, reflecting the average income level of rural population in a given area.

Total Expenditure refers to total expenses of rural households on production, consumption and redistribution, including expenditure on household operations; purchase of productive fixed assets; taxes and fees; consumption expenditure; expenses on properties; and expenses on transfers.

III. Social Insurance

Basic Pension Insurance

1. Number of staff and workers covered refer to staff and workers participating in the basic pension insurance programme according to national laws, regulations and related policies at the end of the reference period, who have already had payment records in social security management agencies, including those who have interrupt payment without terminating the insurance programme. Those who have registered in the programme but with no payment records are not included.

2. Number of retirees participating in the basic pension

insurance programme refer to the number of retirees participating in basic pension insurance programmes by the end of the reference period.

3.Revenue of the basic pension insurance programme refers to payments made by employers and individuals participating in the pension insurance programme in accordance with the basis and proportion stipulated in State regulations, and income from other sources that become source of pension insurance fund, including the premium paid by employers and staff and workers, interest income, subsidies from higher level agencies, income as transfer from subordinate agencies, transferred income, government financial subsidies and other income.

4.Expenditure of basic pension insurance programme refer to payment made on pensions and funeral subsidies to those retired and resigned people covered in pension insurance programmes according to related national policies on scope and standard of expenditure. Also included are expenditure which arises due to shift of the insurance relationship or adjustment of funds among agencies. More specifically, included are pensions for resigned people, pensions for retired people, pension for people quitting jobs, various subsidies, medical fees, funeral subsidies, compensation payments, management fees for social security agencies, expenses on subsidies to lower subordinates, expenses as transfer to agencies at higher level, transferred expenditure and other expenditure.

5.Balance of basic pension insurance programme refers to the balance of basic pension insurance funds at the end of the reference period after deducting expenses from revenue.

Basic Medical Care Insurance

1.Number of people participating in the insurance programme refers to people participating in the basic medical care insurance programme according to related regulations at the end of the reference period.

2.Revenue of the insurance programme refers to payments made by employers and individuals participating in the medical care insurance programme in accordance with the basis and proportion stipulated in State regulations, and income from other sources that become source of medical insurance fund, including income paid by units, individual paid income, financial assistance's income (including individual income from medicaid), financial subsidies' income, interest income and other income.

3.Expenditure of the insurance programme refers to payment made to people covered in basic medical care insurance programme within the scope and standards of expenditure according to related national policies, and medical care payment and other expenses, including medical expenses of hospital inpatients, medical expenses for outpatients and emergency patients, payment from individual accounts and other expenditure.

4.Balance of the basic medical care insurance programme refers to the balance of medical care insurance funds at the end of the reference period.

Unemployment Insurance

1. Number of people covered refers to staff and workers in urban enterprises or institutions who have participated in the unemployment insurance programme according to relevant policies and regulations, and other people who have participated according to local government regulations at the end of the reference period.

2. Revenue of the unemployment insurance programme refers to the total unemployment insurance funds raised in the reference period, including unemployment insurance premium, interest income, financial subsidies, other income, transferred income, subsidies from higher level agencies and income as transfer from subordinate agencies.

3.Expenditure of the unemployment insurance programme refers to total expenses during the reference period to guarantee the basic livelihood of unemployed people, and to encourage their re-employment. Included are unemployment relief, medical fees, funeral subsidies, compensation payments, training expenses, management fees for unemployment insurance agencies, subsidies to lower level agencies, expenses as transfer to higher level agencies, transferred expenditure and other expenditure.

4.Balance of the unemployment insurance programme refers to the balance of revenue of the programme after deducting expenses at the end of the reference period.

Work Injury Insurance

1.Number of people covered refers to staff and workers who have participated in the work injury insurance programme and number of employees in private business according to relevant national regulations at the end of the reference period.

2.Number of beneficiaries refers to number of people benefited from work injury insurance, as a result of work injury or occupational disease. It is the sum of beneficiaries from the work injury medical treatment without rating, disabilities and deaths at work places.

3.Revenue of the work injury insurance programme refers to payments made by employers participating in the work injury insurance programme in accordance with the basis and proportion stipulated in State regulations, and income from other sources that become source of work injury insurance fund, including income of social comprehensive funds paid by employers, government financial subsidies, interest income and other income.

4. Expenditure of the work injury insurance programme refers to payments made from work injury insurance funds to those who participated in the work injury insurance programme and their direct dependents within the scope and standards of expenditure according to related national policies, and other expenditure, including medical fees for work injury, injury and disability subsidies, death subsidies, nursing fees, funeral subsidies, injury prevention fees, occupational rehabilitation fees and other expenditure.

5.Balance of the work injury insurance programme refers to the balance of the work injury funds at the end of the reference period.

Maternity Insurance

1.Number of people covered refers to people who have participated in the maternity insurance programme according to relevant regulation at the end of the reference period.

2.Revenue of maternity insurance refers to payments made by employers participating in the maternity insurance programme in accordance with the basis and proportion stipulated in State regulations, and income from other sources that become source of maternity insurance fund, including income of funds paid by employers, interest income and other income.

3.Expenditure of the maternity insurance programme refers to payments made from maternity insurance funds to staff and workers who participate in the maternity insurance programme within the scope and standards of expenditure in accordance with related national policies, expenses paid for pregnancy, child delivery or surgeries related to family planning, and other expenditure, including allowance for child bearing, medical fees and other expenditure.

4.Balance of the maternity programme refers to the balance of the maternity insurance funds at the end of the reference period.

新疆统计年鉴
XINJIANG STATISTICAL YEARBOOK

10

城市概况

GENERAL SURVEY OF CITIES

简要说明

本篇资料的主要内容及来源

城市概况资料主要包括城市公用事业基本情况、主要经济指标、市政设施、园林绿化、环境卫生、供水供气等。

本篇资料由新疆维吾尔自治区统计局国民经济综合统计处根据新疆维吾尔自治区建设厅和新疆维吾尔自治区统计局相关处室提供的年度数据整理。

Brief Introduction

Main Content and Source of Data

Data on the general survey cities include the basic condition of urban public facilities, main economic indicators, civil facilities, urban greenery, environment and sanitation, supply of gas and heating, public transportation, etc.

Data on this chapter are compiled by the Department of National Accounts of the Xinjiang Bureau of Statistics according to the data of yearly statistics, which are provided by the Construction Bureau of Xinjiang Uygur Autonomous Region and related departments of Statistics Bureau of Xinjiang Uygur Autonomous Region.

10-1 城市公用事业基本情况
Basic Statistics on City Public Utilities

项 目	Item	2011	2012
城市及建筑物面积	**City Areas and Floor Space of Buildings**		
建成区面积(平方公里)	Area of Built Districts(sq.km)	922	960
征用土地面积(平方公里)	Land Put in Requisition for State Construction Projects (sq. km)	15.7	32.4
城市人口密度(人/平方公里)	Population Density of City Districts(persons/sq.km)	4563	4312
供水、供气及供热	**Water Supply, Gas Supply and Heating**		
自来水年供水量(万立方米)	Annual Volume of Tap Water Supply (10 000 cu.m)	80894	85851
#生活用水量	Water Consumption for Residential use	28091	30814
平均每人日生活用水量(升)	Per -Capita Water Consumption for Residential Use (litre)	160	171
用水普及率(%)	Coverage Rate of Population with Access to Tap Water (%)	99.2	99.1
人工煤气供气量(万立方米)	Gaswork Gas Supply (10 000 cu.m)	1999	2190
#家庭用量	Consumption of Gaswork Gas for Residential Use	1999	2190
天然气供气量(万立方米)	Natural Gas Supply (10 000 cu.m)	174413	262670
#家庭用量	Consumption of Coal Gas for Residential Use	45859	62431
液化石油气供气量(吨)	Liquefied Petroleum Gas (ton)	82993	73123
#家庭用量	Consumption of Liquefied Gas for Residential Use	67827	56695
天然气、煤气管道长度(公里)	Length of Gas Pipelines (km)	8765	10124
燃气普及率(%)	Goverage Rate of Urban Population with Access to Gas (%)	96.2	96.6
集中供热面积(万平方米)	Area of Centralized Heating (10 000 sq.m)	21064	21844
#住 宅	Residential Buildings	14716	15491
市政工程	**Municipal Engineering**		
道路长度(公里)	Length of Roads (km)	5476	5813
平均每万人拥有 (公里)	Length of Paved Roads per 10 000 Population (km)	6.7	6.9
道路面积(万平方米)	Area of Paved Roads (10 000 sq.m)	8964	9517
平均每人拥有(平方米)	Area of Paved Roads per Population (sq.m)	10.9	11.2
下水道长度(公里)	Length of Sewer Pipelines (km)	4592	4956
平均每万人拥有 (公里)	Length of Sewer Pipelines per 10 000 Population (km)	5.6	5.8
城市绿化	**City Greening**		
建成区绿化覆盖面积(公顷)	Green Areas of Completed Area (hectare)	33772	34428
每万人建成区绿地面积(公顷)	Green Areas of Completed Area per 10 000 Population (hectare)	41.1	40.6
公园数(个)	Number of Parks and Zoos(unit)	137	139
公园面积(公顷)	Area of Parks (hectare)	3274	3681
环境卫生	**Environmental Sanitation**		
清运生活垃圾(万吨)	Volume of Garbage Disposal (10 000 tons)	344	353
清运粪便(万吨)	Volume of Disposal of Excrement and Urine (10 000 tons)	3.4	0.4
每万人拥有公共厕所(座)	Number of Public Lavatories per 10 000 Population (unit)	2.6	2.6

10-2 各城市主要经济指标
Major Economic Indicators by Cities

单位: 万元 (2012 年) (10 000 yuan)

城市名称	City	地区生产总值(当年价格) Gross Region Production (current-year price)	第一产业 Primary Industry	第二产业 Secondary Industry	#工业 Industry
乌鲁木齐市	Urumqi City	20017386	250218	8290099	7140099
克拉玛依市	Karamay City	8107054	46245	7130736	6920736
吐鲁番市	Turpan City	637696	143733	200401	158901
哈 密 市	Hami [Kumul] City	2094376	206609	1026957	675450
昌 吉 市	Changji City	2603609	331988	1302901	1103014
阜 康 市	Fukang City	1188902	218894	729718	650821
伊 宁 市	Yining [Gulja] City	1367965	63567	363570	184220
奎 屯 市	Kuytun City	1059646	57238	565341	452905
塔 城 市	Tacheng [Qoqek] City	594874	132881	162171	86113
乌 苏 市	Usu City	1534588	455638	810562	672084
阿勒泰市	Altay City	453683	71260	90685	43985
博 乐 市	Bole [Bortala] City	1268844	293470	300914	205866
库尔勒市	Korla City	5914147	353996	4692684	4193313
阿克苏市	Aksu City	1625336	310572	489118	356799
阿图什市	Artux City	279690	44560	65594	42615
喀 什 市	Kashgar [Kaxgar] City	1320127	52000	453675	326589
和 田 市	Hotan City	382731	32412	128163	68086
石河子市	Shi Hezi City	2081934	113665	1198688	917676
阿拉尔市	Aral City				
图木舒克市	Tumxuk City				
五家渠市	Wujiaqu City				

城市名称	City	第三产业 Tertiary Industry	#交通运输、仓储和邮政业 Transport, Storage and Post	人均地区生产总值(元) Per Capita GDP (yuan)
乌鲁木齐市	Urumqi City	11477069	2509580	59576
克拉玛依市	Karamay City	930073	144554	135018
吐鲁番市	Turpan City	293562	75928	23566
哈 密 市	Hami [Kumul] City	860810	234976	45361
昌 吉 市	Changji City	968720	185679	54017
阜 康 市	Fukang City	240290	31388	71924
伊 宁 市	Yining [Gulja] City	940828	70579	27246
奎 屯 市	Kuytun City	437067	77972	69439
塔 城 市	Tacheng [Qoqek] City	299822	36704	35836
乌 苏 市	Usu City	268388	33875	45684
阿勒泰市	Altay City	291738	27047	23928
博 乐 市	Bole [Bortala] City	674461	99404	47917
库尔勒市	Korla City	867467	108043	103336
阿克苏市	Aksu City	825646	93716	33793
阿图什市	Artux City	169536	18446	10951
喀 什 市	Kashgar [Kaxgar] City	814452	89417	24042
和 田 市	Hotan City	222156	18322	6489
石河子市	Shi Hezi City	769582	69400	64346
阿拉尔市	Aral City			
图木舒克市	Tumxuk City			
五家渠市	Wujiaqu City			

10-2 续表 Continued

单位：万元 (10 000 yuan)

城市名称	City	城镇固定资产投资总额 Investment in Fixed Assets in Urban Area	规模以上工业总产值（当年价格） Gross Industrial Output Value above Designated Size (At Current Prices)	公共财政预算收入 General Budgetary Revenue in Local Finance	公共财政预算支出 General Budgetary Expenditure in Local Finance
乌鲁木齐市	Urumqi City	5812238	21508375	2520052	2956004
克拉玛依市	Karamay City	3016611	16938759	572603	701753
吐鲁番市	Turpan City	335671	442497	49222	139574
哈 密 市	Hami [Kumul] City	1851445	1571717	222574	311838
昌 吉 市	Changji City	1085526	2507933	205356	297840
阜 康 市	Fukang City	1140798	1220568	110723	193288
伊 宁 市	Yining [Gulja] City	1019719	416394	172123	326906
奎 屯 市	Kuytun City	1141756	1131640	133614	190875
塔 城 市	Tacheng [Qoqek] City	186263	97984	29407	140461
乌 苏 市	Usu City	574724	415957	80073	199352
阿勒泰市	Altay City	395846	135153	33777	182813
博 乐 市	Bole [Bortala] City	909624	392810	53849	155861
库尔勒市	Korla City	2715379	6223936	261012	368606
阿克苏市	Aksu City	780126	959460	126117	238065
阿图什市	Artux City	259354	124096	20013	171621
喀 什 市	Kashgar [Kaxgar] City	958522	451555	131406	410178
和 田 市	Hotan City	398444	92534	38113	201614
石河子市	Shi Hezi City	1751156	3699463	217520	269061
阿拉尔市	Aral City	583934	187101	32269	48056
图木舒克市	Tumxuk City	250296	109391	14252	27441
五家渠市	Wujiaqu City	1142507	1475814	68623	85556

城市名称	City	居民消费价格指数（上年=100） Consumer Price Index (preceding year=100)	社会消费品零售总额 Total Retail Sales of Consumer Goods	在岗职工平均货币工资（元） Average Money Wage of Staff and Workers (yuan)
乌鲁木齐市	Urumqi City	103.4	7396900	52418
克拉玛依市	Karamay City	102.9	480039	73510
吐鲁番市	Turpan City	104.3	164053	43272
哈 密 市	Hami [Kumul] City	103.7	495812	46103
昌 吉 市	Changji City	104.1	647122	44705
阜 康 市	Fukang City		214813	44918
伊 宁 市	Yining [Gulja] City	103.7	512532	38169
奎 屯 市	Kuytun City	102.4	186019	41006
塔 城 市	Tacheng [Qoqek] City	103.9	145715	39646
乌 苏 市	Usu City	103.9	104592	28692
阿勒泰市	Altay City	104.3	182065	32933
博 乐 市	Bole [Bortala] City	103.1	183538	37207
库尔勒市	Korla City	102.6	597768	50482
阿克苏市	Aksu City	102.2	475204	45613
阿图什市	Artux City	105.1	74137	39582
喀 什 市	Kashgar [Kaxgar] City	104.6	515000	40553
和 田 市	Hotan City	104.8	124646	51671
石河子市	Shi Hezi City	102.8	649839	44227
阿拉尔市	Aral City			38148
图木舒克市	Tumxuk City			36937
五家渠市	Wujiaqu City			46566

10-3 各城市市区设施水平

Level of Urban Public Facilities in Cities

(2012 年)

城市名称	City	城市用水普及率(%) Coverage Rate of Urban Population with Access to Tap Water (%)	城市燃气普及率(%) Coverage Rate of Population with Access to Gas (%)	人均铺装道路面积(平方米) Per Capital Area of Paved Roads (sq.m)	人均公园绿地面积(平方米) Per Capital Area of Parks and Green Land (sq.m)	排水管道密度(公里/平方公里) Density of Sewage Pipelines (km/sq.km)
总 计	**Total**	**99.13**	**96.60**	**14.16**	**10.00**	**5.16**
乌鲁木齐市	Urumqi City	99.95	99.83	7.45	9.20	3.53
克拉玛依市	Karamay City	100.00	100.00	24.07	9.58	6.87
吐鲁番市	Turpan City	98.70	94.79	25.71	26.44	5.28
哈 密 市	Hami [Kumul] City	100.00	95.33	14.94	9.08	10.33
昌 吉 市	Changji City	100.00	100.00	13.38	9.78	3.78
阜 康 市	Fukang City	96.11	99.33	16.70	10.60	6.86
伊 宁 市	Yining [Gulja] City	99.97	94.40	18.89	9.41	13.49
奎 屯 市	Kuytun City	100.00	93.33	15.06	8.65	9.44
塔 城 市	Tacheng [Qoqek] City	93.58	79.63	15.52	12.47	8.70
乌 苏 市	Usu City	88.46	72.53	17.57	6.81	7.24
阿勒泰市	Altay City	96.23	82.71	9.29	18.69	3.51
博 乐 市	Bole [Bortala] City	98.88	66.20	12.77	11.21	6.08
库尔勒市	Korla City	100.00	100.00	27.11	10.46	4.29
阿克苏市	Aksu City	100.00	99.92	12.97	14.64	6.76
阿图什市	Artux City	95.50	94.13	21.80	1.77	6.14
喀 什 市	Kashgar [Kaxgar] City	100.00	98.02	18.62	11.11	2.94
和 田 市	Hotan City	97.19	98.98	16.90	7.67	4.03
石河子市	Shihezi City	100.00	98.97	28.09	10.69	10.05
阿拉尔市	Aral City	95.45	75.76	29.33	11.52	2.66
图木舒克市	Tumxuk City	64.01	66.88	47.56	25.80	7.15
五家渠市	Wujiaqu City	100.00	98.53	22.26	11.32	2.29
北 屯 市	Beitun City	80.14	62.06	33.60	0.71	5.17

10-4 主要年份城市自来水情况

Basic Statistics on Tap Water Supply in Cities in Main Years

指 标	Item	2000	2010	2012
年末水厂生产能力(万吨/日)	Production Capacity of TapWater Supply (10 000 tons/day)	292	373	426
年末供水管道总长度(公里)	Length of Water Supply Piplines (km)	4448	6507	7450
全年供水总量(亿立方米)	Total Annual Volume of Water supply (100 millon cu.m)	5.0	7.7	8.6
#生活用水	For Residential Use	2.5	2.6	3.1
生产用水	For Productive Use	2.0	2.1	2.5
平均每人日生活用水量(升)	Per-Capitall Daily Consumption of Tap Water for Residential Use (litre)	165.1	150.8	171.0
用水人口(万人)	Number of Residents with Access to Tap Water (10 000 persons)	418	626	666

10-5 主要年份城市市政建设情况
Statistics on City Construction in Cities in Main Years

指　标	Item	2000	2010	2012
实有道路长度(公里)	Length of Paved Roads (km)	2809	5178	5813
实有道路面积(万平方米)	Area of Paved Roads (10 000 sq.m)	3654	8323	9517
城市桥梁(座)	Number of City Bridges (unit)	253	384	436
防洪堤长度(公里)	Length of Dyke for Control of Flood (km)	130	262	277
城市下水道总长度(公里)	Length of Sewer Pipelines (km)	2008	4372	4956
城市污水日处理能力(万立方米)	Daily Disposal Capacity of Sewage (10 000 cu.m)	46	157	195
城市路灯盏数(千盏)	Number of Street Light (1 000 units)	72.9	400.1	412.3

注：城市污水日处理能力指污水处理厂处理能力，不包括其他污水处理设施处理量。
Note: The daily treatment capacity in urban area refers to the treatment capacity of a waste- water treatment plant, excluding the volume handled by other polluted-water treatment facility.

10-6 主要年份城市园林绿化情况
Basic Statistics on Parks and Green Areas in Cities in Main Years

指　标	Item	2000	2010	2012
城市园林绿地面积(公顷)	Area of Park and Green Land (hectare)	19124	37686	49512
#建成区绿地面积	Green Land of Completed Area		27773	31355
每万人建成区绿地面积(公顷)	Green Areas of Completed Area Per 10 000 Population (hectare)	53.4	35.7	40.6
建成区绿化覆盖率(%)	Green Covrage Rate of Completed Area (%)	29.1	36.4	35.9
平均每人公园绿地面积(平方米)	Per Capita Parks Green Areas (sq.m)	6.4	8.6	10.0
公园数(个)	Number of Parks and Zoos (unit)	84	131	139
公园面积(公顷)	Area of Parks (hectare)	1568	3156	3681

10-7 主要年份城市环境卫生情况
Basic Statistics on Urban Environment in Cities in Main Years

指　标	Item	2000	2010	2012
环卫专用车辆设备数量(辆)	Number of Special Vehicles for Environmental Sanitation (unit)	767	1690	3365
公共厕所(座)	Number of Public Lavatories (unit)	1684	2119	2162
每万人拥有公共厕所(座)	Number of Public Lavatories Per 10 000 Population (unit)	4.7	2.5	2.6
道路清扫面积(万平方米)	Area under Cleaning Program (10 000 sq.m)	3224	8080	10445
#机械化	Mechanization		3163	4597
清运生活垃圾(万吨)	Volum of Garbage Disposal (10 000 tons)	259	317	353
清运粪便 (万吨)	Volum of Excrement and Urine Disposal (10 000 tons)	16.0	4.0	0.4

10-8 主要年份城市煤气、液化石油气、天然气情况

Basic Statistics on Supply of Gas, Liquefied Petroleum Gas and Natural Gas in Cities in Main Years

指　　标	Item	2000	2010	2012
人工煤气生产能力(万立方米/日)	Production Capacity of Gaswork Gas (10 000 cu.m/day)		49	46
管道长度(公里)	Length of Gas Pipelines (km)	385	7298	10124
人工煤气	Coal Gas		71	71
液化石油气	Liquefied Petroleum Gas		82	81
天然气	Natural Gas	385	7145	9972
全年供气总量(万立方米)	Volume of Gas Supply (10 000 cu.m)			
人工煤气	Coal Gas		1752	2190
液化石油气(吨)	Liquefied Petroleum Gas (ton)	244018	79617	73123
天然气	Natural Gas	5385	134711	262670
用气人口(万人)	Population with Access to Gas (10 000 persons)		604.37	649.25
人工煤气	Coal Gas		8.75	7.00
液化石油气	Liquefied Petroleum Gas	305.70	150.64	94.57
天然气	Natural Gas	27.00	444.98	547.68

10-9 主要年份城市集中供热情况

Basic Statistics on Heating in Cities in Main Years

指　　标	Item	2000	2010	2012
供应能力	**Heating Capacity**			
蒸汽(吨/小时)	Steam (ton/hour)	1638	1376	1959
热水(兆瓦)	Hot Water (1 billion kw)	6145	18897	23675
供热总量(万吉焦)	**Quantity of Heating Supplied (10 000 gigajoules)**			
蒸 汽	Steam		1242	1302
热 水	Hot Water		16866	16691
管道长度(公里)	**Length of Heating Pipelines (km)**			
蒸 汽	Steam	250	207	155
热 水	Hot Water	2064	5912	7376
供热面积(万平方米)	**Area of Centralized Heating (10 000 sq.m)**	**5170**	**19162**	**21844**
#住 宅	Residential Buildings		13298	15491

主要统计指标解释

供水综合生产能力 指按供水设施取水、净化、送水、出厂输水干管等环节设计能力计算的综合生产能力。包括在原设计能力的基础上，经挖、革、改增加的生产能力。计算时，以四个环节中最薄弱的环节为主确定能力。

年末供水管道长度 指从送水泵到用户水表之间所有管道的长度。不包括新安装尚未使用、水厂内以及用户建筑物内的管道。

城市供水总量 指报告期供水企业(单位)供出的全部水量。包括有效供水量和漏损水量。

生产运营用水 指在城区范围内生产、运营的农、林、牧、渔业、工业、建筑业、交通运输业等单位在生产、运营过程中的用水。

公共服务用水 指为城区社会公共生活服务的用水。包括行政事业单位、部队营区和公共设施服务、批发零售贸易业、旅馆饮食业以及社会服务业等单位的用水。

居民家庭用水 指城市范围内所有居民家庭的日常生活用水。包括城市居民、农民家庭、公共供水站用水。

用水普及率 指报告期末城区用水人口数与城市人口总数的比率。计算公式为：

用水普及率＝城区用水人口数（含暂住人口）／城区人口+城区暂住人口×100%

人工煤气生产能力 指报告期末人工煤气生产厂制气、净化、输送等环节的综合生产能力，不包括备用设备能力。一般按设计能力计算，如果实际生产能力大于设计能力时，应按实际测定的生产能力计算。测定时应以制气、净化、输送三个环节中最薄弱的环节为主。

供气管道长度 指报告期末从气源厂压缩机的出口或门站出口至各类用户引入管之间的全部已经通气投入使用的管道长度。不包括煤气生产厂、输配站、液化气储存站、灌瓶站、储配站、气化站、混气站、供应站等厂(站)内的管道。

城市供气总量 指全年燃气企业(单位)向用户供应的燃气数量。包括销售量和损失量。

燃气普及率 指报告期末城区用气的人口数与城市人口总数的比率。计算公式为：

燃气普及率＝城区用气人口（含暂住人口）／城区人口+城区暂住人口×100%

城市供热能力 指供热企业（单位）向城市热用户输送热源的设计能力。

城市供热总量 指在报告期供热企业（单位）向城市热用户输送全部蒸汽和热水的总热量。

城市供热管道长度 指从各种热源到热用户建筑物接入口之间的全部蒸汽和热水的管道长度。不包括各类热源厂内部的管道长度。

道路长度 指年末道路长度和与道路相通的桥梁、隧道的长度，按车行道中心线计算。

城市桥梁 指为跨越天然或人工障碍物而修建的构筑物。包括跨河桥、立交桥、人行天桥以及人行地下通道等。

城市排水道总长度 指所有排水总管、干管、支管、检查井及连接井进出口等长度之和。

城市污水日处理能力 指污水处理厂(污水处理处理装置）每昼夜处理污水量的设计能力。

城市绿地面积 指报告期末用作园林和绿化的各种绿地面积。包括园林绿地、公共绿地、防护绿地、附属绿地和其他绿地面积。

公园绿地 城市中向公众开放的、以游憩为主要功能，有一定的游憩设施和服务设施，同时兼有健全生态、美化景观，防灾减灾等综合作用的绿化用地。包括综合公园、社区公园、专类公园、带状公园和街旁绿地。其中综合公园、专类公园和带状公园面积之和为公园面积。

道路清扫保洁面积 指报告期末对城市道路和公共场所（主要包括城市行车道、人行道、车行隧道、人行过街地下通道、道路附属绿地、地铁站、高架路、人行过街天桥、立交桥、广场、停车场及其他设施等）进行清扫保洁的面积。一天清扫多次的，按清扫保洁面积最大的一次计算。

市容环卫专用车辆 指用于环境卫生作业、监察的专用车辆和设备，包括用于道路清扫、冲洗、洒水、除雪、垃圾粪便清运、市容监察以及与其配套使用的车辆和设备。

Explanatory Notes on Main Statistical Indicators

Production Capacity of Water Supply refers to the designed overall production capacity of water facilities, covering the four segments of water collection, purification, conveyance, and outflow through trunk pipelines. Increased capacity through transformation and innovation projects is included as well. The capacity is determined mainly on the weakest of the above-mentioned four segments.

Length of Water Supply Pipelines at Year-end refers to the total length of all the pipelines between the water pumps and the user water meters, excluding pipelines newly installed but not used yet, pipeline in the water factory, and pipeline in the user's buildings.

Total Volume of Urban Water Supply refers to the total volume of water supplied by water-works (units) during the reference period, including both the effective water supply and loss during the water supply.

Consumption of Water for Production and Operation Use refers to water consumption in the process of production and operation by production and operation units of agriculture, forestry, animal husbandry, fisheries, industry, construction industry, and transportation industry, etc. in urban areas.

Consumption of Water for Public Service Use refers to water consumption for public service in the urban areas. It includes water consumption of administrative institutions, army camps, public facilities, wholesale and retail trades, accommodation and catering industry and social service industry, etc.

Consumption of Water for Households Use refers to consumption of water for daily life of all households in cities, including households of urban residents and farmers, and public water supply stations.

Coverage Rate of Urban Population with Access to Tap Water refers to the ratio of the urban population with access to tap water to the total urban population at the end of reference period. The formula is:

$$\text{Coverage of urban population with access to tap water} = \frac{\text{Urban population with access to tap water}}{\text{Urban population}} \times 100\%$$

Production Capacity of Gaswork Gas refers to the overall production capacity of the urban gasworks in gas generation, purification and delivery at the end of the reference period, excluding capacity of the reserved facilities. In general, it is determined by the designed capacity, and when actual production capacity is larger than the designed capacity, the capacity is determined by the actual measurement on the weakest segment in the production, purification and delivery.

Length of Gas Pipelines refers to the total length of pipelines in use between the outlet of the compressor of gas-work or outlet of gas stations and the leading pipe of users, excluding pipelines within gasworks, delivery stations, LPG storage stations, refilling stations, gas-mixing stations and supply stations.

Volume of Gas Supply refers to the total volume of gas provided to users by gas-producing enterprises (units) in a year, including the volume sold and the volume lost.

Coverage Rate of Urban Population with Access to Gas refers to the ratio of the urban population with access to gas to the total urban population at the end of the reference period. The formula is:

$$\text{Coverage rate of urban population with access to gas} = \frac{\text{Urban population with access to gas}}{\text{Urban population}} \times 100\%$$

Heating Capacity in Urban Areas refers to the designed capacity of heating enterprises (units) in supplying heating energy to urban users during the reference period.

Quantity of Heat Supplied in Urban Areas refers to the total quantity of heat from steam and hot water supplied to urban users by heating enterprises (units) during the reference period.

Length of Urban Heating Pipelines refers to the total length of steam or hot water pipelines for sources of heat to the leading pipelines of the buildings of the users, excluding internal pipelines in heat generating enterprises.

Length of Paved Roads refers to the length of roads with paved surface including bridges and tunnels connected with roads by the end of the year. Length of the roads is measured by the central lines.

Urban Bridges refer to bridges built to cross over natural or man-made barriers, including bridges over rivers, overpasses for traffic and for pedestrians, underpasses for pedestrians, etc.

Length of Urban Sewage Pipes refers to the total length of general drainage, trunks, branch and inspection wells, connection wells, inlets and outlets, etc.

Daily Disposal Capacity of Urban Sewage refers to the designed 24-hour capacity of sewage disposal by the sewage treatment works or facilities.

Area of Urban Green Land refers to the total area occupied for green projects at the end of the reference period, including park green land, production green land, public green land, green land attached to institutions, and other green areas.

Park Green Area refers to green areas open to the public for amusement and rest with the facilities of amusement, rest and services. Its function includes perfecting ecology, beautifying landscape, and preventing and reducing disaster. Park green areas include comprehensive park, community park, theme park, linear park and roadside green space. Total areas of comprehensive park, topic park and belt-shaped is the area of park.

Road Area Cleaned refers to the area which are regularly cleaned, as at the end of the reference period, at urban roads and public places (mainly including urban roadways, pedestrian walkways, vehicular tunnels, pedestrian underpasses, underground railway stations, lifted roads, pedestrians walk bridges, overpasses, plazas, parking lots and other facilities). If there are several times of cleaning with the largest area cleaned will be taken.

Vehicles and Facilities Dedicated to Urban Cleanliness and Environmental Sanitation refer to vehicles and facilities dedicated for use in the operation, management and monitoring of environmental hygiene work. They include vehicles for road cleaning, washing, showering, ice removal, disposal of garbage and human wastes, cleanliness monitoring and related activities.

新疆统计年鉴
XINJIANG STATISTICAL YEARBOOK

11

自然资源与环境保护

NATURAL RESOURCES AND ENVIRONMENT PROTECTION

简要说明

本篇资料的主要内容及来源

本篇主要反映新疆维吾尔自治区自然资源、自然状况及环境保护事业发展情况等资料。主要内容包括自然资源储量和自然状况及水环境、大气环境、固体废物、声环境、生态环境、环境污染治理投资等内容。

水资源、城市生活垃圾清运及处理、地质灾害、矿产资源资料、土地资源和土地利用情况、林木资源等资料分别由新疆维吾尔自治区水利厅、建设厅、地震局、国土资源厅、林业厅提供；气象资料由新疆维吾尔自治区气象局提供。环境污染与治理、声环境、工业污染治理投资等情况由新疆维吾尔自治区环境保护厅依据年报资料整理提供。

2009年国家进行了第二次全国土地调查，我区调查数据目前国土资源部尚未反馈，为此，2013年年鉴中涉及土地资源及相关内容表式仍然沿用2008年度数据。

Brief Introduction

Main Content and Source of Data

This chapter contain information that reflect the natural conditions and natural resources and data on development of environment protection in Xinjiang Uygur Autonomous Region, including natural resources and natural condition, total water resources, atmosphere environment, solid wastes, environmental noise, eco-environment protection, natural disaster and investments in the treatment of environmental pollution etc.

Data on water resource, collection and disposal of urban consumption wastes, geological disasters, land use, forest resource, etc. are provided respectively by Bureau of Water Conservancy, Bureau of Construction, Seismological Bureau, Bureau of Land and Resources, Forestry Bureau in Xinjiang Uygur Autonomous Region; Meteorological data are provided by the Xinjiang Uygur Autonomous Region Meteorological Bureau. Data on environment pollution and treatment, noise monitoring and on investment in the treatment of industrial pollution are provided by the Xinjiang Environmental Protection Bureau.

For the second National Land Survey 2009 national survey data, the Ministry of land and resources has not yet been feedback, therefore, relates to mineral resources and related contents of land resources, table type still 2008 annual data from 2013 yearbook.

11-1 自 然 资 源
Natural Resources

指 标	Item	2012
自然状况	**State of the Nature**	
经纬度	Longitude and Latitude	
东 经	East Longitude	73° 40′ ～96° 23′
北 纬	North Latitude	34° 25′ ～49° 10′
气 候	Climate	
年平均气温(摄氏度)	Annual Average Temperature (℃)	
北 疆	North Xinjiang	9.5
南 疆	South Xinjiang	7.4
东 疆	East Xinjiang	12.0
年平均降水量(毫米)	Annual Average Precipitation (mm)	12.8
北 疆	North Xinjiang	163.7
南 疆	South Xinjiang	218.0
东 疆	East Xinjiang	114.8
平均日照时数(小时)	Average Sunny Hours (hour)	41.8
北 疆	North Xinjiang	2872.4
南 疆	South Xinjiang	2850.2
东 疆	East Xinjiang	2836.0
自然资源	**Natural Resources**	
土地资源(万公顷)	Land Resources (10 000 hectares)	
土地总面积	Total Land Area	16648.97
农用地	Land for farm use	6308.48
耕地面积	Area of Cultivated Land	412.46
园地面积	Garden Area	36.42
林地面积	Woodland Area	676.48
牧草地面积	Pastureland Area	5111.38
其他农用地	Other Land for Agriculture	71.75
建设用地	Land for Construction	123.98
未利用地	Land yet to be Used	10216.51
土地利用率(%)	Land utilization rate (%)	38.64
林木资源	Forest resources	
活立木总蓄积量(万立方米)	Total Standing Stock Volume (10 000 cu.m)	38679
森林蓄积量(万立方米)	Woodland Stock Volume (10 000 cu.m)	33654

11-1 续表 Continued

指　　标	Item	2012
有林地面积(万公顷)	Woodland Area (10 000 hectares)	539.80
灌木林地面积(万公顷)	Bush Woodland Area (10 000 hectares)	495.10
四旁树(万株)	Surrounding Woods (10 000 trees)	25095.00
森林覆盖率(%)	Forest coverage Rate (%)	4.24
水资源(亿立方米)	Water Resources (100 million cu.m)	
水资源总量	Total Water Resources Volume	885.70
地表水水资源量	Surface Water Volume	841.00
地下水水资源量	Underground Water Volume	539.80
重复计算量	Volume of Repeated Computation	495.10
主要矿产资源保有储量	**Reserve of Main Mineral Resources**	
铁矿(万吨)	Iron Ore (10 000 tons)	170527.32
铬矿(万吨)	Chromium Ore (10 000 tons)	90.46
铜矿(金属)(万吨)	Copper Ore (10 000 tons)	536.98
铅矿(金属)(万吨)	Lead Ore (10 000 tons)	261.75
锌矿(金属)(万吨)	Zinc Ore (10 000 tons)	415.01
铝土矿(万吨)	Bauxite(10 000 tons)	55.26
镍矿(金属)(万吨)	Nickel Ore (10 000 tons)	150.49
煤(亿吨)	Coal (100 million tons)	3145.31
耐火粘土(万吨)	Fire-proof Clay (10 000 tons)	703.40
钠硝石(万吨)	Nitratite (10 000 tons)	6266.81
芒硝(Na2SO4) (万吨)	Mirabilite(Na2SO4) (10 000 tons)	1640576.72
盐矿(NaCl) (万吨)	Solidum Salt(NaCI) (10 000 tons)	1178569.72
钾盐(KCl) (万吨)	Potassium(KCI) (10 000 tons)	15945.27
石棉(万吨)	Asbest (10 000 tons)	835.55
云母（工业原料）(吨)	Mica（Industrial raw materials） (ton)	54416.75
蛭石(万吨)	Roseite (10 000 tons)	1543.79
水泥用灰岩(万吨)	Limestone Used for Cement (10 000 tons)	197483.36
膨润土(万吨)	Bentonite (10 000 tons)	36550.41
饰面用花岗岩(万立方米)	Granite as Veneer (10 000 cu.m)	13471.53

注：1.水资源为 2011 年数据。2. 林木资源为 2011 年第八次全国森林资源清查、自治区森林资源第六次复查数据（2012 年公布）。3.因 2009 年第二次全国土地调查数据国家尚未反馈，土地资源仍沿用 2008 年度数据。

Note: a) Water-resources is based on the data in 2011.b) Figures of 2011 forest resources were form the fifth Autonomous Region Forest Survey(2012 announced).c) Because data of the Second National Land Survey in 2009 don't feedback, so data of land resources followed in 2008.

11-2 主要城市平均气温
Monthly Average Temperature of Major Cities

单位：摄氏度 (2012 年) (℃)

城 市	City	一月 Jan.	二月 Feb.	三月 Mar.	四月 Apr.	五月 May	六月 June	七月 July
乌鲁木齐市	Urumqi City	-15.0	-12.0	0.5	14.0	18.7	23.7	24.6
克拉玛依市	Karamay City	-19.7	-13.9	-2.1	16.6	21.2	26.8	27.4
石河子市	Shihezi City	-18.4	-12.7	1.2	16.5	21.1	26.0	26.1
阜康市	Fukang City	-18.1	-13.0	1.3	15.6	20.6	26.3	26.6
米泉市	Miquan City	-16.2	-11.5	1.9	16.2	21.1	26.2	27.1
伊宁市	Yining [Gulja] City	-10.8	-7.9	2.8	16.4	19.7	23.2	24.5
塔城市	Tacheng [Qoqek] City	-12.6	-9.4	2.1	14.5	17.9	22.5	24.2
阿勒泰市	Altay City	-20.2	-15.8	-2.2	11.3	16.1	22.5	21.9
博乐市	Bole [Bor tala] City	-19.1	-14.3	0.1	15.1	19.3	24.2	24.9
库尔勒市	Korla City	-9.2	-1.3	8.3	17.4	22.6	25.9	26.9
阿克苏市	Aksu City	-10.9	-3.0	6.8	17.3	20.6	23.4	23.9
阿图什市	Artux City	-9.2	-2.6	6.7	17.9	20.7	24.9	25.8
喀什市	Kashgar [Kaxgar] City	-9.0	-2.5	6.8	17.8	20.1	24.4	25.3
和田市	Hotan City	-7.0	-0.2	8.9	18.5	21.3	24.3	26.1
吐鲁番市	Turpan City	-8.2	0.7	11.7	21.7	27.4	32.3	33.5
哈密市	Hami [Kumul] City	-12.1	-3.9	5.8	15.2	21.8	26.2	27.2

城 市	City	八月 Aug.	九月 Sept.	十月 Oct.	十一月 Nov.	十二月 Dec.	全年平均 Annual Average
乌鲁木齐市	Urumqi City	23.7	18.1	8.9	-3.9	-12.6	7.4
克拉玛依市	Karamay City	25.5	20.0	10.2	-2.4	-16.4	8.1
石河子市	Shi Hezi City	24.4	18.4	9.1	-3.9	-16.1	7.6
阜康市	Fukang City	24.4	17.6	8.6	-4.7	-16.3	7.4
米泉市	Miquan City	25.6	19.4	10.0	-3.1	-14.2	8.5
伊宁市	Yining [Gulja] City	23.6	18.2	9.1	0.8	-9.6	9.2
塔城市	Tacheng [Qoqek] City	22.2	17.5	8.2	-3.1	-13.4	7.6
阿勒泰市	Altay City	19.8	15.5	5.7	-6.3	-19.5	4.1
博乐市	Bole [Bor tala] City	23.1	17.3	8.5	-4.1	-17.0	6.5
库尔勒市	Korla City	27.2	21.8	11.2	1.1	-6.8	12.1
阿克苏市	Aksu City	24.4	20.2	10.6	0.6	-6.6	10.6
阿图什市	Artux City	26.6	21.9	13.5	4.0	-3.1	12.3
喀什市	Kashgar [Kaxgar] City	25.7	21.0	12.7	3.9	-3.1	11.9
和田市	Hotan City	26.1	22.3	14.1	5.0	-1.1	13.2
吐鲁番市	Turpan City	32.4	24.2	13.6	3.0	-6.3	15.5
哈密市	Hami [Kumul] City	25.3	17.5	8.2	-1.9	-9.9	10.0

11-3 主要城市降水量
Monthly Precipitation of Major Cities

单位：毫米 (2012 年) (millimeter)

城　　市	City	一月 Jan.	二月 Feb.	三月 Mar.	四月 Apr.	五月 May	六月 June	七月 July
乌鲁木齐市	Urumqi City	9.2	18.4	25.6	5.9	25.9	24.9	27.6
克拉玛依市	Karamay City	0.4	0.9		21.8	7.1	22.6	71.3
石河子市	Shi Hezi City	6.2	16.4	5.9	14.6	10.6	10.5	21.4
阜康市	Fukang City	3.6	8.0	12.1	8.0	12.9	3.5	16.6
米泉市	Miquan City	7.4	12.4	18.7	5.1	30.8	16.8	25.2
伊宁市	Yining [Gulja] City	17.7	23.7	20.6	8.0	11.8	9.8	11.9
塔城市	Tacheng [Qoqek] City	7.1	3.0	18.9	15.8	9.8	36.5	11.8
阿勒泰市	Altay City	2.9	2.0	2.9	11.8	6.5	20.8	56.0
博乐市	Bole [Bortala] City	5.8	16.6	7.9	5.1	23.6	10.5	36.1
库尔勒市	Korla City	1.1	0.1			1.5	91.8	15.1
阿克苏市	Aksu City	6.3	1.1	13.3		18.5	11.9	10.3
阿图什市	Artux City	5.0	25.1	43.9	3.2	15.7	20.8	36.6
喀什市	Kashgar [Kaxgar] City	4.6	23.0	14.5	0.2	15.7	9.4	36.2
和田市	Hotan City	2.4	3.1	11.1		5.5	33.4	3.5
吐鲁番市	Turpan City	1.5					1.7	4.2
哈密市	Hami [Kumul] City	2.8			1.3	6.2	29.6	1.4

城　　市	City	八月 Aug.	九月 Sept.	十月 Oct.	十一月 Nov.	十二月 Dec.	全年合计 Annual Total
乌鲁木齐市	Urumqi City	10.1	34.2	32.3	44.2	28.6	286.9
克拉玛依市	Karamay City	23.8	9.2	2.0	0.6	9.5	169.2
石河子市	Shihezi City	7.6	8.2	14.0	43.5	14.5	173.4
阜康市	Fukang City	26.6	17.0	30.1	22.6	17.1	178.1
米泉市	Miquan City	13.5	33.4	32.1	24.0	23.6	243.0
伊宁市	Yining [Gulja] City	12.7	4.2	23.2	31.4	60.0	235.0
塔城市	Tacheng [Qoqek] City	36.7	5.5	26.3	35.6	49.3	256.3
阿勒泰市	Altay City	47.8	15.9	20.9	17.4	48.5	253.4
博乐市	Bole [Bortala] City	13.4	18.8	8.7	14.9	4.9	166.3
库尔勒市	Korla City	3.7		0.3	6.9	6.9	127.4
阿克苏市	Aksu City	15.2	2.7		0.5	1.0	80.8
阿图什市	Artux City	2.3	9.9			5.0	167.5
喀什市	Kashgar [Kaxgar] City	3.3	9.0			4.6	120.5
和田市	Hotan City	15.7				3.1	77.8
吐鲁番市	Turpan City	0.5	1.0	1.2		11.5	21.6
哈密市	Hami [Kumul] City	1.5	2.4	1.6	5.9	9.2	61.9

11-4 主要城市日照时数
Monthly Sunshine Hours of Major Cities

单位：小时　　(2012 年)　　(hour)

城　　市	City	一月 Jan.	二月 Feb.	三月 Mar.	四月 Apr.	五月 May	六月 June	七月 July
乌鲁木齐市	Urumqi City	116.0	115.4	220.4	302.9	337.7	300.7	312.7
克拉玛依市	Karamay City	176.1	194.9	238.3	322.5	349.4	312.8	278.9
石河子市	Shi Hezi City	71.4	102.9	207.1	319.7	359.9	336.2	342.8
阜康市	Fukang City	29.0	105.5	224.2	307.8	346.5	306.3	328.6
米泉市	Miquan City	22.1	48.7	170.3	303.2	343.1	301.4	307.3
伊宁市	Yining [Gulja] City	153.5	149.7	202.5	305.0	342.6	332.3	365.5
塔城市	Tacheng [Qoqek] City	204.0	212.7	225.6	320.9	340.4	315.7	308.5
阿勒泰市	Altay City	207.5	231.2	255.7	291.5	352.5	337.0	321.6
博乐市	Bole [Bortala] City	149.4	173.0	200.2	300.3	314.9	290.7	317.5
库尔勒市	Korla City	189.9	221.0	257.0	282.3	325.6	278.4	333.0
阿克苏市	Aksu City	170.1	174.7	157.7	217.5	289.6	291.4	313.8
阿图什市	Artux City	154.3	124.4	159.3	211.3	253.6	304.9	320.8
喀什市	Kashgar [Kaxgar] City	166.9	136.8	182.4	263.1	287.5	360.9	361.7
和田市	Hotan City	187.0	149.6	199.0	207.8	252.1	249.5	240.6
吐鲁番市	Turpan City	42.3	151.0	209.0	281.6	321.8	295.4	314.9
哈密市	Hami [Kumul] City	233.5	258.0	315.3	352.1	389.6	357.7	377.2

城　　市	City	八月 Aug.	九月 Sept.	十月 Oct.	十一月 Nov.	十二月 Dec.	全年合计 Annual Total
乌鲁木齐市	Urumqi City	346.8	273.8	256.6	151.5	130.1	2864.6
克拉玛依市	Karamay City	324.5	276.5	237.7	152.5	92.5	2956.6
石河子市	Shi Hezi City	357.7	280.4	257.9	150.7	55.7	2842.4
阜康市	Fukang City	344.6	272.7	236.6	115.3	69.9	2687.0
米泉市	Miquan City	345.7	259.2	231.6	93.5	19.5	2445.6
伊宁市	Yining [Gulja] City	352.5	276.3	239.1	161.5	133.5	3014.0
塔城市	Tacheng [Qoqek] City	306.8	283.7	210.7	122.9	117.5	2969.4
阿勒泰市	Altay City	319.3	299.5	191.5	125.9	110.8	3044.0
博乐市	Bole [Bortala] City	318.6	262.4	225.5	149.7	126.4	2828.6
库尔勒市	Korla City	327.7	293.1	277.5	207.8	158.7	3152.0
阿克苏市	Aksu City	309.6	279.7	287.4	196.2	183.3	2871.0
阿图什市	Artux City	281.4	217.7	252.5	154.8	136.1	2571.1
喀什市	Kashgar [Kaxgar] City	334.7	254.1	286.9	186.1	157.8	2978.9
和田市	Hotan City	222.1	253.7	285.4	184.9	175.4	2607.1
吐鲁番市	Turpan City	325.7	260.5	195.6	71.3	43.9	2513.0
哈密市	Hami [Kumul] City	349.3	314.9	281.5	211.1	172.8	3613.0

11-5 环境保护基本情况
Basic Statistics on Environmental Protection

项　　目	Item	2011	2012
水环境	**Water**		
废水排放总量(亿吨)	Volume of Waste Water Discharged (100 million tons)	9.09	9.37
#工业废水排放量	Volume of Industrial Waste Water Discharged	2.88	2.97
城镇生活废水排放量	Volume of Non-industrial Waste Water Discharged	6.21	6.40
集中式治理设施废水排放量	Volume of Centralized Treatment for Waste Water Facilities	0.0038	0.0041
化学需氧量排放量(万吨)	Amount of COD Discharged (10 000 tons)	67.29	67.92
#工业化学需氧量排放量	Amount of COD Discharged by industry	18.76	18.63
城镇生活化学需氧量排放量	Amount of COD Discharged by Non-industry	12.97	12.12
农业化学需氧量排放量	Amount of COD Discharged by Agricutral	35.10	36.72
集中式治理设施化学需氧量排放量	Amount of Centralized Treatment for COD Facilities	0.45	0.45
氨氮排放量(万吨)	Ammonia Nitrogen Discharged (10 000 tons)	4.68	4.73
#工业氨氮排放量	Industrial Ammonia Nitrogen Discharged	1.21	1.18
城镇生活氨氮排放量	Non-industrial Ammonia Nitrogen Discharged	2.21	2.24
农业氨氮排放量	Agricultural Ammonia Nitrogen Discharged	1.23	1.28
集中式治理设施氨氮排放量	Amount of Centralized Treatment for Ammonia Nitrogen Facilities	0.03	0.03
大气环境	**Atmosphere Environment**		
工业废气排放量(亿标立方米)	Industrial Waste Air Emission (100 million cu.m)	11867.99	15869.86
二氧化硫排放量(万吨)	Volume of Sulphur Dioxide Emission (10 000 tons)	76.31	79.61
#工业二氧化硫排放量	Volume of Sulphur Dioxide Emission by Industry	66.91	70.47
城镇生活二氧化硫排放量	Volume of Sulphur Dioxide Emission by Consumption	9.40	9.14
集中式治理设施二氧化硫排放量	Amount of Centralized Treatment for Sulphur Dioxide Facilities	0.0002	0.0001
氮氧化物排放量(万吨)	Ammonia Nitrogen Discharged (10 000 tons)	75.51	81.95

注：2011、2012 年自然保护区只包含自治区及国家级自然保护区。
Note: The nature reserves contain the municipality and state leuel nature protection area.

11-5 续表 1 Continued

项　　目	Item	2011	2012
#工业氮氧化物排放量	Industrial Ammonia Nitrogen Discharged	45.23	50.57
城镇生活氮氧化物排放量	Non-industrial Ammonia Nitrogen Discharged	1.64	1.58
机动车氮氧化物排放量	Agricultural Ammonia Nitrogen Discharged	28.64	29.80
集中式治理设施氮氧化物排放量	Amount of Centralized Treatment for Ammonia Nitrogen Facilities	0.0006	0.0004
烟(粉)尘排放量(万吨)	Volume of Soot Emission (10 000 tons)	53.27	69.61
#工业烟(粉)尘排放量	Volume of Industrial Soot Emission	44.13	60.60
城镇生活烟(粉)尘排放量	Volume of Soot Emission by Consumption	6.97	6.74
机动车烟(粉)尘排放量(总颗粒物排放量)	Volume of Soot Emission by Consumption	2.16	2.26
集中式治理设施氮氧化物排放量	Amount of Centralized Treatment for Ammonia Nitrogen Facilities	0.01	0.01
固体废物	**Solid Wastes**		
一般工业固体废物产生量(万吨)	Industrial Solid Wastes Produced (10 000 tons)	5219.09	7884.03
一般工业固体废物综合利用量(万吨)	Industrial Solid Wastes Utilized (10 000 tons)	2838.11	4064.13
一般工业固体废物处置量(万吨)	Ratio of Industrial Solid Wastes Utilized (%)	620.92	532.65
一般工业固体废物储存量(万吨)	Industrial Solid Wastes Discharged (10 000 tons)	1702.43	3252.65
一般工业固体废物倾倒丢弃量(万吨)	General volume of industrial solid wastes dumping of discarded (10 000 tons)	88.731	35.520
危险废物产生量（万吨）	Amount of hazardous waste generated (10 000 tons)	470.14	444.17
生态环境	**Eco-Environment Protection**		
当年造林面积(万公顷)	Area of Reforestation of the Year (10 000 hectares)	20.58	20.50
自然保护区数(个)	Number of Nature Reserves (unit)	28	28
#国家级	National Level	9	9
自然保护区面积(万公顷)	Area of Nature Reserves (10 000 hectares)	2096.00	2140.56
#国家级	National Level	1365.53	1365.53

11-5 续表 2 Continued

项　目	Item	2011	2012
自然保护区面积占辖区面积比重(%)	Area of Nature Reserves in Regions (%)	12.63	12.86
农村生态示范建设个数(个)	Number of Demonstration Zones of Ecology (unit)	84	151
国家级生态乡镇数(个)	Number of National Eco-towns (unit)	15	37
国家级生态村数(个)	Number of National Eco-village (unit)	7	7
自然灾害	**Natural Disaster**		
发生地质灾害起数(次)	Geological Disaster(case)	24	44
发生地震灾害次数(次)	Seismic Disaster(case)	8	11
#5.0 级以上	Magnitude above 5 Richter Scale	8	11
森林火灾次数(次)	Forest Fire (case)	59	41
森林火灾受灾面积 (公顷)	Fire-Affected Forest Area (hectare)	150.16	17.35
森林病虫害发生面积(万公顷)	Forest Area Affected by Disease and Pests (10 000 hectares)	122.36	126.14
森林病虫害防治面积(万公顷)	Forest Area Provented and Cured from Disease and Pests (10 000 hectares)	54.72	53.90
森林病虫害防治率(%)	Rate of Prevention and Cure (%)	45.0	42.7
环境污染治理投资	**Investment in the Treaiment of Environmental Pollution**		
环境污染治理投资总额(亿元)	Total Investment in Pollution Treatment (10 000 yuan)	194.04	237.09
城镇环境基础设施建设投资额	Investment in Urban Environment Infrastructure	122.61	170.80
工业污染治理项目年完成投资总额	Investment Completed in Treatment Projects Industrial Pollution	23.17	7.91
当年完成环保验收项目环保投资总额	Investment Completed in Treatment Projects Industrial Pollution	48.26	58.39
环境污染治理投资总额相当于新疆生产总值比例(%)	Investment in Pollution Treatment Out of XJ GDP (%)	2.95	3.15
当年施工工业污染治理项目数(个)	Number of Projects in Industrial Pollution Treatment under Construction of The Year (unit)	154	72
当年竣工工业污染治理项目数(个)	Number of Projects Completed in Industrial Pollution Treatment of the Year Projects (unit)	92	54

11-6 水资源情况

Water Resource

年份 Year	地区 Region	水资源总量(亿立方米) Total Amount Of Water Resources (100 million cu.m)	地表水资源量 Surface Water Resources	地下水资源量 Ground Water Resources	地下水与地下水资源重复量 Duplicated Measurement Between surface Water and Groundwater	人均水资源量(立方米/人) Per Capita Water Resources (cu.m/person)
	2000	952.40	897.10	636.29	580.99	5255
	2001	1024.40	966.90	692.31	634.81	5500
	2002	1068.60	1006.00	724.85	662.25	5652
	2003	920.10	863.20	604.30	547.40	4793
	2004	855.40	809.20	502.60	456.40	4390
	2005	962.82	910.66	562.57	510.41	4789
	2006	953.12	903.84	554.13	504.85	4695
	2007	863.80	816.60	514.10	466.90	4168
	2008	802.60	759.50	518.50	475.36	3798
	2009	754.29	713.64	470.47	429.82	3517
	2010	1124.00	1063.00	624.30	563.20	5120
	2011	885.70	841.00	539.80	495.10	4035
乌鲁木齐市	Urumqi City	9.85	9.56	4.58	4.28	351
克拉玛依市	Karamay City	0.58	0.05	1.14	0.62	172
石河子市	Shihezi City	0.15	0.07	0.77	0.69	30
吐鲁番地区	Turpan Administrative Offices	6.94	5.27	6.22	4.55	1106
哈密地区	Hami [Kumul] Administrative Offices	11.03	9.14	7.37	5.48	1908
昌吉回族自治州	Changji Hui Autonomous Prefecture	33.36	29.55	20.55	16.74	2363
伊犁州直属县(市)	Counties (Cities) Direct Under Ili Prefecture	190.60	187.50	90.75	87.61	7102
塔城地区	Tacheng [Tarbagatai] Administrative Offices	51.43	47.72	31.03	27.32	4543
阿勒泰地区	Altay Administrative Offices	92.92	89.14	43.98	40.19	14608
博尔塔拉蒙古自治州	Bortala Mongol Autonomous Prefecture	30.41	27.95	17.90	15.43	6533
巴音郭楞蒙古自治州	Bayangol Mongol Autonomous Prefecture	128.40	122.70	71.51	65.87	9711
阿克苏地区	Aksu Administrative Offices	72.91	65.87	81.99	74.95	3063
克孜勒苏柯尔克孜自治州	Kizilsu Kirgiz Autonomous Prefecture	75.82	74.59	42.32	41.09	14041
喀什地区	Kashgar [Kaxgar] Administrative Offices	73.00	68.38	68.62	64.00	1807
和田地区	Hotan Administrative Offices	108.20	103.50	51.06	46.28	5291

11-7 供水和用水情况
Water Supply and Water Used

单位：亿立方米　　(2011 年)　　(100 million cu.m)

年 份 Year	地 区 Region	供水总量 Water Supply	地表水 Surface Water	地下水 Ground Water	中水利用量 Use of Intermediate Water	用水总量 Water Used	生 产 Production
总 计	**Total**	**523.51**	**424.97**	**97.75**	**0.79**	**523.51**	**507.19**
乌鲁木齐市	Urumqi City	10.68	4.96	5.26	0.46	10.68	8.77
克拉玛依市	Karamay City	4.18	3.54	0.41	0.23	4.18	2.66
石河子市	Shihezi City	15.00	11.80	3.20		15.00	14.53
吐鲁番地区	Turpan Administrative Offices	13.55	5.12	8.42	0.01	13.55	12.68
哈密地区	Hami [Kumul] Administrative Offices	10.17	3.81	6.35	0.01	10.17	9.29
昌吉回族自治州	Changji Hui Autonomous Prefecture	37.31	22.24	15.04	0.03	37.31	35.74
伊犁州直属县(市)	Counties (Cities) Direct Under Ili Prefecture	53.59	49.46	4.13		53.59	51.98
塔城地区	Tacheng [Tarbagatai] Administrative Offices	25.14	14.38	10.76		25.14	24.28
阿勒泰地区	Altay Administrative Offices	34.45	33.95	0.50		34.45	34.20
博尔塔拉蒙古自治州	Bortala Mongol Autonomous Prefecture	14.56	10.42	4.14		14.56	14.31
巴音郭楞蒙古自治州	Bayangol Mongol Autonomous Prefecture	41.40	32.34	9.01	0.05	41.40	39.70
阿克苏地区	Aksu Administrative Offices	101.75	94.90	6.85		101.75	100.47
克孜勒苏柯尔克孜自治州	Kizilsu Kirgiz Autonomous Prefecture	8.40	7.40	1.00		8.40	8.19
喀什地区	Kashgar [Kaxgar] Administrative Offices	110.04	89.99	20.05		110.04	108.25
和田地区	Hotan Administrative Offices	43.29	40.66	2.63		43.29	42.13

年 份 Year	地 区 Region	第一产业 Primary Industry	第二产业 Secondary Industry	第三产业 Tertiary Industry	居民生活 Consumption	生态环境 Ecological Protection	人均用水量(立方米/人) Per Capita Water Used (cu.m/person)
总 计	**Total**	**491.91**	**14.05**	**1.23**	**7.63**	**8.69**	**2385**
乌鲁木齐市	Urumqi City	6.25	2.32	0.20	1.48	0.43	381
克拉玛依市	Karamay City	1.38	1.23	0.05	0.10	1.42	1242
石河子市	Shihezi City	13.28	1.21	0.04	0.25	0.22	2987
吐鲁番地区	Turpan Administrative Offices	12.11	0.51	0.06	0.21	0.66	2160
哈密地区	Hami [Kumul] Administrative Offices	8.87	0.40	0.02	0.28	0.60	1759
昌吉回族自治州	Changji Hui Autonomous Prefecture	33.85	1.80	0.09	0.57	1.00	2643
伊犁州直属县(市)	Counties (Cities) Direct Under Ili Prefecture	49.74	2.11	0.13	0.93	0.68	1997
塔城地区	Tacheng [Tarbagatai] Administrative Offices	23.67	0.50	0.11	0.38	0.48	2221
阿勒泰地区	Altay Administrative Offices	33.86	0.33	0.01	0.14	0.11	5416
博尔塔拉蒙古自治州	Bortala Mongol Autonomous Prefecture	14.10	0.20	0.01	0.19	0.06	3128
巴音郭楞蒙古自治州	Bayangol Mongol Autonomous Prefecture	38.43	1.14	0.13	0.56	1.14	3131
阿克苏地区	Aksu Administrative Offices	99.23	1.10	0.14	0.84	0.44	4275
克孜勒苏柯尔克孜自治州	Kizilsu Kirgiz Autonomous Prefecture	8.10	0.07	0.02	0.15	0.06	1556
喀什地区	Kashgar [Kaxgar] Administrative Offices	107.22	0.94	0.09	0.91	0.88	2723
和田地区	Hotan Administrative Offices	41.81	0.19	0.13	0.64	0.51	2117

11-8 主要年份环保系统机构、人员数
Number of Environmental Protection Agencies and Persons Engaged in Main Years

年 份 Year	机构数 (个) Number of Agencies (unit)	人员数 (人) Total Number of Staff & Workers (person)	#科技人员 Scientific and Technical Personnel	#监测人员 Monitoring Personnel	#监察人员 Supervising and Administrative Personnel
2000	208	1965	110	654	416
2001	208	2096	109	636	420
2002	238	2386	99	692	523
2003	275	2588	107	766	671
2004	288	2694	107	763	701
2005	304	2796	120	758	790
2006	326	2968	125	777	923
2007	326	2962	77	786	955
2008	296	2962	100	812	993
2009	319	3197	103	857	998
2010	324	3237	109	936	1126
2011	335	3372	121	967	1194
2012	324	3459	111	995	1112

注：本表数据从 2009 年开始不包含兵团数据。(11-12、11-13、11-14 同)
Note: The date of this table don't cover the date of XJPCC from 2009.(the same as the table of 11-12,11-13,11-14)

11-9 工业按行业重点调查工业企业废气及污染物排放情况
Emission and Treatment of Waste Water and Pollutant in Industrial Enterprises by Sector

单位：吨 (2012 年) (ton)

行 业	Sector	工业废气排放量(亿立方米) Total Volume of Industrial Waste Gas Emission (100 million cu.m)	工业二氧化硫排放量 Volume of Sulphur Dioxide Emission by Industry	工业氮氧化物排放量 Volume of Nitrogen Dioxide Emission by Industry	工业烟(粉)尘排放量 Volume of Industrial Soot Emission
合 计	**Total**	**15869.86**	**669152.87**	**491647.95**	**573494.87**
农副食品加工业	Processing of Ferrous Metals Ores	45.97	953.10	190.43	5023.07
食品制造业	Processing of Nonferrous Metals Ores	16.37	659.10	287.68	1566.67
酒、饮料和精制茶制造业	Processing of Food from Agricultural Products	101.96	10852.40	6668.33	5071.00
纺织业	Paper and Paper Products Manufacturing	30.85	4948.42	1379.34	1442.39
造纸及纸制品业	Oil Processing, Coking and Nuclear Fuel Processing	1626.11	89441.35	44761.73	43957.64
石油加工、炼焦及核燃料加工业	Raw Chemical Material and Chemical Products	1228.45	27098.31	24058.99	11913.86
化学原料及化学制品制造业	Nonmetal Mineral Products Manufacturing	2652.12	30429.37	68173.92	80194.96
化学纤维制造业	Cement Industry	2214.76	11338.84	62064.83	52443.71
黑色金属冶炼及压延加工业	Smelting and Pressing of Ferrous Metals	2734.67	73514.87	30629.26	46181.89
电力、热力的生产和供应业	Iron and Steel Industry	2730.03	73385.22	30628.23	46179.60
其他行业	Smelting and Pressing of Nonferrous Metals	1052.64	131642.19	9251.91	12875.55
电力、热力的生产和供应业	Electricity and Thermal Production and Supply	4915.76	268624.77	281653.63	153182.07
其他行业	Ohters	1464.97	30989.00	24592.74	212085.79

11-10 工业按行业重点调查工业企业废水及污染物排放情况
Emission and Treatment of Waste Water and Pollutant in Industrial Enterprises by Sector

(2012 年)

行业	Sector	工业废水排放量(万吨) Volume Of Waste Water Discharged (10 000 tons)	工业废水中化学需氧量排放量(吨) COD Discharge From Industral WasteWater (ton)	工业废水中氨氮排放量(吨) Ammonia Nitrogen Discharge form Industrial Waste Water (ton)
合　计	**Total**	**28278.62**	**177224.89**	**11514.20**
农副食品加工业	Processing of Food from Agricultural Products	1780.33	11614.73	277.86
食品制造业	Food Manufacturing	1942.51	10158.95	413.42
酒、饮料和精制茶制造业	Processing of Food from Agricultural Products	899.13	18951.96	305.17
纺织业	Textile Industry	621.18	3192.25	96.29
造纸及纸制品业	Paper and Paper Products Manufacturing	1928.39	9231.47	147.50
石油加工、炼焦及核燃料加工业	Oil Processing, Coking and Nuclear Fuel Processing	2351.98	2563.13	637.82
化学原料及化学制品制造业	Raw Chemical Material and Chemical Products	3562.73	7416.28	7969.11
化学纤维制造业	Chemical Fiber Manufacturing	5935.35	104509.56	1283.12
黑色金属冶炼及压延加工业	Smelting and Pressing of Ferrous Metals	1651.22	1281.26	113.46
电力、热力的生产和供应业	Electricity and Thermal Production and Supply	3086.56	1003.82	38.56
其他行业	Ohters	4519.25	7301.46	231.89

11-11 工业按行业重点调查工业企业固体废物产生量及处理利用情况
Production and Treatment of Waste Solid in Industrial Enterprises by Region

单位：万吨　　(2012 年)　　(10 000 ton)

行业 Sector	一般工业固体废物产生量 Volume of Industrial Solid Wastes Produced	一般工业固体废物综合利用量 Volume of Industrial Solid Wastes Utilized	一般工业固体废物贮存量 Volume of Industrial Solid Wastes in Stocks	一般工业固体废物处置量 Volume of Industrial Solid Wastes Treated	一般工业固体废物倾倒丢弃量 General Volume of Industrial Solid Wastes Dumping of Discarded (10 000 tons)
合　计 **Total**	7757.25	3949.87	3171.51	588.72	48.08
煤炭开采和洗选业 Mining and Washing of Coal	2458.71	1189.33	1120.91	145.09	3.38
黑色金属矿采选业 Processing of Ferrous Metals Ores	1305.99	35.92	1243.08	26.99	
有色金属矿采选业 Processing of Nonferrous Metals Ores	850.40	119.07	606.20	125.13	
黑色金属冶炼及压延加工业 Smelting and Pressing of Ferrous Metals	805.91	753.47		52.44	
电力、热力的生产和供应业 Electricity and Thermal Production and Supply	958.93	808.73	41.37	107.02	1.81
化学原料及化学制品制造业 Raw Chemical Material and Chemical Products	448.44	412.52	7.77	28.11	0.05
非金属矿物制品业 Nonmetal Mineral Products Manufacturing	244.53	188.86	7.49	47.97	0.20
石油加工、炼焦及核燃料加工业 OilProcessing,CokingandNuclearFuel Processing	197.65	167.76		29.89	0.01
有色金属冶炼及压延加工业 Smelting and Pressing of Nonferrous Metals	155.02	74.41	78.86	2.65	
非金属矿采选业 Mining and Processing of Nonmetal Ores	141.60	54.17	58.87	8.00	20.57
其他行业 Ohters	190.06	145.62	6.97	15.44	22.07

11-12 环境污染治理投资
Investment in the Treatment of Environment Pollution

项　　目	Item	2011	2012
环境污染治理投资总额(万元)	**Total Investment in the Treatment of Environment Pollution (10 000 yuan)**	**1940403.95**	**2370935.73**
城镇环境基础设施建设投资	Investment in Urban Environmental Infrastructure	1226067.00	1707970.00
#污水处理	Volume of Waste Water	31296.00	56115.00
垃圾处理	Volume of Garbage Disposal	53631.00	41937.00
燃　气	Gas Supply	220336.00	225918.00
集中供热	Centralized Heating	524178.00	959439.00
园林绿化	Gardening and Greening	396626.00	424561.00
工业污染源治理投资	Investment in the Treatment of Industrial Pollution	231696.35	79106.23
#工业废水治理项目	Number of Project in Industrial Waste water Treatment	36027.88	37904.80
工业废气脱硫治理项目	Number of Project in Industrial Waste Gas Treatment	42003.92	25349.43
工业废气脱硝治理项目	Number of Project in Industrial Waste Gas Treatment	135456.55	9225.00
污染物自动在线监测仪器安装项目	Number of Project Installation　Pollution	146.00	248.00
当年完成环保验收项目环保投资	Investment in the Treatment of Industrial Pollution	482640.60	583859.50
#废水治理环保投资	Investment of Pollution in Waste Water Treatment	153260.30	159631.40
废气治理环保投资	Investment of Pollution in Waste Gas Treatment	153914.40	108311.60
固体废物治理环保投资	Investment of Pollution in Solid Wastes Treatment	31987.80	24523.80
噪声治理环保投资	Investment of Pollution in Noise Treatment	23337.80	15035.60
绿化及生态环保投资	Investment of Pollution in Landscape and Greening	120140.30	276357.10
环境污染治理投资总额相当于新疆生产总值比例(%)	**Investment in the Treatment of Environmental Pollution as Percent of GDP (%)**	**2.95**	**3.15**

11-13 主要年份工业污染治理投资完成情况
Investment Completed in the Treatment of Industrial Pollution in Main Years

年 份 Year	汇总工业企业数(个) Number of Industrial Enterprises (unit)	污染治理项目本年完成投资(万元) Investment In the Treatment of Industrial Pollution (10 000 yuan)	治理废水 Treatment of Waste Water	治理废气 Treatment of Waste Gas	治理固体废物 Treatment of Solid Waste	治理噪声 Treatment of Noise Pollution	治理其他 Treatment of Other Pollution	本年施工项目数(个) Projects Under Construction (unit)	本年竣工项目数(个) Projects Completed (unit)
2000	154	22311	8528	9116	349	4109	209	203	198
2001	113	32009	25917	4886	723	66	416	113	106
2002	89	16952	5015	8241	2206	261	1229	129	85
2003	83	26509	9298	9514	4865	21	2811	104	94
2004	94	29622	12334	13114	2756	92	1327	146	110
2005	97	44008	23549	9656	371	321	10111	162	153
2006	92	45229	26876	12036	2582	32	3703	143	132
2007	90	60138	29958	23891	1676	219	4394	117	103
2008	72	68004	33123	31999	1964	270	648	120	120
2009	99	125435	22242	99849	600	170	2574	109	100
2010	66	66813	19687	46276	800		50	56	48
2011	81	231693	36028	195202			317	154	92
2012	79	79106	37905	40483			718	72	54

11-14 工业污染治理投资来源
Source of Investment in the Treatment of Industrial Pollution

单位：万元 (10 000 yuan)

项　　目	Item	2011	2012
施工项目本年投资来源	Source of Current Investment	231693	79106
排污费补助	Pollution Charges Subsidies	402	890
政府其他补助	Other Government Subsidies	3876	6050
企业自筹	Self-raising Funds	227415	72166
#银行贷款	Bank Loans		1500

11-15 主要城市空气质量指标
Ambient Air Quality in Main Cities

单位:毫克/立方米 (2012 年) (milligram/cu.m)

城　市	City	可吸入颗粒物 (PM10) Paticulate Matters	二氧化硫 (SO_2)	二氧化氮 (NO_2)	空气质量达到及好于二级的天数(天) Days of Air Quality Equal to or Above Grade II (day)
乌鲁木齐市	Urumqi City	0.146	0.058	0.068	292
克拉玛依市	Karamay City	0.065	0.017	0.028	359
石河子市	Shihezi City	0.090	0.035	0.033	340
吐鲁番市	Turpan City	0.203	0.019	0.028	222
哈 密 市	Hami [Kumul] City	0.109	0.025	0.021	330
昌 吉 市	Changji City	0.086	0.040	0.059	340
阜 康 市	Fukang City	0.093	0.031	0.031	316
奎 屯 市	Kuytun City	0.091	0.020	0.027	317
伊 宁 市	Yining [Gulja] City	0.089	0.035	0.038	341
塔 城 市	Tacheng [Qoqek] City	0.053	0.019	0.018	357
乌 苏 市	Usu City	0.073	0.018	0.020	359
阿勒泰市	Altay City	0.036	0.016	0.016	359
博 乐 市	Bole [Bortala] City	0.051	0.019	0.013	364
库尔勒市	Korla City	0.110	0.016	0.034	312
阿克苏市	Aksu City	0.204	0.022	0.023	231
阿图什市	Artux City	0.196	0.015	0.016	193
喀 什 市	Kashgar [Kaxgar] City	0.260	0.036	0.022	146
和 田 市	Hotan City	0.275	0.029	0.032	159
五家渠市	Wujiaqu City	0.094	0.018	0.020	340

11-16 主要城市道路交通噪声监测情况
Monitoring of Urban Road Traffic Noise in Major Cities

(2012 年)

城 市	City	等效声级 dB(A) Average Noise ValuedB(A)
乌鲁木齐市	Urumqi City	67.4
克拉玛依市	Karamay City	65.2
石河子市	Shihezi City	66.1
吐鲁番市	Turpan City	67.3
哈 密 市	Hami [Kumul] City	65.1
昌 吉 市	Changji City	67.2
阜 康 市	Fukang City	65.5
奎 屯 市	Kuytun City	66.2
伊 宁 市	Yining [Gulja] City	63.5
塔 城 市	Tacheng [Qoqek] City	63.3
阿勒泰市	Altay City	67.2
博 乐 市	Bole [Bortala] City	62.1
库尔勒市	Korla City	64.3
阿克苏市	Aksu City	67.8
阿图什市	Artux City	64.8
喀 什 市	Kashgar [Kaxgar] City	69.2
和 田 市	Hotan City	70.4

11-17 主要城市区域环境噪声监测情况
Monitoring of Urban Environment Noise in Major Cities under National Control Programme

(2012 年)

城 市	City	等效声级 dB(A) Average Noise ValuedB(A)
乌鲁木齐市	Urumqi City	54.4
克拉玛依市	Karamay City	53.2
石河子市	Shihezi City	54.1
吐鲁番市	Turpan City	51.7
哈 密 市	Hami [Kumul] City	53.6
昌 吉 市	Changji City	53.4
阜 康 市	Fukang City	51.7
奎 屯 市	Kuytun City	51.3
伊 宁 市	Yining [Gulja] City	51.0
塔 城 市	Tacheng [Qoqek] City	53.5
阿勒泰市	Altay City	54.0
博 乐 市	Bole [Bortala] City	50.2
库尔勒市	Korla City	52.0
阿克苏市	Aksu City	52.0
阿图什市	Artux City	59.4
喀 什 市	Kashgar [Kaxgar] City	57.5
和 田 市	Hotan City	50.9

11-18 主要年份自然保护区基本情况

Basic Situation of Natural Protection in Main Years

年 份 Year	自然保护区个数 (个) Number of Nature Reserves (unit)	#国家级 Nation level	自然保护区面积 (万公顷) Area of Nature Reserves (10 000 hectares)	#国家级 Nation Level	自然保护区占辖区面积比重 (%) Percentage of Nature Reserves in the Region (%)
2000	23	5	1594.05	869.08	9.6
2001	26	7	2042.40	1105.50	12.3
2005	28	8	2183.49	1275.86	13.1
2006	28	8	2162.49	1275.86	13.0
2007	34	8	2257.60	1275.86	13.6
2008	34	8	2257.60	1275.86	13.6
2009	34	8	2257.60	1275.86	13.6
2010	34	8	2257.60	1275.86	13.6
2011	28	9	2096.00	1365.53	12.6
2012	28	9	2140.56	1365.53	12.9

11-19 各地区城市生活垃圾清运和处理情况

Collection, Transport and Disposal of Consumption Wastes in Cities by Region

(2012 年)

城 市	City	生活垃圾清运量 (万吨) Consumption Wastes Collected and Transported (10 000 tons)	生活垃圾处理量 (万吨) Disposal of Consumption Wastes Treatment (10 000 tons)	无害化处理厂数 (座) Number of Factories for Wastes Treatment (unit)	无害化处理能力 (吨/日) Treatment Capacity (m ton/day)	无害化处理量 (万吨) Volume of Wastes Disposed (10 000 tons)	生活垃圾处理率 (%) Treatment Rate of Consumption Wastes (%)
总 计	**Total**	352.69	331.29	21	7880	301.56	93.93
乌鲁木齐市	Urumqi City	136.11	124.45	3	3301	124.45	91.43
克拉玛依市	Karamay City	16.88	16.88	3	450	16.65	100.00
吐鲁番市	Turpan City	7.66	7.58	1	300	7.58	98.96
哈 密 市	Hami [Kumul] City	18.10	17.90	1	350	17.90	98.90
昌 吉 市	Changji City	19.77	19.50	1	420	19.50	98.63
阜 康 市	Fukang City	2.93	2.80	1	150	2.80	95.56
伊 宁 市	Yining [Gulja] City	22.46	22.46	1	600	22.46	100.00
奎 屯 市	Kuytun City	4.87	4.87	1	200	4.87	100.00
塔 城 市	Tacheng [Qoqek] City	6.60	6.30	1	190	6.30	95.45
乌 苏 市	Usu City	4.70	4.40	1	120	4.40	93.62
阿勒泰市	Altay City	3.20	3.04	1	140	3.04	95.00
博 乐 市	Bole [Bortala] City	8.96	8.00	1	149	8.00	89.29
库尔勒市	Korla City	26.88	25.71	1	500	25.71	95.65
阿克苏市	Aksu City	12.70	12.70				100.00
阿图什市	Artux City	3.00	2.90	1	80	2.90	96.67
喀 什 市	Kashgar [Kaxgar] City	19.00	17.00	1	500	17.00	89.47
和 田 市	Hotan City	17.00	15.00	1	180	15.00	88.24
石河子市	Shihezi City	12.70	12.70				100.00
阿拉尔市	Aral City	2.50	2.50				100.00
图木舒克市	Tumxuk City	1.15					
五家渠市	Wujiaqu City	3.65	3.00	1	250	3.00	82.19
北 屯 市	Beitur City	1.87	1.60				85.56

注：表中无害化处理数据均为二级以上无害化处理厂数据。

Note: Data on wastes disposed are provided by secondary and above factories for wastes treatment.

11-20 各地区土地利用情况
Land Use by Region

单位:万公顷 (10 000 hectares)

年份 Year / 地区 Region	土地调查面积 Area under Land Survey	农用地 Land for Agriculture Use	#园 地 Garden Land	#牧草地 Grazing and Pasture Land	建设用地 Land for Construction	居民点及工矿用地 Land for Living Quarters, Mining and Manufacturing Sites	交通用地 Land for Transport Facilities	水利设施用地 Land for Water Conservancy Facilities
2000	16648.97	6346.21	19.22	5136.05	154.38	88.69	22.3	43.39
2001	16648.97	6295.64	19.68	5135.35	112.11	88.88	5.25	17.98
2002	16648.97	6297.36	22.21	5135.75	118.2	94.63	5.49	18.08
2003	16648.97	6301.54	29.58	5131.49	119.96	96.12	5.76	18.08
2004	16648.97	6304.57	33.59	5121.58	121.05	97.02	5.89	18.14
2005	16648.97	6306.07	35.43	5116.07	122.07	97.62	6.12	18.33
2006	16648.97	6307.61	36.37	5112.47	122.66	98.15	6.16	18.35
2007	16648.97	6308.05	36.45	5111.92	123.43	98.86	6.21	18.36
2008	16648.97	6308.48	36.42	5111.38	123.98	99.33	6.27	18.38
乌鲁木齐市 Urumqi City	113.84	90.75	0.34	78.05	4.41	3.88	0.35	0.18
克拉玛依市 Karamay City	86.54	35.99	0.03	23.13	6.5	5.91	0.37	0.22
石河子市 Shihezi City	4.60	3.44	0.07	0.61	0.62	0.57	0.05	…
吐鲁番地区 Turpan Administrative Offices	675.63	84.37	2.19	72.97	2.95	2.49	0.35	0.11
哈密地区 Hami [Kumul] Administrative Offices	1420.95	443.06	1.34	374.21	18.57	17.94	0.51	0.12
昌吉回族自治州 Changji Hui Autonomous Prefecture	776.39	602.96	0.87	497.76	11.69	9.89	0.71	1.1
伊犁州直属县(市) Counties (Cities) Direct Under Ili Prefecture	563.81	476.23	2.14	360.56	9.15	8.31	0.51	0.33
塔城地区 Tacheng [Tarbagatai] Administrative Offices	946.98	765.34	0.57	643.19	9.86	8.13	0.52	1.22
阿勒泰地区 Altay Administrative Offices	1176.99	1069.72	0.03	962.91	4.43	3.08	0.31	1.03
博尔塔拉蒙古自治州 Bortala Mongol Autonomous Prefecture	249.34	192.61	0.36	159.74	2.22	1.92	0.17	0.13
巴音郭楞蒙古自治州 Bayangol Mongol Autonomous Prefecture	4709.54	970.86	7.43	824.19	11.37	8.89	0.84	1.64
阿克苏地区 Aksu Administrative Offices	1313.41	542.5	6.32	403.7	12.67	8.00	0.41	4.26
克孜勒苏柯尔克孜自治州 Kizilsu Kirgiz Autonomous Prefecture	724.68	324.82	0.63	298.14	1.55	1.20	0.16	0.19
喀什地区 Kashgar [Kaxgar] Administrative Offices	1394.8	302.46	10.55	160.61	18.61	13.08	0.53	5.00
和田地区 Hotan Administrative Offices	2491.47	403.37	3.55	251.61	9.38	6.04	0.48	2.85

11-21 造林面积
Area of Afforestation

单位:公顷 (hectare)

年份 Year / 地区 Region	造林总面积 Total Area of Afforestation	按造林方式分 By Approach			按林种用途分 By Function of Forest				
		人工造林 Manual Planting	飞机播种 Airplane Planting	无林地和疏林地新封 Area without Forest or of Sparse Forest	用材林 Timber Forests	经济林 By-product Forests	防护林 Protection Forests	薪炭林 Fuel Forests	特种用途林 Forests for Special Purpose
2000	64173	63793	200		1605	44564	16512	1012	480
2001	106771	106771			2149	78203	24536	1424	459
2002	216924	216924			3034	78302	134723	706	159
2003	263781	253781	10000		10152	59777	191380	2390	82
2004	176540	176540			3897	73103	96897	2638	5
2005	136990	130323	6667		3226	40523	92449	738	54
2006	97424	97424			1780	38495	56548	588	13
2007	146632	124642		21990	2991	71667	71325	589	60
2008	239951	217429		22522	8744	136046	94820	341	
2009	301438	266301		35137	9387	155503	135584	954	10
2010	199629	156964		42665	1996	104527	90546	2298	262
2011	186197	140262		45935	823	92656	89942	2356	420
2012	187321	114287		73034	3702	51435	128692	3309	183
乌鲁木齐市 Urumqi City	4096	4096				130	3866		100
克拉玛依市 Karamay City	1214	547		667		7	1207		
石河子市 Shihezi City	233	233					233		
吐鲁番地区 Turpan Administrative Offices	7551	4684		2867	73	1504	4907	1067	
哈密地区 Hami [Kumul] Administrative Offices	8000	666		7334		34	7966		
昌吉回族自治州 Changji Hui Autonomous Prefecture	18935	11734		7201	27	2679	15962	267	
伊犁州直属县(市) Counties (Cities) Direct Under Ili Prefecture	20637	11173		9464	3044	3780	13759	54	
塔城地区 Tacheng [Tarbagatai] Administrative Offices	19326	7658		11668	445	674	17885	245	77
阿勒泰地区 Altay Administrative Offices	20532	7864		12668		1107	18758	667	
博尔塔拉蒙古自治州 Bortala Mongol Autonomous Prefecture	10379	3545		6834		258	10121		
巴音郭楞蒙古自治州 Bayangol Mongol Autonomous Prefecture	16057	9724		6333		6421	9222	414	
阿克苏地区 Aksu Administrative Offices	9144	5946		3198		167	8977		
克孜勒苏柯尔克孜自治州 Kizilsu Kirgiz Autonomous Prefecture	8592	8059		533	113	2540	5939		
喀什地区 Kashgar [Kaxgar] Administrative Offices	26240	25573		667		23243	2959	32	6
和田地区 Hotan Administrative Offices	16200	12600		3600		8891	6746	563	
自治区直属单位 Autonomous regions directly under the unit	185	185					185		

11-22 林业重点工程造林面积
Area of Key Afforestation Projects

单位:公顷 (hectare)

年 份 Year	地区 Region	造林总面积 Total Area of Afforestation	#退耕还林工程 Grain for Green Projects	#三北及长江流域等防护林工程 Project on Protection Forests in North China and Yangtze River Basin
	2001	102317	13173	
	2002	199324	113010	
	2003	235924	175314	
	2004	152967	82838	70129
	2005	133778	62457	71321
	2006	88744	38160	50584
	2007	138700	32926	105774
	2008	187318	50977	136341
	2009	270997	48120	222877
	2010	177674	38034	139640
	2011	186197	31066	107390
	2012	187321	47091	113213
乌鲁木齐市	Urumqi City	4096	667	4093
克拉玛依市	Karamay City	1214		167
石河子市	Shihezi City	233		
吐鲁番地区	Turpan Administrative Offices	7551	2771	4780
哈密地区	Hami [Kumul] Administrative Offices	8000	3000	5000
昌吉回族自治州	Changji Hui Autonomous Prefecture	18935	4734	14201
伊犁州直属县(市)	Counties (Cities) Direct Under Ili Prefecture	20637	4557	16079
塔城地区	Tacheng [Tarbagatai] Administrative Offices	19326	7726	10933
阿勒泰地区	Altay Administrative Offices	20532	7733	12799
博尔塔拉蒙古自治州	Bortala Mongol Autonomous Prefecture	10379	3255	7124
巴音郭楞蒙古自治州	Bayangol Mongol Autonomous Prefecture	16057	3097	11666
阿克苏地区	Aksu Administrative Offices	9144	2424	6720
克孜勒苏柯尔克孜自治州	Kizilsu Kirgiz Autonomous Prefecture	8592	993	6799
喀什地区	Kashgar [Kaxgar] Administrative Offices	26240	797	7253
和田地区	Hotan Administrative Offices	16200	5337	5599
自治区直属单位	Autonomous regions directly under the unit	185		

11-23 各地区天然湿地面积

Area of Wetlands by Region

单位:百公顷 (2008 年) (100 hectares)

地区 Region	天然湿地面积 Area of Natural Wetlands	河流 Rivers	湖泊 Lakes	沼泽 Marshland	天然湿地面积占土地总面积比重(%) Proportion of Natural Wetlands in Total Area of Territory(%)
总计 Total	**12673.56**	**4732.99**	**4763.91**	**3176.66**	**0.76**
乌鲁木齐市 Urumqi City	74.72	20.98	39.37	14.37	0.66
克拉玛依市 Karamay City	214.69	23.59	154.58	36.52	2.48
石河子市 Shihezi City	4.92	4.77		0.15	1.07
吐鲁番地区 Turpan Administrative Offices	127.84	5.99	0.18	121.67	0.19
哈密地区 Hami [Kumul] Administrative Offices	179.00	35.73	122.34	20.93	0.13
昌吉回族自治州 Changji Hui Autonomous Prefecture	264.46	50.27	2.58	211.61	0.34
伊犁州直属县(市) Counties (Cities) Direct Under Ili Prefecture	543.92	246.61	6.59	290.72	0.96
塔城地区 Tacheng [Tarbagatai] Administrative Offices	352.75	113.36	5.98	233.41	0.37
阿勒泰地区 Altay Administrative Offices	1353.84	353.78	845.49	154.57	1.15
博尔塔拉蒙古自治州 Bortala Mongol Autonomous Prefecture	1331.27	28.88	1176.41	125.98	5.34
巴音郭楞蒙古自治州 Bayangol Mongol Autonomous Prefecture	4034.70	979.74	2098.16	956.80	0.86
阿克苏地区 Aksu Administrative Offices	1018.86	709.19	68.68	240.99	0.78
克孜勒苏柯尔克孜自治州 Kizilsu Kirgiz Autonomous Prefecture	326.89	94.18	46.61	186.10	0.45
喀什地区 Kashgar [Kaxgar] Administrative Offices	1056.83	556.60	88.55	411.68	0.76
和田地区 Hotan Administrative Offices	1788.87	1509.32	108.39	171.16	0.72

11-24 森林火灾情况

Forest Fires

年份 Year	地区 Region	森林火灾次数(次) Forest Fires (case)	一般火灾 Ordinary Fires	较大火灾 Large Fires	火场总面积(公顷) Total Area of Fires (hectare)
	2005	28	1		42.33
	2006	35	5		258.27
	2007	47	13		137.09
	2008	67	19		191.38
	2009	51	35	16	83.58
	2010	34	27	7	65.95
	2011	59	46	13	713.72
	2012	41	40	1	19.16
乌鲁木齐市	Urumqi City				
克拉玛依市	Karamay City				
石河子市	Shihezi City				
吐鲁番地区	Turpan Administrative Offices	2	2		0.360
哈密地区	Hami [Kumul] Administrative Offices	3	3		1.050
昌吉回族自治州	Changji Hui Autonomous Prefecture				
伊犁州直属县(市)	Counties (Cities) Direct Under Ili Prefecture	9	9		1.440
塔城地区	Tacheng [Tarbagatai] Administrative Offices				
阿勒泰地区	Altay Administrative Offices	18	17	1	5.778
博尔塔拉蒙古自治州	Bortala Mongol Autonomous Prefecture				
巴音郭楞蒙古自治州	Bayangol Mongol Autonomous Prefecture	5	5		1.594
阿克苏地区	Aksu Administrative Offices	1	1		4.080
克孜勒苏柯尔克孜自治州	Kizilsu Kirgiz Autonomous Prefecture				
喀什地区	Kashgar [Kaxgar] Administrative Offices				
和田地区	Hotan Administrative Offices				
五家渠市	Wujiaqu City	3	3		4.860

年份 Year	地区 Region	受灾森林总面积(公顷) Destructed Forest Area (hectare)	#天然林 Natural Forest	#人工林 Man-made Forest	经济损失(万元) Economic Loss (10 000 yuan)
	2005	11.62	10.63	0.99	12.52
	2006	94.10	78.28	1.39	9.26
	2007	75.34	31.44	39.37	19.47
	2008	122.74	58.39	65.64	145.53
	2009	72.66	8.24	49.86	52.29
	2010	43.82	17.56	15.70	5.48
	2011	150.16	114.36	35.80	1426.91
	2012	17.35	4.66	12.70	45.88
乌鲁木齐市	Urumqi City				
克拉玛依市	Karamay City				
石河子市	Shihezi City				
吐鲁番地区	Turpan Administrative Offices	0.360		0.360	37.00
哈密地区	Hami [Kumul] Administrative Offices	0.468		0.468	1.97
昌吉回族自治州	Changji Hui Autonomous Prefecture				
伊犁州直属县(市)	Counties (Cities) Direct Under Ili Prefecture	1.224	0.002	1.222	1.55
塔城地区	Tacheng [Tarbagatai] Administrative Offices				
阿勒泰地区	Altay Administrative Offices	4.773	0.573	4.200	5.36
博尔塔拉蒙古自治州	Bortala Mongol Autonomous Prefecture				
巴音郭楞蒙古自治州	Bayangol Mongol Autonomous Prefecture	1.587		1.587	
阿克苏地区	Aksu Administrative Offices	4.080	4.080		
克孜勒苏柯尔克孜自治州	Kizilsu Kirgiz Autonomous Prefecture				
喀什地区	Kashgar [Kaxgar] Administrative Offices				
和田地区	Hotan Administrative Offices				
五家渠市	Wujiaqu City	4.860		4.860	

11-25 森林病虫害防治情况
Prevention of Forest Diseases and Pests

单位：公顷 (hectare)

年份 Year	地区 Region	合计 Total			森林病害 Forest Diseases		
		发生面积 Area of Occurrence	防治面积 Area of Prevention	防治率(%) Prevention Rate (%)	发生面积 Area of Occurrence	防治面积 Area of Prevention	防治率(%) Prevention Rate (%)
	2005	241713	221720	91.7	4467	3440	77.0
	2006	400127	344146	86.0	21993	19273	87.6
	2007	787087	441533	56.1	30194	23393	77.5
	2008	1066659	609457	57.1	147035	92811	63.1
	2009	990580	572735	57.8	82273	68525	83.3
	2010	1051060	570973	54.3	80820	73573	91.0
	2011	1223633	547200	45.0	73747	61240	83.0
	2012	1261386	539040	42.7	68426	57025	83.3
乌鲁木齐市	Urumqi City	6922	6806	98.3			
吐鲁番地区	Turpan Administrative Offices	4312	3836	89.0			
哈密地区	Hami [Kumul] Administrative Offices	12316	11512	93.5	1100	1066	96.9
昌吉回族自治州	Changji Hui Autonomous Prefecture	606856	8585	1.4	1228	1220	99.3
伊犁州直属县(市)	Counties (Cities) Direct Under Ili Prefecture	19264	18033	93.6	2825	2316	81.9
塔城地区	Tacheng [Tarbagatai] Administrative Offices	2829	1963	69.4	343	283	82.6
阿勒泰地区	Altay Administrative Offices	69190	894	1.3	1019		
博尔塔拉蒙古自治州	Bortala Mongol Autonomous Prefecture	3965	3743	94.4	13	13	100.0
巴音郭楞蒙古自治州	Bayangol Mongol Autonomous Prefecture	17688	16624	94.0	539	532	98.7
阿克苏地区	Aksu Administrative Offices	180182	177993	98.8	10043	9847	98.0
克孜勒苏柯尔克孜自治州	Kizilsu Kirgiz Autonomous Prefecture	8366	10	0.1	3198		
喀什地区	Kashgar [Kaxgar] Administrative Offices	208759	185441	88.8	25421	22929	90.2
和田地区	Hotan Administrative Offices	104565	95781	91.6	19676	18656	94.8
自治区林业厅	Xinjiang Forestry Bureau	16172	7819	48.3	3021	163	5.3

年份 Year	地区 Region	森林虫害 Forest Diseases			森林鼠害 Forest Rat Plague		
		发生面积 Area of Occurrence	防治面积 Area of Prevention	防治率(%) Prevention Rate (%)	发生面积 Area of Occurrence	防治面积 Area of Prevention	防治率(%) Prevention Rate (%)
	2005	221500	199700	89.9	21747	18580	85.4
	2006	340320	290693	85.4	37813	34180	90.4
	2007	350592	331735	94.6	406301	86405	21.3
	2008	527465	446766	84.7	392159	69880	17.8
	2009	474213	431197	90.9	434093	73013	16.8
	2010	470961	432316	91.8	499279	65084	13.0
	2011	582653	457627	79.0	567233	28333	5.0
	2012	518263	455652	87.9	674697	26363	3.9
乌鲁木齐市	Urumqi City	4856	4740	97.6	2066	2066	100.0
吐鲁番地区	Turpan Administrative Offices	4312	3836	89.0			
哈密地区	Hami [Kumul] Administrative Offices	9940	9276	93.3	1276	1170	91.7
昌吉回族自治州	Changji Hui Autonomous Prefecture	5348	5119	95.7	600280	2246	0.4
伊犁州直属县(市)	Counties (Cities) Direct Under Ili Prefecture	13701	13119	95.8	2738	2598	94.9
塔城地区	Tacheng [Tarbagatai] Administrative Offices	1792	1252	69.9	694	428	61.7
阿勒泰地区	Altay Administrative Offices	21393	894	4.2	46778		
博尔塔拉蒙古自治州	Bortala Mongol Autonomous Prefecture	3952	3730	94.4			
巴音郭楞蒙古自治州	Bayangol Mongol Autonomous Prefecture	15330	14282	93.2	1819	1810	99.5
阿克苏地区	Aksu Administrative Offices	170139	168146	98.8			
克孜勒苏柯尔克孜自治州	Kizilsu Kirgiz Autonomous Prefecture	5046	10	0.2	122		
喀什地区	Kashgar [Kaxgar] Administrative Offices	164855	146839	89.1	18483	15673	84.8
和田地区	Hotan Administrative Offices	84623	76859	90.8	266	266	100.0
自治区林业厅	Xinjiang Forestry Bureau	12976	7550	58.2	175	106	60.6

注：自治区林业厅数据中包括石河子市和克拉玛依市的数据。
Note: The data on Bureau of Forestry include the data of Shihezi City and Karamay City.

11-26 地震灾害情况
Earthquake Disasters

年 份 Year		地 区 Region	地震次数(次) Number of Earthquakes (case)	5.0-5.9 级 5.0-5.9 Richterscale	6.0-6.9 级 6.0-6.9 Richterscale	7.0 级以上 Over 7.0 Richterscale
2005			4	3	1	
2006			2	2		
2007			1	1		
2008			4	2	1	1
2009			6	6		
	察布查尔县、昭苏县	Qapqai Xibe Autonomous County, Zhaosu [Mongolrure] County	1	1		
	柯坪县、阿合齐县	Kalpin County, Akqi County	1	1		
	阿合齐县、乌什县	Akqi County, Wushi[Uxtnrpan] County	1	1		
	阿图什市	Artux City	1	1		
	叶城县、皮山县	Yecheng[Kagilik] County, Pishan[Guma] County	1	1		
	哈密市	Hami[Kumul] City	1	1		
2010			2	2		
	乌恰县	Wuqia [Ulugqat] County	2	2		
2011			8	7	1	
	乌恰县	Wuqia [Ulugqat] County	1	1		
	托克逊县	Toksun County	1	1		
	青河县	Qinghe[Qinggil]County	1	1		
	阿图什-伽师交界	Artux City border on Jiashi[payzawat] County	1	1		
	于田县	Yutian[Keriya] County	1	1		
	精河县	Jinghe[Jing] County	1	1		
	尼勒克、巩留交界	Nilka County border on Gongliu[Tokkuztara] County	1		1	
	莎车县	Shache[Yarkant]County	1	1		
2012			11	8	3	
	和硕县	Hoxud County	1	1		
	巴里坤县	Barkol Kazak Autonomous County	1	1		
	乌恰县	Wuqia [Ulugqat] County	1	1		
	洛浦县	Lop County	1		1	
	乌恰县	Wuqia [Ulugqat] County	1	1		
	轮台县	Luntai [Bugur] County	1	1		
	新源、和静交界	Xinyuan [Kunes] County border on Hejing County	1		1	
	于田县	Yutian [Keriya] County	1		1	
	阿图什、伽师交界	Artux City border on Jiashi [Payzawat] County	1	1		
	若羌	Ruoqiang [Qarkilik] County	1	1		
	若羌	Ruoqiang [Qarkilik] County	1	1		

注：本表数据由自治区地震局提供。
Note: The data in this table is Provided by theBureau of Earthquake.

11-26 续表 Continued

年 份 Year	地 区 Region	人员伤亡(人) Casualties (person)	#死亡人数 Deaths	经济损失(万元) Economic Losses (10 000 yuan)	失去住所(户) Homeless (household)
2005				16316	5823
2006				126	
2007				11060	5074
2008				38437	5702
2009				20498	4393
察布查尔县、昭苏县	Qapqai Xibe Autonomous County, Zhaosu [Mongolrure] County			4612	1396
柯坪县、阿合齐县	Kalpin County, Akqi County			9068	1706
阿合齐县、乌什县	Akqi County, Wushi[Uxtnrpan] County			4636	708
阿图什市	Artux City			2182	583
叶城县、皮山县	Yecheng[Kagilik] County, Pishan[Guma] County				
哈密市	Hami[Kumul] City				
2010				2408	675
乌恰县	Wuqia [Ulugqat] County			2408	675
2011				105059	15964
乌恰县	Wuqia [Ulugqat] County				
托克逊县	Toksun County			9225	4757
青河县	Qinghe[Qinggil]County			3330	915
阿图什-伽师交界	Artux City border on Jiashi[payzawat] County			18322	1994
于田县	Yutian[Keriya] County			292	
精河县	Jinghe[Jing] County			1185	324
尼勒克-巩留交界	Nilka County border on Gongliu[Tokkuztara] County			67846	7598
莎车县	Shache[Yarkant]County			4859	376
2012				272095	25713
和硕县	Hoxud County			4208	482
巴里坤哈萨克自治县	Barkol Kazak Autonomous County				
乌恰县	Wuqia [Ulugqat] County				
洛浦县	Lop County			52325	1751
乌恰县	Wuqia [Ulugqat] County				
轮台县	Luntai [Bugur] County			4547	578
新源-和静交界	Xinyuan [Kunes] County border on Hejing County			199032	22083
于田县	Yutian [Keriya] County			4958	573
阿图什-伽师交界	Artux City border on Jiashi [Payzawat] County				
若羌县	Ruoqiang [Qarkilik] County			636	
若羌县	Ruoqiang [Qarkilik] County			6388	246

11-27 林业系统营林固定资产投资完成情况
Completed Investment in Fixed Assets for Afforestation in Forest System

单位：万元 (10 000 yuan)

年份 Year	地区 Region	本年完成投资 Investment Completed During the Year	#国家投资 State Investment	本年新增固定资产 Newly Increased Fixed Assets
	2000	23582	11686	4542
	2001	45890	23725	12492
	2002	68861	35835	
	2003	71277	40821	27223
	2004	60631	43475	23047
	2005	80150	57680	24988
	2006	96062	82235	31047
	2007	115523	94094	33091
	2008	158416	129294	55295
	2009	193818	153538	52765
	2010	168930	142678	28725
	2011	85365	39304	41378
	2012	97849	39318	35863
克拉玛依市	Karamay City	38104	4331	
石河子市	Shihezi City	12487	11083	12487
吐鲁番地区	Turpan Administrative Offices	6124		
哈密地区	Hami [Kumul] Administrative Offices	5848	3892	2678
昌吉回族自治州	Changji Hui Autonomous Prefecture	3332	700	3332
伊犁州直属县(市)	Counties (Cities) Direct Under Ili Prefecture	2854	2354	2854
塔城地区	Tacheng [Tarbagatai] Administrative Offices			
阿勒泰地区	Altay Administrative Offices			
博尔塔拉蒙古自治州	Bortala Mongol Autonomous Prefecture	1817	1817	
巴音郭楞蒙古自治州	Bayangol Mongol Autonomous Prefecture	4823	4823	1439
阿克苏地区	Aksu Administrative Offices	13073	2284	13073
克孜勒苏柯尔克孜自治州	Kizilsu Kirgiz Autonomous Prefecture			
自治区林业厅	Xinjiang Forestry Bureau	5426	5426	

注：自 2011 年起固定资产投资统计范围为单项投资 500 万元以上项目，2010 年及以前年份统计范围是只要形成固定资产的投资均需统计。
Note: In 2011,Statistical range of investment in fixed assets is above of 5million yuan single investment project.Before 2010,Statistical range is the formation of the investment fixed assets required statistics.

主要统计指标解释

自然资源　指人类可以直接从自然界获得，并用于生产和生活的物质资源。自然资源一般可以分成可再生资源和非再生资源两大类。可再生资源指在较短时间内可以再生、可以循环利用的资源，包括土地资源、水资源、气候资源、生物资源和海洋资源等。非再生资源指在使用后不能再生的资源，包括矿产资源和地热能源。

土地资源　土地指陆地的表层部分，它主要由岩石、岩石的风化物和土壤构成。土地资源按利用类型可以分为农用地、建筑用地和未利用地。农用地包括耕地、园地、林地、牧草地和水面。建筑用地包括居民点及工矿用地、交通用地和水利设施用地。未利用地指农用地和建筑用地以外的土地，包括滩涂、荒漠、戈壁、冰川和石山等。

耕地面积　指经过开垦用以种植农作物并经常进行耕耘的土地面积。包括种有作物的土地面积、休闲地、新开荒地和抛荒未满三年的土地面积。

林业用地面积　指生长乔木、竹类、灌木、沿海红树林等林木的土地面积，包括有林地、灌木林、疏林地、未成林造林地、迹地、苗圃等。

草地面积　指牧区和农区用于放牧牲畜或割草，植被盖度在5%以上的草原、草坡、草山等面积。包括天然的和人工种植或改良的草地面积。

森林面积　包括郁闭度0.2以上的乔木林地面积和竹林面积，国家特别规定的灌木林地面积，农田林网以及村旁、路旁、水旁、宅旁林木的覆盖面积。

森林蓄积量　指一定森林面积上存在着的林木树干部分的总材积。它是反映一个国家或地区森林资源总规模和水平的基本指标之一，也是反映森林资源的丰富程度、衡量森林生态环境优劣的重要依据。

森林覆盖率　以行政区域为单位，森林面积占区域土地总面积的百分比。计算公式为：

森林覆盖率(%)=森林面积／土地总面积×100%

活立木总蓄积量　指一定范围内土地上全部树木蓄积的总量，包括森林蓄积、疏林蓄积、散生木蓄积和四旁树蓄积。

矿产资源　矿产指由地质作用形成，富集于地壳中或出露于地表达到工农业利用要求的有用矿物。矿产是一种重要的自然资源，是社会发展的重要物质基础。从某种意义上讲，一个国家对矿产资源开发利用的广度和深度，可以作为这个国家经济发展水平的标志。

矿产保有储量　指探明的矿产储量(包括工业储量和远景储量)，扣除已开采部分和地下损失量后的年末实有储量，是反映国家矿产资源现状的重要指标。

气温　指空气的温度，我国一般以摄氏度(℃)为单位表示。气象观测的温度表是放在离地面约1.5米处通风良好的百叶箱里测量的，因此，通常说的气温指的是离地面1.5米处百叶箱中的温度。其统计计算方法为：

月平均气温是将全月各日的平均气温相加，除以该月的天数而得。

年平均气温是将12个月的月平均气温累加后除以12而得。

降水量　指从天空降落到地面的液态或固态(经融化后)水，未经蒸发、渗透、流失而在地面上积聚的深度。其统计计算方法为：

月降水量是将全月各日的降水量累加而得。

年降水量是将12个月的月降水量累加而得。

日照时数　指太阳实际照射地面的时间。其统计方法与降水量相同。

水资源总量　指评价区内降水形成的地表和地下产水总量，即地表产流量与降水入渗补给地下水量之和，不包括过境水量。

地表水资源量　指评价区内河流、湖泊、冰川等地表水体中可以逐年更新的动态水量，即当地天然河川径流量。

地下水资源量　指评价区内降水和地表水对饱水岩土层的补给量，包括降水入渗补给量和河道、湖库、渠系、渠灌田间等地表水体的入渗补给量。

地表水与地下水资源重复计算量　指地表水和地下水相互转化的部分，即天然河川径流量中的地下水排泄量和地下水补给量中来源于地表水的入渗量。

供水总量　指各种水源工程为用户提供的包括输水损失在内的毛供水量之和。

地表水源供水量　指地表水体工程的取水量，按蓄、引、提、调四种形式统计。从水库、塘坝中引水或提水，均属蓄水工程供水量；从河道或湖泊中自流引水的，无论有闸或无闸，均属引水工程供水量；利用扬水站从河道或湖泊中直接取水的，属提水工程供水量；跨流域调水指水资源一级区或独立流域之间的跨流域调配水量，不包括在蓄、引、提水量中。

地下水源供水量　指水井工程的开采量，按浅层谈水、深层承压水和微咸水分别统计。城市地下水源供水量包括自来水厂的开采量和工矿企业自备井的开采量。

其他水源供水量　包括污水处理再利用、集雨工程、海水淡化等水源工程的供水量。

用水总量　指分配给各类用户的包括输水损失在内的毛用水量之和。

农业用水　指农田灌溉用水、林果地灌溉用水、草地灌溉用水和鱼塘补水。

工业用水　指工矿企业在生产过程中用于制造、加工、冷却、空调、净化、洗涤等方面的用水，按新水取用量计，不包括企业内部的重复利用水量。

生活用水 包括城镇生活用水和农村生活用水。城镇生活用水由居民用水和公共用水(含第三产业及建筑业等用水)组成；农村生活用水除居民生活用水外，还包括畜用水在内。

生态环境补水 仅包括人为措施供给的城镇环境用水和部分河湖、湿地补水，而不包括降水、径流自然满足的水量。

工业废水排放量 指经过企业厂区所有排放口排到企业外部的工业废水量。包括生产废水、外排的直接冷却水、超标排放的矿井地下水和与工业废水混排的厂区生活污水，不包括外排的间接冷却水(清污不分流的间接冷却水应计算在内)。

工业废水排放达标量 指报告期内废水中各项污染物指标都达到国家或地方排放标准的外排工业废水量，包括未经处理外排达标的，经废水处理设施处理后达标排放的，以及经污水处理厂处理后达标排放的。

工业废水排放达标率 指工业废水排放达标量占工业废水排放量的百分率，计算公式为：

工业废水排放达标率=工业废水排放达标量/工业废水排放量×100%

化学需氧量(COD) 只指用化学氧化剂氧化水中有机污染物时所需要的氧量。COD值越高，表示水中有机污染物污染越重。

工业废气排放量 指报告期内企业厂区内燃料燃烧和生产工艺过程中产生的各种排入大气的含有污染物的气体的总量，以标准状态(273K，101325Pa)计算。测算公式为：

工业废气排放量=燃料燃烧过程中废气排放量+生产工艺过程中废气排放量

工业烟尘排放量 指企业厂区内燃料燃烧过程中产生的烟气中夹带的颗粒物排放量。

工业粉尘排放量 指企业在生产工艺过程中排放的能在空气中悬浮一定时间的固体颗粒物排放量。如钢铁企业的耐火材料粉尘、焦化企业的筛焦系统粉尘、烧结机的粉尘、石灰窑的粉尘、建材企业的水泥粉尘等。不包括电厂排入大气的烟尘。

工业固体废物产生量 指报告期内企业在生产过程中产生的固体状、半固体状和高浓度液体状废弃物的总量，包括危险废物、冶炼废渣、粉煤灰、炉渣、煤矸石、尾矿、放射性废物和其他废物等；不包括矿山开采的剥离废石和掘进废石(煤矸石和呈酸性或碱性的废石除外)。酸性或碱性废石指采掘的废石其流经水、雨淋水的pH值小于4或pH值大于10.5者。

工业固体废物综合利用量 指报告期内企业通过回收、加工、循环、交换等方式，从固体废物中提取或者使其转化为可以利用的资源、能源和其他原材料的固体废物量(包括当年利用往年的工业固体废物贮存量)，如用作农业肥料、生产建筑材料、筑路等。综合利用量由原产生固体废物的单位统计。

工业固体废物综合利用率 指工业固体废物综合利用量占工业固体废物产生量(包括综合利用往年贮存量)的百分率。计算公式为：

工业固体废物综合利用率=工业固体废物综合利用量/(工业固体废物产生量+综合利用往年贮存量)×100%

工业固体废物贮存量 指报告期内企业以综合利用或处置为目的，将固体废物暂时贮存或堆存在专设的贮存设施或专设的集中堆存场所内的数量。专设的固体废物贮存场所或贮存设施必须有防扩散、防流失、防渗漏、防止污染大气、水体的措施。

工业固体废物处置量 指报告期内企业将固体废物焚烧或者最终置于符合环境保护规定要求的场所，并不再回取的工业固体废物量(包括当年处置往年的工业固体废物贮存量)。处置方式有填埋(其中危险废物应安全填埋)、焚烧、专业贮存场(库)封场处理、深层灌注、回填矿井及海洋处置(经海洋管理部门同意投海处置)等。

工业固体废物排放量 指报告期内企业将所产生的固体废物排到固体废物污染防治设施、场所以外的数量，不包括矿山开采的剥离废石和掘进废石(煤矸石和呈酸性或碱性的废石除外)。

生活垃圾清运量 指报告期内收集和运送到垃圾处理厂(场)的生活垃圾数量。生活垃圾指城市日常生活或为城市日常生活提供服务的活动中产生的固体废物以及法律行政规定的视为城市生活垃圾的固体废物。包括：居民生活垃圾、商业垃圾、集市贸易市场垃圾、街道清扫垃圾、公共场所垃圾和机关、学校、厂矿等单位的生活垃圾。

生活垃圾无害化处理率 指报告期生活垃圾无害化处理量与生活垃圾产生量比率。在统计上，由于生活垃圾产生量不易取得，可用清运量代替。计算公式为：

生活垃圾无害化处理率=生活垃圾无害化处理量/生活垃圾产生量×100%

农用地 指直接用于农业生产的土地，包括耕地、园地、林地、牧草地及其他农用地。

人工林面积 指由人工播种、植苗或扦插造林形成的生长稳定，(一般造林3-5年后或飞机播种5-7年后)每公顷保存株数大于或等于造林设计植树株数80%或郁闭度0.20以上(含02.0)的林分面积。

造林总面积 指在宜林荒山荒地、宜林沙荒地、无立木林地、疏林地和退耕地等其它宜林地上通过人工措施形成或恢复森林、林木、灌木林的过程。用材林 指以生产木材为主要目的的森林和林木，包括以生产竹材为主要目的的竹林。

经济林 指以生产果品，食用油料、饮料、调料，工业原料和药材为主要目的的林木。经济林是人们为了取得林木的果实、叶片、皮层、胶液等产品作为工业原料或者供食用所营造的林木，如油茶、油桐、核桃、樟树、花椒、茶、桑、果等。

防护林 指以防护为主要目的的森林、林木和灌木丛。包括水源涵养林，水土保持林，防风固沙林，农田、牧场防护林，护岸林，护路林等。

薪炭林 指以生产燃料为主要目的的林木。

天然林保护工程 是我国林业的“天”字号工程、一号工程,也是投资最大的生态工程。具体包括三个层次:全面停止长江上游、黄河上中游地区天然林采伐;大幅度调减东北、内蒙古等重点国有林区的木材产量;同时保护好其他地区的天然林资源。主要解决这些区域天然林资源的休养生息和恢复发展问题。

退耕还林还草工程 是我国林业建设上涉及面最广、政策性最强、工序最复杂、群众参与度最高的生态建设工程。主要解决重点地区的水土流失问题。

三北和长江流域等重点防护林体系建设工程 三北和长江中下游地区等重点防护林体系建设工程,是我国涵盖面最大、内容最丰富的防护林体系建设工程。具体包括三北防护林四期工程、长江中下游及淮河太湖流域防护林二期工程、沿海防护林二期工程、珠江防护林二期工程、太行山绿化二期工程和平原绿化二期工程。主要解决三北地区的防沙治沙问题和其他区域各不相同的生态问题。

野生动植物保护及自然保护区建设工程 野生动植物保护及自然保护区建设工程,是一个面向未来,着眼长远,具有多项战略意义的生态保护工程,也是呼应国际大气候、树立中国良好国际形象的“外交工程”。主要解决基因保存、生物多样性保护、自然保护、湿地保护等问题。

湿地 指天然或人工、长久或暂时性的沼泽地、泥炭地或水域地带，包括静止或流动、淡水、半咸水、咸水体，低潮时水深不超过6米的水域以及海岸地带地区的珊瑚滩和海草床、滩涂、红树林、河口、河流、淡水沼泽、沼泽森林、湖泊、盐沼及盐湖。

自然保护区 指为了保护自然环境和自然资源，促进国民经济的持续发展，将一定面积的陆地和水体划分出来，并经各级人民政府批准而进行特殊保护和管理的区域个数。根据保护对象，自然保护区分为自然生态系统类、野生生物类、自然遗迹类。风景名胜区、文物保护区不计在内。

突发环境事件 指突然发生，造成或可能造成重大人员伤亡、重大财产损失和对全国或者某一地区的经济社会稳定、政治安定构成重大威胁和损害，有重大社会影响的涉及公共安全的环境事件。

环境污染治理投资 指在污染源治理和城市环境基础设施建设的资金投入中，用于形成固定资产的资金，其中污染源治理投资包括工业污染源治理投资和“三同时”项目环保投资两部分。环境污染治理投资为城市环境基础设施投资、工业污染源治理投资与“三同时”项目环保投资之和。

林业建设到位资金 报告期内林业建设项目实施单位专项账户上实际收到的用于林业建设的资金合计。

林业建设本年完成投资 指从本年1月1日起至本年最后一天止完成的全部投资额。本年完成投资是反映本年的实际投资规模，计算有关投资效果，进行年度国民经济平衡分析的重要指标。

Explanatory Notes on Main Statistical Indicators

Natural Resources refer to material resources that could be obtained from the nature by human being and used for production and living. Natural resources in general can be classified as renewable resources and non-renewable resources. Renewable resources refer to resources that could be renewed and recycled during a relatively short period of time, including land resource, water resource, climate resource, biology resource and marine resource. Non-renewable resources include resources that could not be renewed, such as minerals and geothermal resource.

Land Resource Land refers to the surface of the earth, consisting of mainly rocks and its weathering and earth. Land resource can be classified, by its utilization, as land for agriculture, land for construction and unused land. Land for agriculture includes cultivated land, plantation land, forestland, grassland and waters. Land for construction includes land for residential purpose, for manufacturing and mining, for transportation and for water-conservancy projects. Unused land refers to land other than land for agriculture and construction, including beaches, deserts, Gobi, glaciers and rock mountains.

Area of Cultivated Land refers to area of land reclaimed for the regular cultivation of various farm crops, including crop-cover land, fallow, newly reclaimed land and land laid idle for less than 3 years.

Area of Afforested Land refers to area for land for trees, bamboo, bushes and mangrove, including forest-covered land, bush-covered land, sparse forest land, land planned for afforestation and nurseries of young trees.

Area of Grassland refers to area of grassland, grass-slopes and grass-covered hills with a vegetation-covering rate of over 5% that are used for animal husbandry or harvesting of grass. It includes natural, cultivated and improved grassland areas.

Forest Area refers to the area of trees and bamboo grow with canopy density above 0.2, the area of shrubby tree according to regulations of the government, the area of forest land inside farm land and the area of trees planted by the side of villages, farm houses and along roads and rivers.

Stock Volume of Forest refers to total stock volume of wood growing in forest area, which shows the total size and level of forest resources of a country or a region. It is also an important indicator illustrating the richness of forest resource and the status of forest ecological environment.

Forest Coverage Rate Taking the administrative jurisdiction as the unit, the percentage of area of afforested land to the area of total land. The formula for calculating forest coverage rate is as follows:

$$\text{Forestry coverage rate (\%)} = \frac{\text{Area of Afforested Land}}{\text{Area of Total Land}} \times 100\ \%$$

Total Standing Stock Volume refers to the total stock volume of trees growing in land, including trees in forest, trees in sparse forest, scattered trees and trees planted by the side of villages, farm houses and along roads and rivers.

Mineral Resources refer to useful minerals that can be used for industrial or agricultural purposes enriched in lithosphere or on earth due to the geological process.

Ensured Mineral Reserves refer to the actual mineral reserves, which equal to the proven mineral reserves (including industrial reserves and prospective reserves) minus extracted parts and underground losses. This indicator shows the current condition of the mineral resources of a Country.

Temperature refers to the air temperature. China uses centigrade as the unit. The thermometry used for weather observation is put in a breezy shutter, which is 1.5 meters high from the ground. Therefore, the commonly used temperature refers to the temperature in the breezy shutter 1.5 meters away from the ground. The calculation method is as follows:

Monthly average temperature is the summation of average daily temperature of one month divided by the actual days of that particular month.

Annual average temperature is the summation of monthly average of a year divided by 12 months.

Volume of Precipitation refers to the deepness of liquid state or solid state (thawed) water falling from the sky to the ground that has not been evaporated, infiltrated or run off. The calculation method is as follows:

Monthly precipitation is the summation of daily precipitation of a month.

Annual precipitation is the summation of 12 months precipitation of a year.

Sunshine Hours refer to the actual hours of sun irradiating the earth. The calculation method is the same as that of the precipitation.

Total Water Resources refers to total volume of water resources measured as run-off for surface water from rainfall and recharge for groundwater in a given area, excluding transit water.

Surface Water Resources refers to total renewable

resources which exist in rivers, lakes, glaciers and other collectors from rainfall and are measured as run-off of rivers..

Groundwater Resources refers to replenishment of aquifers with rainfall and surface water.

Duplicated Measurement between Surface Water and Groundwater refers to mutual exchange between surface water and groundwater, i.e. run-off of rivers includes some depletion into groundwater while groundwater includes some replenishment from surface water.

Water Supply refers to gross water supply by supply systems from sources to consumers, including losses during distribution.

Surface Water Supply refers to withdrawals by surface water supply system, broken down with storage, flow, pumping and transfer. Supply from storage projects includes withdrawals from reservoirs; supply from flow includes withdrawals from rivers and lakes with natural flows no matter if there are locks or not; supply from pumping projects includes withdrawals from rivers or lakes with pumping stations; and supply from transfer refers to water supplies transferred from first-level regions of water resources or independent river drainage areas to others, and should not be covered under supplies of storage, flow and pumping.

Groundwater Supply refers to withdrawals from supplying wells, broken down with shallow layer freshwater, deep layer freshwater and slightly brackish water. Groundwater supply for urban areas includes water mining by both waterworks and own wells of enterprises.

Other Water Supply Sources include supplies by waste-water treatment, rain collection, seawater desalinization and other water projects.

Water Use refers to gross water use distributed to users, including loss during transportation, broken down into use by agriculture, industry, living consumption and ecological protection.

Water Use by Agriculture includes uses of water by irrigation of farming fields and by forestry, animal husbandry and fishing. Water use by forestry, animal husbandry and fishery includes irrigation of forestry and orchards, irrigation of grassland and replenishment of fishing farms.

Water Use by Industry refers to new withdrawals of water, excluding reuse of water within enterprises.

Water Use by Living Consumption includes use of water for living consumption in both urban and rural areas. Urban water use by living consumption is composed of household use and public use (including services, commerce, restaurants, cargo transportation, posts, telecommunications and construction). Rural water use by living consumption includes both households and animals.

Water Use by Ecological Protection includes replenishment of rivers and lakes and use for urban environment.

Waste Water Discharged by Industry refers to the volume of waste water discharged by industrial enterprises through all their outlets, including waste water from production process, directly cooled water, groundwater from mining wells which does not meet discharge standards and sewage from households mixed with waste water produced by industrial activities, but excluding indirectly cooled water discharged (It should be included if the discharge is not separated from waste water).

Industrial Waste Water Meeting Discharge Standards refers to volume of industrial waste water discharge which, with or without treatment, reaches national or local standards with regard to all pollutants.

Ratio of Industrial Waste Water Meeting Discharge Standards refers to percentage of industrial waste water meeting discharge standards over total industrial waste water discharge. It is calculated as:

$$\text{Ratio of industrial waste water meeting discharge standards} = \frac{\text{industrial waste water meeting discharge standards}}{\text{total industrial waste water discharge}}$$

Chemical Oxygen Demand (COD) refers to the amount of oxygen required when chemical oxidants are used to oxidize organic pollutants in water. A higher value of COD corresponds to more serious pollution by organic pollutants.

Industrial Waste Air Emission refers to discharge into atmosphere of waste air containing pollutants generated from fuel burning and production process in enterprises within a given period of time. It is converted into standard (273K, 101325Pa) with the following formula:

Emission=emission from fuel burning+ emission through production process

Industrial Soot Emission refers to the volume of soot in smoke emitted in the process of fuel burning in the premises of enterprises.

Industrial Dust Emission refers to volume of dust emitted by production process of enterprises and suspended in the air for a given period of time, including dust from refractory material of iron and steel works, dust from coke-screening systems and sintering machines of coke plants, dust from lime kilns and dust from cement production in building material enterprises, but excluding soot and dust emitted from power plants.

Industrial Solid Wastes Produced refers to total volume of solid, semi-solid and high concentration liquid residues produced by industrial enterprises from production process in a given period of time, including hazardous wastes, slag, coal ash, gangue, tailings, radioactive residues and other wastes, but excluding stones stripped or dug out in mining - gangue and acid or alkaline stones not included (a stone is acid or alkaline according to the pH value of the water being below 4 or above 10.5 when the stone is in, or soaked by water).

Industrial Solid Wastes Utilized refers to volume of solid wastes from which useful materials can be extracted or which can be converted into usable resources, energy or other materials by means of reclamation, processing, recycling and exchange (including utilizing in the year the stocks of industrial solid wastes of the previous year). Examples of such utilizations include fertilizers, building materials and road materials. The information shall be collected by the producing units of the wastes.

Rate of Utilization of Industrial Solid Wastes refers to the percentage of industrial solid wastes utilized over industrial solid wastes produced (including stocks of the previous years). It is calculated as:

$$\text{Rate of utilization of industrial solid wastes} = \frac{\text{volume of industrial solid wastes utilized}}{\text{industrial solid wastes produced} + \text{stock of previous years}} \times 100\%$$

Stock of Industrial Solid Wastes refers to the volume of solid wastes placed in special facilities or special sites for purposes of utilization or disposal. The sites or facilities should take measures against dispersion, loss, seepage, and air and water contamination.

Industrial Solid Wastes Disposed refers to the quantity of industrial solid wastes which are burnt or placed ultimately in the sites meeting the requirements for environmental protection and not salvaged or recycled (including disposition in the year of those wastes of previous years). The disposition includes landfill (Safe landfills should be conducted for hazardous wastes), incineration, containment spaces, deep underground disposal, backfill in mining pits and disposal at sea.

Industrial Solid Wastes Discharged refers to the volume of industrial solid wastes discharged by producing enterprises to disposal facilities or to other sites. The wastes exclude stones stripped or dug from mining (gangue and acid or alkaline waste stones not included).

Consumption Wastes Transported refers to volume of consumption wastes collected and transported to disposal factories or sites. Consumption wastes are solid wastes produced from urban households or from service activities for urban households, and solid wastes regarded by laws and regulations as urban consumption wastes, including those from households, commercial activities, markets, cleaning of streets, public sites, offices, schools, factories, mining units and other sources.

Ratio of Consumption Wastes Treated refers to consumption wastes treated over that produced. In practical statistics, as it is difficult to estimate, the volume of consumption wastes produced is replaced with that transported. It is calculated as:

$$\text{Ratio of consumption wastes treated} = \frac{\text{consumption wastes treated}}{\text{consumption wastes produced}} \times 100\%$$

Land for Agriculture Use refers to land directly used for agriculture production, including land for cultivation, gardening, forests, herbage and other agriculture activities.

Area of Man-made Forests refer to the area of stable growing forests, planted manually or by airplanes, with a survival rate of 80% or higher of the designed number of trees per hectare, or with a canopy density of or above 0.20 after 3-5 years of manual planting or 5-7 years of airplane planting.

Total Area of Afforestation refers to the total area of land suitable for afforestation, including barren hills, idle land, sand dunes, "grain for green" land, on which acres of arbores or bushes are planted through manual planting, airplane planting, plant seedlings, etc. in accordance with the required density standards of the Technical Procedures of Afforestation, and with a survival rate of over 85% in line with the Implementing Rules of the Forest Law of the People's Republic of China (or a survival rate of 75% in areas with less that 400 mm of annual rainfall and without irrigation facilities). Included in the this category are trees planted alone the roadsides, riversides, or next to houses that occupy an area over 0.066 hectares, or where more than 4 lines of trees are planted. Total area of afforestation is further classified by ownership (state-owned, state-collective, collective or private), by approach of planting (manual, airplane), and by type of forests (timber, by-products, protection, fuel, special use, etc.).

By-product Forests refer to forests that mainly produce fruits, nuts, edible oil, beverages, indigents, raw materials and medicine materials. By-product forests are planted to harvest the fruits, leaves, bark or liquid of trees, and consume them as food or raw materials for the manufacturing industry, such as tea-oil trees, tung oil trees, walnut trees, camphor trees, tea bushes, mulberry trees, fruit trees, etc.

Protection Forests refer to forests, trees and bushes planted mainly for protection or preservation purpose, including water resource conservation forests, water and soil conservation forests, windbreak and dune-fixing forests, farmland and pasture protection forests, riverside protection forests, roadside protection forests, etc.

Fuel Forests refer to forests planted mainly for fuels.

Project on Preservation of Natural Forests is the Number One ecological project in China's forest industry that involves the largest investment. It consists of 3 components: 1) Complete halt of all cutting and logging activities in the natural forests at the upper stream of Yangtze River and the upper and middle streams of the Yellow River. 2) Significant reduction of timber production of key state forest zones in northeast provinces and in Inner Mongolia. 3) Better protection of natural forests in other regions through rehabilitation programmes.

Projects on Converting Cultivated Land to Forests and Grassland (Grain for Green Projects) aiming at preventing soil erosion in key regions, these projects are ecological construction projects in the development of forest industry that have the widest coverage and most sophisticated procedures, with strong policy implications and most active participation of the people.

Projects on Protection Forests in North China and Yangtze River Basin covering the widest areas in China with a rich variety of contents, these projects aim at solving the problem of sand and dust in northeastern China, northern China and northwestern China and the ecological issues in other areas. More specifically, they include phase IV of Project on North China protection forests, phase II of Project on protection forests at the middle and lower streams of Yangtze River and at the Huihe River and Taihu Lake valley, phase II of Project on coastal protection forests, phase II of Project on Pearl River protection forests, phase II Project on greenery of Taihang Mountain and phase II Projects on greenery of plains.

Projects on Preserving Wild Animals and Plants and on Construction of Natural Reserves aiming at gene preservation and protection of bio-diversity, nature and wetlands, these projects are forward-looking with strategic perspectives in line with international trends and practices.

Wetlands refers to marshland and peat bog, whether natural or man-made, permanent or temporary; water covered areas, whether stagnant or flowing, with fresh or semi-fresh or salty water that is less than 6 meters deep at low tide; as well as coral beach, weed beach, mud beach, mangrove, river outlet, rivers, fresh-water marshland, marshland forests, lakes, salty bog and salt lakes along the coastal areas.

Natural Reserves refer to certain areas of land, waters or sea demarked and approved by relevant governments at all levels to put under special protection and management in order to protect the natural environment and natural resources and to promote the sustainable development of the national economy. According to the objects be protected, the natural reserves are classified into classes of natural ecosystem, wild life and natural heritage. Scenic spots and cultural preservation zones are not included.

Environmental Emergencies refers to environmental emergencies that caused or likely to cause significant causalities, serious property damages and pose a major threat and damage to the economic, social or political stability of the country or a region, or have significant social impact that related to the public safety.

Environment Pollution and Destruction Accidents refers to sudden accidents, due to economic or social activities that are contrary to environment protection laws or due to unforeseen factors or natural disasters, that lead to environment pollution, destruction of protected wild animals, plants or nature reserves, damage to human health, economic and property losses, and other negative impacts on the society.

Funds Allocated to Afforestation refers to the total funds which have been transfered into the specific accounts of the agencies responsible for afforestation projects at reporting period.

Completed Investment for Afforestation during the Year reflecting the actual size of investment completed during January 1 and December 31 of the reference year, this indicator is important in estimating investment efficiency and in making annual analysis of the performance of the national economy.

新疆统计年鉴

XINJIANG STATISTICAL YEARBOOK

12

农　业

AGRICULTURE

简要说明

本篇资料的主要内容及来源

本篇资料反映新疆维吾尔自治区农业生产和农村经济基本情况，主要内容包括农村基层组织情况、乡村从业人员、国有农、林、牧、渔场情况、主要农业生产条件、耕地、农林牧渔业产值、主要农产品生产情况、特色农作物生产情况、乡镇企业情况等。

本篇资料除表12-4来自新疆维吾尔自治区国土资源厅，表12-10、12-11、12-12来自新疆维吾尔自治区水利厅，乡镇企业主要指标来自新疆维吾尔自治区乡镇企业局外，其余资料均由新疆维吾尔自治区统计局农村统计处提供。

Brief Introduction

Main Content and Source of Data

The data in this chapter show the basic conditions of agricultural production and rural economy in Xinjiang Uygur Autonomous Region, including mainly rural grassroots units rural population, rural employed labor force, basic conditions of township enterprises, statistic on forest products, cultivated land, gross output value farming, forest, animal husbandry and fishery, output of major farm products and condition on the township enterprises, ect.

Data on table 12-4 are provided by the Xinjiang Bureau Department of land and resources.Data on this chapter are provided by the Xinjiang Bureau of Water Resources except 12-10,12-11,12-12, the data on the township enterprises are from the Xinjiang Bureau of Township Enterprises. Others are provided by the Department of Rural statistics, Xinjiang Bureau of Statistics.

12-1 主要年份农村基层组织情况
Basic Conditions of Rural Grass-roots Unit in Main Years

指　　标	Item	2000	2010	2012
乡镇政府(个)	**Number of Township and Town Governments (unit)**	**794**	**801**	**811**
#镇政府	Number of Township Governments	124	183	204
村民委员会(个)	Number of Villager's Committees (unit)	9378	8796	8670
乡村户数(户)	Number of Rural Households (household)	2008794	2551479	2702112
乡村人口(人)	Rural Population (person)	9131922	10737179	11213136
乡村从业人员(人)	**Number of Rural Laborers (person)**	**3540789**	**4650560**	**5393265**
按性别分	Grouped by Gender			
男	Male	1950559	2558491	2949696
女	Female	1590230	2092069	2443569
按行业分	Grouped by Sector			
农林牧渔业	Agriculture, Forestry, Animal Husbandry & Fishery	3144461	3758972	4319000
工　业	Industry	84766	161325	202757
建筑业	Construction	49126	162427	211391
交通运输、仓储和邮政业	Transportation,Storage, Postal and Telecommunication Services		145132	170919
信息传输、计算机服务和软件业	Information Transmission, Computer Service and Software Sector		13915	19091
批发与零售业	Wholesale and Retail Trades	76727	157457	177864
住宿和餐饮业	Hotels and Catering Serives	109217	106191	126338
其　他	Others	76492	145141	165905

12-2 国有农林牧渔场基本情况
Basic Conditions of State Agriculture, Forestry, Animal Husbandry and Fishery

指　　标	Item	2011	2012
场数合计(个)	**Total (unit)**	**484**	**451**
农　场	Number of Farms	287	262
林　场	Number of Forest Farms	52	51
牧　场	Number of Ranch	133	126
渔　场	Number of Fishing Ground	12	12
场内户数(户)	**Number of Households on a Farm (household)**	**831339**	**835021**
#牧业户数	Number of Stock-breeding Household	72561	71747
场内人口(人)	**Farm Population (person)**	**2532728**	**2502030**
#牧业人口	Stock-breeding Population	257247	254847
场内实有从业人员(人)	**Persons Actually Engaged on a Farm (person)**	**1087919**	**1114625**
男	Male	602929	613982
女	Female	484990	500643
农　业	Employed Persons in Agriculture	783833	764847
工　业	Employed Persons in Industry	66877	81147
建筑业	Employed Persons in Construction	29834	34506
交通运输、仓储和邮政业	Transportation,Storage, Post and Telecommunications Services	34944	40159
信息传输、计算机服务和软件业	Information Transmission, Computer Service and Software Sector	1160	1355
批发与零售业	Wholesale and Retail Trades	53556	64501
住宿和餐饮业	Hotels and Catering Serives	25268	29099
其　他	Others	92447	99011

12-3 各地、州、市、县(市)农村基层组织情况

(2012 年)

地 区	Region	乡镇数(个) Number of Township and Town Governments (unit)	#镇 town	村民委员会(个) Number of Villager's Committees (unit)	乡村户数(户) Number of Rural House-Holds (household)	#牧业户数 Stock-breeding households
总 计	**Total**	**811**	**204**	**8670**	**2702112**	**366916**
乌鲁木齐市	**Urumqi City**	**22**	**8**	**176**	**67107**	**8026**
#乌鲁木齐县	Urumqi County	6	1	41	12035	3627
克拉玛依市	**Karamay City**	**2**		**6**	**682**	**263**
吐鲁番地区	**Turpan Administrative Offices**	**25**	**8**	**175**	**108282**	**3400**
吐鲁番市	Turpan City	9	1	60	43216	2042
鄯善县	Shanshan [piqan]County	9	4	65	39526	352
托克逊县	Toksun County	7	3	50	25540	1006
哈密地区	**Hami [Kumul]Administrative Offices**	**31**	**7**	**170**	**53389**	**14655**
哈密市	Hami [Kumul]City	15	4	91	32156	7536
巴里坤哈萨克自治县	Barkol KazakAutonomous County	10	2	47	18443	6084
伊吾县	Yiwu [Araturuk]County	6	1	32	2790	1035
昌吉回族自治州	**Changji Hui Autonomous Prefecture**	**67**	**35**	**453**	**188980**	**31992**
昌吉市	Changji City	10	7	83	35245	6080
阜康市	Fukang City	6	3	60	19225	2946
呼图壁县	Hutubi County	6	5	50	20762	4004
玛纳斯县	Manas County	11	6	85	27265	3620
奇台县	Qitai County	15	6	60	35401	4752
吉木萨尔县	Jimsar County	9	6	55	28885	3121
木垒哈萨克自治县	Mori Kazak Autonomous County	10	2	60	22197	7469
伊犁哈萨克自治州	**Ili Kazak Autonomous Prefecture**	**211**	**60**	**1942**	**570900**	**94969**
伊犁州直属县(市)	**Counties (Cities) Direct Under Ili Prefecture**	**99**	**23**	**656**	**336571**	**46006**
伊宁市	Yining [Gulja]City	9	1	46	33734	661
奎屯市	Kuytun City	1		4	426	380
伊宁县	Yining [Gulja]County	18	2	130	72488	4673
察布查尔锡伯自治县	Qapqal Xibe Autonomous County	13	2	64	33843	2146
霍城县	Huocheng [korgas]County	10	5	75	52480	2367
巩留县	Gongliu [Tokkuzlara]County	8	2	53	25332	4428
新源县	Xinyuan [kunes]County	11	7	77	39386	7363
昭苏县	Zhaosu [mongolkure]County	10	1	73	26883	7258
特克斯县	Tekes County	8	2	59	22208	8163
尼勒克县	Nilka County	11	1	75	29791	8567
塔城地区	**Tacheng [Tarbagatai] Administrative Offices**	**60**	**23**	**781**	**147157**	**17907**
塔城市	Tacheng [Qoqek] City	5	1	115	20421	1576
乌苏市	Usu City	14	7	134	31667	831
额敏县	Emin [Dorbiljin] County	11	2	139	19590	1269
沙湾县	Shawan County	12	9	227	45919	1923
托里县	Toli County	7	3	66	16148	8286
裕民县	Yumin [Qagantokay] County	5		45	7312	2247
和布克赛尔蒙古自治县	Hoboksar Mongol Autonomous County	6	1	55	6100	1775
阿勒泰地区	**Altay Administrative Offices**	**52**	**14**	**505**	**87172**	**31056**
阿勒泰市	Altay City	10	3	102	16018	3508
布尔津县	Burqin County	7	2	63	15175	5648
富蕴县	Fuyun [Koktokay] County	10	4	71	11514	4048
福海县	Fuhai [Burultokay] County	5		62	9171	3476
哈巴河县	Habahe [Kaba] County	7	1	114	19363	7477
青河县	Qinghe [Qinggil] County	7	3	52	8874	5032
吉木乃县	Jeminay County	6	1	41	7057	1867

Basic Conditions of Rural Grass-roots Units by Prefecture, Autonomous Prefecture, City and County

乡村人口数(人) Rural Population (person)	#牧业人口数 Population Engaged in Livestocks	乡村从业人员(人) Number of Rural Laborers (person)	#男 Male	农林牧渔业 Agriculture, Forestry, Animal Husbandry & Fishery	工业 Industry	建筑业 Construction	交通仓储和邮政业 Transport, Storage, Post and Telecommunication Services	信息传输、计算机服务和软件业 Information Transmission, Computer Servcie and Software Industries	批发与零售业 Retail and Wholesale Trades	住宿和餐饮业 Hotels and Catering Serives	其他 Others
11213136	1465214	5393265	2949696	4319000	202757	211391	170919	19091	177864	126338	165905
225616	27106	138212	73997	83646	10974	1927	12884	246	9364	9746	9425
41818	14103	22376	11730	17014	142	108	1363	26	784	929	2010
2099	934	1327	695	1208			15		17	87	
438968	13814	257862	140876	208701	6568	6526	10799	1127	11662	8762	3717
182070	9430	102898	57758	79086	2431	2966	5682	303	5825	5380	1225
161966	1308	98334	53064	84326	1244	2402	3037	701	3967	2208	449
94932	3076	56630	30054	45289	2893	1158	2080	123	1870	1174	2043
180566	55688	103071	54925	75718	4435	4011	7625	649	3927	3026	3680
113137	26486	65164	34828	50728	2382	1571	3904	437	2532	1670	1940
59554	24943	32936	17373	20662	1967	2403	3652	204	1293	1292	1463
7875	4259	4971	2724	4328	86	37	69	8	102	64	277
683468	118376	385651	209182	302530	17356	7955	14834	786	13049	10621	18520
123998	21075	66420	35923	48404	3667	1706	3143	113	2267	2049	5071
65735	12229	38768	21403	27278	2720	1507	1201	44	1490	1771	2757
82800	16183	45217	23977	37808	1295	196	1796	126	1444	1053	1499
95072	12635	52772	28386	39242	5478	661	2614	109	1947	1151	1570
151313	20739	83514	46116	66662	1725	1972	3292	202	3127	2755	3779
93830	10366	56972	31477	45343	1466	1246	2183	143	1980	1504	3107
70720	25149	41988	21900	37793	1005	667	605	49	794	338	737
2352807	409428	1174676	661593	905020	57003	55376	40378	6162	44295	31453	34989
1501789	222301	718267	410149	536709	33920	41681	30196	4924	30006	21247	19584
148224	3551	73643	40830	37645	6118	8161	7857	369	6377	3735	3381
1469	1369	936	502	860	19	29	9		16	3	
335879	24795	169979	101061	128529	8659	10087	5480	2133	6144	4746	4201
125936	9257	64250	37990	53700	2569	1940	1209	171	1794	1114	1753
211823	11830	123630	66069	97700	3303	4961	5856	882	3720	4225	2983
121882	22188	43229	25504	37384	1395	1011	1408	32	1785	169	45
206314	37901	85526	49782	62783	5828	4410	3383	514	3655	2256	2697
111814	33454	44031	27622	34180	1595	3043	1586	193	1694	772	968
110172	41309	57728	30019	43470	2387	4993	813	437	2344	2181	1103
128276	36647	55315	30770	40458	2047	3046	2595	193	2477	2046	2453
535521	66327	306510	167037	257684	13357	6581	6158	667	8500	5915	7648
66216	4893	42717	22612	33975	1105	666	940	124	1598	711	3598
117108	2711	63585	34345	52893	3661	1212	1122	89	1885	1825	898
83845	5103	48298	28980	42905	1049	638	1026	90	1538	524	528
154812	6833	92452	49311	75786	5714	2132	1873	297	2497	2160	1993
59364	33370	35618	19233	30746	1353	1638	747	44	510	360	220
35528	8536	18005	9435	16185	265	215	368	5	396	315	256
18648	4881	5835	3121	5194	210	80	82	18	76	20	155
315497	120800	149899	84407	110627	9726	7114	4024	571	5789	4291	7757
63528	15218	31906	19360	24024	2511	1029	816	184	1116	566	1660
49515	18650	23258	12845	16759	549	1065	434	118	1129	1236	1968
43739	16066	21223	11995	12276	2965	1388	878	89	954	416	2257
35924	16404	19091	10419	15176	663	1691	578	51	413	342	177
65426	26773	26155	13583	20568	1144	1158	514	49	1153	1016	553
39557	22606	18400	9792	13012	1876	783	782	80	878	579	410
17808	5083	9866	6413	8812	18		22		146	136	732

12-3 续表

地　区	Region	乡镇数（个） Number of Township and Town Governments (unit)	#镇 town	村民委员会（个） Number of Villagers' Committees (unit)	乡村户数（户） Number of Rural Households (unit)	#牧业户数 Stock-Breeding households
博尔塔拉蒙古自治州	**Bortala Mongol Autonomous Prefecture**	**13**	**5**	**227**	**58964**	**6296**
博乐市	Bole [Bortala] City	5	3	107	23518	2553
精河县	Jinghe [Jing] County	4	1	55	22565	1858
温泉县	Wenquan [Araxang] County	4	1	65	12881	1885
巴音郭楞蒙古自治州	**Bayangol Mongol Autonomous Prefecture**	**73**	**14**	**409**	**125130**	**11954**
库尔勒市	Korla City	10	1	59	19415	465
轮台县	Luntai [Bugur] County	10	3	65	18527	934
尉犁县	Yuli [Lopnur] County	7		50	13479	1755
若羌县	Ruoqiang [Qarkilik] County	5	1	26	5644	213
且末县	Qiemo [Qarqan] County	11	0	53	8790	1530
焉耆回族自治县	Yanqi Hui Autonomous County	7	3	49	20622	592
和静县	Hejing County	11	5	55	20148	3973
和硕县	Hoxud County	6		26	10236	1982
博湖县	Bohu [Bagrax] County	6	1	26	8269	510
阿克苏地区	**Aksu Administrative Offices**	**76**	**22**	**1105**	**349913**	**30238**
阿克苏市	Aksu City	6	2	122	35950	6738
温宿县	Wensu [Onsu] County	9	4	104	36462	3584
库车县	Kuqa County	14	8	210	69856	4572
沙雅县	Xayar County	9	3	150	47735	3878
新和县	Xinhe [Toksu] County	7	1	110	34065	4560
拜城县	Baicheng [Bay] County	12	2	150	37591	3500
乌什县	Wushi [Uxturpan] County	8		107	42843	1610
阿瓦提县	Awat County	7	2	119	37647	1057
柯坪县	Kalpin County	4		33	7764	739
克孜勒苏柯尔克孜自治州	**Kizilsu Kirgiz Autonomous Prefecture**	**35**	**4**	**238**	**96492**	**29739**
阿图什市	Artux City	7	1	77	38983	8477
阿克陶县	Akto County	13	2	109	40488	9033
阿合奇县	Akqi County	6	1	18	7755	4652
乌恰县	Wuqia [Ulugqat] County	9		34	9266	7577
喀什地区	**Kashgar [Kaxgar] Administrative Offices**	**163**	**27**	**2360**	**649021**	**101637**
喀什市	Kashgar [Kaxgar] City	8	2	106	37275	2900
疏附县	Shufu County	13	3	165	63114	9460
疏勒县	Shule County	14	2	223	56614	2800
英吉沙县	Yengisar County	14	1	163	53984	5748
泽普县	Zepu [Poskam] County	11	1	138	27631	1647
莎车县	Shache [Yarkant] County	28	6	502	131503	36279
叶城县	Yecheng [Kagilik] County	21	3	319	73196	11443
麦盖提县	Makit County	10	1	129	30728	979
岳普湖县	Yopurga County	9	2	87	28118	5237
伽师县	Jiashi [Payzawat] County	13	2	297	77338	8180
巴楚县	Bachu [Maralbexi] County	11	3	186	63146	11200
塔什库尔干塔吉克自治县	Taxkorgan Tajik Autonomous County	11	1	45	6374	5764
和田地区	**Hotan Administrative Offices**	**91**	**14**	**1384**	**427119**	**33284**
和田市	Hotan City	8	2	111	43343	3280
和田县	Hotan County	12	2	206	62954	2877
墨玉县	Moyu [Karakax] County	16	2	364	112012	9597
皮山县	Pishan [Guma] County	16	3	169	47975	2411
洛浦县	Lop County	9	1	207	54541	4800
策勒县	Qira County	8	1	123	40309	5624
于田县	Yutian [Keriya] County	15	2	170	58408	3177
民丰县	Minfeng [Niya] County	7	1	34	7577	1518
生产建设兵团	**Xinjiang Production and Construction Group**	**2**		**25**	**6133**	**463**

Continued

乡村人口数(人) Rural Population (person)	#牧业人口数 Population Engaged in Live-stocks	乡村从业人员(人) Number of Rural Laborers (person)	#男 Male	农林牧渔业 Agriculture, Forestry, Animal Husbandry & Fishery	工业 Industry	建筑业 Construction	交通仓储和邮政业 Transport, Storage, Post and Telecommunication Services	信息传输、计算机服务和软件业 Information Transmission, Computer Servcie and Software Industries	批发与零售业 Retail and Wholesale Trades	住宿和餐饮业 Hotels and Catering Serives	其他 Others
200489	**22767**	**100685**	**53344**	**73079**	**4170**	**4298**	**3356**	**256**	**4326**	**3508**	**7692**
89162	10139	46798	24513	33163	2377	1932	1867	155	2100	1972	3232
71360	6232	31092	16941	22817	894	971	696	21	1480	1088	3125
39967	6396	22795	11890	17099	899	1395	793	80	746	448	1335
490072	**44430**	**251947**	**145258**	**202316**	**16772**	**6469**	**6901**	**657**	**8533**	**5393**	**4906**
74774	1310	39709	23303	32550	94	649	1284	153	3250	1336	393
74459	3071	33624	18492	30494	354	409	295	68	733	446	825
49900	7166	21036	11623	19347	57	215	357	92	414	206	348
22508	730	16724	11338	8430	5722	1013	953	18	311	277	
40181	5875	17915	10440	15065	257	1122	697	68	394	208	104
78441	2915	41562	24498	30567	3810	1536	1658	33	1179	1339	1440
78148	14183	46532	25632	35381	5931	1130	791	79	1120	1038	1062
38003	7191	17105	9843	14746	172	132	377	116	619	366	577
33658	1989	17740	10089	15736	375	263	489	30	513	177	157
1502681	**108564**	**772590**	**415044**	**665826**	**13396**	**25072**	**17103**	**2825**	**18031**	**11630**	**18707**
159993	22951	68190	38194	47438	1851	5924	4541	589	2998	2767	2082
149853	12321	82529	44199	76023	867	818	736	151	1300	635	1999
314353	16484	166356	86505	132801	3984	8699	5998	1015	5046	2849	5964
200027	14288	98384	57931	90477	1033	3196	465	121	1656	870	566
134004	14590	67973	35501	60541	309	1486	1154	292	583	805	2803
157983	13200	74509	41601	66969	1270	1321	1251	174	1402	769	1353
173151	6715	112500	56824	100200	2142	1957	1277	265	2709	1275	2675
178379	5023	84658	44378	75839	1588	1123	1353	198	1962	1395	1200
34938	2992	17491	9911	15538	352	548	328	20	375	265	65
418410	**122133**	**174577**	**96980**	**135811**	**7814**	**6971**	**6521**	**152**	**6623**	**4477**	**6208**
182965	34365	81889	46049	56893	5461	3375	4573	134	4605	3542	3306
168065	35103	69920	38651	59999	1451	2672	1340		1145	630	2683
30365	23265	8018	4300	7056	99	180	93	18	309	44	219
37015	29400	14750	7980	11863	803	744	515		564	261	
2980801	**422752**	**1365532**	**737297**	**1155810**	**25652**	**57671**	**31710**	**2762**	**38226**	**26236**	**27465**
175431	9700	66050	37680	41310	1700	7200	4100		5200	6540	
278100	38750	96500	56600	71894	3120	5806	3090		5740	2800	4050
283697	6800	218212	130927	195514	3178	7560	3470	250	2280	3500	2460
244824	28465	116285	60468	108150	930	1745	1395	90	1977	1512	486
118090	6168	36785	18430	30192	542	2009	1368	142	1327	100	1105
657345	159084	246819	132056	203664	5625	13269	5835	1246	9325	1880	5975
322992	43403	193626	100406	158217	5373	10248	4923	311	3753	2285	8516
126859	4339	57902	30581	50701	1385	2113	396	91	870	298	2048
122774	27759	53138	26515	44776	869	2096	1465	370	1476	1913	173
359999	36712	137988	71063	125369	1547	2471	3085	201	2597	2610	108
263342	34224	131632	66874	117552	1320	2578	1863	61	3446	2744	2068
27348	27348	10595	5697	8471	63	576	720		235	54	476
1716048	**117331**	**658332**	**356156**	**501882**	**38252**	**34965**	**18738**	**3469**	**19550**	**11314**	**30162**
187884	13837	61385	33473	38523	5676	3568	2465	597	3339	1091	6126
265465	9823	95740	49737	71766	12808	3005	2439	80	1852	2043	1747
476464	31210	158538	84622	113855	10096	12249	5307	634	7499	4653	4245
191539	7136	74533	37392	59182	1057	2096	1696	40	1038	514	8910
221304	15112	97877	51365	81584	3444	5502	2095	796	1881	823	1752
132573	21703	60410	31991	51849	1183	3119	773	144	1782	1014	546
215861	12978	101913	62936	79669	3870	4550	3479	1146	1778	941	6480
24958	5532	7936	4640	5454	118	876	484	32	381	235	356
21111	**1891**	**8803**	**4349**	**7453**	**365**	**150**	**55**		**261**	**85**	**434**

12-4 各地、州、市、县(市)耕地面积

Area of Cultivated land by Prefecture, Autonomous Prefecture, City and County

单位：公顷 (2008 年) (hectare)

地　　区	Region	年末耕地面　　积 Cultivated Land at Year-end	#水浇地 # Irrigable Land	#旱　地 Arid Land
总　计	**Total**	**4124563.70**	**3812247.55**	**204501.81**
乌鲁木齐市	**Urumqi City**	**96950.66**	**78328.45**	**4035.06**
#乌鲁木齐县	Urumqi County	55412.44	48787.55	2206.13
克拉玛依市	**Karamay City**	**41926.31**	**41150.26**	**34.34**
石河子市	**Shihezi City**	**21886.21**	**21444.27**	
吐鲁番地区	**TurpanAdministrative Offices**	**48182.08**	**47560.93**	
吐鲁番市	Turpan City	17365.34	16883.43	
鄯善县	Shanshan [piqan]County	13707.94	13577.23	
托克逊县	Toksun County	17108.80	17100.27	
哈密地区	**Hami [Kumul]Administrative Offices**	**87087.69**	**83783.52**	**2617.09**
哈密市	Hami [Kumul]City	48101.16	47484.37	0.91
巴里坤哈萨克自治县	Barkol KazakAutonomous County	33793.67	31248.76	2494.56
伊吾县	Yiwu [Araturuk]County	5192.86	5050.39	121.62
昌吉回族自治州	**Changji Hui Autonomous Prefecture**	**629255.41**	**575551.19**	**48255.72**
昌吉市	Changji City	81216.70	79559.30	
阜康市	Fukang City	45008.84	43705.99	438.04
呼图壁县	Hutubi County	108240.93	107083.42	
玛纳斯县	Manas County	142651.23	140149.81	1646.14
奇台县	Qitai County	141463.80	125593.52	15405.67
吉木萨尔县	Jimsar County	59196.71	54743.95	4118.61
木垒哈萨克自治县	Mori Kazak Autonomous County	51477.20	24715.20	26647.26
伊犁哈萨克自治州	**Ili Kazak Autonomous Prefecture**	**1370619.63**	**1206934.23**	**147541.35**
伊犁州直属县(市)	**Counties (Cities) Direct Under Ili Prefecture**	**565724.94**	**462766.85**	**93380.19**
伊宁市	Yining [Gulja]City	13143.75	12397.65	157.73
奎屯市	Kuytun City	13830.81	13416.21	
伊宁县	Yining [Gulja]County	91060.36	87325.21	3074.98
察布查尔锡伯自治县	Qapqal Xibe Autonomous County	78010.92	67482.83	8691.95
霍城县	Huocheng [korgas]County	90103.57	86672.14	2627.72
巩留县	Gongliu [Tokkuzlara]County	42300.77	34067.58	5769.73
新源县	Xinyuan [kunes]County	69968.00	64130.84	3631.87
昭苏县	Zhaosu [mongolkure]County	89646.90	46655.06	42897.45
特克斯县	Tekes County	29857.44	23166.80	6399.81
尼勒克县	Nilka County	47802.42	27452.53	20128.95
塔城地区	**Tacheng [Tarbagatai] Administrative Offices**	**623638.56**	**574819.09**	**44346.27**
塔城市	Tacheng [Qoqek] City	116362.76	111668.61	4375.15
乌苏市	Usu City	90090.34	88675.34	
额敏县	Emin [Dorbiljin] County	147338.60	125362.73	21758.60
沙湾县	Shawan County	189499.02	186954.94	254.66
托里县	Toli County	24924.02	24791.30	70.37
裕民县	Yumin [Qagantokay] County	44247.45	26309.92	17887.49
和布克赛尔蒙古自治县	Hoboksar Mongol Autonomous County	11176.37	11056.25	
阿勒泰地区	**Altay Administrative Offices**	**181256.13**	**169348.29**	**9814.89**
阿勒泰市	Altay City	40931.04	40585.26	24.04
布尔津县	Burqin County	20584.37	16887.53	3469.38
富蕴县	Fuyun [Koktokay] County	14892.11	11654.88	2860.36
福海县	Fuhai [Burultokay] County	48402.20	47386.39	105.63
哈巴河县	Habahe [Kaba] County	31714.03	29103.31	2462.77
青河县	Qinghe [Qinggil] County	9825.27	8902.88	892.71
吉木乃县	Jeminay County	14907.11	14828.04	

12-4 续表 Continued

单位：公顷 (hectare)

地　区	Region	年末耕地面积 Cultivated Land at Year-end	#水浇地 # Irrigable Land	#旱　地 Arid Land
博尔塔拉蒙古自治州	**Bortala Mongol Autonomous Prefecture**	**135223.32**	**133774.95**	**23.79**
博乐市	Bole [Bortala] City	65574.44	64586.74	
精河县	Jinghe [Jing] County	36147.89	35728.97	23.79
温泉县	Wenquan [Araxang] County	33500.99	33459.24	
巴音郭楞蒙古自治州	**Bayangol Mongol Autonomous Prefecture**	**322556.95**	**312340.71**	
库尔勒市	Korla City	63399.62	55645.29	
轮台县	Luntai [Bugur] County	32947.41	32914.37	
尉犁县	Yuli [Lopnur] County	68263.86	67857.08	
若羌县	Ruoqiang [Qarkilik] County	7132.15	7070.05	
且末县	Qiemo [Qarqan] County	15088.73	15059.49	
焉耆回族自治县	Yanqi Hui Autonomous County	36128.76	35999.77	
和静县	Hejing County	45540.81	45088.93	
和硕县	Hoxud County	36168.43	35167.26	
博湖县	Bohu [Bagrax] County	17887.18	17538.47	
阿克苏地区	**Aksu Administrative Offices**	**614943.17**	**585562.62**	**1674.65**
阿克苏市	Aksu City	168847.83	161536.10	394.20
温宿县	Wensu [Onsu] County	78711.69	67549.42	831.61
库车县	Kuqa County	65204.00	63182.13	6.41
沙雅县	Xayar County	56653.34	56359.21	
新和县	Xinhe [Toksu] County	37933.16	34910.01	
拜城县	Baicheng [Bay] County	72601.88	71028.51	
乌什县	Wushi [Uxturpan] County	46465.29	43538.75	
阿瓦提县	Awat County	79372.13	78323.46	442.43
柯坪县	Kalpin County	9153.85	9135.03	
克孜勒苏柯尔克孜自治州	**Kizilsu Kirgiz Autonomous Prefecture**	**52859.60**	**50149.91**	**252.68**
阿图什市	Artux City	15715.38	15293.50	223.54
阿克陶县	Akto County	29250.53	27006.77	11.71
阿合奇县	Akqi County	6164.41	6140.43	
乌恰县	Wuqia [Ulugqat] County	1729.28	1709.21	17.43
喀什地区	**Kashgar [Kaxgar] Administrative Offices**	**530457.07**	**516515.12**	**66.56**
喀什市	Kashgar [Kaxgar] City	7165.97	6271.21	
疏附县	Shufu County	51747.77	48541.95	
疏勒县	Shule County	49364.21	47766.47	
英吉沙县	Yengisar County	5718.17	5537.15	60.69
泽普县	Zepu [Poskam] County	37625.15	36203.14	
莎车县	Shache [Yarkant] County	98935.41	95867.11	
叶城县	Yecheng [Kagilik] County	53928.82	52503.91	4.67
麦盖提县	Makit County	50533.09	50138.07	
岳普湖县	Yopurga County	22224.51	22149.50	
伽师县	Jiashi [Payzawat] County	52288.15	51455.31	0.54
巴楚县	Bachu [Maralbexi] County	96950.39	96108.71	0.66
塔什库尔干塔吉克自治县	Taxkorgan Tajik Autonomous County	3975.44	3972.59	
和田地区	**Hotan Administrative Offices**	**172615.60**	**159151.39**	**0.57**
和田市	Hotan City	5996.45	5300.40	
和田县	Hotan County	30130.79	27035.19	
墨玉县	Moyu [Karakax] County	34013.32	28767.52	
皮山县	Pishan [Guma] County	27499.96	27193.71	
洛浦县	Lop County	26977.43	26784.99	
策勒县	Qira County	16489.41	16046.82	0.57
于田县	Yutian [Keriya] County	27445.86	24235.45	
民丰县	Minfeng [Niya] County	4062.38	3787.31	

12-5 农、林、牧、渔业总产值

Gross Output Value of Agriculture, Forestry, Animal Husbandry and Fishery

单位：万元 (10 000 yuan)

年份 Year	地区 Region	农林牧渔业总产值 Total	农业产值 Farming	林业产值 Forestry	牧业产值 Animal Husbandry	渔业产值 Fishery	农林牧渔服务业产值 Output Value of Services for Farming, Forestry, Animal Husbandary and Fishery
1978		191184	142460	3397	44990	337	
1980		220135	164187	5394	50148	406	
1985		565699	429519	25906	108598	1676	
1990		1446535	1104742	38152	294963	8678	
1995		4057332	3150055	56381	823351	27545	
1996		4309617	3340735	61940	875560	31382	
1997		4764743	3738602	64913	925923	35305	
1998		4992355	3873616	74394	1008783	35562	
1999		4611503	3409380	75565	1092279	34279	
2000		4872005	3605405	83451	1145142	38007	
2001		4968125	3488409	100847	1340236	38633	
2002		5250446	3627669	110897	1480382	31498	
2003		6883187	4827597	136936	1619823	32065	266766
2004		7506792	5150018	138204	1874660	42985	300925
2005		8310614	5958464	152851	1835206	43405	320688
2006		8835409	6385954	171994	1890700	46945	339816
2007		10634648	7669468	208623	2315097	70149	371311
2008		11766907	7841922	231830	3182256	99097	411802
2009		12976109	8986167	266451	3183730	111403	428358
2010		18461828	13768852	352701	3757905	126663	455707
2011		19553884	14378900	380808	4150000	141653	502523
2012		22756726	16750000	430407	4853719	152600	570000
乌鲁木齐市	Urumqi City	344293	152160	7518	176096	6965	1554
克拉玛依市	Karamay City	105852	35312	20572	35751	825	13392
吐鲁番地区	Turpan Administrative Offices	567752	464487	3923	91193	481	7668
哈密地区	Hami [Kumul] Administrative Offices	410827	211397	16131	176215	2212	4872
昌吉回族自治州	Changji Hui Autonomous Prefecture	2716179	1179846	25870	1465733	17728	27002
伊犁哈萨克自治州	Ili Kazak Autonomous Prefecture	4245590	2391838	76791	1696808	20686	59467
伊犁州直属县(市)	Counties (Cities) Direct Under Ili Prefecture	1857766	896597	52227	867031	11084	30827
塔城地区	Tacheng [Tarbagatai] Administrative Offices	1809269	1214454	10892	564072	2210	17641
阿勒泰地区	Altay Administrative Offices	578555	280787	13672	265705	7392	10999
博尔塔拉蒙古自治州	Bortala Mongol Autonomous Prefecture	632774	478235	7606	112847	1893	32193
巴音郭楞蒙古自治州	Bayangol Mongol Autonomous Prefecture	2216920	1733792	49684	360004	12163	61277
阿克苏地区	Aksu Administrative Offices	2123094	1670648	30524	334891	13372	73659
克孜勒苏柯尔克孜自治州	Kizilsu Kirgiz Autonomous Prefecture	210021	118668	4277	74173	230	12673
喀什地区	Kashgar [Kaxgar] Administrative Offices	3601391	2491614	79864	941636	12052	76225
和田地区	Hotan Administrative Offices	985305	658061	29166	279843	3403	14832
生产建设兵团	Xinjiang Production and Construction Group	8020942	6194701	92688	1145271	47578	540704

注：本表按当年价格计算。
Note: The number in this form is caculated by current price.

12-6 主要年份农、林、牧、渔业总产值指数
Indices of Gross Output Value of Agriculture, Forestry, Animal Husbandry and Fishery in Main Years

年 份 Year	农林牧渔业总产值 Total	#农业产值 Farming	#林业产值 Forestry	#牧业产值 Animal Husbandry	#渔业产值 Fishery
(上年=100) (preceding year=100)					
1978	113.0	118.6	108.8	105.4	106.7
1980	108.9	108.4	151.2	104.4	112.7
1985	110.9	111.5	131.3	104.6	135.1
1990	115.1	119.2	95.2	102.0	111.3
1995	107.1	107.0	88.5	109.0	127.0
1996	104.2	103.3	101.0	107.7	112.3
1997	109.5	109.6	100.5	110.2	108.6
1998	110.8	111.5	105.5	109.0	102.0
1999	104.8	103.9	100.9	108.1	106.3
2000	105.3	104.2	110.3	108.0	116.4
2001	104.5	103.9	116.1	105.8	104.2
2002	105.2	103.9	111.5	108.9	102.1
2003	106.3	105.2	120.7	108.7	101.7
2004	106.4	104.5	100.7	112.0	108.2
2005	107.4	107.0	105.8	109.0	105.3
2006	107.5	107.7	106.5	107.8	105.3
2007	108.2	108.9	108.6	106.0	115.2
2008	106.7	106.1	107.5	109.4	107.5
2009	105.1	107.8	106.5	98.5	106.9
2010	104.9	104.7	106.4	105.1	105.5
2011	106.9	108.3	105.9	102.0	107.1
2012	107.4	106.8	107.6	109.8	104.1
(1978 年=100) (1978=100)					
1978	100.0	100.0	100.0	100.0	100.0
1980	115.9	115.5	158.8	111.1	120.5
1985	188.4	194.3	245.4	160.0	140.9
1990	303.7	322.6	244.4	243.7	442.4
1995	420.7	453.3	247.4	325.5	863.7
1996	438.4	468.1	249.8	350.6	970.0
1997	480.2	512.8	251.1	386.4	1053.2
1998	531.8	571.7	265.1	421.1	1073.9
1999	557.1	593.8	267.5	455.3	1141.6
2000	586.3	618.8	295.0	491.9	1328.4
2001	612.9	642.8	342.5	520.6	1384.1
2002	644.8	668.1	381.9	566.9	1413.2
2003	685.4	702.6	460.9	616.0	1437.2
2004	729.3	734.2	464.1	689.9	1555.1
2005	783.3	785.6	491.0	752.0	1637.5
2006	842.0	846.1	522.9	810.7	1724.3
2007	911.0	921.4	567.9	859.3	1986.4
2008	972.0	977.6	610.5	940.1	2135.4
2009	1021.6	1053.9	650.2	926.0	2282.7
2010	1071.7	1103.4	691.8	973.2	2408.2
2011	1145.6	1195.0	732.6	992.7	2579.2
2012	1230.4	1276.3	788.3	1090.0	2684.9

12-7 各地、州、市、县(市)农林牧渔业总产值
Gross Output Value of Agriculture, Forestry, Animal Husbandry and Fishery by Prefecture, Autonomous Prefecture, City and County

单位：万元　　(2012 年)　　(10 000 yuan)

地　　区	Region	农林牧渔业总产值 Total	农业产值 Farming	林业产值 Forestry	牧业产值 Animal Husbandry	渔业产值 Fishery	农林牧渔服务业产值 Output Value of Services for Farming, Forestry, Animal Husbandary and Fishery
总　计	**Total**	**22756726**	**16750000**	**430407**	**4853719**	**152600**	**570000**
乌鲁木齐市	**Urumqi City**	**344293**	**152160**	**7518**	**176096**	**6965**	**1554**
#乌鲁木齐县	Urumqi County	87974	28986	1804	55351	333	1500
克拉玛依市	**Karamay City**	**105852**	**35312**	**20572**	**35751**	**825**	**13392**
吐鲁番地区	**TurpanAdministrative Offices**	**567752**	**464487**	**3923**	**91193**	**481**	**7668**
吐鲁番市	Turpan City	239737	201360	1745	32104	360	4168
鄯善县	Shanshan [piqan]County	207646	174348	1181	30503	94	1520
托克逊县	Toksun County	120369	88779	997	28586	27	1980
哈密地区	**Hami [Kumul]Administrative Offices**	**410827**	**211397**	**16131**	**176215**	**2212**	**4872**
哈密市	Hami [Kumul]City	208780	139872	7031	57542	1951	2384
巴里坤哈萨克自治县	Barkol KazakAutonomous County	139981	48382	320	89828	243	1208
伊吾县	Yiwu [Araturuk]County	62066	23143	8780	28845	18	1280
昌吉回族自治州	**Changji Hui Autonomous Prefecture**	**2716179**	**1179846**	**25870**	**1465733**	**17728**	**27002**
昌吉市	Changji City	407152	173283	3634	216567	10079	3589
阜康市	Fukang City	315795	140229	2291	171269	486	1520
呼图壁县	Hutubi County	476980	181182	3721	277151	3519	11407
玛纳斯县	Manas County	524664	298228	3261	212505	2304	8366
奇台县	Qitai County	571350	227651	6009	337420		270
吉木萨尔县	Jimsar County	226197	97320	5558	120929	1340	1050
木垒哈萨克自治县	Mori Kazak Autonomous County	194041	61953	1396	129892		800
伊犁哈萨克自治州	**Ili Kazak Autonomous Prefecture**	**4245590**	**2391838**	**76791**	**1696808**	**20686**	**59467**
伊犁州直属县(市)	**Counties (Cities) Direct Under Ili Prefecture**	**1857766**	**896597**	**52227**	**867031**	**11084**	**30827**
伊宁市	Yining [Gulja]City	112612	67651	855	39567	1769	2770
奎屯市	Kuytun City	15536	7784	96	6406		1250
伊宁县	Yining [Gulja]County	351818	188128	3124	148160	6686	5720
察布查尔锡伯自治县	Qapqal Xibe Autonomous County	201008	133848	3843	59435	579	3303
霍城县	Huocheng [korgas]County	229431	120515	3372	99709	393	5442
巩留县	Gongliu [Tokkuzlara]County	176552	91989	2865	80573	814	311
新源县	Xinyuan [kunes]County	309137	123603	32589	148375	693	3877
昭苏县	Zhaosu [mongolkure]County	158797	61018	734	95111	7	1927
特克斯县	Tekes County	129492	48188	1492	78772	60	980
尼勒克县	Nilka County	173383	53873	3257	110923	83	5247

注：本表按当年价格计算。
Note: The number in this form is caculated by current price.

12-7 续表 1 Continued

单位：万元 (10 000 yuan)

地　区	Region	农林牧渔业总产值 Total	农业产值 Farming	林业产值 Forestry	牧业产值 Animal Husbandry	渔业产值 Fishery	农林牧渔服务业产值 Output Value of Services for Farming, Forestry, Animal Husbandary and Fishery
塔城地区	**Tacheng [Tarbagatai] Administrative Offices**	**1809269**	**1214454**	**10892**	**564072**	**2210**	**17641**
塔城市	Tacheng [Qoqek] City	247873	169631	1232	75447		1563
乌苏市	Usu City	452193	339472	2808	104478	896	4539
额敏县	Emin [Dorbiljin] County	271777	174483	1107	95062		1125
沙湾县	Shawan County	600841	430839	2454	159196	1272	7080
托里县	Toli County	83415	30079	1581	49995		1760
裕民县	Yumin [Qagantokay] County	79212	43737	1230	33428	42	775
和布克赛尔蒙古自治县	Hoboksar Mongol Autonomous County	73958	26213	480	46466		799
阿勒泰地区	**Altay Administrative Offices**	**578555**	**280787**	**13672**	**265705**	**7392**	**10999**
阿勒泰市	Altay City	101574	50765	740	47851	630	1588
布尔津县	Burqin County	56401	23452	1445	29551	263	1690
富蕴县	Fuyun [Koktokay] County	102081	36540	1763	62210	118	1450
福海县	Fuhai [Burultokay] County	137403	84527	2511	41245	5844	3276
哈巴河县	Habahe [Kaba] County	102975	54341	4067	43201	388	978
青河县	Qinghe [Qinggil] County	52685	23834	2976	24862	98	915
吉木乃县	Jeminay County	25436	7328	170	16785	51	1102
博尔塔拉蒙古自治州	**Bortala Mongol Autonomous Prefecture**	**632774**	**478235**	**7606**	**112847**	**1893**	**32193**
博乐市	Bole [Bortala] City	264588	196665	2311	54760	272	10580
精河县	Jinghe [Jing] County	267325	221429	3383	28690	840	12983
温泉县	Wenquan [Araxang] County	100861	60141	1912	29397	781	8630
巴音郭楞蒙古自治州	**Bayangol Mongol Autonomous Prefecture**	**2216920**	**1733792**	**49684**	**360004**	**12163**	**61277**
库尔勒市	Korla City	464391	400003	370	52971	1262	9785
轮台县	Luntai [Bugur] County	286331	241610	431	40646	350	3294
尉犁县	Yuli [Lopnur] County	231116	190085	3516	20752		16763
若羌县	Ruoqiang [Qarkilik] County	258858	243491	2592	10651	5	2119
且末县	Qiemo [Qarqan] County	144764	106299	2864	27301	570	7730
焉耆回族自治县	Yanqi Hui Autonomous County	196394	109080	24341	53906	786	8281
和静县	Hejing County	256783	135741	7372	107532	405	5733
和硕县	Hoxud County	247569	214177	2136	25645	84	5527
博湖县	Bohu [Bagrax] County	130714	93306	6062	20600	8701	2045
阿克苏地区	**Aksu Administrative Offices**	**2123094**	**1670648**	**30524**	**334891**	**13372**	**73659**
阿克苏市	Aksu City	332726	258350	2876	55833	2672	12995
温宿县	Wensu [Onsu] County	342663	256905	6584	55213	3570	20391
库车县	Kuqa County	367429	267256	8327	87957	523	3366

12-7 续表 2 Continued

单位：万元 (10 000 yuan)

地 区	Region	农林牧渔业总产值 Total	农业产值 Farming	林业产值 Forestry	牧业产值 Animal Husbandry	渔业产值 Fishery	农林牧渔服务业产值 Output Value of Services for Farming, Forestry, Animal Husbandary and Fishery
沙雅县	Xayar County	248942	214220	4851	23627	290	5954
新和县	Xinhe [Toksu] County	216127	181418	1508	19648	208	13345
拜城县	Baicheng [Bay] County	170777	118659	2929	41764	5040	2385
乌什县	Wushi [Uxturpan] County	125289	97510	1483	21711	975	3610
阿瓦提县	Awat County	276229	246306	1415	18591	94	9823
柯坪县	Kalpin County	42912	30024	551	10547		1790
克孜勒苏柯尔克孜自治州	**Kizilsu Kirgiz Autonomous Prefecture**	**210021**	**118668**	**4277**	**74173**	**230**	**12673**
阿图什市	Artux City	88995	50500	1345	31750	195	5205
阿克陶县	Akto County	89996	59932	2340	22289	35	5400
阿合奇县	Akqi County	15346	3905	367	10113		961
乌恰县	Wuqia [Ulugqat] County	15684	4331	225	10021		1107
喀什地区	**Kashgar [Kaxgar] Administrative Offices**	**3601391**	**2491614**	**79864**	**941636**	**12052**	**76225**
喀什市	Kashgar [Kaxgar] City	147895	70795	5170	66956	774	4200
疏附县	Shufu County	363233	236337	6510	108936	1050	10400
疏勒县	Shule County	320332	206709	10515	102057	600	451
英吉沙县	Yengisar County	176700	117215	2269	51632	84	5500
泽普县	Zepu [Poskam] County	235004	169839	1812	59153	3600	600
莎车县	Shache [Yarkant] County	684232	511623	32682	116437	3598	19892
叶城县	Yecheng [Kagilik] County	522669	378843	4859	132827	1040	5100
麦盖提县	Makit County	254295	190424	3474	52492	255	7650
岳普湖县	Yopurga County	156470	97695	5171	50835	189	2580
伽师县	Jiashi [Payzawat] County	386456	265845	6985	103964	462	9200
巴楚县	Bachu [Maralbexi] County	334665	243685	417	80503	400	9660
塔什库尔干塔吉克自治县	Taxkorgan Tajik Autonomous County	19440	2604		15844		992
和田地区	**Hotan Administrative Offices**	**985305**	**658061**	**29166**	**279843**	**3403**	**14832**
和田市	Hotan City	86876	53662	1440	28973	770	2031
和田县	Hotan County	174058	132122	2430	36854	1179	1473
墨玉县	Moyu [Karakax] County	219754	144099	5887	65972	851	2945
皮山县	Pishan [Guma] County	114599	79139	2592	29587	33	3248
洛浦县	Lop County	118608	83743	5326	27664	255	1620
策勒县	Qira County	93931	65360	3221	24332	45	973
于田县	Yutian [Keriya] County	152932	91935	6730	51966	219	2082
民丰县	Minfeng [Niya] County	24547	8001	1540	14495	51	460
生产建设兵团	**Xinjiang Production and ConstructionGroup**	**8020942**	**6194701**	**92688**	**1145271**	**47578**	**540704**

12-8 各地、州、市、县(市)农业机械拥有量
Agricultural Machinery by Prefecture, Autonomous Prefecture, City and County

(2012 年)

地区	Region	农业机械总动力(千瓦) Total Power of Agricultural Machinery (kw)	农用大中型拖拉机 Large and Medium Agricultural Tractors 数量(台) Number (unit)	动力(千瓦) Capacity (kw)	小型拖拉机 Small Tractors 数量(台) Number (unit)	动力(千瓦) Capacity (kw)
总计	**Total**	**19682735**	**342644**	**10379185**	**334935**	**4138964**
乌鲁木齐市	**Urumqi City**	**299395**	**3265**	**98672**	**5560**	**67056**
#乌鲁木齐县	Urumqi County	53396	1093	25868	1139	16012
克拉玛依市	**Karamay City**	**30126**	**451**	**14950**	**96**	**1212**
吐鲁番地区	**TurpanAdministrative Offices**	**518343**	**2361**	**81820**	**9619**	**110874**
吐鲁番市	Turpan City	208628	694	23074	3595	40342
鄯善县	Shanshan [piqan]County	210569	834	30029	3828	46774
托克逊县	Toksun County	99146	833	28717	2196	23758
哈密地区	**Hami [Kumul]Administrative Offices**	**341761**	**3536**	**113286**	**10635**	**126618**
哈密市	Hami [Kumul]City	182839	2173	66610	4530	55487
巴里坤哈萨克自治县	Barkol KazakAutonomous County	127579	1049	34498	5192	59050
伊吾县	Yiwu [Araturuk]County	31343	314	12178	913	12081
昌吉回族自治州	**Changji Hui Autonomous Prefecture**	**1912928**	**19864**	**777172**	**45578**	**556881**
昌吉市	Changji City	324939	2511	141407	9188	118931
阜康市	Fukang City	153792	1565	66083	3418	36671
呼图壁县	Hutubi County	321443	4491	152455	5539	81887
玛纳斯县	Manas County	304386	4358	145462	7467	89150
奇台县	Qitai County	468409	3526	142593	10353	114523
吉木萨尔县	Jimsar County	190278	1562	63418	5008	59809
木垒哈萨克自治县	Mori Kazak Autonomous County	149681	1851	65754	4605	55910
伊犁哈萨克自治州	**Ili Kazak Autonomous Prefecture**	**4173679**	**75263**	**2354897**	**73136**	**923825**
伊犁州直属县(市)	**Counties (Cities) Direct Under Ili Prefecture**	**1550457**	**26791**	**885687**	**26601**	**330976**
伊宁市	Yining [Gulja]City	76280	1136	39761	1483	15398
奎屯市	Kuytun City	10532	290	10161	49	370
伊宁县	Yining [Gulja]County	278855	4478	167753	5391	67051
察布查尔锡伯自治县	Qapqal Xibe Autonomous County	187860	3392	117067	2343	33753
霍城县	Huocheng [korgas]County	200219	4589	115933	4262	43511
巩留县	Gongliu [Tokkuzlara]County	185916	2486	85482	4981	65872
新源县	Xinyuan [kunes]County	243590	4890	156932	1581	19753
昭苏县	Zhaosu [mongolkure]County	141742	1843	73084	2775	36760
特克斯县	Tekes County	98417	1873	53072	1339	17347
尼勒克县	Nilka County	127046	1814	66442	2397	31161
塔城地区	**Tacheng [Tarbagatai] Administrative Offices**	**1938879**	**36038**	**1129136**	**30101**	**380211**
塔城市	Tacheng [Qoqek] City	260949	4595	145539	4200	53711
乌苏市	Usu City	572850	12000	400176	9702	121275
额敏县	Emin [Dorbiljin] County	263933	3274	94816	3633	48101
沙湾县	Shawan County	568692	12159	361445	8952	113510
托里县	Toli County	95574	1320	39619	976	12082
裕民县	Yumin [Qagantokay] County	134830	1893	65748	2035	24078
和布克赛尔蒙古自治县	Hoboksar Mongol Autonomous County	42051	797	21793	603	7454
阿勒泰地区	**Altay Administrative Offices**	**684343**	**12434**	**340074**	**16434**	**212638**
阿勒泰市	Altay City	150884	2260	63616	4050	51840
布尔津县	Burqin County	88451	1511	38678	2697	35061
富蕴县	Fuyun [Koktokay] County	117365	2645	67490	2394	35191
福海县	Fuhai [Burultokay] County	126388	3197	81865	1624	21112
哈巴河县	Habahe [Kaba] County	127755	1572	51269	3786	46593
青河县	Qinghe [Qinggil] County	50135	715	20235	1449	17518
吉木乃县	Jeminay County	23365	534	16921	434	5323

12-8 续表 1 Continued

地　　区	Region	农业机械总动力(千瓦) Total Power of Agricultural Machinery (kw)	农用大中型拖拉机 Large and Medium Agricultural Tractors		小型拖拉机 Small Tractors	
			数量(台) Number (unit)	动力(千瓦) Capacity (kw)	数量(台) Number (unit)	动力(千瓦) Capacity (kw)
博尔塔拉蒙古自治州	**Bortala Mongol Autonomous Prefecture**	**569834**	**9193**	**282179**	**14087**	**172772**
博乐市	Bole [Bortala] City	234606	4126	120431	5110	62105
精河县	Jinghe [Jing] County	218147	3499	112826	6570	81526
温泉县	Wenquan [Araxang] County	117081	1568	48922	2407	29141
巴音郭楞蒙古自治州	**Bayangol Mongol Autonomous Prefecture**	**1626559**	**31534**	**919569**	**28719**	**368026**
库尔勒市	Korla City	434564	7557	221140	10334	136822
轮台县	Luntai [Bugur] County	136085	2352	65508	3905	47812
尉犁县	Yuli [Lopnur] County	236300	6811	201664	1373	18863
若羌县	Ruoqiang [Qarkilik] County	54828	1452	34665	284	3622
且末县	Qiemo [Qarqan] County	89216	2148	54934	2159	29828
焉耆回族自治县	Yanqi Hui Autonomous County	209863	3045	102382	3674	45640
和静县	Hejing County	188918	4082	107736	2174	28784
和硕县	Hoxud County	130688	1855	63612	1314	16417
博湖县	Bohu [Bagrax] County	146097	2232	67928	3502	40238
阿克苏地区	**Aksu Administrative Offices**	**2300326**	**45335**	**1268676**	**64176**	**772434**
阿克苏市	Aksu City	228811	4405	114474	7360	91158
温宿县	Wensu [Onsu] County	362512	8226	239969	7024	80846
库车县	Kuqa County	312240	5792	159869	9313	116400
沙雅县	Xayar County	279297	5882	177812	6781	76398
新和县	Xinhe [Toksu] County	177462	3227	100452	5103	61236
拜城县	Baicheng [Bay] County	349132	6068	156556	9601	124938
乌什县	Wushi [Uxturpan] County	214381	5453	118969	5390	78933
阿瓦提县	Awat County	336485	5428	178204	13033	135102
柯坪县	Kalpin County	40006	854	22371	571	7423
克孜勒苏柯尔克孜自治州	**Kizilsu Kirgiz Autonomous Prefecture**	**331289**	**9636**	**221788**	**5816**	**74143**
阿图什市	Artux City	100545	2568	61482	1409	17750
阿克陶县	Akto County	187542	5319	123703	3942	50067
阿合奇县	Akqi County	21822	877	19637	143	2037
乌恰县	Wuqia [Ulugqat] County	21380	872	16966	322	4289
喀什地区	**Kashgar [Kaxgar] Administrative Offices**	**2658519**	**80154**	**1797350**	**36054**	**440211**
喀什市	Kashgar [Kaxgar] City	69294	2481	46190	887	10502
疏附县	Shufu County	307567	7840	165711	6066	74075
疏勒县	Shule County	365062	8671	193438	4911	59453
英吉沙县	Yengisar County	136493	4003	88153	2814	34317
泽普县	Zepu [Poskam] County	173624	6418	131194	2302	28028
莎车县	Shache [Yarkant] County	510905	14809	347521	8041	98807
叶城县	Yecheng [Kagilik] County	201784	7844	156774	1967	23594
麦盖提县	Makit County	208315	6353	167125	2131	26315
岳普湖县	Yopurga County	119322	4385	95964	1428	17022
伽师县	Jiashi [Payzawat] County	226711	7175	155662	3449	42618
巴楚县	Bachu [Maralbexi] County	315206	9213	232469	1874	23209
塔什库尔干塔吉克自治县	Taxkorgan Tajik Autonomous County	24236	962	17149	184	2271
和田地区	**Hotan Administrative Offices**	**676374**	**19280**	**466396**	**7255**	**86212**
和田市	Hotan City	69626	2046	58810	441	5292
和田县	Hotan County	86686	2492	47384	1141	12551
墨玉县	Moyu [Karakax] County	156608	4585	112558	937	9546
皮山县	Pishan [Guma] County	70542	2378	47537	548	7041
洛浦县	Lop County	96734	2918	68991	938	11631
策勒县	Qira County	69373	1461	43373	1481	18210
于田县	Yutian [Keriya] County	101590	2770	70510	1320	16553
民丰县	Minfeng [Niya] County	25215	630	17233	449	5388
生产建设兵团	**Xinjiang Production and Construction Group**	**4243602**	**42772**	**1982430**	**34204**	**438700**

12-8 续表 2 Continued

地　区	Region	大中型拖拉机配套农具(部) Number of Large and Medium Tractor Towing Farm Machinery (unit)	小型拖拉机配套农具(部) Number of Small Tractor Towing Farm Machinery (unit)	农用排灌柴油机 Diesel Engines	
				数　量(台) Number (unit)	动　力(千瓦) Capacity (kw)
总　计	**Total**	**600839**	**634680**	**13603**	**205697**
乌鲁木齐市	**Urumqi City**	**3943**	**4684**	**5**	**33**
#乌鲁木齐县	Urumqi County	1214	2162	5	33
克拉玛依市	**Karamay City**	**892**	**165**	**1**	**15**
吐鲁番地区	**TurpanAdministrative Offices**	**4739**	**17545**	**13**	**158**
吐鲁番市	Turpan City	945	4417		
鄯善县	Shanshan [piqan]County	1792	5874		
托克逊县	Toksun County	2002	7254	13	158
哈密地区	**Hami [Kumul]Administrative Offices**	**9338**	**19406**		
哈密市	Hami [Kumul]City	5958	6451		
巴里坤哈萨克自治县	Barkol KazakAutonomous County	2796	11121		
伊吾县	Yiwu [Araturuk]County	584	1834		
昌吉回族自治州	**Changji Hui Autonomous Prefecture**	**38782**	**67634**	**129**	**2318**
昌吉市	Changji City	6470	12285		
阜康市	Fukang City	3787	4161		
呼图壁县	Hutubi County	9898	19313		
玛纳斯县	Manas County	6182	16823	15	183
奇台县	Qitai County	7769	7782		
吉木萨尔县	Jimsar County	2697	3864		
木垒哈萨克自治县	Mori Kazak Autonomous County	1979	3406	114	2135
伊犁哈萨克自治州	**Ili Kazak Autonomous Prefecture**	**157471**	**126645**	**5474**	**72329**
伊犁州直属县(市)	**Counties (Cities) Direct Under Ili Prefecture**	**49968**	**23306**	**820**	**8537**
伊宁市	Yining [Gulja]City	2702	853	28	570
奎屯市	Kuytun City	659	64		
伊宁县	Yining [Gulja]County	6020	5198	236	2281
察布查尔锡伯自治县	Qapqal Xibe Autonomous County	6883	3542	45	793
霍城县	Huocheng [korgas]County	8240	5040	219	1642
巩留县	Gongliu [Tokkuzlara]County	3626	2552	34	746
新源县	Xinyuan [kunes]County	9290	2812	75	1011
昭苏县	Zhaosu [mongolkure]County	3003	290	73	
特克斯县	Tekes County	5042	1587	8	382
尼勒克县	Nilka County	4503	1368	102	1112
塔城地区	**Tacheng [Tarbagatai] Administrative Offices**	**93711**	**91740**	**2625**	**37966**
塔城市	Tacheng [Qoqek] City	12292	12580	31	732
乌苏市	Usu City	34800	32020	1050	12084
额敏县	Emin [Dorbiljin] County	11170	10899	1374	22589
沙湾县	Shawan County	28071	31372	82	1017
托里县	Toli County	1953	985	60	1283
裕民县	Yumin [Qagantokay] County	4599	3603		
和布克赛尔蒙古自治县	Hoboksar Mongol Autonomous County	826	281	28	261
阿勒泰地区	**Altay Administrative Offices**	**13792**	**11599**	**2029**	**25826**
阿勒泰市	Altay City	3510	1980	51	601
布尔津县	Burqin County	960	2020	173	2249
富蕴县	Fuyun [Koktokay] County	3779	1052	669	8897
福海县	Fuhai [Burultokay] County	3418	2612	350	5250
哈巴河县	Habahe [Kaba] County	718	1827	551	5099
青河县	Qinghe [Qinggil] County	879	1228	217	3417
吉木乃县	Jeminay County	528	880	18	313

12-8 续表 3 Continued

地　区	Region	大中型拖拉机配套农具(部) Number of Large and Medium Tractor Towing Farm Machinery (unit)	小型拖拉机配套农具(部) Number of Small Tractor Towing Farm Machinery (unit)	农用排灌柴油机 Diesel Engines	
				数　量(台) Number (unit)	动　力(千瓦) Capacity (kw)
博尔塔拉蒙古自治州	**Bortala Mongol Autonomous Prefecture**	**14030**	**11427**	**8**	**187**
博乐市	Bole [Bortala] City	7112	3475	3	33
精河县	Jinghe [Jing] County	4809	6943		
温泉县	Wenquan [Araxang] County	2109	1009	5	154
巴音郭楞蒙古自治州	**Bayangol Mongol Autonomous Prefecture**	**55453**	**68336**	**2319**	**32776**
库尔勒市	Korla City	14223	28118	1268	13314
轮台县	Luntai [Bugur] County	4384	8332		
尉犁县	Yuli [Lopnur] County	7271	5424	735	12810
若羌县	Ruoqiang [Qarkilik] County	2211	1852	206	5532
且末县	Qiemo [Qarqan] County	2367	3760		
焉耆回族自治县	Yanqi Hui Autonomous County	9657	8482		
和静县	Hejing County	8806	4970	50	760
和硕县	Hoxud County	3828	2894	60	360
博湖县	Bohu [Bagrax] County	2706	4504		
阿克苏地区	**Aksu Administrative Offices**	**92247**	**141273**	**771**	**8554**
阿克苏市	Aksu City	17040	18279	38	558
温宿县	Wensu [Onsu] County	9569	12460	51	630
库车县	Kuqa County	13115	20292	50	670
沙雅县	Xayar County	14200	16265	560	5694
新和县	Xinhe [Toksu] County	5781	11240	14	154
拜城县	Baicheng [Bay] County	10591	19347	8	113
乌什县	Wushi [Uxturpan] County	8653	11166		
阿瓦提县	Awat County	12054	31346	50	735
柯坪县	Kalpin County	1244	878		
克孜勒苏柯尔克孜自治州	**Kizilsu Kirgiz Autonomous Prefecture**	**10840**	**9935**	**1**	**4**
阿图什市	Artux City	4170	3794		
阿克陶县	Akto County	5271	5107		
阿合奇县	Akqi County	1236	828		
乌恰县	Wuqia [Ulugqat] County	163	206	1	4
喀什地区	**Kashgar [Kaxgar] Administrative Offices**	**119689**	**120155**	**1535**	**24234**
喀什市	Kashgar [Kaxgar] City	970	2733		
疏附县	Shufu County	6590	32750		
疏勒县	Shule County	15477	26151		
英吉沙县	Yengisar County	9165	6185		
泽普县	Zepu [Poskam] County	9159	8779		
莎车县	Shache [Yarkant] County	17522	11017	380	6883
叶城县	Yecheng [Kagilik] County	17660	11773		
麦盖提县	Makit County	12461	8307	136	1999
岳普湖县	Yopurga County	7783	4146	30	264
伽师县	Jiashi [Payzawat] County	11997	6546	225	3094
巴楚县	Bachu [Maralbexi] County	9767	1187	764	11994
塔什库尔干塔吉克自治县	Taxkorgan Tajik Autonomous County	1138	581		
和田地区	**Hotan Administrative Offices**	**15636**	**16535**	**30**	**603**
和田市	Hotan City	1429	468		
和田县	Hotan County	1936	1833	14	180
墨玉县	Moyu [Karakax] County	4447	1191		
皮山县	Pishan [Guma] County	1674	3906	9	117
洛浦县	Lop County	1823	2695		
策勒县	Qira County	1101	2860	3	159
于田县	Yutian [Keriya] County	2750	3100		
民丰县	Minfeng [Niya] County	476	482	4	147
生产建设兵团	**Xinjiang Production and Construction Group**	**77779**	**30940**	**3317**	**64486**

12-9 各地、州、市、县(市)农村电气化和农田水利情况
Statistics on Water Conservancy and Electrification in Rural Areas by Prefecture, Autonomous Prefecture, City and County

(2012 年)

地区	Region	有效灌溉面积(千公顷) Irrigated Area (1000 hectares)	化肥施用量(吨)(折纯) Consumption of Chemical Fertilizer (ton) (100% Purity)	#氮肥 Nitrogenous Fertilizer	#磷肥 Phosphate Fertilizer	#钾肥 Potash Fertilizer
总计	**Total**	**4280.08**	**1926968**	**888894**	**489170**	**131537**
乌鲁木齐市	**Urumqi City**	**45.01**	**8612**	**5410**	**1468**	**970**
#乌鲁木齐县	Urumqi County	12.35	1743	830	468	330
克拉玛依市	**Karamay City**	**10.50**	**3922**	**1309**	**1090**	**322**
吐鲁番地区	**TurpanAdministrative Offices**	**34.56**	**22943**	**10450**	**3884**	**2782**
吐鲁番市	Turpan City	10.40	11620	5062	595	1576
鄯善县	Shanshan [piqan]County	6.72	6048	3776	628	391
托克逊县	Toksun County	17.44	5275	1612	2661	815
哈密地区	**Hami [Kumul]Administrative Offices**	**43.74**	**18136**	**8558**	**3331**	**1440**
哈密市	Hami [Kumul]City	21.13	9913	5259	2051	865
巴里坤哈萨克自治县	Barkol KazakAutonomous County	17.33	5007	2333	222	23
伊吾县	Yiwu [Araturuk]County	5.28	3216	966	1058	552
昌吉回族自治州	**Changji Hui Autonomous Prefecture**	**455.04**	**141289**	**72383**	**33764**	**7287**
昌吉市	Changji City	94.72	29170	12177	6743	2058
阜康市	Fukang City	39.93	8961	5066	1911	4
呼图壁县	Hutubi County	75.29	32348	17406	9615	1662
玛纳斯县	Manas County	70.25	31539	16765	8685	780
奇台县	Qitai County	115.30	22101	12004	3937	707
吉木萨尔县	Jimsar County	40.25	12566	7335	1470	1418
木垒哈萨克自治县	Mori Kazak Autonomous County	19.30	4604	1630	1403	658
伊犁哈萨克自治州	**Ili Kazak Autonomous Prefecture**	**901.63**	**279289**	**114613**	**60482**	**16146**
伊犁州直属县(市)	**Counties (Cities) Direct Under Ili Prefecture**	**326.68**	**105482**	**33272**	**17980**	**5487**
伊宁市	Yining [Gulja]City	14.83	3739	1775	136	44
奎屯市	Kuytun City	4.67	3163	1259	1266	90
伊宁县	Yining [Gulja]County	70.84	29089	8794	4353	1473
察布查尔锡伯自治县	Qapqal Xibe Autonomous County	57.32	14180	4880	4026	1132
霍城县	Huocheng [korgas]County	40.10	12735	3173	3094	1300
巩留县	Gongliu [Tokkuzlara]County	34.81	9425	4109		
新源县	Xinyuan [kunes]County	36.92	11569	3240	1459	586
昭苏县	Zhaosu [mongolkure]County	24.67	6772	2594	1444	637
特克斯县	Tekes County	19.96	3069	707	825	
尼勒克县	Nilka County	22.56	11741	2741	1377	225
塔城地区	**Tacheng [Tarbagatai] Administrative Offices**	**404.96**	**145829**	**65243**	**34349**	**8307**
塔城市	Tacheng [Qoqek] City	85.37	22514	10115	7213	1488
乌苏市	Usu City	82.68	31664	16535	3458	1669
额敏县	Emin [Dorbiljin] County	78.70	24686	7985	7213	562
沙湾县	Shawan County	105.28	52781	24635	13689	4500
托里县	Toli County	24.68	5600	2600	1700	
裕民县	Yumin [Qagantokay] County	18.77	4846	1943	806	7
和布克赛尔蒙古自治县	Hoboksar Mongol Autonomous County	9.48	3738	1430	270	81
阿勒泰地区	**Altay Administrative Offices**	**169.99**	**27978**	**16098**	**8153**	**2352**
阿勒泰市	Altay City	28.42	5431	3360	1918	81
布尔津县	Burqin County	17.33	1739	860	879	
富蕴县	Fuyun [Koktokay] County	18.66	1581	974	513	27
福海县	Fuhai [Burultokay] County	58.80	13129	6890	3178	1836
哈巴河县	Habahe [Kaba] County	28.22	3352	2385	841	126
青河县	Qinghe [Qinggil] County	12.60	2344	1378	691	270
吉木乃县	Jeminay County	5.96	402	251	133	12

12-9 续表 1 Continued

地　区	Region	有效灌溉面积(千公顷) Irrigated Area(1000 hectares)	化肥施用量(吨)(折纯) Consumption of Chemical Fertilizer (ton) (100% Purity)	#氮肥 Nitrogenous Fertilizer	#磷肥 Phosphate Fertilizer	#钾肥 Potash Fertilizer
博尔塔拉蒙古自治州	**Bortala Mongol Autonomous Prefecture**	**130.13**	**47603**	**22533**	**14554**	**2424**
博乐市	Bole [Bortala] City	48.25	16545	6948	4863	1003
精河县	Jinghe [Jing] County	48.50	17902	9020	4596	613
温泉县	Wenquan [Araxang] County	33.38	13156	6565	5095	808
巴音郭楞蒙古自治州	**Bayangol Mongol Autonomous Prefecture**	**254.62**	**135761**	**70196**	**37556**	**8986**
库尔勒市	Korla City	55.15	28535	15776	8560	2178
轮台县	Luntai [Bugur] County	31.85	21100	11490	4147	458
尉犁县	Yuli [Lopnur] County	40.67	23864	11088	8251	2473
若羌县	Ruoqiang [Qarkilik] County	7.27	7405	3875	1639	356
且末县	Qiemo [Qarqan] County	16.85	8423	5680	845	48
焉耆回族自治县	Yanqi Hui Autonomous County	27.16	13977	6450	2192	1269
和静县	Hejing County	27.82	10394	4499	4043	1178
和硕县	Hoxud County	32.47	12830	6847	5143	213
博湖县	Bohu [Bagrax] County	15.38	9233	4491	2736	813
阿克苏地区	**Aksu Administrative Offices**	**505.89**	**254462**	**107691**	**89265**	**17503**
阿克苏市	Aksu City	62.53	58060	23705	25326	2092
温宿县	Wensu [Onsu] County	67.26	23045	2072	5675	7896
库车县	Kuqa County	72.27	43877	19008	12794	1340
沙雅县	Xayar County	79.67	39981	18393	16790	1599
新和县	Xinhe [Toksu] County	45.20	21629	8855	10264	1727
拜城县	Baicheng [Bay] County	56.07	19831	6763	8417	1763
乌什县	Wushi [Uxturpan] County	30.01	12671	9022	840	
阿瓦提县	Awat County	82.33	32117	18179	7602	1086
柯坪县	Kalpin County	10.55	3251	1694	1557	
克孜勒苏柯尔克孜自治州	**Kizilsu Kirgiz Autonomous Prefecture**	**38.76**	**19219**	**9600**	**7111**	**1073**
阿图什市	Artux City	12.69	9592	4671	4921	
阿克陶县	Akto County	19.63	9494	4834	2152	1073
阿合奇县	Akqi County	4.06	51	32	19	
乌恰县	Wuqia [Ulugqat] County	2.38	82	63	19	
喀什地区	**Kashgar [Kaxgar] Administrative Offices**	**606.27**	**318144**	**150658**	**106892**	**15192**
喀什市	Kashgar [Kaxgar] City	11.24	5018	1784	1784	
疏附县	Shufu County	40.00	27775	13750	12760	1100
疏勒县	Shule County	51.00	23300	11800	8100	1900
英吉沙县	Yengisar County	60.74	17999	9522	6955	218
泽普县	Zepu [Poskam] County	25.93	20801	8786	8696	1460
莎车县	Shache [Yarkant] County	110.38	73058	28256	18078	1782
叶城县	Yecheng [Kagilik] County	75.68	32201	17261	7600	4077
麦盖提县	Makit County	61.33	17451	11850	4968	62
岳普湖县	Yopurga County	33.54	34268	15460	10214	3319
伽师县	Jiashi [Payzawat] County	63.56	30525	17052	9684	924
巴楚县	Bachu [Maralbexi] County	67.97	35748	15137	18053	350
塔什库尔干塔吉克自治县	Taxkorgan Tajik Autonomous County	4.90				
和田地区	**Hotan Administrative Offices**	**168.55**	**68555**	**38379**	**19167**	**4158**
和田市	Hotan City	10.42	5919	3918	1513	353
和田县	Hotan County	24.43	9849	5232	2787	921
墨玉县	Moyu [Karakax] County	35.30	14212	6091	2706	1350
皮山县	Pishan [Guma] County	29.16	11707	7819	2795	528
洛浦县	Lop County	21.23	8856	5671	3185	
策勒县	Qira County	16.76	6223	4264	1831	81
于田县	Yutian [Keriya] County	28.33	10258	4655	3653	870
民丰县	Minfeng [Niya] County	2.91	1531	729	697	55
生产建设兵团	**Xinjiang Production and Construction Group**	**1085.38**	**609033**	**277114**	**110606**	**53254**

12-9 续表 2 Continued

地　　区	Region	乡村及村以下办水电站 Hydropower Station inVillage or Below		农村用电量 (万千瓦小时) Electricity Consumed in Rural Areas (10 000 kwh)
		装机容量(万千瓦) Installed Capacity (10 000 kw)	发电量(万千瓦) Generating Capacity (10 000 kw)	
总　计	**Total**	**19.04**	**27843**	**758081**
乌鲁木齐市	**Urumqi City**			**19648**
#乌鲁木齐县	Urumqi County			721
克拉玛依市	**Karamay City**			**438**
吐鲁番地区	**TurpanAdministrative Offices**			**44000**
吐鲁番市	Turpan City			17639
鄯善县	Shanshan [piqan]County			20759
托克逊县	Toksun County			5602
哈密地区	**Hami [Kumul]Administrative Offices**			**22678**
哈密市	Hami [Kumul]City			18962
巴里坤哈萨克自治县	Barkol KazakAutonomous County			3090
伊吾县	Yiwu [Araturuk]County			626
昌吉回族自治州	**Changji Hui Autonomous Prefecture**			**85623**
昌吉市	Changji City			20505
阜康市	Fukang City			6096
呼图壁县	Hutubi County			18316
玛纳斯县	Manas County			9410
奇台县	Qitai County			23616
吉木萨尔县	Jimsar County			2922
木垒哈萨克自治县	Mori Kazak Autonomous County			4758
伊犁哈萨克自治州	**Ili Kazak Autonomous Prefecture**	**2.16**	**3418**	**79697**
伊犁州直属县(市)	**Counties (Cities) Direct Under Ili Prefecture**	**0.92**	**2060**	**32577**
伊宁市	Yining [Gulja]City			1770
奎屯市	Kuytun City			2450
伊宁县	Yining [Gulja]County	0.08	84	4109
察布查尔锡伯自治县	Qapqal Xibe Autonomous County			1853
霍城县	Huocheng [korgas]County			12818
巩留县	Gongliu [Tokkuzlara]County	0.09	350	1009
新源县	Xinyuan [kunes]County	0.24	1441	3681
昭苏县	Zhaosu [mongolkure]County	0.51	20	1081
特克斯县	Tekes County		165	917
尼勒克县	Nilka County			2889
塔城地区	**Tacheng [Tarbagatai] Administrative Offices**			**32227**
塔城市	Tacheng [Qoqek] City			6218
乌苏市	Usu City			4372
额敏县	Emin [Dorbiljin] County			2579
沙湾县	Shawan County			9600
托里县	Toli County			3800
裕民县	Yumin [Qagantokay] County			3665
和布克赛尔蒙古自治县	Hoboksar Mongol Autonomous County			1993
阿勒泰地区	**Altay Administrative Offices**	**1.24**	**1358**	**14894**
阿勒泰市	Altay City	1.00	201	821
布尔津县	Burqin County			1880
富蕴县	Fuyun [Koktokay] County	0.04	57	3795
福海县	Fuhai [Burultokay] County			2661
哈巴河县	Habahe [Kaba] County			892
青河县	Qinghe [Qinggil] County	0.20	1100	4324
吉木乃县	Jeminay County			521

12-9 续表 3 Continued

地　区	Region	乡村及村以下办水电站 HydroPower Station inVillage or Below 装机容量(万千瓦) Installed Capacity (10 000 kw)	发电量(万千瓦) Generating Capacity (10 000 kw)	农村用电量(万千瓦小时) Electricity Consumed in Rural Areas (10 000 kwh)
博尔塔拉蒙古自治州	**Bortala Mongol Autonomous Prefecture**	**0.52**	**1477**	**22523**
博乐市	Bole [Bortala] City	0.15	485	8690
精河县	Jinghe [Jing] County	0.37	992	12082
温泉县	Wenquan [Araxang] County			1751
巴音郭楞蒙古自治州	**Bayangol Mongol Autonomous Prefecture**			**58117**
库尔勒市	Korla City			16563
轮台县	Luntai [Bugur] County			10209
尉犁县	Yuli [Lopnur] County			5410
若羌县	Ruoqiang [Qarkilik] County			1735
且末县	Qiemo [Qarqan] County			790
焉耆回族自治县	Yanqi Hui Autonomous County			3300
和静县	Hejing County			1748
和硕县	Hoxud County			15300
博湖县	Bohu [Bagrax] County			3062
阿克苏地区	**Aksu Administrative Offices**	**6.00**	**96**	**48571**
阿克苏市	Aksu City			4025
温宿县	Wensu [Onsu] County	6.00	96	2515
库车县	Kuqa County			9238
沙雅县	Xayar County			10667
新和县	Xinhe [Toksu] County			12156
拜城县	Baicheng [Bay] County			1600
乌什县	Wushi [Uxturpan] County			2110
阿瓦提县	Awat County			4391
柯坪县	Kalpin County			1869
克孜勒苏柯尔克孜自治州	**Kizilsu Kirgiz Autonomous Prefecture**	**0.12**	**253**	**4120**
阿图什市	Artux City	0.12	253	1828
阿克陶县	Akto County			1717
阿合奇县	Akqi County			320
乌恰县	Wuqia [Ulugqat] County			255
喀什地区	**Kashgar [Kaxgar] Administrative Offices**	**3.00**	**25**	**43031**
喀什市	Kashgar [Kaxgar] City			687
疏附县	Shufu County	3.00	25	1950
疏勒县	Shule County			1200
英吉沙县	Yengisar County			3212
泽普县	Zepu [Poskam] County			3197
莎车县	Shache [Yarkant] County			4159
叶城县	Yecheng [Kagilik] County			1299
麦盖提县	Makit County			8398
岳普湖县	Yopurga County			2383
伽师县	Jiashi [Payzawat] County			6447
巴楚县	Bachu [Maralbexi] County			10100
塔什库尔干塔吉克自治县	Taxkorgan Tajik Autonomous County			
和田地区	**Hotan Administrative Offices**	**1.61**	**2486**	**31030**
和田市	Hotan City	0.08		4179
和田县	Hotan County			4290
墨玉县	Moyu [Karakax] County	1.00	1225	6620
皮山县	Pishan [Guma] County			1455
洛浦县	Lop County	0.36	901	5350
策勒县	Qira County	0.16	360	4043
于田县	Yutian [Keriya] County			2850
民丰县	Minfeng [Niya] County	0.01		2243
生产建设兵团	**Xinjiang Production and Construction Group**	**5.63**	**20088**	**298606**

12-10 灌溉、水库和除涝、治水情况
Irrigation, Reservoirs, Flood Prevention, Water and Soil Conservation

项　　目	Item	2011	2012
灌溉面积(千公顷)	Irrigated Areas (1000 hectares)	4184.45	4311.71
有效灌溉面积	Effective Irrigated Areas	2877.45	3003.57
林地灌溉面积	Irrigated Wooded-land Areas	506.47	479.32
园地灌溉面积	Irrigated Orchard Areas	430.44	463.03
牧草灌溉面积	Irrigated Pasture-land Areas	325.33	322.94
其他灌溉面积	Other Irrigated Areas	44.76	42.85
水库(座)	Number of Reservoirs (unit)	451	457
大型水库	Large Reservoir	14	14
中型水库	Medium-sized Reservoir	86	87
小型水库	Small Reservoir	351	356
水库库容量 (亿立方米)	Capacity of Reservoirs (100 million cu.m)	111.68	112.11
大型水库	Large Reservoir	78.84	78.84
中型水库	Medium-sized Reservoir	25.34	25.47
小型水库	Small Reservoir	7.50	7.79
节水灌溉面积 (千公顷)	Water-saving Irrigated Areas (1000 hectares)	2327.85	2539.30
除涝面积　(千公顷)	Areas wish Flood Prevention Measures (1000 hectares)	42.92	42.92
水土流失治理面积(千公顷)	Area of Soil Erosion under Control (1000 hectares)	383.81	465.46
堤防长度 (公里)	Total Length of Dikes (km)	7233.33	7764.76
堤防保护耕地面积 (千公顷)	Area of Land Protected by Dikes (1000 hectares)	1603.51	1645.74

注: 1.大型水库库容: 1 亿立方米以上; 中型水库库容: 1 千万至 1 亿立方米;小型水库库容: 10 万至 1 千万立方米。2.本表和 12-11，12-12 表资料由水利厅提供。

Note: a) The capacity of the large reservoirs is over 100 million cubic meters, while that of the medium ones is from 10 million to 100 million cubic meters, and that of the small ones is from 100 000 to 10 million cubic meters. b) The data in the table is offered by the Bureau of Water Conservancy, together with table 12-11,12-12.

12-11 各地、州、市水利设施和节水灌溉面积

Water Conservancy Facilities and Water-saving Irrigated Area by Prefecture, Autonomous Prefecture and City

(2012 年)

地 区	Region	水库数 (座) Number of Reservoirs (unit)	水库总库容量 (万立方米) Capacity of Reservoirs (10 000 cu.m)	节水灌溉面积 (千公顷) Water-saving Irrigated Area (1 000 hectares)	水土流失治理面积 (千公顷) Area of Soil Erosion under Control (1 000 hectares)
总 计	**Total**	**457**	**1121112**	**2539.30**	**465.46**
乌鲁木齐市	Urumqi City	32	16536	26.56	18.45
克拉玛依市	Karamay City	7	28710	18.60	7.58
吐鲁番地区	Turpan Administrative Offices	15	10448	92.43	9.80
哈密地区	Hami [Kumul]Administrative Offices	38	10683	77.10	22.92
昌吉回族自治州	Changji HuiAutonomous Prefecture	82	36898	347.47	35.01
伊犁州直属县(市)	Counties (Cities) Direct Under Ili Prefecture	13	255520	197.38	58.52
塔城地区	Tacheng [Tarbagatai] Administrative Offices	60	26754	336.61	11.20
阿勒泰地区	Altay Administrative Offices	65	101495	147.53	12.45
博尔塔拉蒙古自治州	Bortala Mongol Autonomous Prefecture	4	6838	93.82	15.26
巴音郭楞蒙古自治州	Bayangol Mongol Autonomous Prefecture	14	10640	272.19	150.37
阿克苏地区	Aksu Administrative Offices	6	22829	418.51	33.85
克孜勒苏柯尔克孜自治州	Kizilsu Kirgiz Autonomous Prefecture	12	10580	38.69	1.63
喀什地区	Kashgar [Kaxgar] Administrative Offices	50	79598	344.65	15.27
和田地区	Hotan Administrative Offices	43	31359	115.80	59.47
其 他	Others	16	472224	11.96	13.68

12-12 各地、州、市农村饮水安全情况

Basic Statistics on Security of Drinking Water in Rural Area by Prefecture, Autonomous Prefecture and City

单位:万人　　(2012 年)　　(10 000 persons)

地 区	Region	农村饮水安全达标人口 Reach the Standards in Security of Drinking Water of Rural Population	本年新增饮水安全达标人口 Increased in Security of Drinking Water of Rural Population This Year	农村饮水安全未达标人口 Not Reach the Standards in Security of Drinking Water of Rural Populaition
总 计	**Total**	**951.94**	**60.12**	**163.80**
乌鲁木齐市	Urumqi City	23.54	1.15	4.45
克拉玛依市	Karamay City	3.11		
吐鲁番地区	Turpan Administrative Offices	28.78	2.41	7.24
哈密地区	Hami [Kumul]Administrative Offices	19.04	1.51	3.05
昌吉回族自治州	Changji HuiAutonomous Prefecture	69.99	5.09	8.67
伊犁州直属县(市)	Counties (Cities) Direct Under Ili Prefecture	127.67	7.16	18.63
塔城地区	Tacheng [Tarbagatai] Administrative Offices	45.56	3.86	14.27
阿勒泰地区	Altay Administrative Offices	33.88	3.69	6.60
博尔塔拉蒙古自治州	Bortala Mongol Autonomous Prefecture	25.64	2.60	2.47
巴音郭楞蒙古自治州	Bayangol Mongol Autonomous Prefecture	47.72	5.58	8.90
阿克苏地区	Aksu Administrative Offices	114.10	7.27	23.53
克孜勒苏柯尔克孜自治州	Kizilsu Kirgiz Autonomous Prefecture	31.31	2.50	8.54
喀什地区	Kashgar [Kaxgar] Administrative Offices	236.45	10.89	30.74
和田地区	Hotan Administrative Offices	127.24	5.05	17.56
其 他	Others	17.91	1.36	9.15

12-13 主要年份农作物播种面积

Total Sown Areas of Farm Crops in Main Years

单位：千公顷 (1 000 hectares)

年 份 Year	农作物播种面积 Total Sown Area	粮食作物播种面积 Sown Area of Grain Crops	谷 物 Cereal	#水 稻 Rice	#小 麦 Wheat	#玉 米 Corn	#大 麦 Barley	豆 类 Soybeans	薯 类 Tubers	棉 花 Cotton
1978	3021.67	2310.71	2297.44	105.59	1348.82	621.39	50.01	13.27	23.09	150.42
1980	2993.71	2162.37	2147.60	98.39	1354.83	555.79	23.24	14.77	17.55	181.22
1985	2846.63	1853.04	1844.47	74.50	1278.43	418.43	13.63	8.57	10.56	253.52
1990	2979.51	1826.61	1813.16	84.13	1180.11	442.40	42.92	13.45	10.67	435.22
1995	3051.44	1593.29	1528.62	73.38	952.58	439.16	41.58	64.67	10.34	742.90
2000	3388.76	1445.77	1353.99	78.15	838.99	382.45	33.50	91.78	22.59	1012.39
2001	3404.12	1394.96	1281.38	73.28	744.27	410.29	34.11	113.58	20.77	1129.72
2002	3478.37	1493.96	1386.81	74.96	749.74	501.93	36.45	107.15	20.65	943.97
2003	3470.28	1307.02	1202.61	67.16	626.09	454.14	38.25	104.41	23.89	1037.05
2004	3571.89	1378.61	1273.03	66.77	658.08	505.69	24.53	105.58	24.23	1127.55
2005	3728.11	1471.76	1371.89	69.07	761.84	497.64	27.42	99.87	20.51	1157.99
2006	4206.28	1465.82	1369.68	68.00	740.11	496.43	50.96	96.14	22.79	1664.43
2007	4394.25	1379.00	1300.58	70.95	634.02	528.91	55.86	78.42	33.15	1782.60
2008	4536.87	1649.97	1554.43	70.12	877.97	545.39	54.68	95.54	36.02	1668.01
2009	4710.26	1993.50	1867.77	73.49	1153.32	598.38	31.73	125.73	37.68	1409.31
2010	4758.64	1991.61	1879.36	66.93	1120.01	653.82	28.94	112.25	36.99	1460.60
2011	4983.48	2000.36	1916.10	70.59	1077.98	728.00	24.81	84.26	47.12	1638.06
2012	5136.74	2103.20	2034.45	69.23	1081.04	855.72	14.13	68.75	27.97	1720.80

年 份 Year	#长绒棉 Long-Staple Cotton	油 料 Oil Bearing Crops	#油 菜 Rapeseeds	#胡 麻 Flax	#葵 花 Helianthus	甜 菜 Beetroots	蔬 菜 Vegetables	果用瓜 Melon	#甜 瓜 Musk-melon	苜 蓿 Lucerne
1978	29.05	202.13	90.90	65.49	23.68	17.67	55.12	41.95		174.90
1980	38.50	269.39	107.47	81.85	50.08	24.27	46.99	39.54		191.65
1985	26.28	294.78	89.82	81.12	111.39	15.51	54.91	53.69	27.95	132.07
1990	62.69	269.27	117.35	46.04	96.11	66.87	58.07	28.84	15.09	159.34
1995	8.35	306.70	130.11	26.75	140.10	71.10	71.54	25.15	9.72	120.25
2000	49.29	310.07	96.23	24.57	157.05	55.75	127.75	55.99	26.01	120.49
2001	67.69	217.64	72.85	17.10	99.76	85.54	125.96	58.19	26.55	165.06
2002	46.30	215.05	70.00	23.84	96.60	85.32	164.21	82.47	48.47	235.11
2003	70.13	226.38	74.48	22.30	100.07	67.31	163.84	62.45	32.82	294.13
2004	70.63	215.47	67.52	13.74	85.55	59.88	185.60	61.29	36.07	301.10
2005	73.38	185.49	59.92	17.37	84.62	69.90	176.66	70.57	36.02	275.91
2006	106.94	151.73	49.25	14.28	64.29	94.42	186.82	74.02	41.27	242.38
2007	142.53	176.47	59.48	12.32	96.41	94.02	234.88	103.40	62.81	231.36
2008	132.18	286.68	83.67	9.51	172.44	71.14	258.04	110.60	68.22	171.42
2009	82.60	270.05	76.95	12.43	155.74	63.74	262.17	143.47	86.70	165.34
2010	96.79	273.37	70.15	8.75	164.87	75.27	303.59	122.78	69.44	150.14
2011	83.87	264.28	64.47	7.83	163.65	75.43	322.61	118.85	57.78	145.29
2012	53.33	242.34	59.64	8.68	148.19	82.63	306.94	130.08	63.12	149.69

注：粮食、棉花播种面积为国家审定数。
Note: Total sown areas of grain,cotton refer to the statistical data of state approved.

12-14 各地、州、市、县(市)农作物播种面积

单位：千公顷 (2012 年)

地 区	Region	农作物播种面积 Total Sown Area	粮食 Grain Crops	谷物 Cereal	#水稻 Rice	#小麦 Wheat	#玉米 Corn	豆类 Soy-beans
总 计	**Total**	**5136.74**	**2103.20**	**2034.45**	**69.23**	**1081.04**	**855.72**	**68.75**
乌鲁木齐市	**Urumqi City**	**50.40**	**21.90**	**20.84**	**6.57**	**7.87**	**4.20**	**1.06**
#乌鲁木齐县	Urumqi County	12.41	3.84	3.54		1.45	0.12	0.30
克拉玛依市	**Karamay City**	**10.34**	**0.52**	**0.52**		**0.01**	**0.51**	**…**
吐鲁番地区	**TurpanAdministrative Offices**	**53.97**	**6.32**	**6.31**		**0.05**	**1.44**	**0.01**
吐鲁番市	Turpan City	14.06	0.54	0.54			0.03	
鄯善县	Shanshan [piqan]County	15.21	0.94	0.94		0.02	0.56	
托克逊县	Toksun County	24.70	4.84	4.83		0.03	0.85	0.01
哈密地区	**Hami [Kumul]Administrative Offices**	**62.25**	**25.26**	**24.87**		**18.91**	**2.42**	**0.39**
哈密市	Hami [Kumul]City	32.25	5.20	5.07		2.33	1.61	0.13
巴里坤哈萨克自治县	Barkol KazakAutonomous County	24.31	18.67	18.62		16.24	0.47	0.05
伊吾县	Yiwu [Araturuk]County	5.70	1.38	1.18		0.34	0.34	0.20
昌吉回族自治州	**Changji Hui Autonomous Prefecture**	**553.23**	**305.83**	**272.90**	**1.35**	**182.37**	**85.46**	**32.93**
昌吉市	Changji City	97.78	40.49	38.70	0.99	23.82	13.75	1.78
阜康市	Fukang City	51.35	25.81	24.05	0.14	16.42	7.49	1.76
呼图壁县	Hutubi County	92.53	32.68	32.56	0.16	20.61	11.44	0.13
玛纳斯县	Manas County	74.48	21.70	21.46	0.07	4.50	16.77	0.24
奇台县	Qitai County	142.44	116.70	99.91		74.10	23.68	16.79
吉木萨尔县	Jimsar County	45.80	27.32	25.60		18.60	6.76	1.72
木垒哈萨克自治县	Mori Kazak Autonomous County	48.85	41.13	30.61		24.31	5.56	10.53
伊犁哈萨克自治州	**Ili Kazak Autonomous Prefecture**	**1115.93**	**655.23**	**603.93**	**16.79**	**321.43**	**258.78**	**51.31**
伊犁州直属县(市)	**Counties (Cities) Direct Under Ili Prefecture**	**480.56**	**351.65**	**312.76**	**15.95**	**180.93**	**111.83**	**38.89**
伊宁市	Yining [Gulja]City	20.72	14.22	12.58	0.56	5.04	6.98	1.65
奎屯市	Kuytun City	4.67	2.47	2.47		2.00	0.47	
伊宁县	Yining [Gulja]County	89.40	77.38	64.46		19.43	45.04	12.92
察布查尔锡伯自治县	Qapqal Xibe Autonomous County	76.28	53.76	50.48	12.89	26.00	11.58	3.28
霍城县	Huocheng [korgas]County	46.94	28.39	27.44	0.03	12.69	14.71	0.95
巩留县	Gongliu [Tokkuzlara]County	54.93	46.51	33.45	0.43	22.73	10.29	13.06
新源县	Xinyuan [kunes]County	62.47	50.46	44.23	2.04	28.01	14.11	6.23
昭苏县	Zhaosu [mongolkure]County	53.67	26.97	26.89		26.68		0.08
特克斯县	Tekes County	33.33	20.92	20.54		15.35	3.23	0.38
尼勒克县	Nilka County	38.16	30.56	30.22		23.00	5.42	0.34
塔城地区	**Tacheng [Tarbagatai] Administrative Offices**	**444.35**	**245.29**	**244.70**	**0.82**	**115.81**	**125.74**	**0.59**
塔城市	Tacheng [Qoqek] City	86.45	75.32	75.32		36.22	38.35	
乌苏市	Usu City	84.62	21.29	21.28	0.82	9.27	11.15	0.01
额敏县	Emin [Dorbiljin] County	93.37	78.84	78.84		40.45	37.83	
沙湾县	Shawan County	106.43	23.66	23.15		12.08	10.94	0.51
托里县	Toli County	24.07	20.96	20.89		7.81	12.23	0.07
裕民县	Yumin [Qagantokay] County	37.01	24.26	24.26		9.29	14.97	
和布克赛尔蒙古自治县	Hoboksar Mongol Autonomous County	12.40	0.96	0.96		0.70	0.26	
阿勒泰地区	**Altay Administrative Offices**	**191.01**	**58.29**	**46.46**	**0.01**	**24.69**	**21.22**	**11.83**
阿勒泰市	Altay City	28.42	8.84	5.95		1.37	4.57	2.88
布尔津县	Burqin County	23.92	6.28	4.52		0.94	3.31	1.75
富蕴县	Fuyun [Koktokay] County	24.97	10.28	8.54		5.76	2.73	1.73
福海县	Fuhai [Burultokay] County	56.95	8.96	8.96	0.01	2.21	6.74	
哈巴河县	Habahe [Kaba] County	35.92	12.26	6.98		3.31	3.47	5.29
青河县	Qinghe [Qinggil] County	14.87	7.80	7.62		7.43	0.18	0.17
吉木乃县	Jeminay County	5.96	3.88	3.88		3.67	0.21	

注:全区农作物播种面积及棉花面积合计不等于地方和生产建设兵团汇总数。

Sown Areas of Farm Crops by Prefecture, Autonomous Prefecture, City and County

(1 000 hectares)

薯类 Tubers	棉花 Cotton	#长绒棉 Longstaple Cotton	油料 Oil Bearing Crops	#油菜 Rapeseeds	#胡麻 Flax	#葵花 Helianthus	甜菜 Beetroots	蔬菜 Vegetables	果用瓜 Melon	#甜瓜 Muskmelon	苜蓿 Lucerne
27.97	**1720.80**	**53.33**	**242.34**	**59.64**	**8.68**	**148.19**	**82.63**	**306.94**	**130.08**	**63.12**	**149.69**
4.61	**1.37**		**3.44**	**0.18**	**0.02**	**2.73**	**0.04**	**12.60**	**0.16**	**0.02**	**2.02**
2.94			0.45	0.12		0.33		2.50	…		1.62
	7.36							**0.45**	**0.39**	**0.03**	**0.33**
	22.54		**0.21**					**6.43**	**8.69**	**5.46**	**0.45**
	4.49							3.31	3.49	1.32	
	7.76							1.84	4.50	3.61	0.07
	10.29		0.21					1.28	0.69	0.52	0.38
1.06	**19.63**		**2.48**	**2.33**	**0.03**	**0.13**		**2.82**	**5.06**	**4.34**	**2.95**
0.04	19.37		1.31	1.16	0.03	0.12		1.91	2.50	1.77	0.66
1.00	0.25		0.12	0.12		0.01		0.88	0.17	0.17	1.47
0.02	0.01		1.05	1.05		…		0.03	2.39	2.39	0.82
7.95	**117.87**		**28.02**	**0.07**	**1.04**	**20.83**	**9.83**	**39.07**	**6.77**	**0.70**	**5.85**
0.11	40.48		3.14			2.48	1.32	6.44	3.77	0.09	0.32
0.86	0.28		6.20			5.73	1.37	9.45	0.36	0.14	0.59
0.55	35.31		1.03			0.90	0.82	9.16	1.36	0.17	2.69
0.60	41.35		2.37			1.84	0.22	4.20	0.42		0.40
2.62			7.71	0.06		5.53	5.45	5.03	0.11	0.05	0.12
2.03	0.45		5.21	…		3.03	0.35	4.20	0.60	0.22	0.52
1.18			2.36		1.04	1.32	0.31	0.59	0.16	0.04	1.21
6.32	**138.80**		**128.69**	**25.53**	**2.48**	**88.45**	**29.33**	**35.66**	**5.00**	**2.69**	**32.56**
2.99	**13.05**		**44.26**	**23.18**	**2.48**	**18.07**	**22.96**	**15.78**	**1.25**	**0.01**	**5.65**
0.12			0.67	0.01	…	0.66	0.62	3.56	0.25		0.04
	2.10		0.07			0.07		0.03			
0.62	0.08		3.60	0.79		2.77	1.83	3.60	0.52		1.25
0.04	8.32		2.25		0.57	1.24	2.42	1.25	0.24		1.44
0.23	2.55		3.54		0.04	3.50	6.70	2.75	0.08		
0.06			1.99	0.07	0.03	1.89	2.68	1.00	0.07		0.58
0.43			3.19	0.26	0.13	2.73	3.13	0.47	0.03		0.05
0.81			21.95	20.77	0.27	0.92	1.99	0.35			
0.04			5.63	1.14	0.32	4.17	1.47	1.69	0.05	0.01	1.68
0.64			1.36	0.14	1.12	0.11	2.13	1.08	0.01		0.60
0.91	**125.75**		**19.76**	**2.36**		**7.09**	**5.04**	**18.24**	**0.76**	**0.07**	**3.05**
0.04			1.24	0.64		0.53	0.93	2.02	0.03		0.32
0.27	53.73		1.34			1.34	0.44	6.02	0.29	0.07	0.17
			2.19	1.27		0.84	2.58	0.63			0.62
0.16	63.62		2.44			2.33	1.09	9.13	0.44		0.21
0.04	0.24		1.56	0.45		0.55		0.03			0.73
0.31			9.49					0.05			0.89
0.09	8.16		1.50			1.50		0.37			0.11
2.42			**64.66**			**63.28**	**1.33**	**1.64**	**3.00**	**2.61**	**23.86**
0.15			9.04			9.04	0.25	0.31	1.31	1.31	3.03
0.06			10.25			10.25	…	0.12	0.12	0.12	3.24
0.43			7.49			7.49		0.44	0.09	0.03	3.20
0.04			23.07			23.07	1.08	0.11	0.97	0.96	6.11
0.74			12.40			12.40		0.50	0.50	0.19	3.85
0.33			2.35			0.97		0.12			3.87
0.67			0.06			0.06		0.03			0.57

Note:Total of sown areas of farm crops and cotton areas by region do not mean that summary number of local and Production&Construction Corps.

12-14 续表

单位：千公顷

地 区	Region	农作物播种面积 Total Sown Area	粮食 Grain Crops	谷物 Cereal	#水稻 Rice	#小麦 Wheat	#玉米 Corn	豆类 Soy-beans
博尔塔拉蒙古自治州	**Bortala Mongol Autonomous Prefecture**	**130.59**	**47.45**	**47.45**	**0.09**	**12.55**	**34.80**	**…**
博乐市	Bole [Bortala] City	48.44	18.97	18.97	0.09	1.13	17.74	
精河县	Jinghe [Jing] County	48.77	2.27	2.27		1.22	1.05	
温泉县	Wenquan [Araxang] County	33.38	26.21	26.21		10.20	16.01	…
巴音郭楞蒙古自治州	**Bayangol Mongol Autonomous Prefecture**	**309.69**	**56.89**	**56.59**	**0.30**	**35.86**	**19.56**	**0.30**
库尔勒市	Korla City	58.74	2.80	2.79		1.90	0.89	0.01
轮台县	Luntai [Bugur] County	52.93	14.82	14.82		8.52	6.30	
尉犁县	Yuli [Lopnur] County	40.06	0.24	0.24		0.12	0.12	
若羌县	Ruoqiang [Qarkilik] County	13.45	3.48	3.41		2.06	1.35	0.07
且末县	Qiemo [Qarqan] County	24.40	7.19	7.09		4.50	2.54	0.10
焉耆回族自治县	Yanqi Hui Autonomous County	31.96	11.54	11.49	0.02	8.58	2.89	0.04
和静县	Hejing County	31.40	8.11	8.04	0.01	4.30	2.89	0.07
和硕县	Hoxud County	33.55	4.52	4.52		3.33	1.19	
博湖县	Bohu [Bagrax] County	23.19	4.19	4.19	0.27	2.54	1.39	
阿克苏地区	**Aksu Administrative Offices**	**597.16**	**207.40**	**206.57**	**15.81**	**112.90**	**77.00**	**0.82**
阿克苏市	Aksu City	74.27	16.31	16.31	2.51	8.23	5.57	
温宿县	Wensu [Onsu] County	75.28	31.80	31.79	10.06	14.95	6.70	0.01
库车县	Kuqa County	94.77	37.72	37.57		22.00	15.56	0.16
沙雅县	Xayar County	94.55	26.07	26.05		15.00	11.05	0.02
新和县	Xinhe [Toksu] County	54.09	17.60	17.60		10.20	7.40	
拜城县	Baicheng [Bay] County	59.42	32.78	32.42	1.24	14.73	15.73	0.37
乌什县	Wushi [Uxturpan] County	33.36	22.77	22.50	2.01	14.80	5.64	0.27
阿瓦提县	Awat County	100.85	18.07	18.07		10.00	8.07	
柯坪县	Kalpin County	10.55	4.27	4.27		3.00	1.27	
克孜勒苏柯尔克孜自治州	**Kizilsu Kirgiz Autonomous Prefecture**	**60.03**	**46.84**	**46.71**	**0.61**	**26.69**	**18.88**	**0.13**
阿图什市	Artux City	19.58	14.38	14.38	0.09	8.96	5.20	
阿克陶县	Akto County	33.13	27.12	27.12	0.52	14.12	12.37	
阿合奇县	Akqi County	4.06	3.16	3.07		2.27	0.58	0.09
乌恰县	Wuqia [Ulugqat] County	3.26	2.18	2.14		1.34	0.74	0.04
喀什地区	**Kashgar [Kaxgar] Administrative Offices**	**900.98**	**421.77**	**398.54**	**7.05**	**220.11**	**169.64**	**23.23**
喀什市	Kashgar [Kaxgar] City	19.72	10.60	10.60	1.17	6.84	2.59	
疏附县	Shufu County	69.81	43.73	43.73	0.20	26.20	17.33	
疏勒县	Shule County	77.20	36.85	36.85	0.15	20.80	15.91	
英吉沙县	Yengisar County	46.25	29.72	29.60		15.90	13.71	0.12
泽普县	Zepu [Poskam] County	44.95	28.60	18.60	0.27	12.33	6.00	10.00
莎车县	Shache [Yarkant] County	190.21	94.05	86.72	4.67	43.42	38.63	7.33
叶城县	Yecheng [Kagilik] County	91.02	53.93	49.33	0.60	26.19	22.54	4.60
麦盖提县	Makit County	104.18	29.75	28.77		16.67	12.10	0.99
岳普湖县	Yopurga County	47.38	16.33	16.33		9.00	7.33	
伽师县	Jiashi [Payzawat] County	85.34	42.63	42.44		23.97	18.47	0.19
巴楚县	Bachu [Maralbexi] County	120.07	31.33	31.33		16.67	14.67	
塔什库尔干塔吉克自治县	Taxkorgan Tajik Autonomous County	4.85	4.22	4.22		2.13	0.36	
和田地区	**Hotan Administrative Offices**	**236.69**	**159.82**	**158.94**	**7.80**	**80.67**	**70.34**	**0.87**
和田市	Hotan City	18.17	13.68	13.68	0.44	7.57	5.67	
和田县	Hotan County	34.17	25.80	25.60	2.42	13.00	10.18	0.20
墨玉县	Moyu [Karakax] County	55.87	41.53	41.53	2.13	21.67	17.73	
皮山县	Pishan [Guma] County	31.20	18.07	17.76		8.88	8.86	0.31
洛浦县	Lop County	31.73	22.01	22.01	0.01	11.00	11.00	
策勒县	Qira County	25.13	14.10	13.74		6.89	6.74	0.36
于田县	Yutian [Keriya] County	35.84	22.23	22.23	2.80	10.33	9.10	
民丰县	Minfeng [Niya] County	4.57	2.39	2.39		1.33	1.06	
生产建设兵团	**Xinjiang Production and Construction Group**	**1126.38**	**269.63**	**261.88**	**22.17**	**131.16**	**102.08**	**7.74**

Continued

(1 000 hectares)

薯类 Tubers	棉花 Cotton	#长绒棉 Longstaple Cotton	油料 Oil Bearing Crops	#油菜 Rapeseeds	#胡麻 Flax	#葵花 Helianthus	甜菜 Beetroots	蔬菜 Vegetables	果用瓜 Melon	#甜瓜 Muskmelon	苜蓿 Lucerne
0.18	**63.76**		**4.73**			**4.73**	**2.86**	**0.74**	**0.16**	**0.03**	**1.32**
0.06	26.82		0.19			0.19	1.66	0.57	0.04		0.07
	36.94						0.17	0.08	0.06	0.03	0.27
0.12			4.54			4.54	1.03	0.09	0.06		0.98
0.48	**179.64**		**3.06**	**0.96**		**2.10**	**6.44**	**41.98**	**5.39**	**4.26**	**1.70**
0.01	54.30							1.26	0.20	0.08	0.13
	36.45		0.02	0.02				0.26	0.81	0.67	0.54
	39.45							0.08	0.25	0.10	
	4.09		0.02	0.01				0.21	3.56	3.24	0.07
0.03	14.67		0.02	0.02				0.38	0.06	0.04	0.78
	4.30		0.84	0.07		0.77	3.95	6.18	0.06	0.05	0.04
0.25	4.85		1.37	0.76		0.62	1.43	12.58	0.13	0.03	0.08
0.19	16.01		0.09	…		0.09	0.44	10.91	0.12		0.06
	5.54		0.70	0.08		0.62	0.61	10.13	0.19	0.05	0.01
2.50	**315.33**	**43.98**	**5.54**	**4.23**	**1.08**	**0.23**	**4.21**	**25.30**	**15.12**	**4.67**	**11.61**
	44.90	9.60					0.36	4.69	2.07	0.86	5.80
0.19	37.01		0.86	0.79	0.07		0.17	2.07	0.98	0.07	1.10
0.28	50.34		0.75	0.75	…		0.11	2.87	2.35	0.76	0.19
0.43	60.93		0.39	0.39		0.01	0.13	1.68	3.93	1.91	0.20
	33.33		0.08	0.08				1.48	1.11	0.33	0.32
1.60			2.88	1.88	0.77	0.22	3.11	5.56	1.91	0.10	3.92
	4.67		0.58	0.33	0.24		0.33	4.36	0.53	0.08	
	78.47	34.38						2.15	2.09	0.42	0.08
	5.69						…	0.44	0.15	0.14	
0.09	**6.67**		**0.79**	**0.47**	**0.24**	**0.05**		**1.50**	**0.63**	**0.30**	**1.59**
0.02	2.11		0.05	0.01	0.01	0.02		0.50	0.26	0.25	0.63
	4.55		0.01			0.01		0.73	0.34	0.05	0.08
0.05			0.55	0.29	0.24	0.03		0.09	…		0.21
0.02	0.01		0.18	0.18				0.19	0.02		0.66
6.78	**214.11**		**7.53**	**3.98**	**1.72**	**1.05**		**61.01**	**66.36**	**31.42**	**28.87**
								6.47	0.47	0.08	0.20
0.53	4.67		0.13		0.13			10.45	9.83	3.37	
	20.89							7.12	10.64	4.62	1.70
	7.00		1.15	1.15				3.59	2.31	1.41	2.20
2.00	7.33		0.03		0.03			1.65	1.83	0.23	1.13
1.87	43.33		3.00	2.66	…	0.02		13.14	12.25	6.73	2.48
2.21	6.67		1.44		0.15	0.83		9.27	1.50	0.43	5.75
	37.12		1.57	0.17	1.41			2.67	4.94	1.28	3.33
	13.33		0.20			0.20		1.38	4.20	2.20	4.60
	20.17							4.21	12.73	10.07	5.33
	53.33							1.07	5.67	1.00	2.00
0.18	0.27										0.15
0.71	**21.04**		**4.27**	**1.12**	**1.64**	**0.78**		**11.12**	**3.81**	**1.85**	**22.24**
	1.31		0.12					2.01	0.43	0.26	0.38
0.42	2.95		0.51	0.27	0.22			1.20	0.69	0.34	1.13
0.02	4.00		0.17	0.12	0.04	0.01		1.83	1.01	0.34	5.20
0.08	2.65		0.36	0.23		0.12		1.75	0.14	0.03	5.58
0.03	2.67		1.38	…	1.32	0.01		0.97	0.52	0.19	3.49
0.04	2.98		1.04	0.03	0.07	0.43		1.20	0.35	0.25	2.99
0.11	4.49		0.69	0.47		0.21		2.01	0.39	0.19	2.71
0.01			…			…		0.16	0.27	0.25	0.75
5.54	**553.64**	**9.35**	**53.57**	**20.77**	**0.41**	**27.11**	**29.91**	**68.25**	**12.53**	**7.35**	**38.19**

12-15 主要年份农作物种植结构
Planting Structure of Major Farm Crops in Main Years

单位：% (%)

项　目	Item	1995	2000	2010	2012
农作物总播种面积	**Total Sown Areas of Farm Crops**	**100**	**100**	**100**	**100**
粮食作物	Grain Crops	52.21	42.66	41.85	40.94
谷　物	Cereal	50.10	39.95	39.49	39.61
稻　谷	Rice	2.40	2.31	1.41	1.35
小　麦	Wheat	31.22	24.75	23.54	21.05
玉　米	Corn	14.39	11.29	13.74	16.66
谷　子	Millet	0.02	0.04	0.02	…
高　粱	Jowar	0.47	0.39	0.12	0.25
其它谷物	Other Cereal	1.59	1.18	0.67	0.30
豆　类	Soybeans	2.12	2.71	2.36	1.34
#大　豆	Soja	0.94	1.85	1.56	1.08
杂　豆	Miscellaneous Beans	1.18	0.20	0.80	0.02
薯　类	Tubers	0.34	0.66	0.78	0.54
油　料	Oil-bearing Crops	10.05	9.15	5.74	4.72
#花　生	Peanuts		0.14	0.08	0.08
油菜籽	Rapeseeds	4.26	2.84	1.47	1.16
芝　麻	Sesame		0.02	0.03	0.20
胡麻籽	Benne	0.88	0.72	0.18	0.17
向日葵	Helianthus	4.59	4.63	3.46	2.88
棉　花	Cotton	24.35	29.87	30.69	33.50
麻　类	Fiber Crops	0.14	0.21	0.05	0.09
甜　菜	Beetroots	2.33	1.65	1.58	1.61
烟　叶	Tobacco	0.03	0.08	0.02	…
药　材	Medicinal Materials	0.22	0.38	0.42	0.79
蔬菜、瓜类	Vegetables and Melon	3.17	5.42	8.96	8.51
#蔬　菜	Vegetables	2.34	3.77	6.38	5.97
其他农作物	Other Farm Crops	7.16	9.92	9.91	9.29
#青饲料	Succulence	3.94	3.56	1.26	1.18

12-16 主要年份农作物产品产量
Output of Major Farm Crops in Main Years

单位：万吨 (10 000 tons)

年 份 Year	粮 食 Grain Crops	谷 物 Cereal	#水 稻 Rice	#小 麦 Wheat	#玉 米 Corn	#大 麦 Barley	豆 类 Soybeans	薯 类 Tubers	棉 花 Cotton	#长绒棉 Long-staple Cotton
1978	370.01	367.71	27.39	180.02	134.45	5.01	2.30	22.91	5.50	1.19
1980	386.13	384.16	25.62	213.19	126.43	3.50	1.97	16.03	7.92	1.74
1985	496.65	495.16	30.63	314.52	139.38	1.93	1.49	15.14	18.78	1.40
1990	676.89	673.18	47.27	390.80	209.42	10.51	3.71	22.57	46.88	3.48
1995	730.16	716.83	48.25	381.21	266.74	12.82	13.33	26.43	93.50	1.13
1996	818.20	808.67	51.49	420.32	312.54	17.39	9.53	32.50	94.04	1.72
1997	825.34	813.07	55.27	437.60	294.31	17.92	12.27	26.73	115.00	3.10
1998	830.00	814.54	49.56	444.00	302.25	11.00	15.46	33.12	140.00	1.39
1999	838.78	821.70	54.14	423.29	323.06	8.00	17.08	46.06	140.75	1.67
2000	808.60	782.93	60.35	405.80	298.22	11.75	25.67	64.01	150.00	6.16
2001	796.00	767.53	56.79	374.14	318.41	11.86	28.47	60.02	157.00	9.71
2002	875.87	849.48	60.62	386.44	379.05	13.78	26.39	62.41	150.00	6.67
2003	801.64	774.62	50.73	335.67	366.25	14.33	27.02	71.80	160.00	10.10
2004	828.53	800.04	51.31	345.94	388.12	8.06	28.49	70.79	175.25	11.22
2005	877.21	852.00	54.18	400.71	380.36	10.23	25.22	65.86	195.70	11.87
2006	895.22	870.21	59.27	400.31	386.80	17.85	25.01	76.50	267.53	18.59
2007	867.04	846.35	62.52	359.22	396.00	24.26	20.69	101.36	290.00	25.02
2008	909.00	885.99	56.50	395.69	416.41	14.75	23.01	107.62	301.55	19.73
2009	1152.00	1119.77	58.30	630.70	439.38	14.30	32.23	126.06	252.40	11.04
2010	1150.20	1121.88	58.98	623.49	421.61	12.54	28.32	102.50	247.90	13.03
2011	1200.75	1171.64	60.64	576.64	517.67	11.06	29.11	119.75	289.77	12.16
2012	1259.83	1234.81	59.36	576.54	592.11	3.46	25.02	65.85	353.95	5.95

年 份 Year	油 料 Oil bearing Crops	#油 菜 Rapeseeds	#胡 麻 Flax	#葵 花 Helianthus	甜 菜 Beetroots	蔬 菜 Vegetables	果用瓜 Melons	#甜 瓜 Muskmelon	苜 蓿 Lucerne
1978	10.33	3.30	3.14	2.29	16.37	91.26	44.05		
1980	17.59	5.59	5.17	4.59	38.52	73.44	55.68		
1985	34.25	7.29	8.10	16.90	40.69	111.08	103.18	47.02	49.69
1990	38.96	12.17	6.32	18.17	224.37	187.42	93.38	37.75	89.29
1995	49.41	15.12	3.79	29.06	288.14	269.56	68.75	18.31	82.62
1996	30.95	10.15	3.12	16.91	354.52	301.94	67.16	17.33	75.42
1997	29.95	8.92	2.53	17.69	388.71	295.59	86.78	25.90	70.05
1998	37.52	12.32	2.53	20.82	513.12	321.79	88.32	29.45	67.56
1999	60.46	16.37	2.75	35.69	354.24	406.18	143.49	46.38	69.98
2000	60.14	14.75	3.60	35.47	292.65	527.84	151.03	51.22	76.32
2001	42.64	12.19	2.47	23.31	455.12	486.74	156.87	56.86	103.12
2002	44.37	12.90	3.69	23.26	466.81	674.96	233.40	107.49	149.93
2003	50.13	15.43	3.49	25.80	381.65	761.00	189.32	77.61	249.60
2004	44.54	12.16	2.10	21.90	344.21	919.13	186.06	92.54	273.04
2005	38.94	9.22	2.39	21.69	419.12	862.23	220.65	95.58	295.74
2006	32.82	9.73	2.52	16.17	555.53	958.04	237.28	109.98	240.15
2007	40.30	9.60	1.58	25.39	586.93	1173.99	338.67	192.63	205.47
2008	56.85	10.67	1.23	42.87	438.88	970.67	404.17	248.81	150.83
2009	63.91	15.72	1.89	41.40	418.41	1383.21	491.20	286.30	154.90
2010	66.62	15.14	1.32	44.11	486.97	1734.40	435.00	222.58	132.93
2011	66.76	15.18	1.23	45.36	518.95	1866.15	434.31	193.06	139.94
2012	59.04	11.20	1.40	41.44	577.19	1656.02	485.35	213.35	149.62

注：粮食、棉花总产量为国家审定数。
Note:Total grain output refers to the number of state approved.

12-17 各地、州、市、县(市)主要农产品产量

单位：吨 (2012 年)

地区	Region	粮食作物 Grain Crops	谷物 Cereal	#水稻 Rice	#小麦 Wheat	#玉米 Corn	豆类 Soy-beans
总计	**Total**	**12598300**	**12348100**	**593600**	**5765400**	**5921100**	**250200**
乌鲁木齐市	**Urumqi City**	**152322**	**148805**	**60025**	**41322**	**41699**	**3517**
#乌鲁木齐县	Urumqi County	12118	11078		5840	637	1040
克拉玛依市	**Karamay City**	**5014**	**5011**		**64**	**4947**	**3**
吐鲁番地区	**TurpanAdministrative Offices**	**27600**	**27584**		**211**	**8053**	**16**
吐鲁番市	Turpan City	2724	2724			274	
鄯善县	Shanshan [piqan]County	4086	4086		68	2918	
托克逊县	Toksun County	20790	20774		143	4861	16
哈密地区	**Hami [Kumul]Administrative Offices**	**126402**	**125178**		**93289**	**21169**	**1224**
哈密市	Hami [Kumul]City	29070	28519		11026	14008	551
巴里坤哈萨克自治县	Barkol KazakAutonomous County	90825	90601		80639	4242	224
伊吾县	Yiwu [Araturuk]County	6507	6058		1624	2919	449
昌吉回族自治州	**Changji Hui Autonomous Prefecture**	**1562650**	**1521841**	**10446**	**909025**	**590235**	**40809**
昌吉市	Changji City	225885	222776	6913	115800	99843	3109
阜康市	Fukang City	138685	134464	1352	84920	48192	4221
呼图壁县	Hutubi County	160435	160076	1423	103000	54137	359
玛纳斯县	Manas County	143991	143345	758	22225	120143	646
奇台县	Qitai County	627628	612772		426856	179776	14856
吉木萨尔县	Jimsar County	147538	145012		88235	55763	2526
木垒哈萨克自治县	Mori Kazak Autonomous County	118488	103396		67989	32381	15092
伊犁哈萨克自治州	**Ili Kazak Autonomous Prefecture**	**4993960**	**4857375**	**159194**	**1639615**	**3040713**	**136585**
伊犁州直属县(市)	**Counties (Cities) Direct Under Ili Prefecture**	**2557140**	**2456354**	**150579**	**971197**	**1324858**	**100786**
伊宁市	Yining [Gulja]City	115135	110677	6294	26550	77833	4458
奎屯市	Kuytun City	10812	10812		6602	4210	
伊宁县	Yining [Gulja]County	704733	670425		116464	553961	34308
察布查尔锡伯自治县	Qapqal Xibe Autonomous County	387349	381241	125260	134550	121393	6108
霍城县	Huocheng [korgas]County	254528	250978	270	81872	168836	3550
巩留县	Gongliu [Tokkuzlara]County	284429	255047	3712	135520	115815	29382
新源县	Xinyuan [kunes]County	375717	355869	15043	161360	179305	19848
昭苏县	Zhaosu [mongolkure]County	137277	137028		136068		249
特克斯县	Tekes County	101208	99539		53867	41703	1669
尼勒克县	Nilka County	185952	184738		118344	61802	1214
塔城地区	**Tacheng [Tarbagatai] Administrative Offices**	**2086334**	**2084430**	**8589**	**557843**	**1510791**	**1904**
塔城市	Tacheng [Qoqek] City	638136	638136		180483	454528	
乌苏市	Usu City	226998	226998	8589	63553	154809	
额敏县	Emin [Dorbiljin] County	647190	647190		192271	452874	
沙湾县	Shawan County	207759	205994		62304	143069	1765
托里县	Toli County	155199	155060		32491	121200	139
裕民县	Yumin [Qagantokay] County	204601	204601		23312	181289	
和布克赛尔蒙古自治县	Hoboksar Mongol Autonomous County	6451	6451		3429	3022	
阿勒泰地区	**Altay Administrative Offices**	**350486**	**316591**	**26**	**110575**	**205064**	**33895**
阿勒泰市	Altay City	55479	46398		6596	39782	9081
布尔津县	Burqin County	39065	33807		3102	30304	5258
富蕴县	Fuyun [Koktokay] County	60207	56853		27184	29509	3354
福海县	Fuhai [Burultokay] County	80487	80487	26	10107	70354	
哈巴河县	Habahe [Kaba] County	63301	47498		15148	32056	15803
青河县	Qinghe [Qinggil] County	40471	40072		38697	1324	399
吉木乃县	Jeminay County	11476	11476		9741	1735	

注：1.地方与生产建设兵团粮食产量合计不等于全区总计数。2.全区总计数为国家统计局审定数。

Output of Major Farm Crops by Prefecture, Autonomous Prefecture, City and County

(ton)

薯类 Tubers	棉花 Cotton	#长绒棉 Longstaple Cotton	油料 Oil Bearing Crops	#油菜 Rapeseeds	#胡麻 Flax	#葵花 Helianthus	甜菜 Beetroots	蔬菜 Vegetables	果用瓜 Melon	#甜瓜 Muskmelon	苜蓿 Lucerne
658500	**3539458**	**59536**	**590436**	**111956**	**13958**	**414414**	**5771889**	**16560227**	**4853531**	**2133452**	**1496189**
105128	**1701**		**9222**	**311**	**32**	**8680**	**2164**	**592550**	**4302**	**930**	**13779**
55765			885	211		674		83778	93	0	7494
	12360							**20091**	**17132**	**1248**	**4071**
	30268		**892**					**261144**	**246863**	**132724**	**15408**
	5047							154965	98984	28000	
	9942							59000	126949	89397	1300
	15279		892					47179	20930	15327	14108
41606	**33300**		**1801**	**1356**	**90**	**355**		**127869**	**172854**	**138249**	**22795**
231	32839		785	349	90	346		85720	90905	56300	9618
40837	447		226	219		7		39717	3134	3134	8254
538	14		790	788		2		2432	78815	78815	4923
148423	**202645**		**79152**	**49**	**1352**	**63911**	**647685**	**2261765**	**388280**	**27193**	**56191**
4075	62700		12145			7778	98771	517058	252668	3779	1621
31786	1041		18637			17005	106480	305602	19999	6320	4385
16827	57520		1960			1704	60050	546460	53956	5583	29839
21625	80849		6351			4554	24328	329643	28103		5627
36228			20936	43		18678	320129	266592	3217	1953	780
24322	535		13935	6		10356	24233	277279	23281	7698	9172
13560			5188		1352	3836	13694	19131	7056	1860	4767
175922	**265943**		**305481**	**59380**	**3704**	**228458**	**1859179**	**1953740**	**195037**	**80158**	**268134**
99432	**15587**		**106187**	**55030**	**3704**	**43768**	**1480185**	**755964**	**56978**	**300**	**56192**
4741			1667	13	1	1635	41611	240995	10160		479
	2617		200			200		2500			
21912	98		9919	2263		7312	137270	116569	27368		9673
1385	9740		6330		748	3061	164362	50695	10869		12673
6790	3132		8884		105	8776	444210	133488	3360		
1501			5049	178	45	4826	175281	48200	1656		2709
17531			6635	349	281	5206	198756	30228	1461		543
21648			52900	49840	442	2618	116142	13138			
1005			11964	1973	241	9750	87350	68310	1740	300	22705
22919			2639	414	1841	384	115203	51841	364		7410
6758	**250356**		**32577**	**4350**		**20576**	**313263**	**1143049**	**40759**	**2625**	**25131**
300			2058	1556		419	56022	103160	981		1442
2785	105427		4534			4534	36585	445140	15743	2625	1253
			3645	1923		1623	154976	41576			5115
1170	131685		9273			8593	65680	547700	24035		1932
138	396		2100	871		682		961			4745
2333			6242					1148			8205
32	12848		4725			4725		3364			2439
69732			**166717**			**164114**	**65731**	**54727**	**97300**	**77233**	**186811**
4736			27807			27807	13041	13778	35359	35341	31763
3006			26066			26066	70	2619	3744	3744	24266
11683			17396			17396		13859	3895	1125	23401
1446			54634			54634	52620	4606	27452	27150	43640
25776			35575			35575		15213	26850	9873	35347
10102			5065			2462		4025			24895
12983			174			174		627			3499

Note:a) The region total output of grain is not equal to the sum of local and Production and Construction Groups.b) The region total data of grain refer to approvable data by NBS.

12-17 续表

单位：吨

地　　区	Region	粮食作物 Grain Crops	谷物 Cereal	#水稻 Rice	#小麦 Wheat	#玉米 Corn	豆类 Soy-beans
博尔塔拉蒙古自治州	**Bortala Mongol Autonomous Prefecture**	**590904**	**590895**	**970**	**67868**	**522057**	**9**
博乐市	Bole [Bortala] City	260431	260431	970	6901	252560	
精河县	Jinghe [Jing] County	19122	19122		5786	13336	
温泉县	Wenquan [Araxang] County	311351	311342		55181	256161	9
巴音郭楞蒙古自治州	**Bayangol Mongol Autonomous Prefecture**	**381420**	**380770**	**1905**	**216659**	**160380**	**650**
库尔勒市	Korla City	12717	12694		8449	4245	23
轮台县	Luntai [Bugur] County	81756	81756		47073	34683	
尉犁县	Yuli [Lopnur] County	1222	1222		483	739	
若羌县	Ruoqiang [Qarkilik] County	16327	16241		10654	5587	86
且末县	Qiemo [Qarqan] County	44364	44092		28056	15885	272
焉耆回族自治县	Yanqi Hui Autonomous County	91415	91312	107	56289	34916	103
和静县	Hejing County	63743	63577	57	27766	34079	166
和硕县	Hoxud County	33703	33703		20147	13556	
博湖县	Bohu [Bagrax] County	36173	36173	1741	17742	16690	
阿克苏地区	**Aksu Administrative Offices**	**1570420**	**1567876**	**166441**	**754984**	**643784**	**2544**
阿克苏市	Aksu City	125078	125078	26684	55568	42826	
温宿县	Wensu [Onsu] County	260751	260741	107978	100262	52300	10
库车县	Kuqa County	252881	252734		149526	103200	147
沙雅县	Xayar County	187096	187072		103372	83700	24
新和县	Xinhe [Toksu] County	117473	117473		69015	48458	
拜城县	Baicheng [Bay] County	306654	305516	10866	97817	194600	1138
乌什县	Wushi [Uxturpan] County	170776	169551	20913	93413	55000	1225
阿瓦提县	Awat County	122195	122195		67695	54500	
柯坪县	Kalpin County	27516	27516		18316	9200	
克孜勒苏柯尔克孜自治州	**Kizilsu Kirgiz Autonomous Prefecture**	**288702**	**288244**	**5218**	**155867**	**125630**	**458**
阿图什市	Artux City	83888	83888	623	50501	32288	
阿克陶县	Akto County	182666	182666	4595	89861	87953	
阿合奇县	Akqi County	12211	11864		8960	2342	347
乌恰县	Wuqia [Ulugqat] County	9937	9826		6545	3047	111
喀什地区	**Kashgar [Kaxgar] Administrative Offices**	**2679201**	**2622140**	**63994**	**1298103**	**1255828**	**57061**
喀什市	Kashgar [Kaxgar] City	65241	65241	9276	37939	18026	
疏附县	Shufu County	287210	287210	1674	167418	118118	
疏勒县	Shule County	245075	245075	1287	124000	119788	
英吉沙县	Yengisar County	189262	189014		92897	96117	248
泽普县	Zepu [Poskam] County	145052	118346	1580	74400	42366	26706
莎车县	Shache [Yarkant] County	604052	592052	44100	260520	287432	12000
叶城县	Yecheng [Kagilik] County	372239	356702	6077	154200	196425	15537
麦盖提县	Makit County	164334	162114		89084	73030	2220
岳普湖县	Yopurga County	110410	110410		52600	57810	
伽师县	Jiashi [Payzawat] County	278333	277983		140597	137386	350
巴楚县	Bachu [Maralbexi] County	204420	204420		97500	106920	
塔什库尔干塔吉克自治县	Taxkorgan Tajik Autonomous County	13573	13573		6948	2410	
和田地区	**Hotan Administrative Offices**	**1062514**	**1060046**	**56280**	**481408**	**521931**	**2468**
和田市	Hotan City	94111	94111	3711	44881	45519	
和田县	Hotan County	163090	162595	16056	78579	67960	495
墨玉县	Moyu [Karakax] County	272012	272012	16480	131674	123858	
皮山县	Pishan [Guma] County	128726	128132		51897	76182	594
洛浦县	Lop County	138937	138937	30	62041	76866	
策勒县	Qira County	98727	97348		41352	55622	1379
于田县	Yutian [Keriya] County	151337	151337	20003	63284	68050	
民丰县	Minfeng [Niya] County	15574	15574		7700	7874	
生产建设兵团	**Xinjiang Production and Construction Group**	**2039496**	**2012563**	**228456**	**733814**	**1018747**	**26933**

Continued

(ton)

薯 类 Tubers	棉 花 Cotton	#长绒棉 Longstaple Cotton	油 料 Oil Bearing Crops	#油 菜 Rapeseeds	#胡 麻 Flax	#葵 花 Helianthus	甜 菜 Beetroots	蔬 菜 Vegetables	果用瓜 Melon	#甜 瓜 Muskmelon	苜 蓿 Lucerne
6933	**138028**		**14072**			**14072**	**169022**	**37808**	**7061**	**851**	**7832**
1980	57513		667			667	101284	28508	1524		434
	80515						7250	2618	2049	851	2217
4953			13405			13405	60488	6682	3488		5181
16273	**372084**		**6359**	**1247**		**5096**	**586230**	**2605841**	**122424**	**72077**	**20287**
450	113694							88601	7455	1340	1889
	75988		58	58				13657	14002	11776	6463
	90238							2269	9716	2900	
	7445		17	9				6020	60328	50783	150
478	29878		31	28				13130	1294	661	9691
	5689		2208	91		2117	375949	503264	2466	1582	559
9497	7710		2446	965		1481	128934	573886	9015	1778	848
5848	31931		196	1		190	28053	793680	6556		627
	9511		1403	95		1308	53294	611334	11592	1257	60
84286	**576730**	**47345**	**11296**	**7552**	**1979**	**669**	**345080**	**1064844**	**378252**	**106652**	**236949**
	96200	15310					20520	298316	81769	37054	114988
2887	66900		1366	1261	105		6377	38789	14714	1102	13422
9527	89555		969	969			4145	73635	54132	15911	5140
17251	112200		640	632		8	1474	21201	60458	27297	4187
	63824		115	115				41541	28206	6935	6576
54621			7037	3883	1397	661	292600	274000	72578	2990	91052
	7091		1169	692	477		19914	268272	13325	3618	
	129930	46035						43470	51960	10710	1584
	11030						50	5620	1110	1035	
678	**10230**		**1155**	**730**	**250**	**126**		**39229**	**18429**	**8136**	**17478**
482	3226		95	11	9	26		17194	6362	6097	7751
	6990		22			22		17207	11602	2039	1523
134			704	385	241	78		1365	15		1752
62	14		334	334				3463	450		6452
248642	**369810**		**14689**	**6574**	**2826**	**3289**		**2599868**	**2668732**	**1256838**	**257054**
								320175	18486	3220	2114
20800	7155		300		300			451600	420090	143925	
	33903							312886	457285	217924	20400
	10604		2336	2336				154634	100277	62191	20790
75000	11134		93		93			67736	82500	10500	13600
42000	68250		4500	3988	4	26		447023	469170	257699	
109230	10966		4860		319	3023		494348	61223	18378	64650
	69455		2360	250	2110			110400	222450	57750	40000
	22031		240			240		44634	147400	83400	34500
	35952							146848	438851	356851	40000
	100000							49584	251000	45000	21000
1612	360										
17885	**38541**		**10595**	**2013**	**2922**	**4215**		**393478**	**124220**	**57332**	**294773**
	2093		400					93633	17469	9838	4618
12652	5652		789	495	242			50445	16130	5380	8135
112	7524		289	245	23	13		54828	21852	7804	64800
1111	5078		2711	161	290	2167		47542	3044	837	43473
1315	4696		2241	4	2179	35		44973	24757	7295	113045
1842	5646		2074	142	188	876		37902	15368	11174	23359
753	7852		2089	966		1123		61413	20250	12429	33418
100			2			1		2742	5350	2575	3925
42892	**1414420**	**12191**	**135722**	**32744**	**803**	**85543**	**2162529**	**4602000**	**509945**	**251064**	**281438**

12-18 各地、州、市、县(市)农作物单位面积产量

Output of Major Farm Products Per Hectare by Prefecture, Autonomous Prefecture, City and County

单位：公斤/公顷 (2012 年) (kg / hectare)

地 区	Region	粮 食 Grain	#谷 物 Cereal	#小 麦 Wheat	#玉 米 Corn	棉 花 Cotton	油 料 Oil-Bearing Crops	甜 菜 Beetroots
总 计	**Total**	**5990**	**6070**	**5333**	**6919**	**2057**	**2436**	**69854**
乌鲁木齐市	**Urumqi City**	**6955**	**7140**	**5248**	**9919**	**1237**	**2681**	**60000**
#乌鲁木齐县	Urumqi County	3155	3130	4034	5170		1951	
克拉玛依市	**Karamay City**	**9641**	**9660**	**5614**	**9751**	**1680**		
吐鲁番地区	**TurpanAdministrative Offices**	**4367**	**4373**	**4100**	**5584**	**1343**	**4198**	
吐鲁番市	Turpan City	5012	5012		8220	1125		
鄯善县	Shanshan [piqan]County	4355	4355	3750	5249	1281		
托克逊县	Toksun County	4297	4305	4290	5700	1485	4198	
哈密地区	**Hami [Kumul]Administrative Offices**	**5005**	**5034**	**4934**	**8758**	**1696**	**725**	
哈密市	Hami [Kumul]City	5585	5625	4740	8700	1695	599	
巴里坤哈萨克自治县	Barkol KazakAutonomous County	4864	4866	4965	9000	1800	1860	
伊吾县	Yiwu [Araturuk]County	4720	5138	4800	8700	1200	751	
昌吉回族自治州	**Changji Hui Autonomous Prefecture**	**5110**	**5577**	**4985**	**6907**	**1719**	**2825**	**65887**
昌吉市	Changji City	5579	5756	4861	7260	1549	3866	74766
阜康市	Fukang City	5374	5590	5171	6435	3690	3004	77912
呼图壁县	Hutubi County	4909	4917	4997	4732	1629	1904	73232
玛纳斯县	Manas County	6636	6679	4938	7164	1955	2681	111426
奇台县	Qitai County	5378	6133	5760	7590		2717	58765
吉木萨尔县	Jimsar County	5401	5664	4745	8253	1180	2677	70065
木垒哈萨克自治县	Mori Kazak Autonomous County	2881	3378	2797	5822		2197	44079
伊犁哈萨克自治州	**Ili Kazak Autonomous Prefecture**	**7622**	**8043**	**5101**	**11750**	**1916**	**2374**	**63392**
伊犁州直属县(市)	**Counties (Cities) Direct Under Ili Prefecture**	**7272**	**7854**	**5368**	**11848**	**1194**	**2399**	**64458**
伊宁市	Yining [Gulja]City	8095	8799	5270	11157		2476	67558
奎屯市	Kuytun City	4380	4380	3300	9000	1245	3000	
伊宁县	Yining [Gulja]County	9107	10400	5996	12300	1205	2758	75000
察布查尔锡伯自治县	Qapqal Xibe Autonomous County	7205	7552	5175	10485	1170	2810	68025
霍城县	Huocheng [korgas]County	8967	9147	6450	11475	1230	2510	66300
巩留县	Gongliu [Tokkuzlara]County	6115	7624	5961	11250		2535	65400
新源县	Xinyuan [kunes]County	7446	8046	5761	12709		2081	63540
昭苏县	Zhaosu [mongolkure]County	5089	5095	5100			2410	58500
特克斯县	Tekes County	4838	4847	3510	12915		2124	59250
尼勒克县	Nilka County	6085	6113	5146	11400		1934	54000
塔城地区	**Tacheng [Tarbagatai] Administrative Offices**	**8506**	**8518**	**4817**	**12016**	**1991**	**1648**	**62191**
塔城市	Tacheng [Qoqek] City	8472	8472	4982	11851		1660	60455
乌苏市	Usu City	10664	10669	6854	13883	1962	3389	83400
额敏县	Emin [Dorbiljin] County	8209	8209	4754	11970		1665	60135
沙湾县	Shawan County	8780	8897	5159	13080	2070	3797	60000
托里县	Toli County	7404	7423	4161	9911	1650	1344	
裕民县	Yumin [Qagantokay] County	8433	8433	2509	12111		658	
和布克赛尔蒙古自治县	Hoboksar Mongol Autonomous County	6740	6740	4931	11549	1575	3150	
阿勒泰地区	**Altay Administrative Offices**	**6013**	**6814**	**4478**	**9664**		**2578**	**49519**
阿勒泰市	Altay City	6279	7794	4800	8700		3075	52500
布尔津县	Burqin County	6225	7474	3300	9150		2542	30000
富蕴县	Fuyun [Koktokay] County	5859	6654	4719	10805		2322	
福海县	Fuhai [Burultokay] County	8981	8981	4582	10436		2369	48873
哈巴河县	Habahe [Kaba] County	5162	6807	4575	9225		2869	
青河县	Qinghe [Qinggil] County	5191	5258	5205	7528		2154	
吉木乃县	Jeminay County	2958	2958	2656	8220		2900	

注：个别县(市)油料等作物种植在边角地头，未计面积，故单产偏高。

Note: The oil-bearing crop planted at the edge or margin of fields in small number of counties (cities), whose area is not calculated, thus per-unit output is relatively higher.

12-18 续表 Continued

单位：公斤/公顷 (kg/ hectare)

地区	Region	粮食 Grain	#谷物 Cereal	#小麦 Wheat	#玉米 Corn	棉花 Cotton	油料 Oil-Bearing Crops	甜菜 Beet-roots
博尔塔拉蒙古自治州	**Bortala Mongol Autonomous Prefecture**	**12453**	**12454**	**5406**	**15001**	**2165**	**2973**	**59074**
博乐市	Bole [Bortala] City	13730	13730	6081	14236	2145	3529	60885
精河县	Jinghe [Jing] County	8422	8422	4735	12719	2180		43500
温泉县	Wenquan [Araxang] County	11879	11880	5412	15999		2950	58669
巴音郭楞蒙古自治州	**Bayangol Mongol Autonomous Prefecture**	**6704**	**6729**	**6042**	**8200**	**2071**	**2075**	**90985**
库尔勒市	Korla City	4539	4550	4447	4772	2094		
轮台县	Luntai [Bugur] County	5516	5516	5524	5505	2085	3799	
尉犁县	Yuli [Lopnur] County	5043	5043	3938	6175	2287		
若羌县	Ruoqiang [Qarkilik] County	4688	4760	5170	4134	1821	973	
且末县	Qiemo [Qarqan] County	6171	6223	6235	6261	2037	1435	
焉耆回族自治县	Yanqi Hui Autonomous County	7924	7944	6559	12075	1323	2629	95103
和静县	Hejing County	7860	7911	6450	11775	1591	1779	89996
和硕县	Hoxud County	7465	7465	6052	11430	1995	2088	63107
博湖县	Bohu [Bagrax] County	8628	8628	6997	12017	1716	2000	86959
阿克苏地区	**Aksu Administrative Offices**	**7572**	**7590**	**6687**	**8361**	**1829**	**2039**	**81884**
阿克苏市	Aksu City	7669	7669	6755	7682	2143		56685
温宿县	Wensu [Onsu] County	8200	8203	6708	7803	1808	1590	37497
库车县	Kuqa County	6704	6728	6797	6632	1779	1289	37500
沙雅县	Xayar County	7176	7180	6891	7572	1841	1639	10967
新和县	Xinhe [Toksu] County	6675	6675	6766	6548	1915	1429	
拜城县	Baicheng [Bay] County	9354	9425	6642	12374		2443	94185
乌什县	Wushi [Uxturpan] County	7499	7535	6312	9755	1519	2020	60849
阿瓦提县	Awat County	6764	6764	6770	6756	1656		
柯坪县	Kalpin County	6439	6439	6105	7227	1939		15000
克孜勒苏柯尔克孜自治州	**Kizilsu Kirgiz Autonomous Prefecture**	**6164**	**6170**	**5839**	**6654**	**1535**	**1465**	
阿图什市	Artux City	5835	5835	5633	6213	1529	1895	
阿克陶县	Akto County	6735	6735	6363	7111	1538	3000	
阿合奇县	Akqi County	3868	3863	3953	4049		1275	
乌恰县	Wuqia [Ulugqat] County	4553	4583	4882	4130	1500	1869	
喀什地区	**Kashgar [Kaxgar] Administrative Offices**	**6352**	**6579**	**5897**	**7403**	**1727**	**1950**	
喀什市	Kashgar [Kaxgar] City	6155	6155	5550	6960			
疏附县	Shufu County	6567	6567	6390	6815	1533	2250	
疏勒县	Shule County	6650	6650	5962	7531	1623		
英吉沙县	Yengisar County	6367	6385	5844	7012	1515	2025	
泽普县	Zepu [Poskam] County	5072	6363	6032	7061	1518	2790	
莎车县	Shache [Yarkant] County	6422	6827	6000	7440	1575	1500	
叶城县	Yecheng [Kagilik] County	6902	7230	5887	8715	1645	3375	
麦盖提县	Makit County	5523	5635	5345	6036	1871	1500	
岳普湖县	Yopurga County	6760	6760	5844	7883	1652	1200	
伽师县	Jiashi [Payzawat] County	6530	6550	5865	7440	1782		
巴楚县	Bachu [Maralbexi] County	6524	6524	5850	7290	1875		
塔什库尔干塔吉克自治县	Taxkorgan Tajik Autonomous County	3213	3213	3270	6645	1350		
和田地区	**Hotan Administrative Offices**	**6648**	**6669**	**5967**	**7420**	**1832**	**2479**	
和田市	Hotan City	6877	6877	5928	8027	1601	3243	
和田县	Hotan County	6322	6352	6047	6675	1918	1553	
墨玉县	Moyu [Karakax] County	6549	6549	6077	6984	1881	1689	
皮山县	Pishan [Guma] County	7124	7215	5843	8599	1919	7464	
洛浦县	Lop County	6313	6313	5640	6988	1761	1629	
策勒县	Qira County	7001	7085	6001	8258	1898	1987	
于田县	Yutian [Keriya] County	6807	6807	6124	7478	1747	3042	
民丰县	Minfeng [Niya] County	6516	6516	5775	7452		1071	
生产建设兵团	**Xinjiang Production and Construction Group**	**7564**	**7685**	**5595**	**9980**	**2555**	**2534**	**72291**

12-19 各地、州、市、县(市)特色农作物播种面积
Sown Areas of Characteristic Farm Crops by Prefecture,Autonomous Prefecture ,City and County

单位：千公顷 (2012 年) (1000 hectares)

地 区	Region	番 茄 Tomato	工业用番 茄 Tonato in Industry	辣 椒 Peppers	工业用辣 椒 Capsicum	打瓜籽 Melon Seeds	啤酒花 Hop
总 计	**Total**	**77.79**	**58.39**	**76.67**	**55.14**	**97.97**	**2.70**
乌鲁木齐市	**Urumqi City**	**0.78**	**0.25**	**0.98**	**0.02**	**0.03**	
#市辖区	Municipal Districts	0.76	0.25	0.63	0.02	0.03	
乌鲁木齐县	Urumqi County	0.02		0.35			
克拉玛依市	**Karamay City**	**0.10**	**0.08**	**0.13**	**0.03**	**0.36**	
吐鲁番地区	**TurpanAdministrative Offices**	**0.84**		**0.47**		**0.07**	
吐鲁番市	Turpan City	0.37		0.09			
鄯善县	Shanshan [piqan]County	0.32		0.19			
托克逊县	Toksun County	0.15		0.19		0.07	
哈密地区	**Hami [Kumul]Administrative Offices**	**0.26**		**0.27**			
哈密市	Hami [Kumul]City	0.21		0.22			
巴里坤哈萨克自治县	Barkol KazakAutonomous County	0.04		0.05			
伊吾县	Yiwu [Araturuk]County	0.01		…			
昌吉回族自治州	**Changji Hui Autonomous Prefecture**	**15.51**	**13.36**	**5.92**	**2.45**	**10.65**	**0.32**
昌吉市	Changji City	4.03	3.79	0.25	0.04	0.20	0.07
阜康市	Fukang City	1.53	0.17	1.39	0.15	3.76	
呼图壁县	Hutubi County	4.49	4.42	1.86	1.76	0.18	0.14
玛纳斯县	Manas County	2.69	2.67	0.39	0.30	0.21	
奇台县	Qitai County	1.02	0.70	1.20		2.42	
吉木萨尔县	Jimsar County	1.71	1.61	0.58	0.08	2.79	0.11
木垒哈萨克自治县	Mori Kazak Autonomous County	0.04		0.25	0.12	1.10	
伊犁哈萨克自治州	**Ili Kazak Autonomous Prefecture**	**6.58**	**4.61**	**6.67**	**0.72**	**50.46**	**0.14**
伊犁州直属县(市)	**Counties (Cities) Direct Under Ili Prefecture**	**1.89**	**0.32**	**2.07**	**0.36**	**1.32**	
伊宁市	Yining [Gulja]City	0.59		0.58			
奎屯市	Kuytun City	0.03	0.03				
伊宁县	Yining [Gulja]County	0.61		0.47		0.02	
察布查尔锡伯自治县	Qapqal Xibe Autonomous County	0.12	0.02	0.58	0.23		
霍城县	Huocheng [korgas]County	0.43	0.27	0.21	0.13	0.74	
巩留县	Gongliu [Tokkuzlara]County	…		0.10			
新源县	Xinyuan [kunes]County	0.04		0.04		0.03	
昭苏县	Zhaosu [mongolkure]County	…		0.01			
特克斯县	Tekes County	0.05		0.05			
尼勒克县	Nilka County	0.01		0.04		0.53	

12-19 续表 1 Continued

单位：千公顷 (1000 hectares)

地　　区	Region	番　茄 Tomato	工业用番　茄 Tonato in Industry	辣　椒 Peppers	工业用辣　椒 Capsicum	打瓜籽 Melon Seeds	啤酒花 Hop
塔城地区	**Tacheng[Tarbagatai] Administrative Officess**	**4.54**	**4.29**	**4.41**	**0.35**	**20.59**	**0.14**
塔城市	Tacheng [Qoqek] City	0.18		0.23		6.41	0.14
乌苏市	Usu City	2.34	2.30	0.12		0.19	
额敏县	Emin [Dorbiljin] County	0.38	0.37			8.52	
沙湾县	Shawan County	1.62	1.62	3.71		2.89	
托里县	Toli County	0.01		…		0.50	
裕民县	Yumin [Qagantokay] County					1.88	
和布克赛尔蒙古自治县	Hoboksar Mongol Autonomous County	0.01		0.35	0.35	0.20	…
阿勒泰地区	**Altay Administrative Offices**	**0.16**		**0.19**		**28.55**	
阿勒泰市	Altay City	0.03		0.03		2.68	
布尔津县	Burqin County	0.01		0.02		3.22	
富蕴县	Fuyun [Koktokay] County	0.03		0.02		2.19	
福海县	Fuhai [Burultokay] County	0.01		0.01		15.45	
哈巴河县	Habahe [Kaba] County	0.06		0.09		4.82	
青河县	Qinghe [Qinggil] County	0.01		0.01		0.20	
吉木乃县	Jeminay County	0.01		0.01			
博尔塔拉蒙古自治州	**Bortala Mongol Autonomous Prefecture**	**0.18**	**0.10**	**0.13**	**0.02**	**0.04**	
博乐市	Bole [Bortala] City	0.11	0.04	0.11	0.02	0.02	
精河县	Jinghe [Jing] County	0.01		0.01		0.03	
温泉县	Wenquan [Araxang] County	0.06	0.06	0.01	…		
巴音郭楞蒙古自治州	**Bayangol Mongol Autonomous Prefecture**	**8.96**	**8.40**	**24.31**	**23.40**	**2.42**	**0.05**
库尔勒市	Korla City	0.13		0.21			
轮台县	Luntai [Bugur] County	0.02		0.01			
尉犁县	Yuli [Lopnur] County	0.01		0.01			
若羌县	Ruoqiang [Qarkilik] County	0.02		0.02			
且末县	Qiemo [Qarqan] County	0.03		0.17	0.14		
焉耆回族自治县	Yanqi Hui Autonomous County	2.64	2.64	2.66	2.66	0.89	
和静县	Hejing County	2.05	1.79	9.90	9.57	0.57	
和硕县	Hoxud County	1.87	1.86	6.14	6.13	0.19	
博湖县	Bohu [Bagrax] County	2.19	2.11	5.19	4.90	0.77	0.05
阿克苏地区	**Aksu Administrative Offices**	**6.74**	**5.33**	**2.08**	**1.02**	**0.36**	**0.10**
阿克苏市	Aksu City	0.43		0.26			
温宿县	Wensu [Onsu] County	0.13		0.10		0.18	
库车县	Kuqa County	0.29	0.02	0.09			

12-19 续表 2 Continued

单位：千公顷 (1000 hectares)

地　区	Region	番　茄 Tomato	工业用番茄 Tonato in Industry	辣　椒 Peppers	工业用辣椒 Capsicum	打瓜籽 Melon Seeds	啤酒花 Hop
沙雅县	Xayar County	0.09		0.07			
新和县	Xinhe [Toksu] County	0.23		0.12			
拜城县	Baicheng [Bay] County	2.03	1.98	1.16	1.02	0.18	0.10
乌什县	Wushi [Uxturpan] County	3.33	3.33	0.08			
阿瓦提县	Awat County	0.20		0.18			
柯坪县	Kalpin County	0.02		0.01			
克孜勒苏柯尔克孜自治州	**Kizilsu Kirgiz Autonomous Prefecture**	**0.21**		**0.16**			
阿图什市	Artux City	0.03		0.02			
阿克陶县	Akto County	0.09		0.08			
阿合奇县	Akqi County	0.02		0.01			
乌恰县	Wuqia [Ulugqat] County	0.07		0.05			
喀什地区	**Kashgar [Kaxgar] Administrative Offices**	**7.33**	**0.53**	**12.66**	**8.79**	**3.22**	
喀什市	Kashgar [Kaxgar] City	0.63		0.06			
疏附县	Shufu County	1.69		1.26			
疏勒县	Shule County	0.60		0.40			
英吉沙县	Yengisar County	0.49		0.55			
泽普县	Zepu [Poskam] County	0.19		0.10			
莎车县	Shache [Yarkant] County	0.67	0.53	8.07	7.26		
叶城县	Yecheng [Kagilik] County	0.20		1.63	1.53		
麦盖提县	Makit County	0.25		0.12		3.22	
岳普湖县	Yopurga County	0.31		0.09			
伽师县	Jiashi [Payzawat] County	2.20		0.25			
巴楚县	Bachu [Maralbexi] County	0.10		0.13			
塔什库尔干塔吉克自治县	Taxkorgan Tajik Autonomous County						
和田地区	**Hotan Administrative Offices**	**1.51**		**0.75**	**0.03**		
和田市	Hotan City	0.19		0.21			
和田县	Hotan County	0.08		0.16			
墨玉县	Moyu [Karakax] County	0.30		0.11	0.03		
皮山县	Pishan [Guma] County	0.17		0.07			
洛浦县	Lop County	0.06		0.03			
策勒县	Qira County	0.04		0.08			
于田县	Yutian [Keriya] County	0.65		0.08			
民丰县	Minfeng [Niya] County	0.02		0.01			
生产建设兵团	**Xinjiang Production and Construction Group**	**28.80**	**25.73**	**22.14**	**18.65**	**30.36**	**2.08**

12-20 各地、州、市、县(市)特色农作物产量
Output of Characteristic Farm Crops by Prefecture,Autonomous Prefectura,City and County

单位：吨 (2012 年) (ton)

地　区	Region	番　茄 Tomato	工业用番　茄 Tonato in Industry	辣　椒 Peppers	工业用辣　椒 Capsicum	枸　杞 Medlar	打瓜籽 Melon Seeds	啤酒花 Hop
总　计	**Total**	**6833522**	**5794582**	**3028514**	**2185963**	**59941**	**168787**	**11019**
乌鲁木齐市	**Urumqi City**	**52681**	**14111**	**43078**	**1149**	**61**	**53**	
#市辖区	Municipal Districts	51533	14111	29270	1149	61	53	
乌鲁木齐县	Urumqi County	1148		13808				
克拉玛依市	**Karamay City**	**8475**	**6200**	**3900**	**1440**		**900**	
吐鲁番地区	**TurpanAdministrative Offices**	**32497**		**8308**			**350**	
吐鲁番市	Turpan City	15437		1308				
鄯善县	Shanshan [piqan]County	10400		2800				
托克逊县	Toksun County	6660		4200			350	
哈密地区	**Hami [Kumul]Administrative Offices**	**12105**		**11767**				
哈密市	Hami [Kumul]City	10380		10269				
巴里坤哈萨克自治县	Barkol KazakAutonomous County	1325		1402				
伊吾县	Yiwu [Araturuk]County	400		96				
昌吉回族自治州	**Changji Hui Autonomous Prefecture**	**1371398**	**1219048**	**235034**	**96721**	**332**	**23071**	**2372**
昌吉市	Changji City	406741	386607	9883	1100		324	900
阜康市	Fukang City	108660	10808	25480	4900		7756	
呼图壁县	Hutubi County	354336	350034	67950	63510		447	1135
玛纳斯县	Manas County	260582	260364	24980	19272	280	463	
奇台县	Qitai County	69072	50325	69704		52	5447	
吉木萨尔县	Jimsar County	169958	160910	27952	3250		6652	337
木垒哈萨克自治县	Mori Kazak Autonomous County	2049		9085	4689		1982	
伊犁哈萨克自治州	**Ili Kazak Autonomous Prefecture**	**606502**	**490087**	**275563**	**9202**	**692**	**80778**	**2028**
伊犁州直属县(市)	**Counties (Cities) Direct Under Ili Prefecture**	**118521**	**20581**	**92746**	**6046**		**2013**	
伊宁市	Yining [Gulja]City	49480		45233				
奎屯市	Kuytun City	2500	2500					
伊宁县	Yining [Gulja]County	23195		14626			62	
察布查尔锡伯自治县	Qapqal Xibe Autonomous County	7081	1281	20194	3446			
霍城县	Huocheng [korgas]County	30306	16800	4020	2600		1104	
巩留县	Gongliu [Tokkuzlara]County	228		2900				
新源县	Xinyuan [kunes]County	2968		2465			76	
昭苏县	Zhaosu [mongolkure]County	154		173				
特克斯县	Tekes County	1800		1775				
尼勒克县	Nilka County	809		1360			771	

12-20 续表 1 Continued

单位：吨 (ton)

地 区	Region	番 茄 Tomato	工业用番茄 Tonato in Industr	辣 椒 Peppers	工业用辣椒 Capsicum	枸 杞 Medlar	打瓜籽 Melon Seeds	啤酒花 Hop
塔城地区	**Tacheng[Tarbagatai] Administrative Officess**	**483361**	**469506**	**177183**	**3156**	**240**	**30721**	**2028**
塔城市	Tacheng [Qoqek] City	9350		10450			8561	2026
乌苏市	Usu City	290531	288531	7200			454	
额敏县	Emin [Dorbiljin] County	36484	34159				12446	
沙湾县	Shawan County	146916	146816	156347		240	6551	
托里县	Toli County	20		30			633	
裕民县	Yumin [Qagantokay] County						1681	
和布克赛尔蒙古自治县	Hoboksar Mongol Autonomous County	60		3156	3156		395	2
阿勒泰地区	**Altay Administrative Offices**	**4620**		**5634**		**452**	**48044**	
阿勒泰市	Altay City	1070		1068			5221	
布尔津县	Burqin County	50		500			4348	
富蕴县	Fuyun [Koktokay] County	1019		586			4111	
福海县	Fuhai [Burultokay] County	281		118		452	25110	
哈巴河县	Habahe [Kaba] County	1826		2890			8962	
青河县	Qinghe [Qinggil] County	257		372			292	
吉木乃县	Jeminay County	117		100				
博尔塔拉蒙古自治州	**Bortala Mongol Autonomous Prefecture**	**12164**	**9116**	**3743**	**342**	**20297**	**75**	
博乐市	Bole [Bortala] City	6675	4130	3178	324	7	27	
精河县	Jinghe [Jing] County	444		523		20290	48	
温泉县	Wenquan [Araxang] County	5045	4986	42	18			
巴音郭楞蒙古自治州	**Bayangol Mongol Autonomous Prefecture**	**934782**	**882589**	**1009859**	**968334**	**88**	**4504**	**626**
库尔勒市	Korla City	10415		15490				
轮台县	Luntai [Bugur] County	1124		585				
尉犁县	Yuli [Lopnur] County	326		110				
若羌县	Ruoqiang [Qarkilik] County	934		484				
且末县	Qiemo [Qarqan] County	1200		5198	4298	88		
焉耆回族自治县	Yanqi Hui Autonomous County	297195	296190	125318	125040		2192	
和静县	Hejing County	226160	195545	313345	301312		879	
和硕县	Hoxud County	202079	201008	304565	304132		325	
博湖县	Bohu [Bagrax] County	195349	189846	244764	233552		1108	626
阿克苏地区	**Aksu Administrative Offices**	**481465**	**434436**	**27824**	**5174**	**29273**	**823**	**250**
阿克苏市	Aksu City	15954		4691				
温宿县	Wensu [Onsu] County	3985		3500			409	
库车县	Kuqa County	6465	324	1886				

12-20 续表 2 Continued

单位：吨 (ton)

地　区	Region	番　茄 Tomato	工业用番　茄 Tonato in Industr	辣　椒 Peppers	工业用辣　椒 Capsicum	枸　杞 Medlar	打瓜籽 Melon Seeds	啤酒花 Hop
沙雅县	Xayar County	836		771		29273		
新和县	Xinhe [Toksu] County	6289		2185				
拜城县	Baicheng [Bay] County	187699	180840	8894	5174		414	250
乌什县	Wushi [Uxturpan] County	253272	253272	305				
阿瓦提县	Awat County	6685		5422				
柯坪县	Kalpin County	280		170				
克孜勒苏柯尔克孜自治州	**Kizilsu Kirgiz Autonomous Prefecture**	**6270**		**3356**				
阿图什市	Artux City	1835		1030				
阿克陶县	Akto County	2096		1471				
阿合奇县	Akqi County	519		220				
乌恰县	Wuqia [Ulugqat] County	1820		635				
喀什地区	**Kashgar [Kaxgar] Administrative Offices**	**301568**	**16000**	**539205**	**418700**		**1208**	
喀什市	Kashgar [Kaxgar] City	36660		2250				
疏附县	Shufu County	79500		18950				
疏勒县	Shule County	16600		9400				
英吉沙县	Yengisar County	20787		23050				
泽普县	Zepu [Poskam] County	8769		4032				
莎车县	Shache [Yarkant] County	20000	16000	363000	326700			
叶城县	Yecheng [Kagilik] County	9649		96631	92000			
麦盖提县	Makit County	10402		6055			1208	
岳普湖县	Yopurga County	10580		2080				
伽师县	Jiashi [Payzawat] County	83785		7500				
巴楚县	Bachu [Maralbexi] County	4836		6257				
塔什库尔干塔吉克自治县	Taxkorgan Tajik Autonomous County							
和田地区	**Hotan Administrative Offices**	**67686**		**22246**	**450**			
和田市	Hotan City	11069		10024				
和田县	Hotan County	3227		5824				
墨玉县	Moyu [Karakax] County	10941		820	450			
皮山县	Pishan [Guma] County	8133		1602				
洛浦县	Lop County	2456		681				
策勒县	Qira County	2361		1691				
于田县	Yutian [Keriya] County	29160		1375				
民丰县	Minfeng [Niya] County	339		229				
生产建设兵团	**Xinjiang Production and Construction Group**	**2945929**	**2722995**	**844631**	**684451**	**9198**	**57025**	**5743**

12-21 各地、州、市林业生产情况

Condition on Forest Products by Prefecture, Autonomous Prefecture, City

单位:公顷 (2012 年) (hectare)

地　区	Region	当年造林面积 Planting Area in the Current Year	用材林 Timber Forest	经济林 Economic Forest	防护林 Windbreak	薪炭林 Firewood Forest	特种用途林 Forest for Special Purpose
总　计	**Total**	**205027**	**4369**	**54203**	**142963**	**3309**	**183**
乌鲁木齐市	Urumqi City	4096		130	3866		100
克拉玛依市	Karamay City	1214		7	1207		
吐鲁番地区	Turpan Administrative Offices	7551	73	1504	4907	1067	
哈密地区	Hami [Kumul]Administrative Offices	8000		34	7966		
昌吉回族自治州	Changji Hui Autonomous Prefecture	18935	27	2679	15962	267	
伊犁哈萨克自治州	Ili Kazak Administrative Prefecture	60495	3489	5561	50402	966	77
伊犁州直属县(市)	Counties (Cities) Direct Under Ili Prefecture	20637	3044	3780	13759	54	
塔城地区	Tacheng [Tarbagatai] Administrative Offices	19326	445	674	17885	245	77
阿勒泰地区	Altay Administrative Offices	20532		1107	18758	667	
博尔塔拉蒙古自治州	Bortala Mongol Autonomous Prefecture	10379		258	10121		
巴音郭楞蒙古自治州	Bayangol Mongol Autonomous Prefecture	16057		6421	9222	414	
阿克苏地区	Aksu Administrative Offices	9144		167	8977		
克孜勒苏柯尔克孜自治州	Kizilsu Kirgiz Autonomous Prefecture	8592	113	2540	5939		
喀什地区	Kashgar [Kaxgar] Administrative Offices	26240		23243	2959	32	6
和田地区	Hotan Administrative Offices	16200		8891	6746	563	
生产建设兵团	Xinjiang Production and Construction Group	17706	667	2768	14271		

地　区	Region	迹地更新面积 Renewing Area in Slash	当年零星植树(万株) Fragmentary Planting (10 000 trees)	年末实有育苗面积 Actual Sapling Breeding Area	幼林抚育作业面积 Tending Area of Young Growth	成林抚育面积 Tending Area of Full Growth	核桃产量(吨) Walnut Output (ton)	村及村以下木材采伐量(立方米) Timber Felling Output in Village or Below (cu.m)
总　计	**Total**	**2231**	**2235.72**	**19931**	**831053**	**1755018**	**313642**	**265200**
乌鲁木齐市	Urumqi City		90.00	489				1232
克拉玛依市	Karamay City		219.00	933	8204	9670		
吐鲁番地区	Turpan Administrative Offices	47	3.21	78	16000	25466	459	4047
哈密地区	Hami[Kumul] Administrative Offices			88	23686	29465		1430
昌吉回族自治州	Changji Hui Autonomous Prefecture		45.91	7582	2902	3788		31009
伊犁哈萨克自治州	Ili Kazak Administrative Prefecture	424	534.64	1565	124719	309745	1068	71604
伊犁州直属县(市)	Counties (Cities) Direct Under Ili Prefecture	281	362.29	1107	51702	64251	1068	46611
塔城地区	Tacheng [Tarbagatai] Administrative Offices	143	89.03	331	29347	162178		24943
阿勒泰地区	Altay Administrative Offices		83.32	127	43670	83316		50
博尔塔拉蒙古自治州	Bortala Mongol Autonomous Prefecture	89	36.00	248	9266	13640	2	14842
巴音郭楞蒙古自治州	Bayangol Mongol Autonomous Prefecture	14	94.69	509	2967	10821	256	21012
阿克苏地区	Aksu Administrative Offices	1092	28.02	1021	229023	309034	105118	43038
克孜勒苏柯尔克孜自治州	Kizilsu Kirgiz Autonomous Prefecture		13.00	302	13800	28747	880	1306
喀什地区	Kashgar [Kaxgar] Administrative Offices	132	556.52	1556	177453	399066	119511	48733
和田地区	Hotan Administrative Offices	176	423.66	1855	76485	159218	78208	26947
生产建设兵团	Xinjiang Production and Construction Group	97	191.07	3351	129370	406346	8140	

12-22 各地、州、市水果种植面积

Planted Area of Fruits by Prefecture, Autonomous Prefecture, City

单位:公顷 (2012 年) (hectare)

地区	Region	合计 Total	苹果 Apples	梨 Pears	葡萄 Grapes	#无核葡萄 Seedless Grapes
总计	**Total**	**1015152**	**83917**	**70234**	**143318**	**44114**
乌鲁木齐市	Urumqi City	668	104		285	
克拉玛依市	Karamay City					
吐鲁番地区	TurpanAdministrative Offices	40674		28	30336	27779
哈密地区	Hami [Kumul] Administrative Offices	29689	34	38	3776	3026
昌吉回族自治州	Changji Hui Autonomous Prefecture	15356	2847	25	7498	7
伊犁哈萨克自治州	Ili Kazak Autonomous Prefecture	73295	46052	165	7329	
伊犁州直属县(市)	Counties (Cities) Direct Under Ili Prefecture	70395	44768	129	5970	
塔城地区	Tacheng [Tarbagatai] Administrative Offices	1913	1266	36	401	
阿勒泰地区	Altay Administrative Offices	986	18		958	
博尔塔拉蒙古自治州	Bortala MongolAutonomous Prefecture	383	101	6	254	
巴音郭楞蒙古自治州	Bayangol Mongol Autonomous Prefecture	101945	336	36995	15230	
阿克苏地区	Aksu Administrative Offices	201148	14317	13306	7507	
克孜勒苏柯尔克孜自治州	Kizilsu Kirgiz Autonomous Prefecture	32557	138	18	6680	
喀什地区	Kashgar [Kaxgar] Administrative Offices	252491	3804	1310	5052	
和田地区	Hotan Administrative Offices	72085	1093	424	11289	3313
生产建设兵团	Xinjiang Production and Construction Group	194860	15089	17919	48083	9990

地区	Region	桃 Peaches	杏 Apricots	红枣 Jujubes	石榴 Pomegraniate	其它 Others
总计	**Total**	**12652**	**189928**	**473672**	**13778**	**27653**
乌鲁木齐市	Urumqi City	45	58	52		124
克拉玛依市	Karamay City					
吐鲁番地区	TurpanAdministrative Offices	13	1995	7861	441	
哈密地区	Hami [Kumul] Administrative Offices	31	2328	21894		1587
昌吉回族自治州	Changji Hui Autonomous Prefecture	696	2460	126		1705
伊犁哈萨克自治州	Ili Kazak Autonomous Prefecture	1937	12337	571		4904
伊犁州直属县(市)	Counties (Cities) Direct Under Ili Prefecture	1822	12328	543		4836
塔城地区	Tacheng [Tarbagatai] Administrative Offices	107	9	28		66
阿勒泰地区	Altay Administrative Offices	8	…			3
博尔塔拉蒙古自治州	Bortala Mongol Autonomous Prefecture	12	7	1		2
巴音郭楞蒙古自治州	Bayangol Mongol Autonomous Prefecture	269	16804	30358		1952
阿克苏地区	Aksu Administrative Offices	418	31796	130431	103	3269
克孜勒苏柯尔克孜自治州	Kizilsu Kirgiz Autonomous Prefecture	503	16645	7117	202	1254
喀什地区	Kashgar [Kaxgar] Administrative Offices	5370	81987	135706	8975	10288
和田地区	Hotan Administrative Offices	1141	18582	33291	4053	2214
生产建设兵团	Xinjiang Production and Construction Group	2218	4927	106265	5	355

12-23 各地、州、市水果产量
Output of Fruits by Prefecture, Autonomous Prefecture, City

单位：吨 (2012 年) (ton)

地 区	Region	合 计 Total	苹 果 Apples	梨 Pears	葡 萄 Grapes	#无核葡萄 Seedless Grapes
总 计	**Total**	**7367446**	**820982**	**950197**	**2090508**	**1032476**
乌鲁木齐市	Urumqi City	8900	1163		5520	
克拉玛依市	Karamay City					
吐鲁番地区	TurpanAdministrative Offices	867381		380	834854	765200
哈密地区	Hami [Kumul] Administrative Offices	107930	157	335	79937	66005
昌吉回族自治州	Changji Hui Autonomous Prefecture	183024	15355	107	148918	8
伊犁哈萨克自治州	Ili Kazak Autonomous Prefecture	328935	160574	1143	84681	
伊犁州直属县(市)	Counties (Cities) Direct Under Ili Prefecture	306813	150966	452	75149	
塔城地区	Tacheng [Tarbagatai] Administrative Offices	21039	9108	691	9126	
阿勒泰地区	Altay Administrative Offices	1083	500		406	
博尔塔拉蒙古自治州	Bortala MongolAutonomous Prefecture	4114	1251	19	2636	
巴音郭楞蒙古自治州	Bayangol Mongol Autonomous Prefecture	531651	3619	308580	33450	
阿克苏地区	Aksu Administrative Offices	1521185	269817	287513	116069	
克孜勒苏柯尔克孜自治州	Kizilsu Kirgiz Autonomous Prefecture	212702	397	45	79722	
喀什地区	Kashgar [Kaxgar] Administrative Offices	1498481	93950	14733	95396	
和田地区	Hotan Administrative Offices	379649	7479	2842	176887	57933
生产建设兵团	Xinjiang Production and Construction Group	1723494	267220	334500	432438	143330

地 区	Region	桃 Peachs	杏 Apricots	红 枣 Jujubes	石 榴 Pomegranate	其 它 Others
总 计	**Total**	**125073**	**1733624**	**1453977**	**57168**	**135917**
乌鲁木齐市	Urumqi City	605	378	240		994
克拉玛依市	Karamay City					
吐鲁番地区	TurpanAdministrative Offices	188	9798	20782	1379	
哈密地区	Hami [Kumul] Administrative Offices	93	1271	26137		
昌吉回族自治州	Changji Hui Autonomous Prefecture	8269	4563	1103		4709
伊犁哈萨克自治州	Ili Kazak Autonomous Prefecture	21539	47785	2012		11201
伊犁州直属县(市)	Counties (Cities) Direct Under Ili Prefecture	20219	47702	1621		10704
塔城地区	Tacheng [Tarbagatai] Administrative Offices	1177	83	391		463
阿勒泰地区	Altay Administrative Offices	143				34
博尔塔拉蒙古自治州	Bortala MongolAutonomous Prefecture	170	6			32
巴音郭楞蒙古自治州	Bayangol Mongol Autonomous Prefecture	1759	88371	88222		7650
阿克苏地区	Aksu Administrative Offices		384758	417473		45555
克孜勒苏柯尔克孜自治州	Kizilsu Kirgiz Autonomous Prefecture	452	125861	1250	944	4031
喀什地区	Kashgar [Kaxgar] Administrative Offices	41949	909620	252641	40215	49977
和田地区	Hotan Administrative Offices	4599	125258	40218	14588	7778
生产建设兵团	Xinjiang Production and Construction Group	45450	35955	603899	42	3990

12-24 主要年份牲畜饲养情况
Number of Livestock in Main Years

单位：万头(只) (10 000 heads)

年 份 Year	大牲畜年底头数 Large Animals (year-end)	牛 Cattle and Buffaloes	马 Horses	驴 Donkeys	骡 Mules	骆驼 Camels	在大牲畜中役畜 Draught Animals
1978	446.19	222.39	112.39	96.61	1.61	13.19	148.34
1980	482.55	250.65	106.89	108.88	1.72	14.41	154.86
1985	517.55	293.26	99.54	106.57	2.17	16.05	197.29
1990	575.88	338.22	104.58	112.96	2.69	17.43	209.95
1995	580.04	343.54	100.47	117.04	2.77	16.22	213.61
1996	589.41	349.78	101.16	119.36	2.76	16.34	215.05
1997	600.12	359.81	100.32	120.74	2.87	16.38	207.15
1998	606.79	364.29	100.26	123.45	2.80	15.99	205.31
1999	615.91	370.52	101.47	124.99	2.78	16.15	189.86
2000	632.93	384.98	102.57	125.94	2.74	16.70	173.37
2001	630.67	386.40	99.38	126.06	2.84	15.99	172.08
2002	654.46	414.13	99.71	122.22	2.59	15.81	169.51
2003	694.53	453.06	99.39	124.02	2.48	15.58	163.72
2004	716.56	482.30	95.78	120.82	2.36	15.30	151.49
2005	739.72	504.16	94.19	123.90	2.38	15.09	134.81
2006	736.33	502.86	92.09	124.94	2.14	14.30	145.97
2007	702.03	486.98	86.09	113.92	1.83	13.20	120.79
2008	543.41	336.00	83.85	109.25	1.45	12.86	96.56
2009	536.83	330.76	84.60	107.17	1.35	12.95	99.48
2010	536.82	330.47	85.29	106.96	1.19	12.91	108.93
2011	523.00	318.20	85.66	104.73	1.08	13.33	158.20
2012	565.77	365.93	86.84	97.97	1.06	13.97	162.00

年 份 Year	猪年底头数 Hogs (year-end)	羊年底只数 Sheep and Goats (year-end)	山羊 Goats	绵羊 Sheep	牲畜出栏头数 Slanghtered Fattened Animals withina Year	#猪 Hogs	#牛 Cattle and Buffaloes	#羊 Sheep and Goats
1978	103.25	1927.34	349.63	1577.91	460.41	50.75	18.75	382.76
1980	84.62	2105.43	388.89	1716.54	584.09	67.32	24.22	477.81
1985	66.58	2431.91	394.79	2037.12	836.39	49.07	42.33	723.51
1990	89.71	2830.81	449.43	2381.38	1242.89	78.93	70.10	1070.43
1995	135.26	3009.02	471.38	2537.64	1709.93	122.32	101.20	1448.72
1996	138.18	3136.21	498.10	2638.11	1859.28	153.75	116.25	1550.65
1997	145.73	3261.81	514.60	2747.21	2096.67	173.06	125.72	1753.88
1998	169.82	3447.38	528.05	2919.33	2222.27	197.39	140.82	1837.57
1999	188.34	3592.29	555.21	3037.08	2223.89	203.87	145.95	1820.71
2000	201.53	3690.21	586.70	3103.51	2455.99	224.46	154.53	2017.36
2001	208.23	3764.88	601.14	3163.74	2633.83	246.00	179.32	2147.31
2002	219.08	3908.23	626.42	3281.81	2878.39	259.05	188.65	2363.02
2003	227.71	4104.30	657.15	3447.15	3201.99	307.74	202.23	2626.94
2004	223.08	4266.73	669.47	3597.26	3437.59	352.83	220.80	2790.53
2005	238.38	4355.50	659.75	3695.75	3756.92	358.71	249.41	3081.88
2006	243.88	4359.50	654.26	3705.24	4063.52	390.82	278.69	3317.99
2007	237.90	4083.44	608.10	3475.34	4108.28	393.70	271.76	3361.99
2008	177.00	3025.70	453.85	2571.85	3388.09	265.50	207.30	2842.30
2009	180.42	3127.50	469.13	2658.37	3135.72	254.23	210.89	2604.48
2010	171.96	3013.37	528.73	2484.64	3498.52	262.72	216.69	2947.22
2011	254.00	3016.40	489.70	2526.70	3606.61	411.94	203.90	2913.83
2012	265.43	3502.05	525.31	2976.74	3737.30	427.60	222.26	3001.24

注：牲畜出栏数 1999 年以后计算口径与 1998 年以前不同。
Note: The calculating norm of cattles out of stock after 1999 was different from that prior to that in 1998.

12-25 各地、州、市、县(市)牲畜年底头数

Number of Livestock at the Year-end by Prefecture, Autonomous Prefecture, City and County

单位：万头(只) (2012 年) (10 000 heads)

地　区	Region	合 计 Total	#牛 Cattle and Buffaloes	#马 Horses	#驴 Donkeys	#猪 Hogs	#山羊 Goats	#绵羊 Sheep
总　计	**Total**	**4333.25**	**365.93**	**86.84**	**97.97**	**265.43**	**525.31**	**2976.74**
乌鲁木齐市	**Urumqi City**	**72.71**	**7.96**	**1.73**	**0.22**	**8.10**	**17.18**	**37.13**
#乌鲁木齐县	Urumqi County	27.45	2.89	1.31	0.11	0.07	3.71	19.27
克拉玛依市	**Karamay City**	**14.16**	**0.70**	**0.07**	**0.01**	**7.12**	**1.98**	**4.25**
吐鲁番地区	**TurpanAdministrative Offices**	**96.46**	**4.00**	**0.39**	**2.27**	**2.72**	**16.56**	**70.03**
吐鲁番市	Turpan City	31.55	1.21	0.03	0.57	1.61	6.15	21.95
鄯善县	Shanshan [piqan]County	31.23	0.53	0.09	0.57	1.05	3.32	25.50
托克逊县	Toksun County	33.68	2.26	0.27	1.13	0.06	7.09	22.58
哈密地区	**Hami [Kumul]Administrative Offices**	**114.40**	**6.30**	**1.22**	**0.70**	**11.35**	**15.91**	**78.03**
哈密市	Hami [Kumul]City	42.93	2.19	0.31	0.29	2.43	6.62	30.79
巴里坤哈萨克自治县	Barkol KazakAutonomous County	54.21	2.90	0.74	0.33	4.42	5.68	39.73
伊吾县	Yiwu [Araturuk]County	17.26	1.21	0.17	0.08	4.50	3.61	7.51
昌吉回族自治州	**Changji Hui Autonomous Prefecture**	**422.63**	**48.81**	**5.11**	**0.89**	**46.80**	**44.04**	**275.02**
昌吉市	Changji City	77.97	11.42	0.71	0.07	15.04	9.90	40.45
阜康市	Fukang City	29.18	4.42	0.38	0.03	3.36	6.77	14.11
呼图壁县	Hutubi County	59.85	9.39	1.27	0.03	6.68	7.08	35.08
玛纳斯县	Manas County	56.21	5.57	0.84	0.14	5.51	1.44	42.51
奇台县	Qitai County	92.62	9.65	0.73	0.15	7.53	7.56	66.66
吉木萨尔县	Jimsar County	54.83	6.20	0.60	0.26	6.80	4.99	35.88
木垒哈萨克自治县	Mori Kazak Autonomous County	51.97	2.16	0.58	0.21	1.88	6.30	40.33
伊犁哈萨克自治州	**Ili Kazak Autonomous Prefecture**	**1362.25**	**229.67**	**60.41**	**2.85**	**51.31**	**124.47**	**886.48**
伊犁州直属县(市)	**Counties (Cities) Direct Under Ili Prefecture**	**636.55**	**130.09**	**39.76**	**2.57**	**30.60**	**23.42**	**409.49**
伊宁市	Yining [Gulja]City	23.11	4.65	0.40	0.20	2.01	1.15	14.67
奎屯市	Kuytun City	3.27	0.14	0.01		2.34	0.17	0.61
伊宁县	Yining [Gulja]County	87.58	17.62	2.55	0.30	10.00	5.76	51.21
察布查尔锡伯自治县	Qapqal Xibe Autonomous County	42.28	7.10	1.40	0.92	2.71	3.30	26.85
霍城县	Huocheng [korgas]County	70.89	11.49	1.53	0.63	4.14	1.50	51.49
巩留县	Gongliu [Tokkuzlara]County	57.51	12.65	3.80	0.37	2.95	2.61	35.09
新源县	Xinyuan [kunes]County	101.45	23.24	8.23	0.05	2.30	2.11	65.51
昭苏县	Zhaosu [mongolkure]County	89.56	16.41	8.92	0.02	2.47	1.40	60.30
特克斯县	Tekes County	70.18	16.50	4.57	0.03	0.66	2.46	45.93
尼勒克县	Nilka County	90.72	20.29	8.35	0.05	1.02	2.96	57.83
塔城地区	**Tacheng [Tarbagatai] Administrative Offices**	**451.01**	**47.38**	**10.46**	**0.24**	**18.98**	**64.66**	**306.98**
塔城市	Tacheng [Qoqek] City	65.99	7.96	1.77	0.08	2.13	5.58	48.24
乌苏市	Usu City	78.82	4.77	0.82	0.06	4.12	12.54	56.10
额敏县	Emin [Dorbiljin] County	72.23	6.30	1.39		1.72	10.80	51.84
沙湾县	Shawan County	63.05	10.16	1.49	0.01	10.31	6.53	34.26
托里县	Toli County	61.35	7.97	1.72	0.07	0.21	10.20	40.68
裕民县	Yumin [Qagantokay] County	61.57	5.89	2.04		0.36	9.01	43.85
和布克赛尔蒙古自治县	Hoboksar Mongol Autonomous County	48.00	4.33	1.23	0.02	0.13	10.00	32.01
阿勒泰地区	**Altay Administrative Offices**	**274.69**	**52.20**	**10.19**	**0.04**	**1.73**	**36.39**	**170.01**
阿勒泰市	Altay City	50.30	12.10	1.97	0.01	0.43	3.10	32.04
布尔津县	Burqin County	32.91	8.45	1.79		0.18	3.81	18.20
富蕴县	Fuyun [Koktokay] County	60.57	7.12	2.70	0.01	0.10	8.35	41.01
福海县	Fuhai [Burultokay] County	41.67	7.21	0.66		0.79	5.71	26.50
哈巴河县	Habahe [Kaba] County	39.53	11.41	1.53		0.11	5.35	20.73
青河县	Qinghe [Qinggil] County	28.37	3.30	0.78	0.02	0.06	6.99	16.95
吉木乃县	Jeminay County	21.34	2.61	0.76		0.06	3.08	14.58

注: 1.全区总计不等于地方与生产建设兵团汇总数。2.全区总计数为国家统计局审定数。

Note:a)The region total data is not equal to the sum of local and Production and Construction Groups.b)The region total data refer to approvable data of NBS.

12-25 续表 Continued

单位：万头(只) (10 000 heads)

地　　区	Region	合 计 Total	#牛 Cattle and Buffaloes	#马 Horses	#驴 Donkeys	#猪 Hogs	#山羊 Goats	#绵羊 Sheep
博尔塔拉蒙古自治州	**Bortala Mongol Autonomous Prefecture**	**108.61**	**6.79**	**1.37**	**0.17**	**5.17**	**13.18**	**81.69**
博乐市	Bole [Bortala] City	36.44	2.77	0.37	0.09	2.76	3.13	27.19
精河县	Jinghe [Jing] County	36.77	1.50	0.35	0.02	0.98	6.75	27.13
温泉县	Wenquan [Araxang] County	35.40	2.52	0.65	0.06	1.43	3.30	27.37
巴音郭楞蒙古自治州	**Bayangol Mongol Autonomous Prefecture**	**309.54**	**15.46**	**3.10**	**2.38**	**27.95**	**58.19**	**201.82**
库尔勒市	Korla City	30.75	1.01	0.07	0.10	7.87	3.68	18.02
轮台县	Luntai [Bugur] County	36.56	1.31	0.02	0.71	1.44	9.25	23.82
尉犁县	Yuli [Lopnur] County	35.06	0.75	0.05	0.16	0.46	19.71	13.92
若羌县	Ruoqiang [Qarkilik] County	9.77	0.37	0.05	0.21	0.50	0.91	7.69
且末县	Qiemo [Qarqan] County	38.35	1.89	0.10	1.07	0.83	9.68	24.54
焉耆回族自治县	Yanqi Hui Autonomous County	25.42	1.83	0.09	0.07	2.18	0.60	20.65
和静县	Hejing County	93.47	6.75	2.03	0.03	2.80	9.01	72.74
和硕县	Hoxud County	22.37	0.91	0.50	0.02	4.40	4.33	12.00
博湖县	Bohu [Bagrax] County	17.79	0.64	0.19	0.01	7.47	1.02	8.44
阿克苏地区	**Aksu Administrative Offices**	**467.14**	**33.89**	**5.11**	**10.02**	**17.09**	**116.83**	**283.19**
阿克苏市	Aksu City	53.02	2.97	0.26	0.52	7.63	5.89	35.75
温宿县	Wensu [Onsu] County	61.39	3.46	1.00	1.04	1.75	12.43	41.66
库车县	Kuqa County	75.33	5.34	0.43	1.12	2.69	20.18	45.42
沙雅县	Xayar County	46.06	2.78	0.48	1.36	1.87	19.45	19.98
新和县	Xinhe [Toksu] County	24.35	3.05	0.47	1.09	0.17	1.47	18.04
拜城县	Baicheng [Bay] County	92.52	7.88	0.81	2.39	2.41	24.02	54.96
乌什县	Wushi [Uxturpan] County	55.38	5.33	1.39	1.79	0.13	19.07	27.49
阿瓦提县	Awat County	39.49	2.78	0.23	0.28	0.44	5.06	30.69
柯坪县	Kalpin County	19.60	0.30	0.04	0.43		9.26	9.20
克孜勒苏柯尔克孜自治州	**Kizilsu Kirgiz Autonomous Prefecture**	**164.67**	**16.36**	**2.79**	**3.07**	**0.60**	**38.38**	**102.61**
阿图什市	Artux City	47.00	4.77	0.35	0.92	0.35	14.51	25.81
阿克陶县	Akto County	52.44	9.35	0.14	1.63	0.16	8.06	32.95
阿合奇县	Akqi County	35.19	0.88	1.80	0.08	0.09	10.20	22.08
乌恰县	Wuqia [Ulugqat] County	30.04	1.36	0.50	0.44		5.61	21.77
喀什地区	**Kashgar [Kaxgar] Administrative Offices**	**831.71**	**92.10**	**1.67**	**45.43**	**14.67**	**40.86**	**636.57**
喀什市	Kashgar [Kaxgar] City	27.00	1.55	0.01	0.86	1.86	0.34	22.38
疏附县	Shufu County	106.10	10.23	0.10	3.87	1.72	3.54	86.59
疏勒县	Shule County	82.19	9.56	0.04	4.47	6.13	0.66	61.28
英吉沙县	Yengisar County	38.50	5.85	0.03	2.41	0.52	0.41	29.26
泽普县	Zepu [Poskam] County	40.14	5.74	0.18	2.30	1.13	1.34	29.45
莎车县	Shache [Yarkant] County	123.70	15.64	0.21	6.04	0.75	2.39	98.67
叶城县	Yecheng [Kagilik] County	121.34	16.31	0.30	6.89	0.72	6.62	90.37
麦盖提县	Makit County	57.82	6.96	0.19	1.96	0.48	4.90	43.32
岳普湖县	Yopurga County	39.39	5.13	0.13	7.98	0.14	3.44	22.54
伽师县	Jiashi [Payzawat] County	103.20	6.10	0.28	6.70	0.20	6.30	83.61
巴楚县	Bachu [Maralbexi] County	72.80	5.43	0.12	1.47	1.02	5.54	59.22
塔什库尔干塔吉克自治县	Taxkorgan Tajik Autonomous County	19.53	3.60	0.08	0.48		5.38	9.88
和田地区	**Hotan Administrative Offices**	**503.45**	**28.35**	**1.35**	**28.79**	**1.97**	**30.04**	**412.28**
和田市	Hotan City	32.26	2.08	0.04	0.89	1.30	0.64	27.29
和田县	Hotan County	79.39	6.06	0.15	5.22	0.08	2.31	65.49
墨玉县	Moyu [Karakax] County	119.05	9.40	0.24	8.01	0.02	2.20	99.16
皮山县	Pishan [Guma] County	51.38	1.26	0.15	3.73	0.13	3.07	42.95
洛浦县	Lop County	52.31	4.27	0.06	2.95	0.17	0.97	43.86
策勒县	Qira County	51.57	1.37	0.24	2.41	0.08	3.73	43.66
于田县	Yutian [Keriya] County	82.70	3.50	0.40	4.50	0.16	8.00	65.96
民丰县	Minfeng [Niya] County	34.79	0.41	0.07	1.08	0.03	9.12	23.91
生产建设兵团	**Xinjiang Production and Construction Group**	**603.06**	**39.23**	**2.52**	**1.17**	**130.53**	**45.03**	**384.20**

12-26 主要年份畜产品产量
Output of Livestock Products in Main Years

年 份 Year	肉类产量 (万吨) Output of meat (10 000 tons)	#牛 Beef	#马 Horse Meat	#骆驼 Camels	#猪 Pork	#羊 Mutton	#禽兔肉 Poultry and Rabbit Meat
1978	9.65	1.85			2.48	5.32	
1980	12.70	2.20	0.60	0.05	3.29	6.48	
1985	18.37	4.23	0.86	0.15	3.09	9.97	
1990	30.46	7.08	1.18	0.18	4.93	15.75	1.22
1995	52.38	13.14	2.05	0.40	8.37	24.48	3.61
1996	60.31	15.18	2.24	0.38	10.43	26.93	4.82
1997	64.40	16.40	2.55	0.38	11.52	27.72	5.38
1998	75.19	19.19	2.82	0.47	13.60	32.49	6.16
1999	81.36	20.61	2.93	0.62	16.02	33.57	6.94
2000	90.00	22.24	3.57	0.63	17.18	37.50	7.76
2001	97.00	23.99	3.55	0.72	18.36	40.48	8.66
2002	105.44	25.90	3.65	0.68	19.70	43.06	10.38
2003	115.00	28.77	3.88	0.69	22.41	45.54	11.46
2004	128.13	30.42	4.34	0.70	24.58	52.65	13.27
2005	141.46	34.22	4.67	0.77	26.18	59.89	13.46
2006	158.21	39.25	4.80	0.90	28.78	66.99	14.92
2007	160.58	42.25	5.09	0.94	31.73	65.02	13.74
2008	114.74	32.40	4.29	0.95	22.30	45.40	7.89
2009	115.31	33.88	4.33	0.73	22.03	43.77	8.52
2010	121.74	35.47	4.67	0.78	23.05	46.95	8.71
2011	127.28	33.80	4.86	0.73	29.80	46.40	9.50
2012	134.23	36.16	4.96	0.80	30.15	48.01	10.54

年 份 Year	羊 毛 (万吨) Wool (10 000 tons)	#绵羊毛 Sheep Wool	山羊绒 (吨) Cashmere (ton)	驼 毛 (吨) Camel Hair (ton)	牛 奶 (万吨) Cow Milk (10 000 tons)	羊 奶 (万吨) Sheep Milk (10 000 tons)	牛 皮 (万张) Oxhide (10 000 sheets)	羊 皮 (万张) Sheep Skin (10 000 sheets)	禽 蛋 (万吨) Poultry Eggs (10 000 tons)
1978	3.08	3.00	324	371	4.50	0.75	17.36	300.05	
1980	3.31	3.21	263	353	5.84	1.44	18.22	338.32	
1985	7.07	3.91	325	530	16.43	3.27	35.72	587.69	4.29
1990	5.09	4.93	607	656	30.81	4.83	56.76	839.69	6.30
1995	5.66	5.45	716	716	45.21	4.60	91.54	1125.72	9.51
1996	5.99	5.77	780	787	48.76	5.46	92.31	1178.39	10.33
1997	6.25	6.01	813	742	54.18	4.60	96.88	1326.69	12.16
1998	6.48	6.22	811	768	59.96	5.06	110.12	1391.77	13.34
1999	6.76	6.50	849	727	64.81	5.62	118.35	1569.50	16.68
2000	6.98	6.67	893	757	72.54	5.69	125.62	1686.03	18.53
2001	7.30	6.99	973	736	81.09	6.76	143.13	1689.24	20.37
2002	7.78	7.44	1034	824	94.87	5.84	139.87	1801.67	22.64
2003	8.21	7.84	1143	793	113.00	6.21	141.57	1692.35	23.62
2004	8.91	8.49	1228	770	133.32	6.41	150.15	1981.82	24.99
2005	9.38	8.98	1258	730	152.22	5.62	169.53	2022.61	24.99
2006	9.62	8.96	1263	746	179.81	5.60	196.97	2300.73	25.80
2007	9.34	8.92	1265	946	196.23	5.54	191.90	2409.84	28.37
2008	9.03	8.40	1157	1040	137.40	4.96	208.07	2441.52	28.92
2009	7.60	7.16	1261	578	120.88	4.27	193.52	2358.98	23.20
2010	8.69	8.40	1324	602	128.60	4.22	204.14	2403.25	24.35
2011	9.01	8.69	1261	610	130.50	3.41	221.35	2535.63	25.60
2012	9.20	8.85	1225	539	132.21	4.11	221.63	2573.07	25.89

12-27 各地、州、市、县(市)总产肉量

Total Output of Meat by Prefecture, Autonomous Prefecture, City and County

单位：吨 (2012 年) (ton)

地区	Region	合计 Total	#牛 Beef	#马 Horse	#骆驼 Camels	#猪 Pork	#山羊 Goats	#绵羊 Sheep	#禽肉 Poultry Meat	#兔肉 Rabbit Meat
总计	**Total**	**134238**	**361576**	**49625**	**8030**	**301500**	**72390**	**407758**	**102100**	**3314**
乌鲁木齐市	**Urumqi City**	**61333**	**17162**	**2161**	**199**	**17418**	**4223**	**12020**	**7947**	**33**
#乌鲁木齐县	Urumqi County	11127	2931	1613	122	82	1002	4499	815	28
克拉玛依市	**Karamay City**	**10714**	**540**	**16**		**8776**	**164**	**551**	**667**	
吐鲁番地区	**TurpanAdministrative Offices**	**40853**	**10283**	**222**	**100**	**1572**	**2790**	**23890**	**1966**	**30**
吐鲁番市	Turpan City	21050	4031	120		710	1462	13527	1200	
鄯善县	Shanshan [piqan]County	10542	1800	60	40	750	1000	6511	381	
托克逊县	Toksun County	9261	4452	42	60	112	328	3852	385	30
哈密地区	**Hami [Kumul]Administrative Offices**	**52729**	**8252**	**523**	**668**	**18684**	**3692**	**18155**	**2398**	**14**
哈密市	Hami [Kumul]City	24442	5000	86	169	4658	1843	10708	1807	13
巴里坤哈萨克自治县	Barkol KazakAutonomous County	20080	2587	259	372	9459	1170	5564	518	1
伊吾县	Yiwu [Araturuk]County	8207	665	178	127	4567	679	1883	73	
昌吉回族自治州	**Changji Hui Autonomous Prefecture**	**530168**	**81584**	**4910**	**2588**	**195350**	**10073**	**78070**	**156544**	**215**
昌吉市	Changji City	103608	15587	794	352	39666	2768	12991	31202	171
阜康市	Fukang City	68317	9791	411	108	14559	2309	10474	30657	
呼图壁县	Hutubi County	92004	20309	1865	1217	21459	716	9855	36553	22
玛纳斯县	Manas County	67985	6175	573	85	27895	562	12955	19731	6
奇台县	Qitai County	124758	13904	204	125	75783	1422	16003	16990	13
吉木萨尔县	Jimsar County	47464	10363	334	55	9939	1036	9364	16278	3
木垒哈萨克自治县	Mori Kazak Autonomous County	26032	5455	729	646	6049	1260	6428	5133	
伊犁哈萨克自治州	**Ili Kazak Autonomous Prefecture**	**495534**	**173765**	**33164**	**2428**	**92904**	**18797**	**132078**	**40939**	**198**
伊犁州直属县(市)	**Counties (Cities) Direct Under Ili Prefecture**	**254717**	**93646**	**22651**	**252**	**51173**	**3787**	**57470**	**24510**	**117**
伊宁市	Yining [Gulja]City	12680	4528	521	30	3472	179	2396	1463	2
奎屯市	Kuytun City	4262	60			3815	6	97	284	
伊宁县	Yining [Gulja]County	46448	20300	1665	32	10662	1170	7395	4800	
察布查尔锡伯自治县	Qapqal Xibe Autonomous County	18163	6048	750		5784	335	3373	1494	41
霍城县	Huocheng [korgas]County	34474	7157	2059		9750	308	7834	7254	21
巩留县	Gongliu [Tokkuzlara]County	28729	11032	2987	30	5159	426	4927	4000	40
新源县	Xinyuan [kunes]County	38038	13572	5085		6259	309	10861	1936	9
昭苏县	Zhaosu [mongolkure]County	24616	10845	2850	32	2359	172	7616	731	3
特克斯县	Tekes County	17784	8260	1470	16	1225	388	5768	648	1
尼勒克县	Nilka County	29523	11844	5264	112	2688	494	7203	1900	

注：同 12-25 表。
Note:The same applies to 12-25 table following.

12-27 续表 1 Continued

单位：吨 (ton)

地区	Region	合计 Total	#牛 Beef	#马 Horse	#骆驼 Camels	#猪 Pork	#山羊 Goats	#绵羊 Sheep	#禽肉 Poultry Meat	#兔肉 Rabbit Meat
塔城地区	**Tacheng [Tarbagatai] Administrative Officess**	**164280**	**44266**	**7309**	**1082**	**37617**	**10698**	**50017**	**13101**	**49**
塔城市	Tacheng [Qoqek] City	13714	3713	701	93	1348	707	5692	1420	7
乌苏市	Usu City	35666	7904	1824	288	12443	3438	8127	1541	10
额敏县	Emin [Dorbiljin] County	26494	5790	1104	180	7250	2154	8708	1308	
沙湾县	Shawan County	44972	11835	285	45	14010	1448	8940	8362	32
托里县	Toli County	18951	6916	1313	224	1225	1265	7903	105	
裕民县	Yumin [Qagantokay] County	11558	3956	912	216	493	510	5117	352	
和布克赛尔蒙古自治县	Hoboksar Mongol Autonomous County	12925	4152	1170	36	848	1176	5530	13	
阿勒泰地区	**Altay Administrative Offices**	**76537**	**35853**	**3204**	**1094**	**4114**	**4312**	**24591**	**3328**	**32**
阿勒泰市	Altay City	16860	9585	936	378	488	444	4780	229	11
布尔津县	Burqin County	11219	7074	282	48	1020	457	1902	436	
富蕴县	Fuyun [Koktokay] County	15077	4680	663	340	217	1066	6700	1395	16
福海县	Fuhai [Burultokay] County	11260	3970	242	60	1981	710	3947	347	3
哈巴河县	Habahe [Kaba] County	11474	7329	336	56	96	633	2779	243	2
青河县	Qinghe [Qinggil] County	6099	1815	425	140	240	805	2120	554	
吉木乃县	Jeminay County	4548	1400	320	72	72	197	2363	124	
博尔塔拉蒙古自治州	**Bortala Mongol Autonomous Prefecture**	**22010**	**4019**	**610**	**54**	**5984**	**933**	**8507**	**1836**	**18**
博乐市	Bole [Bortala] City	10369	1862	142	33	3576	248	3310	1176	
精河县	Jinghe [Jing] County	5823	834	122	1	1128	523	2797	411	6
温泉县	Wenquan [Araxang] County	5818	1323	346	20	1280	162	2400	249	12
巴音郭楞蒙古自治州	**Bayangol Mongol Autonomous Prefecture**	**83977**	**14138**	**1384**	**289**	**24068**	**6721**	**26563**	**9604**	**183**
库尔勒市	Korla City	18818	2074	2		5687	536	4256	6124	43
轮台县	Luntai [Bugur] County	8783	582	12		2761	1130	3668	508	3
尉犁县	Yuli [Lopnur] County	4972	864	10		442	1543	1738	342	15
若羌县	Ruoqiang [Qarkilik] County	2013	211	18	6	760	138	672	120	9
且末县	Qiemo [Qarqan] County	7619	1667	107	105	884	1112	3275	101	30
焉耆回族自治县	Yanqi Hui Autonomous County	10866	3663	70		2258	1080	2811	852	75
和静县	Hejing County	19821	4072	1053	38	5436	332	8169	416	6
和硕县	Hoxud County	6005	544	70	140	2342	638	1393	863	
博湖县	Bohu [Bagrax] County	5080	461	42		3498	212	581	278	2
阿克苏地区	**Aksu Administrative Offices**	**192881**	**43097**	**3307**	**448**	**31947**	**15092**	**51291**	**33439**	**34**
阿克苏市	Aksu City	49142	11710	210		14975	1320	8330	12220	
温宿县	Wensu [Onsu] County	20324	5706	432	25	2582	1739	5334	4204	2
库车县	Kuqa County	50412	9047	658		4673	4178	18346	6711	

12-27 续表 2 Continued

单位：吨 (ton)

地区	Region	合计 Total	#牛 Beef	#马 Horse	#骆驼 Camels	#猪 Pork	#山羊 Goats	#绵羊 Sheep	#禽肉 Poultry Meat	#兔肉 Rabbit Meat
沙雅县	Xayar County	11261	2285	80		2212	1884	2562	2160	32
新和县	Xinhe [Toksu] County	7241	2335	210		256	160	2098	1836	
拜城县	Baicheng [Bay] County	21141	4636	415	15	5712	1925	5396	2455	
乌什县	Wushi [Uxturpan] County	17215	4672	1209	198	360	2443	4120	3262	
阿瓦提县	Awat County	13430	2386	49		1177	812	4120	172	
柯坪县	Kalpin County	2715	320	44	210		631	985	419	
克孜勒苏柯尔克孜自治州	**Kizilsu Kirgiz Autonomous Prefecture**	**37981**	**13749**	**1565**	**375**	**760**	**3522**	**13582**	**4424**	**4**
阿图什市	Artux City	14743	5778	282	45	549	1279	5210	1600	
阿克陶县	Akto County	13239	6088	137	47	96	685	4495	1691	
阿合奇县	Akqi County	4576	928	876	42	115	627	1890	98	
乌恰县	Wuqia [Ulugqat] County	5423	955	270	241		931	1987	1035	4
喀什地区	**Kashgar [Kaxgar] Administrative Offices**	**359609**	**81603**	**564**	**190**	**21402**	**3625**	**155292**	**88310**	**121**
喀什市	Kashgar [Kaxgar] City	24324	5880			3004	109	13375	1909	
疏附县	Shufu County	40218	13038	30	15	2916	365	18939	4370	
疏勒县	Shule County	36948	8897	15	30	4418	80	13469	8806	
英吉沙县	Yengisar County	19839	7906	27	9	221	76	7332	3774	
泽普县	Zepu [Poskam] County	23622	3111	24		4059	97	6997	9098	
莎车县	Shache [Yarkant] County	51366	7963	20		2400	380	24495	15697	121
叶城县	Yecheng [Kagilik] County	51727	11480	144	48	1063	463	20494	16345	
麦盖提县	Makit County	19635	3973	50		1154	322	9906	3940	
岳普湖县	Yopurga County	14993	3413	36	3	168	227	5917	4319	
伽师县	Jiashi [Payzawat] County	41177	5775	108		240	600	19727	12477	
巴楚县	Bachu [Maralbexi] County	30621	7105	80		1759	486	13241	7575	
塔什库尔干塔吉克自治县	Taxkorgan Tajik Autonomous County	5139	3062	30	85		420	1400		
和田地区	**Hotan Administrative Offices**	**97192**	**23751**	**396**	**340**	**2005**	**2473**	**51798**	**16347**	**82**
和田市	Hotan City	12390	3484	11		1635	35	4752	2473	
和田县	Hotan County	13280	3614	66	68	38	167	6719	2606	2
墨玉县	Moyu [Karakax] County	22291	7176	11	17	53	155	12176	2690	13
皮山县	Pishan [Guma] County	10051	858	44	51	30	341	6019	2685	23
洛浦县	Lop County	9585	2808	11	17	38	89	5054	1566	2
策勒县	Qira County	7642	546	55	51	105	165	5286	1429	5
于田县	Yutian [Keriya] County	17263	5005	187	68	68	792	8948	2161	34
民丰县	Minfeng [Niya] County	4690	260	11	68	38	729	2844	737	3
生产建设兵团	**Xinjiang Production and Construction Group**	**324583**	**44214**	**1495**	**340**	**160923**	**7599**	**69441**	**36519**	**2381**

12-28 水产品产量和养殖面积
Output of Aquatic Products and Cultured Area

年 份 Year	地 区 Region	水产品产量(吨) Aquatic Products (ton)	#养殖产量 Cultured Output	养殖面积(公顷) Culture Area (hectare)
1985		8958	3403	32775
1990		23217	15401	68838
1995		44432	35341	72538
1996		47890	38876	79006
1997		52366	42656	75895
1998		53391	44557	67473
1999		55840	48068	70524
2000		60065	50974	69806
2001		60876	50902	63340
2002		63906	55159	62629
2003		67278	57244	67374
2004		73296	60405	74996
2005		79320	65571	76037
2006		84539	71440	76606
2007		88879	78639	77590
2008		92587	82040	73909
2009		97037	87863	73433
2010		101063	90913	73289
2011		116916	103315	74000
2012		125283	112590	71108
乌鲁木齐市	Urumqi City	7264	7264	2292
克拉玛依市	Karamay City	623	373	70
吐鲁番地区	Turpan Administrative Offices	400	400	43
哈密地区	Hami [Kumul] Administrative Offices	1146	1103	771
昌吉回族自治州	Changji Hui Autonomous Prefecture	17715	17715	3040
伊犁哈萨克自治州	Ili Kazak Autonomous Prefecture	23359	19950	14024
伊犁州直属县(市)	Counties (Cities) Direct Under Ili Prefecture	13241	13087	934
塔城地区	Tacheng [Tarbagatai] Administrative Offices	3069	2494	2957
阿勒泰地区	Altay Administrative Offices	7049	4369	10133
博尔塔拉蒙古自治州	Bortala Mongol Autonomous Prefecture	1569	815	1123
巴音郭楞蒙古自治州	Bayangol Mongol Autonomous Prefecture	11559	5037	3084
阿克苏地区	Aksu Administrative Offices	13643	13263	1223
克孜勒苏柯尔克孜自治州	Kizilsu Kirgiz Autonomous Prefecture	300	150	220
喀什地区	Kashgar [Kaxgar] Administrative Offices	10069	9666	8632
和田地区	Hotan Administrative Offices	2267	2044	475
生产建设兵团	Xinjiang Production and Construction Group	35369	34810	36111

12-29 乡镇企业主要指标
Main Indicators of Township Enterprises

单位：万元 (10 000 yuan)

年份 Year	地区 Region	企业个数（个） Number of Enterprises (unit)	从业人数（人） Employees of Enterprises (person)	总产值 Total Output Value
	1985	98826	367753	75179
	1990	144281	464027	222218
	1991	145762	472332	314765
	1992	155711	498132	402139
	1993	202274	600687	553616
	1994	250037	686425	924082
	1995	281130	745291	1319217
	1996	282733	781784	1622442
	1997	43548	355585	1219032
	1998	269048	712490	2457410
	1999	297147	749205	2736766
	2000	316524	806368	3022076
	2001	334694	824499	3316049
	2002	307963	866661	3629499
	2003	354640	880874	4119555
	2004	368553	933473	4562898
	2005	366883	954411	4994156
	2006	368724	990365	5574730
	2007	377385	1037023	4265895
	2008	378343	1063023	8629234
	2009	378983	1115703	8486719
	2010	383653	1167548	9574341
	2011	391680	1219552	12067084
	2012	398340	1271549	14102422
乌鲁木齐市	Urumqi City	20133	69075	1167342
克拉玛依市	Karamay City	141	591	10553
石河子市	Shihezi City	3020	21685	156172
吐鲁番地区	Turpan Administrative Offices	21103	50655	370546
哈密地区	Hami [Kumul] Administrative Offices	10461	30360	249062
昌吉回族自治州	Changji Hui Autonomous Prefecture	39170	148511	3578065
伊犁州直属县(市)	Counties (Cities) Direct Under Ili Prefecture	52543	167159	1916993
塔城地区	Tacheng [Tarbagatai] Administrative Offices	26660	110291	1738612
阿勒泰地区	Altay Administrative Offices	25018	60237	435633
博尔塔拉蒙古自治州	Bortala Mongol Autonomous Prefecture	8852	36821	397272
巴音郭楞蒙古自治州	Bayangol Mongol Autonomous Prefecture	26062	85786	2327079
阿克苏地区	Aksu Administrative Offices	47237	141170	651136
克孜勒苏柯尔克孜自治州	Kizilsu Kirgiz Autonomous Prefecture	9398	22208	93557
喀什地区	Kashgar [Kaxgar] Administrative Offices	64200	172955	665809
和田地区	Hotan Administrative Offices	44342	154045	344591

12-29 续表 Continued

单位：万元 (10 000 yuan)

年份 Year	地区 Region	营业收入 Business Income	利润总额 Total Profits	上缴税金 Total Taxes
	1985	105072	9357	3136
	1990	249906	8614	5206
	1991	299890	25974	13747
	1992	374810	34644	16976
	1993	584089	51880	27354
	1994	957701	75439	69494
	1995	1493924	110656	76479
	1996	1927425	136410	76479
	1997	1128271	43337	48945
	1998	2455629	156578	82365
	1999	2742029	164949	93490
	2000	3071497	191764	100444
	2001	3377589	211439	108864
	2002	3739524	225723	126732
	2003	4276322	264661	137880
	2004	4757808	304998	152243
	2005	5164593	294021	164604
	2006	5806803	332070	190833
	2007	6776709	318943	228386
	2008	7548573	563293	249122
	2009	8547580	671806	271759
	2010	9596967	756277	306105
	2011	12287481	937847	374096
	2012	14250102	1083776	420174
乌鲁木齐市	Urumqi City	1180860	57510	29005
克拉玛依市	Karamay City	10553	1474	580
石河子市	Shihezi City	210130	6318	2815
吐鲁番地区	Turpan Administrative Offices	353909	37993	18195
哈密地区	Hami [Kumul] Administrative Offices	226572	15439	12868
昌吉回族自治州	Changji Hui Autonomous Prefecture	3500310	245530	95557
伊犁州直属县(市)	Counties (Cities) Direct Under Ili Prefecture	2036573	153766	37801
塔城地区	Tacheng [Tarbagatai] Administrative Offices	1522736	171676	44251
阿勒泰地区	Altay Administrative Offices	492128	40368	15943
博尔塔拉蒙古自治州	Bortala Mongol Autonomous Prefecture	385717	13019	8479
巴音郭楞蒙古自治州	Bayangol Mongol Autonomous Prefecture	2633129	177169	100616
阿克苏地区	Aksu Administrative Offices	634313	49110	21357
克孜勒苏柯尔克孜自治州	Kizilsu Kirgiz Autonomous Prefecture	95120	6510	3471
喀什地区	Kashgar [Kaxgar] Administrative Offices	671840	66877	16470
和田地区	Hotan Administrative Offices	296212	41017	12766

主要统计指标解释

农林牧渔业总产值 指以货币表现的农、林、牧、渔业全部产品和对农林牧渔业生产活动进行的各种支持性服务活动的价值总量，它反映一定时期内农林牧渔业生产总规模和总成果。1957年以前的农林牧渔业总产值中包括了厩肥和农民自给性手工业(如农民自制衣服、鞋、袜，自己从事粮食初步加工等)。1958年及以后，林业中增加了村及村以下竹木采伐产值；牧业中取消了厩肥产值；副业中取消了农民自给性手工业产值，增加了村及村以下办的工业产值；渔业中增加了海洋捕捞水产品产值。1980年及以后，在副业中增加了农民家庭兼营工业商品部分的产值。从1984年起村及村以下工业产值划归工业。从1993年起取消副业，将野生动物的捕猎划入牧业，野生植物采集和农民家庭兼营商品性工业划归农业。从2003年起，执行新的国民经济行业分类标准，农林牧渔业总产值中包括了农林牧渔服务业产值。林业中增加了森林采运业产值。农业中取消了家庭兼营商品性工业产值，将野生林产品的采集划归林业。

农林牧渔业总产值的计算方法通常是按农、林、牧、渔业产品及其副产品的产量分别乘以各自单位产品价格求得；少数生产周期较长，当年没有产品或产品产量不易统计的，则采用间接方法匡算其产值；然后将四业产品产值及农林牧渔服务业产值相加即为农林牧渔业总产值。

粮食产量 指全社会的产量。包括国有经济经营的、集体统一经营的和农民家庭经营的粮食产量，还包括工矿企业办的农场和其他生产单位的产量。粮食除包括稻谷、小麦、玉米、高粱、谷子及其他杂粮外，还包括薯类和豆类。其产量计算方法，豆类按去豆荚后的干豆计算；薯类(包括甘薯和马铃薯，不包括芋头和木薯)1963年以前按每4公斤鲜薯折1公斤粮食计算，从1964年开始改为按5公斤鲜薯折1公斤粮食计算。城市郊区作为蔬菜的薯类(如马铃薯等)按鲜品计算，并且不作粮食统计。其他粮食一律按脱粒后的原粮计算。1989年以前全国粮食产量数据主要靠全面报表取得，1989年开始使用抽样调查数据。

棉花产量 指全社会的产量。包括春播棉和夏播棉。产量按皮棉计算。不包括木棉。

油料产量 指全部油料作物的生产量。包括花生、油菜籽、芝麻、向日葵籽、胡麻籽(亚麻籽)和其他油料。不包括大豆、木本油料和野生油料。花生以带壳干花生计算。

水产品产量 指人工养殖的水产品和天然生长的水产品的捕捞量。包括海水的鱼类、虾蟹类、贝类和藻类以及内陆水域的鱼类、虾蟹类和贝类，不包括淡水生植物。水产品产量是通过各级水产和统计部门逐级上报取得数据。1995年及以前，贝类中牡蛎按鲜肉计算；蚶、蛤、蛙按5斤鲜品折1斤计算。1996 年以后则统一按鲜品计算。

猪、牛、羊肉产量 指当年出栏并已屠宰、除去头蹄下水后带骨肉(即胴体重)的重量。包括全社会范围内的产量。1996年以前为全面统计并逐级上报数据。1999年以后，国家统计局在部分地区开展了猪、牛、羊、禽等主要畜禽品种的抽样调查，并用抽样数据作为国家定案数据使用。2008年，建立了主要畜禽监测调查制度，猪、牛、羊、禽等主要畜禽数据均以抽样调查数为法定数据。

期初(末)畜禽存栏头(只)数 指报告期初(末)农村各种合作经济组织和国营农场、农民个人、机关、团体、学校、工矿企业、部队等单位以及城镇居民饲养的大牲畜、猪、羊、家禽等畜禽的存栏数。数据上报方式及数据调整情况同猪、牛、羊肉产量。

农作物播种面积 指实际播种或移植有农作物的面积。凡是实际种植农作物的面积，不论种植在耕地上还是种植在非耕地上，均包括在农作物播种面积中。在播种季节基本结束后，因遭灾而重新改种和补种的农作物面积，也包括在内。目前，农作物播种面积主要包括粮食、棉花、油料、糖料、麻类、烟叶、蔬菜和瓜类、药材和其它农作物等十大类。

有效灌溉面积 指具有一定的水源，地块比较平整，灌溉工程或设备已经配套，在一般年景下能够进行正常灌溉的耕地面积。在一般情况下，有效灌溉面积应等于灌溉工程或设备已经配备，能够进行正常灌溉的水田和水浇地面积之和。它是反映我国农田水利建设的重要指标。

农用化肥施用量 指本年内实际用于农业生产的化肥数量，包括氮肥、磷肥、钾肥和复合肥。化肥施用量要求按折纯量计算数量。折纯量是指把氮肥、磷肥、钾肥分别按含氮、含五氧化二磷、含氧化钾的百分之百成份进行折算后的数量。复合肥按其所含主要成分折算。公式为:

折纯量= 实物量×某种化肥有效成份含量的百分比

农业机械总动力 指全部农业机械动力的额定功率之和。农业机械是指用于种植业、畜牧业、渔业、农产品初加工、农用运输和农田基本建设等活动的机械及设备。农机总动力按使用能源不同分为以下四部分：

柴油发动机动力：指全部柴油发动机额定功率之和；

汽油发动机动力：指全部汽油发动机额定功率之和；

电动机动力：指全部电动机（含潜水电泵的电动机）额定功率之和；

其他机械动力：指采用柴油、汽油、电力之外的其他能源，如水力、风力、煤炭、太阳能等动力机械功率之和。这个指标的统计数据主要来源于农机部门。

Explanatory Notes on Main Statistical Indicators

Gross Output Value of Agriculture, Forestry, Animal Husbandry and Fishery refers to the total value of products of agriculture, forestry, animal husbandry and fishery, and total value of services in support of agriculture, forestry, animal husbandry and fishery activities. It reflects the total scale and results of agricultural production during a given period. Prior to 1957, China's gross agricultural output value included barnyard manure and handicraft products for self-consumption (clothes, shoes, stockings, and initial grain processing undertaken by peasants). Since 1958, cutting and felling of bamboo and trees by villages and other cooperative organizations under villages have been included in forestry; value of barnyard manure has been excluded from animal husbandry; self consumed handicrafts have not been included from sideline occupations, while the output value of industries run by villages and cooperative organizations under village has been included in sideline occupations; and the output value of fish catches by motor fishing boats has been added to fishery. Since 1980, the value of handicraft products made for sale by individuals in households has been added to sideline occupations. Since 1984, industries run by villages and under villages have been included in the sector of industry. Since 1993, the subdivision of sideline occupations has been cancelled, and the hunting of wild animals has been classified into animal husbandry, and the gathering of wild plants and commodity industry run by rural household have been included in farming. A new industrial classification of economic activities was introduced in 2003. Under the new classification, value of services to agriculture, forestry, animal husbandry and fishery is included in the gross output value of agriculture, value of wood felling and transport is included in forestry, value of industrial output by rural households is not included in agriculture. The First Agriculture Census of China revealed some discrepancy between the production of animal products from the annual reports and that from the census. According to the result of the First Agriculture census, efforts were made to adjust the annual reports of animal husbandry output and the output value of animal husbandry to make the figures from the annual reports consistent with the census data. "The Classification of Products for Statistical Purposes" implemented in 2010 made relevant revision on the output value of agriculture and forestry in 2009.

Gross output value of agriculture is obtained by multiplying the output of each product or by-product by its price, resulting in the output value of each single item. For a small number of products, annual output of which is not available or difficult to get due to the long production (growing) process involved, the output value is estimated through an indirect approach. The sum of output values of all products of agriculture, forestry, animal husbandry and fishery and services in support to those industries is then equal to the gross output value of agriculture.

Grain Output refers to the total output in the whole country including grains produced by State farms, collective units, rural households, as well as by farms affiliated to industrial and mining enterprises and other production units. Grain includes rice, wheat, corn, sorghum, millet and other miscellaneous grains as well as tubers and beans. Output of beans refers to dry beans without pods. The output of tubers (sweet potatoes and potatoes, not including taros and cassava) are converted into that of grain at the ratio 4:1, i.e. 4 kilograms of fresh tubers were equivalent to 1 kilogram of grain up to 1963. Since 1964 the ratio for conversion has been 5:1. Tubers supplied as vegetables (such as potatoes) in cities and suburbs are calculated as fresh vegetables and their output is not included in the output of grain. Output of all other grains refers to husked grain. Data on grain production before 1989 were obtained through the Comprehensive Statistical Reporting System. Since 1989, data from sample surveys are used..

Cotton Output refers to cotton production in the whole country including cotton planted in spring and in autumn. Output is measured as the weight of ginned cotton. Ceiba is not included.

Output of Oil-bearing Crops refers to the total production of oil-bearing crops of various kinds, including peanuts (dry, in shell), rapeseeds, sesame, sunflower seeds, flax seeds, and other oil-bearing crops. Soybeans, oil-bearing woody plants, and wild oil-bearing crops are not included.

Output of Aquatic Products refers to catches of both artificially cultured and naturally grown aquatic products, including fish, shrimps, crabs and shellfish in sea and inland water as well as seaweed. Freshwater plants are not included. Data on output of aquatic products are reported by aquatic product and statistical agencies level by level. Before 1995, among the shellfish, oyster was counted as fresh meat; 5 kilograms of ark shell, clams and frogs are equivalent to 1 kilogram of fresh aquatic products; they have all been counted as fresh aquatic products since 1996.

Output of Pork, Beef, and Mutton refers to the meat of slaughtered hogs, cattle, sheep and goats with head, feet, and offal taken away. Data refers to the production of the whole country. Before 1996, it was a comprehensive reporting from the lower level to the upper one. The First Agricultural Census of China in 1996 revealed some discrepancy between the production of animal products from the annual reports and that from the census. Efforts were made to adjust the output value of animal husbandry to make the figures from the annual reports consistent with the census data. Since 1999, the NBS conducted sample surveys for the major animal husbandry products, such as hogs, cattle, sheep and goats and fowls, and the data from sample surveys are used as national finalized data. Those products, which are not covered by the sample survey, are still reported by statistical agencies level by level. In 2007, the data on animal husbandry from 2000 to 2006 were revised according to the results of the Second Agriculture Census of China. In 2008, A Monitoring and Survey Program was set up on main livestock, the data on the main livestock such as hog, cattle, sheep and poultry became the official data based on the sampling survey.

Number of Livestock or Poultry in Stock at Beginning (or End) of Period refers to the total number of large animals, pigs, sheep, fowls, etc. raised by rural cooperative organizations, State farms, rural individuals, government agencies, schools, industrial and mining enterprises, army, and urban residents at the beginning (or end) of the reference period. Data reporting system and data adjustment are the same as that in the output of pork, beef and mutton.

Sown Area of Crops refers to area of land sown or transplanted with crops regardless of being in cultivated area or non-cultivated area. Area of land re-sown due to natural disasters is also included. At present, the sown area of crops mainly include the following 10 categories of crops: grain, oil-bearing crops, cotton, hemp, sugar crops, tobacco, medicinal materials, vegetables, melons and other farm crops.

Effective Irrigated Area refers to area of land that are effectively irrigated, i.e. relatively level land, where there are water sources or complete sets of irrigation facilities to lift and move adequate water for irrigation purpose under normal conditions. Under normal situations, irrigated area is the sum of watered fields and irrigated fields where irrigation systems orequipment have been installed for regular irrigation purpose. It is an important indicator to reflect the farmland water conservancy construction in China.

Consumption of Chemical Fertilizers in Agriculture refers to the quantity of chemical fertilizers applied in agriculture in the year, including nitrogenous fertilizer, phosphate fertilizer, potash fertilizer, and compound fertilizer. The consumption of chemical fertilizers is calculated in terms of volume of effective components by means of converting the gross weight of the respective fertilizers into weight containing effective component (e.g. nitrogen content in nitrogenous fertilizer, phosphorous pentoxide contents in phosphate fertilizer, and potassium oxide contents in potash fertilizer). Compound fertilizer is converted in regard to its major components. The formula is:

Volume of effective component= physical quantity× effective component of certain chemical fertilizer (%)

Total Power of Agricultural Machinery refers to the total rated capacity of all agricultural machinery. Agricultural machinery refers to the machineries and equipments which are used for activities of planting, animal husbandry, fishery, primary processing of agricultural products, agricultural transport and infrastructure construction of farmland. Total power of agricultural machinery is grouped into four parts according to the energy used:

Diesel engine power refers to the total rated capacity of all diesel engines.

Gasoline engine power refers to the total rated capacity of all gasoline engines.

Motor power refers to the total rated capacity of all motors (include submersible pump motors).

Other mechanical powers refer to the total mechanical capacity of the sources of energy besides diesel, gasoline and motor power, such as hydro power, wind power, coal and solar energy.

Data are mainly from agricultural machinery agencies.

新疆统计年鉴
XINJIANG STATISTICAL YEARBOOK

13

工 业

INDUSTRY

简要说明

本篇资料的主要内容及来源

本篇资料反映了新疆工业的基本情况，主要包括：按登记注册类型、轻重工业、企业规模、工业行业大类等分组的主要经济指标，指标包括：单位数、工业总产值、资产总计、负债合计、主营业务收入、主营业务成本、主营业务税金及附加、利润总额、应交增值税、总资产贡献率、资产负债率、成本费用利润率、全员劳动生产率、主要工业产品产量等。

本章还包括国有控股工业企业、大中型工业企业的主要经济指标，按工业行业大类、轻重工业、企业规模等主要分组数据。

本篇资料中工业行业分类按2011年《国民经济行业分类标准》划分；2010年以前企业大中小型划分执行《统计上大中小型企业划分办法（暂行）》标准；自2011年开始，大中小微型企业划分标准执行《国家统计局关于印发统计上大中小微型企业划分办法的通知》（国统字[2011]75号）。

本篇资料由新疆维吾尔自治区统计局工业交通统计处根据工业统计年度报表中有关资料整理提供。

Brief Introduction

Main Content and Source of Data

Data in this chapter reflect the basic condition of industrial sector including the gross industrial output and indices of industrial enterprises; Main indicator on economic and economic benefit of industrial enterprises above designated size by status of registration, light & heavy industries, size of enterprises, industrial sector. Main indicators including number of enterprises, gross industrial output value, value added of industry, total assets, total liabilities, revenue from principal business, cost of principle business, taxes and other charges on principal business, total profits, value added tax payable, ratio of total assets to industrial output value, assets liability ration, ratio of profits to cost, output of major industrial products, main economic indicator of state-owned and non-state-owned industrial enterprises.

This chapter covers main indicators on economic and economic benefit of all state-owned and non-state-owned industrial enterprises, cooperative enterprises, industrial enterprises with funds from Hong Kong, Macao and Taiwan, foreign funded industrial enterprises, and large & medium-sized enterprises.

In this chapter,industrial sectors are classified in accordance with Classification Standards of Industrial Sectors in National Economy 2011;Piror to 2010 industrial sectors are classified in accordance with Classification Standards;From 2010,the classification of medium- and Iarge-sized enterprises complies with the Notification of National Bureau of Statistics on Printing and Issuing the Measures for Statistical Classification of Mini-,Small- Medium-and Large-sized Entrprises(Gtz[2011]No.75).

Data in this chapter are collected and compiled by the Department of Industry and transport, XBS in accordance with the annual report of industrial statistics.

13-1 主要年份工业总产值
Gross Industrial Output Value in Main Years

单位:亿元 (100 million yuan)

年 份 Year	工业总产值 Gross Industrial Output Value	国有工业 State-owned Enterprises	集体工业 Collective-owned Enterprises	其它经济类型工业 Enterprises of Other Types of Ownership
1978	33.91	30.22	3.69	
1980	40.71	36.20	4.50	0.01
1985	86.78	73.18	11.93	1.67
1990	219.92	176.52	36.72	6.68
1995	593.43	461.31	89.24	42.88
2000	1061.29	258.93	72.78	729.58
2005	2358.83	236.18	17.29	2105.36
2006	2894.88	272.06	16.14	2606.68
2007	3471.51	358.28	17.29	3095.94
2008	4639.02	387.53	15.70	4235.79
2009	4184.50	404.01	15.61	3764.88
2010	5766.51	382.00	25.54	5358.97
2011	7105.31	654.79	29.44	6421.08
2012	7886.25	713.43	20.41	7152.41

13-2 主要年份工业总产值指数
Indices of Gross Industrial Output Value in Main Years

(1978 年=100)

年 份 Year	工业总产值 Gross Industrial Output Value	国有工业 State-owned Enterprises	集体工业 Collective-owned Enterprises	其它经济类型工业 Enterprises of Other Types of Ownership
1978	100.0	100.0	100.0	
1980	117.7	118.0	113.2	(1981 年=100)
1985	220.6	199.5	428.2	851.7
1990	380.3	326.0	915.9	2096.1
1995	670.8	506.1	2104.5	7441.5
2000	1000.4	227.3	1763.6	66265.2
2005	1821.8	218.2	388.9	160072.4
2006	2057.1	246.3	344.8	180922.4
2007	2322.8	319.9	339.3	201240.8
2008	2707.5	336.5	272.4	237624.5
2009	2942.2	353.4	289.2	259031.4
2010	3331.8	325.7	431.9	298801.3
2011	3721.3	527.1	451.7	323156.5
2012	4271.9	576.4	328.3	373388.6

13-3 规模以上工业企业分行业工业增加值

Value-added of Industrial Enterprises above Designated Size by Sector

单位: 万元

行　业	Sector	2011	2012
总　计	**Total**	**25635749.7**	**27241641.4**
按行业分	**Grouped by Industrial Sector**		
煤炭开采和洗选业	Mining and Washing of Coal	1125752.9	1421680.7
石油和天然气开采业	Extraction of Petroleum and Natural Gas	13118622.6	12000740.1
黑色金属矿采选业	Mining and Processing of Ferrous Metals Ores	493050.7	510977.7
有色金属矿采选业	Mining and Processing of Nonferrous Metals Ores	417964.0	411084.2
非金属矿采选业	Mining and Processing of Nonmetal Ores	69693.0	70077.1
开采辅助活动	Mining Activities	543976.1	780382.0
农副食品加工业	Processing of Food from Agricultural Products	407736.7	490161.9
食品制造业	Manufacture of Food	228323.5	279449.2
酒、饮料和精制茶制造业	Manufacture of Beverage	278720.3	370536.8
烟草制品业	Manufacture of Tobacco	236486.5	276304.7
纺织业	Manufacture of Textile	259999.1	240076.8
纺织服装、服饰业	Manufacture of Textile Wearing Apparel, Footware and Caps	8119.5	15727.3
皮革、毛皮、羽毛(绒)及其制品业	Leather, Fur, Feather and Related Products Manufacturing	18521.1	15855.5
木材加工及木、竹、藤、棕、草制品业	Processing of Timber, Wood, Bamboo, Cane, Grass Products	12561.8	16489.0
家具制造业	Manufacture of Furniture	26916.6	10222.3
造纸及纸制品业	Manufacture of Paper and Paper Products	47117.2	52812.4
印刷业和记录媒介的复制	Printing and Copying of Medium for Record	14617.8	16297.5
文教、工美、体育和娱乐用品制造业	Manufacture of Articles for Culture,Education,Sports and Entertainment	1372.8	13306.7
石油加工、炼焦及核燃料加工业	Oil Processing, Coking and Nuclear Fuel Processing	2022820.5	2135694.8

13-3 续表 Continued

单位: 万元

行　　业	Sector	2011	2012
化学原料及化学制品制造业	Raw Chemical Material and Chemical Products	1382059.8	2020278.1
医药制造业	Manufacture of Medicine	40289.0	52322.7
化学纤维制造业	Manufacture of Chemical Fiber	151251.4	128137.1
橡胶和塑料制品业	Manufacture of Rubber Products	130528.3	187141.1
非金属矿物制品业	Manufacture of Nonmetal Mineral Products	811437.1	818196.0
黑色金属冶炼及压延加工业	Smelting and Pressing of Ferrous Metals	868133.9	899757.0
有色金属冶炼及压延加工业	Smelting and Pressing of Nonferrous Metals	312094.1	564780.3
金属制品业	Manufacture of Metal Products	103312.9	88202.6
通用设备制造业	Manufacture of General Purpose Machinery	17264.7	29255.8
专用设备制造业	Manufacture of Special Purpose Machinery	62778.8	74051.7
汽车制造业	Manufacture of Automobile	1070.4	6058.5
铁路、船舶、航空航天和其他运输设备制造业	Manufouture of Railroads,Ships,Aerospace and Other Transportation Equipment	1085.3	1310.6
电气机械及器材制造业	Manufacture of Electric Equipment and Machinery	460713.4	345111.3
计算机、通信和其他电子设备制造业	Manufalture of Communication Equipment Computers and Other Electronic Equipment	60933.0	472.7
仪器仪表制造业	Manufacture of Measuring Instruments	1547.9	1226.7
其他制造业	Others	10027.4	-2970.9
废弃资源综合利用业	Recycling and Disposal of Waste	21707.3	24600.6
金属制品、机械和设备修理业	Manufacture and Repair of Metal Products and Machinery	2856.4	5290.6
电力、热力生产和供应业	Production and Supply of Electricity and Therma	1769022.4	2717733.4
燃气生产和供应业	Production and Supply of Gas	72113.9	118854.7
水的生产和供应业	Production and Supply of Water	23149.8	33954.1

13-4 规模以上工业企业主要经济指标

单位：万元 (2012 年)

项 目	Item	企业单位数(个) Number of Enterprises (unit)	#亏损企业 Loss- Suffering Enterprises	工业总产值(当年价格) Gross Industrial Output Value (At Current Prices)
总 计	**Total**	**1959**	**524**	**75326674.0**
按登记注册类型分	**By Status of Registration**			
内资企业	Domestic Funded Enterprises	1878	503	73694670.8
国有企业	State-owned Enterprises	124	43	6836834.7
#中央企业	Central Enterprises	63	17	5209041.2
地方企业	Local Enterprises	61	26	1627793.5
#自治区属企业	Autonomous	20	8	822944.2
地区(州、市)属企业	Prefecture or City	7	3	309384.4
县(市)属企业	County or City	24	11	179484.1
集体企业	Collective-owned Enterprises	12	3	175972.8
#自治区属企业	Autonomous	4	2	94502.4
地区(州、市)属企业	Prefecture or City	1		3913.0
县(市)属企业	County or City	4		34715.0
镇属企业	Town	1		18139.5
乡属企业	Village			
股份合作企业	Cooperative Enterprises	5	1	22571.3
联营企业	Joint Ownership Enterprises	10	3	41879.6
#国有联营企业	State Joint Ownership Enterprises	5	2	17821.2
集体联营企业	Collective Joint Ownership Enterprises			
国有与集体联营企业	Joint State-collective Enterprises	1		8203.1
其他联营企业	Other Joint Ownership Enterprises	4	1	15855.3
有限责任公司	Limited Liability Corporations	887	244	23201123.0
#国有独资公司	State Sole funded Corporations	57	24	3611266.5
其他有限责任公司	Other Limited Liability Corporations	830	220	19589856.5
股份有限公司	Share-holding Corporations Ltd.	88	27	34055482.8
私营企业	Private Enterprises	730	180	9153719.5
#私营独资企业	Private-funded Enterprises	43	6	512853.3
私营合伙企业	Private Partnership Enterprises	6		57207.1
私营有限责任公司	Private Limited Liability Corporations	651	165	6931386.7
私营股份有限公司	Private Share-holding Corporations Ltd.	30	9	1652272.4
港、澳、台商投资企业	Enterprises with Funds from Hong Kong, Macao and Taiwan	28	6	597645.5
外商投资企业	Foreign Funded Enterprises	53	15	1034357.7
在总计中：国有控股企业	Of the Total : State-owned and State-holding Enterprises	522	148	53466765.1
在总计中：农村工业	Of the Total : Rural Industry	6	1	22158.7
按轻、重工业分	**Grouped by Light & Heavy Industry**			
轻工业	Light Industry	671	180	8926259.0
以农产品为原料	Using Farm Produces as Raw Materials	621	165	8516325.5
以非农产品为原料	Using Non-Farm Produces as Raw Materials	50	15	409933.5
重工业	Heavy Industry	1288	344	66400415.0
采掘工业	Mining and Quarrying	264	71	20013038.2
原料工业	Raw Material Industry	505	178	38158478.2
加工工业	Manufacturing Industry	519	95	8228898.6
按企业规模分	**Grouped by Size of Enterprises (New Standard)**			
大型企业	Large Enterprises	84	20	48657141.4
中型企业	Medium-sized Enterprises	312	98	11712361.0
小型企业	Small Enterprises	1431	352	14263677.7
微型企业	Min Enterprises	132	54	693493.9

Main Economic Indicators of Industrial Enterprises above Designated Size

(10 000 yuan)

工业销售产值(当年价) Sales Value of Industry Products (At Current Prices)	出口交货值 Delivery Value of Industry Export	实收资本 Total Capital Hold	资产合计 Total Assets	流动资产合计 Total Working Capitals	#产成品 Finished Product	固定资产原价 Net Value of Fixed Assets
73484359.9	**419562.7**	**34363194.1**	**116691728.3**	**36801594.1**	**3796867.5**	**85721657.0**
71992441.9	369317.1	33573068.1	114403670.2	35836126.1	3616819.1	84452308.3
6658353.6	10439.4	2661959.2	12451324.4	3202787.3	135905.6	8891912.5
5187954.8	5149.7	1815531.5	8522001.3	2337922.5	55737.0	6142596.4
1470398.8	5289.7	846427.7	3929323.1	864864.8	80168.6	2749316.1
710802.4		285411.5	1473386.0	321528.3	23349.4	1031175.0
284926.4		29869.8	542557.6	231385.3	20947.9	358304.8
178551.8		499893.4	1556088.4	171361.9	7421.9	1182434.1
175577.3		19380.8	117753.5	69500.0	7142.8	61774.5
95500.6		4359.2	41682.6	30299.5	2370.6	9233.2
4264.6		272.1	1005.7	864.9	71.4	396.6
32969.7		6409.1	32767.3	23785.4	4093.0	12875.9
18139.5			10181.6	6823.3		3779.7
21694.7		6877.9	39162.0	19560.2	7960.1	32369.2
40905.1		25530.3	98596.7	33664.7	1931.3	64141.4
17821.2		16097.4	42433.5	15284.3	593.6	26620.6
8203.1		6700.0	33839.5	7439.0		26351.6
14880.8		2732.9	22323.7	10941.4	1337.7	11169.2
22476297.5	103611.8	8669178.4	41154951.2	13705159.6	1816070.8	26441741.9
3512369.0	194.5	1474287.0	5959521.5	1885852.4	112343.1	3948331.1
18963928.5	103417.3	7194891.4	35195429.7	11819307.2	1703727.7	22493410.8
33993038.4	144003.1	19595888.8	45611948.7	11317070.3	865359.2	44136715.6
8425391.0	109147.1	2569998.0	14777261.3	7409067.1	776093.1	4749953.0
471044.5	5920.1	98403.2	403904.4	172280.6	30245.7	194992.4
55232.0		4813.2	18089.4	8867.0	188.9	10794.0
6366839.6	43833.4	1877230.1	10192508.2	4773004.6	688694.5	3998369.2
1532274.9	59393.6	589551.5	4162759.3	2454914.9	56964.0	545797.4
529957.0	30197.8	340861.5	858066.0	359788.3	76332.7	461071.3
961961.0	20047.8	449264.5	1429992.1	605679.7	103715.7	808277.4
52928947.5	159536.9	27474452.4	78386247.9	19595857.8	1796749.8	71918451.0
20654.2	220.1	56044.2	78117.5	10771.2	760.8	10073.7
8459834.2	270261.3	2559757.0	12184700.9	6107587.6	1284052.7	5533351.3
8078915.1	265212.9	2335784.3	11014925.0	5628847.2	1247944.8	4998952.4
380919.1	5048.4	223972.7	1169775.9	478740.4	36107.9	534398.9
65024525.7	149301.4	31803437.1	104507027.4	30694006.5	2512814.8	80188305.7
19871136.0	6436.0	16775436.7	36234524.7	7902797.2	517356.8	37151132.9
37309315.7	48008.9	12438642.2	52546371.0	14647794.5	1437178.3	38307666.8
7844074.0	94856.5	2589358.2	15726131.7	8143414.8	558279.7	4729506.0
48232524.3	113213.5	24448480.6	67826697.7	17128612.1	1315962.8	58821017.1
10894835.4	114672.5	4415813.5	23713706.3	9762016.0	1046703.9	14346560.6
13677303.5	183863.6	5250189.8	23965806.4	9284455.7	1373292.4	12048101.7
679696.7	7813.1	248710.2	1185517.9	626510.3	60908.4	505977.6

13-4 续表

单位：万元

项目	Item	流动负债合计 Total Working Liabilities	长期负债合计 Long-term Liabilities	所有者权益合计 Total Owners' Equities
总计	**Total**	**42078931.7**	**23318022.5**	**49856070.2**
按登记注册类型分	**By Status of Registration**			
内资企业	Domestic Funded Enterprises	40981624.2	23098135.5	48907128.7
国有企业	State-owned Enterprises	4341152.4	2947565.1	4671894.9
#中央企业	Central Enterprises	3237485.0	1644716.9	3594278.4
地方企业	Local Enterprises	1103667.4	1302848.2	1077616.5
#自治区属企业	Autonomous	395247.7	691104.4	386313.7
地区(州、市)属企业	Prefecture or City	193059.1	287543.9	55931.9
县(市)属企业	County or City	317123.5	266898.2	543549.5
集体企业	Collective-owned Enterprises	48108.4	11377.5	57767.9
#自治区属企业	Autonomous	18483.4	741.8	21957.9
地区(州、市)属企业	Prefecture or City	452.2		553.5
县(市)属企业	County or City	10268.8	635.7	21862.6
镇属企业	Town	3721.9		6459.7
乡属企业	Village			
股份合作企业	Cooperative Enterprises	26501.3	7092.2	5568.5
联营企业	Joint Ownership Enterprises	40672.3	27930.9	28255.7
#国有联营企业	State Joint Ownership Enterprises	25947.4	1819.2	13328.6
集体联营企业	Collective Joint Ownership Enterprises			
国有与集体联营企业	Joint State-collective Enterprises	-1763.5	25000.0	10603.0
其他联营企业	Other Joint Ownership Enterprises	16488.4	1111.7	4324.1
有限责任公司	Limited Liability Corporations	18684246.3	8490838.3	13542498.9
#国有独资公司	State Sole funded Corporations	2101826.2	1677408.1	2143599.4
其他有限责任公司	Other Limited Liability Corporations	16582420.1	6813430.2	11398899.5
股份有限公司	Share-holding Corporations Ltd.	10936419.7	9610399.4	25007460.6
私营企业	Private Enterprises	6820906.7	1997252.3	5538385.2
#私营独资企业	Private-funded Enterprises	217637.2	46725.8	139541.3
私营合伙企业	Private Partnership Enterprises	8478.9	768.6	8792.0
私营有限责任公司	Private Limited Liability Corporations	5091917.2	1348917.8	3370232.8
私营股份有限公司	Private Share-holding Corporations Ltd.	1502873.4	600840.1	2019819.1
港、澳、台商投资企业	Enterprises with Funds from Hong Kong, Macao and Taiwan	389746.2	35477.6	421583.0
外商投资企业	Foreign Funded Enterprises	707561.3	184409.4	527358.5
在总计中：国有控股企业	Of the Total : State-owned and State-holding Enterprises	24174320.7	17378962.2	36150759.2
在总计中：农村工业	Of the Total : Rural Industry	8815.2	13109.5	56192.8
按轻、重工业分	**Grouped by Light & Heavy Industry**			
轻工业	Light Industry	6548694.0	976446.6	4296915.2
以农产品为原料	Using Farm Produces as Raw Materials	6094025.5	760498.9	3819080.0
以非农产品为原料	Using Non-Farm Produces as Raw Materials	454668.5	215947.7	477835.2
重工业	Heavy Industry	35530237.7	22341575.9	45559155.0
采掘工业	Mining and Quarrying	10144076.8	7544076.6	18442841.5
原料工业	Raw Material Industry	18986265.0	12074275.7	20625775.9
加工工业	Manufacturing Industry	6399895.9	2723223.6	6490537.6
按企业规模分	**Grouped by Size of Enterprises (New Standard)**			
大型企业	Large Enterprises	21107413.9	14611070.8	31840777.8
中型企业	Medium-sized Enterprises	9945712.4	4252659.1	8862048.7
小型企业	Small Enterprises	10317264.4	4315174.9	8841757.8
微型企业	Min Enterprises	708541.0	139117.7	311485.9

Continued

(10 000 yuan)

主营业务收入 Revenue from Principal Business	#主营业务成本 Cost of Principal Business	主营业务税金及附加 Taxes and Other Charges on Principal Business	营业利润 Business Profit	利润总额 Total Profit	亏损企业亏损总额 Losses Value of Loss-Suffering Enterprises	利税总额 Total Profits and Taxes	本年应交增值税 Value-added Taxes Payable	全部从业人员年平均人数（人） Annual Average Employed Persons (person)
75106656.0	**56971516.2**	**3222977.0**	**8361907.0**	**8886377.7**	**1176981.7**	**15388184.9**	**3278830.2**	**664797**
73476672.2	55678429.4	3207810.3	8237914.5	8754428.4	1153734.2	15183338.7	3221100.0	644109
6696769.1	6008590.4	181624.8	139321.1	199455.6	144781.8	622254.3	241173.9	82776
5215753.8	4683739.8	175806.0	137584.6	181518.7	71982.5	553110.7	195786.0	65394
1481015.3	1324850.6	5818.8	1736.5	17936.9	72799.3	69143.6	45387.9	17382
688654.4	633322.2	1277.5	6961.8	8855.0	24909.0	20526.1	10393.6	7507
311189.5	317605.9	472.9	-25347.3	-16415.5	24409.8	-12667.2	3275.4	2934
181464.3	123181.6	3120.7	-4023.7	-952.2	20511.7	15673.3	13504.8	3723
177704.0	153727.2	2027.7	14203.8	15792.4	2411.9	28410.0	10589.9	2774
96618.0	92945.6	453.2	209.7	-54.1	1671.6	3650.0	3250.9	1743
4264.6	4071.6	10.7	22.4	20.9		113.7	82.1	98
33671.5	23616.7	892.5	7733.3	8135.0		11217.6	2190.1	378
18139.5	7728.5	558.0	6527.4	6526.2		10556.1	3471.9	156
23142.1	19788.4	69.8	749.6	706.1	144.0	1508.6	732.7	658
36547.9	26302.8	170.7	3319.8	4679.9	1895.5	5593.9	743.3	914
14716.7	13726.6	73.2	-1412.9	-1.3	918.5	224.2	152.3	434
7014.8	1728.4	0.0	3409.5	3409.5		3409.5		2
14816.4	10847.8	97.5	1323.2	1271.7	977.0	1960.2	591.0	478
21982828.1	18293512.2	430590.1	1415795.9	1669403.7	395196.3	2964562.2	864568.4	272025
3598272.4	2921703.3	277964.9	174899.6	211260.4	54209.6	636886.0	147660.7	41739
18384555.7	15371808.9	152625.2	1240896.3	1458143.3	340986.7	2327676.2	716907.7	230286
35402823.8	23657888.3	2530091.4	5958939.9	6061024.3	500811.8	10445944.7	1854829.0	177061
8961810.7	7346393.2	62598.9	688325.1	784531.5	107751.6	1092526.1	245395.7	105995
470174.9	377504.9	3361.4	52828.9	55352.7	3447.4	90744.9	32030.8	7131
56178.7	36316.9	369.4	9153.0	8212.7		17184.5	8602.4	679
6569981.9	5481343.9	51905.5	410809.1	493923.9	91565.8	732619.0	186789.6	89191
1865475.2	1451227.5	6962.6	215534.1	227042.2	12738.4	251977.7	17972.9	8994
544659.8	433048.9	2444.8	31544.4	38263.9	4263.3	64678.2	23969.5	9312
1085324.0	860037.9	12721.9	92448.1	93685.4	18984.2	140168.0	33760.7	11376
53793148.3	39433712.1	3056835.5	6752829.8	7091412.9	876796.1	12740928.0	2592679.6	398174
22199.4	17234.6	33.0	1132.8	1260.4	377.3	1795.4	502.0	354
8922486.8	7344699.3	232022.2	422865.0	553585.3	186962.0	1062713.6	277106.1	135256
8518370.0	7025364.6	229258.2	426583.6	546791.6	155720.1	1037426.0	261376.2	124032
404116.8	319334.7	2764.0	-3718.6	6793.7	31241.9	25287.6	15729.9	11224
66184169.2	49626816.9	2990954.8	7939042.0	8332792.4	990019.7	14325471.3	3001724.1	529541
20624454.3	10015457.9	1261552.1	6530145.6	6612468.2	142133.5	9764806.0	1890785.7	205706
37194528.7	32976517.0	1674344.1	542191.7	736864.5	786800.4	3347895.9	936687.3	235568
8365186.2	6634842.0	55058.6	866704.7	983459.7	61085.8	1212769.4	174251.1	88267
48911629.8	35822754.6	2843055.2	6307371.1	6585743.4	637993.5	11689074.7	2260276.1	322757
11474623.6	9004786.8	253324.3	1014292.6	1117481.9	245064.7	1887663.9	516857.7	175139
14015149.7	11525902.6	122317.6	1015624.6	1150172.2	272804.9	1757724.1	485234.3	162306
705252.9	618072.2	4279.9	24618.7	32980.2	21118.6	53722.2	16462.1	4595

13-5 按行业分规模以上工业企业主要经济指标

单位：万元 (2012 年)

行业	Sector	企业单位数(个) Number of Enterprises (unit)	#亏损企业 Loss- Suffering Enterprises	工业总产值(当年价格) Gross Industrial Output Value (At Current Prices)
总计	**Total**	**1959**	**524**	**75326674.0**
煤炭开采和洗选业	Mining and Washing of Coal	115	25	2347353.4
石油和天然气开采业	Extraction of Petroleum and Natural Gas	5		13736414.3
黑色金属矿采选业	Mining and Processing of Ferrous Metals Ores	66	33	1216929.3
有色金属矿采选业	Mining and Processing of Nonferrous Metals Ores	33	7	626231.1
非金属矿采选业	Mining and Processing of Nonmetal Ores	22	4	157574.7
#采盐	Extraction of Salt	4		46621.5
农副食品加工业	Processing of Food from Agricultural Products	279	56	3208192.5
#谷物磨制	Grain Grinding	52	8	432512.6
饲料加工	Fodder Processing	30	5	487695.0
制糖	Sugar Making	13	4	303078.1
食品制造业	Manufacture of Food	116	41	1266942.4
#罐头制造	Manufacture of can	53	28	298119.1
酒、饮料和精制茶制造业	Manufacture of Wine,Beverages and Refined Tea	63	10	878001.7
#酒的制造	Manufacture of Wine	47	8	605170.7
烟草制品业	Manufacture of Tobacco	1		357066.4
纺织业	Manufacture of Textile	81	36	1306516.2
#棉、化纤纺织及印染精加工	Cotton, Chemical Fiber, Dyeing, Printing and Processing	70	31	1206935.5
毛纺织和染整精加工	Wool Textile, Dyeing and Printing	3	2	18357.4
纺织服装、鞋、帽制造业	Manufacture of Textile Wearing Apparel, Footware and Caps	8	1	52796.8
皮革、毛皮、羽毛(绒)及其制品业	Leather, Fur, Feather and Related Products Manufacturing	4	1	62703.3
#皮革鞣制加工	Leather Tanning and Processing	4	1	62703.3
木材加工及木、竹、藤、棕、草制品业	Processing of Timber, Wood, Bamboo, Cane, Grass Products	9		73098.8
家具制造业	Manufacture of Furniture	6	4	80961.5
造纸及纸制品业	Manufacture of Paper and Paper Products	26	8	211025.2
印刷业和记录媒介的复制	Printing and Copying of Medium for Record	11	1	49337.1
石油加工、炼焦及核燃料加工业	Oil Processing, Coking and Nuclear Fuel Processing	92	28	16731304.5
#炼焦	Coking	56	15	1114209.7
化学原料及化学制品制造业	Raw Chemical Material and Chemical Products	131	20	5155131.1
#基础化学原料制造	Basic Chemical Material	35	12	1166513.6
肥料制造	Fertilizer Making	32		1036081.1
合成材料制造	Manufacture of Synthetic Materials	15	3	2487151.1
医药制造业	Manufacture of Medicine	22	2	188396.2
化学纤维制造业	Manufacture of Chemical Fiber	14	8	884342.6
橡胶和塑料制品业	Manufacture of Rubber Products	95	14	1080572.1
非金属矿物制品业	Manufacture of Nonmetal Mineral Products	294	92	3187246.6
#水泥制造	Manufacture of Cement	78	31	1459341.1
黑色金属冶炼及压延加工业	Smelting and Pressing of Ferrous Metals	73	44	7407811.5
有色金属冶炼及压延加工业	Smelting and Pressing of Nonferrous Metals	35	6	2402504.4
金属制品业	Manufacture of Metal Products	63	13	767767.2
通用设备制造业	Manufacture of General Purpose Machinery	22	3	117167.0
专用设备制造业	Manufacture of Special Purpose Machinery	23	1	310418.2
汽车制造业	Manufacture of Automobile	7	6	311841.4
电气机械及器材制造业	Manufacture of Electric Equipment and Machinery	38	3	2192035.4
计算机、通信和其他电子设备制造业	Telecom Equipment, Computer and Other Electronic Equipment	2		223724.2
仪器仪表制造业	Measuring Instruments and Machinery for Cultunal Activify and Office Work	2		4375.8
金属制品、机械和设备修理业	Manufacture and Repairing of Metal Prodults,Mouhinery and Equipment	3		21048.4
电力、热力的生产和供应业	Electricity and Thermal Production and Supply	132	47	6192713.3
#电力生产和电力供应	Electricity Production and Supply	95	26	5958993.6
燃气生产和供应业	Gas Production and Supply	24	1	360904.1
水的生产和供应业	Water Production and Supply	10	6	62183.9

Main Economic Indicators of Industrial Enterprises above Designated Size by Sectors

(10 000 yuan)

工业销售产值(当年价) Sales Value of Industry Products (At Current Prices)	出口交货值 Delivery Value of Industry Export	实收资本 Total Capital Hold	资产合计 Total Assets	流动资产合计 Total Working Capitals	#产成品 Finished Product	固定资产原价 Original Value of Fixed Assets
73484359.9	**419562.7**	**34363194.1**	**116691728.3**	**36801594.1**	**3796867.5**	**85721657.0**
2253440.1		1666083.8	6710292.7	1643277.7	146736.3	2473151.9
13754165.9		13123235.8	23266281.5	3482260.0	127039.4	31634951.2
1136832.8		400802.4	2244893.0	1090020.1	163691.3	701000.4
651312.0		363156.0	1471915.7	391584.0	51665.6	716995.2
151727.3	1536.9	53067.2	193127.3	104401.7	14540.3	85412.7
41545.0		16307.1	53559.0	33428.2	4910.9	18568.0
3020397.1	17966.1	575141.5	3121264.5	1916723.8	530074.7	1103442.6
429296.0		58780.1	272494.2	145797.7	10859.6	98953.8
479324.0		59127.1	384138.0	201015.7	28290.3	121913.4
232929.7		68144.3	415655.3	258744.1	139021.1	261572.8
1226852.1	177125.7	468175.1	1974228.1	978289.9	249105.1	1145270.4
320757.9	147645.2	194907.7	1048429.6	590792.0	203155.7	618609.6
852938.1	1795.0	285521.7	1177645.9	548007.1	76464.4	512743.4
583644.9		217398.9	940339.1	470786.6	64804.2	350674.2
354589.7		18741.7	445764.0	272738.0		128081.0
1274052.6	25312.2	635966.2	2310427.5	1039806.6	222102.6	1191579.4
1180872.3	13163.0	542415.1	2123460.8	977245.9	211321.1	1075260.5
18239.1	440.5	18605.5	24744.3	13698.9	2943.2	19169.7
50937.3	7605.9	11609.8	63500.9	44389.5	4423.0	16798.4
55975.7		6556.5	40387.0	32229.6	3879.6	10543.6
55975.7		6556.5	40387.0	32229.6	3879.6	10543.6
69301.0		17369.1	70008.9	33577.0	10393.7	35283.8
55763.4	33826.0	70994.0	304977.8	48679.7	4617.7	33252.6
203662.5		47048.1	352496.6	169906.3	31220.5	183512.8
49944.5		19726.4	81968.8	34937.6	3873.6	65838.3
16444524.0		5005193.6	8863962.8	2940028.8	536078.2	8300659.4
967070.4		491634.4	1860624.5	770294.3	145262.1	843722.0
5074994.4	27933.3	2346264.0	11384370.0	2957083.2	370356.2	5442731.3
1108872.2	16809.1	754028.5	5006427.9	1139855.6	85330.5	1311557.2
1024719.5	1354.4	488373.9	2627193.6	804246.8	77101.1	1477594.2
2473895.8	8830.7	992141.7	3216767.4	717281.1	184910.7	2492429.6
179989.4	2451.0	70628.1	326081.3	212720.1	26396.6	91426.4
789621.3		162507.8	989485.3	438468.5	107671.7	564167.4
1019323.0	10990.3	268961.1	1069290.4	598587.6	154298.6	437220.6
3043849.1		1620921.9	7767656.7	3191008.9	169353.2	7069869.2
1377289.8		1127495.0	5249560.0	1905685.4	70059.4	6018212.0
7213198.2	16449.0	1297715.5	7147345.4	2666251.6	326975.7	3720602.9
2250337.1	5920.1	546970.6	5719038.1	2187726.5	202020.7	1815065.6
649543.8	3325.2	173667.1	667567.5	394955.3	41231.9	174011.9
111487.2	1025.3	35857.2	118330.5	84297.3	12245.9	30545.8
293873.0	2756.3	74071.6	449103.6	280426.3	53439.8	103452.7
281273.6	108.3	55478.1	273750.9	122902.0	31117.2	61545.3
2136078.8	31072.5	698651.5	6312301.7	3911014.0	77265.7	463209.6
217746.9	43495.3	54435.5	717391.3	220689.0	18876.5	438877.5
3700.0		3000.0	12243.3	6937.0	260.3	264.3
20977.0		10924.9	60156.5	38720.0	3540.8	10498.8
6123886.1		2646888.5	16975333.6	2902813.4	3646.8	14489021.2
5892711.7		2495876.8	15901042.3	2491283.4	3530.5	13584022.5
331252.3		137407.3	726914.5	317158.3	1472.4	424278.3
59978.7		105192.7	654888.2	206662.6		329365.9

13-5 续表

单位: 万元

行业	Sector	流动负债合计 Total Working Liabilities	长期负债合计 Long-term Liabilities	所有者权益合计 Total Owners' Equities
总计	**Total**	**42078931.7**	**23318022.5**	**49856070.2**
煤炭开采和洗选业	Mining and Washing of Coal	2806839.7	1305832.0	2518348.6
石油和天然气开采业	Extraction of Petroleum and Natural Gas	4164659.0	5595340.0	13506282.4
黑色金属矿采选业	Mining and Processing of Ferrous Metals Ores	1317022.7	210857.8	702788.5
有色金属矿采选业	Mining and Processing of Nonferrous Metals Ores	488612.8	228482.6	754549.8
非金属矿采选业	Mining and Processing of Nonmetal Ores	108619.9	6001.3	75508.0
#采盐	Extraction of Salt	13016.9	2643.8	37750.3
农副食品加工业	Processing of Food from Agricultural Products	1910370.2	145427.5	1020290.8
#谷物磨制	Grain Grinding	131498.0	8718.4	129745.1
饲料加工	Fodder Processing	148240.2	39689.9	195640.6
制糖	Sugar Making	239054.2	5425.8	166639.6
食品制造业	Manufacture of Food	1276329.5	92789.5	575977.9
#罐头制造	Manufacture of can	865176.3	56407.5	112219.2
酒、饮料和精制茶制造业	Manufacture of Wine,Beverages and Refined Tea	560323.7	196764.8	402323.2
#酒的制造	Manufacture of Wine	430959.8	189781.1	314025.3
烟草制品业	Manufacture of Tobacco	128861.0		316903.0
纺织业	Manufacture of Textile	1050300.2	175594.5	850578.7
#棉、化纤纺织及印染精加工	Cotton, Chemical Fiber, Dyeing, Printing and Processing	978622.5	165004.6	750639.7
毛纺织和染整精加工	Wool Textile, Dyeing and Printing	10787.5	145.7	13158.7
纺织服装、鞋、帽制造业	Manufacture of Textile Wearing Apparel, Footware and Caps	43436.0	9290.6	8774.3
皮革、毛皮、羽毛(绒)及其制品业	Leather, Fur, Feather and Related Products Manufacturing	25542.0	3389.0	11456.0
#皮革鞣制加工	Leather Tanning and Processing	25542.0	3389.0	11456.0
木材加工及木、竹、藤、棕、草制品业	Processing of Timber, Wood, Bamboo, Cane, Grass Products	37894.9	431.0	31682.9
家具制造业	Manufacture of Furniture	43992.9	10074.8	250910.1
造纸及纸制品业	Manufacture of Paper and Paper Products	204282.3	32796.2	105531.1
印刷业和记录媒介的复制	Printing and Copying of Medium for Record	30695.5	8867.5	41227.1
石油加工、炼焦及核燃料加工业	Oil Processing, Coking and Nuclear Fuel Processing	2933537.7	702211.3	5137028.9
#炼焦	Coking	975704.5	189447.6	607682.2
化学原料及化学制品制造业	Raw Chemical Material and Chemical Products	3099018.3	3518169.6	4721990.5
#基础化学原料制造	Basic Chemical Material	1557980.8	1507491.4	1916185.2
肥料制造	Fertilizer Making	652770.8	961641.5	995410.3
合成材料制造	Manufacture of Synthetic Material	640632.5	1025282.4	1550852.3
医药制造业	Manufacture of Medicine	137474.0	25823.0	154168.6
化学纤维制造业	Manufacture of Chemical Fiber	737813.8	77947.4	171965.2
橡胶和塑料制品业	Manufacture of Rubber Products	504241.0	106068.3	446406.0
非金属矿物制品业	Manufacture of Nonmetal Mineral Products	3123567.6	1229880.6	3270891.4
#水泥制造	Manufacture of Cement	1661650.0	1035787.3	2455742.0
黑色金属冶炼及压延加工业	Smelting and Pressing of Ferrous Metals	4697145.3	452877.5	1888074.7
有色金属冶炼及压延加工业	Smelting and Pressing of Nonferrous Metals	2739379.7	1291085.6	1654782.4
金属制品业	Manufacture of Metal Products	355871.1	47436.5	262543.5
通用设备制造业	Manufacture of General Purpose Machinery	72274.8	976.8	45077.7
专用设备制造业	Manufacture of Special Purpose Machinery	211918.5	10168.7	222022.0
汽车制造业	Manufacture of Automobile	230208.7	11112.5	32429.6
电气机械及器材制造业	Manufacture of Electric Equipment and Machinery	2494419.5	983849.5	2830918.6
计算机、通信和其他电子设备制造业	Telecom Equipment, Computer and Other Electronic Equipment	116443.5	233233.7	367714.1
仪器仪表制造业	Measuring Instruments and Machinery for Cultural Activify and Office Work	1916.7	401.1	9925.5
金属制品、机械和设备修理业	Manufacture and Repairing of Metal Products, Machinery and Equipment	26638.9		33517.6
电力、热力的生产和供应业	Electricity and Thermal Production and Supply	4538433.6	6031256.8	5879180.5
#电力生产和电力供应	Electricity Production and Supply	4161911.0	5590941.7	5638915.8
燃气生产和供应业	Gas Production and Supply	278787.4	146716.6	296805.5
水的生产和供应业	Water Production and Supply	162453.6	201508.9	281888.4

Continued

(10 000 yuan)

主营业务收入 Revenue from Principal Business	#主营业务成本 Cost of Principal Business	主营业务税金及附加 Taxes and Other Charges on Principal Business	营业利润 Business Profit	利润总额 Total Profit	亏损企业亏损总额 Losses Value of Loss-Suffering Enterprises	利税总额 Total Profits and Taxes	本年应交增值税 Value-added Taxes Payable	全部从业人员年平均人数(人) Annual Average Employed Persons (person)
75106656.0	**56971516.2**	**3222977.0**	**8361907.0**	**8886377.7**	**1176981.7**	**15388184.9**	**3278830.2**	**664797**
2320586.7	1580550.7	58368.4	316188.7	319905.8	51496.7	619285.2	241011.0	59104
14472223.3	5458507.7	1139220.8	5785453.2	5845595.9		8352044.9	1367228.2	77384
1168768.1	772125.8	31660.6	204155.0	201429.1	28429.9	333341.5	100251.8	12316
630439.7	312082.9	9897.2	224850.8	222087.3	9556.4	302772.6	70788.1	8769
148201.7	87549.8	4340.5	8097.8	10016.5	3414.5	28540.9	14183.9	3604
43417.8	12309.4	3425.9	5059.2	6312.2		14740.8	5002.7	1116
3202641.9	2775653.4	5123.6	181006.2	207620.9	30339.9	269751.6	57007.1	28450
431183.8	391064.1	402.2	21413.7	26603.8	1186.7	29201.0	2195.0	2908
494726.0	407344.6	365.8	34174.1	39310.7	570.5	48930.4	9253.9	3153
237037.2	192233.4	1643.5	8952.3	9362.2	4583.9	26772.2	15766.5	6158
1246173.8	992819.1	3258.7	42668.3	63076.2	63067.9	107767.4	41432.5	20190
325992.1	273841.3	603.2	-49331.8	-36111.5	53518.4	-23238.5	12269.8	6310
896363.5	570528.0	57626.4	151925.5	157809.6	3806.9	266709.8	51273.8	12959
580630.8	337665.9	56878.2	108799.4	114483.4	3403.5	216904.0	45542.4	10280
354588.7	121438.7	155886.8	55009.2	54751.4		250038.2	39400.0	941
1398990.8	1320434.8	3964.7	-37347.2	13133.5	39638.6	57940.2	40842.0	40245
1312102.2	1246380.8	3627.6	-40575.1	5635.5	35985.6	48583.3	39320.2	36136
18899.7	17092.1	97.1	-539.8	-699.4	1200.0	-103.1	499.2	1205
69320.9	66870.7	40.8	3638.6	4017.3	67.9	5462.1	1404.0	2062
58667.0	53541.1	114.3	3716.1	4065.1	194.9	5006.2	826.8	422
58667.0	53541.1	114.3	3716.1	4065.1	194.9	5006.2	826.8	422
66082.2	54660.4	326.9	6526.4	7739.7		10754.0	2687.4	942
56409.5	49838.8	250.8	-3134.8	-1867.8	2174.0	-990.0	627.0	1250
199097.3	164009.7	742.7	16408.3	18967.7	5740.2	24835.1	5124.7	5476
50180.8	40766.6	212.5	882.4	2432.1	72.2	4285.1	1640.5	1638
16558185.9	14421091.1	1609892.1	-180760.8	-189190.3	457410.2	1766075.7	345373.9	46489
967184.8	794516.9	20696.0	82812.1	83688.3	21625.8	140394.5	36010.2	13418
4753071.5	3702914.3	46963.4	570685.1	636413.1	59021.9	848407.5	165031.0	58208
1353080.8	1156871.5	6839.5	88810.6	104925.0	27923.9	147232.0	35467.5	22110
1031500.1	548971.8	27719.3	316486.5	355929.3		425754.2	42105.6	12767
1894561.1	1637608.9	8317.3	105326.9	113818.1	30881.8	186869.6	64734.2	16496
159873.4	99724.1	1016.5	15103.8	25661.6	350.2	35440.3	8762.2	3727
849536.4	770235.8	1689.9	-5157.8	1141.2	10754.7	20914.4	18083.3	8943
994214.1	849451.2	4091.7	59917.0	70876.7	8007.4	89934.5	14966.1	13341
3044375.5	2556491.4	15115.7	135252.9	177575.6	82186.5	310001.6	117310.3	56240
1359095.7	1122684.0	8110.8	69721.2	104368.9	39490.3	172796.9	60317.2	27935
7510035.1	7186263.0	16760.2	4646.9	38757.1	81829.2	189149.0	133631.7	44009
2066163.9	1829199.5	2301.3	114131.0	109927.5	7625.0	174932.6	62703.8	17862
660154.8	594483.0	2502.7	23853.8	27541.2	1881.7	39785.2	9741.3	8314
113151.1	91163.9	609.8	10008.7	11521.7	1694.8	14982.1	2850.6	2209
335618.7	269424.6	755.7	32746.0	35706.9	801.5	40923.4	4460.8	3989
338465.7	334020.1	323.9	-8607.6	-8234.4	8343.9	-6954.3	956.2	1934
2565093.5	2074075.1	8559.6	260586.1	309063.6	869.6	342262.6	24639.4	9297
208067.1	170117.6	173.6	10247.6	14752.6		14937.9	11.7	4460
3812.0	2565.0	25.0	960.8	960.8		1195.8	210.0	23
20347.8	18006.8	91.8	679.1	834.9		1578.0	651.3	504
6130160.5	5369053.3	18803.2	317325.2	428461.8	138267.3	667311.0	220046.0	55645
5863570.4	5094097.6	18147.6	364425.7	443648.5	109690.7	679809.4	218013.3	48849
344144.7	219262.1	3060.2	55263.0	53648.8	928.9	65739	9029.8	3786
66755.3	45606.0	382.7	-4341.7	-889.6	7018.6	2704.8	3211.7	2743

13-6 各地、州、市、县(市)规模以上工业企业主要经济指标

单位：万元 (2012 年)

地 区	Region	企业单位数(个) Number of Enterprises (unit)	#亏损企业 Loss- Suffering Enterprises	工业总产值(当年价格) Gross Industrial Output Value (At Current Prices)
总 计	**Total**	**1959**	**524**	**75326674.0**
乌鲁木齐市	**Urumqi City**	**370**	**101**	**21508375.4**
天山区	Tianshan District	18	4	2631710.2
沙依巴克区	Shayibak District	26	11	511310.6
新市区	Xinshi District	152	40	6790486.3
水磨沟区	Shui Mogou District	20	4	213865.3
头屯河区	Tou Tunhe District	47	12	5576215.4
达坂城区	Da Bancheng District	10	1	204968.5
米东区	Midong District	93	29	5542064.6
乌鲁木齐县	Urumqi County	4		37754.5
克拉玛依市	**Karamay City**	**66**	**11**	**16938759.3**
独山子区	Dushanzi District	10	5	6490152.9
克拉玛依区	Karamay District	46	5	10305337.6
白碱滩区	Bai Jiantan District	8	1	120845.9
乌尔河区	Urhe District	2		22422.9
吐鲁番地区	**Turpan Administrative Offices**	**84**	**30**	**2718117.0**
吐鲁番市	Turpan City	25	8	442497.1
鄯善县	Shanshan [Piqan] County	34	11	1777627.4
托克逊县	Toksun County	25	11	497992.5
哈密地区	**Hami [Kumul] Administrative Offices**	**97**	**27**	**1881062.4**
哈密市	Hami [Kumul] City	78	23	1571717.4
巴里坤哈萨克自治县	Barkol Kazak Autonomous County	14	3	174260.2
伊吾县	Yiwu [Araturuk] County	5	1	135084.8
昌吉回族自治州	**Changji Hui Autonomous Prefecture**	**324**	**63**	**6042233.4**
昌吉市	Changji City	113	11	2507933.1
阜康市	Fukang City	53	16	1220568.0
呼图壁县	Hutubi County	53	7	501606.2
玛纳斯县	Manas County	37	15	739451.8
奇台县	Qitai County	35	3	506150.7
吉木萨尔县	Jimsar County	28	9	518845.1
木垒哈萨克自治县	Mori Kazak Autonomous County	5	2	47678.5
伊犁哈萨克自治州	**Ili Kazak Autonomous Prefecture**	**376**	**119**	**6137119.2**
伊犁州直属县(市)	**Counties (Cities) Direct Under Ili Prefecture**	**215**	**68**	**3667857.5**
伊宁市	Yining [Gulja] City	29	8	416393.6
奎屯市	Kuytun City	48	20	1131640.0
伊宁县	Yining [Gulja] County	36	11	411057.4
察布查尔锡伯自治县	Qapqal Xibe Autonomous County	15	5	182673.7
霍城县	Huocheng [Korgas] County	31	6	267126.3
巩留县	Gongliu [Tokkuztara] County	15	7	193377.6
新源县	Xinyuan [Kunes] County	17	5	730796.4
昭苏县	Zhaosu [Mongolkure] County	12	4	87215.4
特克斯县	Tekes County	4	1	36737.1
尼勒克县	Nilka County	8	1	210840.0
塔城地区	**Tacheng [Tarbagatai] Administrative Offices**	**98**	**32**	**1367052.3**
塔城市	Tacheng [Qoqek] City	5	2	97983.6
乌苏市	Usu City	18	5	415956.8
额敏县	Emin [Dorbiljin] County	12	4	108582.4

Main Economic Indicators of Industrial Enterprises above Designated Size by Prefecture, Autonomous Prefecture, City and County

(10 000 yuan)

工业销售产值(当年价) Sales Value of Industry Products (At Current Prices)	出口交货值 Delivery Value of Industry Export	实收资本 Total Capital Hold	资产合计 Total Assets	流动资产合计 Total Working Capitals	#产成品 Finished Product	固定资产原价 Original Value of Fixed Assets
73484359.9	**419562.7**	**34363194.1**	**116691728.3**	**36801594.1**	**3796867.5**	**85721657.0**
21103424.1	**214090.0**	**7679508.8**	**32418321.7**	**10198222.8**	**667664.2**	**20402130.2**
2657586.7	35453.4	370496.5	4913758.8	1038532.1	60214.2	4111000.0
476866.4	12934.2	364505.8	3905439.6	1232550.2	23664.9	680813.7
6569558.3	134543.5	3500037.1	12511321.9	4447735.6	268655.8	8334426.7
213488.2		71762.1	423175.9	135130.8	24895.5	448839.0
5384879.9	22322.6	904373.2	4894900.7	1620388.6	84254.1	2699747.9
202146.8		136663.9	562554.3	99469.2	13085.0	331014.7
5561838.9	8836.3	2282495.4	4950506.9	1573941.4	191995.8	3560885.2
37058.9		49174.8	256663.6	50474.9	898.9	235403.0
16787472.4	**5497.8**	**11440519.9**	**18171866.4**	**4724951.7**	**312986.7**	**19852745.0**
6483395.6	4827.8	2880746.3	4374454.4	1108278.7	126601.8	4616776.7
10165005.8		8540503.7	13634643.1	3509141.6	180131.2	15175393.0
118685.1	670.0	18009.9	138695.3	91842.8	5583.9	50391.6
20385.9		1260.0	24073.6	15688.6	669.8	10183.7
2543866.2	**3813.3**	**704002.1**	**4978498.6**	**1543739.9**	**223715.3**	**4700063.5**
391348.9	2458.9	164017.8	777175.4	334800.5	71051.6	393292.7
1706327.3	1354.4	223221.2	2632304.8	830791.6	124175.2	3617400.0
446190.0		316763.1	1569018.4	378147.8	28488.5	689370.8
1760054.6	**1167.0**	**1269998.0**	**4930024.0**	**1563103.9**	**172180.5**	**2202007.9**
1490987.6	1167.0	884253.4	3441423.1	1375316.0	136116.8	1786520.7
144491.3		58129.6	349980.3	126526.2	24842.5	146000.1
124575.7		327615.0	1138620.6	61261.7	11221.2	269487.1
5701990.4	**70934.2**	**2105808.9**	**12355701.1**	**4616722.4**	**521754.2**	**4194786.1**
2425381.4	40996.2	599521.4	4158590.9	1844951.9	173953.6	1251702.7
1162936.1	3960.0	571129.9	2977700.5	843281.1	99205.2	1250562.4
473262.6	822.5	118753.0	440075.7	191675.7	40105.4	197980.8
679714.1	9229.5	196773.5	1034210.8	529097.5	78112.4	660620.2
449678.9	2940.4	110329.5	734546.5	291724.9	82989.5	201633.0
480585.2	12985.6	503501.6	2957993.6	884778.3	43157.1	614612.5
30432.1		5800.0	52583.1	31213.0	4231.0	17674.5
5874399.4	**39381.9**	**2476645.4**	**11577448.5**	**3726238.2**	**522428.3**	**10612169.3**
3529167.1	**22592.4**	**1582702.9**	**7295158.6**	**2293586.0**	**300421.5**	**8066864.1**
407618.7	5979.7	68342.9	560543.6	181987.1	10965.6	501102.1
1130615.6	5246.5	409737.4	2042449.3	726579.4	67656.7	1265065.5
381004.9		160276.6	756335.2	317264.9	38844.3	296535.7
177282.1		54110.0	325669.6	99193.5	15905.1	3946808.9
235527.8	10323.3	105311.3	355389.1	158546.8	47745.8	198682.1
193207.7		349887.9	1087088.3	120408.8	7531.2	717030.9
666046.7	1042.9	219685.3	1146841.0	487521.0	101113.6	479826.8
89937.3		15710.0	74709.2	49029.2	3327.3	29488.9
37265.8		28600.0	99258.2	52955.9	2775.3	50775.7
210660.5		171041.5	846875.1	100099.4	4556.6	581547.5
1252306.8	**16789.5**	**486452.6**	**2336942.7**	**936572.9**	**141704.8**	**1343203.6**
95465.5		13443.3	142555.9	20651.9	1106.0	154911.6
344454.6	16789.5	98984.2	580013.0	282579.7	42573.7	287879.5
99922.6		71529.3	237007.6	100080.9	27981.1	170513.0

13-6 续表 1

单位: 万元

地　区	Region	流动负债合计 Total Working Liabilities	长期负债合计 Long-term Liabilities	所有者权益合计 Total Owners' Equities
总　计	**Total**	**42078931.7**	**23318022.5**	**49856070.2**
乌鲁木齐市	**Urumqi City**	**12170084.2**	**5812752.8**	**14318847.8**
天山区	Tianshan District	1635448.3	1329440.2	1947578.7
沙依巴克区	Shayibak District	1073676.9	1224648.6	1603830.0
新市区	Xinshi District	4528328.1	1711309.1	6188622.0
水磨沟区	Shui Mogou District	98652.2	23840.2	287373.5
头屯河区	Tou Tunhe District	3100251.3	407896.3	1372501.9
达坂城区	Da Bancheng District	232441.5	69224.8	264110.0
米东区	Midong District	1390521.1	953040.9	2602285.7
乌鲁木齐县	Urumqi County	110764.8	93352.7	52546.0
克拉玛依市	**Karamay City**	**4303031.7**	**3128097.9**	**10728226.5**
独山子区	Dushanzi District	1179990.8	283803.8	2900729.1
克拉玛依区	Karamay District	3027524.8	2840735.0	7764885.2
白碱滩区	Bai Jiantan District	85851.4	3131.4	48631.2
乌尔河区	Urhe District	9664.7	427.7	13981.0
吐鲁番地区	**Turpan Administrative Offices**	**1478837.3**	**1086348.5**	**2258138.6**
吐鲁番市	Turpan City	402698.5	48941.2	322986.2
鄯善县	Shanshan [Piqan] County	638942.8	586337.2	1285192.0
托克逊县	Toksun County	437196.0	451070.1	649960.4
哈密地区	**Hami [Kumul] Administrative Offices**	**2111211.4**	**1233835.7**	**1573658.0**
哈密市	Hami [Kumul] City	1543139.1	805848.4	1084899.6
巴里坤哈萨克自治县	Barkol Kazak Autonomous County	116107.0	109256.0	124615.3
伊吾县	Yiwu [Araturuk] County	451965.3	318731.3	364143.1
昌吉回族自治州	**Changji Hui Autonomous Prefecture**	**5075113.5**	**2692550.9**	**4463080.0**
昌吉市	Changji City	1601847.5	590106.2	1963393.8
阜康市	Fukang City	1121617.7	532120.1	1312819.7
呼图壁县	Hutubi County	244078.8	41661.5	146404.9
玛纳斯县	Manas County	477270.7	320945.8	206457.8
奇台县	Qitai County	386148.3	52477.1	295607.0
吉木萨尔县	Jimsar County	1215189.2	1151240.2	518775.0
木垒哈萨克自治县	Mori Kazak Autonomous County	28961.3	4000.0	19621.8
伊犁哈萨克自治州	**Ili Kazak Autonomous Prefecture**	**4468187.7**	**2253007.9**	**4303355.1**
伊犁州直属县(市)	**Counties (Cities) Direct Under Ili Prefecture**	**2579264.4**	**1534084.8**	**2716433.3**
伊宁市	Yining [Gulja] City	182456.2	154614.4	222243.6
奎屯市	Kuytun City	643152.1	567862.7	829598.1
伊宁县	Yining [Gulja] County	342193.5	128363.2	257362.2
察布查尔锡伯自治县	Qapqal Xibe Autonomous County	118365.5	61350.4	136376.5
霍城县	Huocheng [Korgas] County	155558.5	43161.9	141826.5
巩留县	Gongliu [Tokkuztara] County	112720.7	200345.0	394251.6
新源县	Xinyuan [Kunes] County	665482.7	30145.3	447622.2
昭苏县	Zhaosu [Mongolkure] County	35546.6	1466.4	25999.1
特克斯县	Tekes County	52234.0	6061.8	26546.8
尼勒克县	Nilka County	271554.6	340713.7	234606.7
塔城地区	**Tacheng [Tarbagatai] Administrative Offices**	**1206591.2**	**344366.9**	**763398.1**
塔城市	Tacheng [Qoqek] City	46913.6	50133.1	41493.1
乌苏市	Usu City	358172.4	27170.4	189466.5
额敏县	Emin [Dorbiljin] County	70048.4	68575.4	97481.4

Continued

(10 000 yuan)

主营业务收入 Revenue from Principal Business	#主营业务成本 Cost of Principal Business	主营业务税金及附加 Taxes and Other Charges on Principal Business	营业利润 Business Profit	利润总额 Total Profit	亏损企业亏损总额 Losses Value of Loss-Suffering Enterprises	利税总额 Total Profits and Taxes	本年应交增值税 Value-added Taxes Payable	全部从业人员年平均人数(人) Annual Average Employed Persons (person)
75106656.0	**56971516.2**	**3222977.0**	**8361907.0**	**8886377.7**	**1176981.7**	**15388184.9**	**3278830.2**	**664797.0**
21647014.6	**17626465.0**	**937374.8**	**1526175.5**	**1752535.4**	**315422.4**	**3367838.6**	**677928.4**	**140455.0**
2661073.1	2457363.7	4594.1	98720.3	136404.0	37935.2	197758.5	56760.4	16695.0
509713.4	407911.6	5682.4	52984.5	70926.6	9757.1	98712.6	22103.6	11586.0
6915980.1	4104977.2	483772.9	1456613.8	1567534.9	52010.2	2377586.7	326278.9	46196.0
226630.6	195963.6	2027.2	1793.1	18094.2	682.9	33563.1	13441.7	3488.0
5386869.1	5182471.0	12136.4	-10436.1	23996.0	20901.7	119312.9	83180.5	21207.0
206214.2	135793.3	2350.1	42506.1	39540.3	448.8	56597.3	14706.9	7095.0
5703382.7	5122632.1	426707.0	-125940.0	-115578.6	193686.5	471658.8	160530.4	34040.0
37151.4	19352.5	104.7	9933.8	11618.0		12648.7	926.0	148.0
17633783.3	**12920544.4**	**1265321.9**	**2179733.2**	**2262140.2**	**330340.5**	**4458755.9**	**931293.8**	**108071.0**
6484066.3	5842956.0	551630.7	-267286.4	-266977.4	279792.9	372443.0	87789.7	19350.0
11001015.4	6955916.1	711921.1	2436545.6	2516913.9	50529.3	4063884.5	835049.5	85351.0
127741.2	104754.1	1095.9	7821.9	9517.7	18.3	17947.5	7333.9	3141.0
20960.4	16918.2	674.2	2652.1	2686.0	0.0	4480.9	1120.7	229.0
2660238.6	**1983882.0**	**67380.1**	**327112.1**	**330559.4**	**33114.1**	**527874.7**	**129935.2**	**39407.0**
410228.3	351549.2	1964.6	9500.7	11246.0	9501.9	31283.3	18072.7	6908.0
1788279.0	1295260.4	58159.8	270840.0	270591.9	6534.2	419130.3	90378.6	23729.0
461731.3	337072.4	7255.7	46771.4	48721.5	17078.0	77461.1	21483.9	8770.0
1824701.6	**1458864.2**	**22052.0**	**140358.3**	**149566.4**	**34789.8**	**265086.9**	**93468.5**	**32800.0**
1556249.9	1295736.2	15436.8	83010.3	91717.2	33113.2	182730.4	75576.4	27162.0
145462.0	77752.1	2704.6	46249.3	46185.7	946.0	63735.6	14845.3	2975.0
122989.7	85375.9	3910.6	11098.7	11663.5	730.6	18620.9	3046.8	2663.0
5722805.5	**4727628.9**	**44981.0**	**495514.9**	**527845.9**	**88202.7**	**773176.5**	**200349.6**	**69489.0**
2568674.6	2086059.9	7458.9	293324.5	310377.2	12374.4	394838.0	77001.9	21205.0
1143591.1	970343.7	3851.7	77990.1	81502.9	28035.9	127547.6	42193.0	17755.0
467941.1	372010.7	2120.3	61092.4	61694.4	3054.3	76567.7	12753.0	5542.0
691937.7	611385.6	5692.7	-451.1	8541.8	13997.3	53211.2	38976.7	8652.0
445697.0	345341.4	6239.3	38886.9	40708.9	3951.0	64037.7	17089.5	4689.0
374967.3	323653.5	18831.1	18424.6	18883.7	25559.6	46842.5	9127.7	10822.0
29996.7	18834.1	787.0	6247.5	6137.0	1230.2	10131.8	3207.8	824.0
5848291.0	**4397423.2**	**230445.7**	**552221.7**	**599545.7**	**176292.7**	**1117344.8**	**287353.4**	**79761.0**
3512966.5	**2730396.6**	**199047.1**	**237402.0**	**266402.4**	**99047.4**	**620027.6**	**154578.1**	**47767.0**
408242.6	361865.2	3649.5	16681.5	26012.3	15823.2	41710.2	12048.4	6859.0
1174364.8	867380.2	157958.1	47802.2	54017.4	25066.8	273140.1	61164.6	9590.0
363967.7	303575.2	2218.8	4181.4	10255.7	20460.1	24614.8	12140.3	7215.0
156952.0	121918.4	439.4	15632.7	18195.7	782.5	21462.0	2826.9	1867.0
250560.7	205550.5	717.3	21060.6	21958.4	4678.8	31190.1	8514.4	3712.0
194391.9	155446.2	483.8	1443.2	1740.0	10199.5	10286.9	8063.1	2440.0
612569.6	460968.0	31170.2	69267.2	72253.9	6141.8	133416.4	29992.3	11398.0
97447.7	79216.8	137.6	13071.9	13886.3	2148.2	15090.9	1067.0	1138.0
39947.1	36410.8	583.3	-2419.3	-2516.2	3103.0	-131.9	1801.0	739.0
214522.4	138065.3	1689.1	50680.6	50598.9	10643.5	69248.1	16960.1	2809.0
1270031.0	**1036968.0**	**12100.1**	**53174.3**	**66284.9**	**47880.6**	**116618.7**	**38233.7**	**20580.0**
92674.5	101957.5	617.5	-13596.3	-9510.8	11750.6	-8395.4	497.9	1493.0
354793.1	287858.8	4002.7	14568.2	16852.2	5904.9	33910.0	13055.1	5084.0
103226.5	78146.4	559.2	15483.1	16663.8	1859.8	20151.9	2928.9	1425.0

13-6 续表 2

单位：万元

地区	Region	企业单位数（个） Number of Enterprises (unit)	#亏损企业 Loss- Suffering Enterprises	工业总产值（当年价格） Gross Industrial Output Value (At Current Prices)
沙湾县	Shawan County	38	15	372619.1
托里县	Toli County	10	3	198121.0
裕民县	Yumin [Qagantokay] County			
和布克赛尔蒙古自治县	Hoboksar Mongol Autonomous County	15	3	173789.4
阿勒泰地区	**Altay Administrative Offices**	**63**	**19**	**1102209.4**
阿勒泰市	Altay City	15	6	135152.7
布尔津县	Burqin County	6	1	52156.2
富蕴县	Fuyun [Koktokay] County	17	9	480492.2
福海县	Fuhai [Burultokay] County	13		73748.7
哈巴河县	Habahe [Kaba] County	8	1	324257.2
青河县	Qinghe [Qinggil] County	3	2	29210.3
吉木乃县	Jeminay County	1		7192.1
博尔塔拉蒙古自治州	**Bortala Mongol Autonomous Prefecture**	**43**	**14**	**471085.7**
博乐市	Bole [Bortala] City	29	7	392809.7
精河县	Jinghe [Jing] County	13	7	75412.5
温泉县	Wenquan [Araxang] County	1	0	2863.5
巴音郭楞蒙古自治州	**Bayangol Mongol Autonomous Prefecture**	**140**	**32**	**8213541.7**
库尔勒市	Korla City	62	11	6223935.8
轮台县	Luntai [Bugur] County	15	5	292697.5
尉犁县	Yuli [Lopnur] County	1		6027.2
若羌县	Ruoqiang [Qarkilik] County	6	2	462204.4
且末县	Qiemo [Qarqan] County	1	1	2510.2
焉耆回族自治县	Yanqi Hui Autonomous County	10	3	72315.6
和静县	Hejing County	33	7	1110291.9
和硕县	Hoxud County	7	2	26995.8
博湖县	Bohu [Bagrax] County	5	1	16563.3
阿克苏地区	**Aksu Administrative Offices**	**171**	**33**	**4499436.7**
阿克苏市	Aksu City	52	6	959459.7
温宿县	Wensu [Onsu] County	20	4	120203.4
库车县	Kuqa County	40	13	2632552.7
沙雅县	Xayar County	14	2	199552.6
新和县	Xinhe [Toksu] County	9		95165.7
拜城县	Baicheng [Bay] County	22	5	403338.1
乌什县	Wushi [Uxturpan] County	5		21619.9

Continued

(10 000 yuan)

工业销售产值(当年价) Sales Value of Industry Products (At Current Prices)	出口交货值 Delivery Value of Industry Export	实收资本 Total Capital Hold	资产合计 Total Assets	流动资产合计 Total Working Capitals	#产成品 Finished Product	固定资产原价 Original Value of Fixed Assets
344925.9		77146.2	411941.6	239687.6	43259.7	182595.8
192220.2		64860.3	356499.5	172801.6	20157.2	155556.8
175318.0		160489.3	608925.1	120771.2	6627.1	391746.9
1092925.5		**407489.9**	**1945347.2**	**496079.3**	**80302.0**	**1202101.6**
129695.0		35096.4	310499.3	66326.1	6650.0	270773.5
52382.4		16801.9	263096.4	43476.3	1072.1	234470.8
474841.7		190245.9	751887.0	208330.2	56811.6	317988.5
70887.4		81107.7	204043.4	63141.8	6686.1	142329.5
339129.0		51160.0	330267.3	83084.4	7439.7	190247.6
18797.9		23500.0	43171.9	23469.3	1642.5	9652.5
7192.1		9578.0	42381.9	8251.2		36639.2
426167.0	**5661.5**	**153217.0**	**829717.9**	**338513.5**	**66887.4**	**560040.2**
358904.4	5661.5	114519.7	654010.7	243553.5	56477.0	494252.6
64524.3		38589.3	173109.8	93375.6	10099.6	64565.1
2738.3		108.0	2597.4	1584.4	310.8	1222.5
8222543.7	**50755.4**	**4681730.6**	**12943484.9**	**3227059.1**	**392603.8**	**12605390.1**
6176862.5	10192.8	4158634.2	9578088.7	1953612.6	161379.7	10767973.6
316413.7	8144.1	111223.6	577277.8	285957.7	41691.6	286289.4
6027.2		3000.0	6259.0	3641.5	509.6	2790.3
484400.6		60599.9	819904.5	355859.6	47929.3	510266.2
2510.2		10.0	77.2	54.8		412.0
75052.2	9253.0	21288.0	126810.4	69264.0	17833.1	80548.3
1111956.0	140.0	308496.1	1745993.2	509349.2	100214.8	890250.4
29297.5	10022.4	10332.1	52346.7	30264.3	10668.4	29212.4
20023.8	13003.1	8146.7	36727.4	19055.4	12377.3	37647.5
4369551.4	**1403.4**	**1478081.9**	**6661812.1**	**2400577.2**	**254235.1**	**3151958.8**
930592.9		390072.8	2759574.6	1006395.6	67329.4	1072362.7
118117.6		73924.5	374126.8	72682.8	16873.3	262454.0
2606988.5	728.9	752112.9	2070408.7	664408.6	75313.6	1113309.9
193327.3	674.5	91306.8	379393.3	163558.6	22458.7	211196.8
68104.0		23300.7	144400.2	70635.6	8927.1	51793.2
367428.7		129264.2	812295.2	361281.2	50414.9	381657.6
18809.6		6100.0	33681.6	19456.9	7672.2	14825.7

13-6 续表 3

单位: 万元

地　区	Region	流动负债合计 Total Working Liabilities	长期负债合计 Long-term Liabilities	所有者权益合计 Total Owners' Equities
沙湾县	Shawan County	255549.6	25090.8	129015.8
托里县	Toli County	200357.3	42277.1	107186.5
裕民县	Yumin [Qagantokay] County			
和布克赛尔蒙古自治县	Hoboksar Mongol Autonomous County	275549.9	131120.1	198754.8
阿勒泰地区	**Altay Administrative Offices**	**682332.1**	**374556.2**	**823523.7**
阿勒泰市	Altay City	104722.1	137354.5	68422.6
布尔津县	Burqin County	124079.6	51613.6	26865.1
富蕴县	Fuyun [Koktokay] County	306492.3	77665.1	367681.8
福海县	Fuhai [Burultokay] County	41617.5	67250.2	91070.9
哈巴河县	Habahe [Kaba] County	63958.8	32682.0	233626.5
青河县	Qinghe [Qinggil] County	13971.5	7990.8	20965.2
吉木乃县	Jeminay County	27490.3		14891.6
博尔塔拉蒙古自治州	**Bortala Mongol Autonomous Prefecture**	**400236.5**	**254769.1**	**173467.7**
博乐市	Bole [Bortala] City	285257.4	240760.9	126747.9
精河县	Jinghe [Jing] County	113385.1	14008.2	45716.4
温泉县	Wenquan [Araxang] County	1594.0		1003.4
巴音郭楞蒙古自治州	**Bayangol Mongol Autonomous Prefecture**	**3929675.6**	**3287838.8**	**5697777.6**
库尔勒市	Korla City	2288681.4	2743359.7	4534876.5
轮台县	Luntai [Bugur] County	282208.1	42189.3	238629.9
尉犁县	Yuli [Lopnur] County	1811.5		4447.5
若羌县	Ruoqiang [Qarkilik] County	304898.4	185610.4	328780.3
且末县	Qiemo [Qarqan] County	522.4		-445.2
焉耆回族自治县	Yanqi Hui Autonomous County	77175.8	3325.7	46197.8
和静县	Hejing County	917815.5	313038.6	513094.5
和硕县	Hoxud County	31513.9	70.5	20762.1
博湖县	Bohu [Bagrax] County	25048.6	244.6	11434.2
阿克苏地区	**Aksu Administrative Offices**	**2733488.1**	**1214926.7**	**2613055.4**
阿克苏市	Aksu City	1066824.3	602633.2	1082623.4
温宿县	Wensu [Onsu] County	156060.8	133298.2	84007.6
库车县	Kuqa County	805647.8	227638.2	997906.0
沙雅县	Xayar County	159133.0	98278.0	121982.3
新和县	Xinhe [Toksu] County	73318.3	9104.5	50141.3
拜城县	Baicheng [Bay] County	391615.0	131375.5	249629.0
乌什县	Wushi [Uxturpan] County	22888.5	460.0	10329.4

Continued

(10 000 yuan)

主营业务收入 Revenue from Principal Business	#主营业务成本 Cost of Principal Business	主营业务税金及附加 Taxes and Other Charges on Principal Business	营业利润 Business Profit	利润总额 Total Profit	亏损企业亏损总额 Losses Value of Loss-Suffering Enterprises	利税总额 Total Profits and Taxes	本年应交增值税 Value-added Taxes Payable	全部从业人员年平均人数(人) Annual Average Employed Persons (person)
363012.3	333615.1	826.3	-3191.3	434.3	9380.0	11567.6	10307.0	5021.0
196122.7	128588.1	2020.2	21679.0	21898.8	14173.1	25881.0	1962.0	3194.0
160201.9	106802.1	4074.2	18231.6	19946.6	4812.2	33503.6	9482.8	4363.0
1065293.5	**630058.6**	**19298.5**	**261645.4**	**266858.4**	**29364.7**	**380698.5**	**94541.6**	**11414.0**
134154.0	128081.1	428.1	-17664.2	-13191.3	15572.6	-10738.0	2025.2	2507.0
56918.9	30211.7	214.4	8762.5	9522.0	683.9	13720.3	3983.9	545.0
435354.0	235517.9	13249.4	108878.3	107348.6	9121.2	170396.8	49798.8	4634.0
69675.1	54211.9	775.1	10387.9	10775.6		14268.2	2717.5	1090.0
338573.1	159415.4	4439.3	149157.6	150289.9	2716.7	189940.6	35211.4	2314.0
23426.3	20299.3	192.2	-1203.3	-1183.0	1270.3	-186.0	804.8	306.0
7192.1	2321.3		3326.6	3296.6		3296.6		18.0
462359.8	**411589.3**	**1828.0**	**2149.6**	**11635.9**	**13611.7**	**29403.2**	**15939.3**	**8082.0**
393280.5	348521.0	1628.0	5804.4	12831.8	9605.1	28737.5	14277.7	6803.0
66819.9	60948.3	198.5	-3668.7	-1373.8	4006.6	479.3	1654.6	1249.0
2259.4	2120.0	1.5	13.9	177.9		186.4	7.0	30.0
8448765.6	**4424426.3**	**345873.7**	**2460108.5**	**2483061.7**	**25242.4**	**3376439.8**	**547504.4**	**58114.0**
6088712.9	2670286.8	300278.1	2133946.3	2118988.1	9879.4	2864281.8	445015.6	36554.0
297769.2	235447.1	6703.0	32793.5	33538.6	2201.8	45588.0	5346.4	2929.0
5489.0	3428.8	0.0	1774.0	1768.0	0.0	2048.6	280.6	61.0
478043.2	173546.8	27388.7	183253.1	218783.8	4321.9	282920.6	36748.1	3695.0
2510.2	2548.5	30.2	-45.4	-45.9	45.9	286.1	301.8	66.0
74894.3	52166.5	1429.5	5513.7	5680.9	4667.2	10531.1	3420.7	1173.0
1449189.3	1243819.4	9946.0	105059.7	105334.9	618.5	169578.7	54297.8	12595.0
29936.8	25623.1	56.7	168.3	1069.3	850.4	1948.7	822.7	670.0
22220.7	17559.3	41.5	-2354.7	-2056.0	2657.3	-743.8	1270.7	371.0
4456782.9	**3578583.4**	**279717.0**	**323669.3**	**345792.6**	**28108.4**	**778498.5**	**152988.9**	**39192.0**
973410.2	827684.6	3237.9	77487.0	94648.1	3720.5	126195.6	28309.6	13432.0
124875.8	87919.4	1439.3	16263.9	16062.5	345.7	23412.1	5910.3	2886.0
2640299.8	2127800.4	266403.4	133926.7	138750.8	10658.4	488684.7	83530.5	9650.0
200079.3	154811.2	153.1	30494.2	28804.3	939.2	30845.7	1888.3	2732.0
75151.7	52477.1	578.9	20221.4	21181.8		22568.5	807.8	1340.0
367068.6	263455.7	6832.5	38111.6	38413.0	12101.0	76037.1	30791.6	7413.0
18361.2	12922.6	691.5	2969.1	3016.5		4493.4	785.4	303.0

13-6 续表 4

单位: 万元

地　区	Region	企业单位数(个) Number of Enterprises (unit)	#亏损企业 Loss- Suffering Enterprises	工业总产值(当年价格) Gross Industrial Output Value (At Current Prices)
阿瓦提县	Awat County	7	3	34684.6
柯坪县	Kalpin County	2		32860.0
克孜勒苏柯尔克孜自治州	**Kizilsu Kirgiz Autonomous Prefecture**	**22**	**10**	**219473.2**
阿图什市	Artux City	11	5	124096.4
阿克陶县	Akto County	7	2	64169.6
阿合奇县	Akqi County	1		17466.0
乌恰县	Wuqia [Ulugqat] County	3	3	13741.2
喀什地区	**Kashgar [Kaxgar] Administrative Offices**	**87**	**36**	**1031071.4**
喀什市	Kashgar [Kaxgar] City	21	10	451555.0
疏附县	Shufu County	3	2	10166.0
疏勒县	Shule County	13	5	53640.6
英吉沙县	Yengisar County	4	4	12334.4
泽普县	Zepu [Poskam] County	6	3	31996.1
莎车县	Shache [Yarkant] County	8		111885.9
叶城县	Yecheng [Kagilik] County	10	2	94203.2
麦盖提县	Makit County	7	2	38134.3
岳普湖县	Yopurga County	2	2	10820.0
伽师县	Jiashi [Payzawat] County	2		133830.6
巴楚县	Bachu [Maralbexi] County	8	5	52036.3
塔什库尔干塔吉克自治县	Taxkorgan Tajik Autonomous County	3	1	30469.0
和田地区	**Hotan Administrative Offices**	**18**	**6**	**194628.9**
和田市	Hotan City	8	4	92533.7
和田县	Hotan County	4	1	40576.1
墨玉县	Moyu [Karakax] County	2	1	45362.6
皮山县	Pishan [Guma] County	1		4716.1
洛浦县	Lop County	2		9500.8
策勒县	Qira County	1		1939.6
于田县	Yutian [Keriya] County			
民丰县	Minfeng [Niya] County			
自治区直辖县级市	**Municpality Country-LevelCity directly under the Central Government**	**161**	**42**	**5471769.7**
石河子市	Shihezi City	87	27	3699463.3
阿拉尔市	Aral City	31	9	187100.9
图木舒克市	Tumxuk City	9	2	109391.2
五家渠市	Wujiaqu City	34	4	1475814.3

Continued

(10 000 yuan)

工业销售产值(当年价) Sales Value of Industry Products (At Current Prices)	出口交货值 Delivery Value of Industry Export	实收资本 Total Capital Hold	资产合计 Total Assets	流动资产合计 Total Working Capitals	#产成品 Finished Product	固定资产原价 Original Value of Fixed Assets
34638.2		11200.0	64048.8	23138.6	2791.1	39105.0
31544.6		800.0	23882.9	19019.3	2454.8	5253.9
200805.7		**215585.8**	**645768.4**	**213986.9**	**30565.1**	**340003.9**
109480.7		158313.8	342425.9	152472.7	18455.4	124110.5
62922.7		55448.0	120188.6	48474.0	11235.8	42583.8
17466.0		0.0	168148.2	5256.7		167176.8
10936.3		1824.0	15005.7	7783.5	873.9	6132.8
1007415.2	**8947.1**	**280230.3**	**1671605.6**	**603750.3**	**93010.9**	**1219926.9**
455042.9	4769.3	102387.0	718176.2	173805.2	16858.3	762685.2
10221.0		2300.0	6344.6	4047.1	298.0	3428.1
51762.5	1795.0	32020.0	128148.8	65103.7	14389.1	40276.5
11733.0		24745.0	69821.5	18024.3	386.4	44631.3
29259.8		12320.0	37793.9	15330.4	3870.7	18884.6
108845.7	2382.8	25570.0	144978.3	77510.3	17173.8	61319.8
87998.0		39299.0	137238.2	43797.4	6442.2	86801.8
39376.7		13462.3	85476.4	67248.6	8148.0	12477.2
6112.1		1005.0	16973.5	7137.0	1143.5	19429.3
127325.9		3900.0	131249.9	66962.8	8001.8	56976.5
52233.3		15010.0	63638.5	39808.0	12659.7	30299.4
27504.3		8212.0	131765.8	24975.5	3639.4	82717.2
199189.8		**189012.0**	**518061.4**	**122375.6**	**7069.7**	**514310.3**
91761.5		16182.8	135786.4	20424.1	869.2	188801.9
39961.7		141537.2	274122.6	52578.9	402.3	258225.3
51880.9		26737.0	73284.3	30589.0	4243.7	48422.9
4716.1		998.0	17154.2	8323.2		9342.8
8930.0		2927.0	14347.4	9516.6	1554.5	7094.7
1939.6		630.0	3366.5	943.8		2422.7
5287480.0	**17911.1**	**1688853.4**	**8989417.7**	**3522352.6**	**531766.3**	**5366124.8**
3537378.3	13941.9	1251002.4	5845221.5	2166445.3	370502.5	3819464.2
202381.4		134738.0	550043.9	172181.7	31340.2	298367.3
113372.8		45298.5	293906.0	145366.7	15259.1	150285.7
1434347.5	3969.2	257814.5	2300246.3	1038358.9	114664.5	1098007.6

13-6 续表 5

单位：万元

地　　区	Region	流动负债合计 Total Working Liabilities	长期负债合计 Long-term Liabilities	所有者权益合计 Total Owners' Equities
阿瓦提县	Awat County	36881.2	12139.1	13672.7
柯坪县	Kalpin County	21119.2		2763.7
克孜勒苏柯尔克孜自治州	**Kizilsu Kirgiz Autonomous Prefecture**	**395053.8**	**22194.3**	**214685.9**
阿图什市	Artux City	151156.6	19302.9	158132.0
阿克陶县	Akto County	61874.0	910.4	57404.1
阿合奇县	Akqi County	166167.2	1981.0	
乌恰县	Wuqia [Ulugqat] County	15856.0		-850.2
喀什地区	**Kashgar [Kaxgar] Administrative Offices**	**623627.0**	**563767.0**	**465119.3**
喀什市	Kashgar [Kaxgar] City	233254.9	312519.9	165158.3
疏附县	Shufu County	4254.6		2089.9
疏勒县	Shule County	54428.6	33630.7	34019.2
英吉沙县	Yengisar County	15607.7	30776.7	23437.1
泽普县	Zepu [Poskam] County	13080.1	4918.9	19065.7
莎车县	Shache [Yarkant] County	75499.6	30263.9	39214.5
叶城县	Yecheng [Kagilik] County	46864.6	53181.6	36299.8
麦盖提县	Makit County	41602.9	100.0	43771.5
岳普湖县	Yopurga County	11180.2	370.3	3293.0
伽师县	Jiashi [Payzawat] County	37204.1	5260.0	88785.8
巴楚县	Bachu [Maralbexi] County	51048.6	6940.8	3624.0
塔什库尔干塔吉克自治县	Taxkorgan Tajik Autonomous County	39601.1	85804.2	6360.5
和田地区	**Hotan Administrative Offices**	**129826.9**	**159263.5**	**225759.1**
和田市	Hotan City	53187.5	75666.6	6679.0
和田县	Hotan County	45106.1	77278.3	148779.7
墨玉县	Moyu [Karakax] County	20260.6	2987.9	50035.7
皮山县	Pishan [Guma] County	4523.7	3330.7	9299.8
洛浦县	Lop County	4789.0		9558.4
策勒县	Qira County	1960.0		1406.5
于田县	Yutian [Keriya] County			
民丰县	Minfeng [Niya] County			
自治区直辖县级市	**Municpality Country-LevelCity directly under the Central Government**	**4260558.0**	**1608669.4**	**2820899.2**
石河子市	Shihezi City	2010210.6	1345625.3	2253906.9
阿拉尔市	Aral City	320721.1	36232.9	136975.7
图木舒克市	Tumxuk City	132980.2	110078.8	50672.0
五家渠市	Wujiaqu City	1796646.1	116732.4	379344.6

Continued

(10 000 yuan)

主营业务收入 Revenue from Principal Business	#主营业务成本 Cost of Principal Business	主营业务税金及附加 Taxes and Other Charges on Principal Business	营业利润 Business Profit	利润总额 Total Profit	亏损企业亏损总额 Losses Value of Loss-Suffering Enterprises	利税总额 Total Profits and Taxes	本年应交增值税 Value-added Taxes Payable	全部从业人员年平均人数(人) Annual Average Employed Persons (person)
32480.8	28794.2	29.4	1826.4	2534.0	343.6	3528.2	964.8	1299.0
25055.5	22718.2	351.0	2369.0	2381.6		2733.2	0.6	137.0
215807.8	**176303.9**	**2467.9**	**7645.4**	**9559.5**	**9659.5**	**25493.1**	**13465.7**	**3856.0**
126268.7	110151.1	325.3	-911.5	628.4	8030.2	6861.7	5908.0	1937.0
62321.7	48835.4	2103.6	4105.7	4284.8	1340.5	13484.8	7096.4	1140.0
17466.3	6438.6	12.6	4740.0	4935.1		5050.7	103.0	126.0
9751.1	10878.8	26.4	-288.8	-288.8	288.8	95.9	358.3	653.0
1043759.5	**918097.8**	**5942.3**	**20478.3**	**41463.6**	**38127.0**	**86806.5**	**39400.6**	**17905.0**
467067.2	452632.7	2849.9	-20228.7	-2514.6	18633.9	19230.5	18895.2	7600.0
9854.0	8629.9	31.1	612.9	607.3	181.7	819.9	181.5	266.0
66295.7	59112.8	115.8	1701.7	1864.1	846.5	2553.9	574.0	1151.0
11721.7	10538.2	19.2	-1162.5	-1182.1	1182.1	-693.2	469.7	425.0
27437.5	23569.4	97.7	1861.1	2180.3	1697.4	2869.0	591.0	921.0
109441.0	94002.5	15.5	10053.8	10999.4		11233.9	219.0	1054.0
91634.6	82579.6	1013.4	-7142.1	-6524.5	8344.9	-4005.4	1505.7	3511.0
55455.4	43926.5	28.7	6522.6	7231.6	1592.6	7800.4	540.1	687.0
4092.7	3628.2	17.3	-301.7	-263.4	263.4	19.8	265.9	203.0
127326.0	84037.4	788.2	32640.4	32661.7		46225.4	12775.5	1185.0
45929.4	42531.6	103.8	-3883.4	-3348.5	3580.8	-2826.0	418.7	531.0
27504.3	12909.0	861.7	-195.8	-247.7	1803.7	3578.3	2964.3	371.0
189997.3	**178967.0**	**1238.9**	**-4366.7**	**2757.8**	**14893.6**	**13377.1**	**9380.4**	**4142.0**
85955.7	94252.8	366.6	-9486.3	-5559.2	9086.7	-3340.4	1852.2	2129.0
40837.2	28438.6	585.2	2095.4	3011.4	3606.5	8320.1	4723.5	634.0
46503.7	40672.5	66.3	2593.0	3866.4	2200.4	5661.8	1729.1	529.0
4125.6	4867.4	159.4	-42.5	65.3		592.6	367.9	154.0
9416.8	8235.3	61.4	221.7	586.2		1355.3	707.7	585.0
3158.3	2500.4		252.0	787.7		787.7		111.0
4952348.5	**4168740.8**	**18353.7**	**331106.9**	**369913.6**	**69176.9**	**568089.3**	**179822.0**	**63523.0**
3279530.4	2781802.6	16314.9	152705.2	183407.8	51225.4	309674.8	109952.1	47911.0
203715.0	172076.1	747.4	20471.9	21276.3	10855.8	23922.4	1898.7	4582.0
113927.8	94981.5	134.7	7281.5	8756.2	620.0	12263.4	3372.5	1779.0
1355175.3	1119880.6	1156.7	150648.3	156473.3	6475.7	222228.7	64598.7	9251.0

13-7 规模以上工业企业主要经济效益指标

单位: % (2012 年)

项 目	Item	产值利税率 Ratio of Profits and Taxes to Industrial Output Value
总 计	**Total**	**20.4**
按登记注册类型分	**Grouped by Registry Type**	
内资企业	Domestic Funded Enterprises	20.6
国有企业	State-owned Enterprises	9.1
#中央企业	Central Enterprises	10.6
地方企业	Local Enterprises	4.2
#自治区属企业	Autonomous	2.5
地区(州、市)属企业	Prefecture or City	-4.1
县(市)属企业	County or City	8.7
集体企业	Collective-owned Enterprises	16.1
#自治区属企业	Autonomous	3.9
地区(州、市)属企业	Prefecture or City	2.9
县(市)属企业	County or City	32.3
镇属企业	Town	58.2
乡属企业	Village	
股份合作企业	Share-holding Cooperative Enterprises	6.7
联营企业	Joint Ownership Enterprises	13.4
#国有联营企业	State Joint Ownership Enterprises	1.3
集体联营企业	Collective Joint Ownership Enterprises	
国有与集体联营企业	Joint State-collective Enterprises	41.6
其他联营企业	Other Joint Ownership Enterprises	12.4
有限责任公司	Limited Liability Corporations	12.8
#国有独资公司	State Sole funded Corporations	17.6
其他有限责任公司	Other Limited Liability Corporations	11.9
股份有限公司	Share-holding Corporations Ltd.	30.7
私营企业	Private Enterprises	11.9
#私营独资企业	Private-funded Enterprises	17.7
私营合伙企业	Private Partnership Enterprises	30.0
私营有限责任公司	Private Limited Liability Corporations	10.6
私营股份有限公司	Private Share-holding Corporations Ltd.	15.3
港、澳、台商投资企业	Enterprises with Funds from Hong Kong, Macao and Taiwan	10.8
外商投资企业	Foreign Funded Enterprises	13.6
在总计中: 国有控股企业	Of the Total: State-owned and State-holding Enterprises	23.8
在总计中: 农村工业	Of the Total: Rural Industry	8.1
按轻、重工业分	**Grouped by Light & Heavy Industry**	
轻工业	Light Industry	11.9
以农产品为原料	Using Farm Produces as Raw Materials	12.2
以非农产品为原料	Using Non-Farm Produces as Raw Materials	6.2
重工业	Heavy Industry	21.6
采掘工业	Mining and Quarrying	48.8
原料工业	Raw Materials Industry	8.8
加工工业	Manufacturing Industry	14.7
按企业规模分	**Grouped by Size of Enterprises (Old Standard)**	
大型企业	Large Enterprises	24.0
中型企业	Medium-sized Enterprises	16.1
小型企业	Small Enterprises	12.3
微型企业	Mini Enterprises	7.7

Main Indicators on Economic Efficiency of Industrial Enterprises above Designated Size

(%)

总资产贡献率 Ratio of Total Assets to Industrial Output Value	资本保值增值率 Ratio of Capital-hold and Rise	资产负债率 Assets Liability Ratio	流动资产周转次数(次/年) Number of Times of Annual TurnoverWorking Capitals (times/year)	成本费用利润率 Ratio of Profits to Industrial Cost	全员劳动生产率 Overall Labour Productivity
14.5	**116.3**	**57.2**	**2.0**	**14.0**	**39.1**
14.6	116.0	57.2	2.1	14.2	39.7
6.5	112.1	62.4	2.1	3.1	24.8
8.0	108.8	57.7	2.2	3.7	25.8
3.3	124.7	72.4	1.7	1.2	21.0
2.3	61.9	73.8	2.1	1.3	19.6
-0.2	75.9	89.6	1.3	-4.9	11.7
2.8	725.8	64.9	1.1	-0.5	21.7
25.0	122.4	50.9	2.6	9.7	19.5
9.2	100.8	47.3	3.2	-0.1	8.2
11.3	95.7	45.0	4.9	0.5	6.9
34.2	146.8	33.3	1.4	32.6	37.0
103.7	204.4	36.6	2.7	59.0	108.9
4.7	2.8	85.8	1.2	3.1	10.5
7.7	262.1	71.3	1.1	14.1	12.8
1.5	144.6	68.6	1.0		6.5
14.9	733.8	68.7	0.9	94.6	1769.5
8.8	3760.1	80.6	1.4	9.5	11.2
8.8	118.4	67.0	1.6	8.1	22.3
12.2	108.6	63.8	1.9	6.6	27.5
8.2	120.5	67.5	1.6	8.4	21.3
24.0	113.7	45.2	3.1	23.2	86.5
8.7	128.5	62.3	1.2	9.5	19.1
24.1	85.2	65.5	2.7	13.3	21.5
95.4	86.8	51.1	6.3	17.6	49.9
8.7	127.8	66.6	1.4	8.0	16.4
7.0	134.7	51.5	0.8	13.9	41.4
8.3	141.7	50.6	1.5	7.4	14.4
11.3	129.5	62.6	1.8	9.4	24.0
17.6	115.2	53.8	2.7	16.3	52.2
2.7	613.5	28.1	2.1	6.0	12.9
10.2	111.7	64.5	1.5	6.6	15.0
11.0	110.2	65.1	1.5	6.9	15.5
3.1	125.2	58.8	0.8	1.7	9.8
15.0	116.8	56.3	2.2	15.1	45.2
27.8	109.8	49.1	2.6	55.0	73.2
8.0	121.5	60.7	2.5	2.1	29.6
9.2	123.9	58.6	1.0	13.0	21.7
18.5	111.8	53.0	2.9	16.8	58.0
9.2	113.0	62.6	1.2	10.7	20.4
8.9	140.6	62.8	1.5	8.8	22.1
6.2	123.0	73.7	1.1	4.8	23.5

13-8 分行业规模以上工业企业主要经济效益指标

单位: %　　　　　　　　　　　　　　　　　　　　　　　　　　　　　　　　　　(2012 年)

行　　业	Sector	产值利税率 Ratio of Profits and Taxes to Industrial Output Value
总　　计	**Total**	**20.4**
煤炭开采和洗选业	Mining and Washing of Coal	26.4
石油和天然气开采业	Extraction of Petroleum and Natural Gas	60.8
黑色金属矿采选业	Mining and Processing of Ferrous Metals Ores	27.4
有色金属矿采选业	Mining and Processing of Nonferrous Metals Ores	48.4
非金属矿采选业	Mining and Processing of Nonmetal Ores	18.1
#采　盐	Extraction of Salt	31.6
农副食品加工业	Processing of Food from Agricultural Products	8.4
#谷物磨制	Grain Grinding	6.8
饲料加工	Fodder Processing	10.0
制　糖	Sugar Making	8.8
食品制造业	Manufacture of Food	8.5
#罐头制造	Manufacture of can	-7.8
酒、饮料和精制茶制造业	Manufacture of Wine,Beverages and Refined Tea	30.4
#酒的制造	Manufacture of Wine	35.8
烟草制品业	Manufacture of Tobacco	70.0
纺织业	Manufacture of Textile	4.4
#棉、化纤纺织及印染精加工	Cotton, Chemical Fiber, Dyeing, Printing and Processing	4.0
毛纺织和染整精加工	Wool Textile, Dyeing and Printing	-0.6
纺织服装、鞋、帽制造业	Manufacture of Textile Wearing Apparel,Footware and Caps	10.4
皮革、毛皮、羽毛(绒)及其制品业	Leather, Fur, Feather and Related Products Manufacturing	8.0
#皮革鞣制加工	Leather Tanning and Processing	8.0
木材加工及木、竹、藤、棕、草制品业	Processing of Timber, Wood, Bamboo, Cane, Grass Products	14.7
家具制造业	Manufacture of Furniture	-1.2
造纸及纸制品业	Manufacture of Paper and Paper Products	11.8
印刷业和记录媒介的复制	Printing and Copying of Medium for Record	8.7
石油加工、炼焦及核燃料加工业	Oil Processing, Coking and Nuclear Fuel Processing	10.6
#炼　焦	Coking	12.6
化学原料及化学制品制造业	Raw Chemical Material and Chemical Products	16.5
#基础化学原料制造	Basic Chemical Material	12.6
肥料制造	Fertilizer Making	41.1
合成材料制造	Manufacture of Synthetic Materials	7.5
医药制造业	Manufacture of Medicine	18.8
化学纤维制造业	Manufacture of Chemical Fiber	2.4
橡胶制品业	Manufacture of Rubber Products	8.3
非金属矿物制品业	Manufacture of Nonmetal Mineral Products	9.7
#水泥制造	Manufacture of Cement	11.8
黑色金属冶炼及压延加工业	Smelting and Pressing of Ferrous Metals	2.6
有色金属冶炼及压延加工业	Smelting and Pressing of Nonferrous Metals	7.3
金属制品业	Manufacture of Metal Products	5.2
通用设备制造业	Manufacture of General Purpose Machinery	12.8
专用设备制造业	Manufacture of Special Purpose Machinery	13.2
汽车制造业	Manufacture of Automobile	-2.2
电气机械及器材制造业	Manufacture of Electric Equipment and Machinery	15.6
计算机、通信和其他电子设备制造业	Telecom Equipment, Computer and Other Electronic Equipment	6.7
仪器仪表制造业	Measuring Instruments and Machinery for Cultunal Activify and OfficeWork	27.3
金属制品、机械和设备修理业	Manufacture of Repairing of Metal Products,Machinery and Equipment	7.5
电力、热力的生产和供应业	Electricity and Thermal Production and Supply	10.8
#电力生产和电力供应	Electricity Production and Supply	11.4
燃气生产和供应业	Gas Production and Supply	18.2
水的生产和供应业	Water Production and Supply	4.4

Main Indicators on Economic Efficiency of Industrial Enterprises above Designated Size by Sectors

(%)

总资产贡献率 Ratio of Total Assets to Industrial Output Value	资本保值增值率 Ratio of Capital-hold and Rise	资产负债率 Assets Liability Ratio	流动资产周转次数(次/年) Number of Times of Annual Turnover Working Capitals (times/year)	成本费用利润率 Ratio of Profits to Industrial Cost	全员劳动生产率 Overall Labour Productivity
14.5	**116.3**	**57.2**	**2.0**	**14.0**	**39.1**
9.9	116.5	62.4	1.4	16.5	24.1
36.8	107.1	42.0	4.2	87.4	153.4
16.7	107.1	68.6	1.1	20.9	41.5
21.4	111.0	48.7	1.6	56.4	46.9
15.6	107.7	60.8	1.4	7.2	19.4
27.7	125.7	29.5	1.3	17.5	20.5
10.4	118.6	67.2	1.7	6.8	17.2
12.4	123.9	52.3	3.0	6.5	15.9
14.3	110.1	49.1	2.5	8.7	23.2
7.2	88.3	59.9	0.9	4.1	12.2
7.2	95.8	70.8	1.3	5.2	13.4
0.3	44.2	89.2	0.6	-9.7	6.5
23.6	130.2	64.8	1.6	22.6	28.6
24.2	138.9	66.6	1.2	26.4	28.6
56.1	115.8	28.9	1.3	37.9	293.6
3.7	117.2	63.1	1.4	0.9	6.0
3.5	119.9	64.5	1.3	0.4	6.0
-0.2	136.1	46.8	1.4	-3.6	3.7
9.1	-195.8	83.0	1.6	5.6	7.6
13.2	139.0	71.6	1.8	7.4	37.6
13.2	139.0	71.6	1.8	7.4	37.6
16.6	107.5	54.7	2.0	13.0	17.5
0.3	98.1	17.7	1.2	-3.1	8.2
8.2	98.1	69.9	1.2	10.4	9.6
6.3	116.8	48.3	1.4	4.9	10.0
20.8	96.3	42.0	5.6	-1.3	56.2
9.3	125.2	67.3	1.3	9.4	21.8
8.9	128.8	58.4	1.6	14.9	25.5
3.9	142.4	61.4	1.2	7.9	14.3
17.5	189.2	62.0	1.3	49.3	43.8
8.4	101.6	51.8	2.6	6.3	28.8
11.8	120.5	51.6	0.8	17.8	14.0
5.2	74.0	82.4	1.9	0.1	14.3
9.7	133.5	58.0	1.7	7.6	14.0
5.4	141.7	57.8	1.0	6.0	14.6
4.7	154.4	53.1	0.7	7.8	15.0
4.9	102.4	73.5	2.8	0.5	13.6
3.5	291.1	71.0	0.9	5.6	25.3
7.3	104.9	60.7	1.7	4.3	10.5
13.1	123.4	61.9	1.3	10.8	13.6
9.7	116.1	50.5	1.2	11.8	18.6
-1.8	165.3	88.2	2.8	-2.4	3.1
7.3	111.4	55.2	0.7	13.3	37.1
4.0	103.7	48.7	0.9	7.5	11.2
9.9	84.8	18.9	0.6	33.2	53.3
3.1	1329.6	44.3	0.5	4.2	10.5
6.0	128.5	65.2	2.1	7.3	36.3
6.4	129.6	64.4	2.4	8.0	40.0
10.4	183.0	58.9	1.1	18.4	31.4
1.2	119.4	57.0	0.3	-1.2	12.4

13-9 各地、州、市、县(市)规模以上工业企业主要经济效益指标

单位: % (2012 年)

地　区	Region	产值利税率 Ratio of Profits and Taxes to Industrial Output Value
总　计	**Total**	**20.4**
乌鲁木齐市	**Urumqi City**	**15.7**
天山区	Tianshan District	7.5
沙依巴克区	Shayibak District	19.3
新市区	Xinshi District	35.0
水磨沟区	Shui Mogou District	15.7
头屯河区	Tou Tunhe District	2.1
达坂城区	Da Bancheng District	27.6
米东区	Midong District	8.5
乌鲁木齐县	Urumqi County	33.5
克拉玛依市	**Karamay City**	**26.3**
独山子区	Dushanzi District	5.7
克拉玛依区	Karamay District	39.4
白碱滩区	Bai Jiantan District	14.9
乌尔河区	Urhe District	20.0
吐鲁番地区	**Turpan Administrative Offices**	**19.4**
吐鲁番市	Turpan City	7.1
鄯善县	Shanshan [Piqan] County	23.6
托克逊县	Toksun County	15.6
哈密地区	**Hami [Kumul] Administrative Offices**	**14.1**
哈密市	Hami [Kumul] City	11.6
巴里坤哈萨克自治县	Barkol Kazak Autonomous County	36.6
伊吾县	Yiwu [Araturuk] County	13.8
昌吉回族自治州	**Changji Hui Autonomous Prefecture**	**12.8**
昌吉市	Changji City	15.7
阜康市	Fukang City	10.5
呼图壁县	Hutubi County	15.3
玛纳斯县	Manas County	7.2
奇台县	Qitai County	12.7
吉木萨尔县	Jimsar County	9.0
木垒哈萨克自治县	Mori Kazak Autonomous County	21.3
伊犁哈萨克自治州	**Ili Kazak Autonomous Prefecture**	**18.2**
伊犁州直属县(市)	**Counties (Cities) Direct Under Ili Prefecture**	**16.9**
伊宁市	Yining [Gulja] City	10.0
奎屯市	Kuytun City	24.1
伊宁县	Yining [Gulja] County	6.0
察布查尔锡伯自治县	Qapqal Xibe Autonomous County	11.8
霍城县	Huocheng [Korgas] County	11.7
巩留县	Gongliu [Tokkuztara] County	5.3

Main Indicators on Economic Benefit of Industrial Enterprises above Designated Size by Prefecture, Autonomous Prefecture, City and County

(%)

总资产贡献率 Ratio of Total Assets to Industrial Output Value	资本保值增值率 Ratio of Capital-hold and Rise	资产负债率 Assets Liability Ratio	流动资产周转次数(次/年) Number of Times of Annual TurnoverWorking Capitals (times/year)	成本费用利润率 Ratio of Profits to Industrial Cost	全员劳动生产率 Overall Labour Productivity
14.5	**116.3**	**57.2**	**2.0**	**14.0**	**39.1**
11.8	**107.6**	**55.8**	**2.1**	**9.0**	**40.0**
5.7	115.5	60.3	2.6	5.3	36.7
3.5	120.2	58.9	0.4	13.3	12.5
20.2	111.0	50.4	1.6	31.4	71.8
11.3	75.5	32.1	1.7	8.1	18.8
4.8	97.9	72.0	3.3	0.4	15.1
10.5	104.1	53.0	2.1	24.5	19.0
10.4	99.7	47.4	3.6	-2.1	29.4
7.9	80.1	79.5	0.7	41.1	157.0
25.3	**102.4**	**40.9**	**3.7**	**16.3**	**63.1**
9.4	89.7	33.6	5.9	-4.3	37.8
30.6	107.9	43.0	3.1	33.2	70.7
14.1	124.1	64.9	1.4	8.0	12.8
18.7	160.8	41.9	1.3	15.1	33.9
11.9	**121.1**	**54.4**	**1.7**	**14.7**	**30.3**
5.7	111.8	58.4	1.2	2.8	14.5
17.0	116.1	50.6	2.2	18.8	38.2
6.4	138.5	58.6	1.2	11.8	21.5
6.5	**124.3**	**68.1**	**1.2**	**8.9**	**20.2**
6.9	133.4	68.4	1.1	6.3	18.2
19.2	118.2	64.4	1.2	48.5	31.7
1.7	105.0	68.0	2.0	10.5	27.1
7.8	**169.5**	**63.8**	**1.2**	**9.9**	**22.8**
12.0	126.3	52.8	1.4	13.3	30.0
5.4	229.9	55.7	1.4	7.6	18.9
19.7	214.4	65.8	2.4	15.2	23.2
7.1	93.6	80.0	1.3	1.2	26.1
10.4	263.5	59.8	1.5	9.9	30.3
1.9	539.2	82.5	0.4	4.8	9.1
19.5	201.2	62.7	1.0	26.7	19.9
11.2	**122.2**	**62.7**	**1.6**	**11.8**	**26.1**
10.0	**130.6**	**62.7**	**1.5**	**8.6**	**24.0**
9.3	126.6	60.3	2.2	6.6	17.0
14.4	143.3	59.3	1.6	5.6	42.5
4.5	113.0	66.0	1.2	2.9	13.0
9.2	212.1	57.8	1.6	12.9	19.9
9.8	122.5	60.0	1.6	9.6	18.0
2.7	146.7	63.7	1.6	0.9	21.5

13-9 续表 1

单位: %

地　　区	Region	产　值 利税率 Ratio of Profits and Taxes to Industrial Output Value
新源县	Xinyuan [Kunes] County	18.3
昭苏县	Zhaosu [Mongolkure] County	17.3
特克斯县	Tekes County	-0.4
尼勒克县	Nilka County	32.8
塔城地区	**Tacheng [Tarbagatai] Administrative Offices**	**8.5**
塔城市	Tacheng [Qoqek] City	-8.6
乌苏市	Usu City	8.2
额敏县	Emin [Dorbiljin] County	18.6
沙湾县	Shawan County	3.1
托里县	Toli County	13.1
裕民县	Yumin [Qagantokay] County	
和布克赛尔蒙古自治县	Hoboksar Mongol Autonomous County	19.3
阿勒泰地区	**Altay Administrative Offices**	**34.5**
阿勒泰市	Altay City	-8.0
布尔津县	Burqin County	26.3
富蕴县	Fuyun [Koktokay] County	35.5
福海县	Fuhai [Burultokay] County	19.4
哈巴河县	Habahe [Kaba] County	58.6
青河县	Qinghe [Qinggil] County	-0.6
吉木乃县	Jeminay County	45.8
博尔塔拉蒙古自治州	**Bortala Mongol Autonomous Prefecture**	**6.2**
博乐市	Bole [Bortala] City	7.3
精河县	Jinghe [Jing] County	0.6
温泉县	Wenquan [Araxang] County	6.5
巴音郭楞蒙古自治州	**Bayangol Mongol Autonomous Prefecture**	**41.1**
库尔勒市	Korla City	46.0
轮台县	Luntai [Bugur] County	15.6
尉犁县	Yuli [Lopnur] County	34.0
若羌县	Ruoqiang [Qarkilik] County	61.2
且末县	Qiemo [Qarqan] County	11.4
焉耆回族自治县	Yanqi Hui Autonomous County	14.6
和静县	Hejing County	15.3
和硕县	Hoxud County	7.2
博湖县	Bohu [Bagrax] County	-4.5
阿克苏地区	**Aksu Administrative Offices**	**17.3**
阿克苏市	Aksu City	13.2
温宿县	Wensu [Onsu] County	19.5
库车县	Kuqa County	18.6

Continued

(%)

总资产贡献率 Ratio of Total Assets to Industrial Output Value	资本保值增值率 Ratio of Capital-hold and Rise	资产负债率 Assets Liability Ratio	流动资产周转次数(次/年) Number of Times of Annual TurnoverWorking Capitals (times/year)	成本费用利润率 Ratio of Profits to Industrial Cost	全员劳动生产率 Overall Labour Productivity
13.2	107.4	60.7	1.3	13.5	19.6
21.0	106.6	65.1	2.0	16.4	18.6
1.9	82.3	73.3	0.8	-6.0	9.8
9.8	133.9	72.3	2.1	30.0	41.8
6.5	**105.8**	**67.1**	**1.4**	**5.5**	**17.8**
-4.1	113.6	70.7	4.5	-8.9	10.7
7.6	80.4	67.0	1.3	5.1	16.7
10.6	97.9	58.9	1.0	18.4	25.0
4.7	102.7	68.1	1.5	0.1	8.6
8.8	81.9	69.6	1.1	13.6	34.7
6.4	213.2	67.3	1.3	14.3	17.7
21.3	**114.3**	**57.5**	**2.2**	**33.9**	**49.7**
-1.3	109.8	78.0	2.0	-8.6	10.8
9.8	82.0	88.2	1.3	19.7	49.3
23.7	105.1	51.1	2.1	34.2	54.1
8.2	384.2	55.4	1.1	17.7	21.9
58.3	98.6	29.3	4.1	82.6	99.4
1.7	631.7	51.4	1.0	-4.8	10.0
11.4	128.8	64.9	0.9	79.5	300.5
6.0	**96.0**	**79.1**	**1.4**	**2.5**	**17.9**
6.9	83.3	80.6	1.6	3.2	17.8
2.9	165.4	73.6	0.7	-1.9	18.7
9.9	112.9	61.4	1.4	7.9	20.4
27.4	**112.1**	**55.9**	**2.6**	**48.0**	**85.6**
31.0	105.6	52.7	3.1	67.0	115.6
9.1	142.3	56.2	1.0	12.7	30.1
33.1	318.8	28.9	1.5	47.6	40.3
36.3	124.7	59.9	1.3	81.2	94.0
370.6		676.7	45.8	-1.8	14.3
10.0	107.4	63.5	1.1	8.4	16.6
11.9	180.5	70.6	2.9	7.8	22.3
5.2	115.9	60.3	1.0	3.6	9.3
-0.3	94.7	68.9	1.2	-8.8	7.6
13.1	**149.7**	**60.7**	**1.9**	**8.8**	**31.6**
6.0	186.4	60.6	1.0	10.1	18.4
7.8	115.5	77.6	1.7	14.3	16.6
24.6	134.6	51.7	4.0	6.1	66.9

13-9 续表 2

单位: %

地　　区	Region	产　值利税率 Ratio of Profits and Taxes to Industrial Output Value
沙雅县	Xayar County	15.5
新和县	Xinhe [Toksu] County	23.7
拜城县	Baicheng [Bay] County	18.9
乌什县	Wushi [Uxturpan] County	20.8
阿瓦提县	Awat County	10.2
柯坪县	Kalpin County	8.3
克孜勒苏柯尔克孜自治州	**Kizilsu Kirgiz Autonomous Prefecture**	**11.6**
阿图什市	Artux City	5.5
阿克陶县	Akto County	21.0
阿合奇县	Akqi County	28.9
乌恰县	Wuqia [Ulugqat] County	0.7
喀什地区	**Kashgar [Kaxgar] Administrative Offices**	**8.4**
喀什市	Kashgar [Kaxgar] City	4.3
疏附县	Shufu County	8.1
疏勒县	Shule County	4.8
英吉沙县	Yengisar County	-5.6
泽普县	Zepu [Poskam] County	9.0
莎车县	Shache [Yarkant] County	10.0
叶城县	Yecheng [Kagilik] County	-4.3
麦盖提县	Makit County	20.5
岳普湖县	Yopurga County	0.2
伽师县	Jiashi [Payzawat] County	34.5
巴楚县	Bachu [Maralbexi] County	-5.4
塔什库尔干塔吉克自治县	Taxkorgan Tajik Autonomous County	11.7
和田地区	**Hotan Administrative Offices**	**6.9**
和田市	Hotan City	-3.6
和田县	Hotan County	20.5
墨玉县	Moyu [Karakax] County	12.5
皮山县	Pishan [Guma] County	12.6
洛浦县	Lop County	14.3
策勒县	Qira County	40.6
于田县	Yutian [Keriya] County	
民丰县	Minfeng [Niya] County	
自治区直辖县级市	**Municpality Country-LevelCity directly under the Central Government**	**10.4**
石河子市	Shihezi City	8.4
阿拉尔市	Aral City	12.8
图木舒克市	Tumxuk City	11.2
五家渠市	Wujiaqu City	15.1

Continued

(%)

总资产贡献率 Ratio of Total Assets to Industrial Output Value	资本保值增值率 Ratio of Capital-hold and Rise	资产负债率 Assets Liability Ratio	流动资产周转次数(次/年) Number of Times of Annual TurnoverWorking Capitals (times/year)	成本费用利润率 Ratio of Profits to Industrial Cost	全员劳动生产率 Overall Labour Productivity
10.8	173.8	67.9	1.2	15.9	23.4
17.3	160.3	64.4	1.1	35.8	24.1
10.8	108.6	69.3	1.0	11.8	24.5
14.7	118.5	69.3	0.9	19.8	21.4
7.0	131.6	78.7	1.4	8.0	8.4
11.7	824.3	88.4	1.3	10.3	24.8
5.8	**176.4**	**66.8**	**1.0**	**4.6**	**20.2**
3.1	243.1	53.8	0.8	0.5	19.8
12.7	103.5	52.2	1.3	7.7	20.5
6.7		100.0	3.3	38.8	82.4
0.6	-70.9	105.7	1.3	-2.3	9.3
7.4	**192.1**	**71.9**	**1.7**	**4.0**	**16.3**
5.1	173.0	77.0	2.7	-0.5	16.7
13.0	-903.2	67.1	2.4	6.8	7.7
4.1	225.9	69.2	1.0	2.8	8.8
0.4	8146.4	66.4	0.7	-8.9	7.0
9.0	236.0	49.6	1.8	8.3	10.1
9.7	492.0	73.0	1.4	11.0	22.0
0.3	116.8	73.6	2.1	-6.6	5.6
10.2	255.4	48.8	0.8	14.5	15.8
0.8	140.2	80.6	0.6	-5.9	15.3
35.3	152.7	32.4	1.9	34.6	46.4
-2.3	50.1	94.3	1.2	-6.7	28.4
7.1	-1234.6	95.2	1.1	-0.9	36.7
4.5	**108.0**	**55.9**	**1.6**	**1.4**	**16.5**
0.8	156.1	95.1	4.2	-5.6	13.0
5.0	99.7	44.7	0.8	7.8	36.3
7.8	137.1	31.7	1.5	8.9	22.3
3.9	97.4	45.8	0.5	1.3	10.6
9.2	101.4	33.4	1.0	6.4	6.1
23.4		58.2	3.4	26.6	6.9
8.0	**128.3**	**68.5**	**1.4**	**8.0**	**19.4**
7.4	129.1	61.3	1.5	5.9	16.9
5.7	181.3	74.9	1.2	11.1	12.2
5.5	127.9	82.8	0.8	8.2	17.4
10.5	112.4	83.5	1.3	13.1	36.5

13-10 国有控股工业企业主要经济指标

单位: 万元 (2012 年)

项目	Item	企业单位数(个) Number of Enterprises (unit)	#亏损企业 Loss- Suffering Enterprises	工业总产值(当年价格) Gross Industrial Output Value (At Current Prices)
总计	**Total**	**522**	**148**	**53466765.1**
按登记注册类型分	**Grouped by Registry Type**			
内资企业	DomesticFunded Enterprises	514	148	53313270.1
国有企业	State-owned Enterprises	124	43	6836834.7
#中央企业	Central Enterprises	63	17	5209041.2
地方企业	Local Enterprises	61	26	1627793.5
#自治区属企业	Autonomous	20	8	822944.2
地区(州、市)属企业	Prefecture or City	7	3	309384.4
县(市)属企业	County or City	24	11	179484.1
股份合作企业	Share-holding Cooperative Enterprises	1		
联营企业	Joint Ownership Enterprises	6	2	26024.3
#国有联营企业	State Joint Enterprises Ownership	5	2	17821.2
国有与集体联营企业	Joint State-collective OwnershipEnterprises	1		8203.1
有限责任公司	Limited Liability Corporations	330	85	14024599.0
#国有独资公司	Sole State-funded Corporations	56	23	3608476.0
其他有限责任公司	Other Limited Liability Corporations	274	62	10416123.0
股份有限公司	Share-holding Corporations Ltd.	53	18	32425812.1
港、澳、台商投资企业	Enterprises with Funds from Hongkong,Macao and Taiwan	2		79551.4
外商投资企业	Foreign Funded Enterprises	6		73943.6
在总计中: 国有控股企业	Of the Total : State-owned and State-holding Enterprises	522	148	53466765.1
按轻、重工业分	**Grouped by Light & Heavy Industry**			
轻工业	Light Industry	146	42	2344301.3
以农产品为原料	Using Farm Produces as Raw Materials	128	34	2209919.7
以非农产品为原料	Using Non-Farm Produces as Raw Materials	18	8	134381.6
重工业	Heavy Industry	376	106	51122463.8
采掘工业	Mining and Quarrying	79	17	17615486.9
原料工业	Raw Material Industry	196	73	30841755.5
加工工业	Manufacturing Industry	101	16	2665221.4
按企业规模分	**Grouped by Size of Enterprises**			
大型企业	Large Enterprises	57	17	43720176.5
中型企业	Medium-sized Enterprises	142	45	5980487.4
小型企业	Small Enterprises	303	80	3646932.6
微型企业	Mini Enterprises	20	6	119168.6

Main Economic Indicators Efficiency of State-holding Industrial Enterprises

(10 000 yuan)

工业销售产值(当年价) Sales Value of Industry Products (At Current Prices)	出口交货值 Delivery Value of Industry Export	实收资本 Total Capital Hold	资产合计 Total Assets	流动资产合计 Total Working Capitals	#产成品 Finished Product	固定资产原价 Original Value of Fixed Assets
52928947.5	**159536.9**	**27474452.4**	**78386247.9**	**19595857.8**	**1796749.8**	**71918451.0**
52807025.0	159536.9	27207873.3	77737353.7	19477641.2	1784983.0	71528238.7
6658353.6	10439.4	2661959.2	12451324.4	3202787.3	135905.6	8891912.5
5187954.8	5149.7	1815531.5	8522001.3	2337922.5	55737.0	6142596.4
1470398.8	5289.7	846427.7	3929323.1	864864.8	80168.6	2749316.1
710802.4		285411.5	1473386.0	321528.3	23349.4	1031175.0
284926.4		29869.8	542557.6	231385.3	20947.9	358304.8
178551.8		499893.4	1556088.4	171361.9	7421.9	1182434.1
		3468.0	9653.9	6619.2	4764.1	6853.4
26024.3		22797.4	76273.0	22723.3	593.6	52972.2
17821.2		16097.4	42433.5	15284.3	593.6	26620.6
8203.1		6700.0	33839.5	7439.0		26351.6
13761829.1	69964.9	5581296.6	24640062.3	7086196.3	918588.2	19963301.5
3509456.8	194.5	1467588.5	5950366.3	1879753.4	111594.3	3938400.1
10252372.3	69770.4	4113708.1	18689696.0	5206442.9	806993.9	16024901.4
32360818.0	79132.6	18938352.1	40560040.1	9159315.1	725131.5	42613199.1
82321.3		136000.0	250732.6	22702.0	9790.6	132822.2
39601.2		130579.1	398161.6	95514.6	1976.2	257390.1
52928947.5	159536.9	27474452.4	78386247.9	19595857.8	1796749.8	71918451.0
2326106.3	107323.9	905350.3	4333135.5	2110142.5	439969.8	2154290.9
2198465.5	107129.4	750982.5	3517512.0	1831305.0	426136.3	1747141.7
127640.8	194.5	154367.8	815623.5	278837.5	13833.5	407149.2
50602841.2	52213.0	26569102.1	74053112.4	17485715.3	1356780.0	69764160.1
17566902.7		15634262.6	31038497.6	6232255.8	341664.5	35293054.9
30580594.6	42088.8	10180515.7	39193590.3	9535303.3	771519.3	32473842.8
2455343.9	10124.2	754323.8	3821024.5	1718156.2	243596.2	1997262.4
43582770.9	58850.4	22682228.9	55610958.0	12941518.3	915801.6	54394007.0
5583793.9	38795.2	2491069.8	11310858.7	3825731.4	570438.2	10571518.8
3651103.4	61891.3	2231969.6	11054898.1	2721147.1	301533.3	6613195.6
111279.3		69184.1	409533.1	107461.0	8976.7	339729.6

13-10 续表

单位: 万元

项　　目	Item	流动负债合计 Total Working Liabilities	长期负债合计 Long-term Liabilities	所有者权益合计 Total Owners' Equities
总　　计	**Total**	**24174320.7**	**17378962.2**	**36150759.2**
按登记注册类型分	**Grouped by Registry Type**			
内资企业	DomesticFunded Enterprises	23950461.0	17236368.1	35868318.9
国有企业	State-owned Enterprises	4341152.4	2947565.1	4671894.9
#中央企业	Central Enterprises	3237485.0	1644716.9	3594278.4
地方企业	Local Enterprises	1103667.4	1302848.2	1077616.5
#自治区属企业	Autonomous	395247.7	691104.4	386313.7
地区(州、市)属企业	Prefecture or City	193059.1	287543.9	55931.9
县(市)属企业	County or City	317123.5	266898.2	543549.5
股份合作企业	Share-holding Cooperative Enterprises	12988.1		-3334.2
联营企业	Joint Ownership Enterprises	24183.9	26819.2	23931.6
#国有联营企业	State Joint Enterprises Ownership	25947.4	1819.2	13328.6
国有与集体联营企业	Joint State-collective OwnershipEnterprises	-1763.5	25000.0	10603.0
有限责任公司	Limited Liability Corporations	10269291.0	5616909.1	8572590.0
#国有独资公司	Sole State-funded Corporations	2099600.3	1677262.4	2137468.2
其他有限责任公司	Other Limited Liability Corporations	8169690.7	3939646.7	6435121.8
股份有限公司	Share-holding Corporations Ltd.	9302845.6	8645074.7	22603236.6
港、澳、台商投资企业	Enterprises with Funds from Hongkong,Macao and Taiwan	94272.8	16566.6	139893.2
外商投资企业	Foreign Funded Enterprises	129586.9	126027.5	142547.1
在总计中: 国有控股企业	Of the Total : State-owned and State-holding Enterprises	24174320.7	17378962.2	36150759.2
按轻、重工业分	**Grouped by Light & Heavy Industry**			
轻工业	Light Industry	2323547.1	355124.6	1623000.8
以农产品为原料	Using Farm Produces as Raw Materials	2026007.4	164187.3	1310690.0
以非农产品为原料	Using Non-Farm Produces as Raw Materials	297539.7	190937.3	312310.8
重工业	Heavy Industry	21850773.6	17023837.6	34527758.4
采掘工业	Mining and Quarrying	7716505.9	6830001.6	16428987.1
原料工业	Raw Material Industry	12567102.8	9473975.8	16568620.6
加工工业	Manufacturing Industry	1567164.9	719860.2	1530150.7
按企业规模分	**Grouped by Size of Enterprises**			
大型企业	Large Enterprises	15900195.1	12241454.0	27457648.2
中型企业	Medium-sized Enterprises	4503499.4	1847568.6	4472099.5
小型企业	Small Enterprises	3575270.9	3181694.8	4115799.1
微型企业	Mini Enterprises	195355.3	108244.8	105212.4

Continued

(10 000 yuan)

主营业务收入 Revenue from Principal Business	#主营业务成本 Cost of Principal Business	主营业务税金及附加 Taxes and Other Charges on Principal Business	营业利润 Business Profit	利润总额 Total Profit	亏损企业亏损总额 Losses Value of Loss-Suffering Enterprises	利税总额 Total Profits and Taxes	本年应交增值税 Value-added Taxes Payable	全部从业人员年平均人数(人) Annual Average Employed Persons (person)
53793148.3	**39433712.1**	**3056835.5**	**6752829.8**	**7091412.9**	**876796.1**	**12740928**	**2592679.6**	**398174**
53655120.1	39323399.7	3055494.6	6741110.6	7078599.2	876796.1	12717111.9	2583018.1	395564
6696769.1	6008590.4	181624.8	139321.1	199455.6	144781.8	622254.3	241173.9	82776
5215753.8	4683739.8	175806.0	137584.6	181518.7	71982.5	553110.7	195786.0	65394
1481015.3	1324850.6	5818.8	1736.5	17936.9	72799.3	69143.6	45387.9	17382
688654.4	633322.2	1277.5	6961.8	8855.0	24909.0	20526.1	10393.6	7507
311189.5	317605.9	472.9	-25347.3	-16415.5	24409.8	-12667.2	3275.4	2934
181464.3	123181.6	3120.7	-4023.7	-952.2	20511.7	15673.3	13504.8	3723
3025.8	2643.5		16.5	16.5		16.5		130
21731.5	15455.0	73.2	1996.6	3408.2	918.5	3633.7	152.3	436
14716.7	13726.6	73.2	-1412.9	-1.3	918.5	224.2	152.3	434
7014.8	1728.4		3409.5	3409.5		3409.5		2
13246621.0	10998727.0	367146.9	819101.5	1016807.2	239437.4	1912808.3	528854.2	156576
3594427.8	2918138.0	277945.1	175287.6	211637.8	53832.2	637154.9	147572.0	41509
9652193.2	8080589.0	89201.8	643813.9	805169.4	185605.2	1275653.4	381282.2	115067
33686972.7	22297983.8	2506649.7	5780674.9	5858911.7	491658.4	10178399.1	1812837.7	155646
60366.1	51160.4	662.1	3661.7	3942.5		9049.1	4444.5	1346
77662.1	59152.0	678.8	8057.5	8871.2		14767	5217.0	1264
53793148.3	39433712.1	3056835.5	6752829.8	7091412.9	876796.1	12740928	2592679.6	398174
2391682.4	1770368.0	196874.3	106419.2	156645.2	89254.9	477563.7	124044.2	46527
2263983.2	1659469.1	195689.2	135302.6	180626.8	59132.2	493498	117182.0	40125
127699.2	110898.9	1185.1	-28883.4	-23981.6	30122.7	-15934.3	6862.2	6402
51401465.9	37663344.1	2859961.2	6646410.6	6934767.7	787541.2	12263364.3	2468635.4	351647
18283861.5	8452150.8	1212628.2	6164561.8	6250717.9	91593.5	9142781.8	1679435.7	164456
30558142.9	27299299.3	1612589.7	154119.8	315529.8	677081.4	2635186.1	707066.6	158316
2559461.5	1911894.0	34743.3	327729.0	368520.0	18866.3	485396.4	82133.1	28875
44186316.8	31871994.2	2826865.4	5941704.9	6160605.6	628351.0	11109654.8	2122183.8	266369
5809511.7	4521494.0	204880.5	511378.9	574692.9	144676.1	1085516.8	305943.4	88435
3685903.9	2981591.6	23625.5	276308.7	328095.4	100787.6	510295.6	158574.7	42880
111415.9	58632.3	1464.1	23437.3	28019.0	2981.4	35460.8	5977.7	490

13-11 分行业国有控股工业企业主要经济指标

单位: 万元 (2012 年)

行业	Sector	企业单位数(个) Number of Enterprises (unit)	#亏损企业 Loss- Suffering Enterprises	工业总产值(当年价格) Gross Industrial Output Value (At Current Prices)
总计	**Total**	**522**	**148**	**53466765.1**
煤炭开采和洗选业	Mining and Washing of Coal	34	8	1225394.8
石油和天然气开采业	Extraction of Petroleum and Natural Gas	4		13668644.7
黑色金属矿采选业	Mining and Processing of Ferrous Metals Ores	12	4	684002.8
有色金属矿采选业	Mining and Processing of Nonferrous Metals Ores	17	3	424743.9
非金属矿采选业	Mining and Processing of Nonmetal Ores	9	1	81816.7
#采盐	Extraction of Salt	4		46621.5
农副食品加工业	Processing of Food from Agricultural Products	51	9	845157.6
#谷物磨制	Grain Grinding	13	2	77915.5
饲料加工	Fodder Processing	5		174720.6
制糖	Sugar Making	11	4	282541.3
食品制造业	Manufacture of Food	33	14	341111.8
#罐头制造	Manufacture of can	17	12	100034.7
酒、饮料和精制茶制造业	Manufacture of Wine,Beverages and Refined Tea	13	2	262504.7
#酒的制造	Manufacture of Wine	11	2	256456.2
烟草制品业	Manufacture of Tobacco	1		357066.4
纺织业	Manufacture of Textile	10	4	203924.3
#棉、化纤纺织及印染精加工	Cotton, Chemical Fiber, Dyeing, Printing and Processing	9	3	181197.9
纺织服装、鞋、帽制造业	Manufacture of Textile Wearing Apparel,Footware and Caps	4	1	34990.1
造纸及纸制品业	Manufacture of Paper and Paper Products	4	2	62203.6
印刷业和记录媒介的复制	Printing and Copying of Medium for Record	6	1	29855.7
石油加工、炼焦及核燃料加工业	Oil Processing, Coking and Nuclear Fuel Processing	14	8	15094212.9
#炼焦	Coking	5	3	261329.4
化学原料及化学制品制造业	Raw Chemical Material and Chemical Products	36	10	3776966.1
#基础化学原料制造	Basic Chemical Material	13	7	639325.8
肥料制造	Fertilizer Making	7		680772.9
合成材料制造	Manufacture of Synthetic Material	9	3	2381070.2
医药制造业	Manufacture of Medicine	8	1	96801.6
化学纤维制造业	Manufacture of Chemical Fiber	2	1	18963.2
橡胶制品业	Manufacture of Rubber Products	20	6	517066.7
非金属矿物制品业	Manufacture of Nonmetal Mineral Products	77	17	1334848.2
#水泥制造	Manufacture of Cement	37	12	905081.1
黑色金属冶炼及压延加工业	Smelting and Pressing of Ferrous Metals	10	4	5796188.9
有色金属冶炼及压延加工业	Smelting and Pressing of Nonferrous Metals	10	2	470141.0
金属制品业	Manufacture of Metal Products	3	1	281084.0
通用设备制造业	Manufacture of General Purpose Machinery	3	1	14255.5
专用设备制造业	Manufacture of Special Purpose Machinery	8	1	101918.2
汽车制造业	Manufacture of Automobile	4	4	293424.8
电气机械及器材制造业	Manufacture of Electric Equipment and Machinery	8		78826.2
仪器仪表制造业	Manufacture of Measuring Instruments and Machinery	1		
电力、热力的生产和供应业	Electric Power and Thermal Production and Supply	101	35	5551418.4
#电力生产和电力供应	Electric Power Production and Supply	82	24	5405783.5
燃气生产和供应业	Gas Production and Supply	5		200959.6
水的生产和供应业	Water Production and Supply	9	6	49606.6

Main Economic Indicators of Stare-holding Industrial Enterprises by Sectors

(10 000 yuan)

工业销售产值(当年价) Sales Value of Industry Products (At Current Prices)	出口交货值 Delivery Value of Industry Export	实收资本 Total Capital Hold	资产合计 Total Assets	流动资产合计 Total Working Capitals	#产成品 Finished Product	固定资产原价 Net Value of Fixed Assets
52928947.5	**159536.9**	**27474452.4**	**78386247.9**	**19595857.8**	**1796749.8**	**71918451.0**
1198907.9		1014763.1	3710113.0	1012456.2	71795.7	1521724.5
13687621.0		13016635.8	23196681.6	3456735.5	125655.2	31578500.2
637054.3		190725.9	1125154.2	590780.1	97100.3	381645.8
439609.8		284789.1	1088952.0	224052.6	29739.0	517081.0
77654.7		25165.7	97582.3	58265.7	6737.3	38737.7
41545.0		16307.1	53559.0	33428.2	4910.9	18568.0
808273.9		179514.7	965199.3	562194.2	199681.6	432992.2
77412.4		17725.1	71008.6	36396.3	3391.7	22834.8
172607.3		32900.8	247366.7	119798.7	15811.1	61762.2
210823.4		61884.3	369964.6	232747.9	126660.4	237903.9
392453.2	89964.6	172558.6	902617.9	475454.5	137830.6	577456.3
156463.3	79386.1	101915.4	606568.3	350071.6	124562.8	408087.9
256241.8	1795.0	113447.2	354894.2	125761.8	17309.0	124736.4
251075.6		108246.2	347254.6	122495.6	15237.7	117611.0
354589.7		18741.7	445764.0	272738.0		128081.0
196118.6	11708.7	185429.1	405245.4	185540.3	44729.7	239904.6
177628.1		149083.5	348906.2	159874.6	43019.9	204397.1
32098.4	3661.1	9283.8	38770.7	23836.5	3929.8	10889.8
59842.5		22911.5	202044.8	83733.0	8077.4	108994.3
31118.2		12418.4	55967.8	24701.0	2690.0	52841.9
14955605.3		4462478.7	6903329.3	1987969.3	342282.4	7609316.0
226453.7		100313.0	524786.0	168043.9	28065.1	338317.7
3762803.3	25639.8	1634653.5	8011402.1	1971839.7	282043.2	4186549.0
631111.1	16809.1	432534.2	3383764.1	773598.8	41207.2	672678.4
688824.6		189384.7	1341076.8	455896.3	56523.4	1032614.7
2367928.8	8830.7	968924.8	3132468.6	673595.6	181827.5	2450991.4
90751.2	194.5	38470.4	175377.2	119407.3	14804.1	47936.1
16610.4		17000.0	64435.4	13309.9	5896.7	56216.4
492317.0	9662.3	157487.8	547391.6	293692.6	104812.3	253754.6
1321973.7		925098.9	4658991.3	1829920.6	37783.1	5629936.0
893086.1		787306.5	3912029.4	1452561.6	25648.5	5343176.9
5755081.1	16449.0	1029580.3	5567919.5	1739183.1	139174.5	3103759.8
471233.7		109780.6	893049.8	362260.2	40828.8	178396.6
170113.4		65549.9	108704.5	31353.3	3111.9	34027.1
13303.7		7491.0	16388.1	11319.5	337.2	3366.3
86270.7	461.9	20241.5	148210.5	103471.2	27357.7	47729.2
258722.1		36048.1	213952.4	85862.9	28502.8	42824.5
80763.6		23538.6	138685.6	99090.4	7649.7	31748.2
5500979.8		2388658.6	15380727.8	2539619.8	2236.8	13115218.5
5357890.2		2297237.9	14625558.4	2242955.0	2236.8	12493127.9
171307.6		73849.9	408471.0	199563.7	337.7	215990.4
47401.4		89825.7	609883.8	200374.3		282832.7

13-11 续表

单位: 万元

行业	Sector	流动负债合计 Total Working Liabilities	长期负债合计 Long-term Liabilities	所有者权益合计 Total Owners' Equities
总计	**Total**	**24174320.7**	**17378962.2**	**36150759.2**
煤炭开采和洗选业	Mining and Washing of Coal	1496944.5	792647.8	1368484.6
石油和天然气开采业	Extraction of Petroleum and Natural Gas	4158042.4	5595340.0	13443299.1
黑色金属矿采选业	Mining and Processing of Ferrous Metals Ores	694070.1	90324.6	339026.2
有色金属矿采选业	Mining and Processing of Nonferrous Metals Ores	360046.8	181997.9	546637.0
非金属矿采选业	Mining and Processing of Nonmetal Ores	41188.1	4351.5	49664.8
#采盐	Extraction of Salt	13016.9	2643.8	37750.3
农副食品加工业	Processing of Food from Agricultural Products	537517.4	50875.1	374163.1
#谷物磨制	Grain Grinding	40945.6	6536.2	23202.8
饲料加工	Fodder Processing	86980.0	26448.2	133880.7
制糖	Sugar Making	211266.6	5425.8	153271.9
食品制造业	Manufacture of Food	676785.0	57110.4	165442.2
#罐头制造	Manufacture of can	548767.6	48050.6	9672.6
酒、饮料和精制茶制造业	Manufacture of Wine,Beverages and Refined Tea	192062.6	3903.3	153512.0
#酒的制造	Manufacture of Wine	196657.5	3873.5	146723.5
烟草制品业	Manufacture of Tobacco	128861.0		316903.0
纺织业	Manufacture of Textile	190907.6	13697.0	196533.0
#棉、化纤纺织及印染精加工	Cotton, Chemical Fiber, Dyeing, Printing and Processing	179836.3	13697.0	155372.8
纺织服装、鞋、帽制造业	Manufacture of Textile Wearing Apparel,Footware and Caps	34064.7	9287.1	-4581.1
造纸及纸制品业	Manufacture of Paper and Paper Products	117204.8	20039.5	64800.3
印刷业和记录媒介的复制	Printing and Copying of Medium for Record	19642.5	4660.2	30486.4
石油加工、炼焦及核燃料加工业	Oil Processing, Coking and Nuclear Fuel Processing	1949187.9	566370.0	4387771.6
#炼焦	Coking	318761.0	86070.1	119954.9
化学原料及化学制品制造业	Raw Chemical Material and Chemical Products	2115404.2	2494481.2	3389865.4
#基础化学原料制造	Basic Chemical Material	1096591.9	1087075.4	1188445.7
肥料制造	Fertilizer Making	374954.7	381070.4	585051.7
合成材料制造	Manufacture of Synthetic Material	598273.0	1018849.4	1515346.0
医药制造业	Manufacture of Medicine	85411.3	7566.3	77370.9
化学纤维制造业	Manufacture of Chemical Fiber	77127.6	1699.8	-14392.0
橡胶制品业	Manufacture of Rubber Products	272683.2	68227.3	204473.3
非金属矿物制品业	Manufacture of Nonmetal Mineral Products	1471031.1	880737.6	2271505.3
#水泥制造	Manufacture of Cement	1157445.5	790230.0	1930071.4
黑色金属冶炼及压延加工业	Smelting and Pressing of Ferrous Metals	3626723.2	413352.9	1527843.3
有色金属冶炼及压延加工业	Smelting and Pressing of Nonferrous Metals	167701.6	14472.5	695183.4
金属制品业	Manufacture of Metal Products	37354.3	6368.6	64981.4
通用设备制造业	Manufacture of General Purpose Machinery	12608.2		3779.9
专用设备制造业	Manufacture of Special Purpose Machinery	83682.3	2683.3	61844.9
汽车制造业	Manufacture of Automobile	185744.8	11081.6	17126.0
电气机械及器材制造业	Manufacture of Electric Equipment and Machinery	75829.2	29638.5	32042.1
仪器仪表制造业	Manufacture of Measuring Instruments and Machinery			
电力、热力的生产和供应业	Electric Power and Thermal Production and Supply	3945990.7	5586220.6	5326251.4
#电力生产和电力供应	Electric Power Production and Supply	3701469.8	5243024.4	5171790.6
燃气生产和供应业	Gas Production and Supply	200070.0	107682.9	100718.0
水的生产和供应业	Water Production and Supply	152427.4	184508.9	263910.2

Continued

(10 000 yuan)

主营业务收入 Revenue from Principal Business	#主营业务成本 Cost of Principal Business	主营业务税金及附加 Taxes and Other Charges on Principal Business	营业利润 Business Profit	利润总额 Total Profit	亏损企业亏损总额 Losses Value of Loss-Suffering Enterprises	利税总额 Total Profits and Taxes	本年应交增值税 Value-added Taxes Payable	全部从业人员年平均人数(人) Ann Employed Persons (person)
53793148.3	**39433712.1**	**3056835.5**	**6752829.8**	**7091412.9**	**876796.1**	**12740928**	**2592679.6**	**398174**
1259594.9	864441.4	36540.5	159184.8	162960.5	28158.5	339580	140079.0	38516
14402827.5	5415657.7	1138900.2	5762379.1	5822514.1		8325443.7	1364029.4	77204
648324.8	440781.7	16013.0	135238.7	135672.2	8576.3	199176.5	47491.3	5098
415415.8	202708.7	6339.8	154555.6	154589.5	5625.2	201523	40593.7	5634
74336.1	35960.7	3751.5	7561.8	9213.8	83.7	19292.5	6327.2	2408
43417.8	12309.4	3425.9	5059.2	6312.2		14740.8	5002.7	1116
819154.4	676406.1	2626.4	55857.8	62292.5	7028.6	88860	23941.1	10749
76218.2	67454.3	223.3	4755.6	6604.4	368.5	7099.9	272.2	1016
171259.7	129143.7	342.3	16722.5	18249.9		21597	3004.8	1176
216337.8	174290.9	1489.4	7872.1	8524.0	4583.9	25022.1	15008.7	5425
404060.2	321491.8	1572.2	-9698.7	2074.3	39657.3	21760.9	18114.4	7934
158967.6	132583.1	277.2	-46484.9	-35895.9	36425.3	-27352	8266.7	3372
243697.3	118929.4	34413.1	49075.4	49829.0	1584.0	107606.2	23364.1	4600
239175.4	115752.8	34388.2	48677.1	49378.9	1584.0	106980.7	23213.6	4424
354588.7	121438.7	155886.8	55009.2	54751.4		250038.2	39400.0	941
248464.1	250764.3	847.6	-21259.7	1555.7	4628.7	11582.3	9179.0	8934
230389.4	232755.0	717.0	-18004.7	3286.7	2897.7	12879.4	8875.7	7749
49021.9	48983.4	30.5	1703.8	1905.8	67.9	2623.8	687.5	1719
54986.7	49625.6	164.7	-1203.2	-140.6	4011.2	701.6	677.5	2731
31195.6	25258.0	151.5	153.1	1365.2	72.2	2426.5	909.8	1201
15059838.5	13165861.8	1567446.7	-289087.1	-300638.7	442075.2	1576957.4	310149.4	34517
234046.2	195632.5	1360.0	7190.5	7135.4	11238.9	19736.9	11241.5	4029
3406113.8	2663009.0	39379.0	404254.7	455307.5	55304.4	623321.2	128634.7	36758
838606.9	760487.5	3563.1	38281.9	49964.6	24422.6	72201.8	18674.1	13052
711871.9	321855.6	26871.9	244217.4	275901.0		342027	39254.1	5698
1780172.7	1530999.0	8191.1	100840.5	108396.5	30881.8	180656.5	64068.9	16067
73755.3	52273.8	368.5	3738.4	4863.3	349.8	8233.3	3001.5	2044
16830.5	15611.9	5.7	1610.2	2869.1	2082.3	2976.7	101.9	663
477241.6	426508.6	2340.5	2207.4	4410.1	6854.6	15905.3	9154.7	6835
1334807.1	1108212.4	7137.9	83434.3	114833.2	25396.4	185691.7	63720.6	24048
861420.8	708954.9	5233.9	53703.7	79898.8	20710.6	131465.9	46333.2	16897
6038923.6	5783463.1	12334.0	22466.4	56667.8	19422.0	170393.6	101391.8	24751
464591.9	373123.1	656.7	54619.9	54958.3	2289.8	60746.1	5131.1	4275
171901.4	169224.7	314.3	-87.8	8.1	658.1	2128.9	1806.5	1060
15035.2	12980.6	132.3	142.2	155.6	1017.4	707.1	419.2	355
109775.4	87671.3	236.0	8154.8	9713.2	801.5	11223.5	1274.3	2002
265356.4	261780.7	241.8	-7346.0	-7278.7	7278.7	-6083.2	953.7	1490
81903.8	69258.9	249.5	4007.3	4675.0		6700.9	1776.4	967
5506781.7	4968440.9	15046.2	175771.3	268812.1	134849.6	444840.3	160982.0	48701
5333662.5	4782370.0	14886.9	213202.9	286533.6	109055.7	461429.6	160009.1	44397
188621.7	129481.3	1693.0	17906.6	17669.7		22093.8	2731.1	1978
54178.0	38651.7	382.7	-6753.6	-3313.7	7018.6	280.7	3211.7	2621

13-12 各地、州、市、县(市)国有控股工业企业主要经济指标

单位：万元 (2012 年)

地 区	Region	企业单位数(个) Number of Enterprises (unit)	#亏损企业 Loss- Suffering Enterprises	工业总产值(当年价格) Gross Industrial Output Value (At Current Prices)
总 计	**Total**	**522**	**148**	**53466765.1**
乌鲁木齐市	**Urumqi City**	**120**	**36**	**17307462.8**
天山区	Tianshan District	13	3	2597576.9
沙依巴克区	Shayibak District	18	6	471342.0
新市区	Xinshi District	46	16	3910084.1
水磨沟区	Shui Mogou District	5		149668.2
头屯河区	Tou Tunhe District	12	3	5106793.7
达坂城区	Da Bancheng District	6	1	188287.3
米东区	Midong District	18	7	4854536.9
乌鲁木齐县	Urumqi County	2		29173.7
克拉玛依市	**Karamay City**	**14**	**6**	**16177595.3**
独山子区	Dushanzi District	7	5	6474085.2
克拉玛依区	Karamay District	7	1	9703510.1
白碱滩区	Bai Jiantan District			
乌尔河区	Urhe District			
吐鲁番地区	**Turpan Administrative Offices**	**20**	**6**	**1410416.2**
吐鲁番市	Turpan City	6	3	111702.1
鄯善县	Shanshan [Piqan] County	6	1	1118498.0
托克逊县	Toksun County	8	2	180216.1
哈密地区	**Hami [Kumul] Administrative Offices**	**41**	**10**	**1152899.7**
哈密市	Hami [Kumul] City	34	9	1023000.4
巴里坤哈萨克自治县	Barkol Kazak Autonomous County	6	1	113800.5
伊吾县	Yiwu [Araturuk] County	1		16098.8
昌吉回族自治州	**Changji Hui Autonomous Prefecture**	**31**	**7**	**977461.5**
昌吉市	Changji City	9	2	373141.8
阜康市	Fukang City	8	1	454439.6
呼图壁县	Hutubi County	4		64091.0
玛纳斯县	Manas County	4	1	17417.8
奇台县	Qitai County	2	1	42752.4
吉木萨尔县	Jimsar County	4	2	25618.9
木垒哈萨克自治县	Mori Kazak Autonomous County			
伊犁哈萨克自治州	**Ili Kazak Autonomous Prefecture**	**117**	**31**	**3460525.8**
伊犁州直属县(市)	**Counties (Cities) Direct Under Ili Prefecture**	**59**	**18**	**2149820.0**
伊宁市	Yining [Gulja] City	6	3	247717.8
奎屯市	Kuytun City	20	8	857876.6
伊宁县	Yining [Gulja] County	8	1	202492.1
察布查尔锡伯自治县	Qapqal Xibe Autonomous County	5		81322.8
霍城县	Huocheng [Korgas] County	6	2	112254.3
巩留县	Gongliu [Tokkuztara] County	3	2	102118.2
新源县	Xinyuan [Kunes] County	6	1	428421.6
昭苏县	Zhaosu [Mongolkure] County	1		9251.9
特克斯县	Tekes County			
尼勒克县	Nilka County	4	1	108364.7
塔城地区	**Tacheng [Tarbagatai] Administrative Offices**	**31**	**7**	**619383.1**
塔城市	Tacheng [Qoqek] City	3	2	79044.6
乌苏市	Usu City	4	1	81514.4
额敏县	Emin [Dorbiljin] County	6	1	77580.9

Main Economic Indicators of State-holding Industrial Enterprises by Prefecture, Autonomous Prefecture, City and County

(10 000 yuan)

工业销售产值(当年价) Sales Value of Industry Products (At Current Prices)	出口交货值 Delivery Value of Industry Export	实收资本 Total Capital Hold	资产合计 Total Assets	流动资产合计 Total Working Capitals	#产成品 Finished Product	固定资产原价 Net Value of Fixed Assets
48307739.5	**384013.6**	**25679116.9**	**64283377.6**	**16723746.3**	**1668703.4**	**58772698.1**
15696008.5	**95181.2**	**6305777.4**	**20871212.4**	**5572774.0**	**490138.5**	**16637880.3**
1988725.4	21371.5	391715.1	4070228.4	757646.8	46436.9	3758719.4
455828.4	28231.4	416527.0	2589366.9	628202.4	14531.9	694560.5
3436948.4	27888.0	2340485.1	4874662.9	1106953.8	134974.4	5911791.0
288199.2		64301.9	512347.5	166045.0	7047.2	489849.0
5114166.2	15267.5	824245.4	4099025.4	1292675.7	185223.1	2341313.6
166221.0		122163.9	406443.3	68914.5	5579.5	222199.4
4216092.7	2422.8	2083572.8	4083536.8	1516713.4	96345.5	3016940.3
29827.2		62766.2	235601.2	35622.4		202507.1
15596119.1	**15609.9**	**10556175.5**	**16235536.3**	**4088244.5**	**166160.5**	**17908286.5**
5737813.8	15609.9	3132115.0	4715926.2	1363646.2	114138.7	4453037.8
9858305.3		7424060.5	11519610.1	2724598.3	52021.8	13455248.7
1128506.8		**936663.3**	**2303656.6**	**368968.7**	**69616.4**	**3366734.4**
47282.3		35296.8	154247.3	18938.8	597.5	134665.0
959718.3		809152.8	1683210.7	262384.6	68244.2	2913886.9
121506.2		92213.7	466198.6	87645.3	774.7	318182.5
919476.8		**525176.0**	**1801817.2**	**719929.5**	**73427.8**	**978534.3**
820167.1		502875.5	1603799.7	638491.0	65450.5	885088.6
86907.7		22200.5	172566.3	59432.8	7237.2	88514.0
12402.0		100.0	25451.2	22005.7	740.1	4931.7
487100.3	**29002.9**	**135458.5**	**723981.9**	**259112.0**	**54839.6**	**397446.0**
60347.6	4914.6	10662.2	57254.0	29534.0	7141.0	26187.3
305071.6		112261.5	453447.0	168314.0	14442.3	207040.0
39214.4		1030.0	16830.7	7381.2	1233.7	13097.8
34602.3	15290.2	2754.8	84361.3	27652.7	14906.7	51783.3
31064.5		1000.0	28625.0	8250.4	4969.5	25638.0
16799.9	8798.1	7750.0	83463.9	17979.7	12146.4	73699.6
3243151.2	**53383.0**	**1196577.9**	**6100581.3**	**1798766.3**	**242300.6**	**3925371.9**
1680814.2	**35435.3**	**871831.2**	**3708335.0**	**1165305.0**	**127069.1**	**2263876.0**
221972.3		33448.1	306033.1	71561.2	2106.4	341917.9
630035.8	35435.3	148723.1	1062660.7	476892.1	52482.9	600410.7
218595.3		86787.6	374107.5	122706.6	8205.9	191873.6
19798.2		27330.0	113800.0	30975.5	4383.5	8158.9
105230.4		35527.8	139189.7	61118.4	24108.2	89532.9
27668.3		291061.8	713417.4	84932.1		436915.8
361925.0		152371.0	505903.3	264470.9	32854.0	226179.2
13870.0		1100.0	7460.1	4764.7	1422.6	3675.7
81718.9		95481.8	485763.2	47883.5	1505.6	365211.3
900001.9	**17947.7**	**179412.0**	**1136048.5**	**314981.6**	**64247.8**	**856026.9**
70443.4		9811.0	96309.0	9878.3	110.4	118764.4
468974.1	12946.6	32476.0	516454.5	78183.3	16112.0	386833.4
63375.9		56208.4	121953.4	48859.6	15854.0	105047.6

13-12 续表 1

单位: 万元

地　　区	Region	企业单位数(个) Number of Enterprises (unit)	#亏损企业 Loss- Suffering Enterprises	工业总产值(当年价格) Gross Industrial Output Value (At Current Prices)
沙湾县	Shawan County	6	2	128907.7
托里县	Toli County	4	1	119898.6
裕民县	Yumin [Qagantokay] County			
和布克赛尔蒙古自治县	Hoboksar Mongol Autonomous County	6		76710.6
阿勒泰地区	**Altay Administrative Offices**	**27**	**3**	**674176.2**
阿勒泰市	Altay City	7	2	100390.2
布尔津县	Burqin County	6		55851.0
富蕴县	Fuyun [Koktokay] County	5	1	221241.6
福海县	Fuhai [Burultokay] County	4		16533.4
哈巴河县	Habahe [Kaba] County	4		275705.7
青河县	Qinghe [Qinggil] County			
吉木乃县	Jeminay County	1		4454.3
博尔塔拉蒙古自治州	**Bortala Mongol Autonomous Prefecture**	**13**	**5**	**154153.6**
博乐市	Bole [Bortala] City	12	5	149900.6
精河县	Jinghe [Jing] County	1		4253.0
温泉县	Wenquan [Araxang] County			
巴音郭楞蒙古自治州	**Bayangol Mongol Autonomous Prefecture**	**34**	**2**	**5672790.3**
库尔勒市	Korla City	20	1	5062540.9
轮台县	Luntai [Bugur] County			
尉犁县	Yuli [Lopnur] County			
若羌县	Ruoqiang [Qarkilik] County	3		413949.9
且末县	Qiemo [Qarqan] County			
焉耆回族自治县	Yanqi Hui Autonomous County	3		28988.5
和静县	Hejing County	5		142756.6
和硕县	Hoxud County	1		4981.3
博湖县	Bohu [Bagrax] County	2	1	19573.1
阿克苏地区	**Aksu Administrative Offices**	**37**	**5**	**2679356.1**
阿克苏市	Aksu City	10	1	369633.8
温宿县	Wensu [Onsu] County	9	1	45369.9
库车县	Kuqa County	9	1	2178236.9
沙雅县	Xayar County			
新和县	Xinhe [Toksu] County			
拜城县	Baicheng [Bay] County	6	2	71658.3
乌什县	Wushi [Uxturpan] County	2		9253.3

Continued

(10 000 yuan)

工业销售产值(当年价) Sales Value of Industry Products (At Current Prices)	出口交货值 Delivery Value of Industry Export	实收资本 Total Capital Hold	资产合计 Total Assets	流动资产合计 Total Working Capitals	#产成品 Finished Product	固定资产原价 Net Value of Fixed Assets
115375.4	5001.1	18289.0	109674.8	56356.9	18378.4	91638.4
110732.7		32000.0	190886.6	84034.7	9516.2	85528.2
71100.4		30627.6	100770.2	37668.8	4276.8	68214.9
662335.1		**145334.7**	**1256197.8**	**318479.7**	**50983.7**	**805469.0**
99918.9		20622.0	187532.4	38024.3	1197.5	184554.3
55868.0		19580.7	233942.9	32050.5	381.5	215294.2
206297.1		38152.0	493869.2	144668.3	46232.2	212243.3
16505.2		17922.0	39413.0	19201.4	1025.9	37058.5
279291.6		39480.0	262301.8	80265.7	2146.6	121397.6
4454.3		9578.0	39138.5	4269.5		34921.1
152726.2		**73909.8**	**445025.0**	**133404.4**	**37172.6**	**374704.7**
148125.2		72983.8	437069.3	131494.4	36865.0	371836.4
4601.0		926.0	7955.7	1910.0	307.6	2868.3
5593093.3	**39146.5**	**3869921.3**	**8242206.6**	**1526935.2**	**145869.6**	**9679528.2**
5067788.6	19854.5	3714429.5	7046783.5	1142884.5	67078.6	8875481.6
339579.4		57899.9	701300.7	258765.0	33894.8	462650.4
35774.0		14186.4	22726.4	8179.9	3719.3	23654.7
124104.6		72869.1	429917.4	90885.5	21954.3	281612.3
7337.6	5313.6	1450.0	7674.3	5323.4	3014.0	5282.6
18509.1	13978.4	9086.4	33804.3	20896.9	16208.6	30846.6
2654293.0	**6354.1**	**759118.3**	**2418214.1**	**567398.4**	**54056.4**	**1511944.9**
334230.4	1666.4	264809.9	815622.0	153922.8	25434.2	486721.2
42664.8		44121.5	234589.4	39879.0	828.8	115086.1
2196820.7		433194.2	1198429.5	308426.0	15616.0	798350.4
70435.9		11992.7	135221.9	45021.9	6743.2	95626.5
6921.8	4687.7	4000.0	17239.9	9491.6	5434.2	9372.0

13-12 续表 2

单位：万元

地　　区	Region	企业单位数（个） Number of Enterprises (unit)	#亏损企业 Loss- Suffering Enterprises	工业总产值（当年价格） Gross Industrial Output Value (At Current Prices)
阿瓦提县	Awat County	1		5203.9
柯坪县	Kalpin County			
克孜勒苏柯尔克孜自治州	**Kizilsu Kirgiz Autonomous Prefecture**	**2**		**26236.4**
阿图什市	Artux City	2		26236.4
阿克陶县	Akto County			
阿合奇县	Akqi County			
乌恰县	Wuqia [Ulugqat] County			
喀什地区	**Kashgar [Kaxgar] Administrative Offices**	**8**	**3**	**248428.0**
喀什市	Kashgar [Kaxgar] City	7	2	244327.8
疏附县	Shufu County	1	1	4100.2
疏勒县	Shule County			
英吉沙县	Yengisar County			
泽普县	Zepu [Poskam] County			
莎车县	Shache [Yarkant] County			
叶城县	Yecheng [Kagilik] County			
麦盖提县	Makit County			
岳普湖县	Yopurga County			
伽师县	Jiashi [Payzawat] County			
巴楚县	Bachu [Maralbexi] County			
塔什库尔干塔吉克自治县	Taxkorgan Tajik Autonomous County			
和田地区	**Hotan Administrative Offices**	**7**	**3**	**89297.5**
和田市	Hotan City	3	1	56745.2
和田县	Hotan County	2	1	12871.3
墨玉县	Moyu [Karakax] County	1		18373.7
皮山县	Pishan [Guma] County	1	1	1307.3
洛浦县	Lop County			
策勒县	Qira County			
于田县	Yutian [Keriya] County			
民丰县	Minfeng [Niya] County			
自治区直辖县级市	**Municpality Country-LevelCity directly under the Central Government**	**56**	**19**	**2588693.6**
石河子市	Shihezi City	37	13	2170942.2
阿拉尔市	Aral City	6	3	171781.3
图木舒克市	Tumxuk City	6		66153.4
五家渠市	Wujiaqu City	7	3	179816.7

Continued

(10 000 yuan)

工业销售产值(当年价) Sales Value of Industry Products (At Current Prices)	出口交货值 Delivery Value of Industry Export	实收资本 Total Capital Hold	资产合计 Total Assets	流动资产合计 Total Working Capitals	#产成品 Finished Product	固定资产原价 Net Value of Fixed Assets
3219.4		1000.0	17111.4	10657.1		6788.7
26062.9		**37733.9**	**65591.9**	**29576.5**	**673.8**	**35646.4**
26062.9		37733.9	65591.9	29576.5	673.8	35646.4
245966.2		**28056.7**	**376142.7**	**55390.3**	**12047.7**	**529665.8**
241877.0		27056.7	374781.7	54745.9	11769.0	528353.0
4089.2		1000.0	1361.0	644.4	278.7	1312.8
88033.6	**406.1**	**154636.8**	**291112.3**	**35625.5**	**1371.1**	**331490.7**
56745.2		10362.6	101429.0	11780.3		144127.3
12412.3		128537.2	143938.7	10899.8	400.9	147657.1
18470.0		15237.0	40384.9	11076.6	42.9	36251.8
406.1	406.1	500.0	5359.7	1868.8	927.3	3454.5
2477201.6	**144929.9**	**1099911.5**	**4408299.3**	**1567621.0**	**321028.8**	**3095464.0**
2098058.2	130285.1	827922.5	3436399.4	1192994.0	229816.1	2456046.4
164997.3		84008.6	316067.1	78353.6	25842.2	258814.9
63008.1		32879.2	182816.4	85791.7	25103.3	98372.5
151138.0	14644.8	155101.2	473016.4	210481.7	40267.2	282230.2

13-12 续表 3

单位: 万元

地　　区	Region	流动负债合计 Total Working Liabilities	长期负债合计 Long-term Liabilities	所有者权益合计 Total Owners' Equities
总　　计	**Total**	**16723746.3**	**1668703.4**	**31388707.3**
乌鲁木齐市	**Urumqi City**	**5572774.0**	**490138.5**	**9780192.3**
天山区	Tianshan District	757646.8	46436.9	1682923.7
沙依巴克区	Shayibak District	628202.4	14531.9	1318961.8
新市区	Xinshi District	1106953.8	134974.4	2468889.9
水磨沟区	Shui Mogou District	166045.0	7047.2	348736.4
头屯河区	Tou Tunhe District	1292675.7	185223.1	1273618.2
达坂城区	Da Bancheng District	68914.5	5579.5	245931.5
米东区	Midong District	1516713.4	96345.5	2375514.4
乌鲁木齐县	Urumqi County	35622.4		65616.4
克拉玛依市	**Karamay City**	**4088244.5**	**166160.5**	**10109531.5**
独山子区	Dushanzi District	1363646.2	114138.7	3200614.7
克拉玛依区	Karamay District	2724598.3	52021.8	6908916.8
白碱滩区	Bai Jiantan District			
乌尔河区	Urhe District			
吐鲁番地区	**Turpan Administrative Offices**	**368968.7**	**69616.4**	**1014537.1**
吐鲁番市	Turpan City	18938.8	597.5	50406.4
鄯善县	Shanshan [Piqan] County	262384.6	68244.2	835558.3
托克逊县	Toksun County	87645.3	774.7	128572.4
哈密地区	**Hami [Kumul] Administrative Offices**	**719929.5**	**73427.8**	**687770.6**
哈密市	Hami [Kumul] City	638491.0	65450.5	625403.1
巴里坤哈萨克自治县	Barkol Kazak Autonomous County	59432.8	7237.2	59041.7
伊吾县	Yiwu [Araturuk] County	22005.7	740.1	3325.8
昌吉回族自治州	**Changji Hui Autonomous Prefecture**	**259112.0**	**54839.6**	**143603.4**
昌吉市	Changji City	29534.0	7141.0	30788.5
阜康市	Fukang City	168314.0	14442.3	81224.4
呼图壁县	Hutubi County	7381.2	1233.7	9014.0
玛纳斯县	Manas County	27652.7	14906.7	18567.2
奇台县	Qitai County	8250.4	4969.5	5085.8
吉木萨尔县	Jimsar County	17979.7	12146.4	-1076.5
木垒哈萨克自治县	Mori Kazak Autonomous County			
伊犁哈萨克自治州	**Ili Kazak Autonomous Prefecture**	**1798766.3**	**242300.6**	**2458242.2**
伊犁州直属县(市)	**Counties (Cities) Direct Under Ili Prefecture**	**1165305.0**	**127069.1**	**1447229.2**
伊宁市	Yining [Gulja] City	71561.2	2106.4	124158.9
奎屯市	Kuytun City	476892.1	52482.9	448699.4
伊宁县	Yining [Gulja] County	122706.6	8205.9	166132.2
察布查尔锡伯自治县	Qapqal Xibe Autonomous County	30975.5	4383.5	27629.6
霍城县	Huocheng [Korgas] County	61118.4	24108.2	67496.4
巩留县	Gongliu [Tokkuztara] County	84932.1		253398.2
新源县	Xinyuan [Kunes] County	264470.9	32854.0	241486.1
昭苏县	Zhaosu [Mongolkure] County	4764.7	1422.6	1932.8
特克斯县	Tekes County			
尼勒克县	Nilka County	47883.5	1505.6	116295.6
塔城地区	**Tacheng [Tarbagatai] Administrative Offices**	**314981.6**	**64247.8**	**461107.8**
塔城市	Tacheng [Qoqek] City	9878.3	110.4	29807.2
乌苏市	Usu City	78183.3	16112.0	162954.3
额敏县	Emin [Dorbiljin] County	48859.6	15854.0	75681.5

Continued

(10 000 yuan)

主营业务收入 Revenue from Principal Business	#主营业务成本 Cost of Principal Business	主营业务税金及附加 Taxes and Other Charges on Principal Business	营业利润 Business Profit	利润总额 Total Profit	亏损企业亏损总额 Losses Value of Loss-Suffering Enterprises	利税总额 Total Profits and Taxes	本年应交增值税 Value-added Taxes Payable	全部从业人员年平均人数(人) Annual Average Employed Persons (person)
58772698.1	**18668510.6**	**13548143.7**	**31388707.3**	**49136691.5**	**34406033.0**	**3225271.7**	**7654407.9**	**349653**
16637880.3	**7443271.5**	**3623028.6**	**9780192.3**	**15985301.0**	**12519006.6**	**1082576.9**	**1296037.5**	**88286**
3758719.4	1336743.2	1048873.5	1682923.7	1960433.1	1769132.9	3049.9	137186.6	14199
694560.5	552468.0	717936.8	1318961.8	481557.3	369867.0	4800.8	56208.5	8583
5911791.0	2015699.9	367280.6	2468889.9	3465480.7	1200764.2	612749.8	1224103.9	19247
489849.0	129340.1	34270.8	348736.4	292313.7	239696.1	1529.5	23593.4	3500
2341313.6	2201705.0	623463.7	1273618.2	5220847.5	4851454.1	13829.1	101748.6	15499
222199.4	133721.1	26790.5	245931.5	167221.1	106378.0	2120.3	35521.6	6440
3016940.3	984129.7	723892.5	2375514.4	4368666.1	3969717.3	444497.5	-293709.3	20751
202507.1	89464.5	80520.2	65616.4	28781.5	11997.0		11384.2	67
17908286.5	**3318196.1**	**2807508.5**	**10109531.5**	**16453201.6**	**11907795.8**	**1291548.5**	**2266414.6**	**92634**
4453037.8	1108545.8	406765.5	3200614.7	5804773.8	5441861.9	544124.8	-501289.6	17690
13455248.7	2209650.3	2400743.0	6908916.8	10648427.8	6465933.9	747423.7	2767704.2	74944
3366734.4	**479289.4**	**780603.0**	**1014537.1**	**1199522.0**	**568226.1**	**57824.2**	**392399.3**	**9274**
134665.0	60276.9	43563.9	50406.4	50141.3	35535.6	426.6	7910.8	1175
2913886.9	323559.1	524093.3	835558.3	1022871.8	440453.0	55748.1	368777.1	5746
318182.5	95453.4	212945.8	128572.4	126508.9	92237.5	1649.5	15711.4	2353
978534.3	**661421.8**	**447535.3**	**687770.6**	**928489.9**	**670104.7**	**15716.8**	**137565.3**	**20511**
885088.6	575426.7	400458.0	625403.1	835993.9	628964.2	11922.2	103093.7	18948
88514.0	63869.7	47077.3	59041.7	80094.0	36998.2	3452.9	29324.1	1364
4931.7	22125.4		3325.8	12402.0	4142.3	341.7	5147.5	199
397446.0	**436946.1**	**143432.4**	**143603.4**	**495872.4**	**438270.4**	**1796.3**	**12112.0**	**8403**
26187.3	21387.4	5078.1	30788.5	77576.3	64521.4	113.0	6483.7	1875
207040.0	260550.0	111672.5	81224.4	305071.6	279501.7	824.2	6363.9	4067
13097.8	7639.9	176.8	9014.0	39250.8	33524.4	22.7	2893.4	246
51783.3	39310.5	26483.7	18567.2	27268.9	20751.5	376.2	-226.3	813
25638.0	23539.2		5085.8	26126.1	19306.7	225.1	3747.8	383
73699.6	84519.1	21.3	-1076.5	20578.7	20664.7	235.1	-7150.5	1019
3925371.9	**2077839.1**	**1078309.7**	**2458242.2**	**3183985.7**	**2130025.5**	**173288.8**	**474307.9**	**43148**
2263876.0	**1071074.0**	**742101.8**	**1447229.2**	**1635503.6**	**1113431.9**	**159562.6**	**182955.2**	**22994**
341917.9	86366.0	81580.8	124158.9	220385.7	173400.7	1246.5	26374.6	3753
600410.7	358937.7	255027.4	448699.4	630870.8	403239.9	136393.3	34046.0	5429
191873.6	127095.1	76829.9	166132.2	216721.7	148458.8	1251.1	38817.6	4067
8158.9	46839.0		27629.6	20499.3	16294.0	273.2	3132.8	547
89532.9	38598.3	33094.9	67496.4	108050.0	86956.6	318.7	11944.9	1925
436915.8	69394.6		253398.2	28156.0	10786.8	167.4	-1134.9	285
226179.2	243974.5	20442.7	241486.1	315940.2	223141.5	18353.9	40628.1	6108
3675.7	5527.3		1932.8	13870.0	9994.8	30.4	3301.6	170
365211.3	94341.5	275126.1	116295.6	81009.9	41158.8	1528.1	25844.5	710
856026.9	**555752.2**	**116928.8**	**461107.8**	**885402.6**	**679111.4**	**4907.6**	**46894.0**	**12585**
118764.4	49169.8	15589.0	29807.2	67178.5	70421.1	135.4	-4527.6	1152
386833.4	311249.8	42250.2	162954.3	488709.1	365700.6	1131.6	10969.8	3680
105047.6	43698.3	2573.5	75681.5	61854.9	48368.1	192.1	10358.4	1175

13-12 续表 4

单位: 万元

地 区	Region	流动负债合计 Total Working Liabilities	长期负债合计 Long-term Liabilities	所有者权益合计 Total Owners' Equities
沙湾县	Shawan County	51779.3	16944.1	40951.3
托里县	Toli County	67642.1	21896.3	100842.1
裕民县	Yumin [Qagantokay] County			
和布克赛尔蒙古自治县	Hoboksar Mongol Autonomous County	32212.9	17675.7	50871.4
阿勒泰地区	**Altay Administrative Offices**	**451012.9**	**219279.1**	**549905.2**
阿勒泰市	Altay City	58295.0	86408.1	42829.2
布尔津县	Burqin County	126805.4	55155.1	29982.3
富蕴县	Fuyun [Koktokay] County	209285.7	54131.3	230452.2
福海县	Fuhai [Burultokay] County	8585.0		16827.6
哈巴河县	Habahe [Kaba] County	40969.1	3084.6	218248.1
青河县	Qinghe [Qinggil] County			
吉木乃县	Jeminay County	7072.7	20500.0	11565.8
博尔塔拉蒙古自治州	**Bortala Mongol Autonomous Prefecture**	**162521.6**	**177615.1**	**102875.3**
博乐市	Bole [Bortala] City	161100.8	175471.9	98483.6
精河县	Jinghe [Jing] County	1420.8	2143.2	4391.7
温泉县	Wenquan [Araxang] County			
巴音郭楞蒙古自治州	**Bayangol Mongol Autonomous Prefecture**	**1630922.3**	**2299992.8**	**4296676.5**
库尔勒市	Korla City	1234555.9	1919973.6	3877698.9
轮台县	Luntai [Bugur] County			
尉犁县	Yuli [Lopnur] County			
若羌县	Ruoqiang [Qarkilik] County	205440.4	229339.1	266461.2
且末县	Qiemo [Qarqan] County			
焉耆回族自治县	Yanqi Hui Autonomous County	8090.0	200.8	14435.7
和静县	Hejing County	155344.8	150232.8	124339.8
和硕县	Hoxud County	4318.7		3355.6
博湖县	Bohu [Bagrax] County	23172.5	246.5	10385.3
阿克苏地区	**Aksu Administrative Offices**	**824767.9**	**482681.4**	**1009764.4**
阿克苏市	Aksu City	225720.0	246453.0	342866.8
温宿县	Wensu [Onsu] County	93956.2	93881.7	46751.4
库车县	Kuqa County	443224.0	87964.1	573093.2
沙雅县	Xayar County			
新和县	Xinhe [Toksu] County			
拜城县	Baicheng [Bay] County	41915.1	53982.6	38248.0
乌什县	Wushi [Uxturpan] County	8125.4	400.0	8714.5

Continued

(10 000 yuan)

主营业务收入 Revenue from Principal Business	#主营业务成本 Cost of Principal Business	主营业务税金及附加 Taxes and Other Charges on Principal Business	营业利润 Business Profit	利润总额 Total Profit	亏损企业亏损总额 Losses Value of Loss-Suffering Enterprises	利税总额 Total Profits and Taxes	本年应交增值税 Value-added Taxes Payable	全部从业人员年平均人数(人) Annual Average Employed Persons (person)
116871.2	100884.2	349.9	7049.3	8721.5	2179.3	12153.6	3082.2	1563
86378.3	60057.9	449.3	10358.2	10962.2	8496.1	12378.1	966.6	2824
64410.6	33679.5	2649.3	12685.9	13912.2		23349.7	6788.2	2191
663079.5	**337482.2**	**8818.6**	**244458.7**	**247966.8**	**3441.8**	**314048.1**	**57262.7**	**7569**
99480.9	90901.5	557.3	2777.7	2850.3	447.5	6304.9	2897.3	1896
55928.3	31811.3	279.0	10644.7	12197.0		16050.1	3574.1	548
207285.8	103010.6	3711.5	69141.0	70559.5	2994.3	94724.5	20453.5	3149
16638.6	11663.1	268.0	3779.7	3787.9		5143.6	1087.7	313
279291.6	98420.1	4001.9	156133.3	156584.3		189836.3	29250.1	1647
4454.3	1675.6	0.9	1982.3	1987.8		1988.7		16
179769.8	**153931.9**	**753.6**	**4671.0**	**5912.1**	**4696.7**	**14823.1**	**8157.4**	**4098**
175725.2	151311.4	656.1	4064.7	5297.6	4696.7	13778.8	7825.1	3878
4044.6	2620.5	97.5	606.3	614.5		1044.3	332.3	220
5558794.2	**1755291.0**	**329577.6**	**2779836.4**	**2811107.9**	**1593.8**	**3641896.1**	**501210.6**	**26567**
5039819.5	1534618.4	308698.5	2588313.2	2585429.2	267.8	3353479.4	459351.7	20885
332792.4	98269.5	18695.6	152190.0	185670.2		235620.5	31254.7	3018
35128.2	25399.4	308.4	6650.2	6665.0		10930.2	3956.8	581
125207.4	76491.8	1755.5	33448.0	34164.6		42281.5	6361.4	1754
7337.6	5601.0	28.1	304.2	304.0		522.6	190.5	73
18509.1	14910.9	91.5	-1069.2	-1125.1	1326.0	-938.1	95.5	256
2674158.8	**2234334.9**	**248378.8**	**88426.2**	**92757.3**	**74289.2**	**430874.5**	**89738.4**	**15182**
334799.5	279286.1	2155.6	37027.3	39966.9	5315.4	59352.6	17230.1	6506
42427.4	25699.8	504.8	7795.0	7714.6	152.9	11050.7	2831.3	1437
2211693.7	1884683.8	243311.1	20416.8	21939.6	66382.2	326706.6	61455.9	4753
75097.8	37602.5	1738.7	22175.7	22127.3	2438.7	31859.8	7993.8	2162
6921.0	4112.9	646.6	920.9	918.4		1788.7	223.7	196

13-12 续表 5

单位：万元

地　区	Region	流动负债合计 Total Working Liabilities	长期负债合计 Long-term Liabilities	所有者权益合计 Total Owners' Equities
阿瓦提县	Awat County	11827.2		90.5
柯坪县	Kalpin County			
克孜勒苏柯尔克孜自治州	**Kizilsu Kirgiz Autonomous Prefecture**	**22887.2**	**1103.5**	**41556.1**
阿图什市	Artux City	22887.2	1103.5	41556.1
阿克陶县	Akto County			
阿合奇县	Akqi County			
乌恰县	Wuqia [Ulugqat] County			
喀什地区	**Kashgar [Kaxgar] Administrative Offices**	**105022.7**	**247239.4**	**23860.4**
喀什市	Kashgar [Kaxgar] City	103430.3	247239.4	24091.8
疏附县	Shufu County	1592.4		-231.4
疏勒县	Shule County			
英吉沙县	Yengisar County			
泽普县	Zepu [Poskam] County			
莎车县	Shache [Yarkant] County			
叶城县	Yecheng [Kagilik] County			
麦盖提县	Makit County			
岳普湖县	Yopurga County			
伽师县	Jiashi [Payzawat] County			
巴楚县	Bachu [Maralbexi] County			
塔什库尔干塔吉克自治县	Taxkorgan Tajik Autonomous County			
和田地区	**Hotan Administrative Offices**	**54564.8**	**72564.1**	**163983.3**
和田市	Hotan City	38882.2	67030.1	-4483.3
和田县	Hotan County	6968.5	5250.4	131719.8
墨玉县	Moyu [Karakax] County	3600.6	283.6	36500.7
皮山县	Pishan [Guma] County	5113.5		246.1
洛浦县	Lop County			
策勒县	Qira County			
于田县	Yutian [Keriya] County			
民丰县	Minfeng [Niya] County			
自治区直辖县级市	**Municpality Country-LevelCity directly under the Central Government**	**1450860.1**	**1386529.9**	**1556114.2**
石河子市	Shihezi City	1001580.4	1072887.8	1353449.1
阿拉尔市	Aral City	175342.5	108903.8	31469.7
图木舒克市	Tumxuk City	60194.7	86733.7	35888.0
五家渠市	Wujiaqu City	213742.5	118004.6	135307.4

Continued

(10 000 yuan)

主营业务收入 Revenue from Principal Business	#主营业务成本 Cost of Principal Business	主营业务税金及附加 Taxes and Other Charges on Principal Business	营业利润 Business Profit	利润总额 Total Profit	亏损企业亏损总额 Losses Value of Loss-Suffering Enterprises	利税总额 Total Profits and Taxes	本年应交增值税 Value-added Taxes Payable	全部从业人员年平均人数(人) Annual Average Employed Persons (person)
3219.4	2949.8	22.0	90.5	90.5		116.1	3.6	128
25375.7	**19601.8**	**60.0**	**3575.1**	**3557.7**		**3806.2**	**188.5**	**365**
25375.7	19601.8	60.0	3575.1	3557.7		3806.2	188.5	365
239268.6	**247696.2**	**1276.8**	**-20113.3**	**-23157.6**	**29598.0**	**-10003.6**	**11877.2**	**5323**
235878.8	244273.1	1262.9	-19968.9	-23012.8	29453.2	-10012.4	11737.5	5159
3389.8	3423.1	13.9	-144.4	-144.8	144.8	8.8	139.7	164
88327.6	**86930.1**	**250.6**	**-13014.1**	**-12268.6**	**18156.3**	**-5067.3**	**6950.7**	**1827**
56710.7	61104.8	187.6	-13608.3	-13558.4	14447.2	-10296.6	3074.2	1213
13227.9	11696.2	24.0	-1680.8	-2443.8	3499.0	2.3	2422.1	363
17999.2	13956.6	39.0	2481.3	3943.7		5437.1	1454.4	212
389.8	172.5		-206.3	-210.1	210.1	-210.1		39
2124624.2	**1674818.0**	**22222.8**	**232190.0**	**255363.0**	**42749.3**	**369457.9**	**91872.1**	**34035**
1735895.1	1339724.5	16034.0	247122.3	269051.6	19186.7	362854.0	77768.4	27754
167681.2	154747.3	589.2	-20494.0	-20450.4	21040.1	-11782.4	8078.8	2070
58787.4	49473.4	45.2	3726.1	3701.7		4978.4	1231.5	941
162260.5	130872.8	5554.4	1835.6	3060.1	2522.5	13407.9	4793.4	3270

13-13 国有控股工业企业主要经济效益指标

单位: %　　(2012 年)

项　　目	Item	产值利税率 Ratio of Profits and Taxes to Industrial Output Value
总　　计	**Total**	**23.8**
按登记注册类型分	**By Status of Registration**	
内资企业	Domestic Funded Enterprises	23.9
国有企业	State-owned Enterprises	9.1
#中央企业	Central Enterprises	10.6
地方企业	Local Enterprises	4.2
#自治区属企业	Autonomous	2.5
地区(州、市)属企业	Prefecture or City	-4.1
县(市)属企业	County or City	8.7
股份合作企业	Share-holding Cooperative Enterprises	
联营企业	Joint Ownership Enterprises	14.0
#国有联营企业	State Joint Enterprises Ownership	1.3
国有与集体联营企业	Joint State-collectiue Enterprises	41.6
有限责任公司	Limited Liability Corporations	13.6
#国有独资公司	Sole State-funded Corporations	17.7
其他有限责任公司	Other Limited Liability Corporations	12.2
股份有限公司	Share-holding Corporations Ltd.	31.4
港、澳、台商投资企业	Enterprises with Funds from Hongkong,Macao and Taiwan	11.4
外商投资企业	Foreign Funded Enterprises	20.0
在总计中:国有控股企业	Of the Total : State-owned and State-holding Enterprises	23.8
按轻、重工业分	**Grouped by Light & Heavy Industry**	
轻工业	Light Industry	20.4
以农产品为原料	Using Farm Produces as Raw Materials	22.3
以非农产品为原料	Using Non-Farm Produces as Raw Materials	-11.9
重工业	Heavy Industry	24.0
采掘工业	Mining and Quarrying	51.9
原料工业	Raw Materials Industry	8.5
加工工业	Manufacturing Industry	18.2
按企业规模分	**Grouped by Size of Enterprises**	
大型企业	Large Enterprises	25.4
中型企业	Medium-sized Enterprises	18.2
小型企业	Small Enterprises	14.0
微型企业	Mini Enterprises	29.8

Main Indicators on Economic Efficiency of State-holding Industrial Enterprises

(%)

总资产贡献率 Ratio of Total Assets to Industrial Output Value	资本保值增值率 Ratio of Capital-hold and Rise	资产负债率 Assets Liability Ratio	流动资产周转次数(次/年) Number of Times of Annual TurnoverWorking Capitals (times/year)	成本费用利润率 Ratio of Profits to Industrial Cost	全员劳动生产率 Overall Labour Productivity
17.6	**115.2**	**53.8**	**2.7**	**16.3**	**52.2**
17.7	114.8	53.8	2.8	16.3	52.4
6.5	112.1	62.4	2.1	3.1	24.8
8.0	108.8	57.7	2.2	3.7	25.8
3.3	124.7	72.4	1.7	1.2	21.0
2.3	61.9	73.8	2.1	1.3	19.6
-0.2	75.9	89.6	1.3	-4.9	11.7
2.8	725.8	64.9	1.1	-0.5	21.7
0.2	-55.7	134.5	0.5	0.6	0.6
7.4	224.4	68.6	1.0	17.3	14.6
1.5	144.6	68.6	1.0		6.5
14.9	733.8	68.7	0.9	94.6	1769.5
9.6	119.5	65.1	1.9	8.2	24.2
12.2	108.3	63.8	1.9	6.6	27.6
8.8	123.7	65.5	1.9	8.8	23.0
26.1	113.7	44.3	3.7	23.8	95.5
4.2	421.1	44.2	2.7	6.8	11.5
4.9	132.9	64.2	0.8	12.5	28.5
17.6	115.2	53.8	2.7	16.3	52.2
12.3	99.0	62.3	1.1	7.4	17.2
15.4	96.0	62.5	1.2	9.2	19.0
-1.1	114.1	61.7	0.5	-15.3	6.3
17.9	116.1	53.3	2.9	16.7	56.8
30.3	109.5	47.0	2.9	61.9	84.1
8.4	123.2	57.7	3.2	1.1	33.8
14.2	118.0	59.9	1.5	16.6	27.3
21.2	108.8	50.6	3.4	17.7	66.1
11.0	123.4	60.4	1.5	11.0	22.4
6.4	173.4	62.5	1.4	9.4	26.5
11.8	72.2	74.3	1.0	31.9	105.2

13-14 分行业国有控股工业企业主要经济效益指标

单位: % (2012 年)

行业	Sector	产值利税率 Ratio of Profits and Taxes to Industrial Output Value
总计	**Total**	**23.8**
煤炭开采和洗选业	Mining and Washing of Coal	27.7
石油和天然气开采业	Extraction of Petroleum and Natural Gas	60.9
黑色金属矿采选业	Mining and Processing of Ferrous Metals Ores	29.1
有色金属矿采选业	Mining and Processing of Nonferrous Metals Ores	47.5
非金属矿采选业	Mining and Processing of Nonmetal Ores	23.6
#采盐	Extraction of Salt	31.6
农副食品加工业	Processing of Food from Agricultural Products	10.5
#谷物磨制	Grain Grinding	9.1
饲料加工	Fodder Processing	12.4
制糖	Sugar Making	8.9
食品制造业	Manufacture of Food	6.4
#罐头制造	Manufacture of can	-27.3
酒、饮料和精制茶制造业	Manufacture of Wine,Beverages and Refined Tea	41.0
#酒的制造	Manufacture of Wine	41.7
烟草制品业	Manufacture of Tobacco	70.0
纺织业	Manufacture of Textile	5.7
#棉、化纤纺织及印染精加工	Cotton, Chemical Fiber, Dyeing, Printing and Processing	7.1
纺织服装、鞋、帽制造业	Manufacture of Textile Wearing Apparel, Footware and Caps	7.5
造纸及纸制品业	Manufacture of Paper and Paper Products	1.1
印刷业和记录媒介的复制	Printing and Copying of Medium for Record	8.1
石油加工、炼焦及核燃料加工业	Oil Processing, Coking and Nuclear Fuel Processing	10.5
#炼焦	Coking	7.6
化学原料及化学制品制造业	Raw Chemical Material and Chemical Products	16.5
#基础化学原料制造	Basic Chemical Material	11.3
肥料制造	Fertilizer Making	50.2
合成材料制造	Manufacture of Synthetic Material	7.6
医药制造业	Manufacture of Medicine	8.5
化学纤维制造业	Manufacture of Chemical Fiber	15.7
橡胶制品业	Manufacture of Rubber Products	3.1
非金属矿物制品业	Manufacture of Nonmetal Mineral Products	13.9
#水泥制造	Manufacture of Cement	14.5
黑色金属冶炼及压延加工业	Smelting and Pressing of Ferrous Metals	2.9
有色金属冶炼及压延加工业	Smelting and Pressing of Nonferrous Metals	12.9
金属制品业	Manufacture of Metal Products	0.8
通用设备制造业	Manufacture of General Purpose Machinery	5.0
专用设备制造业	Manufacture of Special Purpose Machinery	11.0
汽车制造业	Manufacture of Automobile	-2.1
电气机械和器材制造业	Manufacture of Electric Equipment and Machinery	8.5
电力、热力的生产和供应业	Electricity and Thermal Production and Supply	8.0
#电力生产和电力供应	Electricity Production and Supply	8.5
水的生产和供应业	Water Production and Supply	0.6

Main Indicators on Economic Efficiency of State-holding Industrial Enterprises by Sectors

(%)

总资产贡献率 Ratio of Total Assets to Industrial Output Value	资本保值增值率 Ratio of Capital-hold and Rise	资产负债率 Assets Liability Ratio	流动资产周转次数(次/年) Number of Times of Annual TurnoverWorking Capitals (times/year)	成本费用利润率 Ratio of Profits to Industrial Cost	全员劳动生产率 Overall Labour Productivity
17.6	**115.2**	**53.8**	**2.8**	**16.3**	**52.2**
9.8	123.4	63.1	1.2	15.2	21.0
36.8	107.0	42.1	4.2	87.7	153.3
19.4	102.3	69.8	1.1	25.5	52.5
19.2	107.1	49.8	1.9	61.3	47.9
20.2	123.0	48.9	1.3	14.0	15.1
27.7	125.7	29.5	1.3	17.5	20.5
10.7	104.8	61.0	1.5	8.1	15.4
11.1	98.6	66.9	2.1	9.1	10.4
10.1	113.5	45.9	1.4	12.2	26.4
7.5	92.6	58.6	0.9	4.1	12.8
4.6	64.2	81.7	0.9	0.5	10.2
-1.7	6.7	98.4	0.5	-18.6	0.4
31.1	97.5	55.2	1.9	30.7	32.7
31.6	93.5	57.8	2.0	31.2	33.6
56.1	115.8	28.9	1.3	37.9	293.6
3.5	104.0	51.5	1.3	0.6	3.9
4.2	106.4	55.5	1.4	1.3	4.0
7.4	95.3	111.8	2.1	3.6	6.4
1.3	98.2	67.9	0.7	-0.2	4.3
5.1	116.1	43.4	1.3	4.3	10.0
23.7	95.0	36.4	7.6	-2.2	66.4
6.8	267.9	77.1	1.4	3.2	17.2
9.5	112.2	57.7	1.7	14.9	29.3
3.0	115.7	64.8	1.1	5.8	10.4
27.3	135.9	56.4	1.6	62.3	77.8
8.4	102.2	51.6	2.6	6.4	28.8
5.5	109.7	55.9	0.6	6.9	11.0
11.2	-61.4	122.3	1.3	12.0	9.4
4.5	114.6	62.7	1.6	0.9	11.1
5.4	163.7	51.2	0.7	8.9	16.6
4.7	185.9	50.7	0.6	9.4	16.2
5.4	123.4	72.6	3.5	0.9	16.2
7.2	473.0	22.2	1.3	13.4	32.0
3.1	68.5	40.2	5.5		7.7
4.6	557.5	76.9	1.3	1.1	12.4
9.0	114.0	58.3	1.1	9.5	11.2
-2.1	336.4	92.0	3.1	-2.7	2.9
5.5	258.7	76.9	0.8	6.0	13.7
5.0	136.7	65.2	2.2	5.0	34.0
5.2	137.7	64.5	2.4	5.5	36.4
0.6	119.9	56.7	0.3	-5.3	10.6

13-15 各地、州、市、县(市)国有控股工业企业主要经济效益指标

单位: %　　(2012 年)

地　区	Region	产值利税率 Ratio of Profits and Taxes to Industrial Output Value
总　计	**Total**	**23.8**
乌鲁木齐市	**Urumqi City**	**17.0**
天山区	Tianshan District	7.5
沙依巴克区	Shayibak District	20.6
新市区	Xinshi District	51.3
水磨沟区	Shui Mogou District	20.6
头屯河区	Tou Tunhe District	2.0
达坂城区	Da Bancheng District	29.4
米东区	Midong District	9.2
乌鲁木齐县	Urumqi County	40.1
克拉玛依市	**Karamay City**	**26.9**
独山子区	Dushanzi District	5.7
克拉玛依区	Karamay District	41.0
白碱滩区	Bai Jiantan District	
乌尔河区	Urhe District	
吐鲁番地区	**Turpan Administrative Offices**	**26.3**
吐鲁番市	Turpan City	1.4
鄯善县	Shanshan [Piqan] County	31.9
托克逊县	Toksun County	7.1
哈密地区	**Hami [Kumul] Administrative Offices**	**16.6**
哈密市	Hami [Kumul] City	13.0
巴里坤哈萨克自治县	Barkol Kazak Autonomous County	46.7
伊吾县	Yiwu [Araturuk] County	33.1
昌吉回族自治州	**Changji Hui Autonomous Prefecture**	**8.2**
昌吉市	Changji City	11.0
阜康市	Fukang City	8.7
呼图壁县	Hutubi County	12.3
玛纳斯县	Manas County	-6.3
奇台县	Qitai County	3.7
吉木萨尔县	Jimsar County	-35.1
木垒哈萨克自治县	Mori Kazak Autonomous County	
伊犁哈萨克自治州	**Ili Kazak Autonomous Prefecture**	**22.2**
伊犁州直属县(市)	**Counties (Cities) Direct Under Ili Prefecture**	**21.5**
伊宁市	Yining [Gulja] City	11.0
奎屯市	Kuytun City	30.2
伊宁县	Yining [Gulja] County	14.2
察布查尔锡伯自治县	Qapqal Xibe Autonomous County	14.9
霍城县	Huocheng [Korgas] County	6.2
巩留县	Gongliu [Tokkuztara] County	2.3
新源县	Xinyuan [Kunes] County	21.9
昭苏县	Zhaosu [Mongolkure] County	32.5
特克斯县	Tekes County	
尼勒克县	Nilka County	25.5
塔城地区	**Tacheng [Tarbagatai] Administrative Offices**	**11.6**
塔城市	Tacheng [Qoqek] City	-14.3
乌苏市	Usu City	9.3
额敏县	Emin [Dorbiljin] County	20.1

Main Indicators on Economic Efficiency of State-holding Industrial Enterprises by Prefecture, Autonomous Prefecture, City and County

(%)

总资产贡献率 Ratio of Total Assets to Industrial Output Value	资本保值增值率 Ratio of Capital-hold and Rise	资产负债率 Assets Liability Ratio	流动资产周转次数(次/年) Number of Times of Annual TurnoverWorking Capitals (times/year)	成本费用利润率 Ratio of Profits to Industrial Cost	全员劳动生产率 Overall Labour Productivity
17.6	**115.2**	**53.8**	**2.8**	**16.3**	**52.2**
13.7	**109.8**	**55.4**	**3.0**	**9.2**	**51.0**
5.7	114.9	60.4	2.6	5.3	37.6
3.4	120.5	58.8	0.4	14.6	12.8
36.8	123.7	45.5	4.4	57.1	134.5
14.2	72.8	19.1	2.0	11.0	27.5
4.7	98.9	72.3	3.6	0.3	16.5
10.7	103.6	52.9	2.3	26.7	20.0
11.7	98.5	42.7	4.7	-2.6	37.7
7.8	76.4	79.6	0.7	53.9	362.9
25.8	**102.4**	**40.4**	**4.0**	**16.8**	**69.5**
9.4	90.3	33.7	5.9	-4.4	38.2
31.4	108.0	42.6	3.3	35.4	77.4
14.7	**125.8**	**54.2**	**2.4**	**21.1**	**35.9**
2.7	163.0	68.8	1.4	-2.6	19.8
18.9	126.5	46.5	2.8	26.8	39.2
5.2	106.9	75.0	1.5	2.9	19.7
7.9	**136.3**	**68.9**	**1.1**	**9.9**	20.3
6.4	135.8	68.8	1.1	6.4	18.2
22.1	142.9	66.9	0.9	70.4	46.3
17.6	106.1	88.3	0.6	18.4	41.8
4.9	**789.5**	**54.2**	**1.5**	**4.4**	**19.8**
8.4	1318.4	41.1	2.7	5.9	31.1
3.7	853.1	54.4	1.1	6.0	19.1
25.7	188.9	50.1	3.5	12.1	17.0
1.0	50.1	86.2	0.9	-11.3	5.6
4.3	220.2	85.0	1.0	0.3	12.6
-7.8	246.9	103.0	1.4	-22.9	-3.1
10.9	**124.0**	**62.4**	**1.6**	**13.7**	**31.7**
10.2	**131.7**	**63.6**	**1.5**	**9.4**	**32.5**
8.5	127.8	61.7	2.6	7.3	20.1
16.3	151.0	60.0	1.7	7.4	58.4
7.1	118.6	59.7	1.0	11.1	17.6
8.6	292.3	53.2	3.3	20.8	27.7
4.7	89.6	65.5	1.2	2.4	14.8
2.0	124.6	67.4	1.2	-5.0	54.9
16.4	97.8	60.9	1.3	16.7	24.9
55.5	83.2	70.3	2.4	47.1	37.7
5.8	152.9	75.0	1.6	19.1	48.9
6.4	**116.4**	**62.7**	**1.3**	**8.1**	**19.5**
-6.8	117.9	72.6	4.8	-12.4	8.1
4.6	65.7	56.8	0.9	0.5	12.3
10.0	106.7	60.4	0.8	23.0	29.4

13-15 续表 1

单位: %

地　　区	Region	产值利税率 Ratio of Profits and Taxes to Industrial Output Value
沙湾县	Shawan County	7.4
托里县	Toli County	16.8
裕民县	Yumin [Qagantokay] County	
和布克赛尔蒙古自治县	Hoboksar Mongol Autonomous County	21.0
阿勒泰地区	**Altay Administrative Offices**	**34.1**
阿勒泰市	Altay City	-11.6
布尔津县	Burqin County	28.4
富蕴县	Fuyun [Koktokay] County	29.6
福海县	Fuhai [Burultokay] County	24.4
哈巴河县	Habahe [Kaba] County	59.2
青河县	Qinghe [Qinggil] County	
吉木乃县	Jeminay County	45.8
博尔塔拉蒙古自治州	**Bortala Mongol Autonomous Prefecture**	**8.0**
博乐市	Bole [Bortala] City	8.9
精河县	Jinghe [Jing] County	-10.6
温泉县	Wenquan [Araxang] County	
巴音郭楞蒙古自治州	**Bayangol Mongol Autonomous Prefecture**	**47.3**
库尔勒市	Korla City	52.0
轮台县	Luntai [Bugur] County	
尉犁县	Yuli [Lopnur] County	
若羌县	Ruoqiang [Qarkilik] County	63.9
且末县	Qiemo [Qarqan] County	11.4
焉耆回族自治县	Yanqi Hui Autonomous County	4.4
和静县	Hejing County	14.5
和硕县	Hoxud County	-32.7
博湖县	Bohu [Bagrax] County	-12.0
阿克苏地区	**Aksu Administrative Offices**	**18.5**
阿克苏市	Aksu City	13.7
温宿县	Wensu [Onsu] County	23.7
库车县	Kuqa County	19.1
沙雅县	Xayar County	
新和县	Xinhe [Toksu] County	
拜城县	Baicheng [Bay] County	25.7
乌什县	Wushi [Uxturpan] County	21.8

Continued

(%)

总资产贡献率 Ratio of Total Assets to Industrial Output Value	资本保值增值率 Ratio of Capital-hold and Rise	资产负债率 Assets Liability Ratio	流动资产周转次数(次/年) Number of Times of Annual TurnoverWorking Capitals (times/year)	成本费用利润率 Ratio of Profits to Industrial Cost	全员劳动生产率 Overall Labour Productivity
9.9	124.2	39.6	2.2	4.5	11.2
12.0	80.2	64.2	1.3	20.2	36.7
6.1	358.0	66.7	1.3	15.1	18.3
18.2	**110.0**	**57.6**	**2.5**	**35.3**	**49.8**
-2.6	104.2	81.7	3.0	-11.0	11.1
10.6	82.7	88.2	1.4	22.6	59.3
15.9	106.0	50.2	2.3	27.4	41.3
4.7	435.2	50.3	0.6	21.2	30.2
56.8	93.1	24.0	4.5	96.6	101.6
11.4	128.8	64.9	0.9	79.5	300.5
6.3	**59.9**	**86.2**	**1.8**	**2.3**	**18.7**
6.7	59.2	85.9	1.9	3.1	19.3
1.3	76.4	89.7	0.8	-12.0	12.5
32.0	**114.7**	**52.8**	**3.2**	**60.9**	**112.4**
35.1	107.0	49.3	3.7	87.2	152.0
39.7	124.7	56.0	1.5	88.4	100.9
370.6		676.7	45.8	-1.8	14.3
4.2	150.2	54.7	1.3	1.7	8.4
11.6	335.9	70.5	3.2	6.7	22.0
-11.7	81.2	48.2	1.1	-18.7	0.6
-3.6	66.6	74.6	1.0	-15.0	4.8
14.9	**174.9**	**58.2**	**2.6**	**7.4**	**44.1**
5.2	239.8	60.3	0.8	10.0	21.2
5.4	108.0	83.0	1.4	15.4	16.7
28.6	141.9	48.5	6.0	5.5	88.9
20.8	191.0	71.4	1.7	21.6	29.1
10.7	86.3	57.8	0.6	11.8	15.7

13-15 续表 2

单位: %

地　区	Region	产值利税率 Ratio of Profits and Taxes to Industrial Output Value
阿瓦提县	Awat County	
柯坪县	Kalpin County	
克孜勒苏柯尔克孜自治州	**Kizilsu Kirgiz Autonomous Prefecture**	**10.4**
阿图什市	Artux City	1.4
阿克陶县	Akto County	
阿合奇县	Akqi County	28.9
乌恰县	Wuqia [Ulugqat] County	
喀什地区	**Kashgar [Kaxgar] Administrative Offices**	**2.2**
喀什市	Kashgar [Kaxgar] City	2.1
疏附县	Shufu County	0.4
疏勒县	Shule County	12.6
英吉沙县	Yengisar County	
泽普县	Zepu [Poskam] County	
莎车县	Shache [Yarkant] County	1.8
叶城县	Yecheng [Kagilik] County	14.6
麦盖提县	Makit County	
岳普湖县	Yopurga County	
伽师县	Jiashi [Payzawat] County	
巴楚县	Bachu [Maralbexi] County	0.3
塔什库尔干塔吉克自治县	Taxkorgan Tajik Autonomous County	-1.3
和田地区	**Hotan Administrative Offices**	**0.6**
和田市	Hotan City	-8.3
和田县	Hotan County	7.0
墨玉县	Moyu [Karakax] County	12.5
皮山县	Pishan [Guma] County	
洛浦县	Lop County	
策勒县	Qira County	
于田县	Yutian [Keriya] County	
民丰县	Minfeng [Niya] County	
自治区直辖县级市	**Municpality Country-LevelCity directly under the Central Government**	**9.0**
石河子市	Shihezi City	9.2
阿拉尔市	Aral City	-0.2
图木舒克市	Tumxuk City	11.5
五家渠市	Wujiaqu City	3.8

Continued

(%)

总资产贡献率 Ratio of Total Assets to Industrial Output Value	资本保值增值率 Ratio of Capital-hold and Rise	资产负债率 Assets Liability Ratio	流动资产周转次数(次/年) Number of Times of Annual TurnoverWorking Capitals (times/year)	成本费用利润率 Ratio of Profits to Industrial Cost	全员劳动生产率 Overall Labour Productivity
4.0	**284.8**	**64.2**	**0.9**	**10.3**	**21.8**
1.1	284.8	26.9	0.6	-1.7	11.4
6.7		100.0	3.3	38.8	82.4
4.7	**274.8**	**85.1**	**3.8**	**-2.9**	**18.0**
4.3	187.0	87.7	4.9	-2.9	18.2
1.1	164.9	133.8	5.1	-5.5	3.7
6.3		-87.5	0.8	20.7	14.1
3.3		37.3	0.7	2.1	7.8
6.9		39.7	0.8	23.4	9.0
0.3		141.2	1.1	0.4	23.7
7.2		104.8	1.3	-16.2	71.9
1.5	**111.6**	**45.9**	**1.8**	**-3.4**	**16.8**
-1.5	-43.8	98.4	5.5	-8.8	12.3
0.8	99.5	10.4	0.6	-8.0	28.8
7.8	137.1	31.7	1.5	8.9	22.3
7.6	**99.6**	**63.8**	**1.3**	**7.4**	**18.4**
8.3	105.1	61.1	1.4	7.8	19.4
1.4	216.7	80.0	0.5	-2.2	6.1
5.9	131.0	81.7	0.8	8.5	21.4
4.6	9.0	58.1	1.7	3.6	7.1

13-16 分行业大中型工业企业主要经济指标

单位：万元 (2012 年)

行业	Sector	企业单位数（个） Number of Enterp-rises (unit)	#亏损企业 Loss- Suffering Enterprises	工业总产值（当年价格） Gross Industrial Output Value (At Current Prices)
总计	**Total**	**396**	**118**	**60369502.4**
煤炭开采和洗选业	Mining and Washing of Coal	45	9	1623757.6
石油和天然气开采业	Extraction of Petroleum and Natural Gas	4		13668644.7
黑色金属矿采选业	Mining and Processing of Ferrous Metals Ores	11	3	697663.8
有色金属矿采选业	Mining and Processing of Nonferrous Metals Ores	10	2	413478.4
非金属矿采选业	Mining and Processing of Nonmetal Ores	3		39802.6
#采盐	Extraction of Salt	2		22889.4
农副食品加工业	Processing of Food from Agricultural Products	27	5	794969.5
#谷物磨制	Grinding Grain	1		9817.7
饲料加工	Fodder Processing	2		181664.8
制糖	Sugar Making	13	4	303078.1
食品制造业	Manufacture of Food	15	5	638902.4
#罐头制造	Manufacture of can	1	1	33054.2
酒、饮料和精制茶制造业	Manufacture of Wine,Beverages and Refined Tea	11		426535.1
#酒的制造	Manufacture of Wine	8		357542.6
烟草制品业	Manufacture of Tobacco	1		357066.4
纺织业	Manufacture of Textile	42	19	1019148.2
#棉、化纤纺织及印染精加工	Cotton, Chemical Fiber, Dyeing, Printing and Processing	37	16	947989.7
毛纺织和染整精加工	Wool Textile, Dyeing and Printing	2	1	15566.9
纺织服装、鞋、帽制造业	Manufacture of Textile Wearing Apparel, Footware and Caps	2		30671.8
家具制造业	Manufacture of Furniture	1	1	60386.0
造纸及纸制品业	Manufacture of Paper and Paper Products	3	1	63029.2
印刷业和记录媒介的复制	Printing and Copying of Medium for Record	1		6677.2
石油加工、炼焦及核燃料加工业	Oil Processing, Coking and Nuclear Fuel Processing	21	11	15524503.6
#炼焦	Coking	15	7	716488.1
化学原料及化学制品制造业	Raw Chemical Material and Chemical Products	36	10	4213148.3
#基础化学原料制造	Basic Chemical Material	16	7	904646.9
肥料制造	Fertilizer Making	7		878381.1
合成材料制造	Manufacture of Synthetic Material	8	3	2321028.3
医药制造业	Manufacture of Medicine	2	1	35704.1
化学纤维制造业	Manufacture of Chemical Fiber	8	3	815197.5
橡胶制品业	Manufacture of Rubber Products	7	3	438212.9
非金属矿物制品业	Manufacture of Nonmetal Mineral Products	36	13	1287826.4
#水泥制造	Manufacture of Cement	26	8	931815.9
黑色金属冶炼及压延加工业	Smelting and Pressing of Ferrous Metals	22	12	6436850.1
有色金属冶炼及压延加工业	Smelting and Pressing of Nonferrous Metals	15	2	2063628.4
金属制品业	Manufacture of Metal Products	6		328616.1
专用设备制造业	Manufacture of Special Purpose Machinery	3	1	49192.4
汽车制造业	Manufacture of Automobile	3	3	288654.3
电气机械和器材制造业	Manufacture of Electric Equipment and Machinery	5		1802405.3
计算机、通信和其他电子设备制造业	Telecom Equipment, Computer and Other Electronic Equipment	1		220758.4
金属制品、机械和设备修理业	Manufacture of Metal Products	1		16900.6
电力、热力的生产和供应业	Electricity and Thermal Production and Supply	37	11	4917974.0
#电力生产和电力供应	Electricity Production and Supply	32	10	4824385.6
水的生产和供应业	Water Production and Supply	1	1	18158.6

Main Indicators of Large-scale and Medium-scale Industrial Enterprises by Sectors

(10 000 yuan)

工业销售产值(当年价) Sales Value of Industry Products (At Current Prices)	出口交货值 Delivery Value of Industry Export	实收资本 Total Capital Hold	资产合计 Total Assets	流动资产合计 Total Working Capitals	#产成品 Finished Product	固定资产原价 Original Value of Fixed Assets
59127359.7	**227886.0**	**28864294.1**	**91540404.0**	**26890628.1**	**2362666.7**	**73167577.7**
1558817.0		1473921.3	5568909.3	1275637.6	114157.4	2073639.6
13687621.0		13016635.8	23196681.6	3456735.5	125655.2	31578500.2
657897.0		199211.9	1183247.2	649863.7	105539.6	410140.8
435367.2		242960.0	948565.1	213141.0	27460.6	452409.9
39826.1		17499.9	46767.4	30389.3	4277.5	19317.0
22213.4		14500.0	40515.1	26154.7	4132.8	13595.8
707610.4	351.6	174190.8	1008853.1	597425.9	200418.0	406199.3
9754.9		4841.1	15133.3	2285.9	689.0	5268.9
178677.6		32900.8	244204.3	114444.3	15883.2	66581.0
232929.7		68144.3	415655.3	258744.1	139021.1	261572.8
611834.8	43811.2	181790.5	882372.6	430857.3	78665.2	530405.4
61242.8	35453.4	43836.0	358840.6	227440.5	55315.1	221014.8
415729.6		141507.2	672070.2	329847.8	18057.3	253439.2
345139.9		120253.5	576667.3	291840.1	12556.0	187263.5
354589.7		18741.7	445764.0	272738.0		128081.0
992997.8	25312.2	562042.6	1931471.2	792904.9	172531.7	1028953.8
927501.5	13163.0	482290.0	1777571.9	750089.1	166409.4	933415.6
15326.9	440.5	11907.0	15589.1	7599.9	2194.4	9238.7
26563.2	3661.1	6303.0	33469.5	20519.6	2523.1	8055.9
34743.3	31289.7	63268.0	276530.0	31130.7	3297.0	27016.9
64556.9		17643.0	178696.6	73572.7	4551.5	85981.6
7444.2		5727.4	25276.3	8831.4	1863.8	27343.9
15309983.7		4635814.3	7643255.2	2319810.7	403182.5	7850355.2
608124.7		278448.6	1294009.4	521405.2	93381.1	595721.0
4139881.7	15633.9	1969378.5	8605354.1	2133926.6	293928.5	5007691.4
848851.0	6411.2	527224.4	2943799.3	743907.1	60594.3	1132885.9
879417.3		442649.7	2367836.0	646840.1	49836.4	1386738.1
2304752.8	8493.8	961424.8	3095073.4	652605.3	180759.3	2435103.4
33013.5	194.5	10960.6	70160.9	48495.8	7075.0	22248.8
745336.6		138507.8	880089.2	375751.2	98304.2	515254.1
408335.9	9662.3	128538.2	445177.0	223514.2	85381.0	210715.9
1241036.7		873972.9	4852179.6	1870456.7	62069.0	5438681.3
888627.0		777832.8	4094668.9	1526370.5	41091.1	5195400.6
6299625.7	16449.0	1100933.4	6340170.0	2151891.6	237807.6	3457538.4
1925869.4	5920.1	477960.0	5406919.8	2034781.1	171864.5	1666419.9
225407.4		72088.0	245179.1	122601.3	5369.8	62169.0
52160.2	461.9	21993.2	134861.6	103489.8	12597.1	16331.8
254024.4		29485.8	206604.8	81229.6	27458.3	38781.2
1757218.5	31072.5	598907.8	5837190.2	3536538.3	58299.7	394198.8
212815.1	39166.9	53435.5	714567.8	219124.1	18716.7	438560.1
16709.1		900.6	22970.4	19325.6	1895.0	4347.1
4857280.8		1347411.1	10562082.1	1952786.1	2236.8	9104795.7
4763692.4		1328421.2	10016147.2	1733042.2	2236.8	8666347.5
18158.6		12000.0	421570.6	164883.0		123101.2

13-16 续表

单位: 万元

行　　业	Sector	流动负债合计 Total Working Liabilities	长期负债合计 Long-term Liabilities
总　　计	**Total**	**31053126.3**	**18863729.9**
煤炭开采和洗选业	Mining and Washing of Coal	2206591.2	1258708.5
石油和天然气开采业	Extraction of Petroleum and Natural Gas	4158042.4	5595340.0
黑色金属矿采选业	Mining and Processing of Ferrous Metals Ores	762237.4	51174.3
有色金属矿采选业	Mining and Processing of Nonferrous Metals Ores	304269.0	130871.9
非金属矿采选业	Mining and Processing of Nonmetal Ores	14456.2	522.5
#采　盐	Extraction of Salt	9879.8	522.5
农副食品加工业	Processing of Food from Agricultural Products	525596.8	44076.0
#谷物磨制	Grinding Grain	5547.1	3204.5
饲料加工	Fodder Processing	84687.8	26448.2
制　糖	Sugar Making	239054.2	5425.8
食品制造业	Manufacture of Food	568408.4	46255.2
#罐头制造	Manufacture of can	335411.4	39558.6
酒、饮料和精制茶制造业	Manufacture of Wine,Beverages and Refined Tea	307664.9	178297.0
#酒的制造	Manufacture of Wine	246720.8	178297.0
烟草制品业	Manufacture of Tobacco	128861.0	
纺织业	Manufacture of Textile	791711.6	145003.4
#棉、化纤纺织及印染精加工	Cotton, Chemical Fiber, Dyeing, Printing and Processing	737176.5	134591.4
毛纺织和染整精加工	Wool Textile, Dyeing and Printing	8561.6	
纺织服装、鞋、帽制造业	Manufacture of Textile Wearing Apparel, Footware and Caps	21123.3	7971.2
家具制造业	Manufacture of Furniture	26639.1	7027.2
造纸及纸制品业	Manufacture of Paper and Paper Products	97084.3	19639.5
印刷业和记录媒介的复制	Printing and Copying of Medium for Record	9227.6	4067.2
石油加工、炼焦及核燃料加工业	Oil Processing, Coking and Nuclear Fuel Processing	2301311.5	630596.7
#炼　焦	Coking	700941.2	150880.8
化学原料及化学制品制造业	Raw Chemical Material and Chemical Products	2234096.3	2778118.8
#基础化学原料制造	Basic Chemical Material	1064852.2	791944.4
肥料制造	Fertilizer Making	521393.2	958626.2
合成材料制造	Manufacture of Synthetic Material	579348.1	1015683.2
医药制造业	Manufacture of Medicine	21932.0	384.1
化学纤维制造业	Manufacture of Chemical Fiber	652218.0	77947.4
橡胶制品业	Manufacture of Rubber Products	224609.4	66073.4
非金属矿物制品业	Manufacture of Nonmetal Mineral Products	1660356.0	943123.6
#水泥制造	Manufacture of Cement	1156012.3	882294.5
黑色金属冶炼及压延加工业	Smelting and Pressing of Ferrous Metals	4117161.3	439867.7
有色金属冶炼及压延加工业	Smelting and Pressing of Nonferrous Metals	2610161.0	1275102.1
金属制品业	Manufacture of Metal Products	122797.4	25046.7
专用设备制造业	Manufacture of Special Purpose Machinery	37195.2	1421.6
汽车制造业	Manufacture of Automobile	184859.4	11081.6
电气机械和器材制造业	Manufacture of Electric Equipment and Machinery	2194674.5	946902.2
计算机、通信和其他电子设备制造业	Telecom Equipment, Computer and Other Electronic Equipment	114868.5	233233.7
金属制品、机械和设备修理业	Manufacture of Metal　Products	20379.1	
电力、热力的生产和供应业	Electricity and Thermal Production and Supply	3028237.2	3478497.0
#电力生产和电力供应	Electricity Production and Supply	2873568.6	3176131.8
水的生产和供应业	Water Production and Supply	115141.0	151789.7

Continued

(10 000 yuan)

所有者权益合计 Total Owners' Equities	主营业务收入 Revenue from Principal Business	#主营业务成本 Cost of Principal Business	主营业务税金及附加 Taxes and Other Charges on Principal Business	营业利润 Business Profit	利润总额 Total Profit	亏损企业亏损总额 Losses Value of Loss-Suffering Enterprises	利税总额 Total Profits and Taxes	本年应交增值税 Value-added Taxes Payable	全部从业人员年平均人数(人) Ann Employed Persons (person)
40702826.5	**60386253.4**	**44827541.4**	**3096379.5**	**7321663.7**	**7703225.3**	**883058.2**	**13576738.6**	**2777133.8**	**497896**
2052718.3	1617637.4	1101977.2	46750.6	206189.0	211728.7	32800.1	429018.5	170539.2	49318
13443299.1	14402827.5	5415657.7	1138900.2	5762379.1	5822514.1		8325443.7	1364029.4	77204
368702.2	692077.9	467183.3	19671.8	144442.0	143742.6	12595.0	218375.7	54961.3	6331
513424.1	407421.0	188364.0	6723.7	167349.3	167078.5	5138.2	219977.0	46174.8	5945
31295.3	36308.6	19810.0	2306.4	3744.2	4887.9		10457.6	3263.3	1511
29964.8	24825.2	8251.3	2285.6	3728.0	4833.1		10333.3	3214.6	880
428763.1	737055.8	594351.4	2392.1	55104.0	60201.6	7389.1	85963.3	23369.6	11509
6381.7	9608.9	9232.6	4.1	159.9	236.5		240.6		322
133062.1	175427.3	129849.0	342.3	18394.0	20035.4		23384.6	3006.9	1188
166639.6	237037.2	192233.4	1643.5	8952.3	9362.2	4583.9	26772.2	15766.5	6158
264506.1	617531.5	465415.9	1403.8	43455.8	54971.1	25255.5	81724.0	25349.1	9590
-16129.4	61723.6	49753.2	69.4	-29035.5	-18669.4	18669.4	-12951.2	5648.8	1566
178863.3	460471.8	265180.3	41102.4	83885.2	86985.6		162485.9	34397.9	7946
151649.4	340473.5	177681.6	40976.2	77218.5	80267.8		153194.8	31950.8	6740
316903.0	354588.7	121438.7	155886.8	55009.2	54751.4		250038.2	39400.0	941
774076.0	1110236.2	1057545.6	3513.2	-45501.2	-951.6	30325.3	37391.7	34830.1	34377
689231.5	1052198.2	1005299.4	3233.3	-44082.6	-1415.9	27159.4	35334.0	33516.6	31098
7027.5	15055.1	13526.8	77.3	-151.8	-322.0	822.6	165.8	410.5	975
4375.0	43396.9	44729.4	16.0	1543.8	1689.7		2031.4	325.7	1493
242863.7	35366.3	31605.9	176.2	-3016.8	-1945.3	1945.3	-1769.1		589
61972.7	61722.8	52233.4	270.0	3143.3	4568.4	3133.4	6611.9	1773.5	2817
11981.5	7444.2	5520.2	104.3	-656.8	160.4		798.0	533.3	489
4645378.7	15379617.0	13426102.3	1568324.4	-254763.6	-267159.1	445245.7	1626088.1	324922.8	39601
376219.0	604810.5	503880.9	2784.8	37221.3	36472.3	18622.5	66930.2	27673.1	9423
3583207.6	3780930.7	2900086.6	40692.4	452395.4	499841.7	55559.8	668970.5	128436.4	48101
1077071.5	1089373.3	937546.1	4670.8	29605.8	37342.2	24678.0	61675.8	19662.8	18562
887816.6	867778.7	420031.3	26870.8	295788.1	328263.5		391702.5	36568.2	10604
1500041.9	1716874.3	1471724.0	8095.0	99635.0	106334.7	30881.8	177502.8	63073.1	15896
42816.4	26608.3	18792.9	191.1	-279.7	360.6	349.8	2149.6	1597.9	1021
148165.0	806389.7	727074.2	1602.6	1927.8	7806.0	4078.8	26529.0	17120.4	7801
154494.2	397403.6	359596.7	2254.7	-1740.1	-654.6	5346.8	8732.4	7132.3	5447
2199220.4	1175854.9	972364.4	5533.5	72135.4	100482.5	25212.4	149062.5	43046.5	25272
2013805.1	828301.8	662776.7	4930.8	67479.0	93405.0	18832.7	134052.6	35716.8	19076
1705204.5	6593921.4	6282058.8	15588.8	31184.6	64125.8	44939.7	200650.8	120936.2	35935
1502359.4	1735347.3	1545950.5	1795.8	86212.9	79553.2	6548.3	136160.5	54811.5	15030
97334.7	235920.8	221803.8	794.4	2759.8	3576.3		9486.4	5115.7	3417
96244.8	69956.7	53555.7	115.6	6082.5	7218.2	801.5	7942.4	608.6	1663
10663.8	260673.0	257455.5	210.3	-7157.4	-7090.2	7090.2	-6116.9	763.0	1359
2694613.1	2177409.4	1720642.8	7727.3	249958.0	297189.2		323629.4	18712.9	6400
366465.6	203155.2	165700.4	173.6	10119.2	14643.8		14829.1	11.7	4367
2591.3	15674.5	14464.0	55.0	71.1	211.1		705.9	439.8	364
3665855.7	4907093.9	4420697.7	13567.2	222061.4	296561.7	91387.8	466839.9	156711.0	43977
3582523.7	4785840.8	4297973.5	13538.0	245194.1	305713.9	74045.7	475679.7	156427.8	41175
154639.9	25096.4	17970.9	145.8	-7710.8	-6011.4	6011.4	-4359.8	1505.8	1252

13-17 分行业大中型工业企业主要经济效益指标

单位: %　　　　(2012 年)

行　　业	Sector	产　值利税率 Ratio of Profits and Taxes to Industrial Output Value
总　　计	**Total**	**22.5**
煤炭开采和洗选业	Mining and Washing of Coal	26.4
石油和天然气开采业	Extraction of Petroleum and Natural Gas	60.9
黑色金属矿采选业	Mining and Processing of Ferrous Metals Ores	31.3
有色金属矿采选业	Mining and Processing of Nonferrous Metals Ores	53.2
非金属矿采选业	Mining and Processing of Nonmetal Ores	26.3
#采　盐	Extraction of Salt	45.1
农副食品加工业	Processing of Food from Agricultural Products	10.8
#谷物磨制	Grinding Grain	2.5
饲料加工	Fodder Processing	12.9
制　糖	Sugar Making	8.8
食品制造业	Manufacture of Food	12.8
#罐头制造	Manufacture of can	-39.2
酒、饮料和精制茶制造业	Manufacture of Wine,Beverages and Refined Tea	38.1
#酒的制造	Manufacture of Wine	42.9
烟草制品业	Manufacture of Tobacco	70.0
纺织业	Manufacture of Textile	3.7
#棉、化纤纺织及印染精加工	Cotton, Chemical Fiber, Dyeing, Printing and Processing	3.7
毛纺织和染整精加工	Wool Textile, Dyeing and Printing	1.1
纺织服装、鞋、帽制造业	Manufacture of Textile Wearing Apparel, Footware and Caps	6.6
家具制造业	Manufacture of Furniture	-2.9
造纸及纸制品业	Manufacture of Paper and Paper Products	10.5
印刷业和记录媒介的复制	Printing and Copying of Medium for Record	12.0
石油加工、炼焦及核燃料加工业	Oil Processing, Coking and Nuclear Fuel Processing	10.5
#炼　焦	Coking	9.3
化学原料及化学制品制造业	Raw Chemical Material and Chemical Products	15.9
#基础化学原料制造	Basic Chemical Material	6.8
肥料制造	Fertilizer Making	44.6
合成材料制造	Manufacture of Synthetic Material	7.7
医药制造业	Manufacture of Medicine	6.0
化学纤维制造业	Manufacture of Chemical Fiber	3.3
橡胶制品业	Manufacture of Rubber Products	2.0
非金属矿物制品业	Manufacture of Nonmetal Mineral Products	11.6
#水泥制造	Manufacture of Cement	14.4
黑色金属冶炼及压延加工业	Smelting and Pressing of Ferrous Metals	3.1
有色金属冶炼及压延加工业	Smelting and Pressing of Nonferrous Metals	6.6
金属制品业	Manufacture of Metal Products	2.9
专用设备制造业	Manufacture of Special Purpose Machinery	16.2
汽车制造业	Manufacture of Automobile	-2.1
电气机械和器材制造业	Manufacture of Electric Equipment and Machinery	18.0
计算机、通信和其他电子设备制造业	Telecom Equipment, Computer and Other Electronic Equipment	6.7
金属制品、机械和设备修理业	Manufacture of Metal Products	4.2
电力、热力的生产和供应业	Electricity and Thermal Production and Supply	9.5
#电力生产和电力供应	Electricity Production and Supply	9.9
水的生产和供应业	Water Production and Supply	-24.0

Main Indicators on Economic Efficiency of Large-scale and Medium-scale Industrial Enterprises by Sectors

(%)

总资产贡献率 Ratio of Total Assets to ndustrial Output Value	资本保值增值率 Ratio of Capital-hold and Rise	资产负债率 Assets Liability Ratio	流动资产周转次数(次/年) Number of Times of Annual TurnoverWorking Capitals (times/year)	成本费用利润率 Ratio of Profits to Industrial Cost	全员劳动生产率 Overall Labour Productivity
16.1	**112.1**	**55.5**	**2.3**	**15.5**	**44.8**
8.4	112.3	63.1	1.3	15.4	21.5
36.8	107.4	42.1	4.2	87.7	153.3
20.5	124.6	68.8	1.1	25.7	44.0
23.7	121.5	45.9	1.9	72.2	47.2
22.3	132.5	33.1	1.2	15.0	14.1
25.4	128.4	26.0	1.0	24.3	17.9
9.9	111.3	57.5	1.2	8.8	14.2
3.6		57.8	4.2	2.2	3.2
10.9	119.1	45.5	1.5	13.1	28.5
7.2	88.3	59.9	0.9	4.1	12.2
11.0	145.4	70.0	1.4	9.6	15.7
-0.5	-69.1	104.5	0.3	-23.2	-0.4
25.3	110.5	72.3	1.4	25.1	27.6
27.8	111.4	73.7	1.2	33.5	29.5
56.1	115.8	28.9	1.3	37.9	293.6
3.1	121.6	59.9	1.4	-0.1	5.3
3.2	125.1	61.2	1.4	-0.1	5.4
1.1	83.5	54.9	2.0	-2.1	3.9
6.8	86.5	86.9	2.1	3.5	5.8
-0.1	98.1	12.2	1.1	-5.0	11.1
4.7	100.2	65.3	0.8	7.6	5.9
4.7	101.0	52.6	0.8	1.9	9.6
22.1	93.8	39.2	6.6	-1.9	60.6
7.2	115.6	70.9	1.2	6.4	19.0
9.5	108.1	58.3	1.8	14.9	26.3
3.4	85.4	63.3	1.5	3.5	13.0
17.8	192.3	62.5	1.3	57.1	48.7
8.3	100.3	51.5	2.6	6.6	28.8
3.6	99.4	39.0	0.6	1.4	7.2
6.2	67.8	83.0	2.2	1.0	15.8
3.5	104.1	65.3	1.8	-0.2	11.1
4.4	148.2	54.7	0.6	8.7	14.1
4.6	161.0	50.8	0.5	11.5	14.7
5.6	98.8	73.1	3.1	1.0	14.7
3.0	298.0	72.2	0.9	4.8	24.0
5.7	102.9	60.3	1.9	1.5	7.5
6.2	102.4	28.6	0.7	11.2	9.5
-2.2	-701.9	94.8	3.2	-2.7	2.4
7.6	109.1	53.8	0.6	15.2	48.1
4.0	103.5	48.7	0.9	7.6	11.3
4.3		88.7	0.8	1.3	9.6
6.2	120.9	65.3	2.5	6.3	33.5
6.5	123.4	64.2	2.8	6.7	35.0
-0.6	102.5	63.3	0.2	-17.7	7.8

13-18 主要工业产品产量
Output of Major Industrial Products

产品名称	Item	2011	2012
原煤(吨)	Raw Coal (ton)	119917064	136469850
天然原油(吨)	Crude Oil (ton)	26156316	26706783
天然气(万立方米)	Natural Gas (10 000 cu.m)	2353798	2530101
铁矿石原矿量(吨)	Crudeiron Ore (ton)	37140482	33656556
铜选矿含铜量(吨)	Cuproaurite (ton)	100967	93675
硫铁矿(折含 S 35%)(吨)	Pyritel with Content of (S35%)(ton)	151684	125250
原盐(吨)	Salt (ton)	2580489	3014047
发电量(万千瓦小时)	Electricity (10 000 kwh)	8751884	11874792
#火 电	Thermalpower	7310090	9987236
水 电	Hydropower	1145669	1586205
供热量(万吉焦)	Heat Supply (10 000 gigajoules)	22990	25531
大米(吨)	Rice (ton)	193579	241189
小麦粉(万吨)	Wheate Flour (10 000 tons)	278	368
精制食用植物油(吨)	Refined Edible Oil (ton)	1144978	1554608
成品糖(吨)	Sugar (ton)	461056	536366
饲料(吨)	Forage (ton)	2035077	2331322
糖果(吨)	Candy (ton)	4510	9884
乳制品(吨)	Dairy Products (ton)	351904	418854
罐头(吨)	Canned Food (ton)	1154128	694119
#番茄酱	Tomato Jam	1125359	628749
味精(吨)	Mono Sodium Glutamate (ton)	21607	16547
酱油(吨)	Soy (ton)	28955	28872
方便面(吨)	Instant Noodles(ton)	47721	62167
发酵酒精(千升)	Zymolytic Alcohol (kilo-liter)	64459	72429
饮料酒(千升)	Alcohol Beverage(kilo-liter)	645919	657637
#白 酒	Liquor	73926	87672
啤 酒	Beer	510960	505600
葡萄酒	Grape Wine	58579	53165
软饮料(吨)	Soft Drink (ton)	1485290	1698214
#碳酸饮料	Carbonic Drink	137139	109127
果汁和蔬菜汁饮料	Fruit Juice and Vegetable Juice Drink	483316	703768
包装饮用水	Bottled Water	672029	703255
冷冻饮品(吨)	Ice Beverage (ton)	47042	54112

注：钢材里包括钢材生产中消耗的外购国内钢。
Note: Rolled steel contain that manufacture of steel consumed outsourcing of internal steel.

13-18 续表 1 Continued

产品名称	Item	2011	2012
卷烟(万支)	Cigarettes (10 000 pieces)	1600081	1700000
纱(吨)	Yarn (ton)	399094	402151
布(万米)	Cloth (10 000 m)	7303	6676
#棉 布	Pure Cotton Cloth	7143	5298
绒线(毛线)(吨)	Knitting Wool (ton)	444	545
呢绒(万米)	Woolen Cloth Goods (10 000 m)	383	332
服装(万件)	Garments (10 000 units)	1821	2826
轻革(平方米)	Light Leather (sq.m)	4791153	5180378
人造板(立方米)	Artificial Board (cu.m)	1299462	1360533
#胶合板	Plywood	364283	397624
纤维板	Fiberboard	529521	532610
刨花板	Chip Board	348831	363785
家具(件)	Furniture (unit)	2659957	2297670
#木制家具	WoodenFurniture	2289328	1964149
金属家具	Steal Furniture	227743	193634
纸浆(吨)	Paper Pulp (ton)	234700	222132
纸制品(吨)	Paper produces (ton)	332095	415192
#瓦楞纸箱(纸箱)	Corrugaled Case	276678	364492
机制纸及纸板(吨)	Machine-made Paper and Paperboard (ton)	422924	410547
原油加工量(吨)	Processed Crude Oil (ton)	23884140	24268959
汽油(吨)	Gasoline (ton)	2334956	2393159
溶剂油(吨)	Megilp (ton)	176213	93023
煤油(吨)	Kerosene (ton)	461274	589508
柴油(吨)	Diesel Oil (ton)	10973746	10590956
润滑油(吨)	Lubricating Oil (ton)	825281	640838
燃料油(吨)	Fuel Oil (ton)	118462	105523
石油沥青(吨)	Petroleum Bitumen (ton)	1734067	1591319
液化石油气(吨)	Liquefied Petroleum Gas (ton)	528859	679463
焦炭(吨)	Coke (ton)	13765167	14408656
#机械化焦炉生产的焦炭	Coke Turned out by Mechanized Coke Oven	9927078	10154319
煤气(万立方米)	Coal Gas (10 000 cu.m)	1269083	1445154
硫酸(折 100%)(吨)	Sulfuric Acid (ton)	361779	389819
盐酸(含量 31%以上)(吨)	Hydrochloric Acid (With Content of 31%) (ton)	274338	301738

13-18 续表 2 Continued

产品名称	Item	2011	2012
氢氧化钠(烧碱)(折 100%)(吨)	Caustic Soda (ton)	1315745	1464433
碳酸钠(纯碱)(吨)	Soda Ash (ton)	151592	109224
碳化钙(电石)(折 300 升/千克)(吨)	Calcium Carbide (ton)	2784380	3125805
合成氨(吨)	Synthetic Ammonia (ton)	1775660	1889044
农用氮、磷、钾化学肥料(折纯)(吨)	Chemical Fertilizers (ton)	2335610	3041687
#氮肥(折含 N 100%)	Nitrogen Fertilizers	1557445	2231963
#尿 素	Carbamide	1451997	2094356
磷肥(折合 P_2O_5 100%)	Phosphate Fertilizers	18182	24564
乙烯(吨)	Ethylene(ton)	1039855	1270893
涂料(吨)	Paint (ton)	72167	104969
合成洗涤剂(吨)	Synthetic Detergents (ton)	34461	41324
化学原料药(吨)	Chemical Medicine (ton)	28	214
中成药(吨)	Traditional Chinese Medicine (ton)	5993	4074
轮胎外胎(条)	Outer Tyres (unit)	1038487	1279426
塑料制品(吨)	Plastic Produces (ton)	1041107	1399683
#塑料薄膜	Plastic Film	187406	227371
#农用薄膜	Farm Plastic Sheet	176028	233812
塑料型材(含板片材)	Plastic Moulding Material	30685	67612
塑料制管子及其附件(吨)	Plastic Pipe and Accessory (ton)	431629	551290
塑料编织袋(吨)	Woven Plastic Bag (ton)	112257	120677
泡沫塑料(吨)	Foamed Plastics (ton)	35399	26050
塑料包装箱及容器(吨)	Plastic Packing Case and Container (ton)	46921	78463
日用塑料制品(吨)	Household Plastic Products (ton)	25775	31218
水泥熟料(万吨)	Cement Chamotte (10 000 ton)	2528	3520
窑外分解窑熟料(预分解窑熟料)(万吨)	Clinker Cement (10 000 tons)	1536	3014
水泥(万吨)	Cement (10 000 tons)	3172	4316
水泥电杆(根)	Cement Electric Pole Piece (unit)	276753	362627
商品混凝土(立方米)	Commercial Concrete (cu.m)	23814641	36173219
预应力混凝土桩 (米)	Prestressed Concrete Piles (m)	4980957	6270284
砖(折标准砖)(万块)	Brick (Standard Brick) (10 000 pieces)	1573813	2226725
瓦(万片)	Tile (10 000 pieces)	9118	14098
大理石板材(平方米)	Marble Slab (sq.m)	1240465	1364368
花岗石板材(平方米)	Granite Sheet (sq.m)	12609309	23250934

13-25 续表 3 Continued

产品名称	Item	2011	2012
石膏板(万平方米)	Plasterboard (sq.m)	845	1174
平板玻璃(重量箱)	Plate Glass (weight case)	2454818	3751856
沥青和改性沥青防水卷材(平方米)	Bitumen and Rolled Waterproof Material (sq.m)	2039281	8243157
中空玻璃(平方米)	Insulating Glass (sq.m)	131772	170845
钢化玻璃(平方米)	Toughened Glass (sq.m)	106297	262782
夹层玻璃(平方米)	Laminated Glass (sq.m)	21829	20184
日用玻璃制品(吨)	Household Glass Products (ton)	55926	64840
玻璃保温容器(万个)	Glass Attemperator (10 000 units)	1031	1058
陶质砖(平方米)	Carbonic Bricks (sq.m)	21282306	26982984
耐火材料制品(吨)	Fire Proof Material (ton)	200069	281938
石墨及碳素制品(吨)	Graphite and Carbon Products (ton)	173344	451038
玻璃纤维增强塑料制品(吨)	Glass Fibre Reinforced Plastices Products (ton)	28527	50167
生铁(吨)	Pig Iron (ton)	10884521	13283217
粗钢(吨)	Crude Steel (ton)	8929755	11382344
钢材(吨)	Rolled Steel (ton)	9851406	12898437
中小型型钢	Medium and Small Fasioned Steel	378595	326079
钢　筋	Concrete Iron	2844017	3307038
盘　条(线材)	Wire Rod	2049975	2885674
铁合金(吨)	Ferroalloy (ton)	160568	173015
铜(吨)	Copper (ton)	16721	27054
镍(吨)	Nickel (ton)	8128	10150
铝(吨)	Aluminium (ton)	294144	970733
铝材(吨)	Aluminium Material (ton)	54773	101841
工业锅炉(蒸发量吨)	Industrial Boiler (evaporating quantity ton)	947	1213
泵(台)	Pump (unit)	10953	20035
风机(台)	Fan (unit)	7559	6511
农作物收获机械(台)	Grop Harvesting Machinery (unit)	9708	7686
汽车(辆)	Motor Vehicles(unit)	1148	3391
#载货汽车	Trucks	1148	3391
改装汽车(辆)	Modified Truck (unit)	1576	2942
发电设备(千瓦)	Power Generating Equipment (kw)	3540500	2933000
变压器(千伏安)	Transformer (kva)	48550052	61945187
电力电缆(公里)	Electric Cable (km)	65961	117789

13-19 各地、州、市主要工业产品产量

年 份 Year	地 区 Region	纱 (吨) Yarn (ton)	布 (万米) Cloth (10 000 m)	绒线 (吨) Knitting Wool (ton)	呢绒 (万米) Woolen Piece Goods (10 000 m)
	1978	28008	15616	1239	189
	1980	31272	16931	1614	240
	1985	39130	21150	2396	680
	1990	101941	30017	2179	1230
	1995	244689	30460	2286	1262
	1996	208526	27186	2202	1361
	1997	247143	29862	2393	1227
	1998	220332	26719	1361	979
	1999	294378	27450	1349	798
	2000	334307	28060	1184	754
	2001	302654	25380	843	399
	2002	316095	20679	811	265
	2003	292713	15239	744	206
	2004	291386	13989	980	206
	2005	340864	14047	1118	284
	2006	357324	15415	799	327
	2007	408870	16000	637	368
	2008	397417	15302	578	412
	2009	386085	15148	533	376
	2010	415783	15069	741	326
	2011	399094	7303	444	383
	2012	402151	6676	545	332
乌鲁木齐市	Urumqi City	21411	584	244	
克拉玛依市	Karamay City				
吐鲁番地区	Turpan Administrative Offices	3546			
哈密地区	Hami [Kumul] Administrative Offices	10653			
昌吉回族自治州	Changji Hui Autonomous Prefecture	18876	324		89
伊犁哈萨克自治州	Ili Kazak Autonomous Prefecture	52274	268	301	
伊犁州直属县(市)	Counties (Cities) Direct Under Ili Prefecture	36869		185	
塔城地区	Tacheng [Tarbagatai] Administrative Offices	15405	268	116	
阿勒泰地区	Altay Administrative Offices				
博尔塔拉蒙古自治州	Bortala Mongol Autonomous Prefecture	21736	25		
巴音郭楞蒙古自治州	Bayangol Mongol Autonomous Prefecture	28105	642		
阿克苏地区	Aksu Administrative Offices	43659			
克孜勒苏柯尔克孜自治州	Kizilsu Kirgiz Autonomous Prefecture				
喀什地区	Kashgar [Kaxgar] Administrative Offices	27833	3		
和田地区	Hotan Administrative Offices	988			
自治区直辖县级市	Municpality Country-LevelCity directly under the Central Government	173072	4830		243
石河子市	Shihezi City	173072	4830		243
阿拉尔市	Aral City				
图木舒克市	Tumxuk City				
五家渠市	Wujiaqu City				

Output of Major Industrial Products by Prefecture, Autonomous Prefecture and City

机制纸及纸板(吨) Machine-made Paper and Paperboard (ton)	原盐(万吨) Salt (10 000 tons)	成品糖(万吨) Sugar (10 000 tons)	饮料酒(千升) Alcohol Beverage (kilo-liter)	卷烟(亿支) Cigarettes (100 million pieces)	原煤(万吨) Coal (10 000 tons)	原油(万吨) Crude Oil (10 000 tons)	天然气(万立方米) Natural gas (10 000 cu.m)	发电量(亿千瓦时) Electricity (100 million kwh)	#水电 Hydropower
19851	51.71	2.08	9336	15.05	1079.01	353.05	25100	21.17	4.64
23838	38.18	4.43	17082	15.55	1136.84	390.58	35298	23.58	5.25
41521	35.09	7.18	74809	40.20	1600.22	499.00	54556	38.11	8.64
90857	159.00	16.84	118585	61.70	2100.00	695.00	50161	69.79	14.25
180440	25.98	30.18	249481	68.05	2720.74	1267.83	114821	120.43	22.82
169789	36.54	36.34	219961	67.80	2986.00	1457.10	140609	136.03	24.49
161659	39.85	42.28	259015	66.05	3021.37	1629.25	213006	150.58	26.97
168799	27.53	47.59	271056	60.20	2926.91	1628.38	237826	157.76	28.23
180138	36.14	46.36	269453	55.00	2778.16	1739.65	310600	169.30	30.06
176477	31.78	30.76	269761	52.50	2798.90	1848.43	353930	182.98	30.53
193389	46.02	41.98	296187	55.20	2819.61	1946.95	417429	197.62	34.10
226950	50.75	51.84	307167	60.00	3098.67	2036.19	485237	212.24	34.67
233365	52.71	45.43	317260	62.50	3482.86	2141.39	502942	234.62	36.20
263066	87.32	37.26	345770	70.00	3749.40	2253.02	574805	266.30	37.08
289318	85.35	42.92	355275	70.00	3898.81	2408.32	1066437	306.92	43.27
295338	153.21	53.79	401771	85.00	4518.52	2474.74	1642099	357.15	53.43
252329	111.53	64.94	438502	100.00	5018.64	2604.31	2103348	416.87	58.78
301606	153.06	53.78	486007	120.00	6763.41	2715.13	2358941	489.17	73.84
355762	129.36	40.77	484936	135.00	8812.55	2512.86	2453887	571.31	79.84
371032	174.67	45.10	565041	150.00	9926.72	2558.16	2499096	679.33	97.07
422924	258.05	46.11	645919	160.00	11991.71	2615.63	2353798	875.19	114.57
410547	301.40	53.64	657637	170.00	13646.99	2670.68	2530101	1187.48	158.62
76176	10.33		136050		1341.36	735.00	164540	255.24	
	0.08		4192			1103.01	310136	46.89	
	99.00		7016		1262.90	156.00	105012	29.16	0.53
1152	4.48		17805		2413.99			62.40	
101878	0.25	6.55	44847		4968.17			154.96	0.48
2100	138.38	32.69	173525	170.00	1376.68	96.50	2281	169.36	86.72
		22.22	86028	170.00	645.29			81.50	51.39
2100	138.37	9.14	85798		726.32	96.50	2281	69.01	21.92
	0.01	1.34	1699		5.07			18.85	13.41
	6.06	2.93	641					7.18	1.18
127310	39.75	8.61	38503		386.18	580.17	1948132	63.05	17.83
	3.08	2.52	33839		1511.96			60.52	12.48
			160		11.10			7.48	7.10
4689		0.33	28228		33.32			25.67	12.55
		0.01	292		82.95			12.15	11.80
97242			172539		258.37			293.42	7.93
97242			172539		258.37			293.42	7.93

13-19 续表

年 份 Year	地 区 Region	生 铁 (万吨) Pig Iron (10 000 tons)	粗钢 (万吨) Crude Steel (10 000 tons)	大理石板材 (平方米) Marble Plate (sq.m.)	钢 材 (万吨) Steel Rolled (10 000 tons)
	1978	17.52	8.46		6.83
	1980	15.81	10.74		8.59
	1985	22.87	19.79		16.73
	1990	40.57	36.49	9589	28.48
	1995	69.53	70.59	34169	66.55
	1996	85.64	87.47	6420	86.70
	1997	93.82	97.21	53588	99.89
	1998	100.40	107.67	9197	116.19
	1999	101.30	105.60	7807	117.30
	2000	106.42	109.70	6294	131.26
	2001	111.73	131.83	22786	134.42
	2002	122.78	175.45	34185	173.07
	2003	144.86	204.12	117306	203.10
	2004	193.89	249.13	109663	238.52
	2005	258.66	306.54	78577	326.96
	2006	324.08	394.19	176025	411.45
	2007	394.97	447.24	119926	470.94
	2008	505.70	536.60	160011	576.62
	2009	764.62	653.32	190480	690.81
	2010	941.12	825.54	328249	891.70
	2011	1088.45	892.98	1240465	985.14
	2012	1328.32	1138.23	1364368	1289.84
乌鲁木齐市	Urumqi City	714.66	770.86	13799	913.58
克拉玛依市	Karamay City				
吐鲁番地区	Turpan Administrative Offices	104.46	13.71	3384	6.97
哈密地区	Hami [Kumul] Administrative Offices	19.03			
昌吉回族自治州	Changji Hui Autonomous Prefecture	78.79			
伊犁哈萨克自治州	Ili Kazak Autonomous Prefecture	153.64	139.86	71385	146.79
伊犁州直属县(市)	Counties (Cities) Direct Under Ili Prefecture	139.16	134.32	3500	141.23
塔城地区	Tacheng [Tarbagatai] Administrative Offices		5.54		5.48
阿勒泰地区	Altay Administrative Offices	14.48		67885	0.09
博尔塔拉蒙古自治州	Bortala Mongol Autonomous Prefecture	4.79		1184055	
巴音郭楞蒙古自治州	Bayangol Mongol Autonomous Prefecture	218.01	213.80	5500	208.94
阿克苏地区	Aksu Administrative Offices	6.90		17500	6.01
克孜勒苏柯尔克孜自治州	Kizilsu Kirgiz Autonomous Prefecture	17.57		8396.28	
喀什地区	Kashgar [Kaxgar] Administrative Offices	10.46			
和田地区	Hotan Administrative Offices				
自治区直辖县级市	Municpality Country-LevelCity directly under the Central Government			60349	3.39
石河子市	Shihezi City			60349	3.39
阿拉尔市	Aral City				
图木舒克市	Tumxuk City				
五家渠市	Wujiaqu City				

Continued

水 泥 (万吨) Cement (10 000 tons)	硫 酸 (吨) Sulfuric Acid (ton)	烧 碱 (吨) Caustic Soda (ton)	合成氨 (吨)(折纯) Synthetic Ammonia (ton)	农用氮、磷、钾化肥(吨) Farm Nitrogen Phophate and Potassium (ton)	碳化钙 (电石)(吨) Calcium Crbide (ton)	塑料制品 (吨) Plastic Products (ton)
78.15	20262	4164	33155	20276	4895	3194
90.89	19153	3542	13762	9207	4486	2051
201.05	23921	5045	85728	58080	5989	17974
285.00	47732	15063	397062	287640	15976	40958
489.88	88491	24732	492754	383279	12344	100739
562.87	76413	28008	488337	372056	15901	129059
628.00	77187	35544	581449	428711	28350	143916
728.94	64836	39614	688069	520681	28999	168372
805.83	68169	42161	896632	685587	40216	139497
895.67	71458	51831	947511	754668	51749	197756
981.29	72511	68589	884340	729034	65763	262873
1029.71	70407	93362	956732	766291	73680	230729
1128.98	85322	114110	1082601	854530	82057	314891
1212.99	114046	174445	1015630	869795	115991	388270
1241.74	126901	295917	1192001	1285346	290591	349151
1334.50	160073	423901	1303586	1290802	501283	412032
1536.77	183484	485880	1325017	1385279	711277	517069
1672.76	201993	630314	1471312	1609409	910659	653230
2049.60	300423	814393	1407674	1591027	1560762	697269
2400.96	326112	916205	1484103	1591043	1845104	830651
3171.71	361779	1315745	1775660	2335610	2784380	1041107
4315.93	389819	1464433	1889044	3041687	3125805	1399683
491.90	6617	591687	761507	593715	169877	382725
						25422
211.33	132649				707206	28
201.20	7228			15280	483663	13673
402.22		87601		386508		310306
951.02	143187			302896	54111	114934
493.65					39800	39150
299.78	25709			270037	14311	67277
157.59	117478			32859		8508
105.68						37073
376.81		4336	713486	1250018		15999
585.15	35369		410391	428154		31517
86.51						2623
416.40	15703					37815
155.24				10		809
332.46	49066	780809	3660	65106	1710948	426759
332.46	49066	780809	3660	65106	1710948	426759

13-20 国有控股企业主要指标占全区规模以上工业比重

Percentage of Main Indicators in State-holding Enterprises to Enterprises above Designated Size

单位：万元 (2012 年) (10 000 yuan)

指　标	Item	全区规模以上工业企业 Enterprises Above Designated Size	国　有 控股企业 State-Holding Enterprises	比 重 (%) Percentage (%)
企业单位数(个)	Number of Enterprises(unit)	1959	522	26.6
从业人员(人)	Employed Person (person)	664797	398174	59.9
工业总产值	Gross Industrial Output Value	75326674.0	53466765.1	71.0
工业销售产值	Sales Value of Industry Products	73484359.9	52928947.5	72.0
出口交货值	Delivery Value of Industry Export	419562.7	159536.9	38.0
资产总计	Total Assets	116691728.3	78386247.9	67.2
负债合计	Total Liabilities	66725988.5	42193620.0	63.2
所有者权益	Owner's Right and Interest	49856070.2	36150759.2	72.5
实收资本	Substantial Capital	34363194.1	27474452.4	80.0
主营业务收入	Revenue from Principal Business	75106656.0	53793148.3	71.6
主营业务税金及附加	Taes and Other Charges on Principal Business	3222977.0	3056835.5	94.8
利润总额	Total Profits	8886377.7	7091412.9	79.8
利税总额	Total Profits and Tax	15388184.9	12740928.0	82.8
亏损单位数(个)	Number of Loss-suffering Enterprises (unit)	524	148	28.2
亏损企业亏损额	Losses Value of Loss-suffering	1176981.7	876796.1	74.5

13-21 重点行业主要指标占全区规模以上工业比重

Percentage of Main Indicators in Key Industrial Sectors to Xinjiang's Industry above Designated Size

(2012 年)

指　标	Item	合　计 Total	占全区比重 (%) Percentage (%)
从业人员(人)	**Employed Person (person)**	**664797**	**100**
石油和天然气开采业	Extraction of Petroleum and Natural Gas	77384	11.6
石油加工、炼焦及核燃料加工业	Petroleum Processing,Coking and Nuclear Fuel Processing	46489	7.0
黑色金属冶炼及压延加工业	Smelting and Pressing of Ferrous Metal	44009	6.6
电力、热力的生产和供应业	Electric Power, Thermal Power Production and Supply	55645	8.4
化学原料及化学制品制造业	Raw Chemical Material and Chemical Products	58208	8.8
纺织业	Textile Industry	40245	6.1
农副食品加工业	Processing of Food from Agricultural Products	28450	4.3
工业总产值(万元)	**Gross Industrial Output Value (10 000 yuan)**	**75326674.0**	**100.0**
石油和天然气开采业	Extraction of Petroleum and Natural Gas	13736414.3	18.2
石油加工、炼焦及核燃料加工业	Petroleum Processing,Coking and Nuclear Fuel Processing	16731304.5	22.2
黑色金属冶炼及压延加工业	Smelting and Pressing of Ferrous Metal	7407811.5	9.8
电力、热力的生产和供应业	Electric Power, Thermal Power Production and Supply	6192713.3	8.2
化学原料及化学制品制造业	Raw Chemical Material and Chemical Products	5155131.1	6.8
纺织业	Textile Industry	1306516.2	1.7
农副食品加工业	Processing of Food from Agricultural Products	3208192.5	4.3
工业销售产值(万元)	**Sales Value of Industry Products (10 000 yuan)**	**73484359.9**	**100.0**
石油和天然气开采业	Extraction of Petroleum and Natural Gas	13754165.9	18.3
石油加工、炼焦及核燃料加工业	Petroleum Processing,Coking and Nuclear Fuel Processing	16444524.0	21.8
黑色金属冶炼及压延加工业	Smelting and Pressing of Ferrous Metal	7213198.2	9.6
电力、热力的生产和供应业	Electric Power, Thermal Power Production and Supply	6123886.1	8.1
化学原料及化学制品制造业	Raw Chemical Material and Chemical Products	5074994.4	6.7
纺织业	Textile Industry	1274052.6	1.7
农副食品加工业	Processing of Food from Agricultural Products	3020397.1	4.0

注：所列行业为工业总产值百亿元以上行业。
Note: Listed sector of gross industrial output value were above ten billion sector.

13-21 续表 Continued

指　标	Item	合　计 Total	占全区比重(%) Percentage (%)
资产总计(万元)	**Total of Assets (10 000 yuan)**	**116691728.3**	**100.0**
石油和天然气开采业	Extraction of Petroleum and Natural Gas	23266281.5	19.9
石油加工、炼焦及核燃料加工业	Petroleum Processing,Coking and Nuclear Fuel Processing	8863962.8	7.6
黑色金属冶炼及压延加工业	Smelting and Pressing of Ferrous Metal	7147345.4	6.1
电力、热力的生产和供应业	Electric Power, Thermal Power Production and Supply	16975333.6	14.5
化学原料及化学制品制造业	Raw Chemical Material and Chemical Products	11384370.0	9.8
纺织业	Textile Industry	2310427.5	2.0
农副食品加工业	Processing of Food from Agricultural Products	3121264.5	2.7
利润总额(万元)	**Total Profits (10 000 yuan)**	**8886377.7**	**100.0**
石油和天然气开采业	Extraction of Petroleum and Natural Gas	5845595.9	65.8
石油加工、炼焦及核燃料加工业	Petroleum Processing,Coking and Nuclear Fuel Processing	-189190.3	-2.1
黑色金属冶炼及压延加工业	Smelting and Pressing of Ferrous Metal	38757.1	0.4
电力、热力的生产和供应业	Electric Power, Thermal Power Production and Supply	428461.8	4.8
化学原料及化学制品制造业	Raw Chemical Material and Chemical Products	636413.1	7.2
纺织业	Textile Industry	13133.5	0.1
农副食品加工业	Processing of Food from Agricultural Products	207620.9	2.3
利税总额(万元)	**Total Profitsand Tax (10 000 yuan)**	**15388184.9**	**100.0**
石油和天然气开采业	Extraction of Petroleum and Natural Gas	8352044.9	54.3
石油加工、炼焦及核燃料加工业	Petroleum Processing,Coking and Nuclear Fuel Processing	1766075.7	11.5
黑色金属冶炼及压延加工业	Smelting and Pressing of Ferrous Metal	189149.0	1.2
电力、热力的生产和供应业	Electric Power, Thermal Power Production and Supply	667311.0	4.3
化学原料及化学制品制造业	Raw Chemical Material and Chemical Products	848407.5	5.5
纺织业	Textile Industry	57940.2	0.4
农副食品加工业	Processing of Food from Agricultural Products	269751.6	1.8
主营业务收入(万元)	**Revenue from Principal Business (10 000 yuan)**	**75106656.0**	**100.0**
石油和天然气开采业	Extraction of Petroleum and Natural Gas	14472223.3	19.3
石油加工、炼焦及核燃料加工业	Petroleum Processing,Coking and Nuclear Fuel Processing	16558185.9	22.0
黑色金属冶炼及压延加工业	Smelting and Pressing of Ferrous Metal	7510035.1	10.0
化学原料及化学制品制造业	Raw Chemical Material and Chemical Products	4753071.5	6.3
电力、热力的生产和供应业	Electric Power, Thermal Power Production and Supply	6130160.5	8.2
纺织业	Textile Industry	1398990.8	1.9
农副食品加工业	Processing of Food from Agricultural Products	3202641.9	4.3

13-22 规模以上工业主要产品生产能力

Production Capacity of Major Industrial Products above Designated Size

产品名称	Item	2011	2012
原煤(吨)	Raw Coal (ton)	107859000	150837000
天然原油(吨)	Crude Oil (ton)	26325400	26297800
发电设备容量(万千瓦)	Generating Capacity (10 000 kw)	1698	2135
卷烟(万支)	Cigarettes (10 000 pieces)	2303316	2376000
化学纤维(吨)	Chemical Fiber (ton)	500000	491000
棉纺锭(环锭纺)(锭)	Cotton Hasp (unit)	4024464	4539522
气流纺锭(转杯纺)(头)	Airflow Hasp (unit)	71416	56088
棉布织机(台)	Calico Spinning Machine (set)	4319	2042
原油加工能力(吨)	Crude Petroleum Oil	27735000	28950000
焦炭(吨)	Coke (ton)	23653088	28941000
烧碱（折 100%）(吨)	Caustic Soda	1512900	1523100
炭化钙(电石)(折 300 升/千克)(吨)	Calcium Carbide (ton)	3708000	5013000
农用氮、磷、钾化学肥料(折纯)(吨)	Chemical Fertilizers (ton)	2755337	4670520
初级形态塑料(吨)	Primary Plastic	4008700	3991600
水泥熟料(吨)	Cement Chamotte (ton)	36593000	51113000
# 窑外分解窑熟料	Decompose Cellar Chamotte	29860000	46820000
水泥(吨)	Cement (ton)	49005000	66765000
平板玻璃(重量箱)	Plate Glass (weight case)	2000000	5200000
浮法玻璃(吨)	Float Glass		3000000
平拉玻璃(重量箱)	Plate Drawing Glass (weight case)	2000000	2200000
生铁(吨)	Pig Iron (ton)	14347402	15026600
粗钢(吨)	Crude Steel (ton)	11440000	13359600
钢材(吨)	Rolled Steel (ton)	13186500	15461960
铁合金(吨)	Ferroalloy (ton)	225000	230000
原铝(电解铝)(吨)	Aluminium (ton)	594700	2344700
汽车(辆)	Motor Vehicles(unit)	5000	20000

主要统计指标解释

工业 指从事自然资源的开采，对采掘品和农产品进行加工和再加工的物质生产部门。具体包括：(1)对自然资源的开采，如采矿、晒盐等(但不包括禽兽捕猎和水产捕捞)；(2)对农副产品的加工、再加工，如粮油加工、食品加工、缫丝、纺织、制革等；(3)对采掘品的加工、再加工，如炼铁、炼钢、化工生产、石油加工、机器制造、木材加工等，以及电力、自来水、煤气的生产和供应等；(4)对工业品的修理、翻新，如机器设备的修理、交通运输工具(如汽车)的修理等。

工业统计调查单位为独立核算法人工业企业。

独立核算法人工业企业指从事工业生产经营活动的单位。独立核算法人工业企业应同时具备以下条件：①依法成立，有自己的名称、组织机构和场所，能够承担民事责任；②独立拥有和使用资产，承担负债，有权与其他单位签订合同；③独立核算盈亏，并能够编制资产负债表。

国有及国有控股企业 指国有企业加上国有控股企业。国有企业(即原全民所有制工业或国营工业)指企业全部资产归国家所有，并按《中华人民共和国企业法人登记管理条例》规定登记注册的非公司制的经济组织。包括国有企业、国有独资公司和国有联营企业。1957年以前的公私合营和私营工业，后均改造为国营工业，1992年改为国有工业，这部分工业的资料不单独分列时，均包括在国有企业内。国有控股企业是对混合所有制经济的企业进行的"国有控股"分类。它是指这些企业的全部资产中国有资产(股份)相对其他所有者中的任何一个所有者占资(股)最多的企业。该分组反映了国有经济控股情况。

本篇涉及的其他企业登记注册类型的解释详见综合篇。

轻工业 指主要提供生活消费品和制作手工工具的工业。按其所使用的原料不同，可分为两大类：(1)以农产品为原料的轻工业，是指直接或间接以农产品为基本原料的轻工业。主要包括食品制造、饮料制造、烟草加工、纺织、缝纫、皮革和毛皮制作、造纸以及印刷等工业；(2)以非农产品为原料的轻工业，是指以工业品为原料的轻工业。主要包括文教体育用品、化学药品制造、合成纤维制造、日用化学制品、日用玻璃制品、日用金属制品、手工工具制造、医疗器械制造、文化和办公用机械制造等工业。

重工业 指为国民经济各部门提供物质技术基础的主要生产资料的工业。按其生产性质和产品用途，可以分为下列三类：(1)采掘(伐)工业，是指对自然资源的开采，包括石油开采、煤炭开采、金属矿开采、非金属矿开采等工业；(2)原材料工业，指向国民经济各部门提供基本材料、动力和燃料的工业。包括金属冶炼及加工、炼焦及焦炭、化学、化工原料、水泥、人造板以及电力、石油和煤炭加工等工业；(3)加工工业，是指对工业原材料进行再加工制造的工业。包括装备国民经济各部门的机械设备制造工业、金属结构、水泥制品等工业，以及为农业提供的生产资料如化肥、农药等工业。

根据上述划分原则，修理业中以重工业产品为修理作业对象的划为重工业，反之划为轻工业。

工业总产值

(1)定义：

工业总产值是工业企业在一定时期内生产的以货币形式表现的工业最终产品和提供工业性劳务活动的总价值量。它反映一定时间内工业生产的总规模和总水平。

(2)计算原则：

工业生产的原则，即凡是企业在报告期内生产的最终产品和提供的劳务，均应包括在内。其中的最终产品，不管是否在报告期内销售，只要是报告期内生产的，就应包括在内。凡不是工业生产的产品，均不得计入工业总产值。

最终产品的原则，即企业生产的成品价值必须是本企业生产的，经检验合格不需再进行任何加工的最终产品。企业对外销售的半成品也应视为最终产品计入工业总产值。而在本企业内各车间转移的半成品和在制品只能计算其期末期初差额价值。

工厂法原则，即以法人工业企业作为一个整体计算工业总产值，是其报告期内生产的最终产品和提供劳务的总价值量。

(3)内容及计算方法：

1995年全国工业普查对工业总产值(原规定)的内容及计算原则和方法做了某些修订，修订后的工业总产值(新规定)包括三项内容：即本期生产成品价值、对外加工费收入、在制品半成品期末期初差额价值三部分。

本期生产成品价值：指企业本期生产，并在报告期内不再进行加工，经检验、包装入库的全部工业成品(半成品)价值合计，包括企业生产的自制设备及提供给本企业在建工程、其他非工业部门和福利部门等单位使用的成品价值。本期生产成品价值为按自备原材料生产的产品的数量乘以本期不含增值税(销项税额)的产品实际销售平均单价计算；会计核算中按成本价格转帐的自制设备和自产自用的成品，按成本价格计算生产成品价值。生产成品价值中不包括用定货者来料加工的成品(半成品)价值。

对外加工费收入：指企业在报告期内完成的对外承接的工业品加工(包括用定货者来料加工产品)的加工费收入和对外工业修理作业所取得的加工费收入。对外加工费收入按不含增值税(销项税额)的价格计算，可根据会计“产品销售收入”科目的有关资料取得。

对于本企业对内非工业部门提供的加工修理、设备安装的劳务收入，如果企业会计核算基础较好，能取得这部分资料，而且这部分价值所占比重较大，应包括在对外加工费收入中。

自制半成品在制品期末期初差额价值：指企业报告期在制品期末减期初的差额价值，本指标一般可以从会计核算资料中取得。如果会计产品成本核算中不计算半成品、在制品的成本，则总产值中也不包括这部分价值，反之则包括。

资产总计 指企业过去的交易或者事项形成的、由企业拥有或者控制的、预期会给企业带来经济利益的资源。资产一般按流动性分为流动资产和非流动资产。其中流动资产可分为货币资金、交易性金融资产、应收票据、应收账款、预付款项、其他应收款、存货等；非流动资产可分为长期股权投资、固定资产、无形资产及其他非流动资产等。根据会计“资产负债表”中“资产总计”项目的期末余额数填报。

流动资产合计 资产满足以下条件之一应归为流动资产：（1）预计在一个正常营业周期中变现、出售或耗用，主要包括存货、应收账款等；（2）主要为交易目的而持有；（3）预计在资产负债表日起一年内（含一年）变现；（4）自资产负债日起一年内，交换其他资产或清偿负债的能力不受限制的现金或现金等价物。包括货币资金、应收票据、应收账款、存货等项目。根据会计“资产负债表”中“流动资产合计”项目的期末余额数填报。

固定资产原价 指固定资产的成本，包括企业在购置、自行建造、安装、改建、扩建、技术改造某项固定资产时所发生的全部支出总额。根据会计“固定资产”科目的期末借方余额填报。

累计折旧 指企业在报告期末提取的历年固定资产折旧累计数。根据会计“累计折旧”科目的期末贷方余额填报。

负债合计 指企业过去的交易或者事项形成的，预期会导致经济利益流出企业的现时义务。负债一般按偿还期长短分为流动负债和非流动负债。根据会计“资产负债表”中“负债合计”项目的期末余额数填报。

流动负债合计 负债满足下列条件之一的应归为流动负债：（1）预计在一个正常营业周期中清偿；（2）主要为交易目的而持有；（3）自资产负债表日起一年内到期应予清偿；（4）企业无权自主地将清偿推迟至资产负债表日后一年以上。包括短期借款、应付票据、应付账款、应付职工薪酬、应交税费等项目。根据会计“资产负债表”中“流动负债合计”项目的期末余额数填报。

所有者权益合计 指企业资产扣除负债后由所有者享有的剩余权益。公司的所有者权益又称股东权益。包括实收资本、资本公积、盈余公积、未分配利润等。根据会计“资产负债表”中“所有者权益合计”项目的期末余额数填报。

主营业务收入 指企业确认的销售商品、提供劳务等主营业务的收入。根据会计“主营业务收入”科目的期末贷方余额填报。

主营业务成本 指企业经营主要业务所发生的成本总额。根据会计“主营业务成本”科目的期末借方余额填报。

主营业务税金及附加 指企业经营主要业务应负担的营业税、消费税、城市维护建设税、教育费附加等。根据会计“主营业务税金及附加”科目的期末借方余额填报。

利润总额 指企业在一定会计期间的经营成果，是生产经营过程中各种收入扣除各种耗费后的盈余，反映企业在报告期内实现的亏盈总额。根据会计“利润表”中“利润总额”项目的本期金额数填报。

应交增值税 指企业按税法规定，从事货物销售或提供加工、修理修配劳务等增加货物价值的活动本期应交纳的税金。计算公式为：

应交增值税=销项税额-（进项税额-进项税额转出）-出口抵减内销产品应纳税额-减免税款+出口退税

进项税额指工业企业在报告期内购入货物或接受应税劳务而支付的、准予从销项税额中抵扣的增值税额。

销项税额指工业企业在报告期内销售货物或提供应税劳务应收取的增值税额。

从业人员年平均人数 是指报告期内平均拥有的从业人员人数。其计算公式为：

年平均人数=报告期内12个月平均人数之和 / 12

总资产贡献率 反映企业全部资产的获利能力，是企业经营业绩和管理水平的集中体现，是评价和考核企业盈利能力的核心指标。计算公式为：

总资产贡献率（%）=（利润总额+税金总额+利息支出）/ 平均资产总额*100%

公式中：税金总额为主营业务税金及附加与应交增值税之和；平均资产总额为期初期末资产之和的算术平均值。

资产负债率 该指标既反映企业经营风险的大小，也反映企业利用债权人提供的资金从事经营活动的能力。计算公式为：

资产负债率（%）=负债总额 / 资产总额 *100%

资产与负债均为报告期期末数。

流动资产周转次数 指一定时期内流动资产完成的周转次数，反映投入工业企业流动资金的周转速度。计算公式为：

流动资产周转次数=主营业务收入 / 全部流动资产平均余额

公式中：全部流动资产平均余额为期初和期末的流动资产之和的算术平均值。

成本费用利润率 反映企业投入的生产成本及费用的经济效益，同时也反映企业降低成本所取得的经济效益。计算公式为：

成本费用利润率（%）=利润总额 / 成本费用总额*100%

公式中：成本费用总额为主营业务成本、销售费用、管理费用、财务费用之和。

产品销售率 该指标反映工业产品已实现销售的程度，是分析工业产销衔接情况，研究工业产品满足社会需求的指标。计算公式为：

产品销售率(%) =工业销售产值 / 工业总产值*100%

Explanatory Notes on Main Statistical Indicators

Industry refers to the material production sector which is engaged in the extraction of natural resources and processing and reprocessing of minerals and agricultural products, including (1) extraction of natural resources, such as mining, salt production (but not including hunting and fishing); (2) processing and reprocessing of farm and sideline produces, such as rice husking, flour milling, wine making, oil pressing, silk reeling, spinning and weaving, and leather making; (3) manufacture of industrial products, such as steel making, iron smelting, chemicals manufacturing, petroleum processing, machine building, timber processing; water and gas production and electricity generation and supply; (4)repairing of industrial products such as the repairing of machinery and means of transport (including cars).

In industrial statistics surveys, the units of enquiry are corporate industrial enterprises with independent accounting systems.

Corporate industrial enterprises with independent accounting systems refer to enterprises engaging in industrial production activities, which meet the following requirements: (1) They are established legally, having their own names, organizations, location and able to take civil liability; (2) They possess and use their assets independently, assume liabilities and are entitled to sign contracts with other units; (3) They are financially independent and compile their own balance sheets.

State-owned and State-holding Enterprises refer to state-owned enterprises plus State-holding enterprises. State-owned enterprises (originally known as State-run enterprises with ownership by the whole society) are non-corporate economic entities registered in accordance with the Regulation of the People's Republic of China on the Management of Registration of Legal Enterprises, where all assets are owned by the State. Included in this category are State-owned enterprises, State-funded corporations and State-owned joint-operation enterprises. Joint State-private industries and private industries, which existed before 1957, were transformed into state-run industries since 1957, and into State-owned industries after 1992. Statistics on those enterprises are included in the State-owned industries instead of being grouped them separately. State-holding enterprises are a sub-classification of enterprises with mixed ownership, referring to enterprises where the percentage of State assets (or shares by the State) is larger than any other single share holder of the same enterprise. This sub-classification illustrates the control of the State over a particular industry.

For explanation of enterprises of other types of registration covered in this chapter, please refer to General Survey.

Light Industry refers to the industry that produces consumer goods and hand tools. It consists of two categories, depending on the materials used:

(1) Industries using farm products as raw materials. These are the branches of light industry which directly or indirectly use farm products as basic raw materials, including the manufacture of food and beverages, tobacco processing, textile, clothing, fur and leather manufacturing, paper making, printing, etc.

(2) Industries using non-farm products as raw materials. These are the branches of light industry which use manufactured goods as raw materials, including the manufacture of cultural, educational articles and sports goods, chemicals, synthetic fibre, chemical products for daily use, glass products for daily use, metal products for daily use, hand tools, medical apparatus and instruments, and the manufacture of cultural and office machinery.

Heavy Industry refers to the industry which produces capital goods, and provides various sectors of the national economy with necessary material and technical basis for production. It consists of the following three branches according to the purpose of production or the use of products:

(1) Mining, quarrying and logging industry, which refers to the industry that extracts natural resources, including extraction of petroleum, coal, metal and non-metal ores.

(2) Raw materials industry refers to the industry that provides various sectors of the national economy with raw materials, fuels and power. It includes smelting and processing of metals, coking and coke chemistry, chemical materials and building materials such as cement, plywood, and power, petroleum refining and coal dressing.

(3) Manufacturing industry which refers to the industry that processes raw materials. It includes machine-building industries which equip sectors of the national economy; industries producing metal structure and cement products; and industries producing means of agricultural production, such as chemical fertilizers and pesticides.

In accordance with the above principles of classification, the repairing trades, which are engaged primarily in repairing products of heavy industry, are classified as heavy industry while those which are engaged in repairing products of light industry are classified as light industry.

Gross Industrial Output Value

(1) Definition: Gross industrial output value is the total volume of final industrial products produced and industrial services provided during a given period in monetary terms. It reflects the total achievements and overall scale of industrial production during a given period.

(2) Principles for calculation:

Statistics on industrial production follow the principle that all final industrial products produced and industrial services provided during the reference period are to be included. The final industrial products are included as long as being produced during the reference period, no matter whether they are sold or not during the reference period. The gross industrial output value will not cover those products that are not from industrial production.

Determination of final products follows the principle that all products that are included in the calculation of gross industrial output value are the final products of the enterprise.

which have been accepted through quality check and require no further processing. The intermediate products sold by enterprises are considered as the final products of the enterprise and counted into the gross industrial output value. However, for the intermediate products being transferred among workshops and the work-in-progress products, only the balance value from the beginning to the end of the period is calculated.

Gross industrial output value is calculated following the principle of factory approach, i.e. industrial enterprise with legal entity is used as a whole in calculating the gross industrial output value, which will cover the total value of final industrial products produced and industrial services provided by these enterprises during the reference period.

(3) Content and method of calculation: The old definition of gross industrial output value was modified during the 1995 National Industrial Census. The revised (new) definition of gross industrial output value consists of 3 components: value of the finished products during the reference period, income from processing for external parties, and value of change in semi-finished products between the end and the beginning of the reference period.

Value of finished products during the reference period: refers to the value of all finished (semi-finished) industrial products that are produced during the reference period without the need for further processing, checked for acceptance, packed and put into the warehouse of the enterprise, including the value of own-produced equipment and the value of products provided to the projects under construction of the enterprise, and to other non-industrial or welfare units. Value of finished products during the reference period is calculated by the quantity of products produced using own materials multiplied by the average unit prices at which products are sold (excluding value-added tax). Own-produced equipment and products produced for own use are valued at cost prices as in the case of enterprise accounting. Value of finished products does not include the value of finished products (semi-finished products) that are produced using the materials from the clients who place the orders.

Income from external processing: refers to income from contracted external processing of industrial products (including processing of industrial products using materials from the clients), and the income from industrial repairing work provided to other parties. Income from external processing is calculated using information from the item "products sales income" in the enterprise accounting at the prices with value-added tax excluded.

For income from services such as processing, repairing and installation of equipment provided to non-industrial units within the enterprise, if the accounting work of the enterprise is good enough to separate it from other records, and the share of such services is significant, it should also be included in the income from external processing.

Value of change in semi-finished products between the end and the beginning of the reference period: refers to the value of change in semi-finished products between the end and the beginning of the reference period, which generally can be obtained from accounting records of enterprises. If the enterprise accounting excludes the cost of semi-finished products, then it should not be included in the gross industrial output value, and the reverse if otherwise.

Total Assets refer to all resources that are owned or controlled by enterprises through previous trades or transactions with expectation of making economic profits. Classified by the degree of liquidity, total assets include current assets, and non-current assets. Current assets can be classified into monetary assets, trading financial assets, notes receivable, accounts receivable, advanced payments, other prepaid money and inventories. Non-current assets can be divided into long-term equity investment, fixed assets, intangible assets and other non-current assets. Data on this indicator can be obtained by the year-end figures of total assets in the Assets and Liability Table of accounting records of enterprises.

Total Current Assets refer to the assets that meet one of the following requirements: (1) expected to be cashed, sold or used in a normal operation cycle, mainly including inventory and accounts receivable; (2) be owned for trading purpose mainly; (3) expected to be cashed in one year (including one year) from the day of the Assets and Liability Table; (4) unlimited cash or cash equivalents that can be exchanged with other assets or being capable of settling debts during one year since the day of Assets and Liability Table. Included are monetary assets, notes receivable, accounts receivable and inventories. Data on this indicator can be obtained by the year-end figures of total current assets in the Assets and Liability Table of the accounting records of enterprises.

Original Value of Fixed Assets refers to the cost of fixed assets, or the total expenditure of an enterprise spent on certain fixed assets, through purchase, construction, installation, transformation, expansion or technical upgrading. It is reported according to the year-end debit balance of fixed assets of accounting records.

Accumulated Depreciation refers to the accumulated figure of fixed assets depreciation over the past years that are extracted by the enterprise at the end of the reference period. It is reported according to the year-end credit balance of accumulated depreciation of accounting records.

Total Liabilities refer to payable liabilities of enterprises that accumulated from previous trades or transactions with expectation of economic profits leaking out. In terms of payment, it can be divided into liquid liabilities and long-term liabilities. Data on this item is obtained from the year-end figures on total liabilities from the Assets and Liability Table of the accounting record of the enterprises.

Total Liquid Liabilities refer to the liabilities that meet one of the following requirements: (1) expected to be repaid in a normal operation cycle; (2) be owned for trading purpose mainly; (3) expected to be repaid in one year from the day of the Assets and Liability Table; (4) enterprise has no right to postpone the settlement of which over a year from the day of the Assets and Liability Table. Included are short-term loans, notes payable, accounts payable, employee compensations, taxes and expenses due. Data on this indicator can be obtained by the year-end figures of total liquid liabilities in the Assets and Liability Table of the accounting records of enterprises.

Total Equity refers to the residual ownership of enterprise investors by deducting total liabilities from the total assets, including the paid-in capital, accumulation of capital, operating surplus and non-distributed profits. Data are obtained from the year-end figures on "total equity" from the Assets and

Liability Table of the accounting record of enterprise.

Revenue from Principal Business refers to the income confirmed of an enterprise from the principal business of selling products and providing labor services. Data on this indicator can be obtained from the year-end credit balance of "revenue from principal business" in the accounting record of enterprise.

Cost of Principal Business refers to the total cost occurred from the principal business of the enterprise. Data can be obtained from the year-end debit balance of "cost of principal business" in the accounting record of enterprise.

Tax and Extra Charges from Principal Business refer to the sales tax, consumption tax, urban maintenance and construction tax and education expenses shouldered by the enterprise from its principal business. Data are obtained from the year-end debit balance of "tax and extra charges from principal business" in the accounting record of enterprise.

Total Profits refers to the operation results in a certain accounting period, and it is the balance of various incomes minus various spendings in the course of operation, reflecting the total profits and losses of enterprises in reporting period. Data are obtained from the amount of "total profits" in the "profit table" of the accounting record of enterprise.

Value-added Tax Payable refers to the payable tax of enterprises which engaged in selling of goods or providing services that bring added value to the goods, such as processing, repairing, fitting and other activities should be paid according to Tax Law. The formula is as follows:

Value-added Tax Payable = tax on sales-(tax on purchase-transferred tax on purchase)-exports deduct tax payable on domestic sales-tax relief+the export tax rebate.

Tax on Purchase in Current Year refers to goods purchased by industrial enterprises or value added tax that should be paid but being granted the right to deduct from the tax on sales.

Tax on Sales in Current Year refers to value added tax on industrial enterprises from sales of goods or taxable services that should be charged value added tax.

Average Annual Number of Employed Persons Employed persons refer to all those who are employed in enterprises and receive remunerations there from, including currently working employees, retirees who are re-employed, teachers of local-run schools, as well as foreigners, staff from Hong Kong, Macao and Taiwan, part-time employees and persons with second job who are employed by the enterprise, and employees of other units temporarily working in the enterprises, but excluding former employees who left the enterprise with their employment records still being kept by the enterprises.

Average number of employed persons refers to the number of employee everyday during the reference period, calculated with the following formula:

calculated as follows:

$$\text{Annual average number} = \frac{\text{sum of monthly average number in reference year}}{12}$$

Ratio of Profits, Taxes and Interests to Average Assets reflects the profit-making capability of all assets of the enterprise and is a key indicator manifesting the performance and management and evaluating the profit-making potential of the enterprise. It is calculated as follows:

$$\text{Ratio of Profits, Taxes and Interests to Average Assets (\%)} = \frac{\text{total profits + total taxes + interest payment}}{\text{average assets}} \times 100\%$$

In the above formula, total taxes is the sum of tax and extra charges on the principal business and value-added tax payable; and average assets is the arithmetic mean of the sum of beginning assets and ending assets.

Ratio of Debts to Assets reflects both the operation risk and the capability of the enterprise in making use of the capital from the creditors. It is

$$\text{Ratio of Debts to Assets (\%)} = \frac{\text{total debts}}{\text{total assets}} \times 100\%$$

Both assets and debts are figures at the end of the reference period.

Turnover of Current Assets refers to the number of times of turnover of current assets in a given period of time, which reflects the speed of the turnover of current assets of industrial enterprises, and is calculated as follows:

$$\text{Turnover of Working assets} = \frac{\text{sales revenue of products}}{\text{average balance of total working assets}}$$

In the above formula, average balance of total current assets refers to the arithmetic mean of the sum of current assets at the beginning and at the end of the reference period.

Ratio of Profits to Total Industrial Costs refers to the ratio of profits realized in a given period to the total costs in the same period, which reflects the economic efficiency of input cost and is calculated as follows:

$$\text{Ratio of Profits to Total Industrial Cost (\%)} = \frac{\text{total profits}}{\text{total costs}} \times 100\%$$

Total costs in the above formula are the sum of cost of principal business, marketing cost,

Sales Ratio of Products is an indicator reflecting the actual sale of industrial products, analyzing the production-selling and supply-demand relations. It is calculated as:

$$\text{Sales Ratio of Products (\%)} = \frac{\text{value of industrial sales}}{\text{gross industrial output value (current prices)}} \times 100\%$$

新疆统计年鉴
XINJIANG STATISTICAL YEARBOOK

14

建筑业

CONSTRUCTION

简要说明

本篇资料的主要内容及来源

本篇资料反映在新疆维吾尔自治区注册的建筑法人企业概况及发展情况，包括建筑业企业基本情况和生产经营情况。主要指标有企业个数、从业人员和建筑企业签定合同情况、承包工程完成情况及总产值、增加值、企业技术装备情况、房屋建筑面积、利润、税金、劳动生产率等。

根据建筑业发展的实际情况，建筑业统计范围从2002年起，由原具有建筑业资质等级四级及四级以上的独立核算的建筑业企业调整为具有施工总承包、专业承包和劳务分包的法人建筑业企业。

本篇建筑业企业统计数据是根据国家统计局制定的《建筑业统计报表制度》整理汇总的。建筑业统计数据采取全面调查的方法。资料由新疆维吾尔自治区统计局固定资产投资统计处提供。

Brief Introduction

Main Content and Source of Data

Data in this chapter show the general situation and the development of the construction in Xinjiang Uygur Autonomous Region. They cover the situation of production and management of the enterprises on construction, including the number of enterprises, number of employed persons, complete and gross output value of construction industry, value added floor space of the buildings, profits and taxes of enterprises and labor productivity, etc.

According to the development of construction industry, starting from 2002,the coverage of construction statistics has been adjusted to include all the construction enterprises of various types of ownership with qualification certificates and with independent accounting system ,instead of the original criteria that required construction enterprises of various types of ownership to have qualification certificates at or above Class 4 with independent accounting system.

Data on construction enterprises are collected in accordance with the Reporting System of Construction Statistics stipulated by the National Bureau of Statistics. Data on the construction industry are collected through comprehensive reporting system and provided by the Department of Investment in Fixed Assets Statistics, Xinjiang Bureau of Statistics.

14-1 建筑企业概况
Main Indicators on Construction Enterprises

年 份 Year	地 区 Region	企业个数(个) Number of Enterprises (unit)				从业人员(万人) Number of Persons Employed (10 000 persons)			
		合 计 Total	国 有 State-owned	集 体 Collec-tive-owned	其 他 Others	合 计 Total	国 有 State-owned	集 体 Collec-tive-owned	其 他 Others
	1985	275	117	158		25.85	19.21	6.64	
	1990	353	183	170		22.86	18.36	4.50	
	1995	928	481	432	15	35.33	26.33	8.72	0.28
	1996	886	478	386	22	24.97	18.53	6.09	0.35
	1997	650	313	312	25	30.75	20.39	8.56	1.80
	1998	682	269	348	65	22.14	14.83	6.42	0.89
	1999	711	272	344	95	19.35	13.00	4.94	1.41
	2000	690	226	293	171	26.16	17.69	4.25	4.22
	2001	594	175	152	267	25.27	14.77	2.68	7.82
	2002	730	146	109	475	23.57	8.64	1.89	13.04
	2003	776	112	77	587	20.81	6.16	1.12	13.53
	2004	932	105	51	776	33.22	7.21	0.84	25.17
	2005	881	107	43	731	34.37	8.70	0.90	24.77
	2006	914	102	39	773	33.84	8.81	0.84	24.19
	2007	967	103	35	829	37.02	9.63	0.92	26.47
	2008	998	99	32	867	42.37	11.28	0.48	30.61
	2009	993	90	28	875	48.18	12.01	0.52	35.65
	2010	1004	81	28	895	56.48	12.66	0.52	43.30
	2011	1025	89	22	914	52.73	9.89	0.40	42.44
	2012	1045	89	20	936	63.81	12.86	0.48	50.47
乌鲁木齐市	Urumqi City	435	40	8	387	24.59	6.92	0.20	17.47
克拉玛依市	Karamay City	61	4	2	55	3.06	0.18	0.04	2.84
吐鲁番地区	Turpan Administrative Offices	18	3		15	0.56	0.05		0.51
哈密地区	Hami [Kumul] Administrative Offices	43	3	1	39	0.36	0.04	0.01	0.31
昌吉回族自治州	Changji Hui Autonomous Prefecture	84	1	1	82	3.26	0.03	0.01	3.22
伊犁哈萨克自治州	Ili Kazak Autonomous Prefecture	119	17	6	96	7.84	1.04	0.13	6.67
伊犁州直属县(市)	Counties (Cities) Direct Under Ili Prefecture	63	7	3	53	4.06	0.54	0.10	3.42
塔城地区	Tacheng [Tarbagatai] Administrative Offices	28	4	3	21	2.54	0.28	0.03	2.23
阿勒泰地区	Altay Administrative Offices	28	6		22	1.24	0.22		1.02
博尔塔拉蒙古自治州	Bortala Mongol Autonomous Prefecture	21	2	1	18	1.01	0.16	0.09	0.76
巴音郭楞蒙古自治州	Bayangol Mongol Autonomous Prefecture	59	5	1	53	5.92	0.73		5.19
阿克苏地区	Aksu Administrative Offices	70	2		68	3.49	0.05		3.44
克孜勒苏柯尔克孜自治州	Kizilsu Kirgiz Autonomous Prefecture	16	1		15	0.35			0.35
喀什地区	Kashgar [Kaxgar] Administrative Offices	51	2		49	3.34	0.10		3.24
和田地区	Hotan Administrative Offices	22	1		21	1.47	0.30		1.17
石河子市	Shihezi City	28	4		24	6.93	2.90		4.03
阿拉尔市	Aral City	7	2		5	0.65	0.31		0.34
图木舒克市	Tumxuk City	5	1		4	0.53	0.01		0.52
五家渠市	Wujiaqu City	6	1		5	0.45	0.04		0.41

注：1.2000 年至 2002 年建筑业所有指标数据均包括克拉玛依石油管理局工业部分，2003 年起将此部分扣除(以下同)。
2.2004 年建筑业所有数据为经济普查数，企业个数及其他指标包括没有工作量或者停业企业，往年未包括(以下同)。
3.根据我区建筑特点，建筑业从业人员为年平均人数。

Note: a) All the quota indices in building sector from 2000 to 2002 include the industrial part of Karamay Oil Administration. From 2003, this part was omitted. (the same as in the following) . b) All the data in architectural sector are the statistics of economic census, enterprise numbers and other quota exclude work volume or closed enterprises except for previous years. (the same as in the following) . c)In view of the features of the construction, the number of employed persons refers to the annual average.

14-2 按登记注册类型分建筑企业总产值

Total Output Value of Construction Enterprises by Registration Status

单位：万元 (10 000 yuan)

年 份 Year	地 区 Region	合 计 Total	国有经济 State-owned Units	集体经济 Collective -owned Units	其他经济 Others Units
	1985	175165	138138	37027	
	1990	273893	220574	53319	
	1995	1070085	816396	238387	15302
	1996	1284669	977358	283776	23535
	1997	1141318	828482	288081	24755
	1998	1434787	1002235	378956	53596
	1999	1569486	1085080	365588	118818
	2000	2349506	1436653	362649	550204
	2001	2742800	1394099	252076	1096625
	2002	3136257	1270601	170319	1695337
	2003	3221502	739953	147256	2334293
	2004	3439968	910264	89189	2440515
	2005	3615674	1138005	102580	2375089
	2006	3856223	1269722	88474	2498027
	2007	4541026	1548285	97418	2895323
	2008	6292562	1879497	86431	4326634
	2009	7913768	2245048	119717	5549003
	2010	9694741	2486878	119917	7087946
	2011	13278310	3302487	104738	9871085
	2012	16331061	3670127	161626	12499308
乌鲁木齐市	Urumqi City	6070064	2272098	57911	3740055
克拉玛依市	Karamay City	1190445	51447	27407	1111591
吐鲁番地区	Turpan Administrative Offices	166986	16353		150633
哈密地区	Hami [Kumul] Administrative Offices	351390	100989	12920	237481
昌吉回族自治州	Changji Hui Autonomous Prefecture	956532	10182	15131	931219
伊犁哈萨克自治州	Ili Kazak Autonomous Prefecture	2167763	381190	26024	1760549
伊犁州直属县(市)	Counties (Cities) Direct Under Ili Prefecture	1208203	191878	21539	994786
塔城地区	Tacheng [Tarbagatai] Administrative Offices	585720	123515	4485	457720
阿勒泰地区	Altay Administrative Offices	373840	65797		308043
博尔塔拉蒙古自治州	Bortala Mongol Autonomous Prefecture	294511	75389	21970	197152
巴音郭楞蒙古自治州	Bayangol Mongol Autonomous Prefecture	1554886	175049	263	1379574
阿克苏地区	Aksu Administrative Offices	932367	18373		913994
克孜勒苏柯尔克孜自治州	Kizilsu Kirgiz Autonomous Prefecture	218966	10482		208484
喀什地区	Kashgar [Kaxgar] Administrative Offices	700241	12149		688092
和田地区	Hotan Administrative Offices	312759	56000		256759
石河子市	Shihezi City	934232	386563		547669
阿拉尔市	Aral City	229487	92906		136581
图木舒克市	Tumxuk City	137331	3600		133731
五家渠市	Wujiaqu City	113101	7357		105744

14-3 按构成分建筑企业总产值

Total Output Value of Construction Enterprises by Composition

单位：万元 (10 000 yuan)

年 份 Year	地 区 Region	总产值 Total Output Value	建筑工程 Output Value of Construction Projects	安装工程 Output Value of Installation Projects	其 他 Others
	1985	175165	154496	18042	2627
	1990	273893	241574	28211	4108
	1995	1070085	942158	106744	21183
	1996	1284669	1124271	132079	28319
	1997	1141318	1009082	105891	26345
	1998	1434787	1270483	139104	25200
	1999	1569486	1398179	146154	25153
	2000	2349506	2073166	214425	61915
	2001	2742800	2403688	279909	59203
	2002	3136257	2637362	405115	93780
	2003	3221502	2708269	336535	176698
	2004	3439968	2836668	396509	206791
	2005	3615674	2981373	487239	147062
	2006	3856223	3209192	510770	136261
	2007	4541026	3822922	564228	153876
	2008	6292562	5359129	804719	128714
	2009	7913768	6924156	867812	121800
	2010	9694741	8450628	1107006	137107
	2011	13278310	11850908	1223095	204307
	2012	16331061	14545263	1420629	365169
乌鲁木齐市	Urumqi City	6070064	5409626	572261	88177
克拉玛依市	Karamay City	1190445	721356	394952	74137
吐鲁番地区	Turpan Administrative Offices	166986	90095	73301	3590
哈密地区	Hami [Kumul] Administrative Offices	351390	343272	1650	6468
昌吉回族自治州	Changji Hui Autonomous Prefecture	956532	839671	90798	26063
伊犁哈萨克自治州	Ili Kazak Autonomous Prefecture	2167763	2085514	69628	12621
伊犁州直属县(市)	Counties (Cities) Direct Under Ili Prefecture	1208203	1170610	31782	5811
塔城地区	Tacheng [Tarbagatai] Administrative Offices	585720	561289	21418	3013
阿勒泰地区	Altay Administrative Offices	373840	353615	16428	3797
博尔塔拉蒙古自治州	Bortala Mongol Autonomous Prefecture	294511	294150	361	
巴音郭楞蒙古自治州	Bayangol Mongol Autonomous Prefecture	1554886	1394265	46474	114147
阿克苏地区	Aksu Administrative Offices	932367	871513	50328	10526
克孜勒苏柯尔克孜自治州	Kizilsu Kirgiz Autonomous Prefecture	218966	203393	4857	10716
喀什地区	Kashgar [Kaxgar] Administrative Offices	700241	640810	48940	10491
和田地区	Hotan Administrative Offices	312759	304580	6118	2061
石河子市	Shihezi City	934232	871299	56761	6172
阿拉尔市	Aral City	229487	228887	600	
图木舒克市	Tumxuk City	137331	133731	3600	
五家渠市	Wujiaqu City	113101	113101		

14-4 按行业和登记注册类型分建筑企业总产值
Total Output Value of Construction Enterprises by Registration Status and Sectors

单位：万元 (10 000 yuan)

项 目	Item	2011	2012
总 计	**Total**	**13278310**	**16331061**
#一、二级企业	First Grade and Second Grade Enterprises	11245324	13620448
#国有及国有控股	State-owned and State-holding	6693556	8290122
按登记注册类型分组	**Grouped by Registration Status**		
内资企业	Domestic Funded	13278168	16330949
国有企业	State-owned Enterprises	2568692	2644686
集体企业	Collective-owned Enterprises	104737	161626
股份合作企业	Share-holding Cooperative		
联营企业	Joint Ownership Enterprises	320	117
有限责任公司	Limited Liability Corporations	7230099	9591250
国有独资公司	Sole State -funded Company	733795	1025443
其他有限责任公司	Other Limited Liability Companies	6496304	8565808
股份有限公司	Share-holding Corporations Ltd	698045	895952
私营企业	Private Enterprises	2594276	3020942
#私营有限责任公司	Private Limited Liability Companies	2531826	2892708
私营股份有限公司	Private Stock Limited Companies	60482	99066
其他企业	Others	81998	16376
港、澳、台及外商企业	Enterprises With Funds from Hong Kong, Macao , Taiwan and Foreign	143	112
#合资经营企业(港或澳、台资)	Joint-Venture	70	85
按国民经济行业分组	**Grouped by National Economic Sectors**		
房屋和土木工程建筑业	Buildings and Civil Engineering Construction	12281746	15500234
房屋工程建筑	Building Construction	8742547	11055872
土木工程建筑	Civil Engineering Construction	3539199	4444362
铁路、道路、隧道和桥梁	Railways, Roads, Tunnels and Bridges	2357550	2267180
水利和港口建筑	Water Conservancy and Seaport Construction	563363	1140935
工矿工程建筑	Mine Project	60574	252386
架线和管道工程建筑	Cabling and Piping Project	484035	744068
其他土木工程建筑	Other Civil Engineering	73677	39793
建筑安装业	Construction and Installation	842619	615302
建筑装饰业	Building Decoration	67103	89647
其他建筑业	Others	86842	125878
按隶属关系分组	**Grouped by Subordination**		
中 央	Central Government	4041765	4973648
地 方	Local	9236545	11357413
按企业资质等级分组	**Grouped by Enterprise's Qualification**		
施工总承包	Undertaking Porjects	12380778	14975525
特 级	Special Grade	200534	226404
一 级	First Grade	5349783	6462209
二 级	Second Grade	5115477	6015910
三级及以下	Third Grade and Below	1714984	2271002
专业承包	Specialized Undertaking	824097	1247620
一 级	First Grade	262226	281384
二 级	Second Grade	268414	579147
三级及以下	Third Grade and Below	293457	387089
劳务分包	Work Subcontractors	73435	107916

14-5 建筑企业增加值

Value-added of Construction Enterprises

单位：万元 (10 000 yuan)

年 份 Year	地 区 Region	合 计 Total	按注册类型分 Grouped by Ownership			按隶属关系分 By Administrative Relationship	
			国有企业 State-owned Enterprise	集体企业 Collective-owned Enterprises	其他企业 Others	中央企业 Central Enterprises	地方企业 Local Enterprises
1985		60152	52022	8130			
1990		109923	91983	17940			
1995		283882	207212	72598	4072	92259	191623
1996		303370	218532	78973	5865	96996	206374
1997		380806	284938	87437	8431	133287	247519
1998		296444	182903	89375	24166	84239	212205
1999		323714	198463	87477	37774	92459	213255
2000		587341	386475	84268	116598	274836	312505
2001		637472	340470	49298	247704	260784	376688
2002		621430	223509	37383	360538	211988	409442
2003		672531	143473	29333	499725	161523	511008
2004		693070	158801	18938	515331	157382	535688
2005		716063	199645	18265	498153	176697	539366
2006		790466	230867	20948	538651	215766	574700
2007		947319	304278	19234	623807	278640	668679
2008		1349429	375318	18888	955223	427287	922142
2009		1627342	417474	19541	1190327	492321	1135021
2010		2053556	451108	21823	1580625	658449	1395107
2011		2745615	564723	18348	2162544	864566	1881049
2012		3806156	770767	39629	2995760	1283740	2522416
乌鲁木齐市	Urumqi City	1422106	424778	16504	980824	594723	827383
克拉玛依市	Karamay City	232591	10269	4189	218133	45735	186856
吐鲁番地区	Turpan Administrative Offices	35752	5676		30076	10301	25451
哈密地区	Hami [Kumul] Administrative Offices	38226	9375	1510	27341	6419	31807
昌吉回族自治州	Changji Hui Autonomous Prefecture	201285	1409	2362	197514	13807	187478
伊犁哈萨克自治州	Ili Kazak Autonomous Prefecture	429772	61699	9183	358890	151796	277976
伊犁州直属县(市)	Counties (Cities) Direct Under Ili Prefecture	244468	33363	8086	203018	108794	135673
塔城地区	Tacheng [Tarbagatai] Administrative Offices	117139	15118	1097	100924	37450	79690
阿勒泰地区	Altay Administrative Offices	68165	13218		54948	5552	62613
博尔塔拉蒙古自治州	Bortala Mongol Autonomous Prefecture	49622	8008	5820	35794	7945	41677
巴音郭楞蒙古自治州	Bayangol Mongol Autonomous Prefecture	392998	55334	60	337603	43838	349160
阿克苏地区	Aksu Administrative Offices	277951	3751		274200	24565	253386
克孜勒苏柯尔克孜自治州	Kizilsu Kirgiz Autonomous Prefecture	14626	768		13858		14626
喀什地区	Kashgar [Kaxgar] Administrative Offices	168503	4583		163920	18269	150234
和田地区	Hotan Administrative Offices	84885	14256		70629	14256	70629
石河子市	Shihezi City	330454	134406		196048	304470	25984
阿拉尔市	Aral City	67691	33312		34379	33276	34415
图木舒克市	Tumxuk City	32387	1034		31353	12232	20155
五家渠市	Wujiaqu City	27309	2109		25200	2109	25200

14-6 建筑企业利税总额

Total Pre-tax Profits of Construction Enterprises

单位：万元 (10 000 yuan)

年份 Year	地区 Region	利税总额合计 Total Pre-tax Profits	利润总额 Total Profits	工程结算税金及附加 Taxes and Extra Charges on Project Settlement Accounts	管理费用中的税金 Taxes in Management Expenses	产值利税率(%) Ratio of Pre-tax Profits to Output Value (%)	资金利税率(%) Ratio of Pre-tax Profits to Assets (%)
	1994	28199	5535	20195	2469	3.81	4.11
	1995	30156	2974	24916	2266	3.44	3.46
	1996	20752	-8625	26816	2561	1.97	-0.93
	1997	31970	-4347	33360	2957	2.80	2.51
	1998	37596	-5875	41162	2309	2.62	2.41
	1999	64777	13359	48995	2423	4.13	3.72
	2000	19274	-48005	64614	2665	0.82	0.63
	2001	28688	-47485	74206	1967	1.05	0.84
	2002	84833	-11089	92484	3438	2.70	2.18
	2003	169594	67146	96888	5560	5.26	5.51
	2004	174255	65037	102990	6228	5.07	5.65
	2005	165236	46909	112565	5762	4.57	4.91
	2006	177102	54570	116426	6106	4.59	4.83
	2007	221117	67796	145119	8202	4.87	5.40
	2008	328484	120146	198718	9620	5.22	6.67
	2009	422062	156541	252547	12974	5.33	7.08
	2010	536197	208372	317056	10769	5.53	7.54
	2011	725740	274797	438927	12016	5.47	7.68
	2012	928871	356595	555058	17218	5.69	8.06
乌鲁木齐市	Urumqi City	324001	111763	206611	5627	5.34	5.68
克拉玛依市	Karamay City	64029	26473	35672	1884	5.38	4.78
吐鲁番地区	Turpan Administrative Offices	9135	3175	5229	731	5.47	5.71
哈密地区	Hami [Kumul] Administrative Offices	19655	8668	10736	251	5.59	7.92
昌吉回族自治州	Changji Hui Autonomous Prefecture	50040	17135	31784	1121	5.23	9.32
伊犁哈萨克自治州	Ili Kazak Autonomous Prefecture	106330	29936	74594	1800	4.91	13.38
伊犁州直属县(市)	Counties (Cities) Direct Under Ili Prefecture	48668	10918	37163	587	4.03	11.36
塔城地区	Tacheng [Tarbagatai] Administrative Offices	35719	12786	22311	622	6.10	21.24
阿勒泰地区	Altay Administrative Offices	21943	6232	15120	591	5.87	11.05
博尔塔拉蒙古自治州	Bortala Mongol Autonomous Prefecture	13017	2527	10295	195	4.42	18.16
巴音郭楞蒙古自治州	Bayangol Mongol Autonomous Prefecture	118125	62318	54004	1803	7.60	19.72
阿克苏地区	Aksu Administrative Offices	81875	44591	35519	1765	8.78	13.62
克孜勒苏柯尔克孜自治州	Kizilsu Kirgiz Autonomous Prefecture	5829	1458	4101	270	2.66	4.87
喀什地区	Kashgar [Kaxgar] Administrative Offices	41722	13778	27058	886	5.96	11.72
和田地区	Hotan Administrative Offices	17162	3636	13332	194	5.49	13.81
石河子市	Shihezi City	51150	21863	28936	351	5.48	8.94
阿拉尔市	Aral City	13602	4524	9006	72	5.93	9.52
图木舒克市	Tumxuk City	7346	2315	4815	216	5.35	9.95
五家渠市	Wujiaqu City	5853	2435	3366	52	5.17	7.19

14-7 建筑企业劳动生产率
Labor Productivity of Construction Enterprises

单位：元/人 (yuan/person)

年 份 Year	地 区 Region	按总产值计算的劳动生产率 Overall Labor Productivity in Terms of Total Output Value	#国有经济 State-owned Enterprises	#集体经济 Collective-owned Enterprises	按增加值计算的劳动生产率 Overall Labor Productivity in Terms of Added-Value	#国有经济 State-owned Enterprises	#集体经济 Collective-owned Enterprises
	1994	29871	32616	23023	9499	10546	7186
	1995	34668	38483	26617	11238	12505	8673
	1996	32606	36557	25291	10648	12286	7719
	1997	38808	40629	33658	12948	13973	10215
	1998	47698	51465	40819	9855	10044	9627
	1999	55593	61196	44235	11466	11766	10584
	2000	74994	87999	48767	25208	32781	14138
	2001	84666	94344	62458	19678	23041	12215
	2002	86302	108857	66231	17100	19149	14537
	2003	94165	98095	86190	19659	19020	17169
	2004	107150	112145	107185	21588	22365	22759
	2005	112214	137966	127587	22223	23971	22718
	2006	121506	149550	118932	24907	27794	28159
	2007	126303	134275	139988	26349	26389	27640
	2008	152795	182536	168023	32767	36451	36718
	2009	173714	204170	233869	35721	37966	38174
	2010	176404	200435	231859	37366	36358	42194
	2011	226848	284263	176207	46906	48609	30867
	2012	249202	245195	286875	58080	51698	70367
乌鲁木齐市	Urumqi City	227007	259422	254667	53184	48829	72603
克拉玛依市	Karamay City	354975	303164	1100699	69356	60516	168334
吐鲁番地区	Turpan Administrative Offices	307240	310888		65781	108222	
哈密地区	Hami [Kumul] Administrative Offices	482944	315099	547436	52537	29249	64053
昌吉回族自治州	Changji Hui Autonomous Prefecture	286550	235152	249680	60299	32525	38978
伊犁哈萨克自治州	Ili Kazak Autonomous Prefecture	260740	309332	191354	51693	50078	67567
伊犁州直属县(市)	Counties (Cities) Direct Under Ili Prefecture	293945	326823	193869	59477	56839	72832
塔城地区	Tacheng [Tarbagatai] Administrative Offices	208027	292899	180129	41604	35851	44079
阿勒泰地区	Altay Administrative Offices	269337	294394		49110	59159	
博尔塔拉蒙古自治州	Bortala Mongol Autonomous Prefecture	270890	252307	244111	45642	26801	64667
巴音郭楞蒙古自治州	Bayangol Mongol Autonomous Prefecture	285510	243124	291778	72163	76926	67139
阿克苏地区	Aksu Administrative Offices	289717	401155		86368	81925	
克孜勒苏柯尔克孜自治州	Kizilsu Kirgiz Autonomous Prefecture	321346	374346		21464	27411	
喀什地区	Kashgar [Kaxgar] Administrative Offices	257224	92318		61897	34830	
和田地区	Hotan Administrative Offices	240232	243479		65201	61983	
石河子市	Shihezi City	145467	148936		51454	51822	
阿拉尔市	Aral City	370380	312395		109250	112011	
图木舒克市	Tumxuk City	274441	782609		64722	224794	
五家渠市	Wujiaqu City	218469	184849		52750	53008	

14-8 建筑企业技术装备情况

Number and Power of Machinery and Equipment Owned by Construction Enterprises

年份 Year	地区 Region	自有机械设备总台数(台) Number of Machinery and Equipment Owned (set)	自有机械设备总功率(万千瓦) Total Power of Equipment and Machinery Owned (10 000 kw)	自有机械设备净值(万元) Net Value of Machinery and Equipment Owned (10 000 yuan)	技术装备率(元/人) Value of Machines Per Laborer (yuan/ person)	动力装备率(千瓦/人) Power of Machines Per Laborer (kw/person)
	1985	30307	105	29308	1332	6
	1990	34806	91	46098	2511	5
	1995	55455	138	106383	4211	5
	1996	60567	129	127572	4478	5
	1997	64252	149	139617	4747	5
	1998	72606	148	164157	7415	7
	1999	73735	155	184559	9543	8
	2000	77975	182	224485	8582	7
	2001	85981	177	238142	9425	7
	2002	96116	207	442787	18996	9
	2003	100913	207	395865	11866	6
	2004	98541	239	358397	11389	8
	2005	99324	190	326360	10372	6
	2006	96674	197	348344	11187	6
	2007	103431	203	374396	10650	6
	2008	102266	230	392371	9692	6
	2009	103285	235	407809	9136	5
	2010	97562	238	383196	7145	4
	2011	98768	246	398762	6812	4
	2012	91704	242	430432	6568	4
乌鲁木齐市	Urumqi City	28667	111	179515	6713	4
克拉玛依市	Karamay City	5020	21	51206	15269	6
吐鲁番地区	Turpan Administrative Offices	997	4	5260	9678	8
哈密地区	Hami [Kumul] Administrative Offices	2170	4	12301	16907	6
昌吉回族自治州	Changji Hui Autonomous Prefecture	4998	10	24994	7488	3
伊犁哈萨克自治州	Ili Kazak Autonomous Prefecture	14813	24	33332	4009	3
伊犁州直属县(市)	Counties (Cities) Direct Under Ili Prefecture	7972	9	19977	4860	2
塔城地区	Tacheng [Tarbagatai] Administrative Offices	4439	11	4439	1577	4
阿勒泰地区	Altay Administrative Offices	2402	4	8916	6422	3
博尔塔拉蒙古自治州	Bortala Mongol Autonomous Prefecture	3323	5	10518	9674	5
巴音郭楞蒙古自治州	Bayangol Mongol Autonomous Prefecture	11712	20	26469	4860	4
阿克苏地区	Aksu Administrative Offices	6556	17	24132	7498	5
克孜勒苏柯尔克孜自治州	Kizilsu Kirgiz Autonomous Prefecture	378	1	2594	3807	1
喀什地区	Kashgar [Kaxgar] Administrative Offices	4318	10	10901	4004	4
和田地区	Hotan Administrative Offices	3493	2	7018	5391	1
石河子市	Shihezi City	3184	8	19779	3080	1
阿拉尔市	Aral City	1114	3	19490	31455	5
图木舒克市	Tumxuk City	549	2	2357	4710	4
五家渠市	Wujiaqu City	412		566	1094	1

14-9 按登记注册类型分建筑企业技术装备情况
Number and Power of Machinery and Equipment Owned by Registration Status

(2012 年)

项　　目	Item	自有机械设备年末总台数(台) Number of Machinery and Equipment Owned Year-end (set)	自有机械设备年末总功率(千瓦) Total Power of Machinery and Equipment Owned Year-end (kw)	自有机械设备年末净值(万元) Net Value of Machinery and Equipment Owned Year-end (10 000 yuan)
总　计	**Total**	**91704**	**2421219**	**430432**
#一、二级企业	First, Second Enterprises	72182	2132537	368497
#国有及国有控股	State-owned and State-holding	36083	1384595	239165
按登记注册类型分组	**Grouped by Registration Status**			
内资企业	Domestic Funede	91704	2421219	430432
国有企业	State-owned Enterprises	17149	612049	74656
集体企业	Collective-owned Enterprises	1058	31671	6524
有限责任公司	Limited Liability Corporations	47798	1124692	207171
国有独资公司	Sole State -funded Company	3363	117551	16241
其他有限责任公司	Other Limited Liability Companies	44435	1007141	190929
股份有限公司	Share-holding Corporations Ltd.	2725	218842	51118
私营企业	Private Enterprises	22867	431797	90752
#私营有限责任公司	Private Limited Liability Companies	21968	423787	88230
私营股份有限公司	Private Stock Limited Companies	885	7375	2128
按国民经济行业分组	**Grouped by National Economic Sectors**			
房屋和土木工程建筑业	Buildings and Givil Engineering	85925	2260966	385438
房屋工程建筑	Building	63296	1194734	190132
土木工程建筑	Civil Engineering	22629	1066232	195306
铁路、道路、隧道和桥梁	Railways, Roads, Tunnels and Bridges	10456	698741	95529
水利和港口建筑	Water Conservancy and Seaport	4950	168264	54899
工矿工程建筑	Mining Project	4296	89616	19561
架线和管道工程建筑	Cabling and Piping Project	2871	107589	25131
其他土木工程建筑	Other Civil Engineering	56	2022	186
建筑安装业	Construction and Installation	4472	123639	35171
建筑装饰业	Building Decoration	873	23076	3891
其他建筑业	Others	434	13538	5932
按隶属关系分组	**Grouped by Subordination**			
中　央	Central Government	18813	675072	156549
地　方	Local	72891	1746147	273883
按企业资质等级分组	**Grouped by Enterprise's Qualification**			
施工总承包	Undertaking Porjects	85792	2282248	402184
特　级	Special Grade	682	28129	1474
一　级	First Grade	31287	1205066	188419
二　级	Second Grade	36734	802136	160636
三　级	Third Grade	17089	246917	51655
专业承包	Specialized Undertaking	5912	138971	28248
一　级	First Grade	2487	69442	11887
二　级	Second Grade	992	27764	6081
三　级	Third Grade	2433	41765	10280

14-10 建筑企业签订合同情况
Contracts Signed by Construction Enterprises

单位：万元 (10 000 yuan)

年 份 Year	地 区 Region	合同总额 Total Value Of Contracts	上年结转合同 Value from Contracts Signed In Last Year	本年新签合同 Value from New Contracts Signed In This Year
	2002	3962086	988485	2973601
	2003	4312515	1236887	3075628
	2004	4725501	1351086	3374415
	2005	4857604	1557300	3300304
	2006	5692120	1483664	4208455
	2007	7220300	1986086	5234214
	2008	9907859	2906991	7000868
	2009	12473691	3859836	8613855
	2010	15883584	5459941	10423643
	2011	21956637	6083819	15872818
	2012	27266741	9965704	17301037
乌鲁木齐市	Urumqi City	10689830	5002560	5687270
克拉玛依市	Karamay City	2926017	1179196	1746821
吐鲁番地区	Turpan Administrative Offices	222935	62048	160887
哈密地区	Hami [Kumul] Administrative Offices	537539	178868	358671
昌吉回族自治州	Changji Hui Autonomous Prefecture	1358123	368542	989581
伊犁哈萨克自治州	Ili Kazak Autonomous Prefecture	3076315	757309	2319006
伊犁州直属县(市)	Counties (Cities) Direct Under Ili Prefecture	1680312	332499	1347813
塔城地区	Tacheng [Tarbagatai] Administrative Offices	918754	302023	616731
阿勒泰地区	Altay Administrative Offices	477249	122787	354462
博尔塔拉蒙古自治州	Bortala Mongol Autonomous Prefecture	393518	85725	307793
巴音郭楞蒙古自治州	Bayangol Mongol Autonomous Prefecture	2369727	644938	1724789
阿克苏地区	Aksu Administrative Offices	1445889	469063	976826
克孜勒苏柯尔克孜自治州	Kizilsu Kirgiz Autonomous Prefecture	245757	44906	200851
喀什地区	Kashgar [Kaxgar] Administrative Offices	1257246	440516	816730
和田地区	Hotan Administrative Offices	565176	92047	473129
石河子市	Shihezi City	1535301	514312	1020989
阿拉尔市	Aral City	295338	66968	228370
图木舒克市	Tumxuk City	188217	39276	148941
五家渠市	Wujiaqu City	159813	19430	140383

注：14-10、14-11 表口径为总承包和专业承包企业。
Note:The data of the table 14-10&14-11 refer to all general construction contractors and professional contractors.

14-11 建筑企业承包工程完成情况
Completion of Contracted Projects by Construction Enterprises

单位：万元 (10 000 yuan)

年份 Year	地区 Region	直接从建设单位承揽工程完成产值 Completed Output Value of Projects Contracted Directly from Investors	自行完成施工产值 Own-Completed Output Value	分包出去工程产值 Output Value Of Out-Sourced Projects	从建设单位以外承揽工程产值 Completed Output Value of Projects Contracted From Non-investors
	2002	3141928	3048086	93842	88171
	2003	3238170	3135725	102445	85777
	2004	3443802	3377532	66270	62436
	2005	3634746	3563947	70799	51727
	2006	3856300	3775975	80325	80248
	2007	4534324	4420958	113366	120068
	2008	6309803	6128312	181492	164251
	2009	7993048	7805261	187787	108507
	2010	9723428	9503630	219798	191111
	2011	13382657	13026735	355922	251577
	2012	16409068	16042803	366265	288258
乌鲁木齐市	Urumqi City	6082463	5979356	103107	90708
克拉玛依市	Karamay City	1344054	1127215	216839	63231
吐鲁番地区	Turpan Administrative Offices	166885	166885		100
哈密地区	Hami [Kumul] Administrative Offices	348459	348459		2931
昌吉回族自治州	Changji Hui Autonomous Prefecture	958225	924653	33572	31879
伊犁哈萨克自治州	Ili Kazak Autonomous Prefecture	2130465	2128750	1715	39014
伊犁州直属县(市)	Counties (Cities) Direct Under Ili Prefecture	1209003	1208203	800	
塔城地区	Tacheng [Tarbagatai] Administrative Offices	585720	585720		
阿勒泰地区	Altay Administrative Offices	335742	334827	915	39014
博尔塔拉蒙古自治州	Bortala Mongol Autonomous Prefecture	294512	294512		
巴音郭楞蒙古自治州	Bayangol Mongol Autonomous Prefecture	1524255	1521026	3229	33859
阿克苏地区	Aksu Administrative Offices	931216	925896	5320	6471
克孜勒苏柯尔克孜自治州	Kizilsu Kirgiz Autonomous Prefecture	218965	218965		
喀什地区	Kashgar [Kaxgar] Administrative Offices	690770	689589	1181	10651
和田地区	Hotan Administrative Offices	312759	311457	1302	1302
石河子市	Shihezi City	926120	926120		8112
阿拉尔市	Aral City	229488	229488		
图木舒克市	Tumxuk City	137331	137331		
五家渠市	Wujiaqu City	113101	113101		

14-12 建筑企业资产及资本金
Assets and Capital Principal of Construction Enterprises

单位：万元 (10 000 yuan)

年份 Year	地区 Region	资产合计 Total Assets	流动资产合计 Total of Circulating Funds	固定资产合计 Total of Fixed Assets	固定资产净值 Net Value of Fixed Assets	本年折旧 Depreciation in the Year	资本金合计 Total of Principal Value	#国家资本金 National Principal
1995		939205	647608	240076	225084	18463	221212	110987
2000		3256421	1855185	1215525	1106384	65383	892851	208214
2001		3740312	2187385	1243161	1048023	82884	1055531	227457
2002		4244587	2527414	1364782	1179599	95565	1327186	227601
2003		3375330	2292828	787690	675947	61335	835618	219826
2004		3810825	2632242	825567	722019	62725	929293	225884
2005		3818087	2665404	826376	700835	72103	936389	184447
2006		4115800	2952267	796558	712740	69191	985436	202670
2007		4611598	3387459	804007	706591	76979	1095997	222967
2008		5527993	4040796	958379	862286	91915	1408249	429579
2009		6565349	4966204	1080129	960338	103188	1528701	396188
2010		7906943	6141713	1078910	939519	99050	1585475	412634
2011		10577644	8275111	1395723	1176365	119913	1960348	1948237
2012		13091083	10327841	1462446	1200685	152195	2149972	2138479
	乌鲁木齐市 Urumqi City	6469297	5168497	624361	538048	64813	964707	954426
	克拉玛依市 Karamay City	1574970	1239043	125446	101413	15714	151786	151786
	吐鲁番地区 Turpan Administrative Offices	171150	144004	16593	16093	2580	37469	37469
	哈密地区 Hami [Kumul] Administrative Offices	268617	217731	31638	30287	2235	43241	42820
	昌吉回族自治州 Changji Hui Autonomous Prefecture	623150	487625	58621	49018	6537	129515	128951
	伊犁哈萨克自治州 Ili Kazak Autonomous Prefecture	879319	699161	112962	95761	22649	206822	206726
	伊犁州直属县(市) Counties (Cities) Direct Under Ili Prefecture	469667	377588	57479	50696	17112	101100	101100
	塔城地区 Tacheng [Tarbagatai] Administrative Offices	196366	147081	27431	21062	3060	46425	46329
	阿勒泰地区 Altay Administrative Offices	213286	174492	28052	24003	2477	59297	59297
	博尔塔拉蒙古自治州 Bortala Mongol Autonomous Prefecture	76265	49805	24910	21886	1034	31879	31879
	巴音郭楞蒙古自治州 Bayangol Mongol Autonomous Prefecture	671935	522362	106514	76761	8927	154838	154838
	阿克苏地区 Aksu Administrative Offices	679380	500737	137107	100182	11531	134343	134343
	克孜勒苏柯尔克孜自治州 Kizilsu Kirgiz Autonomous Prefecture	127684	102849	19677	16837	852	27633	27502
	喀什地区 Kashgar [Kaxgar] Administrative Offices	462106	320516	39110	35411	2369	85621	85621
	和田地区 Hotan Administrative Offices	143136	101838	25669	22389	2132	46708	46708
	石河子市 Shihezi City	614127	506011	89785	66101	3560	101338	101338
	阿拉尔市 Aral City	150689	116736	28476	26161	6364	15009	15009
	图木舒克市 Tumxuk City	88089	70153	12353	3706	778	7794	7794
	五家渠市 Wujiaqu City	91169	80773	9224	631	120	11269	11269

14-13 建筑企业负债及所有者权益

Liabilities and Owner's Equity of Construction Enterprises

单位：万元 (10 000 yuan)

年 份 Year	地 区 Region	负债合计 Total Liabilities	所有者权益 Owners' Equity
	1994	540403	192618
	1995	699997	239208
	1996	815330	324051
	1997	1018007	350659
	1998	1175839	385913
	1999	1325825	415026
	2000	2068439	1187982
	2001	2300621	1439690
	2002	2717728	1526859
	2003	2327382	1047948
	2004	2631252	1174864
	2005	2651255	1159206
	2006	2886203	1220298
	2007	3240248	1359137
	2008	3806899	1707855
	2009	4553885	1996439
	2010	5798936	2089888
	2011	7857731	2707722
	2012	9797466	3167556
乌鲁木齐市	Urumqi City	5057360	1398596
克拉玛依市	Karamay City	1221381	242426
吐鲁番地区	Turpan Administrative Offices	128682	42468
哈密地区	Hami [Kumul] Administrative Offices	208928	59204
昌吉回族自治州	Changji Hui Autonomous Prefecture	428711	193634
伊犁哈萨克自治州	Ili Kazak Autonomous Prefecture	628639	250545
伊犁州直属县(市)	Counties (Cities) Direct Under Ili Prefecture	349272	120394
塔城地区	Tacheng [Tarbagatai] Administrative Offices	129016	67216
阿勒泰地区	Altay Administrative Offices	150351	62935
博尔塔拉蒙古自治州	Bortala Mongol Autonomous Prefecture	40921	35344
巴音郭楞蒙古自治州	Bayangol Mongol Autonomous Prefecture	379897	292038
阿克苏地区	Aksu Administrative Offices	427341	252039
克孜勒苏柯尔克孜自治州	Kizilsu Kirgiz Autonomous Prefecture	96974	30579
喀什地区	Kashgar [Kaxgar] Administrative Offices	343352	118754
和田地区	Hotan Administrative Offices	87751	55385
石河子市	Shihezi City	474811	139315
阿拉尔市	Aral City	120098	30591
图木舒克市	Tumxuk City	77012	11077
五家渠市	Wujiaqu City	75608	15561

14-14 建筑企业总收入
Total Income of Construction Enterprises

单位：万元 (10 000 yuan)

年份 Year	地区 Region	企业总收入 Total Income of Enterprises	工程结算收入 Revenue of Project Settlement Accounts	#工程结算成本 Costs of Project Settlement Accounts	其他业务收入 Revenue from Other Business	#其他业务利润 Profits from Other Business
	1994	813369	714469	627830	98900	9332
	1995	898810	821713	713940	77097	9445
	1996	983170	904800	799183	78370	8765
	1997	1210813	1081666	950091	129147	17368
	1998	1454758	1346748	1193276	108010	19146
	1999	1595986	1500818	1320898	95167	14882
	2000	2659696	2514011	2252154	145686	30012
	2001	2961754	2807549	2521902	154205	34532
	2002	3360613	3199880	2854350	160733	30853
	2003	3221521	3090768	2716009	130753	21692
	2004	3395793	3276421	2900842	119372	21601
	2005	3685197	3566042	3202712	119155	23629
	2006	3766819	3643783	3255171	123036	20730
	2007	4584374	4431221	3983622	153154	22186
	2008	6382510	6225083	5635311	157427	33187
	2009	7958865	7788105	7074708	170760	39289
	2010	9849630	9610000	8752747	239630	46564
	2011	13467486	13201119	12045042	266367	39679
	2012	17359472	17075648	15598630	283824	64353
乌鲁木齐市	Urumqi City	6754619	6588062	5990554	166557	47351
克拉玛依市	Karamay City	1605151	1554533	1449945	50618	9358
吐鲁番地区	Turpan Administrative Offices	173997	173068	159016	929	655
哈密地区	Hami [Kumul] Administrative Offices	349410	348302	315785	1108	581
昌吉回族自治州	Changji Hui Autonomous Prefecture	977873	967826	880182	10047	-251
伊犁哈萨克自治州	Ili Kazak Autonomous Prefecture	2141992	2135893	1988018	6099	1032
伊犁州直属县(市)	Counties (Cities) Direct Under Ili Prefecture	1227823	1224546	1153640	3277	886
塔城地区	Tacheng [Tarbagatai] Administrative Offices	545598	544433	495509	1165	-304
阿勒泰地区	Altay Administrative Offices	368571	366914	338869	1657	450
博尔塔拉蒙古自治州	Bortala Mongol Autonomous Prefecture	290107	279998	263331	10109	180
巴音郭楞蒙古自治州	Bayangol Mongol Autonomous Prefecture	1463319	1452173	1304531	11146	1722
阿克苏地区	Aksu Administrative Offices	912483	908913	795682	3570	188
克孜勒苏柯尔克孜自治州	Kizilsu Kirgiz Autonomous Prefecture	135808	133533	123854	2275	1241
喀什地区	Kashgar [Kaxgar] Administrative Offices	737012	735600	672232	1412	348
和田地区	Hotan Administrative Offices	404707	403527	371741	1180	2
石河子市	Shihezi City	922138	915494	843128	6644	1273
阿拉尔市	Aral City	239528	235920	216378	3608	300
图木舒克市	Tumxuk City	140436	132105	121703	8331	280
五家渠市	Wujiaqu City	110892	110701	102550	191	93

14-15 建筑企业亏损额及从业人数

Losses and Employed Persons of Construction Enterprises

(2012 年)

项　　目	Item	企业数（个） Number of Enterprises (unit)	#亏损企业个数 Number of Losssuffering Enterprises	亏损企业亏损额（万元） Amount of Total Loss (10000 yuan)	计算劳动生产率的平均人数（人） Average Number of Staff for Calculation of Labour Productivity (person)	期末从业人数（人） Employees atYear- end (person)
总　　计	**Total**	**1045**	**255**	**58596**	**655333**	**309305**
#一、二级企业	First, Second Enterprises	489	106	46791	540268	252997
#国有及国有控股	State-owned and State-holding	167	30	34973	347969	151596
按登记注册类型分组	**Grouped by Registration Status**					
内资企业	Domestic Funede	1042	253	58588	655324	309295
国有企业	State-owned Enterprises	62	12	11042	106606	52184
集体企业	Collective-owned Enterprises	20	5	244	5634	2654
股份合作企业	Share-holding Cooperative					
有限责任公司	Limited Liability Corporations	409	84	31420	379709	160466
国有独资公司	Sole State -funded Company	27	3	2383	43076	21362
其他有限责任公司	Other Limited Liability Companies	382	81	29037	336633	139104
股份有限公司	Share-holding Corporations Ltd	12	1	2467	36425	16582
私营企业	Private Enterprises	534	150	13414	126310	76328
#私营有限责任公司	Private Limited Liability Companies	522	146	13359	122252	73566
私营股份有限公司	Private Stock Limited Companies	6	2	24	2975	2501
港、澳、台及外商企业	Enterprises With Funds from Hong Kong, Macao , Taiwan and Foreign	3	2	8	9	10
按国民经济行业分组	**Grouped by National Economic Sectors**					
房屋和土木工程建筑业	Buildings and Givil Engineering	707	149	50919	618058	281916
房屋工程建筑	Building	489	107	34466	469016	198613
土木工程建筑	Civil Engineering	218	42	16453	149042	83303
铁路、道路、隧道和桥梁	Railways, Roads, Tunnels and Bridges	84	18	12999	71706	44856
水利和港口建筑	Water Conservancy and Seaport	42	6	1119	43366	15490
工矿工程建筑	Mining Project	20	3	48	11195	6556
架线和管道工程建筑	Cabling and Piping Project	51	9	2156	21765	15734
其他土木工程建筑	Other Civil Engineering	21	6	131	1010	667
建筑安装业	Construction and Installation	164	46	6260	23994	17944
建筑装饰业	Building Decoration	107	37	1061	6494	4507
其他建筑业	Others	67	23	356	6787	4938
按隶属关系分组	**Grouped by Subordination**					
中 央	Central Government	67	5	17565	238058	82316
地 方	Local	978	250	41032	417275	226989
按企业资质等级分组	**Grouped by Enterprise's Qualification**					
施工总承包	Undertaking Porjects	642	134	53009	590029	275187
特　级	Special Grade	1			9000	1924
一　级	First Grade	61	10	32775	256843	120373
二　级	Second Grade	271	47	11057	227863	108651
三　级及以下	Third Grade	309	77	9177	96323	44239
专业承包	Specialized Undertaking	303	81	5032	59531	28256
一　级	First Grade	20	6	347	13379	7283
二　级	Second Grade	88	23	2395	28386	10085
三级及以下	Third Grade	195	52	2290	17766	10888
劳务分包	Work Subcontractors	100	40	555	5773	5862

14-16 建筑企业工程施工情况
Condition of Building Works by Construction Enterprise

单位：万平方米 (10 000 sq.m)

年 份 Year	地 区 Region	房屋建筑施工面积 Floor Space of Buildings Under Construction	#本年新开工面积 New-opened Works for This Year	施工面积中实行投标承包面积 Space of Building and Contracting	#本年新开工面积 New-opened Works for This Year	房屋建筑竣工面积 Floor Space of Buildings Completed
	1995	1212.45	657.34	214.65	148.22	609.84
	1996	1207.45	673.17	397.83	272.22	645.89
	1997	1400.28	778.14	653.90	400.75	747.24
	1998	1662.36	1032.15	1023.88	678.42	879.67
	1999	1943.05	1068.05	1210.90	807.87	1042.51
	2000	2241.48	1448.34	1666.87	1110.04	1261.42
	2001	2659.69	1679.41	2056.30	1380.07	1467.54
	2002	2572.62	1489.38	2133.56	1274.07	1469.59
	2003	2719.22	1735.19	2411.27	1527.79	1450.80
	2004	2812.30	1791.50	2426.79	1613.19	1483.35
	2005	2767.64	1639.80	2512.79	1517.41	1429.36
	2006	2889.64	1854.91	2687.63	1751.99	1645.02
	2007	3552.36	2421.17	3299.73	2277.87	1849.64
	2008	4234.71	2862.31	3982.24	2784.92	2155.98
	2009	5151.60	3560.54	4812.84	3378.63	2517.79
	2010	6620.14	4449.78	6119.70	4235.58	2891.45
	2011	8947.71	5796.89	8318.62	5446.50	3465.49
	2012	11026.49	6247.32	9563.64	5678.19	4553.97
乌鲁木齐市	Urumqi City	3144.63	1468.91	2918.08	1354.00	945.98
克拉玛依市	Karamay City	329.52	139.95	304.83	117.85	87.60
吐鲁番地区	Turpan Administrative Offices	97.80	48.53	78.75	43.78	45.49
哈密地区	Hami [Kumul] Administrative Offices	281.39	215.96	237.57	181.46	115.73
昌吉回族自治州	Changji Hui Autonomous Prefecture	786.45	479.95	627.57	450.97	419.66
伊犁哈萨克自治州	Ili Kazak Autonomous Prefecture	1577.86	938.01	1314.23	849.20	766.33
伊犁州直属县(市)	Counties (Cities) Direct Under Ili Prefecture	743.93	458.40	656.04	417.08	352.06
塔城地区	Tacheng [Tarbagatai] Administrative Offices	502.39	260.27	360.05	221.82	274.79
阿勒泰地区	Altay Administrative Offices	331.54	219.34	298.14	210.30	139.48
博尔塔拉蒙古自治州	Bortala Mongol Autonomous Prefecture	205.51	140.23	176.40	116.11	149.41
巴音郭楞蒙古自治州	Bayangol Mongol Autonomous Prefecture	1359.41	902.57	1139.00	782.06	597.07
阿克苏地区	Aksu Administrative Offices	816.01	450.76	701.98	395.70	390.58
克孜勒苏柯尔克孜自治州	Kizilsu Kirgiz Autonomous Prefecture	145.21	109.43	127.16	106.72	81.43
喀什地区	Kashgar [Kaxgar] Administrative Offices	936.09	424.94	734.86	403.80	419.81
和田地区	Hotan Administrative Offices	347.13	256.29	324.39	247.37	154.44
石河子市	Shihezi City	648.82	401.47	581.13	372.08	215.77
阿拉尔市	Aral City	163.07	121.08	126.05	121.08	69.38
图木舒克市	Tumxuk City	105.87	70.24	105.87	70.24	55.31
五家渠市	Wujiaqu City	81.72	79.00	65.77	65.77	39.98

注：该表口径为总承包和专业承包企业，以下同。
Note: The data of the table refer to all general construction contractors and professional contractors. (the same as in the following)

14-17 按登记注册类型分建筑企业工程施工情况
Condition of Building Works by Construction Enterprise by Registration Status

单位：万平方米 (2012 年) (10 000 sq.m)

项目	Item	房屋建筑施工面积 Floor Space of Buildings Under Construction	#本年新开工面积 New-opened Works for This Year	施工面积中实行投标承包面积 Space of Buildings and Contracting	#本年新开工面积 New-opened Works for This Year	房屋建筑竣工面积 Floor Space of Buildings Completed
总计	**Total**	**11026.49**	**6247.32**	**9563.64**	**5678.19**	**4553.97**
#一、二级企业	First, Second Enterprises	8978.20	4878.96	7828.44	4462.65	3511.48
#国有及国有控股	State-owned and State-holding	4546.12	2504.96	4270.94	2400.90	1584.78
按登记注册类型分组	**Grouped by Registration Status**					
内资企业	Domestic Funede	11026.49	6247.32	9563.64	5678.19	4553.97
国有企业	State-owned Enterprises	1123.53	651.64	1021.86	618.22	416.11
集体企业	Collective-owned Enterprises	50.60	28.05	50.57	28.02	25.58
股份合作企业	Share-holding Cooperative					
有限责任公司	Limited Liability Corporations	6872.24	3837.66	6061.62	3565.74	2894.02
国有独资公司	Sole State -funded Company	519.61	300.43	513.70	300.43	164.82
其他有限责任公司	Other Limited Liability Companies	6352.63	3537.23	5547.92	3265.31	2729.21
股份有限公司	Share-holding Corporations Ltd	460.34	260.58	355.22	226.04	143.16
私营企业	Private Enterprises	2509.08	1461.67	2066.66	1232.46	1071.85
#私营有限责任公司	Private Limited Liability Companies	2398.48	1386.53	2012.14	1203.41	991.61
私营股份有限公司	Private Stock Limited Companies	88.89	64.13	51.29	26.53	64.53
按国民经济行业分组	**Grouped by National Economic Sectors**					
房屋和土木工程建筑业	Buildings and Givil Engineering	10952.46	6209.53	9494.90	5643.24	4522.52
房屋工程建筑	Building	10446.64	5833.88	9182.40	5367.46	4330.26
土木工程建筑	Civil Engineering	505.82	375.65	312.50	275.78	192.26
铁路、道路、隧道和桥梁	Railways, Roads, Tunnels and Bridges	190.32	136.11	75.46	61.44	64.88
水利和港口建筑	Water Conservancy and Seaport	269.26	201.94	197.83	183.77	99.33
工矿工程建筑	Mine Project	34.90	26.27	27.88	19.25	27.33
建筑安装业	Construction and Installation	70.85	35.03	65.98	32.19	28.96
其他建筑业	Others	3.18	2.76	2.76	2.76	2.49
按隶属关系分组	**Grouped by Subordination**					
中央	Central Government	2832.34	1524.89	2723.45	1492.70	1002.29
地方	Local	8194.15	4722.43	6840.19	4185.49	3551.68
按企业资质等级分组	**Grouped by Enterprise's Qualification**					
施工总承包	Undertaking Porjects	10528.69	6066.98	9086.18	5509.55	4451.48
特级	Special Grade	276.20	143.84	276.20	143.83	58.17
一级	First Grade	3494.62	1733.90	3120.79	1623.15	1115.79
二级	Second Grade	4763.18	2855.63	3987.25	2550.08	2265.34
三级及以下	Third Grade	1994.69	1333.61	1701.94	1192.49	1012.18
专业承包	Specialized Undertaking	497.80	180.34	477.46	168.64	102.49
一级	First Grade	18.45		18.45		10.90
二级	Second Grade	425.75	145.59	425.75	145.59	61.28
三级及以下	Third Grade	53.60	34.75	33.26	23.05	30.31

14-18 按登记注册类型分建筑企业竣工房屋建筑面积

Floor Space of Buildings Constructed of Construction Enterprises by Registration Status

单位：平方米　　　　(2012 年)　　　　(sq.m)

项　　目	Item	合　计 Total	住宅用房 Workshop	商业、居民服务业用　房 Residential Building	办公用房 Office Occupancy
总　　计	**Total**	**4553.97**	**3351.68**	**247.86**	**241.48**
#一、二级企业	First, Second Enterprises	3511.48	2594.15	183.85	188.56
#国有及国有控股	State-owned and State-holding	1584.78	1205.09	92.45	50.82
按登记注册类型分组	**Grouped by Registration Status**				
内资企业	Domestic Funede	4553.97	3351.68	247.86	241.48
#国有企业	State-owned Enterprises	416.11	298.35	23.74	10.78
集体企业	Collective-owned Enterprises	25.58	22.65	0.28	1.45
有限责任公司	Limited Liability Corporations	2894.02	2144.76	132.84	153.59
国有独资公司	Sole State -funded Company	164.82	123.38	4.32	12.41
其他有限责任公司	Other Limited Liability Companies	2729.21	2021.38	128.53	141.18
股份有限公司	Share-holding Corporations Ltd	143.16	69.28	40.40	3.32
私营企业	Private Enterprises	1071.85	814.33	50.56	72.27
私营有限责任公司	Private Limited Liability Companies	991.61	748.19	42.83	70.54
私营股份有限公司	Private Stock Limited Companies	64.53	57.47	4.78	1.71
按国民经济行业分组	**Grouped by National Economic Sectors**				
房屋和土木工程建筑业	Buildings and Givil Engineering	4522.52	3332.21	240.05	240.28
房屋工程建筑	Building	4330.26	3180.45	229.27	235.12
土木工程建筑	Civil Engineering	192.26	151.77	10.77	5.16
铁路、道路、隧道和乔梁工程建筑	Railways, Roads, Tunnels and Bridges	64.88	52.21	7.34	1.24
水利和港口工程建筑	Water Conservancy and Seaport	99.33	82.93	2.71	2.66
工矿工程建筑	Mine Project	27.33	16.63		1.26
架线和管道工程建筑	Stringing and Pipeline Constrnction Proiect	0.72		0.72	
建筑安装业	Construction and Installation	28.96	19.47	7.81	1.20
其他建筑业	Others	2.49			
按隶属关系分组	**Grouped by Subordination**				
中央	Central Government	1002.28	792.38	28.69	35.40
地方	Local	3551.68	2559.30	219.16	206.08
按企业资质等级分组	**Grouped by Enterprise's Qualification**				
施工总承包	Undertaking Porjects	4451.48	3277.36	238.06	240.35
特级	Special Grade	58.17	35.31	3.22	1.73
一级	First Grade	1115.79	813.51	66.80	68.63
二级	Second Grade	2265.34	1690.48	104.56	117.07
三级及以下	Third Grade	1012.18	738.06	63.48	52.92
专业承包	Specialized Undertaking	102.49	74.32	9.80	1.13
一级	First Grade	10.90	5.93	1.01	0.48
二级	Second Grade	61.29	48.92	8.25	0.65
三级及以下	Third Grade	30.30	19.47	0.54	

14-18 续表 Continued

单位：平方米 (sq.m)

项目	Item	科研、教育、医疗用房 House for Commerce and Residential Services	文化、体育、娱乐用房 House for Culture and Education	厂房及建筑物用房 House for Medical Care	仓库 House for Scientific Research	其他 Others
总计	**Total**	**270.98**	**34.02**	**187.43**	**23.57**	**196.95**
#一、二级企业	First, Second Enterprises	204.35	26.52	150.99	19.63	143.42
#国有及国有控股	State-owned and State-holding	62.12	6.38	84.82	11.88	71.22
按登记注册类型分组	**Grouped by Registration Status**					
内资企业	Domestic Funede	270.98	34.02	187.43	23.57	196.95
#国有企业	State-owned Enterprises	22.89	2.24	38.32	2.57	17.23
集体企业	Collective-owned Enterprises	0.34				0.84
有限责任公司	Limited Liability Corporations	197.09	26.54	92.04	13.85	133.31
国有独资公司	Sole State -funded Company	10.79		7.05	3.68	3.20
其他有限责任公司	Other Limited Liability Companies	186.30	26.54	84.99	10.17	130.11
股份有限公司	Share-holding Corporations Ltd	5.86	1.62	9.69	3.16	9.84
私营企业	Private Enterprises	44.21	3.62	47.38	3.99	35.48
私营有限责任公司	Private Limited Liability Companies	41.88	3.61	45.67	3.99	34.91
私营股份有限公司	Private Stock Limited Companies					0.57
按国民经济行业分组	**Grouped by National Economic Sectors**					
房屋和土木工程建筑业	Buildings and Givil Engineering	270.98	34.02	186.28	22.26	196.44
房屋工程建筑	Building	261.42	34.01	177.01	22.16	190.83
土木工程建筑	Civil Engineering	9.56	0.01	9.27	0.10	5.62
铁路、道路、隧道和桥梁工程建筑	Railways, Roads, Tunnels and Bridges	2.44	0.01	0.14		1.50
水利和港口工程建筑	Water Conservancy and Seaport	4.71		2.11	0.09	4.12
工矿工程建筑	Mine Project	2.41		7.02		
架线和管道工程建筑	Stringing and Pipeline Constrnction Project					
建筑安装业	Construction and Installation			0.40		0.08
其他建筑业	Others			0.75	1.31	0.43
按隶属关系分组	**Grouped by Subordination**					
中央	Central Government	36.10	3.44	46.58	7.75	51.93
地方	Local	234.88	30.57	140.85	15.82	145.02
按企业资质等级分组	**Grouped by Enterprise's Qualification**					
施工总承包	Undertaking Porjects	267.47	34.02	178.97	21.82	193.43
特级	Special Grade	3.39		14.10		0.42
一级	First Grade	63.52	11.18	64.21	8.40	19.54
二级	Second Grade	135.75	15.34	71.94	9.49	120.71
三级及以下	Third Grade	64.81	7.50	28.72	3.93	52.76
专业承包	Specialized Undertaking	3.51		8.46	1.75	3.52
一级	First Grade	1.42				2.06
二级	Second Grade	0.27		0.75	1.75	0.70
三级及以下	Third Grade	1.82		7.71		0.76

主要统计指标解释

建筑业统计单位　指从事房屋、构筑物建造和设备安装活动的法人企业。建筑业法人企业应具有建筑业资质并能够独立核算，同时其应具备以下条件：①依法成立，有自己的名称、组织机构和场所，能够承担民事责任；②独立拥有和使用资产，承担负债，有权与其他单位签订合同；③独立核算盈亏，能够编制资产负债表。

建筑业总产值　是以货币表现的建筑业企业在一定时期内生产的建筑业产品和提供服务的总和。建筑业总产值包括：

(1)建筑工程产值：指列入建筑工程预算内的各种工程价值。

(2)安装工程产值：指设备安装工程价值，不包括被安装设备本身价值。

(3)其他产值：建筑业总产值中除建筑工程、安装工程以外的产值。包括房屋构筑物修理产值、非标准设备制造产值、总包企业向分包企业收取的管理费以及不能明确划分的施工活动所完成的产值。

a.房屋构筑物修理产值：指房屋和构筑物修理所完成的产值，但不包括被修理房屋、构筑物本身价值和生产设备的修理价值。

b.非标准设备制造产值：指加工制造没有定型的非标准生产设备的加工费和原材料价值(如化工厂、炼油厂用的各种罐、槽，矿井生产统一使用的各种漏斗、三角槽、阀门等)以及附属加工厂为本企业承建工程制作的非标准设备的价值。

建筑业增加值　指建筑业企业在报告期内以货币形式表现的建筑业生产经营活动的最终成果。

从 2004 年第一次全国经济普查开始，建筑业现价增加值按生产法和分配法(收入法)两种方法计算，以收入法的计算结果为准，即从收入的角度出发，根据生产要素在生产过程中应得的收入份额计算。具体计算方法：经济普查年度建筑业增加值按照《经济普查年度 GDP 核算方案》计算，非经济普查年度建筑业增加值按照《非经济普查年度 GDP 核算方案》计算

房屋施工面积　指在报告期内施工的全部房屋建筑面积，包括本期新开工的面积、上期跨入本期继续施工的房屋面积、上期停缓建在本期恢复施工的房屋面积、本期竣工的房屋面积及本期施工后又停缓建的房屋面积。

房屋竣工面积　指在报告期内房屋建筑按照设计要求已全部完工，达到住人和使用条件，经验收鉴定合格或达到竣工验收标准，可正式移交使用单位的各栋房屋建筑面积的总和。

自有机械设备年末总台数　指归本企业所有，属于本企业固定资产的生产性机械设备年末总台数。包括施工机械、生产设备、运输设备以及其他设备。

自有机械设备年末总功率　指本企业自有施工机械、生产设备、运输设备以及其他设备等列为在册固定资产的生产性机械设备年末总功率，按设定能力或查定能力计算。包括机械本身的动力和为该机械服务的单独动力设备，如电动机等。计算单位用千瓦，动力换算可按 1 马力＝0.735 千瓦折合成千瓦数。电焊机、变压器、锅炉不计算动力。

工程结算收入　指企业承包工程实现的工程价款结算收入，以及向发包单位收取的除工程价款以外的按规定列作营业收入的各种款项，如临时设施费、劳动保险费、施工机械调迁费等以及向发包单位收取的各种索赔款。

工程结算利润　指已结算工程实现的利润，如亏损以“－”号表示。计算公式为：

工程结算利润＝工程结算收入－工程结算成本－工程结算税金及附加

企业总收入　指与企业生产经营直接有关的各项收入，包括工程结算收入和其他业务收入。计算公式为：

企业总收入＝工程结算收入＋其他业务收入

Explanatory Notes on Main Statistical Indicators

Statistical Unit in the Construction Industry refers to a corporate enterprise engaged in the construction of buildings and structures and in the installation of equipment. A corporate construction enterprise should have qualification certificates with independent accounting system, and should meet the following 3 requirements: a) being set up in line with relevant legal basis, having its full name, organization and location, and capable of taking civil liabilities; b) independently possessing and using its assets and assuming its liabilities, and entitled to sign contracts with other institutions; and c) making independent accounts of its profits and losses, and capable of compiling its own balance sheet.

Gross Output Value of Construction refers to total of construction products and services, expressed in money terms, produced or rendered by construction and installation enterprises during a given period of time. It includes:

(1) Output value of construction projects: the value of projects covered by the project budgets;

(2) Output value of installation projects: the value of the installation of equipment, (excluding the value of the equipment to be installed);

(3) Other output values: the output value of construction industry apart from that of construction projects and installation projects. It includes: output value of repair of buildings and structures; output value of non-standard equipment manufacture-ing; overhead expenses received by contracted enterprises from the sub-contracted enterprises and the completed output value of construction activities for which there is no clear definition.

a. Output value of repair of buildings and structures: the value created through the repairs of buildings or structures. It does not include the value of buildings or structures being repaired and the value of the repair of production equipment;

b. Output value of manufactured non-standard equipment: the value of non-standard production equipment, including raw materials and manufacturing cost, made for the construction project (i.e., chemical plant; kettles or tanks used by refineries; various fillers, triangle tanks, valves used by mines). It also includes the output value of equipment manufactured by subsidiary workshops.

Value-added of Construction refers to the final result of the activities of production and operation of enterprises of the construction industry in monetary terms during the reference period.

Starting from the 2004 economic census, value-added of construction is calculated by both production approach and income approach, with the figures from the income approach as the final figures., Under the income approach,, calculation starts from the perspective of income and is based on the share of income derived from the production process by the relevant factors of production.. Specifically, value-added of construction for the Census years is calculated in accordance with the Programme of Compilation of GDP and National Accounts for the Year of Economic Census, and value-added of construction for other years is calculated in accordance with the Programme of Compilation of GDP and National Accounts for the Non Economic Census Years.

Floor Space of Buildings Under Construction refers to floor space of buildings under construction during the reference period, including the floor space of buildings for which construction has newly started; buildings for which construction has started earlier and is continuing during the reference period; and buildings for which construction has been suspended earlier but has restarted during the reference period; buildings completed during the reference period; and buildings under construction but construction has subsequently been during the reference period.

Floor Space of Buildings Completed refers to the floor space of buildings that are completed in the reference period in accordance with the requirements of the design, up to the standard for being put into use, and having been checked and accepted by departments concerned as qualified ones.

Total Number of Machinery and Equipment Owned by the End of Year refers to the number of machines and equipment owned by the enterprises, and listed as the fixed assets of the enterprises by the end of the year, including machinery and equipment for construction, production and transportation.

Total Power of Machinery and Equipment Owned by the End of Year refers to the total power of machinery and equipment owned by the enterprises,and listed as the fixed assets of the enterprises by the end of the year, including machinery and equipment for construction,production and transportation.The power of the machinery is calculated on basis of the designed or verified capacity,covering the power of the machinery/equipment and the separate power equipment serving the machinery/equipment (such as electric motors), but excluding welders, transformers and boilers.The unit used for the calculation of power is kilowatt, with horsepower converted to kilowatt by 1 horsepower=0.735 kilowatt.

Income from Settlement of Projects refers to the income received by the construction enterprise from the contracted project through settlement procedures, and other charges to the contractoree as operational costs in addition to the value of the project, such as temporary facility fee,labour insurance premium, moving cost of construction equipment,as well as various types of claims to the contractee.

Profit from Settlement of Projects refers to profit realized through settled projects. It is calculated with the following formula:

Profit from Settlement of Projects=Income from Settlement of Projects−Settled Cost−Settled Taxes and Other Cost

Total Revenue of Enterprises refers to the sum of income from production and operation of enterprises, including income from settlement of projects and other operational income, namely:

Total Revenue of Enterprises=Income from Settlement of Projects+Other Operational Incom

新疆统计年鉴
XINJIANG STATISTICAL YEARBOOK

15

运输和邮电

POSTAL AND TELECOMMUNICATION SERVICES

简要说明

本篇资料的主要内容及来源

本篇资料反映新疆维吾尔自治区交通运输业和邮政、电信业发展的基本状况。

运输业资料主要包括：铁路、公路、民航、管道四种运输方式的线路条数、里程、总运量及周转量、货物运输平均运距、铁路运输主要技术经济指标；民用机动车辆情况。

邮政、电信业资料主要包括：邮政、电信业务完成情况，邮政、电信业务发展水平等资料。

铁路资料来自乌鲁木齐铁路局；公路资料来自新疆维吾尔自治区交通厅；民航运输数据资料来自中国南方航空股份有限公司新疆分公司；电信资料来自新疆维吾尔自治区通信管理局；邮政数据来自新疆维吾尔自治区邮政公司。

本篇资料由新疆维吾尔自治区统计局工业交通统计处收集整理。

Brief Introduction

Main Content and Source of Data

Data in this chapter cover mainly the basic condition of the development of transportation, post and telecommunications in Xinjiang Uygur Autonomous Region.

Data on transport cover mainly the length of the routes of four means of railway, highways, civil aviation and pipeline. total fright traffic, total freight ton-kilometers, average transport distance of fright, principal economic and technical indicators of railway transport, possession of civil vehicles.

Data on post and telecommunication cover mainly the complete business volume of post and telecommunication services, and the development of the post and telecommunication service, ect.

Data on railways transportation come from the Urumqi Bureau of the Transport. Data on the highways come from the Bureau of Transportation. Data on the civil aviation transport come from the China Southwest Airlines, Xinjiang Branch. Data on telecommunication services come from telecommunication Bureau. Data on post are provided by the Post Bureau.

Data in this chapter are collected and compiled by the Division of Industry and Transport Statistics, Xinjiang Bureau of Statistics.

15-1 主要年份运输业基本情况
Basic Conditions of Transport in Main Years

指 标	Item	2000	2010	2012
运输线路长度(公里)	**Length of Transport Routes (km)**			
铁路营业里程	Railways in Operation	3010	4393	4914
公路里程	Highways	80875	152843	165909
民用航线里程	Total Civil Aviation Routes	152941	176992	179054
管道输油（气）里程	Petroleum and Gas Pipelines	2696	11464	12843
客运量(万人)	**Total Passenger Traffic (10 000 persons)**	**23191**	**46346**	**55298**
铁 路	Railways	1147	1523	2162
公 路	Highways	21877	44333	52473
民用航空	Civil Aviation	167	490	663
旅客周转量(亿人公里)	**Total Passenger-Kilometers (100 million passenger-km)**	**292.80**	**670.75**	**849.25**
铁 路	Railways	97.40	170.10	236.72
公 路	Highways	158.20	404.00	478.50
民用航空	Civil Aviation	37.20	96.65	134.03
货运量(万吨)	**Total Freight Traffic (10 000 tons)**	**33090.5**	**64596.7**	**78248.8**
铁 路	Railways	4199	6853	6933
公 路	Highways	27048	50448	61850
民用航空	Civil Aviation	3.5	3.7	5.8
输油(气)管道	Petroleum and Gas Pipelines	1840	7292	9460
货物周转量(亿吨公里)	**Total Freight Ton-kilometers (100 million ton-km)**	**660.88**	**2053.82**	**2558.68**
铁 路	Railways	355.00	814.03	910.58
公 路	Highways	272.90	767.14	946.90
民用航空	Civil Aviation	0.98	0.98	1.44
输油(气)管道	Petroleum and Gas Pipelines	32.00	471.67	699.76
民用汽车拥有量(万辆)	**Possession of Civil Motor Vehicles (10 000 units)**	**37.0**	**135.9**	**211.1**
#载客汽车辆数	Buses and Cars	18.0	87.6	149.1
载货汽车辆数	Trucks	17.5	37.0	51.2
#私人汽车拥有量	Privat Vehicles	13.9	85.8	147.5

注：1.2000 年以后公路里程包括兵团数据。2.2006 年起新疆公路通车里程包含村道里程(以下同)。
Note: a) Since 2000 the highway mileage cover the data of XJPCC. b) Length of highways include lenth of backroad since 2006.(the same as in the following table)

15-2 主要年份运输线路长度
Length of Transport Routes in Main Years

单位:公里 (km)

年份 Year	铁路营业里程 Length of Railways in Operation	#新疆境内 Inside Xinjiang	公路 Length of Highways	#高级次高级公路 High Grade & Seond High Grade Highways	民用航空 Length of the Civil Aviation	#新疆境内 Inside Xinjiang	管道输油(气)里程 Petrolurn and Gas Pipelines
1978	1031	796	23818	5810	4783	4783	443
1980	1103	868	21148	6390	4412	4412	443
1985	1579	1344	22232	8369	4527	4527	473
1990	1578	1343	25425	12566	36465	5159	740
1995	2038	1803	30298	19013	69789	6693	875
1996	2038	1803	31609	20461	122089	9183	928
1997	2038	1803	32053	21495	123664	9717	1373
1998	2038	1803	32762	22485	150473	9717	1955
1999	3008	2780	33484	23214	141872	9719	2496
2000	3010	2775	80875	31059	152941	9719	2696
2001	3010	2774	80947	31635	161814	9719	2965
2002	3010	2775	82929	32541	132483	9898	3153
2003	3009	2775	83633	33891	141456	9898	3008
2004	2999	2763	86824	40679	111768	8664	3003
2005	2925	2761	89531	43803	119481	8664	3003
2006	2925	2761	143736	50119	138564	9064	4631
2007	2925	2761	145219	55080	160354	11363	6793
2008	2925	2925	146652	60233	147753	10560	9455
2009	3837	3673	150683	67684	152392	10754	11235
2010	4393	4228	152843	72887	176992	9939	11464
2011	4480	4316	155150	80974	175797	9939	11077
2012	4914	4315	165909	92456	179054	11727	12843

15-3 主要年份运输线路质量
Quality of Transport Routes in Main Years

单位：公里 (km)

指标	Item	1995	2000	2010	2012
铁路营业里程	Length of National Railways in Operation	2038	3010	4393	4914
#复线里程	Double-Tracking Length		986	1324	1759
#自动闭塞里程	Automatic Blocking Length	273	685	1408	1875
公路线路里程	Length of Highways	30298	80875	152843	165909
#水泥沥青路面	Lenth of bituminous Pavement	27982	33035	72887	92456

注：铁路上述里程是新疆境内里程。
Note: Length of railways refers to length of railway inside in Xinjiang.

15-4 主要年份客运量及周转量

Passenger Traffic and Passenger kilometers in Main Years

年份 Year	客运量(万人) Passenger Traffic (10 000 persons)				旅客周转量(亿人公里) Passenger-Kilometers (100 million passenger-km)			
	总计 Total	铁路 Railways	公路 Highways	民用航空 Civil Aviation	总计 Total	铁路 Railways	公路 Highways	民用航空 Civil Aviation
1978	941	148	786	7	25.23	13.72	10.96	0.55
1980	1356	193	1152	10	30.49	18.83	10.83	0.83
1985	3728	320	3399	9	63.16	33.16	29.13	0.87
1986	4058	362	3674	22	73.87	36.40	34.00	3.74
1987	4439	377	4327	34	83.67	37.14	39.44	7.09
1988	5205	459	4698	48	99.17	42.86	46.35	9.96
1989	8740	453	8240	47	120.69	44.52	66.37	9.80
1990	9602	388	9161	53	103.80	37.96	55.11	10.73
1991	14582	383	14142	56	122.08	41.94	68.05	12.09
1992	14997	425	14490	82	138.24	44.48	75.38	18.38
1993	16352	513	15749	90	174.23	50.04	103.51	20.73
1994	17181	670	16405	106	195.58	58.08	112.50	25.00
1995	17533	672	16739	122	204.89	58.00	117.17	29.68
1996	18858	610	18110	138	218.79	57.80	128.58	32.20
1997	20237	748	19360	129	233.39	64.70	139.00	29.69
1998	21747	878	20735	134	256.90	76.90	149.60	30.40
1999	22763	1000	21618	145	270.74	81.90	157.05	31.79
2000	23191	1147	21877	167	292.80	97.40	158.20	37.20
2001	24344	932	23255	157	309.70	104.10	170.30	35.30
2002	26016	950	24883	183	330.80	106.00	185.60	39.20
2003	26972	879	25878	215	342.00	106.10	195.00	40.90
2004	29782	1023	28473	286	423.80	121.90	249.00	52.90
2005	33220	1134	31747	339	457.42	125.20	271.20	61.02
2006	34471	1272	32835	364	498.30	138.90	292.10	67.30
2007	38434	1873	36159	402	548.10	144.46	326.70	76.94
2008	42111	1311	40392	408	594.60	149.89	363.60	81.11
2009	43410	1371	41604	435	614.66	152.90	376.30	85.46
2010	46346	1523	44333	490	670.75	170.10	404.00	96.65
2011	50461	2002	47927	532	758.26	216.16	437.90	104.16
2012	55298	2162	52473	663	849.25	236.72	478.50	134.03

注：2012 年民航旅客吞吐量为 1334.7 0 万人。
Note: Air passenger handling capacity is 133470million persons in 2012.。

15-5 主要年份货运量及货物周转量

Freight Traffic and Ton-kilometers in Main Years

年 份 Year	货运量(万吨) Freight Traffic (10 000 tons)				
	总 计 Total	铁 路 Railways	公 路 Highways	民用航空 Civil Aviation	输油(气)管道 Petroleum and Gas Pipelines
1978	6064.12	923	4843	0.12	298
1980	8422.16	884	7209	0.16	329
1990	13919.87	1691	11551	0.87	677
1995	25406.00	2733	21754	2.00	917
2000	33090.50	4199	27048	3.50	1840
2001	33589.00	3904	27751	2.00	1932
2002	34966.70	4121	28861	2.70	1982
2003	37485.20	4602	30881	2.20	2000
2004	38885.50	5083	31700	2.50	2100
2005	40600.20	5397	33000	3.20	2200
2006	43096.40	6001	34835	3.40	2256
2007	49009.62	7430	38427	3.62	3149
2008	57187.80	6120	44987	3.80	6077
2009	60162.80	6413	46787	3.80	6959
2010	64596.70	6853	50448	3.70	7292
2011	70361.90	6904	55965	3.90	7489
2012	78248.80	6933	61850	5.80	9460

年 份 Year	货物周转量(亿吨公里) Freight Ton-kilometers (100 million ton-km)				
	总 计 Total	铁 路 Railways	公 路 Highways	民用航空(万吨公里) Civil Aviation (10 000 ton-km)	输油(气)管道 Petroleum and Gas Pipelines
1978	106.96	67.76	32.06	98.10	7.13
1980	121.14	67.27	45.89	137.80	7.97
1990	262.29	141.16	108.09	2048.00	12.84
1995	474.39	240.88	219.72	5744.00	13.22
2000	660.88	355.00	272.90	9776.00	32.00
2001	714.43	403.90	275.90	6300.00	34.00
2002	759.62	425.30	298.00	8238.00	35.50
2003	837.04	475.00	325.00	6400.00	36.40
2004	947.24	548.50	361.00	7400.00	37.00
2005	1032.75	586.90	405.00	8500.00	40.00
2006	1143.31	647.10	425.68	8921.00	69.64
2007	1264.31	678.53	468.80	9085.78	116.07
2008	1656.88	758.74	672.30	9285.43	224.91
2009	1815.81	751.09	705.90	9700.00	357.85
2010	2053.82	814.03	767.14	9837.00	471.67
2011	2199.52	857.01	852.17	9700.00	488.38
2012	2558.68	910.58	946.90	14400.00	699.76

15-6 主要年份货物运输平均运距
Average Transport Distance of Freight in Main Years

单位：公里 (km)

年份 Year	合计 Total	铁路 Railways	公路 Highways	民用航空 Civil Aviation	输油(气)管道 Petroleum and Gas Pipelines
1978	168	565	66	818	239
1980	139	566	64	861	242
1985	158	624	69	945	206
1990	188	835	94	2354	190
1995	187	881	101	2872	144
2000	200	845	101	2857	174
2001	211	1023	99	3150	176
2002	217	1032	103	3051	179
2003	224	865	105	2909	182
2004	244	904	114	2960	176
2005	254	901	122	2656	182
2006	265	894	122	2598	308
2007	257	913	122	2528	368
2008	289	926	149	2456	370
2009	301	873	151	2552	518
2010	317	934	152	2637	514
2011	312	935	152	2480	652
2012	327	945	153	2486	646

15-7 主要年份铁路运输主要财务指标
Main Financial Indicators of Railway Transport in Main Years

单位：万元 (10 000 yuan)

指标	Item	1990	1995	2000	2010	2012
运输总收入	**Total Transport Revenue**	**86686**	**192555**	**509480**	**1926749**	**2224145**
#客运收入	Revenue from Passenger Traffic	18763	33560	82121	234979	386231
货运收入	Revenue from Freight Traffic	62516	142168	318485	1197619	1458362
运输清算收入	**Transportation Claring Revenue**	**59765**		**467142**	**1311275**	**1654636**
运输总支出	**Toatl Transport Expenditure**	**51875**	**193693**	**418497**	**1552877**	**1999989**
#工资	Wages and Salaries	11163	38429	98293	238570	350822
材料	Materials	6702	23183	36210	79181	97217
燃料	Fuel	9308	32996	74487	340960	402260
电力	Electricity	666	2433	4701	8022	25433
折旧	Depreciation	17174	13137	60859	127368	153085
营业外收支净额	**Non-operating Net Revenue or Expenditure**	**6886**	**14503**	**23236**	**-21947**	**30637**
实现利润	**Profits**	**6291**	**-12591**	**34130**	**-273121**	**-417331**
#运输利润	Transport Profits	5501	-11649	33195	-266910	-418406

注：运输总收入、旅客票价收入、货物运费收入是运送到全国范围的客、货运输收入。
Note: Revenue from transport,passenger traffic and freight traffic refer to revenue from transport to allover China.

15-8 铁路运输技术经济主要指标
Main Technical and Economic Indicators of Railway Transport

指 标	Item	2011	2012
货运机车日产量(万吨公里)	Average Daily Ton-kilometers of Freight Locomotives (10 000 ton-km)	120.0	113.9
#内燃机车	Diesel Locomotives	119.3	110.9
货运列车平均总重(吨)	Average Total Tonnage of Freight Locomotives (ton)	2779	2846
#内燃机车	Diesel Locomotives	2787	2857
货运机车日车公里(公里)	Daily Distance per Freight Locomotive (km)	620	550
客运机车日车公里(公里)	Daily Distance per Passenger Locomotive (km)	973	871
内燃机车每万吨公里耗油(公斤)	Oil Consumption of Diesel Locomotives (kg/10 000 ton-km)	28.2	28.9
货物列车出发正点率(%)	Punctuality Rate of Freight Trains at Departure (%)	98.7	98.5
货物列车运行正点率(%)	Punctuality Rate of Freight Trains in Running (%)	98.4	98.4
旅客列车出发正点率(%)	Punctuality Rate of Passenger Trains at Departure (%)	99.5	98.6
旅客列车运行正点率(%)	Punctuality Rate of Passenger Trains in Running (%)	94.0	96.8
旅客列车技术速度(公里/小时)	Technical Speed of Passenger Trains (km/hr)	72.2	70.5
旅客列车旅行速度(公里/小时)	Travelling Speed of Passenger Trains (km/hr)	63.4	62.7
客运密度(万人公里/公里)	Density of Passenger Transport (10 000 passenger-km/km)	540.3	593.7
货物列车技术速度(公里/小时)	Technical Speed of Freight Trains (km/hr)	47.2	47.2
货物列车旅行速度(公里/小时)	Running Speed of Freight Trains (km/hr)	37.5	36.3
货运密度(万吨公里/公里)	Density of Freight Transport (10 000 ton-km/km)	2325.7	1998.6
货车周转时间(天)	Turning Around Time of Freight Cars (day)	4.2	4.5
一次货物作业时间(小时)	Handling Time of Freight (hour)	18.1	17.7
货车中转停留时间(小时)	Transfer Waiting Time per Car (hour)	3.2	3.2
货车静载重(准轨) (吨)	Static Load of Freight Cars (Standard Gauge) (ton)	56.1	56.9

15-9 民用车辆拥有量
Number of Civil Vehicles

单位：辆 (unit)

指 标	Item	2011		2012	
		总 计 Total	#私 人 Private	总 计 Total	#私 人 Private
民用汽车	**Civil Vehicles**	**1697862**	**1131929**	**2110700**	**1474576**
载客汽车	Passenger Vehicles	1147873	896048	1490810	1205254
#大 型	Large	29518	1377	31864	1553
中 型	Medium	31282	10123	34172	11703
小 型	Small	1054529	856243	1391403	1162239
微 型	Minicar	32544	28305	33371	29759
载货汽车	Trucks	437870	171797	511776	211872
#重 型	Large	134918	13393	153855	14659
中 型	Medium	52061	12917	53133	13053
轻 型	Light	247015	142688	301913	181994
微 型	Mini	3876	2799	2875	2166
其它汽车	Others	112119	64084	108114	57450

15-10 主要年份邮电事业情况

Basic Conditions of Postal and Telecommunication Services in Main Years

指　　标	Item	2000	2010	2012
邮政局营业网点(处)	**Number of Post Offices (unit)**		**1276**	**1239**
邮路长度(单程)(公里)	**Length of Postal Routes (km)**	**134109**	**75571**	**72972**
#农 村	Rural	55852	18238	19953
邮政业务总量(万元)	Business Volume of Postal Services	59370	165794	181720
电信业务总量(万元)	Business Volume of Telecommunication Services	413630	5654665	2466653
函件(万件)	Number of Letters (10 000 pieces)	7148	2926	2529
包件(万件)	Number of Parcels (10 000 pieces)	163	174	261
特快专递(万件)	Pieces of Express Mail Services (10 000 pieces)	124	487	583
报刊期发数(万份)	Number of Newspapers and Magazines Circulation (10 000 copies)	535	307	310
长途电话(万分钟)	Number of Long-distance Calls (10 000 minutes)	34712	105001	14025
固定电话年末用户(万户)	Local Telephone Subscribers at Year-end (10 000 subscribers)	191.0	547.5	540.1
#城市电话年末数	Urban Telephone Subscribers at Year-end	136.3	395.8	391.0
乡村电话年末数	Number of Rural Telephones Subscribers at Year-end	54.7	132.1	126.9
#住宅电话年末数	Residential Telephone Subscribers	149.3	346.6	337.0
移动电话年末用户(万户)	Number of Mobile Telephones Subscribers at Year-end (10 000 subscribers)	78.0	1359.8	2008.5
长途电信线路	**Telecommunication Lines**			
光缆线路长度(公里)	Length of Long Distance Optical Cable Lines (km)	10828	259307	368525
邮电通信设备	**Telecommunication Facilities**			
固定长途交换机容量(路端)	Capacity of long-distance Telephone Exchanges (circuit)	102540	315982	284632
本地电话局用交换机容量(万门)	Capacity of Local Office Telephone Exchange (10 000 line)	241.7	928.2	623.6
邮电通信水平	**Level of Postal and Telecommunication Services**			
平均每百人每年发函件数(件)	Annual Arerage Number of Letters Mailed Per 100 persons (piece)	387.0	122.0	114.0
平均每百人每年订报刊数(份)	Annual Arerage Number of Newspaper Subscribed Per 100 Persons (piece)	28.9	12.6	14.0
平均每百人拥有电话机数(固定)(部)	Number of Telephone Sets Owned per 100 Persons(stable) (set)	15.0	25.4	24.5
平均每百人拥有电话机数(移动)(部)	Number of Telephone Sets Owned per 100 Persons (mobile) (set)		63.0	90.9
农村邮电通信水平	**Rural Level**			
通电话的乡(镇)比重(%)	Percentage of Townships with Telephone Communication (%)	100	100	100

15-11 主要年份邮电业务情况
Conditions of Postal and Telecommunication Services in Main Years

年份 Year	邮政业务总量(万元) Business Volume of Postal Services (10000 yuan)	电信业务总量(万元) Business Volume of Telecommunication Services (10000 yuan)	函件(万件) Number of Letters (10 000 pieces)
1978			4842.7
1980			5890.8
1985			7032.6
1990	8203	8312	7380.5
1995	17322	71220	9041.8
2000	59370	413630	7148.0
2001	62265	572073	5601.0
2002	68032	878968	6814.0
2003	72007	1072831	5987.0
2004	74835	1457000	4756.7
2005	80500	1643259	4450.0
2006	94188	2195000	4129.8
2007	100498	2936000	3177.0
2008	113802	3673709	2900.0
2009	133535	4663000	2800.0
2010	165794	5654665	2926.0
2011	138398	2126602	3202.4
2012	181720	2466653	2529.0

年份 Year	特快专递(万件) Pieces of Express Mail Services (10 000 pieces)	报刊期发数(万份) Issue of Newspapers and Magazines (10 000 copies)	集邮业务(万枚) Stamps for Collection (10 000 pieces)	长途电话(万分钟) Length of Long-distance Calls (10 000 minutes)
1978		223.8		258.8
1980		329.6		276.5
1985		578.9		425.1
1990	…	805.7	1034.5	762.5
1995	93.6	478.1	3086.6	11705.9
2000	124.0	534.5	5766.0	34712.0
2001	147.0	358.0	5491.0	89844.0
2002	163.0	399.0	4620.0	45769.0
2003	199.0	587.3	3112.8	35554.2
2004	238.1	283.0	3141.3	62526.0
2005	266.0	293.0	2072.0	52482.0
2006	291.0	341.7	2205.1	46478.0
2007	324.0	305.0	2134.0	67660.0
2008	362.0	296.0	2335.0	42550.0
2009	412.0	296.0	2520.0	48816.0
2010	487.0	307.0	2672.0	105001.0
2011	579.0	296.4	2306.8	91298.0
2012	583.0	310.0	2253.5	14024.8

注：从 1997 年起，市内电话户数统计口径有了较大调整，故农村电话户数增幅较大。
Note: Since 1997, greater adjustment has been made on the Statistic Method about the number of telephone subscribers and the number of rural subscribers has gone up by a bigger margin.

15-11 续表 Continued

年 份 Year	移动电话用户(万户) Number of Mobile Telephone Subscribers (10 000 subscribers)	国际互联网络用户(万户) Number of Subscribers of Internet Services (10 000 subscribers)	固定电话年末用户(万户) Number of Subscribers of Local Telephone at Year-end (10 000 subscribers)	#城市电话用户 Number of Urban Telephone Subscribers
1978			2.9	1.9
1980			3.2	2.1
1985			4.7	3.7
1990			8.9	7.9
1995	2.7		44.6	42.0
2000	78.0		191.0	136.3
2001	180.9	12.8	262.6	196.1
2002	297.0	17.3	337.5	238.3
2003	421.2	60.8	431.0	293.9
2004	489.7	78.0	516.7	387.0
2005	531.3	105.8	612.2	457.5
2006	671.1	123.7	706.9	533.6
2007	808.3	157.8	678.1	520.6
2008	1051.3	142.8	634.9	462.2
2009	1119.6	133.7	573.1	409.6
2010	1359.8	161.1	547.5	395.8
2011	1670.9	208.8	540.5	390.8
2012	2008.5	255.0	540.1	391.0

年 份 Year	#住宅电话 Household Fixed Telephone Subscribers	#乡村电话用户 Rural Fixed Telephone Subscribers	#住宅电话 Household Fixed Telephone Subscribers	公用电话(户) Public Telephone (subscriber)
1978		1.1		
1980		1.0		
1985		1.0		
1990	1.2	1.1		257
1995	26.0	2.6	1.2	5612
2000	101.1	54.7	48.2	70753
2001	124.3	66.5	57.8	84309
2002	179.9	79.5	73.4	166000
2003	180.0	93.5	88.6	281632
2004	194.0	108.2	103.4	432000
2005	318.9	135.2	115.4	570047
2006	369.9	154.5	131.7	668335
2007	359.6	157.5	136.1	675309
2008	310.6	150.0	126.3	597000
2009	234.6	140.8	117.2	570982
2010	237.4	132.1	109.2	529322
2011	236.8	127.5	104.9	476633
2012	234.6	126.9	102.4	436471

主要统计指标解释

铁路营业里程　又称营业长度，指投入客货运输营业或临时营业的线路长度。

铁路自动、半自动闭塞里程　为保证列车安全运行，在一个区间、同一时间内，一般只允许一列列车运行，这种保证列车在这个区间安全间隔运行的技术方法称为“闭塞”。自动闭塞是根据列车运行及有关闭塞分区状态，自动变换通过信号机显示而司机凭信号显示行车的闭塞方法，采用此方式的闭塞公里为自动闭塞里程。

公路里程　指报告期末公路的实际长度。统计范围：包括城间、城乡间、乡（村）间能行驶汽车的公共道路，公路通过城镇街道的里程，公路桥梁长度、隧道长度、渡口宽度。不包括城市街道里程，断头路里程，农（林）业生产用道路里程，工（矿）企业等内部道路里程。统计原则：按已竣工验收或交付使用的实际里程计算；两条或多条公路共同经由同一路段的重复里程，只计算一次。

民用航空航线里程　指统计期间内全部民用航空航线的航线总长度。航线长度指民用航空航线的计费距离。计算航线里程可按重复和不重复两种方法，前者是指各航线长度相加的总和；后者则要扣除各航线之间相同航段重复计算的部分。

输油(气)管道里程　指油、气、成品油等各类介质实际输送距离，是反映运输管线长度的指标，也是计算周转量的依据。对于有复线和备用线的地段，原则上按单线计算管输里程。双线同时输送又不能分开计量的情况下，管输里程为双线长度之和除以2。

货(客)运量　指在一定时期内，各种运输工具实际运送的货物重量(旅客数量)。该指标是反映运输业为国民经济和人民生活服务的数量指标，也是制定和检查运输生产计划、研究运输发展规模和速度的重要指标。货运按吨计算，客运按人计算。货物不论运输距离长短、货物类别，均按实际重量统计。旅客不论行程远近或票价多少，均按一人一次客运量统计；半价票、小孩票也按一人统计。

货物(旅客)周转量　指在一定时期内，由各种运输工具运送的货物(旅客)数量与其相应运输距离的乘积之总和。该指标可以反映运输业生产的总成果，也是编制和检查运输生产计划，计算运输效率、劳动生产率以及核算运输单位成本的主要基础资料。计算货物周转量通常按发出站与到达站之间的最短距离，也就是计费距离计算。计算公式为：

货物(旅客)周转量=∑（货物（旅客）运输量×运输距离）

铁路货车平均静载重　为货物在装车时的静止装载重载重力的利用情况。计算公式为：

货车平均静载重=货物发送吨数/装车数

静载重的多少取决于运送货物的性质、种类、车辆的类型和装载技术的高低。根据货车的平均标记载重与静载重量。等于货物发送吨数除以装车数。

静载重的多少取决于运送货物的性质、种类、车辆的类型和装载技术的高低。

铁路货运机车日产量　指在一定时期内，平均每台货运机车在一昼夜内所完成的总重吨公里数，包括载运货物的重量和车辆本身的自重。该指标从时间和牵引能力两方面反映了机车运用效率。计算公式为：

货运机车平均日产量=货运总重吨公里数/货运机车台日数

民用汽车拥有量　指报告期末，在公安交通管理部门按照《机动车注册登记工作规范》，已注册登记领有民用车辆牌照的全部汽车数量。汽车拥有量统计的主要分类：根据汽车结构分为载客汽车、载货汽车及其他汽车；根据汽车所有者不同分为个人(私人)汽车、单位汽车；根据汽车的使用性质分为营运汽车、非营运汽车和特种汽车；根据汽车大小规格不同载客汽车分为大型、中型、小型和微型，载货汽车分为重型、中型、轻型和微型。

邮电业务总量　指以货币形式表示的邮政、电信企业为社会提供各类邮政通信服务的总数量。

邮电业务总量={各类邮政电信业务量*不变价} + 出租代维及其他业务收入

移动电话用户　指在电信运营企业营业网点办理开户登记手续，通过移动电话交换机进入移动电话网，占用移动电话号码的各类电话用户。包括各类签约用户、智能网预付费用户、无线上网卡用户。

互联网上网人数　指过去半年内使用过互联网的 6 周岁及以上中国居民人数。

固定电话用户　指在电信企业营业网点办理开户登记手续并已接入固定电话网上的全部电话用户。包括普通电话用户、无线市话用户、公用电话用户、窄带综合业务数字网（N—ISDN）用户、智能网专用接入终端用户等。按行政区划分为城市电话用户和农村电话用户。

住宅电话用户　指私人付费或安装在居民住宅并按照私人或住宅电话用户登记注册和收费的各类电话用户。

长途电话交换机容量　指电信企业用于接入长途电话网的电话交换机的设备额定容量。

局用交换机容量　指安装在电信运营企业内用于接续本地固定电话的电话交换机容量，包括接入网设备容量（安装在电信运营企业用于连接语音用户的远端节点的设备容量）。

Explanatory Notes on Main Statistical Indicators

Length of Railways in Operation refers to the total length of the trunk line for passenger and freight transportation in full operation or temporary operation.

Length of Automatic-blocking and Semi- automatic-blocking Railways Blocking is a spacing technique by which a section of the railway only allows one train to pass at a time with the aim of ensuring traffic safety. Automatic-blocking is the blocking method that signal display transforms automatically based on the state of train operation and related block partition, while the driver operates according to the signal display. The section which is blocked using the above method is called as length of automatic-blocking railways. Semi-blocking is realized manually. After the train departs based on signal display, the departure signal machine will perform automatic shutdown blocking, while the station attendant will conduct restoration of section blocking with arrival confirmation of the entire train. The section which is blocked using the above method is called as length of semi-automatic-blocking railways.

Length of Highways refers to the actual length of highways at the end of reference period. It covers public roads running vehicles among cities, city and rural areas, township (villages), highways passing through streets at small cities and towns, length of bridges and tunnels, width of ferry piers. It does not include the length of streets in cities, dead end highways, the length of streets built for agricultural (forest) production and inside factories (mines). It can only be calculated with the actual mileage having been completed, checked and accepted or put into operation. If two or more highways go the same section of the way, the length of the section is only calculated for once.

Length of Routes with Scheduled Flights refers to the total length of all routes for scheduled flights, which is calculated using million kilometres as the unit. There are usually two ways to calculate the route length: duplicated calculation and non-duplicated calculation. Duplicated calculation means that the same segment of different routes can be added duplicately, while the non-duplicated calculation allows the same segment of different routes be counted once only.

Length of Oil (Gas) Pipelines refers to the actual transport distance of oil, gas and oil products, an indicator reflecting the length of transportation routes and a reference to calculate the freight-kilometers. For those sections with double pipelines and alternate pipeline, the length will be calculated according to the length of single pipeline in principle. If the double pipelines perform the transportation at the same time and unable to be counted separately, the length of pipelines will be the length of double pipelines divided by 2.

Freight (Passenger) Traffic refers to the weight of freight (number of passenger) transported with various means within a specific period of time. This indicator reflects the service of the transport industry towards the national economy and people's living conditions, as well as an important indicator used in formulating and monitoring transport production plans and research into the scale and pace of transport development. Freight transport is calculated in tons and passenger traffic is calculated in terms of number of persons. Freight transport is calculated in terms of the actual weight of the goods and takes no account of the type of freight and distance of travel. Passenger traffic is calculated by the principle that one person can be counted only once in one trip and takes no account of the travelling distance and ticket price. The passengers who travel with a half price ticket or a child's ticket is also calculated as one person.

Freight Ton-kilometres (Passenger-kilometres) refers to the sum of the product of the volume of transported cargo (passengers) multiplied by the transport distance. It is an important indicator to reflect the achievement of the transportation industry. This is an important indicator to show the total results of the transport industry; to prepare and examine the transport plan; and to serve as the main basic data for calculating the efficiency, labour productivity and unit cost of transport. Normally, the shortest distance between the departure station and the destination station (i.e., the payable distance) is the basis in calculating the freight ton-kilometres. The formula is as follows:

$$\begin{matrix}\text{Freight ton}-\text{kilometres}\\(\text{passenger}-\text{kilometres})\end{matrix}=\sum\begin{matrix}\text{freight}\\(\text{passenger})\text{traffic}\end{matrix}\times\begin{matrix}\text{distance of}\\\text{transportation}\end{matrix}$$

A Average Static Load of Freight Cars refers to the average cargo weight when loaded onto each freight car under the static condition. It equals to the tonnage of goods dispatched divided by the number of freight cars loaded.

The static load of freight cars is determined by the nature and type of goods loaded the type of vehicles, and the technique of loading. Comparison of the average marked load with the static load of freight cars provides indication on the degree of utilization of loading capacity of freight cars. For its calculation the following formula is applied:

$$\begin{matrix}\text{Utilization rate of}\\\text{capacity of freight cars (\%)}\end{matrix}=\frac{\text{Average static load}}{\text{Average marked load}}\times 100\%$$

Average Daily Haul of Freight Locomotives refers to the average total ton-kilometres accomplished by each freight transport locomotive over one day and night during a given period of time. It includes both the weight of the goods carried and the dead weight of the train itself. It is a comprehensive indicator reflecting the locomotive efficiency in terms of both time and the pulling force.

$$\begin{matrix}\text{Average daily haul of}\\\text{freight transport locomotive}\\(\text{ton}-\text{kilometre})\end{matrix}=\frac{\text{Total ton}-\text{kilometres of freight}}{\text{Daily number of freight transport locomotive}}$$

Possession of Civil Motor Vehicles refer to the total numbers of vehicles that are registered and received vehicles license tags according to the Work Standard for Motor Vehicles Registration formulated by the Transport Management Office under the department of public security at the end of the reference period. They are divided into categories. According to the structure of motor vehicles, they are divided into passenger vehicles, trucks and others; according to ownership into private vehicles and vehicles for the unit's use; according to kind of usage into working vehicles and non-working vehicles; and according to size of vehicles into large passenger vehicles, medium-sized passenger vehicles, small passenger vehicles and mini passenger vehicles, heavy trucks, light-heavy trucks, light trucks and mini-trucks.

Business Volume of Post and Telecommunications refers to the total amount of postal and telecommunication services, expressed in value terms, provided by the post and telecommunications departments for society. This indicator reflects the overall results of development of postal and telecommunication services. It can be classificated as postal services and telecommunication services. Business volume of post and telecommunications is the sum of each service in kind multiplying with its correspondent unit price (constant price).

Mobile Telephone Subscribers refers to persons who have gone through registration procedures in the operation points of enterprises engaged in telecommunications and are hence connected with the mobile telephone communication network through the mobile telephone switchboards and occupy mobile phone numbers. Included are various types of subscriber, prepaid users for intelligent network and wireless network card users.

Internet Users refer to the number of Chinese citizens aged 6 and over who use the Internet in the past six months.

Local Telephone Subscribers refer to all subscribers who have gone through registration procedures in the operation points of enterprises engaged in telecommunications and are hence connected to the local telecommunications service provider through fixed line network. Included are general subscribers, wireless local telephone subscribers, public telephones subscribers, N-ISDN subscribers and intelligent network terminal subscribers.

Household Telephone Subscribers refers to all kinds of subscribers with telephone sets paid privately or installed in the dwelling units of residents, and registered as private subscribers or residence subscribers for payment.

Capacity of Long Distance Telephone Exchanges refers to the rated capacity of telephone exchanges to connect long distance telephone network by enterprises engaged in telecommunications.

Capacity of Office Telephone Exchanges refers to the capacity of telephone exchanges installed in the offices of telecommunication service providers in communication between fixed telephones.It includes the capacity of access network equipment.

新疆统计年鉴
XINJIANG STATISTICAL YEARBOOK

16

批发和零售业、住宿和餐饮业

WHOLESALE & RETAIL TRADES, HOTELS AND CATERING SERVICES

简要说明

本篇资料的主要内容及来源

本篇资料反映新疆维吾尔自治区商品流通市场发展及批发和零售业、住宿和餐饮业经营情况。主要内容有社会消费品零售额；限额以上批发和零售业、住宿和餐饮业情况；限额以上批发和零售业商品销售及商品分类销售情况；限额以上批发和零售贸易企业及住宿和餐饮企业主要财务情况；亿元商品交易市场成交情况；连锁经营情况等。

限额以上批发和零售业、住宿和餐饮业统计限额标准：批发业年销售额2000万元及以上；零售业年销售额500万元及以上；餐饮业年营业额200万元及以上；住宿业为年主营业务收入200万元以上企业。

本篇资料由新疆维吾尔自治区统计局贸易外经统计处提供。

Brief Introduction

Main Content and Source of Data

Data in this chapter reflect the development of Xinjiang's circulation of domestic market and the management situation of wholesale and retail & hotels and catering services, etc. Main contents include the total retail sales, condition of wholesales & retail trades and hotels and catering services above designated size; condition of sale value of enterprises above designated size of wholesales and retail trade and sale value of trade by category of main commodities.

Criteria for wholesale and retail sale trades, hotels and catering services above designated size is defined as follows: wholesale trade has annual sales over 20 million yuan; retail sale trade have annual sale over 5 million yuan; catering services have annual income over 2 million yuan. Enterprise above designated size in accommodation refers to star-rated unit.

Data in this chapter are provided by the Division of Trade Statistics, the Xinjiang Bureau of Statistics.

16-1 主要年份国内贸易基本情况
Basic Conditions of Domestic Trade in Main Years

指　　标	Item	2000	2005	2010	2012
法人企业(个)	**Number of Corporation Enterprises (unit)**	**394**	**1097**	**1449**	**1697**
批发和零售业	Wholesale and Retail Trades	370	800	1175	1388
住宿和餐饮业	Hotels and Catering Servicess	24	297	274	309
#餐饮业	Catering Services	24	65	53	75
产业活动单位(个)	**Number of Establishments (unit)**	**431**	**2396**	**4563**	**4655**
批发和零售业	Wholesale and Retail Trades	382	1998	4137	4145
住宿和餐饮业	Hotels and Catering Services	49	398	426	510
#餐饮业	Catering Services	49	96	122	171
批发和零售业	**Wholesale and Retail Trades**				
商品销售总额（亿元)	Total Sales (100 million yuan)	478.3	1182.0	4230.9	7487.6
社会消费品零售总额(亿元)	**Total Retail Sales of Consumer Goods (100 million yuan)**	**374.5**	**640.2**	**1324.5**	**1799.0**
按销售单位所在地分	By Location of Establishments				
城　镇	City	233.7	443.9	1181.3	1642.3
#城　区	County	65.2	95.6	945.0	1406.7
乡　村	Under County Level	75.6	100.7	143.2	156.7
按行业分	By Sector				
批发和零售业	Wholesale and Retail Trades	242.3	509.3	1156.6	1553.4
住宿和餐饮业	Hotels and Catering Services	38.2	92.8	167.9	245.6
其他行业	Others	94.0	38.1		

注：1.法人企业、产业活动单位统计范围为限额以上企业(单位)。2.商品销售总额、社会消费品零售总额为全口径数据。3.2008 年限额以上住宿业数据为年主营业务收入 200 万元以上企业。4.从 2010 年开始,按销售单位所在地分组由市、县、县以下调整为城镇、城区、乡村。5.从 2010 年开始,按行业分组取消其他行业。

Note: a) Scope of corporation enterprises,industrial activity units covers enterprises(units)above designated size. b) Data of total sales and total retail sales of consumer goods are those of full coverage. c) Data of hotels and catering services above designated size in 2008 are figures from enterprises of annual income over 2 million yuan. d) Since 2010,By the sales units of the group was adjusted,from city,county and under county level to town,city and country.e) Since 2010,by the sector of the group canceled oter sectors.

16-2 主要年份社会消费品零售总额

Total Retail Sales of Consumer Goods in Main Years

单位：亿元 (100 million yuan)

年份 Year	社会消费品零售总额 Total Retail Sales of Consumer Goods	按销售单位所在地分 By Location		
		城镇 City	#城区 County	乡村 Under County Level
1978	21.89	7.44	4.80	9.65
1980	29.36	11.06	6.05	12.25
1985	57.38	24.55	10.70	22.13
1990	104.30	57.17	24.27	22.86
1995	253.65	145.74	50.03	57.88
1996	295.36	171.51	55.38	68.47
1997	310.42	186.37	57.54	66.51
1998	327.52	197.89	59.89	69.74
1999	347.40	213.96	61.51	71.93
2000	374.50	233.66	65.15	75.69
2001	406.35	256.58	69.73	80.04
2002	442.88	284.74	74.32	83.82
2003	421.16	311.33	49.20	60.63
2004	563.41	385.81	85.79	91.81
2005	640.20	443.95	95.60	100.65
2006	733.20	513.12	107.68	112.40
2007	857.50	606.74	123.64	127.12
2008	1041.50	740.85	150.78	149.87
2009	1177.53	834.42	171.76	171.35
2010	1324.48	1181.27	945.03	143.21
2011	1557.09	1411.01	1165.29	146.08
2012	1798.99	1642.24	1406.67	156.75

年份 Year	按行业分 By Sector		
	批发和零售业 Wholesale and Retail Trades	住宿和餐饮业 Hotels and Catering Services	其他行业 Others
1978	17.34	0.57	3.98
1980	22.95	0.94	5.47
1985	40.83	2.51	14.04
1990	72.68	6.06	25.56
1995	169.16	17.27	67.22
1996	191.14	19.44	84.78
1997	198.73	22.22	89.47
1998	206.92	27.84	92.76
1999	222.57	32.76	92.07
2000	242.29	38.21	94.00
2001	266.38	44.57	95.40
2002	296.13	53.04	93.71
2003	341.90	60.64	18.62
2004	450.65	76.22	36.54
2005	509.25	92.82	38.13
2006	582.28	111.55	39.37
2007	685.94	130.51	41.05
2008	841.65	156.49	43.36
2009	956.64	177.21	43.68
2010	1156.62	167.86	
2011	1351.36	205.73	
2012	1553.37	245.62	

16-3 分类型、分地区限额以上批发和零售业、住宿和餐饮业基本情况

Basic Conditions of Enterprises above Designated Size in Wholesale and Retail Trades, Hotels and Catering Services by Category and Region

(2012 年)

指　标	Item	法人企业数（个）Number of Corporation Enterprises (unit)	产业活动单位数（个）Number of Establishments (unit)	从业人员数（人）Engaged Persons (person)
总　计	**Total**	**1697**	**4655**	**160827**
批发业	**Wholesale Trades**	**862**	**2312**	**66390**
内资企业	Domestic Funded Enterprises	858	2295	65540
国有企业	State-owned Enterprises	118	672	20440
集体企业	Collective-owned Enterprises	21	78	1971
股份合作企业	Cooperative Enterprises	1	1	200
联营企业	Joint Ownership Enterprises	1	1	15
集体联营企业	Collective Joint Ownership Enterprises	1	1	15
有限责任公司	State Sole Funded Corporations	264	708	20152
国有独资公司	State Sole Funded Corporations	35	104	5211
其他有限责任公司	Other Limited Liability Corporations	229	604	14941
股份有限公司	Share-holding Corporations Ltd.	27	354	7353
私营企业	Private Enterprises	419	473	14978
私营独资企业	Private-funded Enterprises	2	2	78
私营合伙企业	Private Partnership Enterprises	2	2	32
私营有限责任公司	Private Limited Liability Corporations	407	460	14314
私营股份有限公司	Private Share-holding Corporation Ltd.	8	9	554
其他企业	Others	7	8	431
港、澳、台商投资企业	Enterprises With Funds from Hong Kong, Macao and Taiwan	1	2	383
港、澳、台商独资经营企业	Enterprises With Sole Funds from Hong Kong, Macao and Taiwan	1	2	383
外商投资企业	Foreign Funded Enterprises	3	15	467
中外合资经营企业	Enterprises with Foreign Investment	2	5	77
外资企业	Enterprises with Sole Fund	1	10	390
零售业	**Retail Trades**	**526**	**1833**	**48356**
内资企业	Domestic Funded Enterprises	517	1820	46230
国有企业	State-owned Enterprises	31	198	2939
集体企业	Collective-owned Enterprises	2	9	85
股份合作企业	Share-holding Cooperative Enterprises	1	1	94
有限责任公司	Limited Liability Corporations	149	484	11663
国有独资公司	State Sole Funded Enterprises	5	14	121
其他有限责任公司	Other Limited Liability Corporations	144	470	11542
股份有限公司	Share-holding Corporations Ltd.	6	101	7039
私营企业	Private Enterprises	323	1012	24262
私营独资企业	Private-funded Enterprises	8	9	492
私营有限责任公司	Private Limited Liability Corporations	314	1002	23761
私营股份有限公司	Private Share-holding Corporation Ltd.	1	1	9
其他企业	Others	5	15	148
港、澳、台商投资企业	Enterprises With Funds from Hong Kong, Macao and Taiwan	4	4	563
港、澳、台商独资经营企业	Enterprises With Sole Funds from Hong Kong, Macao and Taiwan	4	4	563
外商投资企业	Foreign Funded Enterprises	5	9	1563
中外合资经营企业	Enterprises with Foreign Investment	4	4	648
外资企业	Enterprises with Sole Fund	1	5	915
住宿业	**Hotels**	**234**	**339**	**33805**
内资企业	Domestic-funded Enterprises	232	336	33266
国有企业	State-owned Enterprises	78	111	11698

16-3 续表 Continued

指　标	Item	法人企业数(个) Number of Corporate Enterprises (unit)	产业活动单位数(个) Number of Economic Active Unit (unit)	从业人员数(人) Engaged Persons (person)
集体企业	Collective-owned Enterprises	6	6	871
联营企业	Joint Ownership Enterprises	1	1	51
国有联营企业	State Joint Ownership Enterprises	1	1	51
有限责任公司	Limited Liability Corporations	64	97	11095
国有独资公司	State Sole Funded Corporations	6	6	722
其他有限责任公司	Other Limited Liability Corporations	58	91	10373
股份有限公司	Share-holding Corporations Ltd.	5	8	967
私营企业	Private Enterprises	73	108	7916
私营独资企业	Private-funded Enterprises	14	26	715
私营合伙企业	Private Partnership Enterprises	2	2	421
私营有限责任公司	Private Limited Liability Corporations	56	78	6535
私营股份有限公司	Private Share-holding Corporation Ltd.	1	2	245
其他企业	Other Enterprises	5	5	668
港、澳、台商投资企业	Enterprises With Funds from Hong Kong, Macao and Taiwan	1	1	26
合资经营企业（港或澳、台资）	Joint-venture Enterprises (Funds from Hong Kong, Macao and Taiwan)	1	1	26
外商投资企业	Foreign Funded Enterprises	1	2	513
中外合资经营企业	Enterprises with Foreign Investment		1	492
外资企业	Enterprises with Sole Fund	1	1	21
餐饮业	**Catering Services**	**75**	**171**	**12276**
内资企业	Domestic Funded Enterprises	74	146	11341
国有企业	State-owned Enterprises	11	18	1859
集体企业	Collective-owned Enterprises	1	1	52
有限责任公司	Limited Liability Corporations	16	30	2176
国有独资公司	State Sole Funded Enterprises	1	1	51
其他有限责任公司	Other Limited Liability Corporations	15	29	2125
股份有限公司	Share-holding Corporations Ltd.	1	1	129
私营企业	Private Enterprises	40	89	6594
私营独资企业	Private-funded Enterprises	6	6	498
私营合伙企业	Private Partnership Enterprises	2	2	239
私营有限责任公司	Private limited Liability Corporations	32	81	5857
其他企业	Others	5	7	531
外商投资企业	Foreign Funded Enterprises	1	25	935
外资企业	Enterprises With Sole Fund	1	25	935
按地区分	**By Region**			
乌鲁木齐市	Urumqi City	566	1531	74986
克拉玛依市	Karamay City	71	148	8241
吐鲁番地区	Turpan Administrative Offices	21	64	1895
哈密地区	Hami [Kumul] Administrative Offices	86	190	5280
昌吉回族自治州	Changji Hui Autonomous Prefecture	73	196	6003
伊犁哈萨克自治州	Ili Kazak Autonomous Prefecture	264	470	14968
伊犁州直属县(市)	Counties (Cities) Direct Under Ili Prefecture	189	246	10084
塔城地区	Tacheng [Tarbagatai] Administrative Offices	41	109	2541
阿勒泰地区	Altay Administrative Offices	34	115	2343
博尔塔拉蒙古自治州	Bortala Mongol Autonomous Prefecture	20	56	1379
巴音郭楞蒙古自治州	Bayangol Mongol Autonomous Prefecture	133	358	10464
阿克苏地区	Aksu Administrative Offices	159	553	9551
克孜勒苏柯尔克孜自治州	Kizilsu Kirgiz Autonomous Prefecture	13	13	817
喀什地区	Kashgar [Kaxgar] Administrative Offices	89	254	8878
和田地区	Hotan Administrative Offices	18	157	1588
生产建设兵团	Production and Construction Corps	184	665	16777

16-4 分行业、分地区限额以上批发和零售业商品销售额

Total Sales Values of Enterprises above Designated Size of Wholesale and Retail Trades by Sector and Region

单位：万元　　(2012 年)　　(10 000 yuan)

指　标	Item	销售总额 Total Sales Value	批　发 Wholesale Value	零　售 Retail Value
总　计	**Total**	**56848355**	**48463848**	**8384507**
批发业	**Wholesale Trade**	**49543512**	**47885242**	**1658270**
农、林、牧产品批发	Wholesale of Farm Produce and Livestock Products	7499519	7461236	38283
谷物、豆及薯类批发	Wholesale of Grain,Bean and Potato	559441	558245	1196
种子批发	Wholesale of Seed	290962	280158	10804
棉、麻批发	Wholesale of Cotton and Liner	6596821	6570538	26283
其他农牧产品批发	Wholesale of Other Farm Produce and Livestock Products	52295	52295	
食品、饮料及烟草制品批发	Wholesale of Food,Beverages and Tobaccos	3548757	3529892	18865
米、面制品及食用油批发	Wholesale of Rice, Flour and Edible Oil	333555	330427	3128
糕点、糖果及糖批发	Wholesale of Pastry,Candy and Sugar	37069	34688	2381
果品、蔬菜批发	Wholesale of Fruit and Vegetable	119684	116944	2740
肉、禽、蛋及水产品批发	Wholesale of Meat,Birds and Equatic Products	36455	36455	
盐及调味品批发	Wholesale of Salt and Condiment Flavoring Material	73898	73448	450
酒、饮料及茶叶批发	Wholesale of Soft Drink and Tea Leaf	79725	79725	
烟草制品批发	Wholesale of Tobaccos	2855100	2848269	6831
其他食品批发	Wholesale of Other Food	13271	9936	3335
纺织、服装及家庭用品批发	Wholesale of Textitle, Garments and Daily Consumer Articles	490416	477277	13139
纺织品、针织品及原料批发	Wholesale of Textile,Hosiery and Raw Material	107529	107529	
服装批发	Wholesale of Garment	120853	110131	10722
化妆品及卫生用品批发	Wholesale of Cosmetics and Health Aids	34850	32781	2069
家用电器批发	Wholesale of Other Covenience Goods	177283	176935	348
其他家庭用品批发	Wholesale of Culture, Sports Appliances and Equipments	49901	49901	
文化、体育用品及器材批发	Wholesale of Books	213446	192484	20962
图书批发	Wholesale of Textitle, Garments and Daily Consumer Articles	160538	147902	12636
首饰、工艺品及收藏品批发	Wholesale of wear、Jewellery、Handicraft、Collectim	6064	5982	82
其他文化用品批发	Wholesale of Other Culture Products	46844	38600	8244
医药及医疗器材批发	Wholesale of Medicines and Medical Appliances	672591	658386	14205
西药批发	Wholesale of Western Medicine	635864	622268	13596
中药批发	Wholesale of Chinese Medicinal Plant	30500	29891	609
医疗用品及器材批发	Wholesale of Medicine and Medical Appliances	6227	6227	
矿产品、建材及化工产品批发	Wholesale of Mineral Products, Building Material and Chemical Products	33655111	32300933	1354178
煤炭及制品批发	Wholesale of Coal and Related Products	601331	601331	
石油及制品批发	Wholesale of Petroleum and Related Products	25031259	23802548	1228711
金属及金属矿批发	Wholesale of Metal and Metal Materials	5029913	4909011	120902
建材批发	Wholesale of Building Materials	551788	549904	1884
化肥批发	Wholesale of Chemical Fertilizer	1763613	1760932	2681
农药批发	Wholesale of Pesticides	18444	18444	

16-4 续表 1 Continued

单位：万元 (10 000 yuan)

指 标	Item	销售总额 Total Sales Value	批 发 Wholesale Value	零 售 Retail Value
其他化工产品批发	Wholesale of Other Chemical Product	658763	658763	
机械设备、五金交电及电子产品批发	Wholesale of Machinery, Hardware and Electronic Equipments	3054523	2866755	187768
农业机械批发	Wholesale of Agriculture Machinery	183201	171448	11753
汽车批发	Wholesale of Motor Vehicles	675076	615889	59187
汽车零配件批发	Wholesale of Motor Vehicles and Parts	300801	222458	78343
摩托车及零配件批发	Wholesale of Motorcycles and Parts	11269	11269	
五金产品批发	Wholesale of Hardware	24974	24974	
电气设备批发	Wholesale of Electric Machinery	310261	310261	
计算机、软件及辅助设备批发	Wholesale of Computer, Software and Assistant Appliances	146238	126945	19293
通讯及广播电视设备批发	Wholesale of Communicating and Broadcasting Television Device	670989	670379	610
其他机械设备及电子产品批发	Wholesale of Other Mechanical Equipment and Electronic Products	731714	713132	18582
贸易经纪与代理	Trades Broker and Agency	88011	77173	10838
贸易代理	Trade Agency	88011	77173	10838
其他批发业	Wholesales of Others	321138	321106	32
再生物资回收与批发	Recovery and Wholesale of Regeneration Material	234412	234380	32
其他未列明的批发	Wholesale of Un-listed	86726	86726	
零售业	**Retail Trades**	**7304843**	**578606**	**6726237**
综合零售	Integrated Retail	1450843	9755	1441088
百货零售	Retail of General Merchandise	1057620	5197	1052423
超级市场零售	Retail of Supermarkets	392073	4558	387515
其他综合零售	Retail of Other Integrate	1150		1150
食品、饮料及烟草制品专门零售	Monopoly Retail of Foods, Beverages and Tobacco	17004	3447	13557
粮油零售	Retail of Grain and Oil	2254		2254
果品、蔬菜零售	Retail of Fruite and Vegetables	1652		1652
肉、禽、蛋及水产品零售	Retail of Meat,Poultry and Eggs	1816		1816
营养和保健品零售	Retail of Health Products	940		940
酒、饮料及茶叶零售	Retail of Soft Drink and Tea Leaf	5084	3447	1637
烟草制品零售	Retail of Tobaccos	5258		5258
纺织、服装及日用品专门零售	Monopoly Retail of Textile, Garments and Daily Consumer Articles	366436	17359	349077
服装零售	Retail of Garment	314538	6159	308379
化妆品及卫生用品零售	Retail of Cosmetics and Health Aids	5920		5920
钟表、眼镜零售	Retail of Timelceeper and Spectacle	12489	11200	1289
其他日用品零售	Retail of Other Covenience Goods	33489		33489
文化、体育用品及器材专门零售	Monopoly Retail of Cultural, Sports Goods And Apparatus	193526	5250	188276
文具用品零售	Retail of Stationery and Office Supplies	4894		4894
图书、报刊零售	Retail of Books,Newspapers	156241	332	155909
珠宝首饰零售	Retail of Jewelry	30792	4680	26112

16-4 续表 2 Continued

单位：万元 (10 000 yuan)

指　标	Item	销售总额 Total Sales Value	批　发 Wholesale Value	零　售 Retail Value
照相器材零售	Retail of Photographic Materials	1599	238	1361
医药及医疗器材专门零售	Monopoly Retail of Medicine and Medical-care Apparatus	788800	117246	671554
药品零售	Retail of Medcine	784389	113924	670465
医疗用品及器材零售	Wholesale of Medical Treatment and Equipment	4411	3322	1089
汽车、摩托车、燃料及零配件专门零售	Monopoly Retail of Car, Motor, Fuel and Parts as Well as Components	3758349	388502	3369847
汽车零售	Retail of Automobiles	2538640	179623	2359017
汽车零配件零售	Retail of Automobiles' Parts	7183		7183
摩托车及零配件零售	Retail of Motorcycle and Fittings	21211	1498	19713
机动车燃料零售	Retail of Auto Fuel	1191315	207381	983934
家用电器及电子产品专门零售	Monopoly Retail of House Hold Electric Appliancesound Electronic Products	417870	35947	381923
家用视听设备零售	Retail of Home audio-visual equipment	221623	19562	202061
日用家电设备零售	Retail of Household Electuic Appliances	87031	4198	82833
计算机、软件及辅助设备零售	Retail of Cumputers,Software and Office Appliances	71158	6341	64817
通信设备零售	Retail of Telecommunication Equipments	38058	5846	32212
五金、家具及室内装修材料专门零售	Monopoly Retail of Hardware, Furniture and Indoor Decorating Material	287707		287707
五金零售	Retail of Hardware	9744		9744
家具零售	Retail of Living Equipment	277963		277963
货摊、无店铺及其他零售业	Non-shop and other Retail	24308	1100	23208
邮购及电视、电话零售	Distribution of Post and E-commerce	553		553
生活用燃料零售	Retail of Life Fuels	23755	1100	22655
按地区分	**By Region**			
乌鲁木齐市	Urumqi City	33412352	28454949	4957403
克拉玛依市	Karamay City	1348368	1054913	293455
吐鲁番地区	Turpan Administrative Offices	419559	329686	89873
哈密地区	Hami [Kumul] Administrative Offices	1192032	924668	267364
昌吉回族自治州	Changji Hui Autonomous Prefecture	1264256	973176	291080
伊犁哈萨克自治州	Ili Kazak Autonomous Prefecture	4429819	3845015	584804
伊犁州直属县(市)	Counties (Cities) Direct Under Ili Prefecture	3372429	2994555	377874
塔城地区	Tacheng [Tarbagatai] Administrative Offices	734341	577034	157307
阿勒泰地区	Altay Administrative Offices	323049	273426	49623
博尔塔拉蒙古自治州	Bortala Mongol Autonomous Prefecture	1094949	1064561	30388
巴音郭楞蒙古自治州	Bayangol Mongol Autonomous Prefecture	1859171	1445981	413190
阿克苏地区	Aksu Administrative Offices	2351188	1860395	490793
克孜勒苏柯尔克孜自治州	Kizilsu Kirgiz Autonomous Prefecture	47216	42045	5171
喀什地区	Kashgar [Kaxgar] Administrative Offices	1780951	1410399	370552
和田地区	Hotan Administrative Offices	248605	223314	25291
生产建设兵团	Production and Construction Group	7399889	6834746	565143

16-5 限额以上餐饮企业经营情况
Operations of Enterprises above Designated Size of Catering Services

单位：万元　　(2012 年)　　(10 000 yuan)

项　目	Item	法人企业数(个) Number of Corporation Enterprises (unit)	产业活动单位数(个) Number of Establishments (unit)	营业额 Business Revenue	#商品零售额 Retail Sales of Commodities
总　计	**Total**	**75**	**171**	**180723**	**157523**
正餐服务	Dinner	71	98	125833	103286
快餐服务	Snack	4	73	54890	54237
按地区分	**By Region**				
乌鲁木齐市	Urumqi City	24	96	114635	106981
克拉玛依市	Karamay City	1	13	7389	7094
吐鲁番地区	Turpan Administrative Offices	1	1	334	187
哈密地区	Hami [Kumul] Administrative Offices	1	1	247	126
昌吉回族自治州	Changji Hui Autonomous Prefecture	2	4	1846	1360
伊犁哈萨克自治州	Ili Kazak Autonomous Prefecture	20	24	24849	16344
伊犁州直属县(市)	Counties (Cities) Direct Under Ili Prefecture	20	23	24614	16190
塔城地区	Tacheng [Tarbagatai] Administrative Offices		1	235	154
巴音郭楞蒙古自治州	Bayangol Mongol Autonomous Prefecture	15	16	17907	14822
阿克苏地区	Aksu Administrative Offices	3	4	3536	2919
喀什地区	Kashgar [Kaxgar] Administrative Offices	2	2	1570	1108
生产建设兵团	Production and Construction Group	6	10	8410	6582

16-6 限额以上住宿企业经营情况
Operation of Enterprises above Designated Size in Hotels Services

单位：万元 (2012 年) (10 000 yuan)

项　　目	Item	营业额 Business Revenue	客房收入 From Hotel Rooms	餐费收入 From Meals
总　计	**Total**	**528395**	**245151**	**221033**
按星级分	**By Stars**			
五　星	Five-Star	140047	49633	66271
四　星	Four-Star	155928	68915	66977
三　星	Three-Star	151044	78504	60095
二　星	Two-Star	24790	16487	6851
一　星	One-Star	1614	680	825
其　他	Others	54972	30932	20014
按行业分	**By Sector**			
旅游饭店	Tourist Hotel	480481	216991	204564
一般旅馆	Fonda	47222	27705	16232
其他住宿服务	Others	692	455	237
按地区分	**By Region**			
乌鲁木齐市	Urumqi City	301304	127404	125433
克拉玛依市	Karamay City	23066	9150	12604
吐鲁番地区	Turpan Administrative Offices	5412	3418	1891
哈密地区	Hami [Kumul] Administrative Offices	20283	8084	11481
昌吉回族自治州	Changji Hui Autonomous Prefecture	13582	5776	6471
伊犁哈萨克自治州	Ili Kazak Autonomous Prefecture	48271	26278	19307
伊犁州直属县(市)	Counties (Cities) Direct Under Ili Prefecture	21742	12496	7680
塔城地区	Tacheng [Tarbagatai] Administrative Offices	7016	2876	3659
阿勒泰地区	Altay Administrative Offices	19513	10906	7968
博尔塔拉蒙古自治州	Bortala Mongol Autonomous Prefecture	3875	1606	2061
巴音郭楞蒙古自治州	Bayangol Mongol Autonomous Prefecture	25356	12239	11434
阿克苏地区	Aksu Administrative Offices	14403	9609	4483
克孜勒苏柯尔克孜自治州	Kizilsu Kirgiz Autonomous Prefecture	2049	1140	830
喀什地区	Kashgar [Kaxgar] Administrative Offices	13962	7295	5472
和田地区	Hotan Administrative Offices	2883	1997	722
生产建设兵团	Production and Construction Group	53949	31155	18844

16-6 续表 Continued

单位：万元 (10 000 yuan)

项　目	Item	商品销售收入 From Commodities	其他收入 Others	床位数（张） Number of beds (unit)
总　计	**Total**	**10938**	**51273**	**77246**
按星级分	**Classified by Star**			
五　星	Five-Star	5985	18158	6323
四　星	Four-Star	1593	18443	21311
三　星	Three-Star	2425	10020	31482
二　星	Two-Star	522	930	6086
一　星	One-Star	98	11	309
其　他	Others	315	3711	11735
按行业分	**By Sector**			
旅游饭店	Tourist Hotel	10527	48399	67996
一般旅馆	Fonda	411	2874	9085
其他住宿服务	Others			165
按地区分	**By Region**			
乌鲁木齐市	Urumqi City	7927	40540	26821
克拉玛依市	Karamay City	82	1230	2932
吐鲁番地区	Turpan Administrative Offices		103	1550
哈密地区	Hami [Kumul] Administrative Offices	213	505	2793
昌吉回族自治州	Changji Hui Autonomous Prefecture	86	1249	2295
伊犁哈萨克自治州	Ili Kazak Autonomous Prefecture	860	1826	13043
伊犁州直属县(市)	Counties (Cities) Direct Under Ili Prefecture	181	1385	5450
塔城地区	Tacheng [Tarbagatai] Administrative Offices	439	42	1571
阿勒泰地区	Altay Administrative Offices	240	399	6022
博尔塔拉蒙古自治州	Bortala Mongol Autonomous Prefecture	208		611
巴音郭楞蒙古自治州	Bayangol Mongol Autonomous Prefecture	631	1052	4917
阿克苏地区	Aksu Administrative Offices	103	208	4350
克孜勒苏柯尔克孜自治州	Kizilsu Kirgiz Autonomous Prefecture		79	269
喀什地区	Kashgar [Kaxgar] Administrative Offices	82	1113	5957
和田地区	Hotan Administrative Offices	79	85	1111
生产建设兵团	Production and Construction Group	667	3283	10597

16-7 各地、州、市、县(市)社会消费品零售总额

Total Retail Sales of Consumer Goods by Prefecture, Autonomous Prefecture, City and County

单位：万元 (2012 年) (10 000 yuan)

地　　区	Region	社会消费品零售总额 Total Retail Sales of Consumer Goods	城　镇 City	城　区 County	乡　村 Under County Level
总　计	**Total**	**17989877**	**16422417**	**14066744**	**1567460**
乌鲁木齐市	**Urumqi City**	**7396900**	**7393122**	**7393122**	**3778**
#乌鲁木齐县	Urumqi County	61327	57627	57627	3700
克拉玛依市	**Karamay City**	**480039**	**477677**	**477677**	**2362**
吐鲁番地区	**TurpanAdministrative Offices**	**294015**	**216166**	**127233**	**77849**
吐鲁番市	Turpan City	164053	141469	127233	22584
鄯善县	Shanshan [piqan]County	96007	58785		37222
托克逊县	Toksun County	33955	15912		18043
哈密地区	**Hami [kumul]Administrative Offices**	**554516**	**525347**	**477281**	**29169**
哈密市	Hami [kumul]City	495812	479825	477281	15987
巴里坤哈萨克自治县	Barkol KazakAutonomous County	44280	31475		12805
伊吾县	Yiwu [Araturuk]County	14424	14047		377
昌吉回族自治州	**Changji Hui Autonomous Prefecture**	**1557170**	**1436896**	**1371810**	**120274**
昌吉市	Changji City	647122	613948	570195	33174
阜康市	Fukang City	214813	197236	175903	17577
呼图壁县	Hutubi County	182619	164357	164357	18262
玛纳斯县	Manas County	200750	180675	180675	20075
奇台县	Qitai County	175966	158369	158369	17597
吉木萨尔县	Jimsar County	84445	76001	76001	8444
木垒哈萨克自治县	Mori Kazak Autonomous County	51455	46310	46310	5145
伊犁哈萨克自治州	**Ili Kazak Autonomous Prefecture**	**2320490**	**1879339**	**1235884**	**441151**
伊犁州直属县(市)	**Counties (Cities) Direct Under Ili Prefecture**	**1363087**	**1123204**	**942456**	**239883**
伊宁市	Yining [Gulja]City	512532	491015	491015	21517
奎屯市	Kuytun City	186019	186019	186019	
伊宁县	Yining [Gulja]County	104641	74379	63048	30262
察布查尔锡伯自治县	Qapqal Xibe Autonomous County	23096	14519	10776	8577
霍城县	Huocheng [korgas]County	150053	110455	63938	39598
巩留县	Gongliu [Tokkuzlara]County	44544	30631	9455	13913
新源县	Xinyuan [kunes]County	178596	97407	49435	81189
昭苏县	Zhaosu [mongolkure]County	39569	29439	16410	10130
特克斯县	Tekes County	68579	44221	31189	24358
尼勒克县	Nilka County	55458	45119	21171	10339
塔城地区	**Tacheng [Tarbagatai] Administrative Offices**	**525214**	**371028**	**164080**	**154186**
塔城市	Tacheng [Qoqek] City	145715	105242	100697	40473
乌苏市	Usu City	104592	84869	46470	19723
额敏县	Emin [Dorbiljin] County	96444	53406		43038
沙湾县	Shawan County	116328	87068	16826	29260
裕民县	Yumin [Qagantokay] County	24183	16388		7795
和布克赛尔蒙古自治县	Hoboksar Mongol Autonomous County	20108	12361	87	7747
托里县	Toli County	17844	11694		6150
阿勒泰地区	**Altay Administrative Offices**	**432189**	**385107**	**129348**	**47082**
阿勒泰市	Altay City	182065	169516	129348	12549
布尔津县	Burqin County	91636	80412		11224
富蕴县	Fuyun [Koktokay] County	46939	39093		7846
福海县	Fuhai [Burultokay] County	44658	39476		5182
哈巴河县	Habahe [Kaba] County	35875	31643		4232
青河县	Qinghe [Qinggil] County	22300	18441		3859
吉木乃县	Jeminay County	8716	6526		2190

16-7 续表 Continued

单位：万元 (10 000 yuan)

地　区	Region	社会消费品零售总额 Total Retail Sales of Consumer Goods	城　镇 City	城　区 County	乡　村 Under County Level
博尔塔拉蒙古自治州	**Bortala Mongol Autonomous Prefecture**	**247064**	**212808**	**128989**	**34256**
博乐市	Bole [Bortala] City	183538	171048	128989	12490
精河县	Jinghe [Jing] County	44119	28073		16046
温泉县	Wenquan [Araxang] County	19407	13687		5720
巴音郭楞蒙古自治州	**Bayangol Mongol Autonomous Prefecture**	**785634**	**670681**	**481375**	**114953**
库尔勒市	Korla City	597768	512646	481375	85122
轮台县	Luntai [Bugur] County	34703	27994		6709
尉犁县	Yuli [Lopnur] County	15849	12535		3314
若羌县	Ruoqiang [Qarkilik] County	6820	5780		1040
且末县	Qiemo [Qarqan] County	8297	7081		1216
焉耆回族自治县	Yanqi Hui Autonomous County	54627	50685		3942
和静县	Hejing County	31303	24426		6877
和硕县	Hoxud County	14476	11866		2610
博湖县	Bohu [Bagrax] County	21791	17668		4123
阿克苏地区	**Aksu Administrative Offices**	**856240**	**730214**	**421696**	**126026**
阿克苏市	Aksu City	475204	458973	385188	16231
温宿县	Wensu [Onsu] County	51462	39412	2652	12050
库车县	Kuqa County	128367	93874	22187	34493
沙雅县	Xayar County	68205	52291	7673	15914
新和县	Xinhe [Toksu] County	29131	20573		8558
拜城县	Baicheng [Bay] County	52702	33080	3996	19622
乌什县	Wushi [Uxturpan] County	12713	5485		7228
阿瓦提县	Awat County	34653	25434		9219
柯坪县	Kalpin County	3803	1092		2711
克孜勒苏柯尔克孜自治州	**Kizilsu Kirgiz Autonomous Prefecture**	**116810**	**106666**	**104826**	**10144**
阿图什市	Artux City	74137	71057	71057	3080
阿克陶县	Akto County	23963	18999	17250	4964
阿合奇县	Akqi County	8270	7880	7880	390
乌恰县	Wuqia [Ulugqat] County	10440	8730	8639	1710
喀什地区	**Kashgar [Kaxgar] Administrative Offices**	**1104713**	**893227**	**466698**	**211486**
喀什市	Kashgar [Kaxgar] City	515000	488167	455480	26833
疏附县	Shufu County	12046	6234		5812
疏勒县	Shule County	54352	47231	10504	7121
英吉沙县	Yengisar County	34100	20135		13965
泽普县	Zepu [Poskam] County	37400	26248		11152
莎车县	Shache [Yarkant] County	106371	72144	500	34227
叶城县	Yecheng [Kagilik] County	88535	54138		34397
麦盖提县	Makit County	72010	49607		22403
岳普湖县	Yopurga County	24828	17658		7170
伽师县	Jiashi [Payzawat] County	55600	36228		19372
巴楚县	Bachu [Maralbexi] County	93000	66297	214	26703
塔什库尔干塔吉克自治县	Taxkorgan Tajik Autonomous County	11471	9140		2331
和田地区	**Hotan Administrative Offices**	**256300**	**189730**	**131176**	**66570**
和田市	Hotan City	124646	107045	92345	17601
和田县	Hotan County	16120	323		15797
墨玉县	Moyu [Karakax] County	31712	22121	15992	9591
皮山县	Pishan [Guma] County	16566	10604		5962
洛浦县	Lop County	18541	13782	7917	4759
策勒县	Qira County	18600	12131		6469
于田县	Yutian [Keriya] County	22129	17180	14045	4949
民丰县	Minfeng [Niya] County	7986	6544	877	1442
生产建设兵团	**Xinjiang Production andConstruction Group**	**2962303**	**2660200**	**1570965**	**302103**

16-8 各地、州、市、县(市)社会消费品零售总额(按行业分)

Total Retail Sales of Consumer Goods by Sector and Prefecture, Autonomous Prefecture, City and County

单位：万元 (2012 年) (10 000 yuan)

地　区	Region	社会消费品零售总额 Total Retail Sales of Consumer Goods	批发和零售业 Wholesale And Retail Sale Trades	住宿和餐饮业 Hotels and Catering Services
总　计	**Total**	**17989877**	**15533734**	**2456143**
乌鲁木齐市	**Urumqi City**	**7396900**	**6529518**	**867382**
#乌鲁木齐县	Urumqi County	61327	12816	48511
克拉玛依市	**Karamay City**	**480039**	**417109**	**62930**
吐鲁番地区	**TurpanAdministrative Offices**	**294015**	**261242**	**32773**
吐鲁番市	Turpan City	164053	151032	13021
鄯善县	Shanshan [piqan]County	96007	82522	13485
托克逊县	Toksun County	33955	27688	6267
哈密地区	**Hami [kumul]Administrative Offices**	**554516**	**449216**	**105300**
哈密市	Hami [kumul]City	495812	406669	89143
巴里坤哈萨克自治县	Barkol KazakAutonomous County	44280	33164	11116
伊吾县	Yiwu [Araturuk]County	14424	9383	5041
昌吉回族自治州	**Changji Hui Autonomous Prefecture**	**1557170**	**1284904**	**272266**
昌吉市	Changji City	647122	536450	110672
阜康市	Fukang City	214813	173286	41527
呼图壁县	Hutubi County	182619	148799	33820
玛纳斯县	Manas County	200750	166399	34351
奇台县	Qitai County	175966	145786	30180
吉木萨尔县	Jimsar County	84445	70881	13564
木垒哈萨克自治县	Mori Kazak Autonomous County	51455	43303	8152
伊犁哈萨克自治州	**Ili Kazak Autonomous Prefecture**	**2320490**	**1950604**	**369886**
伊犁州直属县(市)	**Counties (Cities) Direct Under Ili Prefecture**	**1363087**	**1166244**	**196843**
伊宁市	Yining [Gulja]City	512532	447771	64761
奎屯市	Kuytun City	186019	167245	18774
伊宁县	Yining [Gulja]County	104641	90462	14179
察布查尔锡伯自治县	Qapqal Xibe Autonomous County	23096	18653	4443
霍城县	Huocheng [korgas]County	150053	119297	30756
巩留县	Gongliu [Tokkuzlara]County	44544	37682	6862
新源县	Xinyuan [kunes]County	178596	151469	27127
昭苏县	Zhaosu [mongolkure]County	39569	34951	4618
特克斯县	Tekes County	68579	60812	7767
尼勒克县	Nilka County	55458	37902	17556
塔城地区	**Tacheng [Tarbagatai] Administrative Offices**	**525214**	**439470**	**85744**
塔城市	Tacheng [Qoqek] City	145715	124070	21645
乌苏市	Usu City	104592	84200	20392
额敏县	Emin [Dorbiljin] County	96444	87335	9109
沙湾县	Shawan County	116328	96127	20201
裕民县	Yumin [Qagantokay] County	24183	20354	3829
和布克赛尔蒙古自治县	Hoboksar Mongol Autonomous County	20108	15998	4110
托里县	Toli County	17844	11386	6458
阿勒泰地区	**Altay Administrative Offices**	**432189**	**344890**	**87299**
阿勒泰市	Altay City	182065	150646	31419
布尔津县	Burqin County	91636	59026	32610
富蕴县	Fuyun [Koktokay] County	46939	39032	7907
福海县	Fuhai [Burultokay] County	44658	38497	6161
哈巴河县	Habahe [Kaba] County	35875	31679	4196
青河县	Qinghe [Qinggil] County	22300	18995	3305
吉木乃县	Jeminay County	8716	7015	1701

16-8 续表 Continued

单位：万元 (10 000 yuan)

地区	Region	社会消费品零售总额 Total Retail Sales of Consumer Goods	批发和零售业 Wholesale And Retail Sale Trades	住宿和餐饮业 Hotels and Catering Services
博尔塔拉蒙古自治州	**Bortala Mongol Autonomous Prefecture**	**247064**	**209639**	**37425**
博乐市	Bole [Bortala] City	183538	162979	20559
精河县	Jinghe [Jing] County	44119	30162	13957
温泉县	Wenquan [Araxang] County	19407	16498	2909
巴音郭楞蒙古自治州	**Bayangol Mongol Autonomous Prefecture**	**785634**	**691384**	**94250**
库尔勒市	Korla City	597768	538600	59168
轮台县	Luntai [Bugur] County	34703	27075	7628
尉犁县	Yuli [Lopnur] County	15849	11295	4554
若羌县	Ruoqiang [Qarkilik] County	6820	4728	2092
且末县	Qiemo [Qarqan] County	8297	5842	2455
焉耆回族自治县	Yanqi Hui Autonomous County	54627	50460	4167
和静县	Hejing County	31303	25737	5566
和硕县	Hoxud County	14476	9370	5106
博湖县	Bohu [Bagrax] County	21791	18277	3514
阿克苏地区	**Aksu Administrative Offices**	**856240**	**772747**	**83493**
阿克苏市	Aksu City	475204	462803	12401
温宿县	Wensu [Onsu] County	51462	47718	3744
库车县	Kuqa County	128367	99222	29145
沙雅县	Xayar County	68205	54604	13601
新和县	Xinhe [Toksu] County	29131	23304	5827
拜城县	Baicheng [Bay] County	52702	45516	7186
乌什县	Wushi [Uxturpan] County	12713	10889	1824
阿瓦提县	Awat County	34653	25492	9161
柯坪县	Kalpin County	3803	3199	604
克孜勒苏柯尔克孜自治州	**Kizilsu Kirgiz Autonomous Prefecture**	**116810**	**102684**	**14126**
阿图什市	Artux City	74137	68052	6085
阿克陶县	Akto County	23963	20114	3849
阿合奇县	Akqi County	8270	7036	1234
乌恰县	Wuqia [Ulugqat] County	10440	7482	2958
喀什地区	**Kashgar [Kaxgar] Administrative Offices**	**1104713**	**962565**	**142148**
喀什市	Kashgar [Kaxgar] City	515000	491355	23645
疏附县	Shufu County	12046	9342	2704
疏勒县	Shule County	54352	48174	6178
英吉沙县	Yengisar County	34100	27055	7045
泽普县	Zepu [Poskam] County	37400	31645	5755
莎车县	Shache [Yarkant] County	106371	91962	14409
叶城县	Yecheng [Kagilik] County	88535	70424	18111
麦盖提县	Makit County	72010	57396	14614
岳普湖县	Yopurga County	24828	16861	7967
伽师县	Jiashi [Payzawat] County	55600	39843	15757
巴楚县	Bachu [Maralbexi] County	93000	67241	25759
塔什库尔干塔吉克自治县	Taxkorgan Tajik Autonomous County	11471	11267	204
和田地区	**Hotan Administrative Offices**	**256300**	**223629**	**32671**
和田市	Hotan City	124646	112819	11827
和田县	Hotan County	16120	12214	3906
墨玉县	Moyu [Karakax] County	31712	28761	2951
皮山县	Pishan [Guma] County	16566	15615	951
洛浦县	Lop County	18541	15554	2987
策勒县	Qira County	18600	14697	3903
于田县	Yutian [Keriya] County	22129	17154	4975
民丰县	Minfeng [Niya] County	7986	6815	1171
生产建设兵团	**Production and Construction Group**	**2962303**	**2422143**	**540160**

16-9 限额以上批发企业资产及负债情况

Assets and Liabilities of Enterprises above Designated Size of Wholesale Trades

单位：万元　　(2012 年)　　(10 000 yuan)

指标	Item	资产合计 Total Assets	#流动资产 Working Capitals	#固定资产 Fixed Assets	负债合计 Total Liabilities
总　计	**Total**	**18060080**	**14113408**	**1325397**	**14256741**
按登记注册类型分	**By Type of Registration**				
内资企业	Domestic Funded Enterprises	18060080	14113408	1325397	14256741
国有企业	State-owned Enterprises	6005405	4793075	469000	4924010
集体企业	Collective-owned Enterprises	790048	688502	55523	661684
股份合作企业	Cooperative Enterprises	44140	40568	3381	35096
联营企业	Joint Ownership Enterprises	883	645	215	298
集体联营企业	Collective Joint Ownership Enterprises	883	645	215	298
有限责任公司	Limited Liability Corporations	5306239	4306809	385357	4182842
国有独资公司	State Sole Funded Corporations	639746	495777	57588	479377
其他有限责任公司	Other Limited Liability Corporations	4666493	3811032	327769	3703465
股份有限公司	Share-holding Corporations Ltd.	2634478	1577546	147411	2006566
私营企业	Private Enterprises	3192678	2626495	263334	2381235
私营独资企业	Private-funded Enterprises	3138	3046	74	1866
私营合伙企业	Private Partnership Enterprises	514	452	61	556
私营有限责任公司	Private Limited Liability Corporations	2974082	2465504	222533	2215845
私营股份有限公司	Private Share-holding Corporation Ltd.	214944	157493	40666	162968
其他企业	Other Enterprises	86209	79768	1176	65010
港、澳、台商投资企业	Enterprises With Funds from Hong Kong, Macao and Taiwan	4630	3624	974	-18
港、澳、台商独资经营企业	Enterprises with Sole Funds from Hong Kong, Macao and Taiwan	4630	3624	974	-18
外商投资企业	Foreign Funded Enterprises	63322	50770	9425	53665
中外合资经营企业	Enterprises with Foreign Investment	10876	9397	948	2546
外资企业	Enterprises with Sole Funds	52446	41373	8477	51119
按批发行业小类分组	**By Sector of Wholesale**				
农、林、牧产品批发	Wholesale of Farm Produce and Livestock Products	6512660	5670596	474002	5634815
谷物、豆及薯类批发	Wholesale of Grain,Bean and Potato	559760	439234	77095	490648
种子批发	Wholesale of Fodder	371682	246680	66788	196495
棉、麻批发	Wholesale of Cotton and Liner	5517037	4927075	327244	4900924
其他农牧产品批发	Wholesale of Other Farm Produce and Livestoclc Products	64181	57607	2875	46748
食品、饮料及烟草制品批发	Wholesale of Food,Beverages and Tobaccos	1600829	1223109	168563	814514
米、面制品及食用油批发	Wholesale of Rice, Flour and Edible Oil	318242	265920	33060	269343
糕点、糖果及糖批发	Wholesale of Pastry,Candy and Sugar	10276	7730	237	5796
果品、蔬菜批发业	Wholesale of Fruit and Vegetable	294766	159131	65890	195561
肉、禽、蛋及水产品批发	Wholesale of Meat,Birds and Equatic Products	9965	3545	768	7038
盐及调味品批发	Wholesale of Salt and Condiment Flavoring Material	88631	47093	8363	54944
酒、饮料及茶叶批发	Wholesale of Soft Drink and Tea Leaf	46515	36844	3155	43859
烟草制品批发	Wholesale of Tobaccos	802873	685372	51751	217191
其他食品批发	Wholesale of Other Food	29561	17474	5339	20782
纺织、服装及日用品批发	Wholesale of Textitle, Garments and Daily Consumer Articles	140179	125216	9503	124216
纺织品、针织品及原料批发	Wholesale of Textile,Hosiery and Raw Material	31455	30925	244	28180
服装批发	Wholesale of Garment	45733	42808	609	37750
化妆品及卫生用品批发	Wholesale of Cosmetics and Health Aids	11163	9236	1452	10169
家用电器批发	Wholesale of Household Elictric Appliances	32244	24898	5625	32103
其他家庭用品批发	Wholesale of Household Goods	19584	17349	1573	16014
文化、体育用品及器材批发	Wholesale of Culture, Sports Goods and Apparatus	136006	96010	21838	85811
图书批发	Wholesale of Books	102804	67555	19202	56770

16-9 续表 Continued

单位：万元 (10 000 yuan)

指 标	Item	资产合计 Total Assets	#流动资产 Working Capitals	#固定资产 Fixed Assets	负债合计 Total Liabilities
首饰、工艺品及收藏品批发	Wholesale of wear、Jewellery、Handicraft、Collectim	6334	5321	1013	5511
其他文化用品批发	Wholesale of Other Culture Products	26868	23134	1623	23530
医药及医疗器械批发	Wholesale of Medicines and Medical Appliances	326729	273404	36643	261214
西药批发	Wholesale of Western Medicine	303518	251958	35281	241228
中药批发	Wholesale of Chinese Medicinal Plant and Chinese Patent Medicine	18730	17199	1175	16892
医疗用品及器材批发	Wholesale of Medicine and Medical Appliances	4481	4247	187	3094
矿产品、建材及化工产品批发	Wholesale of Mineral Products, Building Material and Chemical Products	7796985	5428725	530861	6179837
煤炭及制品批发	Wholesale of Coal and Related Products	1694641	936721	25470	746044
石油及制品批发	Wholesale of Petroleum and Related Products	3189056	1973262	416978	3070423
金属及金属矿批发	Wholesale of Metal and Metal Materials	1420652	1193776	25961	1124767
建材批发	Wholesale of Building Materials	196728	181295	4089	158959
化肥批发	Wholesale of Fertilizer	1078191	950829	49058	911085
农药批发	Wholesale of Pesticides	13990	10897	1653	9074
其他化工产品批发	Wholesale of Other Chemical Product	203727	181945	7652	159485
机械设备、五金交电及电子产品批发	Wholesale of Machinery, Hardware and Electronic Equipments	1454256	1235615	78593	1085248
农业机械批发	Wholesale of Agriculture Machinery	144316	116033	17924	97558
汽车批发	Wholesale of Motor Vehicles, Motorcycles and Parts	424759	389477	15057	325803
汽车零配件批发	Retail of Automobiles' Parts	156972	127248	8780	93739
摩托车及零配件批发	Retail of Motorcycle and Fittings	3604	3561	43	2667
五金产品批发	Wholesale of Hardware and Electronic Equipment	14844	12365	764	10337
电气设备批发	Wholesale of Household Electrical Appliances	126868	116318	7329	111293
计算机、软件及辅助设备批发	Wholesale of Computer, Software and Accessory Equipment	42303	38108	2191	25468
通讯及广播电视设备批发	Wholesale of Communicating and Broadcasting Television Device	21644	19494	373	17232
其他机械设备及电子产品批发	Wholesale of Other Mechanical Equipment and Electromic Products	518946	413011	26132	401151
贸易经纪与代理	Trades Broker and Agent	46277	37260	6126	33451
贸易代理	Trades Broker and Agency	46257	37250	6115	33418
其他贸易经纪与代理	Other Trade Broker and Agency	20	10	11	33
其他批发业	Wholesales of Others	114111	77867	9667	91282
再生物资回收与批发业	Recovery and Wholesale of Regeneration Material	90172	62019	6281	76098
其他未列明的批发业	Wholesale of Un-listed	23939	15848	3386	15184
按地区分	**By Region**				
乌鲁木齐市	Urumqi City	7576335	6020542	318217	5195006
克拉玛依市	Karamay City	703189	172728	86775	346309
吐鲁番地区	Turpan Administrative Offices	99456	75399	17397	72298
哈密地区	Hami [Kumul] Administrative Offices	286472	230491	33592	221858
昌吉回族自治州	Changji Hui Autonomous Prefecture	545989	392013	71789	566690
伊犁哈萨克自治州	Ili Kazak Autonomous Prefecture	1124576	804706	99727	1146829
伊犁州直属县(市)	Counties (Cities) Direct Under Ili Prefecture	581055	445231	59710	583786
塔城地区	Tacheng [Tarbagatai] Administrative Offices	494320	331078	22806	420289
阿勒泰地区	Altay Administrative Offices	49201	28397	17211	142754
博尔塔拉蒙古自治州	Bortala Mongol Autonomous Prefecture	204434	171196	14153	126998
巴音郭楞蒙古自治州	Bayangol Mongol Autonomous Prefecture	702006	495423	137690	551977
阿克苏地区	Aksu Administrative Offices	1152270	950056	125331	1133516
克孜勒苏柯尔克孜自治州	Kizilsu Kirgiz Autonomous Prefecture	36284	31002	3036	25046
喀什地区	Kashgar [Kaxgar] Administrative Offices	750556	608748	122819	623637
和田地区	Hotan Administrative Offices	96477	23331	17361	81208
生产建设兵团	Production and Construction Group	4849988	4192167	287909	4219016

16-10 限额以上零售企业资产及负债情况
Assets and Liabilities of Enterprises above Designated Size of Retail Trades

单位：万元 (2012 年) (10 000 yuan)

指 标	Item	资产合计 Total Asset	#流动资产 Working Capitals	#固定资产 Fixed Asset	负债合计 Total Liabilities
总 计	**Total**	**3524670**	**2413706**	**557840**	**2773465**
按登记注册类型分	**By Status of Registration**				
内资企业	Domestic funded Enterprises	3366406	2287770	534135	2665423
国有企业	State-owned Enterprises	207470	109704	53084	104160
集体企业	Collective-owned Enterprises	4181	2910	484	3353
股份合作企业	Share-holding Cooperative Enterprises	1404	630	567	710
有限责任公司	Limited Liability Corporations	1025595	786509	125337	693471
国有独资公司	State Sole Funded Corporations	13689	8114	1672	8422
其他有限责任公司	Other Limited Liability Corporations	1011906	778395	123665	685049
股份有限公司	Share-holding Corporations Ltd.	629910	228102	153560	765809
私营企业	Private Enterprises	1488684	1152981	200057	1090388
私营独资企业	Private-funded Enterprises	41770	35245	2471	36777
私营有限责任公司	Private Limited Liability Corporations	1446806	1117637	197577	1053409
私营股份有限公司	Private Share-holding Corporation Ltd.	108	99	9	202
其他企业	Others	9162	6934	1046	7532
港、澳、台投资企业	Enterprises With Funds from Hong Kong, Macao and Taiwan	64066	49738	8220	45612
港、澳、台商独资经营企业	Enterprises with Sole Funds from Hong Kong, Macao and Taiwan	64066	49738	8220	45612
外商投资企业	Foreign Funded Enterprises	94198	76198	15485	62430
中外合资经营企业	Enterprises with Foreign Investment	66872	51427	13411	47528
外资企业	Enterprises with Sole Fund	27326	24771	2074	14902
按零售行业小类分组	**By Sector of Retail**				
综合零售	Integrated Retail	1019071	543498	218520	799775
百货零售	Retail of Merchandile	823344	393954	190474	651872
超级市场零售	Retail of Supermarket	194882	148869	27876	147649
其他综合零售	Retail of other integrate	845	675	170	254
食品、饮料及烟草制品专门零售	Monopoly Retail of Foods, Beverages and Tobacco	20970	14192	2480	13499
粮油零售	Retail of Grain and Oil	4239	3654	577	4558
果品、蔬菜零售	Retail of Fruit and Vegetables	4016	3080	620	1231
肉、禽、蛋及水产品零售	Retail of Meat,Poultry and Eggs	3461	2911	549	1689
酒、饮料及茶叶零售	Retail of Soft Drink and Tea Leaf	2808	2239	330	2738
烟草制品零售	Retail of Tobauos	6446	2308	404	3283
纺织、服装及日用品专门零售	Monopoly Retail of Textile, Garments and Daily Consumer Articles	175584	103079	35061	164660
服装零售	Garment Retail	164630	93152	34914	154821
钟表、眼镜零售	Retail of Timekeeper and Spectacle	9793	8855	58	8767
其他日用品零售	Retail of Other Covenience Goods	1161	1072	89	1072
文化、体育用品及器材专门零售业	Monopoly Retail of Cultural, Sports Appliances And Equipments	213836	128447	45534	94762
文具用品零售	Retail of Stationery and Office Supplies	2465	2429	36	1335
图书、报刊零售	Retail of Books	153982	70700	44530	72969

16-10 续表 Continued

单位：万元 (10 000 yuan)

指 标	Item	资产合计 Total Assets	#流动资产 Working Capitals	#固定资产 Fixed Assets	负债合计 Total Liabilities
珠宝首饰零售	Retail of Jewelry	56841	54796	965	20051
照相器材零售	Retail of Photographic Materials	548	522	3	407
医药及医疗器材专门零售	Monopoly Retail of Medicine and Medical-care Apparatus	467806	414684	19768	295442
药品零售	Retail of Medcine	465628	412613	19666	293754
医疗用品及器材零售	Wholesale of Medical Treatment and Equipment	2178	2071	102	1688
汽车、摩托车、燃料及零配件专门零售	Monopoly Retail of Car, Motor, Fuel and Parts as Well as Components	1203202	877704	187805	1184231
汽车零售	Retail of Car	1036051	806214	135343	783736
汽车零配件零售	Retail of Automobiles' Accessories	5282	4193	535	3895
摩托车及零配件零售	Retail of Motorcycle and Fittings	10829	10332	469	8486
机动车燃料零售	Retail of Auto Fuel	151040	56965	51458	388114
家用电器及电子产品专门零售	Monopoly Retail of House hold Electric Appliancesound Electronic Products	174235	161113	3984	117549
家用视听设备零售	Retail of Electric Appliances	106984	98927	1534	77846
日用家电设备零售	Retail of Household Electric Equipment	29027	26451	1098	18424
计算机、软件及辅助设备零售	Retail of Cumputers,Software and Office Appliances	30518	28653	1055	17768
通讯设备零售	Retail of Telecommunication Equipments	7706	7082	297	3511
五金、家具及室内装修材料专门零售	Monopoly Retail of Hardware, Furniture and Indoor Decorating Material	222272	155288	36016	84477
五金零售	Retail of Hardware	4918	4776	99	3382
家具零售	Retail of Living equipment	217354	150512	35917	81095
货摊、无店铺及其他零售业	Retail of Storeless and others	27694	15701	8672	19070
邮购及电视、电话零售	Distribution of Post and E-commerce	4057	2389	149	3771
生活用燃料零售业	Retail of Life Fuels	23637	13312	8523	15299
按地区分	**By Region**				
乌鲁木齐市	Urumqi City	2491067	1710285	373656	2017221
克拉玛依市	Karamay City	120617	95621	14762	103872
吐鲁番地区	Turpan Administrative Offices	14520	7876	2899	8235
哈密地区	Hami [Kumul] Administrative Offices	85712	57250	10472	63519
昌吉回族自治州	Changji Hui Autonomous Prefecture	102385	67758	18091	85630
伊犁哈萨克自治州	Ili Kazak Autonomous Prefecture	150309	105579	22333	102443
伊犁州直属县(市)	Counties (Cities) Direct Under Ili Prefecture	129750	94372	16241	91361
塔城地区	Tacheng [Tarbagatai] Administrative Offices	13802	7429	4634	6921
阿勒泰地区	Altay Administrative Offices	6757	3778	1458	4161
博尔塔拉蒙古自治州	Bortala Mongol Autonomous Prefecture	5861	3276	1587	3134
巴音郭楞蒙古自治州	Bayangol Mongol Autonomous Prefecture	154694	115590	24372	124937
阿克苏地区	Aksu Administrative Offices	161347	98166	39941	131656
克孜勒苏柯尔克孜自治州	Kizilsu Kirgiz Autonomous Prefecture	3817	2072	1346	1670
喀什地区	Kashgar [Kaxgar] Administrative Offices	88675	64306	15333	64527
和田地区	Hotan Administrative Offices	10689	6411	2277	4868
生产建设兵团	Production and Construction Group	134977	79516	30771	61753

16-11 限额以上餐饮企业资产及负债情况
Assets and Liabilities of Enterprises above Designated Size of Catering Services

单位：万元 (2012 年) (10 000 yuan)

指　　标	Item	资产合计 Total Asset	#流动资产 Working Capitals	#固定资产 Fixed Asset	负债合计 Total Liabilities
总　计	**Total**	**216096**	**74010**	**75020**	**131937**
按登记注册类型分	**By Status of Registration**				
内资企业	Domestic-funded Enterprises	207431	70527	73762	129020
国有企业	State – owned Enterprises	50197	8481	11106	4792
集体企业	Collective-owned Enterprises	43	33	7	41
有限责任公司	Limited Liability Corporations	55346	15287	34925	57168
国有独资公司	Enterprise with Sole Funds	3365	385	2981	179
其他有限责任公司	Other Limited Liability Corporations	51981	14902	31944	56989
股份有限公司	Share-holding Corporations Ltd.	28910	14446	2856	15948
私营企业	Private Enterprises	67560	27754	24236	46997
私营独资企业	Private-funded Enterprises	2575	690	1804	1919
私营合伙企业	Private Partnership Enterprises	3908	2642	691	620
私营有限责任公司	Private Limited Liability Corporations	61077	24422	21741	44458
其他企业	Others	5375	4526	632	4074
外商投资企业	Foreign Funded Enterprises	8665	3483	1258	2917
外资企业	Enterprises with Sole Fund	8665	3483	1258	2917
按餐饮行业小类分组	**By Sector of Catering**				
正餐服务	Dinner	190110	64571	66201	123172
快餐服务	Snack	25986	9439	8819	8765
按地区分	**By Region**				
乌鲁木齐市	Urumqi City	92719	25993	21939	34755
克拉玛依市	Karamay City	894	875	20	565
吐鲁番地区	Turpan Administrative Offices	43	33	7	41
哈密地区	Hami [Kumul] Administrative Offices	510	78	300	844
昌吉回族自治州	Changji Hui Autonomous Prefecture	573	115	378	165
伊犁哈萨克自治州直属县(市)	Ili Kazak Autonomous Prefecture	64864	17235	41000	61688
巴音郭楞蒙古自治州	Bayangol Mongol Autonomous Prefecture	15832	9009	3339	11427
阿克苏地区	Aksu Administrative Offices	3759	1620	2113	1588
喀什地区	Kashgar [Kaxgar] Administrative Offices	2519	1874	583	1933
生产建设兵团	Production and Construction Group	34383	17178	5341	18931

16-12 限额以上住宿企业资产及负债情况

Assets and Liabilities of Enterprises above Designated Size of Accommodation Services

单位：万元 (2012 年) (10 000 yuan)

指标	Item	资产合计 Total Assets	#流动资产 Working Capitals	#固定资产 Fixed Assets	负债合计 Total Liabilities
总计	**Total**	**1030030**	**365370**	**460490**	**701807**
按登记注册类型分	**By Status of Registration**				
内资企业	Domestic-funded Enterprises	1029377	365199	460034	701734
国有企业	State-owned Enterprises	260423	71696	153974	130577
集体企业	Collective-owned Enterprises	54063	4215	8064	53364
联营企业	Joint Ounership Enterprises	2429	1503	926	1063
国有联营企业	State Ounership Enterprises	2429	1503	926	1063
有限责任公司	Limited Liability Corporations	372381	125993	199473	228578
国有独资公司	State Sole Funded Corporations	14696	6452	7192	11855
其他有限责任公司	Other Limited Liability Corporations	357685	119541	192281	216723
股份有限公司	Share-holding Corporations Ltd.	22257	5738	12844	15444
私营企业	Private Enterprises	249662	109758	77260	209681
私营独资企业	Private-funded Enterprises	14349	6223	5257	8094
私营合伙企业	Private Partnership Enterprises	11762	7640	3192	12852
私营有限责任公司	Private Limited Liability Corporations	221287	95617	68571	187892
私营股份有限公司	Private Limited Liability Corporations	2264	278	240	843
其他企业	Others	68162	46296	7493	63027
港、澳、台商投资企业	Enterprises With Funds from Hong Kong, Macao and Taiwan	510	40	444	90
合资经营企业（港或澳、台资）	Joint-venture Enterprises (Funds from Hong Kong, Macao and Taiwan)	510	40	444	90
外商投资企业	Foreign funded Enterprises	143	131	12	-17
外资企业	Enterprises with Sole Fund	143	131	12	-17
按住宿行业分组	**By Sector of**				
旅游饭店	Tourist Hotel	965045	341075	427122	666150
一般旅馆	Ordinary Hotel	64985	24295	33368	35657
按星级等级分	**Classified by Stars**				
五　星	Five-Star	285651	105181	164479	202303
四　星	Four-Star	205578	62830	120065	127321
三　星	Three-Star	380443	113950	138235	253410
二　星	Two-Star	41318	14999	17197	19304
一　星	One-Star	1587	349	619	1217
其　他	Other	115453	68061	19895	98252
按地区分	**By Region**				
乌鲁木齐市	Urumqi City	462312	194602	163147	296688
克拉玛依市	Karamay City	47933	2480	44224	55155
吐鲁番地区	Turpan Administrative Offices	11071	3212	5019	10785
哈密地区	Hami [Kumul] Administrative Offices	43116	7444	26761	23338
昌吉回族自治州	Changji Hui Autonomous Prefecture	9930	3859	5473	10779
伊犁哈萨克自治州	Ili Kazak Autonomous Prefecture	124849	30626	73669	64016
伊犁州直属县(市)	Counties (Cities) Direct Under Ili Prefecture	69408	16294	39852	34030
塔城地区	Tacheng [Tarbagatai] Administrative Offices	13499	4485	7158	9782
阿勒泰地区	Altay Administrative Offices	41942	9847	26659	20204
博尔塔拉蒙古自治州	Bortala Mongol Autonomous Prefecture	3502	2327	391	3245
巴音郭楞蒙古自治州	Bayangol Mongol Autonomous Prefecture	68174	13874	48150	59527
阿克苏地区	Aksu Administrative Offices	42880	8813	21620	29747
克孜勒苏柯尔克孜自治州	Kizilsu Kirgiz Autonomous Prefecture	6972	698	6073	3794
喀什地区	Kashgar [Kaxgar] Administrative Offices	117162	75588	17928	102117
和田地区	Hotan Administrative Offices	10852	2754	5376	3757
生产建设兵团	Production and Construction Group	81277	19093	42659	38859

16-13 限额以上批发企业主要财务指标

Main Financial Indicators of Wholesale Enterprises above Designated Size

单位：万元 (2012 年) (10 000 yuan)

指　　标	Item	商品销售收入 Revenue of Product Sales	商品销售成本 Cost of Product Sales	商品销售税金及附加 Sales Tax and Extra Changes	商品销售利润 Profits of Product Sales
总　计	**Total**	**48876257**	**46820229**	**106268**	**1949760**
按登记注册类型分	**By Status of Registration**				
内资企业	Domesticfunded Enterprises	48815547	46764671	106182	1944694
国有企业	State-owned Enterprises	9228585	8656640	63843	508102
集体企业	Collective-owned Enterprises	785354	732380	662	52312
股份合作企业	Cooperative Enterprises	65080	58812		6268
联营企业	Joint Ounership Enterprises	3361	3212	1	148
集体联营企业	Collective Joint Ounership Enterprises	3361	3212	1	148
有限责任公司	Limited Liability Corporations	21693211	21026705	28738	637768
国有独资公司	State Sole Funded Corporations	1984165	1825210	19969	138986
其他有限责任公司	Other Limited Liability Corporations	19709046	19201495	8769	498782
股份有限公司	Share-holding Corporations Ltd.	10473180	10133311	6930	332939
私营企业	Private Enterprises	6405702	6003687	5832	396183
私营独资企业	Private-funded Enterprises	10359	9662	13	684
私营合伙企业	Private Partnership Enterprises	4710	4589	3	118
私营有限责任公司	Private Limited Liability Corporations	6140544	5768399	5445	366700
私营股份有限公司	Private Share-holding Corporation Ltd.	250089	221037	371	28681
其他企业	Other Enterprises	161074	149924	176	10974
港、澳、台商投资企业	Enterprises With Funds from Hong Kong, Macao and Taiwan	3288	3029		259
港、澳、台商独资经营企业	Enterprises with Sole Funds from Hong Kong, Macao and Taiwan	3288	3029		259
外商投资企业	Foreign funded Enterprises	57422	52529	86	4807
中外合资经营企业	Enterprises with Foreign Investment	5391	4546	28	817
外资企业	Enterprises with Sole Fund	52031	47983	58	3990
按批发行业小类分组	**By Sector of Wholesale**				
农、林、牧产品批发	Wholesale of Farm Produce and Livestock Products	6984629	6502351	1748	480530
谷物、豆及薯类批发	Wholesale of Grain,Bean and Potato	472247	440781	296	31170
种子批发	Wholesale of Seed and Fodder	277325	204116	45	73164
棉、麻批发	Wholesale of Cotton and Lliner	6183700	5809741	1398	372561
其他农牧产品批发	Wholesale of Other Farm Produce and Livestoclc Products	51357	47713	9	3635
食品、饮料及烟草制品批发	Wholesale of Food,Beverages and Tobaccos	3119035	2717271	79348	322416
米、面制品及食用油批发	Wholesale of Rice, Flour and Edible Oil	318225	298892	212	19121
糕点、糖果及糖批发	Wholesale of Pastry,Candy and Sugar	19540	16006	54	3480
果品、蔬菜批发	Wholesale of Fruit and Vegetable	115632	100865	246	14521
肉、禽、蛋及水产品批发	Wholesale of Meat,Birds and Equatic Products	35929	33760	74	2095
盐及调味品批发	Wholesale of Salt and Condiment Flavoring Material	63019	51845	198	10976
酒、饮料及茶叶批发	Wholesale of Soft Drink and Tea Leaf	85179	66833	385	17961
烟草制品批发	Wholesale of Tobaccos	2456077	2126239	78162	251676
其他食品批发	Wholesale of Other Food	25434	22831	17	2586
纺织、服装及家庭用品批发	Wholesale of Textitle, Garments and Daily Consumer Articles	354207	326980	436	26791
纺织品、针织品及原料批发	Wholesale of Textile,Hosiery and Raw Material	107244	105439	32	1773
服装批发	Wholesale of Garment	108418	95840	167	12411
化妆品及卫生用品批发	Wholesale of Cosmetics and Health Aids	31968	30000	32	1936
家用电器批发	Wholesale of Electrical Appliances	62029	55489	140	6400
其他家庭用品批发	Wholesale of Other Covenience Goods	44548	40212	65	4271
文化、体育用品及器材批发	Wholesale of Culture, Sports Goods and Apparatus	150372	133453	396	16523
图书批发	Wholesale of Books	104209	89996	335	13878

16-13 续表 Continued

单位：万元 (10 000 yuan)

指　　标	Item	商品销售收　　入 Revenue of Product Sales	商品销售成　　本 Cost of Product Sales	商品销售税金及附加 Sales Tax and Extra Changes	商品销售利　　润 Product Sales Profits
首饰、工艺品及收藏品批发	Wholesale of wear、Jewellery、Handicraft、Collectim	6126	5681	43	402
其他文化用品批发	Wholesale of Other Culture Products	40037	37776	18	2243
医药及医疗器械批发	Wholesale of Medicines and Medical Appliances	590326	544901	1046	44379
西药批发	Wholesale of Western Medicine	557962	515378	974	41610
中药批发	Wholesale of Chinese Medicinal Plant and Chinese Patent Medicine	26859	24754	65	2040
医疗用品及器材批发	Wholesale of Medicine and Medical Appliances	5505	4769	7	729
矿产品、建材及化工产品批发	Wholesale of Mineral Products, Building Material and Chemical Products	34638458	33772489	19734	846235
煤炭及制品批发	Wholesale of Coal and Related Products	546919	406792	3890	136237
石油及制品批发	Wholesale of Petroleum and Related Products	27159192	26712504	12956	433732
金属及金属矿批发	Wholesale of Metal and Metal Materials	4389462	4227269	1607	160586
建材批发	Wholesale of Building Materials	457025	441913	326	14786
化肥批发	Wholesale of Fertilizer	1508711	1443648	214	64849
农药批发	Wholesale of Pesticides	17252	15478	0	1774
其他化工产品批发	Wholesale of Other Chemical Product	559897	524885	741	34271
机械设备、五金交电及电子产品批发	Wholesale of Machinery, Hardware and Electronic Equipments	2706799	2506634	2709	197456
农业机械批发	Wholesale of Agriculture Machinery	175303	160161	58	15084
汽车批发	Wholesale of Motor Vehicles	579872	484192	769	94911
汽车零配件批发	Wholesale of Motor Vehicles Parts	241244	232553	268	8423
摩托车及零配件批发	Wholesale of Motorcycles	9632	8889	18	725
五金产品批发	Wholesale of Hardware and Electromic Equipment	22936	21420	16	1500
电气设备批发	Wholesale of Electric Equipments	265181	261566	66	3549
计算机、软件及辅助设备批发	Wholesale of Computer, Software and Accessory Equipment	95659	87547	393	7719
通讯及广播电视设备批发	Wholesale of Communicating and Broadcasting Television Device	634998	632510	21	2467
其他机械设备及电子产品批发	Wholesale of Other Mechanical Equipment and Electromic Products	681974	617796	1100	63078
贸易经纪与代理	Trades Broker and Agent	84636	79867	185	4584
贸易代理	Trades Agent	84636	79867	185	4584
其他批发业	Wholesales of Others	247795	236283	666	10846
再生物资回收与批发业	Recovery and Wholesale of Regeneration Material	200299	200600	472	-773
其他未列明的批发业	Wholesale of Un-listed	47496	35683	194	11619
按地区分	**By Region**				
乌鲁木齐市	Urumqi City	30072472	29227181	39139	806152
克拉玛依市	Karamay City	924409	862249	4114	58046
吐鲁番地区	Turpan Administrative Offices	393783	370662	2692	20429
哈密地区	Hami [Kumul] Administrative Offices	940498	867472	4742	68284
昌吉回族自治州	Changji Hui Autonomous Prefecture	944204	865738	7704	70762
伊犁哈萨克自治州	Ili Kazak Autonomous Prefecture	3665087	3504129	16057	144901
伊犁州直属县(市)	Counties (Cities) Direct Under Ili Prefecture	2730929	2629909	7734	93286
塔城地区	Tacheng [Tarbagatai] Administrative Offices	662725	628617	5495	28613
阿勒泰地区	Altay Administrative Offices	271433	245603	2828	23002
博尔塔拉蒙古自治州	Bortala Mongol Autonomous Prefecture	1040490	953545	2310	84635
巴音郭楞蒙古自治州	Bayangol Mongol Autonomous Prefecture	1338377	1253411	8712	76254
阿克苏地区	Aksu Administrative Offices	1875086	1727653	8439	138994
克孜勒苏柯尔克孜自治州	Kizilsu Kirgiz Autonomous Prefecture	47040	42810	42	4188
喀什地区	Kashgar [Kaxgar] Administrative Offices	1525081	1341330	8049	175702
和田地区	Hotan Administrative Offices	204888	188215	2181	14492
生产建设兵团	Production and Construction Group	5904842	5615834	2087	286921

16-14 限额以上零售企业主要财务指标

Main Financial Indicators of Retail Enterprises above Designated Size

单位：万元 (2012 年) (10 000 yuan)

指 标	Item	商品销售收入 Revenue of Product Sales	商品销售成本 Cost of Product Sales	商品销售税金及附加 Sales Tax and Extra Changes	商品销售利润 Product Sales Profits
总 计	**Total**	**6192494**	**5544519**	**14756**	**633219**
按登记注册类型分	**By Status of Registration**				
内资企业	Domestic Funded Enterprises	5812549	5217443	12920	582186
国有企业	State-owned Enterprises	290787	242244	536	48007
集体企业	Collective-owned Enterprises	6495	5598	33	864
股份合作企业	Share-holding Cooperative Enterprises	1519	1325		194
有限责任公司	Limited Liability Corporations	2037965	1877434	3393	157138
国有独资公司	State Sole Funded Corporations	18035	14582	16	3437
其他有限责任公司	Other Limited Liability Corporations	2019930	1862852	3377	153701
股份有限公司	Share-holding Corporations Ltd.	1015926	896583	753	118590
私营企业	Private Enterprises	2440099	2175700	8190	256209
私营独资企业	Private-funded Enterprises	45350	79242	530	-34422
私营有限责任公司	Private Limited Liability Corporations	2393040	2094800	7658	290582
私营股份有限公司	Private Share-holding Corporation Ltd.	1709	1658	2	49
其他企业	Others	19758	18559	15	1184
港、澳、台投资企业	Enterprises With Funds from Hong Kong, Macao and Taiwan	150236	129515	747	19974
港、澳、台商独资经营企业	Enterprises with Sole Funds from Hong Kong, Macao and Taiwan	150236	129515	747	19974
外商投资企业	Foreign funded Enterprises	229709	197561	1089	31059
中外合资经营企业	Enterprises with Foreign Investment	176344	152982	1089	22273
外资企业	Enterprises with Sole Fund	53365	44579		8786
按零售行业小类分组	**By Sector of Retail**				
综合零售	Integrated Retail	1239944	1044442	4763	190739
百货零售	Retail of General Merchandise	896218	743553	3342	149323
超级市场零售	Retail of Supermarket	342576	299904	1415	41257
其他综合零售	Retail of Other Integrate	1150	985	6	159
食品、饮料及烟草制品专门零售	Monopoly Retail of Foods, Beverages and Tobacco	14287	13759	17	511
粮油零售	Retail of Grain and Oil	2127	3136	1	-1010
果品、蔬菜零售	Retail of Fruite and Vegetables	1506	1485		21
肉、禽、蛋及水产品零售	Retail of Meat,Poultry and Eggs	1816	1227		589
酒、饮料及茶叶零售	Retail of Soft Drink and Tea Leaf	4344	3993	4	347
烟草制品零售	Retail of Tobaccos	4494	3918	12	564
纺织、服装及日用品专门零售	Monopoly Retail of Textile, Garments and Daily Consumer Articles	239645	235183	2360	2102
服装零售	Garment Retail	225524	223302	2348	-126
钟表、眼镜零售	Retail of Timelceeper and Spectacle	12901	10863	11	2027
其他日用品零售	Retail of other Covenience Goods	1220	1018	1	201
文化、体育用品及器材专门零售	Monopoly Retail of Cultural, Sports Goods And Apparatus	175678	122869	972	51837
文具用品零售	Retail of Stationery and Office Supplies	4600	4333	6	261
图书、报刊零售业	Retail of Books	142903	108638	162	34103

16-14 续表 Continued

单位：万元 (10 000 yuan)

指 标	Item	商品销售收入 Revenue of Product Sales	商品销售成本 Cost of Product Sales	商品销售税金及附加 Sales Taxes and Extra Changes	商品销售利润 Product Sales Profits
珠宝首饰零售	Retail of Bijouterie	26750	8546	800	17404
照相器材零售	Retail of Photographic Materials	1425	1352	4	69
医药及医疗器材专门零售	Monopoly Retail of Medicine and Medical-care Apparatus	678661	611180	1277	66204
药品零售	Retail of Medcine	674733	608059	1264	65410
医疗用品及器材零售	Wholesale of Medical Treatment and Equipment	3928	3121	13	794
汽车、摩托车、燃料及零配件专门零售	Monopoly Retail of Car, Motor, Fuel and Parts as Well as Components	3284134	3083224	3266	197644
汽车零售	Retail of Automobiles	2279178	2129038	2310	147830
汽车零配件零售	Retail of Automobiles' Parts	6428	5568	14	846
摩托车及零配件零售	Retail of Motorcycle and Fittings	19203	17678	14	1511
机动车燃料零售	Retail of Auto Fuel	979325	930940	928	47457
家用电器及电子产品专门零售	Monopoly Retail of House hold Electric Appliancesound Electronic Products	387192	347888	909	38395
家用视听设备零售	Retail of Electric Appliances	212477	189857	519	22101
日用家电设备零售	Retail of Household Elctric Appliances	78141	69251	166	8724
计算机、软件及辅助设备零售	Retail of Cumputers,Software and Office Appliances	64373	59949	121	4303
通讯设备零售	Retail of Telecommunication Equipments	32201	28831	103	3267
五金、家具及室内装修材料专门零售	Monopoly Retail of Hardware, Furniture and Indoor Decorating Material	152943	72352	1068	79523
五金零售	Retail of Hardware	8328	7782	7	539
家具零售	Retail of Living Equipment	144615	64570	1061	78984
货摊、无店铺及其他零售业	Retail of Storeless and Others	20010	13622	124	6264
邮购及电视、电话零售	Distribution of Post and E-commerce	503	436		67
生活用燃料零售	Retail of Life Fuels	19507	13186	124	6197
按地区分	**By Region**				
乌鲁木齐市	Urumqi City	4238904	3727955	10132	500817
克拉玛依市	Karamay City	203590	185266	719	17605
吐鲁番地区	Turpan Administrative Offices	15263	13138	33	2092
哈密地区	Hami [Kumul] Administrative Offices	135069	123335	301	11433
昌吉回族自治州	Changji Hui Autonomous Prefecture	111470	138013	656	-27199
伊犁哈萨克自治州	Ili Kazak Autonomous Prefecture	239292	214240	628	24424
伊犁州直属县(市)	Counties (Cities) Direct Under Ili Prefecture	204999	184788	534	19677
塔城地区	Tacheng [Tarbagatai] Administrative Offices	24044	20673	89	3282
阿勒泰地区	Altay Administrative Offices	10249	8779	5	1465
博尔塔拉蒙古自治州	Bortala Mongol Autonomous Prefecture	10266	8601	14	1651
巴音郭楞蒙古自治州	Bayangol Mongol Autonomous Prefecture	282670	259609	782	22279
阿克苏地区	Aksu Administrative Offices	216915	193054	363	23498
克孜勒苏柯尔克孜自治州	Kizilsu Kirgiz Autonomous Prefecture	3748	2949		799
喀什地区	Kashgar [Kaxgar] Administrative Offices	149303	134156	193	14954
和田地区	Hotan Administrative Offices	16421	13630	10	2781
生产建设兵团	Production and Construction Group	569583	530573	925	38085

16-15 限额以上餐饮企业主要财务指标
Main Financial Indicators of Catering Enterprises above Designated Size

单位：万元　　　(2012 年)　　　(10 000 yuan)

指　　标	Item	主营业务收入 Revenue from Principal Business	主营业务成本 Cost of Principal Business	主营业务税金及附加 Tax and Addition of Major Business	主营业务利润 Profit From Principal Business
总　计	**Total**	**140624**	**63781**	**7682**	**69161**
按登记注册类型分	**By Status of Registration**				
内资企业	Domestic-funded Enterprises	111293	50755	6147	54391
国有企业	State – owned Enterprises	14269	5205	680	8384
集体企业	Collective-owned Enterprises	334	295	19	20
有限责任公司	Limited Liability Corporations	23632	11590	1292	10750
国有独资公司	State Sole Funded Corporations	957	396	53	508
其他有限责任公司	Other Limited Liability Corporations	22675	11194	1239	10242
股份有限公司	Share-holding Corporations Ltd	1099	252	59	788
私营企业	Private Enterprises	64297	29128	3674	31495
私营独资企业	Private-funded Enterprises	4256	2535	176	1545
私营合伙企业	Private Partnership Enterprises	3051	1375	156	1520
私营有限责任公司	Private Limited Liability Corporations	56990	25218	3342	28430
其他企业	Others	7662	4285	423	2954
外商投资企业	Foreign Funded Enterprises	29331	13026	1535	14770
外资企业	Enterprises with Sole Fund	29331	13026	1535	14770
按餐饮行业小类分组	**By Sector of Catering**				
正餐服务	Dinner	92817	43400	5166	44251
快餐服务	Snack	47807	20381	2516	24910
按地区分	**By Region**				
乌鲁木齐市	Urumqi City	86326	39365	4746	42215
克拉玛依市	Karamay City	3653		241	3412
吐鲁番地区	Turpan Administrative Offices	333	295	18	20
哈密地区	Hami [Kumul] Administrative Offices	201	61	11	129
昌吉回族自治州	Changji Hui Autonomous Prefecture	950	818	10	122
伊犁哈萨克自治州直属县(市)	Ili Kazak Autonomous Prefecture	24486	11166	1009	12311
巴音郭楞蒙古自治州	Bayangol Mongol Autonomous Prefecture	14809	6920	1140	6749
阿克苏地区	Aksu Administrative Offices	3018	1362	227	1429
喀什地区	Kashgar [Kaxgan] Administratine Offices	1378	462	71	845
生产建设兵团	Production and Construction Group	5470	3332	209	1929

16-16 限额以上住宿企业主要财务指标
Main Financial Indicators of Hotels Enterprises above Designated

单位：万元 (2012 年) (10 000 yuan)

指标	Item	主营业务收入 Revenue from Principal Business	主营业务成本 Cost of Principal Business	主营业务税金及附加 Tax and Addition of Major Business	主营业务利润 Profit From Principal Business
总计	**Total**	**374085**	**160525**	**21186**	**192374**
按登记注册类型分	**By Status of Registration**				
内资企业	Domestic-funded Enterprises	373581	160521	21158	191902
国有企业	State-owned Enterprises	117441	53362	6407	57672
集体企业	Collective-owned Enterprises	13395	3608	681	9106
联营企业	Joint Ownership Enterprises	453	39	25	389
国有联营企业	State Joint Ownership Enterprises	453	39	25	389
有限责任公司	Limited Liability Corporations	142280	69637	8245	64398
国有独资公司	State Sole Funded Corporations	11133	3113	617	7403
其他有限责任公司	Other Limited Liability Corporations	131147	66524	7628	56995
股份有限公司	Share-holding Corporations Ltd.	6785	4097	396	2292
私营企业	Private Enterprises	88971	27087	5089	56795
私营独资企业	Private-funded Enterprises	14570	2657	869	11044
私营合伙企业	Private Partnership Enterprises	4073	976	180	2917
私营有限责任公司	Private Limited Liability Corporation	70007	23454	4022	42531
私营股份有限公司	Private Share-holding Corporation Ltd.	321		18	303
其他企业	Others	4256	2691	315	1250
港、澳、台商投资企业	Enterprises With Funds from Hong Kong, Macao and Taiwan	277	4	16	257
合资经营企业（港或澳、台资）	Joint-venture Enterprises (Funds from Hong Kong, Macao and Taiwan)	277	4	16	257
外商投资企业	Foreign Funded Enterprises	227		12	215
外资企业	Enterprises with Sole Fund	227		12	215
按住宿行业小类分组	**By Sector of National Economic**				
旅游饭店	Tourist Hotel	333177	138295	18815	176067
一般旅馆	Ordinary Hotel	40908	22230	2371	16307
按星级等级分	**Classified by Stars**				
五星	Five-Star	101303	58232	5955	37116
四星	Four-Star	87779	34830	5148	47801
三星	Three-Star	123112	46285	6955	69872
二星	Two-Star	21886	8178	1024	12684
一星	One-Star	1605	581	92	932
其他	Other	38400	12419	2012	23969
按地区分	**By Region**				
乌鲁木齐市	Urumqi City	202846	80553	11826	110467
克拉玛依市	Karamay City	10336	10853	574	-1091
吐鲁番地区	Turpan Administrative Offices	5412	3092	325	1995
哈密地区	Hami [Kumul] Administrative Offices	20322	10606	1014	8702
昌吉回族自治州	Changji Hui Autonomous Prefecture	6783	2455	351	3977
伊犁哈萨克自治州	Ili Kazak Autonomous Prefecture	40240	19422	2343	18475
伊犁州直属县(市)	Counties (Cities) Direct Under Ili Prefecture	21232	8935	1204	11093
塔城地区	Tacheng [Tarbagatai] Administrative Offices	6007	3889	411	1707
阿勒泰地区	Altay Administrative Offices	13001	6598	728	5675
博尔塔拉蒙古自治州	Bortala Mongol Autonomous Prefecture	3875	1403	197	2275
巴音郭楞蒙古自治州	Bayangol Mongol Autonomous Prefecture	24359	8630	1385	14344
阿克苏地区	Aksu Administrative Offices	11672	3842	660	7170
克孜勒苏柯尔克孜自治州	Kizilsu Kirgiz Autonomous Prefecture	2289	888	143	1258
喀什地区	Kashgar [Kaxgar] Administrative Offices	13135	6785	654	5696
和田地区	Hotan Administrative Offices	2850	1426	148	1276
生产建设兵团	Production and Construction Group	29966	10570	1566	17830

16-17 限额以上批发和零售业商品销售类值

Total Sales of Enterprises above Designated Size in Wholesale and Retail Trades by Category of Commodities

单位：万元 (10 000 yuan)

项目	Item	销售总额 Value		批发 Wholesale Trades		零售 Retail Trades	
		2011	2012	2011	2012	2011	2012
总计	**Total**	**51087375**	**55903055**	**44152710**	**48292313**	**6934665**	**7610742**
食品、饮料、烟酒类	Foods, Beverages, Tobacco and Liquor	3814777	4578501	3339677	4010565	475100	567936
服装、鞋帽类、针纺织品类	Garments, Shoes and Hats, Knitted Goods and Textiles	852503	937247	214780	169382	637723	767865
化妆品类	Cosmetics	135089	162853	31996	39726	103093	123127
金银珠宝类	Gold and Silver Jewelry	185515	231914	2539	4952	182976	226962
日用品类	Commodity Categories	218831	259894	56086	62730	162745	197164
五金、电料类	Hardwares, Electrical Materials	45557	45126	35068	34182	10489	10944
体育、娱乐用品类	Sports and Recreational Articles	24422	21438	1607	1345	22815	20093
书报杂志类	Books and Newspapers	281857	316247	136198	149004	145659	167243
电子出版物及音像制品类	E-journal and Video Products	19987	3612	32	307	19955	3305
家用电器及音像器材类	Household Appliances and Video Equipments	457559	514645	167511	201636	290048	313009
中西药品类	Chinese Traditional Medicine and Western Medicines	1169320	1335187	390973	468655	778347	866532
文化办公用品类	Office Articles	256063	269342	149050	160530	107013	108812
家具类	Furnitures	158285	168902	1417	988	156868	167914
通讯器材类	Communication Appliances	99913	82007	44136	22097	55777	59910
煤炭及制品类	Coal and Related Products	203513	473298	199984	467784	3529	5514
木材及制品类	Wood and Wooden Products	1	108	1	108		
石油及制品类	Petroleum and Related Products	26927041	27872855	25330826	26208355	1596215	1664500
化工材料及制品类	Raw Chemical Materials and Related Products	1946394	2566121	1946394	2566121		
金属材料类	Metal Materials	3954438	4441222	3954438	4441222		
建筑装潢材料类	Building and Decoration Materials	87550	128112	85604	128103	1946	9
机电产品及设备类	Mechanical and Electrical Products and Accessories	1265313	1063169	1248659	1045518	16654	17651
汽车类	Automobile	2925083	3244532	808837	972235	2116246	2272297
种子饲料类	Seed and Fddestuff	192480	244854	192480	244854		
棉麻类	Cotton and Hemp	5250189	6402834	5250183	6401011	6	1823
其他类	Others	615695	539035	564234	490903	51461	48132

16-18 亿元以上商品交易市场总体情况
Statistics on Commodity Exchange Markets of Transaction Value over 100 Million Yuan

项 目	Item	市场数(个) Number of Markets (unit)		总摊位数(个) Number of Booths (unit)		年末出租摊位数(个) Number of Rental Booths at Year-end (unit)	
		2011	2012	2011	2012	2011	2012
总 计	**Total**	**68**	**76**	**57514**	**72012**	**51665**	**66674**
按市场类别分组	**By Market Categories**						
综合市场	**Integrated Markets**	**25**	**28**	**31288**	**43123**	**27983**	**39486**
生产资料综合市场	roduction Comprehensive Market	3	3	6062	3752	6062	3695
工业消费品综合市场	Industrial Consumable Comprehensive Markets	8	10	11238	25980	11015	25615
农产品综合市场	Farm Produce Comprehensive Markets	7	8	6513	5779	5972	5136
其他综合市场	Other Comprehensive Markets	7	7	7475	7612	4934	5040
专业市场	**Special Markets**	**43**	**48**	**26226**	**28889**	**23682**	**27188**
生产资料市场	Production Markets	9	9	6299	6652	5427	6172
农业生产用具市场	Agricultural Production Equiment Markets		1		548		296
农用生产资料	Agricultural Production Markets	3	2	818	238	626	179
煤炭市场	Coal and Charcoal Markets	1	1	45	45	45	45
金属材料市场	Metal Materials Markets	2	2	654	1113	654	1113
机械设备市场	Mechanical Equipments Markets	1	1	1100	1000	500	1000
其他生产资料市场	Others	2	2	3682	3708	3602	3539
农产品市场	Farm Produce Markets	13	13	3962	4888	2951	3858
粮油市场	Grain and Oil Markets	1	1	181	181	96	106
肉禽蛋市场	Meat, Poultry and Eggs Markets	3	3	225	225	225	215
水产品市场	Aquatic Products Markets	1	1	400	500	400	500
蔬菜市场	Vegetables Markets	4	3	1514	998	1162	687
干鲜果市场	Dried and Fresh Melons and Fruits Markets	2	3	1212	2554	663	1945
其他农产品市场	Others	2	2	430	430	405	405
食品、饮料及烟酒市场	Food, Beverages, Tobacco and Liquor Markets	3	2	1263	438	717	343
食品饮料市场	Food and Beverages Markets	2	1	1025	200	479	105
其他食品饮料及烟酒市场	Others	1	1	238	238	238	238
纺织、服装、鞋帽市场	Textiles, Clothing, Shoes and Hats Markets	9	12	11293	12068	11206	12055
服装市场	Clothing Markets	6	7	7045	7086	6958	7073
其他纺织服装鞋帽市场	Others	3	5	4248	4982	4248	4982
日用品及文化用品市场	Daily Use Articles and Cultural Goods Markets		1		315		271
小商品市场	Merchandise Markets		1		315		271
黄金、珠宝、玉器等首饰市场	Gold, Jeweller, Jade Markets		1		712		712
黄金、珠宝、玉器等首饰市场	Gold, Jeweller, Jade Markets		1		712		712
电器、通讯器材、电子设备市场	Electrical Appliances, Communication Appliances and Electronical Appliances Markets	2	3	778	1035	771	1035
计算机及辅助设备市场	Computer and Auxillary Equipments Markets	2	2	778	755	771	755
其他电器、通讯器材、电子设备市场市场	Others		1		280		280
家具、五金及装饰材料市场	Furniture, Hardware and Decoration Materials Markets	3	3	1429	1635	1429	1635
家具市场	Furniture Markets	1	1	416	510	416	510
装饰材料市场	Decoration Materials Markets	1	1	325	325	325	325
其他装饰市场	Others	1	1	688	800	688	800
汽车、摩托车及零配件市场	Cars, Motorcycles and Spare Parts Markets	3	3	702	824	681	807
汽车市场	Cars Markets	3	3	702	824	681	807
花、鸟、鱼、虫市场	Flower, Bird, Fish and Insects Markets	1	1	500	322	500	300
花卉市场	Flower Markets	1	1	500	322	500	300
按营业状态分组	**By Operating State**						
常年营业	Business Year	66	75	54669	71967	48820	66629
季节性营业	Seasonal Business	2	1	2845	45	2845	45
按经营方式分组	**By Mode of Operating**						
以批发为主	Mainly in the Wholesale	46	49	38587	55748	33576	51071
以零售为主	Mainly in the Retail	22	27	18927	16264	18089	15603
按经营环境分组	**By Operating Environment**						
露天式	Open Type	17	17	12090	9664	9209	8954
封闭式	Closed Type	46	54	43289	60335	40391	55777
其 他	Others	5	5	2135	2013	2065	1943

16-18 续表 Continued

项　　目	Item	营业面积(平方米) Operating Area (sq.m)		成交额(万元) Turnouer (100 million yuan)	
		2011	2012	2010	2012
总　计	**Total**	**5243876**	**6186284**	**7787385**	**9097630**
按市场类别分组	**By Market Categories**				
综合市场	**Integrated Markets**	**2386997**	**3151599**	**2556501**	**3099824**
生产资料综合市场	Production Comprehensive Market	725348	463756	451772	290213
工业消费品综合市场	Industrial Consumable Comprehensive Markets	822892	1867700	542081	1562819
农产品综合市场	Farm Produce Comprehensive Markets	379776	361162	1224917	887648
其他综合市场	Other Comprehensive Markets	458981	458981	337731	359144
专业市场	**Special Markets**	**2856879**	**3034685**	**5230884**	**5997806**
生产资料市场	Production Markets	777122	741679	2840163	2534830
农业生产用具市场	Agricultural Production Equiment Markets		45436		15860
农用生产资料	Agricultural Production Markets	86090	56090	142912	36057
煤炭市场	Coal and Charcoal Markets	2000	2000	175120	16390
金属材料市场	Metal Materials Markets	320029	320150	2289500	1705650
机械设备市场	Mechanical Equipments Markets	100000	49000	30000	500000
其他生产资料市场	Others	269003	269003	202631	260873
农产品市场	Farm Produce Markets	985269	1090069	825516	1502443
粮油市场	Grain and Oil Markets	10000	10000	71820	53000
肉禽蛋市场	Meat, Poultry and Eggs Markets	708671	708671	188920	186316
水产品市场	Aquatic Products Markets	5200	100000	100000	220000
蔬菜市场	Vegetables Markets	78998	48998	271746	215489
干鲜果市场	Dried and Fresh Melons and Fruits Markets	115000	155000	114672	741282
其他农产品市场	Others	67400	67400	78358	86356
食品、饮料及烟酒市场	Food, Beverages, Tobacco and Liquor Markets	57450	24503	85112	60782
食品饮料市场	Food and Beverages Markets	39960	7013	52428	24667
其他食品饮料及烟酒市场	Others	17490	17490	32684	36115
纺织、服装、鞋帽市场	Textiles, Clothing, Shoes and Hats Markets	319534	388507	753825	1175111
服装市场	Clothing Markets	203512	214685	569557	958542
其他纺织服装鞋帽市场	Others	116022	173822	184268	216569
日用品及文化用品市场	Daily Use Articles and Cultural Goods Markets		6000		11707
小商品市场	Merchandise Markets		6000		11707
黄金、珠宝、玉器等首饰市场	Gold, Jeweller, Jade Markets		57420		28361
黄金、珠宝、玉器等首饰市场	Gold, Jeweller, Jade Markets		57420		28361
电器、通讯器材、电子设备市场	Electrical Appliances, Communication Appliances and Electronical Appliances Markets	17098	26098	44040	58820
计算机及辅助设备市场	Computer and Auxillary Equipments Markets	17098	17098	44040	42020
其他电器、通讯器材、电子设备市场市场	Others		9000		16800
家具、五金及装饰材料市场	Furniture, Hardware and Decoration Materials Markets	212653	212656	111560	126377
家具市场	Furniture Markets	44053	44056	31077	36420
装饰材料市场	Decoration Materials Markets	70000	70000	15477	20257
其他装饰市场	Others	98600	98600	65006	69700
汽车、摩托车及零配件市场	Cars, Motorcycles and Spare Parts Markets	387753	387753	538668	484375
汽车市场	Cars Markets	387753	387753	538668	484375
花、鸟、鱼、虫市场	Flower, Bird, Fish and Insects Markets	100000	100000	32000	15000
花卉市场	Flower Markets	100000	100000	32000	15000
按营业状态分组	**By Operating State**				
常年营业	Business Year	5161876	6184284	7481473	9081240
季节性营业	Seasonal Business	82000	2000	305912	16390
按经营方式分组	**By Mode of Operating**				
以批发为主	Mainly in the Wholesale	3997593	5191885	6619651	7909383
以零售为主	Mainly in the Retail	1246283	994399	1167734	1188247
按经营环境分组	**By Operating Environment**				
露天式	Open Type	1550986	1590706	1471101	1415690
封闭式	Closed Type	3522224	4424912	5954996	7284659
其　他	Others	170666	170666	361288	397281

16-19 亿元以上商品交易市场成交情况(按摊位分)

Basic Statistics on Commodity Exchange Markets of Transaction Value over 100 Million Yuan (by Booths)

项目	Item	年末出租摊位数(个) Number of Booths at Year-end (unit)		成交额(万元) Turnover (100 million yuan)	
		2011	2012	2011	2012
总计	**Total**	**51665**	**66674**	**7787385**	**9097630**
食品、饮料、烟酒类	Food, Beverages, Tobacco and Liquor	12108	12353	2242385	2600267
粮油、食品类	Food,Grain and Oil	11185	11329	2147558	2492113
粮油类	Grain and Oil	912	835	133453	116821
肉禽蛋类	Meat, Poultry and Eggs	1220	1422	348554	415677
水产品类	Aquatic Products	765	663	212328	286103
蔬菜类	Vegetables	4345	4367	609506	824294
干鲜果品类	Dried and Fresh Melons and Fruits	2847	2939	447654	785805
饮料类	Beverages	510	593	52591	61900
烟酒类	Tobacco and Liquor	413	431	42236	46254
服装、鞋帽、针纺织品类	Clothing, Shoes, Hats and Textiles	14396	14248	768499	1203758
服装类	Clothing	9019	9973	510830	913006
鞋帽类	Footwear and Hats	3091	2447	211140	238508
针纺织品类	Knitwear and Textiles	2286	1828	46529	52244
化妆品类	Cosmetics	734	730	35933	39368
金银珠宝类	Gold, Silver and Jewellery	185	4005	62122	114704
日用品类	Articles for Daily Use	2610	2739	131255	168632
洗涤用品类	Washing Articles	765	644	60009	75351
儿童玩具类	Children Toys	368	246	8833	7888
五金、电料类	Hardware & Electrical Materials	2672	2637	135130	120789
体育、娱乐用品类	Sports & Recreational Articles	379	396	18849	18709
书报杂志类	Newspapers and Magazines	262	262	12974	13013
电子出版物及音像制品类	E-journal and Video Products	329	792	14946	26678
家用电器和音像器材类	Household Appliances and Video Equipments	1243	1139	102991	115556
中西药品类	Traditional Chinese and Western Medicine	192	140	9951	10521
西药类	Western Medicine	79	67	4242	4539
中草药及中成药类	Traditional Chinese	61	21	4026	5010
文化办公用品类	Cultural and Official Goods	1550	1475	91453	96603
家具类	Furniture	2962	3527	148344	335091
通讯器材类	Communication Appliances	292	490	16313	22781
煤炭及制品类	Coal and Related Products	259	192	186916	19309
木材及制品类	Wood and Wooden Products	689	716	23360	18492
石油及制品类	Petroleum and Related Products	176	1	12044	27
化工材料及制品类	Raw Chemical Materials and Related Products	1347	1690	228923	300765
化肥类	Fertilizer	624	741	172189	215867
金属材料类	Metal Materials	1284	2009	2406791	1720917
建筑及装潢材料类	Building and Decoration Materials	2034	5223	188105	200884
机电产品及设备类	Mechanical & Electrical Products	1306	3575	86721	649357
农机类	Agricultural Machinery	125	252	12040	50346
汽车类	Automobile	877	1013	619942	630626
种子饲料类	Seed and Feedstuff	336	386	24546	26774
棉麻类	Cotton and Hemp	18	20	346	383
其他类	Others	3425	6916	218546	643626

16-20 各地区亿元以上商品交易市场总体情况

Basic Statistics on Commodity Exchange Markets of Transaction Value over 100 Million Yuan by Region

项 目	Item	市场数(个) Number of Markets (unit)		总摊位数(个) Number of Booths (unit)		年末出租摊位数(个) Number of Rental booths at Year-end (unit)	
		2011	2012	2011	2012	2011	2012
总 计	**Total**	**68**	**76**	**57514**	**72012**	**51665**	**66674**
乌鲁木齐市	Urumqi City	25	25	23097	35883	21994	35201
克拉玛依市	Karamay City	1	1	516	510	416	436
吐鲁番地区	Turpan Administrative Offices	1	1	650	650	650	650
哈密地区	Hami [Kumul] Administrative Offices	1	1	896	896	896	896
昌吉回族自治州	Changji Hui Autonomous Prefecture	2	2	3998	3998	3521	3571
伊犁哈萨克自治州直属县(市)	Ili Kazak Autonomous Prefecture	10	12	5605	6818	5528	6272
巴音郭楞蒙古自治州	Bayangol Mongol Autonomous Prefecture	9	9	8031	8185	4744	4912
阿克苏地区	Aksu Administrative Offices	3	5	1555	2693	1322	2452
喀什地区	Kashgar [Kaxgar] Administrative Offices	4	8	6757	6551	6757	6551
和田地区	Hotan Administrative Offices	2	2	2187	2187	2117	2117
生产建设兵团	Xinjiang Production and Construction Group	10	10	4222	3641	3720	3616

项 目	Item	营业面积(平方米) Operating Area (sq.m)		成交额(万元) Turnover (100 million Yuan)	
		2011	2012	2011	2012
总 计	**Total**	**5243876**	**6186284**	**7787385**	**9097630**
乌鲁木齐市	Urumqi City	2235670	3031178	5538383	6154367
克拉玛依市	Karamay City	30000	30000	64949	69450
吐鲁番地区	Turpan Administrative Offices	15000	15000	94230	97057
哈密地区	Hami [Kumul] Administrative Offices	20000	20000	25437	28297
昌吉回族自治州	Changji Hui Autonomous Prefecture	320303	320303	118523	123817
伊犁哈萨克自治州直属县(市)	Ili Kazak Autonomous Prefecture	756894	803891	493238	590655
巴音郭楞蒙古自治州	Bayangol Mongol Autonomous Prefecture	653164	653164	339443	396055
阿克苏地区	Aksu Administrative Offices	357000	408000	387138	364709
喀什地区	Kashgar [Kaxgar] Administrative Offices	513750	585170	289780	776327
和田地区	Hotan Administrative Offices	99859	99859	115111	119975
生产建设兵团	Production and Construction Group	242236	219719	321153	376921

16-21 连锁零售企业总体情况
Total Conditions of Chain Retail Enterprises

项 目 Item	合 计 Total		直营店 Straight Camp Shop		加盟店 Join in Store	
	2011	2012	2011	2012	2011	2012
连锁总店数(个) **Number of Head Stores (unit)**		**95**				
连锁门店总数(个) Number of Stores (unit)	3629	3711	3016	3063	613	648
年末从业人员数(人) Engaged Persons at Year-end (person)	30351	30983	28239	28826	2112	2157
年末零售营业面积(平方米) Operating Area of Retail Enterprises at Year-end (sq.m)	3247347	2919672	3142563	2812467	104784	107205
连锁门店商品购进总额(万元) Total Purchases Value of Chain Stores (100 million yuan)	5468981	6593447	5402074	6453929	66907	139519
其中:统一配送商品购进额(万元) Centralized Purchase and Delivery (100 million yuan)	4619018	5777005	4563361	5655014	55657	121991
其中:自有配送中心配送商品购进额(万元) Own Purchase and Delivery (100 million yuan)	3237638	3724544	3188791	3613481	48847	111063
非自有配送中心配送商品购进额(万元) Public Puchase and Delivery (100 million yuan)	1127658	1628702	1120848	1617774	6810	10928
商品销售额(万元) Total Sales of Commodities (100 million yuan)	6081912	7138861	5925956	6982697	155956	156164
其中:零售额(万元) Of which:Retail of value	2657259	2834992	2581266	2748425	75992	86568

16-22 连锁零售企业基本情况
Basic Condition of Chain Retail Enterprises

项　　目	Item	连锁总店数 Number of Chain Stores	门店数合计(个) Total Stores (unit)	
			2011	2012
总　计	**Total**	**95**	**3629**	**3711**
按登记注册类型分组	**by Status of Registration**			
内资企业	Domestic Funded Enterprises	94	3626	3708
国有企业	State-owned Enterprises	35	1974	1996
集体企业	Collective-owned Enterprises	1	8	8
有限责任公司	Limited Liability Corporations	18	407	376
其他有限责任公司	Other Limited Liability Corporations	18	407	376
股份有限公司	Share-holding Corporations Ltd.	9	386	394
私营企业	Private Enterprises	30	806	910
私营有限责任公司	Private-funded Enterprises	30	806	910
其他企业	Other Enterprises	1	45	24
外商投资企业	Foreign Funded Enterprises	1	3	3
外资企业	Enterprises with Sole Fund	1	3	3
按行业分组	**By Sector**			
批发业	**Wholesale**	**30**	**2163**	**2192**
食品、饮料及烟草制品批发	Special Wholesale of Food, Beverages and Tobaccos	4	25	24
医药及医疗器材批发	Wholesale of Medicines and Medical Appliances	2	7	7
矿产品、建材及化工产品批发	Wholesale of Minerals、Building Materials and Chemical Materiac	23	2128	2158
其他批发	Others	1	3	3
零售业	**Wholesale**	**65**	**1466**	**1519**
综合零售	Wholesale of Farm Produce and Livestock Products	12	356	402
食品、饮料及烟草制品专门零售	Special Wholesale of Food, Beverages and Tobaccos	1	6	6
纺织、服装及日用品专门零售	Wholesale of Medicines and Medical Appliances	1	3	3
文化、体育用品及器材专门零售	Wholesale	14	114	114
医药及医疗器材专门零售	Wholesale of Farm Produce and Livestock Products	24	734	732
汽车、摩托车、燃料及零配件专门零售	Special Wholesale of Food, Beverages and Tobaccos	3	124	121
家用电器及电子产品专门零售	Wholesale of Medicines and Medical Appliances	9	88	87
五金、家具及室内装修材料专门零售	Wholesale	1	41	54
按业态分组	**By Business Categories**			
便利店	Convenience Store	1	80	121
超　市	Supermarket	4	41	49
大型超市	Hypermarket	4	34	20
百货店	Department Store	1	82	82
专业店	Specialty Store	58	2453	2458
其中：加油站	Gas Station	19	837	867
专卖店	Franchised Store	7	74	86
其　他	Other Store	1	28	28

16-22 续表 1 Continued

项　目	Item	年末从业人员数(人) Engaged Persons at Year-end (person)		年末零售营业面积(平方米) Operating Area of Retail Enterprises at Year-end (sq.m)	
		2011	2012	2011	2012
总　计	**Total**	**30351**	**30983**	**3247347**	**2919672**
按登记注册类型分组	**by Status of Registration**				
内资企业	Domestic Funded Enterprises	29423	30135	3218605	2890930
国有企业	State-owned Enterprises	8910	9382	1615518	1302616
集体企业	Collective-owned Enterprises	50	56	45000	200
有限责任公司	Limited Liability Corporations	5472	4865	256214	278583
其他有限责任公司	Other Limited Liability Corporations	5472	4865	256214	278583
股份有限公司	Share-holding Corporations Ltd.	6243	6817	945001	935547
私营企业	Private Enterprises	8576	8892	352626	369698
私营有限责任公司	Private-funded Enterprises	8576	8892	352626	369698
其他企业	Other Enterprises	172	123	4246	4286
外商投资企业	Foreign Funded Enterprises	928	848	28742	28742
外资企业	Enterprises with Sole Fund	928	848	28742	28742
按行业分组	**By Sector**				
批发业	**Wholesale**	**11007**	**11903**	**2068172**	**1926511**
食品、饮料及烟草制品批发	Special Wholesale of Food, Beverages and Tobaccos	659	628	88747	6401
医药及医疗器材批发	Wholesale of Medicines and Medical Appliances	117	113	961	961
矿产品、建材及化工产品批发	Wholesale of Minerals、Building Materials and Chemical Materiac	10116	11021	1975464	1916149
其他批发	Others	115	141	3000	3000
零售业	**Wholesale**	**19344**	**19080**	**1179175**	**993161**
综合零售	Wholesale of Farm Produce and Livestock Products	5671	6421	263054	294351
食品、饮料及烟草制品专门零售	Special Wholesale of Food, Beverages and Tobaccos	23	21	445	445
纺织、服装及日用品专门零售	Wholesale of Medicines and Medical Appliances	9	7	150	150
文化、体育用品及器材专门零售	Wholesale	1822	1758	100631	99349
医药及医疗器材专门零售	Wholesale of Farm Produce and Livestock Products	3914	4367	86926	100955
汽车、摩托车、燃料及零配件专门零售	Special Wholesale of Food, Beverages and Tobaccos	2071	2105	503968	253638
家用电器及电子产品专门零售	Wholesale of Medicines and Medical Appliances	2577	1779	148968	144532
五金、家具及室内装修材料专门零售	Wholesale	3257	2622	75033	99741
按业态分组	**By Business Categories**				
便利店	Convenience Store	374	460	26359	30000
超　市	Supermarket	1398	1937	95171	108904
大型超市	Hypermarket	3301	3327	128913	142213
百货店	Department Store	96	96	3175	3175
专业店	Specialty Store	9484	9206	707749	661633
其中：加油站	Gas Station	11512	12388	2112885	1857968
专卖店	Franchised Store	4147	3531	171931	115643
其　他	Other Store	39	38	1164	136

16-22 续表 2 Continued

项　　目	Item	直营店门店数(个) Straight Camp Shop (unit)		年末从业人员数(人) Engaged Persons at Year-end (person)	
		2011	2012	2011	2012
总　计	**Total**	**3016**	**3063**	**28239**	**28826**
按登记注册类型分组	**by Status of Registration**				
内资企业	Domestic Funded Enterprises	3013	3060	27311	27978
国有企业	State-owned Enterprises	1687	1709	8781	9253
集体企业	Collective-owned Enterprises	8	8	50	56
有限责任公司	Limited Liability Corporations	370	327	5368	4791
其他有限责任公司	Other Limited Liability Corporations	370	327	5368	4791
股份有限公司	Share-holding Corporations Ltd.	386	394	6243	6817
私营企业	Private Enterprises	528	598	6719	6938
私营有限责任公司	Private-funded Enterprises	528	598	6719	6938
其他企业	Other Enterprises	34	24	150	123
外商投资企业	Foreign Funded Enterprises	3	3	928	848
外资企业	Enterprises with Sole Fund	3	3	928	848
按行业分组	**By Sector**				
批发业	**Wholesale**	**1942**	**1942**	**10957**	**11809**
食品、饮料及烟草制品批发	Special Wholesale of Food, Beverages and Tobaccos	25	24	659	628
医药及医疗器材批发	Wholesale of Medicines and Medical Appliances	7	7	117	113
矿产品、建材及化工产品批发	Wholesale of Minerals、Building Materials and Chemical Materiac	1907	1908	10066	10927
其他批发	Others	3	3	115	141
零售业	**Wholesale**	**1074**	**1121**	**17282**	**17017**
综合零售	Wholesale of Farm Produce and Livestock Products	180	204	4018	4703
食品、饮料及烟草制品专门零售	Special Wholesale of Food, Beverages and Tobaccos	6	6	23	21
纺织、服装及日用品专门零售	Wholesale of Medicines and Medical Appliances	3	3	9	7
文化、体育用品及器材专门零售	Wholesale	114	114	1822	1758
医药及医疗器材专门零售	Wholesale of Farm Produce and Livestock Products	518	532	3505	4022
汽车、摩托车、燃料及零配件专门零售	Special Wholesale of Food, Beverages and Tobaccos	124	121	2071	2105
家用电器及电子产品专门零售	Wholesale of Medicines and Medical Appliances	88	87	2577	1779
五金、家具及室内装修材料专门零售	Wholesale	41	54	3257	2622
按业态分组	**By Business Categories**				
便利店	Convenience Store	23	23	138	140
超　市	Supermarket	27	33	1223	1748
大型超市	Hypermarket	9	11	2166	2217
百货店	Department Store	16	16	17	17
专业店	Specialty Store	2002	1999	8997	8747
其中：加油站	Gas Station	837	867	11512	12388
专卖店	Franchised Store	74	86	4147	3531
其　他	Other Store	28	28	39	38

16-22 续表 3 Continued

项 目	Item	年末零售营业面积(平方米) Operating Area of Retail Enterprises at Year-end (sq.m)		加盟店门店数(个) Number of Join in Stores (unit)	
		2011	2012	2011	2012
总 计	**Total**	**3142563**	**2812467**	**613**	**648**
按登记注册类型分组	**by Status of Registration**				
内资企业	Domestic Funded Enterprises	3113821	2783725	613	648
国有企业	State-owned Enterprises	1610367	1297465	287	287
集体企业	Collective-owned Enterprises	45000	200		
有限责任公司	Limited Liability Corporations	251914	275983	37	49
其他有限责任公司	Other Limited Liability Corporations	251914	275983	37	49
股份有限公司	Share-holding Corporations Ltd.	945001	935547		
私营企业	Private Enterprises	258025	270244	278	312
私营有限责任公司	Private-funded Enterprises	258025	270244	278	312
其他企业	Other Enterprises	3514	4286	11	
外商投资企业	Foreign Funded Enterprises	28742	28742		
外资企业	Enterprises with Sole Fund	28742	28742		
按行业分组	**By Sector**				
批发业	**Wholesale**	**2065189**	**1923528**	**221**	**250**
食品、饮料及烟草制品批发	Special Wholesale of Food, Beverages and Tobaccos	88747	6401		
医药及医疗器材批发	Wholesale of Medicines and Medical Appliances	961	961		
矿产品、建材及化工产品批发	Wholesale of Minerals、Building Materials and Chemical Materiac	1972481	1913166	221	250
其他批发	Others	3000	3000		
零售业	**Wholesale**	**1077374**	**888939**	**392**	**398**
综合零售	Wholesale of Farm Produce and Livestock Products	174841	202737	176	198
食品、饮料及烟草制品专门零售	Special Wholesale of Food, Beverages and Tobaccos	445	445		
纺织、服装及日用品专门零售	Wholesale of Medicines and Medical Appliances	150	150		
文化、体育用品及器材专门零售	Wholesale	100631	99349		
医药及医疗器材专门零售	Wholesale of Farm Produce and Livestock Products	73338	88347	216	200
汽车、摩托车、燃料及零配件专门零售	Special Wholesale of Food, Beverages and Tobaccos	503968	253638		
家用电器及电子产品专门零售	Wholesale of Medicines and Medical Appliances	148968	144532		
五金、家具及室内装修材料专门零售	Wholesale	75033	99741		
按业态分组	**By Business Categories**				
便利店	Convenience Store	7681	10000	57	98
超 市	Supermarket	62004	73737	14	16
大型超市	Hypermarket	95213	108213	25	9
百货店	Department Store	1007	1007	66	66
专业店	Specialty Store	690678	645763	451	459
其中：加油站	Gas Station	2112885	1857968		
专卖店	Franchised Store	171931	115643		
其 他	Other Store	1164	136		

16-22 续表 4 Continued

项　　目	Item	年末从业人员数(人) Engaged Persons at Year-end (person)		年末零售营业面积(平方米) Operating Area of Retail Enterprises at Year-end (sq.m)	
		2011	2012	2011	2012
总　计	**Total**	**2112**	**2157**	**104784**	**107205**
按登记注册类型分组	**by Status of Registration**				
内资企业	Domestic Funded Enterprises	2112	2157	104784	107205
国有企业	State-owned Enterprises	129	129	5151	5151
集体企业	Collective-owned Enterprises				
有限责任公司	Limited Liability Corporations	104	74	4300	2600
其他有限责任公司	Other Limited Liability Corporations	104	74	4300	2600
股份有限公司	Share-holding Corporations Ltd.				
私营企业	Private Enterprises	1857	1954	94601	99454
私营有限责任公司	Private-funded Enterprises	1857	1954	94601	99454
其他企业	Other Enterprises	22		732	
外商投资企业	Foreign Funded Enterprises				
外资企业	Enterprises with Sole Fund				
按行业分组	**By Sector**				
批发业	**Wholesale**	**50**	**94**	**2983**	**2983**
食品、饮料及烟草制品批发	Special Wholesale of Food, Beverages and Tobaccos				
医药及医疗器材批发	Wholesale of Medicines and Medical Appliances				
矿产品、建材及化工产品批发	Wholesale of Minerals、Building Materials and Chemical Materiac	50	94	2983	2983
其他批发	Others				
零售业	**Wholesale**	**2062**	**2063**	**101801**	**104222**
综合零售	Wholesale of Farm Produce and Livestock Products	1653	1718	88213	91614
食品、饮料及烟草制品专门零售	Special Wholesale of Food, Beverages and Tobaccos				
纺织、服装及日用品专门零售	Wholesale of Medicines and Medical Appliances				
文化、体育用品及器材专门零售	Wholesale				
医药及医疗器材专门零售	Wholesale of Farm Produce and Livestock Products	409	345	13588	12608
汽车、摩托车、燃料及零配件专门零售	Special Wholesale of Food, Beverages and Tobaccos				
家用电器及电子产品专门零售	Wholesale of Medicines and Medical Appliances				
五金、家具及室内装修材料专门零售	Wholesale				
按业态分组	**By Business Categories**				
便利店	Convenience Store	236	320	18678	20000
超　市	Supermarket	175	189	33167	35167
大型超市	Hypermarket	1135	1110	33700	34000
百货店	Department Store	79	79	2168	2168
专业店	Specialty Store	487	459	17071	15870
其中：加油站	Gas Station				
专卖店	Franchised Store				
其　他	Other Store				

16-23 连锁住宿和餐饮企业总体情况
Total Conditions of Chain Hotels and Catering Enterprises

项　目	Item	合　计 Total 2011	合　计 Total 2012	直营店 Straight Camp Shop 2011	直营店 Straight Camp Shop 2012
连锁总店数(个)	Number of Chain Stores (unit)		10		
门店总数(个)	Number of Stores (unit)	163	167	105	107
年末从业人员数(人)	Engaged Persons at Year-end (person)	4628	5076	3892	4329
年末餐饮营业面积(平方米)	Operating Area of Catering Enterprises at Year-end (sq.m)	49640	61194	43540	54294
客房数(间)	Number of Hotel Rooms (unit)	227	339	204	339
床位数(个)	Number of Beds (unit)	361	456	326	456
餐位数(位)	Number of Dining-seats (unit)	1750	1567	1450	1253
连锁门店商品购进（采购）额(万元)	Total Purchases Value of Chain Stores (100 million yuan)	16681	18543	15425	17091
其中:统一配送商品购进（采购）额(万元)	Of which:Centralized Purchase and Delivery (100 million yuan)	15835	17603	14595	16170
其中:自有配送中心配送商品购进（采购）额(万元)	Purchases Value of Its Own Distribution Center	12570	11326	11330	9893
非自有配送中心配送商品购进（采购）额(万元)	Purchases Value of Non Its Own Distribution Center	3265	6277	3265	6277
连锁门店营业额(万元)	Business Revenue of Chain Store (100 million yuan)	67760	82467	62070	77046
其中:餐费收入(万元)	Of which:From Meals (100 million yuan)	54490	65606	50264	60714
商品销售额（万元）	Total Sales of Commodities (100 million yuan)	59	361	52	361

项　目	Item	加盟店 Join in Store 2011	加盟店 Join in Store 2012
连锁总店数(个)	Number of Chain Stores (unit)		
门店总数(个)	Number of Stores (unit)	58	60
年末从业人员数(人)	Engaged Persons at Year-end (person)	736	747
年末餐饮营业面积(平方米)	Operating Area of Catering Enterprises at Year-end (sq.m)	6100	6900
客房数(间)	Number of Hotel Rooms (unit)	23	
床位数(个)	Number of Beds (unit)	35	
餐位数(位)	Number of Dining-seats (unit)	300	314
连锁门店商品购进（采购）额(万元)	Total Purchases Value of Chain Stores (100 million yuan)	1257	1452
其中:统一配送商品购进（采购）额(万元)	of which:Centralized Purchase and Delivery (100 million yuan)	1240	1433
其中:自有配送中心配送商品购进（采购）额(万元)	Purchases Value of Its Own Distribution Center	1240	1433
非自有配送中心配送商品购进（采购）额(万元)	Purchases Value of Non Its Own Distribution Center		
连锁门店营业额(万元)	Business Revenue of Chain Store (100 million yuan)	5690	5421
其中:餐费收入(万元)	of which:From Meals (100 million yuan)	4225	4892
商品销售额（万元）	Total Sales of Commodities (100 million yuan)	8	

16-24 连锁住宿和餐饮企业基本情况
Basic Condition of Chain Hotels and Catering Enterprises

项 目	Item	连锁总店数 Number of Head Stores (unit)	门店数合计(个) Total Stores (unit)		年末从业人员数(人) Engaged Persons at Year-end (person)	
			2011	2012	2011	2012
总 计	**Total**	**10**	**163**	**167**	**4628**	**5076**
住宿业	**Hotels**	**2**	**18**	**19**	**1243**	**1617**
按登记注册类型分组	**By Status of Registration**					
内资企业	Domestic Funded Enterprises	2	18	19	1243	1617
有限责任公司	Limited Liability Corporations	1	9	9	973	1077
其他有限责任公司	Other Limited Liability Corporations	1	9	9	973	1077
私营企业	Private Enterprises	1	9	10	270	540
私营有限责任公司	Private-funded Enterprises	1	9	10	270	540
行业中类分组	**By Sector**					
旅游饭店	Travel Hotels	2	18	19	1243	1617
餐饮业	**Catering Enterprises**	**8**	**145**	**148**	**3385**	**3459**
按登记注册类型分组	**By Status of Registration**					
内资企业	Domestic Funded Enterprises	7	123	123	2584	2588
有限责任公司	Limited Liability Corporations	1	3	3	181	165
其他有限责任公司	Other Limited Liability Corporations	1	3	3	181	165
股份有限公司	Share-holding Corporations Ltd.	1	39	36	1343	1185
私营企业	Private Enterprises	5	81	84	1060	1238
私营有限责任公司	Private-funded Enterprises	5	81	84	1060	1238
外商投资企业	Foreign Funded Enterprises	1	22	25	801	871
外资企业	Enterprises with Sole Fund	1	22	25	801	871
按行业分组	**By Sector**					
正餐服务	Restaurant Services	3	15	15	406	545
快餐服务	Fast Food Services	5	130	133	2979	2914

16-24 续表 1 Continued

项目	Item	年末餐饮营业面积(平方米) Operating Area of Catering Enterprises at Year-end (sq.m)		#直营店门店数(个) Number of Straight Camp Shop (unit)	
		2011	2012	2011	2012
总计	**Total**	**49640**	**61194**	**105**	**107**
住宿业	**Hotels**	**14900**	**14400**	**16**	**19**
按登记注册类型分组	**By Status of Registration**				
内资企业	Domestic Funded Enterprises	14900	14400	16	19
有限责任公司	Limited Liability Corporations	14000	14000	9	9
其他有限责任公司	Other Limited Liability Corporations	14000	14000	9	9
私营企业	Private Enterprises	900	400	7	10
私营有限责任公司	Private-funded Enterprises	900	400	7	10
行业中类分组	**By Sector**				
旅游饭店	Travel Hotels	14900	14400	16	19
餐饮业	**Catering Enterprises**	**34740**	**46794**	**89**	**88**
按登记注册类型分组	**By Status of Registration**				
内资企业	Domestic Funded Enterprises	25597	36432	67	63
有限责任公司	Limited Liability Corporations	3824	3824	3	3
其他有限责任公司	Other Limited Liability Corporations	3824	3824	3	3
股份有限公司	Share-holding Corporations Ltd.	11385	19436	39	36
私营企业	Private Enterprises	10388	13172	25	24
私营有限责任公司	Private-funded Enterprises	10388	13172	25	24
外商投资企业	Foreign Funded Enterprises	9143	10362	22	25
外资企业	Enterprises with Sole Fund	9143	10362	22	25
按行业分组	**By Sector**				
正餐服务	Restaurant Services	6212	7872	15	15
快餐服务	Fast Food Services	28528	38922	74	73

16-24 续表 2 Continued

项　　目	Item	年末从业人员数(人) Engaged Persons at Year-end (person)		年末餐饮营业面积(平方米) Operating Area of Catering Enterprises at Year-end (sq.m)		#加盟店门店数(个) Number of Join in Store (unit)	
		2011	2012	2011	2012	2011	2012
总　计	**Total**	**3892**	**4329**	**43540**	**54294**	**58**	**60**
住宿业	**Hotels**	**1183**	**1617**	**14700**	**14400**	**2**	
按登记注册类型分组	**By Status of Registration**						
内资企业	Domestic Funded Enterprises	1183	1617	14700	14400	2	
有限责任公司	Limited Liability Corporations	973	1077	14000	14000		
其他有限责任公司	Other Limited Liability Corporations	973	1077	14000	14000		
私营企业	Private Enterprises	210	540	700	400	2	
私营有限责任公司	Private-funded Enterprises	210	540	700	400	2	
行业中类分组	**By Sector**						
旅游饭店	Travel Hotels	1183	1617	14700	14400	2	
餐饮业	**Catering Enterprises**	**2709**	**2712**	**28840**	**39894**	**56**	**60**
按登记注册类型分组	**By Status of Registration**						
内资企业	Domestic Funded Enterprises	1908	1841	19697	29532	56	60
有限责任公司	Limited Liability Corporations	181	165	3824	3824		
其他有限责任公司	Other Limited Liability Corporations	181	165	3824	3824		
股份有限公司	Share-holding Corporations Ltd.	1343	1185	11385	19436		
私营企业	Private Enterprises	384	491	4488	6272	56	60
私营有限责任公司	Private-funded Enterprises	384	491	4488	6272	56	60
外商投资企业	Foreign Funded Enterprises	801	871	9143	10362		
外资企业	Enterprises with Sole Fund	801	871	9143	10362		
按行业分组	**By Sector**						
正餐服务	Restaurant Services	406	545	6212	7872		
快餐服务	Fast Food Services	2303	2167	22628	32022	56	60

16-24 续表 3 Continued

项　　目	Item	年末从业人员数(人) Engaged Persons at Year-end (person)		年末餐饮营业面积(平方米) Operating Area of Catering Enterprises at Year-end (sq.m)	
		2011	2012	2011	2012
总　计	**Total**	**736**	**747**	**6100**	**6900**
住宿业	**Hotels**	**60**		**200**	
按登记注册类型分组	**By Status of Registration**				
内资企业	Domestic Funded Enterprises	60		200	
有限责任公司	Limited Liability Corporations				
其他有限责任公司	Other Limited Liability Corporations				
私营企业	Private Enterprises	60		200	
私营有限责任公司	Private-funded Enterprises	60		200	
行业中类分组	**By Sector**				
旅游饭店	Travel Hotels	60		200	
餐饮业	**Catering Enterprises**	**676**	**747**	**5900**	**6900**
按登记注册类型分组	**By Status of Registration**				
内资企业	Domestic Funded Enterprises	676	747	5900	6900
有限责任公司	Limited Liability Corporations				
其他有限责任公司	Other Limited Liability Corporations				
股份有限公司	Share-holding Corporations Ltd.				
私营企业	Private Enterprises	676	747	5900	6900
私营有限责任公司	Private-funded Enterprises	676	747	5900	6900
外商投资企业	Foreign Funded Enterprises				
外资企业	Enterprises with Sole Fund				
按行业分组	**By Sector**				
正餐服务	Restaurant Services				
快餐服务	Fast Food Services	676	747	5900	6900

主要统计指标解释

批发业 指批发商向批发、零售单位及其他企事业、机关单位批量销售生活用品和生产资料的活动，以及从事进出口贸易和贸易经纪与代理的活动。批发商可以对所批发的货物拥有所有权，并以本单位、公司的名义进行交易活动；也可以不拥有货物的所有权，而以中介身份做代理销售商。还包括各类商品批发市场中固定摊位的批发活动。

零售业 指百货商店、超级市场、专门零售商店、品牌专卖店、售货摊等主要面向最终消费者（如居民等）的销售活动。包括以互联网、邮政、电话、售货机等方式的销售活动，还包括在同一地点，后面加工生产，前面销售的店铺（如前店后厂的面包房）。不包括：谷物、种子、饲料、牲畜、矿产品、生产用原料、化工原料、农用化工产品、机械设备（乘用车、计算机及通信设备等除外）等生产资料的销售（列入批发业）；非零售单位附带的零售活动，如汽车修理单位销售汽车零件（列入单位主业所对应的行业类别中）；商业零售单位所在商厦的物业管理（列入物业管理）；商业零售单位所在的商品市场、商业大厦的市场管理活动（列入市场管理）。

批发和零售业商品购进、销售、库存额 指各种登记注册类型的批发和零售业企业(单位)以本企业(单位)为总体的，从国内、国外市场购进的商品总量，销售和出口的商品总量、库存的商品总量等情况。该指标可以反映商品流转过程中商品的购进、销售、库存之间的比例关系和存在的问题。

商品购进额 指从本企业以外的单位和个人购进（包括从国外直接进口）作为转卖或加工后转卖的商品金额（含增值税）。商品购进包括：（1）从工农业生产者、批发和零售业企业、住宿和餐饮业企业、出版社或报社的出版发行部门和其他服务业企业购进的商品；（2）从机关团体、事业单位购进的商品；（3）从海关、市场管理部门购进的缉私和没收的商品；（4）从居民收购的废旧商品等。不包括：（1）企业为本单位自身经营用，不是作为转卖而购进的商品，如材料物资、包装物、低值易耗品、办公用品等；（2）未通过买卖行为而收入的商品，如接受其他部门移交的商品、借入的商品、收入代其他单位保管的商品、其他单位赠送的样品、加工回收的成品等；（3）经本单位介绍，由买卖双方直接结算，本单位只收取手续费的业务；（4）销售退回和买方拒付货款的商品；（5）商品溢余。

商品销售额 指对本单位以外的单位和个人出售的商品金额（包括售给本单位消费用的商品，含增值税）。商品销售包括（1）售给城乡居民和社会集团消费用的商品；（2）售给农业、工业、建筑业、运输邮电业、服务业、公用事业等国民经济各行业用于生产、经营用的商品，包括售予批发和零售业作为转卖或加工后转卖的商品；（3）对国（境）外直接出口的商品，不包括：（1）未通过买卖行为付出的商品，如随机构变动移交给其他企业单位的商品、借出的商品、归还受其他单位委托代保管的商品、付出的加工原料和赠送给其他单位的样品等；（2）经本单位介绍，由买卖双方直接结算，本单位只收取手续费的业务；（3）购货退回的商品；（4）商品损耗和损失；（5）出售本单位自用的废旧物资。

商品库存额 指报告期末各种登记注册类型的批发和零售业企业(单位)已取得所有权的商品。它反映批发和零售业企业(单位)的商品库存情况和对市场商品供应的保证程度。商品库存包括: (1)存放在批发和零售业经营单位(如门市部、批发站、采购站、经营处)的仓库、货场、货柜和货架中的商品; (2)挑选、整理、包装中的商品; (3)已记入购进而尚未运到本单位的商品，即发货单或银行承兑凭证已到而货未到的商品; (4)寄放他处的商品，如因购货方拒绝承付款而暂时存在购货方的商品; (5)委托其他单位代销(未作销售或调出)尚未售出的商品; (6)代其他单位购进尚未交付的商品。不包括：所有权不属于本单位的商品；委托外单位加工的商品；外贸企业代理其他单位从国外进口尚未付给订货单位的商品；代国家物资储备部门保管的商品等。

连锁总店（总部） 指负责连锁企业资源（商号、商誉、经营模式、服务标准、管理模式等等）的开发、配置、控制或使用等功能的企业核心管理机构。连锁经营是指经营同类商品或服务，使用统一商号的若干店铺，在同一总店（总部）的管理下，采取统一采购或特许经营等方式，实现规模效益的组织形式，包括直营连锁、特许连锁和自愿连锁三种形式。其中，直营连锁是指连锁店铺由连锁公司全资或控股开设，在总部的直接控制下，开展统一经营的连锁经营形式；特许连锁是指拥有注册商标、企业标志、专利、专有技术等经营资源的企业（特许人），以合同形式将其拥有的经营资源许可其他经营者（被特许人）使用，被特许人按合同约定在统一的经营模式下开展经营，并向特许人支付特许经营费用的连锁经营形式；自愿连锁是指若干个店铺或企业自愿组合起来，在不改变各自资产所有权关系的情况下，以同一个品牌形象面对消费者，以共同进货为纽带开展的连锁经营形式。

亿元商品交易市场 指年成交额在亿元及以上的商品交易市场。商品交易市场是指经有关部门和组织批准设立，有固定场所、设施，有经营管理部门和监管人员，若干市场经营者入内，常年或实际开业三个月以上，集中、公开、独立地进行生活消费品、生产资料等现货商品交易以及提供相关服务的交易场所，包括各类消费品市场、生产资料市场等。

社会消费品零售总额 指企业（单位、个体户）通过交易直接售给个人、社会集团非生产、非经营用的实物商品金额，以及提供餐饮服务所取得的收入金额。个人包括城乡居民和入境人员，社会集团包括机关、社会团体、部队、学校、企事业单位、居委会或村委会等。

住宿业 指有偿为顾客提供临时住宿的服务活动。不包括提供长期住宿场所的活动，如出租房屋、公寓等（列入房地产开发经营）。

餐饮业 指在一定场所，对食物进行现场烹饪、调制，并出售给顾客主要供现场消费的服务活动。

营业额 指住宿和餐饮业单位在经营活动中因提供服务或销售商品等取得的收入。包括：客房收入、餐费收入、商品销售额和其他收入。其中，客房收入指住宿和餐饮业单位在经营活动中因提供住宿服务取得的收入。餐费收入指住宿和餐饮业单位因为顾客提供就餐服务取得的收入，包括经烹饪、调制加工后出售的各种食品，如主食、炒菜、凉拌菜等的收入.

Explanatory Notes on Main Statistical Indicators

Wholesale Trade refers to the activities of wholesaler selling at wholesale commodities for daily use and capital goods to enterprises of wholesale and retail trades and other enterprises, institutions and government offices, including the activities of wholesaler engaged in import and export and acting as a trade agent. The wholesaler may have the right of ownership over the commodities of wholesale and trade in the name of its own's or a company, the wholesaler may not have the right of ownership, only acts an agent. The wholesale trade also include the activities of wholesaler at the fixed stalls of the wholesale market of different commodities.

Retail Trade refers to the activities of department store, supermarket, franchised store, brand store, retail stall and on-the-spot-making-selling store selling commodities to the final consumers (citizens) by any means including internet, post, telephone, sales machine. Retail trade excludes the activities of sales of capital goods such a grain, seed, feed, livestock, mineral products, raw material for production, industrial chemicals, chemical products for farm, machine and equipment (vehicle, computer and communication equipment), and the activities of supplementary sales of non-retailer such as the sales of spareparts of car repair business (listed as branch in correspondence with principle business), property management of buildings of retail units (listed as property management); market management of commercial markets and buildings of retail units (listed as market management) .

Purchase, Sales and Stock of Commodities by Wholesale and Retail Trades refers to the total volume of commodities purchased, total volume of sales and exports, and the stock of commodities by wholesale and retail enterprises (establishments) of different status of registration from domestic and overseas markets. This indicator reflects the relationship among purchase, sales and stock of commodities in the circulation of goods and reveals the existing problems.

Total Purchases of Commodities refers to the total value of purchases of commodities by enterprises (establishments) from other establishments or individuals (including direct import from abroad) for the purpose of re-selling, either with or without further processing of the commodities purchased. The commodities include: (1)commodities purchased from agricultural and industrial producer, wholesaler, retailer, publishing house and other service business, (2) commodities purchased from institutions and government departments, (3) confiscated goods purchased from the customs authorities or market management agencies, (4) second-hand goods and wastes purchased from residents. The commodities exclude (1).commodities purchased by enterprises (establishments) for use in their own business operation, commodities obtained without buying or selling procedures such as materials, consumable goods of low value, office appliance,etc. (2). received goods without trading, such as goods handed over from others, borrowed goods, preserved goods for others, donated goods from others, processed and retrieved goods, etc. (3). goods of direct settlement between buyer and seller with handling fees introduced by others, (4).goods returned or refused to pay by the buyer,(5). excessive goods.

Total Sales of Commodities refer to value of commodities sold by the establishments to other establishments and individuals (including goods sold for self consumption, including the value-added tax). The commodities include: (1) commodities sold to urban and rural residents and social groups for their consumption; (2) commodities sold to establishments in all industries for their production and operation, including agriculture, industry, construction, transportation, post and telecommunications, catering services, and public utility including commodities sold to wholesale and retail establishments for re-selling, with or without further processing; and (3) commodities for direct export to abroad. Excluded are (1) extended commodities without trading, such as goods handed over to other enterprises and institutions because of the change of organizations, lent goods, returned goods preserved for others, extended processing materials and samples donated to others, (2) goods of direct settlement between buyer and seller with handling fees introduced by others,(3). goods returned after purchase, (4) damaged and spoiled goods, (5) waste and used goods of self use,

Total Stock of Commodities refers to total commodities possessed by wholesaler and retailer of various types of registration status at the end of the reference period, reflecting the commodity stock level of various wholesaler and retailer and the potential for market supply. It includes: (1) commodities located in storage, garages, counters, and shelves of operating places (such as sale stores, wholesale centres, and operating offices), (2) commodities in the process of being selected, sorted, and packed, (3) commodities not arrived but recorded as purchase in the account, i.e. commodities not arrived but payment receipts for the commodities from the sellers or the banks arrived , (4) commodities deposited in other places rather than places mentioned above, for instance: commodities in the hold of purchasers temporarily due to the refusal of payment and commodities not taken back after going through the formalities, (5) commodities entrusted to other units to sell but not sold yet, (6) commodities purchased for other units but not delivered yet. Commodities not included as stock are those not owned by the enterprises (units), commodities on commission for processing but not yet delivered, imported commodities of agency of foreign trade enterprise but not yet delivered to ordering units and finally those put in stock on behalf of the state material reserves units.

Chain Head Stores (headquarter) refer to the core leading stores responsible for development, allocation, administration and utilization of resources (name of stores, brand of stores, operation model, service standard, management way, etc.) of chain stores. Chain stores refers to the stores engaged in providing homogeneous commodities or services, with the central leadership of head store and guided by common policies, conduct centralized purchase and distributed selling of commodities, in order to gain better efficiency through standardized operation. The chain stores include regular chain stores, franchise chain stores and voluntary chain stores.

Regular Chain store refers to chain stores that are invested or controlled by the headquarters. They operate under direct and unified management from the headquarters.

Franchise chain store refers to the chain stores (franchisees) which are franchised with operation resources such as trade marks, names, patent and operation know-how by the franchisors in form of contract and pay the operation fees to the franchisors.

Voluntary chain store refers to the stores operate jointly on the voluntary bases while maintaining their status of independent legal entities with full ownership of their assets. They sell goods of same brand from same channel of resource to the consumers.

Large Commodity Markets with Transaction Value over 100 Million Yuan refers to the commodity markets with an annual transaction of over 100 million. The commodity market refers to the markets approved and managed by related departments, where there are fixed sites, facilities, managers and administration offices, where there are a certain number of traders to operate for three month and above or all the year, where the commodities including the articles for daily consumption and capital goods and services are traded in a centralized, independent and open way. Such market includes markets of daily goods and market of capital goods, etc.

Total Retail Sales of Consumer Goods refers to the amount obtained by enterprises (units, self-employed individuals) through direct sales of non-production and non-business physical commodity to individuals, social institutions, and revenue from providing catering services. Individuals include rural and urban households, population from abroad, social institutions include government agencies, social organizations, military units, schools, institutions, neighbourhood (village) committees.

Hotel Services refer to the charged accommodation services provided to customers, excluding the long term accommodation service activities such as rental housing and apartments(it is under real estate development and management).

Catering Services refer to the activities of enterprises providing on-the-spot services of selling food cooked and prepared to the customer in certain sites.

Business Revenue of Hotels and Catering Services refers to revenue received from providing services or selling commodities by corporate enterprises and establishments engaged in hotels and catering services, including income from hotels, from catering services, from selling of commodities and from other services. Income from hotels refers to income of corporate enterprises and establishments engaged in hotels and catering services by providing lodging services. Income from catering services refers to income of corporate enterprises and establishments engaged in hotels and catering services by providing catering services, including selling of cooked or prepared foods such as staple food, cooked dishes or cold dishes. Income from selling of commodities refers to income of corporate enterprises and establishments engaged in hotels and catering services by selling commodities (including value-added tax) that accompany the services they provide. Income from other activities refers to income received other than income from hotels, catering services or selling of commodities, such as income from providing recreation, fitness or business services.

新疆统计年鉴
XINJIANG STATISTICAL YEARBOOK

17

教育、科技和文化

EDUCATION,SCIENCE & TECHNOLOGY AND CULTURE

简要说明

本篇资料的主要内容及来源

教育统计资料包括研究生教育（高等学校研究生教育、科研机构研究生教育）；普通高等学校本专科教育；普通中等教育(中等专业教育、技工学校、普通中学、职业高中、工读学校)；初等教育(小学)、特殊教育(盲聋哑和弱智儿童学校等)以及教育经费等资料。

教育部分资料由新疆维吾尔自治区教育厅依据年报资料整理提供。

科技统计资料包括科技活动基本情况、县级以上政府部门属研究与开发机构及科技信息与文献机构人员数、重大科学技术研究成果及奖励、专利申请和批准情况、高等学校科技活动情况、企事业单位专业技术人员情况、大中型工业企业科技活动情况、各类技术合同鉴定及执行情况、技术经济合同成交情况、技术流向地域情况等。

科技部分资料由新疆维吾尔自治区统计局社会科技统计处根据科技年报和新疆维吾尔自治区科技厅提供资料整理。

文化部分主要包括艺术表演团体、艺术表演场所、公共图书馆、博物馆、文化馆（站）、广播、电影、电视以及文物等文化单位的机构、人员、经费和业务活动情况。

文化部分资料是由新疆维吾尔自治区统计局社会科技统计处根据部门统计报表资料加工整理而成。

Brief Introduction

Main Content and Source of Data

The data on education cover the situation on postgraduate (regular institutions of higher education,research institutions), regular institution of higher education(universities and colleges), regular secondary education, (professional secondary schools, technical schools, regular secondary school,vocational senior secondary schools,schools for juvenile delinquents);primary education (primary schools),special education(schools for the blind, deaf-mutes and the retarded) and expenditure on education.

Statistical data on education compiled by the Statistics Bureau of Xinjiang in accordance with the data from the Bureau of Education.

Data on technology mainly include: condition of scientific and technological activities, state-owned research and development institutions and information and literature institutions at and above county level and persons engaged; the situation of science and technological achievements & prizes and patent applications, basic statistics on scientific and technological activities of high education, condition of professional scientific and technological personnel of enterprises and institutions, statistics on signing and implementing technical contracts, statistics on transaction intechnical and economic contract, statistics on location of technical contract.

Data on technology compiled by the Statistics Bureau of Xinjiang in accordance with the data from the Bureau of Science &Technology.

Data on culture cover mainly the situations on institutions, personal and business activities of arts (performing groups and venues), libraries, museums, cultural centers, archives, cultural stations, broadcasting, films, televisions, news and publication.

Data on culture are collected and tabulated in accordance with the statistical reporting schemes stipulated by the Statistical Bureau of Xinjiang.

17-1 主要年份各级各类学校数

Number of Schools by Level and Type in Main Years

单位：所 (unit)

年 份 Year	普通高等学校 Regular Institutions of Higher Education	中等学校 Secondary Schools	普通中等专业学校 Specialized Secondary Schools	普通中学 Regular Secondary Schools	#高中 Senior Secondary Schools	职业高中 Vocational Secondary Schools	技工学校 Technical Schools	小学 Primary Schools	特殊教育学校 Special Schools
1978	10	2078	78	1997	673		10	9891	1
1980	12	2197	96	2032	720	21	48	9006	2
1985	14	2360	97	2147	794	65	51	8104	3
1990	21	2274	112	1958	766	134	70	7247	6
1995	21	2121	115	1792	554	145	69	7086	6
2000	20	2000	112	1711	484	112	65	6718	7
2001	21	2179	99	1929	472	89	62	6221	7
2002	24	2173	87	1945	507	83	58	6043	7
2003	26	2154	78	1932	500	86	58	5832	8
2004	28	2186	78	1965	498	84	59	5451	8
2005	31	2185	79	1961	503	87	58	5209	10
2006	31	2101	67	1891	486	84	59	4815	9
2007	32	2040	74	1830	454	75	61	4589	9
2008	32	1973	75	1759	444	82	57	4159	10
2009	32	1832	80	1610	413	82	60	3651	10
2010	32	1772	81	1545	385	83	63	3598	13
2011	32	1766	96	1525	368	71	74	3536	15
2012	34	1744	95	1497	366	69	83	3535	19

注：从 2006 年起，职业初中并入普通中学统计。（以下同）
Note: Number of regular secondary schools include the number of junion vocational secondary schools from 2006.(The same follows)

17-2 主要年份各级各类学校教师数

Number of Teachers by Level and Type of School in Main Years

单位：人 (person)

年 份 Year	普通高等学校 Regular Institutions of Higher Education	中等学校 Secondary Schools	普通中等专业学校 Specialized Secondary Schools	普通中学 Regular Secondary Schools	#高中 Senior Secondary Schools	职业高中 Vocational Secondary Schools	技工学校 Technical Schools	小学 Primary Schools	特殊教育学校 Special Schools
1978	2458	44417	2543	41661	8064		213	82616	28
1980	3149	50056	3459	45232	9292	77	1288	98027	54
1985	5473	69185	4554	60942	15059	1567	2122	98294	67
1990	7002	78596	6158	65814	19318	3117	3507	95060	139
1995	7687	76584	6540	62934	14434	3494	3616	106001	162
2000	7924	89211	6786	75895	16069	3104	3426	131259	183
2001	9123	93126	6842	79419	17025	2546	4319	132137	187
2002	10369	96469	6031	84714	19031	2399	3325	132435	200
2003	11237	103156	5157	89332	20976	2440	6227	132284	237
2004	12239	106839	5494	94381	22809	3079	3885	134915	257
2005	12733	112941	4993	102168	25153	1696	4084	134768	262
2006	13783	120777	4339	106975	26815	2832	6631	134718	286
2007	15096	123246	5553	108232	27970	2295	7166	133626	298
2008	15755	121898	5381	108729	28735	2586	5202	132797	313
2009	16234	125152	6086	110842	29402	2464	5760	134263	319
2010	16506	128306	6232	113990	30231	2708	5706	133963	347
2011	17256	132748	7210	116501	31258	2255	6782	135182	316
2012	17570	134900	7173	118299	32375	2347	7081	136130	452

17-3 主要年份各级各类学校在校学生数

Number of Students Enrollment by Level and Type of School in Main Years

单位：人 (person)

年 份 Year	普通高等学校 Regular Institutions of Higher Education	中等学校 Secondary Schools	普通中等专业学校 Specialized Secondary Schools	普通中学 Regular Secondary Schools	#高 中 Senior Secondary Schools	职业高中 Vocational Secondary Schools	技工学校 Technical Schools	小 学 Primary Schools	特殊教育学校 Special Schools
1978	10229	838560	23696	806386	128376		8478	2028771	270
1980	14308	886740	42362	823161	147446	1416	19801	2055513	371
1985	26500	1054293	33251	955356	223405	41825	23861	1966306	706
1990	31271	1015214	45985	863118	251067	65862	40249	1857246	610
1995	44918	912597	68586	749788	141330	54122	40101	2301274	643
2000	74063	1311845	105255	1132912	198639	51270	22408	2477413	674
2001	109815	1390360	97321	1228566	225411	47673	16800	2435667	922
2002	134831	1493580	83902	1338836	272381	50787	20055	2359788	3876
2003	151256	1584700	71499	1448531	315178	45330	19340	2289066	1863
2004	168247	1676971	71324	1517948	359147	61502	26197	2218109	2549
2005	188752	1717403	86744	1587850	387763	63158	26219	2143833	4961
2006	207672	1739422	108131	1572502	402321	23488	35301	2097975	4843
2007	226012	1742947	141162	1529092	413452	31741	40952	2058884	6396
2008	241288	1722667	150715	1483550	418701	41611	46791	2012004	5574
2009	253272	1695984	147439	1444836	417139	54777	48932	1973890	5991
2010	263835	1684027	152227	1422419	419141	59593	49788	1935798	5974
2011	272818	1675169	161657	1409293	432724	60734	43485	1919457	4733
2012	284172	1651618	159069	1383886	440717	57269	51394	1900844	4909

注：1.17-3、17-4、17-5 表中高等学校含研究生数。2.特殊教育学校 2002 年新增随班就读。(以下同)

Note: a) Institntions of higher education include the number of postgraduates with table 17-3,17-4,17-5.

b) In Special Schools for the blind,deaf, mute, new comers may follow the classes accordingly from the year 2002 (The same as follows).

17-4 主要年份各级各类学校招生数

Number of New Students Enrollment by Level and Type of School in Main Years

单位：人 (person)

年 份 Year	普通高等学校 Regular Institutions of Higher Education	中等学校 Secondary Schools	普通中等专业学校 Specialized Secondary Schools	普通中学 Regular Secondary Schools	#高 中 Senior Secondary Schools	职业高中 Vocational Secondary Schools	技工学校 Technical Schools	小 学 Primary Schools	特殊教育学校 Special Schools
1980	3767	336402	14688	310931	73959	792	10531	433089	90
1985	9298	386074	13919	341123	93692	20429	10603	374643	91
1990	8034	356615	15586	297641	84567	27968	15420	335552	103
1995	12307	356814	25260	286318	58203	25643	19593	419717	165
2000	30689	486763	38866	418790	76744	20027	9080	364193	175
2001	42253	510469	26763	459878	93519	16621	7207	352975	135
2002	42808	551353	22241	501824	113366	16746	10442	346386	874
2003	44733	583033	24016	532987	126163	15378	10652	347619	369
2004	53204	606666	27990	536405	138315	27585	14686	347364	390
2005	58653	602335	34882	539922	145044	12416	15115	338539	847
2006	62395	599748	45536	522425	142853	13017	18770	337994	780
2007	68999	619218	65290	510080	146449	19201	24647	340108	1158
2008	74670	603352	62098	497579	147914	21610	22065	328647	840
2009	73904	593290	53692	489838	148869	28243	21517	318488	869
2010	79216	597621	60418	489356	153238	28767	19080	311861	1055
2011	79337	581939	60669	482450	156497	21777	17043	322436	939
2012	83732	571006	56096	469674	155276	22229	23007	331734	1137

17-5 主要年份各级各类学校毕业生数

Number of Graduates by Level and Type of School in Main Years

单位：人 (person)

年 份 Year	普通高等学校 Regular Institutions of Higher Education	中等学校 Secondary Schools	普通中等专业学校 Specialized Secondary Schools	普通中学 Regular Secondary Schools	#高 中 Senior Secondary Schools	职业高中 Vocational Secondary Schools	技工学校 Technical Schools	小 学 Primary Schools	特殊教育学校 Special Schools
1978	1509	205862	8801	195542	53970		1519	388359	195
1980	814	264626	11946	246382	60370	341	5957	292515	37
1981	779	280171	17039	257478	67114	367	5287	397524	37
1982	4108	269927	17201	244853	69504	385	7488	310025	32
1983	4823	283120	11584	260906	77546	1144	9486	317227	27
1984	3426	275788	8130	257833	72191	2764	7061	295993	48
1985	3511	290077	8097	267302	68096	7424	7254	289045	73
1986	4797	296360	11551	268402	58585	8543	7864	307047	52
1987	8001	321981	10623	289556	73947	12280	9522	317820	101
1988	7792	346072	12026	311224	85718	12758	10064	288594	68
1989	6900	347719	12441	308467	86489	14650	12161	249888	57
1990	8603	343313	14260	297235	81062	17938	13880	259301	98
1991	7919	324031	15571	274913	79664	17505	16042	183350	159
1992	8402	310076	14950	260953	84518	18999	15174	268074	157
1993	7741	312284	16760	261502	78675	18558	15464	259468	104
1994	7734	250909	16206	198839	57090	18100	17764	262215	55
1995	10505	271992	18981	215756	44589	16490	20765	271227	57
1996	12272	271267	21701	215295	43478	15424	18847	279866	39
1997	10908	284580	21936	228287	37966	17181	17176	294420	71
1998	11401	313807	23090	259910	49702	18038	12769	321044	100
1999	11886	341434	25118	282486	52403	18826	15004	357801	84
2000	11220	363503	25879	308225	54985	17341	12058	371758	70
2001	16121	380946	26403	329801	59251	13881	10861	395010	104
2002	16380	410299	31598	356203	61932	15087	7411	411626	848
2003	25785	434523	31304	379269	70824	15685	8265	421443	264
2004	31013	468849	24758	420583	84418	15475	8033	417588	382
2005	37920	520798	19559	474621	103928	19492	7126	397592	714
2006	45810	541729	22515	501697	115422	5510	12007	373862	684
2007	48372	557512	25735	515494	127129	5943	10340	361921	716
2008	57076	557655	32537	507098	135240	6454	11566	349300	859
2009	60092	554905	41866	492259	137290	8883	11897	339836	935
2010	66903	547288	44478	473216	135706	14442	15152	334362	728
2011	67219	526007	47371	457944	129478	10256	10436	327704	652
2012	68664	529246	45833	454590	135089	16677	12146	321020	522

17-6 主要年份研究生数
Number of Postgraduates in Main Years

单位：人 (person)

年份 Year	招生数 New Enrollment	在校学生数 Total Enrollment	攻读博士学位 Working for Doctor's Degree	攻读硕士学位 Working for Master's Degree	毕业生数 Graduates	攻读博士学位 Working for Doctor's Degree	攻读硕士学位 Working for Master's Degree
1978	16	16		16			
1980	15	66		66			
1985	120	179		174	21		21
1990	73	256	3	253	112		112
1995	180	509	14	295	91		91
2000	544	1196	48	1148	235	5	230
2001	827	1749	80	1669	277	8	269
2002	1104	2495	112	2383	355	11	344
2003	1664	3629	186	3443	521	18	503
2004	2336	5120	283	4837	832	30	802
2005	2902	6938	415	6523	1066	35	1031
2006	3147	8421	489	7932	1628	90	1538
2007	3491	9623	549	9074	2244	110	2134
2008	3523	10317	595	9722	2786	132	2654
2009	4189	11635	653	10982	3021	121	2900
2010	4595	12675	713	11962	3360	158	3202
2011	4972	14099	840	13259	3421	133	3288
2012	5701	15456	844	14612	4073	159	3914

17-7 高等学校基本情况
Basic Statistics on Institutions of Higher Education

单位：人 (2012 年) (person)

项目	Item	学校数(所) Schools (unit)	毕业生数 Graduates	招生数 New Enrollment	在校学生数 Total Enrollment	教职工数 Staff and Teachers	#专任教师 Full-time Teachers
总计	**Total**		**64591**	**78031**	**268716**	**33192**	**20829**
普通高等学校	Regular Institutionsof Higher Education	34	63709	76646	264002	27885	17570
综合大学	Multiversity	6	16204	18906	68761	8144	4934
理工院校	Science Engineering	12	16748	23125	66001	6088	4035
农业院校	Agriculture	4	10466	12419	44646	3905	2505
医药院校	Medicine	3	4730	4883	20356	2889	1906
师范院校	Normal Institutions	4	9805	10245	39965	3905	2425
财经学院	Economics and Finance	1	3587	4128	15611	1661	1045
政法院校	Politics & Law	2	1437	2011	5142	715	366
体育院校	Sport	1		57	57	145	92
艺术院校	Art	1	732	872	3463	433	262
总计中：高职学校	In total Vocational Training	18	22407	29455	85622	8202	5536
成人高等学校	Ordinary Class for Adult Higher Education		882	1385	4714	5307	3259

17-8 中等专业学校基本情况
Basic Statistics on Specialized Secondary Schools

单位：人 (2012 年) (person)

项　目	Item	毕业生数 Graduates	招生数 New Student Enrollment	在校学生数 Student Enrollment	专业课教师 Teachers of Various Subjects
总　计	**Total**	**71288**	**86751**	**235277**	**5591**
农林牧渔类	Agriculture	12102	16164	40902	810
资源环境类	Resource and Environment	608	812	2187	36
能源与新能源类	Energy	2078	1704	5646	168
土木水利类	Civil and Hydraulic Engineering	4120	5917	14854	149
加工制造类	Processing and Manufacturing	6256	7529	20022	457
石油化工类	Petroleum and Chemical	3027	2720	8806	114
轻纺食品类	Textile and Food	3020	2635	7375	123
交通运输类	Transportation and Communication	4249	8518	19734	218
信息技术类	Information Technologies	3766	4679	11751	410
医药卫生类	Medcine and Health	10716	10696	36002	445
休闲保健类	Recreation and Health Care	737	875	2134	18
财经商贸类	Economics and Finance	3972	3581	9478	360
旅游服务类	Trades and Tourism	2678	3962	9556	174
文化艺术类	Culture Arts and Physical Education	5761	5253	16424	520
体育与健身类	Sports and Fitness	1002	1274	3808	212
教育类	Teacher Training	4912	8849	22510	867
司法服务类	Justice and Services	985	1211	2221	86
公共管理与服务类	Scoial and Public Affairs	473	135	864	50
其　他	Others	826	237	1003	374

17-9 普通中学和其他学校基本情况
Basic Statistics on Regular Secondary Schools and Other Schools

单位：人 (2012 年) (person)

项　目	Item	学校数(所) Schools (unit)	毕业生数 Graduates	招生数 New Enrollment	在校学生数 Total Enrollment	教职工数 Staff and Teachers	#专任教师 Full-time Teachers
普通中学	Regular Secondary Schools	1497	454590	469674	1383886	134043	118299
高　中	Senior Secondary Schools	366	135089	155276	440717		32375
初　中	Junior Secondary Schools	1131	319501	314398	943169		85924
职业高中	Vocational Secondary Schools	69	16677	22229	57269	3167	2347
技工学校	Technical Shools	83	12146	23007	51394	9345	7081
小　学	Primary Schools	3535	321020	331734	1900844	149927	136130
特殊教育学校	Special Schools	19	522	1137	4909	574	452

17-10 各类成人教育情况
Basic Statistics on Adult Education by Type

单位：人 (2012年) (person)

项目	Item	学校数(所) Schools (unit)	毕业生数 Graduates	在校学生数 Total Enrollment	教职工数 Staff and Teachers	#专任教师 Full-time Teachers
成人高等教育	Adult Education Schools	8	16837	68329	5307	3259
广播电视大学	Radio and TV Universities	2	1120	2820	3584	2078
职工大学	Schools of Higher Education for Staff Workers	1	19	252	108	80
教育学院	Pedagogical Colleges	5	1048	3175	1615	1101
普通高校办的成人班	Adult Classes run by Ordinary Colleges and Universities		14650	62082		
成人中等教育	Secondary Schools for Adults	17	8778	18939	1047	832
成人中学	Secondary Schools for Adults	15	813	1998	190	179
成人技术培训学校	Technical adult college	2058	1319232	1536390	3792	1938
成人初等学校	Primary Schools for Adults	478	61624	74283	1745	735
#扫盲班	Literacy Courses		48698	61754	1202	464

17-11 主要年份教育发展水平
Development Level of Education in Main Years

年份 Year	各类学校在校生占全区人口比重(%) Students as Percentage of Total Population (%)	平均每万人口中(人) Number of Students per 10 000 Population (person)			大中小学生各占普通学校学生总数的比重(%) Students of Different Level as Percentage of Total Students(%)		
		大学生 University and College Students	中学生 Secondary School students	小学生 Primary School Students	大学生 University and College Students	中学生 Secondary School Students	小学生 Primary School Students
1978	23.34	8.30	654.00	1645.38	0.36	28.02	70.50
1980	23.04	11.15	641.47	1601.82	0.48	27.80	69.52
1985	22.39	19.47	701.88	1444.60	0.87	31.35	64.52
1990	18.99	20.45	564.44	1208.01	1.08	29.72	63.94
1995	19.61	26.84	453.23	1330.61	1.38	23.00	70.60
2000	22.84	41.05	638.26	1395.72	1.82	27.93	61.09
2001	20.98	58.53	654.84	1298.22	2.79	31.21	61.87
2002	23.14	70.04	702.72	1238.61	3.21	31.87	56.18
2003	22.53	76.33	749.00	1183.62	3.39	33.25	52.54
2004	21.91	83.09	773.23	1129.89	4.18	38.92	56.90
2005	21.96	90.44	766.67	1066.40	4.70	39.86	55.44
2006	21.78	97.20	767.07	1023.40	5.10	40.64	54.26
2007	21.21	103.20	729.77	982.65	5.69	40.19	54.12
2008	20.68	108.44	696.24	911.60	6.20	39.81	54.00
2009	20.57	111.94	669.33	914.42	6.60	39.47	53.93
2010	20.62	115.13	652.09	887.34	6.96	39.41	53.63
2011	20.65	117.14	638.06	869.04	7.21	39.28	53.51
2012	20.48	120.35	619.80	851.34	7.56	38.94	53.49

17-12 主要年份各级学校教师负担学生数

Student-teacher Ratio by Level of School in Main Years

单位：人 (person)

年份 Year	高等学校 University and College		普通中学 Secondary Schools		小学 Primary Schools	
	教师数 Number of Teachers	平均每个教师负担学生数 Student-Teacher Ratio	教师数 Number of Teachers	平均每个教师负担学生数 Student-Teacher Ratio	教师数 Number of Teachers	平均每个教师负担学生数 Student-Teacher Ratio
1978	2458	4.16	41661	19.36	82616	24.56
1980	3149	4.54	45232	18.20	89027	23.09
1985	5473	4.84	60942	15.68	98294	20.00
1990	7002	4.47	65814	13.12	95060	19.54
1995	7687	5.78	62934	11.91	106001	20.77
2000	7924	9.34	75895	14.92	131259	18.87
2005	12733	14.82	101701	15.16	134768	15.91
2006	13783	15.07	106975	14.70	134718	15.57
2007	15096	14.33	108232	14.13	133626	15.41
2008	15755	14.66	108729	13.64	132797	15.15
2009	16234	14.88	110842	13.04	134263	14.70
2010	16506	15.22	113990	12.48	133963	14.45
2011	17256	14.99	116501	12.10	135182	14.20
2012	17570	15.29	118299	11.70	136130	13.96

17-13 主要年份各级学校女学生和女教师数

Number of Female Students and Teachers by Level of School in Main Years

单位：人 (person)

项目	Item	2000	2010	2011	2012
女学生	**Number of Female Students**	**1889552**	**1911185**	**1908102**	**1891395**
高等学校	Institutions of Higher Education	38419	136071	142360	149116
中等专业学校	Specialized Secondary Schools	49892	82554	87298	86008
普通中学	Regular Secondary Schools	568060	718438	714429	703294
职业高中	Vocational Secondary Schools	23670	26234	26138	22536
技工学校	Technical Shools	8740	13228	11553	13655
小　学	Primary Schools	1200513	932296	924510	914822
特殊教育学校	Special Schools for the Blind, Mute and Deaf	258	2364	1814	1964
女学生占学生总数的比重(%)	**Percentage of Female Students to Total Students (%)**	**48.9**	**49.3**	**49.5**	**49.2**
女教师	**Number of Female Teachers**	**134563**	**178259**	**183690**	**187720**
高等学校	Institutions of Higher Education	3192	8362	8831	9044
中等专业学校	Specialized Secondary Schools	3408	3421	3998	4027
普通中学	Regular Secondary Schools	40030	67901	70273	72125
职业高中	Vocational Secondary Schools	1601	1458	1239	1289
技工学校	Technical Schools	1264	3937	4500	4698
小　学	Primary Schools	84944	92917	94609	96208
特殊教育学校	Special Schools for the Blind, Mute and Deaf	124	263	240	329
女教师占教师总数的比重(%)	**Percentage of Female Teachers to Total Teachers (%)**	**58.9**	**63.1**	**64.3**	**64.9**

17-14 主要年份初中毕业生和小学生升学率及小学学龄儿童入学率

Percentage of Graduates of Junior Secondary Schools and Primary Schools Entering Higher Level Schools, Enrollment Rate of School-age Children in Main Years

单位：人、% (person,%)

年份 Year	初中毕业生升高中情况 Student of Graduates of Junior Secondary Schools Entering Senior Secondary Schools			小学毕业生升初中情况 Student of Graduates of Primary Schools Entering Junior Secondary Schools			小学学龄儿童入学情况 Student of School-Age Children Enrolled		
	初中毕业生数 Graduates of Junior Secondary Schools	高中招生数 Students Entering Senior Secondary Schools	升学率 Percentage of Graduates of Primary Schools Entering Junior Secondary Schools	小学毕业生数 Graduates of Primary Schools	初中招生数 Students Entering Junior Secondary Schools	升学率 Percentage of Graduates of Primary Schools Entering Junior Secondary Schools	学龄儿童数 School-Age Children	已入学学龄儿童数 School-Age Children Enrolled in Schools	入学率 Enrollment Rate
1978	141572	68261	48.22	788359	255687	88.67	1541148	1480400	96.00
1980	186012	73989	39.76	292515	236432	80.83	1637610	1548653	94.57
1985	199206	93692	47.03	289045	247431	85.60	1645055	1569328	95.40
1990	216173	84567	39.12	259301	213074	82.17	1502163	1465325	97.50
1995	171167	58203	34.00	271227	228115	84.10	2036541	1976120	97.03
2000	253240	76744	30.30	371758	342046	92.01	2313890	2245190	97.03
2005	370693	145044	39.13	397592	394878	99.33	2007742	1981569	98.70
2006	386275	142853	36.98	373862	379572	101.53	1957604	1941068	99.15
2007	388365	146449	37.71	361921	363631	100.47	1930074	1916265	99.28
2008	371858	147914	39.78	349300	349665	100.10	1865105	1856800	99.55
2009	354969	148869	41.94	339836	340969	100.33	1839775	1829016	99.41
2010	337510	153238	45.40	334362	336118	100.53	1801872	1797853	99.78
2011	328466	156497	47.64	327704	325953	99.47	1785583	1780729	99.73
2012	319501	155276	48.60	321020	314398	97.94	1767028	1763249	99.79

17-15 主要年份各级各类学校少数民族在校学生数

Number of Students Enrollment of Minority Nationalities by Level and Type of School in Main Years

单位：人 (person)

年份 Year	高等学校 Institutions of Higher Education	中等学校 Secondary Schools	中等专业学校 Specialized Secondary Schools	职业高中 Vocational Secondary Schools	技工学校 Technical Schools	普通中学 Regular Secondary Schools	#高中 Senior Secondary Schools	#初中 Junior Secondary Schools	小学（万人） Primary Schools (10 000 persons)
1978	7890	310987	10807			300180	38837	261343	106.58
1980	6455	311213	22263	592	4514	283844	50340	233504	101.73
1985	13996	346833	17888	4915	7649	316381	71199	245182	116.43
1990	17542	439140	23897	13577	13685	387981	94579	293402	126.78
1995	24125	477379	33264	20013	16040	408012	52570	355492	157.84
2000	31989	834390	62572	34992	12260	724566	91843	632723	171.44
2005	75744	993338	32698	54773	13371	892501	152244	740257	136.94
2006	77627	975346	36393	13216	18002	907735	149963	757772	132.94
2007	81978	958643	55224	19181	20476	863762	156478	707284	131.32
2008	85942	935350	62337	28387	23396	821230	160238	660992	130.44
2009	91243	927939	66502	41666	24466	795305	160720	634585	130.31
2010	94708	933338	75924	49388	24894	783132	162687	620445	129.37
2011	102358	940729	82524	54357	21743	782105	173913	608192	129.25
2012	106893	939713	85099	50841	25697	778076	185331	592745	130.10

17-16 各地、州、市各级各类学校数
Number of Schools by Level, Type and by Prefecture, Autonomous Prefecture and City

单位：所　　(2012 年)　　(unit)

地　区	Region	普通高等学校 Regular Institutions of Higher Education	中等职业学校 Specialized Secondary Schools	#中等师范学校 Teacher Training Secondary Schools
总　计	**Total**	**34**	**181**	**13**
乌鲁木齐市	Urumqi City	18	34	2
克拉玛依市	Karamay City	1	3	1
吐鲁番地区	Turpan Administrative Offices		3	1
哈密地区	Hami [Kumul] Administrative Offices		5	
昌吉回族自治州	Changji Hui Autonomous Prefecture	3	8	
伊犁哈萨克自治州	Ili Kazak Autonomous Prefecture	3	39	3
伊犁州直属县(市)	Counties (Cities) Direct Under Ili Prefecture	3	19	1
塔城地区	Tacheng [Tarbagatai] Administrative Offices		10	1
阿勒泰地区	Altay Administrative Offices		10	1
博尔塔拉蒙古自治州	Bortala Mongol Autonomous Prefecture		1	1
巴音郭楞蒙古自治州	Bayangol Mongol Autonomous Prefecture	1	8	1
阿克苏地区	Aksu Administrative Offices	1	8	
克孜勒苏柯尔克孜自治州	Kizilsu Kirgiz Autonomous Prefecture		9	1
喀什地区	Kashgar [Kaxgar] Administrative Offices	1	27	1
和田地区	Hotan Administrative Offices	2	11	1
生产建设兵团	Production and Construction Group	3	23	
自治区直辖县级市	Municpality Country-LevelCity directly under the Central Govern-ment	1	2	1
石河子市	Shihezi City	1	2	1
阿拉尔市	Aral City			

地　区	Region	普通中学 Regular Secondary Schools	#高　中 Senior Secondary Schools	小　学 Primary Schools	特殊教育学校 Special Schools
总　计	**Total**	**1497**	**366**	**3535**	**19**
乌鲁木齐市	Urumqi City	134	54	142	3
克拉玛依市	Karamay City	17	13	29	1
吐鲁番地区	Turpan Administrative Offices	49	14	83	
哈密地区	Hami [Kumul] Administrative Offices	45	13	60	1
昌吉回族自治州	Changji Hui Autonomous Prefecture	48	20	101	1
伊犁哈萨克自治州	Ili Kazak Autonomous Prefecture	323	65	533	4
伊犁州直属县(市)	Counties (Cities) Direct Under Ili Prefecture	183	31	358	3
塔城地区	Tacheng [Tarbagatai] Administrative Offices	77	21	103	1
阿勒泰地区	Altay Administrative Offices	63	13	72	
博尔塔拉蒙古自治州	Bortala Mongol Autonomous Prefecture	31	9	28	1
巴音郭楞蒙古自治州	Bayangol Mongol Autonomous Prefecture	61	22	93	1
阿克苏地区	Aksu Administrative Offices	139	40	584	1
克孜勒苏柯尔克孜自治州	Kizilsu Kirgiz Autonomous Prefecture	36	10	174	1
喀什地区	Kashgar [Kaxgar] Administrative Offices	211	44	976	3
和田地区	Hotan Administrative Offices	148	14	666	1
生产建设兵团	Production and Construction Group	241	45	60	
自治区直辖县级市	Municpality Country-LevelCity directly under the Central Govern-ment	14	3	6	1
石河子市	Shihezi City	13	3	6	1
阿拉尔市	Aral City	1			

17-17 各地、州、市各级各类学校教职工数

Number of Teachers and Staff by Level and Type of School and by Prefecture, Autonomous Prefecture and City

单位：人　　(2012 年)　　(person)

地　区	Region	普通高等学校 Regular Institutions of Higher Education	中等职业学校 Specialized Secondary Schools
总　计	**Total**	**27885**	**14739**
乌鲁木齐市	Urumqi City	17057	4463
克拉玛依市	Karamay City	553	584
吐鲁番地区	Turpan Administrative Offices		314
哈密地区	Hami [Kumul] Administrative Offices		632
昌吉回族自治州	Changji Hui Autonomous Prefecture	1635	700
伊犁哈萨克自治州	Ili Kazak Autonomous Prefecture	1797	2173
伊犁州直属县(市)	Counties (Cities) Direct Under Ili Prefecture	1797	1037
塔城地区	Tacheng [Tarbagatai] Administrative Offices		566
阿勒泰地区	Altay Administrative Offices		570
博尔塔拉蒙古自治州	Bortala Mongol Autonomous Prefecture		187
巴音郭楞蒙古自治州	Bayangol Mongol Autonomous Prefecture	550	498
阿克苏地区	Aksu Administrative Offices	437	436
克孜勒苏柯尔克孜自治州	Kizilsu Kirgiz Autonomous Prefecture		407
喀什地区	Kashgar [Kaxgar] Administrative Offices	940	1853
和田地区	Hotan Administrative Offices	640	586
生产建设兵团	Production and Construction Group	3892	1805
自治区直辖县级市	Municpality Country-LevelCity directly under the Central Govern-ment	384	101
石河子市	Shihezi City	384	101
阿拉尔市	Aral City		

地　区	Region	普通中学 Regular Secondary Schools	小　学 Primary Schools	特殊教育学　校 Special Schools
总　计	**Total**	**134043**	**149927**	**574**
乌鲁木齐市	Urumqi City	12602	10728	187
克拉玛依市	Karamay City	2771	2089	9
吐鲁番地区	Turpan Administrative Offices	3670	4635	
哈密地区	Hami [Kumul] Administrative Offices	3130	3272	47
昌吉回族自治州	Changji Hui Autonomous Prefecture	7472	7714	33
伊犁哈萨克自治州	Ili Kazak Autonomous Prefecture	24610	32880	65
伊犁州直属县(市)	Counties (Cities) Direct Under Ili Prefecture	13958	19647	26
塔城地区	Tacheng [Tarbagatai] Administrative Offices	6454	7747	39
阿勒泰地区	Altay Administrative Offices	4198	5486	
博尔塔拉蒙古自治州	Bortala Mongol Autonomous Prefecture	2721	3502	
巴音郭楞蒙古自治州	Bayangol Mongol Autonomous Prefecture	7268	9414	51
阿克苏地区	Aksu Administrative Offices	12630	14373	30
克孜勒苏柯尔克孜自治州	Kizilsu Kirgiz Autonomous Prefecture	4192	6153	
喀什地区	Kashgar [Kaxgar] Administrative Offices	23595	27405	77
和田地区	Hotan Administrative Offices	10770	12358	54
生产建设兵团	Production and Construction Group	17315	14675	
自治区直辖县级市	Municpality Country-LevelCity directly under the Central Govern-ment	1297	729	21
石河子市	Shihezi City	1278	691	21
阿拉尔市	Aral City	19	38	

17-18 各地、州、市各级各类学校教师数
Number of Teachers by Level and Type of School and by Prefecture, Autonomous Prefecture and City

单位：人 (2012 年) (person)

地区	Region	普通高等学校 Regular Institutions of Higher Education	中等职业学校 Specialized Secondary Schools
总计	**Total**	**17570**	**10352**
乌鲁木齐市	Urumqi City	10268	2843
克拉玛依市	Karamay City	282	287
吐鲁番地区	Turpan Administrative Offices		238
哈密地区	Hami [Kumul] Administrative Offices		473
昌吉回族自治州	Changji Hui Autonomous Prefecture	1155	569
伊犁哈萨克自治州	Ili Kazak Autonomous Prefecture	1089	1572
伊犁州直属县(市)	Counties (Cities) Direct Under Ili Prefecture	1089	763
塔城地区	Tacheng [Tarbagatai] Administrative Offices		380
阿勒泰地区	Altay Administrative Offices		429
博尔塔拉蒙古自治州	Bortala Mongol Autonomous Prefecture		103
巴音郭楞蒙古自治州	Bayangol Mongol Autonomous Prefecture	510	384
阿克苏地区	Aksu Administrative Offices	337	376
克孜勒苏柯尔克孜自治州	Kizilsu Kirgiz Autonomous Prefecture		348
喀什地区	Kashgar [Kaxgar] Administrative Offices	720	1435
和田地区	Hotan Administrative Offices	365	486
生产建设兵团	Production and Construction Group	2539	1171
自治区直辖县级市	Municpality Country-LevelCity directly under the Central Govern-ment	305	67
石河子市	Shihezi City	305	67
阿拉尔市	Aral City		

地区	Region	普通中学 Regular Secondary Schools	#高中 Senior Secondary Schools	小学 Primary Schools	特殊教育学校 Special Schools
总计	**Total**	**118299**	**32375**	**136130**	**452**
乌鲁木齐市	Urumqi City	10408	3908	9742	129
克拉玛依市	Karamay City	2340	908	1857	7
吐鲁番地区	Turpan Administrative Offices	3293	868	4366	
哈密地区	Hami [Kumul] Administrative Offices	2713	1119	3020	31
昌吉回族自治州	Changji Hui Autonomous Prefecture	6349	2398	7287	28
伊犁哈萨克自治州	Ili Kazak Autonomous Prefecture	21896	6669	29517	54
伊犁州直属县(市)	Counties (Cities) Direct Under Ili Prefecture	12553	3514	17858	19
塔城地区	Tacheng [Tarbagatai] Administrative Offices	5576	2017	6731	35
阿勒泰地区	Altay Administrative Offices	3767	1138	4928	
博尔塔拉蒙古自治州	Bortala Mongol Autonomous Prefecture	2378	749	3190	
巴音郭楞蒙古自治州	Bayangol Mongol Autonomous Prefecture	6324	2309	8468	47
阿克苏地区	Aksu Administrative Offices	11401	2871	13383	24
克孜勒苏柯尔克孜自治州	Kizilsu Kirgiz Autonomous Prefecture	3922	1088	5602	
喀什地区	Kashgar [Kaxgar] Administrative Offices	21852	3658	25049	64
和田地区	Hotan Administrative Offices	9883	950	11176	50
生产建设兵团	Production and Construction Group	14379	4311	12810	
自治区直辖县级市	Municpality Country-LevelCity directly under the Central Govern-ment	1161	569	663	18
石河子市	Shihezi City	1143	569	629	18
阿拉尔市	Aral City	18		34	

17-19 各地、州、市各级各类学校在校学生数

Number of Students Enrollment by Level and Type of School and by Prefecture, Autonomous Prefecture and City

单位：人 (2012 年) (person)

地区	Region	普通高等学校 Regular Institutions of Higher Education	中等职业学校 Specialized Secondary Schools
总计	**Total**	**268716**	**235277**
乌鲁木齐市	Urumqi City	158680	72770
克拉玛依市	Karamay City	4198	802
吐鲁番地区	Turpan Administrative Offices		3761
哈密地区	Hami [Kumul] Administrative Offices		3366
昌吉回族自治州	Changji Hui Autonomous Prefecture	21869	13171
伊犁哈萨克自治州	Ili Kazak Autonomous Prefecture	14478	22081
伊犁州直属县(市)	Counties (Cities) Direct Under Ili Prefecture	14478	12699
塔城地区	Tacheng [Tarbagatai] Administrative Offices		3126
阿勒泰地区	Altay Administrative Offices		6256
博尔塔拉蒙古自治州	Bortala Mongol Autonomous Prefecture		802
巴音郭楞蒙古自治州	Bayangol Mongol Autonomous Prefecture	4369	12911
阿克苏地区	Aksu Administrative Offices	2891	13285
克孜勒苏柯尔克孜自治州	Kizilsu Kirgiz Autonomous Prefecture		2496
喀什地区	Kashgar [Kaxgar] Administrative Offices	11552	28749
和田地区	Hotan Administrative Offices	5472	22767
生产建设兵团	Production and Construction Group	39140	36490
自治区直辖县级市	Municpality Country-LevelCity directly under the Central Govern-ment	6067	1826
石河子市	Shihezi City	6067	1826
阿拉尔市	Aral City		

地区	Region	普通中学 Regular Secondary Schools	#高中 Senior Secondary Schools	小学 Primary Schools	特殊教育学校 Special Schools
总计	**Total**	**1383886**	**440717**	**1900844**	**4909**
乌鲁木齐市	Urumqi City	150991	58326	184287	616
克拉玛依市	Karamay City	25031	9311	22641	54
吐鲁番地区	Turpan Administrative Offices	31962	9876	50791	81
哈密地区	Hami [Kumul] Administrative Offices	32440	13850	32268	204
昌吉回族自治州	Changji Hui Autonomous Prefecture	82173	34729	79023	183
伊犁哈萨克自治州	Ili Kazak Autonomous Prefecture	243434	90616	335122	768
伊犁州直属县(市)	Counties (Cities) Direct Under Ili Prefecture	151483	52037	218657	522
塔城地区	Tacheng [Tarbagatai] Administrative Offices	60763	25456	69627	186
阿勒泰地区	Altay Administrative Offices	31188	13123	46838	60
博尔塔拉蒙古自治州	Bortala Mongol Autonomous Prefecture	22014	9636	27201	79
巴音郭楞蒙古自治州	Bayangol Mongol Autonomous Prefecture	70736	27879	96616	209
阿克苏地区	Aksu Administrative Offices	140231	37848	215103	291
克孜勒苏柯尔克孜自治州	Kizilsu Kirgiz Autonomous Prefecture	34427	11643	56367	98
喀什地区	Kashgar [Kaxgar] Administrative Offices	249006	54883	411061	1094
和田地区	Hotan Administrative Offices	112491	13197	188250	880
生产建设兵团	Production and Construction Group	169141	58877	189662	302
自治区直辖县级市	Municpality Country-LevelCity directly under the Central Govern-ment	19809	10046	12452	50
石河子市	Shihezi City	19704	10046	12113	50
阿拉尔市	Aral City	105		339	

17-20 各地、州、市各级各类学校招生数

Number of New Students Enrollment by Level and Type of School and by Prefecture, Autonomous Prefecture and City

单位：人 (2012 年) (person)

地 区	Region	普通高等学校 Regular Institutions of Higher Education	中等职业学校 Specialized Secondary Schools
总 计	**Total**	**78031**	**86751**
乌鲁木齐市	Urumqi City	46060	25326
克拉玛依市	Karamay City	1484	169
吐鲁番地区	Turpan Administrative Offices		1476
哈密地区	Hami [Kumul] Administrative Offices		1313
昌吉回族自治州	Changji Hui Autonomous Prefecture	7238	5745
伊犁哈萨克自治州	Ili Kazak Autonomous Prefecture	4378	8923
伊犁州直属县(市)	Counties (Cities) Direct Under Ili Prefecture	4378	5515
塔城地区	Tacheng [Tarbagatai] Administrative Offices		1315
阿勒泰地区	Altay Administrative Offices		2093
博尔塔拉蒙古自治州	Bortala Mongol Autonomous Prefecture		214
巴音郭楞蒙古自治州	Bayangol Mongol Autonomous Prefecture	1645	3973
阿克苏地区	Aksu Administrative Offices	1046	5103
克孜勒苏柯尔克孜自治州	Kizilsu Kirgiz Autonomous Prefecture		657
喀什地区	Kashgar [Kaxgar] Administrative Offices	2591	10997
和田地区	Hotan Administrative Offices	1732	8016
生产建设兵团	Production and Construction Group	9744	14087
自治区直辖县级市	Municpality Country-LevelCity directly under the Central Govern-ment	2113	752
石河子市	Shihezi City	2113	752
阿拉尔市	Aral City		

地 区	Region	普通中学 Regular Secondary Schools	#高 中 Senior Secondary Schools	小 学 Primary Schools	特殊教育学 校 Special Schools
总 计	**Total**	**469674**	**155276**	**331734**	**1137**
乌鲁木齐市	Urumqi City	52285	20135	32785	122
克拉玛依市	Karamay City	8320	3068	3742	5
吐鲁番地区	Turpan Administrative Offices	10650	3161	9301	9
哈密地区	Hami [Kumul] Administrative Offices	10969	4831	5250	32
昌吉回族自治州	Changji Hui Autonomous Prefecture	26683	11039	12984	39
伊犁哈萨克自治州	IliKazak Autonomous Prefecture	83999	31902	60812	154
伊犁州直属县(市)	Counties (Cities) Direct Under Ili Prefecture	52877	18928	40442	126
塔城地区	Tacheng [Tarbagatai] Administrative Offices	20402	8537	11831	20
阿勒泰地区	Altay Administrative Offices	10720	4437	8539	8
博尔塔拉蒙古自治州	Bortala Mongol Autonomous Prefecture	7259	3214	4789	13
巴音郭楞蒙古自治州	Bayangol Mongol Autonomous Prefecture	24294	9591	19602	64
阿克苏地区	Aksu Administrative Offices	50043	15128	39013	42
克孜勒苏柯尔克孜自治州	Kizilsu Kirgiz Autonomous Prefecture	11070	3951	9939	75
喀什地区	Kashgar [Kaxgar] Administrative Offices	84202	20683	69612	245
和田地区	Hotan Administrative Offices	36908	5517	31788	261
生产建设兵团	Production and Construction Group	56273	19759	30148	35
自治区直辖县级市	Municpality Country-LevelCity directly under the Central Govern-ment	6719	3297	1969	41
石河子市	Shihezi City	6679	3297	1902	41
阿拉尔市	Aral City	40		67	

17-21 各地、州、市各级各类学校毕业生数

Number of Graduates by Level and Type of School and by Prefecture, Autonomous Prefecture and City

单位：人 (2012 年) (person)

地区	Region	普通高等学校 Regular Institutions of Higher Education	中等职业学校 Specialized Secondary Schools
总计	**Total**	**64591**	**71288**
乌鲁木齐市	Urumqi City	37384	24776
克拉玛依市	Karamay City	1087	315
吐鲁番地区	Turpan Administrative Offices		1048
哈密地区	Hami [Kumul] Administrative Offices		558
昌吉回族自治州	Changji Hui Autonomous Prefecture	5929	4111
伊犁哈萨克自治州	Ili Kazak Autonomous Prefecture	3421	5969
伊犁州直属县(市)	Counties (Cities) Direct Under Ili Prefecture	3421	3077
塔城地区	Tacheng [Tarbagatai] Administrative Offices		691
阿勒泰地区	Altay Administrative Offices		2201
博尔塔拉蒙古自治州	Bortala Mongol Autonomous Prefecture		584
巴音郭楞蒙古自治州	Bayangol Mongol Autonomous Prefecture	982	3967
阿克苏地区	Aksu Administrative Offices	910	2848
克孜勒苏柯尔克孜自治州	Kizilsu Kirgiz Autonomous Prefecture		353
喀什地区	Kashgar [Kaxgar] Administrative Offices	2582	7291
和田地区	Hotan Administrative Offices	1599	7904
生产建设兵团	Production and Construction Group	8883	10859
自治区直辖县级市	Municpality Country-LevelCity directly under the Central Govern-ment	1814	705
石河子市	Shihezi City	1814	705
阿拉尔市	Aral City		

地区	Region	普通中学 Regular Secondary Schools	#高中 Senior Secondary Schools	小学 Primary Schools	特殊教育学校 Special Schools
总计	**Total**	**454590**	**135089**	**321020**	**522**
乌鲁木齐市	Urumqi City	47114	18346	30462	107
克拉玛依市	Karamay City	7945	3003	4126	8
吐鲁番地区	Turpan Administrative Offices	10886	3509	8389	10
哈密地区	Hami [Kumul] Administrative Offices	10422	4315	5804	25
昌吉回族自治州	Changji Hui Autonomous Prefecture	26658	10973	14777	43
伊犁哈萨克自治州	Ili Kazak Autonomous Prefecture	79827	27841	53670	51
伊犁州直属县(市)	Counties (Cities) Direct Under Ili Prefecture	48050	15346	34313	39
塔城地区	Tacheng [Tarbagatai] Administrative Offices	20845	8307	12390	5
阿勒泰地区	Altay Administrative Offices	10932	4188	6967	7
博尔塔拉蒙古自治州	Bortala Mongol Autonomous Prefecture	7520	3380	4292	1
巴音郭楞蒙古自治州	Bayangol Mongol Autonomous Prefecture	22421	8668	15004	50
阿克苏地区	Aksu Administrative Offices	43348	10082	35793	13
克孜勒苏柯尔克孜自治州	Kizilsu Kirgiz Autonomous Prefecture	11181	3476	7545	
喀什地区	Kashgar [Kaxgar] Administrative Offices	83045	14297	66320	54
和田地区	Hotan Administrative Offices	38447	4084	34284	112
生产建设兵团	Production and Construction Group	59610	19879	38082	48
自治区直辖县级市	Municpality Country-LevelCity directly under the Central Govern-ment	6166	3236	2472	
石河子市	Shihezi City	6109	3236	2432	
阿拉尔市	Aral City	57		40	

17-22 各类学校教育经费情况
Educational Funds in Various Schools

单位：万元 (2012 年) (10 000 yuan)

指标	Item	合计 Total	国家财政性教育经费 Government Appropriation for Education	#预算内教育经费 Budgetary Education Expense	民办学校中举办者投入 Investor Derotion	社会捐资 Donations	事业收入 Income from Under-takings	其他 Others
总计	**Total**	**5390033.1**	**4908565.9**	**4560898.4**	**2268.0**	**9718.9**	**302062.2**	**167418.1**
高等学校	**Institutions of Higher Education**	**680905.6**	**489116.8**	**480257.2**		**2273.4**	**135137.8**	**54377.6**
普通高等学校	Regular Institutions of Higher Education	615724.2	441716.6	433159.0		1134.7	119651.1	53221.8
普通高等本科学校	Universities with Full Undergraduate Course	453990.7	335549.2	334591.0		1011.6	80089.2	37340.7
普通高职高专学校	Regular Institutions of Specialized Course	161733.5	106167.4	98568.0		123.1	39561.9	15881.1
#:高等职业学校	Universities With High Vocational Course	152236.7	97477.7	89878.3		122.7	38780.6	15855.7
成人高等学校	Institutions of Higher Education for Adults	65181.4	47400.2	47098.2		1138.7	15486.7	1155.8
中等职业学校	**Vocational Secondary Schools**	**350003.9**	**291416.6**	**257383.4**	**53.7**	**544.7**	**31987.0**	**26001.9**
中等专业学校	Specialized Secondary Schools	214021.4	175249.2	167098.5	53.7	111.4	22084.9	16522.2
职业高中	Vocational Senior Secondary Schools	85899.1	77643.5	58372.5		344.3	2584.3	5327.0
#:农村	Rural Areas	362.7	340.7	340.7			22.0	
技工学校	Technical Schools	39658.0	30031.6	24115.1		75.0	6068.2	3483.2
成人中等专业学校	Specialized Secondary Schools for Adults	10425.4	8492.3	7797.3		14.0	1249.6	669.5
中学	**Secondary Schools**	**1828102.0**	**1717803.6**	**1591485.0**	**89.0**	**4842.9**	**77321.3**	**28045.2**
普通中学	Regular Secondary Schools	1827802.1	1717523.1	1591204.5	89.0	4842.9	77301.9	28045.2
普通高中	Regular Senior Secondary Schools	555302.0	466590.6	431155.0	84.5	3883.2	70873.7	13870.0
#:农村	Rural Areas	14823.1	14000.0	13286.6		37.3	389.0	396.8
普通初中	Regular Junior Secondary Schools	1272500.1	1250932.5	1160049.5	4.5	959.7	6428.2	14175.2
#:农村	Rural Areas	688653.3	681980.1	645744.2		689.8	620.7	5362.7
成人中学	Secondary Schools for Adults	299.9	280.5	280.5			19.4	
小学	**Primary Schools**	**1688933.3**	**1666999.3**	**1577638.0**	**403.5**	**1161.7**	**6203.9**	**14164.9**
普通小学	Regular Primary Schools	1688933.3	1666999.3	1577638.0	403.5	1161.7	6203.9	14164.9
#农村	Rural Areas	1055463.8	1046271.1	1006747.1		938.8	635.7	7618.2
特殊教育	**Special Education**	**9001.7**	**7985.3**	**6869.7**		**4.1**	**95.5**	**916.8**
特殊教育学校	Special Education Schools	9001.7	7985.3	6869.7		4.1	95.5	916.8
幼儿园	**Kindergartens**	**261492.8**	**213247.3**	**204510.9**	**1721.8**	**452.9**	**39030.9**	**7039.9**
#农村	Rural Areas	99449.2	92503.8	89332.5	566.6	244.0	2841.7	3293.1
教育行政单位	**Education Administrative Unit**	**278065.7**	**250404.4**	**205826.0**		**144.2**	**1144.6**	**26372.5**
教育事业单位	**Education Institution**	**224413.5**	**207376.8**	**172925.8**		**295.0**	**8322.9**	**8418.8**
其他	**Others**	**69114.6**	**64215.8**	**64002.4**			**2818.3**	**2080.5**

补充资料：其他收入中联合办学（班）收入 11883 千元。
Other income (class) income 11883000 yuan. comed from Joint school .
注：本表按隶属关系填列 Note: Data in The table according to the membership listed.

17-23 科技活动基本情况
Basic Statistics on Scientific and Technological Activities

指 标	Item	2010	2011
研究与试验发展（R&D）投入情况	**Statistics on R&D Input**		
R&D 人员折合全时当量(人・年)	**Full-time Equivalent of Rearch and Development Personnel (person.year)**	**14367**	**15440**
#基础研究	Basic Research	1578	1926
应用研究	Applied Research	3924	4283
试验发展	Experimental Development	8865	9231
R&D 经费支出(万元)	**Expenditure on R&D (10000 yuan)**	**266545**	**330030**
#基础研究	Basic Research	14325	20890
应用研究	Applied Research	63005	65632
试验发展	Experimental Development	189215	243509
日常性支出	Daily Expenditure	233522	286961
资产性支出	Capital Expenditure	33023	43069
#政府资金	Government Funds	79754	88065
企业资金	Self-raised Funds by Enterprises	180506	229449
研究与试验发展经费支出相当于新疆生产总值比例(%)	**Proportion of Expenditure on R&D to GDP of Xinjiang**	**0.49**	**0.50**
科技产出及成果情况	Statistics on S&T Outputs and Results		
发表科技论文（篇）	Scientific Papers Issued (pieces)	18136	20018
出版科技著作（种）	Publication on Science and Technology (kind)	276	428
专利申请受理数（件）	Number of Patents Application Accepted (piece)	1220	1872
#发明专利	Inventions	465	619
专利申请授权数（件）	Number of Patents Application Granted (piece)	160	232
#发明专利	Inventions	76	124

17-24 县级以上政府部门属研究与开发机构及科技信息与文献机构数、人员数
State-owned Research and Development Institutions and Information and Literature Institutions at and above County Level and Persons Engaged

(2011 年)

指 标	Item	合 计 Total	自然科学技术领域 Field of Natural Sciences and Technology	社会、人文科学技术领域 Field of Social Sciences and Humanities	科技信息和文献机构 Scientific-technical Information and Document Institutions
机构数(个)	**Institutions (unit)**	**109**	**95**	**6**	**8**
科技活动人员(人)	**Personal Engaged in Scientific and Technological Activities (person)**	**6436**	**5807**	**399**	**230**
#大学本科及以上学历	University Graduate or above	4229	3775	279	175
研究与试验发展全时人员(人·年)	**Full-time Equivalent of Rearch and Development Personnel (person.year)**	**3133**	**2815**	**278**	**40**
科技活动收入(万元)	**Sources of Funds for S&T(10 000 yuan)**	**155083.4**	**142601.4**	**6903.0**	**5579.0**
#政府拨款	Government Funds	130055.6	120765.0	4159.8	5130.8
科技经费内部支出额(万元)	**Internal Expenditures on Scientific and Technological Activities (10 000 yuan)**	**141748.0**	**131035.0**	**6457.2**	**4255.8**
#劳务费	Service Fees	44633.8	40876.1	1899.7	1858.0
固定资产购建费	Purchases or Construction of Fixed Assets	26334.5	25298.5	648.7	387.3
#研究与发展经费支出	Expenditure on Research and Development	69409.8	65998.4	2466.1	945.3
#基础研究	Basic Research	15322.3	13101.9	2220.4	
应用研究	Applied Research	20942.9	20255.6	221.1	466.2
试验发展	Experimental Development	33144.6	32640.9	24.6	479.1

17-25 重大科学技术研究成果及奖励数

Number of Major Achievements in Scientific and Technological Research and Awarded Prizes

单位：项 (item)

年 份 Year	自治区级重大科技成果 Number of Major Achievements in Science and Technology of Autonomous Region	奖励情况 Awarded Prizes					
		国家级 National	自治区级 Autonomous Regional	一等奖 Frist Class Awards	二等奖 Second Class Awards	三等奖 Third Class Awards	四等奖 Fourth Class Awards
1978 年以前	1551	88	610				
1980-1985	1173	16	356	5	31	102	218
1990	444	3	129		18	56	55
1995	218	3	137	4	26	53	54
2000	250	2	90	5	18	67	
2001	285	6	92	4	23	65	
2002	207	5	99	5	30	64	
2003	232	3	111	8	34	69	
2004	218	4	108	4	33	71	
2005	225	3	101	6	27	68	
2006	212	3	107	8	37	62	
2007	220	8	118	10	42	66	
2008	69	8	108	9	40	59	
2009	166	12					
2010	228	9	130	15	47	68	
2011	205	6	121	14	46	61	
2012	236	6	126	15	45	66	

17-26 专利申请和批准数

Number of Patent Applications Examined and Approved

单位：件 (case)

年 份 Year	申请数 Number of Patent Applications Examined				批准数 Number of Patent Applications Granted				代理机构(个) Agency (unit)
	合 计 Total	发 明 Inventions	实用新型 Utility Models	外观设计 Designs	合 计 Total	发 明 Inventions	实用新型 Utility Models	外观设计 Designs	
1990	250	38	203	9	139	3	135	1	5
1995	609	92	467	50	312	11	285	16	6
2000	1088	179	699	210	717	66	475	176	7
2001	1088	189	683	216	755	90	522	143	5
2002	1239	216	779	244	627	61	407	159	4
2003	1472	253	940	279	751	75	520	156	5
2004	1492	272	870	350	792	75	530	187	5
2005	1851	320	1117	414	921	88	537	296	5
2006	2256	381	1166	709	1187	107	805	275	5
2007	2270	476	1255	539	1534	90	1035	409	5
2008	2412	482	1408	522	1493	82	1100	311	6
2009	2872	662	1865	345	1867	120	1261	486	6
2010	3560	914	2272	374	2562	189	2012	361	6
2011	4736	1273	2732	731	2642	302	1974	366	6
2012	7044	1679	3375	1990	3440	451	2383	606	6

17-27 高等学校科技活动情况
Basic Statistics on Higher Education for Science and Technology Activities

指　　标	Item	2010	2011
高等学校基本情况	**Basic Statistics on Higher Education**		
学校数（个）	Number of Institutions (unit)	68	68
#理工农医	Natural Sciences & Technology	31	31
#人文社科	Social Sciences & Humanities	37	37
R&D 机构（个）	R&D Institutions (unit)	44	45
研究与试验发展（R&D）投入情况	**Statistics on R&D Input**		
R&D 人员折合全时当量(人·年)	Full-time Equivalent of R&D Personnel (man-years)	2341	2748
#基础研究	Basic Research	990	1329
应用研究	Applied Research	1229	1327
试验发展	Experimental Development	120	97
R&D 经费支出(万元)	Expenditure on R&D(10 000 yuan)	18285	21358
#基础研究	Basic Research	5775	9618
应用研究	Applied Research	10717	10041
试验发展	Experimental Development	1792	1698
#日常性支出	Daily Expenditure	15623	19153
资产性支出	Capital Expenditure	2663	2204
#政府资金	Government Funds	15063	19329
企业资金	Self-raised Funds by Enterprises	2662	1367
R&D 项目（课题）情况	**Statistics on R&D Topics**		
R&D 项目（课题）数（项）	R&D Projects (item)	3330	4076
R&D 项目（课题）人员全时当量（人年）	Participants (man-years)	2411	2746
R&D 项目（课题）经费支出（万元）	Expenditure (10000 yuan)	15419	17374
科技产出及成果情况	**Statistics on S&T Outputs and Results**		
发表科技论文（篇）	Scientific Papers Issued (piece)	10642	12113
出版科技著作（种）	Publication on Science and Technology (kind)	156	268
专利申请受理数（件）	Number of Patents Applications Accepted (piece)	103	153
#发明专利	Inventions	60	98
专利申请授权数（件）	Number of Patents Applications Granted (piece)	40	73
#发明专利	Inventions	13	34

17-28 主要年份企事业单位主要专业技术人员数
Number of Main Scientific and Technical Personnel in Enterprises and Institutions in Main Years

单位：人 (person)

年 份 Year	合 计 Total	工程技术人员 Engineering	农业技术人员 Agriculture	卫生技术人员 Health Care	科学研究人员 Scientific Researcn	教学人员 Teaching
1978.6 月末	85063	22198	13141	31741	3042	14941
1985	158709	51636	20730	57559	3416	25368
1990	241524	92383	25089	71906	4326	47820
2000	368262	58576	27764	62338	2409	217175
2001	385129	59913	30043	65585	2492	227096
2002	387726	58011	31867	65364	2337	230147
2003	385705	57506	30808	65622	2236	229533
2004	398318	55421	32831	68604	2928	238534
2005	402404	51915	32744	67945	2451	247349
2006	412977	52702	34131	68231	2460	255453
2007	411590	50680	33859	69101	2453	255497
2008	414277	49175	31799	71104	2261	259938
2009	411628	47525	30126	72827	2518	258632
2010	407651	47734	28433	77357	2071	252056
2011	421372	47357	27921	80290	6728	259076
2012	454975	47755	30422	85615	2224	288959

注：1.1991 年起专业技术人员包括企事业单位(不含行政机关)人员数,教学人员包括社会和自然科技领域及小学教师人数。
2.1996 年后数据不包括中央单位的专业技术人员数，故人员减少较多。

Note: a) The Specialezed and technical personnel include those who work in enterprises and institutions (excluding administrative organs), teaching Staff, those work in social and nature scientific fields as well as elementary school teachers since 1991.
b) After 1996, the data exclude the figure of professionals with national establishments stationed to Xinjiang and thus the number of staff is reduced a lot.

17-29 主要年份企事业单位主要专业技术人员比重
Proportion of Scientific and Technical Personnel in Enterprises and Institutions in Main Years

单位：% (%)

年 份 Year	合 计 Total	工程技术 Engineering	农业技术 Agriculture	卫生技术 Health Care	科学研究 Scientific Research	教 学 Teaching
1978.6 月末	100	26.10	15.45	37.31	3.58	17.56
1985	100	32.54	13.06	36.27	2.15	15.98
1990	100	38.25	10.39	29.77	1.79	19.80
2000	100	15.91	7.54	16.93	0.65	58.97
2001	100	15.55	7.80	17.03	0.65	58.97
2002	100	14.96	8.22	16.86	0.60	59.36
2003	100	14.91	7.99	17.01	0.58	59.51
2004	100	13.91	8.24	17.22	0.74	59.89
2005	100	12.90	8.14	16.89	0.61	61.46
2006	100	12.76	8.26	16.52	0.60	61.86
2007	100	12.31	8.22	16.79	0.60	62.08
2008	100	11.87	7.68	17.16	0.55	62.74
2009	100	11.55	7.32	17.69	0.61	62.83
2010	100	11.71	6.97	18.98	0.51	61.83
2011	100	11.24	6.63	19.05	1.60	61.48
2012	100	10.50	6.68	18.82	0.49	63.51

17-30 规模以上工业企业科技活动情况

(2011 年)

项　　目	Item	企业数(个) Nnmber of Industrial Enterprises (unit)	#有研究与试验发展活动的企业数 Number of Enterprises Having R & D Activities	科技机构(个) Number of Scientific Technological Agencies (unit)	研究与试验发展人员数(人) Number of R & D Persons	研究人员 Research personal
总　计	**Total**	**1738**	**87**	**126**	**8838**	**4541**
按登记注册类型分	**Grouped by Ownership**					
内资企业	Domestic-funded Enterprises	1663	84	124	8811	4525
国有企业	State-owned Enterprises	104	7	12	813	531
集体企业	Collective-owned Enterprises	13	1		23	2
有限责任公司	Limited Liability Corporations	795	35	63	1650	500
国有独资公司	State Sole funded Corporations	54	4	7	65	21
其他有限责任公司	Other Limited Liability Corporations	741	31	56	1585	479
股份有限责任公司	Share-holding Corporations Ltd	87	22	28	5969	3393
私营企业	Private Enterprises	636	19	21	356	99
私营独资企业	Private-funded Enterprises	46				
私营有限责任公司	Private Limited Liability Corporations	553	14	16	204	58
私营股份有限公司	Private Stock Ltd. Co.	28	5	5	152	41
港澳台商投资企业	Enterprises With Funds from Hong Kong, Macao and Taiwan	27	1		10	6
#合资经营企业(港或澳、台资)	Joint-ventures Enterprises	16	1		10	6
港、澳、台商独资经营企业	Enterprises with Funds from Hong Kong, Macao and Taiwan	10				
外商投资企业	Foreign Funded Enterprises	48	2	2	17	10
#外资企业	Enterprises with Sole Fund	12	1	1	14	8
外商投资股份有限公司	Share-holding Corporation Ltd.	7	1	1	3	2
按工业行业大类分	**Grouped by Sector**					
采矿业	Mining and Quarrying	261	11	16	4702	3172
煤炭开采和洗选业	Coal Extracting and Dressing	109	3	5	67	44
石油和天然气开采业	Petroleum and Natural Gas Extraction	25	6	9	4616	3122
黑色金属矿采选业	Processing of Ferrous Metals Ores	74				
有色金属矿采选业	Processing of Nonferrous Metals Ores	30	2	2	19	6
非金属矿采选业	Processing of Nonmetal Ores	23				
制造业	Manufacturing	1332	74	104	4059	1301
农副食品加工业	Processing of Food from Agricultural Products	256	4	7	82	24
食品制造业	Food Manufacturing	118	9	11	328	78
饮料制造业	Beverage Manufacturing	57	2	4	143	58
烟草制品业	Tobacco Manufacturing	1				
纺织业	Textile Industry	85	4	5	380	62
纺织服装、鞋、帽制造业	Leather, Fur, Feather and Related Products Manufacturing	2	1	1	40	7
家具制造业	Furniture Manufacturing	6				
造纸及纸制品业	Paper and Paper Products Manufacturing	23		4		
印刷业和记录媒介的复制	Printing, Reproduction of Recording Media	10				

Statistics on Technical Activities of Large and Medium-sized Industrial Enterprises above Designated Size

研究与试验发展人员折合全时当量(人.年) Full-time Equivalent of R & D personnel	研究人员 Research personal	研究与试验发展经费(万元) Expenditure on R & D	其中 Of which 基础研究 Basic Research	应用研究 Applied Research	试验发展 Experimental Development	其中 Of which 政府资金 Government Appropriation Funds	企业资金 Self-raised Funds by Enterprises	研究与试验发展项目数(项) Projects to R & D	新产品开发项目数(项) Number of New Produots
6723	**3542**	**223352**		**23821**	**199531**	**4891**	**216820**	**757**	**731**
6704	3531	222812		23821	198891	4881	216417	753	729
722	483	8976			8976	35	8893	85	97
23	2	87			87		47	1	2
883	305	56676		19	56657	1183	54200	142	175
50	13	755			755	23	733	5	8
833	292	55921		19	55902	1160	53468	137	167
4774	2652	152491		23562	128929	2483	149590	461	387
304	89	4581		240	4341	780	3687	64	67
164	50	2707			2707	366	2227	25	41
140	39	1874		240	1634	414	1460	39	26
6	4	181			181		54	1	1
6	4	181			181		54	1	1
13	8	359			359	10	349	3	1
10	6	308			308	10	298	2	
3	2	51			51		51	1	1
3622	2509	99607		23017	76591	2029	97578	369	275
51	36	914			914	9	905	3	4
3566	2471	98388		23017	75371	2020	96368	364	269
5	2	305			305		305	2	2
3040	977	115681		804	114876	2793	111245	380	426
36	12	1003			1003	76	927	5	15
189	39	2892		259	2632	119	2883	41	17
115	30	1008			1008	60	948	6	7
254	51	1941			1941	15	1926	9	15
40	7	216			216	17	199	1	1

17-30 续表

(2011 年)

项目	Item	企业数(个) Nnmber of Industrial Enterprises (unit)	#有研究与试验发展活动的企业数 Number of Enterprises Having R & D Activities	科技机构(个) Number of Scientific Technological Agencies (unit)	研究与试验发展人员数(人) Number of R & D Persons	研究人员 Research personal
石油加工、炼焦及核燃料加工业	Oil Processing, Coking and Nuclear Fuel Processing	87	7	8	359	285
化学原料及化学制品制造业	Raw Chemical Material and Chemical Products	108	17	20	1139	406
医药制造业	Medicine Manufacturing	19	2	5	13	6
化学纤维制造业	Chemical Fiber Manufacturing	14				
橡胶制品业	Rubber Products Manufacturing	2	1	1	33	12
塑料制品业	Plastic Products Manufacturing	82	5	8	180	17
非金属矿物制品业	Nonmetal Mineral Products Manufacturing	215	5	9	210	73
黑色金属冶炼及压延加工业	Manufacture and Processing of Ferrous Metals	59	2	3	130	130
有色金属冶炼及压延加工业	Manufalture and Processing of Non-ferrous Metals	27		1		
金属制品业	Metal Products Manufacturing	58	2	2	140	4
通用设备制造业	General Purpose Machinery Manufacturing	20	1	3	18	2
专用设备制造业	Special Purpose Machinery Manufacturing	22	5	6	77	36
交通运输设备制造业	Transport Equipment Manufacturing	8		2		
电气机械及器材制造业	Electric Equipment and Machinery Manufacturing	30	5	3	304	58
通信设备、计算机及其他电子设备制造业	Telecom Equipment, Computer and Other Electronic Equipment	2	1	1	474	37
仪器仪表及文化、办公用机械制造业	Manufacture of Measuring Instrument and Machinery for Cultural Activity & Office Work	2	1		9	5
电力、燃气及水的生产和供应业	Production and Suppoly of Electric Power,Gas and Water	145	2	6	77	68
电力、热力的生产和供应业	Electric Power and Thermal Production and Supply	117	2	6	77	68
燃气生产和供应业	Gas Production and Supply	20				
水的生产和供应业	Water Production and Supply	8				
按企业所在地区划分	**Grouped by Region**					
乌鲁木齐市	Urumqi City	342	26	35	1353	420
克拉玛依市	Karamay City	63	18	21	4067	2686
吐鲁番地区	Turpan Administrative Offices	66	1	2	780	709
哈密地区	Hami [Kumul] Administrative Offices	84	2	2	91	42
昌吉回族自治州	Changji Hui Autonomous Prefecture	292	9	14	516	130
伊犁州直属县(市)	Counties (Cities) Direct Under Ili Prefecture	189	5	11	140	44
塔城地区	Tacheng [Tarbagatai] Administrative Offices	96		1		
阿勒泰地区	Altay Administrative Offices	72	2	1	19	6
博尔塔拉蒙古自治州	Bortala Mongol Autonomous Prefecture	38		1		
巴音郭楞蒙古自治州	Bayangol Mongol Autonomous Prefecture	119	8	12	1028	280
阿克苏地区	Aksu Administrative Offices	141	2	5	49	22
克孜勒苏柯尔克孜自治州	Kizilsu Kirgiz Autonomous Prefecture	18				
喀什地区	Kashgar [Kaxgar] Administrative Offices	58	1	1	108	2
和田地区	Hotan Administrative Offices	16				
自治区直辖县级市	Municpality Country-LevelCity directly under the Central Govern-ment	144	13	20	687	200

Continued

研究与试验发展人员折合全时当量(人.年) Full-time Equivalent of R & D personnel	研究人员 Research personal	研究与试验发展经费(万元) Expenditure on R & D	其中 Of which 基础研究 Basic Research	应用研究 Applied Research	试验发展 Experimental Development	其中 Of which 政府资金 Government Appropriation Funds	企业资金 Self-raised Funds by Enterprises	研究与试验发展项目数(项) Projects to R & D	新产品开发项目数(项) Number of New Produots
289	224	13322			13322	211	13312	65	70
838	320	21351		545	20806	1241	18587	64	54
10	5	152			152	22	130	3	14
23	8	765			765		765	24	19
156	12	3323			3323	208	3115	23	26
113	43	2258			2258	10	2158	17	16
97	97	31948			31948		31948	45	45
30	1	2593			2593	166	2427	2	1
12	1	191			191	16	145	4	18
74	34	2594			2594	281	2290	10	9
285	52	13670			13670	315	13355	9	25
474	37	16287			16287		16287	51	51
6	3	169			169	8	169	1	2
61	56	8064			8064	69	7995	8	30
61	56	8064			8064	69	7995	8	30
1053	300	58134			58134	447	57561	151	222
3053	2040	79245		659	78586	1212	78033	333	354
780	709	17687		17570	117	1442	16245	79	2
32	14	523			523		523	8	9
430	90	15676		240	15436	383	15236	40	18
134	41	1559			1559	76	1389	11	15
									1
5	2	305			305		305	2	1
670	187	28272		5352	22920	554	27697	72	35
31	8	1528			1528	3	1525	3	13
4		687			687		687	1	1
533	151	19736			19736	774	17620	57	60

17-31 各类技术合同签定及执行情况

Statistics on Signing and Implementing Technical Contracts by Type

单位：项、万元 (item,10 000 yuan)

项　目	Item	合同数 Number of Contracts		合同金额 Contract Amount		#技术交易额 Transaction Value in Technical Market	
		2011	2012	2011	2012	2011	2012
总　计	**Total**	**1473**	**1532**	**43778.69**	**54910.48**	**43045.15**	**53326.15**
技术开发合同	Technology Development	305	323	20955.88	21269.51	20843.54	20792.04
技术转让合同	Technology Transfer	39	62	1244.08	4541.55	1219.08	4073.80
技术咨询合同	Technology Consultation	532	524	8674.78	8980.15	8674.78	8847.15
技术服务合同	Technology Service	597	623	12903.95	20119.27	12307.75	19613.16

17-32 各级技术计划项目进入技术市场情况

Statistics on Projects for Technical Plan Entering Technical Market by Level

单位：项、万元 (2012 年) (item,10 000 yuan)

项　目	Item	合　计 Total		国家计划 National Plans		部门计划 Department Plans	
		项　数 Number of Items	金　额 Values	项　数 Number of Items	金　额 Values	项　数 Number of Items	金　额 Values
总　计	**Total**	**1532**	**54910.48**	**6**	**73.00**	**72**	**1375.90**
机关法人	Government Agency Legal Person	1	3.00	1	3.00		
事业法人	Institntion Legal Person	869	17273.00	5	70.00		
企业法人	Business Entity	658	37247.48			72	1375.90
自然人	Person	1	380.00				
其他组织	Others	3	7.00				

项　目	Item	省、自治区计划 单列市计划 Provinces, Municipality Plans		地、市、县计划 Area City and County Plans		计划外 Out of Plan	
		项　数 Number of Items	金　额 Values	项　数 Number of Items	金　额 Values	项　数 Number of Items	金　额 Values
总　计	**Total**	**26**	**2158.11**	**41**	**2844.74**	**1387**	**48458.75**
机关法人	Government Agency Legal Person						
事业法人	Institntion Legal Person	16	698.86	35	2481.76	813	14022.38
企业法人	Business Entity	9	1458.25	6	362.98	571	34050.36
自然人	Person					1	380.00
其他组织	Others	1	1.00			2	6.00

17-33 技术流向地域情况

Statistics on Location of Technical Contract

单位：项、万元 (2012 年) (item, 10 000 yuan)

地 区 Region	合同类别合计 Contracts of Classification Total		技术开发 Technology Development		技术转让 Technology Transfer		技术咨询 Technology Consultation		技术服务 Technology Service	
	项 数 Number of Items	金 额 Values	项 数 Number of Items	金 额 Values	项 数 Number of Items	金 额 Values	项 数 Number of Items	金 额 Values	项 数 Number of Items	金 额 Values
总 计 Total	**1532**	**54910.48**	**323**	**21269.51**	**62**	**4541.55**	**524**	**8980.15**	**623**	**20119.27**
北 京 Beijing	14	1635.16	6	1005.01	2	480.00	2	80.00	4	70.15
天 津 Tianjing	1	2.40							1	2.40
河 北 Hebei	3	105.80	1	26.00					2	79.80
内蒙古 Inner Mongolia	5	320.00					5	320.00		
辽 宁 Liaoning	10	361.60	2	70.00			8	291.60		
吉 林 Jilin	2	38.50					1	38.00	1	0.50
黑龙江 Heilongjiang	3	94.00	1	14.00			2	80.00		
上 海 Shanghai	5	93.55	3	91.00					2	2.55
江 苏 Jiangsu	4	47.26	2	44.80					2	2.46
浙 江 Zhejiang	1	2.00	1	2.00						
安 徽 Aanhui	2	14.40							2	14.40
福 建 Fujian	2	187.00	2	187.00						
山 东 Shandong	2	7.13							2	7.13
河 南 Henan	4	6.00					4	6.00		
湖 北 Hubei	1	2.00							1	2.00
湖 南 Hunan	1	100.00					1	100.00		
广 东 Guangdong	4	471.95	3	416.95					1	55.00
重 庆 Chongqing	1	27.00	1	27.00						
四 川 Sichuan	1	4.80							1	4.80
云 南 Yunnan	1	6.00							1	6.00
西 藏 Xizang	2	50.00	2	50.00						
陕 西 Shaanxi	7	477.90	1	59.40			6	418.50		
甘 肃 Gansu	6	387.80	1	18.00			5	369.80		
新 疆 Xinjiang	1448	49395.38	296	19243.35	59	3003.69	490	7276.25	603	19872.08

17-34 技术经济合同成交情况
Statistics on Transaction in Technical and Economic Contract

单位：项、万元 (2012 年) (item, 10 000 yuan)

买方类别 Classification of Buyers \ 卖方类别 Classification of Sellers		合计 Total		#机关法人 Government Agency Legal Person		#事业法人 Institntion Legal Person	
		项数 Number of Items	金额 Values Number	项数 of Items	金额 Values Number	项数 of Items	金额 Values
总计	**Total**	**1532**	**54910.48**	**1**	**3.00**	**869**	**17273.00**
机关法人	Government Agency Legal Person	241	10613.43			91	4625.73
事业法人	Institntion Legal Person	199	4297.46	1	3.00	122	2643.64
社团法人	Corporation Aggregate	3	16.21				
企业法人	Business Entity	1073	39675.80			653	9833.33
自然人	Person	1	0.30			1	0.30
其他组织	Others	15	307.30			2	170.00

买方类别 Classification of Buyers \ 卖方类别 Classification of Sellers		#企业法人 Business Entity		#自然人 Person		#其他组织 Others	
		项数 Number of Items	金额 Values Number	项数 of Items	金额 Values Number	项数 of Items	金额 Values
总计	**Total**	**658**	**37247.48**	**1**	**380.00**	**3**	**7.00**
机关法人	Government Agency Legal Person	150	5987.70				
事业法人	Institntion Legal Person	76	1650.82				
社团法人	Corporation Aggregate	3	16.21				
企业法人	Business Entity	416	29455.46	1	380.00	3	7.00
自然人	Person						
其他组织	Others	13	137.30				

17-35 主要年份文化产业基本情况
Basic Statistics on Culture in Main Years

项目	Item	2005	2010	2012
文化产业机构数(个)	**Number of Culture Institutions (unit)**	**11777**	**9430**	**7466**
文化部门	Culture Departments	2404	1826	1915
其他部门	Other Departments	9373	7604	5551
文化产业人员数(人)	**Number of Person in Culture (person)**	**34001**	**37711**	**35442**
文化部门	Culture Departments	11515	13310	15072
其他部门	Other Departments	22486	24401	20370
各类文化艺术事业单位数(个)	**Number of Institutions on Various Culture and Art (unit)**			
文化馆	Cultural Centers	110	112	116
公共图书馆	Public Libraries	94	103	105
博物馆	Museums	28	71	72
艺术表演场所	Art Performance Places	47	15	12
艺术表演团体	Art Performance Troupes	89	132	109

17-36 文化艺术、文物事业机构和人员情况
Number of Institutions and Personnel in Culture, Art and Cultural Relics

(2012 年)

项　目	Item	机构数 (个) Number of Institutions (unit)	从业人员数 (人) Number of Persons Engaged (person)
艺术事业	**Art Institutions**	**124**	**5240**
艺术表演团体	Art Performance Troupes	109	4926
#话剧、儿童剧、滑稽剧团	Drama, Children Plays and Comedy Troupes	2	134
歌剧、舞剧、歌舞剧团	Opera, Ballet and Dance Troupes	5	315
歌舞团、轻音乐团	Song and Dance Troupe, Light Music Troupe	51	2409
文工团、文宣队、乌兰牧骑	Cultural and Performance Troupes and Ulanmuchi (equestrain art troupes)	36	1277
戏曲剧团	Local Opera Troupes	5	225
#京 剧	Local Beijing Opera Troupes	2	93
曲艺、杂技、木偶、皮影团	Recitation and Ballad Troupes, Acrobatics and Circus Troupes, Puppet Show Troupes and Shadow Play Troupes	2	142
艺术表演场所	Art Centers	12	273
#剧场、影剧院	Theaters and Music Halls	11	259
艺术创作机构	Art Creation Institutions	3	41
图书馆事业	**Libraries**	**105**	**1070**
群众文化事业	**Mass Culture**	**1259**	**3885**
文化馆	Cultural Centers	116	1353
文化站	Cultural Stations	1143	2532
#乡镇文化站	Township Cultural Stations	1024	2268
艺术教育事业	**Culture and Education**	**2**	**139**
艺术科研机构	**Art Research Institutions**	**2**	**51**
文化市场经营单位	**Entertainment Operators**	**5548**	**20051**
文化娱乐业	Entertainment Operators	3050	10459
文化市场其他经营单位	Cultural Market Operators	2498	9592
其他文化事业	**Other Cultural Units**	**3**	**41**
文物事业合计	**Cultural Relics**	**173**	**2032**
文物机构	Historical Relics Agency	100	1151
文物保护管理机构	Agency of Historical Relics Preservation	97	685
文物科研机构	Scientific and Research Historical Relics Agency	2	135
其他文物机构	Other Historical Relics Agency	1	331
博物馆	Museums	72	852
#历史类	History Museum	30	338
文物商店	Cultural Relics Store	1	29

17-37 电影、电视、广播事业基本情况

Basic Statistics on Feature Film, Television and Broadcasting

项　　目	Item	2011	2012
电影制片厂(个)	**Number of Film Studios (unit)**	**1**	**1**
广播电台(座)	**Number of Broadcasting Stations (unit)**	**6**	**6**
中短波发射台及转播台(座)	Transmission and Relaying Stations of MW&SW (unit)	53	64
中短波广播发射功率(千瓦)	Power of MW & SW Transmitters (kw)	2819	2886
调频发射台及转播台(座)	FM Transmission and Relaying Stations (unit)	976	961
调频发射功率(千瓦)	Power of FM Transmitters (kw)	495.43	521.80
节目(套)	Program (set)	159	159
制作广播节目(小时)	Production of Broadcasting (hour)	270895	288223
#新闻资讯类节目	News Programs	57718	58932
专题服务类节目	Feature Programs	83144	91908
综艺类节目	Variety Show	78111	82531
广播剧类节目	Radio Play	9494	8304
广告类节目	Advertisement Programs	21262	22084
其他类节目	Other Programs	21163	24464
广播人口覆盖率((%)	Listener Rate (%)	94.90	95.34
电视台(座)	**Number of Television Stations (unit)**	**8**	**8**
广播电视台(座)	**Radio and TV Stations (unit)**	**88**	**88**
#县级广播电视台(座)	Radio and TV Station at County-Level (unit)	80	80
电视发射台及转播台(座)	TV Transmission Stations and Relaying Stations (unit)	911	883
电视发射机功率(千瓦)	Power of TV Transmitters (kw)	909.89	935.62
节目(套)	Program (set)	198	198
制作电视节目(小时)	Production of TV Programs (hour)	85002	92503
#新闻资讯类节目	News Programs	30949	32173
专题服务类节目	Feature Programs	18391	19808
综艺类节目	Variety Show	9975	10250
影视剧类节目	Film and TV Play Programs	4238	7454
广告类节目	Advertisement Programs	14125	16058
其他类节目	Other Programs	7323	6760
电视人口覆盖率(%)	Viewer Rate (%)	95.29	95.62
有线电视用户(万户)	Numbe of Users of CATV (10 000 households)	208.02	216.81
#数字电视用户	Number of users Digital TV	188.45	200.28
农村直播卫星用户(万户)	Numbe of Users of Rural Live Statellite(10 000 households)	55.43	121.55

主要统计指标解释

普通高等学校　指按照国家规定的设置标准和审批程序批准举办的，通过全国普通高等学校统一招生考试，招收高中毕业生为主要培养对象，实施高等学历教育的全日制大学、独立设置的学院和高等专科学校、高等职业学校和其他机构(独立学院和分校、大专班)。

大学、独立设置的学院主要实施本科层次以上教育。高等专科学校、高等职业学校实施专科层次教育。其他机构是承担国家普通招生计划任务不计校数的机构，包括独立学院、普通高等学校分校、大专班和批准筹建的普通高等学校等。独立学院指由普通本科高校按新机制、新模式举办的本科层次的二级学院，一些普通本科高校按公办机制和模式建立的二级学院,"分校"或其他类似的二级办学机构不属此范畴。

小学学龄儿童净入学率　指调查范围内已入小学学习的学龄儿童占校内外学龄儿童总数(包括弱智儿童，不包括盲聋哑儿童)的比重。计算公式为：

小学学龄儿童净入学率=已入学的小学学龄儿童数/校内外小学学龄儿童总数*100%

科技活动　指在自然科学、农业科学、医药科学、工程与技术科学、人文与社会科学领域(简称科学技术领域)中，与科技知识的产生、发展、传播和应用密切相关的有组织的活动。可分为研究与试验发展(R&D)、研究与试验发展成果应用及相关的科技服务三类活动。该定义是联合国教科文组织考虑成员国特别是发展中国家开展科技统计工作的需要，而对科技活动所作的统计界定。

科技活动人员　指直接从事科技活动、以及专门从事科技活动管理和为科技活动提供直接服务，累计的实际工作时间占全年制度工作时间10%及以上的人员。(1)直接从事科技活动的人员包括：在独立核算的科学研究与技术开发机构、高等学校、各类企业及其他事业单位内设的研究室、实验室、技术开发中心及中试车间(基地)等机构中从事科技活动的研究人员、工程技术人员、技术工人及其它人员；虽不在上述机构工作，但编入科技活动项目(课题)组的人员；科技信息与文献机构中的专业技术人员；从事论文设计的研究生等。(2)专门从事科技活动管理和为科技活动提供直接服务的人员，包括：独立核算的科学研究与技术开发机构、科技信息与文献机构、高等学校、各类企业及其他事业单位主管科技工作的负责人，专门从事科技活动的计划、行政、人事、财务、物资供应、设备维护、图书资料管理等工作的各类人员，但不包括保卫、医疗保健人员、司机、食堂人员、茶炉工、水暖工、清洁工等为科技活动提供间接服务的人员。该指标用来反映投入科技活动人力的规模。

科学家与工程师　指科技活动人员中具有高、中级技术职称(职务)的人员和不具有高、中级技术职称(职务)的大学本科及以上学历人员。该指标用来反映投入科技活动人力的素质。

研究与试验发展(R&D)　指在科学技术领域，为增加知识总量、以及运用这些知识去创造新的应用进行的系统的创造性的活动，包括基础研究、应用研究、试验发展三类活动。国际上通常采用R&D 活动的规模和强度指标反映一国的科技实力和核心竞争力。

基础研究　指为了获得关于现象和可观察事实的基本原理的新知识(揭示客观事物的本质、运动规律，获得新发现、新学说)而进行的实验性或理论性研究，它不以任何专门或特定的应用或使用为目的。其成果以科学论文和科学著作为主要形式。用来反映知识的原始创新能力。

应用研究　指为获得新知识而进行的创造性研究，主要针对某一特定的目的或目标。应用研究是为了确定基础研究成果可能的用途，或是为达到预定的目标探索应采取的新方法(原理性)或新途径。其成果形式以科学论文、专著、原理性模型或发明专利为主。用来反映对基础研究成果应用途径的探索。

研究与试验发展人员　指参与研究与试验发展项目研究、管理和辅助工作的人员，包括项目(课题)组人员，企业科技行政管理人员和直接为项目(课题)活动提供服务的辅助人员。反映投入从事拥有自主知识产权的研究开发活动的人力规模。

研究与试验发展人员全时当量　指全时人员数加非全时人员按工作量折算为全时人员数的总和。例如：有两个全时人员和三个非全时人员(工作时间分别为2０%、3０% 和70%)，则全时当量为2+0.2+0.3+0.7=3.2 人年。为国际上比较科技人力投入而制定的可比指标。

专业技术人员　指从事专业技术工作和专业技术管理工作的人员，即企事业单位中已经聘任专业技术职务从事专业技术工作和专业技术管理工作的人员，以及未聘任专业技术职务，现在专业技术岗位上工作的人员。包括工程技术人员，农业技术人员，科学研究人员，卫生技术人员，教学人×100%员，经济人员，会计人员，统计人员，翻译人员，图书资料、档案、文博人员，新闻出版人员，律师、公证人员，广播电视播音人员，工艺美术人员，体育人员，艺术人员及企业政治思想工作人员，共十七个专业技术职务类别。用来反映科技人力资源情况。

科技活动经费筹集　指从各种渠道筹集到的计划用于科技活动的经费，包括政府资金、企业资金、事业单位资金、金融机构贷款、国外资金和其他资金等。反映各社会经济主体对促进科技进步所做的努力。

政府资金　指从各级政府部门获得的计划用于科技活动的经费，包括科学事业费、科技三项费、科研基建费、科学基金、教育等部门事业费中计划用于科技活动的经费以及政府部门预算外资金中计划用于科技活动的经费等。

企业资金 指从自有资金中提取或接受其他企业委托的、科研院所和高校等事业单位接受企业委托获得的，计划用于科研和技术开发的经费。不包括来自政府、金融机构及国外的计划用于科技活动的资金。

科技活动经费内部支出 指报告年内用于科技活动的实际支出，包括劳务费、科研业务费、科研管理费，非基建投资购建的固定资产、科研基建支出以及其他用于科技活动的支出。不包括生产性活动支出、归还贷款支出及转拨外单位支出。反映科技投入实际完成情况。

劳务费 指以货币或实物形式直接或间接支付给从事科技活动人员的劳动报酬及各种费用。包括各种形式的工资、津贴、奖金、福利、离退休人员费用、人民助学金等。反映改善科技人员待遇情况。

固定资产购建费 指报告年内使用非基建投资购建的固定资产和用于科研基建投资的实际支出额，即固定资产实际支出和科研基建投资实际完成额之和。固定资产是指长期使用而不改变原有实物形态的主要物资设备、图书资料、实验材料和标本以及其他设备和家具、房屋、建筑物。反映用于改善科研条件和科研手段方面的投入情况。

新产品 指采用新技术原理、新设计构思研制、生产的全新产品，或在结构、材质、工艺等某一方面比原有产品有明显改进，从而显著提高了产品性能或扩大了使用功能的产品。既包括政府有关部门认定并在有效期内的新产品，也包括企业自行研制开发，未经政府有关部门认定，从投产之日起一年之内的新产品。用来反映科技产出及对经济增长的直接贡献。

专利 是专利权的简称，是对发明人的发明创造经审查合格后，由专利局依据专利法授予发明人和设计人对该项发明创造享有的专有权。包括发明、实用新型和外观设计。反映拥有自主知识产权的科技和设计成果情况。

发明(专利) 指对产品、方法或者其改进所提出的新的技术方案。是国际通行的反映拥有自主知识产权技术的核心指标。

实用新型(专利) 指对产品的形状、构造或者其结合所提出的适于实用的新的技术方案。反映具有一定技术含量的技术成果情况。

外观设计(专利) 指对产品的形状、图案、色彩或者其结合所作出的富有美感并适于工业上应用的新设计。反映拥有自主知识产权的外观设计成果情况。

文化及相关产业 指为社会公众提供文化、娱乐产品和服务的活动以及与这些活动有关联的活动的集合。根据提供文化、娱乐产品和服务活动的属性特点，划分为公益性文化活动和经营性文化活动两大类。

文化及相关产业是第三产业的重要组成部分。是在我国《国民经济行业分类》基础上的派生分类，有文化服务和相关文化服务两大类：

文化服务 主要指新闻服务，出版发行和版权服务，广播、电视、电影服务，文化艺术服务，网络文化服务，文化休闲娱乐服务，其他文化服务。

艺术表演团体 由文化部门主办或实行行业管理（经文化市场行政部门审批或已申报登记并领取相关许可证），专门从事表演艺术等活动的各类专业艺术表演团体，含民间职业剧团。如话剧团、方言话剧团、滑稽剧团、儿童剧团、歌剧团、木偶团、皮影团等以及由若干剧种组成的综合性专业艺术表演团体。不包括半工半艺、半农半艺的剧团。

艺术表演场馆 指由文化部门主办或实行行业管理（经文化市场行政部门审批或已申报登记并领取相关许可证），有观众席、舞台、灯光设备，公开售票、专供文艺团体演出的文化活动场所。包括剧院（场）、音乐厅、歌剧院（场）、舞剧院（场）、话剧院(场)、戏院、马戏场、影剧院等进行文艺表演的场所。不包括电影院、礼堂、体育场馆、美术馆及绘画、雕塑等艺术馆。

文化市场经营机构 经文化市场行政部门审批或已申报登记并领取相关许可证的、从事文化经营和文化服务活动的机构。

广播节目综合人口覆盖率 指根据国家广电总局制定的《广播电视人口覆盖率统计技术标准和方法》进行统计调查的，在对象区内采用无线、有线、卫星等技术手段能够收听到包括中央、省、地市、县广播节目其中任意一套的人口数占全国总人口数的百分比。

电视节目综合人口覆盖率 指根据国家广电总局制定的《广播电视人口覆盖率统计技术标准和方法》进行统计调查的，在对象区内采用无线、有线、卫星等技术手段能够收看到包括中央、省、地市、县级电视节目中任意一套的人口数占全国总人口数的百分比。

Explanatory Notes on Main Statistical Indicators

Regular Institutions of Higher Education refer to educational establishments set up according to the government evaluation and approval procedures, recruiting graduates from senior secondary schools as the main target by National Matriculation TEST. They include full-time universities, colleges, institutions of higher professional education, institutions of higher vocational education, institutions of higher vocational education and others (non-university tertiary, branch schools and undergraduate classes).

Universities and colleges primarily provide undergraduate courses; institutions of higher professional education and institutions of higher vocational education primarily provide professional trainings; and others refer to educational establishments, which are responsible for enrolling higher education students under the State Plan but not enumerated in the total number of schools, including: branch schools of universities and colleges, and universities and colleges that have been approved and under plan for construction. Non-university tertiary refers to the regular undergraduate branch college which is running in new mechanism and mode, excluding the branch schools and other similar branches of educational institutions.

Net Enrolment Ratio of Primary Schools refers to the proportion of school age children enrolled at schools to the total number of school age children both in and outside schools (including retarded children, but excluding blind, deaf and mute children). The formula is:

$$\text{Net Enrolment Ratio of Primary Schools} = \frac{\text{Total Primary School}-\text{age Children at Schools}}{\text{Total Primary School}-\text{age Children Whether or Not Attending School}} \times 100\,\%$$

Scientific and Technological Activities (S&T Activities) refer to organized activities which are closely related with the creation, development, dissemination and application of the scientific and technical knowledge in the fields of natural sciences, agricultural science, medical science, engineering and technological science, humanities and social sciences (referred to as scientific and technological fields). S&T activities can be classified into 3 categories: research and development (R&D) activities, application of R&D results, and related S&T services. This statistical definition is made by UNICHIEF for scientific and technological activities to meet the need of carrying out statistical work in this field for its member countries particularly the developing countries.

Personnel Engaged in S&T Activities refers to personnel directly engaged in S&T activities, in the management of S&T activities, and in providing direct service to S&T activities, with over 10% of the total working hours in a year spent on S&T activities. (1) Personnel directly engaged in S&T activities include researchers, engineers, technicians and other related personnel engaged in S&T activities in independent-accounting R&D institutions, institutions of higher learning, and in research institutes, laboratories, technology development centres and central experiment workshops under enterprises and institutions. Also included are people working in S&T research project teams, professional and technical personnel working in S&T information archiving institutes, and graduate students working on the design of their thesis. (2) Personnel engaged in the management of S&T activities and in providing direct service to S&T activities include senior management people responsible for S&T activities in independent-accounting R&D institutions, S&T information archiving institutes, institutions of higher learning and in enterprises and institutions where S&T activities are undertaken. Also included are people responsible for the planning, administration, personnel management, financial management, logistics supply, equipment maintenance, information and library management that are related with S&T activities. People providing indirect services are excluded, such as security, medical service, drivers, plumbers, cleaners and those providing catering and related service. This indicator reflects the size of personnel engaged in S&T activities.

Scientists and Engineers refer to persons engaged in S&T activities either having obtained titles of senior and middle level professional positions, or those without such positions but have completed university or higher education. This indicator reflects the quality of personnel engaged in S&T activities.

Research and Development (R&D) refers to systematic and creative activities in the field of science and technology aiming at increasing the knowledge and using the knowledge for new application. R&D includes 3 categories of activities: basic research, applied research and experimentation for development. The scale and intensity of R&D are widely used internationally to reflect the strength of S&T and the core competitiveness of a country in the world.

Basic Research refers to empirical or theoretical research aiming at obtaining new knowledge on the fundamental principles regarding phenomena or observable facts to reveal the intrinsic nature and underlying laws and to acquire new discoveries or new theories. Basic research takes no specific or designated application as the aim of the research. Results of basic research are mainly released or disseminated in the form of scientific papers or monographs. This indicator reflects the innovation capacity for original knowledge.

Applied Research refers to creative research aiming at obtaining new knowledge on a specific objective or target. Purpose of the applied research is to identify the possible uses of results from basic research, or to explore new (fundamental) methods or new approaches. Results of applied research are expressed in the form of scientific papers, monographs, fundamental models or invention patents. This indicator reflects the exploration of ways to apply the results of basic research.

R&D Personnel refers to persons engaged in research, management and supporting activities of R&D, including persons in the project teams, persons engaged in the management of S&T activities of enterprises and supporting staff providing direct service to the research projects. This indicator reflects the size of personnel engaged in R&D activities with independent intellectual property.

Full-time Equivalent of R&D Personnel refers to the sum of the full-time persons and the full-time equivalent of part-time persons converted by workload. For instance, if there are 2 full-time persons and 3 part-time workers (20%, 30% and 70% of working hours respectively on R&D activities), the full-time equivalent are 2+0.2+0.3+0.7=3.2 person-years. This is an internationally comparable indicator of S&T manpower input.

Professional and Technical Personnel refer to persons engaged in professional and technical work or in the management of professional and technical activities, i.e., people with professional or technical positions who are engaged in professional and technical work or in the management of professional and technical activities, and people without professional or technical positions but are working on professional or technical posts. They include professionals and technicians working in 17 categories of technical occupations including engineering, agriculture, scientific researches, medical service, teaching, economic research and application, accounting, statistics, translation, libraries, archives, cultural and museum service, journalism and publication, lawyers, notarization service, radio and television broadcasting, handicraft and fine arts, sports, performing art, and political workers in enterprises. This indicator reflects the condition of human resources in S&T.

Funding for S&T Activities refers to funds obtained from various sources for S&T activities, including government funds, self-raised funds by enterprises, self-raised funds by institutions, loans from financial institutions, foreign funds and other funds. This indicator reflects the efforts made by various social economic entities in promoting the development of S&T.

Government Funds refers to funds obtained from government agencies at all levels to be used for S&T activities, including fund for scientific undertakings, 3 kinds of fund for S&T activities, fund for capital construction for scientific researches, science fund, funds from education expenditures by education departments for S&T activities, and extra-budget fund from government agencies for S&T activities.

Funds of Enterprises refers to funds of enterprises from their own budget; funds from other enterprises; or funds received by universities or research institutions from enterprises for scientific research or technical development projects. Excluded from this category are funds from government agencies, financial institutions or from foreign institutions.

Internal Expenditure on S&T activities refers to the actual expenditure on S&T activities during the reference year, including service fees, expenditure on research activities, expenditure on research management, purchase or construction of fixed assets not included in the investment for capital construction, expenditure on capital construction for scientific researches, and other expenditure on S&T activities. Not included are expenditure on production activities, repayment of loans and transfer expenditure. This indicator reflects the net investment in S&T more accurately.

Service Fees refer to direct or indirect payment, in cash or in kind, made to personnel engaged in S&T activities as remuneration and other fees. They include, in various forms, salaries, subsidies, bonus, benefits, retirement pension, stipend, etc. This indicator reflects the improvement of the remuneration package for S&T personnel.

Purchase or Construction of Fixed Assets refers to the fixed assets purchased or constructed using funds other than the investment in capital construction, and the actual expenditure on capital construction for scientific researches. In other words, it is the sum of the actual expenditure on fixed assets and the accomplished investment in capital construction for scientific researches. Fixed assets refer to main materials and equipment, literatures and documents in libraries, materials for experiments, specimen, instruments, furniture, buildings and constructions that can be used for a long time without changing the form and shape of those articles or constructions. This indicator reflects the input in improving the condition of S&T and the means of scientific research.

New Products refer to brand new products produced with new technology and new design, or products that represent noticeable improvement in terms of structure, material, or production process for improving significantly the character or function of the older versions. They include new products certified by relevant government agencies within the period of certification, as well as new products designed and produced by enterprises within a year without certification by government agencies. This indicator reflects the direct contribution of S&T output to economic growth.

Patent is an abbreviation for the patent right and refers to the exclusive right of ownership by the inventors or designers for the creation or inventions, given from the patent offices after due process of assessment and approval in accordance with the Patent Law. Patents are granted for inventions, utility models and designs. This indicator reflects the achievements of S&T and design with independent intellectual property.

Patented Inventions refer to new technical proposals to the products or methods or their modifications. This is universal core indicator reflecting the technologies with independent intellectual property.

Patented Utility Models refer to the practical and new technical proposals on the shape and structure of the product or the combination of both. This indicator reflects the condition of technological results with certain technical content.

Designs refer to the aesthetics and industrially applicable new designs for the shape, pattern and colour of the product, or their combinations. This indicator reflects the appearance design achievements with independent intellectual property.

Culture and Related Industries refer to the aggregate of activities, providing the mass with culture goods, amusement goods and services. According to the characteristics of culture goods, amusement goods and services, they can be classified into two categories, or nonprofit cultural activities and profit cultural activities.

Culture and related industries is the important component of the tertiary industry. These are the derivative sector from the Industrial Classification of the National Economy and are composed of two categories of culture services and related cultural services.

Culture services mainly include news services, publishing and copyright services, radio, television, film, arts, network, recreation, and other cultural services

Arts Performance Troupes refer to the various professional performing arts groups, which sponsored by the cultural sectors or guided by the cultural society (approved by the cultural market administration, or registered and permitted with the relative certificate), including non-governmental troupes, such as drama troupes, dialect troupes, comedy troupes, children troupes, Opera troupes, puppetry troupes, Shadowgraph troupes, etc., comprehensive professional arts performance troupes. The semi-working and semi-farming arts troupes are not included.

Arts Performance Places refer to the various sites for cultural activities, which sponsored by the cultural sectors or guided by the cultural society (approved by the cultural market administration, or registered and permitted with the relative certificate), with the facility of auditorium, stage, and lighting, and selling tickets in public, specially performed by arts troupes, including theatre, concert halls, opera halls, dance halls, drama halls, cinemas, circus fields, and other showplaces for the performing arts. The cinemas, auditoriums, stadiums, and arts museums, such as art galleries, painting houses, sculpture houses, are not included.

Cultural Market Operating Units refer to the units deal -ing in culture and cultural services, which registered and perm- itted with the relative certificate by cultural market administra- tion.

Radio Coverage of Population refers to the percentage of population, which can listen to one of central, provincial, city, prefecture, and county radio programs by wireless, cable, satellite and other technical means, in the surveying area, to national total population, according to Statistical Standard and Method on Television and Radio Coverage of Population established by the State Administration of Broadcasting, Film and Television.

Television Coverage of Population refers to the perce- ntage of population, which can watch one of central, provincial, city, prefecture, and county television programs by wireless, cable, satellite and other technical means, in the surveying area, to national total population, according to Statistical Standard and Method on Television and Radio Coverage of Population e- stablished by the State Administration of Broadcasting, Film and Televisio.

新疆统计年鉴
XINJIANG STATISTICAL YEARBOOK

18

体育、卫生及其他

SPORTS, PUBLIC HEALTH AND OTHERS

简要说明

本篇资料的主要内容及来源

本篇资料主要包括卫生事业、体育事业、民政事业、公安机关案件受理处治情况、安全生产情况、道路交通事故和火灾事故等内容，除卫生、体育事业外其他部门数据由新疆维吾尔自治区统计局社会科技处与综合处根据有关部门资料整理。

卫生部门资料是由新疆维吾尔自治区卫生厅依据年报资料整理提供。体育资料是由新疆维吾尔自治区体育局提供。民政部分资料由新疆维吾尔自治区民政厅提供，治安、刑事案件资料由新疆维吾尔自治区公安厅提供，安全生产情况来自新疆维吾尔自治区安全生产监督管理局，道路交通事故和火灾事故分别由新疆维吾尔自治区公安交通管理局和新疆维吾尔自治区消防总队提供。

Brief Introduction

Main Content and Source of Data

Data in this chapter mainly include the development of public health, sports, civil affairs, labor and society protection, offense cases against public order handled by public Security organs, traffic accidents and fires. These statistics are provided by Department of Population and Social Science &Technology in Statistics Bureau of Xinjiang according to the data from the related Department of Statistics Bureau.

Data on public health are from the Bureau of Public Health, these statistics are according to the data of yearly statistics; increased the data of condition of village clinic and basic condition of institution on new cooperative health care of agricultural and pastoral areas. Data on sports are from the Bureau of Sports; Data on civil affairs and labor protection are provided respectively by the Bureau of Civil Affairs and the Bureau of Labor and Social Security. Data on public security, statistics on procuratorial, legal and judicial affairs are provided by the Bureau of Public Security. Data on production safety are come from Xinjiang Administration of Work Safety. Data on traffic accident and fire are respectively provided by the Xinjiang Traffic Management Bureau and the Xinjiang Fire Department.

18-1 体育局系统从业人员情况
Statistics on Staff and Workers in Physical Education System

单位：人 (2012 年) (person)

项　目	Item	合　计 Total	公务员 Civil Servants	教练员 Coaches	运动员 Athletes	科研人员 Scientific and Technical Personnel
总　计	**Total**	**3006**	**402**	**515**	**598**	**21**
体育行政机关	Administrative of Physical Culture and Sports	650	402			
运动项目管理部门	Sports Events Mangement	870		66	598	1
体育运动学校	Physical Education and Sports Schools	505		135		4
业余体校	Spare-time Sports Schools	514		293		2
体育场馆	Stadium and Gymnasium	193		5		
体育科研机构	Sport Scientific Research Institutions	20				14
其　他	Others	254		16		

项　目	Item	医务人员 Medical Personnel	文化教师 Culture Teachers	管理人员 Administrative Personnel	工勤人员 Logistics Workers	其他人员 Others
总　计	**Total**	**27**	**228**	**544**	**365**	**306**
体育行政机关	Administrative of Physical Culture and Sports			134	77	37
运动项目管理部门	Sports Events Mangement	20		86	61	38
体育运动学校	Physical Education and Sports Schools	7	212	60	58	29
业余体校	Spare-time Sports Schools		6	106	49	58
体育场馆	Stadium and Gymnasium			64	90	34
体育科研机构	Sport Scientific Research Institutions		10	4		2
其　他	Others			90	30	108

18-2 按项目分等级裁判员发展人数
Number of Referees in Levels by Type of Sports

单位：人 (2012 年) (person)

项　目	Item	合　计 Total	国家级裁判员 National Referee 小　计 Sub-total	#男 Male	一级裁判员 First Level Referee 小　计 Sub-total	#男 Male	二级裁判员 Second Level Referee 小　计 Sub-total	#男 Male
总　计	**Total**	**599**	**7**	**7**	**97**	**66**	**495**	**369**
田　径	Track and Field Events	1					1	
国际式摔跤	Internationa Wrestling	5					5	5
中国式摔跤	Chinese Wrestling	3	3	3				
柔道	Judo	1					1	1
跆拳道	Taekwondo	33	2	2			31	20
足球	Football	75					75	62
篮球	Basketball	65					65	65
排球	Volleyball	93					93	37
乒乓球	Table Tennis	73			61	38	12	6
羽毛球	Badminton	69					69	47
国际象棋	Chess	6						
中国象棋	Chinese Chess	13						
桥牌	Bridge	6						
汽车	Motor Vehicles	57			12	8	45	36
台球	Billiards	3					3	3
门球	Gateball	12	1	1			11	9
信鸽	Carrier Pigeon	32			24	20	8	8
健美	Bodybuilding	1	1	1				
拔河	Tug of War	13			13	10		
健身气功	Qigong	38					38	35

18-3 按项目分等级运动员发展人数
Number of Athletes at Levels by Type of Sports

单位：人　　(2012 年)　　(person)

项目	Item	合计 Total	国际、国家级运动健将 International and National Level		一级运动员 First Grade		二级运动员 Second Grade	
			小计 Sub-total	#男 Male	小计 Sub-total	#男 Male	小计 Sub-total	#男 Male
总计	**Total**	**728**	**20**	**10**	**79**	**56**	**629**	**388**
田径	Track and Field Events	171			5	5	166	101
游泳	Swimming	10			1		9	4
举重	Weightlifting	7					7	7
拳击	Boxing	16					16	11
国际式摔跤	Internationa Wrestling	21	1	1	3	3	17	8
柔道	Judo	5					5	
跆拳道	Taekwondo	105	7	5	25	18	73	44
自行车	Bicycles	5			5	3		
射击	Shooting	5	2		1		2	2
射箭	Archery	6			2	2	4	2
足球	Football	75					75	51
篮球	Basketball	199	1	1	17	12	181	114
沙滩排球	Beach Volleyball	9			3	2	6	
乒乓球	Table Tennis	33			3	1	30	16
网球	Tennis	8					8	4
手球	Handball	7	4		3			
垒球	Softball	7	5	3	2	2		
速度滑冰	Speed Skating	1					1	1
健美操	Aerobics	4					4	
武术	Wushu	24			3	2	21	19
围棋	Weiqi	2					2	2
橄榄球	Rugby	6			6	6		
航空模型	Model Aeroplane	2					2	2

18-4 各地、州、市体育局系统机构数

Number of Institutions in Sports Committees by Prefecture,Autonomous Prefecture and City

单位：个 (2012 年) (unit)

地区	Region	合计 Total	行政机关 Administrative Agencies	运动项目管理部门 Sports Events Mangement	体育运动学校 Physical Education and Sports Schools
总计	**Total**	**222**	**110**	**6**	**5**
自治区直属	Under Autonomous Region	19	1	6	1
乌鲁木齐市	Urumqi City	19	9		1
克拉玛依市	Karamay City	6	5		
石河子市	Shihezi City	2	1		
吐鲁番地区	Turpan Administrative Offices	8	4		
哈密地区	Hami [Kumul] Administrative Offices	9	4		
昌吉回族自治州	Changji Hui Autonomous Prefecture	10	8		
伊犁哈萨克自治州	Ili Kazak Autonomous Prefecture	45	27		1
伊犁州直属县(市)	Counties (Cities) Direct Under Ili Prefecture	18	11		1
塔城地区	Tacheng [Tarbagatai] Administrative Offices	10	8		
阿勒泰地区	Altay Administrative Offices	17	8		
博尔塔拉蒙古自治州	Bortala Mongol Autonomous Prefecture	8	4		
巴音郭楞蒙古自治州	Bayangol Mongol Autonomous Prefecture	16	10		
阿克苏地区	Aksu Administrative Offices	22	10		1
克孜勒苏柯尔克孜自治州	Kizilsu Kirgiz Autonomous Prefecture	12	5		
喀什地区	Kashgar [Kaxgar] Administrative Offices	28	13		1
和田地区	Hotan Administrative Offices	18	9		

地区	Region	业余体校 Spare-time Sports Schools	体育场馆 Stadium and Gymnasium	体育科研机构 Sport Scientific Research Institutions	其他 Others
总计	**Total**	**72**	**11**	**2**	**16**
自治区直属	Under Autonomous Region		1	1	9
乌鲁木齐市	Urumqi City	5	2	1	1
克拉玛依市	Karamay City	1	1		
石河子市	Shihezi City	1			
吐鲁番地区	Turpan Administrative Offices	4			
哈密地区	Hami [Kumul] Administrative Offices	3			2
昌吉回族自治州	Changji Hui Autonomous Prefecture	1			
伊犁哈萨克自治州	Ili Kazak Autonomous Prefecture	13	2		
伊犁州直属县(市)	Counties (Cities) Direct Under Ili Prefecture	5	1		
塔城地区	Tacheng [Tarbagatai] Administrative Offices	1			1
阿勒泰地区	Altay Administrative Offices	7	1		1
博尔塔拉蒙古自治州	Bortala Mongol Autonomous Prefecture	4			
巴音郭楞蒙古自治州	Bayangol Mongol Autonomous Prefecture	5	1		
阿克苏地区	Aksu Administrative Offices	9	2		
克孜勒苏柯尔克孜自治州	Kizilsu Kirgiz Autonomous Prefecture	5	1		1
喀什地区	Kashgar [Kaxgar] Administrative Offices	12	1		1
和田地区	Hotan Administrative Offices	9			

18-5 各地、州、市体育局系统机构从业人员数
Number of Staff and Workers in Sports Bureau by Region

单位：人　　(2012 年)　　(person)

地　区	Region	合　计 Total	行政机关 Administrative Agencies	运动项目管理部门 Sports Events Mangement	体育运动学　校 Physical Education and Sports Schools	业余体校 Spare-time Sports Schools	体育场馆 Stadium and Gymnasium	体育科研机构 Sport Scientific Research Institutions	其　他 Others
总　计	**Total**	**3006**	**650**	**870**	**505**	**514**	**193**	**20**	**254**
自治区直属	Under Autonomous Region	1322	54	870	146		32	15	205
乌鲁木齐市	Urumqi City	357	43		161	73	75	5	
克拉玛依市	Karamay City	44	34			10			
石河子市	Shihezi City	40	7			33			
吐鲁番地区	Turpan Administrative Offices	37	17			20			
哈密地区	Hami [Kumul] Administrative Offices	65	25			32			8
昌吉回族自治州	Changji Hui Autonomous Prefecture	29	20			3	6		
伊犁哈萨克自治州	Ili Kazak Autonomous Prefecture	380	149		61	118			18
伊犁州直属县(市)	Counties (Cities) Direct Under Ili Prefecture	227	79		61	76	11		
塔城地区	Tacheng [Tarbagatai] Administrative Offices	52	52						
阿勒泰地区	Altay Administrative Offices	101	18			42	23		18
博尔塔拉蒙古自治州	Bortala Mongol Autonomous Prefecture	40	15			25			
巴音郭楞蒙古自治州	Bayangol Mongol Autonomous Prefecture	84	38			32	9		5
阿克苏地区	Aksu Administrative Offices	173	57		55	47	14		
克孜勒苏柯尔克孜自治州	Kizilsu Kirgiz Autonomous Prefecture	66	22			28	10		6
喀什地区	Kashgar [Kaxgar] Administrative Offices	262	84		82	71	13		12
和田地区	Hotan Administrative Offices	107	85			22			

18-6 卫生机构、床位、人员数

(2012 年)

项　目	Item	机构数(个) Number of Institutions (unit)	实有床位数(张) Beds (unit)	在岗职工合计(人) Total Number of Medical Personnel (person)	卫生技术人员小计 Medical Technical Personnel
总　计	**Total**	**18320**	**131542**	**177085**	**136691**
按经济类型分	**Grouped by Economic Type**				
公　立	Public	12202	117390	151059	115959
国 有	State-owned	8984	114167	141497	111409
集 体	Collective-owned	3218	3223	9562	4550
民　营	Non-public	6118	14152	26026	20732
联　营	Joint Ownership	31	112	175	135
私　营	Private	5287	11969	21969	18143
其　他	Others	800	2071	3882	2454
按设置主办单位分	**Grouped by sponsors**				
政府办	Run by Government	8167	111069	136218	106361
社会办	Run by Society	4996	8035	18161	11332
个人办	Run by Private	5157	12438	22706	18998
按市县分	**Guouped by Ctiy and County**				
市	City	6874	78608	110635	89400
县	County	11446	52934	66450	47291
按城乡分	**Grouped by Rural and Urban**				
城　市	Urban	2114	34994	53667	42987
农　村	Rural	16206	96548	123418	93704
按营利性质分	**Grouped by Profit**				
非营利性	Non-profit	13327	118666	146022	110829
营利性	Profit	4583	12876	22126	18736
其　他	Others	410		8937	7126
按机构分	**Grouped By Organizations**				
医院	Total Number of Hospitals	836	103074	109537	89510
综合医院	Comprehensive Hospitals	648	79908	89954	74257
中医医院	Hospitals of Traditional Chinese Medicine	50	6910	6477	5261
中西医结合医院	TCM and Western Medicine Hospital	4	542	523	470
民族医院	Hospitals for Nationalities	47	6543	4736	3829
专科医院	Specialist Hospitals	87	9171	7847	5693

注：1.本表人员合计中包括乡村医生 11548 人和卫生员 1308 人；
　　2.不含乡镇卫生院在村卫生室工作的执业（助理）医师、注册护士数。

Number of Health Institutions, Beds and Persons Engaged by Type of Institutons

执业（助理）医师 Lecensed Assistant Doctor	执业医师 Lecensed Doctors	注册护士 Registered Nurses	药剂人员 Pharmacist	技师(士) Technician (artificer)	检验人员 Laboratory Technicians	其他 Others	见习医师	其他技术人员 Other Technicians	管理人员 Administrative Personnel	工勤人员 Logistics Workers
50540	**41358**	**52449**	**6557**	**7984**	**5539**	**19161**	**4888**	**6972**	**6631**	**13935**
40692	32966	45481	5540	6976	4928	17270	4459	6198	5705	11938
38851	31563	43806	5324	6780	4775	16648	4314	6010	5406	11636
1841	1403	1675	216	196	153	622	145	188	299	302
9848	8392	6968	1017	1008	611	1891	429	774	926	1997
56	49	46	12	8	7	13	2	4	7	16
8787	7448	5925	873	855	507	1703	383	587	777	1608
1005	895	997	132	145	97	175	44	183	142	373
36500	29510	41871	5041	6437	4576	16512	4170	5868	5149	11078
4862	4053	4335	617	647	426	871	338	460	692	1151
9178	7795	6243	899	900	537	1778	380	644	790	1706
33550	29912	36261	4274	5079	3596	10236	2998	4647	4567	9621
16990	11446	16188	2283	2905	1943	8925	1890	2325	2064	4314
16266	15216	18219	1990	2237	1614	4275	1495	2396	2416	5868
34274	26142	34230	4567	5747	3925	14886	3393	4576	4215	8067
38916	31615	45503	5596	6106	4081	14708	4435	5849	5201	11413
8859	7573	6344	881	894	538	1758	397	650	813	1801
2765	2170	602	80	984	920	2695	56	473	617	721
30186	26509	38675	4805	5225	3338	10619	3672	4951	4682	10394
24566	21607	32633	3639	4416	2806	9003	3256	3688	3910	8099
2170	2026	2062	396	256	185	377	71	410	279	527
102	71	182	21	18	12	147	40	7	34	12
1470	1069	1167	505	211	133	476	120	297	155	455
1878	1736	2631	244	324	202	616	185	549	304	1301

Note: a). Total data in this table included 11548 doctors and 1308 medical personels.
b). Total data in this table didn't include licensed doctors and registered nurses in county health centers.

18-6 续表 1

(2012 年)

项　目	Item	机构数(个) Number of Institutions (unit)	床位数(张) Beds (unit)	卫生人员合计(人) Total Number of Medical Personnel (person)	卫生技术人员 Medical Technical Personnel
口腔医院	Nonnasality Hospitals	4	52	263	212
眼科医院	Ophthalmology Hospitals	6	170	259	152
耳鼻喉科医院	Otolaryngology Hospitals	2	150	226	171
肿瘤医院	Tumour Hospital	2	1370	2055	1462
心血管病医院	Cardiovascular Hospitals	2	250	635	362
胸科医院	Chest Hospital	1	516	454	377
妇产(科)医院	Hospitals for Gynaecology and Obsterics	16	511	563	446
儿童医院	Children Hospital	1	30	54	34
精神病医院	Mental Hospitals	13	3856	1582	1160
传染病医院	Infectous Diseases Hospitals	4	620	485	359
皮肤病医院	Skin disease hospital	1	49	33	27
结核病医院	Tubercuiosis Hospitals	1	486	175	154
骨科医院	Hospital of Orthopedics	5	160	122	98
康复医院	Recovery Hospitals	3	168	92	70
整形外科医院	Plastic surgical holpital	1	20	44	23
其他专科医院	Other Specialist Hospitals	25	763	805	586
基层医疗卫生机构	Basic Medical Institutions	16970	25461	54076	36436
社区卫生服务中心(站)	Community Health Service Center	744	3084	7695	6558
社区卫生服务中心	Community Health Service Center	165	2637	4577	3850
社区卫生服务站	Community Health Service Station	579	447	3118	2708
卫生院	Total Number of Public Health Center	923	21990	20926	17731
街道卫生院	Public Health Center in Neighbourhood	4		124	103
乡镇卫生院	Public Health Center in Township and Towns	919	21990	20802	17628
中心卫生院	Public Health Center in Rural Area	139	4700	4028	3458
乡卫生院	Public Health Center in Township	780	17290	16774	14170
村卫生室	Village Clinics	10500		14146	1290
门诊部	Outpatients Department	278	387	1992	1747
综合门诊部	Comprehensive Department	211	347	1553	1387
中医门诊部	Department of Traditional Chinese Medicine	6	5	25	20
中西医结合门诊部	TCM and Western Medicine Department	6	5	21	20
民族医门诊部	Department for Nationalities	5		40	30
专科门诊部	Specialist Department	50	30	353	290
诊所.卫生所.医务室	Clinics, Health Centers	4525		9317	9110
诊所	Clinics	3834		8041	7868
卫生所、医务室	Health Centers,Health Rooms	682		1264	1230

Continued

执业（助理）医师 Lecensed Assistant Doctor	执业医师 Lecensed Doctors	注册护士 Registered Nurses	药剂人员 Pharmacist	技师(士) Technician (artificer)	检验人员 Laboratory Technicians	其　他 Others	见习医师 Intern Doctor	其他技术人员 Other Technicians	管理人员 Administrative Personnel	工勤人员 Logistics Workers
116	109	71	4	4	1	17	9	8	17	26
46	39	76	9	7	7	14	5	21	14	72
68	60	58	11	6	4	28	12	20	4	31
411	408	749	43	58	21	201	52	124	30	439
112	108	218	13	15	12	4		78	34	161
132	130	176	19	16	15	34	13	29	5	43
150	127	176	22	41	26	57	15	37	41	39
11	5	14	4	5	4			4	11	5
317	294	619	53	59	41	112	33	142	65	215
142	127	134	16	27	15	40	5	38	10	78
12	10	12	1	2	1				3	3
64	58	64	7	11	9	8	8	6	6	9
22	19	29	6	11	3	30	29	5	4	15
39	37	20	2	6	3	3		7	6	9
14	10	7	1	1	1				2	19
222	195	208	33	55	39	68	4	30	52	137
16045	11451	11804	1526	1484	1060	5577	1106	1324	982	2478
2733	2352	2476	413	380	259	556	128	306	394	437
1459	1215	1456	265	278	182	392	93	205	241	281
1274	1137	1020	148	102	77	164	35	101	153	156
5873	2895	5542	786	950	688	4580	888	1018	588	1589
42	28	34	9	8	6	10	4	5	1	15
5831	2867	5508	777	942	682	4570	884	1013	587	1574
1140	588	1089	148	207	142	874	177	143	108	319
4691	2279	4419	629	735	540	3696	707	870	479	1255
982	524	308								
908	780	494	101	106	74	138	21			245
681	595	417	87	88	63	114	16			166
9	6	5	3			3				5
11	10	4	3	2	1					1
15	10	6	1	3	1	5				10
192	159	62	7	13	9	16	5			63
5549	4900	2984	226	48	39	303	69			207
4782	4321	2595	195	36	27	260	64			173
766	579	378	31	12	12	43	5			34

18-6 续表 2

(2012 年)

项　目	Item	机构数(个) Number of Institutions (unit)	床位数(张) Beds (unit)	卫生人员合计(人) Total Number of Medical Personnel (person)	卫生技术人员 Medical Technical Personnel
护理站	Nursing Department	9		12	12
专业公共卫生机构	Specialized Public Health Institution	506	2631	13175	10591
疾病预防控制中心	Center for Disease Control and Prevetion	224		6351	4894
自治区属	Autonoumous Areas	1		490	333
区辖市(地区)属	District Municipal	24		1337	1019
地辖市属	administer the municipal	27		1168	922
县属	County	76		2155	1612
其他	Others	96		1201	1008
专科疾病防治院(所、站)	Specialized Disease Prevention & Treatment Institution	5	89	102	55
专科疾病防治院	Specialized Disease Prevention & Treatment Centers	1	5	26	23
其他	Others	1	5	26	23
专科疾病防治所(站、中心)	Specialized Disease Prevention & Treatment Stations	4	84	76	32
药物戒毒所(中心)	The drug detoxificatio Center	3	84	76	32
其他	Others	1			
妇幼保健院(所、站)	Women and Children Care Agencies	91	2542	4041	3318
省辖市(地区)属	District Municipal	5	504	760	643
地辖市属	administer the municipal	19	763	1386	1129
县属	County	64	1235	1759	1424
其他	Others	3	40	136	122
妇幼保健院	Women and Children Care Hospitals	39	1841	2600	2159
妇幼保健所	Women and Children Care Center	4		116	93
妇幼保健站	Women and Children Care Stations	48	701	1325	1066
急救中心(站)	Urgent Care Center	4		151	116
采供血机构	Blood transfusion services	21		513	352
卫生监督所(中心)	Health Inspection Institution (center)	158		1976	1831
自治区属	Autonoumous Areas	1		80	80
省辖市(地区)属	District Municipal	20		440	420
地辖市属	administer the municipal	36		557	507
县属	County	79		739	697
其他	Others	22		160	127
计划生育技术服务机构	The family planning technical service institutions	3		41	25
其他卫生机构	Others	8	376	297	154
疗养院	Sanatoriums	4	376	241	130
卫生监督检验(监测、检测)所(站)	Health Inspection Institution (center)	1		6	6
其他	Others	3		50	18

Continued

执业（助理）医师 Lecensed Assistant Doctor	执业医师 Lecensed Doctors	注册护士 Registered Nurses	药剂人员 Pharmacist	技师(士) Technician (artificer)	检验人员 Laboratory Technicians	其 他 Others	见习医师 Intern Doctor	其他技术人员 Other Technicians	管理人员 Administrative Personnel	工勤人员 Logistics Workers
1		11								
4248	3347	1908	217	1265	1134	2953	104	674	919	991
2672	2091	486	73	843	781	820	51	385	465	607
185	183	3		67	67	78		53	20	84
552	484	80	15	225	219	147	12	102	102	114
521	449	68	12	175	164	146	2	53	81	112
791	535	172	34	291	248	324	18	122	178	243
623	440	163	12	85	83	125	19	55	84	54
32	20	10	2	6	4	5	5		45	2
17	12	2	1	1		2	2		1	2
17	12	2	1	1		2	2		1	2
15	8	8	1	5	4	3	3		44	
15	8	8	1	5	4	3	3		44	
1414	1121	1242	135	271	208	256	43	206	261	256
211	201	323	25	57	43	27		15	76	26
500	422	436	49	93	71	51	6	103	72	82
640	444	440	56	113	86	175	37	82	108	145
63	54	43	5	8	8	3		6	5	3
879	760	900	100	170	132	110	18	142	168	131
52	41	17	1	12	11	11		5	10	8
483	320	325	34	89	65	135	25	59	83	117
49	46	60	1	6	3			10	7	18
65	54	105	5	136	135	41	5	44	44	73
						1831		22	90	33
						80				
						420		1	12	7
						507		17	25	8
						697		4	23	15
						127			30	3
16	15	5	1	3	3			7	7	2
61	51	62	9	10	7	12	6	23	48	72
49	41	56	8	8	6	9	6	8	37	66
3	3	1		2	1					
9	7	5	1			3		15	11	6

18-7 主要年份卫生机构数(不含村卫生室)

Number of Health Institutions in Main Years(Excluding Village Clinics)

单位：个 (unit)

年 份 Year	合 计 Total	医院、卫生院 Hospitals And Township Hospitals	#医院 Hospitals	疗养院 Sanitarium	门诊部 Clinics	专科防治所、站 Specialized Prevention & Treatment Centers or Stations	疾病防控中心 Sanitation and Antiepidemic Agencies	妇幼保健所、站 Maternity and Child Care Centers	社区卫生服务中心（站） Health Service Center for Community	卫生监督所（中心） Research Institutes of Medical Science	其他卫生机构 Other Institutions	诊所、医务保健室、医务室 Clinics Health Care Room Infirmary	#私营、个体机构 Institutions of Privately Owned & Individual
1978	2581	806	204	2	1609	1	104	12			47		
1980	2818	884	270	4	1756	4	102	12			56		
1985	3320	947	389	5	2125	2	139	27			75		
1990	3945	1049	435	6	2536	13	191	59			91		
1995	3932	1292	507	8	2247	16	216	69			84		
2000	7314	1352	522	8	154	16	210	74			96	5404	3653
2005	8087	1516	685	6	224	8	197	88	46	30	113	5859	4183
2006	8175	1560	699	6	220	7	211	92	62	49	83	5885	4227
2007	7465	1629	756	7	240	7	214	87	250	112	30	4889	4093
2008	6739	1629	741	4	217	6	213	89	264	121	31	4165	3756
2009	7288	1669	763	5	221	5	214	90	405	128	30	4521	3678
2010	7650	1712	802	4	259	4	221	90	641	133	31	4555	3796
2011	7587	1742	820	4	247	4	216	90	683	128	30	4443	3745
2012	7820	1759	836	4	278	5	224	91	744	158	32	4525	3827

注：1.2002 年起卫生部新制度规定持有"医疗执业许可证"所有卫生机构算为一个机构,兵团连队卫生室统计到卫生所中,所以卫生机构总数增加。2.从 2007 年开始卫生部门实行网络直报。

Note: a) From 2002, in line with new regulations of ministry of public health,all the health institutions that have medical service permit shall be counted as one and health care rooms shall be counted in health clinics,therefore the total number of health institutions increased.

b) Since 2007, health care institution have carried out direct network report.

18-8 主要年份卫生人员数(不含村卫生室)

Number of Persons Engaged in Health Institutions in Main Years(Excluding Village Clinics)

单位：人 (person)

年 份 Year	合 计 Total	#卫生技术人员 Medical Technical Personnel	#医 生 Doctors	执业医师 Lecensed Doctors	执业助理医师 Lecensed Assistant Doctor	#注册护士 Registered Nurses	平均每万人医生数 Number of Doctors per 10 000 Population	在合计中私人个体开业人员 Persons of Privately Owned & Individual
1978	66252	51050	16898	7368	9530	10765	13.70	
1980	74627	57949	20614	10092	10522	12077	16.06	
1985	88460	68961	25721	13330	12391	17136	18.90	188
1990	102053	79853	33683	24967	8716	23386	22.03	2034
1995	116856	92028	39636	30038	9598	26350	23.86	4252
2000	122064	98093	45402	34892	10510	30850	24.55	5835
2005	117165	96266	41426	32563	8863	30657	20.61	13562
2006	121400	99839	42775	33988	8787	32119	20.87	13256
2007	127621	104671	43551	34838	8713	34662	20.79	14689
2008	130174	106853	43456	35320	8136	36084	20.39	14560
2009	138344	114521	45616	37223	8393	40425	21.13	16616
2010	149069	122860	48166	39301	8865	44238	22.25	19330
2011	155701	129354	48618	39763	8855	48422	22.49	19947
2012	150083	135401	49558	40834	8724	52141	22.63	22604

注：2002 年以前执业医师为中医师、西医师、中西医结合医师，执业助理医师为中医士、西医士、中西医结合医士，注册护士为护师、护士。(以下同)

Note: Prior to 2002,doctors with license were doctors trained in western medicine,assistant doctors are practioners with secondary western medical education,and registered nurses are master nurses and nurses (The following is the same as below) .

18-9 主要年份卫生机构床位数
Number of Sick-Beds in Health Institutions in Main Years

单位：张 (unit)

年份 Year	合计 Total	医院卫生院 Hospitals And Health Centers	#医院 Hospitals	社区服务中心(站) Sanitarium	其他卫生机构 Other Health Institutions	每万人医院、卫生院床位数 Number of Hospital Beds per 10 000 Population
1978	57647	39179	25514		18468	31.78
1980	61075	47236	32944		13839	36.81
1985	60930	55298	42486		5632	40.63
1990	67414	60707	47924		6707	39.70
1995	72955	66696	53336		6259	40.15
2000	70542	65916	52438		4626	35.64
2005	79753	76002	63013	209	3542	37.81
2006	83722	80090	65589	445	3187	39.07
2007	90329	87131	71496	343	2855	41.59
2008	96852	93253	76321	843	2756	43.76
2009	107193	102620	83776	1851	2722	47.54
2010	116230	109851	89871	3588	2791	50.36
2011	125391	118781	97436	3691	2919	53.93
2012	131542	125064	103074	3084	3394	56.01

18-10 医疗机构病床使用情况
Utilization of Beds in Medical Institutions

(2012 年)

项目	Item	实有床位(张) Number of Beds (bed)	实际开放总床日数(日) Beds Open to Patients (day)	实际占用总床日数(床日) Turnover of Beds (times)	平均开放病床(张) Number of Days per Bed in Use in a Year (day)
总计	**Total**	**131542**	**46410431**	**40074515**	**126804**
医院	Total Number of Hospitals	103074	36708615	33809607	100297
综合医院	General Hospital	79908	28510025	26475355	77896
中医医院	Hospital Specialized in Traditional Chinese Medicine	6910	2489767	2509925	6803
中西医结合医院	Hospital Specialized in Combination Of Traditional Chinese and Western Medicine	542	154440	140166	422
民族医院	National Hospital	6543	2263406	1956110	6184
专科医院	Specialized Hospital	9171	3290977	2728051	8992
基层医疗卫生机构	Basic Medical Institutions	25461	8712613	5716915	23805
社区卫生服务中心(站)	Health Service Center for Community	3084	1068163	516167	2918
社区卫生服务中心	Health Service Center for Community	2637	926197	466072	2531
社区卫生服务站	Health Service Center for Community	447	141966	50095	388
卫生院	Total Number of Public Health Center	21990	7644450	5200748	20886
#乡镇卫生院	Township Health Center	21990	7644450	5200748	20886
专业公共卫生机构	Specialized Public Health Institution	2631	851945	501550	2328
专科疾病防治院(所、站)	Specialized Disease Prevention & Treatment Institute	89	32509	11987	89
妇幼保健院(所、站)	Hospitals for Maternity and Child Care	2542	819436	489563	2239
#妇幼保健院	Women and Children Care Agencies	1841	581316	372303	1588
其他机构	Other Institutions	376	137258	46443	375
疗养院	Sanatorium	376	137258	46443	375

18-10 续表 Continued

项　目	Item	病床周转次数(次) Utilization Rate of Beds (%)	病床工作日(日) Number of Days per Bed in Use in a Year (day)	病床使用率(%) Utilization Rate of Beds (%)	出院者平均住院日(日) Average Stay Days in Hospital (day)
总　计	**Total**	**35.2**	**316.0**	**86.35**	**9.0**
医　院	Hospitals	34.9	337.1	92.10	9.8
综合医院	General Hospital	37.7	339.9	92.86	9.2
中医医院	Hospital Specialized in Traditional Chinese Medicine	34.6	369.0	100.81	10.8
中西医结合医院	Hospital Specialized in Combination Of Traditional Chinese and Western Medicine Medicine	25.4	332.2	90.76	12.9
民族医院	National Hospital	27.1	316.3	86.42	12.0
专科医院	Specialized Hospital	16.2	303.4	82.89	15.9
基层医疗卫生机构	Basic Medical Institutions	37.0	240.2	65.62	6.1
社区卫生服务中心(站)	Health Service Center for Community	20.2	176.9	48.32	7.7
社区卫生服务中心	Health Service Center for Community	21.5	184.2	50.32	7.6
社区卫生服务站	Health Service Center for Community	11.7	129.1	35.29	8.9
卫生院	Total Number of Public Health Center	39.2	249.0	68.03	6.0
#乡镇卫生院	Township Health Center	39.2	249.0	68.03	6.0
专业公共卫生机构	Specialized Public Health Institution	35.5	215.5	58.87	5.6
专科疾病防治院(所、站)	Specialized Disease Prevention & Treatment Institute	11.0	135.0	36.87	10.5
妇幼保健院(所、站)	Hospitals for Maternity and Child Care	36.4	218.7	59.74	5.5
#妇幼保健院	Women and Children Care Agencies	38.0	234.4	64.04	5.9
其他机构	Other Institutions	2.8	123.8	33.84	40.9
疗养院	Sanatorium	2.8	123.8	33.84	40.9

18-11 各地、州、市卫生机构、床位和人员数

年份 Year	地区 Region	机构数(个) Number of Institutions (unit)	床位数(张) Beds (unit)	在岗职工合计(人) Total Number of Medical Personnel (person)
	2005	8087	79753	117165
	2006	8175	83722	121400
	2007	7465	90329	127621
	2008	6739	96852	130174
	2009	7288	107193	138344
	2010	7650	116230	149069
	2011	17412	125391	167828
	2012	18320	131542	177085
乌鲁木齐市	Urumqi City	1777	26518	41796
克拉玛依市	Karamay City	94	1648	3612
吐鲁番地区	Turpan Administrative Offices	369	2405	3868
哈密地区	Hami [Kumul] Administrative Offices	477	3462	5252
昌吉回族自治州	Changji Hui Autonomous Prefecture	1441	9930	13305
伊犁哈萨克自治州	Ili Kazak Autonomous Prefecture	4109	23723	33155
伊犁州直属县(市)	Counties (Cities) Direct Under Ili Prefecture	2118	15434	19970
塔城地区	Tacheng [Tarbagatai] Administrative Offices	1228	4897	7923
阿勒泰地区	Altay Administrative Offices	763	3392	5262
博尔塔拉蒙古自治州	Bortala Mongol Autonomous Prefecture	662	2762	4433
巴音郭楞蒙古自治州	Bayangol Mongol Autonomous Prefecture	1271	8271	11188
阿克苏地区	Aksu Administrative Offices	1522	12210	12501
克孜勒苏柯尔克孜自治州	Kizilsu Kirgiz Autonomous Prefecture	305	3207	3923
喀什地区	Kashgar [Kaxgar] Administrative Offices	3475	18514	22100
和田地区	Hotan Administrative Offices	1785	11776	12383
自治区直辖县级市	Municpality Country-LevelCity directly under the Central Govern-ment	1033	7116	9569
石河子市	Shihezi City	746	5539	7260
阿拉尔市	Aral City	191	556	876
图木舒克市	Tumxuk City	2	153	153
五家渠市	Wujiaqu City	94	868	1280

注：1.本表 2012 年数据含乡村医生 11548 人和卫生员 1308 人。
2.不含乡镇卫生院在村卫生室工作的执业（助理）医师、注册护士数。

Number of Health Institutions，Beds and Personnel by Prefecture, Autonomous Prefecture and City

卫生技术人员 Medical Technical Personnel	其他技术人员 Other Technicians	管理人员 Administrative Personnel	工勤人员 Logistics Workers	平均每万人床位数(张) Number of Beds per 10 000 Population (unit)
96266	4626	6330	9943	39.71
99839	5168	6258	10135	39.07
104671	5276	7143	10531	43.11
106853	5694	6419	11208	45.45
114521	6111	6453	11259	49.66
122860	6979	7089	12141	53.28
130604	6904	6837	12606	56.93
136691	6972	6631	13935	58.91
32720	1877	1962	5049	102.86
2937	158	159	356	57.66
3054	114	167	261	38.46
4491	202	164	262	58.44
10919	523	401	804	70.82
26074	1410	1204	2047	51.26
15928	834	755	1346	52.91
6016	378	265	498	46.74
4130	198	184	203	51.13
3526	85	253	330	57.01
9422	452	374	486	60.17
9137	555	403	836	50.94
3125	129	96	185	57.21
16139	560	854	1440	44.60
7173	529	281	1382	55.46
7974	378	313	497	67.33
6070	316	240	413	89.34
678	10	34	35	29.80
139	8	4	2	9.59
1087	44	35	47	95.70

Note: a).Total data in this table included 11548 doctors and 1308 medical personnel.
b).Total data in this table didn't include licensed doctors and registered nurses in tounship in county health Centers.

18-12 各地、州、市卫生技术人员数

单位:人

年 份 Year	地 区 Region	卫生技术人员合计 Number of Medical Technical Personnel	执业医师 Doctors with Licence	执业助理医 师 Lecensed Assistant Doctor
	2005	96266	32563	8863
	2006	99839	33988	8787
	2007	104671	34838	8713
	2008	106853	35320	8136
	2009	114521	37223	8393
	2010	122860	39301	8865
	2011	130604	40265	9265
	2012	136691	41358	9182
乌鲁木齐市	Urumqi City	32720	11897	623
克拉玛依市	Karamay City	2937	1101	35
吐鲁番地区	Turpan Administrative Offices	3054	987	237
哈密地区	Hami [Kumul] Administrative Offices	4491	1478	306
昌吉回族自治州	Changji Hui Autonomous Prefecture	10919	3365	741
伊犁哈萨克自治州	Ili Kazak Autonomous Prefecture	26074	7906	2184
伊犁州直属县(市)	Counties (Cities) Direct Under Ili Prefecture	15928	4880	1207
塔城地区	Tacheng [Tarbagatai] Administrative Offices	6016	1673	571
阿勒泰地区	Altay Administrative Offices	4130	1353	406
博尔塔拉蒙古自治州	Bortala Mongol Autonomous Prefecture	3526	1078	321
巴音郭楞蒙古自治州	Bayangol Mongol Autonomous Prefecture	9422	2801	709
阿克苏地区	Aksu Administrative Offices	9137	2358	797
克孜勒苏柯尔克孜自治州	Kizilsu Kirgiz Autonomous Prefecture	3125	787	342
喀什地区	Kashgar [Kaxgar] Administrative Offices	16139	3529	1628
和田地区	Hotan Administrative Offices	7173	1609	757
自治区直辖县级市	Municpality Country-LevelCity directly under the Central Govern-ment	7974	2462	502
石河子市	Shihezi City	6070	1950	368
阿拉尔市	Aral City	678	145	65
图木舒克市	Tumxuk City	139	31	10
五家渠市	Wujiaqu City	1087	336	59

注：1.本表人员合计中包括乡村医生 11548 人和卫生员 1308 人；
2.不含乡镇卫生院在村卫生室工作的执业（助理）医师、注册护士数

Number of Medical Technical Personnel by Prefecture, Autonomous Prefecture and City

(person)

注册护士 Registered Nurses	药剂人员 Pharmacist	技师(士) Technician (artificer)	检验人员 Laboratory Technicians	其他 Others	平均每万人医生数 Number of Doctors per 10 000 Population
30657	5848	4773		13562	20.61
32119	5948	4980		14017	20.87
34662	5647	6701	4746	14110	20.79
36084	5721	6876	4803	14716	20.39
40425	5989	7164	4977	15327	21.13
44238	6364	7742	5301	16350	22.25
48760	6483	7726	5391	18105	22.49
52449	6557	7984	5539	19161	22.63
13911	1516	1658	1196	3115	48.56
1194	178	178	130	251	39.75
1161	151	210	137	308	19.57
1815	234	230	178	428	30.11
4247	614	633	416	1319	29.28
9769	1112	1733	1233	3370	21.80
5968	699	1112	799	2062	20.87
2260	256	388	254	868	21.42
1541	157	233	180	440	26.51
1295	193	207	150	432	28.88
3595	379	525	359	1413	25.53
3481	432	622	413	1447	13.16
1066	147	146	98	637	20.14
5410	816	999	675	3757	12.42
2214	463	427	253	1703	11.14
3291	322	416	301	981	28.04
2430	249	305	225	768	37.39
313	26	39	26	90	11.25
67	5	10	5	16	2.57
481	42	62	45	107	43.55

Note: a). Total data in this table included 11548 doctors and 1308 medical personels.
b). Total data in this table didn't include licensed doctors and registered nurses in county health centers.

18-13 2000-2012 年历年分市县医院床位和专业卫生技术人员数
Hospital Beds and Medical Technical Personnel by City and County Areas(2000-2012)

年 份 Year	医院床位(张) Number of Hospital Beds (unit)		专业卫生技术人员(人) Number of Medical Technical Personnel (person)		#执业医师、执业助理医师 Lecensed Doctors & Assistant Doctors		#注册护士 Registered Nurses	
	市 City	县 County	市 City	县 County	市 City	县 County	市 City	县 County
2000	38398	27518	44115	31138	18408	13225	16805	9918
2001	38323	27685	44113	31055	18811	13271	16714	10105
2002	38700	26178	41850	27932	16689	10578	15965	8840
2003	42880	26915	44678	28228	17883	10916	17015	9087
2004	46300	27722	46956	28552	19207	10583	17185	9054
2005	50238	29515	54188	31132	23191	12323	18240	9289
2006	52275	31125	56701	32178	24033	13049	19365	9538
2007	54595	32536	68546	36125	28896	14655	24174	10488
2008	57242	36011	69292	37561	28215	15241	24976	11108
2009	58373	25403	54356	19490	20044	7242	22453	6979
2010	61157	28714	56706	21500	20953	7637	23777	8037
2011	65905	31531	61309	22893	21481	7881	26559	8964
2012	70217	32857	65326	24184	22081	8105	28960	9715

18-14 2000-2012 年历年分市县卫生院床位和专业卫生技术人员数
Hospital Beds and Medical Technical Personnel by City and County Areas(2000-2012)

年 份 Year	卫生院床位(张) Number of Hospital Beds (unit)		专业卫生技术人员(人) Number of Medical Technical Personnel (person)		#执业医师、执业助理医师 Lecensed Doctors & Assistant Doctors		#注册护士 Registered Nurses	
	市 City	县 County	市 City	县 County	市 City	县 County	市 City	县 County
2000	2138	11119	3442	13131	1622	6299	1021	3756
2001	2141	11247	3602	13129	1782	6300	1095	3808
2002	2180	9991	4021	11215	1611	4370	970	2829
2003	2471	10147	3645	10901	1364	4227	946	2950
2004	2351	10479	3703	10936	1429	3963	992	2746
2005	5061	11679	10345	13646	5004	5704	2056	3024
2006	4732	13079	10930	14105	5370	6048	2207	3213
2007	2832	12803	18725	18220	9548	8000	4771	4182
2008	3037	13895	17745	19239	8888	8446	4710	4626
2009	3313	15531	3684	12578	1595	4435	1161	3527
2010	3383	16597	3641	13240	1536	4381	1180	3741
2011	3674	17671	3672	13653	1538	4334	1195	4097
2012	3768	18222	3694	14037	1466	4407	1241	4301

18-15 社区卫生服务中心(站)工作量

Medical Services in Health Service Centers for Community

年 份 Year	社区卫生服务中心 Health Service Centers for Community				社区卫生服务站诊疗人次(万人) Health Service Stations for Community (10 000 patients)
	诊疗人次(万人次) Visits (10 000 patient-times)	入院人数(万人) Inpatients (10 000 patients)	病床使用率(%) Utilization Rate (%)	平均住院日(日) Average Stay Days (day)	
2002	76.84	0.16	53.86	10.16	34.41
2003	88.10	0.60	89.51	16.13	33.75
2004	85.62	0.03	36.42	10.00	82.67
2005	67.04	0.03	16.71	11.08	152.68
2006	107.49	0.35	11.71	6.94	179.32
2007	105.73	0.24	59.77	11.70	109.22
2008	156.05	0.94	51.68	11.30	121.92
2009	232.95	2.36	49.93	9.90	207.23
2010	298.47	4.24	61.07	10.40	355.78
2011	323.93	4.37	53.51	9.80	351.28
2012	330.09	4.85	50.32	7.60	341.43

18-16 乡村卫生室基本情况

Basic Conditions of Country Health Room

(2012 年)

项 目	Item	合 计 Total	中 医 Traditional Chinese Medicine	西 医 Western Medicine	中西医结合 Combination Traditional and Western Medicine
机构数(个)	Number of Institutions(unit)	10500	84	8982	1286
执业(助理)医师(人)	Lecensed (Assistant) Doctors (person)	982	30	1837	169
注册护士(人)	Registered Nurses(person)	308	3	781	64
乡村医生和卫生员(人)	Country Doctor and Assistant Nurse(person)	12856	94	11063	1699
乡村医生	Country Doctor	11548	87	9866	1595
卫生员	Assistant Nurse	1308	7	1197	104
诊疗人次数(万人次)	Number of Patients Treated(10 000 patient-times)	788.72	12.06	697.86	78.80
#出 诊	Out-call	66.05	1.64	56.75	7.67

18-17 新型农牧区合作医疗基本情况

Basic Statistics on New Cooperative Health Care in Agricultural and Pastoral Areas

项　　目	Item	2011	2012
开展县(市)数(个)	Number of Counties(citys) to Carry Out(unit)	89	89
覆盖农牧业人口数(万人)	Population Coverage of Agriculture and Animal Husbandry(10 000 persons)	1054.18	1081.61
参合农牧业人口数(万人)	Livestok Population Parameters(10 000 persons)	1050.93	1078.30
参合率(%)	Ratio of Participation(%)	99.70	99.70
当年筹集基金(万元)	Paise Funds This Year(10 000 yuan)	250295.47	339771.84
#中央补助	Central Subsidy	130308.00	165111.00
自治区补助	Autonpmous Region Subsidy	66294.18	87090.00
地方补助	Local Subsidy	20516.50	31048.10
个人缴费	Individual Pay	31636.49	54131.77
当年人均筹集资金(元/人·年)	Annual per Capita Raise Funds(yuan/persons.year)	236.70	320.33
当年基金支出(万元)	Expenditure of Fund This Yesr(10 000 yuan)	210775.48	318926.04
当年基金使用率(%)	Ratio of Fund Utilization This Yesr(%)	84.21	93.86
当年补偿受益人次(万人次)	Benefit of Compensation Population this Year(10 000 person-times)	1140.04	1389.99
住　院	Inpatients	168.48	234.52
门　诊	Out-patient Services	719.37	948.47
体　检	Physical Examination	27.59	19.77
其　他	Others	224.60	187.24
当年总体受益率(%)	Ratio of Total Benefit(%)	108.48	128.91
住院受益率	Benefit Ratio of be in Hospital	16.03	21.75
门诊受益率	Benefit Ratio of out-patient Services	68.45	87.96
当年总补偿比(%)	Total Compensation Ratio(%)	50.01	55.67
#住院平均补偿比	Average Compensation Ratio of be in Hospital	50.00	55.04
新农合管理机构实有人数(人)	Number of Employed Persons in Institution on New Cooperative Health Care of Agriculturial and Pastoral Areas(person)	1275.00	1248.00
新农合管理机构经费收入(万元)	Income of Institution on New Cooperative Health Care of Agriculturial and Pastoral Areas(10 000 yuan)	5393.61	6660.40
新农合管理机构经费支出(万元)	Expenditure of Institution on New Cooperative Health Care of Agriculturial and Pastoral Areas(10 000 yuan)	5532.31	6501.82
每实有人员管理参合人数(人)	Number of Participated Persons by per Practical Employed Persons(person)	15100	14900

18-18 医疗卫生机构门诊服务情况

Basic Conditions of Outpatient service medical and health institutions

项目	Item	总诊疗人次数（万人次） Number of Visits(10000 times)	门、急诊 Outpatients with Emergency Treatment 小计 Total	门诊 Outpatients	急诊 Emergency Treatment	家庭卫生服务人次数 Vistits
总计	**Total**	**8386.56**	**8054.50**	**7739.57**	**314.94**	**37.22**
医院	Hospitals	4207.58	4079.51	3798.53	280.98	20.42
综合医院	General Hospital	3490.62	3380.50	3119.93	260.58	19.55
中医医院	Hospital Specialized in Traditional Chinese Medicine	400.38	393.59	379.56	14.03	0.30
中西医结合医院	Hospital Specialized in Combination Of Traditional Chinese and Western Medicine Medicine	20.66	20.54	20.39	0.15	
民族医院	National Hospital	142.23	134.75	131.45	3.30	0.29
专科医院	Specialized Hospital	153.70	150.13	147.19	2.93	0.28
基层医疗卫生机构	Basic Medical Institutions	3887.53	3698.00	3671.42	26.58	14.79
社区卫生服务中心(站)	Health Service Center for Community	671.52	651.52	644.05	7.47	6.68
卫生院	Health Center	1194.52	1133.09	1113.97	19.11	8.11
村卫生室	Village Clinics	788.72	722.67	722.67		
门诊部	Out-patients Department	115.92	108.38	108.38		
诊所.卫生所.医务室	Clinics Health Care Room Infirmary	1116.86	1082.34	1082.34		
专业公共卫生机构	Specialized Public Health Institution	289.46	275.01	267.63	7.37	2.01
专科疾病防治院(所、站)	Specialized Disease Prevention & Treatment Institute	3.36	3.36	2.75	0.60	
妇幼保健院(所、站)	Hospitals for Maternity and Child Care	280.56	266.11	264.88	1.23	2.01
内：妇幼保健院	Women and Children Care Agencies	179.52	171.62	170.67	0.95	0.87
急救中心(站)	Emergency center	5.54	5.54		5.54	
其他机构	Other Institutions	1.99	1.98	1.98		
疗养院	Sanatorium	1.99	1.98	1.98		

项目	Item	观察室留观病例数（万人） Cases in Observation Room(10000 persons)	健康检查人数（万人） Number of Health Examinations (10000 persons)	急诊病死率（%） Fatality Rate among Emergency Admissions(%)	观察室病死率（%） Fatality Rate in Observation Room (%)
总计	**Total**	**91.17**	**572.99**	**0.17**	**0.10**
医院	Hospitals	61.43	297.87	0.18	0.15
综合医院	General Hospital	52.65	268.56	0.18	0.17
中医医院	Hospital Specialized in Traditional Chinese Medicine	8.19	20.87	0.16	
中西医结合医院	Hospital Specialized in Combination Of Traditional Chinese and Western Medicine Medicine	0.02	0.03		
民族医院	National Hospital	0.23	3.80	0.03	0.18
专科医院	Specialized Hospital	0.35	4.61	0.03	
基层医疗卫生机构	Basic Medical Institutions	25.08	229.65	0.06	0.01
社区卫生服务中心(站)	Health Service Center for Community	16.35	55.23	0.12	0.01
卫生院	Health Center	8.73	174.42	0.04	0.01
村卫生室	Village Clinics				
门诊部	Out-patients Department				
诊所.卫生所.医务室	Clinics Health Care Room Infirmary				
专业公共卫生机构	Specialized Public Health Institution	4.67	45.35	…	
专科疾病防治院(所、站)	Specialized Disease Prevention & Treatment Institute		0.03		
妇幼保健院(所、站)	Hospitals for Maternity and Child Care	4.67	45.33	0.01	
内：妇幼保健院	Women and Children Care Agencies	4.21	21.12	0.01	
急救中心(站)	Emergency center				
其他机构	Other Institutions		0.12		
疗养院	Sanatorium		0.12		

18-19 医疗卫生机构住院服务情况
Basic Conditions of Service in medical and health institutions

项　目	Item	入院人数（人）Number of Inpatients (Person)	出院人数（人）Patients Discharged (Person)
总　计	**Total**	**4467178**	**4464571**
医　院	Hospitals	3514353	3499080
综合医院	General Hospital	2948766	2939956
中医医院	Hospital Specialized in Traditional Chinese Medicine	238045	235128
中西医结合医院	Hospital Specialized in Combination Of Traditional Chinese and Western Medicine Medicine	10749	10733
民族医院	National Hospital	170013	167772
专科医院	Specialized Hospital	146780	145491
基层医疗卫生机构	Basic Medical Institutions	868596	881925
社区卫生服务中心(站)	Health Service Center for Community	53036	59066
卫生院	Health Center	812464	819763
门诊部	Village Clinics	3096	3096
专业公共卫生机构	Specialized Public Health Institution	83133	82527
专科疾病防治院(所、站)	Specialized Disease Prevention & Treatment Institute		980
妇幼保健院(所、站)	Hospitals for Maternity and Child Care	83133	81547
内：妇幼保健院	Women and Children Care Agencies	60790	60372
其他机构	Other Institutions	1096	1039
疗养院	Sanatorium	1096	1039

项　目	Item	住院病人手术人次数（人次）Surgical Operation of Hospitalized (person-times)	每百门急诊的入院人数（人）Inpatients per 100 Outpatient and Emergency Visits (person)	入院病人死亡率(%) Inpatient mortality (%)
总　计	**Total**	**718166**	**7.28**	**0.23**
医　院	Hospitals	701449	8.61	0.28
综合医院	General Hospital	628680	8.72	0.30
中医医院	Hospital Specialized in Traditional Chinese Medicine	34467	6.05	0.11
中西医结合医院	Hospital Specialized in Combination Of Traditional Chinese and Western Medicine Medicine	50	5.23	1.84
民族医院	National Hospital	8157	12.62	0.02
专科医院	Specialized Hospital	30095	9.78	0.44
基层医疗卫生机构	Basic Medical Institutions		4.85	0.03
社区卫生服务中心(站)	Health Service Center for Community		0.81	0.31
卫生院	Health Center		7.17	0.01
门诊部	Village Clinics			
专业公共卫生机构	Specialized Public Health Institution	16717	3.09	0.02
专科疾病防治院(所、站)	Specialized Disease Prevention & Treatment Institute			
妇幼保健院(所、站)	Hospitals for Maternity and Child Care	16717	3.12	0.02
内：妇幼保健院	Women and Children Care Agencies	14224	3.54	0.02
其他机构	Other Institutions		5.52	0.29
疗养院	Sanatorium		5.52	0.29

18-20 医疗卫生机构门诊病人人均医疗费用

The per capita medical expenses of patients hospitalized in the medical and health institutions

项　目	Item	门诊病人次均诊疗费用(元) The per capita medical expenses of outpatient	挂号费 registered fee	诊察费 Diagnostic Fee	检查费 Inspection fee	化验费 Laboratory fee
总　计	**Total**	**106.3**	**0.6**	**1.6**	**22.7**	**9.8**
医　院	Hospitals	161.6	0.9	2.5	37.1	15.1
综合医院	General Hospital	159.0	0.9	2.3	39.4	15.8
中医医院	Hospital Specialized in Traditional Chinese Medicine	180.3	1.1	1.9	25.8	10.1
中西医结合医院	Hospital Specialized in Combination Of Traditional Chinese and Western Medicine Medicine	150.2	0.1	0.1	2.8	1.7
民族医院	National Hospital	102.4	0.9	2.1	14.1	5.1
专科医院	Specialized Hospital	229.0	1.2	7.4	40.0	24.6
基层医疗卫生机构	Basic Medical Institutions	31.1	0.2		3.4	1.3
社区卫生服务中心(站)	Health Service Center for Community	82.3	0.1		7.8	2.5
社区卫生服务中心	Health Service Center for Community	106.2	0.2		13.9	4.1
社区卫生服务站	Health Service Center for Community	59.1	0.1		1.8	0.9
卫生院	Total Number of Public Health Center	34.0	0.4		4.3	2.0
街道卫生院	Public Health Center in Neighbourhood	27.2			9.5	0.3
乡镇卫生院	Public Health Center in Township and Towns	34.0	0.4		4.3	2.0
中心卫生院	Public Health Center in Rural Area	31.7	0.3		5.5	2.3
乡卫生院	Public Health Center in Township	34.7	0.5		3.9	2.0
门诊部	Village Clinics	75.3				
护理站	Nursing Hospital	36.9				
专业公共卫生机构	Specialized Public Health Institution	99.8	0.6	5.6	19.4	22.7
专科疾病防治院(所、站)	Specialized Disease Prevention & Treatment Institute	83.2	0.1			
妇幼保健院(所、站)	Hospitals for Maternity and Child Care	101.9	0.6	5.8	20.0	23.4
内：妇幼保健院	Women and Children Care Agencies	125.4	0.7	7.7	23.2	30.3
其他机构	Other Institutions	239.4	0.1	0.2	4.0	1.6
疗养院	Sanatorium	239.4	0.1	0.2	4.0	1.6

项　目	Item	治疗费 Treatment costs	手术费 Operation Fee	卫生材料费 Sanitary materials fee	药　费 expenses for medicine	药事服务费 Pharmaceutical service fee
总　计	**Total**	**8.7**	**1.8**	**1.8**	**55.2**	**0.2**
医　院	Hospitals	13.5	2.9	2.8	81.5	0.3
综合医院	General Hospital	12.3	2.6	3.0	77.1	0.2
中医医院	Hospital Specialized in Traditional Chinese Medicine	12.5	1.4	1.4	124.3	0.3
中西医结合医院	Hospital Specialized in Combination Of Traditional Chinese and Western Medicine Medicine	11.4	1.1		131.5	0.8
民族医院	National Hospital	7.2	0.6	0.8	69.5	0.4
专科医院	Specialized Hospital	49.1	16.3	4.0	74.8	0.6
基层医疗卫生机构	Basic Medical Institutions	2.3	0.2	0.4	21.3	
社区卫生服务中心(站)	Health Service Center for Community	4.1	0.6	0.8	61.8	
社区卫生服务中心	Health Service Center for Community	5.2	0.9	0.9	75.8	
社区卫生服务站	Health Service Center for Community	3.2	0.2	0.6	48.4	
卫生院	Total Number of Public Health Center	3.5	0.2	0.7	20.1	
街道卫生院	Public Health Center in Neighbourhood	2.5			11.1	
乡镇卫生院	Public Health Center in Township and Towns	3.5	0.2	0.7	20.2	
中心卫生院	Public Health Center in Rural Area	2.9	0.2	0.5	17.3	
乡卫生院	Public Health Center in Township	3.7	0.2	0.7	21.0	
门诊部	Village Clinics					
护理站	Nursing Hospital	19.7		1.6	14.4	
专业公共卫生机构	Specialized Public Health Institution	7.7	3.2	1.9	31.6	0.1
专科疾病防治院(所、站)	Specialized Disease Prevention & Treatment Institute	50.5			32.3	
妇幼保健院(所、站)	Hospitals for Maternity and Child Care	7.3	3.3	2.0	32.2	0.1
内：妇幼保健院	Women and Children Care Agencies	8.1	4.6	2.6	38.1	0.2
其他机构	Other Institutions	24.0		0.2	179.4	
疗养院	Sanatorium	24.0		0.2	179.4	

18-21 医疗卫生机构住院病人人均医疗费用

The per capita medical expenses of patients hospitalized in the medical and health institutions

项目	Item	合计 Total	床位费 Bed fee	检查费 Inspection fee
总计	**Total**	**4353**	**143**	**498**
医院	Hospitals	5283	165	608
综合医院	General Hospital	5097	155	596
中医医院	Hospital Specialized in Traditional Chinese Medicine	6427	179	705
中西医结合医院	Hospital Specialized in Combination Of Traditional Chinese and Western Medicine Medicine	9257	463	1372
民族医院	National Hospital	2644	140	209
专科医院	Specialized Hospital	9963	364	1095
基层医疗卫生机构	Basic Medical Institutions	838	46	89
社区卫生服务中心(站)	Health Service Center for Community	1750	55	159
社区卫生服务中心	Health Service Center for Community	1650	54	160
社区卫生服务站	Health Service Center for Community	2958	64	143
卫生院	Total Number of Public Health Center	775	46	84
乡镇卫生院	Public Health Center in Township and Towns	775	46	84
中心卫生院	Public Health Center in Rural Area	806	50	106
乡卫生院	Public Health Center in Township	766	44	77
专业公共卫生机构	Specialized Public Health Institution	2391	198	179
专科疾病防治院(所、站)	Specialized Disease Prevention & Treatment Institute	578		
妇幼保健院(所、站)	Hospitals for Maternity and Child Care	2412	200	181
内：妇幼保健院	Women and Children Care Agencies	2819	256	216
其他机构	Other Institutions	11233	1871	271
疗养院	Sanatorium	11233	1871	271

项目	Item	化验费 Laboratory fee	治疗费 Treatment costs	手术费 Operation Fee	药费 expenses for medicine
总计	**Total**	**515**	**554**	**271**	**1727**
医院	Hospitals	631	674	333	2079
综合医院	General Hospital	621	573	348	2003
中医医院	Hospital Specialized in Traditional Chinese Medicine	753	1461	262	2132
中西医结合医院	Hospital Specialized in Combination Of Traditional Chinese and Western Medicine Medicine	1656	1959	21	3509
民族医院	National Hospital	269	468	58	1259
专科医院	Specialized Hospital	974	1589	484	4365
基层医疗卫生机构	Basic Medical Institutions	68	95	12	446
社区卫生服务中心(站)	Health Service Center for Community	156	234	79	824
社区卫生服务中心	Health Service Center for Community	152	219	74	746
社区卫生服务站	Health Service Center for Community	206	416	141	1753
卫生院	Total Number of Public Health Center	62	86	7	421
乡镇卫生院	Public Health Center in Township and Towns	62	86	7	421
中心卫生院	Public Health Center in Rural Area	86	95	3	406
乡卫生院	Public Health Center in Township	55	83	9	425
专业公共卫生机构	Specialized Public Health Institution	345	310	422	527
专科疾病防治院(所、站)	Specialized Disease Prevention & Treatment Institute				289
妇幼保健院(所、站)	Hospitals for Maternity and Child Care	349	314	427	530
内：妇幼保健院	Women and Children Care Agencies	404	362	476	602
其他机构	Other Institutions	426	4670		2109
疗养院	Sanatorium	426	4670		2109

18-22 法定报告传染病发病及死亡情况
Confirmed Incidence and Death from Infectious Diseases

项　目	Item	发病率 (1/10 万) Disease Incidence (1/100 000)		死亡率 (1/10 万) Death Rate (1/100 000)	
		2011	2012	2011	2012
总　计	**Total**	**590.9152**	**624.4794**	**2.8511**	**3.1557**
鼠　疫	The Plague				
霍　乱	Cholera				
传染性非典	SARS				
艾滋病	AIDS	3.1766	11.0925	2.0536	2.3362
肝　炎	Viral Hepatitis	276.3316	273.1557	0.0917	0.1041
脊　灰	Epidemic Cerebrospinal Meningitis	0.0917		0.0046	
人禽流感	Highly Pathogenic Bird Flu				
甲型 H1N1 流感	A(H1N1) Flu	1.256	0.7968	0.0046	0.0045
麻　疹	Measles	8.6864	2.6441		0.0091
出血热	Hemorrhage Fever	0.0046	0.0045		
狂犬病	Hydrophobia	0.0092		0.0092	
乙　脑	Encephalitis B				
登革热	Dengue Fever				
炭　疽	Anthrax	0.2063	0.1313		
痢　疾	Dysentery	41.2774	33.0194		
肺结核	Plumonary Tuberculosis	157.8304	181.1651	0.6509	0.6384
伤寒+副伤寒	Typhoid	1.1597	1.1817		
流 脑	Encephalitis B	0.11	0.1177	0.0092	0.0181
百 日 咳	Pertussis	2.6632	3.4726	0.0046	
白 喉	Diphtheria				
新生儿破伤风	Newborn Baby Tetanus	0.1384	0.1463	0.0031	0.0061
猩 红 热	Scarlet Fever	11.8217	10.0285		
布鲁氏菌病	Brucellosis	6.0232	9.7976		0.0045
淋 病	Gonorrhea	9.7452	10.1236		
梅 毒	Syphilis	70.2839	87.4857	0.0183	0.0272
钩 体 病	Leptospirosis		0.0045		
血吸虫病	Schistosomiasis	0.0092	0.0091		
疟　疾	Malaria	0.0229	0.0317		0.0045

注: 1.2012 年度按发病日期统计中，涉及与艾滋病相关的发病数/率的计算，包括既往已报告 HIV 感染者转化为艾滋病病例。2.新生儿破伤风死亡率单位为千分率。
Note: The unit of incidence disease rate and death rate of newborn baby tetanus is 1‰.

18-23 城市前十位疾病死亡原因及构成
Death Causes and Percentage of 10 Major Diseases in Urban Areas

(2012 年)

疾病死亡原因	Cause of Death	死亡总人数 (人) Total Deaths (person)	占死亡总人数的比重 (%) Percentage to Total Deaths (%)
十种死因合计	**Total**	**8360**	**100**
循环系统	Circulatory system	3134	37.49
肿　瘤	Malignant Tumour	2094	25.05
呼吸系统	Diseases of the Respiratory System	1122	13.42
损伤和中毒外部原因	Trauma and Toxicosis	513	6.14
传染病	Infections Disease	322	3.85
消化系统	Disease of the Digestive System	275	3.29
内分泌	Internal secretion	223	2.67
其它疾病	Others	129	1.54
诊断不明	Diagnosis in nubibus	108	1.29
神经系统疾病	Diseases of the Nervous System	107	1.28
泌尿生殖系统	Disease of the Genifourinary system	97	1.16
起源于围生期的某些情况	Diseases of the Nervous system	83	0.99

注：统计范围包括乌鲁木齐市及辖区资料。
Note: Statistics in data covers Urumqi and its Districts.

18-24 安全生产情况
Basic Statistics on Work Safety

单位：人 (person)

项　　目	Item	2011	2012
亿元新疆生产总值生产安全事故死亡人数	Mortality Rate of Work Safety Accident Average 100 Billion Yuan GDP	0.36	0.31
工矿商贸企业就业人员生产安全事故十万人死亡人数	Mortality Rate of Work Safety Accident of Employment in Industrial & Mining and Commercial & Tradal Enterprises Average 100 000 Persons	7.10	6.20
煤矿百万吨死亡人数	Mortality Rate of Coal Procuction Average 1 Million Tons	0.77	0.39
道路交通万车死亡人数	Mortality Rate of Highway Traffic Accident Average 10 000 Vehicles	6.47	5.07

18-25 社会福利事业单位基本情况
Basic Statistics on Social Welfare Institutions

(2012 年)

指　标	Item	院　数(个) Number of Homes (unit)	工作人员数(人) Number of Persons Engaged (person)	床位数(张) Number of Beds (unit)	年末收养人数(人) Number of Persons Housed (person)	#女　性 Female
总　计	**Total**	**565**	**4332**	**41376**	**30575**	**7756**
社会福利院	Social Welfare Homes	52	761	8153	5160	1070
儿童福利院	Children Welfare Homes	47	594	6321	4526	1426
光荣院	Homes for Disabled Veterans	9	72	492	364	89
社会福利医院	Psychopathy Welfare Homes	8	560	2317	2222	623
城镇老年性福利机构	Urban Elderly Welfare Units	80	1015	8277	6151	1343
农村老年性福利机构	Rural Elderly Welfare Units	363	1278	15646	12079	3171
荣誉军人康复医院	Recuperative Hospital for Soldiers with Honour	1	37	80	9	
其他收养性机构	Other Residential Institutions	5	15	90	64	34

18-26 社会福利事业、企业单位数和工作人员数
Number of Social Welfare Institutions and Enterprises and Persons Engaged

(2012 年)

项　目	Item	机构数(个) Number of Institutions or Enterprises (unit)	工作人员数(人) Number of Persons Engaged (person)
收养性福利事业单位	Adopting Social Welfare Institutions	565	4332
工商部门登记	Administravie Office of Industry and Commerce	2	26
编制部门登记	Organization Department	355	2953
民政部门登记	Civil Administration Department	198	1300
未登记	Un-register	10	53
社会福利企业	Social Welfare Enterprises	153	11856
优抚安置事业单位	Administration Agencies for Martyrs	42	432
救助类单位	Salvaged Deparement	69	440
殡葬服务事业单位	Funeral and Interment Institutions	157	849
福利彩票发行单位	Welfare Lottery-Ticked Issuance Unit	24	218
社区服务中心	Community Service Institutions	238	1161

18-27 社会救济情况
Basic Statistics on Social Relief Funds

指　　标	Item	2012
城镇居民最低生活保障人数(人)	**Number of Persons Receiving Lowest Cost-of-living in Urban Area (person)**	**857002**
老年人	Old Folks	103665
成年人	Adult	468066
在职人员	Full Employed Staff and Workers	12293
灵活就业人员	Flexible Employed Persons	144878
登记失业人员	Registered Employed Persons	120196
未登记失业人员	Unregistered Employed Persons	190699
未成年人	Minors	285271
在校生	Enrollment	176387
其　他	Others	108884
城镇居民最低生活保障家庭数(户)	**Number of Family Receiving Lowest Cost-of-living in Urban Area (household)**	**366463**
农村最低生活保障人数(人)	**Number of Persons Receiving Lowest Cost-of-living in Rural Area (person)**	**1358341**
农村最低生活保障家庭数(户)	**Number of Family Receiving Lowest Cost-of-living in Rural Area (household)**	**545848**

18-28 主要年份工会组织情况
Basic Statistics on Trades Unions in Main Years

年　份 Year	工会基层组织个数(个) Number of Grassroots Unions (unit)	全区已建工会组织的基本单位职工与会员人数(万人) Membership and Number of Staff and Workers in Grassroots Unions (10 000 persons)				专职工会干　部(万人) Number of Full-time Personnel of Unions (10 000 persons)
		职工人数 Number of Staff and Workers	#女 Female	会员人数 Number of Membership	#女 Female	
1980	3255	84.20	30.25	67.13	20.42	0.48
1990	10685	231.48	90.64	196.58	76.97	0.79
1995	14457	271.43	114.13	254.49	104.97	1.19
2000	13016	211.73	90.80	200.80	84.93	0.59
2001	18219	234.84	100.71	215.31	91.07	0.73
2002	20806	236.58	99.65	220.85	93.11	0.49
2003	11263	230.24	93.43	220.55	87.05	0.45
2004	11979	224.52	94.49	219.35	90.62	0.48
2005	11721	232.78	97.50	232.03	97.20	0.41
2006	13163	302.05	130.12	263.80	115.64	0.69
2007	15040	323.37	139.45	289.65	124.23	0.60
2008	16880	337.80	147.31	308.81	134.71	0.55
2009	17849	351.69	146.56	326.91	136.48	0.70
2010	19668	371.23	153.55	342.07	147.54	0.60
2011	21023	386.47	159.54	355.78	150.67	0.72
2012	22682	393.94	165.98	371.14	157.39	1.07

18-29 残疾人事业基本情况
Basic Information of People with Disabilities

项　　目	Item	2011	2012
康　复	**Rehabilitation**		
白内障复明	Sight-restoring of Cataract Surgery		
白内障复明手术(万例)	Sight-restoring of Cataract Surgeries (10 000 cases)	0.69	1.26
低视力配用助视器(人)	Vision-aids Provided for Individuds with Low-vision (person)	807	1415
聋儿康复	Rehabilitation of Children With Hearing Disability		
年收训聋儿(人)	Hearing and Speech Training (person)	198	195
聋儿入普幼普小率(%)	Enrollment Rate to General Infant School or Elementary School (%)	18.7	24.1
培训家长(人)	Parents Trained (person)	1152	1510
精神病防治康复	Prevention and Treatment of Psychiatric Diseases		
开展精神病防治康复工作市县数(个)	Number of Counties Carried on the Works (unit)	68	68
综合防治康复精神病人数(万人)	Number of Psychosis Sicks Synthetically Prevented, Cured and Rehabilitated (10 000 persons)	1.52	1.60
监护率(%)	Guardianship Rate (%)	69.00	63.90
显好率(%)	Rate of Getting Better (%)	35.30	51.22
社会参与率(%)	Social Participation Rate (%)	23.80	34.36
肇事率(%)	Violent Everds Rate (%)	0.05	0.08
救济贫困患者数(人)	Number of Poor Sufferer Relieved (person)	3441	4634
用品用具供应件数(万件)	Number of Appliances Supplied (10 000 units)	1.42	1.59
康复训练与服务	Rehabilitation Training and Service		
肢体残疾康复训练数(人)	Rehabilitation Training of Body Disabilities (person)	2360	5136
智力残疾儿童康复训练数(人)	Rehabilitation Training of Mental Disabilities Children (person)	217	1398
教　育	**Education**		
未入学适龄残疾儿童(万人)	Number of Uneducated Children (10 000 persons)	0.42	0.37
残疾人中等职业学校(班)	Secondary Vocational Schools for PWDS		
残联系统办	Run by Institution of Disabled Person's	1	1
教育部门办	Run by Education	1	1
在校学生(万人)	Number of Enrollments	0.0586	0.0584

18-29 续表 Continued

项　目	Item	2011	2012
就　业	**Employment**		
城镇残疾人就业状况(万人)	Employment of Urban Handicappeds (10 000 persons)		
当年安排就业	Persons Employed in the Year	0.48	0.41
按比例就业	Employment by Quota Scheme	0.16	0.15
集中就业	Employment at Welfare Enterprises	0.14	0.10
个体就业	Individual Employment	0.14	0.11
未安排就业	Unemployment	1.62	1.43
农村残疾人就业状况(万人)	Employment of Rural Handicapped (10 000 persons)		
就　业	Employed	21.04	21.60
未就业	Unemployed	4.93	4.30
残疾人就业服务机构(个)	Number of Institutions Engaging in Handicappeds Employment (unit)		
省	Provinces	1	1
地	Prefectures	14	14
市(含县级市)	Cities (Cities at County Level)	16	16
县	County	68	68
市辖区	Districts under the Jurisdiction of Cities	11	11
实施分散按比例就业的地区数(个)	Number of Regions Implemented the Policy of the Disperse Employment by Proportion (unit)		
省	Provinces	1	1
地	Prefectures	14	14
市(含县级市)	Cities (Cities at County Level)	16	16
县	County	68	68
市辖区	Districts under the Jurisdiction of Cities	11	11
残联组织建设	**Organization of Association for the Handicapped**		
残疾人工作者(万人)	Number of Workers for the Handicappeds (10 000 persons)	0.28	0.31

18-30 历届全区人民代表大会代表人数

Number of Deputies to all the Previous People's Congresses of Xinjiang

项　目 Item	第一届 (1954) First Congress	第二届 (1959) Second Congress	第三届 (1964) Third Congress	第四届 (1975) Fourth Congress	第五届 (1978) Fifth Congress	第六届 (1983) Sixth Congress	第七届 (1988) Seventh Congress	第八届 (1993) Eighth Congress	第九届 (1998) Ninth Congress	第十届 (2003) Tenth Congress	第十一届 (2008) Eleventh Congress
代表总数(人) **Total Number of All Deputies (person)**	**376**	**386**	**453**	**809**	**672**	**550**	**550**	**542**	**550**	**550**	**550**
#中国共产党党员 Deputies from the Communist Party of China	178		240			374	357	381	396	396	352
占总数比重(%) Percentage to Total (%)	47.3		53.0			68.0	64.9	70.3	72.0	72.0	64.0
#少数民族 Deputies from National Minorities	331		383	510	430	357	363	355	363	363	363
占总数比重(%) Percentage to Total(%)	88.0		84.5	63.8	64.0	64.9	66.0	65.5	66.0	66.0	66.0
#妇　女 Female Deputies	52	61	89	200	146	17	126	123	135	135	143
占总数比重(%) Percentage to Total(%)	13.8	15.8	19.6	24.7	21.7	21.3	22.9	22.7	24.5	24.5	26.0

18-31 历届全区政治协商会议委员人数

Number of Deputies to all the Previous People's Political Consultative Conferences of Xinjiang

项　目 Item	第一届 (1954) First Congress	第二届 (1959) Second Congress	第三届 (1964) Third Congress	第四届 (1978) Fourth Congress	第五届 (1983) Fifth Congress	第六届 (1988) Sixth Congress	第七届 (1993) Seventh Congress	第八届 (1998) Eighth Congress	第九届 (2003) Ninth Congress	第十届 (2008) Tenth Congress
委员总数(人) **Total Number of All Deputies (person)**	**141**	**275**	**303**	**407**	**441**	**429**	**416**	**444**	**470**	**515**
#中国共产党党员 Deputies from the Communist Party of China	28	57	65	149	158	157	161	183	196	225
占总数比重(%) Percentage to Total(%)	19.9	20.7	21.5	36.6	35.8	36.6	38.7	41.2	41.7	43.7
#少数民族 Deputies from National Minorities	121	196	205	221	253	245	204	246	246	263
占总数比重(%) Percentage to Total(%)	85.8	71.3	67.7	54.3	57.4	57.0	49.0	55.4	52.3	51.1
#妇　女 Female Deputies	10	28	28	40	49	63	66	82	95	125
占总数比重(%) Percentage to Total(%)	7.1	10.2	9.2	9.8	11.1	14.7	15.9	18.5	20.2	24.3

18-32 主要年份律师、公证、调解工作基本情况
Basic Statistics on Lawyers, Notarization and Mediation in Main Years

项　　目	Item	1995	2000	2005	2010	2012
律师工作	**Lawyers**					
律师事务所(个)	Number of Law Offices (unit)	169	227	243	318	321
律师(人)	Number of Lawyers (person)	1705	2414	2088	2900	2931
#专职律师(人)	Full-time Lawyers (person)	1209	1508	1987	2704	2771
兼职和特邀律师(人)	Part-time Lawyers (person)	336	418	101	114	92
聘请担任常年法律顾问的单位(处)	Number of Units with Permanent Legal Advisors (unit)	2560	2613	2663	3858	3333
民事诉讼代理(件)	Agent of Civil Cases (case)	6380	16165	23389	38822	29371
刑事辩护及代理(件)	Defender and Agent of Criminal Cases (case)	5850	5826	7716	8510	7603
非诉讼法律事务(件)	Agent of Non-Litigious Legal Affairs (case)	5357	4810	7066	2450	2213
解答法律咨询(万件)	Agent of Legal Advisory Services (10 000 cases)	4.21	7.45	8.14	10.13	9.56
代写法律事务文书(万件)	Agent of Legal Documents Written on Behalf of Clients (10 000 cases)	1.06	1.94	3.00	2.16	2.29
公证工作	**Notarization**					
公证处(个)	Number of Notary Offices (unit)	126	131	126	125	125
公证员(人)	Notaries (person)	266	332	457	416	433
公证员助理(人)	Assistant Notaries (person)	49	43	61	144	284
办理公证文书(万件)	Number of Notarized Document (10 000 cases)	10.11	18.85	18.05	30.93	37.21
人民调解工作	**Number of People's Mediation**					
专职司法助理员(人)	Number of Full-time Judicial Assistants (person)	1515	1750	1706	1662	1903
人民调解委员会(个)	Number of People's Mediation Committees (unit)	19045	22294	15852	14157	13454
调解人员(万人)	Number of Mediators (10 000 persons)	12.04	10.04	7.86	7.62	6.88
调解民间纠纷(万件)	Number of Civil Disputes Mediated (10 000 cases)	9.18	8.09	6.83	17.21	22.27

18-33 调解民间纠纷分类

Number of Civil Disputes Mediated by Type

(2012 年)

项 目	Item	调解纠纷(件) Civil Disputes (case)	各类纠纷所占比重(%) Percentage (%)
总 计	**Total**	**222682**	**100**
婚姻家庭	Marriage and Family	56371	25.31
合 同	Contract	12792	5.74
劳 动	Labor	10504	4.72
村务管理	Village-affair Management	1936	0.87
土 地	Land	18206	8.18
征地拆迁	Requisitioned Land Demolition	1902	0.85
房屋宅基地	Housing and Housing Sites	6807	3.06
计划生育	Family Planning	292	0.13
邻 里	Neighbour	47257	21.22
损害赔偿	Compensation for Damages	16399	7.36
环境保护	Environment Protection	696	0.31
道路交通事故	Road Traffic Accidents	10198	4.58
物 业	Property Management	2952	1.33
医 疗	Medical Treatment	320	0.14
生产经营	Production and Operation	5457	2.45
其 他	Others	30593	13.74

18-34 火灾事故发生情况

Basic Statistics on Fire Accidents

(2012 年)

指 标	Item	合 计 Total	按事故发生程度分 By Serious Dgree of Fires			
			特 大 Extraordinarily Serious	重 大 Serious	较 大 Comparatively Serious	一 般 Ordinary
发生起数(起)	Fires (case)	7201			2	7199
死亡(人)	Death (person)	18			5	13
受伤(人)	Injuries (person)	35				35
损失折款(万元)	Losses Converted into Cash (10 000 yuan)	8589.09			2369.02	6220.07
平均每起事故损失(元)	Average Loss per Fire (yuan)	11927.63			11845100	8640

18-35 2010-2012 年历年交通事故发生情况

Basic Statistics on Traffic Accidents (2010-2012)

指 标	Item	2010	2011	2012
发生起数(起)	Traffic Accidents (case)	4949	5182	4942
死亡(人)	Death (person)	1851	1992	1932
受伤(人)	Injuries (person)	5859	5903	5422
损失折款(万元)	Losses Converted into Cash (10 000 yuan)	864	1036	1233
平均每起事故损失(元)	Average Loss per Fire (yuan)	1746	2000	2494

18-36 公安机关受理查处治安案件情况
Offense Cases Against Public Order Handled by Public Security Organs

单位：起 (2012 年) (case)

案件类别	Category of Cases	受理 Number of Cases Accepted to be Treated	查处 Number of Cases Investigated and Treated
总计	**Total**	**108831**	**103282**
扰乱公共秩序	Disturbing Work or Public Order	3193	3140
扰乱单位秩序	Disturbing Business Orders	596	579
扰乱公共场所秩序	Disturbing the Orders in Public Places	359	357
寻衅滋事	Causing Quarrels and Making Troubles	885	861
其他	Others	1353	1343
妨害公共安全	Disorderly Cordnct	594	580
非法携带枪支、弹药、管制刀具	Violation of Firearms Control Regulations	210	209
盗窃、损毁公共设施	Stealing and Damaging Public Facilities	89	83
其他	Others	295	288
侵犯他人人身权利、财产权利	Offences Against, Citizens'Personal and Property Rights	78601	73259
侮辱、诽谤、诬告陷害	Insult, Slander and Circumvention	803	721
殴打他人	Beating Other Body	56739	53901
故意伤害	Wilfully Injuring Others	3259	3033
盗窃	Stealing Property	10369	8842
诈骗	Swindling, Seizing and Extorting Property	792	602
抢夺	Robbery and Snatch	167	147
敲诈勒索	Extertion and Blackmail	68	60
其他	Others	6404	5953
妨害社会管理	Disorderly Social Management	26443	26303
阻碍执行职务	Obstructing Government Workers in Performing Their Duties	782	765
违反旅馆业管理	Violating the Hotel Management Regulations	2453	2453
违反房屋出租管理	Violating the Rent Control Regulations	7603	7609
卖淫、嫖娼	Prostitution or Going Whoring	878	876
赌博或为赌博提供条件	Gambling	1456	1419
毒品违法活动	Illegal Drug Related Action	10199	10186
其他	Others	3072	2995

18-37 2008-2012 年历年刑事案件中青少年犯罪情况
Juvenile Delinquency Among Criminal Cases(2008-2012)

单位：人 (person)

年份 Year	刑事罪犯总数 Offenders	#青少年罪犯 Young Offenders	不满 18 岁 Less than 18	18 岁至 25 岁 Between 18 to 25	青少年罪犯占刑事罪犯 (%) Percentage to Total (%)
2008	37222	18317	5899	12418	49.20
2009	33121	15989	4538	11451	48.27
2010	29257	13299	4012	9287	45.45
2011	29690	12627	3697	8930	42.53
2012	30775	12738	3613	9125	41.39

主要统计指标解释

等级运动员人数 指经考核正式批准授予等级运动员称号的人数。运动员等级分为国际级运动健将、运动健将、一级运动员、二级运动员、三级运动员、少年级运动员。该指标主要反映运动员队伍的技术质量水平。

等级裁判员人数 指经考核正式批准授予等级裁判员称号的人数。裁判员等级分为国际裁判、国家级裁判、一级裁判、二级裁判。该指标主要反映裁判员队伍的技术质量水平。

体育场 指有 400 米跑道(中心含足球场),有固定道牙,跑道 6 条以上，并有固定看台的室外田径场地。体育场按看台容纳观众人数分为: 甲级 25000 人以上,乙级 15000-25000 人，丙级 5000-15000 人，丁级 5000 人以下。该指标主要反映大中型体育场数量水平。

体育馆 指有固定看台，可供篮球、排球、羽毛球、乒乓球、体操等项目训练比赛活动用的室内运动场地。体育馆按看台容纳观众人数分为: 甲级 6000 人以上，乙级 4000-6000 人，丙级 2000-4000 人，丁级 2000 人以下。该指标主要反映大中型体育馆数量水平。

医疗卫生机构 指从卫生行政部门取得《医疗机构执业许可证》，或从民政、工商行政、机构编制管理部门取得法人单位登记证书，为社会提供医疗保健、疾病控制、卫生监督服务或从事医学科研和医学在职培训等工作的单位。医疗卫生机构包括医院、基层医疗卫生机构、专业公共卫生机构、其他医疗卫生机构。

医院 包括综合医院、中医医院、中西医结合医院、民族医院、各类专科医院和护理院。

基层医疗卫生机构 包括社区卫生服务中心(站)、街道卫生院、乡镇卫生院、村卫生室、门诊部、诊所(医务室)。

专业公共卫生机构 包括疾病预防控制中心、专科疾病防治机构、妇幼保健机构、健康教育机构、急救中心(站)、采供血机构、卫生监督机构、卫生部门主管的计划生育技术服务中心。

其他医疗卫生机构 包括疗养院、临床检验中心、医学科研机构、医学在职教育机构、医学考试中心、农村改水中心、人才交流中心、统计信息中心等卫生事业单位。

卫生人员 指在医院、基层医疗卫生机构、专业公共卫生机构及其他医疗卫生机构工作的职工，包括卫生技术人员、乡村医生和卫生员、其他技术人员、管理人员和工勤人员。

卫生技术人员 包括执业医师、执业助理医师、注册护士、药师（士）、检验技师（士）、影像技师、卫生监督员和见习医（药、护、技）师（士）等卫生专业人员。不包括从事管理工作的卫生技术人员。

执业医师 指《医师执业证》“级别”为“执业医师”且实际从事医疗、预防保健工作的人员，不包括实际从事管理工作的执业医师。执业医师类别分为临床、中医、口腔和公共卫生四类。

执业助理医师 指《医师执业证》“级别”为“执业助理医师”且实际从事医疗、预防保健工作的人员，不包括实际从事管理工作的执业助理医师。执业助理医师类别分为临床、中医、口腔和公共卫生四类。

每万人口执业(助理)医师 每万人口执业(助理)医师=（执业医师数+执业助理医师数)/人口数×10000。人口数系公安部户籍人口。

每万人口卫生技术人员 每万人口卫生技术人员=卫生技术人员数/人口数×10000。人口数系公安部户籍人口。

每万人口医疗卫生机构床位 每万人口医疗卫生机构床位=医疗卫生机构床位/人口数×10000。人口数系公安部户籍人口。

甲乙类法定报告传染病发病率 是指某年某地区每 10 万人口中甲、乙类法定报告传染病发病情况。即法定报告传染病发病率=甲、乙类法定报告传染病发病人数/人口数 × 100000。

甲乙类法定报告传染病死亡率 是指某年某地区每 10 万人口中甲、乙类法定报告传染病死亡情况。即甲乙类法定报告传染病死亡率=甲、乙类法定报告传染病死亡人数/人口数 × 100000。

甲乙类法定报告传染病病死率 是指某年某地区甲、乙类法定报告传染病死亡人数与发病人数之比。即法定报告传染病病死率=甲、乙类法定报告传染病死亡人数/发病人数 × 100%。

参加新农合人数 指根据本地新农合实施方案到年内新农合筹资截止时已缴纳新农合资金的人口数。

新农合当年基金支出 指本年度实际从新农合基金帐户中支出用于新农合补偿的资金。

新农合补偿支出受益人次 指年内新农合参合人员因病就医获得补偿的人次数，包括住院、家庭帐户形式、门诊、特殊病种大额门诊、住院正常分娩、体检和其他补偿人次之和。

新农合本年度筹资总额 指为本年度筹集的、实际进入新农合专用帐户的基金数额。包括本年度中央及地方财政配套资金、农民个人交纳资金（含民政部门及其他相关部门代缴的救助资金）、新农合基金本年度产生的全部利息收入及其他渠道实际筹集到的新农合基金额。筹资数额以进入新农合专用帐户的基金数额为准，不含上年结转额资金。

卫生总费用 是以货币形式作为综合计量手段，全面反映一个国家或地区在一定时期内（通常指一年），全社会在医疗卫生服务上所消耗的资金总额。卫生费用核算结果及其基础数据，不仅为政府调整和制定卫生经济政策提供宏观经济信息，同时也是评价全社会对人类健康的重视程度，分析卫生保健体制公平与效率的重要依据。

政府卫生支出 指各级政府用于医疗卫生服务、医疗保障补助、卫生和医疗保险行政管理、人口与计划生育事务支出等各项事业的经费。

社会卫生支出　指政府支出外的社会各界对卫生事业的资金投入。包括社会医疗保障支出、商业健康保险费、社会办医支出、社会捐赠援助、行政事业性收费收入等。

个人现金卫生支出　指城乡居民在接受各类医疗卫生服务时的现金支付，包括享受多种医疗保险制度的居民就医时自付的费用。

人均卫生费用　即某年卫生总费用与同期平均人口数之比。

社会福利事业单位　指集中收养社会孤老、残、幼的机构，包括由民政部门管理的社会福利院、儿童福利院、精神病人福利院和城镇集体举办的福利院及农村集体举办的敬老院以及优抚医院和具有收养能力的社区服务中心等。该指标主要反映我国在社会福利性单位投入的水平。

社会福利事业单位收养人数　包括民政部门管理和城镇、农村集体举办的社会福利事业单位中收养的老人、少年儿童、缺乏生活自理能力的残疾人员和精神病人。该指标主要反映收养性社会福利单位的收养能力。

社会福利企业　指以集中安置有一定劳动能力的残疾人员就业为目（残疾职工占生产人员 10%以上）、带有社会福利性质的企业总称。主要包括福利工厂、假肢厂和其他福利企业。

城市居民最低生活保障人数　指在报告期末家庭平均收入在当地规定的最低生活保障线以下的城镇居民数。包括“三无”对象，失业人员和在职、下岗、退休人员等。

农村居民最低生活保障人数　指报告期末在建立农村最低生活保障制度的地区，得到当地政府或集体给予最低生活保障的农业人口家庭人数。

五保户　指无法定抚养义务人，或者虽有法定抚养义务人，但是抚养人无抚养能力的；无劳动能力的；无生活年人来源的老年人、残疾人和未成年人。

聋儿入普幼普小率　指本年度内经康复训练后进入普通幼儿园、普通小学的聋儿数与在训聋儿数(不含当年新收训聋儿数)之比。

综合防治康复精神病人数　指在开展精神病防治康复工作地区，采取不同形式，接受综合性防治康复措施、开放式管理的精神病人数。该指标主要反映精神病患者接受治疗康复情况。

监护率　指通过监护小组、家庭病床、工疗站、社会就业以及精神卫生机构，接受社会化、综合性、开放式治疗与康复的精神病人占经调查摸底、登记在册的精神病人数的百分比。该指标主要反映对精神病患者落实治疗康复措施的情况。

社会参与率　指生活能自理，并参加生产劳动和社会生活的精神病人数占监护精神病人数的百分比。该指标主要反映精神病人康复状况和参与社会的情况。

未入学学龄残疾儿童少年　指截止到本年度 12 月 31 日，在省级人民政府依照《义务教育法》规定的入学年龄段内的，因各种原因未能入学的各类残疾儿童少年人数。

律师　指依法取得律师执业证书，担任法律顾问，民事(刑事、行政)案件代理人、刑事案件辩护人、办理非诉讼业务，解答法律询问，代写法律事务文书等，为社会提供法律服务的人员。

公证人员　指在公证处工作的人员总称，包括公证处主任、副主任、公证员、公证员助理(助理公证员)和其他从事辅助性工作的人员。

公证文书　指公证处根据当事人申请，依照事实和法律，按照法定程序制作的，具有法律效力的司法证明文书。

调解员　指在人民调解委员会担负调解民间纠纷工作的人员，包括调解委员会的委员和调解小组的调解员。该指标主要反映从事人民调解工作的人员数量。

调解民间纠纷　指调解委员会按照法律规定，根据自愿原则，用说服教育的方法调解民间发生的有关民事权利和义务争执的件数，包括调解成功数和调解未成功数。该指标主要反映人民调解委员会的工作量。

特大交通事故　指一次造成死亡 3 人以上，或者重伤 11 人以上，或者死亡 1 人，同时重伤 8 人以上，或者死亡 2 人，同时重伤 5 人以上，或者财产损失 6 万元以上的交通事故。

重大交通事故　指一次造成死亡 1 至 2 人，或者重伤 3 人以上 10 人以下，或者财产损失 3 万元以上不足 6 万元的交通事故。

特大火灾　指造成 30 人以上死亡，或者 100 人以上重伤，或者 1 亿元以上直接财产损失的火灾。

重大火灾　指造成 10 人以上 30 人以下死亡，或者 50 人以上 100 人以下重伤，或者 5000 万元以上 1 亿元以下直接财产损失的火灾。

较大火灾　指造成 3 人以上 10 人以下死亡，或者 10 人以上 50 人以下重伤，或者 1000 万元以上 5000 万元以下直接财产损失的火灾。

一般火灾　指造成3人以下死亡，或者10人以下重伤，或者1000万元以下直接财产损失的火灾。

Explanatory Notes on Main Statistical Indicators

Number of Athletes in Grades refers to the number of athletes who have been given titles through examination. The titles of athletes include international masters of sports, masters of sports, first-grade, second- grade and third-grade sportsmen and young athletes. This indicator reflects skill of the athletes.

Number of Referees in Grades refers to the number of referees who have been given titles after examination. They are classified as international referees, national referees and referees of the first, second and third grades. This indicator reflects the skill of referees.

Stadiums refers to stadiums for track and field events with six lane 400-meter tracks around soccer fields, permanent track marks and permanent bleachers. Stadiums are classified according to seating capacity. They include: Class A stadiums have the capaCity of seating 25000 people each. Class B stadiums have the capaCity of seating 15000 to 25000 people each. Class C stadiums have the capaCity of s eating 5000 to 15000 people each, and Class D stadiums have the capaCity of seating fewer than 5000 people. This indicator reflects numbers of large and medium-sized stadiums.

Gymnasiums refers to indoor sports grounds with permanent seats in which basketball, volleyball, Badminton, table tennis and gymnastics competitions can be held. Gymnasiums are classified according to seating capaCity. They include: Class Agymnasiums with seating over 6000 people. Class B gymnasiums with seating 4000 to 6000 people. Class Cgymnasiums with seating 2000 to 4000 people, and Class D gymnasiums with eating fewer than 2000 people. This indicator reflects the total number of large and medium-sized gymnasiums.

Medical and Health Care Institutions refer to the units which have been qualified the Certification of Health Care Institution by the administration of public health, or qualified the Certification of Corporate Unit by the civil affairs, administration for industry and commerce, commission office for public sector reform, and engaging in medical care, disease prevention and control, health supervision and inspection, medicine research and on-job training, etc., including: hospitals, health care institutions at grass-root level, specialized public health institutions, and other medical and health care institutions.

Hospitals include general hospitals, hospitals specialized in traditional Chinese medicine, hospitals of integrated traditional Chinese and western medicine, nationalities hospitals, specialized hospitals and nursing hospitals.

Health Care Institutions at Grass-root Level include community health service centers, urban health centers, township health centers, village clinics, outpatient departments and clinics (health centers).

Specialized Public Health Institutions include centers for disease control and prevention, specialized disease prevention and treatment institutions, women and children care agencies, health education institutions, first aid centers, blood gathering and supplying institutions, health supervision and inspection agencies, and family planning technical service centers supervised by health institutions.

Other Medical and Health Care Institutions include sanatoriums, clinical laboratory centers, medicinal scientific research institutions, on-job training institutions, medical examination centers, rural water improvement centers, talent exchange centers, and statistical information centers, etc.

Health Care Employees refer to all employees engaged in the health care institutions, such as hospitals, health care institutions at grass-root level, specialized public health institutions, and other medical and health care institutions, including medical technical personnel, village doctors and assistants, other technical personnel, managerial and service staff.

Medical Technical Personnel refer to the professional staff engaged in health care, including licensed doctors, licensed assistant doctors, registered nurses, pharmacists, laboratory technicians, imaging staff, health care supervisors and intern doctors, pharmacists, nurses, and technical personnel, excluding the medical technical personnel engaged in managerial job.

Licensed Doctors refer to the medical workers who have obtained the licenses of qualified doctors and are employed in medical treatment, disease prevention or healthcare institutions, excluding the licensed doctors engaged in management job. The licensed doctors are divided into 4 categories: clinician, Chinese medicine physicians, dentist and public health physicians.

Licensed Assistant Doctors refer to the medical workers who have obtained the licenses of qualified assistant doctors and are employed in medical treatment, disease prevention or healthcare institutions, excluding the licensed assistant doctors engaged in management job. The classification of licensed assistant doctors is clinician, Chinese medicine, dentist and public health.

Number of Licensed (Assistant) Doctors per 10000 Population The formula is:

Number of Licensed Doctors per 10000 Population = (Number of Licensed Doctors + Number of Licensed Assistant Doctors) / Population *10000

The population is the figure of household registration from the Ministry of Public Security.

Number of Medical Technical Personnel per 10000 Population The formula is:

Number of Medical Technical Personnel per 10000 Population = Number of Medical Technical Personnel / Population *10000

Number of Beds of Medical and Health Care Institutions per 10000 Population the formula is:

Number of Beds of Medical and Health Care Institutions per 10000 Population = Number of Beds of Medical and Health Care Institutions / Population *10000

Incidence Rate of A and B Type of Notifiable Infectious Diseases refer to the incidence cases notifiable class A and class B infectious diseases per 100 thousand population in the reference region in the reference year. The formula is:

Incidence Rate of A and B Type of Notifiable Infectious Diseases = Incidence Cases Notifiable Class A and Class B Infectious Diseases / Population *100000

Death Rate of A and B Type of Notifiable Infectious Diseases refer to the death cases notifiable class A and class B infectious diseases per 100 thousand population in the reference region in the reference year. The formula is:

Death Rate of A and B Type of Notifiable Infectious Diseases= Death Cases Notifiable Class A and Class B Infectious Diseases / Population *100000

Mortality Rate of A and B Type Notifiable Infectious Diseases refer to the ratio of death cases notifiable class A and class B infectious diseases to the incidence cases in the reference region in the reference year. The formula is:

Mortality Rate of A and B Type Notifiable Infectious Diseases = Death Cases Notifiable Class A and Class B Infectious Diseases / Incidence Cases *100%

Number of Persons Participated in the New Rural Cooperative Medical System refers to the number of persons who have given payment to the new cooperative medical system by the deadline of fundraising during the year according to the implementation plan of the new system.

Expenditure of Funds for the New Rural Cooperative Medical System This Year refers to expenditures on compensation funds for the new rural cooperative medical system from the fund account of new cooperative medical system this year.

Persons Benefited from the Compensation Expenditure of New Rural Cooperative Medical System refers to the number of persons participated in the new system who have been compensated for medical treatment in the year, including hospitalization, family account form, out-patient, large special diseases out-patient, normal childbirth in hospital, medical examination and other compensations

Funds Raised for the New Rural Cooperative Medical System this Year refers to the amount of funds raised this year and put into the special new rural cooperative medical account, including the matching funds of central and local governments, paid money by farmers (including relief funds paid by the civil affairs department and other relevant departments), all the interest income generated this year of the funds and funds actually raised from other channels this year. The amount of funding equals to the funds entering into the special new rural cooperative medical account, excluding the carry-over funds from the previous year.

Total Expenditure on Health reflects the total expenditure on medical and health care services of a country in a year, estimated using funding source method. It includes government expenditure, social expenditure and individual cash expenditure.

Government Budgetary Expenditure for Public Health refers to budgetary allocation for health undertakings by governments at all levels, including health expenditure, Chinese medicine practitioners' operating expenses, food and drug supervision and management fees, operating expenses of family planning, medical research funding, budget for capital construction funding, health administration and health insurance management fees, health costs of other government departments, medical expenses of administrative departments and institutions, subsidies for basic medical insurance fund.

Social Expenditure for Public Health refers to non-government budgetary capital input, mainly referring to social basic medical care insurance, other social medical care insurance, commercial health insurance, expenditure of non-health-department administrations for health care, expenditure of enterprises for health care, rural household expense on health care, extra-budgetary expenditure for health care in capital investment, private investment on practicing of health care, and extra-budgetary funds of public health institutions, etc.

Individual Cash Expenditure for Public Health refers to cash expenditure for various health services by rural and urban household paid from the disposable income, including urban individual cash expenditure for public health and rural individual cash expenditure for public health.

Average Expenditure on Health refers to the ratio of total expenditure on health in a year to the average population.

Social Welfare Institutions refer to institutions taking care of old pople without children, handicapped people and orphans. They include social welfare institutions run by civil affairs departments, children welfare institutions, social welfare institutions for mental patients, collective-owned old peoples homes in rural areas, convalescent homes and community service centers with the capaCity of receiving those people. This indicator reflects the input in social welfare institutions.

Number of People Taken in by Social Welfare Institutions refers to the number of old people, children, totally dependent handicapped people and mental patients taken in by social welfare institutions run by civil affairs departments and those run by collective units in urban and rural areas. This indicator reflects the cap a City of social welfare institutions.

Social Welfare Enterprises are collective owned enterp-rises which employ the blind, deaf-mute, and other handicapped people who are able to work in cities and towns and enjoy exemption from state taxes, including welfare plants, welfare commercial services, artificial limb plants and farms, etc. This indicator reflects the preferential policies toward disabled persons.

Number of Urban Residents Entitled to Minimum Living Allowances refers to the number of those whose average family income is below a minimum local standard by the end of the reporting period, including both the employed and unemployed, laid off and retired, and those jobless people without stable residence or valid IDs.

Number of Rural Residents Entitled to Minimum Living Allowances refers to the number of those receiving the minimum living allowances from the local government or community in the rural areas where this allowances system is in place as of the end of the reference period.

Households Enjoying Five Guarantees refers to those senior citizens, handicapped or under-aged who, without labour ability, can not make a living by themselves and whose statutory providers are unable to support them or who have no statutory providers at all.

Proportion of Deaf Children Enrolled in Ordinary Pr-eschool and Primary Education refers to the proportion of deaf children who are enrolled in ordinary kindergartens or primary schools during the year in the total number of deaf children under rehabilitation programs (not including new comers into the rehabilitation programs during the year). This indicator mainly reflects number of rehabilitated deaf children entering ordinary kindergartens or primary schools.

Number of Mental Patients under Integrated Prevention and Rehabilitation Program refers to mental disease patients receiving integrated prevention and rehabilitation treatment of various forms under open environment in areas with mental disease rehabilitation programs. This indicator reflects the condition of metal patients receiving rehabilitation treatment.

Supervision Rate refers to the percentage of patients among the total number of registered mental disease patients, who participate in social integrated and open treatment and rehabilitation programs through various forms such as supervision groups, family treatment, employment or guidance from psychiatric institutions. This indicator reflects the implementation of various measures aimed at rehabilitating those metal patients.

Social Participation Rate of Mental Patients refers to proportion of mental disease patients who are able to manage their daily life and participate in economic activities to the total number of mental disease patients under supervision. This indicator reflects the condition of recovery of those metal patient sand their participation in social activities.

School-age Disabled Children not in Schools refer to children with disability in sight, listening, speaking, mentality, limbs or multi-disability who are obliged to compulsory education by law but have not been enrolled in schools due to various reasons. The definition of school age for disabled children is decided by the definition of school age as specified by provincial governments in line wit h the local laws on compulsory education.

Lawyers are certified legal workers according to law, and who are employed by legal counseling firms to act as legal advisers, agents in criminal or civil lawsuits, or defenders in criminal lawsuits, or to handle non-litigious legal affairs, to advise on matters of law or t o write legal papers for others, and provide service to the public.

Notary Personnel refers to people working for notary offices including: directors, deputy direct or, notaries, assistant notaries, and other people providing assistance.

Notary Documents refer to the judicatory notary documents drawn up by the request of the party and are in accordance with facts and laws and following certain legal proceedings. According to usage and locality, the notary documents are divided into following 4 types: domestic notary documents, domestic economic notary documents, foreign-related civil notary documents and foreign-related economic notary documents.

Mediators refer to workers on peoples mediation committees responsible for mediating in civil disputes and cases of slight infraction of the law. They include members of the mediation committees and mediators of mediation groups. This indicator reflects the number of people engaged in meditation.

Mediation of Civil Disputes refers to number of cases made by mediation committees in mediating in civil disputes concerning civil rights and duties through persuasion and education in accordance witht he provisions of lawona voluntary basis, so as to solve disputes by helping the parties involved come to an agreement and understanding, including those unsuccessful ones. This indicator reflects the workload of the mediation committees.

Extraordinarily Serious Traffic Accident refers to an accident which has caused three or more deaths; or over 11 serious injuries; or one death and over 8 serious injuries; or two deaths and over 5 serious injuries; or a loss over 60 thousand yuan.

Serious Traffic Accident refers to an accident which has caused one or two deaths; or three to ten serious injuries; or a loss over 30 thousand yuan to 60 thousand yuan.

Extraordinarily Serious Fire Case refers to a case which has caused over 30 deaths; or over 100 serious injuries; or a direct property loss over 100 million yuan.

Serious Fire Case refers to a case which has caused over 10 to 30 deaths; or over 50 to 100 serious injuries; or a direct property loss over 50 million to 100 million yuan.

Comparatively Serious Fire Case refers to a case which has caused over three to ten deaths; or over 10 to 50 serious injuries; or a direct property loss over 10 million to 50 million yuan.

Ordinary Fire Case refers to a case which has caused less than three deaths; or less than 10 serious injuries; or a direct property loss less than 10 million yuan.

新疆统计年鉴
XINJIANG STATISTICAL YEARBOOK

19

各地州市主要经济指标排序

RANKING OF MAIN ECONOMIC INDICATORS BY REGION OF XINJIANG

简要说明

本篇资料的主要内容及来源

本篇反映2012年新疆各地州（市）主要经济指标排序情况。

本篇资料由新疆维吾尔自治区统计局国民经济综合统计处根据新疆维吾尔自治区统计局各相关专业处提供资料整理。

Brief Introduction

Main Content and Source of Data

Data in this chapter mainly include main social economic statistics by prefecture, autonomous prefecture, city and county in 2012.

Data on this chapter are compiled by the Department of Comprehensive Statistic, XBS according to the data provided by the related department of Statistics Bureau of Xinjiang Uygur Autonomous Region.

19-1 各地、州、市生产总值

Gross Regional Product by Prefecture, Autonomous Prefecture and City

单位：万元 (2012 年) (10 000 yuan)

地 区	Region	地区生产总值 Gross Regional Product	位次 Rank	第一产业增加值 Primary Industry	位次 Rank
乌鲁木齐市	Urumqi city	20017386	1	250218	12
克拉玛依市	Karamay city	8107054	4	46245	15
石河子市	Shihezi city	2081934	11	113665	13
吐鲁番地区	Turpan Administrative Offices	2433907	10	339060	10
哈密地区	Hami [Kumul] Administrative Offices	2682518	9	331154	11
昌吉回族自治州	Changji Hui Autonomous Prefecture	8185631	3	2167200	1
伊犁哈萨克自治州	Ili Kazak Autonomous Prefecture	12519627		3454578	
伊犁州直属县(市)	Counties (Cities) Direct Under Ili Prefecture	5776226	6	1368794	6
塔城地区	Tacheng [Tarbagatai] Administrative Offices	4862311	8	1711173	4
阿勒泰地区	Altay Administrative Offices	1881090	12	374611	9
博尔塔拉蒙古自治州	Bortala Mongol Autonomous Prefecture	1854011	13	570228	7
巴音郭楞蒙古自治州	Bayangol Mongol Autonomous Prefecture	9075401	2	1554446	5
阿克苏地区	Aksu Administrative Offices	6121381	5	1918479	2
克孜勒苏柯尔克孜自治州	Kizilsu Kirgiz Autonomous Prefecture	610309	15	104520	14
喀什地区	Kashgar [Kaxgar] Administrative Offices	5173492	7	1752279	3
和田地区	Hotan Administrative Offices	1472873	14	457209	8

地 区	Region	第二产业增加值 Secondary Industry	位次 Rank	第三产业增加值 Tertiary Industry	位次 Rank	人均地区生产总值（元） Per-capital GDP (yuan)	位次 Rank
乌鲁木齐市	Urumqi city	8290099	1	11477069	1	59576	4
克拉玛依市	Karamay city	7130736	2	930073	9	135018	1
石河子市	Shihezi city	1198688	11	769582	11	64346	3
吐鲁番地区	Turpan Administrative Offices	1542558	8	552289	14	39068	7
哈密地区	Hami [Kumul] Administrative Offices	1337700	10	1013664	8	45613	6
昌吉回族自治州	Changji Hui Autonomous Prefecture	3887740	4	2130691	4	51211	5
伊犁哈萨克自治州	Ili Kazak Autonomous Prefecture	4648820		4416229		26801	
伊犁州直属县(市)	Counties (Cities) Direct Under Ili Prefecture	1976460	6	2430972	2	21187	12
塔城地区	Tacheng [Tarbagatai] Administrative Offices	1788906	7	1362232	7	36550	9
阿勒泰地区	Altay Administrative Offices	883454	12	623025	13	30602	10
博尔塔拉蒙古自治州	Bortala Mongol Autonomous Prefecture	427976	13	855808	10	38141	8
巴音郭楞蒙古自治州	Bayangol Mongol Autonomous Prefecture	5839043	3	1681912	6	65394	2
阿克苏地区	Aksu Administrative Offices	2009284	5	2193618	3	24248	11
克孜勒苏柯尔克孜自治州	Kizilsu Kirgiz Autonomous Prefecture	174526	15	331263	15	10887	14
喀什地区	Kashgar [Kaxgar] Administrative Offices	1431277	9	1989936	5	12817	13
和田地区	Hotan Administrative Offices	290112	14	725552	12	7015	15

19-2 各地、州、市人口状况

Population Status by Prefecture, Autonomous Prefecture and City

单位：万人　　(2012 年)　　(10 000 persons)

地　区	Region	总人口 Total Population	位 次 Rank	城镇人口 Urban Population	位 次 Rank
乌鲁木齐市	Urumqi City	257.80	3	250.50	1
克拉玛依市	Karamay City	28.58	15	28.58	15
石河子市	Shihezi City	62.00	11	62.00	9
吐鲁番地区	Turpan Administrative Offices	62.53	10	47.75	11
哈密地区	Hami [Kumul] Administrative Offices	59.24	12	52.38	10
昌吉回族自治州	Changji Hui Autonomous Prefecture	140.21	6	119.97	5
伊犁哈萨克自治州	Ili Kazak Autonomous Prefecture	462.84		273.62	
伊犁州直属县(市)	Counties (Cities) Direct Under Ili Prefecture	291.72	2	158.02	2
塔城地区	Tacheng [Tarbagatai] Administrative Offices	104.78	8	78.93	7
阿勒泰地区	Altay Administrative Offices	66.34	9	36.67	13
博尔塔拉蒙古自治州	Bortala Mongol Autonomous Prefecture	48.45	14	38.82	12
巴音郭楞蒙古自治州	Bayangol Mongol Autonomous Prefecture	137.47	7	109.46	6
阿克苏地区	Aksu Administrative Offices	239.69	4	154.82	3
克孜勒苏柯尔克孜自治州	Kizilsu Kirgiz Autonomous Prefecture	56.06	13	32.84	14
喀什地区	Kashgar [Kaxgar] Administrative Offices	415.13	1	143.47	4
和田地区	Hotan Administrative Offices	212.34	5	69.91	8

地　区	Region	乡村人口 Rural Population	位 次 Rank	人口自然增长率(‰) Natural Growth Rate (‰)	位 次 Rank
乌鲁木齐市	Urumqi City	7.30	12	6.00	9
克拉玛依市	Karamay City			4.77	14
石河子市	Shihezi City			-0.82	15
吐鲁番地区	Turpan Administrative Offices	14.78	10	12.07	5
哈密地区	Hami [Kumul] Administrative Offices	6.86	13	5.30	12
昌吉回族自治州	Changji Hui Autonomous Prefecture	20.24	9	5.44	11
伊犁哈萨克自治州	Ili Kazak Autonomous Prefecture	189.22		11.95	
伊犁州直属县(市)	Counties (Cities) Direct Under Ili Prefecture	133.70	3	15.11	3
塔城地区	Tacheng [Tarbagatai] Administrative Offices	25.85	7	5.13	13
阿勒泰地区	Altay Administrative Offices	29.67	5	8.87	7
博尔塔拉蒙古自治州	Bortala Mongol Autonomous Prefecture	9.63	11	5.82	10
巴音郭楞蒙古自治州	Bayangol Mongol Autonomous Prefecture	28.01	6	6.29	8
阿克苏地区	Aksu Administrative Offices	84.87	4	10.77	6
克孜勒苏柯尔克孜自治州	Kizilsu Kirgiz Autonomous Prefecture	23.22	8	28.20	2
喀什地区	Kashgar [Kaxgar] Administrative Offices	271.66	1	39.98	1
和田地区	Hotan Administrative Offices	142.43	2	12.09	4

注：城镇、乡村人口按公安年报口径计算。
Note: The urban and rural population in Prefecture, Autonomous Prefecture and City are calculated on the annals of public security.

19-3 各地、州、市全社会固定资产投资
Total Investment in Fixed Assets by Prefecture, Autonomous Prefecture and City

单位：万元 (2012 年) (10 000 yuan)

地 区	Region	合 计 Total	位 次 Rank	建筑工程 Construction Works	位 次 Rank
乌鲁木齐市	Urumqi City	8276320	1	5231929	1
克拉玛依市	Karamay City	3274858	7	2136746	7
石河子市	Shihezi City	1978613	10	712412	14
吐鲁番地区	Turpan Administrative Offices	1756596	12	881686	13
哈密地区	Hami [Kumul] Administrative Offices	3017682	8	1319046	9
昌吉回族自治州	Changji Hui Autonomous Prefecture	7334746	2	4398201	2
伊犁哈萨克自治州	Ili Kazak Autonomous Prefecture	10925718		7271042	
伊犁州直属县(市)	Counties (Cities) Direct Under Ili Prefecture	6143187	3	3861187	3
塔城地区	Tacheng [Tarbagatai] Administrative Offices	2822109	9	2117206	8
阿勒泰地区	Altay Administrative Offices	1960422	11	1292649	10
博尔塔拉蒙古自治州	Bortala Mongol Autonomous Prefecture	1556881	13	1005827	12
巴音郭楞蒙古自治州	Bayangol Mongol Autonomous Prefecture	5444520	4	3789920	4
阿克苏地区	Aksu Administrative Offices	4005680	6	2326357	6
克孜勒苏柯尔克孜自治州	Kizilsu Kirgiz Autonomous Prefecture	792344	15	589314	15
喀什地区	Kashgar [Kaxgar] Administrative Offices	4963534	5	3645634	5
和田地区	Hotan Administrative Offices	1512085	14	1282489	11

地 区	Region	安装工程 Installation Works	位 次 Rank	设备工具器具购置 Purchase of Equipment and Instruments	位 次 Rank	其他费用 Others	位 次 Rank
乌鲁木齐市	Urumqi City	584060	1	1641669	2	818662	1
克拉玛依市	Karamay City	356777	7	543850	10	237485	5
石河子市	Shi Hezi City	273428	8	846172	6	146601	10
吐鲁番地区	Turpan Administrative Offices	160542	11	615621	9	98747	14
哈密地区	Hami [Kumul] Administrative Offices	248299	9	1275901	3	174436	9
昌吉回族自治州	Changji Hui Autonomous Prefecture	412514	5	2126130	1	397901	3
伊犁哈萨克自治州	Ili Kazak Autonomous Prefecture	710725		1982580		961371	
伊犁州直属县(市)	Counties (Cities) Direct Under Ili Prefecture	455218	3	1194789	4	631993	2
塔城地区	Tacheng [Tarbagatai] Administrative Offices	175580	10	402129	11	127194	11
阿勒泰地区	Altay Administrative Offices	79927	12	385662	12	202184	7
博尔塔拉蒙古自治州	Bortala Mongol Autonomous Prefecture	61920	13	368199	13	120935	12
巴音郭楞蒙古自治州	Bayangol Mongol Autonomous Prefecture	498317	2	806047	7	350236	4
阿克苏地区	Aksu Administrative Offices	413485	4	1083461	5	182377	8
克孜勒苏柯尔克孜自治州	Kizilsu Kirgiz Autonomous Prefecture	32800	15	150631	14	19599	15
喀什地区	Kashgar [Kaxgar] Administrative Offices	386230	6	714891	8	216779	6
和田地区	Hotan Administrative Offices	34852	14	95600	15	99144	13

19-4 各地、州、市农林牧渔业总产值

Gross Output Value of Farming, Forestry, Animal Husbandry and Fishery by Prefecture, Autonomous Prefecture and City

单位：万元 (2012 年) (10 000 yuan)

地 区	Region	农林牧渔业总产值 Total	位 次 Rank	农 业 Farming	位 次 Rank	林 业 Forestry	位 次 Rank
乌鲁木齐市	Urumqi City	344293	12	152160	12	7518	12
克拉玛依市	Karamay City	105852	14	35312	14	20572	7
吐鲁番地区	Turpan Administrative Offices	567752	10	464487	9	3923	14
哈密地区	Hami [Kumul] Administrative Offices	410827	11	211397	11	16131	8
昌吉回族自治州	Changji Hui Autonomous Prefecture	2716179	2	1179846	5	25870	6
伊犁哈萨克自治州	Ili Kazak Autonomous Prefecture	4245590		2391838		76791	
伊犁州直属县(市)	Counties (Cities) Direct Under Ili Prefecture	1857766	5	896597	6	52227	2
塔城地区	Tacheng [Tarbagatai] Administrative Offices	1809269	6	1214454	4	10892	10
阿勒泰地区	Altay Administrative Offices	578555	9	280787	10	13672	9
博尔塔拉蒙古自治州	Bortala Mongol Autonomous Prefecture	632774	8	478235	8	7606	11
巴音郭楞蒙古自治州	Bayangol Mongol Autonomous Prefecture	2216920	3	1733792	2	49684	3
阿克苏地区	Aksu Administrative Offices	2123094	4	1670648	3	30524	4
克孜勒苏柯尔克孜自治州	Kizilsu Kirgiz Autonomous Prefecture	210021	13	118668	13	4277	13
喀什地区	Kashgar [Kaxgar] Administrative Offices	3601391	1	2491614	1	79864	1
和田地区	Hotan Administrative Offices	985305	7	658061	7	29166	5

地 区	Region	牧 业 Animal Husbandry	位 次 Rank	渔 业 Fishery	位 次 Rank	农林牧渔服务业 Farming, Forestry, Animal Husbandary and Fishery	位 次 Rank
乌鲁木齐市	Urumqi City	176096	10	6965	7	1554	14
克拉玛依市	Karamay City	35751	14	825	12	13392	9
吐鲁番地区	Turpan Administrative Offices	91193	12	481	13	7668	12
哈密地区	Hami [Kumul] Administrative Offices	176215	9	2212	9	4872	13
昌吉回族自治州	Changji Hui Autonomous Prefecture	1465733	1	17728	1	27002	6
伊犁哈萨克自治州	Ili Kazak Autonomous Prefecture	1696808		20686		59467	
伊犁州直属县(市)	Counties (Cities) Direct Under Ili Prefecture	867031	3	11084	5	30827	5
塔城地区	Tacheng [Tarbagatai] Administrative Offices	564072	4	2210	10	17641	7
阿勒泰地区	Altay Administrative Offices	265705	8	7392	6	10999	11
博尔塔拉蒙古自治州	Bortala Mongol Autonomous Prefecture	112847	11	1893	11	32193	4
巴音郭楞蒙古自治州	Bayangol Mongol Autonomous Prefecture	360004	5	12163	3	61277	3
阿克苏地区	Aksu Administrative Offices	334891	6	13372	2	73659	2
克孜勒苏柯尔克孜自治州	Kizilsu Kirgiz Autonomous Prefecture	74173	13	230	14	12673	10
喀什地区	Kashgar [Kaxgar] Administrative Offices	941636	2	12052	4	76225	1
和田地区	Hotan Administrative Offices	279843	7	3403	8	14832	8

注：本表按当年价格计算。
Notes: The number in this table is computed at current price.

19-5 各地、州、市主要农产品产量

Yield of Major Farm Crops by Prefecture, Autonomous Prefecture and City

单位：吨　　(2012 年)　　(ton)

地　区	Region	粮 食 Grain	位 次 Rank	棉 花 Cotton	位 次 Rank
乌鲁木齐市	Urumqi City	152322	11	1701	13
克拉玛依市	Karamay City	5014	14	12360	11
吐鲁番地区	Turpan Administrative Offices	27600	13	30268	9
哈密地区	Hami [Kumul] Administrative Offices	126402	12	33300	8
昌吉回族自治州	Changji Hui Autonomous Prefecture	1562650	5	202645	5
伊犁哈萨克自治州	Ili Kazak Autonomous Prefecture	4993960		265943	
伊犁州直属县(市)	Counties (Cities) Direct Under Ili Prefecture	2557140	2	15587	10
塔城地区	Tacheng [Tarbagatai] Administrative Offices	2086334	3	250356	4
阿勒泰地区	Altay Administrative Offices	350486	9		
博尔塔拉蒙古自治州	Bortala Mongol Autonomous Prefecture	590904	7	138028	6
巴音郭楞蒙古自治州	Bayangol Mongol Autonomous Prefecture	381420	8	372084	2
阿克苏地区	Aksu Administrative Offices	1570420	4	576730	1
克孜勒苏柯尔克孜自治州	Kizilsu Kirgiz Autonomous Prefecture	288702	10	10230	12
喀什地区	Kashgar [Kaxgar] Administrative Offices	2679201	1	369810	3
和田地区	Hotan Administrative Offices	1062514	6	38541	7

地　区	Region	油 料 Oil Bearing Crops	位 次 Rank	甜 菜 Beetroots	位 次 Rank
乌鲁木齐市	Urumqi City	9222	9	2164	8
克拉玛依市	Karamay City				
吐鲁番地区	Turpan Administrative Offices	892	13		
哈密地区	Hami [Kumul] Administrative Offices	1801	11		
昌吉回族自治州	Changji Hui Autonomous Prefecture	79152	3	647685	2
伊犁哈萨克自治州	Ili Kazak Autonomous Prefecture	305481		1859179	
伊犁州直属县(市)	Counties (Cities) Direct Under Ili Prefecture	106187	2	1480185	1
塔城地区	Tacheng [Tarbagatai] Administrative Offices	32577	4	313263	5
阿勒泰地区	Altay Administrative Offices	166717	1	65731	7
博尔塔拉蒙古自治州	Bortala Mongol Autonomous Prefecture	14072	6	169022	6
巴音郭楞蒙古自治州	Bayangol Mongol Autonomous Prefecture	6359	10	586230	3
阿克苏地区	Aksu Administrative Offices	11296	7	345080	4
克孜勒苏柯尔克孜自治州	Kizilsu Kirgiz Autonomous Prefecture	1155	12		
喀什地区	Kashgar [Kaxgar] Administrative Offices	14689	5		
和田地区	Hotan Administrative Offices	10595	8		

19-6 各地、州、市规模以上工业企业主要经济指标

Main Indicators on Economic of Industrial Enterprises above Designated Size by Prefecture, Autonomous Prefecture and City

单位：% (2012 年) (%)

地 区	Region	工业总产值(万元) Gross Industrial Output Value (10 000 yuan)	位次 Rank	工业销售产值(万元) Sales Value of Industry Products (10 000 yuan)	位次 Rank
乌鲁木齐市	Urumqi City	21508375.4	1	21103424.1	1
克拉玛依市	Karamay City	16938759.3	2	16787472.4	2
石河子市	Shihezi City	3699463.3	6	3537378.3	6
吐鲁番地区	Turpan Administrative Offices	2718117.0	8	2543866.2	8
哈密地区	Hami [Kumul] Administrative Offices	1881062.4	9	1760054.6	9
昌吉回族自治州	Changji Hui Autonomous Prefecture	6042233.4	4	5701990.4	4
伊犁哈萨克自治州	Ili Kazak Autonomous Prefecture	6137119.2		5874399.4	
伊犁州直属县(市)	Counties (Cities) Direct Under Ili Prefecture	3667857.5	7	3529167.1	7
塔城地区	Tacheng [Tarbagatai] Administrative Offices	1367052.3	10	1252306.8	10
阿勒泰地区	Altay Administrative Offices	1102209.4	11	1092925.5	11
博尔塔拉蒙古自治州	Bortala Mongol Autonomous Prefecture	471085.7	13	426167.0	13
巴音郭楞蒙古自治州	Bayangol Mongol Autonomous Prefecture	8213541.7	3	8222543.7	3
阿克苏地区	Aksu Administrative Offices	4499436.7	5	4369551.4	5
克孜勒苏柯尔克孜自治州	Kizilsu Kirgiz Autonomous Prefecture	219473.2	14	200805.7	14
喀什地区	Kashgar [Kaxgar] Administrative Offices	1031071.4	12	1007415.2	12
和田地区	Hotan Administrative Offices	194628.9	15	199189.8	15

地 区	Region	总资产贡献率 Ratio of Total Assets to Industrial OutputValue	位次 Rank	资本保值增值率 Ratio of Capital Holding And Rise	位次 Rank
乌鲁木齐市	Urumqi City	11.8	6	107.6	12
克拉玛依市	Karamay City	25.3	2	102.4	14
石河子市	Shihezi City	7.4	10	129.1	6
吐鲁番地区	Turpan Administrative Offices	11.9	5	121.1	8
哈密地区	Hami [Kumul] Administrative Offices	6.5	12	124.3	7
昌吉回族自治州	Changji Hui Autonomous Prefecture	7.8	8	169.5	3
伊犁哈萨克自治州	Ili Kazak Autonomous Prefecture	11.2		122.2	
伊犁州直属县(市)	Counties (Cities) Direct Under Ili Prefecture	10.0	7	130.6	5
塔城地区	Tacheng [Tarbagatai] Administrative Offices	6.5	11	105.8	13
阿勒泰地区	Altay Administrative Offices	21.3	3	114.3	9
博尔塔拉蒙古自治州	Bortala Mongol Autonomous Prefecture	6.0	13	96.0	15
巴音郭楞蒙古自治州	Bayangol Mongol Autonomous Prefecture	27.4	1	112.1	10
阿克苏地区	Aksu Administrative Offices	13.1	4	149.7	4
克孜勒苏柯尔克孜自治州	Kizilsu Kirgiz Autonomous Prefecture	5.8	14	176.4	2
喀什地区	Kashgar [Kaxgar] Administrative Offices	7.4	9	192.1	1
和田地区	Hotan Administrative Offices	4.5	15	108.0	11

19-6 续表 Continued

单位：% (%)

地　区	Region	资产负债率 Assets Liability Ratio	位次 Rank	成本费用利润率 Ratio of Profits to Industrial Cost	位次 Rank
乌鲁木齐市	Urumqi City	55.8	13	9.0	6
克拉玛依市	Karamay City	40.9	15	16.3	3
石河子市	Shihezi City	61.3	8	5.9	10
吐鲁番地区	Turpan Administrative Offices	54.4	14	14.7	4
哈密地区	Hami [Kumul] Administrative Offices	68.1	3	8.9	7
昌吉回族自治州	Changji Hui Autonomous Prefecture	63.8	6	9.9	5
伊犁哈萨克自治州	Ili Kazak Autonomous Prefecture	62.7		11.8	
伊犁州直属县(市)	Counties (Cities) Direct Under Ili Prefecture	62.7	7	8.6	9
塔城地区	Tacheng [Tarbagatai] Administrative Offices	67.1	4	5.5	11
阿勒泰地区	Altay Administrative Offices	57.5	10	33.9	2
博尔塔拉蒙古自治州	Bortala Mongol Autonomous Prefecture	79.1	1	2.5	14
巴音郭楞蒙古自治州	Bayangol Mongol Autonomous Prefecture	55.9	11	48.0	1
阿克苏地区	Aksu Administrative Offices	60.7	9	8.8	8
克孜勒苏柯尔克孜自治州	Kizilsu Kirgiz Autonomous Prefecture	66.8	5	4.6	12
喀什地区	Kashgar [Kaxgar] Administrative Offices	71.9	2	4.0	13
和田地区	Hotan Administrative Offices	55.9	12	1.4	15

地　区	Region	产值利税率 Ratio of Profits and Taxes to Industrial Output Value	位次 Rank	流动资产周转次数(次/年) Number of Times of Annual Turnover Working Capitals (times/year)	位次 Rank
乌鲁木齐市	Urumqi City	15.7	7	2.1	4
克拉玛依市	Karamay City	26.3	3	3.7	1
石河子市	Shihezi City	8.4	13	1.5	10
吐鲁番地区	Turpan Administrative Offices	19.4	4	1.7	7
哈密地区	Hami [Kumul] Administrative Offices	14.1	8	1.2	14
昌吉回族自治州	Changji Hui Autonomous Prefecture	12.8	9	1.2	13
伊犁哈萨克自治州	Ili Kazak Autonomous Prefecture	18.2		1.6	
伊犁州直属县(市)	Counties (Cities) Direct Under Ili Prefecture	16.9	6	1.5	9
塔城地区	Tacheng [Tarbagatai] Administrative Offices	8.5	11	1.4	12
阿勒泰地区	Altay Administrative Offices	34.5	2	2.2	3
博尔塔拉蒙古自治州	Bortala Mongol Autonomous Prefecture	6.2	15	1.4	11
巴音郭楞蒙古自治州	Bayangol Mongol Autonomous Prefecture	41.1	1	2.6	2
阿克苏地区	Aksu Administrative Offices	17.3	5	1.9	5
克孜勒苏柯尔克孜自治州	Kizilsu Kirgiz Autonomous Prefecture	11.6	10	1.0	15
喀什地区	Kashgar [Kaxgar] Administrative Offices	8.4	12	1.7	6
和田地区	Hotan Administrative Offices	6.9	14	1.6	8

19-7 各地、州、市主要工业产品产量

Output of Major Industrial Products by Prefecture, Autonomous Prefecture and City

(2012 年)

地 区	Region	纱(吨) Yarn (ton)	位次 Rank	布(万米) Cloth (10 000 m)	位次 Rank	呢绒(万米) Woolen Piece Goods (10 000 m)	位次 Rank
乌鲁木齐市	Urumqi City	21411	7	584	3		
克拉玛依市	Karamay City						
石河子市	Shihezi City	173072	1	4830	1	243	1
吐鲁番地区	Turpan Administrative Offices	3546	11				
哈密地区	Hami [Kumul] Administrative Offices	10653	10				
昌吉回族自治州	Changji Hui Autonomous Prefecture	18876	8	324	4	89	2
伊犁哈萨克自治州	Ili Kazak Autonomous Prefecture	52274		268			
伊犁州直属县(市)	Counties (Cities) Direct Under Ili Prefecture	36869	3				
塔城地区	Tacheng [Tarbagatai] Administrative Offices	15405	9	268	5		
阿勒泰地区	Altay Administrative Offices						
博尔塔拉蒙古自治州	Bortala Mongol Autonomous Prefecture	21736	6	25	6		
巴音郭楞蒙古自治州	Bayangol Mongol Autonomous Prefecture	28105	4	642	2		
阿克苏地区	Aksu Administrative Offices	43659	2				
克孜勒苏柯尔克孜自治州	Kizilsu Kirgiz Autonomous Prefecture						
喀什地区	Kashgar [Kaxgar] Administrative Offices	27833	5	3	7		
和田地区	Hotan Administrative Offices	988	12				

地 区	Region	成品糖(万吨) Sugar (10 000 tons)	位次 Rank	饮料酒(千升) Alcohol Beverage (kilo-liter)	位次 Rank	塑料制品(吨) Plastic Products (ton)	位次 Rank
乌鲁木齐市	Urumqi City			136050	2	382725	2
克拉玛依市	Karamay City			4192	11	25422	9
石河子市	Shihezi City			172539	1	426759	1
吐鲁番地区	Turpan Administrative Offices			7016	10	28	15
哈密地区	Hami [Kumul] Administrative Offices			17805	9	13673	11
昌吉回族自治州	Changji Hui Autonomous Prefecture	6.55	4	44847	5	310306	3
伊犁哈萨克自治州	Ili Kazak Autonomous Prefecture	32.69		173525		114934	
伊犁州直属县(市)	Counties (Cities) Direct Under Ili Prefecture	22.22	1	86028	3	39150	5
塔城地区	Tacheng [Tarbagatai] Administrative Offices	9.14	2	85798	4	67277	4
阿勒泰地区	Altay Administrative Offices	1.34	7	1699	12	8508	12
博尔塔拉蒙古自治州	Bortala Mongol Autonomous Prefecture	2.93	5	641	13	37073	7
巴音郭楞蒙古自治州	Bayangol Mongol Autonomous Prefecture	8.61	3	38503	6	15999	10
阿克苏地区	Aksu Administrative Offices	2.52	6	33839	7	31517	8
克孜勒苏柯尔克孜自治州	Kizilsu Kirgiz Autonomous Prefecture			160	15	2623	13
喀什地区	Kashgar [Kaxgar] Administrative Offices	0.33	8	28228	8	37815	6
和田地区	Hotan Administrative Offices	0.01	9	292	14	809	14

19-7 续表 Continued

地 区	Region	机制纸及纸板(吨) Machine-made Paper and Paper board (ton)	位次 Rank	原煤(万吨) Coal (10 000 tons)	位次 Rank	原油(万吨) Crude Oil (10 000 tons)	位次 Rank
乌鲁木齐市	Urumqi City	76176	4	1341.36	4	735.00	2
克拉玛依市	Karamay City					1103.01	1
石河子市	Shihezi City	97242	3	258.37	9		
吐鲁番地区	Turpan Administrative Offices			1262.90	5	156.00	4
哈密地区	Hami [Kumul] Administrative Offices	1152	7	2413.99	2		
昌吉回族自治州	Changji Hui Autonomous Prefecture	101878	2	4968.17	1		
伊犁哈萨克自治州	Ili Kazak Autonomous Prefecture	2100		1376.68		96.50	
伊犁州直属县(市)	Counties (Cities) Direct Under Ili Prefecture			645.29	7		
塔城地区	Tacheng [Tarbagatai] Administrative Offices	2100	6	726.32	6	96.50	5
阿勒泰地区	Altay Administrative Offices			5.07	13		
博尔塔拉蒙古自治州	Bortala Mongol Autonomous Prefecture						
巴音郭楞蒙古自治州	Bayangol Mongol Autonomous Prefecture	127310	1	386.18	8	580.17	3
阿克苏地区	Aksu Administrative Offices			1511.96	3		
克孜勒苏柯尔克孜自治州	Kizilsu Kirgiz Autonomous Prefecture			11.10	12		
喀什地区	Kashgar [Kaxgar] Administrative Offices	4689	5	33.32	11		
和田地区	Hotan Administrative Offices			82.95	10		

地 区	Region	水泥(万吨) Cement (10 000 tons)	位次 Rank	发电量(亿千瓦小时) Electricity (100 million kwh)	位次 Rank	农用化肥(吨) Chemical Fertilizers (ton)	位次 Rank
乌鲁木齐市	Urumqi City	491.90	3	255.24	2	593715	2
克拉玛依市	Karamay City			46.89	9		
石河子市	Shihezi City	332.46	7	293.42	1	65106	6
吐鲁番地区	Turpan Administrative Offices	211.33	9	29.16	10		
哈密地区	Hami [Kumul] Administrative Offices	201.20	10	62.40	7	15280	8
昌吉回族自治州	Changji Hui Autonomous Prefecture	402.22	5	154.96	3	386508	4
伊犁哈萨克自治州	Ili Kazak Autonomous Prefecture	951.02		169.36		302896	
伊犁州直属县(市)	Counties (Cities) Direct Under Ili Prefecture	493.65	2	81.50	4		
塔城地区	Tacheng [Tarbagatai] Administrative Offices	299.78	8	69.01	5	270037	5
阿勒泰地区	Altay Administrative Offices	157.59	11	18.85	12	32859	7
博尔塔拉蒙古自治州	Bortala Mongol Autonomous Prefecture	105.68	13	7.18	15		
巴音郭楞蒙古自治州	Bayangol Mongol Autonomous Prefecture	376.81	6	63.05	6	1250018	1
阿克苏地区	Aksu Administrative Offices	585.15	1	60.52	8	428154	3
克孜勒苏柯尔克孜自治州	Kizilsu Kirgiz Autonomous Prefecture	86.51	14	7.48	14		
喀什地区	Kashgar [Kaxgar] Administrative Offices	416.40	4	25.67	11		
和田地区	Hotan Administrative Offices	155.24	12	12.15	13	10	9

19-8 各地、州、市社会消费品零售总额

Total Retail Sales of Consumer Goods by Prefecture, Autonomous Prefecture and City

单位：万元　　(2012 年)　　(10 000 yuan)

地区	Region	社会消费品零售总额 Total Retail Sales of Consumer Goods	位次 Rank	城镇 City	位次 Rank
乌鲁木齐市	Urumqi City	7396900	1	7393122	1
克拉玛依市	Karamay City	480039	9	477677	8
吐鲁番地区	Turpan Administrative Offices	294015	11	216166	11
哈密地区	Hami [Kumul] Administrative Offices	554516	7	525347	7
昌吉回族自治州	Changji Hui Autonomous Prefecture	1557170	2	1436896	2
伊犁哈萨克自治州	Ili Kazak Autonomous Prefecture	2320490		1879339	
伊犁州直属县(市)	Counties (Cities) Direct Under Ili Prefecture	1363087	3	1123204	3
塔城地区	Tacheng [Tarbagatai] Administrative Offices	525214	8	371028	10
阿勒泰地区	Altay Administrative Offices	432189	10	385107	9
博尔塔拉蒙古自治州	Bortala Mongol Autonomous Prefecture	247064	13	212808	12
巴音郭楞蒙古自治州	Bayangol Mongol Autonomous Prefecture	785634	6	670681	6
阿克苏地区	Aksu Administrative Offices	856240	5	730214	5
克孜勒苏柯尔克孜自治州	Kizilsu Kirgiz Autonomous Prefecture	116810	14	106666	14
喀什地区	Kashgar [Kaxgar] Administrative Offices	1104713	4	893227	4
和田地区	Hotan Administrative Offices	256300	12	189730	13

地区	Region	城区 County	位次 Rank	乡村 Under County Level	位次 Rank
乌鲁木齐市	Urumqi City	7393122	1	3778	13
克拉玛依市	Karamay City	477677	5	2362	14
吐鲁番地区	Turpan Administrative Offices	127233	13	77849	7
哈密地区	Hami [Kumul] Administrative Offices	477281	6	29169	11
昌吉回族自治州	Changji Hui Autonomous Prefecture	1371810	2	120274	5
伊犁哈萨克自治州	Ili Kazak Autonomous Prefecture	1235884		441151	
伊犁州直属县(市)	Counties (Cities) Direct Under Ili Prefecture	942456	3	239883	1
塔城地区	Tacheng [Tarbagatai] Administrative Offices	164080	9	154186	3
阿勒泰地区	Altay Administrative Offices	129348	11	47082	9
博尔塔拉蒙古自治州	Bortala Mongol Autonomous Prefecture	128989	12	34256	10
巴音郭楞蒙古自治州	Bayangol Mongol Autonomous Prefecture	481375	4	114953	6
阿克苏地区	Aksu Administrative Offices	421696	8	126026	4
克孜勒苏柯尔克孜自治州	Kizilsu Kirgiz Autonomous Prefecture	104826	14	10144	12
喀什地区	Kashgar [Kaxgar] Administrative Offices	466698	7	211486	2
和田地区	Hotan Administrative Offices	131176	10	66570	8

19-9 各地、州、市海关进出口总额
Total Value of Imports and Exports by Prefecture, Autonomous Prefecture and City

单位：万美元　　(2012 年)　　(USD 10 000)

地　　区	Region	进出口总额 Total Imports and Exports	位 次 Rank	出口额 Exports	位 次 Rank	进口额 Imports	位 次 Rank
乌鲁木齐市	Urumqi City	1039689	1	806398	1	233291	1
克拉玛依市	Karamay City	23896	11	14146	11	9750	5
石河子市	Shihezi City	76842	7	72791	7	4051	7
吐鲁番地区	Turpan Administrative Offices	3459	13	2272	13	1187	11
哈密地区	Hami [Kumul] Administrative Offices	2624	14	1683	14	941	12
昌吉回族自治州	Changji Hui Autonomous Prefecture	210932	4	199254	3	11678	4
伊犁哈萨克自治州	Ili Administrative Offices	706758		505848		200910	
伊犁州直属县(市)	Counties (Cities) Direct Under Ili Prefecture	571024	2	375891	2	195133	2
塔城地区	Tacheng [Tarbagatai] Administrative Offices	44822	9	39328	9	5494	6
阿勒泰地区	Altay Administrative Offices	90912	6	90629	6	283	14
博尔塔拉蒙古自治州	Bortala Mongol Autonomous Prefecture	245749	3	134605	4	111144	3
巴音郭楞蒙古自治州	Bayangol Mongol Autonomous Prefecture	16687	12	13348	12	3339	9
阿克苏地区	Aksu Administrative Offices	55347	8	53573	8	1774	10
克孜勒苏柯尔克孜自治州	Kizilsu Kirgiz Autonomous Prefecture	26066	10	22720	10	3346	8
喀什地区	Kashgar [Kaxgar] Administrative Offices	108297	5	107358	5	939	13
和田地区	Hotan Administrative Offices	729	15	690	15	39	15

19-10 各地、州、市在岗职工工资总额和平均工资
Total Wages of Employed Staff and Workers and Average Wage by Prefecture, Autonomous Prefecture and City

(2012 年)

地　　区	Region	在岗职工工资总额(万元) Total Wages of Staff and Workers (10 000 yuan)	位 次 Rank	在岗职工平均货币工资(元) Average of Staff and Workers Wage (yuan)	位 次 Rank
乌鲁木齐市	Urumqi City	3845062	1	52418	2
克拉玛依市	Karamay City	1245479	2	73510	1
石河子市	Shihezi City	617312	9	44227	7
吐鲁番地区	Turpan Administrative Offices	395416	11	51343	3
哈密地区	Hami [Kumul] Administrative Offices	395047	12	44480	6
昌吉回族自治州	Changji Hui Autonomous Prefecture	909379	5	42707	8
伊犁哈萨克自治州	Ili Kazak Autonomous Prefecture	2225596		34435	
伊犁州直属县(市)	Counties (Cities) Direct Under Ili Prefecture	1086007	3	36525	12
塔城地区	Tacheng [Tarbagatai] Administrative Offices	763184	8	32926	14
阿勒泰地区	Altay Administrative Offices	376404	13	32116	15
博尔塔拉蒙古自治州	Bortala Mongol Autonomous Prefecture	331083	14	33823	13
巴音郭楞蒙古自治州	Bayangol Mongol Autonomous Prefecture	1009348	4	45609	5
阿克苏地区	Aksu Administrative Offices	884094	7	41760	9
克孜勒苏柯尔克孜自治州	Kizilsu Kirgiz Autonomous Prefecture	169011	15	40090	11
喀什地区	Kashgar [Kaxgar] Administrative Offices	898442	6	41604	10
和田地区	Hotan Administrative Offices	429215	10	48887	4

19-11 各地、州、市公共财政预算收支

The General Budgetary Revenue and Expenditures of Local Finance by Prefecture, Autonomous Prefecture and City

单位：万元 (2012 年) (10 000 yuan)

地 区	Region	公共财政预算收入 Local Financial Revenue	位 次 Rank	公共财政预算支出 Local Financial Expenditure	位 次 Rank
乌鲁木齐市	Urumqi City	2520052	1	2956004	1
克拉玛依市	Karamay City	572603	5	701753	11
石河子市	Shihezi City	217520	12	269061	15
吐鲁番地区	Turpan Administrative Offices	252207	11	521607	13
哈密地区	Hami [Kumul] Administrative Offices	303845	9	681438	12
昌吉回族自治州	Changji Hui Autonomous Prefecture	642809	3	1437355	7
伊犁哈萨克自治州	Ili Kazak Autonomous Prefecture	1136329		4263143	
伊犁州直属县(市)	Counties (Cities) Direct Under Ili Prefecture	561683	6	2094391	3
塔城地区	Tacheng [Tarbagatai] Administrative Offices	320435	8	1122564	8
阿勒泰地区	Altay Administrative Offices	254211	10	1046188	9
博尔塔拉蒙古自治州	Bortala Mongol Autonomous Prefecture	103878	14	478568	14
巴音郭楞蒙古自治州	Bayangol Mongol Autonomous Prefecture	604892	4	1501148	6
阿克苏地区	Aksu Administrative Offices	721656	2	1869077	4
克孜勒苏柯尔克孜自治州	Kizilsu Kirgiz Autonomous Prefecture	70862	15	716335	10
喀什地区	Kashgar [Kaxgar] Administrative Offices	377973	7	2921788	2
和田地区	Hotan Administrative Offices	111841	13	1512549	5

19-12 分城镇居民消费价格指数和商品零售价格指数

General Retail Price and Consumer Price Index by City/County

(上年=100) (2012 年)(抽样调查) (Sampled Survey) (preceding year=100)

地 区	Region	商品零售价格指数 General Retail Price Index	位 次 Rank	居民消费价格指数 General Consumer Price Index	位 次 Rank
乌鲁木齐市	Urumqi City	102.9	13	103.4	13
喀什市	Kashgar [Kaxgar] City	103.9	6	104.6	4
伊宁市	Yining [Gulja] City	103.5	8	103.7	11
和田市	Hotan City	104.1	2	104.8	3
克拉玛依市	Karamay City	102.7	15	102.9	16
哈密市	Hami [Kumul] City	103.1	10	103.7	11
昌吉市	Changji City	104.1	2	104.1	8
库尔勒市	Korla City	102.0	17	102.6	18
阿克苏市	Aksu City	101.4	19	102.2	20
焉耆回族自治县	Yanqi Hui Autonomous County	103.1	10	103.4	13
塔城市	Tacheng [Qoqek] City	102.6	16	103.9	9
阿勒泰市	Altay City	103.9	6	104.3	5
乌苏市	Usu City	102.8	14	103.9	9
博乐市	Bole [Bortala] City	103.2	9	103.1	15
吐鲁番市	Turpan City	104.0	4	104.3	5
库车县	Kuqa County	101.8	18	104.2	7
阿图什市	Artux City	104.0	4	105.1	2
莎车县	Shache [Yarkant] County	105.1	1	105.4	1
奎屯市	Kuytun City	101.4	20	102.4	19
石河子市	Shihezi City	103.1	10	102.8	17

19-13 各地、州、市各类学校在校学生数

Number of Students Enrollment by Type of School and by Prefecture, Autonomous Prefecture and City

单位：人 (2012 年) (person)

地 区	Region	普通高等学校 Regular Institutions of Higher Education	位次 Rank	中等职业学校 Specialized Secondary Schools	位次 Rank
乌鲁木齐市	Urumqi City	158680	1	72770	1
克拉玛依市	Karamay City	4198	8	802	14
石河子市	Shihezi City	6067	5	1826	13
吐鲁番地区	Turpan Administrative Offices			3761	9
哈密地区	Hami [Kumul] Administrative Offices			3366	10
昌吉回族自治州	Changji Hui Autonomous Prefecture	21869	2	13171	5
伊犁哈萨克自治州	Ili Kazak Autonomous Prefecture	14478		22081	
伊犁州直属县(市)	Counties (Cities) Direct Under Ili Prefecture	14478	3	12699	7
塔城地区	Tacheng [Tarbagatai] Administrative Offices			3126	11
阿勒泰地区	Altay Administrative Offices			6256	8
博尔塔拉蒙古自治州	Bortala Mongol Autonomous Prefecture			802	14
巴音郭楞蒙古自治州	Bayangol Mongol Autonomous Prefecture	4369	7	12911	6
阿克苏地区	Aksu Administrative Offices	2891	9	13285	4
克孜勒苏柯尔克孜自治州	Kizilsu Kirgiz Autonomous Prefecture			2496	12
喀什地区	Kashgar [Kaxgar] Administrative Offices	11552	4	28749	2
和田地区	Hotan Administrative Offices	5472	6	22767	3

地 区	Region	普通中学 Regular Secondary Schools	位次 Rank	小学 Primary Schools	位次 Rank
乌鲁木齐市	Urumqi City	150991	3	184287	5
克拉玛依市	Karamay City	25031	13	22641	14
石河子市	Shihezi City	19704	15	12113	15
吐鲁番地区	Turpan Administrative Offices	31962	11	50791	10
哈密地区	Hami [Kumul] Administrative Offices	32440	10	32268	12
昌吉回族自治州	Changji Hui Autonomous Prefecture	82173	6	79023	7
伊犁哈萨克自治州	Ili Kazak Autonomous Prefecture	243434		335122	
伊犁州直属县(市)	Counties (Cities) Direct Under Ili Prefecture	151483	2	218657	2
塔城地区	Tacheng [Tarbagatai] Administrative Offices	60763	8	69627	8
阿勒泰地区	Altay Administrative Offices	31188	12	46838	11
博尔塔拉蒙古自治州	Bortala Mongol Autonomous Prefecture	22014	14	27201	13
巴音郭楞蒙古自治州	Bayangol Mongol Autonomous Prefecture	70736	7	96616	6
阿克苏地区	Aksu Administrative Offices	140231	4	215103	3
克孜勒苏柯尔克孜自治州	Kizilsu Kirgiz Autonomous Prefecture	34427	9	56367	9
喀什地区	Kashgar [Kaxgar] Administrative Offices	249006	1	411061	1
和田地区	Hotan Administrative Offices	112491	5	188250	4

19-14 各地、州、市每万人口医院床位数和医生数
Number of Doctors and Hospital Beds Per 10 000 Population by Prefecture, Autonomous Prefecture and City

(2012 年)

地 区	Region	每万人床位数(张) Number of Beds per 10 000 Population (unit)	位 次 Rank	平均每万人医生数(人) Number of Doctors Per 10 000 Population (person)	位 次 Rank
乌鲁木齐市	Urumqi City	102.86	1	48.56	1
克拉玛依市	Karamay City	57.66	6	39.75	2
石河子市	Shihezi City	89.34	2	37.39	3
吐鲁番地区	Turpan Administrative Offices	38.46	15	19.57	12
哈密地区	Hami [Kumul] Administrative Offices	58.44	5	30.11	4
昌吉回族自治州	Changji Hui Autonomous Prefecture	70.82	3	29.28	5
伊犁哈萨克自治州	Ili Kazak Autonomous Prefecture	51.26		21.80	
伊犁州直属县(市)	Counties (Cities) Direct Under Ili Prefecture	52.91	10	20.87	10
塔城地区	Tacheng [Tarbagatai] Administrative Offices	46.74	13	21.42	9
阿勒泰地区	Altay Administrative Offices	51.13	11	26.51	7
博尔塔拉蒙古自治州	Bortala Mongol Autonomous Prefecture	57.01	8	28.88	6
巴音郭楞蒙古自治州	Bayangol Mongol Autonomous Prefecture	60.17	4	25.53	8
阿克苏地区	Aksu Administrative Offices	50.94	12	13.16	13
克孜勒苏柯尔克孜自治州	Kizilsu Kirgiz Autonomous Prefecture	57.21	7	20.14	11
喀什地区	Kashgar [Kaxgar] Administrative Offices	44.60	14	12.42	14
和田地区	Hotan Administrative Offices	55.46	9	11.14	15

19-15 各地、州、市卫生技术人员和医生数
Medical Technical Personnel and Doctors by Prefecture, Autonomous Prefecture and City

单位：人 (2012 年) (person)

地 区	Region	卫生技术人员 Medical Technical Personnel	位 次 Rank	执业医师 Doctors with Licence	位 次 Rank	执业助理医师 Assistant Doctors with Licence	位 次 Rank
乌鲁木齐市	Urumqi City	32720	1	11897	1	623	7
克拉玛依市	Karamay City	2937	15	1101	12	35	15
石河子市	Shihezi City	6070	8	1950	7	368	10
吐鲁番地区	Turpan Administrative Offices	3054	14	987	14	237	14
哈密地区	Hami [Kumul] Administrative Offices	4491	10	1478	10	306	13
昌吉回族自治州	Changji Hui Autonomous Prefecture	10919	4	3365	4	741	5
伊犁哈萨克自治州	Ili Kazak Autonomous Prefecture	26074		7906		2184	
伊犁州直属县(市)	Counties (Cities) Direct Under Ili Prefecture	15928	3	4880	2	1207	2
塔城地区	Tacheng [Tarbagatai] Administrative Offices	6016	9	1673	8	571	8
阿勒泰地区	Altay Administrative Offices	4130	11	1353	11	406	9
博尔塔拉蒙古自治州	Bortala Mongol Autonomous Prefecture	3526	12	1078	13	321	12
巴音郭楞蒙古自治州	Bayangol Mongol Autonomous Prefecture	9422	5	2801	5	709	6
阿克苏地区	Aksu Administrative Offices	9137	6	2358	6	797	3
克孜勒苏柯尔克孜自治州	Kizilsu Kirgiz Autonomous Prefecture	3125	13	787	15	342	11
喀什地区	Kashgar [Kaxgar] Administrative Offices	16139	2	3529	3	1628	1
和田地区	Hotan Administrative Offices	7173	7	1609	9	757	4

新疆统计年鉴
XINJIANG STATISTICAL YEARBOOK

附录

各省市区主要经济指标排序

RANKING OF MAIN ECONOMIC INDICATORS BY REGION

各省市区主要经济指标排序
Ranking of Main Economic Indicators by Region

(2012 年)

省市区	Region	地区生产总值(亿元) Gross Regional Product (100 million yuan)	位次 Rank	地区生产总值比上年增长(%) Increase Rate of Gross Region Production over the previous year(%)	位次 Rank
全　国	**China**	**519322.1**		**7.8**	
北　京	Beijing	17801.0	13	7.7	30
天　津	Tianjin	12885.2	20	13.8	1
河　北	Hebei	26575.0	6	9.6	25
山　西	Shanxi	12112.8	21	10.1	20
内蒙古	Inner Mongolia	15988.3	15	11.7	13
辽　宁	Liaoning	24801.3	7	9.5	26
吉　林	Jilin	11937.8	22	12.0	10
黑龙江	Heilongjiang	13691.6	17	10.0	23
上　海	Shanghai	20101.3	11	7.5	31
江　苏	Jiangsu	54058.2	2	10.1	20
浙　江	Zhejiang	34606.3	4	8.0	29
安　徽	Anhui	17212.1	14	12.1	9
福　建	Fujian	19701.8	12	11.4	15
江　西	Jiangxi	12948.5	19	11.0	19
山　东	Shandong	50013.2	3	9.8	24
河　南	Henan	29810.1	5	10.1	20
湖　北	Hubei	22250.2	9	11.3	16
湖　南	Hunan	22154.2	10	11.3	16
广　东	Guangdong	57067.9	1	8.2	28
广　西	Guangxi	13031.0	18	11.3	16
海　南	Hainan	2855.3	28	9.1	27
重　庆	Chongqing	11459.0	23	13.6	2
四　川	Sichuan	23849.8	8	12.6	6
贵　州	Guizhou	6802.2	26	13.6	2
云　南	Yunnan	10309.8	24	13.0	4
西　藏	Tibet	695.6	31	11.8	12
陕　西	Shaanxi	14451.2	16	12.9	5
甘　肃	Gansu	5650.2	27	12.6	6
青　海	Qinghai	1884.5	30	12.3	8
宁　夏	Ningxia	2326.6	29	11.5	14
新　疆	Xinjiang	7505.3	25	12.0	10

续表 1

省市区	Region	第一产业增加值(亿元) Value Added of the Primary Industry (100 million yuan)	位次 Rank	第二产业增加值(亿元) Value Added of the Secondary Industry (100 million yuan)	位次 Rank	第三产业增加值(亿元) Value Added of the Tertiary Industry (100 million yuan)	位次 Rank
全　国	**China**	**52377.0**		**235318.6**		**231626.5**	
北　京	Beijing	150.3	29	4058.3	24	13592.5	5
天　津	Tianjin	171.5	28	6663.7	18	6050.0	14
河　北	Hebei	3186.7	5	14001.0	6	9387.3	7
山　西	Shanxi	697.9	25	7009.1	16	4405.9	21
内蒙古	Inner Mongolia	1447.4	17	9032.5	13	5508.4	16
辽　宁	Liaoning	2155.8	11	13338.7	7	9306.8	8
吉　林	Jilin	1412.1	18	6374.5	20	4151.3	24
黑龙江	Heilongjiang	2113.7	12	6456.4	19	5121.4	17
上　海	Shanghai	127.8	30	7912.8	15	12060.8	6
江　苏	Jiangsu	3418.3	3	27121.9	2	23518.0	2
浙　江	Zhejiang	1669.5	14	17312.4	4	15624.4	4
安　徽	Anhui	2178.7	9	9404.0	12	5629.3	15
福　建	Fujian	1776.5	13	10288.6	11	7636.7	13
江　西	Jiangxi	1520.2	16	6967.5	17	4460.8	20
山　东	Shandong	4281.7	1	25735.7	3	19995.8	3
河　南	Henan	3772.3	2	17020.2	5	9017.6	9
湖　北	Hubei	2848.8	8	11190.5	9	8210.9	11
湖　南	Hunan	3004.2	6	10506.4	10	8643.6	10
广　东	Guangdong	2848.9	7	27825.3	1	26393.7	1
广　西	Guangxi	2172.4	10	6333.1	21	4525.6	19
海　南	Hainan	711.5	24	803.7	30	1340.1	28
重　庆	Chongqing	940.0	21	6172.3	22	4346.7	22
四　川	Sichuan	3297.2	4	12587.8	8	7964.8	12
贵　州	Guizhou	890.0	22	2655.4	26	3256.8	25
云　南	Yunnan	1654.6	15	4419.1	23	4236.1	23
西　藏	Tibet	80.4	31	241.7	31	373.5	31
陕　西	Shaanxi	1370.2	19	8075.4	14	5005.6	18
甘　肃	Gansu	780.4	23	2600.6	27	2269.2	27
青　海	Qinghai	176.8	27	1092.0	29	615.8	30
宁　夏	Ningxia	200.2	26	1158.6	28	967.9	29
新　疆	Xinjiang	1320.6	20	3481.6	25	2703.2	26

Continued

第一产业占GDP比重(%) Composition of Primary Industry Product to GDP(%)	位 次 Rank	第二产业占GDP比重(%) Composition of Secondary Industry Product to GDP(%)	位 次 Rank	第三产业占GDP比重(%) Composition of Tertiary Industrial Product to GDP(%)	位 次 Rank
10.1		**45.3**		**44.6**	
0.8	30	22.8	31	76.4	1
1.3	29	51.7	14	47.0	5
12.0	13	52.7	12	35.3	22
5.8	26	57.9	1	36.4	20
9.1	19	56.5	4	34.5	26
8.7	21	53.8	8	37.5	17
11.8	14	53.4	10	34.8	23
15.4	5	47.2	23	37.4	18
0.6	31	39.4	27	60.0	2
6.3	25	50.2	17	43.5	9
4.8	28	50.0	18	45.1	8
12.7	11	54.6	6	32.7	29
9.0	20	52.2	13	38.8	15
11.7	15	53.8	8	34.5	26
8.6	22	51.5	15	40.0	13
12.7	11	57.1	3	30.3	31
12.8	10	50.3	16	36.9	19
13.6	8	47.4	22	39.0	14
5.0	27	48.8	20	46.2	7
16.7	3	48.6	21	34.7	24
24.9	1	28.1	30	46.9	6
8.2	24	53.9	7	37.9	16
13.8	6	52.8	11	33.4	28
13.1	9	39.0	28	47.9	4
16.0	4	42.9	26	41.1	11
11.6	16	34.7	29	53.7	3
9.5	17	55.9	5	34.6	25
13.8	6	46.0	25	40.2	12
9.4	18	57.9	1	32.7	29
8.6	22	49.8	19	41.6	10
17.6	2	46.4	24	36.0	21

续表 2

省市区	Region	人均地区生产总值(元) Per Capita GDP (yuan)	位 次 Rank	总人口(万人) Total Population (10 000 persons)	位 次 Rank
全 国	**China**	**38449**		**135404**	
北 京	Beijing	87091	2	2069	26
天 津	Tianjin	93110	1	1413	27
河 北	Hebei	36584	15	7288	6
山 西	Shanxi	33628	19	3611	18
内蒙古	Inner Mongolia	64319	5	2490	23
辽 宁	Liaoning	56547	7	4389	14
吉 林	Jilin	43412	11	2750	21
黑龙江	Heilongjiang	35711	17	3834	15
上 海	Shanghai	85033	3	2380	24
江 苏	Jiangsu	68347	4	7920	5
浙 江	Zhejiang	63266	6	5477	10
安 徽	Anhui	28792	26	5988	8
福 建	Fujian	52763	9	3748	17
江 西	Jiangxi	28799	25	4504	13
山 东	Shandong	51768	10	9685	2
河 南	Henan	31723	23	9406	3
湖 北	Hubei	38572	13	5779	9
湖 南	Hunan	33480	20	6639	7
广 东	Guangdong	54095	8	10594	1
广 西	Guangxi	27943	27	4682	11
海 南	Hainan	32374	22	887	28
重 庆	Chongqing	39083	12	2945	20
四 川	Sichuan	29579	24	8076	4
贵 州	Guizhou	19566	31	3484	19
云 南	Yunnan	22195	29	4659	12
西 藏	Tibet	22757	28	308	31
陕 西	Shaanxi	38557	14	3753	16
甘 肃	Gansu	21978	30	2578	22
青 海	Qinghai	33023	21	573	30
宁 夏	Ningxia	36166	16	647	29
新 疆	Xinjiang	33796	18	2233	25

Continued

全社会固定资产投资（亿元）Total Investment in Fixed Assets in the Whole Country (100 million yuan)	位 次 Rank	居民消费价格指数 Consumer Price Index	位 次 Rank	城镇居民人均可支配收入(元) Per Capita Annual Disposable Income of Urban households (yuan)	位 次 Rank	城镇居民人均消费性支出(元) Per Capita Annual Living Expenditures for Consumption (yuan)	位 次 Rank
374675.7		**102.6**		**24564.7**		**16674.3**	
6111.7	24	103.3	3	36468.8	2	24045.9	2
7934.8	21	102.7	14	29626.4	6	20024.2	5
19661.3	5	102.6	19	20543.4	19	12531.1	28
8863.3	19	102.5	22	20411.7	21	12211.5	30
11858.2	14	103.1	7	23150.3	10	17717.1	8
21836.3	3	102.8	10	23222.7	9	16593.6	9
9711.4	17	102.5	22	20208.0	23	14613.5	15
9695.4	18	103.2	4	17759.8	29	12983.6	24
5117.6	27	102.8	10	40188.3	1	26253.5	1
30807.7	2	102.6	19	29677.0	5	18825.3	6
17554.4	7	102.2	28	34550.3	3	21545.2	4
15384.3	10	102.3	27	21024.2	15	15011.7	14
12423.1	12	102.4	26	28055.2	7	18593.2	7
11784.7	15	102.7	14	19860.4	24	12775.7	26
31256.0	1	102.1	29	25755.2	8	15778.2	11
21761.5	4	102.5	22	20442.6	20	13733.0	23
15591.8	9	102.9	9	20839.6	17	14496.0	17
14523.2	11	102.0	30	21318.8	12	14609.0	16
18749.4	6	102.8	10	30226.7	4	22396.4	3
9808.6	16	103.2	4	21242.8	13	14244.0	19
2126.3	28	103.2	4	20917.7	16	14456.6	18
8732.3	20	102.6	19	22968.1	11	16573.1	10
17036.5	8	102.5	22	20307.0	22	15049.5	13
5517.8	25	102.7	14	18700.5	26	12585.7	27
7831.1	22	102.7	14	21074.5	14	13883.9	22
670.5	31	103.5	2	18028.3	27	11184.3	31
12044.5	13	102.8	10	20733.9	18	15332.8	12
5145.5	26	102.7	14	17156.9	31	12847.1	25
1848.4	30	103.1	7	17566.3	30	12346.3	29
2096.9	29	102.0	30	19831.4	25	14067.2	20
6258.4	23	103.8	1	17920.7	28	13891.7	21

续表 3

省市区	Region	农民人均纯收入(元) Annual Per Capita Disposable Income of Rural Households (yuan)	位次 Rank	农民人均现金收入(元) Annual Per Capita Cash Income of Rural Households (yuan)	位次 Rank	农民人均生活消费支出(元) Annual Per Capita Living Expenditure of Rural Households (yuan)	位次 Rank
全　国	**China**	**7916.6**		**9787.2**		**5908.0**	
北　京	Beijing	16475.7	2	18902.1	1	11878.9	2
天　津	Tianjin	14025.5	4	17609.1	4	8336.5	5
河　北	Hebei	8081.4	12	10226.3	14	5364.1	18
山　西	Shanxi	6356.6	23	7066.3	26	5566.2	15
内蒙古	Inner Mongolia	7611.3	15	11064.5	13	6382.0	9
辽　宁	Liaoning	9383.7	9	14171.2	6	5998.4	11
吉　林	Jilin	8598.2	11	12675.0	9	6186.2	10
黑龙江	Heilongjiang	8603.8	10	13397.3	7	5718.0	14
上　海	Shanghai	17803.7	1	18868.0	2	11971.5	1
江　苏	Jiangsu	12202.0	5	14523.9	5	9138.2	4
浙　江	Zhejiang	14551.9	3	18381.8	3	10652.7	3
安　徽	Anhui	7160.5	20	8505.1	19	5556.0	16
福　建	Fujian	9967.2	7	11374.4	12	7401.9	7
江　西	Jiangxi	7829.4	14	8797.2	17	5129.5	22
山　东	Shandong	9446.5	8	12758.1	8	6776.0	8
河　南	Henan	7524.9	16	8444.6	20	5032.1	24
湖　北	Hubei	7851.7	13	9337.0	16	5726.7	13
湖　南	Hunan	7440.2	17	8726.9	18	5870.1	12
广　东	Guangdong	10542.8	6	11777.2	11	7458.6	6
广　西	Guangxi	6007.5	25	7380.5	24	4933.6	26
海　南	Hainan	7408.0	18	9337.1	15	4776.3	27
重　庆	Chongqing	7383.3	19	8122.4	22	5018.6	25
四　川	Sichuan	7001.4	21	8090.6	23	5366.7	17
贵　州	Guizhou	4753.0	30	5078.3	31	3901.7	30
云　南	Yunnan	5416.5	28	6693.1	27	4561.3	28
西　藏	Tibet	5719.4	27	5395.3	30	2967.6	31
陕　西	Shaanxi	5762.5	26	7209.0	25	5114.7	23
甘　肃	Gansu	4506.7	31	5668.4	29	4146.2	29
青　海	Qinghai	5364.4	29	6154.9	28	5338.9	20
宁　夏	Ningxia	6180.3	24	8247.0	21	5351.4	19
新　疆	Xinjiang	6393.7	22	12596.1	10	5245.3	21

注：现金收支为不含储蓄借贷后的现金收支。

Continued

农林牧渔业总产值(亿元) Gross Output Value of Farming, Forestry, Animal Husbandry and Fishery (100 million yuan)	位次 Rank	农林牧渔业总产值比上年增长(%) Output Value Increase Rate in 2011 over 2010 of Farming,Forestry, Animal Husbandry and Fishery(%)	位次 Rank	粮食产量(万吨) Grain (10 000 tons)	位次 Rank	棉花产量(万吨) Cotton (10 000 tons)	位次 Rank	油料产量(万吨) Oil bearing Crops (10 000 tons)	位次 Rank
89453.0		**4.9**		**58958.0**		**683.6**		**3436.8**	
395.7	26	2.9	29	113.8	29			1.3	30
375.6	28	3.2	27	161.8	27	5.8	12	0.6	31
5340.1	5	4.0	24	3246.6	8	56.4	3	142.8	9
1304.3	24	5.6	12	1274.1	17	4.7	13	19.6	25
2449.3	17	5.7	10	2528.5	10	0.2	19	145.1	8
4062.4	9	4.9	17	2070.5	13	0.1	21	120.9	10
2502.0	16	5.9	9	3343.0	5	0.8	16	80.7	14
3952.3	10	6.7	4	5761.5	1			22.5	24
321.7	29	0.5	31	122.4	28	0.4	17	1.7	29
5808.8	3	4.8	18	3372.5	4	22.0	8	146.9	7
2658.7	15	1.8	30	769.8	23	3.0	14	38.3	21
3728.3	11	5.6	12	3289.1	7	29.4	5	227.7	5
3007.4	13	4.3	23	659.3	24			28.1	23
2399.3	18	4.6	19	2084.8	12	15.2	9	117.1	11
7945.8	1	4.5	20	4511.4	3	69.8	2	351.0	2
6679.0	2	4.5	20	5638.6	2	25.7	6	569.5	1
4732.1	7	5.6	12	2441.8	11	54.5	4	319.7	3
4904.1	6	3.0	28	3006.5	9	25.1	7	207.8	6
4656.8	8	3.7	25	1396.3	16			96.6	12
3490.7	12	5.7	10	1484.9	15	0.2	18	54.5	19
1082.1	25	6.3	6	199.5	26			10.4	27
1402.0	22	5.1	16	1138.5	20			50.1	20
5433.1	4	4.5	20	3315.0	6	1.3	15	287.8	4
1436.6	21	9.3	1	1079.5	22	0.1	20	87.4	13
2680.2	14	7.0	3	1749.1	14			62.8	16
118.3	31	3.6	26	94.9	31			6.3	28
2303.2	19	6.0	7	1245.1	19	6.7	11	60.3	17
1358.2	23	6.4	5	1109.7	21	8.1	10	67.0	15
263.9	30	5.4	15	101.5	30			35.2	22
385.1	27	6.0	7	375.0	25			18.0	26
2275.7	20	7.4	2	1259.8	18	354.0	1	59.0	18

Note: The cash income and expenditure refer to the one abscent of deposit loan.

续表 4

省市区	Region	工业增加值(亿元) Value-added of Industry (100 million yuan)	位次 Rank	天然气(亿立方米) Natural Gas (100 million cu. m)	位次 Rank	原油(万吨) Crude Oil (10 000 tons)	位次 Rank
全国	**China**	**199859.6**		**1072.2**		**20747.8**	
北京	Beijing	3294.3	24				
天津	Tianjin	6122.9	17	18.7	8	3098.3	3
河北	Hebei	12511.6	6	13.4	9	584.0	9
山西	Shanxi	6302.7	16				
内蒙古	Inner Mongolia	7966.6	13				
辽宁	Liaoning	11712.7	7	7.2	10	1000.0	7
吉林	Jilin	5582.5	20	22.2	7	810.4	8
黑龙江	Heilongjiang	5659.3	19	33.7	6	4001.5	1
上海	Shanghai	7159.4	14	2.9	13	5.3	17
江苏	Jiangsu	23908.4	2	0.6	17	194.5	12
浙江	Zhejiang	15336.3	5				
安徽	Anhui	8025.8	12				
福建	Fujian	8644.2	11				
江西	Jiangxi	5854.6	18				
山东	Shandong	22798.3	3	6.0	11	2774.7	4
河南	Henan	15357.4	4	5.0	12	476.6	10
湖北	Hubei	9735.2	9	1.7	15	78.9	13
湖南	Hunan	9140.0	10				
广东	Guangdong	25937.2	1	83.5	4	1209.3	6
广西	Guangxi	5364.9	21			2.3	18
海南	Hainan	521.2	30	1.8	14	19.0	15
重庆	Chongqing	5181.0	22	0.4	18		
四川	Sichuan	10800.5	8	242.1	3	17.5	16
贵州	Guizhou	2196.1	26				
云南	Yunnan	3450.7	23				
西藏	Tibet	55.1	31				
陕西	Shaanxi	6847.4	15	311.3	1	3527.6	2
甘肃	Gansu	2074.2	27	0.2	19	69.9	14
青海	Qinghai	895.9	28	63.5	5	205.0	11
宁夏	Ningxia	878.6	29	1.5	16	2.3	18
新疆	Xinjiang	2850.1	25	253.0	2	2670.7	5

Continued

社会消费品零售总额(亿元) Total Retail Sales of Consumer Goods (100 million yuan)	位次 Rank	社会消费品零售总额比上年增长(%) Increase Rate in 2011over 2010 of Total Retail Sales of Consumer Goods(%)	位次 Rank	进出口总额(亿美元) Total Value of Imports and Exports (USD 100 million)	位次 Rank	#出口总额(亿美元) Total Exports (USD 100 million)	位次 Rank
210307.0		**14.3**		**38667.6**		**20489.3**	
7702.8	11	11.6	30	4079.2	4	596.5	7
3921.4	23	15.5	15	1156.2	8	483.1	9
9254.0	9	15.2	20	505.5	13	296.0	13
4506.8	19	15.5	15	150.4	23	70.2	23
4572.5	17	14.6	26	112.6	26	39.7	26
9346.6	7	15.5	15	1039.9	9	579.5	8
4772.9	16	15.9	4	245.7	20	59.8	24
5491.0	15	15.6	10	378.2	15	144.4	19
7412.3	12	8.8	31	4365.4	3	2067.4	4
18331.3	3	14.7	24	5480.9	2	3285.4	2
13588.3	4	13.0	28	3122.3	5	2245.7	3
5736.6	14	15.8	5	393.3	14	267.5	14
7256.5	13	15.6	10	1559.3	7	978.4	6
4027.2	22	15.6	10	334.1	16	251.1	15
19651.9	2	14.6	26	2455.4	6	1287.3	5
10915.6	5	15.5	15	517.5	12	296.8	12
9562.5	6	15.6	10	319.6	17	194.0	16
7921.9	10	15.1	22	219.4	21	126.0	20
22677.1	1	11.7	29	9838.2	1	5741.4	1
4516.6	18	15.6	10	294.7	18	154.7	18
870.8	28	14.7	24	143.3	25	31.4	29
4033.7	21	15.7	7	532.0	11	385.7	10
9268.6	8	15.2	20	591.3	10	384.6	11
2027.6	25	15.8	5	66.3	28	49.5	25
3511.6	24	17.1	1	210.0	22	100.2	21
254.6	31	16.3	2	34.2	29	33.6	28
4383.8	20	15.7	7	148.0	24	86.5	22
1906.5	26	15.7	7	89.0	27	35.7	27
476.0	30	16.0	3	11.6	31	7.3	31
548.8	29	14.9	23	22.2	30	16.4	30
1799.0	27	15.5	15	251.7	19	193.5	17

续表 5 Continued

省市区	Region	入境旅游人数(万人) Total Number of Overseas Visitor Arrivals (10 000 persons)	位次 Rank	#外国人 Foreigners	位次 Rank	旅游外汇收入(亿美元) Earnings from International Tourism (USD 100 million)	位次 Rank
全　国	**China**	**13240.5**		**2719.2**		**500.30**	
北　京	Beijing	500.9	5	434.4	5	51.49	5
天　津	Tianjin	73.7	26	63.7	24	22.26	9
河　北	Hebei	129.3	23	106.7	21	5.45	23
山　西	Shanxi	189.2	19	120.4	19	7.20	20
内蒙古	Inner Mongolia	159.2	20	151.5	16	7.72	19
辽　宁	Liaoning	473.1	7	388.6	6	32.64	7
吉　林	Jilin	118.3	24	100.9	22	4.95	24
黑龙江	Heilongjiang	207.6	17	194.7	10	8.35	17
上　海	Shanghai	651.2	4	539.6	4	54.93	3
江　苏	Jiangsu	791.5	3	575.2	2	63.00	2
浙　江	Zhejiang	865.9	2	570.5	3	51.52	4
安　徽	Anhui	331.5	12	190.4	13	15.63	12
福　建	Fujian	493.7	6	167.0	14	42.26	6
江　西	Jiangxi	156.2	21	50.4	26	4.85	25
山　东	Shandong	469.9	8	342.2	7	29.24	8
河　南	Henan	190.8	18	118.7	20	6.11	21
湖　北	Hubei	264.7	13	193.0	11	12.03	14
湖　南	Hunan	224.6	15	90.6	23	9.28	16
广　东	Guangdong	3489.4	1	773.0	1	156.11	1
广　西	Guangxi	350.3	10	192.7	12	12.79	13
海　南	Hainan	81.6	25	52.0	25	3.48	26
重　庆	Chongqing	224.3	16	152.6	15	11.68	15
四　川	Sichuan	227.3	14	151.3	17	7.98	18
贵　州	Guizhou	70.5	27	30.4	27	1.69	27
云　南	Yunnan	457.8	9	329.8	8	19.47	10
西　藏	Tibet	19.5	28	17.5	28	1.06	28
陕　西	Shaanxi	335.2	11	233.7	9	15.97	11
甘　肃	Gansu	10.2	29	6.7	29	0.22	30
青　海	Qinghai	4.7	30	3.8	30	0.24	29
宁　夏	Ningxia	1.9	31	1.4	31	0.05	31
新　疆	Xinjiang	149.8	22	136.3	18	5.51	22

《新疆统计年鉴——2013》特邀编委

（排名不分先后）

新疆维吾尔自治区林业厅

中共中央政治局委员、自治区党委书记张春贤书记参加义务植树

自治区党委副书记、自治区主席努尔·白克力主席参加义务植树

自治区林业厅厅长艾则孜·克尤木调研林业工作

2012年，在自治区党委、人民政府正确领导下，在国家林业局大力支持下，新疆林业各项工作取得可喜成绩。全区完成造林264万亩，其中人工造林179万亩，封育85万亩。义务植树1.3亿株，育苗9.1亿株。特色林果总面积突破2000万亩，各种果树有效株数13亿株，产量700万吨，产值350多亿元。全区农民人均来自林果业收入达到1000多元，林果业收入占全区农民人均收入20%以上，林果业主产区达40%以上，发展好的县市达70%以上，全区农民人均林果业增收190元，超额完成自治区党委提出的全区农民林果业人均增收180元目标。新增3个“全国生态文化村”，温泉县、裕民县、泽普县、博湖县、哈巴河县获批全国生态文明示范工程试点县市。积极配合中央电视台在《新闻直播间》现场直播“中国首次向外国提供野马种源，四匹野马赴蒙古国安家”专题片。切实履行“严管林”职责，逐级签订森林资源管理目标责任状，森林资源得到有效保护。集体林权制度改革主体改革任务基本完成。全面启动国有林场体制改革工作，39个天保工程区国有林场改为全额预算管理事业单位。国有林区棚户区改造工程19个项目全部开工，落实投资1818万元，建成585户。国有林场危旧房2540户改造任务全部开工建设，落实投资2.2亿元，完工1619户，入住712户。启动第二批185个乡镇林业站建设，投资5550万元。落实国有林场危旧房改造基础设施配套资金3146万元和扶贫资金1100万元，配备管护所站卫星接收设备4679套。全区120个森林公安派出所有104个完成主体建设。退耕还林工程到位补助资金5.2亿元，下拨原补助政策资金7633万元，完善政策补助资金2.27亿元。林业厅机关连续16年被评为自治区级精神文明单位。

2013年，新疆林业将以建设生态文明为总要求，以改善生态兴林富民为总任务，全力推进林业三大体系建设，大力实施林业十大生态工程，为建设生态文明和大美新疆作出新的更大贡献。一是加强生态保护和修复，大力实施林业十大生态工程，完成250万亩造林任务。二是继续推进特色林果业提质增效和市场开拓向纵深发展，大力发展种苗花卉产业，加快发展天保后续产业、沙产业和森林旅游业。三是以现代文化为引领，牢固树立尊重自然、顺应自然、保护自然的生态文明理念，营造爱护生态环境的良好氛围。四是继续实施“民生建设年”活动，大力实施民生工程，使林业改革发展成果更多地惠及于民。五是深化林业改革，扎实推进集体林权制度改革，进一步深化国有林场和国有林区体制改革，不断增强林业发展活力。六是改进工作作风，密切联系群众，深入调查研究，用求真务实的精神推动林业科学发展。

新疆河谷林保护

轮台县大力发展小白杏产业。图为农民正在凉晒小白杏。

农村防护林建设成效

铺设沙障

石河子市国家森林城市

2011 年 7 月 4 日，国家林业局、新疆维吾尔自治区人民政府在乌鲁木齐签订加快新疆林业发展合作共建框架协议

新疆野生动物保护宣传月暨爱鸟周启动仪式

新疆特色林果产品广州交易会开幕式

林业系统建党 90 周年文艺汇演

新疆维吾尔自治区信息中心
新疆维吾尔自治区电子政务外网管理中心

自治区信息中心成立于1988年，是隶属于自治区发展和改革委员会管理的副厅级事业单位，核定事业编制85名，专业技术人员占75%，其中高级、中级专业技术人才占50%以上。其主要职责是承担全区经济信息资源开发利用的规划和管理，为自治区党委、人民政府及经济综合管理部门宏观经济决策提供信息服务；承担全区电子政务外网规划、建设、运行、维护及相关管理工作；为党政机关、事业单位提供信息化技术支持与服务。

近年来，在自治区党委、人民政府和自治区发改委党组的正确领导下，我中心紧紧围绕"一个中心、两大任务、三大建设"的工作部署，按照以电子政务外网建设为主线，以实现信息化建设和信息服务两翼齐飞为目标，创新思路，加强管理，改进方法，提高效能，不断提升服务水平和服务质量，各项工作取得积极进展。2010年-2012年先后获得"自治区级文明单位"、"巾帼文明岗"、"自治区级青年文明号"、"自治区级模范职工之家"等荣誉称号。

在自治区党委和自治区人民政府的高度重视和正确领导下，自治区电子政务外网一期建设项目于2009年正式启动，经过多方积极共同努力，我区政务外网建设和应用工作取得突破性进展，建成了上联国家、下联近100个地县、横联近90个区级政务部门和单位的纵横向网络，初步具备承载各政务部门纵向业务应用系统和横向部门间信息交换、共享与业务协同的能力，为实现满足各级政务部门社会管理和公共服务的需要，促进政府监管能力和服务水平的提高的应用目标奠定了良好的基础。我区电子政务外网建设和应用工作得到了国家的积极肯定，作为抓落实、抓管理后发赶超的典型省区在国家会议上做指定发言，并于2010-2012年连续三年获国家电子政务外网管理中心的通报表彰。

我中心在今后的发展中，将紧紧围绕自治区党委、人民政府和发改委的中心工作，积极贯彻落实"十八大"精神，按照《新疆维吾尔自治区电子政务外网"十二五"发展规划》确定的目标，开拓创新，狠抓落实，努力践行新疆效率，为推动新疆跨越式发展和长治久安做出更大的贡献。

自治区信息中心主任、自治区电子政务外网管理中心主任　赵若平

国家信息中心、国家电子政务外网管理中心副主任沈大风一行莅临布尔津县检查指导工作

国家电子政务外网网络与安全技术研讨会在布尔津隆重召开

自治区电子政务外网应用系统视频会议调度平台建设项目验收会

新疆维吾尔自治区奶业办公室

奶业办公室召开 2013 年度党风廉政建设和党建工作会议。会议由书记向天江主持，主任齐新林在大会做重要讲话。

奶业办公室主任齐新林赴南昌参加中国奶业大会

奶业办公室主任齐新林与参加奶业大会的内地相关单位共商合作事宜

新疆维吾尔自治区奶业办公室成立于 1994 年，位于乌鲁木齐市南湖西路北一巷 25 号，是隶属于自治区畜牧厅的县处级事业单位。现有五块牌子，一是自治区奶业办公室，二是自治区学生饮用奶计划协调办公室，三是自治区乳品质量监测中心（科级），四是自治区奶业协会，五是自治区奶牛生产性能测定中心，编制 19 名，领导职数 3 名，实有人员 27 人。

根据国家《乳品质量安全监督管理条例》和《新疆维吾尔自治区奶业条例》，我办承担自治区奶业行业管理、指导、协调、监督和服务工作；具体负责奶业生产和市场调查研究，为自治区党委、政府和主管部门提供制定奶业发展的政策依据；负责对生鲜乳生产、收购、运输等环节的质量安全监管；负责协调“学生饮用奶计划”推广工作，组织评定学生饮用奶奶源基地，会同有关部门对学生饮用奶产品质量安全实施监管监测；建立奶业信息系统，开展奶业统计、奶价监测、生鲜乳质量安全第三方监测工作；承担全疆奶牛生产性能测定工作；组织开展奶业新技术推广、技术咨询、科普宣传，行业宣传，开展国（区）内外奶业界科技交流与经济技术合作。

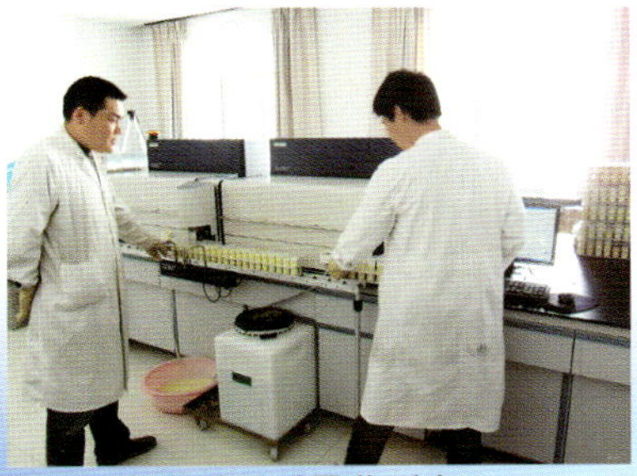

新疆乳品质量监测中心

奶业办公室 2013 年 5 月正式成立学雷锋志愿服务队

奶业办公室办公楼全貌

八师石河子市

争当兵团"三化"建设的排头兵、领头羊

兵团党委常委、副政委、八师石河子市党委书记、八师政委卢晓峰(图右)在团场调研

八师党委副书记、师长、石河子市市长徐志新(右二)在天山铝业视察

中央新疆工作座谈会以来，八师石河子市党委按照中央"三化"要求，以提高经济增长质量和效益为中心，不断转变经济发展方式、推动科学跨越发展，经济社会保持了平稳健康发展。2010年至2012年，师市生产总值由188.51亿元增加到276.12亿元，年均增长15.7%，三次产业结构为25.5∶42.1∶32.4。

在城镇化建设上，师市坚持高起点规划，高标准建设，编制了石河子市未来20年城市总体规划。按照"北进南扩"思路，启动北疆铁路石河子段以南75平方公里的南山新区建设。城市发展空间有效拓展，综合功能进一步完善，建设品位明显提升，承载能力和辐射带动作用明显增强。

在新型工业化建设中，师市注重加快新兴产业的培育、升级，在继续保持氯碱化工产业优势的基础上，积极发展现代煤化工产业、新材料产业，装备制造业和农副产品精深加工等产业，推动初级产品向高精端延伸，不断提高产品附加值。工业对经济增长的贡献率达到41.4%。

在农业现代化建设中，师市按照"稳粮、优棉、增果、兴牧、大力发展农产品加工"要求，围绕龙头企业和市场需求，优化农业结构，提高综合效益。2012年，籽棉平均单产突破400公斤，国家公检率达到100%。同时，师市依托龙头企业，稳步推进酿酒葡萄种植和生猪、奶牛标准化规模化养殖基地建设，畜牧业、林果业占农业经济总量的比重逐年提高。

八师石河子市农业机械化率达到93%，农业现代化全国领先

八师石河子市纺锭规模已达250万锭，荣获"中国绵织名城"称号

近年来，八师石河子市新型工业化发展迅猛，工业对经济增长的贡献率达到 41.4%。图为天业工业园一角。

八师石河子市加大民生建设投入力度，近三年来，民生方面的资金投入占到一般预算支出的 70%以上。图为石河子总场明珠花园社区。

新疆大学
XINJIANG UNIVERSITY

只有努力才能改变　只要努力就能改变

校党委书记李中耀、校长塔西甫拉提·特依拜为新疆大学文化讲堂揭牌

清华大学等 10 所高校对口支援新疆大学 2011 年度工作会议举行

新疆大学辩论队在第十届海峡两岸大学生辩论赛中获得佳绩

新疆大学是全国重点综合性大学，是国家“211 工程”建设高校、国家教育部与新疆维吾尔自治区人民政府共建高校，在新疆高等教育发展中发挥着龙头和示范作用。在近 90 年的发展历程中，新疆大学扎根边疆、艰苦创业、服务边疆，积淀形成了“爱国爱疆、团结进步”的新大精神，特别是近两年来，在自治区党委“只有努力才能改变，只要努力就能改变”的理念指导下，新疆大学领导班子勇于担当，创新求变，凝聚建设发展力量，学校各项事业呈现良好发展势头。

抓实思想政治工作，筑牢学校发展基础。一是理顺“大思政”工作格局，明确由一名副书记、一名副校长共同分管思政和校园稳定工作，这在自治区高校中尚属首例。二是坚持以现代文化占领思想教育高地。2011 年，举办“新疆大学文化讲堂”，获得教育部校园文化建设优秀奖。三是实施班主任和辅导员队伍“细胞工程”建设。自 2011 年起，设立优秀辅导员、班主任专项奖励基金；在推免研究生名额中划拨单独名额，用于从本科学生干部中选聘辅导员。2012 年，被五部委授予“热爱伟大祖国 建设美好家园”主题教育活动先进单位荣誉称号。

抓实教育教学工作，全面提高办学质量。一是加强高水平师资队伍建设。2011 年，信息与工程学院吾守尔·斯拉木当选中国工程院院士。刘浪获第八届“中国青年女科学家奖”。2012 年，选聘教育部“长江学者”特聘教授 1 名，实现零突破。二是推进本科生教育教学改革，创新人才培养模式。2012 年，6 项共 42 人次获省部级一等奖以上奖励。2012 年，获批 2 门国家级精品视频公开课程，1 名教师在全国高校青年教师课堂教学竞赛中获二等奖。获批 2 个教育部本科专业综合改革项目。入选全国首批卓越法律人才教育基地。三是推进学科学位点建设。18 个自治区重点学科有序发展。2011 年，一级学科博士点实现零的突破达到 8 个，二级学科博士点达到 47 个。

抓实科研创新工作，提升学校综合实力。一是提升协同创新能力。获批 2 个自治区级协同创新中心，获批 1 个教育部创新团队。科研项目经费连续两年破亿元，2012 年达到 1.5 亿元。二是深化校地校企合作。已与和田等多个地方政府签署合作协议，与新疆有色集团等区内外大型知名企业及中国科学院等科研院所的合作有序推进。与地方合作组建“新疆大学信息技术创新园”，入驻企业达 34 家。

当前，新疆大学正以“中西部高校基础能力建设工程”和“中西部高校综合实力提升工程”建设为契机，全力推进西部先进、中亚一流、国际知名的高水平大学建设。

新疆大学召开质量建设年总结暨 2011 年度吴泰青年教师优秀教学奖颁奖大会

水韵森林之城—阿克苏市

地委委员、市委书记　高国飞

市长库尔班·吐逊

阿克苏市是阿克苏地区政治、经济、文化中心，及兵团第一师师部所在地。位于塔里木河上游，因水得名，维吾尔语意为“白水城”，古为秦汉之际西域三十六国的姑墨、温宿两国属地，是古丝绸之路上的重要驿站，也是龟兹文化和多浪文化的发源地，素有“塞外江南”之美誉。阿克苏市总面积2.33万平方公里，建城区面积42平方公里。市辖4乡2镇1场、6个街道办事处，总人口62.8万人，由维吾尔、汉、回、哈萨克等30个民族组成。近年来，阿克苏市先后荣获“国家森林城市”、“全国园林绿化先进城市”、“中国优秀旅游城市”、“国家卫生城市”、“中国人居最佳环境范例城市”、“全国双拥模范城” 五连冠、“全国科技进步先进市”、“中国西部大开发新疆十座投资环境最佳城市”、“中国民营经济最佳投资县(市)”、“绿动·2011中国经济十大领军城市”、“中国十大边疆重镇”、“阿克苏多浪河国家湿地公园”、“中国西部百强县市” “中国红富士苹果之乡”、“国家级优质商品棉基地”和“自治区文明城市”七连冠等荣誉称号。

2012年，阿克苏市实现地区生产总值124亿元，比上年增长20.5%；三次产业比重优化为13.41:30.66:55.93；地方财政一般预算收入完成12.61亿元，增长53%；完成固定资产投资95.3亿元，增长53%；社会消费品零售总额48.1亿元，增长18.8%；镇居民人均可支配收入达到18850元，增长15%；农牧民人均纯收入达到10142元，增收1633元，增长19.2%。全年实现工业增加值25.2亿元，增长36.8%。荣获“中国最具区域带动力中小城市百强县（市）”、“中国十佳最具投资潜力文化旅游目的地城市”称号，位列“中国最具投资潜力中小城市百强县(市)”第75位。阿克苏市已步入了历史发展最好最快的时期。

多浪河二期景观带

核桃

红枣

苹果

葡萄

香梨

吉木萨尔县

县委书记彭国春慰问残疾人

县委副书记、县长王燕到工业园区调研

县委、县人民政府签约经济项目

中央新疆工作座谈会以来，吉木萨尔县委通过第十一次党代会，确定了今后五年实现“三大核心目标”和“四大突破”的总体奋斗目标。围绕这一总体目标，2012 年全县实现地区生产总值 48.5 亿元，比 2010 年增长 57%，一二三产比重由 37：36：27 到 31：45：24，二产超过一产成为主导产业，三产新产业不断增加；全社会固定资产投资 185 亿元，比 2010 年增长 6.7 倍；地方公共财政预算收入 6.98 亿元，比 2010 年增长 1.4 倍（每年净增 2 亿多元）；社会消费品零售总额 8.45 亿元，比 2010 年增长 35.9%；农民人均纯收入 10855 元，比 2010 年增加 2993 元。经济社会发展呈现出：一个突破，农民人均纯收入突破万元。四个领先，全社会固定资产投资总额，地区生产总值、工业增加值、地方公共财政预算收入增速在昌吉州领先。

新型工业化取得新成绩。以新型工业化为第一推动力，全年完成工业总产值 71.04 亿元，工业增加值 21.03 亿元，比 2010 年增长 1.5 倍。准东五彩湾希望、神东电力、西部建设等一批重点项目相继建成或投产。成大宝明页岩油、“吉七井”区域勘探开发等加快推进。北庭工业园创建为自治区级工业园，完成基础设施建设投入 1.23 亿元。

城镇化迈上新台阶。以新区开发建设为主、老城改造提升为辅，全年投入城市建设资金 20.78 亿元，比 2010 年增长 2.1 倍。启动新区成大宝明、宜化等 4 家企业生活基地建设。大奇高速公路、吉北大道等一批重点工程如期完工。完成土地征收 3700 亩，公益性征收 111 户。完成安居富民 2852 户，定居兴牧 100 户。北庭故城遗址列入联合国跨国申遗“丝绸之路”中国段首批名单。

农业现代化实现新突破。以“六篇文章”为重点，2012 年，地方公共财政投入农业农村资金 1.73 亿元，比 2010 年增长 3. 2 倍。创新水利投融资体系，启动水溪沟水库、新地乡红土崖子水库建设。东大龙口、西大龙口水库通过验收。定居兴牧水源工程二工河水库下闸蓄水。农村劳动力转移 2.54 万人次，比 2010 年增长 52.1%；农民人均收入中外出务工收入占增收比重 29%，比 2010 年增长 8.9%。牲畜出栏 88.92 万头只，比 2010 年增长 22.07%，农民人均入中畜牧业收入占增收比重达到 34%。

群众幸福指数实现新提高。全年地方公共财政用于民生的支出 10.6 亿元，比 2010 年增长 2.7 倍。完成廉租房 70 套，公租房 115 套，棚户区改造 720 户。3 个自治区级、13 个县级扶贫村投入帮扶资金 140.43 万元，受益群众 1350 人。争创“自治区优秀平安县”取得阶段性成效。投资 420 万元，建成大有镇无线地面数字电视发射台，覆盖山区农民 3.5 万人。

2013 年，县委、县人民政府站在更高的起点上，以学习宣传贯彻十八大精神为主线，以科学发展观为指导，以幸福社区、欢乐广场、美丽乡村、绿色园区为载体，紧紧围绕“三大核心目标”和“四大突破”，坚定不移地推进新型工业化、信息化、城镇化和农业现代化融合协调发展，为率先在昌吉州建成小康社会夯实基础。预期目标是：地区生产总值 66 亿元，同比增长 30%；全社会固定资产投资 251 亿元，同比增长 35%；地方公共财政预算收入 9.42 亿元，同比增长 35%；社会消费品零售总额 9.9 亿元，同比增长 17%；农民人均纯收入 12485 元，增加 1600 元以上。

阿克苏地区发展和改革委员会

地区发改委主任周春阳在拜城县实地查看文冠果种植情况

地区发展和改革委员会是综合研究制订地区经济和社会发展战略、规划和政策，进行总量平衡、结构调整，指导地区经济体制改革，主管重点项目和固定资产投资的宏观调控部门。

近年来，地区发展和改革委员会按照地委、行署的要求，以科学发展观统领各项工作，上下一心，积极进取，扎实工作，在研究制定地区国民经济和社会发展规划，努力扩大固定资产投资规模，积极推进经济结构战略性调整，促进经济社会协调快速发展，以及开展重大课题调查研究，发挥参谋助手作用等方面做了大量卓有成效的工作，特别是在重大项目建设、项目招商引资、争取自治区项目和国家补助投资等方面，取得了突出的成绩，促使一大批关系地区长远发展的重大基础设施建设和基础产业项目相继建成或开工建设，极大增强了地区国民经济和社会发展的后劲。制度建设、作风建设、廉政建设和干部队伍建设有了长足的进步，各项工作得到了自治区发改委和地委、行署的肯定，树立了发展改革部门的权威。2005 年 -2012 年连续八年评为国民经济和社会发展先进单位，连续多年评为社会管理综合治理优秀单位、自治区级精神文明单位，先后荣获国家收费工作先进集体、自治区发改系统先进集体、自治区价格监测先进单位、地区政府系统政务信息先进集体、实施环境保护目标责任书先进单位、人口与计划生育目标责任优秀单位。

地区发改委党组书记卡米力·赛买提、纪检组长侯冠东、地区价格认定局局长陈光荣慰问共建单位阿克苏地区军分区弹药库

地区发改委主任周春阳 、党组书记卡米力·赛买提扶贫慰问

地区发改委《勇立潮头发改人》一书首发仪式

塞外江南 伊宁市

伊犁州党委常委、伊宁市委书记李宁平参加冰雪运动会

伊宁市委常委、市长阿不都沙拉木·沙德克在农村调研

伊宁市是伊犁州的首府城市，是伊犁河谷的政治、经济、文化、交通中心。最早建城于清朝乾隆年间(1762年)，1952年5月23日经国务院批准设市，是新疆解放后最早设市的三个城市之一。全市总面积755平方公里，其中建成区面积37平方公里，现辖11个乡镇(场)、8个街道，有驻市系统单位100多家。全市有37个民族、52万人口，其中世居民族13个，维吾尔族占49.4%，是一个多民族聚居城市。伊宁市气候宜人，水源充足，生态优势和自然优势独特，素有"花城"、"苹果城"、"白杨城"等诸多美誉。2010年被南方人物周刊评选为中国十座宜居中小城市之一，并先后荣获"中国优秀旅游城市"、"国家园林城市"的称号。

伊宁市是东西陆路交通的要冲，地缘优势突出，对外开放的条件优越，距霍尔果斯口岸88公里，距中亚重镇哈萨克斯坦最大城市阿拉木图460公里，具备完整的公路、铁路、民航三位一体的立体交通体系，是新亚欧大陆桥西部桥头堡和连接中亚的重要枢纽，是新疆和全国向西开放的重要门户。早在汉代，就已形成了一条古丝绸通道，不仅沟通中亚各地和西亚，也有许多支线联接南亚和欧洲各地，历史上的伊宁是中国西部的一个繁华商埠。1989年元月，伊宁市被国务院定为开放城市，1992年又被确定为沿边进一步开放城市，并在市区内设立国家级边境经济合作区。2010年5月，国家设立霍尔果斯经济开发区，伊宁市35平方公里被划入霍尔果斯经济开发区，成为"一区三园"中重要的一园——伊宁产业配套园区。

近年来，特别是自治区第八次党代会以来，伊宁市按照建设"天山北坡西部中心城市、对外开放门户城市和区域中心城市"要求，进一步发挥区位优势、比较优势和后发优势，加快推进新型工业化、新型城镇化、现代服务业和现代农牧业进程，以"伊犁河两岸"为重点的"一带、三心、六区"开发建设已拉开序幕，35平方公里经济开发区建设已经进入开发建设阶段，庆华、国投、科伦等一批大企业大项目已落地建设，伊宁市已经进入了新型工业化、新型城镇化和农业现代化的"三化建设"加速推进的新时期。

伊宁市苏拉宫工业园区

即将投入生产的川宁药业抗生素项目

根据自治区、自治州和“十二五”发展的战略部署，伊宁市今后一个时期发展战略和奋斗目标是：以科学发展为主题，以转变经济发展方式为主线，以增加城乡居民收入和财政收入为核心，以改善民生为出发点和落脚点，坚持“资源开发可持续、生态环境可持续”的原则，大力实施文化立市、城建强市、产业富市、科教兴市战略，加快推进新型工业化、新型城镇化、现代服务业和现代农牧业进程，进一步统筹经济社会、城乡、区域、人与自然协调发展，努力打造天山北坡西部的重要增长极、中心城市和向西开放的桥头堡，把伊宁市建设成为充满生机的活力城市、民富市强的实力城市、环境优美的生态城市、安居乐业的幸福城市、团结稳定的和谐城市。到 2015 年地区生产总值达到 225 亿元，年均增长 16.8%，人均生产总值达到 38800 元，在河谷率先超过全国平均水平；财政一般预算收入达到 24 亿元，年均增长 20.3%；城镇居民人均可支配收入达到 2.5 万元以上，农牧民人均纯收入达到 1.3 万元，城镇居民收入和基本公共服务能力超过西部平均水平。

伊宁市城市道路

新疆友好集团伊犁天百国际购物中心

伊宁市达达木图乡富民安居项目

呼图壁县

“呼图壁”一词源于蒙语，寓意为吉祥如意的地方，东距乌鲁木齐市68公里，312国道、201省道、乌奎高速公路、北疆铁路横贯全境，是“乌昌核心经济圈”的重要组成部分和通往北疆各地及霍尔果斯、阿拉山口等边贸口岸的重要交通枢纽。全县南北长258公里，东西最大宽度52公里，总面积9721平方公里，总人口22万，其中县属人口14万，生活着汉族、哈萨克族、回族、维吾尔族等25个民族。县辖六镇、一乡，有兵团农六师芳草湖农场等24家驻县单位。境内呼图壁河、雀尔沟河两大水系年均径流量达4.87亿立方米，历年平均降水量167毫米，无霜期177天，年有效积温稳定在3500摄氏度以上。有宜农荒地130万亩，已耕种面积116万亩，盛产棉花、番茄、西甜瓜、葡萄、苗木花卉等多种特色农产品。石油、天然气、煤炭、蛇纹岩、石灰石、有色金属等矿产资源富集，已探明煤储量100亿吨，天然气储量347亿立方米，石灰岩储量8550万吨，蛇纹岩储量3亿吨。历史文化旅游资源丰富，是3000年前赛人文化的重要发源地和“新疆曲子”的传承地，拥有“天下第一岩画”之称的康家石门子大型生殖崇拜岩画、南部山区侏罗纪山系等旅游景点，具有较高的人文研究和旅游开发价值。先后获得全国文明县城、国家卫生县城、全国科技进步先进县、全国科普示范县、全国牛奶生产强县、国家优质棉基地、国家现代农业示范区、国家现代农业示范区改革与建设试点县、全国农田水利基本建设先进县、全国蔬菜产业重点县、全国农村集体“三资”管理示范县、国家级苗木交易市场、全国农村劳动力转移就业示范县、全国计划生育优质服务先进县，自治区旅游强县、自治区双拥模范县、自治区教育收费示范县、自治区敬老模范县、自治区残疾人工作先进县、自治区粮食生产大县、自治区农业产业化优秀县、自治区首批农业高效节水示范区、自治区农业水价综合改革示范县、自治区国土资源节约集约模范县、自治区第五次乡村百日文体竞赛先进县、自治区安居富民工程先进县、自治区平安县、自治区园林城市等荣誉称号。

中共中央政治局委员、自治区党委书记张春贤在呼图壁县调研

自治区党委副书记、自治区主席努尔·白克力在呼图壁县调研

呼图壁县委书记曾春雷走访慰问社区群众

呼图壁县委副书记、县长郝拥军在石梯子乡双语幼儿园调研

呼图壁工业园

呼图壁现代化养牛场

呼图壁冬捕鱼大丰收

呼图壁鸿新百汇商厦

优质有机稻米生产基地

发展中的奇台县

中共中央政治局委员、自治区党委书记张春贤在奇台县调研

昌吉州党委书记李建国在奇台县调研

奇台县位于新疆维吾尔自治区东北部，昌吉回族自治州东部。县城距乌鲁木齐市195公里，县域总面积1.93万平方公里。全县辖6镇9乡，总人口29万人，有22个民族，少数民族占总人口的25%。有全国唯一的塔塔尔族乡。

奇台县历史悠久。清乾隆三十八年(公元1773年)建县，是古丝绸之路北道上的交通枢纽和重要商埠，曾与哈密、乌鲁木齐、伊犁并称新疆四大商业都会，有"金奇台""旱码头"之美誉。

农业资源优势突出。有可耕地200万亩，是自治区认证的绿色无公害农产品基地县，是全国优质大麦、小麦之乡，国家级商品粮基地县和全国粮食生产先进县标兵。

矿产开发前景广阔。有煤、金、铜、铁、石灰石、花岗岩等20多种矿产资源。预测煤炭资源量3000亿吨，是目前已探明全国最大的整装煤田，现已入驻煤炭煤电煤化工企业40多家。花岗岩石材质地优良，"卡拉麦里金"品牌享誉区内外，被命名为中国石材(花岗岩)产业基地县。

旅游资源独具特色。南部有国家森林公园和江布拉克国家4A级旅游景区；中部有国家级工业旅游示范点－古城酒史馆和汉疏勒城、唐朝墩古城、清东地大庙等人文景观；北部有硅化木·恐龙国家地质公园，被誉为"恐龙之乡"。

近年来，县委、县人民政府以科学发展观为统领，以"科学跨越、富民强县"为己任，团结带领全县各族干部群众，抢抓西部大开发、中央新疆工作座谈会、对口援疆等重大历史机遇，按照"农业稳县、工业强县、三产活县、项目兴县"的发展思路，大力实施

县委书记王炳炬与中石化集团公司领导对接煤制天然气项目

县长孟凡刚在企业调研

国家 4A 级景区江布拉克

"大产业、大园区、大城区"三大发展战略，解放思想、变化变革、敢于担当、务求实效，坚持以新型工业化为第一推动力，全力推动资源大县向经济强县、传统农业向现代农业、传统服务业向现代服务业、自给自足型县城向辐射周边的区域中心城市"四大转变"，各项主要经济指标实现历史性突破，开创了跨越式发展和长治久安的新局面。特别是 2008 年以来，奇台步入"科学跨越、后发赶超"的快车道，综合经济实力大幅提升、城乡面貌发生巨大变化、各族群众生活水平不断提高，先后被确定为新疆绿洲中心城市和昌吉州支点城市。2012 年，实现地区生产总值 87.6 亿元，增长 22.0 %，是 2007 年的 3.2 倍；完成全社会固定资产投资 110 亿元，增长 56.7%，是 2007 年的 17.6 倍；完成地方财政收入 8.42 亿元，增长 36.6%，是 2007 年的 11.2 倍；实现社会消费品零售总额 17.6 亿元，增长 17.2%，是 2007 年的 2.4 倍；农牧民人均纯收入突破万元大关，达到 11133 元，较 2007 年增加 5791 元。

新型工业化迅速崛起

农业现代化发展水平不断提升

现代服务业蓬勃发展

西域明珠 霍城县

伊犁州党委常委、霍城县委书记王进健在伊犁玉龙钢管有限公司向中央和自治区领导介绍情况

霍城县在无锡市举行招商引资暨旅游产业推介会

万亩葡萄长廊

霍城县作为祖国的西大门,是伊犁的门户,也是通往中西亚等国的"咽喉",素有"西域明珠"之美誉。全县总人口 40.75 万人,聚集着维、汉、回、哈等 30 个民族,少数民族人口占 58.2%,总面积 5720 平方公里,耕地面积 60.15 万亩。2012 年,实现地区生产总值 73.8 亿元,增长 18.8%;全社会固定资产投资 35.64 亿元,增长 79.6%;社会消费品零售总额 12 亿元,增长 15.7%;公共财政预算收入 3.01 亿元,增长 27%;城镇居民可支配收入 1.47 万元,增长 14%;农牧民人均收入达到 9597 元,增长 17.5%。

自然资源丰富。这里四季分明,气候温和,地势平坦,盛产苹果、薰衣草、樱桃李、树上干杏、甜菜、小麦、油料等绿色天然农作物、果品植物和香料药材,是享誉全国的"薰衣草之乡"。境内已探明有煤、铁、铜、石灰石、冰州石、大理石等 33 种矿产资源。

旅游资源独特。境内的惠远古城、阿里玛力古城历史悠久,文化灿烂;果子沟、赛里木湖风光无限,令人神往;汇集了大漠风情和天山秀色的新疆唯一绿洲沙漠 – 图开沙漠,独具神韵;著名的东方小夜曲 –《草原之夜》不仅诞生于此,而且享誉中外。历史名城、自然风光、草原文化、民族风情,使霍城这片热土到处散发着神奇的魅力,成为西部旅游的一颗璀璨明珠!

区位优势凸显。霍城是我国和中亚、西亚等 46 个国家和地区的商品集散地和中转站,是新疆各地区和祖国各地进入伊犁河谷和霍尔果斯口岸的必经之路。1989 年国务院批准霍城县为对外开放县,1992 年国务院有关部门先后批准霍城享有边贸权、建立霍尔果斯边民互市、设置清水河经济开发区;2002 年被中组部确定为援疆试点县,2010 年国家科技部批准成立伊犁国家农业科技园区(核心区设在霍城县清水河经济开发区)。

得天独厚的区位优势、丰富的自然资源、良好的投资环境和广阔的市场前景,使霍城逐渐成为我国与哈萨克斯坦等中亚各国开展经济文化交流的中心和连接欧亚大陆的桥头堡,近期的发展将成为伊犁河谷经济发展的带动区,优势特色产业的培育区,体制创新,机制创新和科技创新的实验区。

高原平湖之美誉的赛里木湖

昌吉国家高新区

中共中央政治局委员、自治区党委书记张春贤，自治区党委副书记、自治区主席努尔·白克力视察高新区企业

昌吉州党委书记李建国在辖区企业调研经济运行工作

昌吉市委常委、管委会主任丁彦明走访施工现场

高新区科技服务中心夜景俯瞰

昌吉高新区前身为昌吉经济技术产业开发区，成立于1992年。2000年由自治区人民政府批准晋升为省级高新区，在昌吉市区长宁路为核心区，规划占地面积11.26平方公里。2006年，为了寻求新的发展空间，州、市党委、人民政府决定在榆树沟镇201省道以南，利用国有荒地规划启动昌吉高新区新区建设。昌吉国家高新区新区位于新疆天山北坡经济带核心区域，是全国14个重点开发区域和西部地区重点培育的重要能源战略基地，距乌鲁木齐市中心50公里，乌鲁木齐国际机场36公里；第二座亚欧大陆桥、312国道、216省道、吐乌大高等级公路、乌奎高速公路穿境而过；乌鲁木齐、玛纳斯两大电网和移动、广电网络覆盖全区。辖区内有国家二类通商口岸1个。在新疆而言，昌吉国家高新区交通优势、区位优势明显，是连接天山南北、沟通内地，西出中亚、联通欧洲的桥头堡和黄金通道。

近年来，在党中央、国务院以及区、州党委、人民政府利好政策的推动下，昌吉国家高新区呈现了经济发展势头突飞猛进、园区面貌日新月异、综合竞争力显著提升的良好发展态势。2012年昌吉高新区实现工业总产值150.9亿元(其中新区实现产值77.7)，是2006年23.5亿元的6.4倍，年均增长36.3%，超过昌吉州的木垒县和呼图壁县，占昌吉市经济总量的份额由2006年的30%增加到2012年的46.4%；GDP实现40.6亿元，是2006年的7.2倍，年均增长39.1%；实现固定资产投资总额47.7亿元，是2006年的13.2倍，年均增长53.8%；财政一般预算收入实现0.78亿元，是2006年0.1亿元的7.8倍，年均增长40.8%；入驻园区企业由2006年的25家增加到206家，其中规模以上企业达52家。高新技术企业8家(全州14家)，其中2012年新认定的高新技术企业2家，高新技术产品13个；高新技术企业产值占高新区工业产值的50.2%。拥有国家级企业技术中心2家，自治区级企业技术中心7家；自治区级工程技术研究中心4家；国家级生产力促进中心1家。拥有国家级名牌产品9个，省级名牌产品17个，在全新疆名牌产品名列第一。先后创建为国家级新型工业化产业示范基地、国家输变电装备高新技术产业化基地、国家农副产品加工示范基地、国家现代节水材料高新技术产业化基地等含金量高的“国字”招牌。

娃哈哈生产车间

图为永城农机生产出来的大型农用拖拉机

新疆昌吉国家农业科技园区

产业富园　项目兴园　科技强园　生态立园

中共中央政治局委员、自治区党委书记张春贤来园区调研

昌吉州党委书记李建国来园区新疆农业博览园视察工作

昌吉国家农业科技园区于2002年5月经国家科技部等六部委联合批准成立，2003年4月29日园区党工委、管委会正式挂牌成立，经自治区批准成立了园区党工委、管委会，分别为昌吉州党委、州人民政府的派出机构，正县级建制，行使县级计划、财政、外贸、规划、建设等经济管理和行政管理权限，内设7个职能部门：办公室、财政局、产业发展局、招商局、规划建设环保局、高新农业发展局、安全生产监督管理局，昌吉州国土资源局、工商局、国税局、地税局、质量技术监督局、公安局在园区设立了分支、派出机构。园区规划总面积340平方公里（51万亩），分为核心区和示范区。核心区28平方公里（4.2万亩，位于昌吉市城市东区），示范区312平方公里（46.8万亩，位于昌吉市以北30公里）。

园区自成立以来，在自治区和昌吉州党委、政府的正确领导及各有关部门的大力关心支持下，全面贯彻落实科学发展观，立足新疆实际，抢抓中央支持新疆"大开发、大发展、大建设"的历史性机遇，充分发挥园区的区位、资源、政策、品牌四大优势，按照自治区提出的"三化"和昌吉州提出的"三个率先"的总体要求，不断改革创新，加快发展步伐，园区综合经济实力不断壮大，基础设施建设日臻完善，科技发展水平显著提升，示范带动作用明显增强。建成了国家科普教育示范基地、国家农业产业化示范基地，培育和建成了一批国家、自治区级农业产业化龙头企业、高新技术企业和科技创新平台，研发、示范、推广了一批高新农业科技项目，为促进新疆现代农业的发展、带动农民增收发挥了积极的作用。2012年在全国65家国家级农业科技园区综合评估考核中，经国家六部委联合评审名列第一。

按照"科学规划，完善功能，因地制宜，适度超前，分步实施"原则，不断加大基础设施建设力度，构建了"一区、两城、四园、七基地"功能格局，园区承载项目、科技研发示范推广、产业带动、综合服务等功能显著提升。

头屯河沿岸综合整治开发区一期（乌昌大道南北各1.6公里范围内）占地总面积1.67平方千米。计划总投资160亿，总建筑面积约250万平米。全力打造以西域文化为核心，兼具旅游观光、休闲娱乐、主题公园、商业、商务、办公等为一体的国际旅游文化产业园。

▲ **新疆科技城**立足新疆、面向中亚、网联全国，建设新疆农业科技创新体系，经过5-10年建成新疆农业科技协同创新中心、农业产业综合服务中心，以协同创新支撑、以现代服务业引领新疆农业向现代农业转变，科技驱动新疆农业跨越式发展。

▲ **"印象西域"国际旅游城** 立足新疆、面向中西亚及世界各国，倾力打造以西域文化为核心，兼具旅游观光、休闲娱乐、主题公园、商业、商务、办公等为一体的国际旅游城。

▲ **新疆农业博览园**占地1.53平方千米，建成了国内最大、技术领先的16座高标准智能温室，展示了一批国内外先进的农业新技术、新品种。最终打造成集农业博览、会展、示范等为一体的现代农业科普教育示范基地和全国农业休闲观光旅游基地。

▲ **高新农业产业园** 占地64平方千米，首期20平方千米的道路、绿化、供排水等基础设施建设全面完成。目前已引进泰昆集团、慧尔农业、麦趣尔集团、大北农等一批龙头企业落户。最终将建成以农副产品精深加工、生物制药等产业为主的、面向中西亚的国际性农副产品生产加工出口基地。

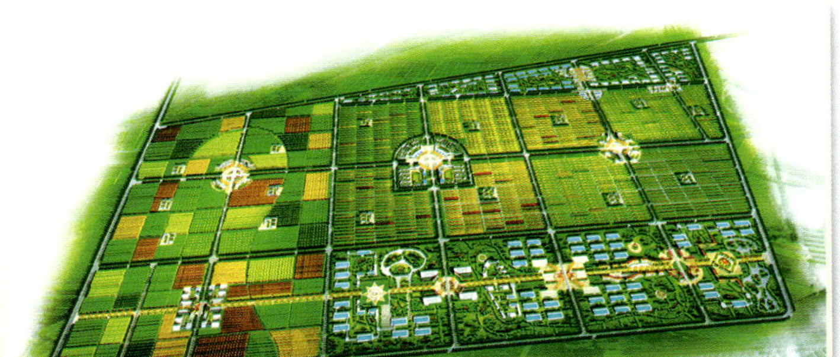

▲ **现代农业示范园**规划面积13.3平方千米，建成了195座高标准日光温室及相关配套设施，中科院、中国农大、上海农科院、新疆农科院等疆内外科研院所相继入驻，实施了一批重点农业科技试验、示范项目，初步建成了现代农业试验示范推广基地和产学研示范基地

▼ **现代科技孵化园**占地1.56平方千米，目前培育引进了西域国家瓜类工程技术研究中心、天康畜牧、泰昆饲料等32家科技研发机构，最终建成新疆现代农业科技研发、示范、推广基地。

7基地

- 农业科普教育基地
- 花卉产业生产基地
- 现代农业休闲观光旅游基地
- 农业产业化基地
- 农业科技研发试验推广基地
- 新型工业化带动农业现代化基地
- 面向中西亚的国际性农副产品生产加工出口基地

乌苏市

乌苏市位于天山北麓、准噶尔盆地西南缘，区域总面积2.07万平方公里，辖区总人口37万余人，其中市属人口22万余人。辖10镇、7乡、3个牧场、1个林场和3个街道办事处。

居伊犁、博州、塔城、阿勒泰、克拉玛依五区（市）之要津，是通往霍尔果斯、巴克图、阿拉山口口岸的重要门户。与新型商贸城奎屯市、国家石化基地独山子区形成北疆“金三角”。国道312线、217线和欧亚第二大陆桥（铁路）横贯东西、贯通天山南北，奎北铁路、奎—赛高等级公路从境内穿过。距乌鲁木齐市260千米、克拉玛依市157千米、奎屯市5千米、独山子区8千米。2012年，全市实现地区生产总值124.1亿元，同比增长24.3%。完成工业增加值53亿元，增长25.4%。完成全社会固定资产投资59.9亿元，增长35.5%。招商引资到位资金34.14亿元。

境内水土、光热、矿产等资源较为丰富，尤以煤炭资源最为丰富，已探明储量7亿吨，远景储量达21亿吨。依托良好的资源和区位、交通优势，规划并建设了49.2平方千米的乌苏化工园，其中一期规划19.2平方千米，现有中电投集团乌苏热电厂、华泰石油化工、乌苏啤酒、新疆天玉、北方新科等68家企业入驻园区，涉及能源、石化上下游产业、农产品、建筑、制造等领域近百种产品，已基本形成门类比较齐全、结构趋向合理的工业体系。

乌苏市以党的十八大精神为指引，坚决贯彻区、地两级党委各项决策部署，围绕“保稳定、促发展、为民生”工作主脉，坚持工业优先发展，大力实施“产业强市、生态美市、文化名市、民生惠市”战略，加快“三化”进程，统筹城乡协调发展，着力改善民生，全力维护社会稳定，不断加强党的建设，以快干、干好的作风奋力推动乌苏实现率先发展。

自治区党委副书记、自治区主席努尔·白克力主席（前排中）在乌苏市委书记梁浩（右一）的陪同下来乌苏调研民生教育等工作

自治区副主席靳诺（左二）在乌苏市委书记梁浩（左一）的陪同下调研我市防震工作

塔城地区地委书记张博（前排右二）在乌苏市委书记梁浩（前排右三）的陪同下来乌苏调研工业企业发展

新区综合服务大楼

啤酒节开幕式。

乌苏市委书记　梁浩

乌苏市市长　马依山·扎合帕尔

伊犁州第 17 届阿肯阿依特斯节在我市隆重开幕，将“草原”搬进了“城市”

石化企业发展迅速

中电投集团公司乌苏热电厂

县委书记　谢强

县长　赛力克·乌拉孜别克

沙湾县

沙湾是天山北坡一颗耀眼的明珠。沙湾区位交通优势突出，是伊犁州和塔城地区的东大门，与8个地州县市，4个陆路通商口岸相连，北疆铁路、115省道、乌奎高速公路自东向西横穿县境，219、223、224三条省道纵贯南北，交通便利、四通八达。沙湾水土光热、矿产旅游资源丰富，辖区面积1.31万平方公里，拥有耕地150万亩、草场830万亩，是全国农业生态县、绿色小康县；境内分布着40多种矿产资源，煤炭、石灰石、石油、天然气储量丰富，已探明储量分别达25亿吨、11.3亿吨、2亿吨、1000亿标准立方米；全县总人口46万人，其中地方人口21万人，由汉、哈萨克、回、维吾尔等24个民族组成，辖9镇、3乡、5个农牧林场和2个管理处，240个村队。沙湾政策人文环境优越，是自治区确定的天山北坡经济区优先发展县市，城乡基础设施完备，经济发展较快，为西部百强县和自治区十强县，先后蝉联七届自治区文明县，两届全国文明县城、全国双拥模范县，先后荣获"中国大盘美食名县"、"中国最佳养生休闲旅游城市"、"国家园林县城"、"中国人居环境范例奖"等50多个国家和自治区级荣誉称号，全县上下处处呈现出经济发展、民族团结、社会和谐、科技进步、各项事业欣欣向荣的喜人景象。

近年来，在自治区党委、政府正确领导下，沙湾县委、政府深入贯彻落实科学发展观，坚持巩固提高抓一产、发展壮大强二产、突出特色活三产、统筹社会促和谐，加速推进新型工业化、农业现代化、新型城镇化、旅游特色化，走出了一条具有沙湾特色、符合县域实际的科学跨越发展之路。2012年，全县完成地区生产总值97.27亿元，增长12.5%；完成地方财政收入6.65亿元，增长21.9%，其中地方公共财政预算收入5.01亿元，增长23.5%；农牧民人均纯收入增加1837元，达到15032元。

棉花收获机正在作业

全民健身运动

瀚海柳浪旅游区

沙湾县世纪大道

美丽的鹿角湾景区

沙湾县举行庆祝建党 90 周年万人红歌会，迎接党的九十华诞

察布查尔锡伯自治县

伊犁州党委书记李学军在伊泰工业园调研

伊犁州党委常委、县委书记王奕文看望边防派出所武警官兵

锡伯族万人贝伦舞展示获大世界吉尼斯之最，县长王春光与工作人员共同展示证书

华夏锡伯第一村

察布查尔，锡伯语为“粮仓”之意，是国家级扶贫开发重点县，同时还是边境县、开放县，还是全国唯一以锡伯族为主体的多民族聚居的自治县。与伊犁哈萨克自治州首府伊宁市隔河相望，西与哈萨克斯坦国接壤，边境线长73.4公里。全县总面积4485平方公里，总人口19.4万人，由25个民族组成，少数民族人口占72%。下辖13个乡镇、1个国营农场、1个农村经济管理中心，驻县有兵团农四师67团、68团、69团等单位。

察布查尔是中国箭乡。完整保留、延续中国传统弓箭礼仪、制作技艺，是国家传统弓和现代弓国家研究培育训练基地。弓箭文化博物馆建成开馆。成功举办第二届全国传统弓射箭比赛，参赛的本县运动员不负“箭乡”美誉，勇夺个人排名赛冠军、团体淘汰赛冠军及个人淘汰赛亚军。

察布查尔是锡伯家园。完整保留、延续了锡伯族语言、文字和传统风俗习惯。近年来，察布查尔县抓紧抢救、深入挖掘、系统整理、大力弘扬加大锡伯文化。锡伯民族博物院完成提升改造，被誉为国内一流的县级博物院。搜集整理锡伯族濒临灭绝的非物质文化遗产项目108个，“西迁节”、“贝伦舞”、“弓箭制作技艺”、“锡伯刺绣”等5个被列入国家级名录，还有18个被列入自治区级名录；中国首部锡伯族民俗数字电影《箭乡少女》拍摄完成，在中央电视台电影频道播映。启动实施国家锡伯族传统文化生态保护区建设项目。

察布查尔矿产丰富。已探明煤炭精查储量303亿吨，是新疆四大煤电煤化工产业基地之一伊犁矿区主战场。自治区级园区伊南工业园区占地160平方公里，现有伊泰、中电投、新汶、中煤、华电、国能等中国500强企业投资，已有煤基多联产、煤制天然气、煤制烯烃等一批项目落地建设，投资总额超3000亿人民币。

察布查尔县物产丰饶。年水径流量166亿立方米，可利用水资源20亿立方米。全县现有灌溉面积138.83万亩。伊犁河流域水土开发将新增150万亩，适合重大项目用地和现代化、集约化、规模化发展。全县天然草场面积300万亩，全县林地面积156万亩，森林覆盖率12%，全年有效光照时数达2846小时，无霜期177天，积温3800℃，年平均降水量222毫米。适宜种植各类农作物，是发展绿色有机食品原料的天然之地。

中央新疆工作座谈会三年来，察布查尔县委、县人民政府在上级党委、政府的正确领导下，按照实现科学跨越发展、确保社会长治久安的要求，变

全疆最大的肉产品生产线——巴口香肉业

察布查尔县万亩榛子基地

锡伯族射箭

伊犁天山水泥有限责任公司

万亩有机水稻基地

化变革、敢于担当、务求实效，科学判断县域经济形势，强势推进“九个坚定不移”发展战略，各项工作在较短时间实现较大突破，2012 年与 2009 年相比，全县地区生产总值翻 0.9 番，地方公共财政预算收入翻 1.3 番、地方规模以上工业增加值翻 1 番，全社会固定资产投资翻 2.4 番，招商引资翻 2.5 番。

2012 年实现地区生产总值 32.78 亿元，增长 22.7%，高于州直平均水平 6.7 个百分点。三次产业比重调整为 48.1：23.4：28.4。完成规模以上工业增加值 2.74 亿元，增长 1.1 倍。地方公共财政预算收入 2.6 亿元，增长 30%。完成固定资产投资 66 亿元，增长 61.6%。城镇居民可支配收入 14052 元，增长 16%。社会消费品零售总额 22946 万元，增长 15%。农牧民人均纯收入净增 1270 元，达到 8676 元，增长 17.1%。地区生产总值、地方公共财政预算收入、固定资产投资、规模以上工业增加值等主要经济指标增速全州第一。

2013 年奋斗目标：实现生产总值 38 亿元，增长 15%。地方工业增加值 5.7 亿元，增长 23 %。地方公共财政预算收入 3.25 亿元，增长 25%。完成全社会固定资产投资 83 亿元，增长 25.8%。城镇居民可支配收入 16300 元，增长 16 %。社会消费品零售总额 2.64 亿元，增长 15 %。农牧民人均纯收入力争增收 1300 元，接近万元，增长 15%。城镇登记失业率控制在 3.6%以内。人口自然增长率控制在 14.10‰以内。

“十二五”时期，是我们抓住重要发展机遇期，统筹城乡、区域、人与社会协调发展的关键时期。我们将以科学发展观为统领，以构建民生、宜居、人文、幸福察布查尔为主题，以新一轮援疆工作为契机，变化变革，敢于担当，狠抓落实，为实现察布查尔县科学跨跃、民生改善、长治久安而不懈奋斗！

国家 AAA 级景区清水湖生态园景区

甜蜜、多彩、宜居 尼勒克

县委书记　周立新

县委副书记、县长　努尔卡·卡那甫

尼勒克，意为“新生命、希望”，地处中天山西段，伊犁河谷东北部，东距乌鲁木齐市516公里，西距伊宁市112公里，交通便利，风光秀丽，气候宜人。全县总面积1.03万平方公里，辖13个乡（镇）场，总人口18.69万人，由哈、汉、维、回、蒙等32个民族构成，其中哈萨克族8.51万人，占总人口的45.6%。

境内资源富饶。尼勒克县是“新疆黑蜂”主要发源地和最大繁育地，其中种蜂场是全国两大黑蜂保护区之一，建成了以“黑蜂”产业为主的“天山黑蜂”产业生态园区，并于2012年成功举办首届中国·新疆“甜蜜尼勒克”蜜蜂文化旅游节。境内有喀什河、巩乃斯河、阿夏勒河三大水系，百余条支流，水能蕴藏量在200万千瓦以上，是新疆水能蕴藏量最丰富、开发潜力最大的地区之一。境内草原辽阔，水草丰茂，草场面积1016万亩，可利用草场面积980.8万亩；林地261.5万亩，拥有河谷湿地古杨林21.3万亩，是西北地区面积最大、保护最好的水土生态林。已发现煤、铁、铜、锰、铅、锌、金、银、石膏、重晶石、石英、石灰石、花岗岩、大理岩、珍珠岩、耐火粘土、膨润土、热泉等20余种矿产资源，建成了150万吨煤焦化产业园区、50万吨铁精粉采选项目、100万吨铁矿开采加工项目和2000万吨群吉萨依有色金属采选项目，逐步形成了以水电、煤焦化、矿产开采加工为主导产业的新型工业化格局。拥有品种繁多的动植物资源百余种，牲畜品种有伊犁马、新疆细毛羊、新疆褐牛等，牲畜存栏数突破百万，初步形成了一批具有规模的乳品、肉制品加工行业龙头企业。野生动物资源、药用动植物资源丰富，是世界上少有的生物多样性天然基因库。尼勒克县旅游资源已经形成5类17种基本类型，形成了“一线三区”的空间格局。这里既有中华民族历史文化的积淀，又有少数民族文化的浓郁风情；既有唐布拉、巴尔盖提温泉、湿地古杨林、吉林台峡谷风景等山川草原风光，又有乔尔玛、奴拉赛古铜矿、草原石人、吉仁台岩画、草原古墓群遗址等众多历史文化古迹，还有百万牲畜转场草原牧业生产的壮丽画卷，是伊犁乃至新疆独具魅力、极具吸引力和开发潜力的旅游宝地。

近年来，尤其是中央新疆工作座谈会召开以来，县委、县人民政府团结带领全县各族干部群众，坚持以邓小平理论、“三个代表”重要思想和科学发展观为指导，全面贯彻落实党的十八大、中央新疆工作座谈会、自治区第八次党代会和州党委工作会议总体部署，坚持以现代文化为引领，瞄准富民强县这一目标，围绕保障和改善民生这一核心，培育煤电煤化工有色金属加工、现代农牧、文化旅游三大产业，推进新型工业化、农牧业现代化、新型城镇化建设，大力实施“生态立县”、“工业强县”、“畜牧大县”、“旅游名县”、“文化兴县”五大战略，加大扶贫和民生建设投入力度，全力维护社会和谐稳定。2012 年，全县实现地区生产总值 35.7 亿元，同比增长 12.3%。其中，一、二、三产业增加值分别为 10.26 亿元、18.71 亿元、6.73 亿元，同比分别增长 6.4%、14.7%、13.5%；三次产业比例为 29:52:19；人均生产总值 19307 元，同比增长 11%；农牧民人均纯收入 8423 元，较上年增加 1400 元，同比增长 20%；城镇居民人均可支配收入 14067 元，较上年增加 1940 元，同比增长 16%；全社会固定资产投资 45 亿元，同比增长 38.9%；社会消费品零售总额 5.6 亿元，同比增长 14.8%；公共财政预算收入 3.61 亿元，同比增长 33.5%。

蜜峰之都

岫玉之城

目前，全县经济发展、社会稳定、民族团结、各族人民安居乐业，各项事业蓬勃发展，已步入了大建设、大开放、大发展的新时期新阶段。在新的起点上，县委、县人民政府将带领全县各族人民群众继续推进尼勒克跨越式发展和长治久安，倾力打造“甜蜜、多彩、宜居”尼勒克，不断谱写科学发展、赶超跨越的豪迈篇章。

蜂农收蜜一景

规模养殖促农富

设施农业基地

跨越发展的富蕴县

县委书记　祁崇江

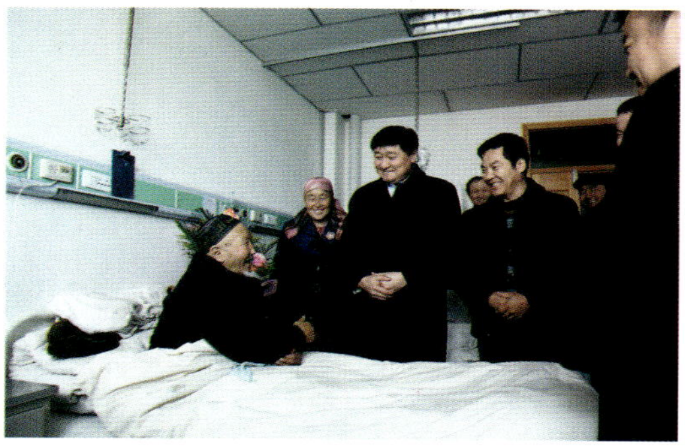

县长沙比提·哈再孜看望老人

富蕴首家钢铁企业金昊铁业奠基

文艺演出

富蕴县地处新疆维吾尔自治区北部，阿勒泰地区东端，额尔齐斯河上游，总面积3.22万平方公里。是新疆矿业基础较好，地质工作程度较高的少数县(市)之一。目前，共发现矿种有四大种，92个品种，尤以黄金，宝石，有色金属闻名遐迩。有色金属，稀有金属储量居全国之首。10种矿产储量居全国前十位，居全疆前列的有：铁、铜、钼、铅、锌。

县域内的水系主要是额尔齐斯河和乌伦古河两大水系。额尔齐斯河是我国唯一流入北冰洋的河流，正常流量为107.31km³/S，年径流量为33.81亿km³。乌伦古河为内流河，富蕴段属于中上游，多年平径流量为9.7亿km³。富蕴县野生动物种类繁多，有100余种。有林地面积503.96万亩，森林覆盖面积420万亩。可可托海景区成功创建为5A级风景名胜区，跻身全疆5个5A级景区之一。县辖六乡四镇，71个行政村。2012年全县总人口9.52万人，由汉族、哈萨克族等26个民族组成，其中:哈萨克族人口6.92万人，占总人口的72.7%；汉族人口2.08万人，占总人口的22.9%。非农业人口3.93万人，占总人口的41.8%。

2012年，地区完成生产总值46.35亿元，增长16.9%。销售收入500万元以上工业企业增加值31.42亿元，增长24.4%；固定资产投资44.37亿元，增长47.5%；地方财政收入达到9.56亿元，增长28.9%，地方财政支出20.03亿元，增长26.4%；金融机构存款余额为29.56亿元，增长10.9%，贷款余额为13.98亿元，增长31.3%。农民人均纯收入达7388元，增长18.5%。全年接待游客88.5万人次，实现旅游收入6.56亿元。

广场文化活动

哈巴河县

中国西部最美的生态边城

中共中央政治局委员、自治区党委书记张春贤在阿克齐镇调研

哈巴河县地处新疆最西北边缘，阿尔泰山南麓，西、北与哈萨克斯坦、俄罗斯接壤，边境线长320公里。全县总面积8185平方公里，辖6乡1镇113个行政村，生活着哈萨克、汉、回等22个民族8.7万人，其中少数民族占69.6%。县内有驻军某部队及兵团第十师185团。

哈巴河水土光热资源充足，矿产资源蕴藏丰富，区位优势得天独厚。哈巴河、别列孜河、阿拉克别克河和额尔齐斯河等四条主要河流，年径流量116亿立方米，有宜农土地142万亩、草场810万亩、林地361万亩。蕴藏的32种矿种中以铜、金的藏量大、品位高而著称，是“阿尔泰有色金属矿带上的一颗璀璨明珠”。正在争取开放的中哈阿黑吐别克口岸、中俄吉克普林口岸，将使哈巴河成为全疆向西开放的“桥头堡”。哈巴河县毗邻喀纳斯景区，自然风光秀美，人文景观丰富，民风高洁淳朴，县内有国家4A级景区——西北最大的天然白桦林。

县委书记　张献成

勤劳智慧的哈巴河人用双手和汗水缔造了国家卫生县城三连冠、国家园林县城、全国双拥模范县两连冠、全国平安建设先进县、自治区优秀平安县等荣誉，正在推进跨越式发展和长治久安的和谐大道上阔步前行，创造更加幸福美好的未来！

2012年，哈巴河县完成地区生产总值38.7亿元，增长12.1%；工业增加值23.8亿元，增长15.0%；地方财政收入5.5亿元，增长44.6%；公共财政预算收入5亿元，增长40.3%；地方固定资产投资28.2亿元，增长39.0%；招商引资到位资金18.1亿元，增长44.1%；农牧民人均纯收入增加1298元，达到7558元。

雅居

县长　阿依丁·托留汗

小麦丰收

阿舍勒铜矿外景

落实科学发展观 构建和谐卫生

博州卫生局

自治区党委常委艾尔肯江·吐拉洪调研我州医药卫生事业发展

卫生工作会议

新疆卫生思想政治工作促进会2012年理事会暨推进加强基层组织建设年研讨会在我州举行

博州卫生局作为全州卫生系统行政主管部门，内设办公室、医政科、妇社科、疾控办、食安办、爱卫办、农卫办、保健办、学会办共3个职能科室和6个业务科室，具体实施卫生全行业管理，负责全州医疗服务、预防保健、卫生监督、爱国卫生等工作。至2012年底，全州共有各级各类卫生机构477所，开放床位1936张，卫生人员总数3270人，每千人拥有病床数5.23张，每千人拥有医护数4.96人，已基本形成州、县(市)、乡、村四级医疗卫生保健网。

过去的一年，全州卫生工作在自治州党委、政府及上级有关部门的领导、关心、支持下，认真贯彻落实中央、自治区、自治州的各项决策部署，坚持保基本、强基层、建机制的基本原则，统筹推进五项重点改革，如期完成确定的各项任务，医改取得重大阶段性成果，全州各族群众看病就医的公平性、可及性和便利性得到改善，看病难、看病贵问题有所缓解。经过近几年的努力，目前已初步建立起符合博州州情的基本医疗保障制度，基本药物制度在基层全部实施，基本公共卫生服务逐步实现均等化，覆盖城乡的医疗卫生服务网络基本建成，国民健康水平不断提高，婴儿死亡率、孕产妇死亡率进一步降低，实现了党和政府得民心、人民群众得实惠、医务人员得鼓舞、卫生事业得发展的多赢局面，积累了坚持党和政府领导、坚持公共医疗卫生公益性、坚持立足博州州情、坚持创新发展的“四坚持”的宝贵经验。今后，我们将进一步增强做好卫生工作的责任感和使命感，坚定信心，务实创新，依靠改革和发展解决存在的问题和困难，依靠改革实现全州卫生事业跨越式发展。

积极开展创建区级文明单位创建活动

参加地震演练救援

霍尔果斯经济开发区

霍尔果斯经济开发区召开一区三园工作会议，伊犁州党委书记、霍尔果斯经济开发区党工委书记李学军现场听取建设工作汇报

霍尔果斯名称源于蒙古语，《西域同文志》表述为"牧地遗矣也，地客游牧，故名"意为水草丰茂的地方。从地理学上来讲，霍尔果斯经济开发区地处东经80° 29′ 、北纬44° 14′ ，因境内有霍尔果斯河而得名。霍尔果斯平均海拔750－840米之间，地势由北向南倾斜。霍尔果斯处在312国道、连霍高速公路、陇海——兰新铁路的最西端。距乌鲁木齐670公里，距伊宁市88公里，距中亚的中心城市阿拉木图市378公里，距哈萨克斯坦最近的城市雅尔肯特市35公里。

党中央、国务院高度重视霍尔果斯的发展，党和国家领导人先后多次到霍尔果斯视察工作，并作出一系列重要决策部署，特别是2004年9月，中哈两国政府签署协议，共同建立中哈霍尔果斯国际边境合作中心，这是我国与周边国家建立的首个跨境国际边境合作区，也是上海合作组织框架下区域合作的示范区。2010年5月，中央召开新疆工作座谈会，决定设立霍尔果斯经济开发区，实行特殊的政策，将其建设成为新疆新的经济增长点和全国向西开放的桥头堡。2011年9月，国务院下发《关于支持喀什霍尔果斯经济开发区建设的若干意见》(国发〔2011〕33号)，明确了霍尔果斯经济开发区的战略定位、总体要求、基本原则、区域范围、产业布局和扶持政策，霍尔果斯经济开发区规划面积73平方公里，"一区三园"空间布局，包括霍尔果斯园区30平方公里(含兵团分区10平方公里)、伊宁配套产业园区35平方公里、清水河配套产业园区8平方公里。为支持霍尔果斯发展，2012年5月，自治区人民政府《关于加快喀什霍尔果斯经济开发区建设的实施意见》(新政发〔2012〕48号)，明确授予霍尔果斯经济开发区行使自治区级管理权。自治州将经济开发区发展列入重要议程，举全州之力加以推进，霍尔果斯迎来了前所未有的发展机遇。

2012年工业总产值20194万元，增长25.0%，工业增加值4587万元；完成全社会固定资产投资16.18亿元，其中基本建设投资14.06亿元；全年进出口贸易额110.01亿美元，其中进口85.96亿美元，出口24.05亿美元；地方财政收入为15728万元，地方财政支出21787万元；全年接待游客110.25万人次，实现旅游综合收入124625万元，中哈霍尔果斯国际边境合作中心出入境旅客27.19万人次，实现收入31969万元；出入境旅客69.2万人，旅购金额91488.56万元。

霍尔果斯经济开发区党工委、管委会挂牌仪式

霍尔果斯经济开发区党工委副书记、管委会主任黄继跃向哈萨克斯坦国际边境合作中心国家股份公司总裁—哈米特·阿斯哈特先生介绍合作中心情况

中哈霍尔果斯－阿腾科里首趟列车对发

江苏产业援疆伊犁州合作项目洽谈签约仪式

敢于争先 担当奋进

开创新和“居中崛起”新局面

新和县位于天山南麓，塔里木盆地北缘，东隔渭干河与库车县相望，西与阿克苏市、阿拉尔市、温宿县接壤，北依却勒塔格山与拜城县相邻，南与沙雅县毗邻；314国道、库阿高速和南疆铁路横贯县境，距库车机场25公里，地理位置优越，交通十分便利。新和县历史悠久、人文荟萃，是古“龟兹国”繁锦之区，享有“汉唐重镇”、“班超府治”、“龟兹故里”的美誉。境内有托乎拉艾肯石窟、唐柘厥关、它乾城、玉奇喀特古城、通古孜巴什古城等宝贵历史文化遗产65处。新和民间艺术文化丰富，非物质文化遗产——木卡姆艺术、民族乐器制作技艺等都彰显出新和独具特色的艺术魅力，塔什艾日克乡被文化部授予“中国民间艺术之乡”称号，境内面积达10万亩的“汉唐屯田遗址”被授予“大世界吉尼斯”之最，新和已成为龟兹旅游的理想目的地。

中共中央政治局委员、自治区党委书记张春贤考察调研职业教育工作

新和是国家优质棉基地县，也是自治区粮食生产基地之一。全县年产优质皮棉6.5万吨，以红枣、核桃为主的特色林果面积达40万亩，红枣、核桃等产品远销国内外。境内石油、天然气资源储量丰富，是中国最大的凝析油及天然气集聚带，境内英买力、羊塔克、玉东三个区块为“西气东输”主气源地之一，已布探井101口，天然气地质储量656.28亿立方米、凝析油及原油地质储量2600万吨。英买力油气群年产天然气25亿立方米、凝析油50万吨、液化气4万吨。

滨湖景观河夜景

近年来，新和县在自治区党委、人民政府及地委、行署的坚强领导下，坚持以邓小平理论、“三个代表”重要思想和科学发展观为指导，以现代文化为引领，围绕“科学跨越，富民强县，实现‘居中崛起’”主题，大力实施“生态立县、工业强县、文化塑县、科教兴县和人才强县”战略，着力打造“能源产业、生态农业、娱乐休闲农家旅游、商贸物流枢纽”四大基地，全力推进优势资源转换，大力发展以“农产品深加工、机械加工制造、石油天然气煤化工深加工、棉花精深加工、商贸物流、新型能源”六大产业，不断深化改革开放，着力提高经济效益，加快社会建设，改善生态环境，经济社会实现了可持续发展。2012年，全县实现地区生产总值25.2亿元，增长19.8%；完成全社会固定资产投资20.1亿元，增长66.0%；完成地方公共财政预算收入4.17亿元；实现社会消费品零售总额2.9亿元，增长18.8%；城镇居民人均可支配收入达17502元，增长15.0%；农民人均纯收入8626元(不含农场)，增长18.6%。

加依村制作的民族乐器知名疆内外

木卡姆艺术被文化部授予“民间艺术之乡”

巴里坤哈萨克自治县

县委书记陈毅士（右二）在三塘湖百万千瓦级风电基地调研

县长叶尔江（左二）检查为民办十件实事进展

巴里坤少数民族传统体育运动会

巴里坤古称蒲类，是古丝绸之路北新道进入新疆的第一重镇。巴里坤哈萨克自治县位于东疆北部，全县总面积3.84万平方公里，与蒙古人民共和国接壤，县城西距乌鲁木齐市570千米，为全国三个哈萨克族自治县之一。2012年，县辖4镇8乡2区1场，年末总人口104106人（少数民族人口39214人），农村人口59830人，人口出生率10.78‰，自然增长率5.94‰。

巴里坤经济以资源型工业、农牧业和旅游业为主。主要农产品有马铃薯、大路菜、大麦、小麦、晚熟哈密瓜、牛羊肉、驼奶等，其中巴里坤"力坤"牌牛羊肉、马铃薯获得了国家"绿色食品"认证；主要工业产品有煤炭、风电、芒硝、硫化碱、原油、黄金等。主要旅游景点有古城景区（国家4A级旅游景区）、巴里坤大草原、地藏寺、仙姑庙、哈萨克文化展馆、兰州湾子古遗址、大河唐城、怪石山、王氏古民宅、月牙湾、马圈沟等，为自治区级旅游强县。巴里坤地形特征为"三山夹两盆"，有"新疆缩影"之称，属温带大陆性冷凉干旱气候区。

2012年，实现县域生产总值36亿元，同比增长20%，其中：一产8.3亿元，同比增长8.5%；二产18.3亿元，同比增长29%；三产9.4亿元，同比增长15%。全社会固定资产投资突破40亿元大关，同比增长64%。招商引资到位资金27.3亿元，同比增长46%。地方财政收入突破3亿元大关，同比增长40%。城镇居民人均可支配收入达到1.63万元，同比增长18%。农牧民人均纯收入达到7189元，同比增长21%。

现代农牧业水平稳步提高，完成农林牧渔业总产值139981万元，同比增长6.05%。其中，种植业产值48382万元、林业产值320万元、牧业产值89828万元、渔业产值243万元、农林牧渔服务业产值1208万元。农林牧渔业增加值74444万元，同比增长5.26%。2012年，粮食产量93903吨、棉花产量447吨、油料产量226吨、蔬菜产量39717吨、瓜类产量3134吨、薯类产量40837吨、饲用玉米产量88470吨。年末牲畜存栏头数54.21万头(只)，全年牲畜出栏53.79万头(只)，肉类总产量20080吨；牛奶产量23245吨。年末农业机械总动力达到12.76万千瓦。

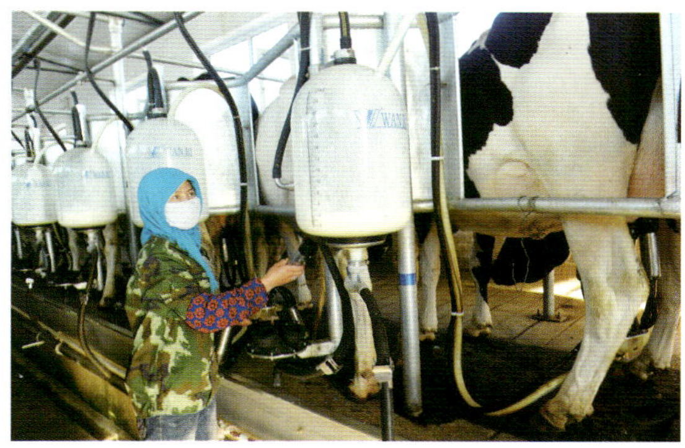

现代畜牧业

2012年，全县完成固定资产投资402662万元，同比增长49.5%。邮电业务收入5409万元，其中，邮政业务收入599万元，增长26.9%；电信业务收入4810万元。年末固定电话（含小灵通）用户12203户、移动电话用户57445户、互联网用户4061户。全年接待国内游客44万人次，增长25.7%。实现国内旅游收入9397万元，增长30.6%。

煤炭化工企业

巴里坤三塘湖百万千瓦风电基地

克拉玛依市>>乌禾尔区

乌尔禾区位于克拉玛依市东北端，北连塔城地区和丰县，西接塔城地区托里县，南枕白杨河，河谷下游为兵团第七师137团，是典型的油、地、兵融合之地。

作为一个依靠石油开发而发展起来的新兴城区，克拉玛依市乌尔禾区兼具石油资源、旅游资源、乡村资源、民俗文化、兵地融合等诸多发展优势。

近年来，随着乌尔禾区总体规划的出台，区委、区政府在市委、市政府的坚强领导下，紧紧围绕市委、市政府中心工作，立足区情，以实现科学跨越为主题，夯基础、练内功，坚持油、地、兵融合发展的理念，坚持“规划统筹、城市共建、产业同布、市场同体、信息共享、交通同网、旅游同线、环境同治、科教同兴”的原则，通过战略研究，明确“东稳、西活、南展、北拓”的阶段性发展思路，确定了“建设生态旅游新城”的发展目标。

乌尔禾区通过在全区上下开展大讨论活动，统一思想，为实现乌尔禾科学跨越，从2009年开始，区委、区政府每年都把阶段性的任务作为全区年度工作主题。2009年“新农村建设年”、2010年“基础工作年”、2011年“基础工作夯实年”、2012年“提速增效年”，通过实施“5321”工程，完善农村基础设施，改善生产生活环境，拓宽农牧民致富渠道，增加农牧民收入，提升农牧民幸福感；摸清家底，土地整合、征收拆迁，制度汇编，完善工作制度和议事规则，规范人财物事管理，在克拉玛依市四个区中率先修定完成总体规划，以稠油开发为契机，加快矿产、旅游、农业资源综合开发利用，提出油地兵融合发展的目标。2012年乌尔禾区积极抢抓风城超稠油和油砂矿开发的历史性机遇，发挥乌尔禾后发优势，实现地区生产总值79.6亿元；农牧民人均纯收入12719元，连续三年增长超过10%；原油总产量首次突破200万吨大关；招商引资实现到位资金1.77亿元，同比增长66.9%；全年地方固定资产投资达1.85亿元，同比增长270%。依据乌尔禾区总体规划，事关乌尔禾长远发展的污水处理厂、青少年活动中心、人力资源服务中心、同兴路和阿腊德路改建、石缘路旅游购物精品一条街、奇石城商业街等基础设施工程、民生工程、招商引资项目陆续开工，乌尔禾经济社会步入科学发展快车道。

旅游节住宿

艾里克湖落日

旅游推介

奇石城项目开工典礼

石油产业蒸蒸日上

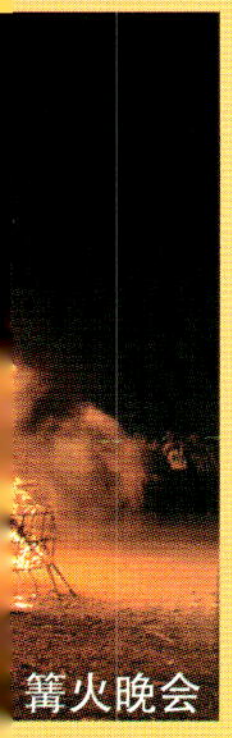

篝火晚会

摔跤

赛马

托克逊县

绿色风城　魅力水乡　幸福驿站

托克逊县位于天山中部、吐鲁番盆地西缘，属南、北、东三疆交汇之地。县城托克逊镇中心大十字海拔0米，是全国唯一的海拔“零点城”。G30线、G3012线、兰新铁路、南疆铁路穿境而过，曾是古丝绸之路上的著名驿站。县域面积1.66万平方公里，辖四乡四镇、45个行政村、12个社区。全县常住人口11.82万人，由维吾尔、汉、回等22个民族构成。

托克逊县光热资源丰富，盛产红枣、哈密瓜、蔬菜、白高粱、孜然、花生等农副产品。畜牧养殖主要有黑羊、西门塔牛、荷斯坦牛等，其中：“托克逊黑羊”被列为《国家优良品种遗传资源保护目录》，通过国家有机食品认证。现已发现矿产46种，优势矿产有煤炭、石灰岩、盐矿、钨、膨润土、蒙皂石矿等。水资源丰富，总量达4.64亿立方米，主要有白杨河、阿拉沟、鱼尔沟、乌斯通沟等六大水系。境内更有雅丹地貌、洄流、盘吉尔怪石林、水系图等多处自然景观。托克逊县全年主导风向为西风，且风速较为平稳，素有“风库”之称。

吐鲁番地区地委书记张文全调研托克逊

近年来，在自治区党委、政府的坚强领导下，深入贯彻落实科学发展观，围绕跨越式发展和长治久安两大历史任务，始终坚持"实力决定一切、创新激发一切、稳定压倒一切"的方针不动摇，以现代文化为引领，科教支撑、转型升级，以新型工业化带动农牧业现代化和新型城镇化，着力打造煤电产业基地、建材基地，结合丰富的自然资源优势，加速推进旅游文化产业升级，统筹全县经济社会各项事业长足发展。2012年，实现地区生产总值40.05亿元，增长18.4%，其中：第一产业增加值7.23亿元，增长7.4%；第二产业增加值24.87亿元，增长24.3%（工业增加值20.33亿元，增长27.5%）；第三产业增加值7.96亿元，增长9.3%。公共财政预算收入48370万元，增长28.0%。全社会固定资产投资42.83亿元，增长25.0%。农牧民人均纯收入6663元，增长19.6%。

百舸争流创示范，千帆竞渡立潮头，托克逊县各族人民立足当下，团结奋斗，勇于创新，以饱满的热情谱写托克逊县明天更加辉煌的诗篇。

托克逊县黑羊

红枣

小白杏

哈密瓜

新疆黑山露天矿有限公司采煤现场

新疆华电吐鲁番发电有限责任公司厂区远景

新疆新冶能源化工股份有限公司石灰窑

新疆圣雄能源股份有限公司 VCM 球罐

雅丹地貌

吐鲁番地区环保局

党风廉政建设暨绩效考评工作会议

吐鲁番地区环保局成立于1991年，局机关下设一室两科，下属3个事业单位，共有在职干部70人，其中聘用专业技术人员23人。地区环保局综合办公楼位于吐鲁番市军民共建路，占地面积9.5亩，建筑面积4100m²，于2004年11月落成使用。

近年来，在吐鲁番地委、行署的正确领导下，吐鲁番地区环保局坚定不移的实施“环保优先、生态立区”和“两个可持续发展”战略，从提高管理水平、强化环保执法、加大资金投入、推进污染防治和广泛宣传教育等方面入手，迎难而上，扎实工作。投入300余万元完成环保系统视频会议、污染源视频监控、环境应急管理系统、OA办公自动化建设，环保系统信息化建设工作走在新疆乃至西北地区的前列；加大重点污染源企业在线监控安装力度，在全疆率先推行污染源自动监控系统委托运营（第三方运营）；加快历史遗留铬渣无害化处置进度，实施倒排机制，抽调业务骨干现场办公，企业投入资金1.6亿元，争取中央配套资金1600万元以及拨付污染治理专项资金1000万元，全面完成25.15万吨历史遗留铬渣处置工作；认真开展专项整治行动，依法拆除艾维尔沟区域9家石灰土窑，12家石灰石开采和加工企业限期整改，艾维尔沟区域环境质量明显改善。环境保护工作取得了较为显著的成绩。目前，吐鲁番地区环保局已先后获得国家环保部“12369”为民服务创先争优优质服务单位、全国污染源普查工作先进集体、自治区级文明单位、自治区级卫生红旗单位等荣誉称号。

环境保护工作事关各族人民的福祉，责任重大，使命光荣。在今后的工作中，吐鲁番地区环保局将全面贯彻落实党的十八大精神，统一思想认识，紧紧围绕“五位一体”总布局，坚持资源开发可持续、生态环境可持续，坚持在发展中保护、在保护中发展，以环境保护优化经济发展，为建设和谐幸福美丽吐鲁番做出新的更大的贡献！

环境应急监控指挥中心

拆除违法排污企业设备

办公楼

东归名城 魅力和静

县委书记汪江华在县五小双语幼儿园调研

县委副书记、县长其米格赴莫呼查汗水库督导调研

和静县位于新疆天山中段南麓，巴州西北部，总面积近4万平方公里，周边与15个县市相邻，是世界上与县市接壤最多的县，载入吉尼斯世界记录。和静县辖6镇6乡，1个自治区工业园区，5个地方国有牧场，1个良种场，1个肉牛场，1个平原林场，境内有兵团二师所属3个团场，自治州一个农场，一个林场，自治区、自治州驻县工矿企业50余个。驻县团级4个，现有规模以上企业20家（主营业务收入2000万以上），有“天山水泥”、“金特钢铁”、“新兴铸管”、“凯宏矿业”、“隆平高科”、“开都河梯级电站”等大中型企业，全县现有人口25万人（含流动人口），共有55个村民委员会和18个居民委员会。

和静县资源丰富，矿产资源众多，其中：铁、菱、镁等矿产资源独树一帜；和静县水能资源优越，目前已开发开都河梯级电站，大山口水电站、小山口水电站、察汗乌苏水电站、柳树沟水电站等，是新疆最大的水电开发基地；和静县农牧业资源雄厚，有我国第一大亚高山寒草甸大草原，现有耕地54万亩（含兵团），是巴州最大的畜牧业、甜菜和番茄酱生产基地，全县牲畜存栏90多万头（只），巴音布鲁克黑头羊被国家农业部认证为优质食品；和静县旅游资源得天独厚，境内自然景观奇特多样，有我国唯一的天鹅自然保护区和国家级巩乃斯森林公园，新疆最大的藏传佛教圣地永安寺（黄庙）、巴音布鲁克大草原、九曲十八弯、天山石林等新疆乃之全国独一无二的旅游景观，国内极品、世界精品，目前巴音布鲁克景区争创5A级景区，巴音布鲁克提名湿地申报世界自然遗产。

和静县“十二五”总体发展思路：“123456”经济社会发展思路即：紧紧围绕一个目标（跨越发展和长治久安），突出两个增长（财政收入大副度增长、城镇居民收入稳定增长），推进“三化建设”（新型工业化、农牧业现代化、新型城镇化），提升四大产业（钢铁产业、电力能源产业、文化旅游产业、现代物流产业）完善五项机制（科学决策、开拓创新、激励约束、优化环境、督查考核），实施六大战略（工业强县、农牧稳县、旅游活县、科教兴县、文化塑县、生态立县），努力把和静打造成为巴州经济强县，文化大县，旅游名县和南北疆交通枢纽。

巴音布鲁克马

和静县天山水泥厂

刺绣作品

天山石林

皮 山 县

县委书记　沈毅

县长　艾斯喀尔·卡斯木

皮山县位于新疆维吾尔自治区的最南端，是一个以维吾尔族为主体，汉族、塔吉克族、柯尔克孜族等12个民族聚居的边境县，与印控克什米尔交界，是和田地区的西大门，距离首府乌鲁木齐1800公里。境内有全军最高的哨所——神仙湾哨卡（海拔5380米）。全县总面积3.98万平方公里（不含兵团农场），辖9个山区乡镇（三个边境乡镇）、7个平原乡镇、一个农业综合开发区和一个良种场、一个国营牧场。皮山县乡村非常分散，全县169个行政村分布在54块绿洲上。2012年底全县总人口270,270人（含兵团农场），少数民族占98.5%。

2012年，在自治区党委、人民政府的亲切关怀和安徽省、三峡集团的大力援助下，在地委、行署的坚强领导下，皮山县委、政府团结带领全县各族干部群众深入实施新时期"富民强县固边"战略，紧紧围绕"果牧富民、资源开发、工业强县、城镇兴县"发展思路，扎实推进经济、政治、文化、社会、生态和党的建设，开创了皮山各项工作的新局面。

——经济社会快速健康发展。2012年，地区生产总值达15.03亿元，同比增长13%（可比价）；全社会固定资产投资11.68亿元，同比增长36.93%；地方财政一般预算收入10423万元，同比增长30.9%；招商引资项目资金4.67亿元，实际到位资金2.02亿元。其中：自治区外到位资金1.92亿元；社会消费品零售总额1.66亿元，同比增长10.36%。农牧民人均纯收入3845元，同比增长13.8%。

——社会事业加快发展，民生工程成效显著。安居工程、教育科技、医疗卫生、社会保障、文化体育、广播影视等各项社会事业全面发展。24类88项重点民生工程顺利实施。新建安居富民房4600户、定居兴牧150户、各类保障性住房2022套；"两基"工作得到进一步巩固，社会保障水平进一步提高；"两证"领证率达30.85%，人口自然增长率为21.05‰。

——基础设施不断完善，生态治理初见成效。2012年，确定重点建设项目36个，完成投资8.1966亿元。涉及国计民生的一大批交通、水利、能源、城市建设等重大项目进展顺利，保障性住房建设、农村公路"畅通富民"工程顺利推进。启动了1902套廉租房、120套公租房建设；深入推进"三北五期"、天然林保护、荒漠植被保护等生态建设工程，人居环境和生态环境逐步得到改善。

——援疆工作全面展开，发展能力不断增强。安徽省、三峡集团对口支援皮山工作深入开展，2012年共安排援疆项目39个、资金2.7亿元，援疆项目的顺利实施极大地改善了群众生产生活条件。在皮山工作的安徽省和三峡集团优秀援疆干部人才真情援疆、无私奉献、忘我工作，展示了良好的精神风貌，激发了皮山各族干部群众对党中央、安徽省和三峡集团的感恩之情，巩固了各民族大团结的良好局面。

2013年是全面实现"十二五"规划总体目标的关键时期，在地委、行署的坚强正确领导下，皮山县委、政府将团结带领全县各族干部群众，全面贯彻落实科学发展观，进一步解放思想、乘势而上，科学发展、扎实工作，维护稳定、促进和谐，以只争朝夕、时不我待的精神风貌，按照"富民强县固边"战略新目标，努力推进皮山县早日实现跨越式发展和长治久安。

皮亚曼石榴

桑株千年古核桃王

建设富民强县和谐幸福——新疏附

广东援疆指挥部领导在疏附县行政服务“六个中心”工地调研

改革农村低保发放办法

新一轮援疆以来，疏附县立足实际，突出强化“责任、创新、效率”意识，坚持“一个龙头、两翼齐飞”的对口援疆工作格局，大力实施广州对口援建疏附县“1336”决策部署(即实现建设一个“富民强县和谐幸福新疏附”的战略目标，强化“民心向党是根本、市场机制是关键、文化引领是方向”三个工作理念，举全市之力推进疏附战略性基础设施、战略性主导产业、战略性发展平台建设三个重大突破，实施好民生工程、基础工程、产业工程、人才工程、融合工程、保障工程六大援建工程)，加快富民强县和谐幸福新疏附建设，民生建设先抓主要矛盾，产业发展依托当地资源，智力援疆重视制度建设，作为广州对口援建的疏附县发生了翻天覆地的变化。2012 年，地区生产总值、固定资产投资额、公共财政预算收入、农民人均纯收入较 2010 年分别增长 57.9%、1.7 倍、2.1 倍和 36.6%，实现了“三年打基础、五年上台阶、十年大发展”援疆工作第一阶段的战略目标。疏附广州援疆工作队分别获得“全国创先争优先进基层党组织”和自治区“2011 年产业援疆先进集体”荣誉称号，是新一轮对口援建以来唯一获此两项殊荣的工作队；成功创建成为全疆唯一同时拥有工业城和商贸物流园两个自治区级产业园区的县；被评为全国、自治区级粮食生产先进县，全国法治城市法治县(市区)创建活动先进单位；县公安局被评为全疆、全国优秀公安局；县企业服务中心被评为自治区中小企业公共服务示范平台。

举办党政领导干部周末大学堂，为干部“充电”

2012 年 9 月，疏附国际商贸物流产业园区被评为自治区级商贸物流园区

2012 年 8 月，疏附广州工业城被评为自治区级工业园区

大规模培训轮训干部　凸显主阵地主渠道作用

中共新疆生产建设兵团第一师委员会党校

常务副校长　蒲必明

理论宣传的阵地　党性锻炼的熔炉

民主协商　沟通无限

中共新疆生产建设兵团第一师委员会党校始建于1960年5月，原系中国人民解放军二军五师干训队，“文革”期间停办。1984年恢复，集农一师行政学院、中央电大农一师分校、兵团农业广播电视学校农一师分校四校合一，一套领导班子。学校实行校委领导制，是一师党委的重要工作部门。全校在职教职员工32人，其中研究生6人。

作为培养党政领导干部的学校，一师党校始终按照师市党委的中心工作，按照培养“靠得住、有本事、留得下、用得上”的培训目标，紧紧围绕师市改革发展稳定大局，充分发挥主渠道作用，坚持改革创新，突出办学特色，全面提升教学科研、管理和后勤服务工作水平，努力提高教育培训质量，在干部培训、理论研究等方面取得了新的成绩。一是教育培训规模逐步扩大。近3年来，围绕师市中心工作及“三化”建设，共举办各类培训班次129余期，培训干部13800余人，有效发挥了党校干部培训主阵地、主渠道作用；二是理论研究水平不断提升。3年来，共发表论文187篇，其中获国家级奖项1篇，省部级72篇。在与组织部、塔里木报社共同编写的纪念建党90周年文丛中收录师党校论文28篇。在《塔里木报》上出了理论专刊9期，刊登论文48篇。这些重大理论研究成果，为师市党委决策提供了重要参考和理论支持；三是努力推进教学模式改革，教学质量不断提高。近年来，全面推广了专题讲授式、研究式、研讨式、互动式、情景模拟式及实地参观考察疆内外亮点工程、示范基地等教学方法，聘请浙江大学、上海市委党校、台州市委党校、兵团党校、地委机关和地委党校专家教授42人次，师领导及师市部局领导65人次赴我校进行专题授课，组织教师参加疆内外培训学习124人次，通过一系列行之有效的教学方式方法，使我校干部教育培训质量有了质的提高。

2012年争取了占地92亩，建筑面积19212m^2，总投资8248万元的兵团第一师党委党校综合教学楼项目，建成后可一次性容纳350人住宿，1500人培训，预计新校区2014年将投入使用并实现校园的整体向阿拉尔搬迁。

多年来，兵团第一师党委党校始终本着“立党育人、求真创新”的校训精神，坚持“四个文明”建设工作。自2008年以来，先后被授予阿克苏地区级文明单位、安全文明小区、“花园式单位”、“无烟单位”、卫生红旗单位和兵团级文明单位等称号，并连续多年被兵团第一师文明委表彰命名为师级文明单位荣誉称号，兵团一类党校。

团结拼搏　奋发向上

共庆生日　构建和谐

红云红河烟草（集团）有限责任公司

新疆卷烟厂

国家局安全检查组由国家经济运行司副司长谢云海带队到新疆卷烟厂检查指导工作

集团董事长姚庆艳视察新疆卷烟厂易地技改工作

集团副总裁黄木忠到新疆卷烟厂视察调研

红云红河烟草(集团)有限责任公司新疆卷烟厂位于新疆维吾尔自治区奎屯市,是新疆唯一的卷烟生产厂家。创建于1960年,于1986年上划国家烟草专卖局(中国烟草总公司),1999年10月,新疆卷烟厂加入将军烟草集团有限公司,2005年12月加入红河卷烟总厂,2008年11月红云红河烟草(集团)有限责任公司成立,新疆卷烟厂成为红云红河集团旗下一员。经过50余年的艰苦创业,新疆卷烟厂已由建成时的小卷烟作坊发展成为现代化的卷烟工业企业,成为奎屯市的经济支柱、自治区的利税大户,是自治区级精神文明建设先进单位、全国烟草系统职业道德先进集体。

企业建成花园式工厂,固定资产12.65亿元,技术装备已达国内烟草行业先进水平。2012年企业年产卷烟34万箱,实现税利25.04亿元。近10年,新疆卷烟厂已累计为国家创造税利96.94亿元,为企业进一步实现更大发展提供了有力保障。2012年新疆卷烟厂生产卷烟34万箱,同比增加2万箱,增长6.3%。销售卷烟33.97万箱,同比增加1.99万箱,增长6.2%;销售收入35.45亿元,同比增加5.25亿元,增长17.4%。实现税金20.76亿元,同比增加2.81亿元,增长15.7%;实现利润总额5.7亿元,同比增加1.74亿元,增长44.0%;实现利税25.04亿元,同比增加4.01亿元,增长19.1%。实现单箱利税7370.89元,同比增加794.85元,增长12.1%;单箱三项费用700.4元,同比增加46.76元,增长7.2%,单箱管理费用571.05元,同比增加88.95元,增长18.5%。

新疆卷烟厂是自治区30家重点扶优扶强工业企业之一,2001年通过ISO9000质量管理体系、2006年通过ISO14000环境管理体系、OHSAS18000职业健康安全管理体系"三标"管理体系认证。企业拥有"云烟"、"红河"、"雪莲"系列品牌卷烟。"雪莲"牌卷烟是新疆"名牌产品",深受广大消费者青睐,也是国家烟草专卖局百牌号之一。2012年初上市的高档新产品"云烟"(软金雪莲),得到消费者的喜爱。

企业的生产经营情况不断攀升,税利连年增长、积极回报社会也赢得了地方政府和民众的支持:2012年5月,企业获得"自治区守合同重信用单位"、6月,获得"自治区创先争优先进基层党组织"、11月,荣获奎屯市"热爱伟大祖国 建设美好家园"主题教育活动先进单位称号、12月,荣获"服务地方发展先进单位"称号。

继往开来,在十二五期间,新疆卷烟厂将继续为国家和新疆维吾尔自治区的经济建设与长治久安做出重要贡献。

集团品牌大重九亮相乌鲁木齐

卷包车间生产线

迎新春文艺汇演

和田市给排水公司

总经理　张嘹

和田市给排水公司位于和田市东巴格路47号，筹建于1984年，其前身是“和田市自来水筹建组”；1988年7月经和田市政府批准，正式成立“和田市自来水公司”；1996年更名为“和田市给排水公司”。29年来，公司在市委、市政府的正确领导下，立足现状，着眼长远，坚持“质量、安全、发展、服务”的管理理念，发扬和田人特有的“特别能吃苦、特别能奉献”精神，迎难而上、团结拼搏、开拓创新，不断推进公司的创新发展，历经了由小到大、由弱到强的艰难发展历程。公司现拥有160多名职工，各类专业技术人员40多名；现公司所属一、二水厂共有水源井16眼、四座清水池，日供水能力6万立方米，日排水处理能力4立方米；截止到2012年底，和田市已铺设供水管网总长度为224公里、排水管网总长度为105公里，供水人数达13.6万余人，供水普及率达96%以上。

近年来，公司秉承“保障供水、真诚服务”宗旨，狠抓安全管理，注重科技创新，充分发挥科技人员和广大职工的聪明才智，极大地提高了供水保障能力；同时，公司注重职工职业道德建设，以“德”塑人，为促进公司科学发展提供强有力的智力支持。1992年获得自治区级“精神文明”单位称号，该称号经2005、2008年度届满复验，我公司属第一批复验合格单位；2000年获自治区安全文明小区和花园式单位称号；2004年评为和田地区“AAA”级企业；2009年获中国水协“特殊贡献奖”。经理张嘹同志荣获2007年度国家人事部、建设部“劳动模范”称号，2013年5月获和田地区“劳动模范”称号。

雄关慢道真如铁，而今迈步从头越。2012年，公司圆满完成了以安全供水为重任、以维护城市供排水管道为己任、以地下街供排水管道铺设改造为重点、以城市排水改扩建二期工程为目标的各项任务。公司自1992年被命名为自治区级文明单位20年来，精神文明建设工作联动效应进一步显现，有力的促进了公司各项工作，使公司职工思想道德建设，民主法制建设不断加强，城市供水、管道维修、城建供排水工程的服务质量不断提升，树立了良好的企业形象。2013年是自治区文明单位“零基启动”的第一年，公司在依“规”创建的基础上，组织力量整理档案500余份，进一步完善了文明创建的软硬件设施，各项创建工作正在稳步推进。

面对公司“建全方位安全体系、保全天候优质供水、推全流程标准服务、创和谐型国有企业”的愿景，公司干部职工有信心、有能力在市委、市政府及住建局的领导下，团结一心，精诚合作，拼搏进取，为企业续写新的辉煌！

美景宜人 前景锦绣

安全生产 保障供水

全程检测 严格把关

辛苦一人 滋润万家

新疆天富电力（集团）有限责任公司

——聚天山之雄魂，铸富企业之精神

自治区党委副书纪、兵团党委书纪、政委车俊(中),兵团党委常委、副政委、八师石河子市党委书记、八师政委卢晓峰(右),兵团党委常委、秘书长、办公厅主任李新明(左)出席天富发电厂 2×660 兆瓦项目奠基仪式

兵团党委副书记、司令员刘新齐来天富调研

新疆天富电力(集团)有限责任公司由原石河子电力工业公司改制组建而成,于 2002 年 2 月 4 日正式在石河子市工商局注册为国有独资公司,注册资本 10.4 亿元。公司下属全资子公司 3 个,控股子公司 3 个,分公司 2 个,其中控股子公司天富热电股份有限公司,于 2002 年 2 月 28 日在上海证券交易所发行上市。

公司主营发电、供电、供热、供天然气及煤炭生产、销售,担负着石河子垦区的电、热、气集中统一经营及大部分煤炭的生产经营管理,也是新疆唯一一家热电联产,水火电并举,发、供、调一体化的能源工业企业。

截止 2012 年底,公司资产总额为 161 亿元,实现主营业务收入 36.31 亿元,利润总额 2.66 亿元,工业增加值 11 亿元,从业人数 8116 人。年供电量突破 65 亿千瓦时,供热量 1462 万吉焦,供天然气 5496 万立方,原煤计划建设产能 210 万吨。

“十二五”期间,天富公司主要围绕师市的发展,不断提升煤、电、网的支撑力,做大增强基础产业,满足八师石河子市经济和社会的发展。“十二五”末,发电装机容量达到 383.1 万千瓦,煤炭产能按规划力争达到 600 万吨。加快推进 220kV 电网建设,力争于 2015 年在石河子城区、工业园区内部以及城区与团场外围形成不完全双环网,2020 年进一步实现双环网结构。

站在新的起点上,天富人将以争创一流的进取之心,埋头苦干的工作作风,百折不挠的意志品格,实现天富电力的科学发展、跨越发展。

庆祝建党 90 周年职工歌咏比赛

争分夺秒抓紧电热源项目建设

兵团首个国家康居示范工程——天富康城全景

职工喜看《天富故事》

兵团首座自建 120 万吨矿井天富煤业公司

明德立新　包容超越

山东能源新汶矿业集团(伊犁)能源开发有限责任公司

总经理王贯东(右)和党委书记亓会平为博士后工作站揭牌

全球最大的煤化工单体工程施工现场

标准化矿井大巷

新汶矿业集团有限责任公司建企于1956年，是一家以国有资产为主体、多种所有制并存，以煤为主、多种产业共同发展的大型企业集团，隶属于世界500强企业山东能源集团公司。先后荣获全国资源综合利用先进单位、全国煤炭行业节能减排先进单位、中国煤炭工业优秀企业管理奖、全国企业文化优秀奖，全国煤炭行业企业文化建设示范基地等称号，被国家发改委等六部委确定为国家第一批循环经济试点企业。在2010年7月党中央、国务院召开的西部大开发工作会议上，被授予"国家西部大开发突出贡献集体"，2013年荣获全国"五一"劳动奖状。

2005年7月，组建成立新汶矿业集团(伊犁)能源开发有限责任公司，2010年，被新疆自治区政府授予"双百"优强企业，连续三年被集团党委授予"党风廉政建设先进单位"、"宣传思想工作先进单位"。

新汶矿业集团伊犁伊宁矿区煤田分布在伊犁河南、北两岸，由伊南、伊北两个煤田组成。伊南煤田位于察布查尔县南部，面积338Km²；伊北煤田位于霍城县东南部，伊宁市北部及伊宁县境内，面积113.4Km²，探明煤炭储量129.6亿吨。该煤田煤种以长焰煤为主，低灰、特低硫、中高发热量，挥发份高、化学活性强，是动力、气化、液化优质原料。

经过近年来的艰辛探索和艰苦创业，构建形成了以煤炭生产为基础、资源转化为主导、机械制造为支撑、商贸物流为引擎的现代产业发展格局。其中：伊犁一号矿井、四号矿井、昭苏矿井都已具备试采条件；国家发改委下发了《关于同意新疆伊犁煤制天然气示范项目开展前期工作的复函》(发改办能源【2013】665号)。全球最大的煤化工单体工程，20亿立方米煤制天然气项目，今年完成设备安装，明年将试车投产。

到"十二五"末，基本建成"世界先进、国内一流"的现代新型煤化基地和循环经济示范园区，为集团公司打造现代新型能源企业，为伊犁打造天山北坡的经济强区、中心城市和向西开放的桥头堡，为全疆跨越式发展和长治久安做出新的更大贡献！

伊犁一矿北立井

伊犁四矿外景

煤化工项目气化炉吊装现场

昭苏煤矿远眺

伊犁一矿南工广鸟瞰图

伊犁能源大厦

中华联合财产保险股份有限公司
CHINA UNITED PROPERTY INSURANCE COMPANY LIMITED

新疆分公司

中华联合财产保险股份有限公司是经中国保监会批准，于2006年12月由中华联合保险控股股份有限公司发起设立的全国性财产保险公司。其前身是由国家财政部、农业部专项拨款，公司成立于1986年7月15日。是新中国之后我国成立的第二家国有保险公司，也是目前全国唯一一家以“中华”冠名的全国性保险公司。2012年10月，经中国保监会审批，中华产险的注册资本金达到145亿元人民币，居国内财险公司第二位，偿付能力充足率达到150%以上，达到偿付能力充足Ⅱ类公司标准。截至2012年底，公司已在全国设立了23家省级分公司、189家中心支公司、1010家支公司、736家营销服务部、机构总计1972家，员工31000余人，形成了比较完整的营销服务网络，建立了一支高素质的保险经营与营销专业队伍。

农业查勘调研

新疆是总公司的发源地，新疆分公司于2011年2月24日成立，是在原新疆区各地州机构的组织架构上新设立的省级分公司，新疆分公司所属各级机构共有246家，其中：省级分公司1家，15家地州分公司，1家省级分公司营业部，12个地州分公司营业部，145家支公司，72个营销服务部，机构网络遍布天山南北。公司的业务经营范围涵盖非寿险业务的各个领域，包括机动车辆保险、企业财产保险、家庭财产保险、工程保险、船舶保险、货物运输保险、责任保险、信用保证保险、农业保险以及短期健康保险和意外伤害保险等。近年又适时开发推出了电话营销专用车险、商务旅行意外伤害险、物流责任险、资产监管责任险、食品安全责任险等符合市场需求的新险种，还开发了一系列适合农村市场的涉农险种，新疆分公司成立以来，广大干部员工充分发扬“敬业、责任、争先、奉献”的八字精神，同心协力，积极进取，为着力打造业外有影响、业内受尊重的保险公司而努力拼搏。公司现保费规模位于全公司首位，当地财险市场位居第二。

公司始终践行“服务至上、创造价值”对客户负责的服务宗旨，遵循“客户为尊、员工为本、效益为先、创新为魂”的经营理念，勇于承担社会责任，通过诚信服务赢得市场，通过提供全方位的保险保障服务社会经济发展大局，得到了社会各界的广泛认可。

合作发展　互利双赢

抓服务　重承诺

加强岗位培训　提高从业人员专业素质

新疆伊珠葡萄酒有限公司

原兵团司令员华士飞来公司参观指导工作

公司新一届领导班子检查生产现场

被誉为“中国冰葡萄酒之乡”的新疆伊珠葡萄酒有限公司，座落在素有“中亚温岛”和“塞外江南”美称的伊犁。这里紧靠天山北坡伊犁河谷平原中部，依傍湿地形成了独特小气候，光照充足，昼夜温差大的自然环境，确属我国种植优质葡萄的最佳地区，有着发展葡萄酿酒业得天独厚的优势。

上个世纪60年代，伊珠人利用伊犁河谷得天独厚的地理环境，在该地区引进了世界上最好的葡萄品种，开始了酿造葡萄酒芬芳之梦。作为新疆自治区、兵团最早生产干葡萄酒、冰葡萄酒的重点企业，三代伊珠人用50年的奋斗和拼搏，由手工操作的团办小厂发展到一座大型现代化企业。公司万亩的原料基地尽显“七分原料”的精髓，意大利引进葡萄加工设备、先进的加工工艺，造就了伊珠葡萄酒的卓越品质。开发研制的冰葡萄酒、干葡萄酒系列产品经自治区鉴定，各项指标均达到国家规定的质量标准，生产技术达到国内先进水平，填补了自治区冰酒生产的空白。公司起草制定的冰葡萄酒标准，成为新疆冰葡萄酒食品安全地方标准，填补了新疆冰葡萄酒产业的空白。产品主要有：冰葡萄酒、干葡萄酒、甜葡萄酒、苹果醋饮料四大系列51个品种。伊珠产品曾获得了国家、自治区等17次荣誉称号和奖励。产品远销全国二十余个省市，市场前景看好。

澳大利亚旺马库钠瓦拉葡萄酒业总裁来厂参观考察

公司员工包装干葡萄酒生产现场

投资 600 多万元新建不锈钢发酵罐

新疆大明矿业集团股份有限公司成立于1997年2月25日，注册股本15000万股，集团公司主要从事黑色金属矿产资源的采选业务。下设鸿源矿业有限责任公司、明盛铜业有限公司、鑫泰化工有限公司、金宏鑫矿业有限责任公司四家子公司。集团公司资产总额达5.65亿余元，净资产额达3.5亿元，职工人数400余人。历经十余年的发展历程，集团公司已成为新疆区域铁矿石采选行业具影响力的中型矿山企业。

大明人始终以“推动行业技术进步，创建本质安全矿山”为指导思想，以矿山资源配置效率最优为经营原则，专注于采矿技术能力进步，在矿山生产中积极推进机械化、数字化、信息化技术的应用，实现了地下矿山生产组织及职能管理等方面实现高效衔接，天湖铁矿已初具现代化矿山的雏形并成为区域内矿产资源采掘行业的安全标准化、信息化建设的标杆企业。

大明矿业在多年的变革过程后，形成了自己特有的企业特质，它专注于技术能力的形成和突破，注重于人才的培养和发展，以超前的战略和企业文化，以持之以恒的诚信理念为基础，以国家产业政策的要求为依据，注重于可持续发展能力的形成。作为矿产资源转化效率最佳的探寻者和实践者，近年来大明矿业在现代采矿理论应用、安全生产及节能减碳等方面均取得了重大的突破。初步形成了以“短流程、低劳动强度、本质安全”为特征的高效采矿模式，以“短距离、高电压输送、变频技术普遍应用”为特征的节能减碳技术应用。天湖铁矿目前在多项生产指标上均以达到甚至超过了国家“安全生产标准化”及“清洁生产一级”的评价指标要求。

经过多年的努力，公司掘进效率台班5.01m3，全员劳动生产率4464吨/年，获得了政府和社会的认可。近几年先后获得各级政府机关部门授予的自治区级“纳税先进企业”、“AAAAA”级诚信单位、“第一批两化融合示范单位”、“节水型企业”、“环境保护优秀企业”、“推动行业进步贡献企业”、自治区重点扶持的100家“成长型企业”、安全标准化一级企业、第三批绿色矿山试点单位、中国矿业行业最具公信力诚信企业、节能减排突出贡献企业等荣誉称号。

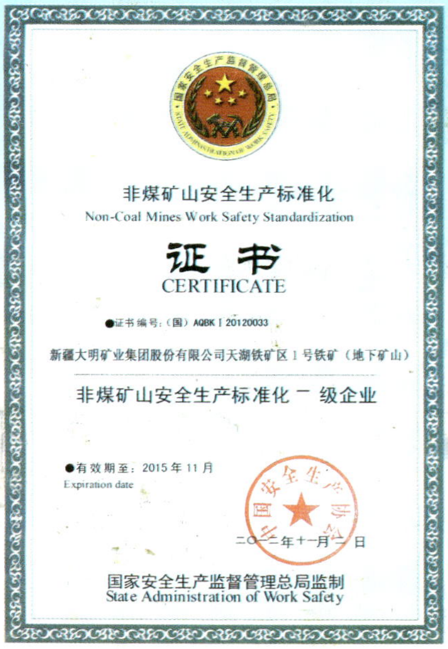
非煤矿山安全生产标准化
Non-Coal Mines Work Safety Standardization
证书
CERTIFICATE
●证书编号：（国）AQBK Ⅰ 20120033
新疆大明矿业集团股份有限公司天湖铁矿区1号铁矿（地下矿山）
非煤矿山安全生产标准化 一 级企业
●有效期至：2015年11月
Expiration date
二〇一二年十一月一日
国家安全生产监督管理总局监制
State Administration of Work Safety

全疆非煤矿安全标准化现场会

天湖环境规划效果图

机械化-3.5米卷扬机井架

肖尔布拉克
酿造新疆酱香型白酒第一品牌
新疆首家引进茅台技术，在天山脚下酿制而成
顺应伊犁河谷气候及节令规律，“道法自然，天人合一”
春季下沙投料，伏天踩曲
要经历九次蒸煮、八次蒸馏、七次取酒的漫长复杂过程
高温制曲、高温堆积、高温蒸馏，道道工序环环相扣
完全寓自然法则与玄妙的掌控之间
1825天长期陈储
流逝的是岁月，积淀的是成熟、完美和气派
疆茅已化为一种艺术的醇香魅力
只为懂得他的人来开启
当您轻吮这杯中的精灵
回味的不仅是这百转千回的美酒和蕴藏在坛中的美景
更收获的是极品、奇香和价值
西域酱酒
肖尔布拉克
疆茅
酱香型
新疆白酒高端市场多年来面对国内知名品牌的强势冲击和占领，新疆白酒还停留在恶性竞争中。2003年，肖尔布拉克酒业战略升级，引进国酒酱香型白酒酿造技术、反复实验、因地制宜、不断的创新，成功的在天山脚下酿造出了酱香型白酒。历经六年精心窖藏，在2010年隆重上市。这款酱香型白酒的上市，是我们新疆各族人民创造的骄傲、荣耀和自豪！填补了新疆白酒业无酱香型白酒的空白，改变了新疆接待外宾无本地高品质、高档次的好酒。受到了新疆各界人士的赞誉。
www.xiaoerbulake.com